Commonly Used Notation

A	Coefficient of risk aversion
A_p	Appraisal ratio of portfolio *p*
AR	Abnormal return
b	Retention or plowback ratio
C	Call option value
CAR	Cumulative abnormal return
CF	Cash flow
D	Duration
E	Exchange rate
E(*x*)	Expected value of random variable *x*
F	Futures price
e	2.718, the base for the natural logarithm, used for continuous compounding
e_{it}	The firm-specific return, also called the residual return, of security *i* in period *t*
f	Forward rate of interest
g	Growth rate of dividends
H	Hedge ratio for an option, also called the option's delta
i	Inflation rate
k	Market capitalization rate, the required rate of return on a firm's stock
ln	Natural logarithm function
M	The market portfolio
N(*d*)	Cumulative normal function, the probability that a standard normal random variable will have value less than *d*
p	Probability
P	Put value

PV	Present value
P/E	Price-to-earnings multiple
r	Rate of return on a security; for fixed-income securities, *r* may denote the rate of interest for a particular period
r_f	The risk-free rate of interest
r_M	The rate of return on the market portfolio
ROE	Return on equity, incremental economic earnings per dollar reinvested in the firm
S_p	Reward-to-volatility ratio of a portfolio, also called Sharpe's measure; the excess expected return divided by the standard deviation
S_t	Stock price at time *t*
t	Time
T_p	Treynor's measure for a portfolio, excess expected return divided by beta
U	Utility function
V	Intrinsic value of a firm, the present value of future dividends per share
X	Exercise price of an option
y	Yield to maturity
α	Rate of return beyond the value that would be forecast from the market's return and the systematic risk of the security
β	Systematic or market risk of a security
ρ_{ij}	Correlation coefficient between returns on securities *i* and *j*
σ	Standard deviation
σ^2	Variance
$\mathbf{Cov}(r_i, r_j)$	Covariance between returns on securities *i* and *j*

FOURTH EDITION

INVESTMENTS

The IRWIN/McGraw-Hill Series in Finance, Insurance, and Real Estate

Stephen A. Ross
Franco Modigliani Professor of Financial Economics
Sloan School of Management
Massachusetts Institute of Technology
Consulting Editor

FOURTH EDITION

INVESTMENTS

ZVI BODIE
BOSTON UNIVERSITY

ALEX KANE
UNIVERSITY OF CALIFORNIA, SAN DEIGO

ALAN J. MARCUS
BOSTON COLLEGE

 **Irwin McGraw-Hill**

Boston   Burr Ridge, IL   Dubuque, IA   Madison, WI   New York   San Francisco   St. Louis
Bangkok   Bogotá   Caracas   Lisbon   London   Madrid
Mexico City   Milan   New Delhi   Seoul   Singapore   Sydney   Taipei   Toronto

To our families with love and gratitude.

Irwin/McGraw-Hill

*A Division of The **McGraw·Hill** Companies*

INVESTMENTS
International Editions 1999

Exclusive rights by McGraw-Hill Book Co – Singapore, for manufacture and export. This book cannot be re-exported from the country to which it is consigned by McGraw-Hill.

4 5 6 7 8 9 10 BJE 2 0 9

ISBN 0-256-24626-2
ISBN 0-256-26192-X (Wall Street Journal edition)

Library of Congress Cataloging-in-Publication Data

Bodie, Zvi.
    Investments / Zvi Bodie, Alex Kane, Alan J. Marcus. – 4th ed.
      p.   cm. (Irwin/McGraw-Hill series in finance, insurance, and real estate)
    Include index.
    ISBN 0-256-24626-2
    1. Investments.   2. Portfolio management.   I. Kane, Alex.
  II. Marcus, Alan, J.   III. Title.   IV. Series.
  HG4521.B564   1999
  332.63'2–dc21   98-8117

www.mhhe.com

When ordering this title, use ISBN 0-07-116097-3

Printed in Singapore

ZVI BODIE
BOSTON UNIVERSITY

Zvi Bodie is Professor of Finance at Boston University School of Management. He holds a Ph.D. from the Massachusetts Institute of Technology and has served on the finance faculty at Harvard University and at MIT. He currently serves as a member of the Pension Research Council at the University of Pennsylvania. He has published widely on pension finance, the management of financial guarantees in both the private and public sector, and investment strategy in an inflationary environment. He has coedited several books on pensions, including *Securing Employer Pensions: An International Perspective, Pensions and the Economy: Sources, Uses and Limitations of Data, Pensions in the U.S. Economy, Issues in Pension Economics,* and *Financial Aspects of the U.S. Pension System.* His research on pensions has focused on the funding and investment policies of private pension plans and on public policies such as the provision of government pension insurance. He has consulted on pension policy for the U.S. Department of Labor, the State of Israel, and Bankers Trust Co.

ALEX KANE
UNIVERSITY OF CALIFORNIA, SAN DIEGO

Alex Kane is professor of finance and economics at the Graduate School of International Relations and Pacific Studies at the University of California, San Diego. He was visiting professor at the Faculty of Economics, University of Tokyo; Graduate School of Business, Harvard; Kennedy School of Government, Harvard; and research associate, National Bureau of Economic Research. An author of many articles in finance and management journals, Professor Kane's research is mainly in corporate finance, portfolio management, and capital markets, most recently in the measurement of market volatility and the pricing of options. Professor Kane is the developer of the *International Simulation Laboratory (ISL)* for training and experimental research in executive decision making.

ALAN J. MARCUS
BOSTON COLLEGE

Alan Marcus is professor of finance and chairman of the finance department in the Wallace E. Carroll School of Management at Boston College. He received his Ph.D. in Economics from MIT in 1981. Professor Marcus recently has been a visiting professor at the Athens Laboratory of Business Administration and at MIT's Sloan School of Management and has served as a research associate at the National Bureau of Economic Research. He also established the Chartered Financial Analysts Review Program at Boston College. Professor Marcus has published widely in the fields of capital markets and portfolio management, with an emphasis on applications of futures and options pricing models. His consulting work has ranged from new product development to provision of expert testimony in utility rate proceedings. He also spent two years at the Federal Home Loan Mortgage Corporation (Freddie Mac), where he developed models of mortgage pricing and credit risk, and he currently serves on the Advisory Council for the Currency Risk Management Alliance of State Street Bank and Windham Capital Management Boston.

In teaching and practice, the field of investments has experienced many changes over the last two decades. This is due in part to an abundance of newly designed securities, in part to the creation of new trading strategies that would have been impossible without concurrent advances in computer technology, and in part to rapid advances in the theory of investments that have come out of the academic community. In no other field, perhaps, is the transmission of theory to real-world practice as rapid as is now commonplace in the financial industry. These developments place new burdens on practitioners and teachers of investments far beyond what was required only a short while ago.

Investments, Fourth Edition, is intended primarily as a textbook for courses in investment analysis. Our guiding principle has been to present the material in a framework that is organized by a central core of consistent fundamental principles. We make every attempt to strip away unnecessary mathematical and technical detail, and we have concentrated on providing the intuition that may guide students and practitioners as they confront new ideas and challenges in their professional lives.

Our primary goal is to present material of practical value, but all three of us are active researchers in the science of financial economics and find virtually all of the material in this book to be of great intellectual interest. Fortunately, we think, there is no contradiction in the field of investments between the pursuit of truth and the pursuit of money. Quite the opposite. The capital asset pricing model, the arbitrage pricing model, the efficient markets hypothesis, the option-pricing model, and the other centerpieces of modern financial research are as much intellectually satisfying subjects of scientific inquiry as they are of immense practical importance for the sophisticated investor.

In our effort to link theory to practice, we have attempted to make our approach consistent with that of the Institute of Chartered Financial Analysts (ICFA), a subsidiary of the Association of Investment Management and Research (AIMR). In addition to fostering research in finance, the AIMR and ICFA administer an education and certification program to candidates seeking the title of Chartered Financial Analyst (CFA). The CFA curriculum represents the consensus of a committee of distinguished scholars and practitioners regarding the core of knowledge required by the investment professional.

There are many features of this text that make it consistent with and relevant to the CFA curriculum. The end-of-chapter problem sets contain questions from past CFA exams, and, for students who will be taking the exam, Appendix B is a useful tool that lists each CFA question in the text and the exam from which it has been taken. Chapter 3 includes excerpts from the "Code of Ethics and Standards of Professional Conduct" of the ICFA. Chapter 26, which discusses investors and the investment process, and is modeled after the ICFA outline.

UNDERLYING PHILOSOPHY

We believe that attention to a few important principles can simplify the study of otherwise difficult material and that fundamental principles should organize and motivate all study. These principles are crucial to understanding the securities already traded in financial markets and in understanding new securities that will be introduced in the future. For this reason, we have made this book thematic, meaning we never offer rules of thumb without reference to the central tenets of the modern approach to finance.

The common theme unifying this book is that *security markets are nearly efficient,* meaning most securities are usually priced appropriately given their risk and return attributes. There are few free lunches found in markets as competitive as the financial market. This simple observation is, nevertheless, remarkably powerful in its implications for the design of investment strategies; as a result, our discussions of strategy are always guided by the implications of the efficient markets hypothesis. While the degree of market efficiency is, and always will be, a matter of debate, we hope our discussions throughout the book convey a good dose of healthy criticism concerning much conventional wisdom.

Distinctive Themes

This edition of *Investments* is organized around several important themes:

1. The central theme is the near-informational-efficiency of well-developed security markets, such as those in the United States, and the general awareness that competitive markets do not offer "free lunches" to participants.

   A second theme is the risk-return trade-off. This too is a no-free-lunch notion, holding that in competitive security markets, higher expected returns come only at a price: the need to bear greater investment risk. However, this notion leaves several questions unanswered. How should one measure the risk of an asset? What should be the quantitative trade-off between risk (properly measured) and expected return? The approach we present to these issues is known as *modern portfolio theory,* which is another organizing principle of this book. Modern portfolio theory focuses on the techniques and implications of *efficient diversification,* and we devote considerable attention to the effect of diversification on portfolio risk as well as the implications of efficient diversification for the proper measurement of risk and the risk-return relationship.

2. This text places greater emphasis on **asset allocation** than most of its competitors. We prefer this emphasis for two important reasons. First, it corresponds to the procedure that most individuals actually follow. Typically, you start with all of your money in a bank account, only then considering how much to invest in something riskier that might offer a higher expected return. The logical step at this point is to consider other risky asset classes, such as stock, bonds, or real estate. This is an asset allocation decision. Second, in most cases, the asset allocation choice is far more important in determining overall investment performance than is the set of security selection decisions. Asset allocation is the primary determinant of the risk-return profile of the investment portfolio, and so it deserves primary attention in a study of investment policy.

3. This text offers a much broader and deeper treatment of futures, options, and other derivative security markets than most investments texts. These markets have become both crucial and integral to the financial universe and are the major sources of innovation in that universe. Your only choice is to become conversant in these markets—whether you are to be a finance professional or simply a sophisticated individual investor.

NEW IN THE FOURTH EDITION

Following is a summary of the content changes in the Fourth Edition:

Market Structure (Chapter 3)

We have updated our treatment of market microstructure in Chapter 3 with additional discussion of IPOs, underpricing, and the recent controversy over trading practices in the Nasdaq market. This discussion brings students up to date on trading practices in various security markets and provides an overview of the advantages and disadvantages of various forms of market organization. The chapter also contains additional material on ethics drawn from the CFA curriculum, and AIMR standards of professional conduct.

New Chapter on Mutual Funds and Other Investment Companies (Chapter 4)

Chapter 4 provides considerable detail on the organization of funds, reviews the costs and benefits associated with investing via mutual funds, examines empirical evidence on the investment performance of funds, and discusses how to find and interpret information on funds such as that presented in *Morningstar's* guide. This chapter thus provides the background necessary to understand this increasingly important market.

Expanded Discussion of Historical Rates of Return (Chapter 5)

In Chapter 5 of this edition, we have added tables of historical data regarding the performance of several asset classes. The new rate of return series give a richer set of benchmarks by which to evaluate investment performance. The expanded discussion of rate of return facilitates the interpretation of these data.

Efficient Diversification (Chapter 8)

Our chapter on Optimal Risky Portfolios (Chapter 8) has a new section in which we present an Excel spreadsheet model for deriving the efficient frontier and efficient portfolios along that frontier. The spreadsheet model makes our discussion of efficient diversification more concrete and shows the student how to build his or her own portfolio optimizer.

Multifactor Index Models (Chapter 10)

Our chapter on index models has been updated with an extensive discussion of multifactor models. The discussion shows why multifactor models can improve on single-factor models in terms of the ability to describe patterns of security returns, and provides an introduction to the potential importance of multiple sources of systematic risk that underlies modern asset pricing theory. We also provide an introduction to how such multifactor models might be tested.

Efficient Markets (Chapter 12)

Chapter 12's review of the empirical literature on the efficient markets hypothesis has been thoroughly updated. The new coverage highlights important new anomalies and attempts to provide balanced interpretations of them.

Empirical Evidence (Chapter 13)

Chapter 13 has been completely rewritten to reflect new research on the determinants of security returns. The chapter considers in detail the problems involved in testing equilibrium risk-return relationships. The new version of the chapter also considerably increases the discussion of the testing of multifactor models of security returns.

Fixed Income Management (Chapter 16)

A new discussion of convexity has been added to Chapter 16 of this edition. The new material highlights some of the problems encountered in fixed-income risk management and provides an introduction to more advanced techniques. The discussion appears in a modular format that can be easily skipped if the intructor views the material as too advanced.

Equity Markets (Chapter 18)

Chapter 18, which covers equity valuation, contains an expanded discussion of P/E ratios. These ratios are crucial to security analysis and the new coverage provides additional insight into how they may be interpreted.

Portfolio Management (Chapter 26)

This material, which focuses on many practical issues in formulating portfolio strategy, has been streamlined in this edition from two chapters into one. The current treatment eliminates duplication of material found elsewhere in the text, and enhances the readability of the material.

In addition to these changes, we have updated and edited our treatment of topics wherever it was possible to improve exposition or coverage.

ORGANIZATION AND CONTENT

The text is composed of seven sections that are fairly independent and may be studied in a variety of sequences. Since there is enough material in the book for a two-semester course, clearly a one-semester course will require the instructor to decide which parts to include.

Part I is introductory and contains important institutional material focusing on the financial environment. We discuss the major players in the financial markets, provide an overview of the types of securities traded in those markets, and explain how and where securities are traded. We also discuss in depth mutual funds and other investment companies, which have become an increasingly important means of investing for individual investors. Chapter 5 is a general discussion of risk and return, making the general point that historical returns on broad asset classes are consistent with a risk-return trade-off.

The material presented in Part I should make it possible for instructors to assign term projects early in the course. These projects might require the student to analyze in detail a particular group of securities. Many instructors like to involve their students in some sort of investment game and the material in these chapters will facilitate this process.

Parts II and III contain the core of modern portfolio theory. We focus more closely in Chapter 6 on how to describe investors' risk preferences. In Chapter 7 we progress to asset allocation and then in Chapter 8 to portfolio optimization.

After our treatment of modern portfolio theory in Part II, we investigate in Part III the implications of that theory for the equilibrium structure of expected rates of return on risky assets. Chapters 9 and 10 treat the capital asset pricing model and its implementation using index models, and Chapter 11 covers the arbitrage pricing theory. We complete Part II with a chapter on the efficient markets hypothesis, including its rationale as well as the evidence for and against it, and a chapter on empirical evidence concerning security returns. The empirical evidence chapter in this edition follows the efficient markets chapter so that the student can use the perspective of efficient market theory to put other studies on returns in context.

Part IV is the first of three parts on security valuation. This Part treats fixed-income securities—bond pricing (Chapter 14), term structure relationships (Chapter 15), and interest-rate risk management (Chapter 16). The next two Parts deal with equity securities and derivative securities. For a course emphasizing security analysis and excluding portfolio theory, one may proceed directly from Part I to Part III with no loss in continuity.

Part V is devoted to equity securities. We proceed in a "top down" manner, starting with the broad macroeconomic environment (Chapter 17), next moving on to equity valuation (Chapter 18), and then using this analytical framework, we treat fundamental analysis including financial statement analysis (Chapter 19).

Part VI covers derivative assets such as options, futures, swaps, callable and convertible securities. It contains two chapters on options and two on futures.

Finally, **Part VII** presents extensions of previous material. Topics covered in this Part include evaluation of portfolio performance (Chapter 24), portfolio management in an international setting (Chapter 25), a general framework for the implementation of investment strategy in a nontechnical manner modeled after the approach presented in CFA study materials (Chapter 26), risk management and hedging techniques (Chapter 27), and an overview of active portfolio management (Chapter 28).

PEDAGOGICAL FEATURES

This book contains several features designed to make it easy for the student to understand, absorb, and apply the concepts and techniques presented. Each chapter begins with an **overview,** which describes the material to be covered, and ends with a detailed **Summary,** which recapitulates the main ideas presented.

Learning investments is in many ways like learning a new language. Before one can communicate, one must learn the basic vocabulary. To facilitate this process, all new terms are presented in **boldface** type the first time we use them, and at the end of each chapter there is a **Key Terms** section listing the most important new terms introduced in that chapter. A **Glossary** of all the terms used appears at the end of the book.

Boxes containing short articles from business periodicals are included throughout the book. We think they enliven the test discussion with examples from the world of current events. We chose the boxed material on the basis of relevance, clarity of presentation, and consistency with good sense.

A unique feature of this book is the inclusion of **Concept Checks** in the body of the text. These self-test questions and problems enable the student to determine whether he or she has understood the preceding material and to reinforce that understanding. Detailed solutions to all these questions are provided at the end of each chapter.

These Concept Checks may be approached in a variety of ways. They may be skipped altogether in a first reading of the chapter with no loss in continuity. They can then be answered with any degree of diligence and application upon the second reading. Finally, they can serve as models for solving the end-of-chapter problems assigned by the instructor.

Each chapter also contains a list of **Selected Readings** that are annotated to guide the student toward useful sources of additional information in specific subject areas.

The **end-of-chapter Problems** progress from the simple to the complex. We strongly believe that practice in solving problems is a critical part of learning investments, so we have provided lots of problems. Many are taken from CFA examinations and therefore represent the kinds of questions that professionals in the field believe are relevant to the "real world." These problems are identified by an icon in the text margin.

ANCILLARY MATERIALS

For the Instructor

Instructor's Manual   The Instructor's Manual, prepared by Richard D. Johnson, Colorado State University, has been revised and improved in this edition. Each chapter includes a chapter overview, a review of learning objectives, an annotated chapter outline (organized to include the Transparency Masters/PowerPoint package), and teaching tips and insights. Transparency Masters are located at the end of each chapter.

PowerPoint Presentation Software   These presentation slides, also developed by Richard D. Johnson, provide the instructor with an electronic format of the Transparency Masters. These slides follow the order of the chapters, but if you have PowerPoint software, you may customize the program to fit your lecture presentation.

Test Bank   The Test Bank, prepared by Marilyn K. Wiley, Florida Atlantic University, has been revised to increase the quantity and variety of questions. Short-answer essay questions are also provided for each chapter to further test student comprehension and critical thinking abilities. The Test Bank is also available in computerized version. Test bank disks are available in Windows and Macintosh-compatible formats.

For the Student

The Wall Street Journal Edition   Available through a unique arrangement with Dow Jones & Company, *The Wall Street Journal* Edition of *Investments* includes a 10-week subscription to *The Wall Street Journal* included in the price of the book. Instructors should contact their sales representative about ordering this special edition.

Solutions Manual   The Solutions Manual, prepared by the authors, includes a detailed solution to each end-of-chapter problem. This manual is available for packaging with the text. Please contact your local Irwin/McGraw-Hill representative for further details on how to order the Solutions manual/textbook package.

Student Problem Manual   An interactive and dynamic web-based student problem manual has been created to build up the quantitative skills of the students through chapter-by-chapter worked out problems; reinforcing of important concepts; internet hot links and corresponding exercises for each chapter; problems that require use of excel spreadsheets and financial calculators; and projects requiring interaction with the Irwin website and the World Wide Web. The package includes a printed component and access to the web-based site.

Morningstar StockTools   Morningstar StockTools is a full-color, Windows-based CD-ROM that contains a database of nearly 8,000 stocks. There are 160 screenable fields for every stock that increases the potential for students to pinpoint the characteristics that they are looking for in an investment.

- Functional tools include screen, format, find, detail, and rank buttons. **Screen** for stocks that meet the criteria that you set, **format** allows you to view and print a custom display that meets your screening and ranking criteria, **find** helps you to cut through the huge database to get to a particular stock, and the **detail** function allows you to analyze an individual stock. The **rank** function helps you to quickly zero in on the stocks with the highest or lowest P/E Ratios or the largest or smallest market caps.
- The portfolio function is a tool that lets you analyze a portfolio of stocks like a mutual fund. It is a way to see how a group of stocks that you create interact together, see how risky the portfolio is, and play "what if" scenarios by moving and removing stocks from the mix.
- The performance tools include total returns and growth rates. They measure the magnitude of a stock's return or of a company's revenue over a given period.
- Segment tools include the business segment analysis and regional breakdown.
- Contextual tools allow you to compare a stock with other stocks, industries, indexes, and a variety of other benchmarks.

The Innovative Investor, Version 2.0   Prepared by Matthew Will, Dennis Foster, and David Shimko, this software is available in Lotus and a new Excel version. These templates are designed to provide students with quick access to difficult calculations associated with the analysis of securities such as stocks, bonds, callable and convertible securities, options, and futures, as well as to facilitate the analytics underlying asset allocation, performance evaluation, and other applications. All spreadsheets come complete with comprehensive "What-if" analysis, in addition to automatic graphing and printing capabilities. These user-friendly capsules are designed to solve many problems a student of investments might encounter, beginning with problems available in the User's Manual, but extending as well to problems you may encounter in a career as a financial analyst or sophisticated investor. Together with the text, the software enables students not only to process calculations, but to ask questions and build upon the intuition established in the text.

ACKNOWLEDGMENTS

Throughout the development of this text, experienced instructors have provided critical feedback and suggestions for improvement. These individuals deserve a special thanks for their valuable insights and contributions. The following instructors played a vital role in the development of this and previous editions of *Investments*:

Scott Besley
University of Florida

John Binder
University of Illinois at Chicago

Paul Bolster
Northeastern University

Phillip Braun
Northwestern University

L. Michael Couvillion
Plymouth State University

Anna Craig
Emory University

David C. Distad
University of California at Berkeley

Craig Dunbar
University of Western Ontario

Michael C. Ehrhardt
University of Tennessee at Knoxville

David Ellis
Babson College

Greg Filbeck
University of Toledo

Jeremy Goh
Washington University

John M. Griffin
Arizona State University

Mahmoud Haddad
Wayne State University

Robert G. Hansen
Dartmouth College

Joel Hasbrouck
New York University

Andrea Heuson
University of Miami

Shalom J. Hochman
University of Houston

A. James Ifflander
A. James Ifflander and Associates

Robert Jennings
Indiana University

Richard D. Johnson
Colorado State University

Susan D. Jordan
University of Kentucky

G. Andrew Karolyi
Ohio State University

Josef Lakonishok
University of Illinois at Champaign/Urbana

Dennis Lasser
Binghamton University

Christopher K. Ma
Texas Tech University

Anil K. Makhija
University of Pittsburgh

Steven Mann
University of South Carolina

Deryl W. Martin
Tennessee Technical University

Jean Masson
University of Ottawa.

Ronald May
St. John's University

Rick Meyer
University of South Florida

Don B. Panton
University of Texas at Arlington

Robert Pavlik
Southwest Texas State

Herbert Quigley
University of D.C.

Speima Rao
University of Southwestern Louisiana

Leonard Rosenthal
Bentley College

Eileen St. Pierre
University of Northern Colorado

Anthony Sanders
Ohio State University

John Settle
Portland State University

Edward C. Sims
Western Illinois University

Steve L. Slezak
University of North Carolina at Chapel Hill

Keith V. Smith
Purdue University

Patricia B. Smith
University of New Hampshire

Laura T. Starks
University of Texas

Manuel Tarrazo
University of San Francisco

Jack Treynor
Treynor Capital Management

Charles A. Trzincka
SUNY Buffalo

Gopala Vasuderan
Suffolk University

Joseph Vu
De Paul University

Simon Wheatley
University of Chicago

Marilyn K. Wiley
Florida Atlantic University

James Williams
California State University at Northridge

Tony R. Wingler
University of North Carolina at Greensboro

Hsiu-Kwang Wu
University of Alabama

Thomas J. Zwirlein
University of Colorado at Colorado Springs

For granting us permission to include many of their examination questions in the text, we are grateful to the Institute of Chartered Financial Analysts.

Much credit is due also to the development and production team: our special thanks go to Shelley Kronzek, Associate Editor; Michele Janicek, Development Editor; Jean Lou Hess, Senior Project Manager; and Crispin Prebys, Senior Designer.

Finally, we thank Judy, Hava, and Sheryl, who contributed to the book with their support and understanding.

Zvi Bodie
Alex Kane
Alan J. Marcus

CONTENTS

INTRODUCTION

THE INVESTMENT ENVIRONMENT

Even a cursory glance at *The Wall Street Journal* reveals a bewildering collection of securities, markets, and financial institutions. Although it may appear so, the financial environment is not chaotic: There is rhyme and reason behind the array of instruments and markets. The central message we want to convey in this chapter is that financial markets and institutions evolve in response to the desires, technologies, and regulatory constraints of the investors in the economy. In fact, we could *predict* the general shape of the investment environment (if not the design of particular securities) if we knew nothing more than these desires, technologies, and constraints. This chapter provides a broad overview of the investment environment. We begin by examining the differences between financial assets and real assets. We proceed to the three broad sectors of the financial environment: households, businesses, and government. We see how many features of the investment environment are natural responses of profit-seeking firms and individuals to opportunities created by the demands of these sectors, and we examine the driving forces behind financial innovation. Next, we discuss recent trends in financial markets. Finally, we conclude with a discussion of the relationship between households and the business sector.

1.1   REAL ASSETS VERSUS FINANCIAL ASSETS

The material wealth of a society is determined ultimately by the productive capacity of its economy—the goods and services that can be provided to its members. This productive capacity is a function of the **real assets** of the economy: the land, buildings, knowledge, and machines that are used to produce goods and the workers whose skills are necessary to use those resources. Together, physical and "human" assets generate the entire spectrum of output produced and consumed by the society.

In contrast to such real assets are **financial assets** such as stocks or bonds. These assets, per se, do not represent a society's wealth. Shares of stock are no more than sheets of paper; they do not directly contribute to the productive capacity of the economy. Instead, financial assets contribute to the productive capacity of the economy *indirectly*, because they allow for separation of the ownership and management of the firm and facilitate the transfer of funds to enterprises with attractive investment opportunities. Financial assets certainly contribute to the wealth of the individuals or firms holding them. This is because financial assets are *claims* to the income generated by real assets or claims on income from the government.

When the real assets used by a firm ultimately generate income, the income is allocated to investors according to their ownership of the financial assets, or securities, issued by the firm. Bondholders, for example, are entitled to a flow of income based on the interest rate and par value of the bond. Equityholders or stockholders are entitled to any residual income after bondholders and other creditors are paid. In this way the values of financial assets are derived from and depend on the values of the underlying real assets of the firm.

Real assets are income-generating assets, whereas financial assets define the allocation of income or wealth among investors. Individuals can choose between consuming their current endowments of wealth today and investing for the future. When they invest for the future, they may choose to hold financial assets. The money a firm receives when it issues securities (sells them to investors) is used to purchase real assets. Ultimately, then, the returns on a financial asset come from the income produced by the real assets that are financed by the issuance of the security. In this way, it is useful to view financial assets as the means by which individuals hold their claims on real assets in well-developed economies. Most of us cannot personally own auto plants, but we can hold shares of General Motors or Ford, which provide us with income derived from the production of automobiles.

Real and financial assets are distinguished operationally by the balance sheets of individuals and firms in the economy. Whereas real assets appear only on the asset side of the balance sheet, financial assets always appear on both sides of balance sheets. Your financial claim on a firm is an asset, but the firm's issuance of that claim is the firm's liability. When we aggregate over all balance sheets, financial assets will cancel out, leaving only the sum of real assets as the net wealth of the aggregate economy.

Another way of distinguishing between financial and real assets is to note that financial assets are created *and destroyed* in the ordinary course of doing business. For example, when a loan is paid off, both the creditor's claim (a financial asset) and the debtor's obligation (a financial liability) cease to exist. In contrast, real assets are destroyed only by accident or by wearing out over time.

The distinction between real and financial assets is apparent when we compare the composition of national wealth in the United States, presented in Table 1.1, with the financial assets and liabilities of U.S. households shown in Table 1.2. National wealth consists of structures, equipment, inventories of goods, and land. (It does not include the value of

Table 1.1   Domestic Net Worth*

Assets	$ Billion
Residential structures	$ 5,856
Plant and equipment	6,061
Inventories	1,221
Consumer durables	2,491
Land	4,364
Gold and SDRs	21
TOTAL	$20,014

*Column sums may differ from total because of rounding error.

Source: Balance Sheets for the U.S. Economy, 1945–94, Board of Governors of the Federal Reserve System, June 1995.

Table 1.2   Balance Sheet of U.S. Households*

Assets	$ Billion	% of Total	Liabilities and Net Worth	$ Billion	% of Total
Tangible assets					
Houses	$ 4,518	15.8%	Mortgages	$ 3,163	11.1%
Land	3,015	10.6	Consumer credit	984	3.4
Durables	2,491	8.7	Bank and other loans	173	0.6
Other	520	1.8	Other	506	1.8
Total tangibles	$10,544	36.9%	Total liabilities	$ 4,826	16.9%
Financial assets					
Deposits	$ 3,102	10.9%			
Life insurance reserves	488	1.7			
Pension reserves	5,010	17.6			
Corporate equity	2,886	10.1			
Equity in noncorporate business	2,511	8.8			
Mutual fund shares	1,067	3.7			
Personal trusts	670	2.3			
Debt securities	1,873	6.6			
Other	388	1.4			
Total financial assets	17,995	63.1	Net worth	23,713	83.1
TOTAL	$28,539	100.0%	TOTAL	$28,539	100.0%

*Column sums may differ from total because of rounding error.

Source: Balance Sheets for the U.S. Economy, 1945–94, Board of Governors of the Federal Reserve System, June 1995.

"human capital"—the value of the earnings potential of the work force.) In contrast, Table 1.2 includes financial assets such as bank accounts, corporate equity, bonds, and mortgages.

Persons in the United States tend to hold their financial claims in an indirect form. In fact, only about one-quarter of the adult U.S. population holds shares directly. The claims of most individuals on firms are mediated through institutions that hold shares on their behalf: institutional investors such as pension funds, insurance companies, mutual funds, and endowment funds. Table 1.3 shows that today approximately half of all U.S. equity is held by institutional investors.

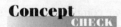

Question 1 • Are the following assets real or financial?

a. **Patents**

b. **Lease obligations**

c. **Customer goodwill**

d. **A college education**

e. **A $5 bill**

Table 1.3   Holdings of Corporate Equities in the United States, 1996

Sector	Share Ownership, $ Billions	% of Total
Private pension funds	$1,255.1	13.4%
State and local pension funds	851.8	9.1
Insurance companies	577.7	6.2
Mutual funds	1,384.2	14.7
Bank personal trusts	213.9	2.3
Foreign investors	575.7	6.1
Households and nonprofit organizations	4,477.3	47.7
Other	51.7	0.6
TOTAL	$9,387.4	100.0%

Source: New York Stock Exchange Fact Book, 1996.

1.2   FINANCIAL MARKETS AND THE ECONOMY

We stated earlier that real assets determine the wealth of an economy, whereas financial assets merely represent claims on real assets. Nevertheless, financial assets and the markets in which they are traded play several crucial roles in developed economies. Financial assets allow us to make the most of the economy's real assets.

Consumption Timing

Some individuals in an economy are earning more than they currently wish to spend. Others—for example, retirees—spend more than they currently earn. How can you shift your purchasing power from high-earnings periods to low-earnings periods of life? One way is to "store" your wealth in financial assets. In high-earnings periods, you can invest your savings in financial assets such as stocks and bonds. In low-earnings periods, you can sell these assets to provide funds for your consumption needs. By so doing, you can shift your consumption over the course of your lifetime, thereby allocating your consumption to periods that provide the greatest satisfaction. Thus financial markets allow individuals to separate decisions concerning current consumption from constraints that otherwise would be imposed by current earnings.

Allocation of Risk

Virtually all real assets involve some risk. When GM builds its auto plants, for example, its management cannot know for sure what cash flows those plants will generate. Financial markets and the diverse financial instruments traded in those markets allow investors with the greatest taste for risk to bear that risk, while other less-risk-tolerant individuals can, to a greater extent, stay on the sidelines. For example, if GM raises the funds to build its auto plant by selling both stocks and bonds to the public, the more optimistic, or risk-tolerant, investors buy shares of stock in GM. The more conservative individuals can buy GM bonds, which promise to provide a fixed payment. The stockholders bear most of the business risk along with potentially higher rewards. Thus capital markets allow the risk that is inherent to all investments to be borne by the investors most willing to bear that risk.

This allocation of risk also benefits the firms that need to raise capital to finance their investments. When investors can self-select into security types with risk–return characteristics that best suit their preferences, each security can be sold for the best possible price. This facilitates the process of building the economy's stock of real assets.

Separation of Ownership and Management

Many businesses are owned and managed by the same individual. This simple organization, well-suited to small businesses, in fact was the most common form of business organization before the Industrial Revolution. Today, however, with global markets and large-scale production, the size and capital requirements of firms have skyrocketed. For example, General Electric has assets worth about $33 billion. Corporations of such size simply could not exist as owner-operated firms. General Electric actually has about one-half million stockholders, whose ownership stake in the firm is proportional to their holdings of shares.

Such a large group of individuals obviously cannot actively participate in the day-to-day management of the firm. Instead, they elect a board of directors, which in turn hires and supervises the management of the firm. This structure means that the owners and managers of the firm are different. This gives the firm a stability that the owner-managed firm cannot achieve. For example, if some stockholders decide they no longer wish to hold shares in the firm, they can sell their shares to other investors, with no impact on the management of the firm. Thus financial assets and the ability to buy and sell those assets in financial markets allow for easy separation of ownership and management.

How can all of the disparate owners of the firm, ranging from large pension funds holding thousands of shares to small investors who may hold only a single share, agree on the objectives of the firm? Again, the financial markets provide some guidance. All may agree that the firm's management should pursue strategies that enhance the value of their shares. Such policies will make all shareholders wealthier and allow them all to better pursue their personal goals, whatever those goals might be. We return to the relationship between owners and managers of the firm at the end of the chapter.

1.3   CLIENTS OF THE FINANCIAL SYSTEM

We start our analysis with a broad view of the major clients that place demands on the financial system. By considering the needs of these clients, we can gain considerable insight into why organizations and institutions have evolved as they have.

We can classify the clientele of the investment environment into three groups: the household sector, the corporate sector, and the government sector. This trichotomy is not perfect; it excludes some organizations such as not-for-profit agencies and has difficulty with some hybrids such as unincorporated or family-run businesses. Nevertheless, from the standpoint of capital markets, the three-group classification is useful.

The Household Sector

Households constantly make economic decisions concerning such activities as work, job training, retirement planning, and savings versus consumption. We will take most of these decisions as being already made and focus on financial decisions specifically. Essentially, we concern ourselves only with what financial assets households desire to hold.

Even this limited focus, however, leaves a broad range of issues to consider. Most households are potentially interested in a wide array of assets, and the assets that are attractive can vary considerably depending on the household's economic situation. Even a limited consideration of taxes and risk preferences can lead to widely varying asset demands, and this demand for variety is, as we shall see, a driving force behind financial innovation.

Taxes lead to varying asset demands because people in different tax brackets "transform" before-tax income to after-tax income at different rates. For example, high-tax-bracket investors naturally will seek tax-free securities, compared with low-tax-bracket investors who want primarily higher-yielding taxable securities. A desire to minimize taxes also leads to demand for securities that are exempt from state and local taxes. This, in turn, causes demand for portfolios that specialize in tax-exempt bonds of one particular state. In other words, differential tax status creates "tax clienteles" that in turn give rise to demand for a range of assets with a variety of tax implications. The demand of investors encourages entrepreneurs to offer such portfolios (for a fee, of course!).

Risk considerations also create demand for a diverse set of investment alternatives. At an obvious level, differences in risk tolerance create demand for assets with a variety of risk–return combinations. Individuals also have particular hedging requirements that contribute to diverse investment demands.

Consider, for example, a resident of New York City who plans to sell her house and retire to Miami, Florida, in 15 years. Such a plan seems feasible if real estate prices in the two cities do not diverge before her retirement. How can one hedge Miami real estate prices now, short of purchasing a home there immediately rather than at retirement? One way to hedge the risk is to purchase securities that will increase in value if Florida real estate becomes more expensive. This creates a hedging demand for an asset with a particular risk characteristic. Such demands lead profit-seeking financial corporations to supply the desired goods: observe Florida real estate investment trusts (REITs) that allow individuals to invest in securities whose performance is tied to Florida real estate prices. If Florida real estate becomes more expensive, the REIT will increase in value. The individual's loss as a potential purchaser of Florida real estate is offset by her gain as an investor in that real estate. This is only one example of how a myriad of risk-specific assets are demanded *and created* by agents in the financial environment.

Risk motives also lead to demand for ways that investors can easily diversify their portfolios and even out their risk exposure. We will see that these diversification motives inevitably give rise to mutual funds that offer small individual investors the ability to invest in a wide range of stocks, bonds, precious metals, and virtually all other financial instruments.

The Business Sector

Whereas household financial decisions are concerned with how to invest money, businesses typically need to raise money to finance their investments in real assets: plant, equipment, technological know-how, and so forth. Table 1.4 presents balance sheets of U.S. corporations as a whole. The heavy concentration on tangible assets is obvious. Broadly speaking, there are two ways for businesses to raise money—they can borrow it, either from banks or directly from households by issuing bonds, or they can "take in new partners" by issuing stocks, which are ownership shares in the firm.

Businesses issuing securities to the public have several objectives. First, they want to get the best price possible for their securities. Second, they want to market the issues to the public at the lowest possible cost. This has two implications. First, businesses might want to farm out the marketing of their securities to firms that specialize in such security issuance, because it is unlikely that any single firm is in the market often enough to justify a full-time security issuance division. Issue of securities requires immense effort. The security issue must be brought to the attention of the public. Buyers then must subscribe to the issue, and records of subscriptions and deposits must be kept. The allocation of the security to each buyer must be determined, and subscribers finally must exchange money for secu-

Table 1.4   Balance Sheet of Nonfinancial U.S. Business*

Assets	$ Billion	% of Total	Liabilities and Net Worth	$ Billion	% of Total
Tangible assets			Liabilities		
Equipment and structures	$ 4,023	49.7%	Bonds and mortgages	$1,522	18.8%
Land	141	1.7	Bank loans	563	6.9
Inventories	1,066	13.2	Other loans	457	5.6
Total tangibles	$5,230	64.6%	Trade debt	800	9.9
			Other	811	10.0
			Total liabilities	$4,152	51.3%
Financial assets					
Deposits and cash	$ 298	3.7%			
Marketable securities	559	6.9			
Consumer credit	90	1.1			
Trade credit	942	11.6			
Other	978	12.1			
Total financial assets	2,867	35.4	Net worth	3,945	48.7
TOTAL	$8,097	100.0%	TOTAL	$8,097	100.0%

*Column sums may differ from total because of rounding error.

Source: Balance Sheets for the U.S. Economy, 1945–94, Board of Governors of the Federal Reserve System, June 1995.

rities. These activities clearly call for specialists. The complexities of security issuance have been the catalyst for creation of an investment banking industry to cater to business demands. We will return to this industry shortly.

The second implication of the desire for low-cost security issuance is that most businesses will prefer to issue fairly simple securities that require the least extensive incremental analysis and, correspondingly, are the least expensive to arrange. Such a demand for simplicity or uniformity by business-sector security issuers is likely to be at odds with the household sector's demand for a wide variety of risk-specific securities. This mismatch of objectives gives rise to an industry of middlemen who act as intermediaries between the two sectors, specializing in transforming simple securities into complex issues that suit particular market niches.

The Government Sector

Like businesses, governments often need to finance their expenditures by borrowing. Unlike businesses, governments cannot sell equity shares; they are restricted to borrowing to raise funds when tax revenues are not sufficient to cover expenditures. They also can print money, of course, but this source of funds is limited by its inflationary implications, and so most governments usually try to avoid excessive use of the printing press.

Governments have a special advantage in borrowing money because their taxing power makes them very creditworthy and, therefore, able to borrow at the lowest rates. The financial component of the federal government's balance sheet is presented in Table 1.5. Notice that the major liabilities are government securities, such as Treasury bonds or Treasury bills.

A second, special role of the government is in regulating the financial environment. Some government regulations are relatively innocuous. For example, the Securities and Exchange Commission is responsible for disclosure laws that are designed to enforce truthfulness in various financial transactions. Other regulations have been much more controversial.

One example is Regulation Q, which for decades put a ceiling on the interest rates that banks were allowed to pay to depositors, until it was repealed by the Depository

Table 1.5   Financial Assets and Liabilities of the U.S. Government

Assets	$ Billion	% of Total	Liabilities	$ Billion	% of Total
Deposits, currency, gold	$100.0	22.9%	Currency	$ 27.5	0.6%
Mortgages	50.3	11.5	Government securities	3,760.6	86.8
Loans	112.5	25.7	Insurance and pension reserves	436.1	10.1
Other	174.7	39.9	Other	106.4	2.5
TOTAL	$437.5	100.0%	TOTAL	$4,330.6	100.0%

Source: Flow of Funds Accounts: Flows and Outstandings, Board of Governors of the Federal Reserve System, 1997.

Institutions Deregulation and Monetary Control Act of 1980. These ceilings were supposedly a response to widespread bank failures during the Great Depression. By curbing interest rates, the government hoped to limit further failures. The idea was that if banks could not pay high interest rates to compete for depositors, their profits and safety margins presumably would improve. The result was predictable: Instead of competing through interest rates, banks competed by offering "free" gifts for initiating deposits and by opening more numerous and convenient branch locations. Another result also was predictable: Bank competitors stepped in to fill the void created by Regulation Q. The great success of money market funds in the 1970s came in large part from depositors leaving banks that were prohibited from paying competitive rates. Indeed, much financial innovation may be viewed as responses to government tax and regulatory rules.

1.4   THE ENVIRONMENT RESPONDS TO CLIENTELE DEMANDS

When enough clients demand and are willing to pay for a service, it is likely in a capitalistic economy that a profit-seeking supplier will find a way to provide and charge for that service. This is the mechanism that leads to the diversity of financial markets. Let us consider the market responses to the disparate demands of the three sectors.

Financial Intermediation

Recall that the financial problem facing households is how best to invest their funds. The relative smallness of most households makes direct investment intrinsically difficult. A small investor obviously cannot advertise in the local newspaper his or her willingness to lend money to businesses that need to finance investments. Instead, **financial intermediaries** such as banks, investment companies, insurance companies, or credit unions naturally evolve to bring the two sectors together. Financial intermediaries sell their own liabilities to raise funds that are used to purchase liabilities of other corporations.

For example, a bank raises funds by borrowing (taking in deposits) and lending that money to (purchasing the loans of) other borrowers. The spread between the rates paid to depositors and the rates charged to borrowers is the source of the bank's profit. In this way, lenders and borrowers do not need to contact each other directly. Instead, each goes to the bank, which acts as an intermediary between the two. The problem of matching lenders with borrowers is solved when each comes independently to the common intermediary. The convenience and cost savings the bank offers the borrowers and lenders allow it to profit from the spread between the rates on its loans and the rates on its deposits. In other words, the problem of coordination creates a market niche for the bank as intermediary. Profit opportunities alone dictate that banks will emerge in a trading economy.

Table 1.6   Balance Sheet of Financial Institutions*

Assets	$ Billion	% of Total	Liabilities and Net Worth	$ Billion	% of Total
Tangible assets			Liabilities		
Equipment and structures	$ 528	3.1%	Deposits	$ 3,462	20.1%
Land	99	0.6	Mutual fund shares	1,564	9.1
Total tangibles	$ 628	3.6%	Life insurance reserves	478	2.8
			Pension reserves	4,651	27.0
			Money market securities	1,150	6.7
			Bonds and mortgages	1,589	9.2
Financial assets			Other	3,078	17.8
Deposits and cash	$ 364	2.1%	Total liabilities	$15,971	92.6%
Government securities	3,548	20.6			
Corporate bonds	1,924	11.2			
Mortgages	2,311	13.4			
Consumer credit	894	5.2			
Other loans	1,803	10.4			
Corporate equity	3,310	19.2			
Other	2,471	14.3			
Total financial assets	16,625	96.4	Net worth	1,281	7.4
TOTAL	$17,252	100.0%	TOTAL	$17,252	100.0%

*Column sums may differ from total because of rounding error.

Source: Balance Sheets for the U.S. Economy, 1945–94, Board of Governors of the Federal Reserve System, June 1995.

Financial intermediaries are distinguished from other businesses in that both their assets and their liabilities are overwhelmingly financial. Table 1.6 shows that the balance sheets of financial institutions include very small amounts of tangible assets. Compare Table 1.6 with Table 1.4, the balance sheet of the nonfinancial corporate sector. The contrast arises precisely because intermediaries are middlemen, simply moving funds from one sector to another. In fact, from a bird's-eye view, this is the primary social function of such intermediaries, to channel household savings to the business sector.

Other examples of financial intermediaries are investment companies, insurance companies, and credit unions. All these firms offer similar advantages, in addition to playing a middleman role. First, by pooling the resources of many small investors, they are able to lend considerable sums to large borrowers. Second, by lending to many borrowers, intermediaries achieve significant diversification, meaning they can accept loans that individually might be risky. Third, intermediaries build expertise through the volume of business they do. One individual trying to borrow or lend directly would have much less specialized knowledge of how to structure and execute the transaction with another party.

Investment companies, which pool together and manage the money of many investors, also arise out of the "smallness problem." Here, the problem is that most household portfolios are not large enough to be spread across a wide variety of securities. It is very expensive in terms of brokerage and trading costs to purchase one or two shares of many different firms, and it clearly is more economical for stocks and bonds to be purchased and sold in large blocks. This observation reveals a profit opportunity that has been filled by *mutual funds* offered by many investment companies.

Mutual funds pool the limited funds of small investors into large amounts, thereby gaining the advantages of large-scale trading; investors are assigned a prorated share of the total funds according to the size of their investment. This system gives small investors advantages that they are willing to pay for in the form of a management fee to the mutual fund operator. Mutual funds are logical extensions of an investment club or cooperative, in which individuals themselves team up and pool funds. The fund sets up shop as a firm that accepts the assets of many investors, acting as an investment agent on their behalf. Again, the advantages of specialization are sufficiently large that the fund can provide a valuable service and still charge enough for it to clear a handsome profit.

Investment companies also can design portfolios specifically for large investors with particular goals. In contrast, mutual funds are sold in the retail market, and their investment philosophies are differentiated mainly by strategies that are likely to attract a large number of clients. Some investment companies manage "commingled funds," in which the monies of different clients with similar goals are merged into a "mini–mutual fund," which is run according to the common preferences of those clients. We discuss investment companies in greater detail in Chapter 4.

Economies of scale also explain the proliferation of analytic services available to investors. Newsletters, databases, and brokerage house research services all exploit the fact that the expense of collecting information is best borne by having a few agents engage in research to be sold to a large client base. This setup arises naturally. Investors clearly want information, but, with only small portfolios to manage, they do not find it economical to incur the expense of collecting it. Hence a profit opportunity emerges: A firm can perform this service for many clients and charge for it.

Investment Banking

Just as economies of scale and specialization create profit opportunities for financial intermediaries, so too do these economies create niches for firms that perform specialized services for businesses. We said before that firms raise much of their capital by selling securities such as stocks and bonds to the public. Because these firms do not do so frequently, however, investment banking firms that specialize in such activities are able to offer their services at a cost below that of running an in-house security issuance division.

Investment bankers such as Merrill Lynch, Salomon Brothers, or Goldman, Sachs advise the issuing firm on the prices it can charge for the securities issued, market conditions, appropriate interest rates, and so forth. Ultimately, the investment banking firm handles the marketing of the security issue to the public.

Investment bankers can provide more than just expertise to security issuers. Because investment bankers are constantly in the market, assisting one firm or another to issue securities, the public knows that it is in the banker's interest to protect and maintain its reputation for honesty. The investment banker will suffer along with investors if it turns out that securities it has underwritten have been marketed to the public with overly optimistic or exaggerated claims, for the public will not be so trusting the next time that investment banker participates in a security sale. The investment banker's effectiveness and ability to command future business thus depends on the reputation it has established over time. Obviously, the economic incentives to maintain a trustworthy reputation are not nearly as strong for firms that plan to go to the securities markets only once or very infrequently. Therefore, investment bankers can provide a certification role—a "seal of approval"—to security issuers. Their investment in reputation is another type of scale economy that arises from frequent participation in the capital markets.

Financial Innovation and Derivatives

The investment diversity desired by households is far greater than most businesses have a desire to satisfy. Most firms find it simpler to issue "plain vanilla" securities, leaving exotic variants to others who specialize in financial markets. This, of course, creates a profit opportunity for innovative security design and repackaging that investment bankers are only too happy to fill.

Consider the astonishing changes in the mortgage markets since 1970, when mortgage pass-through securities were first introduced by the Government National Mortgage Association (GNMA, or Ginnie Mae). These pass-throughs aggregate individual home mortgages into relatively homogenous pools. Each pool acts as backing for a GNMA **pass-through security.** GNMA securityholders receive the principal and interest payments made on the underlying mortgage pool. For example, the pool might total $100 million of 10 percent, 30-year conventional mortgages. The purchaser of the pool receives all monthly interest and principal payments made on the pool. The banks that originated the mortgages continue to service them but no longer own the mortgage investments; these have been passed through to the GNMA securityholders.

Pass-through securities were a tremendous innovation in mortgage markets. The *securitization* of mortgages meant that mortgages could be traded just like other securities in national financial markets. Availability of funds no longer depended on local credit conditions; with mortgage pass-throughs trading in national markets, mortgage funds could flow from any region to wherever demand was greatest.

The next round of innovation came when it became apparent that investors might be interested in mortgage-backed securities with different effective times to maturity. Thus was born the *collateralized mortgage obligation*, or CMO. The CMO meets the demand for mortgage-backed securities with a range of maturities by dividing the overall pool into a series of classes called tranches. The so-called fast-pay tranche receives all the principal payments made on the entire mortgage pool until the total investment of the investors in the tranche is repaid. In the meantime, investors in the other tranches receive only interest on their investment. In this way, the fast-pay tranche is retired first and is the shortest-term mortgage-backed security. The next tranche then receives all of the principal payments until it is retired, and so on, until the slow-pay tranche, the longest-term class, finally receives payback of principal after all other tranches have been retired.

Although these securities are relatively complex, the message here is that security demand elicited a market response. The waves of product development in the last two decades are responses to perceived profit opportunities created by as-yet unsatisfied demands for securities with particular risk, return, tax, and timing attributes. As the investment banking industry becomes ever more sophisticated, security creation and customization become more routine. Most new securities are created by dismantling and rebundling more basic securities. For example, the CMO is a dismantling of a simpler mortgage-backed security into component tranches. A Wall Street joke asks how many investment bankers it takes to sell a light bulb. The answer is 100—one to break the bulb and 99 to sell off the individual fragments.

This discussion leads to the notion of primitive versus derivative securities. A **primitive security** offers returns based only on the status of the issuer. For example, bonds make stipulated interest payments depending only on the solvency of the issuing firm. Dividends paid to stockholders depend as well on the board of directors' assessment of the firm's financial position. In contrast, **derivative securities** yield returns that depend on additional factors pertaining to the prices of other assets. For example, the payoff to stock options depends on the price of the underlying stock. In our mortgage examples, the derivative mortgage-backed securities offer payouts that depend on the original mortgages, which are the primitive securities. Much of the innovation in security design may be viewed as the continual creation of new types of derivative securities from the available set of primitive securities.

Derivatives have become an integral part of the investment environment. One use of derivatives, perhaps the primary use, is to hedge risks. However, derivatives also can be used to take highly speculative positions. Moreover, when complex derivatives are misunderstood, firms that believe they are hedging might in fact be increasing their exposure to various sources of risk. This seemed to be the case in 1994 when several firms lost large sums on their derivatives positions. Among the more spectacular losses were those of Procter & Gamble, which took a $157 million pretax charge on two interest-rate–related derivative products, and Piper Jaffray Companies, a financial services firm which suffered a loss of $700 million in its fixed income portfolios, many of which were believed by clients to be very conservatively invested.

While these losses attracted considerable attention, they were in fact the exception to the more common use of such securities as risk-management tools. Derivatives will continue to play an important role in portfolio management and the financial system. We will return to this topic later in the text. For the time being, however, we direct you to the primer on derivatives in the nearby box.

Concept
CHECK

Question 2 • If you take out a car loan, is the loan a primitive security or a derivative security?
Question 3 • Explain how a car loan from a bank creates both financial assets and financial liabilities.

Response to Taxation and Regulation

We have seen that much financial innovation and security creation may be viewed as a natural market response to unfulfilled investor needs. Another driving force behind innovation is the ongoing game played between governments and investors on taxation and regulation. Many financial innovations are direct responses to government attempts either to regulate or to tax investments of various sorts. We can illustrate this with several examples.

We have already noted how Regulation Q, which limited bank deposit interest rates, spurred the growth of the money market industry. It also was one reason for the birth of the Eurodollar market. Because Regulation Q did not apply to dollar-denominated time deposits in foreign accounts, many U.S. banks and foreign competitors established branches in London and other cities outside the United States, where they could offer competitive rates outside the jurisdiction of U.S. regulators. The growth of the Eurodollar market was also the result of another U.S. regulation: reserve requirements. Foreign branches were exempt from such requirements and were thus better able to compete for deposits. Ironically, despite the fact that Regulation Q no longer exists, the Eurodollar market continues to thrive, thus complicating the lives of U.S. monetary policymakers.

Another innovation attributable largely to tax avoidance motives is the long-term deep discount, or zero-coupon, bond. These bonds, often called *zeros*, pay little or no interest, instead providing returns to investors through a redemption price that is higher than the initial sales price. Corporations were allowed for tax purposes to impute an implied interest expense based on this built-in price appreciation. The government's technique for imputing tax-deductible interest expenses, however, proved to be too generous in the early years of the bonds' lives, so corporations issued these bonds widely to exploit the resulting tax benefit. Ultimately, the Treasury caught on and amended its interest imputation procedure, and the flow of new zeros dried up.

Meanwhile, however, the financial markets had discovered that zeros were useful ways to lock in a long-term investment return. When the supply of primitive zero-coupon bonds ended, financial innovators created derivative zeros by purchasing U.S. Treasury bonds, "stripping" off the coupons, and selling them separately as zeros.

Another tax-induced innovation is the *dual fund*. Under U.S. tax law, capital gains are taxed at lower rates than dividends. The differential means high-tax-bracket investors

UNDERSTANDING THE COMPLEX WORLD OF DERIVATIVES

What are derivatives anyway, and why are people saying such terrible things about them?

Some critics see the derivatives market as a multi-trillion-dollar house of cards composed of interlocking, highly leveraged transactions. They fear that the default of a single large player could stun the world financial system.

But others, including Federal Reserve Chairman Alan Greenspan, say the risk of such a meltdown is negligible. Proponents stress that the market's hazards are more than outweighed by the benefits derivatives provide in helping banks, corporations and investors manage their risks.

Because the science of derivatives is relatively new, there's no easy way to gauge the ultimate impact these instruments will have. There are now more than 1,200 different kinds of derivatives on the market, most of which require a computer program to figure out. Surveying this complex subject, dozens of derivatives experts offered these insights:

Q: What is the broadest definition of derivatives?

A: Derivatives are financial arrangements between two parties whose payments are based on, or "derived" from, the performance of some agreed-upon benchmark. Derivatives can be issued based on currencies, commodities, government or corporate debt, home mortgages, stocks, interest rates, or any combination.

Company stock options, for instance, allow employees and executives to profit from changes in a company's stock price without actually owning shares. Without knowing it, homeowners frequently use a type of privately traded "forward" contract when they apply for a mortgage and lock in a borrowing rate for their house closing, typically for as many as 60 days in the future.

Q: What are the most common forms of derivatives?

A: Derivatives come in two basic categories, option-type contracts and forward-type contracts. These may be exchange-listed, such as futures and stock options, or they may be privately traded.

Options give buyers the right, but not the obligation, to buy or sell an asset at a preset price over a specific period. The option's price is usually a small percentage of the underlying asset's value.

Forward-type contracts, which include forwards, futures and swaps, commit the buyer and the seller to trade a given asset at a set price on a future date. These are "price fixing" agreements that saddle the buyer with the same price risks as actually owning the asset. But normally, no money changes hands until the delivery date, when the contract is often settled in cash rather than by exchanging the asset.

Q: In business, what are they used for?

A: While derivatives can be powerful speculative instruments, businesses most often use them to hedge. For instance, companies often use forwards and exchange-listed futures to protect against fluctuations in currency or commodity prices, thereby helping to manage import and raw-materials costs. Options can serve a similar purpose; interest-rate options such as caps and floors help companies control financing costs in much the same way that caps on adjustable-rate mortgages do for homeowners.

Q: How do over-the-counter derivatives generally originate?

A: A derivatives dealer, generally a bank or securities firm, enters into a private contract with a corporation, investor or another dealer. The contract commits the dealer to provide a return linked to a desired interest rate, currency or other asset. For example, in an interest-rate swap, the dealer might receive a floating rate in return for paying a fixed rate.

Q: Why are derivatives potentially dangerous?

A: Because these contracts expose the two parties to market moves with little or no money actually changing hands, they involve leverage. And that leverage may be vastly increased by the terms of a particular contract. In the derivatives that hurt P&G, for instance, a given move in U.S. or German interest rates was multiplied 10 times or more.

When things go well, that leverage provides a big return, compared with the amount of capital at risk. But it also causes equally big losses when markets move the wrong way. Even companies that use derivatives to hedge, rather than speculate, may be at risk, since their operation would rarely produce perfectly offsetting gains.

Q: If they are so dangerous, why are so many businesses using derivatives?

A: They are among the cheapest and most readily available means at companies' disposal to buffer themselves against shocks in currency values, commodity prices and interest rates. Donald Nicoliasen, a Price Waterhouse expert on derivatives, says derivatives "are a new tool in everybody's bag to better manage business returns and risks."

Source: Lee Berton, "Understanding the Complex World of Derivatives," *The Wall Street Journal*, June 14, 1994. Excerpted by permission of *The Wall Street Journal* © 1994 Dow Jones & Company, Inc. All Rights Reserved Worldwide.

prefer capital gains, whereas tax-exempt investors are happy to receive dividends. Entrepreneurs therefore created dual funds (the derivative asset) in which *income* and *capital* shares on a portfolio of stocks (the primitive assets) were sold separately. The income shareholders receive the dividends on the portfolio, plus their share of the initial value when the portfolio is cashed in. The capital shareholders receive their share of initial value plus any accumulated capital gains.

There are plenty of other examples. The Eurobond market came into existence as a response to changes in U.S. tax law. Financial futures markets were stimulated by abandonment in the early 1970s of the system of fixed exchange rates and by new federal regulations that overrode state laws treating some financial futures as gambling arrangements.

The general tendency is clear: Tax and regulatory pressures on the financial system very often lead to unanticipated financial innovations when profit-seeking investors make an end run around the government's restrictions. The constant game of regulatory catch-up sets off another flow of new innovations.

1.5   MARKETS AND MARKET STRUCTURE

Just as securities and financial institutions come into existence as natural responses to investor demands, so too do markets evolve to meet needs. Consider what would happen if organized markets did not exist. Households that wanted to borrow would need to find others that wanted to lend. Inevitably, a meeting place for borrowers and lenders would be settled on, and that meeting place would evolve into a financial market. In old London a pub called Lloyd's launched the maritime insurance industry. A Manhattan curb on Wall Street became synonymous with the financial world.

We can differentiate four types of markets: direct search markets, brokered markets, dealer markets, and auction markets.

A **direct search market** is the least organized market. Here, buyers and sellers must seek each other out directly. One example of a transaction taking place in such a market would be the sale of a used refrigerator in which the seller advertises for buyers in a local newspaper. Such markets are characterized by sporadic participation and low-priced and nonstandard goods. It does not pay most people or firms to seek profits by specializing in such an environment.

The next level of organization is a **brokered market.** In markets where trading in a good is sufficiently active, brokers can find it profitable to offer search services to buyers and sellers. A good example is the real estate market, where economies of scale in searches for available homes and for prospective buyers make it worthwhile for participants to pay brokers to conduct the searches for them. Brokers in given markets develop specialized knowledge on valuing assets traded in that given market.

An important brokered investment market is the so-called *primary market*, where new issues of securities are offered to the public. In the primary market investment bankers act as brokers; they seek out investors to purchase securities directly from the issuing corporation.

Another brokered market is that for large *block transactions*, in which very large blocks of stock are bought or sold. These blocks are so large (technically more than 10,000 shares but usually much larger) that brokers or "block houses" often are engaged to search directly for other large traders, rather than bringing the trade directly to the stock exchange where relatively smaller investors trade.

When trading activity in a particular type of asset increases, **dealer markets** arise. Here, dealers specialize in various assets, purchasing them for their own inventory and selling them for a profit from their inventory. Dealers, unlike brokers, trade assets for their own accounts. The dealer's profit margin is the "bid–asked" spread—the difference between the price at which the dealer buys for and sells from inventory. Dealer markets save traders on search costs because market participants can easily look up prices at which they can buy from or sell to dealers. Obviously, a fair amount of market activity is required before dealing in a market is an attractive source of income. The over-the-counter securities market is one example of a dealer market.

Trading among investors of already issued securities is said to take place in *secondary markets*. Therefore, the over-the-counter market is one example of a secondary market. Trading in secondary markets does not affect the outstanding amount of securities; ownership is simply transferred from one investor to another.

The most integrated market is an **auction market,** in which all transactors in a good converge at one place to bid on or offer a good. The New York Stock Exchange (NYSE) is an example of an auction market. An advantage of auction markets over dealer markets is that one need not search to find the best price for a good. If all participants converge, they can arrive at mutually agreeable prices and thus save the bid–asked spread.

Continuous auction markets (as opposed to periodic auctions such as in the art world) require very heavy and frequent trading to cover the expense of maintaining the market. For this reason, the NYSE and other exchanges set up listing requirements, which limit the shares traded on the exchange to those of firms in which sufficient trading interest is likely to exist.

The organized stock exchanges are also secondary markets. They are organized for investors to trade existing securities among themselves.

Question 4 • Many assets trade in more than one type of market. In what types of markets do the following trade?

a. **Used cars**
b. **Paintings**
c. **Rare coins**

1.6   ONGOING TRENDS

Several important trends have changed the contemporary investment environment:

1. Globalization
2. Securitization
3. Credit enhancement
4. Financial engineering

Each is the logical consequence of the demand and supply forces that give rise to specialized markets and instruments.

Globalization

If a wider range of investment choices can benefit investors, why should we limit ourselves to purely domestic assets? **Globalization** requires efficient communication technology and the dismantling of regulatory constraints. These tendencies in worldwide investment environments have encouraged international investing in recent years.

U.S. investors commonly participate in foreign investment opportunities in several ways: (1) purchase foreign securities using American Depositary Receipts (ADRs), which

ADR HOLDERS FEEL HEAT FROM CRISIS IN MEXICO

NEW YORK—Surprise!

You might have been buying stocks like Telefonos de Mexico on the New York Stock Exchange with dollars and receiving your dividends in dollars. But you were never protected from the risk either that the stock might tumble or that the Mexican currency might collapse.

Investors who have been active buyers of foreign stocks through the purchase of American depositary receipts on U.S. exchanges are finding out the hard way that it's easy to buy them, but well nigh impossible to escape the risks—including the currency risk—foreign shares represent.

Double Whammy

ADRs are negotiable certificates or electronic entries that certify that the holder owns shares of a foreign company that are on deposit in the company's home market. Because they trade on U.S. exchanges and are priced in dollars they are a very convenient way for American investors to buy foreign shares. But their prices reflect not only the underlying value of the company in its home market, but also the relative value of the company's home-market currency against the dollar. In the worst case, both the stock price at home and the home currency could fall, as they did in the case of Mexican stocks in 1994, dealing U.S. holders of ADRs a double whammy.

Foreign companies like ADRs because they can be used to gain additional exposure for their stocks and, less frequently, to actually raise new capital in the U.S. The booming ADR growth for the past few years—a record 7.2 billion ADR shares were traded in the U.S. in 1994—has given American investors access to stocks in countries as disparate as Germany and Belize.

The tremendous growth in ADRs has meant big business for the U.S. exchanges, depositary institutions (usually banks) and brokerage firms that deal in ADRs. At the end of 1994, there were 1,397 depositary receipt programs in the U.S., according to Citicorp. Of the 254 new stocks listed on the Big Board in 1994, 52 were foreign companies, most of which used ADRs. The National Association of Securities Dealers has seven sales representatives scouring the globe to persuade foreign companies to list their shares in the U.S.

But Mexico's financial crisis, and the resulting losses to U.S. investors, is likely to slow the pace at which foreign companies come to U.S. markets, at least in the near term.

"We're cautious about Latin America in the short term," said Mark A. Bach, vice president and ADR global sales director at Citibank. "And the pace of activity from China has been slowing, and I don't see it increasing dramatically. But, in the long term, we still think the globalization of markets and the need for global capital raising won't go away."

Source: Dave Kansas, *The Wall Street Journal*, January 12, 1995. Excerpted by permission of *The Wall Street Journal* © 1994 Dow Jones & Company, Inc. All Rights Reserved Worldwide.

are domestically traded securities that represent claims to shares of foreign stocks; (2) purchase foreign securities that are offered in dollars; (3) buy mutual funds that invest internationally; and (4) buy derivative securities with payoffs that depend on prices in foreign security markets.

U.S. investors who wish to purchase foreign shares can often do so using American Depositary Receipts. Brokers who act as intermediaries for such transactions purchase an inventory of stock of some foreign issuer. The broker then issues an ADR that represents a claim to some number of those foreign shares held in inventory. The ADR is denominated in dollars and can be traded on U.S. stock exchanges but is in essence no more than a claim on a foreign stock. Thus, from the investor's point of view, there is no more difference between buying a French versus a U.S. stock than there is in holding a Massachusetts-backed stock compared with a California-based stock. Of course, the investment implications may differ: The nearby box emphasizes that ADRs still expose investors to exchange rate risk.

Many foreign firms are so eager to lure U.S. investors that they will save these investors the expense of paying the higher commissions that are associated with the ADRs. Figure 1.1 shows a case in point. Cadbury Schweppes is a United Kingdom–based corporation that

Figure 1.1

Globalization and
American depositary
receipts.

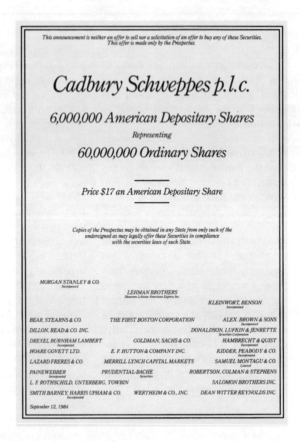

marketed its stock directly to U.S. investors in ADRs. Each ADR represents a claim to 10 shares of Cadbury Schweppes stock.

An example of how far globalization has progressed appears in Figure 1.2. Here, Walt Disney is selling debt claims denominated in European currency units (ECUs), an index of a basket of European currency values. Indeed, with European monetary union scheduled to take effect shortly, there soon should be a single European currency, the euro, that will replace the currencies of participating nations. Such monetary union obviously will be a major milestone in the globalization of markets.

Securitization

Until recently, financial intermediaries served to channel funds from national capital markets to smaller local ones. **Securitization,** however, now allows borrowers to enter capital markets directly. In this procedure pools of loans typically are aggregated into pass-through securities, such as mortgage pool pass-throughs. Then, investors can invest in securities backed by those pools. The transformation of these pools into standardized securities enables issuers to deal in a volume large enough that they can bypass intermediaries. We have already discussed this phenomenon in the context of the securitization of the mortgage market. Today, most conventional mortgages are securitized by government mortgage agencies.

Another example of securitization is the collateralized automobile receivable (CAR), a pass-through arrangement for car loans. Figure 1.3 shows an example of such a note. The

Figure 1.2

Globalization: a debt issue denominated in European currency units.

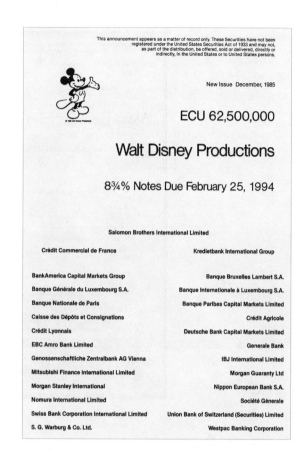

loan originator passes the loan payments through to the holder of the CAR. Aside from mortgages, the biggest asset-backed securities are for credit card debt, car loans, home equity loans, and student loans.

Securitization also has been used to allow U.S. banks to unload their portfolios of shaky loans to developing nations. So-called Brady bonds (named after Nicholas Brady, former secretary of the Treasury) are formed by securitizing bank loans to several countries in shaky fiscal condition. The U.S. banks exchange their loans to developing nations for bonds backed by those loans. The payments that the borrowing nation would otherwise make to the lending bank are directed instead to the holder of the bond. These bonds are traded in capital markets. Therefore, if they choose, banks can remove these loans from their portfolios simply by selling the bonds. In addition, the United States in many cases has enhanced the credit quality of these bonds by designating a quantity of Treasury bonds to serve as partial collateral for the loans. In the event of a foreign default, the holders of the Brady bonds would have claim to the collateral.

Concept **CHECK**   **Question 5** • **When mortgages are pooled into securities, the pass-through agencies (Freddie Mac and Fannie Mae) typically guarantee the underlying mortgage loans. If the homeowner defaults on the loan, the pass-through agency makes good on the loan; the investor in the mortgage-backed security does not bear the credit risk.**

a. Why does the allocation of risk to the pass-through agency rather than the securityholder make economic sense?

b. Why is the allocation of credit risk less of an issue for Brady bonds?

Figure 1.3
Securitization of
automobile loans.

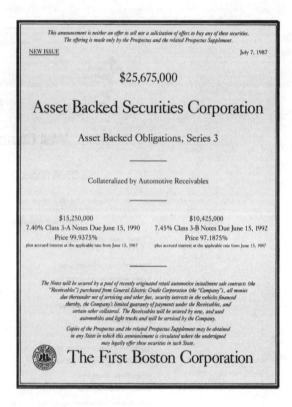

Credit Enhancement

In the past, a corporation that was not in the best financial condition would be able to obtain loans only through commercial banks. The banks' credit departments scrutinized each customer. A business shopping around for a loan might be sized up simultaneously by several different banks.

Today, the credit-hungry corporation can arrange for **credit enhancement.** It engages an insurance company to put its credit behind the corporation's, for a fee. The firm can then float a bond of "enhanced" credit rating directly to the public.

Figure 1.4 shows an example of credit enhancement in a joint financial venture between the Rockefeller Group and Aetna Casualty and Surety. The Rockefeller Group is a privately held corporation and thus exempt from a large part of typical disclosure rules. It cannot issue publicly traded bonds at reasonably low yields without revealing information to the public that it wishes to keep private. Instead, it purchases Aetna's backing. Aetna can perform its own credit analysis, keeping the information revealed confidential.

Financial Engineering

Disparate investor demands elicit a supply of exotic securities. Creative security design often calls for **bundling** primitive and derivative securities into one composite security. One such example appears in Figure 1.5. The Chubb Corporation, with the aid of Goldman, Sachs, has combined three primitive securities—stocks, bonds, and preferred stock—into one hybrid security. Chubb is issuing preferred stock that is convertible into common stock, at the option of the holder, and exchangeable into convertible bonds at the option of the firm. Hence this security is a bundling of preferred stock with several options.

Figure 1.4

Aetna's credit
enhancement of the
Rockefeller Group's
bond.

Offering Circular

$100,000,000

Rockefeller Group International Finance N.V.

13¼% Notes Due 1989

Unconditionally Guaranteed as to Payment of Principal and Interest by

Rockefeller Group, Inc.

and under a Surety Bond Issued by

The Ætna Casualty and Surety Company

Issue Price 99¾%

Principal of, premium, if any, and interest on the Notes will be payable without deduction for, or on account of, United States or Netherlands Antilles withholding taxes, all as set forth herein. Interest will be payable annually on June 21, commencing in 1985.

The Notes will mature on June 21, 1989. The Notes are redeemable (i) as a whole or from time to time in part, on or after June 21, 1987 at a redemption price equal to 101¼% of the principal amount of the Notes if made prior to June 21, 1988 and 100½% of the principal amount of the Notes if made on or after June 21, 1988, plus, in each case, accrued interest to the date fixed for redemption, and (ii) as a whole at any time in the event of certain developments involving United States or Netherlands Antilles withholding taxes, at their principal amount plus accrued interest to the date fixed for redemption. See "Description of the Notes". The Notes may also be redeemed as a whole, at a redemption price equal to their principal amount plus accrued interest to the date fixed for redemption, at the option of The Ætna Casualty and Surety Company ("Ætna") upon the occurrence of certain events. See "Description of the Surety Bond".

The Notes will be unconditionally guaranteed as to the payment of principal, premium, if any, and interest and certain other amounts by Rockefeller Group, Inc. As a private corporation, Rockefeller Group, Inc., does not disclose financial information to the public. Accordingly, arrangements have been made for payments of principal of, premium, if any, and interest on, and certain other amounts with respect to, the Notes to be guaranteed under a Surety Bond issued by Ætna. See "Description of the Notes" and "Description of the Surety Bond".

Application has been made to list the Notes on the Luxembourg Stock Exchange.

The Notes have not been registered under the United States Securities Act of 1933 and may not be offered or sold, directly or indirectly, in the United States of America, or its territories or possessions or to citizens, nationals or residents thereof, except as set forth herein. See "Underwriting".

A temporary global Note without interest coupons in the amount of $100,000,000 will be delivered to a depositary in London for the account of participants in Euro-clear and CEDEL S.A. on or about June 21, 1984 and will be exchangeable for definitive Notes not earlier than 90 days after the completion of the distribution upon certification that such Notes are not beneficially owned by United States citizens, nationals or residents, as set forth herein. Interest on the Notes will not be payable until issuance of the definitive Notes. See "Description of the Notes—Denomination and Transfer".

MORGAN GUARANTY LTD

AMRO INTERNATIONAL LIMITED	CHASE MANHATTAN LIMITED
CREDIT SUISSE FIRST BOSTON LIMITED	DEUTSCHE BANK AKTIENGESELLSCHAFT
DRESDNER BANK AKTIENGESELLSCHAFT	ENSKILDA SECURITIES
	SKANDINAVISKA ENSKILDA LIMITED
LEHMAN BROTHERS INTERNATIONAL	SAMUEL MONTAGU & CO. LIMITED
SHEARSON LEHMAN/AMERICAN EXPRESS INC	
ORION ROYAL BANK LIMITED	SOCIÉTÉ GÉNÉRALE
SOCIÉTÉ GÉNÉRALE DE BANQUE S.A.	SWISS BANK CORPORATION INTERNATIONAL LIMITED
UNION BANK OF SWITZERLAND (SECURITIES) LIMITED	S. G. WARBURG & CO. LTD.

May 25, 1984

Quite often, creating a security that appears to be attractive requires **unbundling** of an asset. An example is given in Figure 1.6. There, a mortgage pass-through certificate is unbundled into two classes. Class 1 receives only principal payments from the mortgage pool, whereas class 2 receives only interest payments. Another example of unbundling was given in the discussion of financial innovation and CMOs in Section 1.4.

The process of bundling and unbundling is called **financial engineering,** which refers to the creation and design of securities with custom-tailored characteristics, often regarding exposures to various source of risk. Financial engineers view securities as bundles of (possibly risky) cash flows that may be carved up and rearranged according to the needs or desires of traders in the security markets. Many of the derivative securities we spoke of earlier in the chapter are products of financial engineering.

Question 6 • How can tax motives contribute to the desire for unbundling?

1.7   ON THE RELATIONSHIP BETWEEN HOUSEHOLDS AND BUSINESSES

Occasional waves of takeovers, particularly with the development of exotic defenses, bring to the surface public misgivings about "unproductive speculation" on Wall Street. Many see a need to curb such activities that purportedly divert funds from productive uses and

Figure 1.5
Bundling creates a
complex security.

3,000,000 Shares
The Chubb Corporation
$4.25 Convertible Exchangeable Preferred Stock
(Stated Value $50 Per Share)

The $4.25 Convertible Exchangeable Preferred Stock (the "Preferred Stock"), $1.00 par value, of The Chubb Corporation (the "Corporation") offered hereby is convertible at the option of the holder at any time, unless previously redeemed, into Common Stock, $1.00 par value, of the Corporation (the "Common Stock") at the rate of .722 shares of Common Stock for each share of Preferred Stock (equivalent to a conversion price of $69.25 per share), subject to adjustment under certain conditions. On March 25, 1985, the last reported sale price of the Common Stock on the New York Stock Exchange was $57¼ per share.

The Preferred Stock also is exchangeable in whole at the sole option of the Corporation on any dividend payment date beginning April 15, 1988 for the Corporation's 8½% Convertible Subordinated Debentures due April 15, 2010 (the "Debentures") at the rate of $50 principal amount of Debentures for each share of Preferred Stock. See "Description of Debentures".

The Preferred Stock is redeemable for cash at any time, in whole or in part, at the option of the Corporation at redemption prices declining to $50 on April 15, 1995, plus accrued and unpaid dividends to the redemption date. However, the Preferred Stock is not redeemable prior to April 15, 1988 unless the closing price of the Common Stock on the New York Stock Exchange shall have equaled or exceeded 140% of the then effective conversion price per share for at least 20 consecutive trading days ending within 5 days prior to the notice of redemption. Dividends on the Preferred Stock will be cumulative and are payable quarterly on January 15, April 15, July 15 and October 15. The initial dividend will be payable on July 15, 1985 and will accrue from the date of issuance. See "Description of Preferred Stock".

Application will be made to list the Preferred Stock on the New York Stock Exchange.

THESE SECURITIES HAVE NOT BEEN APPROVED OR DISAPPROVED BY THE SECURITIES AND EXCHANGE COMMISSION NOR HAS THE COMMISSION PASSED UPON THE ACCURACY OR ADEQUACY OF THIS PROSPECTUS. ANY REPRESENTATION TO THE CONTRARY IS A CRIMINAL OFFENSE.

	Initial Public Offering Price	Underwriting Discount	Proceeds to Corporation(1)
Per Share	$50.00	$1.375	$48.625
Total	$150,000,000	$4,125,000	$145,875,000

(1) Before deducting expenses payable by the Corporation estimated at $500,000.

The shares of Preferred Stock are offered severally by the Underwriters, as specified herein, subject to receipt and acceptance by them and subject to their right to reject any order in whole or in part. It is expected that certificates for the shares of Preferred Stock will be ready for delivery at the offices of Goldman, Sachs & Co., New York, New York on or about April 2, 1985.

Goldman, Sachs & Co.

The date of this Prospectus is March 26, 1985.

cause plant shutdowns and unemployment. An important related issue that may not come up in the public debate is the inherent conflict among households, the direct and indirect shareholders of businesses, and the professional managers who run them. This issue is an important feature of the investment environment.

The control structure of a typical, publicly traded firm is modeled on a democratic arrangement. Its main features are, in principle, as follows:

1. No one has to own shares. Willing investors buy shares, satisfied shareholders can buy more, and unsatisfied shareholders can unload the stock at any time.

2. Management has to disclose to the public a great deal of information, which is audited by independent experts.

3. Important decisions of management must be approved by voting in shareholder meetings.

4. In any election, the rule is one-share/one-vote; thus shareholder voting power is proportional to the shareholder's stake in the corporation. Absentee shareholders can vote by proxy.

5. Corporate management, from the president down, is subject to control by the board of directors led by the chairperson. Individual directors are elected by shareholders, who can unseat directors in any meeting. Shareholder meetings can be called by shareholders, as well as by management. One annual meeting is mandatory.

Figure 1.6
Unbundling of mortgages into principal- and interest-only securities.

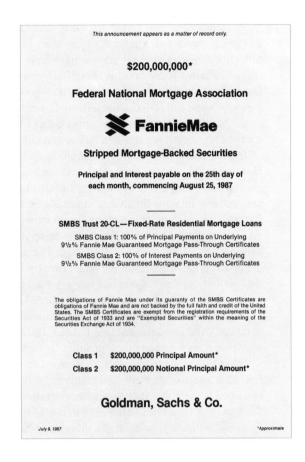

Given such a system, what can go wrong? If management is unsatisfactory, the board should oust it. If the board members are not on their toes, shareholders will oust them. In the end, if all works as intended, the corporation will be run by management that executes the (aggregate) will of shareholders.

Management, however, can hurt shareholders in two ways. First, incompetent managers may be very expensive to shareholders (and to corporate employees, who also are stakeholders). Second, management's control of pecuniary rewards and other perquisites comes directly from the pockets of shareholders. This creates a conflict between management and shareholders, which is called the **agency problem.** A great deal of financial theory is dedicated to the analysis of this problem. Corporate executives are probably the best-compensated professionals in the nation, which is fine as long as the shareholders are happy. After all, competition itself should ensure that managerial resource compensation is allocated as efficiently as any production factor in the economy.

This is not a minor issue, because a lot of money is at stake. The size of modern corporations and the uncertainties associated with complex and changing environments and technologies mean a large amount of wealth is put at risk every day.

When we have large corporations and many diversified investors, however, control is very dispersed. In many cases even the largest shareholder holds less than 2% of the shares. Managers, through executive stock options and compensation shares, may become major shareholders. By and by, one often finds that management seems to control the board, rather than vice versa.

What about proxy fights to wrest control of the firm from current management? Evidence shows that the cost of an average proxy fight is in the millions of dollars. Shareholders who attempt such a fight have to use their own funds. Management that defends against it uses corporate coffers in addition to already existing communication channels to shareholders at large. Little wonder that few such attempts are made. When they are, most fail. Dissidents win some seats on the board of directors in a majority of cases, but seldom enough to assume control of the company. Ousting the management of a large corporation is a modern-day version of David's battle with Goliath.

In fact, shareholders' greatest protection is the hunger and might of other businesses. How does this sword of Damocles work? A bad management team, whether incompetent or excessively greedy, causes the firm's shares to sell at a price that reflects its poor performance. Now imagine the management of one business observing another that is underperforming. All it has to do is acquire the underperforming business, fire current management, and put in place its own (presumably better) people; the stock price then should reflect expectations of improved performance. The acquiring firm might therefore be willing to bid up the price of shares of the target firm by as much as 50% to acquire it. In the process, the economy gets rid of one bad management team and becomes more efficient.

Just the threat of this mechanism ought to keep management on its toes. However, give management the ability to engage in expensive takeover defenses (at shareholder expense, of course), and its vulnerability is limited. The danger of antitakeover regulation that allows poor managers to protect their positions is clear.

What about the arguments that takeovers lead to shutdowns and unemployment, and that funds for takeovers are diverted from productive resources? A firm that takes over another one must believe that it can improve operations. If it pays a premium for the acquisition, the acquiring firm must believe it can create additional value to justify the purchase price. Potential efficiency gains might therefore be expected to be an impetus for mergers and acquisitions. Of course, one might argue that some acquisitions are motivated more by tax motives than true economic efficiency, but this seems more a reason to modify tax law than intrude in the market for corporate control.

The argument that takeover funds are diverted from productive uses is without merit. After all, the money that is paid by the acquirer to the target firm's shareholders does not disappear; it is reinvested in financial markets. In the end, the displacement of bad management ought to bring in, if anything, more investment funds in this newly created opportunity.

SUMMARY

1. Real assets are used to produce the goods and services created by an economy. Financial assets are claims to the income generated by real assets. Securities are financial assets. Financial assets are part of an investor's wealth, but not part of national wealth. Instead, financial assets determine how the "national pie" is split up among investors.

2. The three sectors of the financial environment are households, businesses, and government. Households decide on investing their funds. Businesses and government, in contrast, typically need to raise funds.

3. The diverse tax and risk preferences of households create a demand for a wide variety of securities. In contrast, businesses typically find it more efficient to offer relatively uniform types of securities. This conflict gives rise to an industry that creates complex derivative securities from primitive ones.

4. The smallness of households creates a market niche for financial intermediaries, mutual funds, and investment companies. Economies of scale and specialization are factors supporting the investment banking industry.

5. Four types of markets may be distinguished: direct search, brokered, dealer, and auction markets. Securities are sold in all but direct search markets.

6. Four recent trends in the financial environment are globalization, securitization, credit enhancement, and financial engineering.

7. Stockholders own the corporation and, in principle, can oust an unsatisfactory management team. In practice, ouster may be difficult because of the advantage that management has in proxy fights. The threat of takeover helps keep management doing its best for the firm.

Key Terms

real assets	derivative security	securitization
financial assets	direct search market	credit enhancement
financial intermediaries	brokered market	bundling
investment company	dealer markets	unbundling
investment bankers	auction market	financial engineering
pass-through security	globalization	agency problem
primitive security		

Selected Readings

Excellent discussions of financial innovation may be found in:
  Miller, Merton H. "Financial Innovation: The Last Twenty Years and the Next." *Journal of Financial and Quantitative Analysis* 21 (December 1986), pp. 459–71.
  Miller, Merton H. "Financial Innovation: Achievements and Prospects." *Journal of Applied Corporate Finance* 4 (Winter 1992).
Several trends in the capital markets are discussed in:
  Economic Report of the President, which is published annually.

Problems

1. Suppose you discover a treasure chest of $10 billion in cash.
   a. Is this a real or financial asset?
   b. Is society any richer for the discovery?
   c. Are you wealthier?
   d. Can you reconcile your answers to *(b)* and *(c)*? Is anyone worse off as a result of the discovery?

2. Lanni Products is a start-up computer software development firm. It currently owns computer equipment worth $30,000 and has cash on hand of $20,000 contributed by Lanni's owners. For each of the following transactions, identify the real and/or financial assets that trade hands. Are any financial assets created or destroyed in the transaction?
   a. Lanni takes out a bank loan. It receives $50,000 in cash and signs a note promising to pay back the loan over three years.
   b. Lanni uses the cash from the bank plus $20,000 of its own funds to finance the development of new financial planning software.
   c. Lanni sells the software product to Microsoft, which will market it to the public under the Microsoft name. Lanni accepts payment in the form of 1,500 shares of Microsoft stock.
   d. Lanni sells the shares of stock for $80 per share, and uses part of the proceeds to pay off the bank loan.

Figure 1.7
A gold-backed
security.

*This announcement is neither an offer to sell nor a solicitation of an offer to buy any of these Certificates.
This offer is made only by the Offering Memorandum.*

NEW ISSUE   **$100,000,000**   July 7, 1987

AMERICAN GOLD CERTIFICATES

Due July 1, 1991

- *American Gold Certificates represent physical allocated gold bullion
insured and held in safekeeping at Bank of Delaware.*
- *Anytime during the four-year period, the certificate holder
may request physical delivery of the gold.*

*Copies of the Offering Memorandum may be obtained in any State from only such of the undersigned
as may legally offer these certificates in such State.*

J. W. KORTH CAPITAL MARKETS, INC.

THE CHICAGO CORPORATION	COWEN & CO.	DOMINICK & DOMINICK INCORPORATED
FIRST ALBANY CORPORATION		GRIFFIN, KUBIK, STEPHENS & THOMPSON, INC.
INTERSTATE SECURITIES CORPORATION		JANNEY MONTGOMERY SCOTT INC.
McDONALD & COMPANY SECURITIES, INC.		PACIFIC SECURITIES, INC.
RONEY & CO.	STEPHENS INC.	UMIC, INC.
VINING-SPARKS SECURITIES, INC.		WESTCAP SECURITIES, INC.
BAKER, WATTS & CO.		BARCLAY INVESTMENTS, INC.
BIRR, WILSON SECURITIES, INC.		D. A. DAVIDSON & CO. INCORPORATED
INDEPENDENCE SECURITIES, INC.		JESUP & LAMONT SECURITIES CO., INC.
EMMETT A. LARKIN CO., INC.		SCOTT & STRINGFELLOW, INC.
SEIDLER AMDEC SECURITIES INC.		UNDERWOOD, NEUHAUS & CO. INCORPORATED

3. Reconsider Lanni Products from Problem 2.
   a. Prepare its balance sheet just after it gets the bank loan. What is the ratio of real assets to total assets?
   b. Prepare the balance sheet after Lanni spends the $70,000 to develop the product. What is the ratio of real assets to total assets?
   c. Prepare the balance sheet after it accepts payment of shares from Microsoft. What is the ratio of real assets to total assets?

4. Examine the balance sheet of the financial sector. What is the ratio of tangible assets to total assets? What is the ratio for nonfinancial firms? Why should this difference be expected?

5. In the 1960s, the U.S. government instituted a 30% withholding tax on interest payments on bonds sold in the United States to overseas investors. (It has since been repealed.) What connection does this have to the contemporaneous growth of the huge Eurobond market, where U.S. firms issue dollar-denominated bonds overseas?

6. Consider Figure 1.7, which describes an issue of American gold certificates.
   a. Is this issue a primary or secondary market transaction?
   b. Are the certificates primitive or derivative assets?
   c. What market niche is filled by this offering?

7. Why would you expect securitization to take place only in highly developed capital markets?

8. Suppose that you are an executive of General Motors, and that a large share of your potential income is derived from year-end bonuses that depend on GM's annual profits.
   a. Would purchase of GM stock be an effective hedging strategy for the executive who is worried about the uncertainty surrounding her bonus?
   b. Would purchase of Toyota stock be an effective hedge strategy?

9. Consider again the GM executive in Problem 8. In light of the fact that the design of the annual bonus exposes the executive to risk that she would like to shed, why doesn't GM instead pay her a fixed salary that doesn't entail this uncertainty?

10. What is the relationship between securitization and the role of financial intermediaries in the economy? What happens to financial intermediaries as securitization progresses?

11. Many investors would like to invest part of their portfolios in real estate, but obviously cannot on their own purchase office buildings or strip malls. Explain how this situation creates a profit incentive for investment firms that can sponsor REITs (real estate investment trusts).

12. Financial engineering has been disparaged as nothing more than paper shuffling. Critics argue that resources that go to *rearranging wealth* (i.e., bundling and unbundling financial assets) might better be spent on *creating* wealth (i.e., creating real assets). Evaluate this criticism. Are there any benefits realized by creating an array of derivative securities from various primary securities?

13. Although we stated that real assets comprise the true productive capacity of an economy, it is hard to conceive of a modern economy without well-developed financial markets and security types. How would the productive capacity of the U.S. economy be affected if there were no markets in which one could trade financial assets?

14. Why does it make sense that the first futures markets introduced in 19th-century America were for trades in agricultural products? For example, why did we not see instead futures for goods such as paper or pencils?

solutions to
Concept CHECKS

1. The real assets are patents, customer relations, and the college education. These assets enable individuals or firms to produce goods or services that yield profits or income. Lease obligations are simply claims to pay or receive income and do not in themselves create new wealth. Similarly, the $5 bill is only a paper claim on the government and does not produce wealth.

2. The car loan is a primitive security. Payments on the loan depend only on the solvency of the borrower.

3. The borrower has a financial liability, the loan owed to the bank. The bank treats the loan as a financial asset.

4. *a.* Used cars trade in direct search markets when individuals advertise in local newspapers, and in dealer markets at used-car lots or automobile dealers.

   b. Paintings trade in broker markets when clients commission brokers to buy or sell art for them, in dealer markets at art galleries, and in auction markets.

   c. Rare coins trade mostly in dealer markets in coin shops, but they also trade in auctions and in direct search markets when individuals advertise they want to buy or sell coins.

5. *a.* The pass-through agencies are far better equipped to evaluate the credit risk associated with the pool of mortgages. They are constantly in the market, have ongoing relationships with the originators of the loans, and find it economical to set up "quality control" departments to monitor the credit risk of the mortgage pools. Therefore, the pass-through agencies are better able to incur the risk; they charge for this "service" via a "guarantee fee."

   b. Investors might not find it worthwhile to purchase these securities if they had to assess the credit risk of these loans for themselves. It is far cheaper for them to allow the agencies to collect the guarantee fee. In contrast to mortgage-backed securities, which are backed by pools of large numbers of mortgages, the Brady bonds are backed by large government loans. It is more feasible for the investor to evaluate the credit quality of a few governments than dozens or hundreds of individual mortgages.

6. Creative unbundling can separate interest or dividend from capital gains income. Dual funds do just this. In tax regimes where capital gains are taxed at lower rates than other income, or where gains can be deferred, such unbundling may be a way to attract different tax clienteles to a security.

MARKETS AND INSTRUMENTS

This chapter covers a range of financial securities and the markets in which they trade. Our goal is to introduce you to the features of various security types. This foundation will be necessary to understand the more analytic material that follows in later chapters. Financial markets are traditionally segmented into **money markets** and **capital markets.** Money market instruments include short-term, marketable, liquid, low-risk debt securities. Money market instruments sometimes are called *cash equivalents*, or just *cash* for short. Capital markets, in contrast, include longer-term and riskier securities. Securities in the capital market are much more diverse than those found within the money market. For this reason, we will subdivide the capital market into four segments: longer-term fixed-income markets, equity markets, and the derivative markets for options and futures. We first describe money market instruments and how to measure their yields. We then move

on to fixed-income and equity securities. We explain the structure of various stock market indexes in this chapter because market benchmark portfolios play an important role in portfolio construction and evaluation. Finally, we survey the derivative security markets for options and futures contracts.

2.1   THE MONEY MARKET

The money market is a subsector of the fixed-income market. It consists of very short-term debt securities that usually are highly marketable. Many of these securities trade in large denominations, and so are out of the reach of individual investors. Money market funds, however, are easily accessible to small investors. These mutual funds pool the resources of many investors and purchase a wide variety of money market securities on their behalf.

Figure 2.1 is a reprint of a money rates listing from *The Wall Street Journal*. It includes the various instruments of the money market that we will describe in detail. Table 2.1 lists outstanding volume in 1996 of the major instruments of the money market.

Figure 2.1

Rates on money market securities.

MONEY RATES

Tuesday, October 14, 1997

The key U.S. and foreign annual interest rates below are a guide to general levels but don't always represent actual transactions.

PRIME RATE: 8.50% (effective 3/26/97). The base rate on corporate loans posted by at least 75% of the nation's 30 largest banks.

DISCOUNT RATE: 5.00%. The charge on loans to depository institutions by the Federal Reserve Banks.

FEDERAL FUNDS: 5 7/8% high, 5 1/2% low, 5 5/8% near closing bid, 5 3/4% offered. Reserves traded among commercial banks for overnight use in amounts of $1 million or more. Source: Prebon Yamane (U.S.A.) Inc.

CALL MONEY: 7.25% (effective 3/27/97). The charge on loans to brokers on stock exchange collateral. Source: Dow Jones.

COMMERCIAL PAPER placed directly by General Electric Capital Corp.: 5.48% 30 to 39 days; 5.48% 40 to 89 days; 5.55% 90 to 270 days.

COMMERCIAL PAPER: High-grade unsecured notes sold through dealers by major corporations: 5.48% 30 days; 5.45% 60 days; 5.50% 90 days.

CERTIFICATES OF DEPOSIT: 5.20% one month; 5.23% two months; 5.28% three months; 5.62% six months; 5.84% one year. Average of top rates paid by major New York banks on primary new issues of negotiable C.D.s, usually on amounts of $1 million and more. The minimum unit is $100,000. Typical rates in the secondary market: 5.57% one month; 5.68% three months; 5.75% six months.

BANKERS ACCEPTANCES: 5.54% 30 days; 5.54% 60 days; 5.56% 90 days; 5.56% 120 days; 5.57% 150 days; 5.57% 180 days. Offered rates of negotiable, bank-backed business credit instruments typically financing an import order.

LONDON LATE EURODOLLARS: 5 5/8% - 5 1/2% one month; 5 11/16% - 5 9/16% two months; 5 3/4% - 5 5/8% three months; 5 25/32% - 5 21/32% four months; 5 13/16% - 5 11/16% five months; 5 27/32% - 5 23/32% six months.

LONDON INTERBANK OFFERED RATES (LIBOR): 5 5/8% one month; 5 25/32% three months; 5 27/32% six months; 6 1/32% one year. The average of interbank offered rates for dollar deposits in the London market based on quotations at five major banks. Effective rate for contracts entered into two days from date appearing at top of this column.

FOREIGN PRIME RATES: Canada 5.25%; Germany 3.60%; Japan 1.625%; Switzerland 3.625 (eff. 10/14/97). %; Britain 7.00%. These rate indications aren't directly comparable; lending practices vary widely by location.

TREASURY BILLS: Results of the Tuesday, October 14, 1997, auction of short-term U.S. government bills, sold at a discount from face value in units of $10,000 to $1 million: 4.98% 13 weeks; 5.12% 26 weeks.

OVERNIGHT REPURCHASE RATE: 5.46%. Dealer financing rate for overnight sale and repurchase of Treasury securities. Source: Dow Jones.

FEDERAL HOME LOAN MORTGAGE CORP. (Freddie Mac): Posted yields on 30-year mortgage commitments. Delivery within 30 days 7.47%, 60 days 7.50%, standard conventional fixed-rate mortgages; 5.625%, 2% rate capped one-year adjustable rate mortgages. Source: Dow Jones.

FEDERAL NATIONAL MORTGAGE ASSOCIATION (Fannie Mae): Posted yields on 30 year mortgage commitments (priced at par) for delivery within 30 days 7.41%, 60 days 7.46%, standard conventional fixed rate-mortgages; 6.60%, 6/2 rate capped one-year adjustable rate mortgages. Source: Dow Jones.

MERRILL LYNCH READY ASSETS TRUST: 5.08%. Annualized average rate of return after expenses for the past 30 days; not a forecast of future returns.

Source: The Wall Street Journal, October 15, 1997. Reprinted by permission of The Wall Street Journal, © 1997 Dow Jones & Company, Inc. All Rights Reserved Worldwide.

Table 2.1   Components of the Money Market (December 1996)

	$ Billion
Repurchase agreements	$191.1
Small-denomination time deposits*	948.6
Large-denomination time deposits[†]	494.3
Eurodollars	109.6
Short-term Treasury securities[‡]	449.4
Bankers' acceptances[‡]	11.6
Commercial paper[‡]	479.1

*Less than $100,000 denomination.

[†]More than $100,000 denomination.

[‡]October 1996.

Source: Data from Economic Report of the President. U.S. Government Printing Office, 1996.

Treasury Bills

U.S. *Treasury bills* (T-bills, or just bills, for short) are the most marketable of all money market instruments. T-bills represent the simplest form of borrowing: The government raises money by selling bills to the public. Investors buy the bills at a discount from the stated maturity value. At the bill's maturity, the holder receives from the government a payment equal to the face value of the bill. The difference between the purchase price and ultimate maturity value constitutes the investor's earnings.

T-bills with initial maturities of 91 days or 182 days are issued weekly. Offerings of 52-week bills are made monthly. Sales are conducted via auction, at which investors can submit competitive or noncompetitive bids.

A competitive bid is an order for a given quantity of bills at a specific offered price. The order is filled only if the bid is high enough relative to other bids to be accepted. If the bid is high enough to be accepted, the bidder gets the order at the bid price. Thus the bidder risks paying one of the highest prices for the same bill (bidding at the top), against the hope of bidding "at the tail," that is, making the cutoff at the lowest price.

A noncompetitive bid is an unconditional offer to purchase bills at the average price of the successful competitive bids. The Treasury ranks bids by offering price and accepts bids in order of descending price until the entire issue is absorbed by the competitive plus noncompetitive bids. Competitive bidders face two dangers: They may bid too high and overpay for the bills or bid too low and be shut out of the auction. Noncompetitive bidders, by contrast, pay the average price for the issue, and all noncompetitive bids are accepted up to a maximum of $1 million per bid. In recent years, noncompetitive bids have absorbed between 10% and 25% of the total auction.

Individuals can purchase T-bills directly at auction or on the secondary market from a government securities dealer. T-bills are highly liquid; that is, they are easily converted to cash and sold at low transaction cost and with not much price risk. Unlike most other money market instruments, which sell in minimum denominations of $100,000, T-bills sell in minimum denominations of only $10,000. The income earned on T-bills is exempt from all state and local taxes, another characteristic distinguishing them from other money market instruments.

Bank Discount Yields   T-bill yields are not quoted in the financial pages as effective annual rates of return. Instead, the **bank discount yield** is used. To illustrate this method, consider a $10,000 par value T-bill sold at $9,600 with a maturity of a half-year, or 182 days. The $9,600 investment provides $400 in earnings. The rate of return on the investment is defined as dollars earned per dollar invested, in this case,

$$\frac{\text{Dollars earned}}{\text{Dollars invested}} = \frac{\$400}{\$9,600} = .0417 \text{ per six-month period, or } 4.17\% \text{ semiannually}$$

Invested funds increase over the six-month period by a factor of 1.0417. If one continues to earn this rate of return over an entire year, then invested funds grow by a factor of 1.0417 in each six-month period; by year-end, each dollar invested grows with compound interest to $1 \times (1.0417)^2 = \$1.0851$. Therefore, we say that the **effective annual rate** on the bill is 8.51%. The effective annual rate is thus defined as the total growth of funds after a year if all funds are reinvested at the same rate they earn during the actual investment period. This approach to annualizing returns is designed to account for compound interest.

Unfortunately, T-bill yields in the financial pages are quoted using the **bank discount method.** In this approach, the bill's discount from par value, $400, is "annualized" based on a 360-day year. The $400 discount is annualized as follows: $\$400 \times (360/182) = \$791.21$.

Figure 2.2

Treasury bill listings.

TREASURY BILLS						TREASURY BILLS					
	Days to				Ask		Days to				Ask
Maturity	Mat.	Bid	Asked	Chg.	Yld.	Maturity	Mat.	Bid	Asked	Chg.	Yld.
Oct 30 '97	1	4.33	4.29	+0.11	4.35	Feb 26 '98	120	5.11	5.09	+0.23	5.25
Nov 06 '97	8	4.72	4.68	+0.10	4.75	Mar 05 '98	127	5.13	5.11	+0.19	5.28
Nov 13 '97	15	5.04	5.00	+0.17	5.08	Mar 12 '98	134	5.10	5.08	+0.18	5.25
Nov 20 '97	22	4.85	4.81	+0.15	4.89	Mar 19 '98	141	5.07	5.05	+0.16	5.22
Nov 28 '97	30	4.93	4.89	+0.19	4.98	Mar 26 '98	148	4.92	4.90	+0.17	5.07
Dec 04 '97	36	5.02	4.98	+0.16	5.07	Apr 02 '98	155	5.11	5.09	+0.18	5.28
Dec 11 '97	43	5.04	5.00	+0.17	5.10	Apr 09 '98	162	5.11	5.09	+0.18	5.28
Dec 18 '97	50	5.04	5.00	+0.18	5.10	Apr 16 '98	169	5.13	5.11	+0.17	5.31
Dec 26 '97	58	5.09	5.05	+0.18	5.16	Apr 23 '98	176	5.13	5.12	+0.17	5.32
Jan 02 '98	65	5.03	5.01	+0.21	5.13	Apr 30 '98	183	5.13	5.11	+0.17	5.32
Jan 08 '98	71	5.14	5.12	+0.19	5.24	**Apr 30 '98**	**183**	**5.12**	**5.11**	**+0.16**	**5.32**
Jan 15 '98	78	5.10	5.08	+0.16	5.21	May 28 '98	211	5.13	5.11	+0.17	5.32
Jan 22 '98	85	5.10	5.09	+0.18	5.22	Jun 25 '98	239	5.13	5.11	+0.17	5.33
Jan 29 '98	92	5.10	5.08	+0.19	5.22	Jul 23 '98	267	5.14	5.12	+0.17	5.35
Jan 29 '98	92	5.11	5.10	+0.20	5.24	Aug 20 '98	295	5.13	5.11	+0.15	5.35
Feb 05 '98	99	6.12	6.10	+1.17	6.29	Sep 17 '98	323	5.12	5.10	+0.15	5.36
Feb 12 '98	106	5.13	5.11	+0.20	5.26	Oct 15 '98	351	5.13	5.12	+0.15	5.39
Feb 19 '98	113	5.13	5.11	+0.21	5.27						

Source: The Wall Street Journal, October 29, 1997. Prices are for October 28, 1997.
Reprinted by permission of The Wall Street Journal, © 1997 Dow Jones & Company,
Inc. All Rights Reserved Worldwide.

This figure is divided by the $10,000 par value of the bill to obtain a bank discount yield of 7.912%.

We can highlight the source of the discrepancy between the bank discount yield and effective annual yield by examining the bank discount formula:

$$r_{BD} = \frac{10,000 - P}{10,000} \times \frac{360}{n} \tag{2.1}$$

where P is the bond price, n is the maturity of the bill in days, and r_{BD} is the bank discount yield. (Actually, because of the convention of *skip-day settlement,* n is reported as though the T-bill sale will not be consummated until one business day after the date on which the T-bill price is quoted. For example, Figure 2.2, which reports prices for October 28, 1997, shows only one day to maturity for the first bill despite the fact that two days remain until maturity.)

The bank discount formula thus takes the bill's discount from par as a fraction of par value and then annualizes by the factor $360/n$. There are three problems with this technique, and they all combine to reduce the bank discount yield compared with the effective annual yield. First, the bank discount yield is annualized using a 360-day year rather than a 365-day year. Second, the annualization technique uses simple interest rather than compound interest. Multiplication by $360/n$ does not account for the ability to earn interest on interest, which is the essence of compounding. Finally, the denominator in the first term in equation 2.1 is the par value, $10,000, rather than the purchase price of the bill, P. We want an interest rate to tell us the income that we can earn per dollar invested, but dollars invested here are P, not $10,000. Less than $10,000 is required to purchase the bill.

Figure 2.2 shows Treasury bill listings from *The Wall Street Journal* for prices on October 28, 1997. The discount yield on the bill maturing on January 29, 1998, is 5.11 based on the bid price of the bond and 5.10% based on the asked price. (The bid price is the price at which a customer can sell the bill to a dealer in the security, whereas the asked price is the price at which the customer can buy a security from a dealer. The difference in bid and asked prices is a source of profit to the dealer.)

To determine the bill's true market price, we must solve equation 2.1 for P. Rearranging equation 2.1, we obtain

$$P = 10,000 \times [1 - r_{BD} \times (n/360)] \tag{2.2}$$

Equation 2.2 in effect first "de-annualizes" the bank discount yield to obtain the actual proportional discount from par, then finds the fraction of par for which the bill sells (which is the expression in brackets), and finally multiplies the result by par value, or $10,000. In the case at hand, n = 92 days for a January 29 maturity bill. The discount yield based on the asked price is 5.10% or .0510, so the asked price of the bill is

$$\$10,000 \times [1 - .0510 \times (92/360)] = \$9,869.667$$

Concept CHECK

Question 1 • Find the bid price of the preceding bill based on the bank discount yield at bid.

The "yield" column in Figure 2.2 is the **bond equivalent yield** of the T-bill. This is the bill's yield over its life, assuming that it is purchased for the asked price. The bond equivalent yield is the return on the bill over the period corresponding to its remaining maturity multiplied by the number of such periods in a year. Therefore, the bond equivalent yield, r_{BEY}, is

$$r_{BEY} = \frac{10,000 - P}{P} \times \frac{365}{n} \tag{2.3}$$

In equation 2.3 the holding period return of the bill is computed in the first term on the right-hand side as the price increase of the bill if held until maturity per dollar paid for the bill. The second term annualizes that yield. Note that the bond equivalent yield correctly uses the price of the bill in the denominator of the first term and uses a 365-day year in the second term to annualize. (In leap years, we use a 366-day year in equation 2.3.) It still, however, uses a simple interest procedure to annualize, also known as *annual percentage rate,* or APR, and so problems still remain in comparing yields on bills with different maturities. Nevertheless, yields on most securities with less than a year to maturity are annualized using a simple interest approach.

Thus, for our demonstration bill,

$$r_{BEY} = \frac{10,000 - 9,869.667}{9,869.667} \times \frac{365}{92} = .0524$$

or 5.24%, as reported in *The Wall Street Journal.*

A convenient formula relating the bond equivalent yield to the bank discount yield is

$$r_{BEY} = \frac{365 \times r_{BD}}{360 - (r_{BD} \times n)}$$

where r_{BD} is the discount yield. Here, r_{BD} = .0510, so that

$$r_{BEY} = \frac{365 \times .0510}{360 - (.0510 \times 92)} = .0524$$

as derived previously.

Finally, the effective annual yield on the bill based on the ask price, $9,869.667, is obtained from a compound interest calculation. The 92-day return equals

$$\frac{10,000 - 9,869.667}{9,869.667} = .0132, \text{ or } 1.32\%$$

Annualizing, we find that funds invested at this rate would grow over the course of a year by the factor $(1.0132)^{365/92} = 1.0534$, implying an effective annual yield of 5.34%.

This example illustrates the general rule that the bank discount yield is less than the bond equivalent yield, which in turn is less than the compounded, or effective, annual yield.

Certificates of Deposit

A **certificate of deposit,** or CD, is a time deposit with a bank. Time deposits may not be withdrawn on demand. The bank pays interest and principal to the depositor only at the end of the fixed term of the CD. CDs issued in denominations greater than $100,000 are usually negotiable, however; that is, they can be sold to another investor if the owner needs to cash in the certificate before its maturity date. Short-term CDs are highly marketable, although the market significantly thins out for maturities of six months or more. CDs are treated as bank deposits by the Federal Deposit Insurance Corporation, so they are insured for up to $100,000 in the event of a bank insolvency.

Commercial Paper

Large, well-known companies often issue their own short-term unsecured debt notes rather than borrow directly from banks. These notes are called **commercial paper.** Very often, commercial paper is backed by a bank line of credit, which gives the borrower access to cash that can be used (if needed) to pay off the paper at maturity.

Commercial paper maturities range up to 270 days; longer maturities would require registration with the Securities and Exchange Commission and so are almost never issued. Most often, commercial paper is issued with maturities of less than one or two months. Usually, it is issued in multiples of $100,000. Therefore, small investors can invest in commercial paper only indirectly, via money market mutual funds.

Commercial paper is considered to be a fairly safe asset, because a firm's condition presumably can be monitored and predicted over a term as short as one month. Many firms issue commercial paper intending to roll it over at maturity, that is, issue new paper to obtain the funds necessary to retire the old paper. If lenders become complacent about a firm's prospects and grant rollovers heedlessly, they can suffer big losses. When Penn Central defaulted in 1970, it had $82 million of commercial paper outstanding. However, the Penn Central episode was the only major default on commercial paper in the past 40 years. Largely because of the Penn Central default, almost all commercial paper today is rated for credit quality by one or more of the following rating agencies: Moody's Investor Services, Standard & Poor's Corporation, Fitch Investor Service, and/or Duff and Phelps.

Bankers' Acceptances

A **banker's acceptance** starts as an order to a bank by a bank's customer to pay a sum of money at a future date, typically within six months. At this stage, it is similar to a postdated check. When the bank endorses the order for payment as "accepted," it assumes responsibility for ultimate payment to the holder of the acceptance. At this point, the acceptance may be traded in secondary markets like any other claim on the bank. Bankers' acceptances are considered very safe assets because traders can substitute the bank's credit standing for their own. They are used widely in foreign trade where the creditworthiness of one trader is unknown to the trading partner. Acceptances sell at a discount from the face value of the payment order, just as T-bills sell at a discount from par value.

Eurodollars

Eurodollars are dollar-denominated deposits at foreign banks or foreign branches of American banks. By locating outside the United States, these banks escape regulation by the Federal Reserve Board. Despite the tag "Euro," these accounts need not be in European banks, although that is where the practice of accepting dollar-denominated deposits outside the United States began.

Most Eurodollar deposits are for large sums, and most are time deposits of less than six months' maturity. A variation on the Eurodollar time deposit is the Eurodollar certificate of deposit. A Eurodollar CD resembles a domestic bank CD except that it is the liability of a non-U.S. branch of a bank, typically a London branch. The advantage of Eurodollar CDs over Eurodollar time deposits is that the holder can sell the asset to realize its cash value before maturity. Eurodollar CDs are considered less liquid and riskier than domestic CDs, however, and thus offer higher yields. Firms also issue Eurodollar bonds, which are dollar-denominated bonds in Europe, although bonds are not a money market investment because of their long maturities.

Repos and Reverses

Dealers in government securities use **repurchase agreements,** also called "repos" or "RPs," as a form of short-term, usually overnight, borrowing. The dealer sells government securities to an investor on an overnight basis, with an agreement to buy back those securities the next day at a slightly higher price. The increase in the price is the overnight interest. The dealer thus takes out a one-day loan from the investor, and the securities serve as collateral.

A *term repo* is essentially an identical transaction, except that the term of the implicit loan can be 30 days or more. Repos are considered very safe in terms of credit risk because the loans are backed by the government securities. A *reverse repo* is the mirror image of a repo. Here, the dealer finds an investor holding government securities and buys them, agreeing to sell them back at a specified higher price on a future date.

The repo market was upset by several failures of government security dealers in 1985. In these cases the dealers had entered into the typical repo arrangements with investors, pledging government securities as collateral. The investors did not take physical possession of the securities as they could have under the purchase and resale arrangement. Some of the dealers, unfortunately, fraudulently pledged the same securities as collateral in different repos; when the dealers went under, the investors found that they could not collect the securities that they had "purchased" in the first phase of the repo transaction. In the wake of the scandal, repo rates for nonprimary dealers increased, whereas rates for some well-capitalized firms fell as investors became more sensitive to credit risk.[1] Investors can best protect themselves by taking delivery of the securities, either directly or through an agent such as a bank custodian.

Federal Funds

Just as most of us maintain deposits at banks, banks maintain deposits of their own at a Federal Reserve bank. Each member bank of the Federal Reserve System, or "the Fed," is required to maintain a minimum balance in a reserve account with the Fed. The required balance depends on the total deposits of the bank's customers. Funds in the bank's reserve account are called **federal funds,** or *fed funds*. At any time, some banks have more funds than required at the Fed. Other banks, primarily big banks in New York and other financial centers, tend to have a shortage of federal funds. In the federal funds market, banks with

---

[1]Stephen A. Lumpkin, "Repurchase and Reverse Repurchase Agreements," in T. Cook and T. Rowe, eds., *Instruments of the Money Market* (Richmond, Va.: Federal Reserve Bank of Richmond, 1986).

excess funds lend to those with a shortage. These loans, which are usually overnight transactions, are arranged at a rate of interest called the federal funds rate.

Although the fed funds market arose primarily as a way for banks to transfer balances to
meet reserve requirements, today the market has evolved to the point that many large banks
use federal funds in a straightforward way as one component of their total sources of funding. Therefore, the fed funds rate is simply the rate of interest on very short-term loans
among financial institutions.

Brokers' Calls

Individuals who buy stocks on margin borrow part of the funds to pay for the stocks from
their broker. The broker in turn may borrow the funds from a bank, agreeing to repay the
bank immediately (on call) if the bank requests it. The rate paid on such loans is usually
about 1% higher than the rate on short-term T-bills.

The LIBOR Market

The **London Interbank Offered Rate** (LIBOR) is the rate at which large banks in London are willing to lend money among themselves. This rate, which is quoted on dollar-
denominated loans, has become the premier short-term interest rate quoted in the European
money market, and it serves as a reference rate for a wide range of transactions. For example, a corporation might borrow at a floating rate equal to LIBOR plus 2%.

Yields on Money Market Instruments

Although most money market securities are of low risk, they are not risk-free. For example, as we noted earlier, the commercial paper market was rocked by the Penn Central
bankruptcy, which precipitated a default on $82 million of commercial paper. Money mar-
ket investors became more sensitive to creditworthiness after this episode, and the yield
spread between low- and high-quality paper widened.

The securities of the money market do promise yields greater than those on default-free
T-bills, at least in part because of greater relative riskiness. In addition, many investors
require more liquidity; thus they will accept lower yields on securities such as T-bills that
can be quickly and cheaply sold for cash. Figure 2.3 shows that bank CDs, for example,
consistently have paid a risk premium over T-bills. Moreover, that risk premium increased
with economic crises such as the energy price shocks associated with the two OPEC dis-
turbances, the failures of Continental Illinois and Penn Square banks, or the stock market
crash in 1987.

2.2   THE FIXED-INCOME CAPITAL MARKET

The fixed-income capital market is composed of longer-term borrowing instruments than
those that trade in the money market. This market includes Treasury notes and bonds, corporate bonds, municipal bonds, mortgage securities, and federal agency debt.

The title "fixed-income" is given to these securities because most of them promise
either a fixed stream of income or a stream of income that is determined according to a
specified formula. Payments are administered by the issuer or a banking agent on the
issuer's behalf. These payments are fixed unless the issuer is declared bankrupt.

Figure 2.3

The spread between three-month CD and Treasury bill rates.

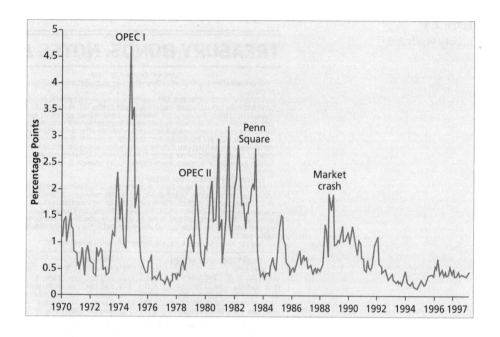

Treasury Notes and Bonds

The U.S. government borrows funds in large part by selling **Treasury notes** and **Treasury bonds.** T-note maturities range up to 10 years, whereas bonds are issued with maturities ranging from 10 to 30 years. Both are issued in denominations of $1,000 or more. Both make semiannual interest payments called *coupon payments*, a name derived from pre-computer days, when investors would literally clip coupons attached to the bond and present a coupon to an agent of the issuing firm to receive the interest payment. Aside from their differing maturities at issuance, the only major distinction between T-notes and T-bonds is that T-bonds may be callable during a given period, usually the last five years of the bond's life. The call provision gives the Treasury the right to repurchase the bond at par value. Although the Treasury hasn't issued these bonds since 1984, several previously issued callable bonds are still outstanding.

Figure 2.4 is an excerpt from a listing of Treasury issues in *The Wall Street Journal.* Note the bond (*arrow*) that matures in October 2000. The coupon income, or interest, paid by the bond is $5\frac{3}{4}\%$ of par value, meaning that a $1,000 face-value bond pays $57.50 in annual interest in two semiannual installments of $28.75 each. The numbers to the right of the colon in the bid and asked prices represent units of $1/32$ of a point.

The bid price of the October 2000 bond is $99\,^{22}/_{32}$, or 99.6875. The asked price is $99\,^{24}/_{32}$, or 99.75. Although bonds are sold in denominations of $1,000 par value, the prices are quoted as a percentage of par value. Thus the bid price of 99.6875 should be interpreted as 99.6875% of par or $996.875 for the $1,000 par value bond. Similarly, the bond could be bought from a dealer for $997.50. The −16 bid change means the closing bid price on this day fell $^{16}/_{32}$ (as a percentage of par value) from the previous day's closing bid price. Finally, the yield to maturity on the bond based on the asked price is 5.84%.

The **yield to maturity** reported in the financial pages is calculated by determining the semiannual yield and then doubling it, rather than compounding it for two half-year

Figure 2.4

Treasury bonds and notes.

TREASURY BONDS, NOTES & BILLS

Tuesday, October 28, 1997
Representative and Indicative Over-the-Counter quotations based on $1 million or more.

Treasury bond, note and bill quotes are as of mid-afternoon. Colons in bond and note bid-and-asked quotes represent 32nds; 101:01 means 101 1/32. Net changes in 32nds. Treasury bill quotes in hundredths, quoted in terms of a rate discount. Days to maturity calculated from settlement date. All yields are based on a one-day settlement and calculated on the offer quote. Current 13-week and 26-week bills are boldfaced. For bonds callable prior to maturity, yields are computed to the earliest call date for issues quoted above par and to the maturity date for issues quoted below par. n-Treasury note. i-Inflation-indexed. wi-When issued. iw-Inflation-indexed when issued; daily change is expressed in basis points.
Source: Dow Jones/Cantor Fitzgerald.

U.S. Treasury strips as of 3 p.m. Eastern time, also based on transactions of $1 million or more. Colons in bid-and-asked quotes represent 32nds; 99:01 means 99 1/32. Net changes in 32nds. Yields calculated on the asked quotation. ci-stripped coupon interest. bp-Treasury bond, stripped principal. np-Treasury note, stripped principal. For bonds callable prior to maturity, yields are computed to the earliest call date for issues quoted above par and to the maturity date for issues below par.
Source: Bear, Stearns & Co. via Street Software Technology Inc.

GOVT. BONDS & NOTES

Rate	Maturity Mo/Yr	Bid	Asked	Chg.	Ask Yld.	Rate	Maturity Mo./Yr	Bid	Asked	Chg.	Ask Yld.
5⅝	Oct 97n	99:31	100:00	....	5.47	11⅞	Nov 03	129:12	129:18	−34	5.98
5¾	Oct 97n	99:31	100:00	....	5.59	5⅞	Feb 04n	99:16	99:18	−30	5.96
7⅜	Nov 97n	100:00	100:02	−1	5.82	7¼	May 04n	106:22	106:24	−32	5.99
8⅞	Nov 97n	100:03	100:05	....	5.27	12¾	May 04	133:28	134:02	−39	6.00
5⅜	Nov 97n	99:30	100:00	....	5.26	7¼	Aug 04n	106:27	106:29	−32	6.00
6	Nov 97n	99:31	100:01	−1	5.50	13¾	Aug 04	142:16	142:22	−40	6.01
5¼	Dec 97n	99:29	99:31	−1	5.34	7⅞	Nov 04n	110:15	110:19	−34	6.01
6	Dec 97n	100:01	100:03	−1	5.34	11⅝	Nov 04	131:19	131:25	−39	6.02
7⅞	Jan 98n	100:15	100:17	−2	5.22	7½	Feb 05n	108:16	108:18	−34	6.03
						6½	May 05n	102:24	102:26	−34	6.03
6¼	Jul 98n	100:15	100:17	−4	5.51	9⅛	May 04-09	115:31	116:03	−28	6.10
5⅞	Aug 98n	100:04	100:06	−5	5.62	10⅜	Nov 04-09	123:31	124:05	−30	6.10
9¼	Aug 98n	102:24	102:26	−5	5.57	11¾	Feb 05-10	132:22	132:28	−32	6.10
4¾	Aug 98n	99:08	99:10	−5	5.59	10	May 05-10	123:01	123:07	−33	6.11
6⅛	Aug 98n	100:12	100:14	−5	5.57	12¾	Nov 05-10	141:18	141:24	−36	6.10
4¾	Sep 98n	99:07	99:09	−5	5.56	13⅞	May 06-11	151:02	151:08	−34	6.09
6	Sep 98n	100:10	100:12	−5	5.57	14	Nov 06-11	154:00	154:06	−40	6.11
7⅛	Oct 98n	101:12	101:14	−5	5.57	10⅜	Nov 07-12	131:00	131:06	−38	6.16
4¾	Oct 98n	99:03	99:05	−5	5.62	12	Aug 08-13	145:04	145:10	−45	6.18
5⅞	Oct 98n	100:06	100:08	−5	5.62	13¼	May 09-14	157:13	157:19	−46	6.19
6¼	Aug 00n	101:01	101:03	−15	5.82						
6⅛	Sep 00n	100:23	100:25	−15	5.83						
5¾	Oct 00n	99:22	99:24	−16	5.84						
8½	Nov 00n	107:09	107:11	−16	5.83						
5⅝	Nov 00n	99:11	99:13	−15	5.84						
5½	Dec 00n	98:30	99:00	−16	5.85						
5¼	Jan 01n	98:09	98:11	−17	5.81						

Source: The Wall Street Journal, October 29, 1997. Reprinted by permission of The Wall Street Journal, © 1997 Dow Jones & Company, Inc. All Rights Reserved Worldwide.

periods. This use of a simple interest technique to annualize means that the yield is quoted on an annual percentage rate (APR) basis rather than as an effective annual yield. The APR method in this context is also called the *bond equivalent yield*.

You can pick out the callable bonds in Figure 2.4 because a range of years appears in the maturity-date column. These are the years during which the bond is callable. Yields on premium bonds (bonds selling above par value) are calculated as the yield to the first call date, whereas yields on discount bonds are calculated as the yield to the maturity date.

Concept CHECK

Question 2 • Why does it make sense to calculate yields on discount bonds to maturity and yields on premium bonds to the first call date?

Federal Agency Debt

Some government agencies issue their own securities to finance their activities. These agencies usually are formed to channel credit to a particular sector of the economy that

Figure 2.5

Government agency issues.

GOVERNMENT AGENCY & SIMILAR ISSUES

Tuesday, October 21, 1997
Over-the-Counter mid-afternoon quotations based on large transactions, usually $1 million or more. Colons in bid-and-asked quotes represent 32nds; 101:01 means 101 1/32.
All yields are calculated to maturity, and based on the asked quote. * – Callable issue, maturity date shown. For issues callable prior to maturity, yields are computed to the earliest call date for issues quoted above par, or 100, and to the maturity date for issues below par.
Source: Bear, Stearns & Co. via Street Software Technology Inc.

GNMA Mtge. Issues Oct97

Rate	Mat.	Bid	Asked	Yld.
6.00	30Yr	95:03	95:05	6.82
6.50	30Yr	97:24	97:26	6.92
7.00	30Yr	99:26	99:28	7.09
7.50	30Yr	101:22	101:24	7.26
8.00	30Yr	103:14	103:16	7.31
8.50	30Yr	104:22	104:24	7.04
9.00	30Yr	106:18	106:20	6.76
9.50	30Yr	108:11	108:13	6.86
10.00	30Yr	109:17	109:19	7.08
10.50	30Yr	109:29	109:31	7.45
11.00	30Yr	111:17	111:19	7.32

Student Loan Marketing

Rate	Mat.	Bid	Asked	Yld.
5.63	12-97*	100:01	100:02	5.16
5.75	1-98*	100:02	100:03	5.21
7.00	3-98	100:16	100:18	5.36
6.25	6-98	100:12	100:14	5.60
5.82	9-98	99:28	99:30	5.87
6.16	12-99*	99:22	99:25	6.28
7.50	3-00	103:04	103:07	6.02
6.05	9-00	99:26	99:29	6.08
5.88	2-01*	98:14	98:18	6.37
6.38	12-01*	99:26	99:30	6.39
7.00	12-02	103:02	103:08	6.25
7.30	8-12	106:17	106:25	6.57
0.00	10-22	17:10	17:18	7.10

FNMA Issues

Rate	Mat.	Bid	Asked	Yld.
6.05	11-97	100:01	100:02	4.60
9.55	11-97	100:06	100:08	3.75
9.55	12-97	100:18	100:19	4.80
6.05	1-98	100:04	100:05	5.24
5.38	1-98*	99:28	99:29	5.72
8.65	2-98	100:16	100:18	6.55
5.01	2-98	99:28	99:30	5.16

Federal Home Loan Bank

Rate	Mat.	Bid	Asked	Yld.
5.45	11-97	100:00	100:01	4.45
5.63	12-97*	100:01	100:02	5.17
5.65	1-98*	100:02	100:03	5.18
5.75	1-98*	100:02	100:03	5.22
5.78	1-98	100:03	100:04	5.23
5.87	1-98	100:04	100:05	5.27
5.99	2-98	100:04	100:06	5.28
5.80	2-98*	100:02	100:04	3.19
4.98	2-98	99:24	99:26	5.50
6.08	4-98	100:07	100:09	5.47

Federal Farm Credit Bank

Rate	Mat.	Bid	Asked	Yld.
5.50	11-97	100:00	100:01	4.32
5.60	11-97	100:00	100:01	3.81
5.68	11-97	100:00	100:01	4.43
5.51	12-97	101:12	101:13	0.00
5.62	12-97	100:02	100:03	4.63
5.40	12-97	100:00	100:01	4.86
5.63	1-98	100:00	100:01	5.37
5.53	2-98	99:31	100:00	5.46

Farm Credit Fin. Asst. Corp.

Rate	Mat.	Bid	Asked	Yld.
9.38	7-03	113:28	114:02	6.40
9.45	11-03*	103:16	103:22	5.84
8.80	6-05	114:16	114:22	6.34
9.20	9-05*	107:04	107:10	6.42

Tennessee Valley Authority

Rate	Mat.	Bid	Asked	Yld.
5.13	3-98	99:24	99:26	5.57
5.95	9-98	100:03	100:05	5.76
6.25	8-99*	100:04	100:07	6.12
8.38	10-99	104:10	104:13	5.93
6.00	11-00	99:22	99:25	6.08
6.50	8-01	100:29	101:01	6.19
7.45	10-01*	102:02	102:06	6.81
6.88	1-02*	100:26	100:30	6.62
6.88	8-02*	100:26	101:00	6.62

Rate	Mat.	Bid	Asked	Yld.
6.38	5-01	101:08	101:12	5.94
6.75	1-02	101:18	101:22	6.28
12.38	10-02	123:24	123:30	6.64
5.25	9-03	96:06	96:12	5.99
6.38	7-05	100:20	100:26	6.24
6.63	8-06	102:06	102:14	6.26
8.25	9-16	114:12	114:20	6.85
8.63	10-16	118:08	118:16	6.86
9.25	7-17	125:14	125:22	6.86
7.63	1-23	110:30	111:06	6.70
8.88	3-26	123:27	124:03	6.92

World Bank Bonds

Rate	Mat.	Bid	Asked	Yld.
8.38	10-99	104:30	105:01	5.61
8.13	3-01	106:28	107:00	5.80

Financing Corporation

Rate	Mat.	Bid	Asked	Yld.
10.70	10-17	137:07	137:15	7.15
9.80	11-17	132:27	133:03	6.76
9.40	2-18	123:28	124:04	7.13
9.80	4-18	132:13	132:21	6.82
10.00	5-18	134:04	134:12	6.86
10.35	8-18	137:22	137:30	6.89
9.65	11-18	131:01	131:09	6.83
9.90	12-18	133:09	133:17	6.87
9.60	12-18	130:00	130:08	6.87
9.65	3-19	130:27	131:03	6.86
9.70	4-19	131:06	131:14	6.88
9.00	6-19	122:22	122:30	6.94
8.60	9-19	118:18	118:26	6.92

Inter-Amer. Devel. Bank

Rate	Mat.	Bid	Asked	Yld.
9.45	9-98	103:04	103:07	5.67
7.13	9-99	102:08	102:11	5.82
8.50	5-01	106:28	107:00	6.25
6.13	3-06	98:24	98:30	6.29
6.63	3-07	101:22	101:28	6.35
12.25	12-08	142:11	142:19	6.75
8.88	6-09	116:30	117:06	6.72
8.40	9-09	113:28	114:04	6.66
8.50	3-11	114:14	114:22	6.81
7.13	3-23*	92:08	92:16	7.81
7.00	6-25	100:27	101:03	6.91
6.80	10-25	98:17	98:25	6.90

Resolution Funding Corp.

Rate	Mat.	Bid	Asked	Yld.
8.13	10-19	114:14	114:22	6.82
8.88	7-20	122:18	122:26	6.88
9.38	10-20	127:09	127:17	6.96
8.63	1-21	119:07	119:15	6.93
8.63	1-30	118:31	119:07	7.10
8.88	4-30	121:14	121:22	7.15

Source: The Wall Street Journal, October 22, 1997. Reprinted by permission of The Wall Street Journal, © 1997 Dow Jones & Company, Inc. All Rights Reserved Worldwide.

Congress believes might not receive adequate credit through normal private sources. Figure 2.5 reproduces listings of some of these securities from *The Wall Street Journal*. The majority of the debt is issued in support of farm credit and home mortgages.

The major mortgage-related agencies are the Federal Home Loan Bank (FHLB), the Federal National Mortgage Association (FNMA, or Fannie Mae), the Government National Mortgage Association (GNMA, or Ginnie Mae), and the Federal Home Loan Mortgage Corporation (FHLMC, or Freddie Mac). The FHLB borrows money by issuing securities and lends this money to savings and loan institutions to be lent in turn to individuals borrowing for home mortgages.

Freddie Mac and Ginnie Mae were organized to provide liquidity to the mortgage market. Until the pass-through securities sponsored by these agencies were established (see the discussion of mortgages and mortgage-backed securities later in this section), the lack of a secondary market in mortgages hampered the flow of investment funds into mortgages and made mortgage markets dependent on local, rather than national, credit availability.

The farm credit agencies consist of

1. The 12 district Banks for Cooperatives, which make seasonal loans to farm cooperatives.
2. The 12 Federal Land Banks, which make mortgage loans on farm properties.
3. The 12 Federal Intermediate Credit Banks, which provide short term financing for production and marketing of crops and livestock.

Some of these agencies are government owned, and therefore can be viewed as branches of the U.S. government. Thus their debt is fully free of default risk. Ginnie Mae is an example of a government-owned agency. Other agencies, such as the farm credit agencies, the Federal Home Loan Bank, Fannie Mae, and Freddie Mac, are merely federally *sponsored*.

Although the debt of federally sponsored agencies is not explicitly insured by the federal government, it is widely assumed that the government would step in with assistance if an agency neared default. Thus these securities are considered extremely safe assets, and their yield spread above Treasury securities is usually small.

Municipal Bonds

Municipal bonds are issued by state and local governments. They are similar to Treasury and corporate bonds except that their interest income is exempt from federal income taxation. The interest income also is exempt from state and local taxation in the issuing state. Capital gains taxes, however, must be paid on "munis," when the bonds mature or if they are sold for more than the investor's purchase price.

There are basically two types of municipal bonds. These are *general obligation* bonds, which are backed by the "full faith and credit" (i.e., the taxing power) of the issuer, and *revenue bonds*, which are issued to finance particular projects and are backed either by the revenues from that project or by the particular municipal agency operating the project. Typical issuers of revenue bonds are airports, hospitals, and turnpike or port authorities. Obviously, revenue bonds are riskier in terms of default than general obligation bonds.

An *industrial development bond* is a revenue bond that is issued to finance commercial enterprises, such as the construction of a factory that can be operated by a private firm. In effect, these private-purpose bonds give the firm access to the municipality's ability to borrow at tax-exempt rates.

Like Treasury bonds, municipal bonds vary widely in maturity. A good deal of the debt issued is in the form of short-term *tax anticipation notes*, which raise funds to pay for expenses before actual collection of taxes. Other municipal debt is long term and used to fund large capital investments. Maturities range up to 30 years.

The key feature of municipal bonds is their tax-exempt status. Because investors pay neither federal nor state taxes on the interest proceeds, they are willing to accept lower yields on these securities. These lower yields represent a huge savings to state and local governments. Correspondingly, they constitute a huge drain of potential tax revenue from the federal government, and the government has shown some dismay over the explosive increase in use of industrial development bonds.

By the mid-1980s, Congress became concerned that these bonds were being used to take advantage of the tax-exempt feature of municipal bonds rather than as a source of funds for publicly desirable investments. The Tax Reform Act of 1986 placed new restrictions on the issuance of tax-exempt bonds. Since 1988, each state is allowed to issue mortgage revenue and private-purpose tax-exempt bonds only up to a limit of $50 per capita or $150 million, whichever is larger. In fact, the outstanding amount of industrial revenue bonds stopped growing after 1986, as evidenced in Figure 2.6.

An investor choosing between taxable and tax-exempt bonds must compare after-tax returns on each bond. An exact comparison requires a computation of after-tax rates of return that explicitly accounts for taxes on income and realized capital gains. In practice, there is a simpler rule of thumb. If we let t denote the investor's marginal tax bracket and r denote the total before-tax rate of return available on taxable bonds, then $r(1 - t)$ is the after-tax rate available on those securities. If this value exceeds the rate on municipal bonds, r_m, the investor does better holding the taxable bonds. Otherwise, the tax-exempt municipals provide higher after-tax returns.

Figure 2.6

Outstanding tax-exempt debt.

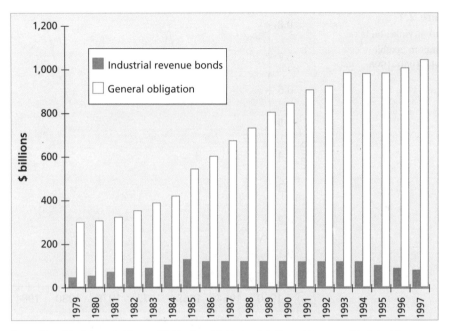

Source: Flow of Funds Accounts: Flows and Outstandings, Washington, D.C.: Board of Governors of the Federal Reserve System, second quarter, 1997.

Table 2.2   Equivalent Taxable Yields Corresponding to Various Tax-Exempt Yields

	Tax-Exempt Yield				
Marginal Tax Rate	**2%**	**4%**	**6%**	**8%**	**10%**
20%	2.5	5.0	7.5	10.0	12.5
30	2.9	5.7	8.6	11.4	14.3
40	3.3	6.7	10.0	13.3	16.7
50	4.0	8.0	12.0	16.0	20.0

One way to compare bonds is to determine the interest rate on taxable bonds that would be necessary to provide an after-tax return equal to that of municipals. To derive this value, we set after-tax yields equal, and solve for the **equivalent taxable yield** of the tax-exempt bond. This is the rate a taxable bond must offer to match the after-tax yield on the tax-free municipal.

$$r(1 - t) = r_m \qquad (2.4)$$

or

$$r = r_m/(1 - t) \qquad (2.5)$$

Thus the equivalent taxable yield is simply the tax-free rate divided by $1 - t$. Table 2.2 presents equivalent taxable yields for several municipal yields and tax rates.

This table frequently appears in the marketing literature for tax-exempt mutual bond funds because it demonstrates to high-tax-bracket investors that municipal bonds offer highly attractive equivalent taxable yields. Each entry is calculated from equation 2.5. If the equivalent taxable yield exceeds the actual yields offered on taxable bonds, the investor is better off after taxes holding municipal bonds. Notice that the equivalent taxable interest rate increases with the investor's tax bracket; the higher the bracket, the more valuable the tax-exempt feature of municipals. Thus high-tax-bracket investors tend to hold municipals.

Figure 2.7

Ratio of yields on tax-exempt to taxable bonds, 1960–1996.

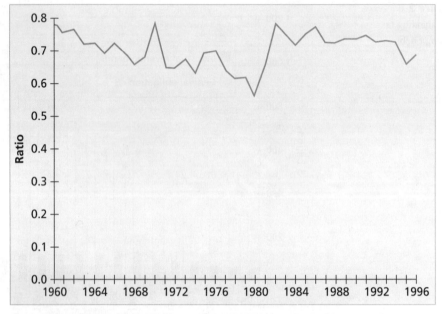

Source: Data from Moody's Municipal and Government Manual, Moody's Investors Service, 1997.

We also can use equation 2.4 or 2.5 to find the tax bracket at which investors are indifferent between taxable and tax-exempt bonds. The cutoff tax bracket is given by solving equation 2.4 for the tax bracket at which after-tax yields are equal. Doing so, we find that

$$t = 1 - \frac{r_m}{r} \tag{2.6}$$

Thus the yield ratio r_m/r is a key determinant of the attractiveness of municipal bonds. The higher the yield ratio, the lower the cutoff tax bracket, and the more individuals will prefer to hold municipal debt. Figure 2.7 graphs the yield ratio since 1960. In recent years, the ratio has hovered at about .73, implying that investors in (federal plus local) tax brackets greater than 27% would derive greater after-tax yields from municipals. Note, however, that it is difficult to control precisely for differences in the risks of these bonds, so the cutoff tax bracket must be taken as approximate.

Concept 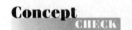 Question 3 • Suppose your tax bracket is 28%. Would you prefer to earn a 6% taxable return or a 4% tax-free return? What is the equivalent taxable yield of the 4% tax-free yield?

Corporate Bonds

Corporate bonds are the means by which private firms borrow money directly from the public. These bonds are similar in structure to Treasury issues—they typically pay semi-annual coupons over their lives and return the face value to the bondholder at maturity. They differ most importantly from Treasury bonds in degree of risk. Default risk is a real consideration in the purchase of corporate bonds, and Chapter 14 discusses this issue in considerable detail. For now, we distinguish only among *secured bonds*, which have specific collateral backing them in the event of firm bankruptcy; unsecured bonds, called *debentures*, which have no collateral; and *subordinated debentures,* which have a lower-priority claim to the firm's assets in the event of bankruptcy.

Figure 2.8
Corporate bond
listings.

Source: The Wall Street Journal, October 28, 1997. Reprinted by permission of The Wall Street Journal, © 1997 Dow Jones & Company, Inc. All Rights Reserved Worldwide.

Corporate bonds usually come with options attached. *Callable bonds* give the firm the option to repurchase the bond from the holder at a stipulated call price. *Convertible bonds* give the bondholder the option to convert each bond into a stipulated number of shares of stock. These options are treated in more detail in Chapter 14.

Figure 2.8 is a partial listing of corporate bond prices from *The Wall Street Journal.* The listings are similar to those for Treasury bonds. The highlighted AT&T bond listed has a coupon rate of 7% and a maturity date of 2005. Its **current yield,** defined as annual coupon income divided by price, is 6.7%. (Note that current yield is a different measure from yield to maturity. The differences are explored in Chapter 14.) A total of 100 bonds traded on this particular day. The closing price of the bond was 104% of par, or $1,040, which was higher than the previous day's close by $1^5/8$% of par value.

Mortgages and Mortgage-Backed Securities

An investments text of 30 years ago probably would not include a section on mortgage loans, because investors could not invest in these loans. Now, because of the explosion in mortgage-backed securities, almost anyone can invest in a portfolio of mortgage loans, and these securities have become a major component of the fixed-income market.

Until the 1970s, almost all home mortgages were written for a long term (15- to 30-year maturity), with a fixed interest rate over the life of the loan, and with equal fixed monthly payments. These so-called conventional mortgages are still the most popular, but a diverse set of alternative mortgage designs has developed.

Fixed-rate mortgages have posed difficulties to lenders in years of increasing interest rates. Because banks and thrift institutions traditionally issued short-term liabilities (the deposits of their customers) and held long-term assets such as fixed-rate mortgages, they suffered losses when interest rates increased and the rates paid on deposits increased while mortgage income remained fixed.

The *adjustable-rate mortgage* was a response to this interest rate risk. These mortgages require the borrower to pay an interest rate that varies with some measure of the current market interest rate. For example, the interest rate might be set at 2 percentage points above the current rate on one-year Treasury bills and might he adjusted once a year. Usually, the contract sets a limit, or cap, on the maximum size of an interest rate change within a year and over the life of the contract. The adjustable-rate contract shifts much of the risk of fluctuations in interest rates from the lender to the borrower.

Because of the shifting of interest rate risk to their customers, banks are willing to offer lower rates on adjustable-rate mortgages than on conventional fixed-rate mortgages. This can be a great inducement to borrowers during a period of high interest rates. As interest rates fall, however, conventional mortgages typically regain popularity.

A *mortgage-backed security* is either an ownership claim in a pool of mortgages or an obligation that is secured by such a pool. These claims represent securitization of mortgage loans. Mortgage lenders originate loans and then sell packages of these loans in the secondary market. Specifically, they sell their claim to the cash inflows from the mortgages as those loans are paid off. The mortgage originator continues to service the loan, collecting principal and interest payments, and passes these payments along to the purchaser of the mortgage. For this reason, these mortgage-backed securities are called *pass-throughs*.

For example, suppose that ten 30-year mortgages, each with a principal value of $100,000, are grouped together into a million-dollar pool. If the mortgage rate is 10%, then the first month's payment for each loan would be $877.57, of which $833.33 would be interest and $44.24 would be principal repayment. The holder of the mortgage pool would receive a payment in the first month of $8,775.70, the total payments of all 10 of the mortgages in the pool.[2] In addition, if one of the mortgages happens to be paid off in any month, the holder of the pass-through security also receives that payment of principal. In future months, of course, the pool will comprise fewer loans, and the interest and principal payments will be lower. The prepaid mortgage in effect represents a partial retirement of the pass-through holder's investment.

Mortgage-backed pass-through securities were first introduced by the Government National Mortgage Association (GNMA, or Ginnie Mae) in 1970. GNMA pass-throughs carry a guarantee from the U.S. government that ensures timely payment of principal and interest, even if the borrower defaults on the mortgage. This guarantee increases the marketability of the pass-through. Thus investors can buy or sell GNMA securities like any other bond.

Other mortgage pass-throughs have since become popular. These are sponsored by FNMA (Federal National Mortgage Association, or Fannie Mae) and FHLMC (Federal

---

[2]Actually, the institution that services the loan and the pass-through agency that guarantees the loan each retain a portion of the monthly payment as a charge for their services. Thus the interest rate received by the pass-through investor is a bit less than the interest rate paid by the borrower. For example, although the 10 homeowners together make total monthly payments of $8,775.70, the holder of the pass-through security may receive a total payment of only $8,740.

Figure 2.9

Mortgage-backed securities outstanding, 1979–1997.

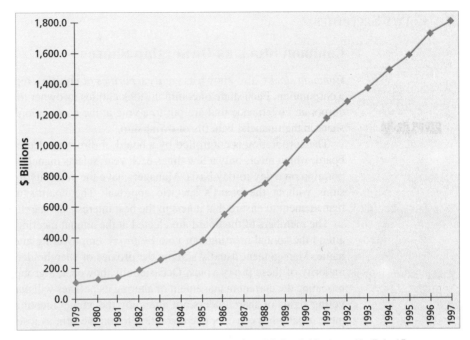

Source: Flow of Funds Accounts: Flows and Outstandings, Washington D.C.: Board of Governors of the Federal Reserve System, September 1997.

Home Loan Mortgage Corporation, or Freddie Mac). As of the second quarter of 1997, roughly $1.76 trillion of mortgages were securitized into mortgage-backed securities. This makes the mortgage-backed securities market bigger than the $1.44 trillion corporate bond market and nearly half the size of the $3.55 trillion market in Treasury securities. Figure 2.9 illustrates the explosive growth of mortgage-backed securities since 1979.

The success of mortgage-backed pass-throughs has encouraged introduction of pass-through securities backed by other assets. For example, the Student Loan Marketing Association (SLMA, or Sallie Mae) sponsors pass-throughs backed by loans originated under the Guaranteed Student Loan Program and by other loans granted under various federal programs for higher education.

Although pass-through securities often guarantee payment of interest and principal, they do not guarantee the rate of return. Holders of mortgage pass-throughs therefore can be severely disappointed in their returns in years when interest rates drop significantly. This is because homeowners usually have an option to prepay, or pay ahead of schedule, the remaining principal outstanding on their mortgages.

This right is essentially an option held by the borrower to "call back" the loan for the remaining principal balance, quite analogous to the option held by government or corporate issuers of callable bonds. The prepayment option gives the borrower the right to buy back the loan at the outstanding principal amount rather than at the present discounted value of the *scheduled* remaining payments. When interest rates fall, so that the present value of the scheduled mortgage payments increases, the borrower may choose to take out a new loan at today's lower interest rate and use the proceeds of the loan to prepay or retire the outstanding mortgage. This refinancing may disappoint pass-through investors, who are liable to "receive a call" just when they might have anticipated capital gains from interest rate declines.

2.3   EQUITY SECURITIES

Common Stock as Ownership Shares

Common stocks, also known as *equity securities* or **equities,** represent ownership shares in a corporation. Each share of common stock entitles its owner to one vote on any matters of corporate governance that are put to a vote at the corporation's annual meeting and to a share in the financial benefits of ownership.[3]

The corporation is controlled by a board of directors elected by the shareholders. The board, which meets only a few times each year, selects managers who actually run the corporation on a day-to-day basis. Managers have the authority to make most business decisions without the board's specific approval. The board's mandate is to oversee the management to ensure that it acts in the best interests of shareholders.

The members of the board are elected at the annual meeting. Shareholders who do not attend the annual meeting can vote by *proxy,* empowering another party to vote in their name. Management usually solicits the proxies of shareholders and normally gets a vast majority of these proxy votes. Occasionally, however, a group of shareholders intent on unseating the current management or altering its policies will wage a proxy fight to gain the voting rights of shareholders not attending the annual meeting. Thus, although management usually has considerable discretion to run the firm as it sees fit—without daily oversight from the equityholders who actually own the firm—both oversight from the board and the possibility of a proxy fight serve as checks on that discretion.

Another related check on management's discretion is the possibility of a corporate takeover. In these episodes, an outside investor who believes that the firm is mismanaged will attempt to acquire the firm. Usually, this is accomplished with a *tender offer*, which is an offer made to purchase at a stipulated price, usually substantially above the current market price, some or all of the shares held by the current stockholders. If the tender is successful, the acquiring investor purchases enough shares to obtain control of the firm and can replace its management.

The common stock of most large corporations can be bought or sold freely on one or more stock exchanges. A corporation whose stock is not publicly traded is said to be closely held. In most closely held corporations, the owners of the firm also take an active role in its management. Therefore, takeovers are generally not an issue.

Thus, although there is substantial separation of the ownership and the control of large corporations, there are at least some implicit controls on management that tend to force it to act in the interests of the shareholders.

Characteristics of Common Stock

The two most important characteristics of common stock as an investment are its **residual claim** and **limited liability** features.

Residual claim means that stockholders are the last in line of all those who have a claim on the assets and income of the corporation. In a liquidation of the firm's assets the shareholders have a claim to what is left after all other claimants such as the tax authorities, employees, suppliers, bondholders, and other creditors have been paid. For a firm not in liquidation, shareholders have claim to the part of operating income left over after interest

---

[3]A corporation sometimes issues two classes of common stock, one bearing the right to vote, the other not. Because of its restricted rights, the nonvoting stock might sell for a lower price.

and taxes have been paid. Management can either pay this residual as cash dividends to shareholders or reinvest it in the business to increase the value of the shares.

Limited liability means that the most shareholders can lose in the event of failure of the corporation is their original investment. Unlike owners of unincorporated businesses, whose creditors can lay claim to the personal assets of the owner (house, car, furniture), corporate shareholders may at worst have worthless stock. They are not personally liable for the firm's obligations.

Concept
CHECK

Question 4
a. **If you buy 100 shares of IBM stock, to what are you entitled?**
b. **What is the most money you can make on this investment over the next year?**
c. **If you pay $50 per share, what is the most money you could lose over the year?**

Stock Market Listings

Figure 2.10 is a partial listing from *The Wall Street Journal* of stocks traded on the New York Stock Exchange. The NYSE is one of several markets in which investors may buy or sell shares of stock. We will examine these markets in detail in Chapter 3.

To interpret the information provided for each traded stock, consider the listing for Home Depot. The first two columns provide the highest and lowest price at which the stock has traded in the last 52 weeks, $56\frac{1}{2}$ and $31\frac{13}{16}$, respectively. The .20 figure means that the last quarter's dividend was $.05 per share, which is consistent with annual dividend payments of $.05 \times 4 = \$.20$. This value corresponds to a dividend yield of .4%, meaning that the dividend paid per dollar of each share is $.004. That is, Home Depot stock is selling at $55\frac{3}{4}$ (the last recorded or "close" price in the next-to-last column), so that the dividend yield is $.20/55.75 = .0036 = .36\%$, or .4% rounded to one decimal place. The stock listings show that dividend yields vary widely among firms. It is important to recognize that high-dividend-yield stocks are not necessarily better investments than low-yield stocks. Total return to an investor comes from dividends and **capital gains,** or appreciation in the value of the stock. Low-dividend-yield firms presumably offer greater prospects for capital gains, or investors would not be willing to hold the low-yield firms in their portfolios.

Figure 2.10   Stock market listings.

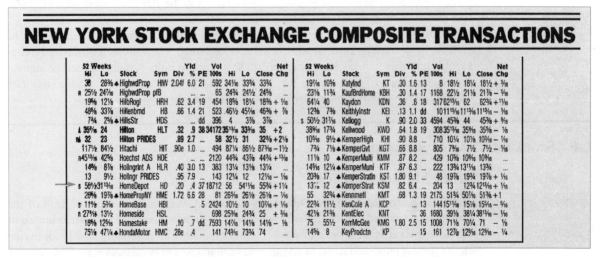

The P/E ratio, or **price–earnings ratio,** is the ratio of the current stock price to last year's earnings per share. The P/E ratio tells us how much stock purchasers must pay per dollar of earnings that the firm generates. The P/E ratio also varies widely across firms. Where the dividend yield and P/E ratio are not reported in Figure 2.10 the firms have zero dividends, or zero or negative earnings. We shall have much to say about P/E ratios in Chapter 18.

The sales column shows that 18,712 hundred shares of the stock were traded. Shares commonly are traded in round lots of 100 shares each. Investors who wish to trade in smaller "odd lots" generally must pay higher commissions to their stockbrokers. The highest price and lowest price per share at which the stock traded on that day were 56 and $54^{11}/_{16}$, respectively. The last, or closing, price of $55^3/_4$ was up $1^1/_4$ from the closing price of the previous day.

Preferred Stock

Preferred stock has features similar to both equity and debt. Like a bond, it promises to pay to its holder a fixed amount of income each year. In this sense preferred stock is similar to an infinite-maturity bond, that is, a perpetuity. It also resembles a bond in that it does not convey voting power regarding the management of the firm. Preferred stock is an equity investment, however. The firm retains discretion to make the dividend payments to the preferred stockholders; it has no contractual obligation to pay those dividends. Instead, preferred dividends are usually *cumulative;* that is, unpaid dividends cumulate and must be paid in full before any dividends may be paid to holders of common stock. In contrast, the firm does have a contractual obligation to make the interest payments on the debt. Failure to make these payments sets off corporate bankruptcy proceedings.

Preferred stock also differs from bonds in terms of its tax treatment for the firm. Because preferred stock payments are treated as dividends rather than interest, they are not tax-deductible expenses for the firm. This disadvantage is somewhat offset by the fact that corporations may exclude 70% of dividends received from domestic corporations in the computation of their taxable income. Preferred stocks therefore make desirable fixed-income investments for some corporations.

Even though preferred stock ranks after bonds in terms of the priority of its claims to the assets of the firm in the event of corporate bankruptcy, preferred stock often sells at lower yields than do corporate bonds. Presumably, this reflects the value of the dividend exclusion, because risk considerations alone indicate that preferred stock ought to offer higher yields than bonds. Individual investors, who cannot use the 70% exclusion, generally will find preferred stock yields unattractive relative to those on other available assets.

Preferred stock is issued in variations similar to those of corporate bonds. It may be callable by the issuing firm, in which case it is said to be *redeemable*. It also may be convertible into common stock at some specified conversion ratio. A relatively recent innovation in the market is adjustable-rate preferred stock, which, similar to adjustable-rate mortgages, ties the dividend to current market interest rates.

2.4   STOCK AND BOND MARKET INDEXES

Stock Market Indexes

The daily performance of the Dow Jones Industrial Average is a staple portion of the evening news report. Although the Dow is the best-known measure of the performance of the stock market, it is only one of several indicators. Other more broadly based indexes are computed and published daily. In addition, several indexes of bond market performance are widely available. The nearby box describes the Dow, gives a bit of its history, and discusses some of its strengths and shortcomings.

WHAT IS THE DOW JONES INDUSTRIAL AVERAGE, ANYWAY?

Quick. How did the market do yesterday? If you're like most people, you'd probably answer by saying that the Dow Jones Industrial Average rose or fell.

At 100 years old, the Dow Jones Industrial Average has acquired a unique place in the collective consciousness of investors. It is the number quoted on the nightly news, and remembered when the market takes a dive.

But enough with the blandishments. What *is* the Dow, exactly, and what does it do?

The first part is easy: The Dow is an average of 30 blue-chip U.S. stocks. As for what it does, perhaps the simplest explanation is this: It's a tool by which the general public can measure the overall performance of the U.S. stock market.

Industry Bellwethers

Even though the industrial average consists of only 30 stocks, the theory is that each one represents a particular sector of the economy and serves as a reliable bellwether for that industry. Thus, the Dow Jones roster is made up of giants such as International Business Machines Corp., J.P. Morgan & Co., and AT&T Corp. Together, the 30 stocks reflect the market as a whole.

Initially, the industrial average comprised 12 companies. Only one, General Electric Co., remains in the average under its original name. Many of the others are extinct today, while some have mutated into companies that are still active. But a century ago, these were the corporate titans of the time. On October 1, 1928, a year before the crash, the Dow was expanded to a 30-stock average.

Marching Higher

As times have changed, so have the makeup and mechanics of the Dow. Back in 1896, all Charles Dow needed was a pencil and paper to compute the industrial average: He simply added up the prices of the 12 stocks and then divided by 12.

Today, the first step in calculating the Dow is still totaling the prices of the component stocks. But the rest of the math isn't so easy anymore, because the divisor is continually being adjusted. The reason? To preserve historical continuity. In the past 100 years, there have been many stock splits, spinoffs, and stock substitutions that, without adjustment, would distort the value of the Dow.

To understand how the formula works, consider a stock split. Say three stocks are trading at $15, $20, and $25; the average of the three is $20. But if the company with the $20 stock has a 2-for-1 split, its shares suddenly are priced at half of their previous level. That's not to say the value of the

investment changed; rather the $20 stock simply sells for $10, with twice as many shares available. The average of the three stocks, meanwhile, falls to $16.66. So, the Dow divisor is adjusted to keep the average at $20 and reflect the continuing value of the investment represented by the gauge.

Minimal Change

Over time, the divisor has been adjusted several times, mostly downward (it now stands at .31143932). This explains why the average can be reported as, say, 8500, though no single stock in the average is close to that price.

Since Charles Dow's time, several stock market indexes have challenged the Dow Jones Industrial Average. In 1928, Standard & Poor's Corp. developed the S&P 90, which by the 1950s evolved into the S&P 500, a benchmark widely used today by professional money managers. And now indexes abound. Wilshire Associates in Santa Monica, California, for example, uses computers to compile an index of nearly 7,000 stocks.

Nevertheless, the Dow remains unique. For one, it isn't market-weighted like other indicators, which means it isn't adjusted to reflect the market capitalization of the component stocks. Because of that, the Dow gives more emphasis to higher-priced stocks than to lower-priced stocks.

So, a stock such as United Technologies Corp. constitutes only 0.26% of the S&P 500. Yet it accounts for a whopping 5.5% of the Dow Jones industrials, because it is one of the highest-priced stocks in the Dow.

Despite the weighting difference, the Dow, by and large, closely tracks other major market indexes. That's because, for one, the stocks in the industrial average do an adequate job of representing their industries.

"There are only 30 stocks in the Dow and 500 stocks in the S&P, but it is the weighting that makes them track closely," says Mr. Dickey of Dain Bosworth. Since the S&P 500 is weighted by market capitalization, "a large part of the movement is determined by the biggest companies," he explains. And these big companies that drive the S&P are invariably also found in the Dow.

In the end, while some indexes may be more closely watched by professionals, the Dow Jones Industrial Average has retained its position as the most popular measure, if for no other reason than that it has stood the test of time. As the oldest continuing barometer of the U.S. stock market, it tells us where we came from, which helps us understand where we are.

The ever-increasing role of international trade and investments has made indexes of foreign financial markets part of the general news. Thus foreign stock exchange indexes such as the Nikkei Average of Tokyo and the Financial Times index of London are fast becoming household names.

Dow Jones Averages

The Dow Jones Industrial Average (DJIA) of 30 large, "blue-chip" corporations has been computed since 1896. Its long history probably accounts for its preeminence in the public mind. (The average covered only 20 stocks until 1928.)

Originally, the DJIA was calculated as the simple average of the stocks included in the index. Thus, if there were 30 stocks in the index, one would add up the value of the 30 stocks and divide by 30. The percentage change in the DJIA would then be the percentage change in the average price of the 30 shares.

This procedure means that the percentage change in the DJIA measures the return on a portfolio that invests one share in each of the 30 stocks in the index. The value of such a portfolio (holding one share of each stock in the index) is the sum of the 30 prices. Because the percentage change in the *average* of the 30 prices is the same as the percentage change in the *sum* of the 30 prices, the index and the portfolio have the same percentage change each day.

To illustrate, consider the data in Table 2.3 for a hypothetical two-stock version of the Dow Jones Average. Stock ABC sells initially at $25 a share, while XYZ sells for $100. Therefore, the initial value of the index would be $(25 + 100)/2 = 62.5$. The final share prices are $30 for stock ABC and $90 for XYZ, so the average falls by 2.5 to $(30 + 90)/2 = 60$. The 2.5 point drop in the index is a 4% decrease: $2.5/62.5 = .04$. Similarly, a portfolio holding one share of each stock would have an initial value of $25 + $100 = 125 and a final value of $30 + $90 = 120, for an identical 4% decrease.

Because the Dow measures the return on a portfolio that holds one share of each stock, it is called a **price-weighted average.** The amount of money invested in each company represented in the portfolio is proportional to that company's share price.

Price-weighted averages give higher-priced shares more weight in determining performance of the index. For example, although ABC increased by 20%, while XYZ fell by only 10%, the index dropped in value. This is because the 20% increase in ABC represented a smaller price gain ($5 per share) than the 10% decrease in XYZ ($10 per share). The "Dow portfolio" has four times as much invested in XYZ as in ABC because XYZ's price is four times that of ABC. Therefore, XYZ dominates the average.

You might wonder why the DJIA is now (in early 1998) at a level of about 8500 if it is supposed to be the average price of the 30 stocks in the index. The DJIA no longer equals the average price of the 30 stocks because the averaging procedure is adjusted whenever

Table 2.3　Data to Construct Stock Price Indexes

Stock	Initial Price	Final Price	Shares (Million)	Initial Value of Outstanding Stock ($ Million)	Final Value of Outstanding Stock ($ Million)
ABC	$ 25	$30	20	$500	$600
XYZ	100	90	1	100	90
TOTAL				$600	$690

a stock splits or pays a stock dividend of more than 10%, or when one company in the group of 30 industrial firms is replaced by another. When these events occur, the divisor used to compute the "average price" is adjusted so as to leave the index unaffected by the event.

For example, if XYZ were to split two for one and its share price to fall to $50, we would not want the average to fall, as that would incorrectly indicate a fall in the general level of market prices. Following a split, the divisor must be reduced to a value that leaves the average unaffected by the split. Table 2.4 illustrates this point. The initial share price of XYZ, which was $100 in Table 2.3, falls to $50 if the stock splits at the beginning of the period. Notice that the number of shares outstanding doubles, leaving the market value of the total shares unaffected. The divisor, d, which originally was 2.0 when the two-stock average was initiated, must be reset to a value that leaves the "average" unchanged. Because the sum of the postsplit stock prices is 75, while the presplit average price was 62.5, we calculate the new value of d by solving $75/d = 62.5$. The value of d, therefore, falls from its original value of 2.0 to $75/62.5 = 1.20$, and the initial value of the average is unaffected by the split: $75/1.20 = 62.5$.

At period-end, ABC will sell for $30, while XYZ will sell for $45, representing the same negative 10% return it was assumed to earn in Table 2.3. The new value of the price-weighted average is $(30 + 45)/1.20 = 62.5$. The index is unchanged, so the rate of return is zero, rather than the –4% return that would be calculated in the absence of a split.

This return is greater than that calculated in the absence of a split. The relative weight of XYZ, which is the poorer-performing stock, is reduced by a split because its price is lower; hence the performance of the average is higher. This example illustrates that the implicit weighting scheme of a price-weighted average is somewhat arbitrary, being determined by the prices rather than by the outstanding market values (price per share times number of shares) of the shares in the average.

Because the Dow Jones Averages are based on small numbers of firms, care must be taken to ensure that they are representative of the broad market. As a result, the composition of the average is changed every so often to reflect changes in the economy. The last change took place on March 12, 1997, when Hewlett-Packard, Johnson & Johnson, Travelers Group, and Wal-Mart were added to the index and Texaco, Bethlehem Steel, Westinghouse, and Woolworth were dropped. The nearby box presents the history of the firms in the index since 1928. The fate of many companies once considered "the bluest of the blue chips" is striking evidence of the changes in the U.S. economy in the last 70 years.

In the same way that the divisor is updated for stock splits, if one firm is dropped from the average and another firm with a different price is added, the divisor has to be updated to leave the average unchanged by the substitution. By now, the divisor for the Dow Jones Industrial Average has fallen to a value of about .311.

Table 2.4   Data to Construct Stock Price Indexes after a Stock Split

Stock	Initial Price	Final Price	Shares (Million)	Initial Value of Outstanding Stock ($ Million)	Final Value of Outstanding Stock ($ Million)
ABC	$25	$30	20	$500	$600
XYZ	50	45	2	100	90
TOTAL				$600	$690

DOW JONES INDUSTRIAL AVERAGE: CHANGES SINCE OCT. 1, 1928

Oct. 1, 1928	1929	1930s	1940s	1950s	1960s	1970s	1980s	May 6, 1991	March 12, 1997
Allied Chemical & Dye							AlliedSignal*('85)		AlliedSignal
Wright Aeronautical	Curtiss-Wright ('29)	Hudson Motor ('30) Coca-Cola ('32) National Steel ('35)		Aluminum Co. of America ('59)					Aluminum Co. of America
North American		Johns-Manville ('30)					Amer. Express ('82)		American Express
Victor Talking Machine	Natl. Cash Register ('29)	IBM ('32) AT&T ('39)							AT&T
International Nickel						Inco Ltd.* ('76)	Boeing ('87)		Boeing
International Harvester							Navistar* ('86)	Caterpillar	Caterpillar
Goodrich		Standard Oil (Calif.) ('30)					Chevron* ('84)		Chevron
Texas Gulf Sulphur		Intl. Shoe ('32) United Aircraft ('33) National Distillers ('34)		Owens-Illinois ('59)			Coca-Cola ('87)		Coca-Cola
U.S. Steel							USX Corp.* ('86)	Walt Disney	Walt Disney
American Sugar		Borden ('30) DuPont ('35)							DuPont
American Tobacco (B)		Eastman Kodak ('30)							Eastman Kodak
Standard Oil (N.J.)						Exxon* ('72)			Exxon
General Electric									General Electric
General Motors									General Motors
Atlantic Refining		Goodyear ('30)							Goodyear
Texas Corp.				Texaco* ('59)					Hewlett-Packard
Chrysler						IBM ('79)			IBM
Paramount Publix		Loew's ('32)		Intl. Paper ('56)					International Paper
Bethlehem Steel									Johnson & Johnson
General Railway Signal		Liggett & Myers ('30) Amer. Tobacco ('32)					McDonald's ('85)		McDonald's
Mack Trucks		Drug Inc. ('32) Corn Products ('33)		Swift & Co. ('59)		Esmark* ('73) Merck ('79)			Merck
American Smelting				Anaconda ('59)		Minn. Mining ('76)			Minn. Mining
American Can							Primerica* ('87)	J.P. Morgan	J.P. Morgan
Postum Inc.	General Foods* ('29)						Philip Morris ('85)		Philip Morris
Nash Motors		United Air Trans. ('30) Procter & Gamble ('32)							Procter & Gamble
Sears Roebuck									Sears Roebuck
Westinghouse Electric									Travelers Group
Union Carbide									Union Carbide
Radio Corp.		Nash Motors ('32) United Aircraft ('39)				United Tech.* ('75)			United Technologies
Woolworth									Wal-Mart Stores

Source: Data from *Economic Report of the President,* U.S. Government Printing Office, 1996.
*Includes overnight Eurodollars.
†Less than $100,000 denomination.
‡More than $100,000 denomination.

Note: Year of change shown in ( ); *denotes name change, in some cases following a takeover or merger. To track changes in the components, begin in the column for 1928 and work across. For instance, American Sugar was replaced by Borden in 1930, which in turn was replaced by Du Pont in 1935. Source: From "How the 30 Stocks in the Dow Jones Industrial Average Have Changed since October 1, 1928," *The Wall Street Journal,* March 13, 1997. Reprinted by permission of *The Wall Street Journal,* © 1997 Dow Jones & Company, Inc. All Rights Reserved Worldwide.

Concept

Question 5 • Suppose XYZ in Table 2.3 increases in price to $110, while ABC falls to $20. Find the percentage change in the price-weighted average of these two stocks. Compare that to the percentage return of a portfolio that holds one share in each company.

Dow Jones & Company also computes a Transportation Average of 20 airline, trucking, and railroad stocks; a Public Utility Average of 15 electric and natural gas utilities; and a Composite Average combining the 65 firms of the three separate averages. Each is a price-weighted average, and thus overweights the performance of high-priced stocks.

Figure 2.11 reproduces some of the data reported on the Dow Jones Averages from *The Wall Street Journal* (which is owned by Dow Jones & Company). The bars show the range of values assumed by the average on each day. The crosshatch indicates the closing value of the average.

Standard & Poor's Indexes

The Standard & Poor's Composite 500 (S&P 500) stock index represents an improvement over the Dow Jones Averages in two ways. First, it is a more broadly based index of 500 firms. Second, it is a **market-value-weighted index.** In the case of the firms XYZ and ABC disclosed above, the S&P 500 would give ABC five times the weight given to XYZ because the market value of its outstanding equity is five times larger, $500 million versus $100 million.

The S&P 500 is computed by calculating the total market value of the 500 firms in the index and the total market value of those firms on the previous day of trading. The percentage increase in the total market value from one day to the next represents the increase in the index. The rate of return of the index equals the rate of return that would be earned by an investor holding a portfolio of all 500 firms in the index in proportion to their market values, except that the index does not reflect cash dividends paid by those firms.

To illustrate, look again at Table 2.3. If the initial level of a market-value-weighted index of stocks ABC and XYZ were set equal to an arbitrarily chosen starting value such as 100, the index value at year-end would be $100 \times (690/600) = 115$. The increase in the index reflects the 15% return earned on a portfolio consisting of those two stocks held in proportion to outstanding market values.

Unlike the price-weighted index, the value-weighted index gives more weight to ABC. Whereas the price-weighted index fell because it was dominated by higher-price XYZ, the value-weighted index rises because it gives more weight to ABC, the stock with the higher total market value.

Note also from Tables 2.3 and 2.4 that market-value-weighted indexes are unaffected by stock splits. The total market value of the outstanding XYZ stock increases from $100 million to $110 million regardless of the stock split, thereby rendering the split irrelevant to the performance of the index.

A nice feature of both market-value-weighted and price-weighted indexes is that they reflect the returns to straightforward portfolio strategies. If one were to buy each share in the index in proportion to its outstanding market value, the value-weighted index would perfectly track capital gains on the underlying portfolio. Similarly, a price-weighted index tracks the returns on a portfolio comprised of equal shares of each firm.

Investors today can purchase shares in mutual funds that hold shares in proportion to their representation in the S&P 500. These **index funds** yield a return equal to that of the S&P 500 index and so provide a low-cost passive investment strategy for equity investors.

Standard & Poor's also publishes a 400-stock Industrial Index, a 20-stock Transportation Index, a 40-stock Utility Index, and a 40-stock Financial Index.

Figure 2.11
The Dow Jones
Industrial Average.

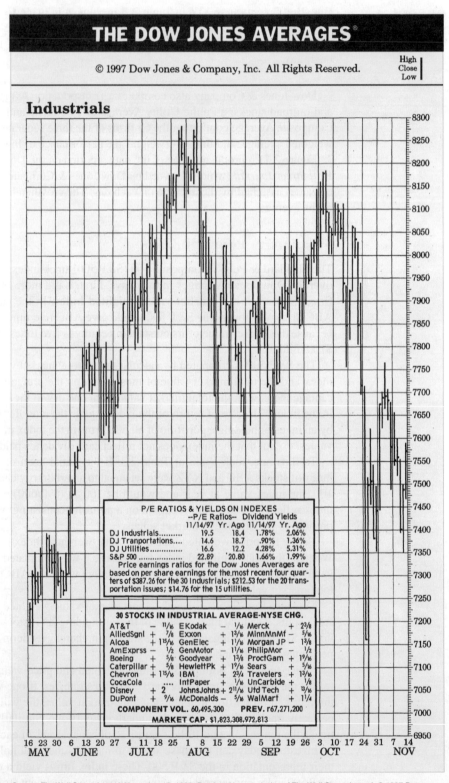

THE DOW JONES AVERAGES®

© 1997 Dow Jones & Company, Inc. All Rights Reserved.

High
Close
Low

Industrials

P/E RATIOS & YIELDS ON INDEXES

	--P/E Ratios--		Dividend Yields	
	11/14/97	Yr. Ago	11/14/97	Yr. Ago
DJ Industrials..........	19.5	18.4	1.78%	2.06%
DJ Tranportations....	14.6	18.7	.90%	1.36%
DJ Utilities..............	16.6	12.2	4.28%	5.31%
S&P 500	22.89	'20.80	1.66%	1.99%

Price earnings ratios for the Dow Jones Averages are based on per share earnings for the most recent four quarters of $387.26 for the 30 Industrials; $212.53 for the 20 transportation issues; $14.76 for the 15 utilities.

30 STOCKS IN INDUSTRIAL AVERAGE-NYSE CHG.

AT&T	−	¹¹⁄₁₆	EKodak	−	¹⁄₁₆	Merck	+	2³⁄₈
AlliedSgnl	+	⁷⁄₈	Exxon	+	1³⁄₈	MinnMnMf	−	⁵⁄₁₆
Alcoa	+	1¹⁵⁄₁₆	GenElec	+	1¹⁄₁₆	Morgan JP	−	1³⁄₈
AmExprss	−	¹⁄₂	GenMotor	−	1¹⁄₁₆	PhilipMor	−	¹⁄₂
Boeing	+	⁵⁄₈	Goodyear	+	1³⁄₈	ProctGam	+	1⁹⁄₁₆
Caterpillar	+	⁵⁄₈	HewlettPk	+	1⁹⁄₁₆	Sears	+	⁵⁄₁₆
Chevron	+	1¹⁵⁄₁₆	IBM	+	2³⁄₄	Travelers	+	1³⁄₁₆
CocaCola	...		IntPaper	+	¹⁄₁₆	UnCarbide	+	¹⁄₈
Disney	+	2	JohnsJohns	+	2¹¹⁄₁₆	Utd Tech	+	¹³⁄₁₆
DuPont	+	⁹⁄₁₆	McDonalds	−	⁵⁄₁₆	WalMart	+	1¹⁄₄

COMPONENT VOL. 60,495,300   **PREV.** r67,271,200

MARKET CAP. $1,823,308,972,813

Concept CHECK **Question 6** • **Reconsider companies XYZ and ABC from question 5. Calculate the percentage change in the market-value-weighted index. Compare that to the rate of return of a portfolio that holds $500 of ABC stock for every $100 of XYZ stock (i.e., an index portfolio).**

Other Market-Value Indexes

The New York Stock Exchange publishes a market-value-weighted composite index of all NYSE-listed stocks, in addition to subindexes for industrial, utility, transportation, and financial stocks. The American Stock Exchange, or, Amex, also computes a market-value-weighted index of its stocks. These indexes are even more broadly based than the S&P 500. The National Association of Securities Dealers publishes an index of nearly 3,000 over-the-counter (OTC) firms using the National Association of Securities Dealers Automatic Quotations (Nasdaq) service.

The ultimate U.S. equity index so far computed is the Wilshire 5000 index of the market value of all NYSE and Amex stocks plus actively traded OTC stocks. Despite its name, the index actually includes about 7,000 stocks. Figure 2.12 reproduces a *Wall Street Journal* listing of stock index performance. Vanguard offers a mutual fund, the Total Stock Market Portfolio, that enables investors to match the performance of the Wilshire 5000 index.

More recently, market-value-weighted indexes of non-U.S. stock markets have been developed and disseminated. A leader in this field has been Morgan Stanley Capital International (MSCI). Table 2.5 presents several of the MSCI indexes.

Equally Weighted Indexes   Market performance is sometimes measured by an equally weighted average of the returns of each stock in an index. Such an averaging technique, by placing equal weight on each return, corresponds to an implicit portfolio strategy that places equal dollar values on each stock. This is in contrast to both price weighting (which requires equal numbers of shares of each stock) and market value weighting (which requires investments in proportion to outstanding value).

Unlike price- or market-value-weighted indexes, equally weighted indexes do not correspond to buy-and-hold portfolio strategies. Suppose that you start with equal dollar investments in the two stocks of Table 2.3, ABC and XYZ. Because ABC increases in value by 20% over the year while XYZ decreases by 10%, your portfolio no longer is equally weighted. It is now more heavily invested in ABC. To reset the portfolio to equal weights, you would need to rebalance: sell off some ABC stock and/or purchase more XYZ stock. Such rebalancing would be necessary to align the return on your portfolio with that on the equally weighted index.

The Value Line Index   The Dow Jones and market-value-weighted indexes all use arithmetic averaging: They all sum up either prices or market values and divide by a divisor. In contrast, the Value Line index is an equally weighted **geometric average** of the performance of about 1,700 firms. To compare geometric and arithmetic averages, suppose that three firms have returns on a trading day as follows:

Stock	Return
A	10%
B	−5%
C	20%

Figure 2.12
Performance of stock indexes.

STOCK MARKET DATA BANK   11/14/97

MAJOR INDEXES

— †12-MO — HIGH	LOW		DAILY HIGH	LOW	CLOSE	NET CHG	% CHG	†12-MO CHG	% CHG	FROM 12/31	% CHG
DOW JONES AVERAGES											
8259.31	6268.35	30 Industrials	7590.16	7467.38	x7572.48 +	84.72 +	1.13	+ 1224.45 +	19.29	+ 1124.21 +	17.43
3368.33	2218.68	20 Transportation	3118.12	3066.49	3106.69 +	38.24 +	1.25	+ 885.24 +	39.85	+ 851.02 +	37.73
247.99	209.47	15 Utilities	246.48	243.74	245.60 +	1.86 +	0.76	+ 10.69 +	4.55	+ 13.07 +	5.62
2620.84	1977.29	65 Composite	2474.54	2438.29	x2468.33 +	27.07 +	1.11	+ 467.41 +	23.36	+ 442.50 +	21.84
929.94	681.02	DJ Global-US	882.03	868.10	879.87 +	10.98 +	1.26	+ 183.67 +	26.38	+ 179.31 +	25.60
NEW YORK STOCK EXCHANGE											
514.21	380.85	Composite	487.17	480.20	487.17 +	6.48 +	1.35	+ 97.15 +	24.91	+ 94.87 +	24.18
643.81	480.94	Industrials	611.16	601.77	611.16 +	8.35 +	1.39	+ 117.88 +	23.90	+ 116.78 +	23.62
310.70	247.87	Utilities	306.60	301.41	306.60 +	5.15 +	1.71	+ 47.54 +	18.35	+ 46.69 +	17.96
481.05	341.87	Transportation	447.82	442.18	447.82 +	4.17 +	0.94	+ 100.56 +	28.96	+ 95.52 +	27.11
493.08	339.08	Finance	454.92	449.69	454.92 +	5.23 +	1.16	+ 110.68 +	32.15	+ 103.75 +	29.54
STANDARD & POOR'S INDEXES											
983.12	720.98	500 Index	930.44	915.34	928.35 +	11.69 +	1.28	+ 190.73 +	25.86	+ 187.61 +	25.33
1146.82	847.68	Industrials	1089.59	1070.51	1087.15 +	14.98 +	1.40	+ 220.48 +	25.44	+ 217.18 +	24.96
211.44	180.93	Utilities	208.75	207.19	208.30 +	0.65 +	0.31	+ 6.21 +	3.07	+ 9.49 +	4.77
339.84	247.16	400 MidCap	317.19	312.92	316.71 +	3.79 +	1.21	+ 64.18 +	25.41	+ 61.13 +	23.92
192.48	134.54	600 SmallCap	177.66	175.64	177.61 +	1.97 +	1.12	+ 37.65 +	26.90	+ 32.13 +	22.09
212.04	155.37	1500 Index	200.21	197.15	199.80 +	2.49 +	1.26	+ 41.03 +	25.84	+ 39.99 +	25.02
NASDAQ STOCK MARKET											
1745.85	1201.00	Composite	1585.44	1557.74	1583.51 +	r24.26 +	1.56	+ 321.71 +	25.50	+ 292.48 +	22.65
1148.21	783.92	Nasdaq 100	1030.58	1002.92	1027.85 +	r22.60 +	2.25	+ 228.41 +	28.57	+ 206.49 +	25.14
1414.11	971.06	Industrials	1256.64	1241.34	1256.43 +	18.99 +	1.53	+ 154.05 +	13.97	+ 146.80 +	13.23
1884.02	1384.41	Insurance	1751.89	1734.82	1740.30 −	7.08 −	0.41	+ 350.97 +	25.26	+ 274.87 +	18.76
1977.59	1227.39	Banks	1896.12	1887.98	1891.25 +	1.50 +	0.08	+ 663.86 +	54.09	+ 617.79 +	48.51
732.03	478.25	Computer	654.18	640.23	652.63 +	r13.73 +	2.15	+ 150.80 +	30.05	+ 133.84 +	25.80
312.80	198.06	Telecommunications	291.36	287.09	291.32 +	4.33 +	1.51	+ 77.59 +	36.30	+ 75.41 +	34.93
OTHERS											
721.90	541.20	Amex Composite*	672.62	666.38	672.62 +	5.76 +	0.86	+ 95.32 +	16.51	+ 100.28 +	17.52
518.94	382.40	Russell 1000	491.20	483.65	490.03 +	6.09 +	1.26	+ 98.51 +	25.16	+ 96.28 +	24.45
465.21	335.85	Russell 2000	428.46	423.39	428.41 +	5.02 +	1.19	+ 81.89 +	23.63	+ 65.80 +	18.15
551.24	407.16	Russell 3000	520.43	512.77	519.35 +	6.42 +	1.25	+ 103.94 +	25.02	+ 99.91 +	23.82
477.08	365.15	Value-Line(geom.)	445.08	440.97	444.76 +	3.54 +	0.80	+ 75.84 +	20.56	+ 69.44 +	18.50
9486.69	6998.62	Wilshire 5000	...	...	8932.58 +	108.97 +	1.24	+ 1804.40 +	25.31	+ 1734.29 +	24.09

†-Based on comparable trading day in preceding year. *-Replaced previous index eff. 1/02/97.

Source: The Wall Street Journal, November 17, 1997. Reprinted by permission of The Wall Street Journal, © 1997 Dow Jones & Company, Inc. All Rights Reserved Worldwide.

Table 2.5   Selected MSCI Stock Indexes

International Indexes	Special Areas	National Indexes	
The World Index	The World Index ex USA	Spain	Australia
North America	Kokusal Index (World ex Japan)	Sweden	Singapore/Malaysia
EAFE	EASEA Index (EAFE ex Japan)	Switzerland	Belgium
Europe 13	Pacific ex Japan	United Kingdom	Netherlands
Nordic Countries	The World Index ex The UK	Italy	Denmark
Pacific	EAFE ex The UK	Japan	Norway
Far East	Europe 13 ex The UK	Hong Kong	Canada
		New Zealand	Germany
		France	Austria
		United States	Finland

Source: Morgan Stanley Capital International Perspective III '90, Geneva, Switzerland.

An equally weighted arithmetic average of these returns would be

$$[.10 + (2 .05) + .20]/3 = .0833 = 8.33\%$$

In contrast, the geometric average, r_G, is computed as

$$1 + r_G = [(1 + .10)(1 2 .05)(1 + .20)]^{1/3} = 1.0784$$

for a geometric average of 7.84%. The general formula for the geometric average is

$$1 + r_G = [(1 + r_1)(1 + r_2) \cdots (1 + r_n)]^{1/n}$$

where r_i is the return on the ith security in the index.

Note that the geometric average is less than the arithmetic average. This is a general property; whenever there is variation in performance among the stocks in an index, the geometric average will be less than the arithmetic average.[4] For this reason the Value Line index provides a downward-biased measure of the rate of return that would be earned by an investor purchasing an equally weighted portfolio of all the stocks in the index. In fact, there is no portfolio strategy that results in a rate of return equal to that of a geometric index.

Foreign and International Stock Market Indexes

Development in financial markets worldwide includes the construction of indexes for these markets. The most important are the Nikkei, FTSE (pronounced "footsie"), and DAX. The Nikkei 225 is a price-weighted average of the largest Tokyo Stock Exchange (TSE) stocks. The Nikkei 300 is a value-weighted index. FTSE is published by the *Financial Times* of London and is a value-weighted index of 100 of the largest London Stock Exchange corporations. The DAX index is the premier German stock index.

Figure 2.13 shows the list of foreign stock exchange indexes published by *The Wall Street Journal*. The indexes are used to measure the return of the stock markets in each country in local currencies as well as in U.S. dollars, accounting for the effect of exchange rate movements. The range of countries for which stock indexes are regularly computed gives a sense of how pervasive the use of this approach to measuring market conditions has become. Other indexes such as Morgan Stanley's (see Table 2.5) provide a rich picture of international indexes for professional investors.

Bond Market Indicators

Just as stock market indexes provide guidance concerning the performance of the overall stock market, several bond market indicators measure the performance of various categories of bonds. The three most well-known groups of indexes are those of Merrill Lynch, Lehman Brothers, and Salomon Brothers. Table 2.6, Panel A lists the components of the fixed-income market at the beginning of 1996. Panel B presents a profile of the characteristics of the three major bond indexes.

The major problem with these indexes is that true rates of return on many bonds are difficult to compute because the infrequency with which the bonds trade make reliable up-to-date prices difficult to obtain. In practice, some prices must be estimated from bond valuation models. These "matrix" prices may differ from true market values.

---

[4]See Chapter 24 for more discussion of this issue.

Figure 2.13

Listing of foreign stock market indexes.

	DOW JONES WORLD STOCK INDEX				

REGION/COUNTRY	DJ EQUITY MARKET INDEX, LOCAL CURRENCY	PCT. CHG.	5:30 P.M. INDEX	CHG.	PCT. CHG.
Americas			157.11	− 0.24	− 0.15
Canada	137.40	− 0.07	116.43	− 0.01	− 0.01
Mexico	230.58	− 0.50	93.68	− 1.04	− 1.10
U.S.	635.93	− 0.15	635.93	− 0.96	− 0.15
Europe/Africa			142.01	+ 0.79	+ 0.56
Austria	114.96	+ 0.12	113.77	− 0.40	− 0.35
Belgium	148.07	+ 0.70	147.17	+ 1.21	+ 0.83
Denmark	115.00	+ 0.05	114.84	+ 0.10	+ 0.09
Finland	244.93	+ 0.85	215.73	+ 2.12	+ 0.99
France	130.97	+ 0.72	130.47	+ 1.04	+ 0.80
Germany	145.05	+ 0.03	143.10	+ 0.22	+ 0.15
Ireland	205.28	+ 0.16	168.57	+ 0.12	+ 0.07
Italy	141.08	− 0.01	112.32	+ 0.10	+ 0.09
Netherlands	187.59	+ 0.45	183.76	+ 0.86	+ 0.47
Norway	156.05	+ 1.97	142.44	+ 3.02	+ 2.17
South Africa	210.03	+ 0.10	132.30	+ 0.44	+ 0.33
Spain	165.05	+ 0.93	123.61	+ 0.87	+ 0.71
Sweden	225.74	+ 1.61	185.60	+ 3.01	+ 1.65
Switzerland	214.06	+ 0.70	228.96	+ 1.96	+ 0.86
United Kingdom	153.46	+ 0.56	126.01	+ 0.58	+ 0.46
Europe/Africa (ex. South Africa)			142.36	+ 0.81	+ 0.57
Europe/Africa (ex. U.K. & S. Africa)			154.81	+ 0.95	+ 0.62
Asia/Pacific			120.69	+ 0.04	+ 0.03
Australia	closed		136.48	+ 0.29	+ 0.21
Hong Kong	247.09	− 0.36	248.06	− 0.96	− 0.39
Indonesia	224.64	− 0.05	191.66	− 0.15	− 0.08
Japan	98.37	− 0.11	112.57	+ 0.09	+ 0.08
Malaysia	228.77	− 0.44	249.05	− 1.31	− 0.52
New Zealand	134.84	+ 0.43	167.72	+ 1.37	+ 0.82
Philippines	364.92	+ 0.18	362.05	+ 0.65	+ 0.18
Singapore	176.52	+ 0.50	203.09	+ 0.89	+ 0.44
South Korea	143.69	− 0.97	137.83	− 1.85	− 1.32
Taiwan	153.37	− 0.67	142.82	− 0.64	− 0.45
Thailand	closed		198.75	− 0.11	− 0.06
Asia/Pacific (ex. Japan)			188.34	− 0.27	− 0.14
World (ex. U.S.)			128.00	+ 0.32	+ 0.25
DJ WORLD STOCK INDEX			140.40	+ 0.11	+ 0.08

Indexes based on 6/30/82=100 for U.S., 12/31/91=100 for World.

Source: From The Wall Street Journal, June 11, 1996. Reprinted by permission of The Wall Street Journal, © 1996 Dow Jones & Company, Inc. All Rights Reserved Worldwide.

Table 2.6   The U.S. Fixed-Income Market and Its Indexes

A. The fixed-income market

Sector	Size ($ Billion)	% of Market
Treasury	$3,548	37.4%
Government-sponsored enterprises	944	10.0
Corporate	1,440	15.2
Tax-exempt*	1,107	11.7
Mortgage backed	1,762	18.6
Asset backed	686	7.2
TOTAL	$9,487	100.0%

B. Profile of bond indexes

	Lehman Brothers	Merrill Lynch	Salomon Brothers
Number of issues	Over 6,500	Over 5,000	Over 5,000
Maturity of included bonds	≥ 1 year	≥ 1 year	≥ 1 year
Excluded issues	Junk bonds Convertibles Flower bonds Floating rate	Junk bonds Convertibles Flower bonds	Junk bonds Convertibles Floating rate
Weighting	Market value	Market value	Market value
Reinvestment of intramonth cash flows	No	Yes (in specific bond)	Yes (at one-month T-bill rate)
Daily availability	Yes	Yes	Yes

*Includes private purpose tax-exempt debt.

Source: Panel A: Flow of Funds Accounts, Flows and Outstandings, Board of Governors of the Federal Reserve System, Second Quarter, 1997. Panel B: Frank K. Reilly, G. Wenchi Kao, and David J. Wright, "Alternative Bond Market Indexes," Financial Analysts Journal (May–June 1992), pp. 44–58.

2.5 DERIVATIVE MARKETS

One of the most significant developments in financial markets in recent years has been the growth of futures, options, and related derivatives markets. These instruments provide payoffs that depend on the values of other assets such as commodity prices, bond and stock prices, or market index values. For this reason these instruments sometimes are called **derivative assets,** or **contingent claims.** Their values derive from or are contingent on the values of other assets.

Options

A **call option** gives its holder the right to purchase an asset for a specified price, called the **exercise** or **strike price,** on or before a specified expiration date. For example, a January call option on Eli Lilly stock with an exercise price of $65 entitles its owner to purchase Lilly stock for a price of $65 at any time up to and including the expiration date in January. Each option contract is for the purchase of 100 shares. However, quotations are made on a per-share basis. The holder of the call need not exercise the option; it will be profitable to exercise only if the market value of the asset that may be purchased exceeds the exercise price.

When the market price exceeds the exercise price, the optionholder may "call away" the asset for the exercise price and reap a payoff equal to the difference between the stock price and the exercise price. Otherwise, the option will be left unexercised. If not exercised before the expiration date of the contract, the option simply expires and no longer has value. Calls therefore provide greater profits when stock prices increase and thus represent bullish investment vehicles.

In contrast, a **put option** gives its holder the right to sell an asset for a specified exercise price on or before a specified expiration date. A January put on Lilly with an exercise price of $65 thus entitles its owner to sell Lilly stock to the put writer at a price of $65 at any time before expiration in January, even if the market price of Lilly is lower than $65. Whereas profits on call options increase when the asset increases in value, profits on put options increase when the asset value falls. The put is exercised only if its holder can deliver an asset worth less than the exercise price in return for the exercise price.

Figure 2.14 presents stock option quotations from *The Wall Street Journal*. The highlighted options are for Lilly. The repeated number under the name of the firm is the current price of Lilly shares, 66^{1}/_{2}$. The two columns to the right of Lilly give the exercise price and expiration month of each option. Thus we see that the paper reports data on call and put options on Lilly with exercise prices ranging from 42^{1}/_{2}$ to $70 per share and with expiration dates in January, November, and December. These exercise prices bracket the current price of Lilly shares.

The next four columns provided trading volume and closing prices of each option. For example, 213 contracts traded on the January expiration call with an exercise price of $65. The last trade price was 5^{7}/_{8}$, meaning that an option to purchase one share of Lilly at an exercise price of $65 sold for $5.875. Each option *contract*, therefore, cost $587.50.

Notice that the prices of call options decrease as the exercise price increases. For example, the January maturity call with exercise price 67^{1}/_{2}$ costs only 4^{1}/_{4}$. This makes sense, because the right to purchase a share at a higher exercise price is less valuable. Conversely, put prices increase with the exercise price. The right to sell a share of Lilly at a price of $65 in November cost 1^{5}/_{16}$ while the right to sell at $70 cost 4^{1}/_{2}$.

Figure 2.14
Options market
listings.

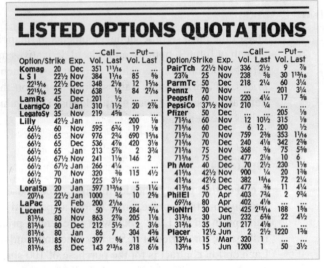

Source: The Wall Street Journal, November 17, 1997. Reprinted by permission of The
Wall Street Journal, © 1997 Dow Jones & Company, Inc. All Rights Reserved Worldwide.

Question 7 • What would be the profit or loss per share of stock to an investor who
bought the November maturity Lilly call option with exercise price 65 if the stock price
at the expiration of the option is 68? What about a purchaser of the put option with
the same exercise price and maturity?

Futures Contracts

A **futures contract** calls for delivery of an asset (or in some cases, its cash value) at a specified delivery or maturity date for an agreed-upon price, called the futures price, to be paid
at contract maturity. The *long position* is held by the trader who commits to purchasing the
commodity on the delivery date. The trader who takes the *short position* commits to delivering the commodity at contract maturity.

Figure 2.15 illustrates the listing of several stock index futures contracts as they appear
in *The Wall Street Journal*. The top line in boldface type gives the contract name, the
exchange on which the futures contract is traded in parentheses, and the contract size. Thus
the second contract listed is for the S&P 500 index, traded on the Chicago Mercantile
Exchange (CME). Each contract calls for delivery of 250 times the value of the S&P 500
stock price index.

The next several rows detail price data for contracts expiring on various dates. The
December 1997 maturity contract opened during the day at a futures price of 919.60 per
unit of the index. (The last line of the entry shows that the S&P 500 index was at 928.35 at
close of trading on the day of the listing.) The highest futures price during the day was 935,
the lowest was 915.10, and the settlement price (a representative trading price during the
last few minutes of trading) was 932.60. The settlement price increased by 13.40 from the
previous trading day. The highest and lowest futures prices over the contract's life to date
have been 992.25 and 753.00, respectively. Finally, open interest, or the number of outstanding contracts, was 383,031. Corresponding information is given for each maturity
date.

Figure 2.15

Financial futures listings.

FUTURES PRICES

INDEX

DJ INDUSTRIAL AVERAGE (CBOT) $10 times average

	Open	High	Low	Settle	Chg	Open High	Low	Open Interest
Dec	7535.0	7615.0	7480.0	7600.0 +	83.0	8252.0	6870.0	9,597
Mr98	7613.0	7675.0	7560.0	7674.0 +	85.0	8335.0	6970.0	1,866
June	7690.0	7752.0	7640.0	7752.0 +	86.0	8320.0	7070.0	111
Sept	7770.0	7833.0	7725.0	7833.0 +	87.0	8410.0	7150.0	46

Est vol 10,500; vol Th 14,677; open int 11,620, +460.
The index: High 7590.16; Low 7467.38; Close 7572.48, +84.72

S&P 500 INDEX (CME) $250 times index

	Open	High	Low	Settle	Chg	Open High	Low	Open Interest
Dec	919.60	935.00	915.10	932.60 +	13.40	992.25	753.00	383,031
Mr98	933.00	944.50	927.70	942.50 +	13.60	100260	854.40	19,727
June	942.50	954.00	937.50	952.30 +	13.80	101200	864.25	4,434
Sept	....	....		962.20 +	14.00	102295	884.00	498
Dec	....	....		973.00 +	14.80	103625	895.00	532
Ju99	....	....		995.50 +	16.10	106115	959.35	176

Est vol 145,501; vol Th 144,181; open int 408,478, +3,928.
Indx prelim High 930.44; Low 915.34; Close 928.35, +11.69

MINI S&P 500 (CME) $50 times index

	Open	High	Low	Settle	Chg	Open High	Low	Open Interest
Dec	920.00	934.75	915.00	932.50 +	13.25	992.25	844.00	16,425

Est vol 11,381; vol Th 14,021; open int 16,710, −31.

S&P MIDCAP 400 (CME) $500 times index

	Open	High	Low	Settle	Chg	Open High	Low	Open Interest
Dec	315.00	319.40	314.40	318.90 +	4.30	343.25	254.20	11,587

Est vol 570; vol Th 578; open int 11,599, −103.
The index: High 317.19; Low 312.92; Close 316.71, +3.79

NIKKEI 225 STOCK AVERAGE (CME)-$5 times index

	Open	High	Low	Settle	Chg	Open High	Low	Open Interest
Dec	15150.	15545.	15000.	15350. −	80	20905.	14905.	19,794

Est vol 3,054; vol Th 1,352; open int 19,839, +80.
The index: High 15371.83; Low 14966.13; Close 15082.52 −344.75

NASDAQ 100 (CME)-$100 times index

	Open	High	Low	Settle	Chg	Open High	Low	Open Interest
Dec	100845	103575	100800	103525 +	22.75	117000	811.35	9,123
Mr98	102600	104925	102600	104925 +	22.75	118600	959.00	233
June	....	....		106400 +	22.7	119275	110275	132

Est vol 2,659; vol Th 3,668; open int 9,488, +94.
The index: High 1030.32; Low 1002.92; Close 1027.85, +24.93

The trader holding the long position profits from price increases. Suppose that at expiration the S&P 500 index is at 935.60. The long position trader who entered the contract at the futures price of 932.60 would pay the previously agreed-upon 932.60 for each unit of the index, which at contract maturity would be worth 935.60. Because each contract calls for delivery of $250 times the index, ignoring brokerage fees, the profit to the long position would equal $250 \times (935.60 − 932.60) = 750. Conversely, the short position must deliver $250 times the value of the index for the previously agreed-upon futures price. The short position's loss equals the long position's profit.

The right to purchase the asset at an agreed-upon price, as opposed to the obligation, distinguishes call options from long positions in futures contracts. A futures contract *obliges* the long position to purchase the asset at the futures price; the call option, in contrast, *conveys the right* to purchase the asset at the exercise price. The purchase will be made only if it yields a profit.

Clearly, a holder of a call has a better position than does the holder of a long position on a futures contract with a futures price equal to the option's exercise price. This advantage, of course, comes only at a price. Call options must be purchased; futures contracts may be entered into without cost. The purchase price of an option is called the *premium*. It represents the compensation the holder of the call must pay for the ability to exercise the option only when it is profitable to do so. Similarly, the difference between a put option and a short futures position is the right, as opposed to the obligation, to sell an asset at an agreed-upon price.

SUMMARY

1. Money market securities are very short-term debt obligations. They are usually highly marketable and have relatively low credit risk. Their low maturities and low credit risk ensure minimal capital gains or losses. These securities trade in large denominations, but they may be purchased indirectly through money market funds.

2. Much of the U.S. government borrowing is in the form of Treasury bonds and notes. These are coupon-paying bonds usually issued at or near par value. Treasury bonds are similar in design to coupon-paying corporate bonds.

3. Municipal bonds are distinguished largely by their tax-exempt status. Interest payments (but not capital gains) on these securities are exempt from federal income taxes. The equivalent taxable yield offered by a municipal bond equals $r_m/(1 - t)$, where r_m is the municipal yield and t is the investor's tax bracket.

4. Mortgage pass-through securities are pools of mortgages sold in one package. Owners of pass-throughs receive the principal and interest payments made by the borrower. The originator that issued the mortgage merely services the mortgage, simply "passing through" the payments to the purchasers of the mortgage. A federal agency may guarantee the payment of interest and principal on mortgages pooled into these pass-through securities.

5. Common stock is an ownership share in a corporation. Each share entitles its owner to one vote on matters of corporate governance and to a prorated share of the dividends paid to shareholders. Stock, or equity, owners are the residual claimants on the income earned by the firm.

6. Preferred stock usually pays fixed dividends for the life of the firm; it is a perpetuity. A firm's failure to pay the dividend due on preferred stock, however, does not precipitate corporate bankruptcy. Instead, unpaid dividends simply cumulate. Newer varieties of preferred stock include convertible and adjustable rate issues.

7. Many stock market indexes measure the performance of the overall market. The Dow Jones Averages, the oldest and best-known indicators, are price-weighted indexes. Today, many broad-based, market-value-weighted indexes are computed daily. These include the Standard & Poor's 500 Stock Index, the NYSE and Amex indexes, the Nasdaq index, and the Wilshire 5000 Index. The Value Line index is a geometrically weighted average of about 1,700 firms.

8. A call option is a right to purchase an asset at a stipulated exercise price on or before a maturity date. A put option is the right to sell an asset at some exercise price. Calls increase in value while puts decrease in value as the price of the underlying asset increases.

9. A futures contract is an obligation to buy or sell an asset at a stipulated futures price on a maturity date. The long position, which commits to purchasing, gains if the asset value increases while the short position, which commits to purchasing, loses.

Key Terms

money market	commercial paper	Treasury notes
capital markets	banker's acceptance	Treasury bonds
bank discount yield	eurodollars	yield to maturity
effective annual rate	repurchase agreements	municipal bonds
bank discount method	federal funds	equivalent taxable yield
bond equivalent yield	London Interbank Offered	current yield
certificate of deposit	Rate	equities

residual claim	market-value-weighted	contingent claims
limited liability	index	call option
capital gains	index funds	exercise (strike) price
price–earnings ratio	geometric average	put option
preferred stock	derivative assets	futures contract
price-weighted average		

Selected Readings

A standard reference to the securities, terminology, and organization of the money market is still:
  Stigum, Marcia. *The Money Market.* Homewood, Ill.: Dow Jones-Irwin, 1983.
A good survey of a wide variety of financial markets and instruments is:
  Logue, Dennis E., ed. *The WG&L Handbook of Financial Markets.* Cincinnati, Ohio: Warren, Gorham & Lamont, 1995.
A survey textbook on capital markets, with emphasis on institutional features, and sections on the money market, as well as debt, equity, and derivative markets is:
  Fabozzi, Frank J.; and Franco Modigliani. *Capital Markets: Institutions and Instruments,* 2d ed. Englewood Cliffs, N.J.: Prentice Hall, 1996.

Problems

1. The following multiple-choice problems are based on questions that appeared in past CFA examinations.
   a. A firm's preferred stock often sells at yields below its bonds because:
      i. Preferred stock generally carries a higher agency rating.
      ii. Owners of preferred stock have a prior claim on the firm's earnings.
      iii. Owners of preferred stock have a prior claim on a firm's assets in the event of liquidation.
      iv. Corporations owning stock may exclude from income taxes most of the dividend income they receive.
   b. A municipal bond carries a coupon of 6¾% and is trading at par; to a taxpayer in a 34% tax bracket, this bond would provide a taxable equivalent yield of:
      i. 4.5%
      ii. 10.2%
      iii. 13.4%
      iv. 19.9%
   c. Which is the *most risky* transaction to undertake in the stock index option markets if the stock market is expected to increase substantially after the transaction is completed?
      i. Write a call option.
      ii. Write a put option
      iii. Buy a call option.
      iv. Buy a put option.

2. A U.S. Treasury bill has 180 days to maturity and a price of $9,600 per $10,000 face value. The bank discount yield of the bill is 8%.
   a. Calculate the bond equivalent yield for the Treasury bill. Show calculations. (Ignore skip-day settlement.)
   b. Briefly explain why a Treasury bill's bond equivalent yield differs from the discount yield.

3. A bill has a bank discount yield of 6.81% based on the asked price, and 6.90% based on the bid price. The maturity of the bill (already accounting for skip-day settlement) is 60 days. Find the bid and asked prices of the bill.

4. Reconsider the T-bill of question 3. Calculate its bond equivalent yield and effective annual yield based on the ask price. Confirm that these yields exceed the discount yield.

5. Which security offers a higher effective annual yield?
   a. i. A three-month bill selling at $9,764.
      ii. A six-month bill selling at $9,539.
   b. Calculate the bank discount yield on each bill.

6. A Treasury bill with 90-day maturity sells at a bank discount yield of 3%.
   a. What is the price of the bill?
   b. What is the 90-day holding period return of the bill?
   c. What is the bond equivalent yield of the bill?
   d. What is the effective annual yield of the bill?

7. Find the price of a six-month (182-day) U.S. Treasury bill with a par value of $100,000 and a bank discount yield of 9.18 percent.

8. Find the after-tax return to a corporation that buys a share of preferred stock at $40, sells it at year-end at $40, and receives a $4 year-end dividend. The firm is in the 30% tax bracket.

9. Consider the three stocks in the following table. P_t represents price at time t, and Q_t represents shares outstanding at time t. Stock C splits two for one in the last period.

	P_0	Q_0	P_1	Q_1	P_2	Q_2
A	90	100	95	100	95	100
B	50	200	45	200	45	200
C	100	200	110	200	55	400

   a. Calculate the rate of return on a price-weighted index of the three stocks for the first period ($t = 0$ to $t = 1$).
   b. What must happen to the divisor for the price-weighted index in year 2?
   c. Calculate the rate of return for the second period ($t = 1$ to $t = 2$).

10. Using the data in problem 9, calculate the first-period rates of return on the following indexes of the three stocks:
    a. A market-value-weighted index.
    b. An equally weighted index.
    c. A geometric index.

11. An investor is in a 28% tax bracket. If corporate bonds offer 9% yields, what must municipals offer for the investor to prefer them to corporate bonds?

12. Short-term municipal bonds currently offer yields of 4%, while comparable taxable bonds pay 5%. Which gives you the higher after-tax yield if your tax bracket is:
    a. Zero.
    b. 10%.
    c. 20%.
    d. 30%.

13. Find the equivalent taxable yield of the municipal bond in the previous question for tax brackets of zero, 10%, 20%, and 30%.

14. The coupon rate on a tax-exempt bond is 5.6 percent, and the rate on a taxable bond is 8 percent. Both bonds sell at par. The tax bracket (marginal tax rate) at which an investor would be indifferent between the two bonds is:
    a. 30.0%.
    b. 39.6%.
    c. 41.7%.
    d. 42.9%.

15. Which security should sell at a greater price?
    a. A 10-year Treasury bond with a 9% coupon rate versus a 10-year T-bond with a 10% coupon.
    b. A three-month maturity call option with an exercise price of $40 versus a three-month call on the same stock with an exercise price of $35.
    c. A put option on a stock selling at $50, or a put option on another stock selling at $60 (all other relevant features of the stocks and options may be assumed to be identical).
    d. A three-month T-bill with a discount yield of 6.1% versus a three-month bill with a discount yield of 6.2%.

16. Why do call options with exercise prices greater than the price of the underlying stock sell for positive prices?

17. Both a call and a put currently are traded on stock XYZ; both have strike prices of $50 and maturities of six months. What will be the profit to an investor who buys the call for $4 in the following scenarios for stock prices in six months? What will be the profit in each scenario to an investor who buys the put for $6?
    a. $40.
    b. $45.
    c. $50.
    d. $55.
    e. $60.

18. Explain the difference between a put option and a short position in a futures contract.

19. Explain the difference between a call option and a long position in a futures contract.

20. What would you expect to happen to the spread between yields on commercial paper and Treasury bills if the economy were to enter a steep recession?

21. Examine the first 50 stocks listed in the stock market listings for NYSE stocks in your local newspaper. For how many of these stocks is the 52-week high price at least 50% greater than the 52-week low price? What do you conclude about the volatility of prices on individual stocks?

1. The discount yield at bid is 5.11. Therefore

$$P = 10,000 \,[1 - .0511 \times (92/360)] = \$9,869.41$$

2. If the bond is selling below par, it is unlikely that the government will find it optimal to call the bond at par, when it can instead buy the bond in the secondary market for less than par. Therefore, it makes sense to assume that the bond will remain alive until its maturity date. In contrast, premium bonds are vulnerable to call because the government can acquire them by paying only par value. Hence it is more likely that the bonds will repay principal at the first call date, and the yield to first call is the statistic of interest.

3. A 6% taxable return is equivalent to an after-tax return of 6(1 − .28) = 4.32%. Therefore, you would be better off in the taxable bond. The equivalent taxable yield of the tax-free bond is 4/(1 − .28) = 5.55%. So a taxable bond would have to pay a 5.55% yield to provide the same after-tax return as a tax-free bond offering a 4% yield.

4. a. You are entitled to a prorated share of IBM's dividend payments and to vote in any of IBM's stockholder meetings.
   b. Your potential gain is unlimited because IBM's stock price has no upper bound.
   c. Your outlay was $50 × 100 = $5,000. Because of limited liability, this is the most you can lose.

5. The price-weighted index increases from 62.5 [i.e., (100 + 25)/2] to 65 [i.e., (110 + 20)/2], a gain of 4%. An investment of one share in each company requires an outlay of $125 that would increase in value to $130, for a return of 4% (i.e., 5/125), which equals the return to the price-weighted index.

6. The market-value-weighted index return is calculated by computing the increase in the value of the stock portfolio. The portfolio of the two stocks starts with an initial value of $100 million + $500 million = $600 million and falls in value to $110 million + $400 million = $510 million, a loss of 90/600 = .15 or 15%. The index portfolio return is a weighted average of the returns on each stock with weights of $\frac{1}{6}$ on XYZ and $\frac{5}{6}$ on ABC (weights proportional to relative investments). Because the return on XYZ is 10%, while that on ABC is −20%, the index portfolio return is $\frac{1}{6} \times 10\% + \frac{5}{6} \times (-20\%) = -15\%$, equal to the return on the market-value-weighted index.

7. The payoff to the call option is $3 per share at maturity. The option cost is $2.75 per share. The dollar profit is therefore $.25. The put option expires worthless. Therefore, the investor's loss is the cost of the put, or $1⁵/₁₆.

HOW SECURITIES ARE TRADED

The first time a security trades is when it is issued. Therefore, we begin our examination of trading with a look at how securities are first marketed to the public by investment bankers, the midwives of securities. Then we turn to the various exchanges where already-issued securities can be traded among investors. We examine the competi-

tion among the New York Stock Exchange, the American Stock Exchange, the regional exchanges, and the over-the-counter market for the patronage of security traders. Next we turn to the mechanics of trading in these various markets. We describe the role of the specialist in exchange markets and the dealer in over-the-counter markets. We also touch briefly on block trading and the SuperDot system of the NYSE for electronically routing orders to the floor of the exchange. We discuss the costs of trading and describe the recent debate between the NYSE and its competitors over which market provides the lowest-

cost trading arena. Finally, we describe the essentials of specific transactions such as buying on margin and selling stock short and discuss relevant regulations governing security trading. We will see that some regulations, such as those governing insider trading, can be difficult to interpret in practice.

3.1   HOW FIRMS ISSUE SECURITIES

When firms need to raise capital they may choose to sell (or *float*) new securities. These new issues of stocks, bonds, or other securities typically are marketed to the public by investment bankers in what is called the **primary market.** Purchase and sale of already-issued securities among private investors takes place in the **secondary market.**

There are two types of primary market issues of common stock. *Initial public offerings,* or *IPOs,* are stocks issued by a formerly privately owned company selling stock to the public for the first time. *Seasoned new issues* are offered by companies that already have floated equity. A sale by IBM of new shares of stock, for example, would constitute a seasoned new issue.

We also distinguish between two types of primary market issues: a *public offering*, which is an issue of stock or bonds sold to the general investing public that can then be traded on the secondary market; and a *private placement,* which is an issue that is sold to a few wealthy or institutional investors at most, and, in the case of bonds, is generally held to maturity.

Investment Bankers and Underwriting

Public offerings of both stocks and bonds typically are marketed via an **underwriting** by investment bankers. In fact, more than one investment banker usually markets the securities. A lead firm forms an *underwriting syndicate* of other investment bankers to share the responsibility for the stock issue.

The bankers advise the firm regarding the terms on which it should attempt to sell the securities. A preliminary registration statement must be filed with the Securities and Exchange Commission (SEC) describing the issue and the prospects of the company. This *preliminary prospectus* is known as a *red herring* because of a statement printed in red that the company is not attempting to sell the security before the registration is approved. When the statement is finalized and approved by the SEC, it is called the **prospectus.** At this time the price at which the securities will be offered to the public is announced.

There are two methods of underwriting a securities issue. In a *firm commitment* underwriting arrangement the investment bankers purchase the securities from the issuing company and then resell them to the public. The issuing firm sells the securities to the underwriting syndicate for the public offering price less a spread that serves as compensation to the underwriters. In such an arrangement the underwriters assume the full risk that the shares cannot in fact be sold to the public at the stipulated offering price. Figure 3.1 depicts the relationship among the firm issuing the security, the underwriting syndicate, and the public.

An alternative to firm commitment is the *best-efforts* agreement. In this case the investment banker agrees to help the firm sell the issue to the public but does not actually purchase the securities. The banker simply acts as an intermediary between the public and the firm and thus does not bear the risk of being unable to resell purchased securities at the offering price. The best-efforts procedure is more common for initial public offerings of common stock, for which the appropriate share price is less certain.

Corporations engage investment bankers either by negotiation or by competitive bidding. Negotiation is far more common. Besides being compensated by the spread between the purchase price and the public offering price, an investment banker may receive shares of common stock or other securities of the firm. In the case of competitive bidding, a firm may announce its intent to issue securities and invite investment bankers to submit bids for the underwriting. Such a bidding process may reduce the cost of the issue; it might also bring fewer services from the investment banker. Many public utilities are required to solicit competitive bids from underwriters.

Figure 3.1

Relationship among a firm issuing securities, the underwriters, and the public.

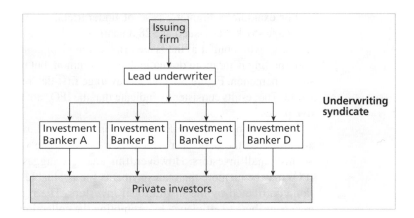

Shelf Registration

An important innovation in the method of issuing securities was introduced in 1982, when the SEC approved Rule 415, which allows firms to register securities and gradually sell them to the public for two years after the initial registration. Because the securities are already registered, they can be sold on short notice with little additional paperwork. In addition, they can be sold in small amounts without incurring substantial flotation costs. The securities are "on the shelf," ready to be issued, which has given rise to the term *shelf registration*.

Question 1 • Why does it make sense for shelf registration to be limited in time?

Initial Public Offerings

Investment bankers manage the issuance of new securities to the public. Once the SEC has commented on the registration statement and a preliminary prospectus has been distributed to interested investors, the investment bankers organize "road shows" in which they travel around the country to publicize the imminent offering. These road shows serve two purposes. First, they attract potential investors and provide them information about the offering. Second, they collect for the issuing firm and its underwriters information about the price at which they will be able to market the securities. Large investors communicate their interest in purchasing shares of the IPO to the underwriters; these indications of interest are called a *book* and the process of polling potential investors is called *bookbuilding*. The book provides valuable information to the issuing firm because large institutional investors often will have useful insights about the market demand for the security as well as the prospects of the firm and its competitors. It is common for investment bankers to revise both their initial estimates of the offering price of a security and the number of shares offered based on feedback from the investing community.

Why would investors truthfully reveal their interest in an offering to the investment banker? Might they be better off expressing little interest in the hope that this will drive down the offering price? Truth is the better policy in this case because truth-telling is rewarded. Shares of IPOs are allocated to investors in part based on the strength of each investor's expressed interest in the offering. If a firm wishes to get a large allocation when it is optimistic about the security, it needs to reveal its optimism. In turn, the underwriter needs to offer the security at a bargain price to these investors to induce them to participate in bookbuilding and share their information. Thus IPOs commonly are underpriced compared to the price at which they could be marketed. Such underpricing is reflected in price jumps on the date when the shares are first traded in public security markets.

For example, a dramatic case of underpricing took place on August 8, 1995, when Netscape stock was issued at $28 a share and closed at $58¼ on the first day of trading. Investors who bought at the issue price earned a *one-day* return of 108%. This degree of underpricing is far more dramatic than is common, but underpricing seems to be a universal phenomenon. Figure 3.2 presents average first-day returns on IPOs of stocks across the world. The results consistently indicate that the IPOs are marketed to the investors at attractive prices.

Underpricing of IPOs makes them appealing to all investors, yet institutional investors are allocated the bulk of a typical new issue. Some view this as unfair discrimination against small investors. However, this analysis suggests that the apparent discounts on IPOs may be no more than fair payments for a valuable service, specifically, the information contributed by the institutional investors. The right to allocate shares in this way may contribute to efficiency by promoting the collection and dissemination of such information.[1]

Appropriate pricing of IPOs can be difficult, and not all IPOs turn out to be underpriced. Some stocks do poorly after the initial issue and others cannot even be fully sold to the market. Underwriters left with unmarketable securities are forced to sell them at a loss on the secondary market. Therefore, the investment banker bears the price risk of an underwritten issue.

Interestingly, despite their dramatic initial investment performance, IPOs have been poor long-term investments. Figure 3.3 compares the stock price performance of IPOs with shares of other firms of the same size for each of the five years after issue of the IPO. The year-by-year underperformance of the IPOs is dramatic, suggesting that on average, the investing public may be too optimistic about the prospects of these firms.

Very small firms may find initial public offerings using underwriters too expensive. The nearby box discusses how one firm used the Internet to do an IPO on its own, thereby avoiding underwriting fees. The box also discusses the growing feasibility of stock trading over the Internet.

Figure 3.2
Average initial returns for IPOs in various countries.

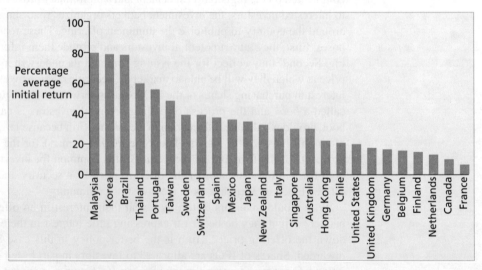

Source: Tim Loughran, Jay Ritter, and Kristian Rydqvist, "Initial Public Offerings: International Insights," Pacific-Basin Finance Journal 2 (1994), pp. 165–99.

---

[1]An elaboration of this point and a more complete discussion of the bookbuilding process is provided in Lawrence Benveniste and William Wilhelm, "Initial Public Offerings: Going by the Book," *Journal of Applied Corporate Finance* 9 (Spring 1997).

SEC SAYS BREWERY MAY USE INTERNET TO OFFER ITS STOCK

Confronting the first real-world collision of free markets and cyberspace, the Securities and Exchange Commission gave a cautious blessing to a New York brewery that has been using the Internet to underwrite and sell its own stock.

The company, Spring Street Brewing Co., faced a classic fund-raising problem of the small company—too small to interest Wall Street underwriters but reluctant to sell itself to venture capitalists. So it came up with a new approach. It posted a page on the World Wide Web to let people interested in buying and selling its stock meet and do deals. It called the system Wit-Trade, after the Wit beer it brews. And it launched an initial public offering, raising $1.6 million without paying a penny to underwriters.

The episode is extraordinary in several respects. For one, it shows the power of the Internet to free companies from their traditional market limitations, says Spring Street President and Chief Executive Andrew Klein.

"We've proved that there is a demand from small investors for illiquid, high-risk, high-potential securities," he says. "My phone's been ringing off the hook from companies that want to know how they can sell a piece of their companies to the public using this technology, without paying underwriters or brokers and without having to give the company away to venture capitalists."

Robert Colby, deputy director of the SEC's market-regulation division, says it's not uncommon for a small company to keep a list of shareholders that want to buy its stock. "What's unusual here," Mr. Colby says, "is that [Mr. Klein] put this list up on the Internet. And he added new elements, such as receiving buyers' funds and holding them."

That, indeed, is how the Wit-Trade system was working before Spring Street suspended it. On its web site, the company posted contracts that buyers and sellers filled out using their home computers. The buyer then mailed a check to Spring Street, which processed the trade as a Wall Street firm would and sent the seller's stock certificate back to the buyer.

That's where the SEC came in. "As you are not a registered broker-dealer, we suggest you modify your system to eliminate the company's control over these funds," the SEC's letter prodded. It asked the company to arrange for the trades to be processed by a bank or escrow agent, which Spring Street plans to do, Mr. Klein says.

While novel, the use of the Internet to trade and underwrite securities is going to increase quickly, says Daniel Weaver, a finance professor at Marquette University. "It's a natural place for small companies," he says. "I think small companies are getting dissatisfied with the service they get from underwriters." He notes that discount brokerage Charles Schwab Corp. plans an Internet trading system and predicts that other brokerage firms will follow suit, allowing companies to market more or less directly to the public.

All the same, the potential explosion of Internet trading is a daunting one for the SEC. So-called self-regulating organizations like the New York Stock Exchange and the National Association of Securities Dealers now take responsibility for policing much of the trading on more conventional securities markets. If trading on the Internet increases, there isn't anyone to monitor it—at least at the moment—except the SEC.

Figure 3.3

Long-term relative performance of initial public offerings.

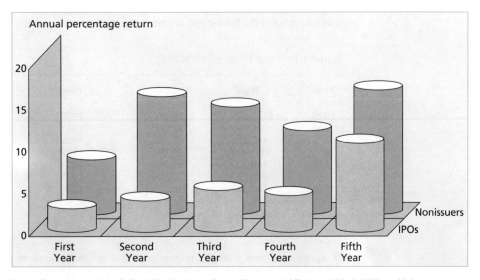

Source: Tim Loughran and Jay R. Ritter, "The New Issues Puzzle," The Journal of Finance 50 (March 1995), pp. 23–51.

Concept   Question 2 • Your broker just called. You can buy 200 shares of Good Time Inc.'s IPO
at the offer price. What should you do? [*Hint:* Why is the broker calling *you?*]

3.2   WHERE SECURITIES ARE TRADED

Once securities are issued to the public, investors may trade them among themselves.
Purchase and sale of already-issued securities take place in the secondary markets, which
consist of (1) national and local securities exchanges, (2) the over-the-counter market, and
(3) direct trading between two parties.

The Secondary Markets

There are several **stock exchanges** in the United States. Two of these, the New York Stock
Exchange (NYSE) and the American Stock Exchange (Amex), are national in scope.[2] The
others, such as the Boston and Pacific exchanges, are regional exchanges, which primarily
list firms located in a particular geographic area. There are also several exchanges for trading of options and futures contracts, which we'll discuss in the options and futures chapters.

An exchange provides a facility for its members to trade securities, and only members
of the exchange may trade there. Therefore memberships, or *seats*, on the exchange are
valuable assets. The majority of seats are *commission broker* seats, most of which are
owned by the large full-service brokerage firms. The seat entitles the firm to place one of
its brokers on the floor of the exchange where he or she can execute trades. The exchange
member charges investors for executing trades on their behalf. The commissions that members can earn through this activity determine the market value of a seat. A seat on the
NYSE has sold over the years for as little as $4,000 in 1878, and as much as $2 million in
1998. See Table 3.1 for a history of seat prices.

The NYSE is by far the largest single exchange. The shares of approximately 3,000 firms
trade there, and more than 3,000 stock issues (common and preferred stock) are listed. Daily
trading volume on the NYSE averaged 264.5 million shares in 1993. Table 3.2 shows the
trading activity of securities listed on the various stock exchanges as of 1996. The table shows
that the NYSE accounts for over 85% of the trading that takes place on stock exchanges.

The Amex also is national in scope, but it focuses on listing smaller and younger firms
than does the NYSE. Regional exchanges provide a market for trading shares of local firms
that do not meet the listing requirements of the national exchanges. The national exchanges

Table 3.1   Seat Prices on the NYSE

Year	High	Low	Year	High	Low
1875	$ 6,800	$ 4,300	1990	$ 430,000	$ 250,000
1905	85,000	72,000	1991	440,000	345,000
1935	140,000	65,000	1992	600,000	410,000
1965	250,000	190,000	1993	775,000	500,000
1975	138,000	55,000	1994	830,000	760,000
1980	275,000	175,000	1995	1,050,000	785,000
1985	480,000	310,000	1996	1,450,000	1,225,000

Source: New York Stock Exchange Fact Book, 1996.

---

[2]As this text went to press, the boards of the Amex and Nasdaq Stock Markets unanimously approved a preliminary merger
agreement to join the two exchanges. However, initial plans are for the two marketplaces to continue to operate largely
independently.

are willing to list a stock (allow trading in that stock on the exchange) only if the firm meets certain criteria of size and stability.

Table 3.3 gives the initial listing requirements for the NYSE. These requirements ensure that a firm is of significant trading interest before the NYSE will allocate facilities for it to be traded on the floor of the exchange. If a listed company suffers a decline and fails to meet the criteria in Table 3.3, it may be delisted from the exchange.

Regional exchanges also sponsor trading of some firms that are traded on national exchanges. This dual listing enables local brokerage firms to trade in shares of large firms without needing to purchase a membership on the NYSE.

The NYSE recently has lost market share to the regional exchanges and, far more dramatically, to the over-the-counter market. Today, approximately two-thirds of the trades in stocks listed on the NYSE are actually executed on the NYSE. In contrast, about 80% of the trades in NYSE-listed shares were executed on the exchange in the early 1980s. The loss is attributed to lower commissions charged on other exchanges, although the NYSE believes that a more inclusive treatment of trading costs would show that it is the most cost-effective trading arena. In any case, many of these non-NYSE trades were for relatively small transactions. The NYSE is still by far the preferred exchange for large traders, and its market share of exchange-listed companies (when measured in share volume rather than number of trades) is still above 80%.

The over-the-counter Nasdaq market (described in detail shortly) has posed a bigger competitive challenge to the NYSE. Its share of trading volume in NYSE-listed firms increased from 2.5% in 1983 to 6.7% in 1996. Moreover, many large firms that would be eligible to list their shares on the NYSE now choose to list on Nasdaq. Some of the well-known firms currently trading on Nasdaq are Microsoft, Intel, Apple Computer, Sun Microsystems, and MCI Communications. Total trading volume in over-the-counter stocks on the computerized Nasdaq system has increased dramatically in the last decade, rising from about 50 million shares per day in 1984 to 543 million shares in 1997. Share volume on Nasdaq now sur-

Table 3.2   Trading in Various Stock Markets, 1996

	Trading Volume during the Year (Billions of Shares)	% of Total*	Dollar Volume of Trading (Billions of dollars)	% of Total*
Exchange trading				
New York	104.64	87.2%	$4,063.7	89.6%
American	5.63	4.7	91.3	2.0
Regional Exchanges†	9.79	8.2	380.3	8.4
TOTAL	120.06	100.0%	$4,535.3	100.0%
Dealer market				
Nasdaq	145.60	100.0%	$3,592.50	100.0%

*Column sums subject to rounding error.
†Regional exchanges include Boston, Chicago, Pacific, and Philadelphia Stock Exchanges.
Source: Nasdaq Fact Book and Company Directory, 1997.

Table 3.3   Initial Listing Requirements for the NYSE

Pretax income in last year	$ 2,500,000
Average annual pretax income in previous two years	$ 2,000,000
Net tangible assets	$40,000,000
Market value of publicly held stock	$40,000,000
Shares publicly held	1,100,000
Number of holders of 100 shares or more	2,000

Source: Data from the New York Stock Exchange Fact Book, 1996.

passes that on the NYSE. However, because Nasdaq-listed firms tend to sell at lower prices, the dollar value of Nasdaq trades is still only about 80% that of NYSE trades.

Other new sources of competition to the NYSE come from abroad. For example, the London Stock Exchange is preferred by some traders because it offers greater anonymity. In addition, new restrictions introduced by the NYSE to limit price volatility in the wake of the market crash of 1987 are viewed by some traders as another reason to trade abroad. These so-called circuit breakers are discussed below.

While most common stocks are traded on the exchanges, most bonds and other fixed-income securities are not. Corporate bonds are traded both on the exchanges and over the counter, but all federal and municipal government bonds are traded only over the counter.

The Over-the-Counter Market

Roughly 35,000 issues are traded on the **over-the-counter** (OTC) **market** and any security may be traded there, but the OTC market is not a formal exchange. There are no member-ship requirements for trading, nor are there listing requirements for securities (although there are requirements to be listed on Nasdaq, the computer-linked network for trading of OTC securities). In the OTC market thousands of brokers register with the SEC as dealers in OTC securities. Security dealers quote prices at which they are willing to buy or sell securities. A broker can execute a trade by contacting the dealer listing an attractive quote.

Before 1971, all OTC quotations of stock were recorded manually and published daily. The so-called *pink sheets* were the means by which dealers communicated their interest in trading at various prices. This was a cumbersome and inefficient technique, and published quotes were a full day out of date. In 1971 the National Association of Securities Dealers Automated Quotation system, or **Nasdaq,** began to offer immediate information on a computer-linked system of bid and asked prices for stocks offered by various dealers. The **bid price** is that at which a dealer is willing to purchase a security; the **asked price** is that at which the dealer will sell a security. The system allows a dealer who receives a buy or sell order from an investor to examine all current quotes, call the dealer with the best quote, and execute a trade. Securities of nearly 5,500 firms are quoted on the system, which is now called the Nasdaq Stock Market.

The Nasdaq market is divided into two sectors, the Nasdaq National Market (comprising a bit more than 4,000 companies) and the Nasdaq SmallCap Market (comprised of about 1,300 smaller companies). The National Market securities must meet more stringent listing requirements and trade in a more liquid market. Some of the more important initial listing requirements for each of these markets are presented in Table 3.4. For even smaller firms, Nasdaq maintains an electronic "OTC Bulletin Board," which is not part of the Nasdaq market but is simply a means for brokers and dealers to get and post current price quotes over a computer network. Finally, the smallest stocks continue to be listed on the pink sheets distributed through the National Association of Securities Dealers.

Nasdaq has three levels of subscribers. The highest, Level 3, is for firms dealing, or "making markets," in OTC securities. These market makers maintain inventories of a security and continually stand ready to buy these shares from or sell them to the public at the quoted bid and asked price. They earn profits from the spread between the bid price and the asked price. Level 3 subscribers may enter the bid and asked prices at which they are willing to buy or sell stocks into the computer network and update these quotes as desired.

Level 2 subscribers receive all bid and asked quotes but cannot enter their own quotes. These subscribers tend to be brokerage firms that execute trades for clients but do not actively deal in the stocks for their own accounts. Brokers attempting to buy or sell shares call the market maker who has the best quote to execute a trade.

Table 3.4   Partial Requirements for Initial Listing on the Amex and Nasdaq Markets

	Amex	Nasdaq National Market	Nasdaq SmallCap Market
Tangible assets	None	$6 million	$4 million
Shares in public hands	500,000	1.1 million	1 million
Market value of shares	$3 million	$8 million	$5 million
Price of stock	$3	$5	$4
Pretax income	$750,000	$1 million	$750,000
Shareholders	800	400	300

Sources: Amex Fact Book, 1997, and Nasdaq World Wide Web page, 1997.

Level 1 subscribers receive only the median, or "representative," bid and asked prices on each stock. Level 1 subscribers are investors who are not actively buying and selling securities, yet the service provides them with general information.

For bonds, the over-the-counter market is a loosely organized network of dealers linked together by a computer quotation system. In practice, the corporate bond market often is quite "thin," in that there are few investors interested in trading a particular bond at any particular time. The bond market is therefore subject to a type of "liquidity risk," because it can be difficult to sell holdings quickly if the need arises.

The Third and Fourth Markets

The **third market** refers to trading of exchange-listed securities on the OTC market. Until the 1970s, members of the NYSE were required to execute all their trades of NYSE-listed securities on the exchange and to charge commissions according to a fixed schedule. This schedule was disadvantageous to large traders, who were prevented from realizing economies of scale on large trades. The restriction led brokerage firms that were not members of the NYSE, and so not bound by its rules, to establish trading in the OTC market on large NYSE-listed firms. These trades took place at lower commissions than would have been charged on the NYSE, and the third market grew dramatically until 1972 when the NYSE allowed negotiated commissions on orders exceeding $300,000. On May 1, 1975, frequently referred to as "May Day," commissions on all orders became negotiable.

The **fourth market** refers to direct trading between investors in exchange-listed securities without benefit of a broker. Large institutions that wish to avoid brokerage fees altogether may engage in direct trading. The fourth market has grown dramatically in recent years as big institutional investors have begun using electronic trading networks to step around brokers. Networks such as Instinet or Posit allow traders to trade stocks directly without ever going through a broker or an exchange. Posit allows for trades in both single stocks and stock portfolios. Both networks allow for much greater anonymity than exchange trading. On some days, Instinet accounts for up to 20% of the total volume of trading on Nasdaq-listed shares.

The National Market System

The Securities Act Amendments of 1975 directed the Securities and Exchange Commission to implement a national competitive securities market. Such a market would entail centralized reporting of transactions and a centralized quotation system, and would result in enhanced competition among market makers. In 1975 a "Consolidated Tape" began reporting trades on the NYSE, the Amex, and the major regional exchanges, as well as on

Nasdaq-listed stocks. In 1977 the Consolidated Quotations Service began providing on-line bid and asked quotes for NYSE securities also traded on various other exchanges. This enhances competition by allowing market participants such as brokers or dealers who are at different locations to interact, and it allows orders to be directed to the market in which the best price can be obtained. In 1978 the Intermarket Trading System was implemented to link seven exchanges by computer (NYSE, Amex, Boston, Cincinnati, Midwest, Pacific, and Philadelphia). Brokers and market makers can thus display quotes on all markets and execute cross-market trades.

The final step in integrating securities markets would be the establishment of a central limit order book. Such an electronic "book" would contain all orders conditional on both prices and dates. All markets would be linked and all traders could compete for all orders. Such a system has not yet been implemented, however, and does not appear to be imminent.

3.3   TRADING ON EXCHANGES

Most of the material in this section applies to all securities traded on exchanges. Some of it, however, applies just to stocks, and in such cases we use the term *stocks* or *shares*.

The Participants

When an investor instructs a broker to buy or sell securities, a number of players must act to consummate the trade. We start our discussion of the mechanics of exchange trading with a brief description of the potential parties to a trade.

The investor places an order with a broker. The brokerage firm owning a seat on the exchange contacts its *commission broker,* who is on the floor of the exchange, to execute the order. *Floor brokers* are independent members of the exchange who own their own seats and handle work for commission brokers when those brokers have too many orders to handle.

Registered traders are frequent traders who perform no public function, but instead use their membership to execute trades for their own accounts. By trading directly, they avoid the commissions that would be incurred if they had to trade through a broker. There are relatively few registered traders.

The **specialist** is central to the trading process. Specialists maintain a market in one or more listed securities. All trading in a given stock takes place at one location on the floor of the exchange called the *specialist's post*. At the specialist's post is a computer monitor that presents all the current offers from interested traders to buy or sell shares at various prices as well as the number of shares these quotes are good for. The specialist manages the trading in the stock. The market-making responsibility for each stock is assigned by the NYSE to one specialist firm. There is only one specialist per stock but most firms will have responsibility for trading in several stocks. The specialist firm also may act as a dealer in the stock, trading for its own account. We will examine the role of the specialist in more detail shortly.

Types of Orders

Market Orders   Market orders are simply buy or sell orders that are to be executed immediately at current market prices. For example, an investor might call his broker and ask for the market price of Exxon. The retail broker will wire this request to the commission broker on the floor of the exchange, who will approach the specialist's post and ask the specialist for best current quotes. Finding that the current quotes are $68 per share bid and $68¼ asked, the investor might direct the broker to buy 100 shares "at market," meaning that he is willing to pay $68¼ per share for an immediate transaction. Similarly, an order to "sell at market" will result in stock sales at $68 per share. When a trade is executed, the specialist's clerk will fill out an order card that reports the time, price, and quantity of shares traded, and the transaction is reported on the exchange's ticker tape.

There are two potential complications to this simple scenario, however. First, as noted earlier, the posted quotes of $68 and $68¼ actually represent commitments to trade up to a specified number of shares. If the market order is for more than this number of shares, the order may be filled at multiple prices. For example, if the asked price is good for orders of up to 600 shares, and the investor wishes to purchase 1,000 shares, it may be necessary to pay a slightly higher price for the last 400 shares than the quoted asked price.

The second complication arises from the possibility of trading "inside the quoted spread." If the broker who has received a market buy order for Exxon meets another broker who has received a market sell order for Exxon, they can agree to trade with each other at a price of $68⅛ per share. By meeting in the middle of the quoted spread, both the buyer and the seller obtain "price improvement," that is, transaction prices better than the best quoted prices. Such "meetings" of brokers are more than accidental. Because all trading takes place at the specialist's post, floor brokers know where to look for counterparties to take the other side of a trade. One study[3] found that when the spread between the quoted bid and asked price was $¼ or greater, approximately one-half of trades on the NYSE were actually executed "inside the quotes." Now that the minimum tick size on the NYSE has been reduced from $⅛ to $1/16, even more trades ought to be executed inside the quotes.

Limit Orders   Investors may also place limit orders, whereby they specify prices at which they are willing to buy or sell a security. If the stock falls below the limit on a *limit-buy order* then the trade is to be executed. If Exxon is selling at $68 bid, $68¼ asked, for example, a limit-buy order may instruct the broker to buy the stock if and when the share price falls below $65. Correspondingly, a *limit-sell order* instructs the broker to sell as soon as the stock price goes above the specified limit.

What happens if a limit order is placed between the quoted bid and ask prices? For example, suppose you have instructed your broker to buy Exxon at a price of $68⅛ or better. The order may not be executed immediately, since the quoted asked price for the shares is $68¼, which is more than you are willing to pay. However, your willingness to buy at $68⅛ is better than the quoted bid price of $68 per share. Therefore, you may find that there are traders who were unwilling to sell their shares at the $68 bid price but are happy to sell shares to you at your higher bid price of $68⅛.

Until recently, the minimum tick size on the New York Stock Exchange was $⅛. In 1997 the NYSE and all other exchanges began allowing price quotes in $1/16 increments. This move could reduce the spread between bid and ask prices and therefore reduce trading costs. The NYSE also voted to eventually quote stock prices in decimals (i.e., in dollars and cents) rather than dollars and sixteenths. In principle, this could reduce the bid–asked spread to as little as one penny, but it is possible that even with decimal pricing, exchanges could mandate a minimum tick size, for example, of 5 cents. Moreover, even with decimal pricing, the typical bid–asked spread on smaller, less actively traded firms (which already exceeds $⅛ and therefore is not constrained by tick size requirements) would not be expected to fall.

Stop-loss orders are similar to limit orders in that the trade is not to be executed unless the stock hits a price limit. In this case, however, the stock is to be sold if its price falls *below* a stipulated level. As the name suggests, the order lets the stock be sold to stop further losses from accumulating. Symmetrically, *stop-buy orders* specify that the stock

---

[3]K. Ross, J. Shapiro, K. Smith, "Price Improvement of SuperDot Market Orders on the NYSE," NYSE Working Paper 96-02, March 1996.

Figure 3.4
Limit orders.

		Condition	
		Price below the limit	**Price above the limit**
Action	**Buy**	Limit-buy order	Stop-buy order
	Sell	Stop-loss order	Limit-sell order

should be bought when its price rises above a given limit. These trades often accompany short sales, and they are used to limit potential losses from the short position. Short sales are discussed in greater detail in Section 3.7. Figure 3.4 organizes these four types of trades in a simple matrix.

Orders also can be limited by a time period. Day orders, for example, expire at the close of the trading day. If it is not executed on that day, the order is canceled. *Open or good-till-canceled orders*, in contrast, remain in force for up to six months unless canceled by the customer. At the other extreme, *fill or kill orders* expire if the broker cannot fill them immediately.

Specialists and the Execution of Trades

A specialist "makes a market" in the shares of one or more firms. This task may require the specialist to act as either a broker or dealer. The specialist's role as a broker is simply to execute the orders of other brokers. Specialists may also buy or sell shares of stock for their own portfolios. When no other broker can be found to take the other side of a trade, specialists will do so even if it means they must buy for or sell from their own accounts. The NYSE commissions these companies to perform this service and monitors their performance. In this role, specialists act as dealers in the stock.

Part of the specialist's job as a broker is simply mechanical. The specialist maintains a "book" listing all outstanding unexecuted limit orders entered by brokers on behalf of clients. (Actually, the book is now a computer console.) When limit orders can be executed at market prices, the specialist executes, or "crosses," the trade.

The specialist is required to use the highest outstanding offered purchase price and lowest outstanding offered selling price when matching trades. Therefore, the specialist system results in an auction market, meaning all buy and all sell orders come to one location, and the best orders "win" the trades. In this role, the specialist acts merely as a facilitator.

The more interesting function of the specialist is to maintain a "fair and orderly market" by acting as a dealer in the stock. In return for the exclusive right to make the market in a specific stock on the exchange, the specialist is required to maintain an orderly market by buying and selling shares from inventory. Specialists maintain their own portfolios of stock and quote bid and asked prices at which they are obligated to meet at least a limited amount of market orders. If market buy orders come in, specialists must sell shares from their own accounts at the asked price; if sell orders come in, they must stand willing to buy at the listed bid price.[4]

---

[4]Actually, the specialist's published price quotes are valid only for a given number of shares. If a buy or sell order is placed for more shares than the quotation size, the specialist has the right to revise the quote.

Ordinarily, however, in an active market specialists can cross buy and sell orders without their own direct participation. That is, the specialist's own inventory of securities need not be the primary means of order execution. Occasionally, however, the specialist's bid and asked prices will be better than those offered by any other market participant. Therefore, at any point the effective asked price in the market is the lower of either the specialist's asked price or the lowest of the unfilled limit-sell orders. Similarly, the effective bid price is the highest of unfilled limit-buy orders or the specialist's bid. These procedures ensure that the specialist provides liquidity to the market. In practice, specialists participate in approximately 10%–20% of transactions on the NYSE.

By standing ready to trade at quoted bid and asked prices, the specialist is exposed somewhat to exploitation by other traders. Large traders with ready access to late-breaking news will trade with specialists only if the specialists' quoted prices are temporarily out of line with assessments of value based on that information. Specialists who cannot match the information resources of large traders will be at a disadvantage when their quoted prices offer profit opportunities to more informed traders.

You might wonder why specialists do not protect their interests by setting a low bid price and a high asked price. A specialist using that strategy would not suffer losses by maintaining a too-low asked price or a too-high bid price in a period of dramatic movements in the stock price. Specialists who offer a narrow spread between the bid and the asked prices have little leeway for error and must constantly monitor market conditions to avoid offering other investors advantageous terms.

There are two reasons why large bid–asked spreads are not viable options for the specialist. First, one source of the specialist's income is derived from frequent trading at the bid and asked prices, with the spread as the trading profit. A too-large spread would make the specialist's quotes noncompetitive with the limit orders placed by other traders. If the specialist's bid and asked quotes are consistently worse than those of public traders, it will not participate in any trades and will lose the ability to profit from the bid–asked spread. Another reason specialists cannot use large bid–ask spreads to protect their interests is that they are obligated to provide *price continuity* to the market.

To illustrate the principle of price continuity, suppose that the highest limit-buy order for a stock is $30 while the lower limit-sell order is at $32. When a market buy order comes in, it is matched to the best limit-sell at $32. A market sell order would be matched to the best limit-buy at $30. As market buys and sells come to the floor randomly, the stock price would fluctuate between $30 and $32. The exchange would consider this excessive volatility, and the specialist would be expected to step in with bid and/or asked prices between these values to reduce the bid–asked spread to an acceptable level, such as ¼ or ½ point.

Specialists earn income both from commissions for acting as brokers for orders and from the spread between the bid and asked prices at which they buy and sell securities. It also appears that specialists' access to their book of limit orders gives them unique knowledge about the probable direction of price movement over short periods of time. For example, suppose the specialist sees that a stock now selling for $45 has limit-buy orders for more than 100,000 shares at prices ranging from $44.50 to $44.75. This latent buying demand provides a cushion of support, because it is unlikely that enough sell pressure could come in during the next few hours to cause the price to drop below $44.50. If there are very few limit-sell orders above $45, some transient buying demand could raise the price substantially. The specialist in such circumstances realizes that a position in the stock offers little downside risk and substantial upside potential. Such immediate access to the trading intentions of other market participants seems to allow a specialist to earn substantial profits on personal transactions. One can easily overestimate such advantages, however, because ever more of the large orders are negotiated "upstairs," that is, as fourth-market deals.

Table 3.5   Block Transactions on the New York Stock Exchange

Year	Shares (Thousands)	Percentage of Reported Volume	Average Number of Block Transactions per Day
1965	48,262	3.1%	9
1970	450,908	15.4	68
1975	778,540	16.6	136
1980	3,311,132	29.2	528
1985	14,222,272	51.7	2,139
1990	19,681,849	49.6	3,333
1995	49,736,912	57.0	7,793
1996	58,510,323	55.9	9,246

Source: Data from the New York Stock Exchange Fact Book, 1996.

Block Sales

Institutional investors frequently trade blocks of several thousand shares of stock. Table 3.5 shows that **block transactions** of over 10,000 shares now account for more than half of all trading on the NYSE. Although a 10,000-share trade is considered commonplace today, large blocks often cannot be handled comfortably by specialists who do not wish to hold very large amounts of stock in their inventory. For example, one huge block transaction in terms of dollar value in 1997 was for $2 billion of shares in British Petroleum. Goldman, Sachs bought the block and resold it overnight to various investors for a reported profit of $15 million. Of course, Goldman was also subject to the risk that BP stock could have fallen in value during the day before the shares could be sold.

In response to this problem, "block houses" have evolved to aid in the placement of block trades. Block houses are brokerage firms that help to find potential buyers or sellers of large block trades. Once a trader has been located, the block is sent to the exchange floor, where the trade is executed by the specialist. If such traders cannot be identified, the block house might purchase all or part of a block sale for its own account. The broker then can resell the shares to the public.

The DOT System

A relatively recent innovation is the Designated Order Turnaround (DOT) system, and its technically improved successor, SuperDot. SuperDot enables exchange members to send orders directly to the specialist over computer lines. The largest market order that can be handled is 30,099 shares. In 1996, SuperDot processed an average of 401,500 orders per day, with an average execution time of 22 seconds.

SuperDot is especially useful to program traders. A **program trade** is a coordinated purchase or sale of an entire portfolio of stocks. Many trading strategies (such as index arbitrage, a topic we will study in Chapter 23) require that an entire portfolio of stocks be purchased or sold simultaneously in a coordinated program. SuperDot is the tool that enables the many trading orders to be sent out at once and executed almost simultaneously.

Approximately 80% of all orders are submitted through SuperDot. However, these tend to be smaller orders, and in 1996 they accounted for only 38% of total trading volume.

Settlement

Since June 1995, an order executed on the exchange must be settled within three working days. This requirement is often called T + 3, for trade date plus three days. The purchaser must deliver the cash, and the seller must deliver the stock to the broker, who in turn delivers it to the buyer's broker. Transfer of the shares is made easier when the firm's clients keep their securities in *street name*, meaning that the broker holds the shares registered in the firm's own name on behalf of the client. This arrangement can speed security transfer. T + 3 settlement has made such arrangements more important: It can be quite difficult for a seller of a security to complete delivery to the purchaser within the three-day period if the stock is kept in a safe deposit box.

Settlement is simplified further by a clearinghouse. The trades of all exchange members are recorded each day, with members' transactions netted out, so that each member need only transfer or receive the net number of shares sold or bought that day. Each member settles only with the clearinghouse, instead of with each firm with whom trades were executed.

3.4   TRADING ON THE OTC MARKET

On the exchanges all trading takes place through a specialist. Trades on the OTC market, however, are negotiated directly through dealers. Each dealer maintains an inventory of selected securities. Dealers sell from their inventories at asked prices and buy for them at bid prices.

An investor who wishes to purchase or sell shares engages a broker, who tries to locate the dealer offering the best deal on the security. This contrasts with exchange trading, where all buy or sell orders are negotiated through the specialist, who arranges for the best bids to get the trade. In the OTC market brokers must search the offers of dealers directly to find the best trading opportunity. In this sense, Nasdaq is largely a price quotation, not a trading system. While bid and asked prices can be obtained from the Nasdaq computer network, the actual trade still requires direct negotiation (usually over the phone) between the broker and the dealer in the security.

However, in the wake of the stock market crash of 1987, Nasdaq instituted a Small Order Execution System (SOES), which is in effect a trading system. Under SOES, market makers in a security who post bid or asked prices on the Nasdaq network may be contacted over the network by other traders and are required to trade at the prices they currently quote. The rules of SOES—for example, how many shares the dealer must commit to trade at the posted bid or asked price—are still evolving, however.

Because the Nasdaq system does not require a specialist, OTC trades do not require a centralized trading floor as do exchange-listed stocks. Dealers can be located anywhere, as long as they can communicate effectively with other buyers and sellers.

One disadvantage of the decentralized dealer market is that the investing public is vulnerable to *trading through,* which refers to the practice of dealers to trade with the public at their quoted bid or asked prices even if other customers have offered to trade at better prices. For example, a dealer who posts a \$20 bid and \$20$\frac{1}{2}$ asked price for a stock may continue to fill market buy orders at this asked price and market sell orders at this bid price, even if there are limit orders by public customers "inside the spread," for example, limit orders to buy at \$20$\frac{1}{8}$, or limit orders to sell at \$20$\frac{3}{8}$. This practice harms the investor whose limit order is not filled (is "traded through"), as well as the investor whose market buy or sell order is not filled at the best available price.

Trading through on Nasdaq sometimes results from imperfect coordination among dealers. A limit order placed with one broker may not be seen by brokers for other traders because computer systems are not linked and only the broker's own bid and asked prices are posted on the Nasdaq system. In contrast, trading through is strictly forbidden on the

NYSE or Amex, where "price priority" requires that the specialist fill the best-priced order first. Moreover, because all traders in an exchange market must trade through the specialist, the exchange provides true *price discovery*, meaning that market prices reflect prices at which *all* participants at that moment are willing to trade. This is the advantage of a centralized auction market.

In October 1994 the Justice Department announced an investigation of the Nasdaq stock market regarding possible collusion among market makers to maintain spreads at artificially high levels. The probe was encouraged by the observation that Nasdaq stocks rarely traded at bid–asked spreads of odd eighths, that is, $\frac{1}{8}$, $\frac{3}{8}$, $\frac{5}{8}$, or $\frac{7}{8}$. Even for the biggest and most active shares trading on Nasdaq, the vast majority of trades seemed to be executed at quarter-point or half-point spreads. Cooperation among Nasdaq dealers to increase their profits by maintaining wide spreads would be a violation of antitrust laws. In addition to the Justice Department investigation, the controversy over spreads in the Nasdaq market generated an SEC investigation as well as private lawsuits alleging that traders suffered losses from excessive spreads maintained through collusion among Nasdaq market makers.

In July 1996 the Justice Department settled with the Nasdaq dealers accused of colluding to maintain wide spreads. While none of the dealer firms had to pay penalties, they agreed to refrain from pressuring any other market maker to maintain wide spreads and from refusing to deal with other traders who try to undercut an existing spread. In addition, the firms agreed to randomly monitor phone conversations among dealers to ensure that the terms of the settlement are adhered to.

In August 1996 the SEC settled with the National Association of Securities Dealers (NASD) as well as with the Nasdaq stock market. The settlement called for NASD to improve surveillance of the Nasdaq market and to take steps to prohibit market makers from colluding on spreads. NASD has proposed a system called OATS (for Order Audit Trail System) that would require Nasdaq dealers to provide a daily record of details (including precise time information) on every transaction they handle, from the moment the order is called in by a customer to the time it is executed. This will allow regulators to determine whether any rules have been broken. In addition, the SEC mandated the following three rules for Nasdaq dealers:

1. *Display publicly all limit orders.* Limit orders from all investors that exceed 100 shares must now be displayed. Therefore, the quoted bid or asked price for a stock must now be the best price quoted by any investor, not simply the best dealer quote. This shrinks the effective spread on the stock and also avoids trading through.

2. *Make public best dealer quotes.* Nasdaq dealers must now disclose whether they have posted better quotes in private trading systems such as Instinet than they are quoting in the Nasdaq market.

3. *Reveal the size of best customer limit orders.* For example, if a dealer quotes an offer to buy 1,000 shares of stock at a quoted bid price and a customer places a limit-buy order for 500 shares at the same price, the dealer must advertise the bid price as good for 1,500 shares.

The private law suit settled in December 1997, when 30 securities firms agreed to pay $910 million in damages. The nearby box reports on the suits, the original study in the *Journal of Finance* that started the controversy, and changes in Nasdaq following the settlements.

COLLUSION IN THE STOCK MARKET

Now that its price-fixing scandal has been laid to rest, has Nasdaq become a more efficient equity market?

It is just possible that William Christie and Paul Schultz have written the first billion-dollar economics article. Last month 30 securities firms paid $910m to settle a class-action suit alleging price-fixing on America's Nasdaq stock exchange. This stemmed directly from a study of pricing patterns by the two economists.

The article* also led to sweeping changes in the rules governing share trading in America, most of which mainly affected Nasdaq, the world's second-largest stockmarket. It was claimed that the new rules would greatly improve the efficiency of trading, ultimately benefiting investors by far more than a paltry $1 billion. And did they? Two new studies revisit the issues at Nasdaq. They find that although the market has become much more efficient, investors are not getting as good a deal as they might.

In their original article, Messrs Christie and Schultz found that in 70 of the 100 most heavily traded stocks, Nasdaq dealers avoided quoting prices in odd eighths of a dollar. Buyers were far more likely to quote shares at 28½ or 28¾ than at 28⅝. This raised the possibility that the dealers, known as market makers, were tacitly colluding to keep the gap between the price they paid for a share and the price at which they sold it wider than it would have been in a truly competitive market.

Setting the Terms

How could the market makers rig the so-called bid–ask spreads in this way? Broadly speaking, stock markets come in two main forms. Some, such as the New York Stock Exchange, are primarily "auction" markets; prices are set by the investors placing orders to trade at a given price, with buyers and sellers being paired off by a "specialist" or a central computer. Nasdaq, by contrast, is primarily a "dealer" market, in which market makers compete for orders by quoting prices at which they are willing to buy or sell. In a pure dealer market, the investor must trade on whatever terms a market maker offers or not at all.

Some of the main rule changes, introduced early last year by the Securities and Exchange Commission (SEC), aimed to end the market makers' dominance of price setting. The SEC directed Nasdaq to make customers' orders public. Moreover, the previously exclusive electronic systems used to trade big orders were opened up, so that prices on these systems, which were often better than those offered by the market makers, would be visible and available to the publc.

The impact of these rules, which initially applied only to 100 companies traded on Nasdaq, has been analysed by five economists, including Messrs Christie and Schultz.** They find that spreads fell by around 30% immediately after the new rules took effect in January 1997. Spreads narrowed most in shares which previously had the widest spreads.

The study concludes that the new rules are not entitled to all the credit for narrower spreads. The extensive publicity given to the price-fixing charges, and the closer regulatory oversight that these charges prompted, also helped reduce spreads to levels similar to those on the New York Stock Exchange.

After the period analysed in that article, another new rule took effect. From June 1997 dealers had to quote prices in sixteenths of a dollar, instead of eighths. David Whitcomb of Rutgers University argues that investors would benefit if Nasdaq stocks were more finely priced, ideally in hundredths of a dollar. However, a plan backed by the SEC to "decimalize" share prices on all America's stock markets seems to have ground to a halt. That is a pity, for the potential gains could be huge. The evidence: immediately after the introduction of sixteenths last June, spreads on Nasdaq narrowed again, by roughly 10%.

*"Why do Nasdaq market makers avoid odd-eighth quotes?" *Journal of Finance*, May 1994.
**"Nasdaq market reform: new evidence that competition from the public lowers trading costs," by Michael Barclay, William Christie, Jeffrey Harris, Eugene Kandel and Paul Schultz, *Journal of Finance*, Forthcoming.
Source: Reprinted from *The Economist*, January 17, 1998.

Market Structure in Other Countries

The structure of security markets varies considerably from one country to another. A full cross-country comparison is far beyond the scope of this text. Therefore, we instead briefly review two of the biggest non-U.S. stock markets: the London and Tokyo exchanges. Figure 3.5 shows the volume of trading in major world markets.

Figure 3.5
Dollar volume of
equity trading in major
world markets, 1996.

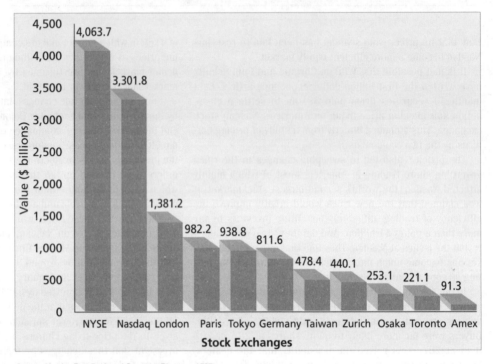

Source: Nasdaq Fact Book and Company Directory, 1997.

The London Stock Exchange

The London Stock Exchange is conveniently located between the world's two largest financial markets, those of the United States and Japan. The trading day in London overlaps with Tokyo in the morning and with New York in the afternoon. Trading arrangements on the London Stock Exchange resemble those on Nasdaq. Competing dealers who wish to make a market in a stock enter bid and asked prices into the Stock Exchange Automated Quotations (SEAQ) computer system. Market orders can then be matched against those quotes. However, negotiation among institutional traders results in more trades being executed inside the published quotes than is true of Nasdaq. As in the United States, security firms are allowed to act both as dealers and as brokerage firms, that is, both making a market in securities and executing trades for their clients.

The London Stock Exchange is attractive to some traders because it offers greater anonymity than U.S. markets, primarily because records of trades are not published for a period of time until after they are completed. Therefore, it is harder for market participants to observe or infer a trading program of another investor until after that investor has completed the program. This anonymity can be quite attractive to institutional traders that wish to buy or sell large quantities of stock over a period of time.

The Tokyo Stock Exchange

The Tokyo Stock Exchange (TSE) is the largest stock exchange in Japan, accounting for about 80% of total trading. There is no specialist system on the TSE. Instead, a *saitori* maintains a public limit-order book, matches market and limit orders, and is obliged to follow certain actions to slow down price movements when simple matching of orders would result in price changes greater than exchange-prescribed limits. In their clerical role of matching orders saitoris are somewhat similar to specialists on the NYSE. However, saitoris do not trade for their own accounts and therefore are quite different from either dealers or specialists in the United States.

Because the saitoris perform an essentially clerical role, there are no market-making services or liquidity provided to the market by dealers or specialists. The limit-order book is the primary provider of liquidity. In this regard, the TSE bears some resemblance to the fourth market in the United States in which buyers and sellers trade directly via networks such as Instinet or Posit. On the TSE, however, if order imbalances would result in price movements across sequential trades that are considered too extreme by the exchange, the saitori may temporarily halt trading and advertise the imbalance in the hope of attracting additional trading interest to the "weak" side of the market.

The TSE organizes stocks into two categories. The First Section consists of about 1,200 of the most actively traded stocks. The Second Section is for about 400 less actively traded stocks. Trading in the larger First Section stocks occurs on the floor of the exchange. The remaining securities in the First Section and the Second Section trade electronically.

3.5   TRADING COSTS

Part of the cost of trading a security is obvious and explicit. Your broker must be paid a commission. Individuals may choose from two kinds of brokers: full-service or discount. Full-service brokers, who provide a variety of services, often are referred to as account executives or financial consultants. Besides carrying out the basic services of executing orders, holding securities for safekeeping, extending margin loans, and facilitating short sales, normally they provide information and advice relating to investment alternatives. Full-service brokers usually are supported by a research staff that issues analyses and forecasts of general economic, industry, and company conditions and often makes specific buy or sell recommendations.

Some customers take the ultimate leap of faith and allow a full-service broker to make buy and sell decisions for them by establishing a *discretionary account*. This step requires an unusual degree of trust on the part of the customer, because an unscrupulous broker can "churn" an account, that is, trade securities excessively, in order to generate commissions.

Discount brokers, on the other hand, provide "no-frills" services. They buy and sell securities, hold them for safekeeping, offer margin loans, and facilitate short sales, and that is all. The only information they provide about the securities they handle consists of price quotations. Increasingly, the line between full-service and discount brokers can be blurred. Some brokers are purely no-frill, some offer limited services, and others charge for specific services.

In recent years, discount brokerage services have become increasingly available. Today, many banks, thrift institutions, and mutual fund management companies offer such services to the investing public as part of a general trend toward the creation of one-stop financial "supermarkets." Table 3.6 presents the commission schedule for one prominent

Table 3.6   Commission Schedule Quoted by a Large Discount Brokerage Firm

Value of Shares	Fixed Charge	plus	Variable Charge (% of purchase or sale)
$0–$2,500	$ 25		1.60%
$2,501–$5,000	$ 35		0.84%
$5,001–$15,000	$ 50		0.40%
$15,001–$50,000	$ 60		0.30%
$50,001–$250,000	$100		0.125%
Above $250,000	$125		0.11%
Minimum commission = $36.25 or $.0275 per share, whichever is greater			
Maximum commission = $.48 per share			

discount broker, which is fairly representative of the industry. Notice that there is a minimum charge regardless of trade size, and that cost as a fraction of the value of traded shares falls as trade size increases.

One recent trend is toward on-line trading either through the Internet or through software that connects a customer directly to a brokerage firm. While there is little conceptual difference between placing your order using a phone call versus a computer link, on-line brokerage firms can process trades more cheaply since they do not have to pay as many brokers. Commissions on such trades can already be below $10 for trades on exchange- or Nasdaq-listed shares.[5]

In addition to the explicit part of trading costs—the broker's commission—there is an implicit part—the dealer's **bid–asked spread**. Sometimes the broker is a dealer in the security being traded and will charge no commission but will collect the fee entirely in the form of the bid–asked spread.

Another implicit cost of trading that some observers would distinguish is the price concession an investor may be forced to make for trading in any quantity that exceeds the quantity the dealer is willing to trade at the posted bid or asked price.

The commission for trading common stocks is generally around 2% of the value of the transaction, but it can vary significantly. Before 1975 the schedule of commissions was fixed, but in today's environment of negotiated commissions there is substantial flexibility. On some trades, full-service brokers will offer even lower commissions than will discount brokers. In general, it pays the investor to shop around.

Total trading costs consisting of the commission, the dealer bid–asked spread, and the price concession can be substantial. According to one study, the round-trip costs (costs of purchase and resale) of trading large blocks of stocks of small companies can be as high as 30%.[6] However, in most cases costs of trades are far smaller. The commissions can be as low as 0.25% of the value of stocks traded for large transactions made through discount houses.

An ongoing controversy between the NYSE and its competitors is the extent to which better execution on the NYSE offsets the generally lower explicit costs of trading in other markets. Execution refers to the size of the effective bid–asked spread and the amount of price impact in a market. The NYSE believes that many investors focus too intently on the costs they can see, despite the fact that quality of execution can be a far more important determinant of total costs. Many trades on the NYSE are executed at a price inside the quoted spread. This can happen because floor brokers at the specialist's post can bid above or sell below the specialist's quote. In this way, two public orders cross without incurring the specialist's spread.

In contrast, in a dealer market such as Nasdaq, all trades go through the dealer, and all trades, therefore, are subject to a bid–asked spread. The client never sees the spread as an explicit cost, however. The price at which the trade is executed incorporates the dealer's spread, but this part of the trading cost is never reported to the investor. Similarly, regional markets are disadvantaged in terms of execution because their lower trading volume means that fewer brokers congregate at a specialist's post, resulting in a lower probability of two public orders crossing.

A controversial practice related to the bid–asked spread and the quality of trade execution is "paying for order flow." This entails paying a broker a rebate for directing the trade

---

[5]These fees are for Web-based trades. Broker-assisted trades still typically cost more than $30.
[6]T. F. Loeb, "Trading Cost: The Critical Link between Investment Information and Results," *Financial Analysts Journal*, May–June 1983.

to a particular dealer rather than to the NYSE. By bringing the trade to a dealer instead of to the exchange, however, the broker eliminates the possibility that the trade could have been executed without incurring a spread. Moreover, a broker that is paid for order flow might direct a trade to a dealer that does not even offer the most competitive price. (Indeed, the fact that dealers can afford to pay for order flow suggests that they are able to lay off the trade at better prices elsewhere and, therefore, that the broker also could have found a better price with some additional effort.)

Such practices raise serious ethical questions, because the broker's primary obligation is to obtain the best deal for the client. Payment for order flow might be justified if the rebate were passed along to the client either directly or through lower commissions, but it is not clear that such rebates are passed through.

3.6   BUYING ON MARGIN

When purchasing securities, investors have easy access to a source of debt financing called *brokers' call loans*. The act of taking advantage of brokers' call loans is called *buying on margin*.

Purchasing stocks on **margin** means the investor borrows part of the purchase price of the stock from a broker. The broker, in turn, borrows money from banks at the call money rate to finance these purchases, and charges its clients that rate plus a service charge for the loan. All securities purchased on margin must be left with the brokerage firm in street name, because the securities are used as collateral for the loan.

The Board of Governors of the Federal Reserve System sets limits on the extent to which stock purchases may be financed via margin loans. Currently, the initial margin requirement is 50%, meaning that at least 50% of the purchase price must be paid for in cash, with the rest borrowed.

The *percentage margin* is defined as the ratio of the net worth, or "equity value," of the account to the market value of the securities. To demonstrate, suppose that the investor initially pays $6,000 toward the purchase of $10,000 worth of stock (100 shares at $100 per share), borrowing the remaining $4,000 from the broker. The account will have a balance sheet as follows:

Assets		Liabilities and Owner's Equity	
Value of stock	$10,000	Loan from broker	$4,000
		Equity	$6,000

The initial percentage margin is

$$\text{Margin} = \frac{\text{Equity in account}}{\text{Value of stock}} = \frac{\$6,000}{\$10,000} = .60$$

If the stock's price declines to $70 per share, the account balance becomes:

Assets		Liabilities and Owner's Equity	
Value of stock	$7,000	Loan from broker	$4,000
		Equity	$3,000

The equity in the account falls by the full decrease in the stock value, and the percentage margin is now

$$\text{Margin} = \frac{\text{Equity in account}}{\text{Value of stock}} = \frac{\$3,000}{\$7,000} = .43, \text{ or } 43\%$$

If the stock value were to fall below $4,000, equity would become negative, meaning that the value of the stock is no longer sufficient collateral to cover the loan from the broker. To guard against this possibility, the broker sets a *maintenance margin*. If the percentage margin falls below the maintenance level, the broker will issue a *margin call* requiring the investor to add new cash or securities to the margin account. If the investor does not act, the broker may sell the securities from the account to pay off enough of the loan to restore the percentage margin to an acceptable level.

An example will show how the maintenance margin works. Suppose the maintenance margin is 30%. How far could the stock price fall before the investor would get a margin call? To answer this question requires some algebra.

Let P be the price of the stock. The value of the investor's 100 shares is then $100P$, and the equity in his or her account is $100P - \$4,000$. The percentage margin is therefore $(100P - \$4,000)/100P$. The price at which the percentage margin equals the maintenance margin of .3 is found by solving for P in the equation

$$\frac{100P - \$4,000}{100P} = .3$$

which implies that $P = \$57.14$. If the price of the stock were to fall below $57.14 per share, the investor would get a margin call.

Concept
CHECK

Question 3 • If the maintenance margin in the example we discussed were 40%, how far could the stock price fall before the investor would get a margin call?

Why do investors buy stocks (or bonds) on margin? They do so when they wish to invest an amount greater than their own money alone would allow. Thus they can achieve greater upside potential, but they also expose themselves to greater downside risk.

To see how, let us suppose that an investor is bullish (optimistic) on IBM stock, which is currently selling at $100 per share. The investor has $10,000 to invest and expects IBM stock to go up in price by 30% during the next year. Ignoring any dividends, the expected rate of return would thus be 30% if the investor spent only $10,000 to buy 100 shares.

But now let us assume that the investor also borrows another $10,000 from the broker and invests it in IBM also. The total investment in IBM would thus be $20,000 (for 200 shares). Assuming an interest rate on the margin loan of 9% per year, what will be the investor's rate of return now (again ignoring dividends) if IBM stock does go up 30% by year's end?

The 200 shares will be worth $26,000. Paying off $10,900 of principal and interest on the margin loan leaves $15,100 ($26,000 − $10,900). The rate of return, therefore, will be

$$\frac{\$15,100 - \$10,000}{\$10,000} = 51\%$$

The investor has parlayed a 30% rise in the stock's price into a 51% rate of return on the $10,000 investment.

Doing so, however, magnifies the downside risk. Suppose that instead of going up by 30% the price of IBM stock goes down by 30% to $70 per share. In that case the 200 shares

Table 3.7   Illustration of Buying Stock on Margin

Change in Stock Price	End of Year Value of Shares	Repayment of Principal and Interest	Investor's Rate of Return*
30% increase	$26,000	$10,900	51%
No change	20,000	10,900	−9%
30% decrease	14,000	10,900	−69%

*Assuming the investor buys $20,000 worth of stock by borrowing $10,000 at an interest rate of 9% per year.

will be worth $14,000, and the investor is left with $3,100 after paying off the $10,900 of principal and interest on the loan. The result is a disastrous rate of return:

$$\frac{\$3,100 - \$10,000}{\$10,000} = -69\%$$

Table 3.7 summarizes the possible results of these hypothetical transactions. Note that if there is no change in IBM's stock price, the investor loses 9%, the cost of the loan.

Concept CHECK

Question 4 • Suppose that in the previous example the investor borrows only $5,000 at the same interest rate of 9% per year. What will be the rate of return if the price of IBM stock goes up by 30%? If it goes down by 30%? If it remains unchanged?

3.7   SHORT SALES

A **short sale** allows investors to profit from a decline in a security's price. An investor borrows a share of stock from a broker and sells it. Later, the short seller must purchase a share of the same stock in the market in order to replace the share that was borrowed. This is called *covering the short position*. Table 3.8 compares stock purchases to short sales.

The short seller anticipates the stock price will fall, so that the share can be purchased at a lower price than it initially sold for; the short seller will then reap a profit. Short sellers must not only replace the shares but also pay the lender of the security any dividends paid during the short sale.

In practice, the shares loaned out for a short sale are typically provided by the short seller's brokerage firm, which holds a wide variety of securities of its other investors in street name. The owner of the shares will not even know that the shares have been lent to the short seller. If the owner wishes to sell the shares, the brokerage firm will simply borrow shares from another investor. Therefore, the short sale may have an indefinite term. However, if the brokerage firm cannot locate new shares to replace the ones sold, the short seller will need to repay the loan immediately by purchasing shares in the market and turning them over to the brokerage firm to close out the loan.

Exchange rules permit short sales only after an *uptick*, that is, only when the last recorded change in the stock price is positive. This rule apparently is meant to prevent waves of speculation against the stock. In other words, the votes of "no confidence" in the stock that short sales represent may be entered only after a price increase.

Finally, exchange rules require that proceeds from a short sale must be kept on account with the broker. The short seller, therefore, cannot invest these funds to generate income. However, large institutional investors typically will receive some income from the proceeds of a short sale being held with the broker. In addition, short sellers are required to

Table 3.8   Cash Flows from Purchasing versus Short Selling Shares of Stock

Time	Action	Cash Flow
	Purchase of Stock	
0	Buy share	– Initial price
1	Receive dividend, sell share	Ending price + dividend
	Profit = (Ending price + dividend) – Initial price	
	Short Sale of Stock	
0	Borrow share; sell it	+ Initial price
1	Repay dividend and buy share to replace the share originally borrowed	– (Ending price + dividend)
	Profit = Initial price – (Ending price + dividend)	

Note: A negative cash flow implies a cash outflow.

post margin (which is essentially collateral) with the broker to ensure that the trader can cover any losses sustained should the stock price rise during the period of the short sale.[7]

To illustrate the actual mechanics of short selling, suppose that you are bearish (pessimistic) on IBM stock, and that its current market price is $100 per share. You tell your broker to sell short 1,000 shares. The broker borrows 1,000 shares either from another customer's account or from another broker.

The $100,000 cash proceeds from the short sale are credited to your account. Suppose the broker has a 50% margin requirement on short sales. This means that you must have other cash or securities in your account worth at least $50,000 that can serve as margin (that is, collateral) on the short sale. Let us suppose that you have $50,000 in Treasury bills. Your account with the broker after the short sale will then be:

Assets		Liabilities and Owner's Equity	
Cash	$100,000	Short position in IBM stock	$100,000
T-bills	$ 50,000	(1,000 shares owed)	
		Equity	$ 50,000

Your initial percentage margin is the ratio of the equity in the account, $50,000, to the current value of the shares you have borrowed and eventually must return, $100,000:

$$\text{Percentage margin} = \frac{\text{Equity}}{\text{Value of stock owed}} = \frac{\$50,000}{\$100,000} = .50$$

Suppose you are right, and IBM stock falls to $70 per share. You can now close out your position at a profit. To cover the short sale, you buy 1,000 shares to replace the ones you borrowed. Because the shares now sell for $70, the purchase costs only $70,000. Because your account was credited for $100,000 when the shares were borrowed and sold, your profit is $30,000: The profit equals the decline in the share price times the number of shares sold short. On the other hand, if the price of IBM stock goes up while you are short, you may get a margin call from your broker.

---

[7]We should note that although we have been describing a short sale of a stock, bonds also may be sold short.

Let us suppose that the broker has a maintenance margin of 30% on short sales. This means that the equity in your account must be at least 30% of the value of your short position at all times. How far can the price of IBM stock go up before you get a margin call?

Let P be the price of IBM stock. Then the value of the shares you must return is $1,000P$, and the equity in your account is $\$150,000 - 1,000P$. Your short position margin ratio is therefore $(\$150,000 - 1,000P)/1,000P$. The critical value of P is thus

$$\frac{\text{Equity}}{\text{Value of shares owed}} = \frac{\$150,000 - 1,000P}{1,000P} = .3$$

which implies that $P = \$115.38$ per share. If IBM stock should rise above $\$115.38$ per share, you will get a margin call, and you will either have to put up additional cash or cover your short position.

Question 5 • If the short position maintenance margin in the preceding example were 40%, how far could the stock price rise before the investor would get a margin call?

3.8   REGULATION OF SECURITIES MARKETS

Government Regulation

Trading in securities markets in the United States is regulated under a myriad of laws. The two major laws are the Securities Act of 1933 and the Securities Exchange Act of 1934. The 1933 act requires full disclosure of relevant information relating to the issue of new securities. This is the act that requires registration of new securities and the issuance of a prospectus that details the financial prospects of the firm. SEC approval of a prospectus or financial report does not mean that it views the security as a good investment. The SEC cares only that the relevant facts are disclosed; investors make their own evaluations of the security's value.

The 1934 act established the Securities and Exchange Commission to administer the provisions of the 1933 act. It also extended the disclosure principle of the 1933 act by requiring firms with issued securities on secondary exchanges to periodically disclose relevant financial information.

The 1934 act also empowered the SEC to register and regulate securities exchanges, OTC trading, brokers, and dealers. The act thus established the SEC as the administrative agency responsible for broad oversight of the securities markets. The SEC, however, shares oversight with other regulatory agencies. For example, the Commodity Futures Trading Commission (CFTC) regulates trading in futures markets, whereas the Federal Reserve has broad responsibility for the health of the U.S. financial system. In this role the Fed sets margin requirements on stocks and stock options and regulates bank lending to securities markets participants.

The Securities Investor Protection Act of 1970 established the Securities Investor Protection Corporation (SIPC) to protect investors from losses if their brokerage firms fail. Just as the Federal Deposit Insurance Corporation provides federal protection to depositors against bank failure, the SIPC ensures that investors will receive securities held for their account in street name by the failed brokerage firm up to a limit of $500,000 per customer. The SIPC is financed by levying an "insurance premium" on its participating, or member, brokerage firms. It also may borrow money from the SEC if its own funds are insufficient to meet its obligations.

In addition to federal regulations, security trading is subject to state laws. The laws providing for state regulation of securities are known generally as *blue sky laws*, because they attempt to prevent the false promotion and sale of securities representing nothing more than blue sky. State laws to outlaw fraud in security sales were instituted before the Securities Act of 1933. Varying state laws were somewhat unified when many states adopted portions of the Uniform Securities Act, which was proposed in 1956.

Self-Regulation and Circuit Breakers

Much of the securities industry relies on self-regulation. The SEC delegates to secondary exchanges much of the responsibility for day-to-day oversight of trading. Similarly, the National Association of Securities Dealers oversees trading of OTC securities. The Association for Investment Management and Research's Code of Ethics and Professional Conduct sets out principles that govern the behavior of Chartered Financial Analysts, more commonly referred to as CFAs. The nearby box presents a brief outline of those principles.

The market collapse of 1987 prompted several suggestions for regulatory change. Among these was a call for "circuit breakers" to slow or stop trading during periods of extreme volatility. Some of the current circuit breakers are as follows:

Trading halts: When the Dow Jones Industrial Average declines by 350 points from its previous day's close, trading is halted for one-half hour. If the average falls by 550 points from its previous day's close, trading is halted for one hour.

Sidecars: If the S&P 500 futures contract falls by 12 points from its previous day's close, all program trades executed through SuperDot must sit unexecuted for 5 minutes. (In addition, a 12-point drop will trigger the Chicago Mercantile Exchange to halt trading in the S&P 500 futures contract for one hour.)

Collars: When the Dow moves 50 points in either direction from the previous day's close, Rule 80A of the NYSE requires that index arbitrage orders pass a "tick test." In a falling market, sell orders may be executed only at a plus tick or zero-plus tick, meaning that the trade may be done at a higher price than the last trade (a plus tick) or at the last price if the last recorded change in the stock price is positive (a zero-plus tick). The rule remains in effect for the rest of the day unless the Dow returns to within 25 points of the previous day's close.

Circuit breakers have been modified from time to time. For example, after trading was halted for the first time (on October 27, 1997, when the Dow fell by more than 500 points) dissatisfaction with the two trading halts that were triggered led the NYSE to revise its policies. In particular, as the level of stock prices have risen over time, the trigger points have been adjusted. A 5% swing in the Dow Jones Industrial Average in 1987 would have corresponded to a movement in the index of about 100 points. In early 1998, with the Dow at about 8,000, a 5% move is about 400 points. The trigger setting off a circuit breaker obviously needed to be reconsidered in the face of such major changes in market prices.

Under rules proposed by the NYSE in February 1998, if the Dow falls by 10%, trading will be halted for one hour if the drop occurs before 2:00 P.M. (Eastern Standard Time), for one-half hour if the drop occurs between 2:00 and 2:30, but not at all if the drop occurs after 2:30. If the Dow falls by 20%, trading will be halted for two hours if the drop occurs before 1:00 P.M., for one hour if the drop occurs between 1:00 and 2:00, and for the rest of the day if the drop occurs after 2:00. A 30% drop in the Dow would close the market for the rest of the day, regardless of the time. In addition, the NYSE is considering widening the 50-point collars that limit program trading.

EXCERPTS FROM AIMR STANDARDS OF PROFESSIONAL CONDUCT

Standard I: Fundamental Responsibilities

Members shall maintain knowledge of and comply with all applicable laws, rules, and regulations including AIMR's Code of Ethics and Standards of Professional Conduct.

Standard II: Responsibilities to the Profession

- Professional Misconduct. Members shall not engage in any professional conduct involving dishonesty, fraud, deceit, or misrepresentation.
- Prohibition against Plagiarism.

Standard III: Responsibilities to the Employer

- Obligation to Inform Employer of Code and Standards. Members shall inform their employer that they are obligated to comply with these Code and Standards.
- Disclosure of Additional Compensation Arrangements. Members shall disclose to their employer all benefits that they receive in addition to compensation from that employer.

Standard IV: Responsibilities to Clients and Prospects

- Investment Process and Research Reports. Members shall exercise diligence and thoroughness in making investment recommendations . . . distinguish between facts and opinions in research reports . . . and use reasonable care to maintain objectivity.

- Interactions with Clients and Prospects. Members must place their clients' interests before their own.
- Portfolio Investment Recommendations. Members shall make a reasonable inquiry into a client's financial situation, investment experience, and investment objectives prior to making appropriate investment recommendations. . . .
- Priority of Transactions. Transactions for clients and employers shall have priority over transactions for the benefit of a member.
- Disclosure of Conflicts to Clients and Prospects. Members shall disclose to their clients and prospects all matters, including ownership of securities or other investments, that reasonably could be expected to impair the members' ability to make objective recommendations.

Standard V: Responsibilities to the Public

- Prohibition against Use of Material Nonpublic [Inside] Information. Members who possess material nonpublic information related to the value of a security shall not trade in that security.
- Performance Presentation. Members shall not make any statements that misrepresent the investment performance that they have accomplished or can reasonably be expected to achieve.

Source: Abridged from *The Standards of Professional Conduct* of the Association for Investment Management and Research, 1997.

The idea behind circuit breakers is that a temporary halt in trading during periods of very high volatility can help mitigate informational problems that might contribute to excessive price swings. For example, even if a trader is unaware of any specific adverse economic news, if he or she sees the market plummeting, he or she will suspect that there might be a good reason for the price drop and will become unwilling to buy shares. In fact, the trader might decide to sell shares to avoid losses. Thus feedback from price swings to trading behavior can exacerbate market movements. Circuit breakers give participants a chance to assess market fundamentals while prices are temporarily frozen. In this way, they have a chance to decide whether price movements are warranted while the market is closed.

Of course, circuit breakers have no bearing on trading in non-U.S. markets. It is quite possible that they simply have induced those who engage in program trading to move their operations into foreign exchanges.

Insider Trading

One of the important restrictions on trading involves *insider trading*. It is illegal for anyone to transact in securities to profit from **inside information,** that is, private information held by officers, directors, or major stockholders that has not yet been divulged to the public. The difficulty is that the definition of *insiders* can be ambiguous. Although it is obvious

BIG WEAPON AGAINST INSIDER TRADING IS UPHELD

In a resounding victory for securities regulators, the Supreme Court upheld one of the government's main weapons in fighting insider trading.

In the case of an attorney convicted of insider trading in Pillsbury Co. stock, the justices endorsed an approach known as the misappropriation theory, which has been used since the early 1980s to nab stock traders who obtain sensitive, nonpublic information but who don't qualify as traditional company insiders.

One Securities and Exchange Commission official estimated that in the past five years, as much as 45% of its insider-trading cases have involved misappropriation. They ranged from a psychiatrist who learned of a planned takeover from a patient to a printer who traded on information from tender-offer documents that had yet to be circulated.

Defense lawyers have long argued that the SEC exceeded its authority by going after people who weren't really insiders or who didn't have a direct fiduciary duty to the company whose stock was traded. Recently, two federal appeals courts agreed.

But yesterday, the Supreme Court rejected that argument by a vote of 6-3. It ruled that the theory is "well-tuned to an animating purpose" of the securities laws: "to insure honest securities markets and thereby promote investor confidence." In a 35-page opinion by Justice Ruth Bader Ginsburg,

the court cautioned that investors might "hesitate to venture their capital in a market where trading based on misappropriated nonpublic information is unchecked by law."

The ruling resolves a long-running debate over the reach of an important securities regulation, Section 10(b) of the Securities Exchange Act of 1934, which is used to prosecute insider traders. The law doesn't mention insider trading; it simply bars the use of "deception" in buying and selling securities. The SEC has contended that the law is violated even if the person being deceived wasn't directly involved in the stock transaction. The justices said that broad interpretation is reasonable so long as a trade has occurred and someone in possession of nonpublic information has been deceived.

The case involved Minneapolis attorney James O'Hagan, who reaped a $4.3 million profit in 1988 after buying shares in Pillsbury. At the time, his law firm was advising Grand Metropolitan PLC on its planned takeover of Pillsbury, although he wasn't involved in the deal. The government claimed he tricked another lawyer into telling him about the takeover bid; he later was convicted of illegally using, or misappropriating, nonpublic information. The main issue before the Supreme Court was whether Mr. O'Hagan violated the law in trading Pillsbury stock, given that his firm didn't represent the company and he therefore didn't have a direct fiduciary duty to it.

Source: Edward Felsenthal, *The Wall Street Journal*, June 26, 1997, p. C1. Reprinted by permission of *The Wall Street Journal*, © Dow Jones & Company, Inc. All Rights Reserved Worldwide.

that the chief financial officer of a firm is an insider, it is less clear whether the firm's biggest supplier can be considered an insider. However, the supplier may deduce the firm's near-term prospects from significant changes in orders. This gives the supplier a unique form of private information, yet the supplier does not necessarily qualify as an insider. These ambiguities plague security analysts, whose job is to uncover as much information as possible concerning the firm's expected prospects. The distinction between legal private information and illegal inside information can be fuzzy.

An important Supreme Court decision in 1997, however, came down on the side of an expansive view of what constitutes illegal insider trading. The decision upheld the so-called misappropriation theory of insider trading, which holds that traders may not trade on nonpublic information even if they are not company insiders. The nearby box discusses the implications of this case.

The SEC requires officers, directors, and major stockholders of all publicly held firms to report all of their transactions in their firm's stock. A compendium of insider trades is published monthly in the SEC's *Official Summary of Securities Transactions and Holdings*. The idea is to inform the public of any implicit votes of confidence or no confidence made by insiders.

Do insiders exploit their knowledge? The answer seems to be, to a limited degree, yes. Two forms of evidence support this conclusion. First, there is abundant evidence of "leakage" of useful information to some traders before any public announcement of that information. For example, share prices of firms announcing dividend increases (which the market interprets as good news concerning the firm's prospects) commonly increase in value a few days *before* the public announcement of the increase.[8] Clearly, some investors are acting on the good news before it is released to the public. Similarly, share prices tend to increase a few days before the public announcement of above-trend earnings growth.[9] At the same time, share prices still rise substantially on the day of the public release of good news, indicating that insiders, or their associates, have not fully bid up the price of the stock to the level commensurate with that news.

The second sort of evidence on insider trading is based on returns earned on trades by insiders. Researchers have examined the SEC's summary of insider trading to measure the performance of insiders. In one of the best known of these studies, Jaffe[10] examined the abnormal return on stock over the months following purchases or sales by insiders. For months in which insider purchasers of a stock exceeded insider sellers of the stock by three or more, the stocks had an abnormal return in the following eight months of about 5%. When insider sellers exceeded inside buyers, however, the stock tended to perform poorly.

SUMMARY

1. Firms issue securities to raise the capital necessary to finance their investments. Investment bankers market these securities to the public on the primary market. Investment bankers generally act as underwriters who purchase the securities from the firm and resell them to the public at a markup. Before the securities may be sold to the public, the firm must publish an SEC-approved prospectus that provides information on the firm's prospects.

2. Issued securities are traded on the secondary market, that is, on organized stock exchanges, the over-the-counter market, or, for large traders, through direct negotiation. Only members of exchanges may trade on the exchange. Brokerage firms holding seats on the exchange sell their services to individuals, charging commissions for executing trades on their behalf. The NYSE and, to a lesser extent, the Amex have fairly strict listing requirements. Regional exchanges provide listing opportunities for local firms that do not meet the requirements of the national exchanges.

3. Trading of common stocks in exchanges takes place through specialists. Specialists act to maintain an orderly market in the shares of one or more firms, maintaining "books" of limit-buy and limit-sell orders and matching trades at mutually acceptable prices. Specialists also will accept market orders by selling from or buying for their own inventory of stocks.

4. The over-the-counter market is not a formal exchange but an informal network of brokers and dealers who negotiate sales of securities. The Nasdaq system provides on-line computer quotes offered by dealers in the stock. When an individual wishes to purchase or sell a share, the broker can search the listing of offered bid and asked prices, call the dealer who has the best quote, and execute the trade.

[8]See, for example, J. Aharony and I. Swary, "Quarterly Dividend and Earnings Announcement and Stockholders' Return: An Empirical Analysis," *Journal of Finance* 35 (March 1980).

[9]See, for example, George Foster, Chris Olsen, and Terry Shevlin, "Earnings Releases, Anomalies, and the Behavior of Security Returns," *The Accounting Review*, October 1984.

[10]Jeffrey F. Jaffe, "Special Information and Insider Trading," *Journal of Business* 47 (July 1974).

5. Block transactions account for about half of trading volume. These trades often are too large to be handled readily by specialists, and thus block houses have developed that specialize in these transactions, identifying potential trading partners for their clients.

6. Buying on margin means borrowing money from a broker in order to buy more securities. By buying securities on margin, an investor magnifies both the upside potential and the downside risk. If the equity in a margin account falls below the required maintenance level, the investor will get a margin call from the broker.

7. Short selling is the practice of selling securities that the seller does not own. The short seller borrows the securities sold through a broker and may be required to cover the short position at any time on demand. The cash proceeds of a short sale are always kept in escrow by the broker, and the broker usually requires that the short seller deposit additional cash or securities to serve as margin (collateral) for the short sale.

8. Securities trading is regulated by the Securities and Exchange Commission, as well as by self-regulation of the exchanges. Many of the important regulations have to do with full disclosure of relevant information concerning the securities in question. Insider trading rules also prohibit traders from attempting to profit from inside information.

9. In addition to providing the basic services of executing buy and sell orders, holding securities for safekeeping, making margin loans, and facilitating short sales, full-service brokers offer investors information, advice, and even investment decisions. Discount brokers offer only the basic brokerage services but usually charge less.

10. Total trading costs consist of commissions, the dealer's bid–asked spread, and price concessions.

Key Terms

primary market	Nasdaq	block transactions
secondary market	bid price	program trades
underwriting	asked price	bid–asked spread
prospectus	third market	margin
stock exchanges	fourth market	short sale
over-the-counter market	specialist	inside information

Selected Readings

An overview of market organization is provided in:

Schwartz, Robert A., ed. *Global Equity Markets: Technological, Competitive, and Regulatory Challenges.* New York: New York University Salomon Center, 1995.

The *Fact Books* of the NYSE, AMEX, and Nasdaq are published annually and contain extensive data on trading in the respective markets.

Problems

1. FBN, Inc., has just sold 100,000 shares in an initial public offering. The underwriter's explicit fees were $70,000. The offering price for the shares was $50, but immediately upon issue the share price jumped to $53.
   a. What is your best guess as to the total cost to FBN of the equity issue?
   b. Is the entire cost of the underwriting a source of profit to the underwriters?

2. Suppose that you sell short 100 shares of IBX, now selling at $70 per share.
   a. What is your maximum possible loss?
   b. What happens to the maximum loss if you simultaneously place a stop-buy order at $78?

3. An expiring put will be exercised and the stock will be sold if the stock price is below the exercise price. A stop-loss order causes a stock sale when the stock price falls below some limit. Compare and contrast the two strategies of purchasing put options versus issuing a stop-loss order.

4. Compare call options and stop-buy orders.

5. Here is some price information on Marriott:

	Bid	Asked
Marriott	$37\frac{1}{4}$	$38\frac{1}{8}$

You have placed a stop-loss order to sell at $38. What are you telling your broker? Given market prices, will your order be executed?

6. Do you think it is possible to replace market-making specialists by a fully automated computerized trade-matching system?

7. Consider the following limit-order book of a specialist. The last trade in the stock took place at a price of $50.

Limit-Buy Orders		Limit-Sell Orders	
Price ($)	Shares	Price ($)	Shares
49.75	500	50.25	100
49.50	800	51.50	100
49.25	500	54.75	300
49.00	200	58.25	100
48.50	600		

a. If a market-buy order for 100 shares comes in, at what price will it be filled?
b. At what price would the next market-buy order be filled?
c. If you were the specialist, would you desire to increase or decrease your inventory of this stock?

8. What purpose does the Designated Order Turnaround system (SuperDot) serve on the New York Stock Exchange?

9. Who sets the bid and asked price for a stock traded over the counter? Would you expect the spread to be higher on actively or inactively traded stocks?

10. Consider the following data concerning the NYSE:

Year	Average Daily Trading Volume (Thousands of Shares)	Annual High Price of an Exchange Membership
1991	178,917	$ 440,000
1992	202,266	600,000
1993	264,519	775,000
1994	291,351	830,000
1995	346,101	1,050,000
1996	411,953	1,450,000

What do you conclude about the short-run relationship between trading activity and the value of a seat?

11. Suppose that Intel currently is selling at $80 per share. You buy 250 shares, using $15,000 of your own money and borrowing the remainder of the purchase price from your broker. The rate on the margin loan is 8%.

    a. What is the percentage increase in the net worth of your brokerage account if the price of Intel *immediately* changes to (i) $88; (ii) $80; (iii) $72? What is the relationship between your percentage return and the percentage change in the price of Intel?

    b. If the maintenance margin is 25%, how low can Intel's price fall before you get a margin call?

    c. How would your answer to (b) change if you had financed the initial purchase with only $10,000 of your own money?

    d. What is the rate of return on your margined position (assuming again that you invest $15,000 of your own money) if Intel is selling *after one year* at (i) $88; (ii) $80; (iii) $72? What is the relationship between your percentage return and the percentage change in the price of Intel? Assume that Intel pays no dividends.

    e. Continue to assume that a year has passed. How low can Intel's price fall before you get a margin call?

12. Suppose that you sell short 250 shares of Intel, currently selling for $80 per share, and give your broker $15,000 to establish your margin account.

    a. If you earn no interest on the funds in your margin account, what will be your rate of return after one year if Intel stock is selling at (i) $88; (ii) $80; (iii) $72? Assume that Intel pays no dividends.

    b. If the maintenance margin is 25%, how high can Intel's price rise before you get a margin call?

    c. Redo parts (a) and (b), now assuming that Intel's dividend (paid at year end) is $2 per share.

13. Here is some price information on Fincorp stock. Suppose first that Fincorp trades in a dealer market.

Bid	Asked
55$\frac{1}{4}$	55$\frac{1}{2}$

    a. Suppose you have submitted an order to your broker to buy at market. At what price will your trade be executed?

    b. Suppose you have submitted an order to sell at market. At what price will your trade be executed?

    c. Suppose an investor has submitted a limit order to sell at 55\frac{3}{8}$. What will happen?

    d. Suppose another investor has submitted a limit order to buy at 55\frac{3}{8}$. What will happen?

14. Now reconsider the previous problem assuming that Fincorp sells in an exchange market like the NYSE.

    a. Is there any chance for price improvement in the market orders considered in parts (a) and (b)?

    b. Is there any chance of an immediate trade at 55\frac{3}{8}$ for the limit-buy order in part (d)?

15. You are bullish on AT&T stock. The current market price is $50 per share, and you have $5,000 of your own to invest. You borrow an additional $5,000 from your broker at an interest rate of 8% per year and invest $10,000 in the stock.

    a. What will be your rate of return if the price of AT&T stock goes up by 10% during the next year? (Ignore the expected dividend.)

    b. How far does the price of AT&T stock have to fall for you to get a margin call if the maintenance margin is 30%?

16. You've borrowed $20,000 on margin to buy shares in Disney, which is now selling at $80 per share. Your account starts at the initial margin requirement of 50%. The maintenance margin is 35%. Two days later, the stock price falls to $75 per share.

    a. Will you receive a margin call?

    b. How low can the price of Disney shares fall before you receive a margin call?

17. You are bearish on AT&T stock and decide to sell short 100 shares at the current market price of $50 per share.

    a. How much in cash or securities must you put into your brokerage account if the broker's initial margin requirement is 50% of the value of the short position?

    b. How high can the price of the stock go before you get a margin call if the maintenance margin is 30% of the value of the short position?

18. On January 1, you sold short one round lot (i.e., 100 shares) of Zenith stock at $14 per share. On March 1, a dividend of $2 per share was paid. On April 1, you covered the short sale by buying the stock at a price of $9 per share. You paid 50 cents per share in commissions for each transaction. What is the value of your account on April 1?

19. Call one full-service broker and one discount broker and find out the transaction costs of implementing the following strategies:

    a. Buying 100 shares of IBM now and selling them six months from now.

    b. Investing an equivalent amount of six-month at-the-money call options (calls with strike price equal to the stock price) on IBM stock now and selling them six months from now.

The following questions are from past CFA examinations:

20. If you place a stop-loss order to sell 100 shares of stock at $55 when the current price is $62, how much will you receive for each share if the price drops to $50?

    a. $50.

    b. $55.

    c. $54⅞.

    d. Cannot tell from the information given.

21. You wish to sell short 100 shares of XYZ Corporation stock. If the last two transactions were at 34⅛ followed by 34³⁄₁₆, you only can sell short on the next transaction at a price of

    a. 34⅛ or higher.

    b. 34³⁄₁₆ or higher.

    c. 34³⁄₁₆ or lower.

    d. 34⅛ or lower.

22. Specialists on the New York Stock Exchange do all of the following except

    a. Act as dealers for their own accounts.

    b. Execute limit orders.

    c. Help provide liquidity to the marketplace.

    d. Act as odd-lot dealers.

1. Limited-time shelf registration was introduced because of its favorable trade-off of saving issue costs against mandated disclosure. Allowing unlimited-time shelf registration would circumvent blue sky laws that ensure proper disclosure.

2. Run for the hills! If the issue were underpriced, it most likely would be oversubscribed by institutional traders. The fact that the underwriters need to actively market the shares to the general public may indicate that better-informed investors view the issue as overpriced.

3. $$\frac{100P - \$4,000}{100P} = .4$$

$$100P - \$4,000 = 40P$$

$$60P = \$4,000$$

$$P = \$66.67 \text{ per share}$$

4. The investor will purchase 150 shares, with a rate of return as follows:

Year-End Change in Price	Year-End Value of Shares	Repayment of Principal and Interest	Investor's Rate of Return
30%	19,500	$5,450	40.5%
No change	15,000	5,450	−4.5
−30%	10,500	5,450	−49.5

5. $$\frac{\$150,000 - 1,000P}{1,000P} = .4$$

$$\$150,000 - 1,000P = 400P$$

$$1,400P = \$150,000$$

$$P = \$107.14 \text{ per share}$$

MUTUAL FUNDS AND OTHER INVESTMENT COMPANIES

The previous chapter introduced you to the mechanics of trading securities and the structure of the markets in which securities trade. Increasingly, however, individual investors are choosing not to trade securities directly for their own accounts. Instead, they direct their funds to investment companies that purchase securities on their behalf.

The most important of these financial intermediaries are open-end investment companies, more commonly known as mutual funds, to which we devote most of this chapter. We also touch briefly on other types of investment companies such as unit investment trusts and closed-end funds. We begin the chapter by describing and comparing the various types of investment companies available to investors. We then examine the functions of mutual funds, their investment styles and policies, and the costs of investing in these funds. Next we take a first look at the investment performance of these funds. We consider the impact of expenses

and turnover on net performance and examine the extent to which performance is consistent from one period to the next. In other words, will the mutual funds that were the best *past* performers be the best *future* performers? Finally, we discuss sources of information on mutual funds, and we consider in detail the information provided in the most comprehensive guide, Morningstar's *Mutual Fund Sourcebook*.

4.1   INVESTMENT COMPANIES

Investment companies are financial intermediaries that collect funds from individual investors and invest those funds in a potentially wide range of securities or other assets. Pooling of assets is the key idea behind investment companies. Each investor has a claim to the portfolio established by the investment company in proportion to the amount invested. These companies thus provide a mechanism for small investors to "team up" to obtain the benefits of large-scale investing.

Investment companies perform several important functions for their investors:

1. *Record keeping and administration.* Investment companies issue periodic status reports, keeping track of capital gains distributions, dividends, investments, and redemptions, and they may reinvest dividend and interest income for shareholders.

2. *Diversification and divisibility.* By pooling their money, investment companies enable investors to hold fractional shares of many different securities. They can act as large investors even if any individual shareholder cannot.

3. *Professional management.* Many, but not all, investment companies have full-time staffs of security analysts and portfolio managers who attempt to achieve superior investment results for their investors.

4. *Lower transaction costs.* Because they trade large blocks of securities, investment companies can achieve substantial savings on brokerage fees and commissions.

While all investment companies pool assets of individual investors, they also need to divide claims to those assets among those investors. Investors buy shares in investment companies, and ownership is proportional to the number of shares purchased. The value of each share is called the **net asset value,** or **NAV.** Net asset value equals assets minus liabilities expressed on a per-share basis:

$$\text{Net asset value} = \frac{\text{Market value of assets minus liabilities}}{\text{Shares outstanding}}$$

Consider a mutual fund that manages a portfolio of securities worth $120 million. Suppose the fund owes $4 million to its investment advisers and owes another $1 million for rent, wages due, and miscellaneous expenses. The fund has 5 million shareholders. Then

$$\text{Net asset value} = \frac{\$120\text{ million} - \$5\text{ million}}{5\text{ million shares}} = \$23\text{ per share}$$

Concept
CHECK

Question 1 • Consider these data from the December 31, 1996, balance sheet of the Index Trust 500 Portfolio mutual fund sponsored by the Vanguard Group. What was the net asset value of the portfolio?

Assets:	$30,376,657,000
Liabilities:	44,805,000
Shares:	438,518,428

4.2   TYPES OF INVESTMENT COMPANIES

In the United States, investment companies are classified by the Investment Company Act of 1940 as either unit investment trusts or managed investment companies. The portfolios of unit investment trusts are essentially fixed and thus are called "unmanaged." In contrast, managed companies are so named because securities in their investment portfolios continually are bought and sold: The portfolios are managed. Managed companies are further classified as either closed-end or open-end. Open-end companies are what we commonly call mutual funds.

Unit Investment Trusts

Unit investment trusts are pools of money invested in a portfolio that is fixed for the life of the fund. To form a unit investment trust, a sponsor, typically a brokerage firm, buys a portfolio of securities which are deposited into a trust. It then sells to the public shares, or "units," in the trust, called *redeemable trust certificates*. All income and payments of principal from the portfolio are paid out by the fund's trustees (a bank or trust company) to the shareholders. Most unit trusts hold fixed-income securities and expire at their maturity, which may be as short as a few months if the trust invests in short-term securities like money market instruments, or as long as many years if the trust holds long-term assets like fixed-income securities. The fixed life of fixed-income securities makes them a good fit for fixed-life unit investment trusts. In fact, about 90% of all unit investment trusts are invested in fixed-income portfolios, and about 90% of fixed-income unit investment trusts are invested in tax-exempt debt.

There is little active management of a unit investment trust because once established, the portfolio composition is fixed; hence these trusts are referred to as *unmanaged*. Trusts tend to invest in relatively uniform types of assets; for example, one trust may invest in municipal bonds, another in corporate bonds. The uniformity of the portfolio is consistent with the lack of active management. The trusts provide investors a vehicle to purchase a pool of one particular type of asset, which can be included in an overall portfolio as desired. The lack of active management of the portfolio implies that management fees can be lower than those of managed funds.

Sponsors of unit investment trusts earn their profit by selling shares in the trust at a premium to the cost of acquiring the underlying assets. For example, a trust that has purchased $5 million of assets may sell 5,000 shares to the public at a price of $1,030 per share, which (assuming the trust has no liabilities) represents a 3% premium over the net asset value of the securities held by the trust. The 3% premium is the trustee's fee for establishing the trust.

Investors who wish to liquidate their holdings of a unit investment trust may sell the shares back to the trustee for net asset value. The trustees can either sell enough securities from the asset portfolio to obtain the cash necessary to pay the investor, or they may instead sell the shares to a new investor (again at a slight premium to net asset value).

Managed Investment Companies

There are two types of managed companies: closed-end and open-end. In both cases, the fund's board of directors, which is elected by shareholders, hires a management company to manage the portfolio for an annual fee that typically ranges from .2% to 1.5% of assets. In many cases the management company is the firm that organized the fund. For example, Fidelity Management and Research Corporation sponsors many Fidelity mutual funds and is responsible for managing the portfolios. It assesses a management fee on each Fidelity fund. In other cases, a mutual fund will hire an outside portfolio manager. For example, Vanguard has hired Wellington Management as the investment adviser for its Wellington Fund. Most management companies have contracts to manage several funds.

Open-end funds stand ready to redeem or issue shares at their net asset value (although both purchases and redemptions may involve sales charges). When investors in open-end funds wish to "cash out" their shares, they sell them back to the fund at NAV. In contrast,

Figure 4.1
Closed-end mutual funds.

CLOSED-END FUNDS

Friday, June 28 1996

Closed-end funds sell a limited number of shares and invest the proceeds in securities. Unlike open-end funds, closed-ends generally do not buy their shares back from investors who wish to cash in their holdings. Instead, fund shares trade on a stock exchange. The following list, provided by Lipper Analytical Services, shows the exchange where each fund trades (A: American; C: Chicago; N: NYSE; O: Nasdaq; T: Toronto; z: does not trade on an exchange). The data also include the fund's most recent net asset value, its closing share price on the day NAV was calculated, and the percentage difference between the market price and the NAV (often called the premium or discount). For equity funds, the final column provides 52-week returns based on market prices plus dividends. For bond funds, the final column shows the past 12 months' income distributions as a percentage of the current market price. Footnotes appear after a fund's name. a: the NAV and market price are ex dividend. b: the NAV is fully diluted. c: NAV, market price and premium or discount are as of Thursday's close. d: NAV, market price and premium or discount are as of Wednesday's close. e: NAV assumes rights offering is fully subscribed. v: NAV is converted at the commercial Rand rate. w: Convertible Note-NAV (not market) conversion value. y: NAV and market price are in Canadian dollars. All other footnotes refer to unusual circumstances; explanations for those that appear can be found at the bottom of this list. N/A signifies that the information is not available or not applicable.

Fund Name	Stock Exch	NAV	Market Price	Prem /Disc	52 week Market Return
General Equity Funds					
Adams Express	N	22.94	19 1/8	− 16.6	20.5
Alliance All-Mkt -a	N	22.57	19	− 15.8	17.1
Avalon Capital	O	10.77	9 3/4	− 9.5	N/A
Baker Fentress	N	23.88	19 1/8	− 19.9	29.2
Bergstrom Cap	A	133.84	116 1/2	− 13.0	31.7
Blue Chip Value	N	9.46	8 1/2	− 10.1	34.5
Central Secs	A	22.67	24	+ 5.9	25.8
Corp Renaissance -c	O	10.36	8 3/8	− 19.2	−9.5
Engex	A	16.25	12 3/4	− 21.5	36.0
Equus II	A	21.18	14 5/8	− 30.9	19.3
Gabelli Equity	N	10.10	9 5/8	− 4.7	8.3
General American	N	26.42	22	− 16.7	23.7
Inefficient Mkt	A	13.44	11 3/8	− 15.4	32.5
Liberty AllStr Eq	N	11.55	10 3/4	− 6.9	18.9
Liberty AllStr Gr	N	11.31	9 5/8	− 14.9	13.6
MicroCap Fund	O	N/A	6	0.0	26.3
Morgan FunShares -c	O	10.50	8 7/8	− 15.5	21.0
Morgan Gr Sm Cap -h	N	12.72	10 3/8	− 18.4	30.8
NAIC Growth -c	C	16.93	17 1/2	+ 3.4	59.4
Royce Value	N	14.52	12 3/8	− 14.8	14.9
Royce,5.75 '04Cv -w	N	109.18	101 1/4	− 7.3	1.8
Salomon SBF	N	16.67	14 1/4	− 14.5	33.7
Source Capital	N	44.53	41 1/4	− 7.4	10.9
Tri-Continental	N	29.57	24	− 18.8	18.1
Zweig	N	11.02	11 1/8	+ 1.0	10.0
Specialized Equity Funds					
Alliance Gl Env	N	16.73	13 1/8	− 21.5	44.1
C&S Realty	A	9.03	9 1/4	+ 2.4	7.4
C&S Total Rtn	N	13.97	13 1/2	− 3.4	15.7
Centrl Fd Canada -c	A	4.74	4 3/4	+ 0.2	−1.1
Counsellors Tand	N	19.40	18 1/4	− 5.9	27.4

Fund Name	Stock Exch	NAV	Market Price	Prem /Disc	52 week Market Return
India Fund	N	9.73	9 1/4	− 4.9	−9.8
India Growth -d	N	13.74	14 5/8	+ 6.4	−16.3
Indonesia	N	9.90	11 1/8	+ 12.4	0.0
Irish Inv	N	16.17	13 1/8	− 18.8	21.8
Italy	N	10.67	8 7/8	− 16.8	14.8
Jakarta Growth	N	9.16	8 3/4	− 4.5	−1.6
Japan Equity	N	11.94	12 5/8	+ 5.7	8.5
Japan OTC Equity	N	9.14	8 5/8	− 5.6	−2.8
Jardine Fl China	N	12.08	10 3/8	− 14.1	−5.1
Jardine Fl India -c	N	9.80	9 1/4	− 5.6	−20.3
Korea	N	18.52	21 1/8	+ 14.1	9.8
Korea Equity	N	8.17	8 1/2	+ 4.0	6.5
Korean Inv	N	10.30	9 7/8	− 4.1	−5.4
Latin Amer Disc	N	14.60	12 5/8	− 13.5	17.2
Latin Amer Eq	N	17.41	15 1/8	− 13.1	9.8
Latin Amer Growth	N	12.74	10 1/2	− 17.6	2.1
Latin Amer Inv	N	19.71	16 3/4	− 15.0	5.9
Malaysia	N	21.54	18 3/4	− 13.0	1.1
Mexico -ac	N	17.90	15	− 16.2	−1.0
Mexico Eqty&Inc -c	N	12.19	9 7/8	− 19.0	−5.7
Morgan St Africa	N	16.06	12 5/8	− 21.4	20.6
Morgan St Asia	N	13.45	12	− 10.8	17.2
Morgan St Em	N	17.44	16 7/8	− 3.2	11.6
Morgan St India	N	11.06	11 1/4	+ 1.7	9.8
New South Africa	N	17.57	13 3/4	− 21.7	1.2
New World Inv	z	N/A	N/A	0.0	N/A
Pakistan Inv	N	7.15	6 3/4	− 5.6	0.1
Portugal	N	15.27	12 1/2	− 18.1	−6.1
ROC Taiwan	N	10.77	11 3/8	+ 5.6	3.0
Schroder Asian	N	14.27	13 1/8	− 8.0	18.0
Scudder New Asia	N	16.06	14 5/8	− 8.9	0.1
Scudder New Eur	N	15.99	12 5/8	− 21.0	23.7
Singapore -c	N	12.91	12 3/4	− 1.2	−8.9
Southern Africa	N	20.84	16 3/4	− 19.6	29.2
Spain	N	12.24	9 7/8	− 19.3	14.8
Swiss Helvetia	N	25.56	21 1/4	− 16.9	8.6
TCW/DW Emer Mkts	N	13.53	11	− 18.7	9.3
Taiwan -c	N	22.74	24	+ 5.5	9.8
Taiwan Equity -c	N	11.23	10 7/8	− 3.2	2.4
Templeton China -c	N	13.33	11 1/8	− 16.5	11.8
Templeton Dragon	N	16.01	13 1/4	− 17.2	13.8
Templeton Em App -c	N	13.99	12 1/2	− 10.7	10.4
Templeton Em Mkt	N	17.52	19	+ 8.4	7.1
Templeton Russia -c	N	22.41	26 1/4	+ 17.1	N/A
Templeton Vietnm	N	13.85	11 1/4	− 18.8	−4.7
Thai	N	24.60	23 5/8	− 4.0	2.3
Thai Capital	N	14.62	13 1/4	− 9.4	−7.2
Third Canadian -cy	T	15.02	14 1/4	− 5.1	17.6
Turkish Inv	N	5.83	6	+ 2.9	−4.0
United Corps Ltd -cy	T	52.03	35 1/2	− 31.8	11.2
United Kingdom -a	N	15.86	12 5/8	− 20.4	17.9
Worldwide Value	N	25.53	21 1/2	− 15.8	42.6
Z-Seven	O	19.38	20	+ 3.2	19.7

Fund Name	Stock Exch	NAV	Market Price	Prem /Disc	12 Mo Yield 5/31/96
U.S. Gov't. Bond Funds					
ACM Govt Inc	N	9.33	9 7/8	+ 5.8	8.5

closed-end funds do not redeem or issue shares. Investors in closed-end funds who wish to cash out must sell their shares to other investors. Shares of closed-end funds are traded on organized exchanges and can be purchased through brokers just like other common stock; their prices therefore can differ from NAV.

Figure 4.1 is a listing of closed-end funds from *The Wall Street Journal*. The first column after the name of the fund indicates the exchange on which the shares trade (A: Amex; C: Chicago; N: NYSE; O: Nasdaq; T: Toronto; z: does not trade on an exchange). The next three columns give the fund's most recent net asset value, the closing share price, and the percentage difference between the two; which is (Price – NAV)/NAV. Notice that there are more funds selling at discounts to NAV (indicated by negative differences) than premiums.

Finally, the 52-week return based on the percentage change in share price plus dividend income is presented in the last column.

The common divergence of price from net asset value, often by wide margins, is a puzzle that has yet to be fully explained. To see why this is a puzzle, consider a closed-end fund that is selling at a discount from net asset value. If the fund were to sell all the assets in the portfolio, it would realize proceeds equal to net asset value. The difference between the market price of the fund and the fund's NAV would represent the per-share increase in the wealth of the fund's investors. Despite this apparent profit opportunity, sizable discounts seem to persist for long periods of time.

Interestingly, while many closed-end funds sell at a discount from net asset value, the prices of these funds when originally issued are typically above NAV. This is a further puzzle, as it is hard to explain why investors would purchase these newly issued funds at a premium to NAV when the shares tend to fall to a discount shortly after issue.

Many investors consider closed-end funds selling at a discount to NAV to be a bargain. Even if the market price never rises to the level of NAV, the dividend yield on an investment in the fund at this price would exceed the dividend yield on the same securities held outside the fund. To see this, imagine a fund with an NAV of $10 per share holding a portfolio that pays an annual dividend of $1 per share; that is, the dividend yield to investors that hold this portfolio directly is 10%. Now suppose that the market price of a share of this closed-end fund is $9. If management pays out dividends received from the shares as they come in, then the dividend yield to those that hold the same portfolio through the closed-end fund will be $1/$9, or 11.1%.

Recent variations on closed-end funds are *interval closed-end funds* and *discretionary closed-end funds*. Interval closed-end funds may purchase from 5% to 25% of outstanding shares from investors at intervals of 3, 6, or 12 months. Discretionary closed-end funds may purchase any or all outstanding shares from investors, but no more frequently than once every two years. The repurchase of shares for either of these funds takes place at net asset value plus a repurchase fee that may not exceed 2%.

In contrast to closed-end funds, the price of open-end funds cannot fall below NAV, because these funds stand ready to redeem shares at NAV. The offering price will exceed NAV, however, if the fund carries a **load.** A load is, in effect, a sales charge, which is paid to the seller. Load funds are sold by securities brokers and directly by mutual fund groups.

Unlike closed-end funds, open-end mutual funds do not trade on organized exchanges. Instead, investors simply buy shares from and liquidate through the investment company at net asset value. Thus the number of outstanding shares of these funds changes daily.

Other Investment Organizations

There are intermediaries not formally organized or regulated as investment companies that nevertheless serve functions similar to investment companies. Two of the more important are commingled funds and real estate investment trusts.

Commingled Funds   Commingled funds are partnerships of investors that pool their funds. The management firm that organizes the partnership, for example, a bank or insurance company, manages the funds for a fee. Typical partners in a commingled fund might be trust or retirement accounts which have portfolios that are much larger than those of most individual investors but are still too small to warrant managing on a separate basis.

Commingled funds are similar in form to open-end mutual funds. Instead of shares, though, the fund offers units, which are bought and sold at net asset value. A bank or insurance company may offer an array of different commingled funds from which trust or retirement accounts can choose. Examples are a money market fund, a bond fund, and a common stock fund.

Real Estate Investment Trusts (REITs)   A REIT is similar to a closed-end fund. REITs invest in real estate or loans secured by real estate. Besides issuing shares, they raise capital by borrowing from banks and issuing bonds or mortgages. Most of them are highly leveraged, with a typical debt ratio of 70%.

There are two principal kinds of REITs. *Equity trusts* invest in real estate directly, whereas *mortgage trusts* invest primarily in mortgage and construction loans. REITs generally are established by banks, insurance companies, or mortgage companies, which then serve as investment managers to earn a fee.

REITs are exempt from taxes as long as at least 95% of their taxable income is distributed to shareholders. For shareholders, however, the dividends are taxable as personal income.

4.3   MUTUAL FUNDS

Mutual funds are the common name for open-end investment companies. This is the dominant investment company today, accounting for roughly 90% of investment company assets. Assets under management in the mutual fund industry surpassed $4 trillion in mid-1997.

Investment Policies

Each mutual fund has a specified investment policy, which is described in the fund's prospectus. For example, money market mutual funds hold the short-term, low-risk instruments of the money market (see Chapter 2 for a review of these securities), while bond funds hold fixed-income securities. Some funds have even more narrowly defined mandates. For example, some fixed-income funds will hold primarily Treasury bonds, others primarily mortgage-backed securities.

Management companies manage a family, or "complex," of mutual funds. They organize an entire collection of funds and then collect a management fee for operating them. By managing a collection of funds under one umbrella, these companies make it easy for investors to allocate assets across market sectors and to switch assets across funds while still benefiting from centralized record keeping. Some of the most well-known management companies are Fidelity, Vanguard, Putnam, and Dreyfus. Each offers an array of open-end mutual funds with different investment policies. There were nearly 6,300 mutual funds at the end of 1996, which were offered by only 400 fund complexes.

Some of the more important fund types, classified by investment policy, are discussed next.

Money Market Funds   These funds invest in money market securities. They usually offer check-writing features, and net asset value is fixed at $1 per share, so that there are no tax implications such as capital gains or losses associated with redemption of shares.

Equity Funds   Equity funds invest primarily in stock, although they may, at the portfolio manager's discretion, also hold fixed-income or other types of securities. Funds commonly will hold at least some money market securities to provide liquidity necessary to meet potential redemption of shares.

Investment Companies, a manual published by Wiesenberger Investment Companies Services, classifies common stock funds according to the following objectives:

1. Maximum capital gain
2. Growth
3. Growth and income
4. Income
5. Income and security

The objectives are arranged according to the manual "in descending order of emphasis on capital appreciation and, consequently, in ascending order of the importance placed on current income and relative price stability."

Fixed-Income Funds   As the name suggests, these funds specialize in the fixed-income sector. Within that sector, however, there is considerable room for specialization. For example, various funds will concentrate on corporate bonds, Treasury bonds, mortgage-backed securities, or municipal (tax-free) bonds. Indeed, some of the municipal bond funds will invest only in bonds of a particular state (or even city!) in order to satisfy the investment desires of residents of that state who wish to avoid local as well as federal taxes on the interest paid on the bonds. Many funds will also specialize by the maturity of the securities, ranging from short-term to intermediate to long-term, or by the credit risk of the issuer, ranging from very safe to high-yield or "junk" bonds.

Balanced and Income Funds   Some funds are designed to be candidates for an individual's entire investment portfolio. Therefore, they hold both equities and fixed-income securities in relatively stable proportions. According to Wiesenberger, such funds are classified as income or balanced funds. *Income funds* strive to maintain safety of principal consistent with "as liberal a current income from investments as possible," while *balanced funds* "minimize investment risks so far as this is possible without unduly sacrificing possibilities for long-term growth and current income."

Asset Allocation Funds   These funds are similar to balanced funds in that they hold both stocks and bonds. However, asset allocation funds may dramatically vary the proportions allocated to each market in accord with the portfolio manager's forecast of the relative performance of each sector. Hence these funds are engaged in market timing and are not designed to be low-risk investment vehicles.

Index Funds   An index fund tries to match the performance of a broad market index. The fund buys shares in securities included in a particular index in proportion to the security's representation in that index. For example, Vanguard Index Trust 500 Portfolio is a mutual fund that replicates the composition of the Standard & Poor's 500 stock price index. Because the S&P 500 is a value-weighted index, the fund buys shares in each S&P 500 company in proportion to the market value of that company's outstanding equity. Investment in an index fund is a low-cost way for small investors to pursue a passive investment strategy—that is, to invest without engaging in security analysis. Of course, index funds can be tied to nonequity indexes as well. For example, Vanguard offers a bond index fund and a real estate index fund.

Specialized Sector Funds   Some funds concentrate on a particular industry. For example, Fidelity markets dozens of "select funds," each of which invests in a specific

Table 4.1   Classification of Mutual Funds (as of December 31, 1996)

Type of Fund	Number of Funds	Assets ($ Million)	% of Total
Common stock			
Maximum capital gain	180	68,395	2.1%
Small company growth	491	109,590	3.4
International equity	995	257,959	8.0
Long-term growth	1,153	509,004	15.8
Growth and current income	618	416,826	12.9
Equity income	189	73,895	2.3
	3,626	1,435,669	44.6%
Bond			
Flexible income	90	69,915	2.2%
Corporate bond	685	137,218	4.3
Corporate high yield	190	79,867	2.5
Government mortgage-backed	165	43,681	1.4
Government securities	540	86,601	2.7
Municipal	502	110,577	3.4
Municipal high yield	67	30,650	1.0
Municipal single state	1,302	113,142	3.5
International	264	26,208	0.8
	3,805	697,859	21.7%
Specialized			
Energy/natural resources	42	6,043	0.2%
Financial services	21	7,300	0.2
Gold and precious metals	50	4,890	0.2
Health care	28	9,344	0.3
Other	56	7,421	0.2
Technology	53	17,466	0.5
Utilities	101	24,544	0.8
	351	77,008	2.4%
Money market			
Taxable	736	761,799	23.7%
Tax-free	396	140,046	4.3
	1,132	901,845	28.0%
Mixed asset classes			
Balanced	320	68,235	2.1%
Asset allocation	178	40,105	1.2
	498	108,340	3.4%
TOTAL	9,412	3,220,721	100.0%

Note: The total number of funds, 9,412, may be overstated to the extent that funds with different classes (Class A shares, B shares, etc.) are treated as separate funds.

Source: Investment Companies Yearbook, 1997, CDA Wiesenberger Investment Companies Service, 1355 Picard Drive, Rockville, MD 20850.

industry such as biotechnology, utilities, precious metals, or telecommunications. Other funds specialize in securities of particular countries.

Table 4.1 breaks down the number of mutual funds by investment orientation as of the end of 1996. Figure 4.2 is part of the listings for mutual funds from *The Wall Street Journal*. Notice that the funds are organized by the fund family. For example, the funds sponsored by the Vanguard Group appear at the right of the figure. The first two columns after the name of each fund present the net asset value of the fund and the change in NAV from the previous day. The last column is the year-to-date return on the fund.

Figure 4.2

Listing of mutual fund quotations.

MUTUAL FUND QUOTATIONS

Templeton Group:
AmerTr2 r 15.42 +0.08 + 8.2
CapAcc 9.12 +0.04 +11.4
DevMktI p 15.02 +0.02 +15.9
DevMkt2 14.89 +0.02 +15.4
ForgnI p 10.01 +0.02 + 9.0
Forgn2 p 9.93 +0.03 + 8.6
GlInfral p 10.65 +0.05 +12.7
GlobOpl p 13.88 +0.01 +12.4
GrowIRcl 11.74 +0.04 + 9.6
GrwthI p 18.89 +0.05 + 8.9
Grwth2 p 18.73 +0.05 + 8.4
GlBond i p 9.70 +0.03 + 2.4
Japan p 10.34 +0.02 + 1.6
LatinAm I p 11.19 −0.02 +12.8
GlRlEstl p 13.59 +0.03 + 5.7
GlSmCol p 8.61 +0.02 +12.8
GlSmCo2 8.55 +0.03 +12.6
WorldI p 16.32 +0.04 + 9.5
World2 16.17 +0.05 + 9.0

Templeton Instit:
EmMS 12.23 +0.02 +14.1
ForEqS 15.44 +0.06 +10.4
GrwthS 12.95 +0.06 +10.4
ThirdAve 23.37 +0.18 + 7.2
ThomWhite r 12.06 +0.03 + 7.7

Van Kamp Amer Cap A:
CATFA p 17.07 +0.09 −1.4k
CmstA p 15.40 +0.11 +10.1
CpBdA p 6.75x +0.01 − 2.8
EmGrA p 35.87 +0.78 +17.6
EntA p 14.45 +0.16 +11.6
EqIncA p 6.51 +0.04 + 5.3
Exch 166.94 +0.62 +10.3

GlEqA p 14.01 +0.09 +10.9
GlGvA p 7.98x ... − 1.6
GlMgdA p 10.82 +0.06 + 7.4
GrIncA p 15.11 +0.08 + 7.2
GvScA p 9.96 +0.06 − 2.3
GvTIA p 8.12 +0.04 − 2.0
GvT97 p 14.36 +0.05 + 0.3
HarbA p 15.44 +0.11 + 6.1
HICpA p 6.29x −0.04 + 5.9
HiYIdA p 9.49 +0.01 +4.1k
HYMuA p 10.96 +0.04 + 0.7
InTFA p 18.73 +0.09 −1.7k
LimMtA p 12.12 +0.03 + 0.3
MunInA p 14.99 +0.07 −0.8k
PA TFA p 17.07 +0.08 −1.2k
PaceA p 11.92 +0.07 + 7.7
ReEstA p 10.62 +0.05 + 8.2
ST GIA p 7.62 +0.01 +3.0k
StgInA p 12.06 +0.06 +3.2k
TxFHA p 14.34 +0.05 −1.2k
TXTFA p 10.06 +0.05 + 0.3
US GvA p 14.24 +0.04 −1.2k
UtilA p 15.43 +0.28 + 3.6

Vanguard Group:
AdmIT 10.06 +0.06 − 2.8
AdmLT 9.99 +0.11 − 6.9
AdmST 9.97 +0.02 + 0.6
AssetA 17.77 +0.12 + 5.4
Convrt 12.26 +0.05 + 7.4
EqInc 17.50 +0.07 + 6.6
Explr 56.01 +0.86 +12.1
HznAgGr 12.04 +0.18 +11.9
HznCpOp 10.80 +0.28 +10.0
HznGAAP 10.85 +0.05 + 3.6

HznGlbEq 11.53 +0.01 + 9.5
LIFEInc 11.39 +0.07 + 1.2
LIFECon 11.84 +0.06 + 3.3
LIFEMod 12.52 +0.08 + 4.8
LIFEGro 13.09 +0.08 + 6.8
Morg 15.44 +0.13 +12.2
Prmcp 28.35 +0.29 + 8.6
Quant 21.33 +0.09 + 9.6
SelValu 10.27 +0.09 NS
STAR 15.69 +0.08 + 6.1
TxMBal 12.26 +0.06 + 4.7
TxMCap 14.65 +0.09 +10.3
TxMGI 14.37 +0.04 +10.1
TrIntl 32.27 +0.13 + 5.7
TrUS 38.13 +0.20 + 8.5
STTsry 10.10 +0.03 + 0.6
STFed 10.05 +0.03 + 0.9
STCorp 10.68 +0.03 + 0.8
ITTsry 10.26 +0.06 − 2.8
GNMA 10.06 +0.06 − 0.2
ITCorp 9.56 +0.05 − 2.6
LTTsry 9.70 +0.11 − 7.1
LTCorp 8.66 +0.08 − 4.7
HYCorp 7.57 +0.01 + 0.6
Prefd 9.32 +0.04 + 1.0
IdxTotB 9.69 +0.05 − 1.4
IdxTBIst 9.69 +0.05 − 1.4
IdxSTB 9.85 +0.03 + 0.7
IdxITB 9.79 +0.05 − 2.6
IdxLTB 9.80 +0.10 − 6.4
Idx Bal 13.27 +0.08 + 5.3
Idx 500 62.89 +0.20 +10.0
IdxExt 26.26 +0.35 +10.5
IdxTot 16.39 +0.10 +10.0

Name	NAV	Chg	Net YTD %ret
IdxGro	15.40	+0.03	+11.4
IdxVal	15.67	+0.06	+ 8.5
IdxSmC	20.58	+0.34	+11.4
IdxEMkt	12.33	+0.01	+14.8
IdxEur	14.98	+0.14	+ 7.0
IdxPac	11.88	−0.03	+ 3.3
IdxIntl	10.21	+0.03	NA
IdxInst	63.24	+0.19	+10.1
MuHY	10.42	+0.05	− 0.5
MuInt	13.02	+0.06	− 0.1
MuLtd	10.62	+0.02	+ 0.9
MuLong	10.73	+0.07	− 0.7
MuInlg	12.12	+0.08	− 1.2
MuSht	15.54	+0.01	+ 1.4
CAInsIT	10.29	+0.05	+ 0.7
CAInsLT	10.98	+0.08	− 0.9
FL Ins	10.68	+0.07	− 1.1
NJIns	11.35	+0.07	− 1.3
NYIns	10.63	+0.06	− 1.0
OHIns	11.32	+0.07	− 0.8
PAIns	10.96	+0.06	− 0.5
SPEnrg r	19.93	+0.21	+15.1
SPGold r	12.73	−0.07	+ 7.2
SPHlth r	55.19	+0.46	+11.6
SP Reit	10.22	+0.04	NA
SPUtil	12.67	+0.22	+ 2.3
USGro	23.30	+0.04	+14.5
IntlGr	16.43	+0.05	+ 9.4
WellsI	19.74	+0.14	− 0.2
WellIn	25.19	+0.12	+ 4.8
Wndsr	15.46	+0.04	+ 7.8
WndsII	22.53	+0.10	+10.0

Source: The Wall Street Journal. Reprinted by permission of The Wall Street Journal, © 1996 Dow Jones & Company, Inc. All Rights Reserved Worldwide.

Often the fund name describes its investment policy. For example, Vanguard's GNMA fund invests in mortgage-backed securities, the municipal intermediate fund (MuInt) invests in intermediate-term municipal bonds, and the high-yield corporate bond fund (HYCorp) invests in large part in speculative grade, or "junk," bonds with high yields. You can see that Vanguard offers more than a dozen index funds, including portfolios indexed to the bond market (IdxTotB), the Wilshire 5000 index (IdxTot), the Russell 2000 Index of small firms (IdxSmC), as well as European- and Pacific Basin–indexed portfolios (IdxEur and IdxPac). However, names of common stock funds frequently reflect little or nothing about their investment policies. Examples are Vanguard's Windsor and Wellington funds.

How Funds Are Sold

Most mutual funds have an underwriter that has exclusive rights to distribute shares to investors. Mutual funds are generally marketed to the public either directly by the fund underwriter or indirectly through brokers acting on behalf of the underwriter. Direct-marketed funds are sold through the mail, various offices of the fund, over the phone, and, increasingly, over the Internet. Investors contact the fund directly to purchase shares. For example, if you look at the financial pages of your local newspaper, you will see several advertisements for funds, along with toll-free phone numbers that you can call to receive a fund's prospectus and an application to open an account with the fund.

A bit less than half of fund sales today are distributed through a sales force. Brokers or financial advisers receive a commission for selling shares to investors. (Ultimately, the commission is paid by the investor. More on this shortly.) In some cases, funds use a "captive" sales force that sells only shares in funds of the mutual fund group they represent.

The trend today, however, is toward "financial supermarkets," which sell shares in funds of many complexes. This approach was made popular by the OneSource program of Charles Schwab & Co. Schwab allows customers of the OneSource program to buy funds from many different fund groups. Instead of charging customers a sales commission, Schwab splits management fees with the mutual fund company. The supermarket approach seems to be proving popular. For example, Fidelity now sells more than 800 non-Fidelity mutual funds through its FundsNetwork even though many of those funds compete with Fidelity products. Like Schwab, Fidelity shares a portion of the management fee from the non-Fidelity funds its sells.

4.4   COSTS OF INVESTING IN MUTUAL FUNDS

Fee Structure

An individual investor choosing a mutual fund should consider not only the fund's stated investment policy and past performance, but also its management fees and other expenses. Comparative data on virtually all important aspects of mutual funds are available in the annual reports prepared by Wiesenberger Investment Companies Services or in Morningstar's *Mutual Fund Sourcebook*, which can be found in many academic and public libraries. You should be aware of four general classes of fees.

Front-End Load   A front-end load is a commission or sales charge paid when you purchase the shares. These charges, which are used primarily to pay the brokers who sell the funds, may not exceed 8.5%, but in practice they are rarely higher than 6.25%. *Low-load funds* have loads that range up to 3% of invested funds. *No-load funds* have no front-end sales charges. Loads effectively reduce the amount of money invested. For example, each $1,000 paid for a fund with an 8.5% load results in a sales charge of $85 and fund investment of only $915. You need cumulative returns of 9.3% of your net investment (85/915 = .093) just to break even.

Back-End Load   A back-end load is a redemption, or "exit," fee incurred when you sell your shares. Typically, funds that impose back-end loads start them at 5% or 6% and reduce them by 1 percentage point for every year the funds are left invested. Thus an exit fee that starts at 6% would fall to 4% by the start of your third year. These charges are known more formally as "contingent deferred sales charges."

Operating Expenses   Operating expenses are the costs incurred by the mutual fund in operating the portfolio, including administrative expenses and advisory fees paid to the investment manager. These expenses, usually expressed as a percentage of total assets under management, may range from 0.2% to 2%. Shareholders do not receive an explicit bill for these operating expenses; however, the expenses periodically are deducted from the assets of the fund. Shareholders pay for these expenses through the reduced value of the portfolio.

12b-1 Charges   The Securities and Exchange Commission allows the managers of so-called 12b-1 funds to use fund assets to pay for distribution costs such as advertising, promotional literature including annual reports and prospectuses, and, most important, commissions paid to brokers who sell the fund to investors. These **12b-1 fees** are named after the SEC rule that permits use of these plans. Funds may use 12b-1 charges instead of, or in addition to, front-end loads to generate the fees with which to pay brokers. As with operating expenses, investors are not explicitly billed for 12b-1 charges. Instead, the fees are deducted from the assets of the fund. Therefore, 12b-1 fees (if any) must be added to operating expenses to obtain the true annual expense ratio of the fund. The SEC now requires that all funds include in the prospectus a consolidated expense table that summarizes all relevant fees. The 12b-1 fees are limited to 1% of a fund's average net assets per year.[1]

A recent innovation in the fee structure of mutual funds is the creation of different "classes"; they represent ownership in the same portfolio of securities but impose different combinations of fees. For example, Class A shares typically are sold with front-end loads of between 4% and 5%. Class B shares impose 12b-1 charges and back-end loads. Because Class B shares pay 12b-1 fees while Class A shares do not, the reported rate of return on the B shares will be less than that of the A shares despite the fact that they represent holdings in the same portfolio. (The reported return on the shares does not reflect the impact of loads paid by the investor.) Class C shares do not impose back-end redemption fees, but they impose 12b-1 fees higher than those in Class B, often as high as 1% annually. Other classes and combinations of fees are also marketed by mutual fund companies. For example, Merrill Lynch introduced Class D shares of some of its funds in 1994, which included front-end loads and 12b-1 charges of .25%.

Each investor must choose the best combination of fees. Obviously, pure no-load no-fee funds distributed directly by the mutual fund group are the cheapest alternative, and these will often make most sense for knowledgeable investors. However, many investors are willing to pay for financial advice, and the commissions paid to advisers who sell these funds are the most common form of payment. Alternatively, investors may choose to hire a fee-only financial manager who charges directly for services and does not accept commissions. These advisers can help investors select portfolios of low- or no-load funds (as well as provide other financial advice). Independent financial planners have become increasingly important distribution channels for funds in recent years.

If you do buy a fund through a broker, the choice between paying a load and paying 12b-1 fees will depend primarily on your expected time horizon. Loads are paid only once for each purchase, whereas 12b-1 fees are paid annually. Thus if you plan to hold your fund for a long time, a one-time load may be preferable to recurring 12b-1 charges.

You can identify funds with various charges by the following letters placed after the fund name in the listing of mutual funds in the financial pages: *r* denotes redemption or exit fees; *p* denotes 12b-1 fees; *t* denotes both redemption and 12b-1 fees. The listings do not allow you to identify funds that involve front-end loads, however; while NAV for each fund is presented, the offering price at which the fund can be purchased, which may include a load, is not.

Fees and Mutual Fund Returns

The rate of return on an investment in a mutual fund is measured as the increase or decrease in net asset value plus income distributions such as dividends or distributions of capital gains expressed as a fraction of net asset value at the beginning of the investment period. If we denote the net asset value at the start and end of the period as NAV_0 and NAV_1, respectively, then

$$\text{Rate of return} = \frac{NAV_1 - NAV_0 + \text{Income and capital gain distributions}}{NAV_0}$$

---

[1]The maximum 12b-1 charge for the sale of the fund is .75%. However, an additional service fee of .25% of the fund's assets also is allowed for personal service and/or maintenance of shareholder accounts.

For example, if a fund has an initial NAV of $20 at the start of the month, makes income distributions of $.15 and capital gain distributions of $.05, and ends the month with NAV of $20.10, the monthly rate of return is computed as

$$\text{Rate of return} = \frac{\$20.10 - \$20.00 + \$.15 + \$.05}{\$20.00} = .015, \text{ or } 1.5\%$$

Notice that this measure of the rate of return ignores any commissions such as front-end loads paid to purchase the fund.

On the other hand, the rate of return is affected by the fund's expenses and 12b-1 fees. This is because such charges are periodically deducted from the portfolio, which reduces net asset value. Thus the rate of return on the fund equals the gross return on the underlying portfolio minus the total expense ratio.

To see how expenses can affect rate of return, consider a fund with $100 million in assets at the start of the year and with 10 million shares outstanding. The fund invests in a portfolio of stocks that provides no income but increases in value by 10%. The expense ratio, including 12b-1 fees, is 1%. What is the rate of return for an investor in the fund?

The initial NAV equals $100 million/10 million shares = $10 per share. In the absence of expenses, fund assets would grow to $110 million and NAV would grow to $11 per share, for a 10% rate of return. However, the expense ratio of the fund is 1%. Therefore, $1 million will be deducted from the fund to pay these fees, leaving the portfolio worth only $109 million, and NAV equal to $10.90. The rate of return on the fund is only 9%, which equals the gross return on the underlying portfolio minus the total expense ratio.

Fees can have a big effect on performance. Table 4.2 considers an investor who starts with $10,000 and can choose between three funds that all earn an annual 12% return on investment before fees but have different fee structures. The table shows the cumulative amount in each fund after several investment horizons. Fund A has total operating expenses of .5%, no load, and no 12b-1 charges. This might represent a low-cost producer like Vanguard. Fund B has no load but has 1% in management expenses and .5% in 12b-1 fees. This level of charges is fairly typical of actively managed equity funds. Finally, Fund C has 1% in management expenses, no 12b-1 charges, but assesses an 8% front-end load on purchases as well as reinvested dividends. We assume the dividend yield on each fund is 5%.

Note the substantial return advantage of low-cost Fund A. Moreover, that differential is greater for longer investment horizons.

Table 4.2   Impact of Costs on Investment Performance

	Cumulative Proceeds (All Dividends Reinvested)		
	Fund A	**Fund B**	**Fund C**
Initial investment*	$10,000	$10,000	$ 9,200
5 years	17,234	16,474	15,225
10 years	29,699	27,141	25,196
15 years	51,183	44,713	41,698
20 years	88,206	73,662	69,006

*After front-end load, if any.
Notes
1. Fund A is no-load with .5% expense ratio.
2. Fund B is no-load with 1.5% expense ratio.
3. Fund C has an 8% load on purchase and reinvested dividends, with a 1% expense ratio. The dividend yield on the fund is 5%. (Thus the 8% load on reinvested dividends reduces net returns by .08 × 5% = .4%.)
4. Gross return on all funds is 12% per year before expenses.

Although expenses can have a big impact on net investment performance, it is sometimes difficult for the investor in a mutual fund to measure true expenses accurately. This is because of the common practice of paying for some expenses in **soft dollars.** A portfolio manager earns soft-dollar credits with a stockbroker by directing the fund's trades to that broker. Based on those credits, the broker will pay for some of the mutual fund's expenses, such as databases, computer hardware, or stock-quotation systems. The soft-dollar arrangement means that the stockbroker effectively returns part of the trading commission to the fund. The advantage to the mutual fund is that purchases made with soft dollars are not included in the fund's expenses, so the fund can advertise an unrealistically low expense ratio to the public. Although the fund may have paid the broker needlessly high commissions to obtain the soft-dollar "rebate," trading costs are not included in the fund's expenses. The impact of the higher trading commission shows up instead in net investment performance. Soft-dollar arrangements make it difficult for investors to compare fund expenses, and periodically these arrangements come under attack.

Concept

Question 2 • The Equity Fund sells Class A shares with a front-end load of 6% and Class B shares with 12b-1 fees of .4% annually as well as back-end load fees that start at 5% and fall by 1% for each full year the investor holds the portfolio (until the fifth year). Assume the rate of return on the fund portfolio net of operating expenses is 10% annually. What will be the value of a $10,000 investment in Class A and Class B shares if the shares are sold after (*a*) one year, (*b*) four years, (*c*) eight years? Which fee structure provides higher net proceeds at the end of the investment horizon?

4.5   TAXATION OF MUTUAL FUND INCOME

Investment returns of mutual funds are granted "pass-through status" under the U.S. tax code, meaning that taxes are paid only by the investor in the mutual fund, not by the fund itself. The income is treated as passed through to the investor as long as the fund meets several requirements, most notably that at least 90% of all income is distributed to shareholders. In addition, the fund must receive less than 30% of its gross income from the sale of securities held for less than three months, and the fund must satisfy some diversification criteria. Actually, the earnings pass-through requirements can be even more stringent than 90%, since to avoid a separate excise tax, a fund must distribute at least 98% of income in the calendar year that it is earned.

A fund's short-term capital gains, long-term capital gains, and dividends are passed through to investors as though the investor earned the income directly. The investor will pay taxes at the appropriate rate depending on the type of income as well as the investor's own tax bracket.[2]

The pass through of investment income has one important disadvantage for individual investors. If you manage your own portfolio, you decide when to realize capital gains and losses on any security; therefore, you can time those realizations to efficiently manage your tax liabilities. When you invest through a mutual fund, however, the timing of the sale of securities from the portfolio is out of your control, which reduces your ability to

---

[2]An interesting problem that an investor needs to be aware of derives from the fact that capital gains and dividends on mutual funds are typically paid out to shareholders once or twice a year. This means that an investor who has just purchased shares in a mutual fund can receive a capital gain distribution (and be taxed on that distribution) on transactions that occurred long before he or she purchased shares in the fund. This is particularly a concern late in the year when such distributions typically are made.

LOW "TURNOVERS" MAY TASTE VERY GOOD TO FUND OWNERS

With lower capital-gains tax rates in store, mutual-fund investors are going to be rewarded by portfolio managers who believe in one of the stock market's most effective strategies: buy and hold.

This is because, under the new federal tax agreement, investors will face far lower taxes from stock mutual funds that pay out little in the way of dividends and hold onto their gains for as long as they can.

So, how can you find such funds? The best way is to track a statistic called "turnover." Turnover rates are disclosed in a fund's annual report, prospectus and, many times, in the semiannual report.

Turnover measures how much trading a fund does. A fund with 100% turnover is one that, on average, holds onto its positions for one year before selling them. A fund with a turnover of 50% "turns over" half of its portfolio in a year; that is, after six months it has replaced about half of its portfolio.

Funds with low turnover generate fewer taxes each year. Consider the nation's top two largest mutual funds, Fidelity Magellan and Vanguard Index Trust 500 Portfolio. The Vanguard fund, with an extremely low turnover rate of 5%, handed its investors less of an annual tax bill the past three years than Magellan, which had a turnover rate of 155%. Diversified U.S. stock funds on average have a turnover rate of close to 90%.

Vanguard Index Trust 500 Portfolio, at $42 billion the second-largest fund in the country, has low turnover, and as an index fund you'd expect it to stay that way. Index funds buy and hold a basket of stocks to try to match the performance of a market benchmark—in this case, the Standard & Poor's 500 Index.

But turnover isn't a constant. Though Fidelity Magellan, at $58 billion the largest fund in the nation, shows a high turnover rate of 155%, that's because its new manager Robert Stansky has been revamping the fund since he took over from Jeffrey Vinik last year. The turnover rate could well go down, along with Magellan's taxable distributions, as Mr. Stansky settles in.

It makes sense that turnover would offer clues about how much tax a fund would generate. Funds that just buy and hold stocks, such as index funds, aren't selling stocks that generate gains. So an investor has to pay taxes only when he sells the low-turnover fund, if the fund has appreciated in value.

On the other hand, a fund that trades in a frenzy could generate lots of short-term gains. For instance, a fund sells XYZ Corp. after three months, realizing a gain of $1 million. Then it buys ABC Corp., and sells it after two months, realizing a gain of, say, $2 million. By law, these gains have to be distributed to investors, who then have to pay taxes on them, and since they're short-term gains, the tax rate is higher.

Fans of low-turnover funds say that, in general, such portfolios have had higher total returns than high-turnover funds. There are always exceptions, of course: Peter Lynch, former skipper of giant Fidelity Magellan fund, racked up huge returns while trading stocks like they were baseball cards. Still, one reason low-turnover funds might have higher returns is that they don't incur the hidden costs of trading, such as commissions paid to brokers, that can drain away a fund's returns.

Source: Robert McGough, "Low 'Turnovers' May Taste Very Good to Fund Owners in Wake of Tax Deal," *The Wall Street Journal*, July 31, 1997, p. C1. Reprinted by permission of *The Wall Street Journal*, © 1997 Dow Jones & Company, Inc. All Rights Reserved Worldwide.

engage in tax management. Of course, if the mutual fund is held in a tax-deferred retirement account such as an IRA or 401(k) account, these tax management issues are irrelevant.

A fund with a high portfolio turnover rate can be particularly "tax inefficient." **Turnover** is the ratio of the trading activity of a portfolio to the assets of the portfolio. It measures the fraction of the portfolio that is "replaced" each year. For example, a $100 million portfolio with $50 million in sales of some securities with purchases of other securities would have a turnover rate of 50%. High turnover means that capital gains or losses are being realized constantly, and therefore that the investor cannot time the realizations to manage his or her overall tax obligation. The nearby box focuses on the importance of turnover rates on tax efficiency.

Concept CHECK

Question 3 • An investor's portfolio currently is worth $1 million. During the year, the investor sells 1,000 shares of Microsoft at a price of $80 per share and 2,000 shares of Ford at a price of $40 per share. The proceeds are used to buy 1,600 shares of IBM at $100 per share.

a. What was the portfolio turnover rate?

b. If the shares in Microsoft originally were purchased for $70 each and those in Ford were purchased for $35, and the investor's tax rate on capital gains income is 20%, how much extra will the investor owe on this year's taxes as a result of these transactions?

4.6   MUTUAL FUND INVESTMENT PERFORMANCE: A FIRST LOOK

We noted earlier that one of the benefits of mutual funds for the individual investor is the ability to delegate management of the portfolio to investment professionals. The investor retains control over the broad features of the overall portfolio through the asset allocation decision: Each individual chooses the percentages of the portfolio to invest in bond funds versus equity funds versus money market funds, and so forth, but can leave the specific security selection decisions within each investment class to the managers of each fund. Shareholders hope that these portfolio managers can achieve better investment performance than they could obtain on their own.

What is the investment record of the mutual fund industry? This seemingly straight-forward question is deceptively difficult to answer because we need a standard against which to evaluate performance. For example, we clearly would not want to compare the investment performance of an equity fund to the rate of return available in the money market. The vast differences in the risk of these two markets dictate that year-by-year as well as average performance will differ considerably. We would expect to find that equity funds outperform money market funds (on average) as compensation to investors for the extra risk incurred in equity markets. How then can we determine whether mutual fund portfolio managers are performing up to par *given* the level of risk they incur? In other words, what is the proper benchmark against which investment performance ought to be evaluated?

Measuring portfolio risk properly and using such measures to choose an appropriate benchmark is an extremely difficult task. We devote all of Parts II and III of the text to issues surrounding the proper measurement of portfolio risk and the trade-off between risk and return. In this chapter, therefore, we will satisfy ourselves with a first look at the question of fund performance by using only very simple performance benchmarks and ignoring the more subtle issues of risk differences across funds. However, we will return to this topic in Chapter 12, where we take a closer look at mutual fund performance after adjusting for differences in the exposure of portfolios to various sources of risk.

Here we use as a benchmark for the performance of equity fund managers the rate of return on the Wilshire 5000 Index. Recall from Chapter 2 that this is a value-weighted index of about 7,000 stocks that trade on the NYSE, Nasdaq, and Amex stock markets. It is the most inclusive index of the performance of U.S. equities. The performance of the Wilshire 5000 is a useful benchmark with which to evaluate professional managers because it corresponds to a simple passive investment strategy: Buy all the shares in the index in proportion to their outstanding market value. Moreover, this is a feasible strategy for even small investors, because the Vanguard Group offers an index fund (its Total Stock Market Portfolio) designed to replicate the performance of the Wilshire 5000 index. The expense ratio of the fund is extremely small by the standards of other equity funds, only .25% per year. Using the Wilshire 5000 Index as a benchmark, we may pose the problem of evaluating the performance of mutual fund portfolio managers this way: How does the typical performance of actively managed equity mutual funds compare to the performance of a passively managed portfolio that simply replicates the composition of a broad index of the stock market?

Figure 4.3

Percent of equity
mutual funds
outperformed by
Wilshire 5000 Index.

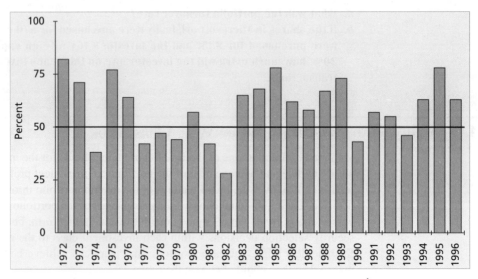

Source: The Vanguard Group.

By using the Wilshire 5000 as a benchmark, we use a well-diversified equity index to evaluate the performance of managers of diversified equity funds. Nevertheless, as noted earlier, this is only an imperfect comparison, as the risk of the Wilshire 5000 portfolio may not be comparable to that of any particular fund.

Casual comparisons of the performance of the Wilshire 5000 index versus that of professionally managed mutual fund portfolios show disappointing results for most fund managers. Figure 4.3 shows the percentage of mutual fund managers whose performance was inferior in each year to the Wilshire 5000. In more years than not, the Index has outperformed the median manager. Figure 4.4 shows the cumulative return since 1971 of the Wilshire 5000 compared to the Lipper General Equity Fund Average. The annualized return of the Wilshire 5000 was 12.97% versus 11.87% for the average fund. The 1.10% margin is substantial.

To some extent, however, this comparison is unfair. Real funds incur expenses which reduce the rate of return of the portfolio, as well as trading costs such as commissions and bid-ask spreads that also reduce returns. John Bogle, former chairman of the Vanguard Group, has estimated that operating expenses reduce the return of typical managed portfolios by about 1% and that transaction fees associated with trading reduce returns by an additional .7%. In contrast, the return to the Wilshire index is calculated as though investors can buy or sell the index with reinvested dividends without incurring any expenses.

These considerations suggest that a better benchmark for the performance of actively managed funds is the performance of index funds, rather than the performance of the indexes themselves. Vanguard's Wilshire 5000 fund was established only recently, and so has a short track record. However, because it is passively managed, its expense ratio is only about 0.25%; moreover because index funds need to engage in very little trading, its turnover rate is about 3% per year, also extremely low. If we reduce the rate of return on the index by about 0.30%, we ought to obtain a good estimate of the rate of return achievable by a low-cost indexed portfolio. This procedure reduces the average margin of superiority of the index strategy over the average mutual fund from 1.10% to .80%, still suggesting that over the past two decades, passively managed (indexed) equity funds would have outperformed the typical actively managed fund.

Figure 4.4

Growth of $1 invested in Wilshire 5000 Index versus Average General Equity Fund.

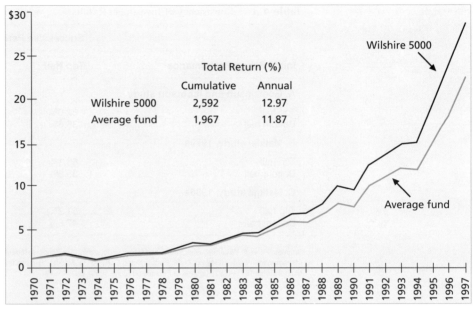

Source: The Vanguard Group.

This result may seem surprising to you. After all, it would not seem unreasonable to expect that professional money managers should be able to outperform a very simple rule such as "hold an indexed portfolio." As it turns out, however, there may be good reasons to expect such a result. We explore them in detail in Chapter 12, where we discuss the efficient market hypothesis.

Of course, one might argue that there are good managers and bad managers, and that the good managers can, in fact, consistently outperform the index. To test this notion, we examine whether managers with good performance in one year are likely to repeat that performance in a following year. In other words, is superior performance in any particular year due to luck, and therefore random, or due to skill, and therefore consistent from year to year?

To answer this question, Goetzmann and Ibbotson[3] examined the performance of a large sample of equity mutual fund portfolios over the 1976–1985 period. Dividing the funds into two groups based on total investment return for different subperiods, they posed the question: "Do funds with investment returns in the top half of the sample in one two-year period continue to perform well in the subsequent two-year period?"

Panel A of Table 4.3 presents a summary of their results. The table shows the fraction of "winners" (i.e., top-half performers) in the initial period that turn out to be winners or losers in the following two-year period. If performance were purely random from one period to the next, there would be entries of 50% in each cell of the table, as top- or bottom-half performers would be equally likely to perform in either the top or bottom half of the sample in the following period. On the other hand, if performance were due entirely to skill, with no randomness, we would expect to see entries of 100% on the diagonals and entries of 0% on the off-diagonals: Top-half performers would all remain in the top half while

[3]William N. Goetzmann and Roger G. Ibbotson, "Do Winners Repeat?" *Journal of Portfolio Management* (Winter 1994), pp. 9–18.

Table 4.3   Consistency of Investment Results

Initial Period Performance	Successive Period Performance	
	Top Half	Bottom Half
A. Goetzmann and Ibbotson study		
Top half	62.0%	38.0%
Bottom half	36.6%	63.4%
B. Malkiel study, 1970s		
Top half	65.1%	34.9%
Bottom half	35.5%	64.5%
C. Malkiel study, 1980s		
Top half	51.7%	48.3%
Bottom half	47.5%	52.5%

Sources: Panel A: William N. Goetzmann and Roger G. Ibbotson, "Do Winners Repeat?" Journal of Portfolio Management (Winter 1994), pp. 9–18; Panels B and C: Burton G. Malkiel, "Returns from Investing in Equity Mutual Funds 1971–1991," Journal of Finance 50 (June 1995), pp. 549–72.

bottom-half performers similarly would all remain in the bottom half. In fact, the table shows that 62.0% of initial top-half performers fall in the top half of the sample in the following period, while 63.4% of initial bottom-half performers fall in the bottom half in the following period. This evidence is consistent with the notion that at least part of a fund's performance is a function of skill as opposed to luck, so that relative performance tends to persist from one period to the next.[4]

On the other hand, this relationship does not seem stable across different sample periods. Malkiel[5] uses a larger sample, but a similar methodology (except that he uses one-year instead of two-year investment returns) to examine performance consistency. He finds that while initial-year performance predicts subsequent-year performance in the 1970s (see Table 4.3, Panel B), the pattern of persistence in performance virtually disappears in the 1980s (Panel C).

To summarize, the evidence that performance is consistent from one period to the next is suggestive, but it is inconclusive. In the 1970s, top-half funds in one year were twice as likely in the following year to be in the top half as the bottom half of funds. In the 1980s, the odds that a top-half fund would fall in the top half in the following year were essentially equivalent to those of a coin flip.

Other studies suggest that bad performance is more likely to persist than good performance. This makes some sense: It is easy to identify fund characteristics that will predictably lead to consistently poor investment performance, notably high expense ratios, and high turnover ratios with associated trading costs. It is far harder to identify the secrets of successful stock picking. (If it were easy, we would all be rich!) Thus the consistency we do observe in fund performance may be due in large part to the poor performers. This suggests that the real value of past performance data is to avoid truly poor funds, even if identifying the future top performers is still a daunting task.

[4]Another possibility is that performance consistency is due to variation in fee structure across funds. We return to this possibility in Chapter 12.
[5]Burton G. Malkiel, "Returns from Investing in Equity Mutual Funds 1971–1991," *Journal of Finance* 50 (June 1995), pp. 549–72.

Concept

Question 4 • Suppose you observe the investment performance of 200 portfolio managers and rank them by investment returns during the year. Of the managers in the top half of the sample, 40% are truly skilled, but the other 60% fell in the top half purely because of good luck. What fraction of these top-half managers would you expect to be top-half performers next year?

4.7   INFORMATION ON MUTUAL FUNDS

The first place to find information on a mutual fund is in its prospectus. The Securities and Exchange Commission requires that the prospectus describe the fund's investment objectives and policies in a concise "Statement of Investment Objectives" as well as in lengthy discussions of investment policies and risks. The fund's investment adviser and its portfolio manager are also described. The prospectus also presents the costs associated with purchasing shares in the fund in a fee table. Sales charges such as front-end and back-end loads as well as annual operating expenses such as management fees and 12b-1 fees are detailed in the fee table.

Despite this useful information, there is widespread agreement that most prospectuses are difficult to read and laden with legalese. Several mutual fund complexes currently are experimenting with a simplified plain-English pamphlet that can be distributed with the formal prospectus. The pamphlets present fees and expenses very clearly and use simple bar charts to present historical returns. It is expected that these simplified profiles, or some variant of them, will be made mandatory in the near future.

Funds provide information about themselves in two other sources. The Statement of Additional Information, also known as Part B of the prospectus, includes a list of the securities in the portfolio at the end of the fiscal year, audited financial statements, and a list of the directors and officers of the fund. The fund's annual report, which is generally issued semiannually, also includes portfolio composition and financial statements, as well as a discussion of the factors that influenced fund performance over the last reporting period.

With more than 6,000 mutual funds to choose from, it can be difficult to find and select the fund that is best suited for a particular need. Several publications now offer "encyclopedias" of mutual fund information to help in the search process. Two prominent sources are Wiesenberger's *Investment Companies* and Morningstar's *Mutual Fund Sourcebook.* The Investment Company Institute, the national association of mutual funds, closed-end funds, and unit investment trusts, publishes an annual *Directory of Mutual Funds* that includes information on fees as well as phone numbers to contact funds. To illustrate the range of information available about funds, we consider Morningstar's report on Vanguard's Windsor Fund, reproduced in Figure 4.5.

Some of Morningstar's analysis is qualitative. The top box on the left-hand side of the page provides a short description of the fund, in particular the types of securities in which the fund tends to invest, and a short biography of the current portfolio manager. The bottom box on the left is a more detailed discussion of the fund's income strategy. The short statement of the fund's investment policy is in the top right-hand corner: Windsor is a growth and income equity fund.

The table on the left labeled "Performance" reports on the fund's returns over the last few years and over longer periods up to 15 years. Comparisons of returns to relevant indexes, in this case, the S&P 500 and the Wilshire 5000 indexes, are provided to serve as a benchmark in evaluating the performance of the fund. (Morningstar uses the Lehman Brothers Aggregate Bond Index as the benchmark for fixed-income funds.) The values

Figure 4.5   Morningstar report.

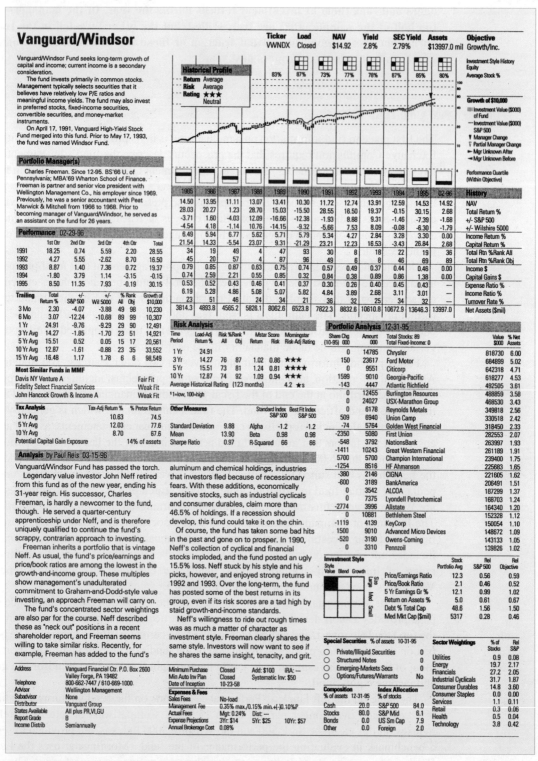

Although data are gathered from reliable sources, Morningstar cannot guarantee completeness and accuracy.

Source: Morningstar Mutual Funds. © 1996 Morningstar, Inc. All rights reserved. 225 W. Wacker Dr., Chicago, IL.

under these columns give the performance of the fund relative to the index. For example, Windsor's return was 4.07% below the S&P 500 over the last 3 months, but 1.17% per year better than the S&P over the past 15 years. The returns reported for the fund are calculated net of expenses, 12b-1 fees, and any other fees automatically deducted from fund assets, but they do not account for any sales charges such as front-end loads or back-end charges. Next appear the percentile ranks of the fund compared to all other funds (see column headed by "All") and to all funds with the same investment objective (see column headed by "Obj"). A rank of 1 means the fund is a top performer. A rank of 80 would mean that it was beaten by 80% of funds in the comparison group. You can see from the table that Windsor has had a very poor year compared to other growth and income funds, but that its longer-term performance, for example, over the past 5 years, has been excellent, better than all but 17% of the funds in the growth and income category. Finally, growth of $10,000 invested in the fund over various periods ranging from the past 3 months to the past 15 years is given in the last column.

More data on the performance of the fund are provided in the graph at the top right of the figure. The curves show how $10,000 invested in 1985 in either Windsor (dotted line) or the S&P 500 (solid line) with all dividends reinvested would have grown through 1996. Below the graph is a box for each year that depicts the relative performance of the fund for that year. The shaded area on the box shows the quartile in which the fund's performance falls relative to other funds with the same objective. If the shaded band is at the top of the box, the firm was a top quartile performer in that period, and so on.

The table below the graph presents historical data on characteristics of the fund. These data include return, return relative to appropriate benchmark indexes such as the S&P 500, the component of returns due to income (dividends) or capital gains, the percentile rank of the fund compared to all funds and funds in its objective class (where, again, 1% is the best performer and 99% would mean that the fund was outperformed by 99% of its comparison group), the expense ratio, and turnover rate of the portfolio.

The table on the right entitled "Portfolio Analysis" presents the 25 largest holdings of the portfolio, showing the change in the holding of each of those securities over the past quarter. Investors can thus get a quick look at the manager's biggest bets.

Below the portfolio analysis is a box labeled "Investment Style." In this box, Morningstar evaluates style along two dimensions: One dimension is the size of the firms held in the portfolio as measured by the market value of outstanding equity; the other dimension is a value/growth continuum. Morningstar defines *value stocks* as those with low ratios of market price per share to earnings per share or book value per share. These are called value stocks because they have a low price relative to these two measures of value. In contrast, *growth stocks* have high ratios, suggesting that investors in these firms must believe that the firm will experience rapid growth to justify the prices at which the stocks sell. The shaded box for Windsor shows that the portfolio tends to hold larger firms (top row) and value stocks (left column). A year-by-year history of Windsor's investment style is presented in the sequence of such boxes at the top of the figure.

The center of the figure, labeled "Risk Analysis," is one of the more complicated but interesting facets of Morningstar's analysis. The column labeled "Load-Adj Return" rates a fund's return compared to other funds with the same investment policy. Returns for periods ranging from 1 to 10 years are calculated with all loads and back-end fees applicable to that investment period subtracted from total income. The return is then divided by the average return for the comparison group of funds to obtain the "Morningstar Return"; therefore, a value of 1.0 in the column "MStar Return" would indicate average performance while a value of 1.10 would indicate returns 10% above the average for the comparison group (e.g., 11% return for the fund versus 10% for the comparison group).

TIPS TO PICK THE RIGHT PONY

Hope springs eternal

Folks keep buying lottery tickets. They keep stuffing quarters into slot machines. And yes, they keep buying actively managed stock funds.

The grim truth, however, is that most actively managed funds fail to beat the market. That is why I am such a big fan of index funds, which simply purchase the stocks in an index in an effort to match the index's performance.

But there is an undeniable allure to buying actively managed stock funds. If you're going to engage in this dubious endeavor, how can you stack the odds in your favor? Here are some pointers from the pros:

Go Long

Mutual-fund analysts do just what the rest of us do. They start by looking for managers with long and venerable track records, preferably extending back 10 or 15 years. "You want people who have created happiness for long periods, and you hope the experience will continue," says Michael Stolper, publisher of Mutual Fund Monthly, a San Diego newsletter.

Invest in Style

But while an impressive record is nice, it is only a starting point. Analysts also want some sense that the record is repeatable. They look for consistency of performance and ignore those whose long-term record is built on one or two years of outsized returns.

Analysts also tend to be leery of market-timing and sector-rotating managers, who aim to bail out of stocks at the right time or astutely switch among stock-market sectors. How come? These managers may have built their entire record on just four or five good calls, so it is difficult to know if they are tremendously skillful, or very lucky. Instead, analysts favor managers with a stellar history of careful stock selection, because such a record typically involves making the right decision on hundreds of different securities.

For instance, you might try to find the best stock-pickers in six fund categories: large-company value, small-company value, large-company growth, small-company growth, developed foreign markets and emerging markets. Value funds look for stocks that are cheap based on market yardsticks such as dividends and earnings, while growth funds hunt for companies with rapid revenue and profit growth.

The trouble is, how do you know if a manager really has stuck to his discipline? My suggestion: See if your local library carries Morningstar Mutual Funds. This newsletter gives detailed information on 1,500 funds, including historical style boxes, which provide a year-by-year look at whether a fund held, say, large-company value stocks or midsize growth stocks. If a fund consistently falls in or near a particular style box, it is a sign that the fund has stuck to its knitting.

Think Small

If you identify a manager who has put together a sparkling record by mining a single part of the stock market, you are unlikely to be alone in this discovery. "The great managers attract money really quickly," says Kenneth Gregory, editor of the No-Load Fund Analyst, a San Francisco newsletter. "It's a real dilemma."

He says there are still a few highly regarded managers who haven't been inundated with money. But these are the exception. What to do? Be prepared to compromise, by buying smaller funds with shorter track records, and don't ignore new offerings.

Pinch Pennies

The more a fund charges, the tougher it is for the manager to beat the market, so pay careful attention to cost.

Don Phillips, president of Morningstar Inc., which publishes Morningstar Mutual Funds, advises sticking with funds that charge annual expenses of less than 1%, and certainly not more than 1.5%. "And that's especially the case if you're retaining an investment adviser, who is charging a fee on top of that," Mr. Phillips says.

Source: Jonathan Clements, "If You're Betting on Managed Funds, Here Are Tips to Pick the Right Pony," *The Wall Street Journal*, July 2, 1996, p. C1. Reprinted by permission of *The Wall Street Journal*, © 1996 Dow Jones & Company, Inc. All Rights Reserved Worldwide.

The risk measure indicates the portfolio's exposure to poor performance, that is, the "downside risk" of the fund. Morningstar focuses on periods in which the fund's return is less than that of risk-free T-bills. The total underperformance compared to T-bills in those months with poor portfolio performance divided by total months sampled is the measure of downside risk. This measure also is scaled by dividing by the average downside risk measure for all firms with the same investment objective. Therefore, the average value in the "MStar Risk" column is 1.0.

The two columns to the left of Morningstar risk and return are the percentile scores of risk and return for each fund. The risk-adjusted rating, ranging from one to five stars, is based on the Morningstar return score minus the risk score.

The tax analysis box on the left provides some evidence on the tax efficiency of the fund by comparing pretax and after-tax returns. The after-tax return, given in the first column, is computed based on the dividends paid to the portfolio as well as realized capital gains, assuming the investor is in the maximum tax bracket at the time of the distribution. State and local taxes are ignored. The "tax efficiency" of the fund is defined as the ratio of after-tax to pretax returns; it is presented in the second column, labeled "% Pretax Return." Tax efficiency will be lower when turnover is higher because capital gains are taxed as they are realized.

The bottom of Morningstar's analysis provides information on the expenses and loads associated with investments in the fund, as well as information on the fund's investment adviser. Thus Morningstar provides a considerable amount of the information you would need to decide among several competing funds. Still, as the nearby box suggests, choosing a fund involves fairly sophisticated analysis. The box gives some reasonable pointers for investors confronting this decision.

SUMMARY

1. Unit investment trusts, closed-end management companies, and open-end management companies are all classified and regulated as investment companies. Unit investment trusts are essentially unmanaged in the sense that the portfolio, once established, is fixed. Managed investment companies, in contrast, may change the composition of the portfolio as deemed fit by the portfolio manager. Closed-end funds are traded like other securities; they do not redeem shares for their investors. Open-end funds will redeem shares for net asset value at the request of the investor.

2. Net asset value equals the market value of assets held by a fund minus the liabilities of the fund divided by the shares outstanding.

3. Mutual funds free the individual from many of the administrative burdens of owning individual securities and offer professional management of the portfolio. They also offer advantages that are available only to large-scale investors, such as discounted trading costs. On the other hand, funds are assessed management fees and incur other expenses, which reduce the investor's rate of return. Funds also eliminate some of the individual's control over the timing of capital gains realizations.

4. Mutual funds are often categorized by investment policy. Major policy groups include money market funds; equity funds, which are further grouped according to emphasis on income versus growth; fixed-income funds; balanced and income funds; asset allocation funds; index funds; and specialized sector funds.

5. Costs of investing in mutual funds include front-end loads, which are sales charges; back-end loads, which are redemption fees or, more properly, contingent-deferred sales charges; fund operating expenses; and 12b-1 charges, which are recurring fees used to pay for the expenses of marketing the fund to the public.

6. Income earned on mutual fund portfolios is not taxed at the level of the fund. Instead, as long as the fund meets certain requirements for pass-through status, the income is treated as being earned by the investors in the fund.

7. The average rate of return of the average equity mutual fund in the last 25 years has been below that of a passive index fund holding a portfolio to replicate a broad-based index like the S&P 500 or Wilshire 5000. Some of the reasons for this disappointing record are the costs incurred by actively managed funds, such as the expense of conducting the research to guide stock-picking activities, and trading costs due to higher portfolio turnover. The record on the consistency of fund performance is mixed. In some

sample periods, the better-performing funds continue to perform well in the following periods; in other sample periods they do not.

Key Terms

investment company	open-end fund	12b-1 fees
net asset value (NAV)	closed-end fund	soft dollars
unit investment trust	load	turnover

Problems

1. Would you expect a typical open-end fixed-income mutual fund to have higher or lower operating expenses than a fixed-income unit investment trust? Why?

2. An open-end fund has a net asset value of $10.70 per share. It is sold with a front-end load of 6%. What is the offering price?

3. If the offering price of an open-end fund is $12.30 per share and the fund is sold with a front-end load of 5%, what is its net asset value?

4. The composition of the Fingroup Fund portfolio is as follows:

Stock	Shares	Price
A	200,000	$35
B	300,000	$40
C	400,000	$20
D	600,000	$25

The fund has not borrowed any funds, but its accrued management fee with the portfolio manager currently totals $30,000. There are 4 million shares outstanding. What is the net asset value of the fund?

5. Reconsider the Fingroup Fund in the previous problem. If during the year the portfolio manager sells all of the holdings of stock D and replaces it with 200,000 shares of stock E at $50 per share and 200,000 shares of stock F at $25 per share, what is the portfolio turnover rate?

6. The Closed Fund is a closed-end investment company with a portfolio currently worth $200 million. It has liabilities of $3 million and 5 million shares outstanding.
   a. What is the NAV of the fund?
   b. If the fund sells for $36 per share, what is the percentage premium or discount that will appear in the listings in the financial pages?

7. Corporate Fund started the year with a net asset value of $12.50. By year end, its NAV equaled $12.10. The fund paid year-end distributions of income and capital gains of $1.50. What was the rate of return to an investor in the fund?

8. A closed-end fund starts the year with a net asset value of $12.00. By year end, NAV equals $12.10. At the beginning of the year, the fund was selling at a 2% premium to NAV. By the end of the year, the fund is selling at a 7% discount to NAV. The fund paid year-end distributions of income and capital gains of $1.50.
   a. What is the rate of return to an investor in the fund during the year?
   b. What would have been the rate of return to an investor who held the same securities as the fund manager during the year?

9. What are some comparative advantages of investing in the following:
   a. Unit investment trusts.

    b. Open-end mutual funds.

    c. Individual stocks and bonds that you choose for yourself.

10. Open-end equity mutual funds find it necessary to keep a significant percentage of total investments, typically around 5% of the portfolio, in very liquid money market assets. Closed-end funds do not have to maintain such a position in "cash-equivalent" securities. What difference between open-end and closed-end funds might account for their differing policies?

11. Balanced funds and asset allocation funds invest in both the stock and bond markets. What is the difference between these types of funds?

12. *a.* Impressive Fund had excellent investment performance last year, with portfolio returns that placed it in the top 10% of all funds with the same investment policy. Do you expect it to be a top performer next year? Why or why not?

    b. Suppose instead that the fund was among the poorest performers in its comparison group. Would you be more or less likely to believe its relative performance will persist into the following year? Why?

13. Consider a mutual fund with $200 million in assets at the start of the year and with 10 million shares outstanding. The fund invests in a portfolio of stocks that provides dividend income at the end of the year of $2 million. The stocks included in the fund's portfolio increase in price by 8%, but no securities are sold, and there are no capital gains distributions. The fund charges 12b-1 fees of 1%, which are deducted from portfolio assets at year-end. What is net asset value at the start and end of the year? What is the rate of return for an investor in the fund?

14. The Investments Fund sells Class A shares with a front-end load of 6% and Class B shares with 12b-1 fees of .5% annually as well as back-end load fees that start at 5% and fall by 1% for each full year the investor holds the portfolio (until the fifth year). Assume the portfolio rate of return net of operating expenses is 10% annually. If you plan to sell the fund after four years, are Class A or Class B shares the better choice for you? What if you plan to sell after 15 years?

15. Suppose you observe the investment performance of 350 portfolio managers for five years, and rank them by investment returns during each year. After five years, you find that 11 of the funds have investment returns that place the fund in the top half of the sample in each and every year of your sample. Such consistency of performance indicates to you that these must be the funds whose managers are in fact skilled, and you invest your money in these funds. Is your conclusion warranted?

16. You are considering an investment in a mutual fund with a 4% load and expense ratio of .5%. You can invest instead in a bank CD paying 6% interest.

    a. If you plan to invest for two years, what annual rate of return must the fund portfolio earn for you to be better off in the fund than in the CD? Assume annual compounding of returns.

    b. How does your answer change if you plan to invest for six years? Why does your answer change?

    c. Now suppose that instead of a front-end load the fund assesses a 12b-1 fee of .75% per year. What annual rate of return must the fund portfolio earn for you to be better off in the fund than in the CD? Does your answer in this case depend on your time horizon?

17. Suppose that every time a fund manager trades stock, transaction costs such as commissions and bid–asked spreads amount to .4% of the value of the trade. If the portfolio turnover rate is 50%, by how much is the total return of the portfolio reduced by trading costs?

18. You expect a tax-free municipal bond portfolio to provide a rate of return of 4%. Management fees of the fund are .6%. What fraction of portfolio income is given up to fees? If the management fees for an equity fund also are .6%, but you expect a portfolio return of 12%, what fraction of portfolio income is given up to fees? Why might management fees be a bigger factor in your investment decision for bond funds than for stock funds? Can your conclusion help explain why unmanaged unit investment trusts tend to focus on the fixed-income market?

solutions to

1. $$\text{NAV} = \frac{\$30,376,657,000 - \$44,805,000}{438,518,428} = \$69.17.$$

2. The net investment in the Class A shares after the 6% commission is \$9,400. If the fund earns a 10% return, the investment will grow after n years to $\$9,400 \times (1.10)^n$. The Class B shares have no front-end load. However, the net return to the investor after 12b-1 fees will be only 9%. In addition, there is a back-end load that reduces the sales proceeds by a percentage equal to (5 – years until sale) until the fifth year, when the back-end load expires.

Horizon	Class A Shares $\$9,400 \times (1.10)^n$	Class B Shares $\$10,000 \times (1.09)^n \times (1 - \text{percentage exit fee})$	
1 year	\$10,340.00	$\$10,000 \times (1.09) \times (1 - .04)$	= \$10,464.00
4 years	\$13,762.54	$\$10,000 \times (1.09)^4 \times (1 - .01)$	= \$13,974.66
8 years	\$20,149.73	$\$10,000 \times (1.09)^8$	= \$19,925.63

For shorter investment horizons (e.g., less than four years), the Class B shares provide the higher proceeds. For longer horizons, the Class A shares, which impose a one-time commission, are better.

3. *a.* Turnover = \$160,000 in trades per \$1 million of portfolio value = 16%.

b. Realized capital gains are $\$10 \times 1,000 = \$10,000$ on Microsoft and $\$5 \times 2,000 = \$10,000$ on Ford. The tax owed on the capital gains is therefore $.20 \times \$20,000 = \$4,000$.

4. Out of the 100 top-half managers, 40 are skilled and will repeat their performance next year. The other 60 were just lucky, but we should expect half of them to be lucky again next year, meaning that 30 of the lucky managers will be in the top half next year. Therefore, we should expect a total of 70 managers, or 70% of the better performers, to repeat their top-half performance.

HISTORY OF INTEREST RATES AND RISK PREMIUMS

Individuals must be concerned with both the expected return and the risk of the assets that might be included in their portfolios. To help us form reasonable expectations for the performance of a wide array of potential investments, this chapter surveys the historical performance of the major asset classes. It uses a risk-free portfolio of Treasury bills as a benchmark to evaluate that performance. Therefore, we start the chapter with a review of the determinants of the risk-free interest rate, the rate available on Treasury bills, paying attention to the distinction between real and nominal returns. We then turn to the measurement of the expected returns and volatilities of risky assets, and show how historical data can be used to construct estimates of such statistics for several broadly diversified portfolios. Finally, we review the historical record of several portfolios of interest to provide a sense of the range of performance in the past several decades.

5.1   DETERMINANTS OF THE LEVEL OF INTEREST RATES

Interest rates and forecasts of their future values are among the most important inputs into an investment decision. For example, suppose you have $10,000 in a savings account. The bank pays you a variable interest rate tied to some short-term reference rate such as the 30-day Treasury bill rate. You have the option of moving some or all of your money into a longer-term certificate of deposit that offers a fixed rate over the term of the deposit.

Your decision depends critically on your outlook for interest rates. If you think rates will fall, you will want to lock in the current higher rates by investing in a relatively long-term CD. If you expect rates to rise, you will want to postpone committing any funds to long-term CDs.

Forecasting interest rates is one of the most notoriously difficult parts of applied macroeconomics. Nonetheless, we do have a good understanding of the fundamental factors that determine the level of interest rates:

1. The supply of funds from savers, primarily households.
2. The demand for funds from businesses to be used to finance investments in plant, equipment, and inventories (real assets or capital formation).
3. The government's net supply and/or demand for funds as modified by actions of the Federal Reserve Bank.

Before we elaborate on these forces and resultant interest rates, we need to distinguish real from nominal interest rates.

Real and Nominal Rates of Interest

Suppose exactly one year ago you deposited $1,000 in a one-year time deposit guaranteeing a rate of interest of 10%. You are about to collect $1,100 in cash.

Is your $100 return for real? That depends on what money can buy these days, relative to what you *could* buy a year ago. The consumer price index (CPI) measures purchasing power by averaging the prices of goods and services in the consumption basket of an average urban family of four. Although this basket may not represent your particular consumption plan, suppose for now that it does.

Suppose the rate of inflation (percent change in the CPI, denoted by i) for the last year amounted to $i = 6\%$. This tells you that the purchasing power of money is reduced by 6% a year. The value of each dollar depreciates by 6% a year in terms of the goods it can buy. Therefore, part of your interest earnings are offset by the reduction in the purchasing power of the dollars you will receive at the end of the year. With a 10% interest rate, after you net out the 6% reduction in the purchasing power of money, you are left with a net increase in purchasing power of about 4%. Thus we need to distinguish between a **nominal interest rate**—the growth rate of your money—and a **real interest rate**—the growth rate of your purchasing power. If we call R the nominal rate, r the real rate, and i the inflation rate, then we conclude

$$r \approx R - i$$

In words, the real rate of interest is the nominal rate reduced by the loss of purchasing power resulting from inflation.

In fact, the exact relationship between the real and nominal interest rate is given by

$$1 + r = \frac{1 + R}{1 + i}$$

This is because the growth factor of your purchasing power, $1 + r$, equals the growth factor of your money, $1 + R$, divided by the new price level, that is, $1 + i$ times its value in the previous period. The exact relationship can be rearranged to

$$r = \frac{R - i}{1 + i}$$

which shows that the approximation rule overstates the real rate by the factor $1 + i$.

For example, if the interest rate on a one-year CD is 8%, and you expect inflation to be 5% over the coming year, then using the approximation formula, you expect the real rate to be $r = 8\% - 5\% = 3\%$. Using the exact formula, the real rate is $r = \frac{.08 - .05}{1 + .05} = .0286$, or 2.86%. Therefore, the approximation rule overstates the expected real rate by only .14% (14 basis points). The approximation rule is more exact for small inflation rates and is perfectly exact for continuously compounded rates. We discuss further details in the appendix to this chapter.

Before the decision to invest, you should realize that conventional certificates of deposit offer a guaranteed *nominal* rate of interest. Thus you can only infer the expected real rate on these investments by subtracting your expectation of the rate of inflation.

It is always possible to calculate the real rate after the fact. The inflation rate is published by the Bureau of Labor Statistics (BLS). The future real rate, however, is unknown, and one has to rely on expectations. In other words, because future inflation is risky, the real rate of return is risky even when the nominal rate is risk-free.

The Equilibrium Real Rate of Interest

Three basic factors—supply, demand, and government actions—determine the *real* interest rate. The nominal interest rate, which is the rate we actually observe, is the real rate plus the expected rate of inflation. So a fourth factor affecting the interest rate is the expected rate of inflation.

Although there are many different interest rates economywide (as many as there are types of securities), economists frequently talk as if there were a single representative rate. We can use this abstraction to gain some insights into determining the real rate of interest if we consider the supply and demand curves for funds.

Figure 5.1 shows a downward-sloping demand curve and an upward-sloping supply curve. On the horizontal axis, we measure the quantity of funds, and on the vertical axis, we measure the real rate of interest.

The supply curve slopes up from left to right because the higher the real interest rate, the greater the supply of household savings. The assumption is that at higher real interest rates households will choose to postpone some current consumption and set aside or invest more of their disposable income for future use.[1]

The demand curve slopes down from left to right because the lower the real interest rate, the more businesses will want to invest in physical capital. Assuming that businesses rank projects by the expected real return on invested capital, firms will undertake more projects the lower the real interest rate on the funds needed to finance those projects.

Equilibrium is at the point of intersection of the supply and demand curves, point E in Figure 5.1.

---

[1]There is considerable disagreement among experts on the issue of whether household saving does go up in response to an increase in the real interest rate.

Figure 5.1

Determination of the equilibrium real rate of interest.

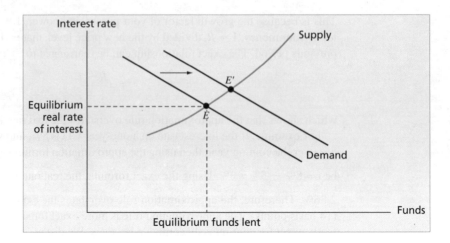

The government and the central bank (Federal Reserve) can shift these supply and demand curves either to the right or to the left through fiscal and monetary policies. For example, consider an increase in the government's budget deficit. This increases the government's borrowing demand and shifts the demand curve to the right, which causes the equilibrium real interest rate to rise to point E'. That is, a forecast that indicates higher than previously expected government borrowing increases expected future interest rates. The Fed can offset such a rise through an expansionary monetary policy, which will shift the supply curve to the right.

Thus, although the fundamental determinants of the real interest rate are the propensity of households to save and the expected productivity (or we could say profitability) of investment in physical capital, the real rate can be affected as well by government fiscal and monetary policies.

The Equilibrium Nominal Rate of Interest

We've seen that the real rate of return on an asset is approximately equal to the nominal rate minus the inflation rate. Because investors should be concerned with their real returns—the increase in their purchasing power—we would expect that as the inflation rate increases, investors will demand higher nominal rates of return on their investments. This higher rate is necessary to maintain the expected real return offered by an investment.

Irving Fisher (1930) argued that the nominal rate ought to increase one for one with increases in the expected inflation rate. If we use the notation $E(i)$ to denote the current expectation of the inflation rate that will prevail over the coming period, then we can state the so-called *Fisher equation* formally as

$$R = r + E(i)$$

This relationship has been debated and empirically investigated. The equation implies that if real rates are reasonably stable, then increases in nominal rates ought to predict higher inflation rates. The results are mixed; although the data do not strongly support this relationship, nominal interest rates seem to predict inflation as well as alternative methods, in part because we are unable to forecast inflation well with any method.

One reason it is difficult to determine the empirical validity of the Fisher hypothesis that changes in nominal rates predict changes in future inflation rates is that the real rate also changes unpredictably over time. Nominal interest rates can be viewed as the sum of the required real rate on nominally risk-free assets, plus a "noisy" forecast of inflation.

Figure 5.2

Interest and inflation rates, 1953–1996.

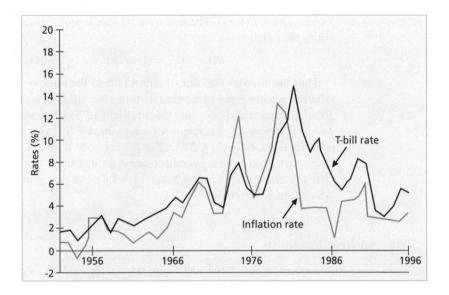

In Part IV we discuss the relationship between short- and long-term interest rates. Longer rates incorporate forecasts for long-term inflation. For this reason alone, interest rates on bonds of different maturity may diverge. In addition, we will see that prices of longer-term bonds are more volatile than those of short-term bonds. This implies that expected returns on longer-term bonds may include a risk premium, so that the expected real rate offered by bonds of varying maturity also may vary.

Concept

Question 1

a. **Suppose the real interest rate is 3% per year and the expected inflation rate is 8%. What is the nominal interest rate?**

b. **Suppose the expected inflation rate rises to 10%, but the real rate is unchanged. What happens to the nominal interest rate?**

Bills and Inflation, 1953–1996

The Fisher equation predicts a close connection between inflation and the rate of return on T-bills. This is apparent in Figure 5.2, which plots both time series on the same set of axes. Both series tend to move together, which is consistent with our previous statement that expected inflation is a significant force determining the nominal rate of interest.

For a holding period of 30 days, the difference between actual and expected inflation is not large. The 30-day bill rate will adjust rapidly to changes in expected inflation induced by observed changes in actual inflation. It is not surprising that we see nominal rates on bills move roughly in tandem with inflation over time.

Taxes and the Real Rate of Interest

Tax liabilities are based on *nominal* income and the tax rate determined by the investor's tax bracket. Congress recognized the resultant "bracket creep" (when nominal income grows due to inflation and pushes taxpayers into higher brackets) and mandated index-linked tax brackets in the Tax Reform Act of 1986.

Index-linked tax brackets do not provide relief from the effect of inflation on the taxation of savings, however. Given a tax rate (t) and a nominal interest rate (R), the after-tax interest rate is $R(1 - t)$. The real after-tax rate is approximately the after-tax nominal rate minus the inflation rate:

$$R(1 - t) - i = (r + i)(1 - t) - i = r(1 - t) - it$$

Thus the after-tax real rate of return falls as the inflation rate rises. Investors suffer an inflation penalty equal to the tax rate times the inflation rate. If, for example, you are in a 30% tax bracket and your investments yield 12%, while inflation runs at the rate of 8%, then your before-tax real rate is 4%, and you *should*, in an inflation-protected tax system, net after taxes $4(1 - .3) = 2.8\%$. But the tax code does not recognize that the first 8% of your return is no more than compensation for inflation—not real income—and hence your after-tax return is reduced by $8\% \times .3 = 2.4\%$, so that your after-tax real interest rate, at .4%, is almost wiped out.

5.2   RISK AND RISK PREMIUMS

Risk means uncertainty about future rates of return. We can quantify that uncertainty using probability distributions.

For example, suppose you are considering investing some of your money, now all invested in a bank account, in a stock market index fund. The price of a share in the fund is currently $100, and your time horizon is one year. You expect the cash dividend during the year to be $4, so your expected *dividend yield* (dividends earned per dollar invested) is 4%.

Your total holding-period return (HPR) will depend on the price you expect to prevail one year from now. Suppose your best guess is that it will be $110 per share. Then your *capital gain* will be $10 and your HPR 14%. The definition of the holding-period return in this context is capital gain income plus dividend income per dollar invested in the stock at the start of the period:

$$\text{HPR} = \frac{\text{Ending price of a share} - \text{Beginning price} + \text{Cash dividend}}{\text{Beginning price}}$$

In our case we have

$$\text{HPR} = \frac{\$110 - \$100 + \$4}{\$100} = .14, \text{ or } 14\%$$

This definition of the HPR assumes the dividend is paid at the end of the holding period. To the extent that dividends are received earlier, the HPR ignores reinvestment income between the receipt of the payment and the end of the holding period. Recall also that the percent return from dividends is called the dividend yield, and so the dividend yield plus the capital gains yield equals the HPR.

There is considerable uncertainty about the price of a share a year from now, however, so you cannot be sure about your eventual HPR. We can try to quantify our beliefs about the state of the economy and the stock market, however, in terms of three possible scenarios with probabilities as presented in Table 5.1.

How can we evaluate this probability distribution? Throughout this book we will characterize probability distributions of rates of return in terms of their expected or mean return, $E(r)$, and their standard deviation, σ. The expected rate of return is a probability-weighted average of the rates of return in all scenarios. Calling $p(s)$ the probability of each scenario and $r(s)$ the HPR in each scenario, where scenarios are labeled or "indexed" by the variable s, we may write the expected return as

$$E(r) = \sum_s p(s)r(s) \tag{5.1}$$

Table 5.1   Probability Distribution of HPR on the Stock Market

State of the Economy	Probability	Ending Price	HPR
Boom	.25	$140	44%
Normal growth	.50	110	14
Recession	.25	80	−16

Applying this formula to the data in Table 5.1, we find that the expected rate of return on the index fund is

$$E(r) = (.25 \times 44\%) + (.5 \times 14\%) + [25 \times (-16\%)] = 14\%$$

The standard deviation of the rate of return (σ) is a measure of risk. It is defined as the square root of the variance, which in turn is the expected value of the squared deviations from the expected return. The higher the volatility in outcomes, the higher will be the average value of these squared deviations. Therefore, variance and standard deviation measure the uncertainty of outcomes. Symbolically,

$$\sigma^2 = \sum_s p(s)\,[r(s) - E(r)]^2 \tag{5.2}$$

Therefore, in our example,

$$\sigma^2 = .25(44 - 14)^2 + .5(14 - 14)^2 + .25(-16 - 14)^2 = 450$$

and

$$\sigma = \sqrt{450} = 21.21\%$$

Clearly, what would trouble potential investors in the index fund is the downside risk of a −16% rate of return, not the upside potential of a 44% rate of return. The standard deviation of the rate of return does not distinguish between these two; it treats both simply as deviations from the mean. As long as the probability distribution is more or less symmetric about the mean, σ is an adequate measure of risk. In the special case where we can assume that the probability distribution is normal—represented by the well-known bell-shaped curve—$E(r)$ and σ are perfectly adequate to characterize the distribution.

Getting back to the example, how much, if anything, should you invest in the index fund? First, you must ask how much of an expected reward is offered for the risk involved in investing money in stocks.

We measure the reward as the difference between the *expected* HPR on the index stock fund and the **risk-free rate,** that is, the rate you can earn by leaving money in risk-free assets such as T-bills, money market funds, or the bank. We call this difference the **risk premium** on common stocks. If the risk-free rate in the example is 6% per year, and the expected index fund return is 14%, then the risk premium on stocks is 8% per year. The difference in any particular period between the *actual* rate of return on a risky asset and the risk-free rate is called **excess return.** Therefore, the risk premium is the expected excess return.

The degree to which investors are willing to commit funds to stocks depends on **risk aversion.** Financial analysts generally assume investors are risk averse in the sense that, if the risk premium were zero, people would not be willing to invest any money in stocks. In theory, then, there must always be a positive risk premium on stocks in order to induce risk-averse investors to hold the existing supply of stocks instead of placing all their money in risk-free assets.

Although this sample scenario analysis illustrates the concepts behind the quantification of risk and return, you may still wonder how to get a more realistic estimate of $E(r)$ and σ for common stocks and other types of securities. Here history has insights to offer.

Table 5.2   Rates of Return, 1926–1996

Year	Small Stocks	Large Stocks	Long–Term T–Bonds	Intermediate– Term T–Bonds	T–Bills	Inflation
1926	−8.91	12.21	4.54	4.96	3.19	−1.12
1927	32.23	35.99	8.11	3.34	3.12	−2.26
1928	45.02	39.29	−0.93	0.96	3.21	−1.16
1929	−50.81	−7.66	4.41	5.89	4.74	0.58
1930	−45.69	−25.90	6.22	5.51	2.35	−6.40
1931	−49.17	−45.56	−5.31	−5.81	0.96	−9.32
1932	10.95	−9.14	11.89	8.44	1.16	−10.27
1933	187.82	54.56	1.03	0.35	0.07	0.76
1934	25.13	−2.32	10.15	9.00	0.60	1.52
1935	68.44	45.67	4.98	7.01	−1.59	2.99
1936	84.47	33.55	6.52	3.77	−0.95	1.45
1937	−52.71	−36.03	0.43	1.56	0.35	2.86
1938	24.69	29.42	5.25	5.64	0.09	−2.78
1939	−0.10	−1.06	5.90	4.52	0.02	0.00
1940	−11.81	−9.65	6.54	2.03	0.00	0.71
1941	−13.08	−11.20	0.99	−0.59	0.06	9.93
1942	51.01	20.80	5.39	1.81	0.26	9.03
1943	99.79	26.54	4.87	2.78	0.35	2.96
1944	60.53	20.96	3.59	1.98	−0.07	2.30
1945	82.24	36.11	6.84	3.60	0.33	2.25
1946	−12.80	−9.26	0.15	0.69	0.37	18.13
1947	−3.09	4.88	−1.19	0.32	0.50	8.84
1948	−6.15	5.29	3.07	2.21	0.81	2.99
1949	21.56	18.24	6.03	2.22	1.10	−2.07
1950	45.48	32.68	−0.96	0.25	1.20	5.93
1951	9.41	23.47	−1.95	0.36	1.49	6.00
1952	6.36	18.91	1.93	1.63	1.66	0.75
1953	−5.68	−1.74	3.83	3.63	1.82	0.75
1954	65.13	52.55	4.88	1.73	0.86	−0.74
1955	21.84	31.44	−1.34	−0.52	1.57	0.37
1956	3.82	6.45	−5.12	−0.90	2.46	2.99
1957	−15.03	−11.14	9.46	7.84	3.14	2.90
1958	70.63	43.78	−3.71	−1.29	1.54	1.76
1959	17.82	12.95	−3.55	−1.26	2.95	1.73
1960	−5.16	0.19	13.78	11.98	2.66	1.36
1961	30.48	27.63	0.19	2.23	2.13	0.67
1962	−16.41	−8.79	6.81	7.38	2.72	1.33
1963	12.20	22.63	−0.49	1.79	3.12	1.64
1964	18.75	16.67	4.51	4.45	3.54	0.97

5.3   THE HISTORICAL RECORD

Bills, Bonds, and Stocks, 1926–1996

The record of past rates of return is one possible source of information about risk premiums and standard deviations. We can estimate the historical risk premium by taking an average of the past differences between the returns on an asset class and the risk-free rate. Table 5.2 presents the annual rates of return on five asset classes for the period 1926–1996.

"Large Stocks" in Table 5.2 refers to Standard & Poor's market-value-weighted portfolio of 500 U.S. common stocks with the largest market capitalization. "Small Stocks" rep-

Table 5.2   *(Continued)*

Year	Small Stocks	Large Stocks	Long–Term T–Bonds	Intermediate– Term T–Bonds	T–Bills	Inflation
1965	37.67	12.50	−0.27	1.27	3.94	1.92
1966	−8.08	−10.25	3.70	5.14	4.77	3.46
1967	103.39	24.11	−7.41	0.16	4.24	3.04
1968	50.61	11.00	−1.20	2.48	5.24	4.72
1969	−32.27	−8.33	−6.52	−2.10	6.59	6.20
1970	−16.54	4.10	12.69	13.93	6.50	5.57
1971	18.44	14.17	17.47	8.71	4.34	3.27
1972	−0.62	19.14	5.55	3.80	3.81	3.41
1973	−40.54	−14.75	1.40	2.90	6.91	8.71
1974	−29.74	−26.40	5.53	6.03	7.93	12.34
1975	69.54	37.26	8.50	6.79	5.80	6.94
1976	54.81	23.98	11.07	14.20	5.06	4.86
1977	22.02	−7.26	0.90	1.12	5.10	6.70
1978	22.29	6.50	−4.16	0.32	7.15	9.02
1979	43.99	18.77	9.02	4.29	10.45	13.29
1980	35.34	32.48	13.17	0.83	11.57	12.52
1981	7.79	−4.98	3.61	6.09	14.95	8.92
1982	27.44	22.09	6.52	33.39	10.71	3.83
1983	34.49	22.37	−0.53	5.44	8.85	3.79
1984	−14.02	6.46	15.29	14.46	10.02	3.95
1985	28.21	32.00	32.68	23.65	7.83	3.80
1986	3.40	18.40	23.96	17.22	6.18	1.10
1987	−13.95	5.34	−2.65	1.68	5.50	4.43
1988	21.72	16.86	8.40	6.63	6.44	4.42
1989	8.37	31.34	19.49	14.82	8.32	4.65
1990	−27.08	−3.20	7.13	9.05	7.86	6.11
1991	50.24	30.66	18.39	16.67	5.65	3.06
1992	27.84	7.71	7.79	7.25	3.54	2.90
1993	20.30	9.87	15.48	12.02	2.97	2.75
1994	−3.34	1.29	−7.18	−4.42	3.91	2.67
1995	33.21	37.71	31.67	18.07	5.58	2.54
1996	16.50	23.00	0.10	2.70	5.20	3.32
Average	19.02	12.50	5.31	5.16	3.76	3.22
Standard deviation	40.44	20.39	7.96	6.47	3.35	4.54
Minimum	−52.71	−45.56	−7.41	−5.81	−1.59	−10.27
Maximum	187.82	54.56	32.68	33.39	14.95	18.13

Source: Inflation data: Bureau of Labor Statistics; security return data for 1926–1996: Center for Research in Security Prices; security return data for 1997: Returns on appropriate index portfolios.

resents the value-weighted portfolio of the lowest-capitalization quintile (that is, the firms in the bottom 20% of all companies traded on the NYSE when ranked by market capitalization). Since 1982, this portfolio has included smaller stocks listed on the Amex and Nasdaq markets as well. The portfolio contains approximately 2,000 stocks with average capitalization of $100 million.

"Long-Term T-Bonds" are represented by a government bond with at least a 20-year maturity and approximately current-level coupon rate.[2] "Intermediate-Term T-Bonds" have at least a seven-year maturity with a current-level coupon rate.

---

[2]The importance of the coupon rate when comparing returns on bonds is discussed in Part III.

Figure 5.3

Rates of return on stocks, bonds, and T-bills, 1926–1996.

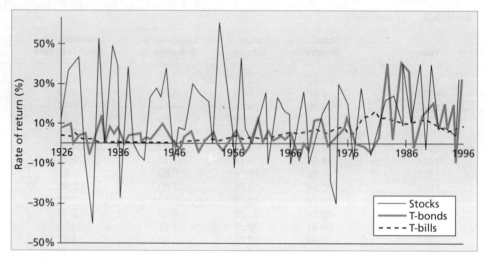

Source: Prepared from data in Table 5.2.

"T-Bills" in Table 5.2 are of approximately 30-day maturity, and the one-year HPR represents a policy of "rolling over" the bills as they mature. Because T-bill rates can change from month to month, the total rate of return on these T-bills is riskless only for 30-day holding periods.[3] The last column of Table 5.2 gives the annual inflation rate as measured by the rate of change in the Consumer Price Index.

At the bottom of each column are four descriptive statistics. The first is the arithmetic mean or average holding period return. For bills, it is 3.76%; for long-term government bonds, 5.31%; and for large stocks, 12.50%. The numbers in that row imply a positive average excess return suggesting a risk premium of, for example, 1.55% per year on long-term government bonds and 8.74% on large stocks (the average excess return is the average HPR less the average risk-free rate of 3.76%).

The second statistic at the bottom of Table 5.2 is the standard deviation. The higher the standard deviation, the higher the variability of the HPR. This standard deviation is based on historical data rather than forecasts of *future* scenarios as in equation 5.2. The formula for historical variance, however, is similar to equation 5.2:

$$\sigma^2 = \frac{n}{n-1} \sum_{t=1}^{n} \frac{(r_t - \bar{r})^2}{n}$$

Here, each year's outcome (r_t) is taken as a possible scenario. [We multiply by $n/(n-1)$ to eliminate statistical bias in the estimate of variance.] Deviations are taken from the historical average, $\bar{r}$, instead of the expected value, $E(r)$. Each historical outcome is taken as equally likely and given a "probability" of $1/n$.

Figure 5.3 gives a graphic representation of the relative variabilities of the annual HPR for the three different asset classes. We have plotted the three time series on the same set of axes, each in a different color. The graph shows very clearly that the annual HPR on stocks is the most variable series. The standard deviation of large-stock returns has been

---

[3]The few negative returns in this column, all dating from before World War II, reflect periods where, in the absence of T-bills, returns on government securities with about 30-day maturity have been used. However, these securities included options to be exchanged for other securities, thus increasing their price and lowering their yield relative to what a simple T-bill would have offered.

Figure 5.4
The normal
distribution.

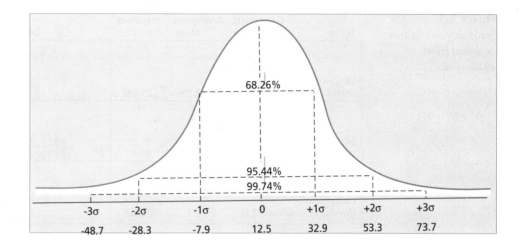

20.39% (and that of small stocks larger still) compared to 7.96% for long-term government bonds and 3.35% for bills. Here is evidence of the risk–return trade-off that characterizes security markets: The markets with the highest average returns also are the most volatile.

The other summary measures at the end of Table 5.2 show the highest and lowest annual HPR (the range) for each asset over the 71-year period. The extent of this range is another measure of the relative riskiness of each asset class. It, too, confirms the ranking of stocks as the riskiest and bills as the least risky of the three asset classes.

An all-stock portfolio with a standard deviation of 20.39% would represent a very volatile investment. For example, if stock returns are normally distributed with a standard deviation of 20.39% and an expected rate of return of 12.50% (the historical average), in roughly one year out of three, returns will be less than 7.89% (12.50 – 20.39) or greater than 32.89% (12.50 + 20.39).

Figure 5.4 is a graph of the normal curve with mean 12.50% and standard deviation 20.39%. The graph shows the theoretical probability of rates of return within various ranges given these parameters.

Figure 5.5 presents another view of the historical data, the actual frequency distribution of returns on various asset classes over the period 1926–1996. Again, the greater range of stock returns relative to bill or bond returns is obvious. The first column of the figure gives the geometric averages of the historical rates of return on each asset class; this figure thus represents the compound rate of growth in the value of an investment in these assets. The second column shows the arithmetic averages that, absent additional information, might serve as forecasts of the future HPRs for these assets. The last column is the variability of asset returns, as measured by standard deviation. The historical results are consistent with the risk–return trade-off: Riskier assets have provided higher expected returns, and historical risk premiums are considerable. The nearby box presents a brief overview of the performance and risk characteristics of a wider range of assets.

We should stress that variability of HPR in the past can be an unreliable guide to risk, at least in the case of the risk-free asset. For an investor with a holding period of one year, for example, a one-year T-bill is a riskless investment, at least in terms of its nominal return, which is known with certainty. However, the standard deviation of the one-year T-bill rate estimated from historical data is not zero: This reflects variation in expected returns rather than fluctuations of actual returns around prior expectations.

Figure 5.5

Frequency distribution of annual HPRs, 1926–1996.

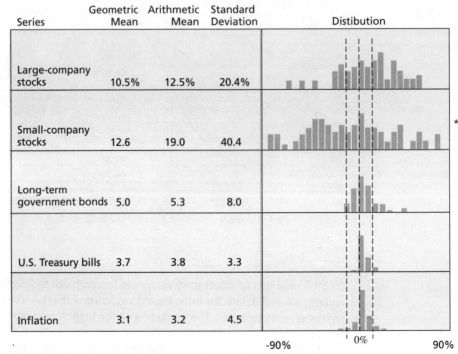

Series	Geometric Mean	Arithmetic Mean	Standard Deviation	Distibution
Large-company stocks	10.5%	12.5%	20.4%	
Small-company stocks	12.6	19.0	40.4	
Long-term government bonds	5.0	5.3	8.0	
U.S. Treasury bills	3.7	3.8	3.3	
Inflation	3.1	3.2	4.5	

*The 1933 small company stock total return was 187.8%.

Source: Prepared from data in Table 5.2.

The risk of cash flows of real assets reflects both *business risk* (profit fluctuations due to business conditions) and *financial risk* (increased profit fluctuations due to leverage). This reminds us that an all-stock portfolio represents claims on leveraged corporations. Most corporations carry some debt, the service of which is a fixed cost. Greater fixed cost makes profits riskier; thus leverage increases equity risk.

Concept CHECK

Question 2 • Compute the average excess return on stocks (over the T-bill rate) and its standard deviation for the years 1926–1934.

5.4   REAL VERSUS NOMINAL RISK

The distinction between the real and the nominal rate of return is crucial in making investment choices when investors are interested in the future purchasing power of their wealth. Thus a U.S. Treasury bond that offers a "risk-free" *nominal* rate of return is not truly a risk-free investment—it does not guarantee the future purchasing power of its cash flow.

An example might be a bond that pays $1,000 on a date 20 years from now but nothing in the interim. Although some people see such a zero-coupon bond as a convenient way for individuals to lock in attractive, risk-free, long-term interest rates (particularly in IRA or Keogh[4] accounts), the evidence in Table 5.3 is rather discouraging about the value of $1,000 in 20 years in terms of today's purchasing power.

[4]A tax shelter for self-employed individuals.

INVESTING: WHAT TO BUY WHEN?

In making broad-scale investment decisions investors may want to know how various types of investments have performed during booms, recessions, high inflation and low inflation. The table shows how 10 asset categories per-formed during representative years since World War II. But history rarely repeats itself, so historical performance is only a rough guide to the figure.

Investment	Average Annual Return on Investment*			
	Recession	Boom	High Inflation	Low Inflation
Bonds (long-term government)	17%	4%	−1%	8%
Commodity index	1	−6	15	−5
Diamonds (1-carat investment grade)	−4	8	79	15
Gold† (bullion)	−8	−9	105	19
Private home	4	6	6	5
Real estate‡ (commercial)	9	13	18	6
Silver (bullion)	3	−6	94	4
Stocks (blue chip)	14	7	−3	21
Stocks (small growth-company)	17	14	7	12
Treasury bills (3-month)	6	5	7	3

*In most cases, figures are computed as follows: Recession—average of performance during calendar years 1946, 1975, and 1982; boom—average of 1951, 1965, and 1984; high inflation—average of 1947, 1974, and 1980; low inflation—average of 1955, 1961, and 1986.

†Gold figures are based only on data since 1971 and may be less reliable than others.

‡Commercial real estate figures are based only on data since 1978 and may be less reliable than others.

Sources: Commerce Dept.; Commodity Research Bureau; DeBeers Inc.; Diamond Registry; Dow Jones & Co.; Dun & Bradstreet; Handy & Harman; Ibbotson Associates; Charles Kroll (Diversified Investor's Forecast); Merrill Lynch; National Council of Real Estate Investment Fiduciaries; Frank B. Russell Co.; Shearson Lehman Bros.; T. Rowe Price New Horizons Fund.

Source: Modified from *The Wall Street Journal*, November 13, 1987. Reprinted by permission of *The Wall Street Journal*, © 1987 Dow Jones & Company, Inc. All Rights Reserved Worldwide.

Table 5.3 Purchasing Power of $1,000 20 Years from Now and 20-Year Real Annualized HPR

Assumed Annual Rate of Inflation	Number of Dollars Required 20 Years from Now to Buy What $1 Buys Today	Purchasing Power of $1,000 to Be Received in 20 Years	Annualized Real HPR
4%	$2.19	$456.39	7.69%
6	3.21	311.80	5.66
8	4.66	214.55	3.70
10	6.73	148.64	1.82
12	9.65	103.67	0.00

Purchasing price of bond is $103.7.
Nominal 20-year annualized HPR is 12% per year.
Purchasing power = $1,000/(1 + inflation rate)^{20}.
Real HPR, r, is computed from the following relationship:

$$r = (1 + R)/(1 + i) - 1$$
$$= 1.12/(1 + i) - 1$$

Suppose the price of the bond is $103.67, giving a nominal rate of return of 12% per year (since $103.67 \times 1.12^{20} = 1,000$). We can compute the real annualized HPR for each inflation rate.

A revealing comparison is at a 12% rate of inflation. At that rate, Table 5.3 shows that the purchasing power of the $1,000 to be received in 20 years would be $103.67, the amount initially paid for the bond. The real HPR in these circumstances is zero. When the rate of inflation equals the nominal rate of interest, the price of goods increases just as fast as the money accumulated from the investment, and there is no growth in purchasing power.

At an inflation rate of only 4% per year, however, the purchasing power of $1,000 will be $456.39 in terms of today's prices; that is, the investment of $103.67 grows to a real value of $456.39, for a real 20-year annualized HPR of 7.69% per year.

Again looking at Table 5.3, you can see that an investor expecting an inflation rate of 8% per year anticipates a real annualized HPR of 3.70%. If the actual rate of inflation turns out to be 10% per year, the resulting real HPR is only 1.82% per year. These differences show the important distinction between expected and actual inflation rates.

Even professional economic forecasters acknowledge that their inflation forecasts are hardly certain even for the next year, not to mention the next 20. When you look at an asset from the perspective of its future purchasing power, you can see that an asset that is risk-less in nominal terms can be very risky in real terms.[5]

Concept

Question 3 • Suppose the rate of inflation turns out to be 13% per year. What will be the real annualized 20-year HPR on the nominally risk-free bond?

SUMMARY

1. The economy's equilibrium level of real interest rates depends on the willingness of households to save, as reflected in the supply curve of funds, and on the expected profitability of business investment in plant, equipment, and inventories, as reflected in the demand curve for funds. It depends also on government fiscal and monetary policy.

2. The nominal rate of interest is the equilibrium real rate plus the expected rate of inflation. In general, we can directly observe only nominal interest rates; from them, we must infer expected real rates, using inflation forecasts.

3. The equilibrium expected rate of return on any security is the sum of the equilibrium real rate of interest, the expected rate of inflation, and a security-specific risk premium.

4. Investors face a trade-off between risk and expected return. Historical data confirm our intuition that assets with low degrees of risk provide lower returns on average than do those of higher risk.

5. Assets with guaranteed nominal interest rates are risky in real terms because the future inflation rate is uncertain.

Key Terms

nominal interest rate	risk-free rate	excess return
real interest rate	risk premium	risk aversion

Selected Readings

The classic work of the determination of the level of interest rates is:

Fisher, Irving. *The Theory of Interest: As Determined by Impatience to Spend Income and Opportunity to Invest It.* New York: Augustus M. Kelley, Publishers, 1965, originally published in 1930.

---

[5]In 1997 the Treasury began issuing inflation-indexed bonds called TIPS (for Treasury Inflation Protected Securities) which offer protection against inflation uncertainty. We discuss these bonds in more detail in Chapter 14. However, the vast majority of bonds make payments that are fixed in dollar terms; the real returns on these bonds are subject to inflation risk.

The standard reference for historical returns on a variety of instruments, updated annually, is:
Stocks, Bonds, Bills and Inflation: 1997 Yearbook. Chicago: Ibbotson Associates, Inc., 1998.

Problems

1. You have $5,000 to invest for the next year and are considering three alternatives:
   a. A money market fund with an average maturity of 30 days offering a current yield of 6% per year.
   b. A one-year savings deposit at a bank offering an interest rate of 7.5%.
   c. A 20-year U.S. Treasury bond offering a yield to maturity of 9% per year.
   What role does your forecast of future interest rates play in your decisions?

2. Use Figure 5.1 in the text to analyze the effect of the following on the level of real interest rates:
   a. Businesses become more pessimistic about future demand for their products and decide to reduce their capital spending.
   b. Households are induced to save more because of increased uncertainty about their future social security benefits.
   c. The Federal Reserve Board undertakes open-market purchases of U.S. Treasury securities in order to increase the supply of money.

3. You are considering the choice between investing $50,000 in a conventional one-year bank CD offering an interest rate of 7% and a one-year "Inflation-Plus" CD offering 3.5% per year plus the rate of inflation.
   a. Which is the safer investment?
   b. Which offers the higher expected return?
   c. If you expect the rate of inflation to be 3% over the next year, which is the better investment? Why?
   d. If we observe a risk-free nominal interest rate of 7% per year and a risk-free real rate of 3.5%, can we infer that the market's expected rate of inflation is 3.5% per year?

4. Look at Table 5.1 in the text. Suppose you now revise your expectations regarding the stock market as follows:

State of the Economy	Probability	Ending Price	HPR
Boom	.35	$140	44%
Normal growth	.30	110	14
Recession	.35	80	−16

   Use equations 5.1 and 5.2 to compute the mean and standard deviation of the HPR on stocks. Compare your revised parameters with the ones in the text.

5. Derive the probability distribution of the one-year HPR on a 30-year U.S. Treasury bond with an 8% coupon if it is currently selling at par and the probability distribution of its yield to maturity a year from now is as follows:

State of the Economy	Probability	YTM
Boom	.20	11.0%
Normal growth	.50	8.0
Recession	.30	7.0

   For simplicity, assume the entire 8% coupon is paid at the end of the year rather than every six months.

6. Using the historical risk premiums as your guide, what would be your estimate of the expected annual HPR on the S&P 500 stock portfolio if the current risk-free interest rate were 8%?

7. Compute the means and standard deviations of the annual HPR of large stocks and Treasury bonds using only the last 30 years of data in Table 5.2, 1967–1996. How do these statistics compare with those computed from the data for the period 1926–1941? Which do you think are the most relevant statistics to use for projecting into the future?

8. During a period of severe inflation, a bond offered a nominal HPR of 80% per year. The inflation rate was 70% per year.
   a. What was the real HPR on the bond over the year?
   b. Compare this real HPR to the approximation $r = R - i$.

9. Suppose that the inflation rate is expected to be 3% in the near future. Using the historical data provided in this chapter, what would be your predictions for:
   a. The T-bill rate?
   b. The expected rate of return on large stocks?
   c. The risk premium on the stock market?

10. An economy is making a rapid recovery from steep recession, and businesses foresee a need for large amounts of capital investment. Why would this development affect real interest rates?

 11. Given $100,000 to invest, what is the expected risk premium in dollars of investing in equities versus risk-free T-bills (U.S. Treasury bills) based on the following table?

Action	Probability	Expected Return
Invest in equities	.6	$50,000
	.4	–$30,000
Invest in risk-free T-bill	1.0	$ 5,000

   a. $13,000.
   b. $15,000.
   c. $18,000.
   d. $20,000.

 12. Based on the scenarios below, what is the expected return for a portfolio with the following return profile?

	Market Condition		
	Bear	Normal	Bull
Probability	.2	.3	.5
Rate of return	–25%	10%	24%

   a. 4%.
   b. 10%.
   c. 20%.
   d. 25%.

Use the following expectations on Stocks X and Y to answer questions 13 through 15 (round to the nearest percent).

	Bear Market	Normal Market	Bull Market
Probability	0.2	0.5	0.3
Stock X	−20%	18%	50%
Stock Y	−15%	20%	10%

 13. What are the expected returns for Stocks X and Y?

	Stock X	Stock Y
a.	18%	5%
b.	18%	12%
c.	20%	11%
d.	20%	10%

 14. What are the standard deviations of returns on Stocks X and Y?

	Stock X	Stock Y
a.	15%	26%
b.	20%	4%
c.	24%	13%
d.	28%	8%

 15. Assume that of your $10,000 portfolio, you invest $9,000 in Stock X and $1,000 in Stock Y. What is the expected return on your portfolio?
a. 18%.
b. 19%.
c. 20%.
d. 23%.

 16. Probabilities for three states of the economy, and probabilities for the returns on a particular stock in each state are shown in the table below.

State of Economy	Probability of Economic State	Stock Performance	Probability of Stock Performance in Given Economic State
Good	.3	Good	.6
		Neutral	.3
		Poor	.1
Neutral	.5	Good	.4
		Neutral	.3
		Poor	.3
Poor	.2	Good	.2
		Neutral	.3
		Poor	.5

The probability that the economy will be neutral *and* the stock will experience poor performance is

a. .06.

b. .15.

c. .50.

d. .80.

17. An analyst estimates that a stock has the following probabilities of return depending on the state of the economy:

State of Economy	Probability	Return
Good	.1	15%
Normal	.6	13
Poor	.3	7

The expected return of the stock is:

a. 7.8%.

b. 11.4%.

c. 11.7%.

d. 13.0%.

Problems 18–19 represent a greater challenge. You may need to review the definitions of call and put options in Chapter 2.

18. You are faced with the probability distribution of the HPR on the stock market index fund given in Table 5.1 of the text. Suppose the price of a put option on a share of the index fund with exercise price of $110 and maturity of one year is $12.

   a. What is the probability distribution of the HPR on the put option?

   b. What is the probability distribution of the HPR on a portfolio consisting of one share of the index fund and a put option?

   c. In what sense does buying the put option constitute a purchase of insurance in this case?

19. Take as given the conditions described in the previous question, and suppose the risk-free interest rate is 6% per year. You are contemplating investing $107.55 in a one-year CD and simultaneously buying a call option on the stock market index fund with an exercise price of $110 and a maturity of one year. What is the probability distribution of your dollar return at the end of the year?

APPENDIX: CONTINUOUS COMPOUNDING

Suppose that your money earns interest at an annual nominal percentage rate (APR) of 6% per year compounded semiannually. What is your *effective* annual rate of return, accounting for compound interest?

We find the answer by first computing the per (compounding) period rate, 3% per half-year, and then computing the future value (FV) at the end of the year per dollar invested at the beginning of the year. In this example, we get

$$FV = (1.03)^2 = 1.0609$$

Table 5A.1   Effective Annual Rates for APR of 6%

Compounding Frequency	n	R_{EFF} (%)
Annually	1	6.00000
Semiannually	2	6.09000
Quarterly	4	6.13636
Monthly	12	6.16778
Weekly	52	6.17998
Daily	365	6.18313

The effective annual rate (R_{EFF}), that is, the annual rate at which your funds have grown is just this number minus 1.0.

$$R_{EFF} = 1.0609 - 1 = .0609 = 6.09\% \text{ per year}$$

The general formula for the effective annual rate is

$$R_{EFF} = \left(1 + \frac{APR}{n}\right)^n - 1$$

where APR is the annual percentage rate and n is the number of compounding periods per year. Table 5A.1 presents the effective annual rates corresponding to an annual percentage rate of 6% per year for different compounding frequencies.

As the compounding frequency increases, $(1 + APR/n)^n$ gets closer and closer to e^{APR}, where e is the number 2.71828 (rounded off to the fifth decimal place). In our example, $e^{.06} = 1.0618365$. Therefore, if interest is continuously compounded, $R_{EFF} = .0618365$, or 6.18365% per year.

Using continuously compounded rates simplifies the algebraic relationship between real and nominal rates of return. To see how, let us compute the real rate of return first using annual compounding and then using continuous compounding. Assume the nominal interest rate is 6% per year compounded annually and the rate of inflation is 4% per year compounded annually. Using the relationship

$$\text{Real rate} = \frac{1 + \text{Nominal rate}}{1 + \text{Inflation rate}} - 1$$

$$r = \frac{(1 + R)}{(1 + i)} - 1 = \frac{R - i}{1 + i}$$

we find that the effective annual real rate is

$$r = 1.06/1.04 - 1 = .01923 = 1.923\% \text{ per year}$$

With continuous compounding, the relationship becomes

$$e^r = e^R/e^i = e^{R-i}$$

Taking natural logarithms, we get

$$r = R - i$$
$$\text{Real rate} = \text{Nominal rate} - \text{Inflation rate}$$

all expressed as annual, continuously compounded percentage rates.

Thus if we assume a nominal interest rate of 6% per year compounded continuously and an inflation rate of 4% per year compounded continuously, the real rate is 2% per year compounded continuously.

To pay a fair interest rate to a depositor, the compounding frequency must be at least equal to the frequency of deposits and withdrawals. Only when you compound at least as frequently as transactions in an account can you assure that each dollar will earn the full interest due for the exact time it has been in the account. These days, on-line computing for deposits is common, so one expects the frequency of compounding to grow until the use of continuous or at least daily compounding becomes the norm.

s o l u t i o n s   t o
Concept
CHECKS

1. *a.* $1 + R = (1 + r)(1 + i) = (1.03)(1.08) = 1.1124$
   $R = 11.24\%$
   b. $1 + R = (1.03)(1.10) = 1.133$
   $R = 13.3\%$

2. The mean excess return for the period 1926–1934 is 4.5 percent (below the historical average), and the standard deviation (dividing by $n - 1$) is 30.79 (above the historical average). These results reflect the severe downturn of the great crash and the unusually high volatility of stock returns in this period.

3. $r = (.12 - .13)/1.13 = -.00885$, or $-.885\%$. When the inflation rate exceeds the nominal interest rate, the real rate of return is negative.

PORTFOLIO THEORY

RISK AND RISK AVERSION

The investment process consists of two broad tasks. One task is security and market analysis, by which we assess the risk and expected-return attributes of the entire set of possible investment vehicles. The second task is the formation of an optimal portfolio of assets. This task involves the determination of the best risk-return opportunities available from feasible investment portfolios and the choice of the best portfolio from the feasible set. We start our formal analysis of investments with this latter task, called *portfolio theory*. We return to the security analysis task in later chapters. This chapter introduces three themes in portfolio theory, all centering on risk. The first is the basic tenet that investors avoid risk and demand a reward for engaging in risky investments. The reward is taken as a risk premium, an expected rate of return higher than that available on alternative risk-free investments. The second theme allows us to summarize and quantify investors' personal trade-offs between portfolio risk and expected return. To do this we introduce the *utility function*, which assumes that investors can assign a welfare, or "utility," score to any investment portfolio depending on its risk and

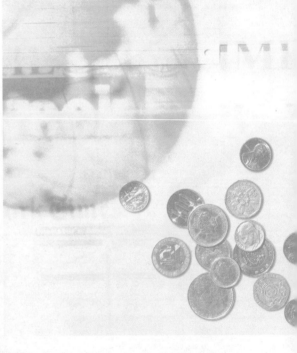

return. Finally, the third fundamental principle is that we cannot evaluate the risk of an asset separate from the portfolio of which it is a part; that is, the proper way to measure the risk of an individual asset is to assess its impact on the volatility of the entire portfolio of investments. Taking this approach, we find that seemingly risky securities may be portfolio stabilizers and actually low-risk assets. Appendix A to this chapter describes the theory and practice of measuring portfolio risk by the variance or standard deviation of returns. We discuss other potentially relevant characteristics of the probability distribution of portfolio returns, as well as the circumstances in which variance is sufficient to measure risk. Appendix B discusses the classical theory of risk aversion.

6.1 RISK AND RISK AVERSION

Risk with Simple Prospects

The presence of risk means that more than one outcome is possible. A *simple prospect* is an investment opportunity in which a certain initial wealth is placed at risk, and there are only two possible outcomes. For the sake of simplicity, it is useful to begin our analysis and elucidate some basic concepts using simple prospects.[1]

Take as an example initial wealth, W, of $100,000, and assume two possible results. With a probability $p = .6$, the favorable outcome will occur, leading to final wealth $W_1 = \$150,000$. Otherwise, with probability $1 - p = .4$, a less favorable outcome, $W_2 = \$80,000$, will occur. We can represent the simple prospect using an event tree:

$$
W = \$100,000 \quad
\begin{matrix}
p = .6 & W_1 = \$150,000 \\
1-p = .4 & W_2 = \$80,000
\end{matrix}
$$

Suppose that an investor is offered an investment portfolio with a payoff in one year that is described by such a simple prospect. How can she evaluate this portfolio?

First, she could try to summarize it using descriptive statistics. For instance, her mean or expected end-of-year wealth, denoted $E(W)$, is

$$
E(W) = pW_1 + (1 - p)W_2
$$
$$
= (.6 \times 150,000) + (.4 \times 80,000)
$$
$$
= \$122,000
$$

The expected profit on the $100,000 investment portfolio is $22,000: $122,000 - 100,000$. The variance, σ^2, of the portfolio's payoff is calculated as the expected value of the squared deviations of each possible outcome from the mean:

$$
\sigma^2 = p[W_1 - E(W)]^2 + (1 - p)[W_2 - E(W)]^2
$$
$$
= .6(150,000 - 122,000)^2 + .4(80,000 - 122,000)^2
$$
$$
= 1,176,000,000
$$

The standard deviation, σ, which is the square root of the variance, is therefore $34,292.86.

Clearly, this is risky business: The standard deviation of the payoff is large, much larger than the expected profit of $22,000. Whether the expected profit is large enough to justify such risk depends on the alternative portfolios.

Let us suppose Treasury bills are one alternative to the risky portfolio. Suppose that at the time of the decision, a one-year T-bill offers a rate of return of 5%; $100,000 can be invested to yield a sure profit of $5,000. We can now draw the decision tree.

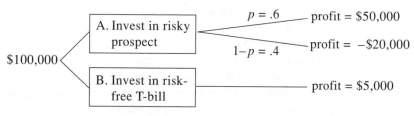

---

[1]Chapters 6 through 8 rely on some basic results from elementary statistics. For a refresher, see the Quantitative Review in the Appendix at the end of the book.

Earlier, we showed the expected profit on the prospect to be $22,000. Therefore, the expected marginal, or incremental, profit of the risky portfolio over investing in safe T-bills is

$$\$22,000 - \$5,000 = \$17,000$$

meaning that one can earn a **risk premium** of $17,000 as compensation for the risk of the investment.

The question of whether a given risk premium provides adequate compensation for the investment's risk is age-old. Indeed, one of the central concerns of finance theory (and much of this text) is the measurement of risk and the determination of the risk premiums that investors can expect of risky assets in well-functioning capital markets.

Concept

Question 1 • **What is the risk premium of Susan's risky portfolio in terms of rate of return rather than dollars?**

Risk, Speculation, and Gambling

One definition of *speculation* is "the assumption of considerable business risk in obtaining commensurate gain." Although this definition is fine linguistically, it is useless without first specifying what is meant by "commensurate gain" and "considerable risk."

By "commensurate gain" we mean a positive expected profit beyond the risk-free alternative. This is the risk premium. In our example, the dollar risk premium is the profit net of the alternative, which is the sure T-bill profit. The risk premium is the incremental expected gain from taking on the risk. By "considerable risk" we mean that the risk is sufficient to affect the decision. An individual might reject a prospect that has a positive risk premium because the added gain is insufficient to make up for the risk involved.

To gamble is "to bet or wager on an uncertain outcome." If you compare this definition to that of speculation, you will see that the central difference is the lack of "commensurate gain." Economically speaking, a gamble is the assumption of risk for no purpose but enjoyment of the risk itself, whereas speculation is undertaken in spite of the risk involved because one perceives a favorable risk-return trade-off. To turn a gamble into a speculative prospect requires an adequate risk premium to compensate risk-averse investors for the risks that they bear. Hence, *risk aversion and speculation are not inconsistent.*

In some cases a gamble may appear to the participants as speculation. Suppose that two investors disagree sharply about the future exchange rate of the U.S. dollar against the British pound. They may choose to bet on the outcome. Suppose that Paul will pay Mary $100 if the value of £1 exceeds $1.70 one year from now, whereas Mary will pay Paul if the pound is worth less than $1.70. There are only two relevant outcomes: (1) the pound will exceed $1.70, or (2) it will fall below $1.70. If both Paul and Mary agree on the probabilities of the two possible outcomes, and if neither party anticipates a loss, it must be that they assign $p = .5$ to each outcome. In that case the expected profit to both is zero and each has entered one side of a gambling prospect.

What is more likely, however, is that the bet results from differences in the probabilities that Paul and Mary assign to the outcome. Mary assigns it $p > .5$, whereas Paul's assessment is $p < .5$. They perceive, subjectively, two different prospects. Economists call this case of differing beliefs "heterogeneous expectations." In such cases investors on each side of a financial position see themselves as speculating rather than gambling.

Both Paul and Mary should be asking, "Why is the other willing to invest in the side of a risky prospect that I believe offers a negative expected profit?" The ideal way to resolve heterogeneous beliefs is for Paul and Mary to "merge their information," that is, for each party to verify that he or she possesses all relevant information and processes the information properly. Of course, the acquisition of information and the extensive communication that is required to eliminate all heterogeneity in expectations is costly, and thus up to a point heterogeneous expectations cannot be taken as irrational. If, however, Paul and Mary enter such contracts frequently, they would recognize the information problem in one of two ways: Either they will realize that they are creating gambles when each wins half of the bets, or the consistent loser will admit that he or she has been betting on the basis of inferior forecasts.

Concept
CHECK

Question 2 • **Assume that dollar-denominated T-bills in the United States and pound-denominated bills in the United Kingdom offer equal yields to maturity. Both are short-term assets, and both are free of default risk. Neither offers investors a risk premium. However, a U.S. investor who holds U.K. bills is subject to exchange rate risk, because the pounds earned on the U.K. bills eventually will be exchanged for dollars at the future exchange rate. Is the U.S. investor engaging in speculation or gambling?**

Risk Aversion and Utility Values

We have discussed risk with simple prospects and how risk premiums bear on speculation. A prospect that has a zero risk premium is called a *fair game*. Investors who are **risk averse** reject investment portfolios that are fair games or worse. Risk-averse investors are willing to consider only risk-free or speculative prospects. Loosely speaking, a risk-averse investor "penalizes" the expected rate of return of a risky portfolio by a certain percentage (or penalizes the expected profit by a dollar amount) to account for the risk involved. The greater the risk the investor perceives, the larger the penalty. One might wonder why we assume risk aversion as fundamental. We believe that most investors would accept this view from simple introspection, but we discuss the question more fully in Appendix B of this chapter.

We can formalize this notion of a risk-penalty system. To do so, we will assume that each investor can assign a welfare, or **utility,** score to competing investment portfolios based on the expected return and risk of those portfolios. The utility score may be viewed as a means of ranking portfolios. Higher utility values are assigned to portfolios with more attractive risk-return profiles. Portfolios receive higher utility scores for higher expected returns and lower scores for higher volatility. Many particular "scoring" systems are legitimate. One reasonable function that is commonly employed by financial theorists assigns a portfolio with expected return $E(r)$ and variance of returns σ^2 the following utility score:

$$U = E(r) - .005A\sigma^2 \tag{6.1}$$

where U is the utility value and A is an index of the investor's aversion. (The factor of .005 is a scaling convention that allows us to express the expected return and standard deviation in equation 6.1 as percentages rather than decimals.)

Equation 6.1 is consistent with the notion that utility is enhanced by high expected returns and diminished by high risk. (Whether variance is an adequate measure of portfolio risk is discussed in Appendix A.) The extent to which variance lowers utility depends on A, the investor's degree of risk aversion. More risk-averse investors (who have the larger As) penalize risky investments more severely. Investors choosing among competing investment portfolios will select the one providing the highest utility level.

Risk aversion obviously will have a major impact on the investor's appropriate risk-return trade-off. The nearby box discusses some techniques that financial advisors use to gauge the risk aversion of their clients.

TIME FOR INVESTING'S FOUR-LETTER WORD

What four-letter word should pop into mind when the stock market takes a harrowing nose dive?

No, not those. R-I-S-K.

Risk is the potential for realizing low returns or even losing money, possibly preventing you from meeting important objectives, like sending your kids to the college of their choice or having the retirement lifestyle you crave.

But many financial advisers and other experts say that these days investors aren't taking the idea of risk as seriously as they should, and they are overexposing themselves to stocks.

"The market has been so good for years that investors no longer believe there's risk in investing," says Gary Schatsky, a financial adviser in New York.

So before the market goes down and stays down, be sure that you understand your tolerance for risk and that your portfolio is designed to match it.

Assessing your risk tolerance, however, can be tricky. You must consider not only how much risk you can *afford* to take but also how much risk you can *stand* to take.

Determining how much risk you can stand—your temperamental tolerance for risk—is more difficult. It isn't quantifiable.

To that end, many financial advisers, brokerage firms and mutual-fund companies have created risk quizzes to help people determine whether they are conservative, moderate or aggressive investors. Some firms that offer such quizzes include Merrill Lynch, T. Rowe Price Associates Inc., Baltimore, Zurich Group Inc.'s Scudder Kemper Investments Inc., New York, and Vanguard Group in Malvern, Pa.

Typically, risk questionnaires include seven to 10 questions about a person's investing experience, financial security and tendency to make risky or conservative choices.

The benefit of the questionnaires is that they are an objective resource people can use to get at least a rough idea of their risk tolerance. "It's impossible for someone to assess their risk tolerance alone," says Mr. Bernstein. "I may say I don't like risk, yet will take more risk than the average person."

Many experts warn, however, that the questionnaires should be used simply as a first step to assessing risk tolerance. "They are not precise," says Ron Meier, a certified public accountant.

The second step, many experts agree, is to ask yourself some difficult questions, such as: How much you can stand to lose over the long term?

"Most people can stand to lose a heck of a lot temporarily," says Mr. Schatsky. The real acid test, he says, is how much of your portfolio's value you can stand to lose over months or years.

As it turns out, most people rank as middle-of-the-road risk-takers, say several advisers. "Only about 10% to 15% of my clients are aggressive," says Mr. Roge.

Source: Reprinted with permission from *The Wall Street Journal* © 1998 by Dow Jones & Company. All Rights Reserved Worldwide.

What's Your Risk Tolerance?

Circle the letter that corresponds to your answer

1. Just 60 days after you put money into an investment, its price falls 20 percent. Assuming none of the fundamentals have changed, what would you do?
   a. Sell to avoid further worry and try something else
   b. Do nothing and wait for the investment to come back
   c. Buy more. It was a good investment before; now it's a cheap investment, too
2. Now look at the previous question another way. Your investment fell 20 percent, but it's part of a portfolio being used to meet investment goals with three different time horizons.

Notice in equation 6.1 that the utility provided by a risk-free portfolio is simply the rate of return on the portfolio, because there is no penalization for risk. This provides us with a convenient benchmark for evaluating portfolios. For example, recall the earlier investment problem, choosing between a portfolio with an expected return of 22% and a standard deviation $\sigma = 34\%$ and T-bills providing a risk-free return of 5%. Although the risk premium on the risky portfolio is large, 17%, the risk of the project is so great that an investor would not need to be very risk averse to choose the safe all-bills strategy. Even for $A = 3$, a moderate risk-aversion parameter, equation 6.1 shows the risky portfolio's utility value as $22 - (.005 \times 3 \times 34^2) = 4.66\%$, which is slightly lower than the risk-free rate. In this case, one would reject the portfolio in favor of T-bills.

The downward adjustment of the expected return as a penalty for risk is $.005 \times 3 \times 34^2 = 17.34\%$. If the investor were less risk averse (more risk tolerant), for example, with $A = 2$, she would adjust the expected rate of return downward by only 11.56%. In that case the

2A. What would you do if the goal were five years away?
   a. Sell
   b. Do nothing
   c. Buy more

2B. What would you do if the goal were 15 years away?
   a. Sell
   b. Do nothing
   c. Buy more

2C. What would you do if the goal were 30 years away?
   a. Sell
   b. Do nothing
   c. Buy more

3. The price of your retirement investment jumps 25% a month after you buy it. Again, the fundamentals haven't changed. After you finish gloating, what do you do?
   a. Sell it and lock in your gains
   b. Stay put and hope for more gain
   c. Buy more; it could go higher

4. You're investing for retirement, which is 15 years away. Which would you rather do?
   a. Invest in a money-market fund or guaranteed investment contract, giving up the possibility of major gains, but virtually assuring the safety of your principal
   b. Invest in a 50-50 mix of bond funds and stock funds, in hopes of getting some growth, but also giving yourself some protection in the form of steady income
   c. Invest in aggressive growth mutual funds whose value will probably fluctuate significantly during the year, but have the potential for impressive gains over five or 10 years

5. You just won a big prize! But which one? It's up to you.

   a. $2,000 in cash
   b. A 50% chance to win $5,000
   c. A 20% chance to win $15,000

6. A good investment opportunity just came along. But you have to borrow money to get in. Would you take out a loan?
   a. Definitely not
   b. Perhaps
   c. Yes

7. Your company is selling stock to its employees. In three years, management plans to take the company public. Until then, you won't be able to sell your shares and you will get no dividends. But your investment could multiply as much as 10 times when the company goes public. How much money would you invest?
   a. None
   b. Two months' salary
   c. Four months' salary

Scoring Your Risk Tolerance

To score the quiz, add up the number of answers you gave in each category a–c, then multiply as shown to find your score

(a)	answers	_____	× 1 =	_____	points
(b)	answers	_____	× 2 =	_____	points
(c)	answers	_____	× 3 =	_____	points

YOUR SCORE _____ points

If you scored...	You may be a:
9–14 points	Conservative investor
15–21 points	Moderate investor
22–27 points	Aggressive investor

Source: Reprinted with permission from *The Wall Street Journal.* © 1998 by Dow Jones & Company. All Rights Reserved Worldwide.

utility level of the portfolio would be 10.44%, higher than the risk-free rate, leading her to accept the prospect.

Question 3 • A portfolio has an expected rate of return of 20% and standard deviation of 20%. Bills offer a sure rate of return of 7%. Which investment alternative will be chosen by an investor whose $A = 4$? What if $A = 8$?

Because we can compare utility values to the rate offered on risk-free investments when choosing between a risky portfolio and a safe one, we may interpret a portfolio's utility value as its "certainty equivalent" rate of return to an investor. That is, the **certainty equivalent rate** of a portfolio is the rate that risk-free investments would need to offer with certainty to be considered equally attractive as the risky portfolio.

Figure 6.1

The trade-off between risk and return of a potential investment portfolio.

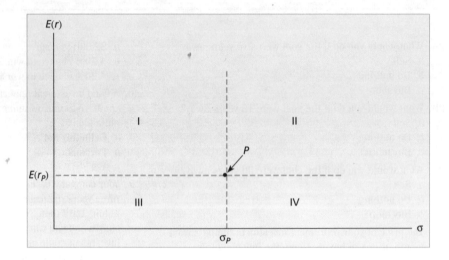

Now we can say that a portfolio is desirable only if its certainty equivalent return exceeds that of the risk-free alternative. A sufficiently risk-averse investor may assign any risky portfolio, even one with a positive risk premium, a certainty equivalent rate of return that is below the risk-free rate, which will cause the investor to reject the portfolio. At the same time, a less risk-averse (more risk-tolerant) investor will assign the same portfolio a certainty equivalent rate that exceeds the risk-free rate and thus will prefer the portfolio to the risk-free alternative. If the risk premium is zero or negative to begin with, any downward adjustment to utility only makes the portfolio look worse. Its certainty equivalent rate will be below that of the risk-free alternative for all risk-averse investors.

In contrast to risk-averse investors, **risk-neutral** investors judge risky prospects solely by their expected rates of return. The level of risk is irrelevant to the risk-neutral investor, meaning that there is no penalization for risk. For this investor a portfolio's certainty equivalent rate is simply its expected rate of return.

A **risk lover** is willing to engage in fair games and gambles; this investor adjusts the expected return upward to take into account the "fun" of confronting the prospect's risk. Risk lovers will always take a fair game because their upward adjustment of utility for risk gives the fair game a certainty equivalent that exceeds the alternative of the risk-free investment.

We can depict the individual's trade-off between risk and return by plotting the characteristics of potential investment portfolios that the individual would view as equally attractive on a graph with axes measuring the expected value and standard deviation of portfolio returns. Figure 6.1 plots the characteristics of one portfolio.

Portfolio P, which has expected return $E(r_P)$ and standard deviation σ_P, is preferred by risk-averse investors to any portfolio in quadrant IV because it has an expected return equal to or greater than any portfolio in that quadrant and a standard deviation equal to or smaller than any portfolio in that quadrant. Conversely, any portfolio in quadrant I is preferable to portfolio P because its expected return is equal to or greater than P's and its standard deviation is equal to or smaller than P's.

This is the mean-standard deviation, or equivalently, **mean-variance (M-V) criterion.** It can be stated as: A dominates B if

$$E(r_A) \geq E(r_B)$$

and

$$\sigma_A \leq \sigma_B$$

and at least one inequality is strict (rules out the equality).

Figure 6.2
The indifference
curve.

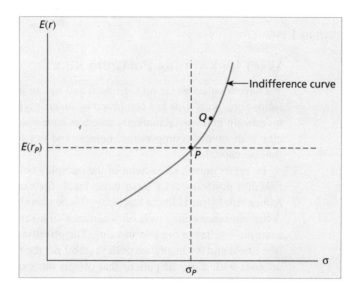

Table 6.1   Utility Values of Possible Portfolios

Expected Return, $E(r)$	Standard Deviation, σ	Utility = $E(r) - .005A\sigma^2$
10%	20.0%	$10 - .005 \times 4 \times 400 = 2$
15	25.5	$15 - .005 \times 4 \times 650 = 2$
20	30.0	$20 - .005 \times 4 \times 900 = 2$
25	33.9	$25 - .005 \times 4 \times 1,150 = 2$

In the expected return–standard deviation graph the preferred direction is northwest, because in this direction we simultaneously increase the expected return *and* decrease the variance of the rate of return. This means that any portfolio that lies northwest of *P* is superior to *P*.

What can be said about portfolios in the quadrants II and III? Their desirability, compared with *P*, depends on the exact nature of the investor's risk aversion. Suppose an investor identifies all portfolios that are equally attractive as portfolio *P*. Starting at *P*, an increase in standard deviation lowers utility; it must be compensated for by an increase in expected return. Thus point *Q* is equally desirable to this investor as *P*. Investors will be equally attracted to portfolios with high risk and high expected returns compared with other portfolios with lower risk but lower expected returns.

These equally preferred portfolios will lie on a curve in the mean–standard deviation graph that connects all portfolio points with the same utility value (Figure 6.2). This is called the **indifference curve.**

To determine some of the points that appear on the indifference curve, examine the utility values of several possible portfolios for an investor with $A = 4$, presented in Table 6.1. Note that each portfolio offers identical utility, because the high-return portfolios also have high risk. Although in practice the exact indifference curves of various investors cannot be known, this analysis can take us a long way in determining appropriate principles for portfolio selection strategy.

Concept

CHECK

Question 4

a. **How will the indifference curve of a less risk-averse investor compare to the indifference curve drawn in Figure 6.2?**

b. **Draw both indifference curves passing through point *P*.**

6.2   PORTFOLIO RISK

Asset Risk versus Portfolio Risk

We have focused so far on the return and risk of an individual's overall investment portfolio. Such portfolios are composed of diverse types of assets. In addition to their direct investment in financial markets, investors have stakes in pension funds, life insurance policies with savings components, homes, and not least, the earning power of their skills (human capital).

Investors must take account of the interplay between asset returns when evaluating the risk of a portfolio. At a most basic level, for example, an insurance contract serves to reduce risk by providing a large payoff when another part of the portfolio is faring poorly. A fire insurance policy pays off when another asset in the portfolio—a house or factory, for example—suffers a big loss in value. The offsetting patterns of returns on these two assets (the house and the insurance policy) stabilizes the risk of the overall portfolio. Investing in an asset with a payoff pattern that offsets our exposure to a particular source of risk is called **hedging.**

Insurance contracts are obvious hedging vehicles. In many contexts financial markets offer similar, although perhaps less direct, hedging opportunities. For example, consider two firms, one producing suntan lotion, the other producing umbrellas. The shareholders of each firm face weather risk of an opposite nature. A rainy summer lowers the return on the suntan-lotion firm but raises it on the umbrella firm. Shares of the umbrella firm act as "weather insurance" for the suntan-lotion firm shareholders in precisely the same way that fire insurance policies insure houses. When the lotion firm does poorly (bad weather), the "insurance" asset (umbrella shares) provides a high payoff that offsets the loss.

Another means to control portfolio risk is **diversification,** by which we mean that investments are made in a wide variety of assets so that the exposure to the risk of any particular security is limited. By placing one's eggs in many baskets, overall portfolio risk actually may be less than the risk of any component security considered in isolation.

To examine these effects more precisely, and to lay a foundation for the mathematical properties that will be used in coming chapters, we will consider an example with less than perfect hedging opportunities, and in the process review the statistics underlying portfolio risk and return characteristics.

A Review of Portfolio Mathematics

Consider the problem of Humanex, a nonprofit organization deriving most of its income from the return on its endowment. Years ago, the founders of Best Candy willed a large block of Best Candy stock to Humanex with the provision that Humanex may never sell it. This block of shares now comprises 50% of Humanex's endowment. Humanex has free choice as to where to invest the remainder of its portfolio.[2]

The value of Best Candy stock is sensitive to the price of sugar. In years when the Caribbean sugar crop fails, the price of sugar rises significantly and Best Candy suffers considerable losses. We can describe the fortunes of Best Candy stock using the following scenario analysis:

---

[2]The portfolio is admittedly unusual. We use this example only to illustrate the various strategies that might be used to control risk and to review some useful results from statistics.

	Normal Year for Sugar		Abnormal Year
	Bullish Stock Market	Bearish Stock Market	Sugar Crisis
Probability	.5	.3	.2
Rate of return	25%	10%	−25%

To summarize these three possible outcomes using conventional statistics, we review some of the key rules governing the properties of risky assets and portfolios.

Rule 1   The mean or **expected return** of an asset is a probability-weighted average of its return in all scenarios. Calling $\Pr(s)$ the probability of scenario s and $r(s)$ the return in scenario s, we may write the expected return, $E(r)$, as

$$E(r) = \sum_s \Pr(s)r(s) \tag{6.2}$$

Applying this formula to the case at hand, with three possible scenarios, we find that the expected rate of return of Best Candy's stock is

$$E(r_{\text{Best}}) = (.5 \times 25) + (.3 \times 10) + .2(-25)$$
$$= 10.5\%$$

Rule 2   The **variance** of an asset's returns is the expected value of the squared deviations from the expected return. Symbolically,

$$\sigma^2 = \sum_s \Pr(s)[r(s) - E(r)]^2 \tag{6.3}$$

Therefore, in our example

$$\sigma^2_{\text{Best}} = .5(25 - 10.5)^2 + .3(10 - 10.5)^2 + .2(-25 - 10.5)^2$$
$$= 357.25$$

The **standard deviation** of Best's return, which is the square root of the variance, is $\sqrt{357.25} = 18.9\%$.

Humanex has 50% of its endowment in Best's stock. To reduce the risk of the overall portfolio, it could invest the remainder in T-bills, which yield a sure rate of return of 5%. To derive the return of the overall portfolio, we apply rule 3.

Rule 3   The rate of return on a portfolio is a weighted average of the rates of return of each asset comprising the portfolio, with portfolio proportions as weights. This implies that the *expected* rate of return on a portfolio is a weighted average of the *expected* rate of return on each component asset.

In this case, the portfolio proportions in each asset are .5, and the portfolio's expected rate of return is

$$E(r_{\text{Humanex}}) = .5E(r_{\text{Best}}) + .5r_{\text{Bills}}$$
$$= (.5 \times 10.5) + (.5 \times 5)$$
$$= 7.75\%$$

The standard deviation of the portfolio may be derived from rule 4.

Rule 4   When a risky asset is combined with a risk-free asset, the portfolio standard deviation equals the risky asset's standard deviation multiplied by the portfolio proportion invested in the asset.

In this case, the Humanex portfolio is 50% invested in Best stock and 50% invested in risk-free bills. Therefore,

$$\sigma_{Humanex} = .5\sigma_{Best}$$
$$= .5 \times 18.9$$
$$= 9.45\%$$

By reducing its exposure to the risk of Best by half, Humanex reduces its portfolio standard deviation by half. The cost of this risk reduction, however, is a reduction in expected return. The expected rate of return on Best stock is 10.5%. The expected return on the one-half T-bill portfolio is 7.75%. This makes the risk premiums over the 5% rate on risk-free bills 5.5% for Best stock and 2.75% for the half T-bill portfolio. By reducing the share of Best stock in the portfolio by one-half, Humanex reduces its portfolio risk premium by one-half, from 5.5% to 2.75%.

In an effort to improve the contribution of the endowment to the operating budget, Humanex's trustees hire Sally, a recent MBA, as a consultant. Investigating the sugar and candy industry, Sally discovers, not surprisingly, that during years of sugar crisis in the Caribbean basin, SugarKane, a big Hawaiian sugar company, reaps unusual profits and its stock price soars. A scenario analysis of SugarKane's stock looks like this:

	Normal Year for Sugar		Abnormal Year
	Bullish Stock Market	Bearish Stock Market	Sugar Crisis
Probability	.5	.3	.2
Rate of return	1%	−5%	35%

The expected rate of return on SugarKane's stock is 6%, and its standard deviation is 14.73%. Thus SugarKane is almost as volatile as Best, yet its expected return is only a notch better than the T-bill rate. This cursory analysis makes SugarKane appear to be an unattractive investment. For Humanex, however, the stock holds great promise.

SugarKane offers excellent hedging potential for holders of Best stock because its return is highest precisely when Best's return is lowest—during a Caribbean sugar crisis. Consider Humanex's portfolio when it splits its investment evenly between Best and SugarKane. The rate of return for each scenario is the simple average of the rates on Best and SugarKane because the portfolio is split evenly between the two stocks (see rule 3).

	Normal Year for Sugar		Abnormal Year
	Bullish Stock Market	Bearish Stock Market	Sugar Crisis
Probability	.5	.3	.2
Rate of return	13.0%	2.5%	5.0%

The expected rate of return on Humanex's hedged portfolio is 8.25% with a standard deviation of 4.83%.

Sally now summarizes the reward and risk of the three alternatives:

Portfolio	Expected Return	Standard Deviation
All in Best Candy	10.50%	18.90%
Half in T-bills	7.575	9.45
Half in SugarKane	8.25	4.83

The numbers speak for themselves. The hedge portfolio including SugarKane clearly dominates the simple risk-reduction strategy of investing in safe T-bills. It has higher expected return *and* lower standard deviation than the one-half T-bill portfolio. The point is that, despite SugarKane's large standard deviation of return, it is a risk reducer for some investors—in this case, those holding Best stock.

The risk of the individual assets in the portfolio must be measured in the context of the effect of their return on overall portfolio variability. This example demonstrates that assets with returns that are inversely associated with the initial risky position are the most powerful risk reducers.

Concept  **Question 5 • Suppose that the stock market offers an expected rate of return of 20%, with a standard deviation of 15%. Gold has an expected rate of return of 18%, with a standard deviation of 17%. In view of the market's higher expected return and lower uncertainty, will anyone choose to hold gold in a portfolio?**

To quantify the hedging or diversification potential of an asset, we use the concepts of covariance and correlation. The **covariance** measures how much the returns on two risky assets move in tandem. A positive covariance means that asset returns move together. A negative covariance means that they vary inversely, as in the case of Best and SugarKane.

To measure covariance, we look at return "surprises," or deviations from expected value, in each scenario. Consider the product of each stock's deviation from expected return in a particular scenario:

$$[r_{Best} - E(r_{Best})][r_{Kane} - E(r_{Kane})]$$

This product will be positive if the returns of the two stocks move together across scenarios, that is, if both returns exceed their expectations or both fall short of those expectations in the scenario in question. On the other hand, if one stock's return exceeds its expected value when the other's falls short, the product will be negative. Thus a good measure of how much the returns move together is the *expected value* of this product across all scenarios, which is defined as the covariance:

$$\text{Cov}(r_{Best}, r_{Kane}) = \sum_s \text{Pr}(s)[r_{Best}(s) - E(r_{Best})][r_{Kane}(s) - E(r_{Kane})] \qquad (6.4)$$

In this example, with $E(r_{Best}) = 10.5\%$ and $E(r_{Kane}) = 6\%$, and with returns in each scenario summarized in the table at the top of the next page, we compute the covariance by applying equation 6.4. The covariance between the two stocks is

$$\text{Cov}(r_{Best}, r_{Kane}) = .5(25 - 10.5)(1 - 6)$$
$$+ .3(10 - 10.5)(-5 - 6) + .2(-25 - 10.5)(35 - 6)$$
$$= -240.5$$

The negative covariance confirms the hedging quality of SugarKane stock relative to Best Candy. SugarKane's returns move inversely with Best's.

	Normal Year for Sugar		Abnormal Year
	Bullish Stock Market	Bearish Stock Market	Sugar Crisis
Probability	.5	.3	.2
		Rate of Return (%)	
Best Candy	25	10	−25
SugarKane	1	−5	35

An easier statistic to interpret than the covariance is the **correlation coefficient,** which scales the covariance to a value between −1 (perfect negative correlation) and +1 (perfect positive correlation). The correlation coefficient between two variables equals their covariance divided by the product of the standard deviations. Denoting the correlation by the Greek letter ρ, we find that

$$\rho(\text{Best, SugarKane}) = \frac{\text{Cov}[r_{\text{Best}}, r_{\text{SugarKane}}]}{\sigma_{\text{Best}}\sigma_{\text{SugarKane}}}$$

$$= \frac{-240.5}{18.9 \times 14.73}$$

$$= -.86$$

This large negative correlation (close to −1) confirms the strong tendency of Best and SugarKane stocks to move inversely, or "out of phase" with one another.

The impact of the covariance of asset returns on portfolio risk is apparent in the following formula for portfolio variance.

Rule 5   When two risky assets with variances σ_1^2 and σ_2^2, respectively, are combined into a portfolio with portfolio weights w_1 and w_2, respectively, the portfolio variance σ_P^2 is given by

$$\sigma_P^2 = w_1^2\sigma_1^2 + w_2^2\sigma_2^2 + 2w_1w_2\text{Cov}(r_1, r_2)$$

In this example, with equal weights in Best and SugarKane, $w_1 = w_2 = .5$, and with $\sigma_{\text{Best}} = 18.9\%$, $\sigma_{\text{Kane}} = 14.73\%$, and $\text{Cov}(r_{\text{Best}}, r_{\text{Kane}}) = -240.5$, we find that

$$\sigma_P^2 = (.5^2 \times 18.9^2) + (.5^2 \times 14.73^2) + [2 \times .5 \times .5 \times (-240.5)] = 23.3$$

so that $\sigma_P = \sqrt{23.3} = 4.83\%$, precisely the same answer for the standard deviation of the returns on the hedged portfolio that we derived earlier from the scenario analysis.

Rule 5 for portfolio variance highlights the effect of covariance on portfolio risk. A positive covariance increases portfolio variance, and a negative covariance acts to reduce portfolio variance. This makes sense because returns on negatively correlated assets tend to be offsetting, which stabilizes portfolio returns.

Basically, hedging involves the purchase of a risky asset that is negatively correlated with the existing portfolio. This negative correlation makes the volatility of the hedge asset a risk-reducing feature. A hedge strategy is a powerful alternative to the simple risk-reduction strategy of including a risk-free asset in the portfolio.

In later chapters we will see that, in a rational market, hedge assets will offer relatively low expected rates of return. The perfect hedge, an insurance contract, is by design perfectly negatively correlated with a specified risk. As one would expect in a "no free lunch" world, the insurance premium reduces the portfolio's expected rate of return.

Concept
CHECK

Question 6 • **Suppose that the distribution of SugarKane stock were as follows:**

Bullish Stock Market	Bearish Stock Market	Sugar Crisis
7%	−5%	20%

a. **What would be its correlation with Best?**
b. **Is SugarKane stock a useful hedge asset now?**
c. **Calculate the portfolio rate of return in each scenario and the standard deviation of the portfolio from the scenario returns. Then evaluate σ_p using rule 5.**
d. **Are the two methods of computing portfolio standard deviations consistent?**

SUMMARY

1. Speculation is the undertaking of a risky investment for its risk premium. The risk premium has to be large enough to compensate a risk-averse investor for the risk of the investment.

2. A fair game is a risky prospect that has a zero-risk premium. It will not be undertaken by a risk-averse investor.

3. Investors' preferences toward the expected return and volatility of a portfolio may be expressed by a utility function that is higher for higher expected returns and lower for higher portfolio variances. More risk-averse investors will apply greater penalties for risk. We can describe these preferences graphically using indifference curves.

4. The desirability of a risky portfolio to a risk-averse investor may be summarized by the certainty equivalent value of the portfolio. The certainty equivalent rate of return is a value that, if it is received with certainty, would yield the same utility as the risky portfolio.

5. Hedging is the purchase of a risky asset to reduce the risk of a portfolio. The negative correlation between the hedge asset and the initial portfolio turns the volatility of the hedge asset into a risk-*reducing* feature. When a hedge asset is perfectly negatively correlated with the initial portfolio, it serves as a perfect hedge and works like an insurance contract on the portfolio.

Key Terms

risk premium	risk lover	expected return
risk averse	mean-variance (M-V)	variance
utility	criterion	standard deviation
certainty equivalent	indifference curve	covariance
rate	hedging	correlation
risk neutral	diversification	coefficient

Selected Readings

A classic work on risk and risk aversion is:
   Arrow, Kenneth. *Essays in the Theory of Risk Bearing*. Amsterdam: North Holland, 1971.
Some good statistics texts with business applications are:
   Levy, Haim; and Moshe Ben-Horim. *Statistics: Decisions and Applications in Business and Economics*. New York: Random House, 1984.
   Wonnacott, Thomas H.; and Ronald J. Wonnacott. *Introductory Statistics for Business and Economics*. New York: Wiley, 1984.

Problems

1. Consider a risky portfolio. The end-of-year cash flow derived from the portfolio will be either $70,000 or $200,000 with equal probabilities of .5. The alternative risk-free investment in T-bills pays 6% per year.

   a. If you require a risk premium of 8%, how much will you be willing to pay for the portfolio?

   b. Suppose that the portfolio can be purchased for the amount you found in (a). What will be the expected rate of return on the portfolio?

   c. Now suppose that you require a risk premium of 12%. What is the price that you will be willing to pay?

   d. Comparing your answers to (a) and (c), what do you conclude about the relationship between the required risk premium on a portfolio and the price at which the portfolio will sell?

2. Consider a portfolio that offers an expected rate of return of 12% and a standard deviation of 18%. T-bills offer a risk-free 7% rate of return. What is the maximum level of risk aversion for which the risky portfolio is still preferred to bills?

3. Draw the indifference curve in the expected return–standard deviation plane corresponding to a utility level of 5% for an investor with a risk aversion coefficient of 3. (Hint: Choose several possible standard deviations, ranging from 5% to 25%, and find the expected rates of return providing a utility level of 5%. Then plot the expected return–standard deviation points so derived.)

4. Now draw the indifference curve corresponding to a utility level of 4% for an investor with risk aversion coefficient $A = 4$. Comparing your answers to questions 3 and 4, what do you conclude?

5. Draw an indifference curve for a risk-neutral investor providing utility level 5%.

6. What must be true about the sign of the risk aversion coefficient, A, for a risk lover? Draw the indifference curve for a utility level of 5% for a risk lover.

Use the following data in answering questions 7, 8, and 9.

Utility Formula Data		
Investment	Expected Return $E(r)$	Standard Deviation σ
1	12%	30%
2	15	50
3	21	16
4	24	21

$$U = E(r) - .005A\sigma^2 \qquad \text{where} \quad A = 4$$

7. Based on the utility formula above, which investment would you select if you were risk averse with A = 4?
   a. 1.
   b. 2.
   c. 3.
   d. 4.

8. Based on the utility formula above, which investment would you select if you were risk neutral?
   a. 1.
   b. 2.
   c. 3.
   d. 4.

9. The variable (A) in the utility formula represents the:
   a. investor's return requirement.
   b. investor's aversion to risk.
   c. certainty-equivalent rate of the portfolio.
   d. preference for one unit of return per four units of risk.

Consider historical data showing that the average annual rate of return on the S&P 500 portfolio over the past 70 years has averaged about 8.5% more than the Treasury bill return and that the S&P 500 standard deviation has been about 20% per year. Assume these values are representative of investors' expectations for future performance and that the current T-bill rate is 5%. Use these values to answer questions 10 to 12.

10. Calculate the expected return and variance of portfolios invested in T-bills and the S&P 500 index with weights as follows:

W_{bills}	W_{index}
0	1.0
0.2	0.8
0.4	0.6
0.6	0.4
0.8	0.2
1.0	0

11. Calculate the utility levels of each portfolio of question 10 for an investor with A = 3. What do you conclude?

12. Repeat question 11 for an investor with A = 5. What do you conclude?

Reconsider the Best and SugarKane stock market hedging example in the text, but assume for questions 13 to 15 that the probability distribution of the rate of return on SugarKane stock is as follows:

	Bullish Stock Market	Bearish Stock Market	Sugar Crisis
Probability	.5	.3	.2
Rate of return	10%	−5%	20%

13. If Humanex's portfolio is half Best stock and half SugarKane, what are its expected return and standard deviation? Calculate the standard deviation from the portfolio returns in each scenario.

14. What is the covariance between Best and SugarKane?

15. Calculate the portfolio standard deviation using rule 5 and show that the result is consistent with your answer to question 13.

1. The expected rate of return on the risky portfolio is $22,000/$100,000 = .22, or 22%. The T-bill rate is 5%. The risk premium therefore is 22% − 5% = 17%.

2. The investor is taking on exchange rate risk by investing in a pound-denominated asset. If the exchange rate moves in the investor's favor, the investor will benefit and will earn more from the U.K. bill than the U.S. bill. For example, if both the U.S. and U.K. interest rates are 5 percent, and the current exchange rate is $1.50 per pound, a $1.50 investment today can buy one pound, which can be invested in England at a certain rate of 5 percent, for a year-end value of 1.05 pounds. If the year-end exchange rate is $1.60 per pound, the 1.05 pounds can be exchanged for 1.05 × $1.60 = $1.68 for a rate of return in dollars of $1 + r = $1.68/$1.50 = 1.12, or 12%, more than is available from U.S. bills. Therefore, if the investor expects favorable exchange rate movements, the U.K. bill is a speculative investment. Otherwise, it is a gamble.

3. For the $A = 4$ investor the utility of the risky portfolio is

$$U = 20 - (.005 \times 4 \times 20^2)$$
$$= 12$$

while the utility of bills is

$$U = 7 - (.005 \times 4 \times 0)$$
$$= 7$$

The investor will prefer the risky portfolio to bills. (Of course, a mixture of bills and the portfolio might be even better, but that is not a choice here.)
   For the $A = 8$ investor, the utility of the risky portfolio is

$$U = 20 - (.005 \times 8 \times 20^2)$$
$$= 4$$

while the utility of bills is again 7. The more risk-averse investor therefore prefers the risk-free alternative.

4. The less risk-averse investor has a shallower indifference curve. An increase in risk requires less increase in expected return to restore utility to the original level.

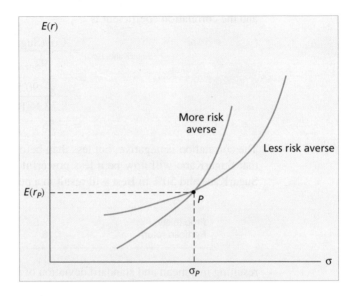

5. Despite the fact that gold investments *in isolation* seem dominated by the stock market, gold still might play a useful role in a diversified portfolio. Because gold and stock market returns have very low correlation, stock investors can reduce their portfolio risk by placing part of their portfolios in gold.

6. *a.* With the given distribution for SugarKane, the scenario analysis looks as follows:

	Normal Year for Sugar		Abnormal Year
	Bullish Stock Market	Bearish Stock Market	Sugar Crisis
Probability	.5	.3	.2
	Rate of Return (%)		
Best Candy	25	10	−25
SugarKane	7	−5	20
T-bills	5	5	5

The expected return and standard deviation of SugarKane is now

$$E(r_{\text{SugarKane}}) = (.5 \times 7) + .3(-5) + (.2 \times 20)$$
$$= 6$$

$$\sigma_{\text{SugarKane}} = [.5(7 - 6)^2 + .3(-5 - 6)^2 + .2(20 - 6)^2]^{1/2}$$
$$= 8.72$$

The covariance between the returns of Best and SugarKane is

$$\text{Cov(SugarKane, Best)} = .5(7 - 6)(25 - 10.5) + .3(-5 - 6)(10 - 10.5)$$
$$+ .2(20 - 6)(-25 - 10.5) = -90.5$$

and the correlation coefficient is

$$\rho_{(SugarKane, Best)} = \frac{Cov(SugarKane, Best)}{\sigma_{SugarKane}\sigma_{Best}}$$

$$= \frac{-90.5}{8.72 \times 18.90}$$

$$= -.55$$

The correlation is negative, but less than before (−.55 instead of −.86) so we expect that SugarKane will now be a less powerful hedge than before. Investing 50% in SugarKane and 50% in Best will result in a portfolio probability distribution of

Probability	.5	.3	.2
Portfolio return	16	2.5	−2.5

resulting in a mean and standard deviation of

$$E(r_{Hedged\ portfolio}) = (.5 \times 16) + (.3 \times 2.5) + .2(-2.5)$$
$$= 8.25$$

$$\sigma_{Hedged\ portfolio} = [.5(16 - 8.25)^2 + .3(2.5 - 8.25)^2 + .2(-2.5 - 8.25)^2]^{1/2}$$
$$= 7.94$$

b. It is obvious that even under these circumstances the hedging strategy dominates the risk-reducing strategy that uses T-bills (which results in $E(r) = 7.75\%$, $\sigma = 9.45\%$). At the same time, the standard deviation of the hedged position (7.94%) is not as low as it was using the original data.

c, d. Using rule 5 for portfolio variance, we would find that

$$\sigma^2 = (.5^2 \times \sigma^2_{Best}) + (.5^2 \times \sigma^2_{Kane}) + [2 \times .5 \times .5 \times Cov(SugarKane, Best)]$$
$$= (.5^2 \times 18.9^2) + (.5^2 \times 8.72^2) + [2 \times .5 \times .5 \times (-90.5)]$$
$$= 63.06$$

which implies that $\sigma = 7.94$, precisely the same result that we obtained by analyzing the scenarios directly.

APPENDIX A: A DEFENSE OF MEAN-VARIANCE ANALYSIS

Describing Probability Distributions

The axiom of risk aversion needs little defense. So far, however, our treatment of risk has been limiting in that it took the variance (or, equivalently, the standard deviation) of portfolio returns as an adequate risk measure. In situations in which variance alone is not adequate to measure risk this assumption is potentially restrictive. Here we provide some justification for mean-variance analysis.

The basic question is how one can best describe the uncertainty of portfolio rates of return. In principle, one could list all possible outcomes for the portfolio over a given period. If each outcome results in a payoff such as a dollar profit or rate of return, then this payoff value is the *random variable* in question. A list assigning a probability to all possible values of the random variable is called the probability distribution of the random variable.

The reward for holding a portfolio is typically measured by the expected rate of return across all possible scenarios, which equals

$$E(r) = \sum_{s=1}^{n} \Pr(s)r(s)$$

where $s = 1, \ldots, n$ are the possible outcomes or scenarios, $r(s)$ is the rate of return for outcome s, and $\Pr(s)$ is the probability associated with it.

Actually, the expected value or mean is not the only candidate for the central value of a probability distribution. Other candidates are the median and the mode.

The *median* is defined as the outcome value that exceeds the outcome values for half the population and is exceeded by the other half. Whereas the expected rate of return is a weighted average of the outcomes, the weights being the probabilities, the median is based on the rank order of the outcomes and takes into account only the order of the outcome values.

The median differs significantly from the mean in cases where the expected value is dominated by extreme values. One example is the income (or wealth) distribution in a population. A relatively small number of households command a disproportionate share of total income (and wealth). The mean income is "pulled up" by these extreme values, which makes it nonrepresentative. The median is free of this effect, since it equals the income level that is exceeded by half the population, regardless of by how much.

Finally, a third candidate for the measure of central value is the *mode*, which is the most likely value of the distribution or the outcome with the highest probability. However, the expected value is by far the most widely used measure of central or average tendency.

We now turn to the characterization of the risk implied by the nature of the probability distribution of returns. In general, it is impossible to quantify risk by a single number. The idea is to describe the likelihood and magnitudes of "surprises" (deviations from the mean) with as small a set of statistics as is needed for accuracy. The easiest way to accomplish this is to answer a set of questions in order of their informational value and to stop at the point where additional questions would not affect our notion of the risk–return trade-off.

The first question is, "What is a typical deviation from the expected value?" A natural answer would be, "The expected deviation from the expected value is _____." Unfortunately, this answer is not helpful because it is necessarily zero: Positive deviations from the mean are offset exactly by negative deviations.

There are two ways of getting around this problem. The first is to use the expected *absolute value* of the deviation which turns all deviations into positive values. This is known as MAD (mean absolute deviation), which is given by

$$\sum_{s=1}^{n} \Pr(s) \times \text{Absolute value}[r(s) - E(r)]$$

The second is to use the expected *squared* deviation from the mean, which also must be positive, and which is simply the variance of the probability distribution:

$$\sigma^2 = \sum_{s=1}^{n} \Pr(s)[r(s) - E(r)]^2$$

Note that the unit of measurement of the variance is "percent squared." To return to our original units, we compute the standard deviation as the square root of the variance, which is measured in percentage terms, as is the expected value. The variance also is called the

Figure 6A.1   Skewed probability distributions for rates of return on a portfolio.

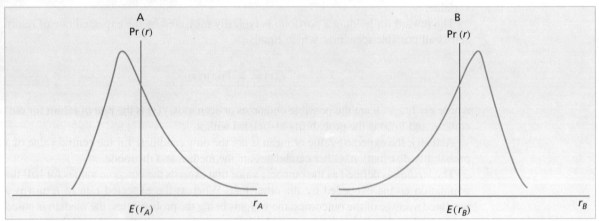

second central moment around the mean, with the expected return itself being the first moment.

Although the variance measures the average squared deviation from the expected value, it does not provide a full description of risk. To see why, consider the two probability distributions for rates of return on a portfolio, in Figure 6A.1.

A and *B* are probability distributions with identical expected values and variances. The graphs show that the variances are identical because probability distribution *B* is the mirror image of *A*.

What is the principal difference between *A* and *B*? *A* is characterized by more likely but small losses and less likely but extreme gains. This pattern is reversed in *B*. The difference is important. When we talk about risk, we really mean "*bad* surprises." The bad surprises in *A*, although they are more likely, are small (and limited) in magnitude. The bad surprises in *B* are more likely to be extreme. A risk-averse investor will prefer *A* to *B* on these grounds; hence it is worthwhile to quantify this characteristic. The asymmetry of the distribution is called *skewness*, which we measure by the third central moment, given by

$$M^3 = \sum_{s=1}^{n} \Pr(s)[r(s) - E(r)]^3$$

Cubing the deviations from expected value preserves their signs, which allows us to distinguish good from bad surprises. Because this procedure gives greater weight to larger deviations, it causes the "long tail" of the distribution to dominate the measure of skewness. Thus the skewness of the distribution will be positive for a right-skewed distribution such as *A* and negative for a left-skewed distribution such as *B*. The asymmetry is a relevant characteristic, although it is not as important as the magnitude of the standard deviation.

To summarize, the first moment (expected value) represents the reward. The second and higher central moments characterize the uncertainty of the reward. All the even moments (variance, M_4, etc.) represent the likelihood of extreme values. Larger values for these moments indicate greater uncertainty. The odd moments (M_3, M_5, etc.) represent measures of asymmetry. Positive numbers are associated with positive skewness and hence are desirable.

We can characterize the risk aversion of any investor by the preference scheme that the investor assigns to the various moments of the distribution. In other words, we can write the utility value derived from the probability distribution as

$$U = E(r) - b_0\sigma^2 + b_1 M_3 - b_2 M_4 + b_3 M_5 - \cdots$$

where the importance of the terms lessens as we proceed to higher moments. Notice that the "good" (odd) moments have positive coefficients, whereas the "bad" (even) moments have minus signs in front of the coefficients.

How many moments are needed to describe the investor's assessment of the probability distribution adequately? Samuelson's "Fundamental Approximation Theorem of Portfolio Analysis in Terms of Means, Variances, and Higher Moments"[3] proves that in many important circumstances:

1. The importance of all moments beyond the variance is much smaller than that of the expected value and variance. In other words, disregarding moments higher than the variance will not affect portfolio choice.

2. The variance is as important as the mean to investor welfare.

Samuelson's proof is the major theoretical justification for mean-variance analysis. Under the conditions of this proof mean and variance are equally important, and we can overlook all other moments without harm.

The major assumption that Samuelson makes to arrive at this conclusion concerns the "compactness" of the distribution of stock returns. The distribution of the rate of return on a portfolio is said to be compact if the risk can be controlled by the investor. Practically speaking, we test for compactness of the distribution by posing a question: Will the risk of my position in the portfolio decline if I hold it for a shorter period, and will the risk approach zero if I hold the portfolio for only an instant? If the answer is yes, then the distribution is compact.

In general, compactness may be viewed as being equivalent to continuity of stock prices. If stock prices do not take sudden jumps, then the uncertainty of stock returns over smaller and smaller time periods decreases. Under these circumstances investors who can rebalance their portfolios frequently will act so as to make higher moments of the stock return distribution so small as to be unimportant. It is not that skewness, for example, does not matter in principle. It is, instead, that the actions of investors in frequently revising their portfolios will limit higher moments to negligible levels.

Continuity or compactness is not, however, an innocuous assumption. Portfolio revisions entail transaction costs, meaning that rebalancing must of necessity be somewhat limited and that skewness and other higher moments cannot entirely be ignored. Compactness also rules out such phenomena as the major stock price jumps that occur in response to takeover attempts. It also rules out such dramatic events as the 25% one-day decline of the stock market on October 19, 1987. Except for these relatively unusual events, however, mean-variance analysis is adequate. In most cases, if the portfolio may be revised frequently, we need to worry about the mean and variance only.

Portfolio theory, for the most part, is built on the assumption that the conditions for mean-variance (or mean–standard deviation) analysis are satisfied. Accordingly, we typically ignore higher moments.

Concept
CHECK

Question A.1 • How does the simultaneous popularity of both lotteries and insurance policies confirm the notion that individuals prefer positive to negative skewness of portfolio returns?

---

[3]Paul A. Samuelson, "The Fundamental Approximation Theorem of Portfolio Analysis in Terms of Means, Variances, and Higher Moments," *Review of Economic Studies* 37 (1970).

Table 6A.1   Frequency Distribution of Rates of Return from a One-Year Investment in Randomly Selected Portfolios from NYSE-Listed Stocks

Statistic	N = 1		N = 8		N = 32		N = 128	
	Observed	Normal	Observed	Normal	Observed	Normal	Observed	Normal
Minimum	−71.1	NA	−12.4	NA	6.5	NA	16.4	NA
5th centile	−14.4	−39.2	8.1	4.6	17.4	16.7	22.7	22.6
20th centile	−.5	6.3	16.3	16.1	22.2	22.3	25.3	25.3
50th centile	19.6	28.2	26.4	28.2	27.8	28.2	28.1	28.2
70th centile	38.7	49.7	33.8	35.7	31.6	32.9	30.0	30.0
95th centile	96.3	95.6	54.3	51.8	40.9	39.9	34.1	33.8
Maximum	442.6	NA	136.7	NA	73.7	NA	43.1	NA
Mean	28.2	28.2	28.2	28.2	28.2	28.2	28.2	28.2
Standard deviation	41.0	41.0	14.4	14.4	7.1	7.1	3.4	3.4
Skewness (M_3)	255.4	0.0	88.7	0.0	44.5	0.0	17.7	0.0
Sample size	1,227	—	131,072	—	32,768	—	16,384	—

Source: Lawrence Fisher and James H. Lorie, "Some Studies of Variability of Returns on Investments in Common Stocks," Journal of Business 43 (April 1970).

Normal and Lognormal Distributions

Modern portfolio theory, for the most part, assumes that asset returns are normally distributed. This is a convenient assumption because the normal distribution can be described completely by its mean and variance, consistent with mean-variance analysis. The argument has been that even if individual asset returns are not exactly normal, the distribution of returns of a large portfolio will resemble a normal distribution quite closely.

The data support this argument. Table 6A.1 shows summaries of the results of one-year investments in many portfolios selected randomly from NYSE stocks. The portfolios are listed in order of increasing degrees of diversification; that is, the numbers of stocks in each portfolio sample are 1, 8, 32, and 128. The percentiles of the distribution of returns for each portfolio are compared to what one would have expected from portfolios identical in mean and variance but drawn from a normal distribution.

Looking first at the single-stock portfolio ($n = 1$), the departure of the return distribution from normality is significant. The mean of the sample is 28.2%, and the standard deviation is 41.0%. In the case of normal distribution with the same mean and standard deviation, we would expect the fifth percentile stock to lose 39.2%, but the fifth percentile stock actually lost 14.4%. In addition, although the normal distribution's mean coincides with its median, the actual sample median of the single stock was 19.6%, far below the sample mean of 28.2%.

In contrast, the returns of the 128-stock portfolio are virtually identical in distribution to the hypothetical normally distributed portfolio. The normal distribution therefore is a pretty good working assumption for well-diversified portfolios. How large a portfolio must be for this result to take hold depends on how far the distribution of the individual stocks is from normality. It appears from the table that a portfolio typically must include at least 32 stocks for the one-year return to be close to normally distributed.

There remain theoretical objections to the assumption that individual stock returns are normally distributed. Given that a stock price cannot be negative, the normal distribution cannot be truly representative of the behavior of a holding-period rate of return because it allows for any outcome, including the whole range of negative prices. Specifically, rates of return lower than −100% are theoretically impossible because they imply the possibility of negative security prices. The failure of the normal distribution to rule out such outcomes must be viewed as a shortcoming.

Figure 6A.2

The lognormal distribution for three values of σ.

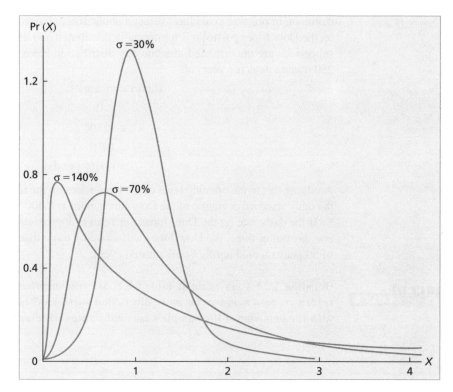

Source: J. Atchison and J. A. C. Brown, The Lognormal Distribution (New York: Cambridge University Press, 1976).

An alternative assumption is that the continuously compounded annual rate of return is normally distributed. If we call this rate r and we call the effective annual rate r_e, then $r_e = e^r - 1$, and because e^r can never be negative, the smallest possible value for r_e is -1, or -100%. Thus this assumption nicely rules out the troublesome possibility of negative prices while still conveying the advantages of working with normal distributions. Under this assumption the distribution of r_e will be *lognormal*. This distribution is depicted in Figure 6A.2.

Call $r_e(t)$ the effective rate over an investment period of length t. For *short* holding periods, that is, where t is small, the approximation of $r_e(t) = e^{rt} - 1$ by rt is quite accurate and the normal distribution provides a good approximation to the lognormal. With rt normally distributed, the effective annual return over short time periods may be taken as approximately normally distributed.

For short holding periods, therefore, the mean and standard deviation of the effective holding-period returns are proportional to the mean and standard deviation of the annual, continuously compounded rate of return on the stock and to the time interval.

Therefore, if the standard deviation of the annual continuously compounded rate of return on a stock is 40% ($\sigma = .40$ and $\sigma^2 = .16$), then the variance of the holding period return for one month, for example, is for all practical purposes

$$\sigma^2(\text{monthly}) = \frac{\sigma^2}{12} = \frac{.16}{12} = .0133$$

and the monthly standard deviation is $\sqrt{.0133} = .1155$.

To illustrate this principle, suppose that the Dow Jones Industrial Average went up one day by 50 points from 8,400 to 8,450. Is this a "large" move? Looking at annual, continuously compounded rates on the Dow Jones portfolio, we find that the annual standard deviation in postwar years has averaged about 16%. Under the assumption that the return on the Dow Jones portfolio is lognormally distributed and that returns between successive subperiods are uncorrelated, the one-day distribution has a standard deviation (based on 250 trading days per year) of

$$\sigma(\text{day}) = \sigma(\text{year})\sqrt{1/250}$$
$$= \frac{.16}{\sqrt{250}}$$
$$= .0101$$
$$= 1.01\% \text{ per day}$$

Applying this to the opening level of the Dow Jones on the trading day, 8,400, we find that the daily standard deviation of the Dow Jones index is $8,400 \times .0101 = 84.8$ points per day.

If the daily rate on the Dow Jones portfolio is approximately normal, we know that in one day out of three, the Dow Jones will move by more than 1% either way. Thus a move of 50 points would hardly be an unusual event.

Concept CHECK

Question A.2 • Look again at Table 6A.1. Are you surprised that the minimum rates of return are less negative for more diversified portfolios? Is your explanation consistent with the behavior of the sample's maximum rates of return?

SUMMARY: APPENDIX A

1. The probability distribution of the rate of return can be characterized by its moments. The reward from taking the risk is measured by the first moment, which is the mean of the return distribution. Higher moments characterize the risk. Even moments provide information on the likelihood of extreme values, and odd moments provide information on the asymmetry of the distribution.

2. Investors' risk preferences can be characterized by their preferences for the various moments of the distribution. The fundamental approximation theorem shows that when portfolios are revised often enough, and prices are continuous, the desirability of a portfolio can be measured by its mean and variance alone.

3. The rates of return on well-diversified portfolios for holding periods that are not too long can be approximated by a normal distribution. For short holding periods (up to one month), the normal distribution is a good approximation for the lognormal.

Problem: Appendix A

1. The Smartstock investment consulting group prepared the following scenario analysis for the end-of-year dividend and stock price of Klink Inc., which is selling now at $12 per share:

		End-of-Year	
Scenario	Probability	Dividend ($)	Price ($)
1	.10	0	0
2	.20	0.25	2.00
3	.40	0.40	14.00
4	.25	0.60	20.00
5	.05	0.85	30.00

Compute the rate of return for each scenario and
a. The mean, median, and mode.
b. The standard deviation and mean absolute deviation.
c. The first moment, and the second and third moments around the mean. Is the probability distribution of Klink stock positively skewed?

A.1. Investors appear to be more sensitive to extreme outcomes relative to moderate outcomes than variance and higher *even* moments can explain. Casual evidence suggests that investors are eager to insure extreme losses and express great enthusiasm for highly positively skewed lotteries. This hypothesis is, however, extremely difficult to prove with properly controlled experiments.

A.2. The better diversified the portfolio, the smaller is its standard deviation, as the sample standard deviations of Table 6A.1 confirm. When we draw from distributions with smaller standard deviations, the probability of extreme values shrinks. Thus the expected smallest and largest values from a sample get closer to the mean value as the standard deviation gets smaller. This expectation is confirmed by the samples of Table 6A.1 for both the sample maximum and minimum annual rate.

APPENDIX B: RISK AVERSION AND EXPECTED UTILITY

We digress here to examine the rationale behind our contention that investors are risk averse. Recognition of risk aversion as central in investment decisions goes back at least to 1738. Daniel Bernoulli, one of a famous Swiss family of distinguished mathematicians, spent the years 1725 through 1733 in St. Petersburg, where he analyzed the following coin-toss game. To enter the game one pays an entry fee. Thereafter, a coin is tossed until the *first* head appears. The number of tails, denoted by n, that appears until the first head is tossed is used to compute the payoff, R, to the participant, as

$$R(n) = 2^n$$

The probability of no tails before the first head ($n = 0$) is $\frac{1}{2}$ and the corresponding payoff is $2^0 = \$1$. The probability of one tail and then heads ($n = 1$) is $\frac{1}{2} \times \frac{1}{2}$ with payoff $2^1 = \$2$, the probability of two tails and then heads ($n = 2$) is $\frac{1}{2} \times \frac{1}{2} \times \frac{1}{2}$, and so forth.

The following table illustrates the probabilities and payoffs for various outcomes:

Tails	Probability	Payoff = $R(n)$	Probability × Payoff
0	$\frac{1}{2}$	$1	$1/2
1	$\frac{1}{4}$	$2	$1/2
2	$\frac{1}{8}$	$4	$1/2
3	$\frac{1}{16}$	$8	$1/2
·	·	·	·
·	·	·	·
·	·	·	·
n	$(1/2)^{n+1}$	$2^n	$1/2

The expected payoff is therefore

$$E(R) = \sum_{n=0}^{\infty} \Pr(n)R(n)$$
$$= 1/2 + 1/2 + \cdots$$
$$= \infty$$

The evaluation of this game is called the "St. Petersburg Paradox." Although the expected payoff is infinite, participants obviously will be willing to purchase tickets to play the game only at a finite, and possibly quite modest, entry fee.

Bernoulli resolved the paradox by noting that investors do not assign the same value per dollar to all payoffs. Specifically, the greater their wealth, the less their "appreciation" for each extra dollar. We can make this insight mathematically precise by assigning a welfare or utility value to any level of investor wealth. Our utility function should increase as wealth is higher, but each extra dollar of wealth should increase utility by progressively smaller amounts.[4] (Modern economists would say that investors exhibit "decreasing marginal utility" from an additional payoff dollar.) One particular function that assigns a subjective value to the investor from a payoff of $R, which has a smaller value per dollar the greater the payoff, is the function $\log(R)$. If this function measures utility values of wealth, the subjective utility value of the game is indeed finite.[5] The certain wealth level necessary to yield this utility value is $2.00, because $\log(2.00) = .693$. Hence the certainty equivalent value of the risky payoff is $2.00, which is the maximum amount that this investor will pay to play the game.

Von Neumann and Morgenstern adapted this approach to investment theory in a complete axiomatic system in 1946. Avoiding unnecessary technical detail, we restrict ourselves here to an intuitive exposition of the rationale for risk aversion.

Imagine two individuals who are identical twins, except that one of them is less fortunate than the other. Peter has only $1,000 to his name while Paul has a net worth of $200,000. How many hours of work would each twin be willing to offer to earn one extra dollar? It is likely that Peter (the poor twin) has more essential uses for the extra money than does Paul. Therefore, Peter will offer more hours. In other words, Peter derives a greater personal welfare or assigns a greater "utility" value to the 1,001st dollar than Paul does to the 200,001st. Figure 6B.1 depicts graphically the relationship between the wealth and the utility value of wealth that is consistent with this notion of decreasing marginal utility.

Individuals have different rates of decrease in their marginal utility of wealth. What is constant is the *principle* that the per-dollar increment to utility decreases with wealth. Functions that exhibit the property of decreasing per-unit value as the number of units grows are called concave. A simple example is the log function, familiar from high school mathematics. Of course, a log function will not fit all investors, but it is consistent with the risk aversion that we assume for all investors.

Now consider the following simple prospect:

---

[4]This utility is similar in spirit to the one that assigns a satisfaction level to portfolios with given risk and return attributes. However, the utility function here refers not to investors' satisfaction with alternative portfolio choices but only to the subjective welfare they derive from different levels of wealth.

[5]If we substitute the "utility" value, $\log(R)$, for the dollar payoff, R, to obtain an expected utility value of the game (rather than expected dollar value), we have, calling $V(R)$ the expected utility,

$$V(R) = \sum_{n=0}^{\infty} \Pr(n)\log[R(n)] = \sum_{n=0}^{\infty} (1/2)^{n+1}\log(2^n) = .693$$

Figure 6B.1

Utility of wealth with a log utility function.

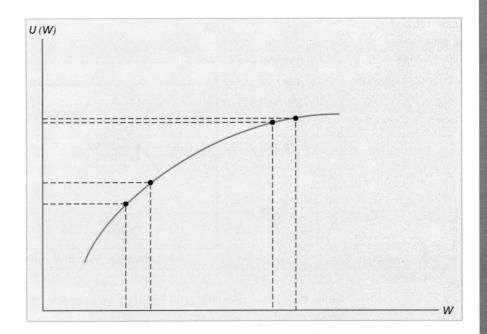

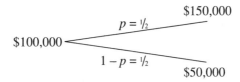

This is a fair game in that the expected profit is zero. Suppose, however, that the curve in Figure 6B.1 represents the investor's utility value of wealth, assuming a log utility function. Figure 6B.2 shows this curve with numerical values marked.

Figure 6B.2 shows that the loss in utility from losing $50,000 exceeds the gain from winning $50,000. Consider the gain first. With probability $p = .5$, wealth goes from $100,000 to $150,000. Using the log utility function, utility goes from $\log(100,000) = 11.51$ to $\log(150,000) = 11.92$, the distance G on the graph. This gain is $G = 11.92 - 11.51 = .41$. In expected utility terms, then, the gain is $pG = .5 \times .41 = .21$.

Now consider the possibility of coming up on the short end of the prospect. In that case, wealth goes from $100,000 to $50,000. The loss in utility, the distance L on the graph, is $L = \log(100,000) - \log(50,000) = 11.51 - 10.82 = .69$. Thus the loss in expected utility terms is $(1 - p)L = .5 \times .69 = .35$, which exceeds the gain in expected utility from the possibility of winning the game.

We compute the expected utility from the risky prospect:

$$E[U(W)] = pU(W_1) + (1 - p)U(W_2)$$
$$= \tfrac{1}{2}\log(50,000) + \tfrac{1}{2}\log(150,000)$$
$$= 11.37$$

If the prospect is rejected, the utility value of the (sure) $100,000 is $\log(100,000) = 11.51$, greater than that of the fair game (11.37). Hence the risk-averse investor will reject the fair game.

Using a specific investor utility function (such as the log utility function) allows us to compute the certainty equivalent value of the risky prospect to a given investor, Mary

Figure 6B.2
Fair games and
expected utility.

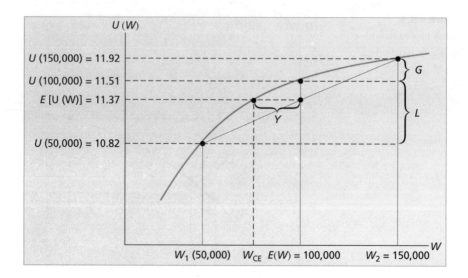

Smith. This is the amount that, if received with certainty, Mary would consider equally attractive as the risky prospect.

If log utility describes Mary's preferences toward wealth outcomes, then Figure 6B.2 can also tell us what is, for her, the dollar value of the prospect. We ask, "What sure level of wealth has a utility value of 11.37 (which equals the expected utility from the prospect)?" A horizontal line drawn at the level 11.37 intersects the utility curve at the level of wealth W_{CE}. This means that

$$\log(W_{CE}) = 11.37$$

which implies that

$$W_{CE} = e^{11.37}$$
$$= \$86,681.87$$

W_{CE} is therefore the certainty equivalent of the prospect. The distance Y in Figure 6B.2 is the penalty, or the downward adjustment, to the expected profit that is attributable to the risk of the prospect.

$$Y = E(W) - W_{CE}$$
$$= \$100,000 - \$86,681.87$$
$$= \$13,318.13$$

Smith views $86,681.87 for certain as being equal in utility value as $100,000 at risk. Therefore, she would be indifferent between the two.

Concept **CHECK**

Question B.1 • Suppose the utility function is $U(W) = \sqrt{W}$.
a. What is the utility level at wealth levels $50,000 and $150,000?
b. What is expected utility if p still equals .5?
c. What is the certainty equivalent of the risky prospect?
d. Does this utility function also display risk aversion?
e. Does this utility function display more or less risk aversion than the log utility function?

Does revealed behavior of investors demonstrate risk aversion? Looking at prices and past rates of return in financial markets, we can answer with a resounding "yes." With remarkable consistency, riskier bonds are sold at lower prices than are safer ones with otherwise similar characteristics. Riskier stocks also have provided higher average rates of return over long periods of time than less risky assets such as T-bills. For example, over the 1926 to 1996 period, the average rate of return on the S&P 500 portfolio exceeded the T-bill return by about 8.5% per year.

It is abundantly clear from financial data that the average, or representative, investor exhibits substantial risk aversion. For readers who recognize that financial assets are priced to compensate for risk by providing a risk premium and at the same time feel the urge for some gambling, we have a constructive recommendation: Direct your gambling desire to investment in financial markets. As Von Neumann once said, "The stock market is a casino with the odds in your favor." A small risk-seeking investment may provide all the excitement you want with a positive expected return to boot!

Problems: Appendix B

1. Suppose that your wealth is $250,000. You buy a $200,000 house and invest the remainder in a risk-free asset paying an annual interest rate of 6%. There is a probability of .001 that your house will burn to the ground and its value will be reduced to zero. With a log utility of end-of-year wealth, how much would you be willing to pay for insurance (at the beginning of the year)? (Assume that, if the house does not burn down, its end-of-year value still will be $200,000.)

2. If the cost of insuring your house is $1 per $1,000 of value, what will be the certainty equivalent of your end-of-year wealth if you insure your house at:
   a. ½ its value.
   b. Its full value.
   c. 1½ times its value.

solution to Concept CHECKS

B.1. *a.*
$$U(W) = \sqrt{W}$$
$$U(50,000) = \sqrt{50,000}$$
$$= 223.61$$
$$U(150,000) = 387.30$$

b. $E(U) = (.5 \times 223.61) + (.5 \times 387.30)$
$$= 305.45$$

c. We must find W_{CE} that has utility level 305.45. Therefore
$$\sqrt{W_{CE}} = 305.45$$
$$W_{CE} = 305.45^2$$
$$= \$93,301$$

d. Yes. The certainty equivalent of the risky venture is less than the expected outcome of $100,000.

e. The certainty equivalent of the risky venture to this investor is greater than it was for the log utility investor considered in the text. Hence this utility function displays less risk aversion.

CAPITAL ALLOCATION BETWEEN THE RISKY ASSET AND THE RISK-FREE ASSET

Portfolio managers seek to achieve the best possible trade-off between risk and return. A top-down analysis of their strategies starts with the broadest choices concerning the makeup of the portfolio.   For example, the **capital allocation decision** is the choice of the proportion of the overall portfolio to place in safe but low-return money market securities versus risky but higher-return securities like stocks. The choice of the fraction of funds apportioned to risky investments is the first part of the investor's **asset allocation decision,** which describes the distribution of risky investments across broad asset classes—stocks, bonds, real estate, foreign assets, and so on. Finally, the **security selection decision** describes the choice of which particular securities to hold within each asset class.   The top-down analysis of portfolio construction has much to recommend it. Most institutional investors follow a top-down approach. Capital allocation and asset allocation decisions will be made at a high organizational level, with the choice of the specific securities to hold within each asset class delegated to particular portfolio managers. Individual investors typically follow a less-structured approach to money management, but they also typically give priority to broader allocation issues. For example, an individual's first decision is usually how much of his or her wealth must be left in a safe bank or money market account.   This chapter treats the broadest part of the asset allocation decision, capital allocation between risk-free assets versus the risky portion of the portfolio. We will take the composition of the risky portfolio as given and refer to it as "the" **risky asset.** In Chapter 8 we will examine how the composition of the risky portfolio may best be determined. For now, however, we start our "top-down journey" by asking how an investor decides how much to invest in the risky versus the risk-free asset.   This capital allocation problem may be solved in two stages. First we determine the risk–return trade-off encountered when choosing between the risky and risk-free assets. Then we show how risk aversion determines the optimal mix of the two assets. This analysis leads us to examine so-called passive strategies, which call for allocation of the portfolio between a (risk-free) money market fund and an index fund of common stocks.

7.1   CAPITAL ALLOCATION ACROSS RISKY AND RISK-FREE PORTFOLIOS

History shows us that long-term bonds have been riskier investments than investments in Treasury bills, and that stock investments have been riskier still. On the other hand, the riskier investments have offered higher average returns. Investors, of course, do not make all-or-nothing choices from these investment classes. They can and do construct their portfolios using securities from all asset classes. Some of the portfolio may be in risk-free Treasury bills, some in high-risk stocks.

The most straightforward way to control the risk of the portfolio is through the fraction of the portfolio invested in Treasury bills and other safe money market securities versus risky assets. This capital allocation decision is an example of an asset allocation choice—a choice among broad investment classes, rather than among the specific securities within each asset class. Most investment professionals consider asset allocation the most important part of portfolio construction. Consider this statement by John Bogle, made when he was chairman of the Vanguard Group of Investment Companies:

> The most fundamental decision of investing is the allocation of your assets: How much should you own in stock? How much should you own in bonds? How much should you own in cash reserves? . . . That decision [has been shown to account] for an astonishing 94% of the differences in total returns achieved by institutionally managed pension funds . . . There is no reason to believe that the same relationship does not also hold true for individual investors.[1]

Therefore, we start our discussion of the risk–return trade-off available to investors by examining the most basic asset allocation choice: the choice of how much of the portfolio to place in risk-free money market securities versus other risky asset classes.

We will denote the investor's portfolio of risky assets as *P* and the risk-free asset as *F*. We will assume for the sake of illustration that the risky component of the investor's overall portfolio is comprised of two mutual funds, one invested in stocks and the other invested in long-term bonds. For now, we take the composition of the risky portfolio as given and focus only on the allocation between it and risk-free securities. In the next chapter, we turn to asset allocation and security selection across risky assets.

When we shift wealth from the risky portfolio to the risk-free asset, we do not change the relative proportions of the various risky assets within the risky portfolio. Rather, we reduce the relative weight of the risky portfolio as a whole in favor of risk-free assets.

---

[1]John C. Bogle, *Bogle on Mutual Funds* (Burr Ridge, IL: Irwin Professional Publishing, 1994), p. 235.

For example, assume that the total market value of an initial portfolio is $300,000, of which $90,000 is invested in the Ready Asset money market fund, a risk-free asset for practical purposes. The remaining $210,000 is invested in risky equity securities—$113,400 in IBM and $96,600 in GM. The IBM and GM holding is "the" risky portfolio, 54% in IBM and 46% in GM:

$$\text{IBM:} \qquad w_1 = \frac{113,400}{210,000} = .54$$

$$\text{GM:} \qquad w_2 = \frac{96,600}{210,000} = .46$$

The weight of the risky portfolio, P, in the **complete portfolio,** including risk-free investments, is denoted by y:

$$y = \frac{210,000}{300,000} = .7 \text{ (risky assets)}$$

$$1 - y = \frac{90,000}{300,000} = .3 \text{ (risk-free assets)}$$

The weights of each stock in the complete portfolio are as follows:

$$\text{IBM:} \qquad \frac{\$113,400}{\$300,000} = .378$$

$$\text{GM:} \qquad \frac{\$96,600}{\$300,000} = .322$$

$$\text{Risky portfolio} \qquad\qquad = .700$$

The risky portfolio is 70% of the complete portfolio.

Suppose that the owner of this portfolio wishes to decrease risk by reducing the allocation to the risky portfolio from $y = .7$ to $y = .56$. The risky portfolio would total only $168,000 (.56 × $300,000 = $168,000), requiring the sale of $42,000 of the original $210,000 risky holdings, with the proceeds used to purchase more shares in Ready Asset (the money market fund). Total holdings in the risk-free asset will increase to $300,000 × $(1 - .56) = $132,000$, or the original holdings plus the new contribution to the money market fund:

$$\$90,000 + \$42,000 = \$132,000$$

The key point, however, is that we leave the proportions of each stock in the risky portfolio unchanged. Because the weights of IBM and GM in the risky portfolio are .54 and .46, respectively, we sell .54 × $42,000 = $22,680 of IBM and .46 × $42,000 = $19,320 of GM. After the sale, the proportions of each stock in the risky portfolio are in fact unchanged:

$$\text{IBM:} \qquad w_1 = \frac{113,400 - 22,680}{210,000 - 42,000} = .54$$

$$\text{GM:} \qquad w_2 = \frac{96,600 - 19,320}{210,000 - 42,000} = .46$$

Rather than thinking of our risky holdings as IBM and GM stock separately, we may view our holdings as if they were in a single fund that holds IBM and GM in fixed proportions. In this sense we treat the risky fund as a single risky asset, that asset being a particular bundle of securities. As we shift in and out of safe assets, we simply alter our holdings of that bundle of securities commensurately.

Given this simplification, we can now turn to the desirability of reducing risk by changing the risky/risk-free asset mix, that is, reducing risk by decreasing the proportion *y*. As long as we do not alter the weights of each security within the risky portfolio, the probability distribution of the rate of return on the risky portfolio remains unchanged by the asset reallocation. What will change is the probability distribution of the rate of return on the *complete* portfolio that consists of the risky asset and the risk-free asset.

Question 1 • What will be the dollar value of your position in IBM, and its proportion in your overall portfolio, if you decide to hold 50% of your investment budget in Ready Asset?

7.2   THE RISK-FREE ASSET

By virtue of its power to tax and control the money supply, only the government can issue default-free bonds. Even the default-free guarantee by itself is not sufficient to make the bonds risk-free in real terms. The only risk-free asset in real terms would be a perfectly price-indexed bond. Moreover, a default-free perfectly indexed bond offers a guaranteed real rate to an investor only if the maturity of the bond is identical to the investor's desired holding period. Even indexed bonds are subject to interest rate risk, because real interest rates change unpredictably through time. When future real rates are uncertain, so is the future price of indexed bonds.

Nevertheless, it is common practice to view Treasury bills as "the" **risk-free asset.** Their short-term nature makes their values insensitive to interest rate fluctuations. Indeed, an investor can lock in a short-term nominal return by buying a bill and holding it to maturity. Moreover, inflation uncertainty over the course of a few weeks, or even months, is negligible compared with the uncertainty of stock market returns.

In practice, most investors use a broader range of money market instruments as a risk-free asset. All the money market instruments are virtually free of interest rate risk because of their short maturities and are fairly safe in terms of default or credit risk.

Most money market funds hold, for the most part, three types of securities—Treasury bills, bank certificates of deposit (CDs), and commercial paper (CP)—differing slightly in their default risk. The yields to maturity on CDs and CP for identical maturity, for example, are always somewhat higher than those of T-bills. The pattern of this yield spread for 90-day CDs is shown in Figure 7.1.

Money market funds have changed their relative holdings of these securities over time but, by and large, T-bills make up only about 15% of their portfolios. Nevertheless, the risk of such blue-chip short-term investments as CDs and CP is minuscule compared with that of most other assets such as long-term corporate bonds, common stocks, or real estate. Hence we treat money market funds as the most easily accessible risk-free asset for most investors.

Figure 7.1

Spread between three-month CD and T-bill rates.

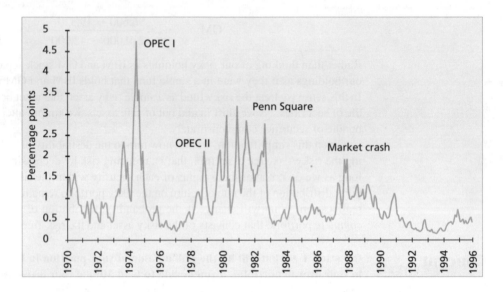

7.3 ## PORTFOLIOS OF ONE RISKY ASSET AND ONE RISK-FREE ASSET

In this section we examine the risk–return combinations available to investors. This is the "technological" part of asset allocation; it deals only with the opportunities available to investors given the features of the broad asset markets in which they can invest. In the next section we address the "personal" part of the problem—the specific individual's choice of the best risk–return combination from the set of feasible combinations.

Suppose that the investor has already decided on the composition of the optimal risky portfolio. The investment proportions in all the available risky assets are known. Now the final concern is with the proportion of the investment budget, y, to be allocated to the risky portfolio, P. The remaining proportion, $1 - y$, is to be invested in the risk-free asset, F.

Denote the risky rate of return by r_P and denote the expected rate of return on P by $E(r_P)$ and its standard deviation by σ_P. The rate of return on the risk-free asset is denoted as r_f. In the numerical example we assume that $E(r_P) = 15\%$, $\sigma_P = 22\%$, and that the risk-free rate is $r_f = 7\%$. Thus the risk premium on the risky asset is $E(r_P) - r_f = 8\%$.

With a proportion, y, in the risky portfolio, and $1 - y$ in the risk-free asset, the rate of return on the *complete* portfolio, denoted C, is r_C where

$$r_C = yr_P + (1 - y)r_f$$

Taking the expectation of this portfolio's rate of return,

$$\begin{aligned} E(r_C) &= yE(r_P) + (1 - y)r_f \\ &= r_f + y[E(r_P) - r_f] \\ &= 7 + y(15 - 7) \end{aligned} \tag{7.1}$$

This result is easily interpreted. The base rate of return for any portfolio is the risk-free rate. In addition, the portfolio is *expected* to earn a risk premium that depends on the risk premium of the risky portfolio, $E(r_P) - r_f$, and the investor's exposure to the risky asset, denoted by y. Investors are assumed to be risk averse and thus unwilling to take on a risky position without a positive risk premium.

As we noted in Chapter 6, when we combine a risky asset and a risk-free asset in a portfolio, the standard deviation of that portfolio is the standard deviation of the risky asset multiplied by the weight of the risky asset in that portfolio. In our case, the complete port-

Figure 7.2

Expected return–
standard deviation
combinations.

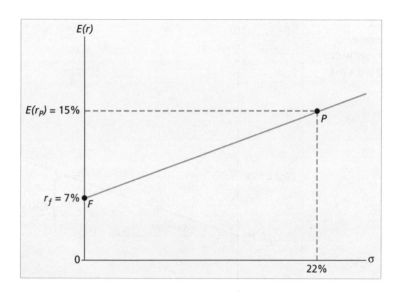

folio consists of the risky asset and the risk-free asset. Because the standard deviation of the risky portfolio is $\sigma_P = 22\%$,

$$\sigma_C = y\sigma_P$$
$$= 22y$$

(7.2)

which makes sense because the standard deviation of the portfolio is proportional to both the standard deviation of the risky asset and the proportion invested in it. In sum, the rate of return of the complete portfolio will have expected return $E(r_C) = r_f + y[E(r_P) - r_f] = 7 + 8y$ and standard deviation $\sigma_C = 22y$.

The next step is to plot the portfolio characteristics (as a function of y) in the expected return–standard deviation plane. This is done in Figure 7.2. The expected return–standard deviation combination for the risk-free asset, F, appears on the vertical axis because the standard deviation is zero. The risky asset, P, is plotted with a standard deviation, $\sigma_P = 22\%$, and expected return of 15%. If an investor chooses to invest solely in the risky asset, then $y = 1.0$, and the resulting portfolio is P. If the chosen position is $y = 0$, then $1 - y = 1.0$, and the resulting portfolio is the risk-free portfolio F.

What about the more interesting midrange portfolios where y lies between zero and 1? These portfolios will graph on the straight line connecting points F and P. The slope of that line is simply $[E(r_P) - r_f]/\sigma_P$ (or rise/run), in this case, 8/22.

The conclusion is straightforward. Increasing the fraction of the overall portfolio invested in the risky asset increases the expected return by the risk premium of equation 7.1, which is 8%. It also increases portfolio standard deviation according to equation 7.2 at the rate 22%. The extra return per extra risk is thus $8/22 = .36$.

To derive the exact equation for the straight line between F and P, we rearrange equation 7.2 to find that $y = \sigma_C/\sigma_P$, and we substitute for y in equation 7.1 to describe the expected return–standard deviation trade-off:

$$E(r_c) = r_f + y[E(r_P) - r_f]$$
$$= r_f + \frac{\sigma_C}{\sigma_P}[E(r_P) - r_f]$$
$$= 7 + \frac{8}{22}\sigma_C$$

Figure 7.3

The investment
opportunity set with a
risky asset and a risk-
free asset.

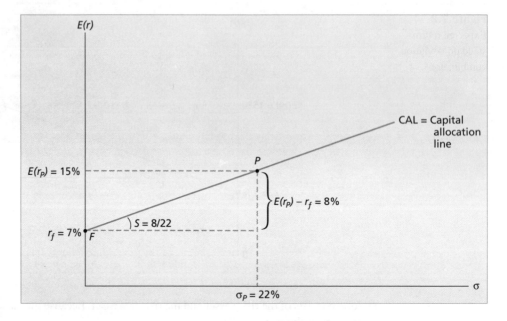

Thus the expected return of the portfolio as a function of its standard deviation is a straight line, with intercept r_f and slope as follows:

$$S = \frac{E(r_P) - r_f}{\sigma_P} = \frac{8}{22}$$

Figure 7.3 graphs the *investment opportunity set,* which is the set of feasible expected return and standard deviation pairs of all portfolios resulting from different values of y. The graph is a straight line originating at r_f and going through the point labeled P.

This straight line is called the **capital allocation line** (CAL). It depicts all the risk–return combinations available to investors. The slope of the CAL, S, equals the increase in the expected return of the chosen portfolio per unit of additional standard deviation—in other words, the measure of extra return per extra risk. For this reason, the slope also is called the **reward-to-variability ratio.**

A portfolio equally divided between the risky asset and the risk-free asset, that is, where $y = .5$, will have an expected rate of return of $E(r_C) = 7 + (.5 \times 8) = 11\%$, implying a risk premium of 4%, and a standard deviation of $\sigma_C = .5 \times 22 = 11\%$. It will plot on the line FP midway between F and P. The reward-to-variability ratio is $S = 4/11 = .36$, precisely the same as that of portfolio P.

Question 2 • **Can the reward-to-variability ratio, $S = [E(r_C - r_f]/\sigma_C$, of any combination of the risky asset and the risk-free asset be different from the ratio for the risky asset taken alone, $[E(r_P) - r_f]/\sigma_P$, which in this case is .36?**

What about points on the line to the right of portfolio P in the investment opportunity set? If investors can borrow at the (risk-free) rate of $r_f = 7\%$, they can construct portfolios that may be plotted on the CAL to the right of P.

Figure 7.4

The opportunity set with differential borrowing and lending rates.

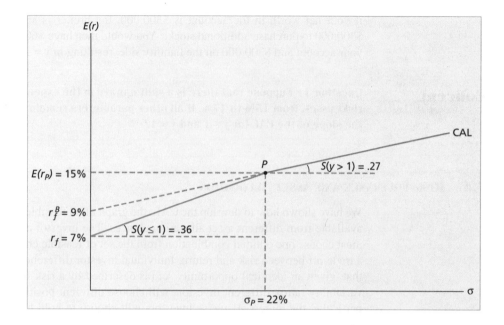

Suppose the investment budget is $300,000 and our investor borrows an additional $120,000, investing the total available funds in the risky asset. This is a *leveraged* position in the risky asset; it is financed in part by borrowing. In that case

$$y = \frac{420,000}{300,000} = 1.4$$

and $1 - y = 1 - 1.4 = -.4$, reflecting a short position in the risk-free asset, which is a borrowing position. Rather than lending at a 7% interest rate, the investor borrows at 7%. The distribution of the portfolio rate of return still exhibits the same reward-to-variability ratio:

$$E(r_C) = 7\% + (1.4 \times 8\%) = 18.2\%$$
$$\sigma_C = 1.45 \times 22\% = 30.8\%$$
$$S = \frac{E(r_C) - r_f}{\sigma_C} = \frac{18.2 - 7}{30.8} = .36$$

As one might expect, the leveraged portfolio has a higher standard deviation than does an unleveraged position in the risky asset.

Of course, nongovernment investors cannot borrow at the risk-free rate. The risk of a borrower's default causes lenders to demand higher interest rates on loans. Therefore, the nongovernment investor's borrowing cost will exceed the lending rate of $r_f = 7\%$. Suppose that the borrowing rate is $r_f^B = 9\%$. Then in the borrowing range, the reward-to-variability ratio, the slope of the CAL, will be $[E(r_P) - r_f^B]/\sigma_P = 6/22 = .27$. The CAL will therefore be "kinked" at point P, as shown in Figure 7.4. To the left of P the investor is lending at 7%, and the slope of the CAL is .36. To the right of P, where $y > 1$, the investor is borrowing at 9% to finance extra investments in the risky asset, and the slope is .27.

In practice, borrowing to invest in the risky portfolio is easy and straightforward if you have a margin account with a broker. All you have to do is tell your broker that you want to buy "on margin." Margin purchases may not exceed 50% of the purchase value. Therefore, if your net worth in the account is \$300,000, the broker is allowed to lend you up to \$300,000 to purchase additional stock.[2] You would then have \$600,000 on the asset side of your account and \$300,000 on the liability side, resulting in $y = 2.0$.

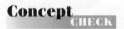

Question 3 • Suppose that there is a shift upward in the expected rate of return on the risky asset, from 15% to 17%. If all other parameters remain unchanged, what will be the slope of the CAL for $y \leq 1$ and $y > 1$?

7.4   RISK TOLERANCE AND ASSET ALLOCATION

We have shown how to develop the CAL, the graph of all feasible risk-return combinations available from different asset allocation choices. The investor confronting the CAL now must choose one optimal combination from the set of feasible choices. This choice entails a trade-off between risk and return. Individual investor differences in risk aversion imply that, given an identical opportunity set (as described by a risk-free rate and a reward-to-variability ratio), different investors will choose different positions in the risky asset. In particular, the more risk-averse investors will choose to hold less of the risky asset and more of the risk-free asset.

In Chapter 6 we showed that the utility an investor derives from a portfolio with a given probability distribution of rates of return can be described by the expected return and variance of the portfolio rate of return. Specifically, we developed the following representation:

$$U = E(r) - .005A\sigma^2$$

where A is the coefficient of risk aversion. We interpret this expression to say that the utility from a portfolio increases as the expected rate of return increases, and it decreases when the variance increases. The relative magnitude of these changes is governed by the coefficient of risk aversion, A. For risk-neutral investors, $A = 0$. Higher levels of risk aversion are reflected in larger values for A.

An investor who faces a risk-free rate, r_f, and a risky portfolio with expected return $E(r_P)$ and standard deviation σ_P will find that, for any choice of y, the expected return of the complete portfolio is given by equation 7.1, part of which we repeat here:

$$E(r_C) = r_f + y[E(r_P) - r_f]$$

From equation 7.2, the variance of the overall portfolio is

$$\sigma_C^2 = y^2\sigma_P^2$$

The investor attempts to maximize his or her utility level, U, by choosing the best allocation to the risky asset, y. Typically, we write this problem as follows:

$$\text{Max}_y \, U = E(r_C) - .005A\sigma_C^2 = r_f + y[E(r_P) - r_f] - .005Ay^2\sigma_P^2$$

where A is the coefficient of risk aversion.

Students of calculus will remember that the maximization problem is solved by setting the derivative of this expression to zero. Doing so and solving for y yields the optimal position for risk-averse investors in the risky asset, y^*, as follows:[3]

$$y^* = \frac{E(r_P) - r_f}{.01A\sigma_P^2} \tag{7.3}$$

This solution shows that the optimal position in the risky asset is, as one would expect, *inversely* proportional to the level of risk aversion and the level of risk, as measured by the variance, and directly proportional to the risk premium offered by the risky asset.

Going back to our numerical example [$r_f = 7\%$, $E(r_P) = 15\%$, and $\sigma_P = 22\%$], the optimal solution for an investor with a coefficient of risk aversion $A = 4$ is

$$y^* = \frac{15 - 7}{.01 \times 4 \times 22^2} = .41$$

In other words, this particular investor will invest 41% of the investment budget in the risky asset and 59% in the risk-free asset.

With 41% invested in the risky portfolio, the rate of return of the complete portfolio will have an expected return and standard deviation as follows:

$$E(r_C) = 7 + [.41 \times (15 - 7)] = 10.28\%$$
$$\sigma_C = .41 \times 22 = 9.02\%$$

The risk premium of the complete portfolio is $E(r_C) - r_f = 3.28\%$, which is obtained by taking on a portfolio with a standard deviation of 9.02%. Notice that 3.28/9.02 = .36, which is the reward-to-variability ratio assumed for this problem.

A graphical way of presenting this decision problem is to use indifference curve analysis. Recall from Chapter 6 that the indifference curve is a graph in the expected return–standard deviation plane of all points that result in a given level of utility. The curve then displays the investor's required trade-off between expected return and standard deviation.

For example, suppose that the initial portfolio under consideration is the risky asset itself, $y = 1$. The dark green curve in Figure 7.5 represents the indifference curve for an investor with a degree of risk aversion, $A = 4$, that passes through the risky asset with $E(r_P) = 15\%$ and $\sigma_P = 22\%$. The black curve, by contrast, shows an indifference curve going through P with a smaller degree of risk aversion, $A = 2$. The light indifference curve is flatter, that is, the more risk-tolerant (less risk-averse) investor requires a smaller increase in expected return to compensate for a given increase in standard deviation. The intercept of the indifference curve with the vertical axis is the *certainty equivalent* of the risky portfolio's expected rate of return because it gives a risk-free return with the same utility as the risky portfolio. Notice in Figure 7.5 that the less risk-averse investor (with $A = 2$) has a higher certainty equivalent for a risky portfolio such as P than the more risk-averse investor ($A = 4$).

Indifference curves can be drawn for many benchmark portfolios, representing various levels of utility. Figure 7.6 shows this set of indifference curves.

---

[3]The derivative with respect to y equals $E(r_P) - r_f - .01yA\sigma_P^2$. Setting this expression equal to zero and solving for y yields equation 7.3.

Figure 7.5
Two indifference
curves through a
risky asset.

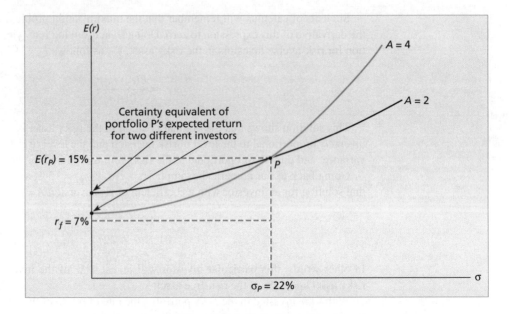

Figure 7.6
A set of indifference
curves.

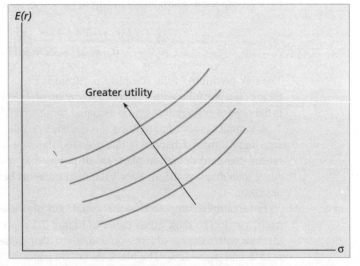

To show how to use indifference curve analysis to determine the choice of the optimal portfolio for a specific CAL, Figure 7.7 superimposes the graphs of the indifference curves on the graph of the investment opportunity set, the CAL.

The investor seeks the position with the highest feasible level of utility, represented by the highest possible indifference curve that touches the investment opportunity set. This is the indifference curve tangent to the CAL.

This optimal overall portfolio is represented by point C on the investment opportunity set. Such a graphical approach yields the same solution as the algebraic approach:

$$E(r_C) = 10.28\%$$

and

$$\sigma_C = 9.02\%$$

which implies that $y^* = .41$.

In summary, the asset allocation process can be broken down into two steps: (1) determine the CAL, and (2) find the point of highest utility along that line.

THE RIGHT MIX: FINE-TUNING A PORTFOLIO

Plunged into doubt?

Amid the recent market turmoil, maybe you are wondering whether you really have the right mix of investments. Here are a few thoughts to keep in mind:

Taking Stock

If you are a bond investor who is petrified of stocks, the wild price swings of the past few weeks have probably confirmed all of your worst suspicions. But the truth is, adding stocks to your bond portfolio could bolster your returns, without boosting your portfolio's overall gyrations.

How can that be? While stocks and bonds often move up and down in tandem, this isn't always the case, and sometimes stocks rise when bonds are tumbling.

Indeed, Chicago researchers Ibbotson Associates figures a portfolio that's 100% in longer-term government bonds has the same risk profile as a mix that includes 83% in longer-term government bonds and 17% in the blue-chip stocks that constitute Standard & Poor's 500 stock index.

The bottom line? Everybody should own some stocks. Even cowards.

Padding the Mattress

On the other hand, maybe you're a committed stock market investor, but you would like to add a calming influence to your portfolio. What's your best bet?

When investors look to mellow their stock portfolios, they usually turn to bonds. Indeed, the traditional balanced portfolio, which typically includes 60% stocks and 40% bonds, remains a firm favorite with many investment experts.

A balanced portfolio isn't a bad bet. But if you want to calm your stock portfolio, I would skip bonds and instead add cash investments such as Treasury bills and money market funds. Ibbotson calculates that, over the past 25 years, a mix of 75% stocks and 25% Treasury bills would have performed about as well as a mix of 60% stocks and 40% longer-term government bonds, and with a similar level of portfolio price gyrations.

Moreover, the stock–cash mix offers more certainty, because you know that even if your stocks fall in value, your cash never will. By contrast, both the stocks and bonds in a balanced portfolio can get hammered at the same time.

Patience Has Its Rewards, Sometimes

Stocks are capable of generating miserable short-run results. During the past 50 years, the worst five-calendar-year stretch for stocks left investors with an annualized loss of 2.4%.

But while any investment can disappoint in the short run, stocks do at least sparkle over the long haul. As a long-term investor, your goal is to fend off the dual threats of inflation and taxes and make your money grow. And on that score, stocks are supreme.

According to Ibbotson Associates, over the past 50 years, stocks gained 5.5% a year after inflation and an assumed 28% tax rate. By contrast, longer-term government bonds waddled along at just 0.8% a year and Treasury bills returned a mere 0.3%.

Source: Jonathan Clements, "The Right Mix: Fine-Tuning a Portfolio to Make Money and Still Sleep Soundly," *The Wall Street Journal*, July 23, 1996. Reprinted by permission of *The Wall Street Journal*, © 1996 Dow Jones & Company, Inc. All Rights Reserved Worldwide.

Figure 7.7

The graphical solution to the portfolio decision.

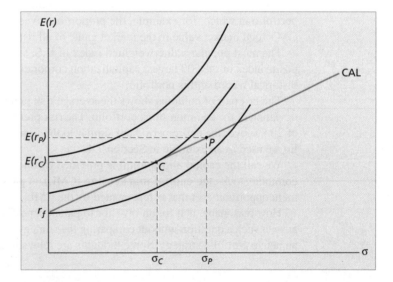

The choice for y^*, the fraction of overall investment funds to place in the risky portfolio versus the safer but lower-expected-return risk-free asset, is in large part a matter of risk aversion. The nearby box provides additional perspective on the problem, characterizing it neatly as a trade-off between making money, but still sleeping soundly.

Question 4

a. If an investor's coefficient of risk aversion is $A = 3$, how does the optimal asset mix change? What are the new $E(r_C)$ and σ_C?

b. Suppose that the borrowing rate, $r_f^B = 9\%$, is greater than the lending rate, $r_f = 7\%$. Show, graphically, how the optimal portfolio choice of some investors will be affected by the higher borrowing rate. Which investors will *not* be affected by the borrowing rate?

7.5   PASSIVE STRATEGIES: THE CAPITAL MARKET LINE

The CAL is derived with the risk-free and "the" risky portfolio, P. Determination of the assets to include in risky portfolio P may result from a passive or an active strategy. A **passive strategy** describes a portfolio decision that avoids *any* direct or indirect security analysis.[4] At first blush, a passive strategy would appear to be naive. As will become apparent, however, forces of supply and demand in large capital markets may make such a strategy a reasonable choice for many investors.

In Chapter 5, we presented a compilation of the history of rates of return on different asset classes. The data are available at many universities from the University of Chicago's Center for Research in Security Prices (CRSP). This database contains rates of return on several asset classes, including 30-day T-bills, long-term T-bonds, long-term corporate bonds, and common stocks. The CRSP tapes provide a monthly rate of return series for the period 1926 to the present and, for common stocks, a daily rate of return series from 1963 to the present. We can use these data to examine various passive strategies.

A natural candidate for a passively held risky asset would be a well-diversified portfolio of common stocks. We have already said that a passive strategy requires that we devote no resources to acquiring information on any individual stock or group of stocks, so we must follow a "neutral" diversification strategy. One way is to select a diversified portfolio of stocks that mirrors the value of the corporate sector of the U.S. economy. This results in a portfolio in which, for example, the proportion invested in GM stock will be the ratio of GM's total market value to the market value of all listed stocks.

The most popular value-weighted index of U.S. stocks is the Standard & Poor's composite index of the 500 largest capitalization corporations (S&P 500).[5] Table 7.1 shows the historical record of this portfolio.

The last pair of columns shows the average risk premium over T-bills and the standard deviation of the common stock portfolio. The risk premium of 8.7% and standard deviation of 20.8% over the entire period are similar to the figures we assumed for the risky portfolio we used as an example in Section 7.4.

We call the capital allocation line provided by one-month T-bills and a broad index of common stocks the **capital market line** (CML). A passive strategy generates an investment opportunity set that is represented by the CML.

How reasonable is it for an investor to pursue a passive strategy? Of course, we cannot answer such a question without comparing the strategy to the costs and benefits accruing to an active portfolio strategy. Some thoughts are relevant at this point, however.

---

[4]By "indirect security analysis" we mean the delegation of that responsibility to an intermediary such as a professional money manager.

[5]Before March 1957 it consisted of 90 of the largest stocks.

Table 7.1   Average Rates of Return and Standard Deviations for Common Stocks and
One-Month Bills, and the Risk Premium over Bills of Common Stock

| | Common Stocks | | One-Month Bills | | Risk Premium of Common Stocks over Bills | |
	Mean	S.D.	Mean	S.D.	Mean	S.D.
1926–1942	7.2	29.6	1.0	1.7	6.2	29.9
1943–1960	17.4	18.0	1.4	1.0	16.0	18.3
1961–1978	8.0	17.3	4.9	1.6	3.1	18.2
1979–1996	17.1	13.1	7.5	3.2	9.6	13.5
1926–1996	12.5	20.4	3.8	3.4	8.7	20.8

First, the alternative active strategy is not free. Whether you choose to invest the time and cost to acquire the information needed to generate an optimal active portfolio of risky assets, or whether you delegate the task to a professional who will charge a fee, constitution of an active portfolio is more expensive than a passive one. The passive portfolio requires only small commissions on purchases of T-bills (or zero commissions if you purchase bills directly from the government) and management fees to a mutual fund company that offers a market index fund to the public. Vanguard, for example, operates the Index Trust 500 Portfolio that mimics the S&P 500 index. It purchases shares of the firms constituting the S&P 500 in proportion to the market values of the outstanding equity of each firm, and therefore essentially replicates the S&P 500 index. The fund thus duplicates the performance of this market index. It has one of the lowest operating expenses (as a percentage of assets) of all mutual stock funds precisely because it requires minimal managerial effort.

A second reason to pursue a passive strategy is the free-rider benefit. If there are many active, knowledgeable investors who quickly bid up prices of undervalued assets and force down prices of overvalued assets (by selling), we have to conclude that at any time most assets will be fairly priced. Therefore, a well-diversified portfolio of common stock will be a reasonably fair buy, and the passive strategy may not be inferior to that of the average active investor. (We will elaborate this argument and provide a more comprehensive analysis of the relative success of passive strategies in later chapters.) Indeed, the nearby box shows that passive index funds have become quite popular investments in the last few years.

To summarize, a passive strategy involves investment in two passive portfolios: virtually risk-free short-term T-bills (or, alternatively, a money market fund) and a fund of common stocks that mimics a broad market index. The capital allocation line representing such a strategy is called the *capital market line*. Historically, based on 1926 to 1996 data, the passive risky portfolio offered an average risk premium of 8.7% and a standard deviation of 20.8%, resulting in a reward-to-variability ratio of .42. Passive investors allocate their investment budgets among instruments according to their degree of risk aversion.

We can use our analysis to deduce a typical investor's risk-aversion parameter. From Table 1.2 in Chapter 1, we estimate that approximately 71% of net worth is invested in a broad array of risky assets.[6] We assume this portfolio has the same reward-risk character-

---

[6]We include in the risky portfolio tangible assets, half of pension reserves, corporate and noncorporate equity, mutual fund shares, and personal trusts. This portfolio sums to $20,183 billion, which is 71% of household net worth.

INVESTORS RUSH TO INDEX FUNDS

Time was when most American investors chose their own stocks, one at a time. More recently they asked mutual fund managers to do the picking for them.

Now, cocky as the longest bull market in history continues without a substantial decline, many are deciding that they no longer need an expert to find the best investments. Instead, they are investing in mutual funds whose sole purpose is to mimic the performance of the stock market.

Known as index funds, these funds simply hold shares in all the companies that make up a popular stock market index—for example, the 500 stocks in the Standard & Poor's 500 index, which, after the Dow Jones Industrial Average, is the most widely followed market barometer. In essence, these funds run on autopilot, giving up the chance to do any better than the market average but also guaranteeing that except for the nominal cost of running the fund, they will do no worse.

Index funds have been growing in popularity far faster than even the mutual fund business as a whole. Over the last decade, the amount of mutual fund money invested in the most widely held stock index funds has risen more than a hundredfold, to $65 billion—a growth rate 18 times that of the rapidly expanding fund industry overall. And much of that money found its way to index funds in just the last two years.

The growth of index funds has created a broader challenge for the mutual fund industry as a whole. Index funds, by their very nature, undermine the central tenet of the mutual fund business—that individual investors who do not have the time to manage their own money should put their trust in a financial professional trading on their behalf.

But if index funds, which are much less profitable for the industry than traditional mutual funds, can consistently outperform professional stock pickers, investors are likely to demand better results to justify the higher fees that most mutual funds charge. Indeed, it is not clear that the industry's

giants will be able to maintain the elaborate marketing and management structure they have built up if much of what they do is put on automatic pilot.

Investors are clearly pouring more and more money into index funds. A decade ago, index funds that tracked the S&P 500 had only $556 million in assets, less than half of 1% of the $146 billion in United States equity funds. Last year, though, assets in those funds topped $65 billion, or 4.4% of the $1.5 trillion in domestic equity funds. And of the $165 billion in new cash that flowed into American stock funds in the first 11 months of last year, index funds took in $15.2 billion, or more than 9 percent—triple the portion of just two years before, according to Lipper Analytical Services.

Institutions, too, have been increasing the portion of their portfolios they devote to indexing. According to Greenwich Associates, a Connecticut investment research company, American pension funds last year devoted nearly 16% of their total assets, a larger portion than ever before, to stock index funds. Those assets accounted for one-third of the funds' holdings of American stocks.

While novices in the market may have misconceptions, certainly most investors understand that if the stock market as a whole goes down, so will their index fund. And some of them vow to keep on investing through the inevitable bumps in the road.

But few neophyte fund investors recall a period like the five years that ended in 1982, when more than 80% of actively managed portfolios performed better than the S&P 500. That was clear to Mr. Brennan of Vanguard this month. After he spent a few days hearing comments from callers to Vanguard, he ordered that a special article be prepared for this month's newsletter for investors.

Under the heading "Remarkable returns may raise unrealistic expectations," the article also warned "Indexing isn't invulnerable."

Source: Abridged from Edward Wyatt, "Riding Wall St. on Autopilot: Investors Rush to Index Funds," *The New York Times*, January 28, 1997, p. A1.

istics as the S&P 500, that is, a risk premium of 8.74% and standard deviation of 20.39% as documented in Table 5.2. Substituting these values in equation 7.3, we obtain

$$y^* = \frac{E(r_M) - r_f}{.01 \times A\sigma_M^2}$$

$$= \frac{8.74}{.01 \times A \times 20.39^2} = .71$$

which implies a coefficient of risk aversion of

$$A = \frac{8.74}{.01 \times .71 \times 20.39^2} = 2.96$$

Of course, this calculation is highly speculative. We have assumed without basis that the average investor holds the naive view that historical average rates of return and standard deviations are the best estimates of expected rates of return and risk, looking to the future. To the extent that the average investor takes advantage of contemporary information in addition to simple historical data, our estimate of $A = 2.96$ would be an unjustified inference. Nevertheless, a broad range of studies, taking into account the full range of available assets, places the degree of risk aversion for the representative investor in the range of 2.0 to 4.0.[7]

Concept
CHECK

Question 5 • **Suppose that expectations about the S&P 500 index and the T-bill rate are the same as they were in 1997, but you find that today a greater proportion is invested in T-bills than in 1997. What can you conclude about the change in risk tolerance over the years since 1997?**

SUMMARY

1. Shifting funds from the risky portfolio to the risk-free asset is the simplest way to reduce risk. Other methods involve diversification of the risky portfolio and hedging. We take up these methods in later chapters.

2. T-bills provide a perfectly risk-free asset in nominal terms only. Nevertheless, the standard deviation of real rates on short-term T-bills is small compared to that of other assets such as long-term bonds and common stocks, so for the purpose of our analysis we consider T-bills as the risk-free asset. Money market funds hold, in addition to T-bills, short-term relatively safe obligations such as CP and CDs. These entail some default risk, but again, the additional risk is small relative to most other risky assets. For convenience, we often refer to money market funds as risk-free assets.

3. An investor's risky portfolio (the risky asset) can be characterized by its reward-to-variability ratio, $S = [E(r_P) - r_f]/\sigma_P$. This ratio is also the slope of the CAL, the line that, when graphed, goes from the risk-free asset through the risky asset. All combinations of the risky asset and the risk-free asset lie on this line. Other things equal, an investor would prefer a steeper-sloping CAL, because that means higher expected return for any level of risk. If the borrowing rate is greater than the lending rate, the CAL will be "kinked" at the point of the risky asset.

4. The investor's degree of risk aversion is characterized by the slope of his or her indifference curve. Indifference curves show, at any level of expected return and risk, the required risk premium for taking on one additional percentage of standard deviation. More risk-averse investors have steeper indifference curves; that is, they require a greater risk premium for taking on more risk.

5. The optimal position, y^*, in the risky asset, is proportional to the risk premium and inversely proportional to the variance and degree of risk aversion:

$$y^* = \frac{E(r_P) - r_f}{.01 A \sigma_P^2}$$

---

[7]See, for example, I. Friend and M. Blume, "The Demand for Risky Assets," *American Economic Review* 64 (1974), or S. J. Grossman and R. J. Shiller, "The Determinants of the Variability of Stock Market Prices," *American Economic Review* 71 (1981).

Graphically, this portfolio represents the point at which the indifference curve is tangent to the CAL.

6. A passive investment strategy disregards security analysis, targeting instead the risk-free asset and a broad portfolio of risky assets such as the S&P 500 stock portfolio. If in 1997 investors took the mean historical return and standard deviation of the S&P 500 as proxies for its expected return and standard deviation, then the values of outstanding assets would imply a degree of risk aversion of about $A = 2.96$ for the average investor. This is in line with other studies, which estimate typical risk aversion in the range of 2.0 through 4.0.

Key Terms

capital allocation decision	complete portfolio	reward-to-variability ratio
asset allocation decision	risk-free asset	passive strategy
security selection decision	capital allocation line	capital market line
risky asset		

Selected Readings

The classic article describing the asset allocation choice, whereby investors choose the optimal fraction of their wealth to place in risk-free assets, is:

Tobin, James. "Liquidity Preference as Behavior towards Risk." *Review of Economic Studies* 25 (February 1958).

Practitioner-oriented approaches to asset allocation may be found in:

Maginn, John L., and Donald L. Tuttle. *Managing Investment Portfolios: A Dynamic Process.* 2nd ed. New York: Warren, Gorham, & Lamont, 1990.

Problems

You manage a risky portfolio with an expected rate of return of 18% and a standard deviation of 28%. The T-bill rate is 8%.

1. Your client chooses to invest 70% of a portfolio in your fund and 30% in a T-bill money market fund. What is the expected value and standard deviation of the rate of return on his portfolio?

2. Suppose that your risky portfolio includes the following investments in the given proportions:

   Stock A: 25%
   Stock B: 32%
   Stock C: 43%

   What are the investment proportions of your client's overall portfolio, including the position in T-bills?

3. What is the reward-to-variability ratio (S) of your risky portfolio? Your client's?

4. Draw the CAL of your portfolio on an expected return–standard deviation diagram. What is the slope of the CAL? Show the position of your client on your fund's CAL.

5. Suppose that your client decides to invest in your portfolio a proportion y of the total investment budget so that the overall portfolio will have an expected rate of return of 16%.

   a. What is the proportion y?

   b. What are your client's investment proportions in your three stocks and the T-bill fund?

   c. What is the standard deviation of the rate of return on your client's portfolio?

6. Suppose that your client prefers to invest in your fund a proportion y that maximizes the expected return on the overall portfolio subject to the constraint that the overall portfolio's standard deviation will not exceed 18%.

    a. What is the investment proportion, y?

    b. What is the expected rate of return on the overall portfolio?

7. Your client's degree of risk aversion is $A = 3.5$.

    a. What proportion, y, of the total investment should be invested in your fund?

    b. What is the expected value and standard deviation of the rate of return on your client's optimized portfolio?

You estimate that a passive portfolio, that is, one invested in a risky portfolio that mimics the S&P 500 stock index, yields an expected rate of return of 13% with a standard deviation of 25%. Continue to assume that $r_f = 8\%$.

8. Draw the CML and your funds' CAL on an expected return–standard deviation diagram.

    a. What is the slope of the CML?

    b. Characterize in one short paragraph the advantage of your fund over the passive fund.

9. Your client ponders whether to switch the 70% that is invested in your fund to the passive portfolio.

    a. Explain to your client the disadvantage of the switch.

    b. Show him the maximum fee you could charge (as a percentage of the investment in your fund deducted at the end of the year) that would still leave him at least as well off investing in your fund as in the passive one. (Hint: The fee will lower the slope of his CAL by reducing the expected return net of the fee.)

10. Consider the client in problem 7 with $A = 3.5$.

    a. If he chose to invest in the passive portfolio, what proportion, y, would he select?

    b. Is the fee (percentage of the investment in your fund, deducted at the end of the year) that you can charge to make the client indifferent between your fund and the passive strategy affected by his capital allocation decision (i.e., his choice of y)?

11. Look at the data in Table 7.1 on the average risk premium of the S&P 500 over T-bills, and the standard deviation of that risk premium. Suppose that the S&P 500 is your risky portfolio.

    a. If your risk-aversion coefficient is 4 and you believe that the entire 1926–1996 period is representative of future expected performance, what fraction of your portfolio should be allocated to T-bills and what fraction to equity?

    b. What if you believe that the 1979–1996 period is representative?

    c. What do you conclude upon comparing your answers to (*a*) and (*b*)?

12. What do you think would happen to the expected return on stocks if investors perceived higher volatility in the equity market? Relate your answer to equation 7.3.

13. Consider the following information about a risky portfolio that you manage, and a risk-free asset: $E(r_P) = 11\%$, $\sigma_P = 15\%$, $r_f = 5\%$.

    a. Your client wants to invest a proportion of her total investment budget in your risky fund to provide an expected rate of return on her overall or complete portfolio equal to 8%. What proportion should she invest in the risky portfolio, P, and what proportion in the risk-free asset?

    b. What will be the standard deviation of the rate of return on her portfolio?

    c. Another client wants the highest return possible subject to the constraint that you limit his standard deviation to be no more than 12%. Which client is more risk averse?

Suppose that the borrowing rate that your client faces is 9%. Assume that the S&P 500 index has an expected return of 13% and standard deviation of 25%, that $r_f = 5\%$, and that your fund has the parameters given in problem 13.

14. Draw a diagram of your client's CML, accounting for the higher borrowing rate. Superimpose on it two sets of indifference curves, one for a client who will choose to borrow, and one who will invest in both the index fund and a money market fund.

15. What is the range of risk aversion for which a client will neither borrow nor lend, that is, for which $y = 1$?

16. Solve problems 14 and 15 for a client who uses your fund rather than an index fund.

17. What is the largest percentage fee that a client who currently is lending $(y < 1)$ will be willing to pay to invest in your fund? What about a client who is borrowing $(y > 1)$?

Use the following graph to answer problems 18 and 19.

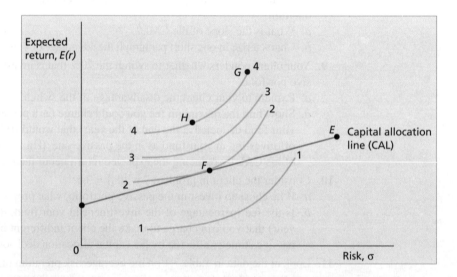

18. Which indifference curve represents the greatest level of utility that can be achieved by the investor?
    a. 1.
    b. 2.
    c. 3.
    d. 4.

19. Which point designates the optimal portfolio of risky assets?
    a. E.
    b. F.
    c. G.
    d. H.

20. Given $100,000 to invest, what is the expected risk premium in dollars of investing in equities versus risk-free T-bills based on the following table?

Action	Probability	Expected Return
Invest in equities	.6	$50,000
	.4	−$30,000
Invest in risk-free T-bills	1.0	$ 5,000

    a. $13,000.
    b. $15,000.
    c. $18,000.
    d. $20,000.

21. The change from a straight to a kinked capital allocation line is a result of the:
    a. Reward-to-variability ratio increasing.
    b. Borrowing rate exceeding the lending rate.
    c. Investor's risk tolerance decreasing.
    d. Increase in the portfolio proportion of the risk-free asset.

22. You manage an equity fund with an expected risk premium of 10% and an expected standard deviation of 14%. The rate on Treasury bills is 6%. Your client chooses to invest $60,000 of her portfolio in your equity fund and $40,000 in a T-bill money market fund. What is the expected return and standard deviation of return on your client's portfolio?

	Expected Return	Standard Deviation of Return
a.	8.4%	8.4%
b.	8.4	14.0
c.	12.0	8.4
d.	12.0	14.0

23. What is the reward-to-variability ratio for the *equity fund* in problem 22?
    a. .71.
    b. 1.00.
    c. 1.19.
    d. 1.91.

s o l u t i o n s t o
Concept
CHECKS

1. Holding 50% of your invested capital in Ready Assets means that your investment proportion in the risky portfolio is reduced from 70% to 50%.

    Your risky portfolio is constructed to invest 54% in IBM and 46% in GM. Thus the proportion of IBM in your overall portfolio is .5 × 54 = 27%, and the dollar value of your position in IBM is $300,000 × .27 = $81,000.

2. In the expected return–standard deviation plane all portfolios that are constructed from the same risky and risk-free funds (with various proportions) lie on a line from the risk-free rate through the risky fund. The slope of the CAL (capital allocation line) is the same everywhere; hence the reward-to-variability ratio is the same for all of these portfolios. Formally, if you invest a proportion, y, in a risky fund with expected return $E(r_P)$ and standard deviation σ_P, and the remainder, $1 - y$, in a risk-free asset with a sure rate r_f, then the portfolio's expected return and standard deviation are

$$E(r_C) = r_f + y[E(r_P) - r_f]$$
$$\sigma_C = y\sigma_P$$

and therefore the reward-to-variability ratio of this portfolio is

$$S_C = \frac{E(r_C) - r_f}{\sigma_C} = \frac{y[E(r_P) - r_f]}{y\sigma_P} = \frac{E(r_P) - r_f}{\sigma_P}$$

which is independent of the proportion y.

3. The lending and borrowing rates are unchanged at $r_f = 7\%$, $r_f^B = 9\%$. The standard deviation of the risky portfolio is still 22%, but its expected rate of return shifts from 15% to 17%.

    The slope of the two-part CAL is

$$\frac{E(r_P) - r_f}{\sigma_P} \quad \text{for the lending range}$$

$$\frac{E(r_P) - r_f^B}{\sigma_P} \quad \text{for the borrowing range}$$

Thus in both cases the slope increases: from 8/22 to 10/22 for the lending range, and from 6/22 to 8/22 for the borrowing range.

4. *a.* The parameters are $r_f = 7$, $E(r_P) = 15$, $\sigma_P = 22$. An investor with a degree of risk aversion A will choose a proportion y in the risky portfolio of

$$y = \frac{E(r_P) - r_f}{.01 \times A\sigma_P^2}$$

With the assumed parameters and with $A = 3$ we find that

$$y = \frac{15 - 7}{.01 \times 3 \times 484} = .55$$

When the degree of risk aversion decreases from the original value of 4 to the new value of 3, investment in the risky portfolio increases from 41% to 55%. Accordingly, the expected return and standard deviation of the optimal portfolio increase:

$$E(r_C) = 7 + (.55 \times 8) = 11.4 \text{ (before: 10.28)}$$
$$\sigma_C = .55 \times 22 = 12.1 \text{ (before: 9.02)}$$

b. All investors whose degree of risk aversion is such that they would hold the risky portfolio in a proportion equal to 100% or less ($y < 1.00$) are lending rather than borrowing, and so are unaffected by the borrowing rate. The least risk-averse of these investors hold 100% in the risky portfolio ($y = 1$). We can solve for the degree of risk aversion of these "cut off" investors from the parameters of the investment opportunities:

$$y = 1 = \frac{E(r_P) - r_f}{.01 \times A\sigma_P^2} = \frac{8}{4.84A}$$

which implies

$$A = \frac{8}{4.84} = 1.65$$

Any investor who is more risk tolerant (that is, $A < 1.65$) would borrow if the borrowing rate were 7%. For borrowers,

$$y = \frac{E(r_P) - r_f^B}{.01 \times A\sigma_P^2}$$

Suppose, for example, an investor has an A of 1.1. When $r_f = r_f^B = 7\%$, this investor chooses to invest in the risky portfolio.

$$y = \frac{8}{.01 \times 1.1 \times 4.84} = 1.50$$

which means that the investor will borrow 50% of the total investment capital. Raise the borrowing rate, in this case to $r_f^B = 9\%$, and the investor will invest less in the risky asset. In that case,

$$y = \frac{6}{.01 \times 1.1 \times 4.84} = 1.13$$

and "only" 13% of his or her investment capital will be borrowed. Graphically, the line from r_f to the risky portfolio shows the CAL for lenders. The dashed part *would* be relevant if the borrowing rate equaled the lending rate. When the borrowing rate exceeds the lending rate, the CAL is kinked at the point corresponding to the risky portfolio.

The following figure shows indifference curves of two investors. The steeper indifference curve portrays the more risk-averse investor, who chooses portfolio C_0, which involves lending. This investor's choice is unaffected by the borrowing rate.

The more risk-tolerant investor is portrayed by the shallower-sloped indifference curves. If the lending rate equaled the borrowing rate, this investor would choose portfolio C_1 on the dashed part of the CAL. When the borrowing rate goes up, this investor chooses portfolio C_2 (in the borrowing range of the kinked CAL), which involves less borrowing than before. This investor is hurt by the increase in the borrowing rate.

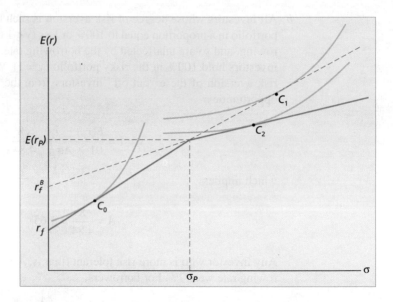

5. If all the investment parameters remain unchanged, the only reason for an investor to decrease the investment proportion in the risky asset is an increase in the degree of risk aversion. If you think that this is unlikely, then you have to reconsider your faith in your assumptions. Perhaps the S&P 500 is not a good proxy for the optimal risky portfolio. Perhaps investors expect a higher real rate on T-bills.

OPTIMAL RISKY PORTFOLIOS

In Chapter 7 we discussed the capital allocation decision. That decision governs how an investor chooses between risk-free assets and "the" optimal portfolio of risky assets. This chapter explains how to construct that optimal risky portfolio. We begin with a discussion of how diversification can reduce the variability of portfolio returns. After establishing this basic point, we examine efficient diversification strategies at the asset allocation and security selection levels. We start with a simple example of asset allocation that excludes the risk-free asset. To that effect we use two risky mutual funds: a long-term bond fund and a stock fund. With this example we investigate the relationship between investment proportions and the resulting portfolio expected return and standard deviation. We then add a risk-free asset to the menu and determine the optimal asset allocation. We do so by combining the principles of optimal allocation between risky assets and risk-free assets (from Chapter 7) with the risky portfolio construction methodology. Moving from asset allocation to security selection we first generalize asset allocation to a universe of many risky securities. We show how the best attainable capital allocation line emerges from the efficient portfolio algorithm, so that portfolio optimization can be conducted in two stages, asset allocation and security selection. We examine common fallacies relating the power of diversification to the insurance principle and to investing for the long run in two appendixes.

8.1   DIVERSIFICATION AND PORTFOLIO RISK

Suppose that your portfolio is composed of only one stock, Compaq Computer Corporation. What would be the sources of risk to this "portfolio"? You might think of two broad sources of uncertainty. First, there is the risk that comes from conditions in the general economy, such as the business cycle, the inflation rate, interest rates, and exchange rates. None of these macroeconomic factors can be predicted with certainty, and all affect the rate of return on Compaq stock. In addition to these macroeconomic factors there are firm-specific influences, such as Compaq's success in research and development, and personnel changes. These factors affect Compaq without noticeably affecting other firms in the economy.

Now consider a naive **diversification** strategy, in which you include additional securities in your portfolio. For example, place half your funds in Exxon and half in Compaq. What should happen to portfolio risk? To the extent that the firm-specific influences on the two stocks differ, we should reduce portfolio risk. For example, when oil prices fall, hurting Exxon, computer prices might rise, helping Compaq. The two effects are offsetting, and they stabilize portfolio return.

But why end diversification at only two stocks? If we diversify into many more securities, we continue to spread out our exposure to firm-specific factors, and portfolio volatility should continue to fall. Ultimately, however, even with a large number of stocks we cannot avoid risk altogether, since virtually all securities are affected by the common macroeconomic factors. For example, if all stocks are affected by the business cycle, we cannot avoid exposure to business cycle risk no matter how many stocks we hold.

When all risk is firm-specific, as in Figure 8.1A, diversification can reduce risk to arbitrarily low levels. The reason is that with all risk sources independent, the exposure to any particular source of risk is reduced to a negligible level. The reduction of risk to very low levels in the case of independent risk sources is sometimes called the **insurance principle**, because of the notion that an insurance company depends on the risk reduction achieved through diversification when it writes many policies insuring against many independent sources of risk, each policy being a small part of the company's overall portfolio. (See Appendix B to this chapter for a discussion of the insurance principle.)

When common sources of risk affect all firms, however, even extensive diversification cannot eliminate risk. In Figure 8.1B, portfolio standard deviation falls as the number of securities increases, but it cannot be reduced to zero.[1] The risk that remains even after extensive diversification is called **market risk**, risk that is attributable to marketwide risk sources. Such risk is also called **systematic risk**, or **nondiversifiable risk**. In contrast, the risk that *can* be eliminated by diversification is called **unique risk, firm-specific risk, nonsystematic risk**, or **diversifiable risk**.

This analysis is borne out by empirical studies. Figure 8.2 shows the effect of portfolio diversification, using data on NYSE stocks.[2] The figure shows the average standard deviation of equally weighted portfolios constructed by selecting stocks at random as a function of the number of stocks in the portfolio. On average, portfolio risk does fall with diversification, but the power of diversification to reduce risk is limited by systematic or common sources of risk.

---

[1]The interested reader can find a more rigorous demonstration of these points in Appendix A. That discussion, however, relies on tools developed later in this chapter.

[2]Meir Statman, "How Many Stocks Make a Diversified Portfolio," *Journal of Financial and Quantitative Analysis* 22 (September 1987).

Figure 8.1

Portfolio risk as a function of the number of stocks in the portfolio.

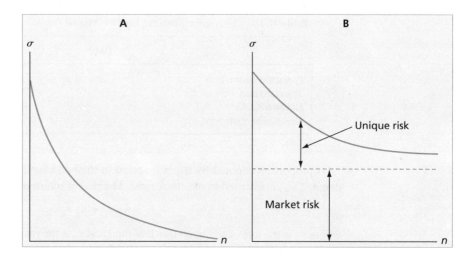

Figure 8.2   Portfolio diversification. The average standard deviation of returns of portfolios composed of only one stock was 49.2%. The average portfolio risk fell rapidly as the number of stocks included in the portfolio increased. In the limit, portfolio risk could be reduced to only 19.2%.

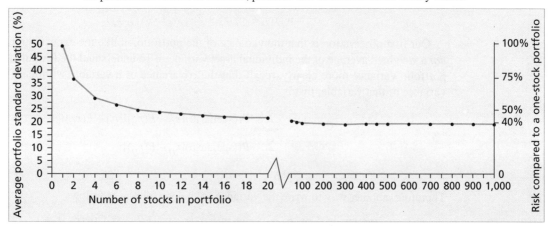

Source: Edwin J. Elton and Martin J. Gruber, Modern Portfolio Theory and Investment Analysis, 5th ed. (New York: John Wiley and Sons, 1995), adapted by Meir Statman, "How Many Stocks Make a Diversified Portfolio." Journal of Financial and Quantitative Analysis 22 (September 1987).

8.2   PORTFOLIOS OF TWO RISKY ASSETS

In the last section we considered naive diversification using equally weighted portfolios of several securities. It is time now to study *efficient* diversification, whereby we construct risky portfolios to provide the lowest possible risk for any given level of expected return.

Portfolios of two risky assets are relatively easy to analyze, and they illustrate the principles and considerations that apply to portfolios of many assets. We will consider a portfolio comprised of two mutual funds, a bond portfolio specializing in long-term debt securities, denoted D, and a stock fund that specializes in equity securities, E. Table 8.1 lists the parameters describing the rate-of-return distribution of these funds. These parameters are representative of those that can be estimated from actual funds.

Table 8.1   Descriptive Statistics for Two Mutual Funds

	Debt	Equity
Expected return, E(r)	8%	13%
Standard deviation, σ	12%	20%
Covariance, Cov(r_D, r_E)	72	
Correlation coefficient, ρ_{DE}	.30	

A proportion denoted by w_D is invested in the bond fund, and the remainder, $1 - w_D$, denoted w_E, is invested in the stock fund. The rate of return on this portfolio, r_p, will be

$$r_p = w_D r_D + w_E r_E$$

where r_D is the rate of return on the debt fund and r_E is the rate of return on the equity fund.

As shown in Chapter 6, the expected return on the portfolio is a weighted average of expected returns on the component securities with portfolio proportions as weights:

$$E(r_p) = w_D E(r_D) + w_E E(r_E) \tag{8.1}$$

The variance of the two-asset portfolio (rule 5 of Chapter 6) is

$$\sigma_p^2 = w_D^2 \sigma_D^2 + w_E^2 \sigma_E^2 + 2 w_D w_E \text{Cov}(r_D, r_E) \tag{8.2}$$

Our first observation is that the variance of the portfolio, unlike the expected return, is *not* a weighted average of the individual asset variances. To understand the formula for the portfolio variance more clearly, recall that the covariance of a variable with itself is the variance of that variable; that is

$$
\begin{aligned}
\text{Cov}(r_D, r_D) &= \sum_{\text{scenarios}} \text{Pr(scenario)}[r_D - E(r_D)][r_D - E(r_D)] \\
&= \sum_{\text{scenarios}} \text{Pr(scenario)}[r_D - E(r_D)]^2 \\
&= \sigma_D^2
\end{aligned}
\tag{8.3}
$$

Therefore, another way to write the variance of the portfolio is as follows:

$$\sigma_p^2 = w_D w_D \text{Cov}(r_D, r_D) + w_E w_E \text{Cov}(r_E, r_E) + 2 w_D w_E \text{Cov}(r_D, r_E) \tag{8.4}$$

In words, the variance of the portfolio is a weighted sum of covariances, and each weight is the product of the portfolio proportions of the pair of assets in the covariance term.

Table 8.2 shows the covariance matrix of the returns on the two mutual funds. On the borders of that matrix, we have placed the portfolio weights invested in each fund. This bordered matrix provides a quick way to compute the portfolio variance, which is easy to program in a spreadsheet: Multiply each element in the covariance matrix by the two portfolio weights given in its row and column. Add up the four resultant terms, and you have the formula for portfolio variance given in equation 8.4.

This procedure works because the covariance matrix is symmetric around the diagonal, that is, $\text{Cov}(r_D, r_E) = \text{Cov}(r_E, r_D)$. Thus each covariance term appears twice. Solving the following concept check question will convince you that this procedure will work for portfolios comprised of any number of assets.

Concept CHECK

Question 1

a. **First confirm that this simple rule for computing portfolio variance from the covariance matrix is consistent with equation 8.2.**

Table 8.2   Bordered Covariance Matrix

Portfolio Weights	Covariances	
	w_D	w_E
w_D	$\text{Cov}(r_D, r_D)$	$\text{Cov}(r_D, r_E)$
w_E	$\text{Cov}(r_E, r_D)$	$\text{Cov}(r_E, r_E)$

b. **Now consider a portfolio of three funds, *X, Y, Z,* with weights w_X, w_Y, and w_Z. Show that the portfolio variance is**

$$w_X^2 \sigma_X^2 + w_Y^2 \sigma_Y^2 + w_Z^2 \sigma_Z^2 + 2w_X w_Y \text{Cov}(r_X, r_Y) + 2w_X w_Z \text{Cov}(r_X, r_Z) + 2w_Y w_Z \text{Cov}(r_Y, r_Z)$$

Equation 8.2 reveals that variance is reduced if the covariance term is negative. It is important to recognize that even if the covariance term is positive, the portfolio standard deviation *still* is less than the weighted average of the individual security standard deviations, unless the two securities are perfectly positively correlated.

To see this, recall from Chapter 6, equation 6.5, that the covariance can be computed from the correlation coefficient as

$$\text{Cov}(r_D, r_E) = \rho_{DE} \sigma_D \sigma_E$$

So that

$$\sigma_p^2 = w_D^2 \sigma_D^2 + w_E^2 \sigma_E^2 + 2w_D w_E \sigma_D \sigma_E \rho_{DE} \tag{8.5}$$

Given the standard deviations of asset returns, portfolio variance is higher when ρ_{DE} is higher. In the case of perfect positive correlation, $\rho_{DE} = 1$, the right-hand side of equation 8.5 is a perfect square and simplifies to

$$\sigma_p^2 = (w_D \sigma_D + w_E \sigma_E)^2$$

or

$$\sigma_p = w_D \sigma_D + w_E \sigma_E$$

Therefore, the standard deviation of the portfolio with perfect positive correlation is just the weighted average of the component standard deviations. In all other cases, the correlation coefficient is less than 1, making the portfolio standard deviation *less* than the weighted average of the component standard deviations.

A hedge asset has *negative* correlation with the other assets in the portfolio. Equation 8.5 shows that such assets will be particularly effective in reducing total risk. Moreover, equation 8.1 shows that expected return is unaffected by correlation between returns. Therefore, other things equal, we will always prefer to add to our portfolios assets with low or, even better, negative correlation with our existing position. The nearby box from *The Wall Street Journal* makes this point when it advises you to find "funds that zig when blue chip [stocks] zag."

Because the portfolio's expected return is the weighted average of its component expected returns, whereas its standard deviation is less than the weighted average of the component standard deviations, *portfolios of less than perfectly correlated assets always offer better risk–return opportunities than the individual component securities on their own.* The lower the correlation between the assets, the greater the gain in efficiency.

FINDING FUNDS THAT ZIG WHEN BLUE CHIPS ZAG

Investors hungry for lower risk are hearing some surprising recommendations from financial advisers:

- mutual funds investing in less-developed nations that many Americans can't immediately locate on a globe.
- funds specializing in small European companies with unfamiliar names.
- funds investing in commodities.

All of these investments are risky by themselves, advisers readily admit. But they also tend to zig when big U.S. stocks zag. And that means that such fare, when added to a portfolio heavy in U.S. blue-chip stocks, actually may damp the portfolio's ups and downs.

Combining types of investments that don't move in lock step "is one of the very few instances in which there is a free lunch—you get something for nothing," says Gary Greenbaum, president of investment counselors Greenbaum & Associates in Oradell, N.J. The right combination of assets can trim the volatility of an investment portfolio, he explains, without reducing the expected return over time.

Getting more variety in one's holdings can be surprisingly tricky. For instance, investors who have shifted dollars into a diversified international-stock fund may not have ventured as far afield as they think, says an article in the most recent issue of *Morningstar Mutual Funds*. Those funds typically load up on European blue-chip stocks that often behave similarly and respond to the same world-wide economic conditions as do U.S. corporate giants.

To get a fund that invests world-wide and that may perform less similarly to U.S. stock funds, Morningstar international editor Tricia Rothschild suggests that investors consider international small-stock funds. "In addition to focusing on small, domestically oriented firms that aren't tied to multinational trends," she writes, "these funds are also more likely to hold emerging-markets stocks."

Many investment professionals use a statistical measure known as a "correlation coefficient" to identify categories of securities that tend to zig when others zag. A figure approaching the maximum 1.0 indicates that two assets have consistently moved in the same direction. A correlation coefficient approaching the minimum, negative 1.0, indicates that the assets have consistently moved in the opposite direction. Assets with a zero correlation have moved independently.

Funds invested in Japan, developing nations, small European companies, and gold stocks have been among those moving opposite to the Vanguard Index 500 over the past several years.

Source: Karen Damato, "Finding Funds That Zig When Blue Chips Zag." *The Wall Street Journal*, June 17, 1997. Excerpted by permission of *The Wall Street Journal*, © 1997 Dow Jones & Company, Inc. All Rights Reserved Worldwide.

How low can portfolio standard deviation be? The lowest possible value of the correlation coefficient is –1, representing perfect negative correlation. In this case, equation 8.5 simplifies to

$$\sigma_p^2 = (w_D\sigma_D - w_E\sigma_E)^2$$

and the portfolio standard deviation is

$$\sigma_p = \text{Absolute value } (w_D\sigma_D - w_E\sigma_E)$$

When $\rho = -1$, a perfectly hedged position can be obtained by choosing the portfolio proportions to solve

$$w_D\sigma_D - w_E\sigma_E = 0$$

The solution to this equation is

$$w_D = \frac{\sigma_E}{\sigma_D + \sigma_E}$$

$$w_E = \frac{\sigma_D}{\sigma_D + \sigma_E} = 1 - w_D$$

These weights drive the standard deviation of the portfolio to zero.[3]

---

[3] It is possible to drive portfolio variance to zero with perfectly positively correlated assets as well, but this would require short sales.

Table 8.3   Expected Return and Standard Deviation with Various Correlation Coefficients

			Portfolio Standard Deviation for Given Correlation			
w_D	w_E	$E(r_P)$	$\rho = -1$	$\rho = 0$	$\rho = .30$	$\rho = 1$
0.00	1.00	13.00	20.00	20.00	20.00	20.00
0.10	0.90	12.50	16.80	18.04	18.40	19.20
0.20	0.80	12.00	13.60	16.18	16.88	18.40
0.30	0.70	11.50	10.40	14.46	15.47	17.60
0.40	0.60	11.00	7.20	12.92	14.20	16.80
0.50	0.50	10.50	4.00	11.66	13.11	16.00
0.60	0.40	10.00	0.80	10.76	12.26	15.20
0.70	0.30	9.50	2.40	10.32	11.70	14.40
0.80	0.20	9.00	5.60	10.40	11.45	13.60
0.90	0.10	8.50	8.80	10.98	11.56	12.80
1.00	0.00	8.00	12.00	12.00	12.00	12.00
			Minimum Variance Portfolio			
	w_D		0.6250	0.7353	0.8200	—
	w_E		0.3750	0.2647	0.1800	—
	$E(r_P)$		9.8750	9.3235	8.9000	—
	σ_P		0.0000	10.2899	11.4473	—

Let us apply this analysis to the data of the bond and stock funds as presented in Table 8.1. Using these data, the formulas for the expected return, variance, and standard deviation of the portfolio are

$$E(r_p) = 8w_D + 13w_E$$
$$\sigma_p^2 = 12^2 w_D^2 + 20^2 w_E^2 + 2 \times 12 \times 20 \times .3 \times w_D w_E$$
$$= 144w_D^2 + 400w_E^2 + 144w_D w_E$$
$$\sigma_p = \sqrt{\sigma_p^2}$$

We can experiment with different portfolio proportions to observe the effect on portfolio expected return and variance. Suppose we change the proportion invested in bonds. The effect on expected return is tabulated in Table 8.3 and plotted in Figure 8.3. When the proportion invested in debt varies from zero to 1 (so that the proportion in equity varies from 1 to zero), the portfolio expected return goes from 13% (the stock fund's expected return) to 8% (the expected return on bonds).

What happens when $w_D > 1$ and $w_E < 0$? In this case portfolio strategy would be to sell the equity fund short and invest the proceeds of the short sale in the debt fund. This will decrease the expected return of the portfolio. For example, when $w_D = 2$ and $w_E = -1$, expected portfolio return falls to $2 \times 8 + (-1) \times 13 = 3\%$. At this point the value of the bond fund in the portfolio is twice the net worth of the account. This extreme position is financed in part by short selling stocks equal in value to the portfolio's net worth.

The reverse happens when $w_D < 0$ and $w_E > 1$. This strategy calls for selling the bond fund short and using the proceeds to finance additional purchases of the equity fund.

Of course, varying investment proportions also has an effect on portfolio standard deviation. Table 8.3 presents portfolio standard deviations for different portfolio weights calculated from equation 8.5 using the assumed value of the correlation coefficient, .30, as well as other values of ρ. Figure 8.4 shows the relationship between standard deviation and portfolio weights. Look first at the solid curve for $\rho_{DE} = .30$. The graph shows that as the portfolio weight in the equity fund increases from zero to 1, portfolio standard deviation first falls with the initial diversification from bonds into stocks, but then rises again as the

Figure 8.3
Portfolio expected
return as a function
of investment
proportions.

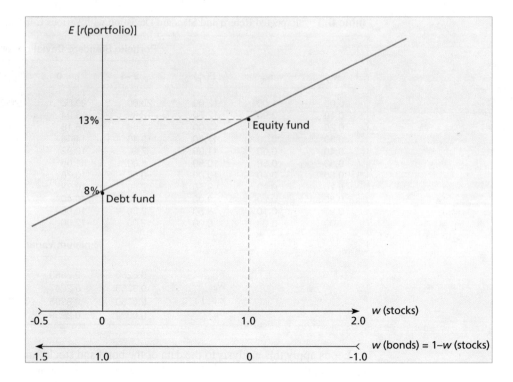

portfolio becomes heavily concentrated in stocks, and again is undiversified. This pattern will generally hold as long as the correlation coefficient between the funds is not too high. For a pair of assets with a large positive correlation of returns, the portfolio standard deviation will increase monotonically from the low-risk asset to the high-risk asset. Even in this case, however, there is a positive (if small) value of diversification.

What is the minimum level to which portfolio standard deviation can be held? For the parameter values stipulated in Table 8.1, the portfolio weights that solve this minimization problem turn out to be:[4]

$$w_{\text{Min}}(D) = .82$$
$$w_{\text{Min}}(E) = 1 - .82 = .18$$

This minimum variance portfolio has a standard deviation of

$$\sigma_{\text{Min}} = [(.82^2 \times 12^2) + (.18^2 \times 20^2) + (2 \times .82 \times .18 \times 72)]^{1/2} = 11.45\%$$

as indicated in the last line of Table 8.3 for the column $\rho = .30$.

The solid green line in Figure 8.4 represents the portfolio standard deviation when $\rho = .30$ as a function of the investment proportions. It passes through the two undiversified portfolios of $w_D = 1$ and $w_E = 1$. Note that the **minimum-variance portfolio** has a standard deviation smaller than that of either of the individual component assets. This illustrates the effect of diversification.

---

[4]This solution uses the minimization techniques of calculus. Write out the expression for portfolio variance from equation 8.2, substitute $1 - w_D$ for w_E, differentiate the result with respect to w_D, set the derivative equal to zero, and solve for w_D to obtain

$$w_{\text{Min}}(D) = \frac{\sigma_E^2 - \text{Cov}(r_D, r_E)}{\sigma_D^2 + \sigma_E^2 - 2\text{Cov}(r_D, r_E)}$$

Alternatively, with a computer spreadsheet, you an obtain an accurate solution by generating a fine grid for Table 8.3 and observing the minimum.

Figure 8.4
Portfolio standard
deviation as a function
of investment
proportions.

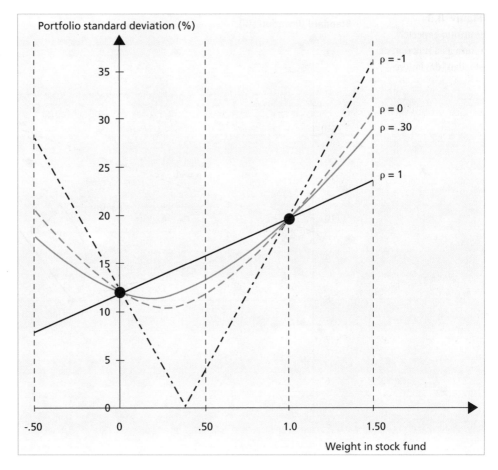

The other three lines in Figure 8.4 show how portfolio risk varies for other values of the correlation coefficient, holding the variances of each asset constant. These lines plot the values in the other three columns of Table 8.3.

The solid black line connecting the undiversified portfolios of all bonds or all stocks, $w_D = 1$ or $w_E = 1$, shows portfolio standard deviation with perfect positive correlation, $\rho = 1$. In this case there is no advantage from diversification, and the portfolio standard deviation is the simple weighted average of the component asset standard deviations.

The dashed green curve depicts portfolio risk for the case of uncorrelated assets, $\rho = 0$. With lower correlation between the two assets, diversification is more effective and portfolio risk is lower (at least when both assets are held in positive amounts). The minimum portfolio standard deviation when $\rho = 0$ is 10.29% (see Table 8.3), again lower than the standard deviation of either asset.

Finally, the upside-down triangular broken line illustrates the perfect hedge potential when the two assets are perfectly negatively correlated ($\rho = -1$). In this case the solution for the minimum-variance portfolio is

$$w_{\text{Min}}(D; \rho = -1) = \frac{\sigma_E}{\sigma_D + \sigma_E}$$

$$= \frac{20}{12 + 20} = .625 \qquad (8.6)$$

$$w_{\text{Min}}(E; \rho = -1) = 1 - .625 = .375$$

and the portfolio variance (and standard deviation) is zero.

Figure 8.5

Portfolio expected return as a function of standard deviation.

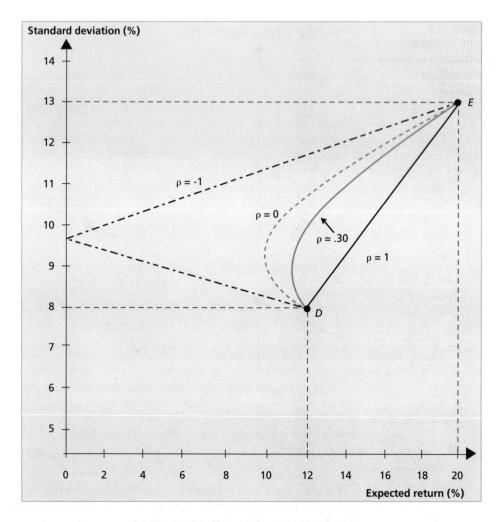

We can combine Figures 8.3 and 8.4 to demonstrate the relationship between portfolio risk (standard deviation) and expected return—given the parameters of the available assets. This is done in Figure 8.5. For any pair of investment proportions, w_D, w_E, we read the expected return from Figure 8.3 and the standard deviation from Figure 8.4. The resulting pairs of expected return and standard deviation are tabulated in Table 8.3 and plotted in Figure 8.5.

The solid green curve in Figure 8.5 shows the **portfolio opportunity set** for $\rho = .30$. We call it the portfolio opportunity set because it shows all combinations of portfolio expected return and standard deviation that can be constructed from the two available assets. The other lines show the portfolio opportunity set for other values of the correlation coefficient. The solid black line connecting the two funds shows that there is no benefit from diversification when the correlation between the two is positive ($\rho = 1$). The opportunity set is not "pushed" to the northwest. The dashed green line demonstrates the greater benefit from diversification when the correlation coefficient is lower than .30.

Finally, for $\rho = -1$, the portfolio opportunity set is linear, but now it offers a perfect hedging opportunity and the maximum advantage from diversification.

To summarize, although the expected return of any portfolio is simply the weighted average of the asset expected returns, this is not true of the standard deviation. Potential benefits from diversification arise when correlation is less than perfectly positive. The lower the correlation, the greater the potential benefit from diversification. In the extreme case of perfect negative correlation, we have a perfect hedging opportunity and can construct a zero-variance portfolio.

Suppose now that an investor wishes to select the optimal portfolio from the opportunity set. The best portfolio will depend on risk aversion. Portfolios to the northeast in Figure 8.5 provide higher rates of return but impose greater risk. The best trade-off among these choices is a matter of personal preference. Investors with greater risk aversion will prefer portfolios to the southwest, with lower expected return but lower risk.[5]

Concept **CHECK**

Question 2 • Compute and draw the portfolio opportunity set for the debt and equity funds when the correlation coefficient between them is $\rho = .25$.

8.3 ASSET ALLOCATION WITH STOCKS, BONDS, AND BILLS

In the previous chapter we examined the simplest asset allocation decision, that involving the choice of how much of the portfolio to leave in risk-free money market securities versus in a risky portfolio. Now we have taken a further step, specifying the risky portfolio as comprised of a stock and bond fund. We still need to show how investors can decide on the proportion of their risky portfolios to allocate to the stock versus the bond market. This, too, is an asset allocation decision. As the nearby box emphasizes, most investment professionals recognize that "the really critical decision is how to divvy up your money among stocks, bonds and supersafe investments such as Treasury bills."

In the last section, we derived the properties of portfolios formed by mixing two risky assets. Given this background, we now reintroduce the choice of the third, risk-free, portfolio. This will allow us to complete the basic problem of asset allocation across the three key asset classes: stocks, bonds, and risk-free money market securities. Once you understand this case, it will be easy to see how portfolios of many risky securities might best be constructed.

The Optimal Risky Portfolio with Two Risky Assets and a Risk-Free Asset

What if our risky assets are still confined to the bond and stock funds, but now we can also invest in risk-free T-bills yielding 5%? We start with a graphical solution. Figure 8.6 shows the opportunity set generated from the joint probability distribution of the bond and stock funds, using the data from Table 8.1.

Two possible capital allocation lines (CALs) are drawn from the risk-free rate ($r_f = 5\%$) to two feasible portfolios. The first possible CAL is drawn through the minimum-variance

---

[5]Given a level of risk aversion, one can determine the portfolio that provides the highest level of utility. Recall from Chapter 7 that we were able to describe the utility provided by a portfolio as a function of its expected return, $E(r_p)$, and its variance, σ_p^2, according to the relationship $U = E(r_p) - .005A\sigma_p^2$. The portfolio mean and variance are determined by the portfolio weights in the two funds, w_E and w_D, according to equations 8.1 and 8.2. Using those equations and some calculus, we find the optimal investment proportions in the two funds:

$$w_D = \frac{E(r_D) - E(r_E) + .01A(\sigma_D^2 - \sigma_D\sigma_E\rho_{DE})}{.01A(\sigma_D^2 + \sigma_E^2 - 2\sigma_D\sigma_E\rho_{DE})}$$

$$w_E = 1 - w_D$$

Figure 8.6

The opportunity set of the debt and equity funds and two feasible CALs.

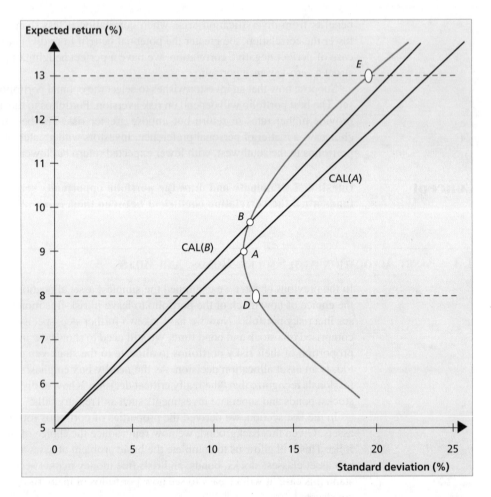

portfolio A, which is invested 82% in bonds and 18% in stocks (Table 8.3, bottom panel). Portfolio A's expected return is 8.90%, and its standard deviation is 11.45%. With a T-bill rate of 5%, the **reward-to-variability ratio**, which is the slope of the CAL combining T-bills and the minimum-variance portfolios, is

$$S_A = \frac{E(r_A) - r_f}{\sigma_A} = \frac{8.9 - 5}{11.45} = .34$$

Now consider the CAL that uses portfolio B instead of A. Portfolio B invests 70% in bonds and 30% in stocks. Its expected return is 9.5% (a risk premium of 4.5%), and its standard deviation is 11.70%. Thus the reward-to-variability ratio on the CAL that is supported by Portfolio B is

$$S_B = \frac{9.5 - 5}{11.7} = .38$$

which is higher than the reward-to-variability ratio of the CAL that we obtained using the minimum-variance portfolio and T-bills. Thus Portfolio B dominates A.

But why stop at Portfolio B? We can continue to ratchet the CAL upward until it ultimately reaches the point of tangency with the investment opportunity set. This must yield the CAL with the highest feasible reward-to-variability ratio. Therefore, the tangency port-

RECIPE FOR SUCCESSFUL INVESTING: FIRST, MIX ASSETS WELL

First things first.

If you want dazzling investment results, don't start your day foraging for hot stocks and stellar mutual funds. Instead, say investment advisers, the really critical decision is how to divvy up your money among stocks, bonds, and supersafe investments such as Treasury bills.

In Wall Street lingo, this mix of investments is called your asset allocation. "The asset-allocation choice is the first and most important decision," says William Droms, a finance professor at Georgetown University. "How much you have in [the stock market] really drives your results."

"You cannot get [stock market] returns from a bond portfolio, no matter how good your security selection is or how good the bond managers you use," says William John Mikus, a managing director of Financial Design, a Los Angeles investment adviser.

For proof, Mr. Mikus cites studies such as the 1991 analysis done by Gary Brinson, Brian Singer and Gilbert Beebower. That study, which looked at the 10-year results for 82 large pension plans, found that a plan's asset-allocation policy explained 91.5% of the return earned.

Designing a Portfolio

Because your asset mix is so important, some mutual fund companies now offer free services to help investors design their portfolios.

Gerald Perritt, editor of the *Mutual Fund Letter*, a Chicago newsletter, says you should vary your mix of assets depending on how long you plan to invest. The further you are from your investment goal, the more you should have in stocks. The closer you get, the more you should lean toward bonds and money-market instruments, such as Treasury bills. Bonds and money-market instruments may generate lower returns than stocks. But for those who need money in the near future, conservative investments make more sense, because there's less chance of suffering a devastating short-term loss.

Summarizing Your Assets

"One of the most important things people can do is summarize all their assets on one piece of paper and figure out their asset allocation," says Mr. Pond.

Once you've settled on a mix of stocks and bonds, you should seek to maintain the target percentages, says Mr. Pond. To do that, he advises figuring out your asset allocation once every six months. Because of a stock-market plunge, you could find that stocks are now a far smaller part of your portfolio than you envisaged. At such a time, you should put more into stocks and lighten up on bonds.

When devising portfolios, some investment advisers consider gold and real estate in addition to the usual trio of stocks, bonds and money-market instruments. Gold and real estate give "you a hedge against hyperinflation," says Mr. Droms. "But real estate is better than gold, because you'll get better long-run returns."

Source: Jonathan Clements, "Recipe for Successful Investing: First, Mix Assets Well," *The Wall Street Journal*, October 6, 1993. Reprinted by permission of *The Wall Street Journal*, © 1993 Dow Jones & Company, Inc. All Rights Reserved Worldwide.

---

folio, labeled P in Figure 8.7, is the optimal risky portfolio to mix with T-bills. We can read the expected return and standard deviation of Portfolio P from the graph in Figure 8.7.

$$E(r_P) = 11\%$$
$$\sigma_P = 14.2\%$$

In practice, we obtain the solution to this problem with a computer program. We can describe the process briefly, however.

The objective is to find the weights w_D and w_E that result in the highest slope of the CAL (i.e., the weights that result in the risky portfolio with the highest reward-to-variability ratio). Therefore, the objective is to maximize the slope of the CAL for any possible portfolio, p. Thus our *objective function* is the slope that we have called S_p:

$$S_p = \frac{E(r_p) - r_f}{\sigma_p}$$

For the portfolio with two risky assets, the expected return and standard deviation of Portfolio p are

Figure 8.7

The opportunity set of the debt and equity funds with the optimal CAL and the optimal risky portfolio.

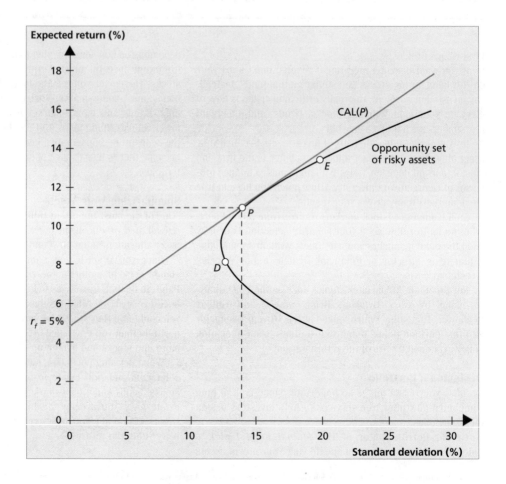

$$E(r_p) = w_D E(r_D) + w_E E(r_E)$$
$$= 8w_D + 13w_E$$
$$\sigma_p = [w_D^2 \sigma_D^2 + w_E^2 \sigma_E^2 + 2w_D w_E \text{Cov}(r_D, r_E)]^{1/2}$$
$$= [144w_D^2 + 400w_E^2 + (2 \times 72 w_D w_E)]^{1/2}$$

When we maximize the objective function, S_p, we have to satisfy the constraint that the portfolio weights sum to one (100%), that is, $w_D + w_E = 1$. Therefore, we solve a mathematical problem formally written as

$$\underset{w_i}{\text{Max }} S_p = \frac{E(r_p) - r_f}{\sigma_p}$$

subject to $\Sigma w_i = 1$. This is a standard problem in calculus.

In the case of two risky assets, the solution for the weights of the **optimal risky portfolio**, P, can be shown to be as follows:[6]

---

[6]The solution procedure for two risky assets is as follows. Substitute for $E(r_p)$ from equation 8.1 and for σ_p from equation 8.5. Substitute $1 - w_D$ for w_E. Differentiate the resulting expression for S_p with respect to w_D, set the derivative equal to zero, and solve for w_D.

$$w_D = \frac{[E(r_D) - r_f]\sigma_E^2 - [E(r_E) - r_f]\text{Cov}(r_D, r_E)}{[E(r_D) - r_f]\sigma_E^2 + [E(r_E) - r_f]\sigma_D^2 - [E(r_D) - r_f + E(r_E) - r_f]\text{Cov}(r_D, r_E)}$$

$$w_E = 1 - w_D \tag{8.7}$$

Substituting our data, the solution is

$$w_D = \frac{(8 - 5)400 - (13 - 5)72}{(8 - 5)400 + (13 - 5)144 - (8 - 5 + 13 - 5)72} = .40$$

$$w_E = 1 - .40 = .60$$

The expected return and standard deviation of this optimal risky portfolio are

$$E(r_P) = (.4 \times 8) + (.6 \times 13) = 11\%$$

$$\sigma_P = [(.4^2 \times 144) + (.6^2 \times 400) + (2 \times .4 \times .6 \times 72)]^{1/2} = 14.2\%$$

The CAL of this optimal portfolio has a slope of

$$S_P = \frac{11 - 5}{14.2} = .42$$

which is the reward-to-variability ratio of Portfolio P. Notice that this slope exceeds the slope of any of the other feasible portfolios that we have considered, as it must if it is to be the slope of the best feasible CAL.

In Chapter 7 we found the optimal *complete* portfolio given an optimal *risky* portfolio and the CAL generated by a combination of this portfolio and T-bills. Now that we have constructed the optimal risky portfolio, P, we can use the individual investor's degree of risk aversion, A, to calculate the optimal proportion of the complete portfolio to invest in the risky component.

An investor with a coefficient of risk aversion $A = 4$ would take a position in Portfolio P of [7]

$$y = \frac{E(r_P) - r_f}{.01 \times A\sigma_P^2} = \frac{11 - 5}{.01 \times 4 \times 14.2^2} = .7439 \tag{8.8}$$

Thus the investor will invest 74.39% of his or her wealth in Portfolio P and 25.61% in T-bills. Portfolio P consists of 40% in bonds, so the percentage of wealth in bonds will be $yw_D = .4 \times .7439 = .2976$, or 29.76%. Similarly, the investment in stocks will be $yw_E = .6 \times .7439 = .4463$, or 44.63%. The graphical solution of this asset allocation problem is presented in Figures 8.8 and 8.9.

Once we have reached this point, generalizing to the case of many risky assets is straightforward. Before we move on, let us briefly summarize the steps we followed to arrive at the complete portfolio.

1. Specify the return characteristics of all securities (expected returns, variances, covariances).
2. Establish the risky portfolio:
   a. Calculate the optimal risky portfolio, P (equation 8.7).
   b. Calculate the properties of Portfolio P using the weights determined in step (*a*) and equations 8.1 and 8.2.

---

[7]As noted earlier, the .01 that appears in the denominator is a scale factor that arises because we measure returns as percentages rather than decimals. If we were to measure returns as decimals (e.g., .07 rather than 7%), we would not use the .01 in the denominator. Notice that switching to decimals would reduce the scale of the numerator by a multiple of .01 and the denominator by $.01^2$.

Figure 8.8
Determination of the optimal overall portfolio.

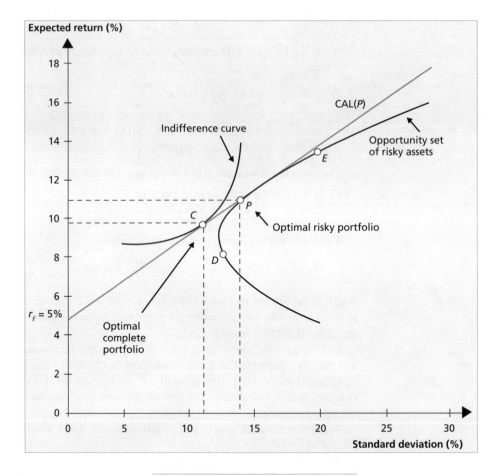

Figure 8.9
The proportions of the optimal overall portfolio.

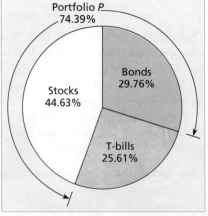

3. Allocate funds between the risky portfolio and the risk-free asset:

a. Calculate the fraction of the complete portfolio allocated to Portfolio P (the risky portfolio) and to T-bills (the risk-free asset) (equation 8.8).

b. Calculate the share of the complete portfolio invested in each asset and in T-bills.

Before moving on, recall that our two risky assets, the bond and stock mutual funds, are already diversified portfolios. The diversification *within* each of these portfolios must be credited for a good deal of the risk reduction compared to undiversified single securities. For example, the standard deviation of the rate of return on an average stock is about 50% (see Figure 8.2). In contrast, the standard deviation of our stock-index fund is only 20%, about equal to the historical standard deviation of the S&P 500 portfolio. This is evidence of the importance of diversification within the asset class. Optimizing the asset allocation between bonds and stocks contributed incrementally to the improvement in the reward-to-variability ratio of the complete portfolio. The CAL with stocks, bonds, and bills (Figure 8.7) shows that the standard deviation of the complete portfolio can be further reduced to 18% while maintaining the same expected return of 13% as the stock portfolio.

Concept
CHECK

Question 3 • The universe of available securities includes two risky stock funds, *A* and *B*, and T-bills. The data for the universe are as follows:

	Expected Return	Standard Deviation
A	10%	20%
B	30	60
T-bills	5	0

The correlation coefficient between funds *A* and *B* is −.2.
a. Draw the opportunity set of Funds *A* and *B*.
b. Find the optimal risky portfolio, *P*, and its expected return and standard deviation.
c. Find the slope of the CAL supported by T-bills and Portfolio *P*.
d. How much will an investor with *A* = 5 invest in Funds *A* and *B* and in T-bills?

8.4   THE MARKOWITZ PORTFOLIO SELECTION MODEL

Security Selection

We can generalize the portfolio construction problem to the case of many risky securities and a risk-free asset. As in the two risky assets example, the problem has three parts. First, we identify the risk–return combinations available from the set of risky assets. Next, we identify the optimal portfolio of risky assets by finding the portfolio weights that result in the steepest CAL. Finally, we choose an appropriate complete portfolio by mixing the risk-free asset with the optimal risky portfolio. Before describing the process in detail, let us first present an overview.

The first step is to determine the risk–return opportunities available to the investor. These are summarized by the **minimum-variance frontier** of risky assets. This frontier is a graph of the lowest possible portfolio variance that can be attained for a given portfolio expected return. Given the set of data for expected returns, variances, and covariances, we can calculate the minimum-variance portfolio for any targeted expected return. The plot of these expected return–standard deviation pairs is presented in Figure 8.10.

Notice that all the individual assets lie to the right inside the frontier, at least when we allow short sales in the construction of risky portfolios.[8] This tells us that risky portfolios

---

[8]When short sales are prohibited, single securities may lie on the frontier. For example, the security with the highest expected return must lie on the frontier, as that security represents the *only* way that one can obtain a return that high, and so it must also be the minimum-variance way to obtain that return. When short sales are feasible, however, portfolios can be constructed that offer the same expected return and lower variance. These portfolios typically will have short positions in low-expected-return securities.

Figure 8.10

The minimum-variance frontier of risky assets.

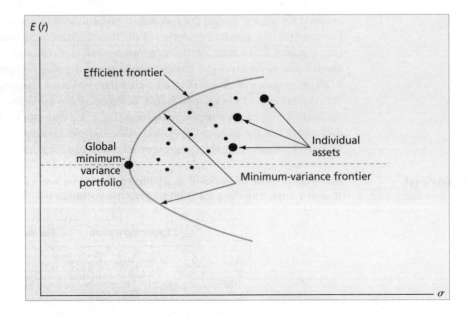

constituted of only a single asset are inefficient. Diversifying investments leads to portfolios with higher expected returns and lower standard deviations.

All the portfolios that lie on the minimum-variance frontier from the global minimum-variance portfolio and upward provide the best risk–return combinations and thus are candidates for the optimal portfolio. The part of the frontier that lies above the global minimum-variance portfolio, therefore, is called the **efficient frontier**. For any portfolio on the lower portion of the minimum-variance frontier, there is a portfolio with the same standard deviation and a greater expected return positioned directly above it. Hence the bottom part of the minimum-variance frontier is inefficient.

The second part of the optimization plan involves the risk-free asset. As before, we search for the capital allocation line with the highest reward-to-variability ratio (that is, the steepest slope) as shown in Figure 8.11.

The CAL that is supported by the optimal portfolio, P, is tangent to the efficient frontier. This CAL dominates all alternative feasible lines (the broken lines that are drawn through the frontier). Portfolio P, therefore, is the optimal risky portfolio.

Finally, in the last part of the problem the individual investor chooses the appropriate mix between the optimal risky portfolio P and T-bills, exactly as in Figure 8.8.

Now let us consider each part of the portfolio construction problem in more detail. In the first part of the problem, risk-return analysis, the portfolio manager needs, as inputs, a set of estimates for the expected returns of each security and a set of estimates for the covariance matrix. (In Part V on security analysis we will examine the security valuation techniques and methods of financial analysis that analysts use. For now, we will assume that analysts already have spent the time and resources to prepare the inputs.)

Suppose that the horizon of the portfolio plan is one year. Therefore, all estimates pertain to a one-year holding period return. Our security analysts cover n securities. As of now, time zero, we observed these security prices: $P_1^0, \ldots, P_n^0$. The analysts derive estimates for each security's expected rate of return by forecasting end-of-year (time 1) prices: $E(P_1^1)$, $\ldots, E(P_n^1)$, and the expected dividends for the period: $E(D_1), \ldots, E(D_n)$. The set of expected rates of return is then computed from

$$E(r_i) = \frac{E(P_i^1) + E(D_i) - P_i^0}{P_i^0}$$

Figure 8.11

The efficient frontier of risky assets with the optimal CAL.

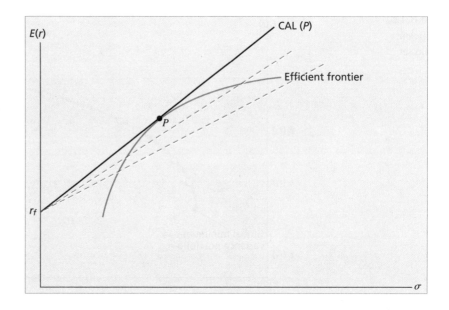

The covariances among the rates of return on the analyzed securities (the covariance matrix) usually are estimated from historical data. Another method is to use a scenario analysis of possible returns from all securities instead of, or as a supplement to, historical analysis.

The portfolio manager is now armed with the n estimates of $E(r_i)$ and the $n \times n$ estimates in the covariance matrix in which the n diagonal elements are estimates of the variances, σ_i^2, and the $n^2 - n = n(n - 1)$ off-diagonal elements are the estimates of the covariances between each pair of asset returns. (You can verify this from Table 8.2 for the case $n = 2$.) We know that each covariance appears twice in this table, so actually we have $n(n - 1)/2$ different covariances estimates. If our portfolio management unit covers 50 securities, our security analysts need to deliver 50 estimates of expected returns, 50 estimates of variances, and $50 \times 49/2 = 1{,}225$ different estimates of covariances. This is a daunting task! (We show later how the number of required estimates can be reduced substantially.)

Once these estimates are compiled, the expected return and variance of any risky portfolio with weights in each security, w_i, can be calculated from the bordered covariance matrix or, equivalently, from the following formulas:

$$E(r_p) = \sum_{i=1}^{n} w_i E(r_i) \tag{8.9}$$

$$\sigma_p^2 = \sum_{i=1}^{n} \sum_{j=1}^{n} w_i w_j \text{Cov}(r_i, r_j) \tag{8.10}$$

An extended worked example showing you how to do this on a spreadsheet is presented in the next section.

We mentioned earlier that the idea of diversification is age-old. The phrase "don't put all your eggs in one basket" existed long before modern finance theory. It was not until 1952, however, that Harry Markowitz published a formal model of portfolio selection embodying diversification principles, thereby paving the way for his 1990 Nobel Prize for economics.[9] His model is precisely step one of portfolio management: the identification of the efficient set of portfolios, or, as it is often called, the *efficient frontier of risky assets*.

---

[9]Harry Markowitz, "Portfolio Selection," *Journal of Finance*, March 1952.

Figure 8.12
The efficient
portfolio set.

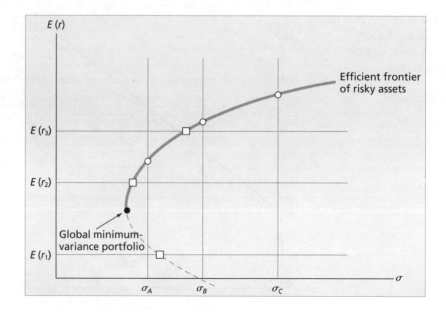

The principal idea behind the frontier set of risky portfolios is that, for any risk level, we are interested only in that portfolio with the highest expected return. Alternatively, the frontier is the set of portfolios that minimize the variance for any target expected return.

Indeed, the two methods of computing the efficient set of risky portfolios are equivalent. To see this, consider the graphical representation of these procedures. Figure 8.12 shows the minimum-variance frontier.

The points marked by squares are the result of a variance-minimization program. We first draw the constraints, that is, horizontal lines at the level of required expected returns. We then look for the portfolio with the lowest standard deviation that plots on each horizontal line—we look for the portfolio that will plot farthest to the left (smallest standard deviation) on that line. When we repeat this for many levels of required expected returns, the shape of the minimum-variance frontier emerges. We then discard the bottom (dashed) half of the frontier, because it is inefficient.

In the alternative approach, we draw a vertical line that represents the standard deviation constraint. We then consider all portfolios that plot on this line (have the same standard deviation) and choose the one with the highest expected return, that is, the portfolio that plots highest on this vertical line. Repeating this procedure for many vertical lines (levels of standard deviation) gives us the points marked by circles that trace the upper portion of the minimum-variance frontier, the efficient frontier.

When this step is completed, we have a list of efficient portfolios, because the solution to the optimization program includes the portfolio proportions, w_i, and the expected return, $E(r_p)$, and standard deviation, σ_p.

Let us restate what our portfolio manager has done so far. The estimates generated by the analysts were transformed into a set of expected rates of return and a covariance matrix. This group of estimates we shall call the **input list**. This input list is then fed into the optimization program.

Before we proceed to the second step of choosing the optimal risky portfolio from the frontier set, let us consider a practical point. Some clients may be subject to additional constraints. For example, many institutions are prohibited from taking short positions in any asset. For these clients the portfolio manager will add to the program constraints that rule out negative (short) positions in the search for efficient portfolios. In this special case it is possible that single assets may be, in and of themselves, efficient risky portfolios. For example, the asset with the highest expected return will be a frontier portfolio because, without the opportunity of short sales, the only way to obtain that rate of return is to hold the asset as one's entire risky portfolio.

Short-sale restrictions are by no means the only such constraints. For example, some clients may want to ensure a minimal level of expected dividend yield from the optimal portfolio. In this case the input list will be expanded to include a set of expected dividend yields $d_1, \ldots, d_n$ and the optimization program will include an additional constraint that ensures that the expected dividend yield of the portfolio will equal or exceed the desired level, d.

Portfolio managers can tailor the efficient set to conform to any desire of the client. Of course, any constraint carries a price tag in the sense that an efficient frontier constructed subject to extra constraints will offer a reward-to-variability ratio inferior to that of a less constrained one. The client should be made aware of this cost and should carefully consider constraints that are not mandated by law.

Another type of constraint is aimed at ruling out investments in industries or countries considered ethically or politically undesirable. This is referred to as *socially responsible investing*, which entails a cost in the form of a lower reward-to-variability on the resultant constrained, optimal portfolio. This cost can be justifiably seen as a contribution to the underlying cause (albeit not a tax-deductible one).

8.5 A SPREADSHEET MODEL

Calculation of Expected Return and Variance

Several software packages can be used to generate the efficient frontier. We will demonstrate the method using Microsoft Excel. Excel is far from the best program for this purpose and is limited in the number of assets it can handle, but working through a simple portfolio optimizer in Excel can illustrate concretely the nature of the calculations used in more sophisticated "black-box" programs. You will find that even in Excel, the computation of the efficient frontier is fairly easy.

We will apply the Markowitz portfolio optimizer to the problem of international diversification. Table 8.4A is taken from Chapter 25, "International Diversification," and shows average returns, standard deviations, and the correlation matrix for the rates of return on the stock indexes of seven countries over the period 1980–1993. Suppose that toward the end of 1979, the analysts of International Capital Management (ICM) had produced an input list that anticipated these results. As portfolio manager of ICM, what set of efficient portfolios would you have considered as investment candidates?

After we input Table 8.4A into our spreadsheet as shown, we create the bordered covariance matrix in Table 8.4B using the relationship $\text{Cov}(r_i, r_j) = \rho_{ij}\sigma_i\sigma_j$. The table shows both cell formulas (upper panel) and numerical results (lower panel).

Next we prepare the data for the computation of the efficient frontier. To establish a benchmark against which to evaluate our efficient portfolios, we use an equally weighted portfolio, that is, the weights for each of the seven countries is equal to $1/7 = .1429$. To compute the properties of this portfolio, these portfolio weights are entered in the border column A53–A59 and border row B52–H52.[10] We calculate the variance of this portfolio

---

[10]You should not enter the portfolio weights in these rows and columns independently, since if a weight in the row changes, the weight in the corresponding column must change to the same value for consistency. Thus you should *copy* each entry from column A to the corresponding element of row 52.

Table 8.4   Performance of Stock Indexes of Seven Countries, 1980–1993

	A	B	C	D	E	F	G	H
1								
2		A. Annualized Standard Deviation, Average Return,						
3		and Correlation Coefficients of International Stocks, 1980–1993						
4								
5		Std. Dev. (%)	Average Ret. (%)					
6	US	21.1	15.7					
7	Germany	25.0	21.7					
8	UK	23.5	18.3					
9	Japan	26.6	17.3					
10	Australia	27.6	14.8					
11	Canada	23.4	10.5					
12	France	26.6	17.2					
13								
14		Correlation Matrix						
15		US	Germany	UK	Japan	Australia	Canada	France
16	US	1.00	0.37	0.53	0.26	0.43	0.73	0.44
17	Germany	0.37	1.00	0.47	0.36	0.29	0.36	0.63
18	UK	0.53	0.47	1.00	0.43	0.50	0.54	0.51
19	Japan	0.26	0.36	0.43	1.00	0.26	0.29	0.42
20	Australia	0.43	0.29	0.50	0.26	1.00	0.56	0.34
21	Canada	0.73	0.36	0.54	0.29	0.56	1.00	0.39
22	France	0.44	0.63	0.51	0.42	0.34	0.39	1.00

	A	B	C	D	E	F	G	H
27		B. Covariance Matrix: Cell Formulas						
28								
29		US	Germany	UK	Japan	Australia	Canada	France
30	US	b6*b6*b16	b7*b6*c16	b8*b6*d16	b9*b6*e16	b10*b6*f16	b11*b6*g16	b12*b6*h16
31	Germany	b6*b7*b17	b7*b7*c17	b8*b7*d17	b9*b7*e17	b10*b7*f17	b11*b7*g17	b12*b7*h17
32	UK	b6*b8*b18	b7*b8*c18	b8*b8*d18	b9*b8*e18	b10*b8*f18	b11*b8*g18	b12*b8*h18
33	Japan	b6*b9*b19	b7*b9*c19	b8*b9*d19	b9*b9*e19	b10*b9*f19	b11*b9*g19	b12*b9*h19
34	Australia	b6*b10*b20	b7*b10*c20	b8*b10*d20	b9*b10*e20	b10*b10*f20	b11*b10*g20	b12*b10*h20
35	Canada	b6*b11*b21	b7*b11*c21	b8*b11*d21	b9*b11*e21	b10*b11*f21	b11*b11*g21	b12*b11*h21
36	France	b6*b12*b22	b7*b12*c22	b8*b12*d22	b9*b12*e22	b10*b12*f22	b11*b12*g22	b12*b12*h22
37								
38		Covariance Matrix: Results						
39								
40		US	Germany	UK	Japan	Australia	Canada	France
41	US	445.21	195.18	262.80	145.93	250.41	360.43	246.95
42	Germany	195.18	625.00	276.13	239.40	200.10	210.60	418.95
43	UK	262.80	276.13	552.25	268.79	324.30	296.95	318.80
44	Japan	145.93	239.40	268.79	707.56	190.88	180.51	297.18
45	Australia	250.41	200.10	324.30	190.88	761.76	361.67	249.61
46	Canada	360.43	210.60	296.95	180.51	361.67	547.56	242.75
47	France	246.95	418.95	318.80	297.18	249.61	242.75	707.56

	A	B	C	D	E	F	G	H
49		C. Bordered Covariance Matrix for the Equally Weighted Portfolio and Portfolio Variance:						
50		Cell Formulas						
51		US	Germany	UK	Japan	Australia	Canada	France
52	Weights	a53	a54	a55	a56	a57	a58	a59
53	0.1429	a53*b52*b41	a53*c52*c41	a53*d52*d41	a53*e52*e41	a53*f52*f41	a53*g52*g41	a53*h52*h41
54	0.1429	a54*b52*b42	a54*c52*c42	a54*d52*d42	a54*e52*e42	a54*f52*f42	a54*g52*g42	a54*h52*h42
55	0.1429	a55*b52*b43	a55*c52*c43	a55*d52*d43	a55*e52*e43	a55*f52*f43	a55*g52*g43	a55*h52*h43
56	0.1429	a56*b52*b44	a56*c52*c44	a56*d52*d44	a56*e52*e44	a56*f52*f44	a56*g52*g44	a56*h52*h44
57	0.1429	a57*b52*b45	a57*c52*c45	a57*d52*d45	a57*e52*e45	a57*f52*f45	a57*g52*g45	a57*h52*h45
58	0.1429	a58*b52*b46	a58*c52*c46	a58*d52*d46	a58*e52*e46	a58*f52*f46	a58*g52*g46	a58*h52*h46
59	0.1429	a59*b52*b47	a59*c52*c47	a59*d52*d47	a59*e52*e47	a59*f52*f47	a59*g52*g47	a59*h52*h47
60	Sum(a53:a59)	sum(b53:b59)	sum(c53:c59)	sum(d53:d59)	sum(e53:e59)	sum(f53:f59)	sum(g53:g59)	sum(h53:h59)
61	Portfolio variance	sum(b60:h60)						
62	Portfolio SD	b61^.5						
63	Portfolio mean	a53*c6+a54*c7+a55*c8+a56*c9+a57*c10+a58*c11+a59*c12						

Table 8.4   (*continued*)

	A	B	C	D	E	F	G	H
64								
65		C. Bordered Covariance Matrix for the Equally Weighted Portfolio and Portfolio Variance:						
66		Results						
67	Portfolio	US	Germany	UK	Japan	Australia	Canada	France
68	weights	0.1429	0.1429	0.1429	0.1429	0.1429	0.1429	0.1429
69	0.1429	9.09	3.98	5.36	2.98	5.11	7.36	5.04
70	0.1429	3.98	12.76	5.64	4.89	4.08	4.30	8.55
71	0.1429	5.36	5.64	11.27	5.49	6.62	6.06	6.51
72	0.1429	2.98	4.89	5.49	14.44	3.90	3.68	6.06
73	0.1429	5.11	4.08	6.62	3.90	15.55	7.38	5.09
74	0.1429	7.36	4.30	6.06	3.68	7.38	11.17	4.95
75	0.1429	5.04	8.55	6.51	6.06	5.09	4.95	14.44
76	1.0000	38.92	44.19	46.94	41.43	47.73	44.91	50.65
77	Portfolio variance	314.77						
78	Portfolio SD	17.7						
79	Portfolio mean	16.5						

	A	B	C	D	E	F	G	H	I
80		D. Bordered Covariance Matrix for the Efficient Frontier Portfolio with Mean of 16.5%							
81		(same mean as the equally weighted portfolio—weights altered by the Solver)							
82									
83	Portfolio	US	Germany	UK	Japan	Australia	Canada	France	
84	weights	0.3759	0.1976	0.0725	0.2073	0.1143	0.0345	−0.0021	
85	0.3759	62.91	14.49	7.17	11.37	10.76	4.67	−0.19	
86	0.1976	14.49	24.39	3.96	9.81	4.52	1.43	−0.17	
87	0.0725	7.17	3.96	2.91	4.04	2.69	0.74	−0.05	
88	0.2073	11.37	9.81	4.04	30.41	4.52	1.29	−0.13	
89	0.1143	10.76	4.52	2.69	4.52	9.95	1.43	−0.06	
90	0.0345	4.67	1.43	0.74	1.29	1.43	0.65	−0.02	
91	−0.0021	−0.19	−0.17	−0.05	−0.13	−0.06	−0.02	0.00	
92	1.0000	111.18	58.43	21.46	61.32	33.80	10.20	−0.61	17.20
93	Portfolio variance	295.76							
94	Portfolio SD	17.2							
95	Portfolio mean	16.5							

	A	B	C	D	E	F	G	H	I	J
96		E. The Unrestricted Efficient Frontier and the Restricted Frontier (with no short sales)								
97										
98		Standard Deviation		Country Weights In Efficient Portfolios						
99	Mean	Unrestricted	Restricted	US	Germany	UK	Japan	Australia	Canada	France
100	9.0	24.2	not feasible	−0.01	−0.29	−0.20	0.22	0.06	0.98	0.22
101	10.5	22.1		0.06	−0.20	−0.15	0.22	0.07	0.81	0.18
102	10.5		23.4	0.00	0.00	0.00	0.00	0.00	1.00	0.00
103	11.0	21.5		0.09	−0.17	−0.13	0.22	0.08	0.75	0.17
104	11.0		22.3	0.00	0.00	0.00	0.07	0.00	0.93	0.00
105	12.0	20.3		0.14	−0.11	−0.10	0.22	0.08	0.63	0.14
106	12.0		20.6	0.00	0.00	0.00	0.16	0.03	0.77	0.04
107	14.0	18.4	18.4	0.23	0.01	−0.03	0.21	0.10	0.40	0.08
108	15.0	17.8	17.8	0.28	0.07	0.00	0.21	0.10	0.28	0.06
109	17.5	17.2	17.2	0.39	0.22	0.09	0.21	0.12	−0.01	−0.01
110	18.0	17.3	17.3	0.42	0.25	0.10	0.21	0.12	−0.07	−0.03
111	18.5	17.4		0.44	0.28	0.12	0.21	0.12	−0.13	−0.04
112	18.5		17.8	0.28	0.36	0.14	0.17	0.04	0.00	0.00
113	21.0	19.0		0.56	0.43	0.20	0.20	0.14	−0.42	−0.11
114	21.0		22.5	0.00	0.80	0.17	0.02	0.00	0.00	0.00
115	22.0	20.0	not feasible	0.61	0.49	0.23	0.20	0.14	−0.53	−0.14
116	26.0	25.4	not feasible	0.79	0.73	0.37	0.19	0.17	−1.00	−0.25

in cell B77 in Table 8.4C. The entry in this cell equals the sum of each element in the covariance matrix where each element is first multiplied by the portfolio weights given in both the row and column borders.[11] We also include two cells to compute the standard deviation and expected return of the equally weighted portfolio (formulas in cells B62, B63) and find that they yield an expected return of 16.5% with a standard deviation of 17.7% (results in cells B78 and B79).

To compute points along the *efficient* frontier we use the Excel Solver in Table 8.4D (which you can find in the Tools menu under Add-Ins). Once you bring up Solver, you are asked to enter the cell of the target (objective) function. In our application, the target is the variance of the portfolio, given in cell B93. Solver will minimize this target. You next must input the cell range of the decision variables (in this case, the portfolio weights, contained in cells B85–B91). Finally, you enter all necessary constraints. For an unrestricted efficient frontier that allows short sales, there are two constraints: first, that the sum of the weights equals 1.0 (cell A92 = 1), and second, that the portfolio expected return equals a target mean return. We will choose a target return equal to that of the equally weighted portfolio, 16.5%, so our second constraint is that cell B95 = 16.5. Once you have entered the two constraints you ask the Solver to find the optimal portfolio weights.

The Solver beeps when it has found a solution and alters automatically the portfolio weight cells in row 84 and column A to show the makeup of the efficient portfolio. It adjusts the entries in the bordered covariance matrix to reflect the multiplication by these new weights, and it shows the mean and variance of this optimal portfolio—the minimum variance portfolio with mean return of 16.5%. These results are shown in Table 8.4D, cells B93–B95. The table shows that the standard deviation of the *efficient* portfolio with same mean as the *equally weighted* portfolio is 17.2%, a reduction of risk of about one-half percentage point. Observe that the weights of the efficient portfolio differ radically from equal weights.

To generate the entire efficient frontier, keep changing the required mean in the constraint (cell B95) and letting the Solver work for you. If you record a sufficient number of points, you will be able to generate a graph of the quality of Figure 8.13.

The outer frontier in Figure 8.13 is drawn assuming that the investor may maintain negative portfolio weights. If shortselling is not allowed, we may impose the additional constraints that each weight (the elements in column A and row 84) must be nonnegative; we would then obtain the restricted efficient frontier curve in Figure 8.13, which lies inside the frontier obtained allowing short sales. The superiority of the unrestricted efficient frontier reminds us that restrictions imposed on portfolio choice may be costly.

The Solver allows you to add short sale and other constraints easily. Once they are entered, you repeat the variance-minimization exercise until you generate the entire restricted frontier. By using macros in Excel or—even better—with specialized software, the entire routine can be accomplished with one push of a button.

Table 8.4E presents a number of points on the two frontiers. The first column gives the required mean and the next two columns show the resultant variance of efficient portfolios with and without short sales. Note that the restricted frontier cannot obtain a mean return less than 10.5% (which is the mean in Canada, the country index with the lowest mean return) or more than 21.7% (corresponding to Germany, the country with the highest mean return). The last seven columns show the portfolio weights of the seven country stock indexes in the opti-

---

[11]We need the sum of each element of the covariance matrix, where each term has first been multiplied by the product of the portfolio weights from its row and column. These values appear in Panel C of Table 8.4. We will first sum these elements for each column and then add up the column sums. Row 60 contains the appropriate column sums. Therefore, the sum of cells B60–H60, which appears in cell B61, is the variance of the portfolio formed using the weights appearing in the borders of the covariance matrix.

Figure 8.13
Efficient frontier with
seven countries.

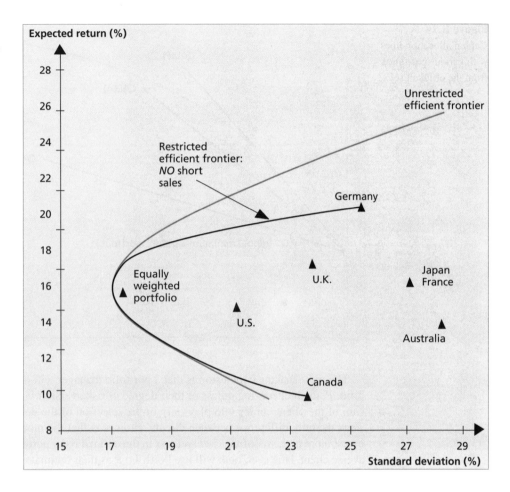

mal portfolios. You can see that the weights in restricted portfolios are never negative. For mean returns in the range from about 14% to 18%, the two frontiers overlap since the optimal weights in the unrestricted frontier turn out to be positive (see also Figure 8.13).

Notice that despite the fact that German stocks offer the highest mean return and even the highest reward-to-variability ratio, the weight of U.S stocks is generally higher in both restricted and unrestricted portfolios. This is due to the lower correlation of U.S. stocks with stocks of other countries, and it illustrates the importance of diversification attributes when forming efficient portfolios. Figure 8.13 presents points corresponding to means and standard deviations of individual country indexes, as well as the equally weighted portfolio. The figure clearly shows the benefits from diversification.

Capital Allocation and the Separation Property

Now that we have the efficient frontier, we proceed to step two and introduce the risk-free asset. Figure 8.14 shows the efficient frontier plus three CALs representing various portfolios from the efficient set. As before, we ratchet up the CAL by selecting different portfolios until we reach Portfolio *P*, which is the tangency point of a line from *F* to the efficient frontier. Portfolio *P* maximizes the reward-to-variability ratio, the slope of the line from *F* to portfolios on the efficient frontier. At this point our portfolio manager is done. Portfolio *P* is the optimal risky portfolio for the manager's clients. This is a good time to ponder our results and their implementation.

Figure 8.14

Capital allocation lines with various portfolios from the efficient set.

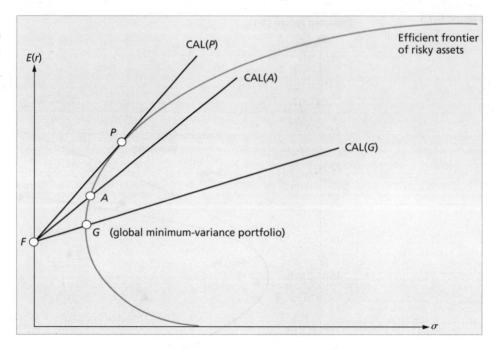

The most striking conclusion is that a portfolio manager will offer the same risky portfolio, *P*, to all clients regardless of their degree of risk aversion.[12] The degree of risk aversion of the client comes into play only in the selection of the desired point on the CAL. Thus the only difference between clients' choices is that the more risk-averse client will invest more in the risk-free asset and less in the optimal risky portfolio than will a less risk-averse client. However, both will use Portfolio *P* as their optimal risky investment vehicle.

This result is called a **separation property**; it tells us that the portfolio choice problem may be separated into two independent tasks. The first task, determination of the optimal risky portfolio, is purely technical. Given the manager's input list, the best risky portfolio is the same for all clients, regardless of risk aversion. The second task, however, allocation of the complete portfolio to T-bills versus the risky portfolio, depends on personal preference. Here the client is the decision maker.

The crucial point is that the optimal portfolio *P* that the manager offers is the same for all clients. This result makes professional management more efficient and hence less costly. One management firm can serve any number of clients with relatively small incremental administrative costs.

In practice, however, different managers will estimate different input lists, thus deriving different efficient frontiers, and offer different "optimal" portfolios to their clients. The source of the disparity lies in the security analysis. It is worth mentioning here that the rule of GIGO (garbage in–garbage out) also applies to security analysis. If the quality of the security analysis is poor, a passive portfolio such as a market index fund will result in a better CAL than an active portfolio that uses low-quality security analysis to tilt portfolio weights toward seemingly favorable (mispriced) securities.

As we have seen, optimal risky portfolios for different clients also may vary because of portfolio constraints such as dividend-yield requirements, tax considerations, or other client

---

[12]Clients who impose special restrictions (constraints) on the manager, such as dividend yield, will obtain another optimal portfolio. Any constraint that is added to an optimization problem leads, in general, to a different and less desirable optimum compared to an unconstrained program.

preferences. Nevertheless, this analysis suggests that a limited number of portfolios may be sufficient to serve the demands of a wide range of investors. This is the theoretical basis of the mutual fund industry.

The (computerized) optimization technique is the easiest part of the portfolio construction problem. The real arena of competition among portfolio managers is in sophisticated security analysis.

Concept
CHECK

Question 4 • Suppose that two portfolio managers who work for competing investment management houses each employ a group of security analysts to prepare the input list for the Markowitz algorithm. When all is completed, it turns out that the efficient frontier obtained by portfolio manager *A* dominates that of manager *B*. By domination we mean that *A*'s optimal risky portfolio lies northwest of *B*'s. Hence, given a choice, investors will all prefer the risky portfolio that lies on the CAL of *A*.
a. What should be made of this outcome?
b. Should it be attributed to better security analysis by *A*'s analysts?
c. Could it be that *A*'s computer program is superior?
d. If you were advising clients (and had an advance glimpse at the efficient frontiers of various managers), would you tell them to periodically switch their money around to the manager with the most northwesterly portfolio?

Asset Allocation and Security Selection

As we have seen, the theories of security selection and asset allocation are identical. Both activities call for the construction of an efficient frontier, and the choice of a particular portfolio from along that frontier. The determination of the optimal combination of securities proceeds in the same manner as the analysis of the optimal combination of asset classes. Why, then, do we (and the investment community) distinguish between asset allocation and security selection?

Three factors are at work. First, as a result of greater need and ability to save (for college educations, recreation, longer life in retirement, health care needs, etc.), the demand for sophisticated investment management has increased enormously. Second, the widening spectrum of financial markets and financial instruments has put sophisticated investment beyond the capacity of many amateur investors. Finally, there are strong economic returns to scale in investment management. The end result is that the size of a competitive investment company has grown with the industry, and efficiency in organization has become an important issue.

A large investment company is likely to invest both in domestic and international markets and in a broad set of asset classes, each of which requires specialized expertise. Hence the management of each asset-class portfolio needs to be decentralized, and it becomes impossible to simultaneously optimize the entire organization's risky portfolio in one stage, although this would be prescribed as optimal on *theoretical* grounds.

The practice is therefore to optimize the security selection of each asset-class portfolio independently. At the same time, top management continually updates the asset allocation of the organization, adjusting the investment budget of each asset-class portfolio. When changed frequently in response to intensive forecasting activity, these reallocations are called *market timing*. The shortcoming of this two-step approach to portfolio construction, versus the theory-based one-step optimization, is the failure to exploit the covariance of the individual securities in one asset-class portfolio with the individual securities in the other asset classes. Only the covariance matrix of the securities within each asset-class portfolio can be used. However, this loss might be small because of the depth of diversification of each portfolio and the extra layer of diversification at the asset allocation level.

8.6   OPTIMAL PORTFOLIOS WITH RESTRICTIONS ON THE RISK-FREE ASSET

The availability of a risk-free asset greatly simplifies the portfolio decision. When all investors can borrow and lend at that risk-free rate, we are led to a *unique* optimal risky portfolio that is appropriate for all investors given a common input list. This portfolio maximizes the reward-to-variability ratio. All investors use the same risky portfolio and differ only in the proportion they invest in it and in the risk-free asset.

What if a risk-free asset is not available? Although T-bills are risk-free assets in nominal terms, their real returns are uncertain. Without a risk-free asset, there is no tangency portfolio that is best for all investors. In this case investors have to choose a portfolio from the efficient frontier of risky assets redrawn in Figure 8.15.

Each investor will now choose an optimal risky portfolio by superimposing a personal set of indifference curves on the efficient frontier as in Figure 8.15. An investor with indifference curves marked U', U'', and U''' in Figure 8.15 will choose Portfolio *P*. More risk-averse investors with steeper indifference curves will choose portfolios with lower means and smaller standard deviations such as Portfolio *Q*, while more risk-tolerant investors will choose portfolios with higher means and greater risk, such as Portfolio *S*. The common feature of all these investors is that each chooses portfolios on the efficient frontier.

Even if virtually risk-free lending opportunities are available, many investors do face borrowing restrictions. They may be unable to borrow altogether, or, more realistically, they may face a borrowing rate that is significantly greater than the lending rate.

When a risk-free investment is available, but an investor cannot borrow, a CAL exists but is limited to the line *FP* as in Figure 8.16. Any investors whose preferences are represented by indifference curves with tangency portfolios on the portion *FP* of the CAL, such as Portfolio *A*, are unaffected by the borrowing restriction. Such investors are net *lenders* at rate r_f.

Aggressive or more risk-tolerant investors, who *would* choose Portfolio *B* in the absence of the borrowing restriction, are affected, however. Such investors will be driven to port-

Figure 8.15

Portfolio selection without a risk-free asset.

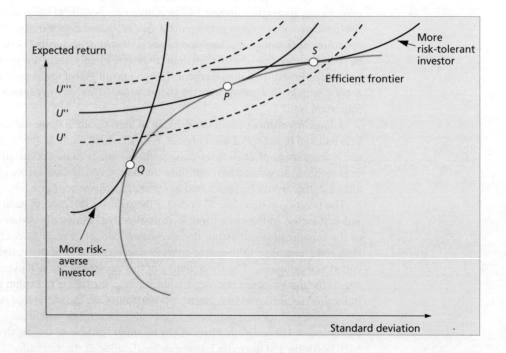

folios such as Portfolio Q, which are on the efficient frontier of risky assets. These investors will not invest in the risk-free asset.

In more realistic scenarios, individuals who wish to borrow to invest in a risky portfolio will have to pay an interest rate higher than the T-bill rate. For example, the call money rate charged by brokers on margin accounts is higher than the T-bill rate.

Investors who face a borrowing rate greater than the lending rate confront a three-part CAL such as in Figure 8.17. CAL_1, which is relevant in the range FP_1, represents the efficient portfolio set for defensive (risk-averse) investors. These investors invest part of their funds in T-bills at rate r_f. They find that the tangency Portfolio is P_1, and they choose a complete portfolio such as Portfolio A in Figure 8.18.

Figure 8.16
Portfolio selection with risk-free lending but no borrowing.

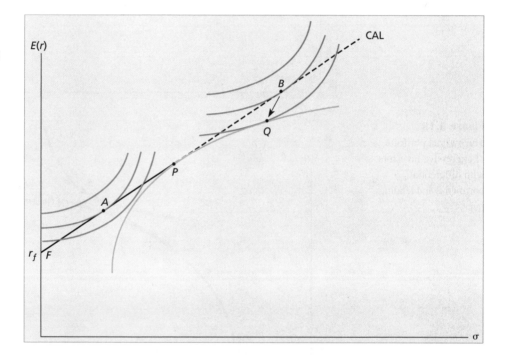

Figure 8.17
The investment opportunity set with differential rates for borrowing and lending.

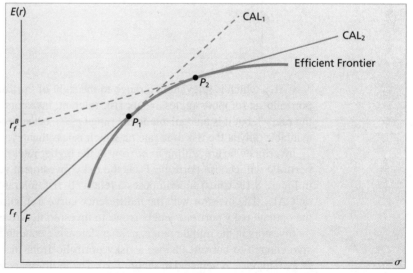

Figure 8.18

The optimal portfolio of defensive investors with differential borrowing and lending rates.

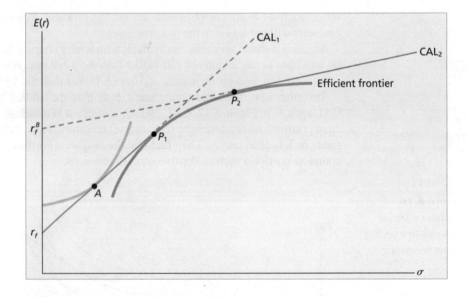

Figure 8.19

The optimal portfolio of aggressive investors with differential borrowing and lending rates.

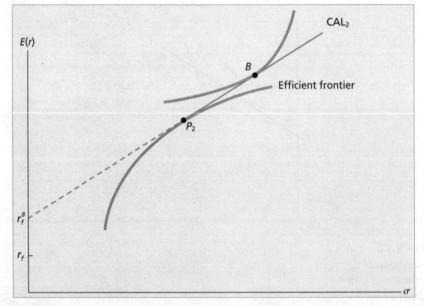

CAL_2, which is relevant in a range to the right of Portfolio P_2, represents the efficient portfolio set for more aggressive, or risk-tolerant, investors. This line starts at the borrowing rate r_f^B, but it is unavailable in the range $r_f^B P_2$, because *lending* (investing in T-bills) is available only at the risk-free rate r_f, which is less than r_f^B.

Investors who are willing to *borrow* at the higher rate, r_f^B, to invest in an optimal risky portfolio will choose Portfolio P_2 as the risky investment vehicle. Such a case is depicted in Figure 8.19, which superimposes a relatively risk-tolerant investor's indifference curve on CAL_2. The investor with the indifference curve in Figure 8.19 chooses Portfolio P_2 as the optimal risky portfolio and borrows to invest in it, arriving at the overall Portfolio B.

Investors in the middle range, neither defensive enough to invest in T-bills nor aggressive enough to borrow, choose a risky portfolio from the efficient frontier in the range $P_1 P_2$. This case is depicted in Figure 8.20. The indifference curve representing the investor in Figure 8.20 leads to a tangency portfolio on the efficient frontier, Portfolio C.

Figure 8.20

The optimal portfolio of moderately risk-tolerant investors with differential borrowing and lending rates

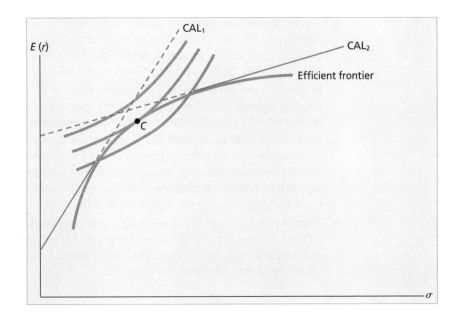

Concept CHECK

Question 5 • With differential lending and borrowing rates, only investors with about average degrees of risk aversion will choose a portfolio in the range P_1P_2 in Figure 8.18. Other investors will choose a portfolio on CAL$_1$ if they are more risk averse, or on CAL$_2$ if they are more risk tolerant.

a. Does this mean that investors with average risk aversion are more dependent on the quality of the forecasts that generate the efficient frontier?

b. Describe the trade-off between expected return and standard deviation for portfolios between P_1 and P_2 in Figure 8.18 compared with portfolios on CAL$_2$ beyond P_2.

SUMMARY

1. The expected return of a portfolio is the weighted average of the component asset expected returns with the investment proportions as weights.

2. The variance of a portfolio is the weighted sum of the elements of the covariance matrix with the product of the investment proportions as weights. Thus the variance of each asset is weighted by the square of its investment proportion. Each covariance of any pair of assets appears twice in the covariance matrix; thus the portfolio variance includes twice each covariance weighted by the product of the investment proportions in each of the two assets.

3. Even if the covariances are positive, the portfolio standard deviation is less than the weighted average of the component standard deviations, as long as the assets are not perfectly positively correlated. Thus portfolio diversification is of value as long as assets are less than perfectly correlated.

4. The greater an asset's covariance with the other assets in the portfolio, the more it contributes to portfolio variance. An asset that is perfectly negatively correlated with a portfolio can serve as a perfect hedge. The perfect hedge asset can reduce the portfolio variance to zero.

5. The efficient frontier is the graphical representation of a set of portfolios that maximize expected return for each level of portfolio risk. Rational investors will choose a portfolio on the efficient frontier.

6. A portfolio manager identifies the efficient frontier by first establishing estimates for the asset expected returns and the covariance matrix. This input list is then fed into an optimization program that reports as outputs the investment proportions, expected returns, and standard deviations of the portfolios on the efficient frontier.

7. In general, portfolio managers will arrive at different efficient portfolios because of differences in methods and quality of security analysis. Managers compete on the quality of their security analysis relative to their management fees.

8. If a risk-free asset is available and input lists are identical, all investors will choose the same portfolio on the efficient frontier of risky assets: the portfolio tangent to the CAL. All investors with identical input lists will hold an identical risky portfolio, differing only in how much each allocates to this optimal portfolio and to the risk-free asset. This result is characterized as the separation principle of portfolio construction.

9. When a risk-free asset is not available, each investor chooses a risky portfolio on the efficient frontier. If a risk-free asset is available but borrowing is restricted, only aggressive investors will be affected. They will choose portfolios on the efficient frontier according to their degree of risk tolerance.

Key Terms

diversification	firm-specific risk	optimal risky portfolio
insurance principle	nonsystematic risk	minimum-variance frontier
market risk	diversifiable risk	efficient frontier
systematic risk	minimum-variance portfolio	input list
nondiversifiable risk	portfolio opportunity set	separation property
unique risk	reward-to-variability ratio	

Selected Readings

Two frequently cited papers on the impact of diversification on portfolio risk are:

Evans, John L.; and Stephen H. Archer. "Diversification and the Reduction of Dispersion: An Empirical Analysis." *Journal of Finance*, December 1968.

Wagner, W. H.; and S. C. Lau. "The Effect of Diversification on Risk." *Financial Analysts Journal*, November–December 1971.

The seminal works on portfolio selection are:

Markowitz, Harry M. "Portfolio Selection." *Journal of Finance*, March 1952.

Markowitz, Harry M. *Portfolio Selection: Efficient Diversification of Investments.* New York: John Wiley & Sons, 1959.

Also see:

Samuelson, Paul A. "Risk & Uncertainty: A Fallacy of Large Numbers." *Scientia* 98 (1963).

Problems

The following data apply to problems 1 through 8:

A pension fund manager is considering three mutual funds. The first is a stock fund, the second is a long-term government and corporate bond fund, and the third is a T-bill money market fund that yields a rate of 8%. The probability distribution of the risky funds is as follows:

	Expected Return	Standard Deviation
Stock fund (S)	20%	30%
Bond fund (B)	12	15

The correlation between the fund returns is .10.

1. What are the investment proportions of the minimum-variance portfolio of the two risky funds, and what is the expected value and standard deviation of its rate of return?

2. Tabulate and draw the investment opportunity set of the two risky funds. Use investment proportions for the stock funds of zero to 100% in increments of 20%.

3. Draw a tangent from the risk-free rate to the opportunity set. What does your graph show for the expected return and standard deviation of the optimal portfolio?

4. Solve numerically for the proportions of each asset and for the expected return and standard deviation of the optimal risky portfolio.

5. What is the reward-to-variability ratio of the best feasible CAL?

6. You require that your portfolio yield an expected return of 14%, and that it be efficient on the best feasible CAL.
   a. What is the standard deviation of your portfolio?
   b. What is the proportion invested in the T-bill fund and each of the two risky funds?

7. If you were to use only the two risky funds, and still require an expected return of 14%, what must be the investment proportions of your portfolio? Compare its standard deviation to that of the optimized portfolio in problem 6. What do you conclude?

8. Suppose that you face the same opportunity set, but you cannot borrow. You wish to construct a portfolio of only stocks and bonds with an expected return of 24%. What are the appropriate portfolio proportions and the resulting standard deviations? What reduction in standard deviation could you attain if you were allowed to borrow at the risk-free rate?

9. Stocks offer an expected rate of return of 18%, with a standard deviation of 22%. Gold offers an expected return of 10% with a standard deviation of 30%.
   a. In light of the apparent inferiority of gold with respect to both mean return and volatility, would anyone hold gold? If so, demonstrate graphically why one would do so.
   b. Given the data above, reanswer (*a*) with the additional assumption that the correlation coefficient between gold and stocks equals 1. Draw a graph illustrating why one would or would not hold gold in one's portfolio. Could this set of assumptions for expected returns, standard deviations, and correlation represent an equilibrium for the security market?

10. Suppose that there are many stocks in the security market and that the characteristics of Stocks *A* and *B* are given as follows:

Stock	Expected Return	Standard Deviation
A	10%	5%
B	15	10
	Correlation = −1	

Suppose that it is possible to borrow at the risk-free rate, r_f. What must be the value of the risk-free rate? (Hint: Think about constructing a risk-free portfolio from Stocks *A* and *B*.)

11. Assume that expected returns and standard deviations for all securities (including the risk-free rate for borrowing and lending) are known. In this case all investors will have the same optimal risky portfolio. (True or false?)

12. The standard deviation of the portfolio is always equal to the weighted average of the standard deviations of the assets in the portfolio. (True or false?)

13. Suppose you have a project that has a .7 chance of doubling your investment in a year and a .3 chance of halving your investment in a year. What is the standard deviation of the rate of return on this investment?

14. Suppose that you have $1 million and the following two opportunities from which to construct a portfolio:

    a. Risk-free asset earning 12% per year.

    b. Risky asset earning 30% per year with a standard deviation of 40%.

    If you construct a portfolio with a standard deviation of 30%, what will be the rate of return?

The following data apply to problems 15 through 17.

Hennessy & Associates manages a $30 million equity portfolio for the multimanager Wilstead Pension Fund. Jason Jones, financial vice president of Wilstead, noted that Hennessy had rather consistently achieved the best record among the Wilstead's six equity managers. Performance of the Hennessy portfolio had been clearly superior to that of the S&P 500 in four of the past five years. In the one less-favorable year, the shortfall was trivial.

Hennessy is a "bottom-up" manager. The firm largely avoids any attempt to "time the market." It also focuses on selection of individual stocks, rather than the weighting of favored industries.

There is no apparent conformity of style among the six equity managers. The five managers, other than Hennessy, manage portfolios aggregating $250 million made up of more than 150 individual issues.

Jones is convinced that Hennessy is able to apply superior skill to stock selection, but the favorable returns are limited by the high degree of diversification in the portfolio. Over the years, the portfolio generally held 40–50 stocks, with about 2%–3% of total funds committed to each issue. The reason Hennessy seemed to do well most years was because the firm was able to identify each year 10 or 12 issues which registered particularly large gains.

Based on this overview, Jones outlined the following plan to the Wilstead pension committee:

> Let's tell Hennessy to limit the portfolio to no more than 20 stocks. Hennessy will double the commitments to the stocks that it really favors, and eliminate the remainder. Except for this one new restriction, Hennessy should be free to manage the portfolio exactly as before.

All the members of the pension committee generally supported Jones's proposal because all agreed that Hennessy had seemed to demonstrate superior skill in selecting stocks. Yet the proposal was a considerable departure from previous practice, and several committee members raised questions. Respond to each of the following questions.

15. *a.* Will the limitations of 20 stocks likely increase or decrease the risk of the portfolio? Explain.

    b. Is there any way Hennessy could reduce the number of issues from 40 to 20 without significantly affecting risk? Explain.

16. One committee member was particularly enthusiastic concerning Jones's proposal. He suggested that Hennessy's performance might benefit further from reduction in the

number of issues to 10. If the reduction to 20 could be expected to be advantageous, explain why reduction to 10 might be less likely to be advantageous. (Assume that Wilstead will evaluate the Hennessy portfolio independently of the other portfolios in the fund.)

17. Another committee member suggested that, rather than evaluate each managed portfolio independently of other portfolios, it might be better to consider the effects of a change in the Hennessy portfolio on the total fund. Explain how this broader point of view could affect the committee decision to limit the holdings in the Hennessy portfolio to either 10 or 20 issues.

The following data are for problems 18 through 20.

The correlation coefficients between pairs of stocks are as follows: Corr(A,B) = .85; Corr(A,C) = .60; Corr(A,D) = .45. Each stock has an expected return of 8% and a standard deviation of 20%.

18. If your entire portfolio is now composed of Stock A and you can add some of only one stock to your portfolio, would you choose (explain your choice):
    a. B.
    b. C.
    c. D.
    d. Need more data.

19. Would the answer to problem 18 change for more risk-averse or risk-tolerant investors? Explain.

20. Suppose that in addition to investing in one more stock you can invest in T-bills as well. Would you change your answers to problems 18 and 19 if the T-bill rate is 8%?

21. Which one of the following portfolios cannot lie on the efficient frontier as described by Markowitz?

	Portfolio	Expected Return (%)	Standard Deviation(%)
a.	W	15	36
b.	X	12	15
c.	Z	5	7
d.	Y	9	21

22. Which statement about portfolio diversification is correct?
    a. Proper diversification can reduce or eliminate systematic risk.
    b. Diversification reduces the portfolio's expected return because it reduces a portfolio's total risk.
    c. As more securities are added to a portfolio, total risk typically would be expected to fall at a decreasing rate.
    d. The risk-reducing benefits of diversification do not occur meaningfully until at least 30 individual securities are included in the portfolio.

23. The measure of risk for a security held in a diversified portfolio is:
 a. Specific risk.
 b. Standard deviation of returns.
 c. Reinvestment risk.
 d. Beta.

24. Portfolio theory as described by Markowitz is most concerned with:
 a. The elimination of systematic risk.
 b. The effect of diversification on portfolio risk.
 c. The identification of unsystematic risk.
 d. Active portfolio management to enhance return.

25. Assume that a risk-averse investor owning stock in Miller Corporation decides to add the stock of either Mac or Green Corporation to her portfolio. All three stocks offer the same expected return and total risk. The covariance of return between Miller and Mac is –.05 and between Miller and Green is +.05. Portfolio risk is expected to:
 a. Decline more when the investor buys Mac.
 b. Decline more when the investor buys Green.
 c. Increase when either Mac or Green is bought.
 d. Decline or increase, depending on other factors.

26. Stocks *A*, *B*, and *C* have the same expected return and standard deviation. The following table shows the correlations between the returns on these stocks.

	Stock *A*	Stock *B*	Stock *C*
Stock A	+1.0		
Stock B	+0.9	+1.0	
Stock C	+0.1	−0.4	+1.0

Given these correlations, the portfolio constructed from these stocks having the lowest risk is a portfolio:
 a. Equally invested in stocks *A* and *B*.
 b. Equally invested in stocks *A* and *C*.
 c. Equally invested in stocks *B* and *C*.
 d. Totally invested in stock *C*.

27. Statistics for three stocks, *A*, *B*, and *C*, are shown in the following tables.

Standard Deviations of Returns

Stock:	A	B	C
Standard deviation:	.40	.20	.40

Correlations of Returns

Stock	A	B	C
A	1.00	0.90	0.50
B		1.00	0.10
C			1.00

Based *only* on the information provided in the tables, and given a choice between a portfolio made up of equal amounts of stocks A and B *or* a portfolio made up of equal amounts of stocks B and C, state which portfolio you would recommend. Justify your choice.

The following table of compound annual returns by decade applies to problems 28 and 29.

	1920s*	1930s	1940s	1950s	1960s	1970s	1980s	1990s†	1987–96
Large company stocks	6.98%	−1.25%	9.11%	19.41%	7.84%	5.90%	17.60%	7.64%	15.30%
Small company stocks	−1.51	7.28	20.63	19.01	13.72	8.75	12.46	8.05	11.11
Long-term T-bonds	1.57	4.60	3.59	0.26	1.14	6.63	11.50	6.79	9.31
Intermediate-term T-bonds	1.49	3.91	1.70	1.11	3.41	6.11	12.01	5.60	8.23
Treasury bills	1.41	0.30	0.37	1.87	3.89	6.29	9.00	2.92	5.48
Inflation	−0.40	−2.04	5.36	2.22	2.52	7.36	5.10	1.99	3.68

*Based on the period 1926–1929.

†Based on the period 1990–1996.

Source: Data in Table 5.2.

28. Input the data from the table into a spreadsheet. Compute the serial correlation in decade returns for each asset class and for inflation. Also find the correlation between the returns of various asset classes. What do the data indicate?

29. Convert the asset returns by decade presented in the table into real rates. Repeat the analysis of problem 28 for the real rates of return.

solutions to
Concept
CHECKS

1. *a.* The first term will be $w_D \times w_D \times \sigma_D^2$, since this is the element in the top corner of the matrix (σ_D^2) times the term on the column border (w_D) times the term on the row border (w_D). Applying this rule to each term of the covariance matrix results in the sum $w_D^2 \sigma_D^2 + w_D w_E \text{Cov}(r_E, r_D) + w_E w_D \text{Cov}(r_D, r_E) + w_E^2 \sigma_E^2$, which is the same as equation 8.2, since $\text{Cov}(r_E, r_D) = \text{Cov}(r_D, r_E)$.

b. The bordered covariance matrix is

	w_X	w_Y	w_Z
w_X	σ_X^2	$\text{Cov}(r_X, r_Y)$	$\text{Cov}(r_X, r_Z)$
w_Y	$\text{Cov}(r_Y, r_X)$	σ_Y^2	$\text{Cov}(r_Y, r_Z)$
w_Z	$\text{Cov}(r_Z, r_X)$	$\text{Cov}(r_Z, r_Y)$	σ_Z^2

There are nine terms in the covariance matrix. Portfolio variance is calculated from these nine terms:

$$\sigma_P^2 = w_X^2 \sigma_X^2 + w_Y^2 \sigma_Y^2 + w_Z^2 \sigma_Z^2$$
$$+ w_X w_Y \text{Cov}(r_X, r_Y) + w_Y w_X \text{Cov}(r_Y, r_X)$$
$$+ w_X w_Z \text{Cov}(r_X, r_Z) + w_Z w_X \text{Cov}(r_Z, r_X)$$
$$+ w_Y w_Z \text{Cov}(r_Y, r_Z) + w_Z w_Y \text{Cov}(r_Z, r_Y)$$
$$= w_X^2 \sigma_X^2 + w_Y^2 \sigma_Y^2 + w_Z^2 \sigma_Z^2$$
$$+ 2w_X w_Y \text{Cov}(r_X, r_Y) + 2w_X w_Z \text{Cov}(r_X, r_Z) + 2w_Y w_Z \text{Cov}(r_Y, r_Z)$$

2. The parameters of the opportunity set are $E(r_D) = 8\%$, $E(r_E) = 13\%$, $\sigma_D = 12\%$, $\sigma_E = 20\%$, and $\rho(D,E) = .25$. From the standard deviations and the correlation coefficient we generate the covariance matrix:

Stock	D	E
D	144	60
E	60	400

The *global minimum-variance* portfolio is constructed so that

$$w_D = \frac{\sigma_E^2 - \text{Cov}(r_D, r_E)}{\sigma_D^2 + \sigma_E^2 - 2\,\text{Cov}(r_D, r_E)}$$

$$= \frac{400 - 60}{(144 + 400) - (2 \times 60)} = .8019$$

$$w_E = 1 - w_D = .1981$$

Its expected return and standard deviation are

$$E(r_P) = (.8019 \times 8) + (.1981 \times 13) = 8.99\%$$
$$\sigma_P = [w_D^2 \sigma_D^2 + w_E^2 \sigma_E^2 + 2 w_D w_E \text{Cov}(r_D, r_E)]^{1/2}$$
$$= [(.8019^2 \times 144) + (.1981^2 \times 400) + (2 \times .8019 \times .1981 \times 60)]^{1/2}$$
$$= 11.29\%$$

For the other points we simply increase w_D from .10 to .90 in increments of .10; accordingly, w_E ranges from .90 to .10 in the same increments. We substitute these portfolio proportions in the formulas for expected return and standard deviation. Note that for w_D or w_E equal to 1.0, the portfolio parameters equal those of the stock.

We then generate the following table:

w_E	w_D	E(r)	σ
0.0	1.0	8.0	12.00
0.1	0.9	8.5	11.46
0.2	0.8	9.0	11.29
0.3	0.7	9.5	11.48
0.4	0.6	10.0	12.03
0.5	0.5	10.5	12.88
0.6	0.4	11.0	13.99
0.7	0.3	11.5	15.30
0.8	0.2	12.0	16.76
0.9	0.1	12.5	18.34
1.0	0.0	13.0	20.00
0.1981	0.8019	8.99	11.29 minimum variance portfolio

You can now draw your graph.

3. *a.* The computations of the opportunity set of the stock and risky bond funds are like those of question 2 and will not be shown here. You should perform these computations, however, in order to give a graphical solution to part *a*. Note that the covariance between the funds is

$$Cov(r_A, r_B) = \rho(A,B) \times \sigma_A \times \sigma_B$$
$$= -.2 \times 20 \times 60 = -240$$

b. The proportions in the optimal risky portfolio are given by

$$w_A = \frac{(10-5)60^2 - (30-5)(-240)}{(10-5)60^2 + (30-5)20^2 - 30(-240)}$$
$$= .6818$$
$$w_B = 1 - w_A = .3182$$

The expected return and standard deviation of the optimal risky portfolio are

$$E(r_P) = (.6818 \times 10) + (.3128 \times 30) = 16.36\%$$
$$\sigma_P = \{(.6818^2 \times 20^2) + (.3182^2 \times 60^2) + [2 \times .6818 \times .3182(-240)]\}^{1/2}$$
$$= 21.13\%$$

Note that in this case the standard deviation of the optimal risky portfolio is smaller than the standard deviation of stock *A*. Note also that portfolio *P* is not the global minimum-variance portfolio. The proportions of the latter are given by

$$w_A = \frac{60^2 - (-240)}{60^2 + 20^2 - 2(-240)} = .8571$$
$$w_B = 1 - w_A = .1429$$

With these proportions, the standard deviation of the minimum-variance portfolio is

$$\sigma(\min) = \{(.8571^2 \times 20^2) + (.1429^2 \times 60^2) + [2 \times .8571 \times .1429 \times (-240)]\}^{1/2}$$
$$= 17.57\%$$

which is smaller than that of the optimal risky portfolio.

c. The CAL is the line from the risk-free rate through the optimal risky portfolio. This line represents all efficient portfolios that combine T-bills with the optimal risky portfolio. The slope of the CAL is

$$S = \frac{E(r_P) - r_f}{\sigma_P} = \frac{16.36 - 5}{21.13} = .5376$$

d. Given a degree of risk aversion, *A*, an investor will choose a proportion, *y*, in the optimal risky portfolio of

$$y = \frac{E(r_P) - r_f}{.01 \times A\sigma_P^2} = \frac{16.36 - 5}{.01 \times 5 \times 21.13^2} = .5089$$

This means that the optimal risky portfolio, with the given data, is attractive enough for an investor with *A* = 5 to invest 50.89% of his or her wealth in it. Since stock *A* makes up 68.18% of the risky portfolio and stock *B* 31.82%, the investment proportions for this investor are

Stock *A*:	.5089 × 68.18 =	34.70%
Stock *B*:	.5089 × 31.82 =	16.19%
Total		50.89%

4. Efficient frontiers derived by portfolio managers depend on forecasts of the rates of return on various securities and estimates of risk, that is, the covariance matrix. The forecasts themselves do not control outcomes. Thus preferring managers with rosier forecasts (northwesterly frontiers) is tantamount to rewarding the bearers of good news and punishing the bearers of bad news. What we should do is reward bearers of *accurate* news. Thus if you get a glimpse of the frontiers (forecasts) of portfolio managers on a regular basis, what you want to do is develop the track record of their forecasting accuracy and steer your advisees toward the more accurate forecaster. Their portfolio choices will, in the long run, outperform the field.

5. *a.* Portfolios that lie on the CAL are combinations of the tangency (risky) portfolio and the risk-free asset. Hence they are just as dependent on the accuracy of the efficient frontier as portfolios that are on the frontier itself. If we judge forecasting accuracy by the accuracy of the reward-to-variability ratio, then all portfolios on a CAL will be exactly as accurate as the tangency portfolio.

   b. All portfolios on CAL_1 are combinations of portfolio P_1 with lending (buying T-bills). This combination of one risky asset with a risk-free asset leads to a linear relationship between the portfolio expected return and its standard deviation:

$$E(r_P) = r_f + \frac{E(r_{P1}) - r_f}{\sigma_{P1}} \sigma_P \qquad (5.b)$$

The same applies to all portfolios on CAL_2; just replace $E(r_{P_1})$, σ_{P_1} in equation 5.b with $E(r_{P_2})$, σ_{P_2}.

An investor who wishes to have an expected return between $E(r_{P_1})$ and $E(r_{P_2})$ must find the appropriate portfolio on the efficient frontier of risky assets between P_1 and P_2 in the correct proportions.

APPENDIX A: THE POWER OF DIVERSIFICATION

Section 8.1 introduced the concept of diversification and the limits to the benefits of diversification resulting from systematic risk. Given the tools we have developed, we can reconsider this intuition more rigorously and at the same time sharpen our insight regarding the power of diversification.

Recall from equation 8.10 that the general formula for the variance of a portfolio is

$$\sigma_p^2 = \sum_{j=1}^{n} \sum_{i=1}^{n} w_i w_j \text{Cov}(r_i, r_j) \qquad (8A.1)$$

Consider now the naive diversification strategy in which an equally weighted portfolio is constructed, meaning that $w_i = 1/n$ for each security. In this case equation 8A.1 may be rewritten as follows, where we break out the terms for which $i = j$ into a separate sum, noting that $\text{Cov}(r_i, r_j) = \sigma_i^2$.

$$\sigma_p^2 = \frac{1}{n} \sum_{i=1}^{n} \frac{1}{n} \sigma_i^2 + \sum_{\substack{j=1 \\ j \neq i}}^{n} \sum_{i=1}^{n} \frac{1}{n^2} \text{Cov}(r_i, r_j) \qquad (8A.2)$$

Note that there are n variance terms and $n(n - 1)$ covariance terms in equation 8A.2.

If we define the average variance and average covariance of the securities as

$$\bar{\sigma}^2 = \frac{1}{n} \sum_{i=1}^{n} \sigma_i^2$$

$$\overline{\text{Cov}} = \frac{1}{n(n-1)} \sum_{\substack{j=1 \\ j \neq i}}^{n} \sum_{i=1}^{n} \text{Cov}(r_i, r_j)$$

we can express portfolio variance as

$$\sigma_p^2 = \frac{1}{n}\bar{\sigma}^2 + \frac{n-1}{n}\overline{\text{Cov}} \tag{8A.3}$$

Now examine the effect of diversification. When the average covariance among security returns is zero, as it is when all risk is firm-specific, portfolio variance can be driven to zero. We see this from equation 8A.3: The second term on the right-hand side will be zero in this scenario, while the first term approaches zero as n becomes larger. Hence when security returns are uncorrelated, the power of diversification to limit portfolio risk is unlimited.

However, the more important case is the one in which economywide risk factors impart positive correlation among stock returns. In this case, as the portfolio becomes more highly diversified (n increases) portfolio variance remains positive. Although firm-specific risk, represented by the first term in equation 8A.3, is still diversified away, the second term simply approaches $\overline{\text{Cov}}$ as n becomes greater. [Note that $(n-1)/n = 1 - 1/n$, which approaches 1 for large n.] Thus the irreducible risk of a diversified portfolio depends on the covariance of the returns of the component securities, which in turn is a function of the importance of systematic factors in the economy.

To see further the fundamental relationship between systematic risk and security correlations, suppose for simplicity that all securities have a common standard deviation, σ, and all security pairs have a common correlation coefficient, ρ. Then the covariance between all pairs of securities is $\rho\sigma^2$, and equation 8A.3 becomes

$$\sigma_p^2 = \frac{1}{n}\sigma^2 + \frac{n-1}{n}\rho\sigma^2 \tag{8A.4}$$

The effect of correlation is now explicit. When $\rho = 0$, we again obtain the insurance principle, where portfolio variance approaches zero as n becomes greater. For $\rho > 0$, however, portfolio variance remains positive. In fact, for $\rho = 1$, portfolio variance equals σ^2 regardless of n, demonstrating that diversification is of no benefit: In the case of perfect correlation, all risk is systematic. More generally, as n becomes greater, equation 8A.4 shows that systematic risk becomes $\rho\sigma^2$.

Table 8A.1 presents portfolio standard deviation as we include ever-greater numbers of securities in the portfolio for two cases, $\rho = 0$ and $\rho = .40$. The table takes σ to be 50%. As one would expect, portfolio risk is greater when $\rho = .40$. More surprising, perhaps, is that portfolio risk diminishes far less rapidly as n increases in the positive correlation case. The correlation among security returns limits the power of diversification.

Note that for a 100-security portfolio, the standard deviation is 5% in the uncorrelated case—still significant when we consider the potential of zero standard deviation. For $\rho = .40$, the standard deviation is high, 31.86%, yet it is very close to undiversifiable systematic risk in the infinite-sized universe, $\sqrt{\rho\sigma^2} = \sqrt{.4 \times 50^2} = 31.62\%$. At this point, further diversification is of little value.

We also gain an important insight from this exercise. When we hold diversified portfolios, the contribution to portfolio risk of a particular security will depend on the *covariance*

Table 8A.1   Risk Reduction of Equally Weighted Portfolios in Correlated and Uncorrelated Universes

Universe Size n	Optimal Portfolio Proportion 1/n (%)	$\rho = 0$		$\rho = .4$	
		Standard Deviation (%)	Reduction in σ	Standard Deviation (%)	Reduction in σ
1	100	50.00	14.64	50.00	8.17
2	50	35.36		41.83	
5	20	22.36	1.95	36.06	0.70
6	16.67	20.41		35.36	
10	10	15.81	0.73	33.91	0.20
11	9.09	15.08		33.71	
20	5	11.18	0.27	32.79	0.06
21	4.76	10.91		32.73	
100	1	5.00	0.02	31.86	0.00
101	0.99	4.98		31.86	

of that security's return with those of other securities, and *not* on the security's variance. As we shall see in Chapter 9, this implies that fair risk premiums also should depend on covariances rather than total variability of returns.

Concept CHECK

Question A.1 • **Suppose that the universe of available risky securities consists of a large number of stocks, identically distributed with $E(r) = 15\%$, $\sigma = 60\%$, and a common correlation coefficient of $\rho = .5$.**

a. **What is the expected return and standard deviation of an equally weighted risky portfolio of 25 stocks?**

b. **What is the smallest number of stocks necessary to generate an efficient portfolio with a standard deviation equal to or smaller than 43%?**

c. **What is the systematic risk in this universe?**

d. **If T-bills are available and yield 10%, what is the slope of the CAL?**

solution to Concept CHECKS

A.1. The parameters are $E(r) = 15$, $\sigma = 60$, and the correlation between any pair of stocks is $\rho = .5$.

a. The portfolio expected return is invariant to the size of the portfolio because all stocks have identical expected returns. The standard deviation of a portfolio with $n = 25$ stocks is

$$\sigma_P = [\sigma^2/n + \rho \times \sigma^2(n-1)/n]^{1/2}$$
$$= [60^2/25 + .5 \times 60^2 \times 24/25]^{1/2} = 43.27$$

b. Because the stocks are identical, efficient portfolios are equally weighted. To obtain a standard deviation of 43%, we need to solve for n:

$$43^2 = \frac{60^2}{n} + .5 \times \frac{60^2(n-1)}{n}$$
$$1{,}849n = 3{,}600 + 1{,}800n - 1{,}800$$
$$n = \underline{1{,}800} = 36.73$$
$$49$$

Thus we need 37 stocks and will come in with volatility slightly under the target.

c. As *n* gets very large, the variance of an efficient (equally weighted) portfolio diminishes, leaving only the variance that comes from the covariances among stocks, that is

$$\sigma_P = \sqrt{\rho \times \sigma^2} = \sqrt{.5 \times 60^2} = 42.43$$

Note that with 25 stocks we came within .84% of the systematic risk, that is, the nonsystematic risk of a portfolio of 25 stocks is .84%. With 37 stocks the standard deviation is 43%, of which nonsystematic risk is .57%.

d. If the risk-free is 10%, then the risk premium on any size portfolio is 15 − 10 = 5%. The standard deviation of a well-diversified portfolio is (practically) 42.43%, hence the slope of the CAL is

$$S = 5/42.43 = .1178$$

APPENDIX B: THE INSURANCE PRINCIPLE: RISK-SHARING VERSUS RISK-POOLING

Mean-variance analysis has taken a strong hold among investment professionals, and insight into the mechanics of efficient diversification has become quite widespread. Common misconceptions or fallacies about diversification still persist, however. Here we will try to put some to rest.

It is commonly believed that a large portfolio of independent insurance policies is a necessary and sufficient condition for an insurance company to shed its risk. The fact is that a multitude of independent insurance policies is neither necessary nor sufficient for a sound insurance portfolio. Actually, an individual insurer who would not insure a single policy also would be unwilling to insure a large portfolio of independent policies.

Consider Paul Samuelson's (1963) story. He once offered a colleague 2-to-1 odds on a $1,000 bet on the toss of a coin. His colleague refused, saying, "I won't bet because I would feel the $1,000 loss more than the $2,000 gain. But I'll take you on if you promise to let me make a hundred such bets."

Samuelson's colleague, like many others, might have explained his position, not quite correctly, as: "One toss is not enough to make it reasonably sure that the law of averages will turn out in my favor. But with a hundred tosses of a coin, the law of averages will make it a darn good bet."

Another way to rationalize this argument is to think in terms of rates of return. In each bet you put up $1,000 and then get back $3,000 with a probability of one-half, or zero with a probability of one-half. The probability distribution of the rate of return is 200% with $p = \frac{1}{2}$ and −100% with $p = \frac{1}{2}$.

The bets are all independent and identical and therefore the expected return is $E(r) = \frac{1}{2}(200) + \frac{1}{2}(-100) = 50\%$, regardless of the number of bets. The standard deviation of the rate of return on the portfolio of independent bets is[13]

$$\sigma(n) = \sigma/\sqrt{n}$$

where σ is the standard deviation of a single bet:

$$\sigma = [\tfrac{1}{2}(200 - 50)^2 + \tfrac{1}{2}(-100 - 50)^2]^{1/2}$$
$$= 150\%$$

---

[13]This follows from equation 8.10, setting $w_i = 1/n$ and all covariances equal to zero because of the independence of the bets.

The average rate of return on a sequence of bets, in other words, has a smaller standard deviation than that of a single bet. By increasing the number of bets we can reduce the standard deviation of the rate of return to any desired level. It seems at first glance that Samuelson's colleague was correct. But he was not.

The fallacy of the argument lies in the use of a rate of return criterion to choose from portfolios *that are not equal in size*. Although the portfolio is equally weighted across bets, each extra bet increases the scale of the investment by $1,000. Recall from your corporate finance class that when choosing among mutually exclusive projects you cannot use the internal rate of return (IRR) as your decision criterion when the projects are of different sizes. You have to use the net present value (NPV) rule.

Consider the dollar profit (as opposed to rate of return) distribution of a single bet:

$$E(R) = \tfrac{1}{2} \times 2,000 + \tfrac{1}{2} \times (-1,000)$$
$$= \$500$$
$$\sigma_R = [\tfrac{1}{2}(2,000 - 500)^2 + \tfrac{1}{2}(-1,000 - 500)^2]^{1/2}$$
$$= \$1,500$$

These are independent bets where the total profit from n bets is the sum of the profits from the single bets. Therefore, with n bets

$$E[R(n)] = \$500n$$
$$\text{Variance } (\sum_{i=1}^{n} R_i) = n\sigma_R^2$$
$$\sigma_R(n) = \sqrt{n\sigma_R^2}$$
$$= \sigma_R\sqrt{n}$$

so that the standard deviation of the dollar return *increases* by a factor equal to the square root of the number of bets, n, in contrast to the standard deviation of the rate of return, which *decreases* by a factor of the square root of n.

As another analogy, consider the standard coin-tossing game. Whether one flips a fair coin 10 times or 1,000 times, the expected percentage of heads flipped is 50%. One expects the actual proportion of heads in a typical running of the 1,000-toss experiment to be closer to 50% than in the 10-toss experiment. This is the law of averages.

But the actual number of heads will typically depart from its expected value by a greater amount in the 1,000-toss experiment. For example, 504 heads is close to 50% and is 4 more than the expected number. To exceed the expected number of heads by 4 in the 10-toss game would require 9 out of 10 heads, which is a much more extreme departure from the mean. In the many-toss case, there is more volatility of the *number* of heads and less volatility of the *percentage* of heads. This is the same when an insurance company takes on more policies: The *dollar* variance of its portfolio increases while the *rate of return* variance falls.

The lesson is this: Rate of return analysis is appropriate when considering mutually exclusive portfolios of equal size, which is what we did in all the examples so far. We applied a fixed investment budget, and we investigated only the consequences of varying investment proportions in various assets. But if an insurance company takes on more and more insurance policies, it is increasing portfolio dollar investments. The analysis called for in that case must be cast in terms of dollar profits, in much the same way that NPV is called for instead of IRR when we compare different-sized projects. This is why risk-pooling (i.e., accumulating independent risky prospects) does not act to eliminate risk.

Samuelson's colleague should have counteroffered: "Let's make 1,000 bets, each with your $2 against my $1." Then he would be holding a portfolio of fixed size, equal to $1,000, which is diversified into 1,000 identical independent prospects. This would make the insurance principle work.

Another way for Samuelson's colleague to get around the riskiness of this tempting bet is to share the large bets with friends. Consider a firm engaging in 1,000 of Paul Samuelson's bets. In each bet the firm puts up $1,000 and receives $3,000 or nothing, as before. Each bet is too large for you. Yet if you hold a 1/1,000 share of the firm, your position is exactly the same as if you were to make 1,000 small bets of $2 against $1. A 1/1,000 share of a $1,000 bet is equivalent to a $1 bet. Holding a small share of many large bets essentially allows you to replace a stake in one large bet with a diversified portfolio of manageable bets.

How does this apply to insurance companies? Investors can purchase insurance company shares in the stock market, so they can choose to hold as small a position in the overall risk as they please. No matter how great the risk of the policies, a large group of individual small investors will agree to bear the risk if the expected rate of return exceeds the risk-free rate. Thus it is the sharing of risk among many shareholders that makes the insurance industry tick.

APPENDIX C: THE FALLACY OF TIME DIVERSIFICATION

The insurance story just discussed illustrates a misuse of rate of return analysis, specifically the mistake of comparing portfolios of different sizes. A more insidious version of this error often appears under the guise of "time diversification."

Consider the case of Mr. Frier, who has $100,000. He is trying to figure out the appropriate allocation of this fund between risk-free T-bills that yield 10% and a risky portfolio that yields an annual rate of return with $E(r_P) = 15\%$ and $\sigma_P = 30\%$.

Mr. Frier took a course in finance in his youth. He likes quantitative models, and after careful introspection estimates that his degree of risk aversion, A, is 4. Consequently, he calculates that his proper allocation to the risky portfolio is

$$y = \frac{E(r_P) - r_f}{.01 \times A\sigma_P^2} = \frac{15 - 10}{.01 \times 4 \times 30^2} = .14$$

that is, a 14% investment ($14,000) in the optimal risky portfolio.

With this strategy, Mr. Frier calculates his complete portfolio expected return and standard deviation as

$$E(r_C) = r_f + y[E(r_P) - r_f] = 10.70\%$$
$$\sigma_C = y\sigma_P = 4.20\%$$

At this point, Mr. Frier gets cold feet because this fund is intended to provide the mainstay of his retirement wealth. He plans to retire in five years, and any mistake will be burdensome.

Mr. Frier calls Ms. Mavin, a highly recommended financial adviser. Ms. Mavin explains that indeed the time factor is all-important. She cites academic research showing that asset rates of return over successive holding periods are independent. Therefore, she argues, returns in good years and bad years will tend to cancel out over the five-year period. Consequently, the average portfolio rate of return over the investment period will be less risky than would appear from the standard deviation of a single-year portfolio return.

Figure 8C.1
Simulated return distributions for the period 1998–2017. Geometric average annual rates.

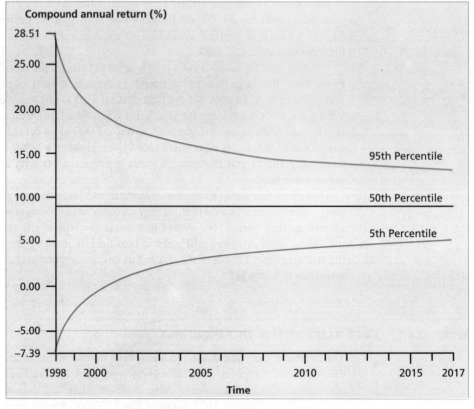

Source: Stocks, Bonds, Bills, and Inflation: 1998 Yearbook (Chicago: Ibbotson Associates, Inc., 1998).

Because returns in each year are independent, Ms. Mavin tells Mr. Frier that a five-year investment is equivalent to a portfolio of five equally weighted independent assets. With such a portfolio, the (five-year) holding period return has a mean of

$$E[r_P(5)] = 15\% \text{ per year}$$

and standard deviation of[14]

$$\sigma_P(5) = \frac{30}{\sqrt{5}}$$

$$= 13.42\% \text{ per year}$$

Mr. Frier is relieved. He believes that the effective standard deviation has fallen from 30% to 13.42%, and that the reward-to-variability ratio is much better than his first assessment.

Is Mr. Frier's newfound sense of security warranted? Specifically, is Ms. Mavin's time diversification really a risk-reducer? It is true that the standard deviation of the annualized *rate* of return over five years really is only 13.42% as Mavin claims, compared with the 30% one-year standard deviation. But what about the volatility of Mr. Frier's total retirement fund? With a standard deviation of the five-year average return of 13.42%, a one-standard-

---

[14]The calculation for standard deviation is only approximate, because it assumes that the five-year return is the sum of each of the five one-year returns, and this formulation ignores compounding. The error is small, however, and does not affect the point we want to make.

Figure 8C.2

Dollar returns on common stocks. Simulated distributions of nominal wealth index for the period 1998–2017 (year-end 1993 equals 1.00).

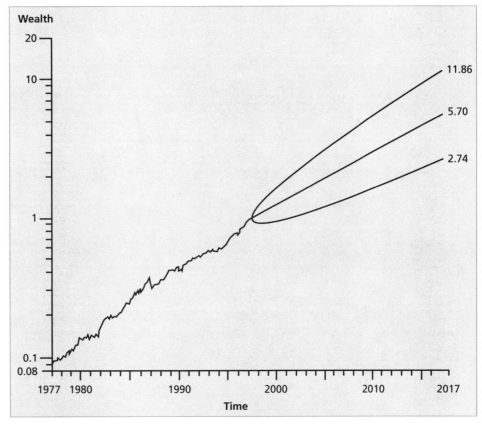

Source: Stocks, Bonds, Bills, and Inflation: 1998 Yearbook (Chicago: Ibbotson Associates, Inc., 1998).

deviation disappointment in Mr. Frier's average return over the five-year period will affect final wealth by a factor of $(1 - .1342)^5 = .487$, meaning that final wealth will be less than one-half of its expected value. This is a larger impact than the 30% one-year swing.

Ms. Mavin is wrong: Time diversification does not reduce risk. Although it is true that the *per year* average rate of return has a smaller standard deviation for a longer time horizon, it also is true that the uncertainty compounds over a greater number of years. Unfortunately, this latter effect dominates in the sense that the *total return* becomes more uncertain the longer the investment horizon.

Figures 8C.1 and 8C.2 show the fallacy of time diversification. They represent simulated returns to a stock investment and show the range of possible outcomes. Although the confidence band around the expected rate of return on the investment narrows with investment life, the dollar confidence band widens.

Again, the coin-toss analogy is helpful. Think of each year's investment return as one flip of the coin. After many years, the average number of heads approaches 50%, but the possible deviation of total heads from one-half the number of flips still will be growing.

The lesson is, once again, that one should not use rate of return analysis to compare portfolios of different size. Investing for more than one holding period means that the amount of risk is growing. This is analogous to an insurer taking on more insurance policies. The fact that these policies are independent does not offset the effect of placing more funds at risk. Focus on the standard deviation of the rate of return should never obscure the more proper emphasis on the possible dollar values of a portfolio strategy.

EQUILIBRIUM IN CAPITAL MARKETS

THE CAPITAL ASSET PRICING MODEL

The capital asset pricing model, almost always referred to as the CAPM, is a centerpiece of modern financial economics. The model gives us a precise prediction of the relationship that we should observe between the risk of an asset and its expected return. This relationship serves two vital functions. First, it provides a benchmark rate of return for evaluating possible investments. For example, if we are analyzing securities, we might be interested in whether the expected return we forecast for a stock is more or less than its "fair" return given its risk. Second, the model helps us to make an educated guess as to the expected return on assets that have not yet been traded in the marketplace. For example, how do we price an initial public offering of stock? How will a major new investment project affect the return investors require on a company's stock? Although the CAPM does not fully withstand empirical tests, it is widely used because of the insight it offers and because its accuracy suffices for many important applications. In this chapter we start with the basic version of the CAPM. We also show how some assumptions of the simple version may be relaxed to allow for greater realism.

9.1   THE CAPITAL ASSET PRICING MODEL

The capital asset pricing model is a set of predictions concerning equilibrium expected returns on risky assets. Harry Markowitz laid down the foundation of modern portfolio management in 1952. The CAPM was developed 12 years later in articles by William Sharpe,[1] John Lintner,[2] and Jan Mossin.[3] The time for this gestation indicates that the leap from Markowitz's portfolio selection model to the CAPM is not trivial.

We will approach the CAPM by posing the question "what if," where the "if" part refers to a simplified world. Positing an admittedly unrealistic world allows a relatively easy leap to the "then" part. Once we accomplish this, we can add complexity to the hypothesized environment one step at a time and see how the conclusions must be amended. This process allows us to derive a reasonably realistic and comprehensible model.

We summarize the simplifying assumptions that lead to the basic version of the CAPM in the following list. The thrust of these assumptions is that we try to ensure that individuals are as alike as possible, with the notable exceptions of initial wealth and risk aversion. We will see that conformity of investor behavior vastly simplifies our analysis.

1. There are many investors, each with an endowment (wealth) that is small compared to the total endowment of all investors. Investors are price-takers, in that they act as though security prices are unaffected by their own trades. This is the usual perfect competition assumption of microeconomics.

2. All investors plan for one identical holding period. This behavior is myopic (short-sighted) in that it ignores everything that might happen after the end of the single-period horizon. Myopic behavior is, in general, suboptimal.

3. Investments are limited to a universe of publicly traded financial assets, such as stocks and bonds, and to risk-free borrowing or lending arrangements. This assumption rules out investment in nontraded assets such as education (human capital), private enterprises, and governmentally funded assets such as town halls and international airports. It is assumed also that investors may borrow or lend any amount at a fixed, risk-free rate.

4. Investors pay no taxes on returns and no transaction costs (commissions and service charges) on trades in securities. In reality, of course, we know that investors are in different tax brackets and that this may govern the type of assets in which they invest. For example, tax implications may differ depending on whether the income is from interest, dividends, or capital gains. Furthermore, trading is costly, and commissions and fees depend on the size of the trade and the good standing of the individual investor.

5. All investors are rational mean-variance optimizers, meaning that they all use the Markowitz portfolio selection model.

6. All investors analyze securities in the same way and share the same economic view of the world. The result is identical estimates of the probability distribution of future cash flows from investing in the available securities; that is, for any set of security prices, they all derive the same input list to feed into the Markowitz model. Given a set of security prices and the risk-free interest rate, all investors use the

---

[1]William Sharpe, "Capital Asset Prices: A Theory of Market Equilibrium," *Journal of Finance,* September 1964.
[2]John Lintner, "The Valuation of Risk Assets and the Selection of Risky Investments in Stock Portfolios and Capital Budgets," *Review of Economics and Statistics,* February 1965.
[3]Jan Mossin, "Equilibrium in a Capital Asset Market," *Econometrica,* October 1966.

same expected returns and covariance matrix of security returns to generate the efficient frontier and the unique optimal risky portfolio. This assumption is often referred to as **homogeneous expectations** or beliefs.

These assumptions represent the "if" of our "what if" analysis. Obviously, they ignore many real-world complexities. With these assumptions, however, we can gain some powerful insights into the nature of equilibrium in security markets.

We can summarize the equilibrium that will prevail in this hypothetical world of securities and investors briefly. The rest of the chapter explains and elaborates on these implications.

1. All investors will choose to hold a portfolio of risky assets in proportions that duplicate representation of the assets in the **market portfolio** (M), which includes all traded assets. For simplicity, we generally refer to all risky assets as *stocks*. The proportion of each stock in the market portfolio equals the market value of the stock (price per share multiplied by the number of shares outstanding) divided by the total market value of all stocks.

2. Not only will the market portfolio be on the efficient frontier, but it also will be the tangency portfolio to the optimal capital allocation line (CAL) derived by each and every investor. As a result, the *capital market line* (CML), the line from the risk-free rate through the market portfolio, M, is also the best attainable capital allocation line. All investors hold M as their optimal risky portfolio, differing only in the amount invested in it versus in the risk-free asset.

3. The risk premium on the market portfolio will be proportional to its risk and the degree of risk aversion of the representative investor. Mathematically,

$$E(r_M) - r_f = \bar{A}\sigma_M^2 \times .01$$

where σ_M^2 is the variance of the market portfolio and $\bar{A}$ is the average degree of risk aversion across investors.[4] Note that because M is the optimal portfolio, which is efficiently diversified across all stocks, σ_M^2 is the systematic risk of this universe.

4. The risk premium on *individual* assets will be proportional to the risk premium on the market portfolio, M, and the *beta coefficient* of the security relative to the market portfolio. Beta measures the extent to which returns on the stock and the market move together. Formally, beta is defined as

$$\beta_i = \frac{\text{Cov}(r_i, r_M)}{\sigma_M^2}$$

and the risk premium on individual securities is

$$E(r_i) - r_f = \frac{\text{Cov}(r_i, r_M)}{\sigma_M^2}[E(r_M) - r_f]$$

$$= \beta_i[E(r_M) - r_f]$$

We will elaborate on these results and their implications shortly.

---

[4]As we pointed out in Chapter 8, the scale factor .01 arises because we measure returns as percentages rather than decimals.

Why Do All Investors Hold the Market Portfolio?

What is the market portfolio? When we sum over, or aggregate, the portfolios of all individual investors, lending and borrowing will cancel out (since each lender has a corresponding borrower), and the value of the aggregate risky portfolio will equal the entire wealth of the economy. This is the market portfolio, M. The proportion of each stock in this portfolio equals the market value of the stock (price per share times number of shares outstanding) divided by the sum of the market values of all stocks.[5] The CAPM implies that as individuals attempt to optimize their personal portfolios, they each arrive at the same portfolio, with weights on each asset equal to those of the market portfolio.

Given the assumptions of the previous section, it is easy to see that all investors will desire to hold identical risky portfolios. If all investors use identical Markowitz analysis (Assumption 5) applied to the same universe of securities (Assumption 3) for the same time horizon (Assumption 2) and use the same input list (Assumption 6), they all must arrive at the same determination of the optimal risky portfolio, the portfolio on the efficient frontier identified by the tangency line from T-bills to that frontier, as in Figure 9.1. This implies that if the weight of GM stock, for example, in each common risky portfolio is 1%, then GM also will comprise 1% of the market portfolio. The same principle applies to the proportion of any stock in each investor's risky portfolio. As a result, the optimal risky portfolio of all investors is simply a share of the market portfolio in Figure 9.1.

Now suppose that the optimal portfolio of our investors does not include the stock of some company, such as Delta Airlines. When all investors avoid Delta stock, the demand is zero, and Delta's price takes a free fall. As Delta stock gets progressively cheaper, it becomes ever more attractive and other stocks look relatively less attractive. Ultimately, Delta reaches a price where it is attractive enough to include in the optimal stock portfolio.

Such a price adjustment process guarantees that all stocks will be included in the optimal portfolio. It shows that *all* assets have to be included in the market portfolio. The only issue is the price at which investors will be willing to include a stock in their optimal risky portfolio.

Figure 9.1

The efficient frontier and the capital market line.

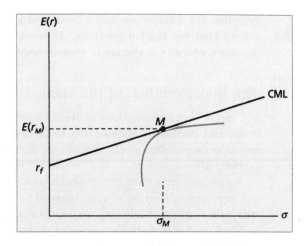

This may seem a roundabout way to derive a simple result: If all investors hold an identical risky portfolio, this portfolio has to be *M*, the market portfolio. Our intention, however, is to demonstrate a connection between this result and its underpinnings, the equilibrating process that is fundamental to security market operation.

The Passive Strategy Is Efficient

In Chapter 7 we defined the CML (capital market line) as the CAL (capital allocation line) that is constructed from a money market account (or T-bills) and the market portfolio. Perhaps now you can fully appreciate why the CML is an interesting CAL. In the simple world of the CAPM, *M* is the optimal tangency portfolio on the efficient frontier, as shown in Figure 9.1.

In this scenario the market portfolio that all investors hold is based on the common input list, thereby incorporating all relevant information about the universe of securities. This means that investors can skip the trouble of doing specific analysis and obtain an efficient portfolio simply by holding the market portfolio. (Of course, if everyone were to follow this strategy, no one would perform security analysis and this result would no longer hold. We discuss this issue in depth in Chapter 12 on market efficiency.)

Thus the passive strategy of investing in a market index portfolio is efficient. For this reason, we sometimes call this result a **mutual fund theorem**. The mutual fund theorem is another incarnation of the separation property discussed in Chapter 8. Assuming that all investors choose to hold a market index mutual fund, we can separate portfolio selection into two components—a technological problem, creation of mutual funds by professional managers—and a personal problem that depends on an investor's risk aversion, allocation of the *complete* portfolio between the mutual fund and risk-free assets.

In reality, different investment managers do create risky portfolios that differ from the market index. We attribute this in part to the use of different input lists in the formation of the optimal risky portfolio. Nevertheless, the significance of the mutual fund theorem is that a passive investor may view the market index as a reasonable first approximation to an efficient risky portfolio.

Question 1 • If there are only a few investors who perform security analysis, and all others hold the market portfolio, *M*, would the CML still be the efficient CAL for investors who do not engage in security analysis? Why or why not?

The Risk Premium of the Market Portfolio

In Chapter 7 we discussed how individual investors go about deciding how much to invest in the risky portfolio. Returning now to the decision of how much to invest in portfolio *M* versus in the risk-free asset, what can we deduce about the equilibrium risk premium of portfolio *M*?

We asserted earlier that the equilibrium risk premium on the market portfolio, $E(r_M) - r_f$, will be proportional to the average degree of risk aversion of the investor population and the risk of the market portfolio, σ_M^2. Now we can explain this result.

Recall that each individual investor chooses a proportion *y*, allocated to the optimal portfolio *M*, such that

$$y = \frac{E(r_M) - r_f}{.01 \times A\sigma_M^2} \tag{9.1}$$

In the simplified CAPM economy, risk-free investments involve borrowing and lending among investors. Any borrowing position must be offset by the lending position of the creditor. This means that net borrowing and lending across all investors must be zero, and in consequence the average position in the risky portfolio is 100%, or $\bar{y} = 1$. Setting $y = 1$ in equation 9.1 and rearranging, we find that the risk premium on the market portfolio is related to its variance by the average degree of risk aversion:

$$E(r_M) - r_f = .01 \times \bar{A}\sigma_M^2 \qquad (9.2)$$

Question 2 • **Data from the period 1926 to 1996 for the S&P 500 index yield the following statistics: average excess return, 8.7%; standard deviation, 20.8%.**
a. **To the extent that these averages approximated investor expectations for the period, what must have been the average coefficient of risk aversion?**
b. **If the coefficient of risk aversion were actually 3.5, what risk premium would have been consistent with the market's historical standard deviation?**

Expected Returns on Individual Securities

The CAPM is built on the insight that the appropriate risk premium on an asset will be determined by its contribution to the risk of investors' overall portfolios. Portfolio risk is what matters to investors and is what governs the risk premiums they demand.

Remember that all investors use the same input list, that is, the same estimates of expected returns, variances, and covariances. We saw in Chapter 8 that these covariances can be arranged in a covariance matrix, so that the entry in the fifth row and third column, for example, would be the covariance between the rates of return on the fifth and third securities. Each diagonal entry of the matrix is the covariance of one security's return with itself, which is simply the variance of that security. We will consider the construction of the input list a bit later. For now we take it as given.

Suppose, for example, that we want to gauge the portfolio risk of GM stock. We measure the contribution to the risk of the overall portfolio from holding GM stock by its covariance with the market portfolio. To see why this is so, let us look again at the way the variance of the market portfolio is calculated. To calculate the variance of the market portfolio, we use the bordered covariance matrix with the market portfolio weights, as discussed in Chapter 8. We highlight GM in this depiction of the n stocks in the market portfolio.

Portfolio Weights	w_1	w_2	...	w_{GM}	...	w_n
w_1	$Cov(r_1,r_1)$	$Cov(r_1,r_2)$	...	$Cov(r_1,r_{GM})$	...	$Cov(r_1,r_n)$
w_2	$Cov(r_2,r_1)$	$Cov(r_2,r_2)$	...	$Cov(r_2,r_{GM})$	...	$Cov(r_2,r_n)$
•	•	•		•		•
•	•	•		•		•
•	•	•		•		•
w_{GM}	$Cov(r_{GM},r_1)$	$Cov(r_{GM},r_2)$	...	$Cov(r_{GM},r_{GM})$	...	$Cov(r_{GM},r_n)$
•	•	•		•		•
•	•	•		•		•
•	•	•		•		•
w_n	$Cov(r_n,r_1)$	$Cov(r_n,r_2)$	...	$Cov(r_n,r_{GM})$	...	$Cov(r_n,r_n)$

Recall that we calculate the variance of the portfolio by summing over all the elements of the covariance matrix, first multiplying each element by the portfolio weights from the row and the column. The contribution of one stock to portfolio variance therefore can be expressed as the sum of all the covariance terms in the row corresponding to the stock where each covariance is multiplied by both the stock's weight from its row and the weight from its column.[6]

For example, the contribution of GM's stock to the variance of the market portfolio is

$$w_{GM}[w_1\text{Cov}(r_1,r_{GM}) + w_2\text{Cov}(r_2,r_{GM}) + \cdots + w_{GM}\text{Cov}(r_{GM},r_{GM}) + \cdots + w_n\text{Cov}(r_n,r_{GM})] \quad (9.3)$$

Equation 9.3 provides a clue about the respective roles of variance and covariance in determining asset risk. When there are many stocks in the economy, there will be many more covariance terms than variance terms. Consequently, the covariance of a particular stock with all other stocks will dominate that stock's contribution to total portfolio risk. We may summarize the terms in brackets in equation 9.3 simply as the covariance of GM with the market portfolio. In other words, we can best measure the stock's contribution to the risk of the market portfolio by its covariance with that portfolio:

$$\text{GM's contribution to variance} = w_{GM}\text{Cov}(r_{GM},r_M)$$

This should not surprise us. For example, if the covariance between GM and the rest of the market is negative, then GM makes a "negative contribution" to portfolio risk: By providing returns that move inversely with the rest of the market, GM stabilizes the return on the overall portfolio. If the covariance is positive, GM makes a positive contribution to overall portfolio risk because its returns amplify swings in the rest of the portfolio.

To prove this more rigorously, note that the rate of return on the market portfolio may be written as

$$r_M = \sum_{k=1}^{n} w_k r_k$$

Therefore, the covariance of the return on GM with the market portfolio is

$$\text{Cov}(r_{GM},r_M) = \text{Cov}(r_{GM}, \sum_{k=1}^{n} w_k r_k) = \sum_{k=1}^{n} w_k \text{Cov}(r_{GM},r_k) \quad (9.4)$$

Comparing the last term of equation 9.4 to the term in brackets in equation 9.3, we can see that the covariance of GM with the market portfolio is indeed proportional to the contribution of GM to the variance of the market portfolio.

Having measured the contribution of GM stock to market variance, we may determine the appropriate risk premium for GM. We note first that the market portfolio has a risk premium of $E(r_M) - r_f$ and a variance of σ_M^2, for a reward-to-risk ratio of

$$\frac{E(r_M) - r_f}{\sigma_M^2} \quad (9.5)$$

[6]An alternative and equally valid approach would be to measure GM's contribution to market variance as the sum of the elements in the row *and* the column corresponding to GM. In this case, GM's contribution would be twice the sum in equation 9.3. The approach that we take in the text allocates contributions to portfolio risk among securities in a convenient manner in that the sum of the contributions of each stock equals the total portfolio variance, whereas the alternative measure of contribution would sum to twice the portfolio variance. This results from a type of double-counting, because adding both the rows and the columns for each stock would result in each entry in the matrix being added twice.

This ratio often is called the **market price of risk**,[7] because it quantifies the extra return that investors demand to bear portfolio risk. The ratio of risk premium to variance tells us how much extra return must be earned per unit of portfolio risk.

Consider an average investor who is currently invested 100% in the market portfolio and suppose he were to increase his position in the market portfolio by a tiny fraction, δ, financed by borrowing at the risk-free rate. Think of the new portfolio as a combination of three assets: the original position in the market with return r_M, plus a short (negative) position of size δ in the risk-free asset that will return $-\delta r_f$, plus a long position of size δ in the market that will return δr_M. The portfolio rate of return will be $r_M + \delta(r_M - r_f)$. Taking expectations and comparing with the original expected return, $E(r_M)$, the incremental expected rate of return will be

$$\Delta E(r) = \delta[E(r_M) - r_f]$$

To measure the impact of the portfolio shift on risk, we compute the new value of the portfolio variance. The new portfolio has a weight of $(1 + \delta)$ in the market and $-\delta$ in the risk-free asset. Therefore, the variance of the adjusted portfolio is

$$\sigma^2 = (1 + \delta)^2 \sigma_M^2 = (1 + 2\delta + \delta^2)\sigma_M^2 = \sigma_M^2 + (2\delta + \delta^2)\sigma_M^2$$

However, if δ is very small, then δ^2 will be negligible compared to 2δ, so we may ignore this term.[8] Therefore, the variance of the adjusted portfolio is $\sigma_M^2 + 2\delta\sigma_M^2$, and portfolio variance has increased by

$$\Delta\sigma^2 = 2\delta\sigma_M^2$$

Summarizing these results, the trade-off between the *incremental risk premium* and *incremental risk*, referred to as the *marginal price of risk*, is given by the ratio

$$\frac{\Delta E(r)}{\Delta\sigma^2} = \frac{E(r_M) - r_f}{2\sigma_M^2}$$

and equals one-half the market price of risk of equation 9.5.

Now suppose that, instead, investors were to invest the increment δ in GM stock, also financed by borrowing at the risk-free rate. The increase in mean excess return is

$$\Delta E(r) = \delta[E(r_{GM}) - r_f]$$

This portfolio has a weight of 1.0 in the market, δ in GM, and $-\delta$ in the risk-free asset. Its variance is $1^2\sigma_M^2 + \delta^2\sigma_M^2 + [2 \times 1 \times \delta \times \text{Cov}(r_{GM}, r_M)]$.

The increase in variance therefore includes the variance of the incremental position in GM *plus* twice its covariance with the market:

$$\Delta\sigma^2 = \delta^2\sigma_{GM}^2 + 2\delta\text{Cov}(r_{GM}, r_M)$$

---

[7]We open ourselves to ambiguity in using this term, because the market portfolio's reward-to-variability ratio

$$\frac{E(r_M) - r_f}{\sigma_M}$$

sometimes is referred to as the market price of risk. Note that since the appropriate risk measure of GM is its covariance with the market portfolio (its contribution to the variance of the market portfolio), this risk is measured in percent squared. Accordingly, the price of this risk, $[E(r_M) - r_f]/\sigma^2$, is defined as the percentage expected return per percent square of variance.

[8]For example, if δ is 1% (.01 of wealth), then its square is .0001 of wealth, one-hundredth of the original value. The term $\delta^2\sigma_M^2$ will be smaller than $2\delta\sigma_M^2$ by an order of magnitude.

Dropping the negligible term involving δ^2, the *marginal price of risk* of GM is

$$\frac{\Delta E(r)}{\Delta \sigma^2} = \frac{E(r_{GM}) - r_f}{2\text{Cov}(r_{GM}, r_M)}$$

In equilibrium, the marginal price of risk of GM stock must equal that of the market portfolio. Otherwise, if the marginal price of risk of GM is greater than the market's, investors can increase their portfolio reward for bearing risk by increasing the weight of GM in their portfolio. Until the price of GM stock rises relative to the market, investors will keep buying GM stock. The process will continue until stock prices adjust so that marginal price of risk of GM equals that of the market. The same process, in reverse, will equalize marginal prices of risk when GM's initial marginal price of risk is less than that of the market portfolio. Equating the marginal price of risk of GM's stock to that of the market results in a relationship between the risk premium of GM and that of the market:

$$\frac{E(r_{GM}) - r_f}{2\text{Cov}(r_{GM}, r_M)} = \frac{E(r_M) - r_f}{2\sigma_M^2}$$

To determine the fair risk premium of GM stock, we rearrange slightly to obtain

$$E(r_{GM}) - r_f = \frac{\text{Cov}(r_{GM}, r_M)}{\sigma_M^2} [E(r_M) - r_f] \tag{9.6}$$

The ratio $\text{Cov}(r_{GM}, r_M)/\sigma_M^2$ measures the contribution of GM stock to the variance of the market portfolio as a fraction of the total variance of the market portfolio. The ratio is called **beta** and denoted by β. Using this measure, we can restate equation 9.6 as

$$E(r_{GM}) = r_f + \beta_{GM}[E(r_M) - r_f] \tag{9.7}$$

This **expected return–beta relationship** is the most familiar expression of the CAPM to practitioners. We will have a lot more to say about the expected return–beta relationship shortly.

We see now why the assumptions that made individuals act similarly are so useful. If everyone holds an identical risky portfolio, then everyone will find that the beta of each asset with the market portfolio equals the asset's beta with his or her own risky portfolio. Hence everyone will agree on the appropriate risk premium for each asset.

Does the fact that few real-life investors actually hold the market portfolio imply that the CAPM is of no practical importance? Not necessarily. Recall from Chapter 8 that reasonably well-diversified portfolios shed firm-specific risk and are left with mostly systematic or market risk. Even if one does not hold the precise market portfolio, a well-diversified portfolio will be so very highly correlated with the market that a stock's beta relative to the market will still be a useful risk measure.

In fact, several authors have shown that modified versions of the CAPM will hold true even if we consider differences among individuals leading them to hold different portfolios. For example, Brennan[9] examined the impact of differences in investors' personal tax rates on market equilibrium, and Mayers[10] looked at the impact of nontraded assets such as human capital (earning power). Both found that although the market portfolio is no longer

---

[9]Michael J. Brennan, "Taxes, Market Valuation, and Corporate Finance Policy," *National Tax Journal*, December 1973.
[10]David Mayers, "Nonmarketable Assets and Capital Market Equilibrium under Uncertainty," in *Studies in the Theory of Capital Markets*, ed. M. C. Jensen (New York: Praeger, 1972).

each investor's optimal risky portfolio, the expected return–beta relationship should still hold in a somewhat modified form.

If the expected return–beta relationship holds for any individual asset, it must hold for any combination of assets. Suppose that some portfolio P has weight w_k for stock k, where k takes on values $1, \ldots, n$. Writing out the CAPM equation 9.7 for each stock, and multiplying each equation by the weight of the stock in the portfolio, we obtain these equations, one for each stock:

$$
\begin{aligned}
w_1 E(r_1) &= w_1 r_f + w_1 \beta_1 [E(r_M) - r_f] \\
+ w_2 E(r_2) &= w_2 r_f + w_2 \beta_2 [E(r_M) - r_f] \\
+ \quad \cdots &= \cdots \\
+ w_n E(r_n) &= w_n r_f + w_n \beta_n [E(r_M) - r_f] \\
\hline
E(r_P) &= r_f + \beta_P [E(r_M) - r_f]
\end{aligned}
$$

Summing each column shows that the CAPM holds for the overall portfolio because $E(r_P) = \sum_k w_k E(r_k)$ is the expected return on the portfolio, and $\beta_P = \sum_k w_k \beta_k$ is the portfolio beta. Incidentally, this result has to be true for the market portfolio itself,

$$
E(r_M) = r_f + \beta_M [E(r_M) - r_f]
$$

Indeed, this is a tautology because $\beta_M = 1$, as we can verify by demonstrating that

$$
\beta_M = \frac{\text{Cov}(r_M, r_M)}{\sigma_M^2} = \frac{\sigma_M^2}{\sigma_M^2}
$$

This also establishes 1 as the weighted average value of beta across all assets. If the market beta is 1, and the market is a portfolio of all assets in the economy, the weighted average beta of all assets must be 1. Hence betas greater than 1 are considered aggressive in that investment in high-beta stocks entails above-average sensitivity to market swings. Betas below 1 can be described as defensive.

A word of caution: We are all accustomed to hearing that well-managed firms will provide high rates of return. We agree this is true if one measures the *firm's* return on investments in plant and equipment. The CAPM, however, predicts returns on investments in the *securities* of the firm.

Let us say that everyone knows a firm is well run. Its stock price will therefore be bid up, and consequently returns to stockholders who buy at those high prices will not be excessive. Security prices, in other words, reflect public information about a firm's prospects, but only the risk of the company (as measured by beta in the context of the CAPM) should affect expected returns. In a rational market investors receive high expected returns only if they are willing to bear risk.

Concept
CHECK

Question 3 • Suppose that the risk premium on the market portfolio is estimated at 8% with a standard deviation of 22%. What is the risk premium on a portfolio invested 25% in GM and 75% in Ford, if they have betas of 1.10 and 1.25, respectively?

The Security Market Line

We can view the expected return–beta relationship as a reward-risk equation. The beta of a security is the appropriate measure of its risk because beta is proportional to the risk that the security contributes to the optimal risky portfolio.

Risk-averse investors measure the risk of the optimal risky portfolio by its variance. In this world we would expect the reward, or the risk premium on individual assets, to depend

Figure 9.2
The security market
line.

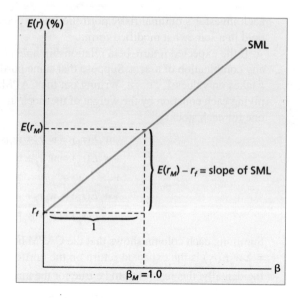

on the contribution of the individual asset to the risk of the portfolio. The beta of a stock measures the stock's contribution to the variance of the market portfolio. Hence we expect, for any asset or portfolio, the required risk premium to be a function of beta. The CAPM confirms this intuition, stating further that the security's risk premium is directly proportional to both the beta and the risk premium of the market portfolio; that is, the risk premium equals $\beta[E(r_M) - r_f]$.

The expected return–beta relationship can be portrayed graphically as the **security market line (SML)** in Figure 9.2. Because the market beta is 1, the slope is the risk premium of the market portfolio. At the point on the horizontal axis where $\beta = 1$ (which is the market portfolio's beta) we can read off the vertical axis the expected return on the market portfolio.

It is useful to compare the security market line to the capital market line. The CML graphs the risk premiums of *efficient* portfolios (i.e., portfolios composed of the market and the risk-free asset) as a function of portfolio standard deviation. This is appropriate because standard deviation is a valid measure of risk for efficiently diversified portfolios that are candidates for an investor's overall portfolio. The SML, in contrast, graphs *individual asset* risk premiums as a function of asset risk. The relevant measure of risk for individual assets held as parts of well-diversified portfolios is not the asset's standard deviation or variance; it is, instead, the contribution of the asset to the portfolio variance, which we measure by the asset's beta. The SML is valid for both efficient portfolios and individual assets.

The security market line provides a benchmark for the evaluation of investment performance. Given the risk of an investment, as measured by its beta, the SML provides the required rate of return from that investment to compensate investors for risk, as well as the time value of money.

Because the security market line is the graphic representation of the expected return–beta relationship, "fairly priced" assets plot exactly on the SML; that is, their expected returns are commensurate with their risk. Given the assumptions we made at the start of this section, all securities must lie on the SML in market equilibrium. Nevertheless, we see here how the CAPM may be of use in the money-management industry. Suppose that the SML relation is used as a benchmark to assess the fair expected return on a risky asset. Then security analysis is performed to calculate the return actually expected. (Notice

Figure 9.3
The SML and a
positive-alpha stock.

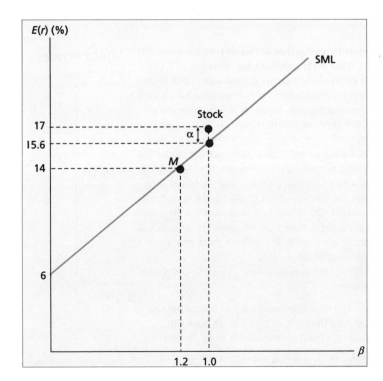

that we depart here from the simple CAPM world in that some investors now apply their own unique analysis to derive an "input list" that may differ from their competitors'.) If a stock is perceived to be a good buy, or underpriced, it will provide an expected return in excess of the fair return stipulated by the SML. Underpriced stocks therefore plot above the SML: Given their betas, their expected returns are greater than dictated by the CAPM. Overpriced stocks plot below the SML.

The difference between the fair and actually expected rates of return on a stock is called the stock's **alpha**, denoted α. For example, if the market return is expected to be 14%, a stock has a beta of 1.2, and the T-bill rate is 6%, the SML would predict an expected return on the stock of $6 + 1.2(14 - 6) = 15.6\%$. If one believed the stock would provide a return of 17%, the implied alpha would be 1.4% (see Figure 9.3).

One might say that security analysis (which we treat in Part V) is about uncovering securities with nonzero alphas. This analysis suggests that the starting point of portfolio management can be a passive market-index portfolio. The portfolio manager will then increase the weights of securities with positive alphas and decrease the weights of securities with negative alphas. We show one strategy for adjusting the portfolio weights in such a manner in Chapter 28.

The CAPM is also useful in capital budgeting decisions. For a firm considering a new project, the CAPM can provide the *required rate of return* that the project needs to yield, based on its beta, to be acceptable to investors. Managers can use the CAPM to obtain this cutoff internal rate of return (IRR), or "hurdle rate" for the project.

The nearby box describes how the CAPM can be used in capital budgeting. It also discusses some empirical anomalies concerning the model, which we address in detail in Chapters 12 and 13. The article asks whether the CAPM is useful for capital budgeting in light of these shortcomings; it concludes that even given the anomalies cited, the model still can be useful to managers who wish to increase the fundamental value of their firms.

TALES FROM THE FAR SIDE

Financial markets' evaluation of risk determines the way firms invest. What if the markets are wrong?

Investors are rarely praised for their good sense. But for the past two decades a growing number of firms have based their decisions on a model which assumes that people are perfectly rational. If they are irrational, are businesses making the wrong choices?

The model, known as the "capital-asset pricing model," or CAPM, has come to dominate modern finance. Almost any manager who wants to defend a project—be it a brand, a factory or a corporate merger—must justify his decision partly based on the CAPM. The reason is that the model tells a firm how to calculate the return that its investors demand. If shareholders are to benefit, the returns from any project must clear this "hurdle rate."

Although the CAPM is complicated, it can be reduced to five simple ideas:

- Investors can eliminate some risks—such as the risk that workers will strike, or that a firm's boss will quit—by diversifying across many regions and sectors.

- Some risks, such as that of a global recession, cannot be eliminated through diversification. So even a basket of all of the stocks in a stockmarket will still be risky.

- People must be rewarded for investing in such a risky basket by earning returns above those that they can get on safer assets, such as Treasury bills.

- The rewards on a specific investment depend only on the extent to which it affects the market basket's risk.

- Conveniently, that contribution to the market basket's risk can be captured by a single measure—dubbed "beta"—which expresses the relationship between the investment's risk and the market's.

Beta is what makes the CAPM so powerful. Although an investment may face many risks, diversified investors should

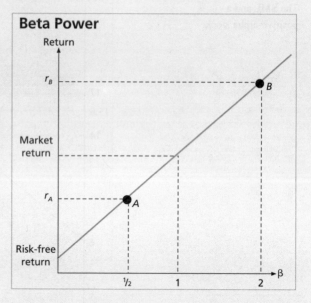

Beta Power

care only about those that are related to the market basket. Beta not only tells managers how to measure those risks, but it also allows them to translate them directly into a hurdle rate. If the future profits from a project will not exceed that rate, it is not worth shareholders' money.

The diagram shows how the CAPM works. Safe investments, such as Treasury bills, have a beta of zero. Riskier investments should earn a premium over the risk-free rate which increases with beta. Those whose risks roughly match the market's have a beta of one, by definition, and should earn the market return.

So suppose that a firm is considering two projects, A and B. Project A has a beta of $1/2$: when the market rises or falls by 10%, its returns tend to rise or fall by 5%. So its risk premium is only half that of the market. Project B's risk premium

---

Yet another use of the CAPM is in utility rate-making cases.[11] In this case the issue is the rate of return that a regulated utility should be allowed to earn on its investment in plant and equipment. Suppose that the equityholders have invested $100 million in the firm and that the beta of the equity is .6. If the T-bill rate is 6% and the market risk premium is 8%, then the fair profits to the firm would be assessed as $6 + .6(8) = 10.8\%$ of the $100 million investment, or $10.8 million. The firm would be allowed to set prices at a level expected to generate these profits.

---

[11]This application is fast disappearing, as many states are in the process of deregulating their public utilities and allowing a far greater degree of free market pricing. Nevertheless, a considerable amount of rate setting still takes place.

is twice that of the market, so it must earn a higher return to justify the expenditure.

Never Knowingly Underpriced

But there is one small problem with the CAPM: Financial economists have found that beta is not much use for explaining rates of return on firms' shares. Worse, there appears to be another measure which explains these returns quite well.

That measure is the ratio of a firm's book value (the value of its assets at the time they entered the balance sheet) to its market value. Several studies have found that, on average, companies that have high book-to-market ratios tend to earn excess returns over long periods, even after adjusting for the risks that are associated with beta.

The discovery of this book-to-market effect has sparked a fierce debate among financial economists. All of them agree that some risks ought to carry greater rewards. But they are now deeply divided over how risk should be measured. Some argue that since investors are rational, the book-to-market effect must be capturing an extra risk factor. They conclude, therefore, that managers should incorporate the book-to-market effect into their hurdle rates. They have labeled this alternative hurdle rate the "new estimator of expected return," or NEER.

Other financial economists, however, dispute this approach. Since there is no obvious extra risk associated with a high book-to-market ratio, they say, investors must be mistaken. Put simply, they are underpricing high book-to-market stocks, causing them to earn abnormally high returns. If managers of such firms try to exceed those inflated hurdle rates, they will forgo many profitable investments. With economists now at odds, what is a conscientious manager to do?

In a new paper,* Jeremy Stein, an economist at the Massachusetts Institute of Technology's business school, offers a paradoxical answer. If investors are rational, then beta cannot be the only measure of risk, so managers should stop using it. Conversely, if investors are irrational, then beta is still the right measure in many cases. Mr. Stein argues that if beta captures an asset's fundamental risk—that is, its contribution to the market basket's risk—then it will often make sense for managers to pay attention to it, even if investors are somehow failing to.

Often, but not always. At the heart of Mr. Stein's argument lies a crucial distinction—that between (a) boosting a firm's long-term value and (b) trying to raise its share price. If investors are rational, these are the same thing: any decision that raises long-term value will instantly increase the share price as well. But if investors are making predictable mistakes, a manager must choose.

For instance, if he wants to increase today's share price—perhaps because he wants to sell his shares, or to fend off a takeover attempt—he must usually stick with the NEER approach, accommodating investors' misperceptions. But if he is interested in long-term value, he should usually continue to use beta. Showing a flair for marketing, Mr. Stein labels this far-sighted alternative to NEER the "fundamental asset risk"—or FAR—approach.

Mr. Stein's conclusions will no doubt irritate many company bosses, who are fond of denouncing their investors' myopia. They have resented the way in which CAPM—with its assumption of investor infallibility—has come to play an important role in boardroom decision-making. But it now appears that if they are right, and their investors are wrong, then those same far-sighted managers ought to be the CAPM's biggest fans.

*Jeremy Stein, "Rational Capital Budgeting in an Irrational World," *The Journal of Business*, October 1996.
Source: "Tales from the FAR Side," *The Economist*, November 16, 1996, p. 8.

Concept CHECK

Question 4 • Stock XYZ has an expected return of 12% and risk of $\beta = 1$. Stock ABC has expected return of 13% and $\beta = 1.5$. The market's expected return is 11%, and $r_f = 5\%$.
  a. According to the CAPM, which stock is a better buy?
  b. What is the alpha of each stock? Plot the SML and each stock's risk-return point on one graph. Show the alphas graphically.

Question 5 • The risk-free rate is 8% and the expected return on the market portfolio is 16%. A firm considers a project that is expected to have a beta of 1.3.
  a. What is the required rate of return on the project?
  b. If the expected IRR of the project is 19%, should it be accepted?

9.2   Extensions of the CAPM

The assumptions that allowed Sharpe to derive the simple version of the CAPM are admittedly unrealistic. Financial economists have been at work ever since the CAPM was devised to extend the model to more realistic scenarios.

There are two classes of extensions to the simple version of the CAPM. The first attempts to relax the assumptions that we outlined at the outset of the chapter. The second acknowledges the fact that investors worry about sources of risk other than the uncertain value of their securities, such as unexpected changes in relative prices of consumer goods. This idea involves the introduction of additional risk factors besides security returns, and we discuss it further in Chapters 11 and 22.

The CAPM with Restricted Borrowing: The Zero-Beta Model

The CAPM is predicated on the assumption that all investors share an identical input list that they feed into the Markowitz algorithm. Thus all investors agree on the location of the efficient (minimum-variance) frontier, where each portfolio has the lowest variance among all feasible portfolios at a target expected rate of return. When all investors can borrow and lend at the safe rate, r_f, all agree on the optimal tangency portfolio and choose to hold a share of the market portfolio.

However, when borrowing is restricted, as it is for many financial institutions, or when the borrowing rate is higher than the lending rate because borrowers pay a default premium, the market portfolio is no longer the common optimal portfolio for all investors.

When investors no longer can borrow at a common risk-free rate, they may choose risky portfolios from the entire set of efficient frontier portfolios according to how much risk they choose to bear. The market is no longer the common optimal portfolio. In fact, with investors choosing different portfolios, it is no longer obvious whether the market portfolio, which is the aggregate of all investors' portfolios, will even be on the efficient frontier. If the market portfolio is no longer mean-variance efficient, then the expected return–beta relationship of the CAPM will no longer characterize market equilibrium.

An equilibrium expected return–beta relationship in the case of restrictions on risk-free investments has been developed by Fischer Black.[12] Black's model is fairly difficult and requires a good deal of facility with mathematics. Therefore, we will satisfy ourselves with a sketch of Black's argument and spend more time with its implications.

Black's model of the CAPM in the absence of a risk-free asset rests on the three following properties of mean-variance efficient portfolios:

1. Any portfolio constructed by combining efficient portfolios is itself on the efficient frontier.

2. Every portfolio on the efficient frontier has a "companion" portfolio on the bottom half (the inefficient part) of the minimum-variance frontier with which it is uncorrelated. Because the portfolios are uncorrelated, the companion portfolio is referred to as the **zero-beta portfolio** of the efficient portfolio.

---

[12]Fischer Black, "Capital Market Equilibrium with Restricted Borrowing," *Journal of Business*, July 1972.

Figure 9.4

Efficient portfolios and their zero-beta companions.

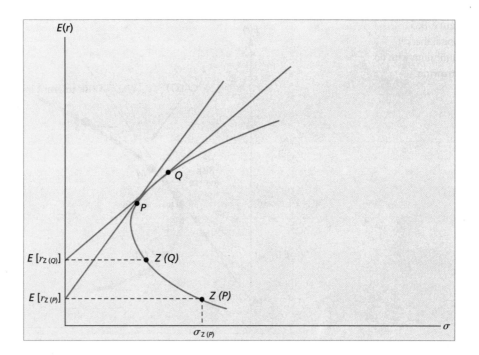

The expected return of an efficient portfolio's zero-beta companion portfolio can be derived by the following graphical procedure. From any efficient portfolio such as P in Figure 9.4 draw a tangency line to the vertical axis. The intercept will be the expected return on portfolio P's zero-beta companion portfolio, denoted $Z(P)$. The horizontal line from the intercept to the minimum-variance frontier identifies the standard deviation of the zero-beta portfolio. Notice in Figure 9.4 that different efficient portfolios such as P and Q have different zero-beta companions.

These tangency lines are helpful constructs only. They do *not* signify that one can invest in portfolios with expected return–standard deviation pairs along the line. That would be possible only by mixing a risk-free asset with the tangency portfolio. In this case, however, we assume that risk-free assets are not available to investors.

3. The expected return of any asset can be expressed as an exact, linear function of the expected return on any two frontier portfolios. Consider, for example, the minimum-variance frontier portfolios P and Q. Black showed that the expected return on any asset i can be expressed as

$$E(r_i) = E(r_Q) + [E(r_P) - E(r_Q)] \frac{\text{Cov}(r_i, r_P) - \text{Cov}(r_P, r_Q)}{\sigma_P^2 - \text{Cov}(r_P, r_Q)} \tag{9.8}$$

Note that Property 3 has nothing to do with market equilibrium. It is a purely mathematical property relating frontier portfolios and individual securities.

With these three properties, the Black model can be applied to any of several variations: no risk-free asset at all, risk-free lending but no risk-free borrowing, and borrowing at a rate higher than r_f. We show here how the model works for the case with risk-free lending but no borrowing.

Figure 9.5

Capital market equilibrium with no borrowing.

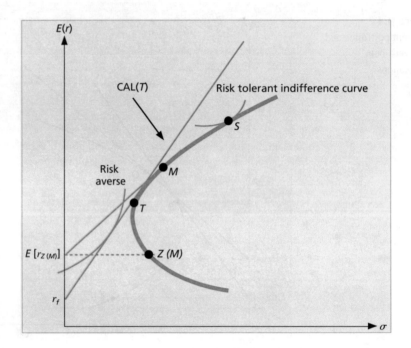

Imagine an economy with only two investors, one relatively risk averse and one risk tolerant. The risk-averse investor will choose a portfolio on the CAL supported by portfolio T in Figure 9.5, that is, he will mix portfolio T with lending at the risk-free rate. T is the tangency portfolio on the efficient frontier from the risk-free lending rate, r_f. The risk-tolerant investor is willing to accept more risk to earn a higher-risk premium; she will choose portfolio S. This portfolio lies along the efficient frontier with higher risk and return than portfolio T. The aggregate risky portfolio (i.e., the market portfolio, M) will be a combination of T and S, with weights determined by the relative wealth and degrees of risk aversion of the two investors. Since T and S are each on the efficient frontier, so is M (from Property 1).

From Property 2, M has a companion zero-beta portfolio on the minimum-variance frontier, $Z(M)$, shown in Figure 9.5. Moreover, by Property 3 we can express the return on any security in terms of M and $Z(M)$ as in equation 9.8. But, since by construction $Cov[r_M, r_{Z(M)}] = 0$, the expression simplifies to

$$E(r_i) = E[r_{Z(M)}] + E[r_M - r_{Z(M)}]\frac{Cov(r_i, r_M)}{\sigma_M^2} \qquad (9.9)$$

where P from equation 9.8 has been replaced by M and Q has been replaced by $Z(M)$. Equation 9.9 may be interpreted as a variant of the simple CAPM, in which r_f has been replaced with $E[r_{Z(M)}]$.

The more realistic scenario, where investors lend at the risk-free rate and borrow at a higher rate, was considered in Chapter 8. The same arguments that we have just employed can also be used to establish the zero-beta CAPM in this situation. Problem 18 at the end of this chapter asks you to fill in the details of the argument for this situation.

Concept    Question 6 • **Suppose that the zero-beta portfolio exhibits returns that are, on average, greater than the rate on T-bills. Is this fact relevant to the question of the validity of the CAPM?**

Lifetime Consumption: The CAPM with Dynamic Programming

One of the restrictive assumptions for the simple version of the CAPM is that investors are myopic—they plan for one common holding period. Investors actually may be concerned with a lifetime consumption plan and a desire to leave a bequest to children. Consumption plans that are feasible for them depend on current wealth and future rates of return on the investment portfolio. These investors will want to rebalance their portfolios as often as required by changes in wealth.

However, Eugene Fama[13] showed that, even if we extend our analysis to a multiperiod setting, the single-period CAPM still may be appropriate. The key assumptions that Fama used to replace myopic planning horizons are that investor preferences are unchanging over time and the risk-free interest rate and probability distribution of security returns do not change unpredictably over time. Of course, this latter assumption is also unrealistic. However, the extension to the CAPM engendered by considering random changes to the so-called investment opportunity set must wait until Chapter 27.

9.3   THE CAPM AND LIQUIDITY: A THEORY OF ILLIQUIDITY PREMIUMS

Liquidity refers to the cost and ease with which an asset can be converted into cash, that is, sold. Traders have long recognized the importance of liquidity, and some evidence suggests that illiquidity can reduce market prices substantially. For example, one study[14] finds that market discounts on closely held (and therefore nontraded) firms can exceed 30%. It also reports on an unusual class of stocks that was issued with a provision that prohibited public trading for two to three years, which sold at a discount of about 30%. Interestingly, such a discount is similar to the three-year risk premium on an average stock, which has been between 8% and 9% per year. This suggests that premiums for illiquidity can be roughly of the same magnitude as risk premiums, and may deserve a comparable amount of attention. The nearby box focuses on the relationship between liquidity and stock returns.

A rigorous treatment of the value of liquidity was developed by Amihud and Mendelson.[15] Recent studies show that liquidity plays an important role in explaining rates of return on financial assets.[16] We believe that liquidity will become an important part of standard valuation, and therefore present here a simplified version of their model.

Recall Assumption 4 of the CAPM, that all trading is costless. In reality, no security is perfectly liquid, in that all trades involve some transaction cost. Investors prefer more liquid assets with lower transaction costs, so it should not surprise us to find that all else equal, relatively illiquid assets trade at lower prices or, equivalently, that the expected return on illiquid assets must be higher. Therefore, an **illiquidity premium** must be impounded into the price of each asset. The impact of liquidity will depend on the distribution of transaction costs across assets, as well as the distribution of investors across investment horizons. We use simplified distributions to illustrate the effect of liquidity on equilibrium expected returns. However, these simplifications are expositional only, and the predicted effect of liquidity on equilibrium returns is quite general.

---

[13]Eugene F. Fama, "Multiperiod Consumption-Investment Decisions," *American Economic Review* 60 (1970).

[14]Shannon P. Pratt, *Valuing a Business: The Analysis of Closely Held Companies*, 2nd ed. (Homewood, Ill.: Dow Jones–Irwin, 1989).

[15]Yakov Amihud and Haim Mendelson, "Asset Pricing and the Bid–Ask Spread," *Journal of Financial Economics* 17 (1986), pp. 223–49.

[16]For example, Venkat Eleswarapu, "Cost of Transacting and Expected Returns in the NASDAQ Market," *Journal of Finance* 2, no. 5 (1993), pp. 2113–27.

STOCK INVESTORS PAY HIGH PRICE FOR LIQUIDITY

Given a choice between liquid and illiquid stocks, most investors, to the extent they think of it at all, opt for issues they know are easy to get in and out of.

But for long-term investors who don't trade often—which includes most individuals—that may be unnecessarily expensive. Recent studies of the performance of listed stocks show that, on average, less-liquid issues generate substantially higher returns—as much as several percentage points a year at the extremes.

"Liquidity is a valuable item that must be, and is, paid for even if it's not used," says Steven Wunch, a vice president at Kidder, Peabody & Co. In terms of investment strategy, he adds, "It only makes sense that if you don't need it or use it, don't pay for it."

Illiquidity Payoff

Among the academic studies that have attempted to quantify this illiquidity payoff is a recent work by two finance professors, Yakov Amihud of New York University and Tel Aviv University, and Haim Mendelson of the University of Rochester. Their study looks at New York Stock Exchange issues over the 1961–1980 period and defines liquidity in terms of bid–asked spreads as a percentage of overall share price.

Market makers use spreads in quoting stocks to define the difference between the price they'll bid to take stock off an investor's hands and the price they'll offer to sell stock to any willing buyer. The bid price is always somewhat lower because of the risk to the broker of tying up precious capital to hold stock in inventory until it can be resold.

If a stock is relatively illiquid, which means there's not a ready flow of orders from customers clamoring to buy it, there's more of a chance the broker will lose money on the trade. To hedge this risk, market makers demand an even bigger discount to service potential sellers, and the spread will widen further.

The study by Profs. Amihud and Mendelson shows that liquidity spreads—measured as a percentage discount from the stock's total price—ranged from less than 0.1 percent, for widely held International Business Machines Corp., to as much as 4 percent to 5 percent. The widest-spread group was dominated by smaller, low-priced stocks.

The study found that, overall, the least-liquid stocks averaged an 8.5 percent-a-year higher return than the most-liquid stocks over the 20-year period. On average, a one percentage point increase in the spread was associated with a 2.5 percent higher annual return for New York Stock Exchange stocks. The relationship held after results were adjusted for size and other risk factors.

An extension of the study of Big Board stocks done at *The Wall Street Journal*'s request produced similar findings. It shows that for the 1980–85 period, a one percentage-point-wider spread was associated with an extra average annual gain of 2.4 percent. Meanwhile, the least-liquid stocks outperformed the most-liquid stocks by almost six percentage points a year.

Cost of Trading

Since the cost of the spread is incurred each time the stock is traded, illiquid stocks can quickly become prohibitively expensive for investors who trade frequently. On the other hand, small, long-term investors needn't worry so much about spreads, since they can amortize them over a longer period.

In terms of investment strategy, this suggests "that the small investor should tailor the types of stocks he or she buys to his expected holding period," Prof. Mendelson says. If the investor expects to sell within three months, he says, it's better to pay up for liquidity and get the lowest spread. If the investor plans to hold the stock for a year or more, it makes sense to aim at stocks with spreads of 3 percent or more to capture the extra return.

We start with the simplest case, in which we ignore systematic risk. Imagine a world with a large number of uncorrelated securities. Because the securities are uncorrelated, well-diversified portfolios of these securities will have standard deviations near zero and the market portfolio will be virtually as safe as the risk-free asset. Moreover, the covariance between any pair of securities also is zero, implying that the beta of any security with the market portfolio is zero. Therefore, according to the CAPM, all assets should have expected rates of return equal to that of the risk-free asset, which we will take to be T-bills.

Assume that investors know in advance for how long they intend to hold their portfolios, and suppose that there are n types of investors, grouped by investment horizon. Type 1 investors intend to liquidate their portfolios in one period, Type 2 investors in two periods, and so on, until the longest-horizon investors (Type n) intend to hold their portfolios for n periods.

Because we are now dealing with a multiperiod model, we should be careful in our comparison with the single-period CAPM. However, we've seen that Fama's work (see footnote 13) implies that even if investors have multiperiod investment horizons, the simple expected return–beta relationship of the CAPM still might describe equilibrium security returns. To maintain Fama's results, we will assume that as investors liquidate their portfolios, just enough investors of each type enter the market to take the place of those who depart. Thus in each period there is identical demand for securities, as Fama required. However, even with these assumptions, the presence of trading costs *in conjunction with* differing investment horizons will require an adaptation of the CAPM.

We assume that there are only two classes of securities: liquid and illiquid. The liquidation cost of a class L (more liquid) stock to an investor with a horizon of h years (a type h investor) will reduce the per-period rate of return by $c_L/h\%$. For example, if the combination of commissions and the bid–asked spread on a security resulted in a liquidation cost of 10%, then the per-period rate of return for an investor who holds stock for five years would be reduced by approximately 2% per year, whereas the return on a 10-year investment would fall by only 1% per year.[17] Class I (illiquid) assets have higher liquidation costs that reduce the per-period return by $c_I/h\%$, where c_I is greater than c_L. Therefore, if you intend to hold a class L security for h periods, your expected rate of return *net* of transaction costs is $E(r_L) - c_L/h$. There is no liquidation cost on T-bills.

The following table presents the expected return investors would realize from the risk-free asset and class L and class I stock portfolios *assuming* that the simple CAPM is correct and all securities have an expected return of r:

Asset:	Risk-Free	Class L	Class I
Gross rate of return:	r	r	r
One-period liquidation cost:	0	c_L	c_I
Investor Type		**Net Rate of Return**	
1	r	$r - c_L$	$r - c_I$
2	r	$r - c_L/2$	$r - c_I/2$
...	...	...	...
n	r	$r - c_L/n$	$r - c_I/n$

These net rates of return are inconsistent with a market in equilibrium, because with equal gross rates of return all investors would prefer to invest in zero-transaction-cost T-bills. As a result, both class L and class I stock prices must fall, causing their expected returns to rise until investors are willing to hold these shares.

Suppose, therefore, that each gross return is higher by some fraction of liquidation cost. Specifically, assume that the gross expected return on class L stocks is $r + xc_L$ and that of class I stocks is $r + yc_I$, where x and y are smaller than 1 (otherwise, diversified stock portfolios would dominate the risk-free asset in term of net returns). The *net* rate of return on

---

[17]This simple structure of liquidation costs allows us to derive a correspondingly simple solution for the effect of liquidity on expected returns. Amihud and Mendelson used a more general formulation, but then needed to rely on complex and more difficult-to-interpret mathematical programming. All that matters for the qualitative results below, however, is that illiquidity costs be less onerous to longer-term investors.

class L stocks to an investor with a horizon of h will be $(r + xc_L) - c_L/h = r + c_L(x - 1/h)$. In general, the rates of return to investors will be:

Asset:	Risk-Free	Class L	Class I
Gross rate of return:	r	$r + xc_L$	$r + yc_I$
One-period liquidation cost:	0	c_L	c_I

Investor Type		Net Rate of Return	
1	r	$r + c_L(x - 1)$	$r + c_I(y - 1)$
2	r	$r + c_L(x - 1/2)$	$r + c_I(y - 1/2)$
. . .	. . .	. . .	. . .
n	r	$r + c_L(x - 1/n)$	$r + c_I(y - 1/n)$

Notice that the liquidation cost has a greater impact on per-period returns for shorter-term investors. This is because the cost is amortized over fewer periods. As the horizon becomes very large, the per-period impact of the transaction cost approaches zero and the net rate of return approaches the gross rate.

Figure 9.6 graphs the net rate of return on the three asset classes for investors of differing horizons. The more illiquid stock has the lowest net rate of return for very short investment horizons because of its large liquidation costs. However, in equilibrium, the stock must be priced at a level that offers a rate of return high enough to induce some investors to hold it, implying that its gross rate of return must be higher than that of the more liquid stock. Therefore, for long enough investment horizons, the net return on class I stocks will exceed that on class L stocks.

Both stock classes underperform T-bills for very short investment horizons, because the transactions costs then have the largest per-period impact. Ultimately, however, because the *gross* rate of return of stocks exceeds r, for a sufficiently long investment horizon, the more liquid stocks in class L will dominate bills. The threshold horizon can be read from Figure 9.6 as H_{rL}. Anyone with a horizon that exceeds H_{rL} will prefer class L stocks to T-bills. Those with horizons below H_{rL} will choose bills. For even longer horizons, because c_I exceeds c_L, the net rate of return on relatively illiquid class I stocks will exceed that on class L stocks. Therefore, investors with horizons greater than H_{LI} will specialize in the most illiquid stocks with the highest gross rate of return. These investors are harmed least by the effect of trading costs.

Now we can determine equilibrium illiquidity premiums. For the marginal investor with horizon H_{LI}, the *net* return from class I and L stocks is the same. Therefore,

$$r + c_L(x - 1/h_{LI}) = r + c_I(y - 1/h_{LI})$$

We can use this equation to solve for the relationship between x and y as follows:

$$y = \frac{1}{h_{LI}} + \frac{c_L}{c_I}\left(x - \frac{1}{h_{LI}}\right)$$

The expected gross return on illiquid stocks is then

$$r_I = r + c_L y = r + \frac{c_I}{h_{LI}} + c_L\left(x - \frac{1}{h_{LI}}\right) = r + c_L x + \frac{1}{h_{LI}}\left(c_I - c_L\right) \tag{9.10}$$

Recalling that the expected gross return on class L stocks is $r_L = r + c_L x$, we conclude that the illiquidity premium of class I versus class L stocks is

Figure 9.6

Net returns as a function of investment horizon.

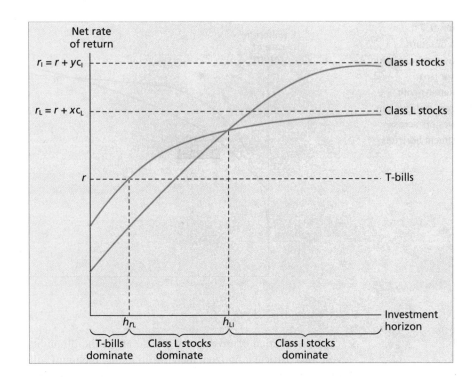

$$r_I - r_L = \frac{1}{h_{LI}}(c_I - c_L) \tag{9.11}$$

Similarly, we can derive the liquidity premium of class L stocks over T-bills. Here, the marginal investor who is indifferent between bills and class L stocks will have investment horizon h_{rL} and a net rate of return just equal to r. Therefore, $r + c_L(x - 1/h_{rL}) = r$, implying that $x = 1/h_{rL}$, and the liquidity premium of class L stocks must be $xc_L = c_L/h_{rL}$. Therefore,

$$r_L - r = \frac{1}{h_{rL}}c_L \tag{9.12}$$

There are two lessons to be learned from this analysis. First, as predicted, equilibrium expected rates of return are bid up to compensate for transaction costs, as demonstrated by equations 9.11 and 9.12. Second, the illiquidity premium is *not* a linear function of transaction costs. In fact, the incremental illiquidity premium steadily declines as transaction costs increase. To see that this is so, suppose that c_L is 1% and $c_I - c_L$ is also 1%. Therefore, the transaction cost increases by 1% as you move out of bills into the more liquid stock class, and by another 1% as you move into the illiquid stock class. Equation 9.12 shows that the illiquidity premium of class L stocks over no-transaction-cost bills is then $1/h_{rL}$, and equation 9.11 shows that the illiquidity premium of class I over class L stocks is $1/h_{LI}$. But h_{LI} exceeds h_{rL} (see Figure 9.6), so we conclude that the incremental effect of illiquidity declines as we move into ever more illiquid assets.

The reason for this last result is simple. Recall that investors will self-select into different asset classes, with longer-term investors holding assets with the highest gross return but that are the most illiquid. For these investors, the effect of illiquidity is less costly because trading costs can be amortized over a longer horizon. Therefore, as these costs increase, the investment horizon associated with the holders of these assets also increases, which mitigates the impact on the required gross rate of return.

Figure 9.7

Rates of return as a function of liquidation cost for two populations with different distributions of investors across investment horizons.

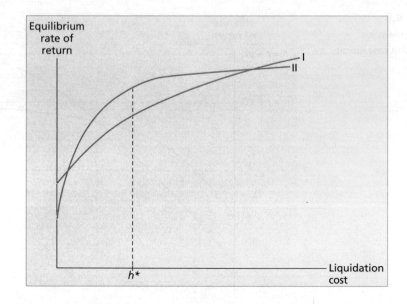

The distribution of investors will also affect the illiquidity premium. If many traders invest for a particular horizon, then the illiquidity premium will rise less rapidly around that horizon. Figure 9.7 illustrates this result. The curve labeled I corresponds to a relatively even distribution of investors across investment horizons. The curve labeled II, which flattens rapidly around the investment horizon h^*, would arise in a case where many investors have horizons of approximately h^*.

Concept

CHECK

Question 7 • Consider a very illiquid asset class of stocks, class V, with $c_V > c_I$. Use a graph like Figure 9.6 to convince yourself that there is an investment horizon, h_{IV}, for which an investor would be indifferent between stocks in illiquidity classes I and V. Analogously to equation 9.11, in equilibrium, the differential in gross returns must be

$$r_V - r_I = \frac{1}{h_{IV}} (c_V - c_I)$$

Our analysis so far has focused on the case of uncorrelated assets, allowing us to ignore issues of systematic risk. This special case turns out to be easy to generalize. If we were to allow for correlation among assets due to common systematic risk factors, we would find that the illiquidity premium is simply additive to the risk premium of the usual CAPM.[18] Therefore, we can generalize the CAPM expected return–beta relationship to include a liquidity effect as follows:

$$E(r_i) - r_f = \beta_i [E(r_M) - r_f] + f(c_i)$$

where $f(c_i)$ is a function of trading costs that measures the effect of the illiquidity premium given the trading costs of security i. We have seen that $f(c_i)$ is increasing in c_i but at a

---

[18]The only assumption necessary to obtain this result is that for each level of beta, there are many securities within that risk class, with a variety of transaction costs. (This is essentially the same assumption used by Modigliani and Miller in their famous capital structure irrelevance proposition.) Thus our earlier analysis could be applied within each risk class, resulting in an illiquidity premium that simply adds on to the systematic risk premium.

Figure 9.8

The relationship between illiquidity and average returns.

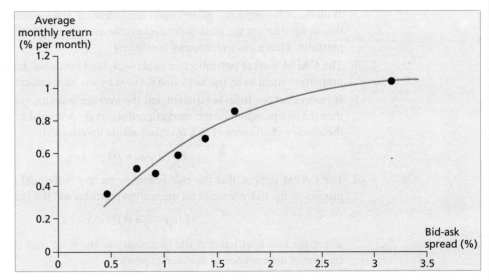

Source: Derived from Yakov Amihud and Haim Mendelson, "Asset Pricing and the Bid–Ask Spread," *Journal of Financial Economics* 17 (1986), pp. 223–49.

decreasing rate. The usual CAPM equation is modified because each investor's optimal portfolio is now affected by liquidation cost as well as risk-return considerations.

The model can be generalized in other ways as well. For example, even if investors do not know their investment horizon for certain, as long as investors do not perceive a connection between unexpected needs to liquidate investments and security returns, the implications of the model are essentially unchanged, with expected horizons replacing actual horizons in equations 9.11 and 9.12.

Amihud and Mendelson provided a considerable amount of empirical evidence that liquidity has a substantial impact on gross stock returns. We will defer our discussion of most of that evidence until Chapter 13. However, for a preview of the quantitative significance of the illiquidity effect, examine Figure 9.8, which is derived from their study. It shows that average monthly returns over the 1961–1980 period rose from .35% for the group of stocks with the lowest bid–asked spread (the most liquid stocks) to 1.024% for the highest-spread stocks. This is an annualized differential of about 8%, nearly equal to the historical average risk premium on the S&P 500 index! Moreover, as their model predicts, the effect of the spread on average monthly returns is nonlinear, with a curve that flattens out as spreads increase.

SUMMARY

1. The CAPM assumes that investors are single-period planners who agree on a common input list from security analysis and seek mean-variance optimal portfolios.

2. The CAPM assumes that security markets are ideal in the sense that:

   a. They are large, and investors are price-takers.

   b. There are no taxes or transaction costs.

   c. All risky assets are publicly traded.

   d. Investors can borrow and lend any amount at a fixed risk-free rate.

3. With these assumptions, all investors hold identical risky portfolios. The CAPM holds that in equilibrium the market portfolio is the unique mean-variance efficient tangency portfolio. Thus a passive strategy is efficient.

4. The CAPM market portfolio is a value-weighted portfolio. Each security is held in a proportion equal to its market value divided by the total market value of all securities.

5. If the market portfolio is efficient and the average investor neither borrows nor lends, then the risk premium on the market portfolio is proportional to its variance, σ_M^2, and to the average coefficient of risk aversion across investors, A:

$$E(r_M) - r_f = .01 \times \overline{A}\sigma_M^2$$

6. The CAPM implies that the risk premium on any individual asset or portfolio is the product of the risk premium on the market portfolio and the beta coefficient:

$$E(r_i) - r_f = \beta_i[E(r_M) - r_f]$$

where the beta coefficient is the covariance of the asset with the market portfolio as a fraction of the variance of the market portfolio

$$\beta_i = \frac{\text{Cov}(r_i, r_M)}{\sigma_M^2}$$

7. When risk-free investments are restricted but all other CAPM assumptions hold, then the simple version of the CAPM is replaced by its zero-beta version. Accordingly, the risk-free rate in the expected return–beta relationship is replaced by the zero-beta portfolio's expected rate of return:

$$E(r_i) = E[r_{Z(M)}] + \beta_i E[r_M - r_{Z(M)}]$$

8. The simple version of the CAPM assumes that investors are myopic. When investors are assumed to be concerned with lifetime consumption and bequest plans, but investors' tastes and security return distributions are stable over time, the market portfolio remains efficient and the simple version of the expected return–beta relationship holds.

9. Liquidity costs can be incorporated into the CAPM relationship. When there is a large number of assets with any combination of beta and liquidity cost c_i, the expected return is bid up to reflect this undesired property according to

$$E(r_i) - r_f = \beta_i[E(r_M) - r_f] + f(c_i)$$

Key Terms

homogeneous expectations	beta	zero-beta portfolio
market portfolio	expected return–beta relationship	liquidity
mutual fund theorem	security market line (SML)	illiquidity premium
market price of risk	alpha	

Selected Readings

A good introduction to the intuition of the CAPM is:

Malkiel, Burton G. *A Random Walk Down Wall Street.* 6th ed. New York: W. W. Norton, 1995.

The four articles that established the CAPM are:

Sharpe, William. "Capital Asset Prices: A Theory of Market Equilibrium." *Journal of Finance*, September 1964.

Lintner, John. "The Valuation of Risk Assets and the Selection of Risky Investments in Stock Portfolios and Capital Budgets." *Review of Economics and Statistics*, February 1965.

Mossin, Jan. "Equilibrium in a Capital Asset Market." *Econometrica*, October 1966.

Treynor, Jack. "Towards a Theory of Market Value of Risky Assets." Unpublished manuscript, 1961.

A review of the simple CAPM and its variants is contained in:

Jensen, Michael C. "The Foundation and Current State of Capital Market Theory." In Jensen, Michael C., ed. *Studies in the Theory of Capital Markets*. New York: Praeger, 1972.

The zero-beta version of the CAPM appeared in:

Black, Fischer. "Capital Market Equilibrium with Restricted Borrowing." *Journal of Business*, July 1972.

Excellent practitioner-oriented discussions of the CAPM are:

Mullins, David. "Does the Capital Asset Pricing Model Work?" *Harvard Business Review*, January/February 1982.

Rosenberg, Barr; and Andrew Rudd. "The Corporate Uses of Beta." In Stern, J. M.; and D. H. Chew, Jr., eds. *The Revolution in Corporate Finance*. New York: Basil Blackwell, 1986.

A good discussion of liquidity, asset prices, and financial policy can be found in:

Amihud Yakov; and Haim Mendelson. "Liquidity, Asset Prices and Financial Policy." *Financial Analysts Journal*, November–December 1991.

Problems

1. What is the beta of a portfolio with $E(r_P) = 18\%$, if $r_f = 6\%$ and $E(r_M) = 14\%$?

2. The market price of a security is $50. Its expected rate of return is 14%. The risk-free rate is 6% and the market risk premium is 8.5%. What will be the market price of the security if its covariance with the market portfolio doubles (and all other variables remain unchanged)? Assume that the stock is expected to pay a constant dividend in perpetuity.

3. You are a consultant to a large manufacturing corporation that is considering a project with the following net after-tax cash flows (in millions of dollars):

Years from Now	After-Tax Cash Flow
0	−40
1–10	15

The project's beta is 1.8. Assuming that $r_f = 8\%$ and $E(r_M) = 16\%$, what is the net present value of the project? What is the highest possible beta estimate for the project before its NPV becomes negative?

4. Are the following true or false?
   a. Stocks with a beta of zero offer an expected rate of return of zero.
   b. The CAPM implies that investors require a higher return to hold highly volatile securities.
   c. You can construct a portfolio with beta of .75 by investing .75 of the investment budget in T-bills and the remainder in the market portfolio.

5. Consider the following table, which gives a security analyst's expected return on two stocks for two particular market returns:

Market Return	Aggressive Stock	Defensive Stock
5%	−2%	6%
25	38	12

   a. What are the betas of the two stocks?
   b. What is the expected rate of return on each stock if the market return is equally
      likely to be 5% or 25%?
   c. If the T-bill rate is 6% and the market return is equally likely to be 5% or 25%, draw
      the SML for this economy.
   d. Plot the two securities on the SML graph. What are the alphas of each?
   e. What hurdle rate should be used by the management of the aggressive firm for a
      project with the risk characteristics of the defensive firm's stock?

   If the simple CAPM is valid, which of the following situations in problems 6 to 12 are
possible? Explain. Consider each situation independently.

6.

Portfolio	Expected Return	Beta
A	20	1.4
B	25	1.2

7.

Portfolio	Expected Return	Standard Deviation
A	30	35
B	40	25

8.

Portfolio	Expected Return	Standard Deviation
Risk-free	10	0
Market	18	24
A	16	12

9.

Portfolio	Expected Return	Standard Deviation
Risk-free	10	0
Market	18	24
A	20	22

10.

Portfolio	Expected Return	Beta
Risk-free	10	0
Market	18	1.0
A	16	1.5

11.

Portfolio	Expected Return	Beta
Risk-free	10	0
Market	18	1.0
A	16	0.9

12.

Portfolio	Expected Return	Standard Deviation
Risk-free	10	0
Market	18	24
A	16	22

In problems 13 to 15 assume that the risk-free rate of interest is 6% and the expected rate of return on the market is 16%.

13. A share of stock sells for $50 today. It will pay a dividend of $6 per share at the end of the year. Its beta is 1.2. What do investors expect the stock to sell for at the end of the year?

14. I am buying a firm with an expected perpetual cash flow of $1,000 but am unsure of its risk. If I think the beta of the firm is .5, when in fact the beta is really 1, how much *more* will I offer for the firm than it is truly worth?

15. A stock has an expected rate of return of 4%. What is its beta?

16. Two investment advisers are comparing performance. One averaged a 19% rate of return and the other a 16% rate of return. However, the beta of the first investor was 1.5, whereas that of the second was 1.

    a. Can you tell which investor was a better predictor of individual stocks (aside from the issue of general movements in the market)?

    b. If the T-bill rate were 6% and the market return during the period were 14%, which investor would be the superior stock selector?

    c. What if the T-bill rate were 3% and the market return were 15%?

17. In 1997 the rate of return on short-term government securities (perceived to be risk-free) was about 5%. Suppose the expected rate of return required by the market for a portfolio with a beta of 1 is 12%. According to the capital asset pricing model (security market line):

    a. What is the expected rate of return on the market portfolio?

    b. What would be the expected rate of return on a stock with $\beta = 0$?

    c. Suppose you consider buying a share of stock at $40. The stock is expected to pay $3 dividends next year and you expect it to sell then for $41. The stock risk has been evaluated by $\beta = -.5$. Is the stock overpriced or underpriced?

18. Suppose that you can invest risk-free at rate r_f but can borrow only at a higher rate, r_f^B. This case was considered in Section 8.6.

    a. Draw a minimum-variance frontier. Show on the graph the risky portfolio that will be selected by defensive investors. Show the portfolio that will be selected by aggressive investors.

    b. What portfolios will be selected by investors who neither borrow nor lend?

    c. Where will the market portfolio lie on the efficient frontier?

    d. Will the zero-beta CAPM be valid in this scenario? Explain. Show graphically the expected return on the zero-beta portfolio.

19. Consider an economy with two classes of investors. Tax-exempt investors can borrow or lend at the safe rate, r_f. Taxed investors pay tax rate t on all interest income, so their net-of-tax safe interest rate is $r_f(1 - t)$. Show that the zero-beta CAPM will apply to this economy and that $(1 - t)r_f < E[r_{Z(M)}] < r_f$.

20. Suppose that borrowing is restricted so that the zero-beta version of the CAPM holds. The expected return on the market portfolio is 17%, and on the zero-beta portfolio it is 8%. What is the expected return on a portfolio with a beta of .6?

21. The security market line depicts:

    a. A security's expected return as a function of its systematic risk.

    b. The market portfolio as the optimal portfolio of risky securities.

    c. The relationship between a security's return and the return on an index.

    d. The complete portfolio as a combination of the market portfolio and the risk-free asset.

22. Within the context of the capital asset pricing model (CAPM), assume:

    • Expected return on the market = 15%.

    • Risk-free rate = 8%.

    • Expected rate of return on XYZ security = 17%.

    • Beta of XYZ security = 1.25.

    Which one of the following is correct?

    a. XYZ is overpriced.

    b. XYZ is fairly priced.

    c. XYZ's alpha is −.25%.

    d. XYZ's alpha is .25%.

23. What is the expected return of a zero-beta security?

    a. Market rate of return.

    b. Zero rate of return.

    c. Negative rate of return.

    d. Risk-free rate of return.

24. Capital asset pricing theory asserts that portfolio returns are best explained by:

    a. Economic factors.

    b. Specific risk.

    c. Systematic risk.

    d. Diversification.

25. According to CAPM, the expected rate of return of a portfolio with a beta of 1.0 and an alpha of 0 is:

    a. Between r_M and r_f.

    b. The risk-free rate, r_f.

    c. $\beta(r_M - r_f)$.

    d. The expected return on the market, r_M.

The following table shows risk and return measures for two portfolios.

Portfolio	Average Annual Rate of Return	Standard Deviation	Beta
R	11%	10%	0.5
S&P 500	14%	12%	1.0

26. When plotting portfolio *R* on the preceding table relative to the SML, portfolio *R* lies:
    a. On the SML.
    b. Below the SML.
    c. Above the SML.
    d. Insufficient data given.

27. When plotting portfolio *R* relative to the capital market line, portfolio *R* lies:
    a. On the CML.
    b. Below the CML.
    c. Above the CML.
    d. Insufficient data given.

28. Briefly explain whether investors should expect a higher return from holding Portfolio A versus Portfolio B under capital asset pricing theory (CAPM). Assume that both portfolios are fully diversified.

	Portfolio A	Portfolio B
Systematic risk (beta)	1.0	1.0
Specific risk for each individual security	High	Low

solutions to Concept CHECKS

1. We can characterize the entire population by two representative investors. One is the "uninformed" investor, who does not engage in security analysis and holds the market portfolio, whereas the other optimizes using the Markowitz algorithm with input from security analysis. The uninformed investor does not know what input the informed investor uses to make portfolio purchases. The uninformed investor knows, however, that if the other investor is informed, the market portfolio proportions will be optimal. Therefore, to depart from these proportions would constitute an uninformed bet, which will, on average, reduce the efficiency of diversification with no compensating improvement in expected returns.

2. *a.* Substituting the historical mean and standard deviation in equation 9.2 yields a coefficient of risk aversion of

$$\bar{A} = \frac{E(r_M) - r_f}{.01 \times \sigma_M^2} = \frac{8.7}{.01 \times 20.8^2} = 2.01$$

b. This relationship also tells us that for the historical standard deviation and a coefficient of risk aversion of 3.5 the risk premium would be

$$E(r_M) - r_f = .01 \times \bar{A}\sigma_M^2 = .01 \times 3.5 \times 20.8^2 = 15.1\%$$

3. For these investment proportions, w_{Ford}, w_{GM}, the portfolio β is

$$\beta_P = w_{\text{Ford}}\beta_{\text{Ford}} + w_{\text{GM}}\beta_{\text{GM}}$$
$$= (.75 \times 1.25) + (.25 \times 1.10) = 1.2125$$

As the market risk premium, $E(r_M) - r_f$, is 8%, the portfolio risk premium will be

$$E(r_P) - r_f = \beta_P[E(r_M) - r_f]$$
$$= 1.2125 \times 8 = 9.7\%$$

4. The alpha of a stock is its expected return in excess of that required by the CAPM.

$$\alpha = E(r) - \{r_f + \beta[E(r_M) - r_f]\}$$
$$\alpha_{XYZ} = 12 - [5 + 1.0(11 - 5)] = 1\%$$
$$\alpha_{ABC} = 13 - [5 + 1.5(11 - 5)] = -1\%$$

ABC plots below the SML, while *XYZ* plots above.

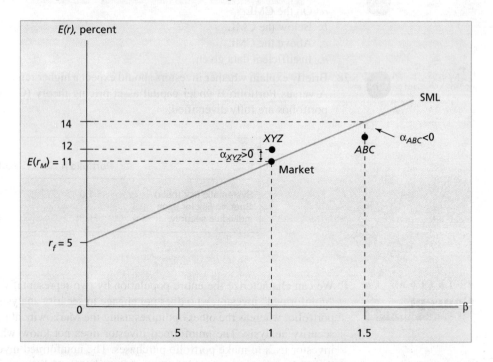

5. The project-specific required return is determined by the project beta coupled with the market risk premium and the risk-free rate. The CAPM tells us that an acceptable expected rate of return for the project is

$$r_f + \beta[E(r_M) - r_f] = 8 + 1.3(16 - 8) = 18.4\%$$

which becomes the project's hurdle rate. If the IRR of the project is 19%, then it is desirable. Any project with an IRR equal to or less than 18.4% should be rejected.

6. If the basic CAPM holds, any zero-beta asset must be expected to earn on average the risk-free rate. Hence the posited performance of the zero-beta portfolio violates the simple CAPM. It does not, however, violate the zero-beta CAPM. Since we know that borrowing restrictions do exist, we expect the zero-beta version of the model is more likely to hold, with the zero-beta rate differing from the virtually risk-free T-bill rate.

7. Consider investors with time horizon h_{IV} who will be indifferent between illiquid (I) and very illiquid (V) classes of stock. Call z the fraction of liquidation cost by which the gross return of class V stocks is increased. For these investors, the indifference condition is

$$[r + y\, c_I] - c_I/h_{LI} = [r + z\, c_V] - c_V/h_{IV}$$

This equation can be rearranged to show that

$$[r + z\, c_V] - [r + y\, c_I] = (c_I - c_V)/h_{IV}$$

SINGLE-INDEX AND MULTIFACTOR MODELS

Chapter 8 introduced the Markowitz portfolio selection model, which shows how to obtain the maximum return possible for any level of portfolio risk. Implementation of the Markowitz portfolio selection model, however, requires a huge number of estimates of covariances between all pairs of available securities. Moreover, these estimates have to be fed into a mathematical optimization program that requires vast computer capacity to perform the necessary calculations for large portfolios. Because the data requirements and computer capacity called for in the full-blown Markowitz procedure are overwhelming, we must search for a strategy that reduces the necessary compilation and processing of data. We introduce in this chapter a simplifying assumption that at once eases our computational burden and offers significant new insights into the nature of systematic risk versus firm-specific risk. This abstraction is the notion of an "index model," specifying the  process by which security returns are generated. Our discussion of the index model also introduces the concept of multifactor models of security returns, a concept at the heart of contemporary investment theory and its applications.

10.1   A SINGLE-INDEX SECURITY MARKET

Systematic Risk versus Firm-Specific Risk

The success of a portfolio selection rule depends on the quality of the input list, that is, the estimates of expected security returns and the covariance matrix. In the long run, efficient portfolios will beat portfolios with less reliable input lists and consequently inferior reward-to-risk trade-offs.

Suppose your security analysts can thoroughly analyze 50 stocks. This means that your input list will include the following:

$$
\begin{aligned}
n = &\quad 50 \text{ estimates of expected returns} \\
n = &\quad 50 \text{ estimates of variances} \\
(n^2 - n)/2 = &\quad \underline{1{,}225} \text{ estimates of covariances} \\
&\quad 1{,}325 \text{ estimates}
\end{aligned}
$$

This is a formidable task, particularly in light of the fact that a 50-security portfolio is relatively small. Doubling n to 100 will nearly quadruple the number of estimates to 5,150. If $n = 2{,}700$, roughly the number of NYSE stocks, we need more than 3.6 *million* estimates.

Covariances between security returns tend to be positive because the same economic forces affect the fortunes of many firms. Some examples of common economic factors are business cycles, interest rates, technological changes, and cost of labor and raw materials. All these (interrelated) factors affect almost all firms. Thus unexpected changes in these variables cause, simultaneously, unexpected changes in the rates of return on the entire stock market.

Suppose that we group all relevant economic factors into one macroeconomic indicator and assume that it moves the security market as a whole. We further assume that, beyond this common effect, all remaining uncertainty in stock returns is firm specific; that is, there is no other source of correlation between securities. Firm-specific events would include new inventions, deaths of key employees, and other factors that affect the fortune of the individual firm without affecting the broad economy in a measurable way.

We can summarize the distinction between macroeconomic and firm-specific factors by writing the holding-period return on security i as

$$r_i = E(r_i) + m_i + e_i \tag{10.1}$$

where $E(r_i)$ is the expected return on the security as of the beginning of the holding period, m_i is the impact of unanticipated macro events on the security's return during the period, and e_i is the impact of unanticipated firm-specific events. Both m_i and e_i have zero expected values because each represents the impact of unanticipated events, which by definition must average out to zero.

We can gain further insight by recognizing that different firms have different sensitivities to macroeconomic events. Thus if we denote the unanticipated components of the macro factor by F, and denote the responsiveness of security i to macroevents by beta β_i, then the macro component of security i is $m_i = \beta_i F$, and then equation 10.1 becomes[1]

$$r_i = E(r_i) + \beta_i F + e_i \tag{10.2}$$

---

[1] You may wonder why we choose the notation β for the responsiveness coefficient because β already has been defined in Chapter 9 in the context of the CAPM. The choice is deliberate, however. Our reasoning will be obvious shortly.

Equation 10.2 is known as a **single-factor model** for stock returns. It is easy to imagine that a more realistic decomposition of security returns would require more than one factor in equation 10.2. We treat this issue later in the chapter. For now, let us examine the simple case with only one macro factor.

Of course, a factor model is of little use without specifying a way to measure the factor that is posited to affect security returns. One reasonable approach is to assert that the rate of return on a broad index of securities such as the S&P 500 is a valid proxy for the common macro factor. This approach leads to an equation similar to the factor model, which is called a **single-index model** because it uses the market index to proxy for the common or systematic factor.

According to the index model, we can separate the actual or realized rate of return on a security into macro (systematic) and micro (firm-specific) components in a manner similar to that in equation 10.2. We write the rate of return on each security as a sum of three components:

	Symbol
1. The stock's expected return if the market is neutral, that is, if the market's excess return, $r_M - r_f$, is zero	α_i
2. The component of return due to movements in the overall market; β_i is the security's responsiveness to market movements	$\beta_i(r_M - r_f)$
3. The unexpected component due to unexpected events that are relevant only to this security (firm specific)	e_i

The holding period excess return on the stock can be stated as

$$r_i - r_f = \alpha_i + \beta_i(r_M - r_f) + e_i$$

Let us denote excess returns over the risk-free rate by capital R and rewrite this equation as

$$R_i = \alpha_i + \beta_i R_M + e_i \tag{10.3}$$

We write the index model in terms of excess returns over r_f rather than in terms of total returns because the level of the stock market return represents the state of the macro economy only to the extent that it exceeds or falls short of the rate of return on risk-free T-bills. For example, in the 1950s, when T-bills were yielding only 1% or 2%, a return of 8% or 9% on the stock market would be considered good news. In contrast, in the early 1980s, when bills were yielding over 10%, that same 8% or 9% would signal disappointing macroeconomic news.[2]

Equation 10.3 says that each security has two sources of risk: *market or systematic risk*, attributable to its sensitivity to macroeconomic factors as reflected in R_M, and *firm-specific risk*, as reflected in e. If we denote the variance of the excess return on the market, R_M, as σ_M^2, then we can break the variance of the rate of return on each stock into two components:

---

[2]Practitioners often use a "modified" index model that is similar to equation 10.3 but that uses total rather than excess returns. This practice is most common when daily data are used. In this case the rate of return on bills is on the order of only about .02% per day, so total and excess returns are almost indistinguishable.

	Symbol
1. The variance attributable to the uncertainty of the common macroeconomic factor	$\beta_i^2\sigma_M^2$
2. The variance attributable to firm-specific uncertainty	$\sigma^2(e_i)$

The covariance between R_M and e_i is zero because e_i is defined as firm specific, that is, independent of movements in the market. Hence the variance of the rate of return on security i is

$$\sigma_i^2 = \beta_i^2\sigma_M^2 + \sigma^2(e_i)$$

The covariance between the excess rates of return on two stocks, for example, R_i and R_j, derives only from the common factor R_M, because e_i and e_j are each firm specific and therefore presumed to be uncorrelated. Hence the covariance between two stocks is

$$\text{Cov}(R_i, R_j) = \text{Cov}(\beta_i R_M, \beta_j R_M) = \beta_i\beta_j\sigma_M^2 \qquad (10.4)$$

These calculations show that if we have

n estimates of the expected excess returns, $E(R_i)$

n estimates of the sensitivity coefficients, β_i

n estimates of the firm-specific variances, $\sigma^2(e_i)$

1 estimate for the variance of the (common) macroeconomic factor, σ_M^2,

then these $(3n + 1)$ estimates will enable us to prepare the input list for this single-index security universe. Thus for a 50-security portfolio we will need 151 estimates rather than 1,325; for the entire New York Stock Exchange, about 2,700 securities, we will need 8,101 estimates rather than approximately 3.6 million!

It is easy to see why the index model is such a useful abstraction. For large universes of securities, the number of estimates required for the Markowitz procedure using the index model is only a small fraction of what otherwise would he needed.

Another advantage is less obvious but equally important. The index model abstraction is crucial for specialization of effort in security analysis. If a covariance term had to be calculated directly for each security pair, then security analysts could not specialize by industry. For example, if one group were to specialize in the computer industry and another in the auto industry, who would have the common background to estimate the covariance *between* IBM and GM? Neither group would have the deep understanding of other industries necessary to make an informed judgment of comovements among industries. In contrast, the index model suggests a simple way to compute covariances. Covariances among securities are due to the influence of the single common factor, represented by the market index return, and can be easily estimated using equation 10.4.

The simplification derived from the index model assumption is, however, not without cost. The "cost" of the model lies in the restrictions it places on the structure of asset return uncertainty. The classification of uncertainty into a simple dichotomy—macro versus micro risk—oversimplifies sources of real-world uncertainty and misses some important sources of dependence in stock returns. For example, this dichotomy rules out industry events, events that may affect many firms within an industry without substantially affecting the broad macroeconomy.

Statistical analysis shows that relative to a single index, the firm-specific components of some firms are correlated. Examples are the nonmarket components of stocks in a single industry, such as computer stocks or auto stocks. At the same time, statistical significance does not always correspond to economic significance. Economically speaking, the question that is more relevant to the assumption of a single-index model is whether portfolios constructed using covariances that are estimated on the basis of the single-factor or single-index assumption are significantly different from, and less efficient than, portfolios constructed using covariances that are estimated directly for each pair of stocks. We explore this issue further in Chapter 28 on active portfolio management.

Concept
CHECK

Question 1 • Suppose that the index model for stocks A and B is estimated with the following results:

$$R_A = 1.0\% + .9R_M + e_A$$
$$R_B = -2.0\% + 1.1R_M + e_B$$
$$\sigma_M = 20\%$$
$$\sigma(e_A) = 30\%$$
$$\sigma(e_B) = 10\%$$

Find the standard deviation of each stock and the covariance between them.

Estimating the Index Model

Equation 10.3 also suggests how we might go about actually measuring market and firm-specific risk. Suppose that we observe the excess return on the market index and a specific asset over a number of holding periods. We use as an example monthly excess returns on the S&P 500 index and GM stock for a one-year period. We can summarize the results for a sample period in a **scatter diagram**, as illustrated in Figure 10.1.

Figure 10.1
Security characteristic line (SCL) for GM.

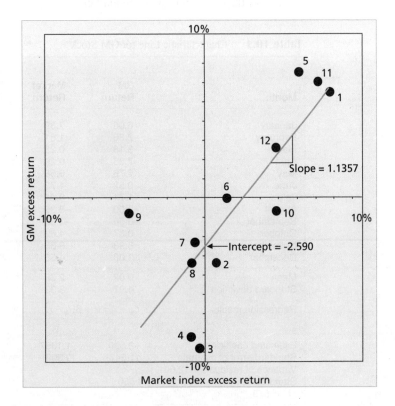

The horizontal axis in Figure 10.1 measures the excess return (over the risk-free rate) on the market index, whereas the vertical axis measures the excess return on the asset in question (GM stock in our example). A pair of excess returns (one for the market index, one for GM stock) constitutes one point on this scatter diagram. The points are numbered 1 through 12, representing excess returns for the S&P 500 and GM for each month from January through December. The single-index model states that the relationship between the excess returns on GM and the S&P 500 is given by

$$R_{GMt} = \alpha_{GM} + \beta_{GM} R_{Mt} + e_{GMt}$$

Note the resemblance of this relationship to a **regression equation.**

In a single-variable linear regression equation, the dependent variable plots around a straight line with an intercept α and a slope β. The deviations from the line, e, are assumed to be mutually uncorrelated as well as uncorrelated with the independent variable. Because these assumptions are identical to those of the index model we can look at the index model as a regression model. The sensitivity of GM to the market, measured by β_{GM}, is the slope of the regression line. The intercept of the regression line is α_{GM}, representing the average firm-specific return. Deviations of particular observations from the regression line in any period are denoted e_{GMt}, and called **residuals.** Each of these residuals is the difference between the actual stock return and the return that would be predicted from the regression equation describing the usual relationship between the stock and the market; therefore, they measure the impact of firm-specific events during the particular month. The parameters of interest, α, β, and Var(e), can be estimated using standard regression techniques.

Estimating the regression equation of the single-index model gives us the **security characteristic line** (SCL), which is plotted in Figure 10.1. (The regression results and raw data appear in Table 10.1.) The SCL is a plot of the typical excess return on a security as a function of the excess return on the market.

Table 10.1   Characteristic Line for GM Stock

Month	GM Return	Market Return	Monthly T-Bill Rate	Excess GM Return	Excess Market Return
January	6.06	7.89	0.65	5.41	7.24
February	−2.86	1.51	0.58	−3.44	0.93
March	−8.18	0.23	0.62	−8.79	−0.38
April	−7.36	−0.29	0.72	−8.08	−1.01
May	7.76	5.58	0.66	7.10	4.92
June	0.52	1.73	0.55	−0.03	1.18
July	−1.74	−0.21	0.62	−2.36	−0.83
August	−3.00	−0.36	0.55	−3.55	−0.91
September	−0.56	−3.58	0.60	−1.16	−4.18
October	−0.37	4.62	0.65	−1.02	3.97
November	6.93	6.85	0.61	6.32	6.25
December	3.08	4.55	0.65	2.43	3.90
Mean	0.02	2.38	0.62	−0.60	1.75
Standard deviation	4.97	3.33	0.05	4.97	3.32
Regression results	$r_{GM} - r_f = \alpha + \beta(r_M - r_f)$				
	α	β			
Estimated coefficient	−2.590	1.1357			
Standard error of estimate	(1.547)	(0.309)			
Variance of residuals = 12.601					
Standard deviation of residuals = 3.550					
$R^2 = .575$					

This sample of holding period returns is, of course, too small to yield reliable statistics. We use it only for demonstration. For this sample period we find that the beta coefficient of GM stock, as estimated by the slope of the regression line, is 1.1357, and that the intercept for this SCL is –2.59% per month.

For each month, t, our estimate of the residual, e_t, which is the deviation of GM's excess return from the prediction of the SCL, equals

$$\text{Deviation} = \text{Actual} - \text{Predicted return}$$

$$e_{\text{GM}t} = R_{\text{GM}t} - (\beta_{\text{GM}} R_{Mt} + \alpha_{\text{GM}})$$

These residuals are estimates of the monthly unexpected *firm-specific* component of the rate of return on GM stock. Hence we can estimate the firm-specific variance by[3]

$$\sigma^2(e_{\text{GM}}) = \frac{1}{10} \sum_{t=1}^{12} e_t^2 = 12.60$$

The standard deviation of the firm-specific component of GM's return, $\sigma(e_{\text{GM}})$, is $\sqrt{12.60} = 3.55\%$ per month, equal to the standard deviation of the regression residual.

The Index Model and Diversification

The index model, first suggested by Sharpe,[4] also offers insight into portfolio diversification. Suppose that we choose an equally weighted portfolio of n securities. The excess rate of return on each security is given by

$$R_i = \alpha_i + \beta_i R_M + e_i$$

Similarly, we can write the excess return on the portfolio of stocks as

$$R_P = \alpha_P + \beta_P R_M + e_P \qquad (10.5)$$

We now show that, as the number of stocks included in this portfolio increases, the part of the portfolio risk attributable to nonmarket factors becomes ever smaller. This part of the risk is diversified away. In contrast, the market risk remains, regardless of the number of firms combined into the portfolio.

To understand these results, note that the excess rate of return on this equally weighted portfolio, for which each portfolio weight $w_i = 1/n$, is

$$R_P = \sum_{i=1}^{n} w_i R_i = \frac{1}{n} \sum_{i=1}^{n} R_i = \frac{1}{n} \sum_{i=1}^{n} (\alpha_i + \beta_i R_M + e_i)$$

$$= \frac{1}{n} \sum_{i=1}^{n} \alpha_i + \left(\frac{1}{n} \sum_{i=1}^{n} \beta_i \right) R_M + \frac{1}{n} \sum_{i=1}^{n} e_i \qquad (10.6)$$

Comparing equations 10.5 and 10.6, we see that the portfolio has a sensitivity to the market given by

$$\beta_P = \frac{1}{n} \sum_{i=1}^{n} \beta_i$$

---

[3]Because the mean of e_i is zero, e_t^2 is the squared deviation from its mean. The average value of e_t^2 is therefore the estimate of the variance of the firm-specific component. We divide the sum of squared residuals by the degrees of freedom of the regression, $n - 2 = 12 - 2 = 10$, to obtain an unbiased estimate of $\sigma^2(e)$.

[4]William F. Sharpe, "A Simplified Model of Portfolio Analysis," *Management Science*, January 1963.

which is the average of the individual β_is, and has a nonmarket return component of a constant (intercept)

$$\alpha_P = \frac{1}{n} \sum_{i=1}^{n} \alpha_i$$

which is the average of the individual alphas, plus the zero mean variable

$$e_P = \frac{1}{n} \sum_{i=1}^{n} e_i$$

which is the average of the firm-specific components. Hence the portfolio's variance is

$$\sigma_P^2 = \beta_P^2 \sigma_M^2 + \sigma^2(e_P) \qquad (10.7)$$

The systematic risk component of the portfolio variance, which we defined as the component that depends on marketwide movements, is $\beta_P^2 \sigma_M^2$ and depends on the sensitivity coefficients of the individual securities. This part of the risk depends on portfolio beta and σ_M^2 and will persist regardless of the extent of portfolio diversification. No matter how many stocks are held, their common exposure to the market will be reflected in portfolio systematic risk.[5]

In contrast, the nonsystematic component of the portfolio variance is $\sigma^2(e_P)$ and is attributable to firm-specific components, e_i. Because these e_is are independent, and all have zero expected value, the law of averages can be applied to conclude that as more and more stocks are added to the portfolio, the firm-specific components tend to cancel out, resulting in ever-smaller nonmarket risk. Such risk is thus termed *diversifiable*. To see this more rigorously, examine the formula for the variance of the equally weighted "portfolio" of firm-specific components. Because the e_is are uncorrelated,

$$\sigma^2(e_P) = \sum_{i=1}^{n} \left(\frac{1}{n}\right)^2 \sigma^2(e_i) = \frac{1}{n} \bar{\sigma}^2(e)$$

where $\bar{\sigma}^2(e)$ is the average of the firm-specific variances. Because this average is independent of n, when n gets large, $\sigma^2(e_P)$ becomes negligible.

To summarize, as diversification increases, the total variance of a portfolio approaches the systematic variance, defined as the variance of the market factor multiplied by the square of the portfolio sensitivity coefficient, β_P^2. This is shown in Figure 10.2.

Figure 10.2 shows that as more and more securities are combined into a portfolio, the portfolio variance decreases because of the diversification of firm-specific risk. However, the power of diversification is limited. Even for very large n, part of the risk remains because of the exposure of virtually all assets to the common, or market, factor. Therefore, this systematic risk is said to be nondiversifiable.

This analysis is borne out by empirical evidence. We saw the effect of portfolio diversification on portfolio standard deviations in Figure 8.2. These empirical results are similar to the theoretical graph presented here in Figure 10.2.

Concept CHECK

Question 2 • Reconsider the two stocks in Concept Check 1. Suppose we form an equally weighted portfolio of *A* and *B*. What will be the nonsystematic standard deviation of that portfolio?

---

[5]Of course, one can construct a portfolio with zero systematic risk by mixing negative β and positive β assets. The point of our discussion is that the vast majority of securities have a positive β, implying that well-diversified portfolios with small holdings in large numbers of assets will indeed have positive systematic risk.

Figure 10.2

The variance of a portfolio with risk coefficient β in the single-factor economy.

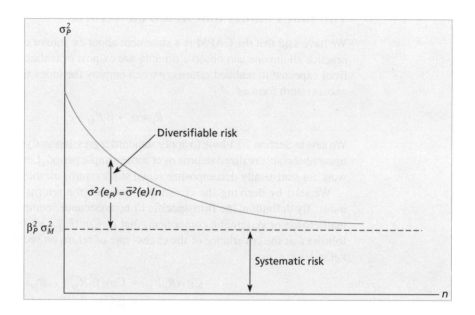

σ_P^2

Diversifiable risk

$\sigma^2(e_P) = \overline{\sigma}^2(e)/n$

$\beta_P^2\,\sigma_M^2$

Systematic risk

n

10.2   THE CAPM AND THE INDEX MODEL

Actual Returns versus Expected Returns

The CAPM is an elegant model. The question is whether it has real-world value—whether its implications are borne out by experience. Chapter 13 provides a range of empirical evidence on this point, but for now we focus briefly on a more basic issue: Is the CAPM testable even in principle?

For starters, one central prediction of the CAPM is that the market portfolio is a mean-variance efficient portfolio. Consider that the CAPM treats all traded risky assets. To test the efficiency of the CAPM market portfolio, we would need to construct a value-weighted portfolio of a huge size and test its efficiency. So far, this task has not been feasible. An even more difficult problem, however, is that the CAPM implies relationships among *expected* returns, whereas all we can observe are actual or realized holding period returns, and these need not equal prior expectations. Even supposing we could construct a portfolio to represent the CAPM market portfolio satisfactorily, how would we test its mean-variance efficiency? We would have to show that the reward-to-variability ratio of the market portfolio is higher than that of any other portfolio. However, this reward-to-variability ratio is set in terms of expectations, and we have no way to observe these expectations directly.

The problem of measuring expectations haunts us as well when we try to establish the validity of the second central set of CAPM predictions, the expected return–beta relationship. This relationship is also defined in terms of expected returns $E(r_i)$ and $E(r_M)$:

$$E(r_i) = r_f + \beta_i[E(r_M) - r_f] \tag{10.8}$$

The upshot is that, as elegant and insightful as the CAPM is, we must make additional assumptions to make it implementable and testable.

The Index Model and Realized Returns

We have said that the CAPM is a statement about ex ante or expected returns, whereas in practice all anyone can observe directly are ex post or realized returns. To make the leap from expected to realized returns, we can employ the index model, which we will use in excess return form as

$$R_i = \alpha_i + \beta_i R_M + e_i \tag{10.9}$$

We saw in Section 10.1 how to apply standard regression analysis to estimate equation 10.9 using observable realized returns over some sample period. Let us now see how this framework for statistically decomposing actual stock returns meshes with the CAPM.

We start by deriving the covariance between the returns on stock i and the market index. By definition, the firm-specific or nonsystematic component is independent of the marketwide or systematic component, that is, $\text{Cov}(R_M, e_i) = 0$. From this relationship, it follows that the covariance of the excess rate of return on security i with that of the market index is

$$\begin{aligned}
\text{Cov}(R_i, R_M) &= \text{Cov}(\beta_i R_M + e_i, R_M) \\
&= \beta_i \text{Cov}(R_M, R_M) + \text{Cov}(e_i, R_M) \\
&= \beta_i \sigma_M^2
\end{aligned}$$

Note that we can drop α_i from the covariance terms because α_i is a constant and thus has zero covariance with all variables.

Because $\text{Cov}(R_i, R_M) = \beta_i \sigma_M^2$, the sensitivity coefficient, β_i, in equation 10.9, which is the slope of the regression line representing the index model, equals

$$\beta_i = \frac{\text{Cov}(R_i, R_M)}{\sigma_M^2}$$

The index model beta coefficient turns out to be the same beta as that of the CAPM expected return–beta relationship, except that we replace the (theoretical) market portfolio of the CAPM with the well-specified and observable market index.

Concept CHECK

Question 3 • The data below describe a three-stock financial market that satisfies the single-index model.

Stock	Capitalization	Beta	Mean Excess Return	Standard Deviation
A	$3,000	1.0	10%	40%
B	$1,940	0.2	2	30
C	$1,360	1.7	17	50

The single factor in this economy is perfectly correlated with the value-weighted index of the stock market. The standard deviation of the market index portfolio is 25%.
a. What is the mean excess return of the index portfolio?
b. What is the covariance between stock *A* and the index?
c. Break down the variance of stock *B* into its systematic and firm-specific components.

The Index Model and the Expected Return–Beta Relationship

Recall that the CAPM expected return–beta relationship is, for any asset i and the (theoretical) market portfolio,

$$E(r_i) - r_f = \beta_i[E(r_M) - r_f]$$

where $\beta_i = \text{Cov}(R_i, R_M)/\sigma_M^2$. This is a statement about the mean of expected excess return of assets relative to the mean excess return of the (theoretical) market portfolio.

If the index M in equation 10.9 represents the true market portfolio, we can take the expectation of each side of the equation to show that the index model specification is

$$E(r_i) - r_f = \alpha_i + \beta_i[E(r_M) - r_f]$$

A comparison of the index model relationship to the CAPM expected return–beta relationship (equation 10.8) shows that the CAPM predicts that α_i should be zero for all assets. The alpha of a stock is its expected return in excess of (or below) the fair expected return as predicted by the CAPM. If the stock is fairly priced, its alpha must be zero.

We emphasize again that this is a statement about *expected* returns on a security. After the fact, of course, some securities will do better or worse than expected and will have returns higher or lower than predicted by the CAPM; that is, they will exhibit positive or negative alphas over a sample period. But this superior or inferior performance could not have been forecast in advance.

Therefore, if we estimate the index model for several firms, using equation 10.9 as a regression equation, we should find that the ex post or realized alphas (the regression intercepts) for the firms in our sample center around zero. If the initial expectation for alpha were zero, as many firms would be expected to have a positive as a negative alpha for some sample period. The CAPM states that the *expected* value of alpha is zero for all securities, whereas the index model representation of the CAPM holds that the *realized* value of alpha should average out to zero for a sample of historical observed returns. Just as important, the sample alphas should be unpredictable, that is, independent from one sample period to the next.

Some interesting evidence on this property was compiled by Michael Jensen,[6] who examined the alphas realized by mutual funds over the period 1945 to 1964. Figure 10.3 shows the frequency distribution of these alphas, which do indeed seem to be distributed around zero.

There is yet another applicable variation on the intuition of the index model, the **market model**. Formally, the market model states that the return "surprise" of any security is proportional to the return surprise of the market, plus a firm-specific surprise:

$$r_i - E(r_i) = \beta_i[r_M - E(r_M)] + e_i$$

This equation divides returns into firm-specific and systematic components somewhat differently from the index model. If the CAPM is valid, however, you can see that, substituting for $E(r_i)$ from equation 10.8, the market model equation becomes identical to the index model. For this reason the terms "index model" and "market model" are used interchangeably.

---

[6]Michael C. Jensen, "The Performance of Mutual Funds in the Period 1945–1964," *Journal of Finance* 23 (May 1968).

Figure 10.3
Frequency distribution
of alphas.

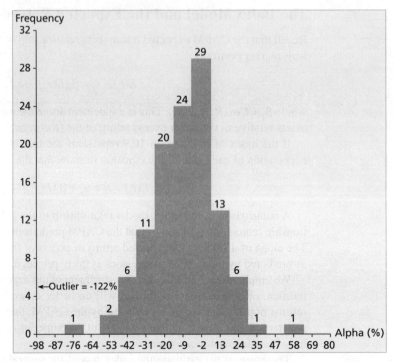

Source: Michael C. Jensen, "The Performance of Mutual Funds in the Period 1945–1964," *Journal of Finance* 23 (May 1968).

Concept CHECK   Question 4 • Can you sort out the nuances of the following maze of models?
a. **CAPM**
b. **Single-factor model**
c. **Single-index model**
d. **Market model**

10.3   THE INDUSTRY VERSION OF THE INDEX MODEL

Not surprisingly, the index model has attracted the attention of practitioners. To the extent that it is approximately valid, it provides a convenient benchmark for security analysis.

A modern practitioner using the CAPM, who has neither special information about a security nor insight that is unavailable to the general public, will conclude that the security is "properly" priced. By properly priced, the analyst means that the expected return on the security is commensurate with its risk, and therefore plots on the security market line. For instance, if one has no private information about GM's stock, then one should expect

$$E(r_{GM}) = r_f + \beta_{GM}[E(r_M) - r_f]$$

A portfolio manager who has a forecast for the market index, $E(r_M)$, and observes the risk-free T-bill rate, r_f, can use the model to determine the benchmark expected return for any stock. The beta coefficient, the market risk, σ_M^2, and the firm-specific risk, $\sigma^2(e)$, can be estimated from historical SCLs, that is, from regressions of security excess returns on market index excess returns.

There are many sources for such regression results. One widely used source is Research Computer Services Department of Merrill Lynch, which publishes a monthly *Security Risk Evaluation* book, commonly called the "beta book."

Security Risk Evaluation uses the S&P 500 index as the proxy for the market portfolio. It relies on the 60 most recent monthly observations to calculate regression parameters. Merrill Lynch and most services[7] use total returns, rather than excess returns (deviations from T-bill rates), in the regressions. In this way they estimate a variant of our index model, which is

$$r = a + br_M + e^* \tag{10.10}$$

instead of

$$r - r_f = \alpha + \beta(r_M - r_f) + e \tag{10.11}$$

To see the effect of this departure, we can rewrite equation 10.11 as

$$r = r_f + \alpha + \beta r_M - \beta r_f + e = \alpha + r_f(1 - \beta) + \beta r_M + e \tag{10.12}$$

Comparing equations 10.10 and 10.12, you can see that if r_f is constant over the sample period, both equations have the same independent variable, r_M, and residual, e. Therefore, the slope coefficient will be the same in the two regressions.[8]

However, the intercept that Merrill Lynch calls alpha is really an estimate of $\alpha + r_f(1 - \beta)$. The apparent justification for this procedure is that, on a monthly basis, $r_f(1 - \beta)$ is small and is apt to be swamped by the volatility of actual stock returns. But it is worth noting that for $\beta \neq 1$, the regression intercept in equation 10.10 will not equal the index model alpha as it does when excess returns are used as in equation 10.11.

Another way the Merrill Lynch procedure departs from the index model is in its use of percentage changes in price instead of total rates of return. This means that the index model variant of Merrill Lynch ignores the dividend component of stock returns.

Table 10.2 illustrates a page from the beta book which includes estimates for GM. The third column, Close Price, shows the stock price at the end of the sample period. The next two columns show the beta and alpha coefficients. Remember that Merrill Lynch's alpha is actually an estimate of $\alpha + r_f(1 - \beta)$.

The next column, R-SQR, shows the square of the correlation between r_i and r_M. The R-square statistic, R^2, which is sometimes called the *coefficient of determination*, gives the fraction of the variance of the dependent variable (the return on the stock) that is explained by movements in the independent variable (the return on the S&P 500 index). Recall from Section 10.1 that the part of the total variance of the rate of return on an asset, σ^2, that is explained by market returns is the systematic variance, $\beta^2\sigma_M^2$. Hence the R-square is systematic variance over total variance, which tells us what fraction of a firm's volatility is attributable to market movements:

$$R^2 = \frac{\beta^2\sigma_M^2}{\sigma^2}$$

---

[7]Value Line is another common source of security betas. Value Line uses weekly rather than monthly data and uses the New York Stock Exchange index instead of the S&P 500 as the market proxy.

[8]Actually, r_f does vary over time and so should not be grouped casually with the constant term in the regression. However, variations in r_f are tiny compared with the swings in the market return. The actual volatility in the T-bill rate has only a small impact on the estimated value of β.

Table 10.2   Market Sensitivity Statistics

Ticker Symbol	Security Name	June 1994 Close Price	Beta	Alpha	R-SQR	RESID STD DEV-N	Standard Error Beta	Alpha	Adjusted Beta	Number of Observations
GBND	General Binding Corp	18.375	0.52	−0.06	0.02	10.52	0.37	1.38	0.68	60
GBDC	General Bldrs Corp	0.930	0.58	−1.03	0.00	17.38	0.62	2.28	0.72	60
GNCMA	General Communication Inc Class A	3.750	1.54	0.82	0.12	14.42	0.51	1.89	1.36	60
GCCC	General Computer Corp	8.375	0.93	1.67	0.06	12.43	0.44	1.63	0.95	60
GDC	General Datacomm Inds Inc	16.125	2.25	2.31	0.16	18.32	0.65	2.40	1.83	60
GD	General Dynamics Corp	40.875	0.54	0.63	0.03	9.02	0.32	1.18	0.69	60
GE	General Elec Co	46.625	1.21	0.39	0.61	3.53	0.13	0.46	1.14	60
JOB	General Employment Enterpris	4.063	0.91	1.20	0.01	20.50	0.73	2.69	0.94	60
GMCC	General Magnaplate Corp	4.500	0.97	0.00	0.04	14.18	0.50	1.86	0.98	60
GMW	General Microwave Corp	8.000	0.95	0.16	0.12	8.83	0.31	1.16	0.97	60
GIS	General MLS Inc	54.625	1.01	0.42	0.37	4.82	0.17	0.63	1.01	60
GM	General MTRS Corp	50.250	0.80	0.14	0.11	7.78	0.28	1.02	0.87	60 ←
GPU	General Pub Utils Cp	26.250	0.52	0.20	0.20	3.69	0.13	0.48	0.68	60
GRN	General RE Corp	108.875	1.07	0.42	0.31	5.75	0.20	0.75	1.05	60
GSX	General SIGNAL Corp	33.000	0.86	−0.01	0.22	5.85	0.21	0.77	0.91	60

Source: Modified from *Security Risk Evaluation*, 1994, Research Computer Services Department of Merrill Lynch, Pierce, Fenner and Smith, Inc., pp. 9–17. Based on S&P 500 index, using straight regression.

The firm-specific variance, $\sigma^2(e)$, is the part of the asset variance that is unexplained by the market index. Therefore, because

$$\sigma^2 = \beta^2 \sigma_M^2 + \sigma^2(e)$$

the coefficient of determination also may be expressed as

$$R^2 = 1 - \frac{\sigma^2(e)}{\sigma^2} \tag{10.13}$$

Accordingly, the column following R-SQR reports the standard deviation of the non-systematic component, $\sigma(e)$, calling it RESID STD DEV-N, in reference to the fact that the e is estimated from the regression residuals. This variable is an estimate of firm-specific risk.

The following two columns appear under the heading of Standard Error. These are statistics that allow us to test the precision and significance of the regression coefficients. The standard error of an estimate is the standard deviation of the possible estimation error of the coefficient. A rule of thumb is that if an estimated coefficient is less than twice its standard error, we cannot reject the hypothesis that the true coefficient is zero. The ratio of the coefficient to its standard error is the t-statistic. A t-statistic greater than 2 is the traditional cutoff for statistical significance. The two columns of the standard error of the estimated beta and alpha allow us a quick check on the statistical significance of these estimates.

The next-to-last column is called Adjusted Beta. The motivation for adjusting beta estimates is that, on average, the beta coefficients of stocks seem to move toward 1 over time. One explanation for this phenomenon is intuitive. A business enterprise usually is established to produce a specific product or service, and a new firm may be more unconventional than an older one in many ways, from technology to management style. As it grows, however, a firm often diversifies, first expanding to similar products and later to more diverse operations. As the firm becomes more conventional, it starts to resemble the rest of the economy even more. Thus its beta coefficient will tend to change in the direction of 1.

Another explanation for this phenomenon is statistical. We know that the average beta over all securities is 1. Thus before estimating the beta of a security our best forecast of the beta would be that it is 1. When we estimate this beta coefficient over a particular sample period, we sustain some unknown sampling error of the estimated beta. The greater the difference between our beta estimate and 1, the greater is the chance that we incurred a large estimation error and that beta in a subsequent sample period will be closer to 1.

The sample estimate of the beta coefficient is the best guess for the sample period. Given that beta has a tendency to evolve toward 1, however, a forecast of the future beta coefficient should adjust the sample estimate in that direction.

Merrill Lynch adjusts beta estimates in a simple way.[9] They take the sample estimate of beta and average it with 1, using the weights of two-thirds and one-third:

$$\text{Adjusted beta} = \tfrac{2}{3}\text{ sample beta} + \tfrac{1}{3}(1)$$

Finally, the last column shows the number of observations, which is 60 months, unless the stock is newly listed and fewer observations are available.

For the 60 months ending in June 1994, GM's beta was estimated at .80. Note that the adjusted beta for GM is .87, taking it a third of the way toward 1.

The sample period regression alpha is .14%. Because GM's beta is less than 1, we know that this means that the index model alpha estimate is somewhat smaller. As in equation 10.12, we have to subtract $(1 - \beta)r_f$ from the regression alpha to obtain the index model alpha. Even so, the standard error of the alpha estimate is 1.02. The estimate of alpha is far less than twice its standard error. Consequently, we cannot reject the hypothesis that the true alpha is zero.

Concept

Question 5 • What was GM's CAPM alpha per month during the period covered by the Merrill Lynch regression if during this period the average monthly rate of return on T-bills was .6%?

Most importantly, these alpha estimates are ex post (after the fact) measures. They do not mean that anyone could have forecasted these alpha values ex ante (before the fact). In fact, the name of the game in security analysis is to forecast alpha values ahead of time. A well-constructed portfolio that includes long positions in future positive alpha stocks and short positions in future negative alpha stocks will outperform the market index. The key term here is "well constructed," meaning that the portfolio has to balance concentration on high alpha stocks with the need for risk-reducing diversification. The beta and residual variance estimates from the index model regression make it possible to achieve this goal. (We examine this technique in more detail in Part VII on active portfolio management.)

Note that GM's RESID STD DEV-N is 7.78% per month and its R^2 is .11. This tells us that $\sigma^2_{GM}(e) = 7.78^2 = 60.53$ and, because $R^2 = 1 - \sigma^2(e)/\sigma^2$, we can solve for the estimate of GM's total standard deviation by rearranging equation 10.13 as follows:

$$\sigma_{GM} = \left[\frac{\sigma_{GM}(e)}{1 - R^2}\right]^{1/2} = \left(\frac{60.53}{.89}\right)^{1/2} = 8.25\% \text{ per month}$$

This is GM's monthly standard deviation for the sample period. Therefore, the annualized standard deviation for that period was $8.25\sqrt{12} = 28.58\%$.

---

[9]A more sophisticated method is described in Oldrich A. Vasicek, "A Note on Using Cross-Sectional Information in Bayesian Estimation of Security Betas," *Journal of Finance* 28 (1973), pp. 1233–39.

In the absence of special information concerning GM, if our forecast for the market index is 14% and T-bills pay 6%, we learn from the Merrill Lynch beta book that the CAPM forecast for the rate of return on GM stock is

$$E(r_{GM}) = r_f + \text{adjusted beta} \times [E(r_M) - r_f]$$
$$= 6 + .87 (14 - 6)$$
$$= 12.96\%$$

Predicting Betas

We saw in the previous section that betas estimated from past data may not be the best estimates of future betas: Betas seem to drift toward 1 over time. This suggests that we might want a forecasting model for beta.

One simple approach would be to collect data on beta in different periods and then estimate a regression equation:

$$\text{Current beta} = a + b \text{ (Past beta)} \qquad (10.14)$$

Given estimates of a and b, we would then forecast future betas using the rule

$$\text{Forecast beta} = a + b \text{ (Current beta)}$$

There is no reason, however, to limit ourselves to such simple forecasting rules. Why not also investigate the predictive power of other financial variables in forecasting beta? For example, if we believe that firm size and debt ratios are two determinants of beta, we might specify an expanded version of equation 10.14 and estimate

$$\begin{aligned}
\text{Current beta} = \ &a \\
&+ b_1 \quad \text{(Past beta)} \\
&+ b_2 \quad \text{(Firm size)} \\
&+ b_3 \quad \text{(Debt ratio)}
\end{aligned}$$

Now we would use estimates of a and b_1 through b_3 to forecast future betas.

Such an approach was followed by Rosenberg and Guy[10] who found the following variables to help predict betas:

1. Variance of earnings.
2. Variance of cash flow.
3. Growth in earnings per share.
4. Market capitalization (firm size).
5. Dividend yield.
6. Debt-to-asset ratio.

Rosenberg and Guy also found that even after controlling for a firm's financial characteristics, industry group helps to predict beta. For example, they found that the beta values of gold mining companies are on average .827 lower than would be predicted based on financial characteristics alone. This should not be surprising; the −.827 "adjustment factor" for the gold industry reflects the fact that gold values are inversely related to market returns.

---

[10]Barr Rosenberg and J. Guy, "Prediction of Beta from Investment Fundamentals, Parts 1 and 2," *Financial Analysts Journal*, May–June and July–August 1976.

Table 10.3   Industry Betas and Adjustment Factors

Industry	Beta	Adjustment Factor
Agriculture	0.99	−.140
Drugs and medicine	1.14	−.099
Telephone	0.75	−.288
Energy utilities	0.60	−.237
Gold	0.36	−.827
Construction	1.27	.062
Air transport	1.80	.348
Trucking	1.31	.098
Consumer durables	1.44	.132

Table 10.3 presents beta estimates and adjustment factors for a subset of firms in the Rosenberg and Guy study.

Question 6 • Compare the first five and last four industries in Table 10.3. What characteristic seems to determine whether the adjustment factor is positive or negative?

10.4   MULTIFACTOR MODELS

The index model's decomposition of returns into systematic and firm-specific components is compelling, but confining systematic risk to a single factor is not. Indeed, when we introduced the index model, we noted that the systematic or macro factor summarized by the market return arises from a number of sources, for example, uncertainty about the business cycle, interest rates, and inflation. It stands to reason that a more explicit representation of systematic risk, allowing for the possibility that different stocks exhibit different sensitivities to its various components, would constitute a useful refinement of the index model.

Empirical Foundation of Multifactor Models

Take another look at the column R-SQR in Table 10.2, which shows a page from the beta book. Recall that the R^2 of the index model regression measures the fraction of the variation in a security's return that can be attributed to variation in the market return. The values in the table range from 0.00 to 0.61, with an average value of .16, indicating that the index model explains only a small fraction of the variance of stock returns. Although this sample is small, it turns out that such results are typical. How can we improve on the single-index model but still maintain the useful dichotomy between systematic and diversifiable risk?

To illustrate the approach, let's start with a two-factor model. Suppose the two most important macroeconomic sources of risk are uncertainties surrounding the state of the business cycle, which we will measure by gross domestic product, GDP, and interest rates, denoted IR. The return on any stock will respond to both sources of macro risk as well as to its own firm-specific risks. We therefore can generalize the single-index model into a two-factor model describing the excess rate of return on a stock in some time period as follows:

$$R_t = \alpha + \beta_{GDP}GDP_t + \beta_{IR}IR_t + e_t$$

The two macro factors on the right-hand side of the equation comprise the systematic factors in the economy; thus they play the role of the market index in the single-index model. As before, e_t reflects firm-specific influences.

Now consider two firms, one a regulated utility, the other an airline. Because its profits are controlled by regulators, the utility is likely to have a low sensitivity to GDP risk, that is, a "low GDP beta." But it may have a relatively high sensitivity to interest rates: When rates rise, its stock price will fall; this will be reflected in a large (negative) interest rate beta. Conversely, the performance of the airline is very sensitive to economic activity, but it is not very sensitive to interest rates. It will have a high GDP beta and a small interest rate beta. Suppose that on a particular day, a news item suggests that the economy will expand. GDP is expected to increase, but so are interest rates. Is the "macro news" on this day good or bad? For the utility this is bad news, since its dominant sensitivity is to rates. But for the airline, which responds more to GDP, this is good news. Clearly a one-factor or single-index model cannot capture such differential responses to varying sources of macroeconomic uncertainty.

Of course the market return reflects macro factors as well as the average sensitivity of firms to those factors. When we estimate a single-index regression, therefore, we implicitly impose an (incorrect) assumption that each stock has the same relative sensitivity to each risk factor. If stocks actually differ in their betas relative to the various macroeconomic factors, then lumping all systematic sources of risk into one variable such as the return on the market index will ignore the nuances that better explain individual-stock returns. Of course, once you see why a two-factor model can better explain stock returns, it is easy to see that models with even more factors—**multifactor models**—can provide even better descriptions of returns.[11]

Another reason that multifactor models can improve on the descriptive power of the index model is that betas seem to vary over the business cycle. In fact, the preceding section on predicting betas pointed out that some of the variables that are used to predict beta are related to the business cycle (e.g., earnings growth). Therefore, it makes sense that we can improve the single-index model by including variables that are related to the business cycle.

One example of the multifactor approach is the work of Chen, Roll, and Ross,[12] who used the following set of factors to paint a broad picture of the macroeconomy. Their set is obviously only one of many possible sets that might be considered.[13]

IP = % change in industrial production
EI = % change in expected inflation
UI = % change in unanticipated inflation
CG = excess return of long-term corporate bonds over long-term government bonds
GB = excess return of long-term government bonds over T-bills

This list gives rise to the following five-factor model of excess security returns during holding period, t, as a function of the change in the set of macroeconomic indicators:

$$R_{it} = \alpha_i + \beta_{iIP}IP_t + \beta_{iEI}EI_t + \beta_{iUI}UI_t + \beta_{iCG}CG_t + \beta_{iGB}GB_t + e_{it} \qquad (10.15)$$

Equation 10.15 is a multidimensional security characteristic line with five factors. As before, to estimate the betas of a given stock we can use regression analysis. Here, however, because there is more than one factor, we estimate a *multiple* regression of the excess

---

[11]It is possible (although unlikely) that even in the multifactor economy, only exposure to market risk will be "priced," that is, carry a risk premium, so that only the usual single-index beta would matter for expected stock returns. Even in this case, however, portfolio managers interested in analyzing the risks to which their portfolios are exposed still would do better to use a multifactor model that can capture the multiplicity of risk sources.

[12]N. Chen, R. Roll, and S. Ross, "Economic Forces and the Stock Market," *Journal of Business* 59 (1986), pp. 383–403.

[13]To date, there is no compelling evidence that such a comprehensive list is necessary, or that these are the best variables to represent systematic risk. We choose this representation to demonstrate the potential of multifactor models. Discussion of the empirical content of this and similar models appears in Chapter 13, "Empirical Evidence on Security Returns."

returns of the stock in each period on the five macroeconomic factors. The residual variance of the regression estimates the firm-specific risk.

The approach taken in equation 10.15 requires that we specify which macroeconomic variables are relevant risk factors. Two principles guide us when we specify a reasonable list of factors. First, we want to limit ourselves to macroeconomic factors with considerable ability to explain security returns. If our model calls for hundreds of explanatory variables, it does little to simplify our description of security returns. Second, we wish to choose factors that seem likely to be important risk factors, that is, factors that concern investors sufficiently that they will demand meaningful risk premiums to bear exposure to those sources of risk. We will see in the next chapter, on the so-called arbitrage pricing theory, that a multifactor security market line arises naturally from the multifactor specification of risk.

An alternative approach to specifying macroeconomic factors as candidates for relevant sources of systematic risk uses firm characteristics that seem on empirical grounds to represent exposure to systematic risk. One such multifactor model was proposed by Fama and French.[14]

$$R_{it} = \alpha_i + \beta_{iM}R_{Mt} + \beta_{iSMB}\text{SMB}_t + \beta_{iHML}\text{HML}_t + e_{it} \qquad (10.16)$$

where

SMB = small minus big: the return of a portfolio of small stocks in excess of the
return on a portfolio of large stocks

HML = high minus low: the return of a portfolio of stocks with high ratios of book
value to market value in excess of the return on a portfolio of stocks with low
book-to-market ratios

Note that in this model the market index does play a role and is expected to capture systematic risk originating from macroeconomic factors.

These two firm-characteristic variables are chosen because of longstanding observations that corporate capitalization (firm size) and book-to-market ratio seem to be predictive of average stock returns, and therefore risk premiums. Fama and French propose this model on empirical grounds: While SMB and HML are not obvious candidates for relevant risk factors, these variables may suggest changes in yet-unknown more fundamental variables. For example, Fama and French point out that firms with high ratios of book-to-market value are more likely to be in financial distress and that small stocks may be more sensitive to changes in business conditions. Thus these variables may capture sensitivity to risk factors in the macroeconomy.

Theoretical Foundations of Multifactor Models

The CAPM presupposes that the only relevant source of risk arises from variations in stock returns, and therefore a representative (market) portfolio can capture this entire risk. As a result, individual-stock risk can be defined by the contribution to overall portfolio risk; hence the risk premium on an individual stock is determined solely by its beta on the market portfolio. But is this narrow view of risk warranted?

Consider a relatively young investor whose future wealth is determined in large part by labor income. The stream of future labor income is also risky and may be intimately tied to the fortunes of the company for which the investor works. Such an investor might choose an investment portfolio that will help to diversify labor-income risk. For that pur-

[14]Eugene F. Fama and Kenneth R. French, "Multifactor Explanations of Asset Pricing Anomalies," *Journal of Finance* 51 (1996), pp. 55–84.

pose, stocks with lower-than-average correlation with future labor income would be favored, that is, such stocks will receive higher weights in the individual portfolio than their weights in the market portfolio. Put another way, using this broader notion of risk, these investors no longer consider the market portfolio as efficient and the rationale for the CAPM expected return–beta relationship no longer applies.

In principle, the CAPM may still hold if the hedging demands of various investors are equally distributed across different types of securities so that deviations of portfolio weights from those of the market portfolio are offsetting. But if hedging demands are common to many investors, the prices of securities with desirable hedging characteristics will be bid up and the expected return reduced, which will invalidate the CAPM expected return–beta relationship.

For example, suppose that important firm characteristics are associated with firm size (market capitalization) and that investors working for small companies therefore diversify by tilting their portfolios toward large stocks. If many more investors work for small rather than large corporations, then demand for large stocks will exceed that predicted by the CAPM while demand for small stocks will be lower. This will lead to a rise in prices and a fall in expected returns on large stocks compared to predictions from the CAPM.

Merton developed a multifactor CAPM (also called the intertemporal CAPM, or ICAPM) by deriving the demand for securities by investors concerned with lifetime consumption.[15] The ICAPM demonstrates how common sources of risk affect the risk premium of securities that help hedge this risk.

When a source of risk has an effect on expected returns, we say that this risk "is priced." While the single-factor CAPM predicts that only market risk will be priced, the ICAPM predicts that other sources of risk also may be priced. Merton suggested a list of possible common sources of uncertainty that might affect expected security returns. Among these are uncertainties in labor income, prices of important consumption goods (e.g., energy prices), or changes in future investment opportunities (e.g., changes in the riskiness of various asset classes). However, it is difficult to predict whether there exists sufficient demand for hedging these sources of uncertainty to affect security returns.

Empirical Models and the ICAPM

The empirical models using proxies for extramarket sources of risk are unsatisfying for a number of reasons. We discuss these models further in Chapter 13, but for now we can summarize as follows:

1. Some of the factors in the proposed models cannot be clearly identified as hedging a significant source of uncertainty.

2. As suggested by Black, the fact that researchers scan and rescan the database of security returns in search of explanatory factors (an activity often called data-snooping) may result in assigning meaning to past, random outcomes. Black observes that return premiums to factors such as firm size largely vanished after they were first discovered.[16]

3. Whether historical return premiums associated (statistically) with firm characteristics such as size and book-to-market ratios represent priced risk factors or are simply unexplained anomalies remains to be resolved. Daniel and Titman argue that the evidence suggests that past risk premiums on these firm-

---

[15]Robert C. Merton, "An Intertemporal Capital Asset Pricing Model," *Econometrica* 41 (1973), pp. 867–87.
[16]Fischer Black, "Beta and Return," *Journal of Portfolio Management* 20 (1993), pp. 8–18.

characteristic variables are not associated with movements in market factors and hence do not represent factor risk.[17] Their findings, if verified, are disturbing because they provide evidence that characteristics that are not associated with systematic risk are priced, in direct contradiction to the prediction of both the CAPM and ICAPM. Indeed, if you turn back to the box in the previous chapter on page 262, you will see that much of the discussion of the validity of the CAPM turns on the interpretation of these results.

SUMMARY

1. A single-factor model of the economy classifies sources of uncertainty as systematic (macroeconomic) factors or firm-specific (microeconomic) factors. The index model assumes that the macro factor can be represented by a broad index of stock returns.

2. The single-index model drastically reduces the necessary inputs into the Markowitz portfolio selection procedure. It also aids in specialization of labor in security analysis.

3. According to the index model specification, the systematic risk of a portfolio or asset equals $\beta^2 \sigma_M^2$ and the covariance between two assets equals $\beta_i \beta_j \sigma_M^2$.

4. The index model is estimated by applying regression analysis to excess rates of return. The slope of the regression curve is the beta of an asset, whereas the intercept is the asset's alpha during the sample period. The regression line is also called the *security characteristic line*. The regression beta is equivalent to the CAPM beta, except that the regression uses actual returns and the CAPM is specified in terms of expected returns. The CAPM predicts that the average value of alphas measured by the index model regression will be zero.

5. Practitioners routinely estimate the index model using total rather than excess rates of return. This makes their estimate of alpha equal to $\alpha + r_f(1 - \beta)$.

6. Betas show a tendency to evolve toward 1 over time. Beta forecasting rules attempt to predict this drift. Moreover, other financial variables can be used to help forecast betas.

7. Multifactor models seek to improve the explanatory power of the single-index model by modeling the systematic component in greater detail. These models use indicators intended to capture a wide range of macroeconomic risk factors and, sometimes, firm-characteristic variables such as size or book-to-market ratio.

8. An extension of the single-factor CAPM, the ICAPM, is a multifactor model of security returns, but it does not specify which risk factors need to be considered.

Key Terms

single-factor model	regression equation	market model
single-index model	residuals	multifactor models
scatter diagram	security characteristic line	

Selected Readings

The seminal paper relating the index model to the portfolio selection problem is:
   Sharpe, William F. "A Simplified Model of Portfolio Analysis." *Management Science*, January 1963.

Papers on the tendency of betas to drift over time are:
   Blume, Marshall. "Betas and Their Regression Tendencies." *Journal of Finance* 10 (June 1975).

---

[17]Kent Daniel and Sheridan Titman, "Evidence on the Characteristics of Cross Sectional Variation in Stock Returns," *Journal of Finance* 52 (1997), pp. 1–33.

Klemkosky. R. C.; and J. D. Martin. "The Adjustment of Beta Forecasts." *Journal of Finance* 10 (September 1975).

Vasicek, O. "A Note on Using Cross-Sectional Information in Bayesian Estimation of Security Betas." *Journal of Finance* 8 (December 1973).

Papers on the relation between beta and firm characteristics are:

Rosenberg, Barr; and J. Guy. "Predictions of Beta from Investment Fundamentals." *Financial Analysts Journal* 32 (May–June 1976).

Robichek, A. A.; and R. A. Cohn. "The Economic Determinants of Systematic Risk." *Journal of Finance*, May 1974.

Problems

1. A portfolio management organization analyzes 60 stocks and constructs a mean-variance efficient portfolio that is constrained to these 60.
   a. How many estimates of expected returns, variances, and covariances are needed to optimize this portfolio?
   b. If one could safely assume that stock market returns closely resemble a single-index structure, how many estimates would be needed?

2. The following are estimates for two of the stocks in problem 1.

Stock	Expected Return	Beta	Firm-Specific Standard Deviation
A	13	0.8	30
B	18	1.2	40

   The market index has a standard deviation of 22% and the risk-free rate is 8%
   a. What is the standard deviation of stocks A and B?
   b. Suppose that we were to construct a portfolio with proportions:

Stock A:	.30
Stock B:	.45
T-bills:	.25

   Compute the expected return, standard deviation, beta, and nonsystematic standard deviation of the portfolio.

3. Consider the following two regression lines for stocks A and B in the following figure.

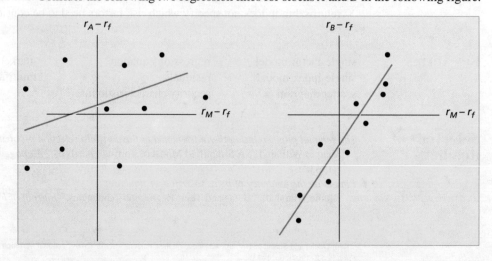

a. Which stock has higher firm-specific risk?
b. Which stock has greater systematic (market) risk?
c. Which stock has higher R^2?
d. Which stock has higher alpha?
e. Which stock has higher correlation with the market?

4. Consider the two (excess return) index model regression results for A and B:

$R_A = 1\% + 1.2R_M$
R-SQR = .576
RESID STD DEV-N = 10.3%

$R_B = -2\% + .8R_M$
R-SQR = .436
RESID STD DEV-N = 9.1%

a. Which stock has more firm-specific risk?
b. Which has greater market risk?
c. For which stock does market movement explain a greater fraction of return variability?
d. Which stock had an average return in excess of that predicted by the CAPM?
e. If r_f were constant at 6% and the regression had been run using total rather than excess returns, what would have been the regression intercept for stock A?

Use the following data for problems 5 through 11. Suppose that the index model for stocks A and B is estimated from excess returns with the following results:

$$R_A = 3\% + .7R_M + e_A$$
$$R_B = -2\% + 1.2R_M + e_B$$
$$\sigma_M = 20\%; \qquad R\text{-}SQR_A = .20; \qquad R\text{-}SQR_B = .12$$

5. What is the standard deviation of each stock?
6. Break down the variance of each stock to the systematic and firm-specific components.
7. What is the covariance and correlation coefficient between two stocks?
8. What is the covariance between each stock and the market index?
9. Are the intercepts of the two regressions consistent with the CAPM? Interpret their values.
10. For portfolio P with investment proportions of .60 in A and .40 in B, rework problems 5, 6, and 8.
11. Rework problem 10 for portfolio Q with investment proportions of .50 in P, .30 in the market index, and .20 in T-bills.
12. In a two-stock capital market, the capitalization of stock A is twice that of B. The standard deviation of the excess return on A is 30% and on B is 50%. The correlation coefficient between the excess returns is .7.
a. What is the standard deviation of the market index portfolio?
b. What is the beta of each stock?
c. What is the residual variance of each stock?
d. If the index model holds and stock A is expected to earn 11% in excess of the risk-free rate, what must be the risk premium on the market portfolio?
13. A stock recently has been estimated to have a beta of 1.24:
a. What will Merrill Lynch compute as the "adjusted beta" of this stock?

b. Suppose that you estimate the following regression describing the evolution of beta over time:

$$\beta_t = .3 + .7\beta_{t-1}$$

What would be your predicted beta for next year?

14. When the annualized monthly percentage rates of return for a stock market index were regressed against the returns for ABC and XYZ stocks over the period 1989–1998 in an ordinary least squares regression, the following results were obtained:

Statistic	ABC	XYZ
Alpha	−3.20%	7.3%
Beta	0.60	0.97
R^2	0.35	0.17
Residual standard deviation	13.02%	21.45%

Explain what these regression results tell the analyst about risk-return relationships for each stock over the 1989–1998 period. Comment on their implications for future risk-return relationships, assuming both stocks were included in a diversified common stock portfolio, especially in view of the following additional data obtained from two brokerage houses, which are based on two years of weekly data ending in December 1998.

Brokerage House	Beta of ABC	Beta of XYZ
A	.62	1.45
B	.71	1.25

15. Based on current dividend yields and expected growth rates, the expected rates of return on stocks A and B are 11% and 14%, respectively. The beta of stock A is .8, while that of stock B is 1.5. The T-bill rate is currently 6%, while the expected rate of return on the S&P 500 index is 12%. The standard deviation of stock A is 10% annually, while that of stock B is 11%.

a. If you currently hold a well-diversified portfolio, would you choose to add either of these stocks to your holdings?

b. If instead you could invest only in bills plus only one of these stocks, which stock would you choose? Explain your answer using either a graph or a quantitative measure of the attractiveness of the stocks.

16. Assume the correlation coefficient between Baker Fund and the S&P 500 Stock Index is .70. What percentage of Baker Fund's total risk is specific (i.e., nonsystematic)?

a. 35%.

b. 49%.

c. 51%.

d. 70%.

17. The correlation between the Charlottesville International Fund and the EAFE Market Index is 1.0. The expected return on the EAFE Index is 11%, the expected return on Charlottesville International Fund is 9%, and the risk-free return in EAFE countries is 3%. Based on this analysis, the implied beta of Charlottesville International is:
    a. Negative.
    b. .75.
    c. .82.
    d. 1.00.

18. The concept of *beta* is most closely associated with:
    a. Correlation coefficients.
    b. Mean-variance analysis.
    c. Nonsystematic risk.
    d. The capital asset pricing model.

19. Beta and standard deviation differ as risk measures in that beta measures:
    a. Only unsystematic risk, while standard deviation measures total risk.
    b. Only systematic risk, while standard deviation measures total risk.
    c. Both systematic and unsystematic risk, while standard deviation measures only unsystematic risk.
    d. Both systematic and unsystematic risk, while standard deviation measures only systematic risk.

s o l u t i o n s t o
Concept
CHECKS

1. The variance of each stock is $\beta^2\sigma_M^2 + \sigma^2(e)$.
   For stock *A*, we obtain

$$\sigma_A^2 = .9^2(20)^2 + 30^2 = 1{,}224$$
$$\sigma_A = 35$$

   For stock *B*,

$$\sigma_B^2 = 1.1^2(20)^2 + 10^2 = 584$$
$$\sigma_B = 24$$

   The covariance is

$$\beta_A\beta_B\sigma_M^2 = .9 \times 1.1 \times 20^2 = 396$$

2. $\sigma^2(e_P) = (1/2)^2[\sigma^2(e_A) + \sigma^2(e_B)]$
   $= (1/4)(30^2 + 10^2)$
   $= 250$

   Therefore

$$\sigma(e_P) = 15.8$$

3. *a.* Total market capitalization is $3{,}000 + 1{,}940 + 1{,}360 = 6{,}300$. Therefore, the mean excess return of the index portfolio is

$$\frac{3{,}000}{6{,}300} \times 10 + \frac{1{,}940}{6{,}300} \times 2 + \frac{1{,}360}{6{,}300} \times 17 = 10$$

b. The covariance between stock A and the index portfolio equals

$$\text{Cov}(R_A, R_M) = \beta_A \sigma_M^2 = .2 \times 25^2 = 125$$

c. The variance of B equals

$$\sigma_B^2 = \text{Var}(\beta_B R_M + e_B) = \beta_B^2 \sigma_M^2 + \sigma^2(e_B)$$

Thus the firm-specific variance of B equals

$$\sigma^2(e_B) = \sigma_B^2 - \beta_B^2 \sigma_M^2 = 30^2 - .2^2 \times 25^2 = 875$$

4. The CAPM is a model that relates expected rates of return to risk. It results in the expected return–beta relationship where the expected risk premium on any asset is proportional to the expected risk premium on the market portfolio with beta as the proportionality constant. As such the model is impractical for two reasons: (i) expectations are unobservable, and (ii) the theoretical market portfolio includes every risky asset and is in practice unobservable. The next three models incorporate additional assumptions to overcome these problems.

    The single-factor model assumes that one economic factor, denoted F, exerts the only common influence on security returns. Beyond it, security returns are driven by independent, firm-specific factors. Thus for any security, i,

$$r_i = a_i + b_i F + e_i$$

    The single-index model assumes that in the single-factor model, the factor F is perfectly correlated with and therefore can be replaced by a broad-based index of securities that can proxy for the CAPM's theoretical market portfolio.

    At this point it should be said that many interchange the meaning of the index and market models. The concept of the market model is that rate of return *surprises* on a stock are proportional to corresponding surprises on the market index portfolio, again with proportionality constant β.

5. Merrill Lynch's alpha is related to the CAPM alpha by

$$\alpha_{\text{Merrill}} = \alpha_{\text{CAPM}} + (1 - \beta) r_f$$

For GM, $\alpha_{\text{Merrill}} = .14\%$, $\beta = .80$, and we are told that r_f was .6%. Thus

$$\alpha_{\text{CAPM}} = .14\% - (1 - .80).6\%$$
$$= .02\%$$

GM still performed well relative to the market and the index model. It beat its "benchmark" return by an average of .018% per month.

6. The industries with positive adjustment factors are most sensitive to the economy. Their betas would be expected to be higher because the business risk of the firms is higher. In contrast, the industries with negative adjustment factors are in business fields with a lower sensitivity to the economy. Therefore, for any given financial profile, their betas are lower.

ARBITRAGE PRICING THEORY

The exploitation of security mispricing in such a way that risk-free economic profits may be earned is called **arbitrage**. It involves the simultaneous purchase and sale of equivalent securities in order to profit from discrepancies in their price relationship. The concept of arbitrage is central to the theory of capital markets. This chapter discusses the nature and use of arbitrage opportunities. We show how to identify arbitrage opportunities and why investors will take the largest possible positions in arbitrage portfolios. Perhaps the most basic principle of capital market theory is that equilibrium market prices are rational in that they rule out (risk-free) arbitrage opportunities. Pricing relationships that guarantee the absence of arbitrage possibilities are extremely powerful. If actual security prices allow for arbitrage, the result will be strong pressure to restore equilibrium. Only a few investors need be aware of arbitrage opportunities to bring about a large volume of trades, and

these trades will bring prices back into balance.   The CAPM gave us the security market line, a relationship between expected return and risk as measured by beta. Arbitrage pricing theory, or APT, also stipulates a relationship between expected return and risk, but it uses different assumptions and techniques. We explore this relationship using well-diversified portfolios, showing in a one-factor setting that these portfolios are priced to satisfy the CAPM expected return–beta relationship. Because all well-diversified portfolios have to satisfy that relationship, we show that all individual securities almost certainly satisfy this same relationship. This reasoning leads to an SML relationship that avoids reliance on the unobservable, theoretical market portfolio that is central to the CAPM. Next we show how the single-factor APT (just like the CAPM) can easily be generalized to a richer multifactor version. Finally, we discuss the similarities and differences between the APT, CAPM, and the index model.

11.1 ARBITRAGE OPPORTUNITIES AND PROFITS

An arbitrage opportunity arises when an investor can construct a **zero investment portfolio** that will yield a *sure* profit. To construct a zero investment portfolio one has to be able to sell short at least one asset and use the proceeds to purchase (go long on) one or more assets. Borrowing may be viewed as a short position in the risk-free asset. Clearly, any investor would like to take as large a position as possible in an arbitrage portfolio.

An obvious case of an arbitrage opportunity arises when the law of one price is violated. When an asset is trading at different prices in two markets (and the price differential exceeds transaction costs), a simultaneous trade in the two markets can produce a sure profit (the net price differential) without any investment. One simply sells short the asset in the high-priced market and buys it in the low-priced market. The net proceeds are positive, and there is no risk because the long and short positions offset each other.

In modern markets with electronic communications and instantaneous execution, arbitrage opportunities have become rare but not extinct. The same technology that enables the market to absorb new information quickly also enables fast operators to make large profits by trading huge volumes the instant an arbitrage opportunity appears. This is the essence of index arbitrage, to be discussed in Part VI and Chapter 21.

From the simple case of a violation of the law of one price, let us proceed to a less obvious (yet just as profitable) arbitrage opportunity. Imagine that four stocks are traded in an economy with only four distinct, possible scenarios. The rates of return of the four stocks for each inflation–interest rate scenario appear in Table 11.1. The current prices of the stocks and rate of return statistics are shown in Table 11.2.

Eyeballing the rate of return data, it is not obvious that an arbitrage opportunity exists. The expected returns, standard deviations, and correlations do not reveal any particular abnormality.

Consider, however, an equally weighted portfolio of the first three stocks (Apex, Bull, and Crush), and contrast its possible future rates of return with those of the fourth stock, Dreck. These returns are derived from Table 11.1 and summarized in Table 11.3, which reveals that the equally weighted portfolio will outperform Dreck in all scenarios. The rate of return statistics of the two alternatives are

	Mean	Standard Deviation	Correlation
Three-stock portfolio	25.83	6.40	.94
Dreck	22.25	8.58	

Because the two investments are not perfectly correlated, there is no violation of the law of one price. Nevertheless, the equally weighted portfolio will fare better under *any* circumstances; thus any investor, no matter how risk averse, can take advantage of this perfect

Table 11.1 Rate of Return Projections

	High Real Interest Rates		Low Real Interest Rates	
	High Inflation	**Low Inflation**	**High Inflation**	**Low Inflation**
Probability:	.25	.25	.25	.25
Stock				
Apex (*A*)	−20	20	40	60
Bull (*B*)	0	70	30	−20
Crush (*C*)	90	−20	−10	70
Dreck (*D*)	15	23	15	36

Table 11.2 Rate of Return Statistics

				Correlation Matrix			
Stock	**Current Price**	**Expected Return**	**Standard Deviation (%)**	**A**	**B**	**C**	**D**
A	$10	25	29.58%	1.00	−0.15	−0.29	0.68
B	10	20	33.91	−0.15	1.00	−0.87	−0.38
C	10	32.5	48.15	−0.29	−0.87	1.00	0.22
D	10	22.25	8.58	0.68	−0.38	0.22	1.00

Table 11.3 Rates of Return on Equally Weighted Portfolio of *A, B,* and *C* and Dreck

	High Real Interest Rates		Low Real Interest Rates	
	High Inflation	**Low Inflation**	**High Inflation**	**Low Inflation**
Equally weighted portfolio (*A, B,* and *C*)	23.33	23.33	20.00	36.67
Dreck	15.00	23.00	15.00	36.00

dominance. Investors will take a short position in Dreck and use the proceeds to purchase the equally weighted portfolio.[1] Let us see how it would work.

Suppose we sell short 300,000 shares of Dreck and use the $3 million proceeds to buy 100,000 shares each of Apex, Bull, and Crush. The dollar profits in each of the four scenarios will be as follows:

		High Real Interest Rates		Low Real Interest Rates	
Stock	**Dollar Investment**	**High Inflation**	**Low Inflation**	**High Inflation**	**Low Inflation**
Apex	$ 1,000,000	$−200,000	$ 200,000	$ 400,000	$ 600,000
Bull	1,000,000	0	700,000	300,000	−200,000
Crush	1,000,000	900,000	−200,000	−100,000	700,000
Dreck	−3,000,000	−450,000	−690,000	−450,000	−1,080,000
Portfolio	0	$ 250,000	$ 10,000	$ 150,000	$ 20,000

---

[1]Short selling is discussed in Chapter 3.

The first column verifies that the net investment is zero. Yet our portfolio yields a positive profit in any scenario. This is a money machine. Investors will want to take an infinite position in such a portfolio because larger positions entail no risk of losses, yet yield ever-growing profits. In principle, even a single investor would take such large positions that the market would react to the buying and selling pressure: The price of Dreck has to come down and/or the prices of Apex, Bull, and Crush have to go up. The arbitrage opportunity will be eliminated.

Concept

Question 1 • **Suppose that Dreck's price starts falling without any change in its per-share dollar payoffs. How far must the price fall before arbitrage between Dreck and the equally weighted portfolio is no longer possible? (Hint: What happens to the amount of the equally weighted portfolio that can be purchased with the proceeds of the short sale as Dreck's price falls?)**

The idea that market prices will move to rule out arbitrage opportunities is perhaps the most fundamental concept in capital market theory. Violation of this restriction would indicate the grossest form of market irrationality.

The critical property of a risk-free arbitrage portfolio is that any investor, regardless of risk aversion or wealth, will want to take an infinite position in it. Because those large positions will force prices up or down until the opportunity vanishes, we can derive restrictions on security prices that satisfy a "no-arbitrage" condition, that is, prices for which no arbitrage opportunities are left in the marketplace.

There is an important difference between arbitrage and risk-return dominance arguments in support of equilibrium price relationships. A dominance argument holds that when an equilibrium price relationship is violated, many investors will make portfolio changes. Individual investors will make limited changes, though, depending on their degree of risk aversion. Aggregation of these limited portfolio changes is required to create a large volume of buying and selling, which in turn restores equilibrium prices. By contrast, when arbitrage opportunities exist each investor wants to take as large a position as possible; hence it will not take many investors to bring about the price pressures necessary to restore equilibrium. Therefore, implications for prices derived from no-arbitrage arguments are stronger than implications derived from a risk-return dominance argument.

The CAPM is an example of a dominance argument, implying that all investors hold mean-variance efficient portfolios. If a security is mispriced, then investors will tilt their portfolios toward the underpriced and away from the overpriced securities. Pressure on equilibrium prices results from many investors shifting their portfolios, each by a relatively small dollar amount. The assumption that a large number of investors are mean-variance sensitive is critical; in contrast, the implication of a no-arbitrage condition is that a few investors who identify an arbitrage opportunity will mobilize large dollar amounts and restore equilibrium.

Practitioners often use the terms "arbitrage" and "arbitrageurs" more loosely than our strict definition. "Arbitrageur" often refers to a professional searching for mispriced securities in specific areas such as merger-target stocks, rather than to one who seeks strict (risk-free) arbitrage opportunities. Such activity is sometimes called **risk arbitrage** to distinguish it from pure arbitrage.

To leap ahead, in Part VI we will discuss "derivative" securities such as futures and options, whose market values are completely determined by prices of other securities. For example, the value of a call option on a stock is determined by the price of the stock. For such securities, strict arbitrage is a practical possibility, and the condition of no-arbitrage leads to exact pricing. In the case of stocks and other "primitive" securities whose values are not determined strictly by another asset or bundle of assets, no-arbitrage conditions must be obtained by appealing to diversification arguments.

11.2   THE APT AND WELL-DIVERSIFIED PORTFOLIOS

Stephen Ross developed the **arbitrage pricing theory** (APT) in 1976.[2] We begin with a simple version of the model, which assumes that only one systematic factor affects security returns. However, the usual discussion of the APT is concerned with the multifactor case, and we treat this richer model in Section 11.5.

Ross starts by examining a single-factor model similar in spirit to the market model introduced in Chapter 10. As in that model, uncertainty in asset returns has two sources: a common or macroeconomic factor, and a firm-specific cause. The common factor is assumed to have zero expected value, since it measures *new* information concerning the macroeconomy which, by definition, has zero expected value. There is no need, however, to assume that the factor can be proxied by the return on a market-index portfolio.

If we call F the deviation of the common factor from its expected value, β_i the sensitivity of firm i to that factor, and e_i the firm-specific disturbance, the factor model states that the actual return on firm i will equal its initially expected return plus a (zero expected value) random amount attributable to unanticipated economywide events, plus another (zero expected value) random amount attributable to firm-specific events.

Formally,

$$r_i = E(r_i) + \beta_i F + e_i$$

where $E(r_i)$ is the expected return on stock i. All the nonsystematic returns, the e_is, are uncorrelated among themselves and uncorrelated with the factor F.

To make the factor model more concrete, consider an example. Suppose that the macro factor, F, is taken to be the unexpected percentage change in gross domestic product (GDP), and that the consensus is that GDP will increase by 4% this year. Suppose also that a stock's β value is 1.2. If GDP increases by only 3%, then the value of F would be -1%, representing a 1% disappointment in actual growth versus expected growth. Given the stock's beta value, this disappointment would translate into a return on the stock that is 1.2% lower than previously expected. This macro surprise together with the firm-specific disturbance, e_i, determine the total departure of the stock's return from its originally expected value.

Well-Diversified Portfolios

Now we look at the risk of a portfolio of stocks. We first show that if a portfolio is well diversified, its firm-specific or nonfactor risk can be diversified away. Only factor (or systematic) risk remains. If we construct an n-stock portfolio with weights w_i, $\Sigma w_i = 1$, then the rate of return on this portfolio is as follows:

$$r_P = E(r_P) + \beta_P F + e_P \tag{11.1}$$

where

$$\beta_P = \Sigma w_i \beta_i$$

[2]Stephen A. Ross, "Return, Risk and Arbitrage," in I. Friend and J. Bicksler, eds., *Risk and Return in Finance* (Cambridge, Mass.: Ballinger, 1976).

is the weighted average of the β_i of the n securities. The portfolio nonsystematic component (which is uncorrelated with F) is

$$e_P = \Sigma w_i e_i$$

which similarly is a weighted average of the e_i of the n securities.

We can divide the variance of this portfolio into systematic and nonsystematic sources, as we saw in Chapter 10. The portfolio variance is

$$\sigma_P^2 = \beta_P^2 \sigma_F^2 + \sigma^2(e_P)$$

where σ_F^2 is the variance of the factor F, and $\sigma^2(e_P)$ is the nonsystematic risk of the portfolio, which is given by

$$\sigma^2(e_P) = \text{Variance}(\Sigma w_i e_i) = \Sigma w_i^2 \sigma^2(e_i)$$

Note that in deriving the nonsystematic variance of the portfolio, we depend on the fact that the firm-specific e_is are uncorrelated and hence that the variance of the "portfolio" of nonsystematic e_is is the weighted sum of the individual nonsystematic variances with the square of the investment proportions as weights.

If the portfolio were equally weighted, $w_i = 1/n$, then the nonsystematic variance would be

$$\sigma^2\left(e_P, w_i = \frac{1}{n}\right) = \Sigma\left(\frac{1}{n}\right)^2 \sigma^2(e_i) = \frac{1}{n} \Sigma \frac{\sigma^2(e_i)}{n} = \frac{1}{n} \overline{\sigma}^2(e_i)$$

In this case, we divide the average nonsystematic variance, $\overline{\sigma}^2(e_i)$, by n, so that when the portfolio gets large in the sense that n is large and the portfolio remains equally weighted across all n stocks, the nonsystematic variance approaches zero.

Concept CHECK

Question 2 • What will be the nonsystematic standard deviation of the equally weighted portfolio if the average value of $\sigma(e_i)$ equals 30%, and (*a*) $n = 10$, (*b*) $n = 100$, (*c*) $n = 1,000$, and (*d*) $n = 10,000$? What do you conclude about the nonsystematic risk of large, diversified portfolios?

The set of portfolios for which the nonsystematic variance approaches zero as n gets large consists of more portfolios than just the equally weighted portfolio. Any portfolio for which each w_i becomes consistently smaller as n gets large (specifically, where each w_i^2 approaches zero as n gets large) will satisfy the condition that the portfolio nonsystematic risk will approach zero as n gets large.

In fact, this property motivates us to define a **well-diversified portfolio** as one that is diversified over a large enough number of securities with proportions w_i, each small enough that for practical purposes the nonsystematic variance, $\sigma^2(e_P)$, is negligible. Because the expected value of e_P is zero, if its variance also is zero, we can conclude that any realized value of e_P will be virtually zero. Rewriting equation 11.1, we conclude that for a well-diversified portfolio for all practical purposes

$$r_P = E(r_P) + \beta_P F$$

and

$$\sigma_P^2 = \beta_P^2 \sigma_F^2; \qquad \sigma_P = \beta_P \sigma_F$$

Large (mostly institutional) investors can hold portfolios of hundreds and even thousands of securities; thus the concept of well-diversified portfolios clearly is operational in contemporary financial markets. Well-diversified portfolios, however, are not necessarily equally weighted.

As an illustration, consider a portfolio of 1,000 stocks. Let our position in the first stock be $w\%$. Let the position in the second stock be $2w\%$, the position in the third $3w\%$, and so on. In this way our largest position (in the thousandth stock) is $1,000w\%$. Can this portfolio possibly be well diversified, considering the fact that the largest position is 1,000 times the smallest position? Surprisingly, the answer is yes.

To see this, let us determine the largest weight in any one stock, in this case, the thousandth stock. The sum of the positions in all stocks must be 100%; therefore,

$$w + 2w + \cdots + 1,000w = 100$$

Solving for w, we find that

$$w = .0002\%$$
$$1,000w = .2\%$$

Our *largest* position amounts to only .2 of 1%. And this is very far from an equally weighted portfolio. Yet for practical purposes this still is a well-diversified portfolio.

Betas and Expected Returns

Because nonfactor risk can be diversified away, only factor risk commands a risk premium in market equilibrium. Nonsystematic risk across firms cancels out in well-diversified portfolios, so that only the systematic risk of a portfolio of securities can be related to its expected returns.

The solid line in Figure 11.1A plots the return of a well-diversified Portfolio A with $\beta_A = 1$ for various realizations of the systematic factor. The expected return of Portfolio A is 10%; this is where the solid line crosses the vertical axis. At this point the systematic factor is zero, implying no macro surprises. If the macro factor is positive, the portfolio's return exceeds its expected value; if it is negative, the portfolio's return falls short of its mean. The return on the portfolio is therefore

$$E(r_A) + \beta_A F = 10\% + 1.0 \times F$$

Compare Figure 11.1A with Figure 11.1B, which is a similar graph for a single stock (S) with $\beta_s = 1$. The undiversified stock is subject to nonsystematic risk, which is seen in a scatter of points around the line. The well-diversified portfolio's return, in contrast, is determined completely by the systematic factor.

Figure 11.1

Returns as a function of the systematic factor. **A**, Well-diversified Portfolio A. **B**, Single stock (S).

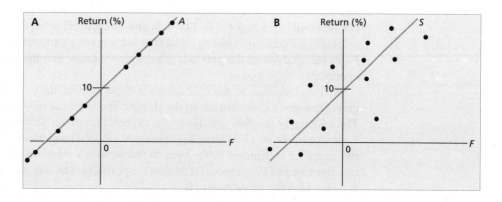

Figure 11.2

Returns as a function of the systematic factor: an arbitrage opportunity.

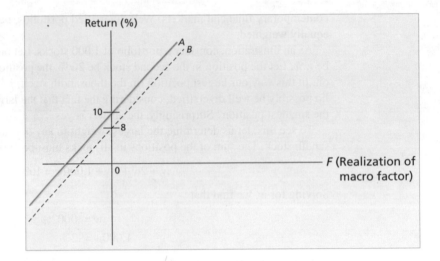

Now consider Figure 11.2, where the dashed line plots the return on another well-diversified portfolio, Portfolio B, with an expected return of 8% and β_B also equal to 1.0. Could Portfolios A and B coexist with the return pattern depicted? Clearly not: No matter what the systematic factor turns out to be, Portfolio A outperforms Portfolio B, leading to an arbitrage opportunity.

If you sell short $1 million of B and buy 1 million of A, a zero net investment strategy, your return would be $20,000, as follows:

$$
\begin{array}{ll}
(.10 + 1.0 \times F) \times \$1 \text{ million} & \text{(from long position in } A\text{)} \\
\underline{-(.08 + 1.0 \times F) \times \$1 \text{ million}} & \underline{\text{(from short position in } B\text{)}} \\
.02 \times \$1 \text{ million} = \$20,000 & \text{(net proceeds)}
\end{array}
$$

You make a risk-free profit because the factor risk cancels out across the long and short positions. Moreover, the strategy requires zero net investment. You should pursue it on an infinitely large scale until the return discrepancy between the two portfolios disappears. Well-diversified portfolios with equal betas must have equal expected returns in market equilibrium, or arbitrage opportunities exist.

What about portfolios with different betas? We show now that their risk premiums must be proportional to beta. To see why, consider Figure 11.3. Suppose that the risk-free rate is 4% and that well-diversified portfolio, C, with a beta of .5, has an expected return of 6%. Portfolio C plots below the line from the risk-free asset to Portfolio A. Consider, therefore, a new portfolio, D, composed of half of Portfolio A and half of the risk-free asset. Portfolio D's beta will be ($\frac{1}{2} \times 0 + \frac{1}{2} \times 1.0$) = .5, and its expected return will be ($\frac{1}{2} \times 4 + \frac{1}{2} \times 10$) = 7%. Now Portfolio D has an equal beta but a greater expected return than Portfolio C. From our analysis in the previous paragraph we know that this constitutes an arbitrage opportunity.

We conclude that, to preclude arbitrage opportunities, the expected return on all well-diversified portfolios must lie on the straight line from the risk-free asset in Figure 11.3. The equation of this line will dictate the expected return on all well-diversified portfolios.

Notice in Figure 11.3 that risk premiums are indeed proportional to portfolio betas. The risk premium is depicted by the vertical arrow, which measures the distance between the risk-free rate and the expected return on the portfolio. The risk premium is zero for $\beta = 0$, and rises in direct proportion to β.

Figure 11.3
An arbitrage
opportunity.

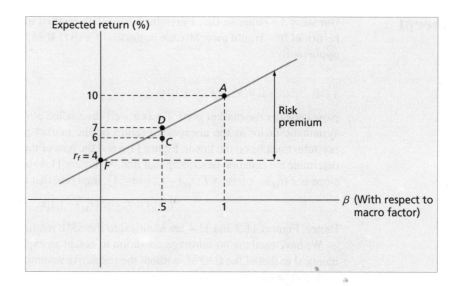

Table 11.4   Portfolio Characteristics and Weights in the Zero-Beta Portfolio

Portfolio	Expected Return	Beta	Portfolio Weight
U	$E(r_U)$	β_U	$\dfrac{\beta_V}{\beta_V - \beta_U}$
V	$E(r_V)$	β_V	$\dfrac{-\beta_U}{\beta_V - \beta_U}$

More formally, suppose that two well-diversified portfolios are combined into a zero-beta portfolio, Z, by choosing the weights shown in Table 11.4. The weights of the two assets in portfolio Z sum to 1, and the portfolio beta is zero:

$$\beta_Z = w_U\beta_U + w_V\beta_V = \frac{\beta_V}{\beta_V - \beta_U}\beta_U + \frac{-\beta_U}{\beta_V - \beta_U}\beta_V = 0$$

Portfolio Z is riskless: It has no diversifiable risk because it is well diversified, and no exposure to the systematic factor because its beta is zero. To rule out arbitrage, then, it must earn only the risk-free rate. Therefore,

$$E(r_Z) = w_U E(r_U) + w_V E(r_V)$$

$$= \frac{\beta_V}{\beta_V - \beta_U} E(r_U) + \frac{-\beta_U}{\beta_V - \beta_U} E(r_V) = r_f$$

Rearranging the last equation, we can conclude that

$$\frac{E(r_U) - r_f}{\beta_U} = \frac{E(r_V) - r_f}{\beta_V} \tag{11.2}$$

which implies that risk premiums be proportional to betas, as in Figure 11.3.

Concept CHECK

Question 3 • Suppose that Portfolio *E* is well diversified with a beta of $^2/_3$ and expected return of 9%. Would an arbitrage opportunity exist? If so, what would be the arbitrage opportunity?

The Security Market Line

Now consider the market portfolio as a well-diversified portfolio, and let us measure the systematic factor as the unexpected return on the market portfolio. Because the market portfolio must be on the line in Figure 11.3 and the beta of the market portfolio is 1, we can determine the equation describing that line. As Figure 11.4 shows, the intercept is r_f and the slope is $E(r_M) - r_f$ [rise = $E(r_M) - r_f$; run = 1], implying that the equation of the line is

$$E(r_P) = r_f + [E(r_M) - r_f]\beta_P \qquad (11.3)$$

Hence, Figures 11.3 and 11.4 are identical to the SML relation of the CAPM.[3]

We have used the no-arbitrage condition to obtain an expected return–beta relationship identical to that of the CAPM, without the restrictive assumptions of the CAPM. This suggests that despite its restrictive assumptions the main conclusion of the CAPM, namely, the SML expected return–beta relationship, should be at least approximately valid.

It is worth noting that in contrast to the CAPM, the APT does not require that the benchmark portfolio in the SML relationship be the true market portfolio. Any well-diversified portfolio lying on the SML of Figure 11.4 may serve as the benchmark portfolio. For example, one might define the benchmark portfolio as the well-diversified portfolio most highly correlated with whatever systematic factor is thought to affect stock returns. Accordingly, the APT has more flexibility than does the CAPM because problems associated with an unobservable market portfolio are not a concern.

Figure 11.4
The security market line.

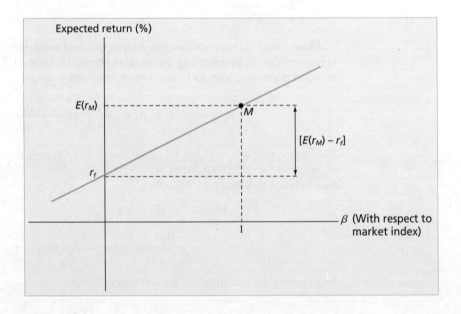

---

[3]Equation 11.3 also can be derived from equation 11.2. If you use the market portfolio, *M*, as portfolio *U* in equation 11.2, and solve for the expected return on portfolio *V* (noting that $\beta_M = 1$), you will find that the expected return on *V* is given by the SML relationship.

In addition, the APT provides further justification for use of the index model in the practical implementation of the SML relationship. Even if the index portfolio is not a precise proxy for the true market portfolio, which is a cause of considerable concern in the context of the CAPM, we now know that if the index portfolio is sufficiently well diversified, the SML relationship should still hold true according to the APT.

So far we have demonstrated the APT relationship for well-diversified portfolios only. The CAPM expected return–beta relationship applies to single assets, as well as to portfolios. In the next section we generalize the APT result one step further.

11.3   INDIVIDUAL ASSETS AND THE APT

We have demonstrated that if arbitrage opportunities are to be ruled out, each well-diversified portfolio's expected excess return must be proportional to its beta. For any two well-diversified portfolios P and Q, this can be written as

$$\frac{E(r_P) - r_f}{\beta_P} = \frac{E(r_Q) - r_f}{\beta_Q} \tag{11.4}$$

The question is whether this relationship tells us anything about the expected returns on the component stocks. The answer is that if this relationship is to be satisfied by all well-diversified portfolios, it must be satisfied by *almost* all individual securities, although the proof of this proposition is somewhat difficult. We note at the outset that, intuitively, we must prove simply that nonsystematic risk does not matter for security returns. The expected return–beta relationship that holds for well-diversified portfolios must also hold for individual securities.

First, we show that if individual securities satisfy equation 11.4, so will all portfolios. If for any two stocks, i and j, the same relationship holds exactly, that is,

$$\frac{E(r_i) - r_f}{\beta_i} = \frac{E(r_j) - r_f}{\beta_j} = K$$

where K is a constant for all securities, then by cross-multiplying, we can write, for any security i,

$$E(r_i) = r_f + \beta_i K$$

Therefore, for any portfolio P with security weights w_i we have

$$E(r_P) = \Sigma w_i E(r_i) = r_f \Sigma w_i + K \Sigma w_i \beta_i$$

Because $\Sigma w_i = 1$ and $\beta_P = \Sigma w_i \beta_i$, we have

$$E(r_P) = r_f + \beta_P K$$

Thus, for all portfolios,

$$\frac{E(r_P) - r_f}{\beta_P} = K$$

and because all portfolios have the same K,

$$\frac{E(r_P) - r_f}{\beta_P} = \frac{E(r_Q) - r_f}{\beta_Q}$$

In other words, if the expected return–beta relationship holds for all single assets, then it will hold for *all* portfolios, well diversified or not.

Question 4 • **Confirm the property expressed in equation 11.4 with a simple numerical example. Suppose that Portfolio *P* has an expected return of 10%, and β of .5, whereas Portfolio *Q* has an expected return of 15% and β of 1. The risk-free rate, r_f, is 5%.**
a. **Find *K* for these portfolios, and confirm that they are equal.**
b. **Find *K* for an equally weighted portfolio of *P* and *Q*, and show that it equals *K* for each individual security.**

Now we show that it also is necessary that almost all securities satisfy the condition. To avoid extensive mathematics, we will satisfy ourselves with a less rigorous argument.

Suppose that the expected return–beta relationship is violated for all single assets. Now create a pair of well-diversified portfolios from these assets. What are the chances that, in spite of the fact that for any pair of assets this relationship,

$$\frac{E(r_i) - r_f}{\beta_i} = \frac{E(r_j) - r_f}{\beta_j}$$

does not hold, the relationship *will* hold for the well-diversified portfolios as follows:

$$\frac{E(r_P) - r_f}{\beta_P} = \frac{E(r_Q) - r_f}{\beta_Q}$$

The chances are small, but it is possible that the relationships among the single securities are violated in offsetting ways so that somehow it holds for the pair of well-diversified portfolios.

Now construct yet another well-diversified portfolio. What are the chances that the violation of the relationships for single securities are such that the third portfolio also will fulfill the no-arbitrage expected return–beta relationship? Obviously, the chances are smaller still, but the relationship is possible. Continue with a fourth well-diversified portfolio, and so on. If the no-arbitrage expected return–beta relationship has to hold for infinitely many different, well-diversified portfolios, it must be virtually certain that the relationship holds for all individual securities.

We use the term "virtually certain" advisedly because we must distinguish this conclusion from the statement that all securities surely fulfill this relationship. The reason we cannot make the latter statement has to do with a property of well-diversified portfolios.

Recall that to qualify as well diversified, a portfolio must have very small positions in all securities. If, for example, only one security violates the expected return–beta relationship, then the effect of this violation on a well-diversified portfolio will be too small to be of importance for any practical purpose, and meaningful arbitrage opportunities will not arise. But if many securities violate the expected return–beta relationship, the relationship will no longer hold for well-diversified portfolios, and arbitrage opportunities will be available.

Consequently, we conclude that imposing the no-arbitrage condition on a single-factor security market implies maintenance of the expected return–beta relationship for all well-diversified portfolios and for all but possibly a *small* number of individual securities.

The APT serves many of the same functions as the CAPM. It gives us a benchmark for rates of return that can be used in capital budgeting, security evaluation, or investment performance evaluation. Moreover, the APT highlights the crucial distinction between non-diversifiable risk (factor risk) that requires a reward in the form of a risk premium and diversifiable risk that does not.

11.4   THE APT AND THE CAPM

The APT is an extremely appealing model. It depends on the assumption that a rational equilibrium in capital markets precludes arbitrage opportunities. A violation of the APT's pricing relationships will cause extremely strong pressure to restore them even if only a limited number of investors become aware of the disequilibrium.

Furthermore, the APT yields an expected return–beta relationship using a well-diversified portfolio that practically can be constructed from a large number of securities. In contrast, the CAPM is derived assuming an inherently unobservable "market" portfolio.

In spite of these appealing advantages, the APT does not fully dominate the CAPM. The CAPM provides an unequivocal statement on the expected return–beta relationship for all assets, whereas the APT implies that this relationship holds for all but perhaps a small number of securities. This is an important difference, yet it is fruitless to pursue because the CAPM is not a readily testable model in the first place. A more productive comparison is between the APT and the index model.

Recall that the index model relies on the assumptions of the CAPM with additional assumptions that (1) a specified market index is virtually perfectly correlated with the (unobservable) theoretical market portfolio; and (2) the probability distribution of stock returns is stationary, so that sample period returns can provide valid estimates of expected returns and variances.

The implication of the index model is that the market index portfolio is efficient and that the expected return–beta relationship holds for all assets. The assumption that the probability distribution of security returns is stationary, and the observability of the index make it possible to test the efficiency of the index portfolio and the expected return–beta relationship. The arguments leading from the assumptions to these implications rely on mean-variance efficiency; that is, if any security violates the expected return–beta relationship, then many investors (each relatively small) will tilt their portfolios so that their combined overall pressure on prices will restore an equilibrium that satisfies the relationship.

In contrast, the APT uses a single-factor security market assumption and arbitrage arguments to obtain the expected return–beta relationship for well-diversified portfolios. Because it focuses on the no-arbitrage condition, without the further assumptions of the market or index model, the APT cannot rule out a violation of the expected return–beta relationship for any particular asset. For this, we need the CAPM assumptions and its dominance arguments.

11.5   A MULTIFACTOR APT

We have assumed so far that there is only one systematic factor affecting stock returns. This simplifying assumption is in fact too simplistic. It is easy to think of several factors driven by the business cycle that might affect stock returns: interest rate fluctuations, inflation rates, oil prices, and so on. Presumably, exposure to any of these factors will affect a stock's risk and hence its expected return. We can derive a multifactor version of the APT to accommodate these multiple sources of risk.

Suppose that we generalize the factor model expressed in equation 11.1 to a two-factor model:

$$r_i = E(r_i) + \beta_{i1}F_1 + \beta_{i2}F_2 + e_i \tag{11.5}$$

Factor 1 might be, for example, departures of GDP growth from expectations, and factor 2 might be unanticipated inflation. Each factor has a zero expected value because each measures the surprise in the systematic variable rather than the level of the variable. Similarly, the firm-specific component of unexpected return, e_i, also has zero expected value. Extending such a two-factor model to any number of factors is straightforward.

Establishing a multifactor APT is similar to the one-factor case. But first we must introduce the concept of a **factor portfolio**, which is a well-diversified portfolio constructed to have a beta of 1 on one of the factors and a beta of 0 on any other factor. This is an easy restriction to satisfy, because we have a large number of securities to choose from, and a relatively small number of factors. Factor portfolios will serve as the benchmark portfolios for a multifactor security market line.

Suppose that the two factor portfolios, called Portfolios 1 and 2, have expected returns $E(r_1) = 10\%$ and $E(r_2) = 12\%$. Suppose further that the risk-free rate is 4%. The risk premium on the first factor portfolio becomes $10\% - 4\% = 6\%$, whereas that on the second factor portfolio is $12\% - 4\% = 8\%$.

Now consider an arbitrary well-diversified portfolio, Portfolio A, with beta on the first factor, $\beta_{A1} = .5$, and beta on the second factor, $\beta_{A2} = .75$. The multifactor APT states that the overall risk premium on this portfolio must equal the sum of the risk premiums required as compensation to investors for each source of systematic risk. The risk premium attributable to risk factor 1 should be the portfolio's exposure to factor 1, β_{A1}, multiplied by the risk premium earned on the first factor portfolio, $E(r_1) - r_f$. Therefore, the portion of Portfolio A's risk premium that is compensation for its exposure to the first factor is $\beta_{A1}[E(r_1) - r_f] = .5(10\% - 4\%) = 3\%$, whereas the risk premium attributable to risk factor 2 is $\beta_{A2}[E(r_2) - r_f] = .75(12\% - 4\%) = 6\%$. The total risk premium on the portfolio should be $3 + 6 = 9\%$. Therefore, the total return on the portfolio should be 13%:

4%	(risk-free rate)
+ 3	(risk premium for exposure to factor 1)
+ 6	(risk premium for exposure to factor 2)
13%	(total expected return)

To see why the expected return on the portfolio must be 13%, consider the following argument. Suppose that the expected return on Portfolio A were 12% rather than 13%. This return would give rise to an arbitrage opportunity. Form a portfolio from the factor portfolios with the same betas as Portfolio A. This requires weights of .5 on the first factor portfolio, .75 on the second factor portfolio, and −.25 on the risk-free asset. This portfolio has exactly the same factor betas as Portfolio A: It has a beta of .5 on the first factor because of its .5 weight on the first factor portfolio, and a beta of .75 on the second factor.

However, in contrast to Portfolio A, which has a 12% expected return, this portfolio's expected return is $(.5 \times 10) + (.75 \times 12) - (.25 \times 4) = 13\%$. A long position in this portfolio and a short position in Portfolio A would yield an arbitrage profit. The total return per dollar long or short in each position would be

$$
\begin{array}{ll}
.13 + .5F_1 + .75F_2 & \text{(long position in factor portfolios)} \\
\underline{- (.12 + .5F_1 + .75F_2)} & \text{(short position in Portfolio A)} \\
.01 &
\end{array}
$$

for a positive, risk-free return on a zero net investment position.

To generalize this argument, note that the factor exposure of any portfolio, P, is given by its betas, β_{P1} and β_{P2}. A competing portfolio formed from factor portfolios with weights β_{P1} in the first factor portfolio, β_{P2} in the second factor portfolio, and $1 - \beta_{P1} - \beta_{P2}$ in T-bills will have betas equal to those of Portfolio P and expected return of

$$
\begin{aligned}
E(r_P) &= \beta_{P1}E(r_1) + \beta_{P2}E(r_2) + (1 - \beta_{P1} - \beta_{P2})r_f \\
&= r_f + \beta_{P1}[E(r_1) - r_f] + \beta_{P2}[E(r_2) - r_f]
\end{aligned}
\tag{11.6}
$$

Hence any well-diversified portfolio with betas β_{P1} and β_{P2} must have the return given in equation 11.6 if arbitrage opportunities are to be precluded. If you compare equations 11.3 and 11.6, you will see that equation 11.6 is simply a generalization of the one-factor SML.

Finally, the extension of the multifactor SML of equation 11.6 to individual assets is precisely the same as for the one-factor APT. Equation 11.6 cannot be satisfied by every well-diversified portfolio unless it is satisfied by virtually every security taken individually. This establishes a multifactor version of the APT. Hence the fair rate of return on any stock with $\beta_1 = .5$ and $\beta_2 = .75$ is 13%. Equation 11.6 thus represents the multifactor SML for an economy with multiple sources of risk.

Concept
CHECK

Question 5 • Find the fair rate of return on a security with $\beta_1 = .2$ and $\beta_2 = 1.4$.

One shortcoming of the multifactor APT is that it gives no guidance concerning the determination of the risk premiums on the factor portfolios. In contrast, the CAPM implies that the risk premium on the market is determined by the market's variance and the average degree of risk aversion across investors. As it turns out, the CAPM also has a multifactor generalization, sometimes called the intertemporal (ICAPM). This model provides some guidance concerning the risk premiums on the factor portfolios. Moreover, recent theoretical research has demonstrated that one may estimate an expected return–beta relationship even if the true factors or factor portfolios cannot be identified. This issue is treated in the papers by Reisman and Shanken cited in the selected readings at the end of this chapter.

SUMMARY

1. A (risk-free) arbitrage opportunity arises when two or more security prices enable investors to construct a zero net investment portfolio that will yield a sure profit.

2. Rational investors will want to take infinitely large positions in arbitrage portfolios regardless of their degree of risk aversion.

3. The presence of arbitrage opportunities and the resulting large volume of trades will create pressure on security prices. This pressure will continue until prices reach levels that preclude arbitrage. Only a few investors need to become aware of arbitrage opportunities to trigger this process because of the large volume of trades in which they will engage.

4. When securities are priced so that there are no risk-free arbitrage opportunities, we say that they satisfy the no-arbitrage condition. Price relationships that satisfy the no-arbitrage condition are important because we expect them to hold in real-world markets.

5. Portfolios are called "well-diversified" if they include a large number of securities and the investment proportion in each is sufficiently small. The proportion of a security in a well-diversified portfolio is small enough so that for all practical purposes a reasonable change in that security's rate of return will have a negligible effect on the portfolio's rate of return.

6. In a single-factor security market, all well-diversified portfolios have to satisfy the expected return–beta relationship of the security market line to satisfy the no-arbitrage condition.

7. If all well-diversified portfolios satisfy the expected return–beta relationship, then all but a small number of securities also must satisfy this relationship.

8. The assumption of a single-factor security market made in the simple version of the APT, together with the no-arbitrage condition, implies the same expected return–beta relationship as does the CAPM, yet it does not require the restrictive assumptions of the

CAPM and its (unobservable) market portfolio. The price of this generality is that the APT does not guarantee this relationship for all securities at all times.

9. A multifactor APT generalizes the single-factor model to accommodate several sources of systematic risk.

Key Terms

arbitrage	risk arbitrage	well-diversified portfolio
zero investment portfolio	arbitrage pricing theory	factor portfolio

Selected Readings

Stephen Ross developed the arbitrage pricing theory in two articles:

Ross, S. A. "Return, Risk and Arbitrage." In *Risk and Return in Finance*, eds. I. Friend and J. Bicksler. Cambridge, Mass.: Ballinger, 1976.

Ross, S. A. "Arbitrage Theory of Capital Asset Pricing." *Journal of Economic Theory*, December 1976.

Articles exploring the factors that influence common stock returns are:

Bower, D. A.; R. S. Bower; and D. E. Logue. "Arbitrage Pricing and Utility Stock Returns." *Journal of Finance*, September 1994.

Chen, N. F.; R. Roll; and S. Ross. "Economic Forces and the Stock Market: Testing the APT and Alternative Asset Pricing Theories." *Journal of Business*, July 1986.

Sharpe, W. "Factors in New York Stock Exchange Security Returns, 1931–1979." *Journal of Portfolio Management*, Summer 1982.

Articles exploring the requirement from reference portfolios necessary to test the expected return–beta relationship are:

Reisman, H. "Reference Variables, Factor Structure, and the Approximate Multibeta Representation." *Journal of Finance*, September 1992.

Shanken, J. "Multivariate Proxies and Asset Pricing Relations: Living with the Roll Critique." *Journal of Financial Economics*, March 1987.

Problems

1. Suppose that two factors have been identified for the U.S. economy: the growth rate of industrial production, IP, and the inflation rate, IR. IP is expected to be 3%, and IR 5%. A stock with a beta of 1 on IP and .5 on IR currently is expected to provide a rate of return of 12%. If industrial production actually grows by 5%, while the inflation rate turns out to be 8%, what is your revised estimate of the expected rate of return on the stock?

2. Suppose that there are two independent economic factors, F_1 and F_2. The risk-free rate is 6%, and all stocks have independent firm-specific components with a standard deviation of 45%. The following are well-diversified portfolios:

Portfolio	Beta on F_1	Beta on F_2	Expected Return
A	1.5	2.0	31
B	2.2	−0.2	27

What is the expected return–beta relationship in this economy?

3. Consider the following data for a one-factor economy. All portfolios are well diversified.

Portfolio	E(r)	Beta
A	12%	1.2
F	6%	0

Suppose that another portfolio, Portfolio E, is well diversified with a beta of .6 and expected return of 8%. Would an arbitrage opportunity exist? If so, what would be the arbitrage strategy?

4. The following is a scenario for three stocks constructed by the security analysts of Pf Inc.

Stock	Price ($)	Scenario Rate of Return (%)		
		Recession	Average	Boom
A	10	−15	20	30
B	15	25	10	−10
C	50	12	15	12

   a. Construct an arbitrage portfolio using these stocks.
   b. How might these prices change when equilibrium is restored? Give an example where a change in Stock C's price is sufficient to restore equilibrium, assuming that the dollar payoffs to Stock C remain the same.

5. Assume that both Portfolios A and B are well diversified, that $E(r_A) = 12\%$, and $E(r_B) = 9\%$. If the economy has only one factor, and $\beta_A = 1.2$, whereas $\beta_B = .8$, what must be the risk-free rate?

6. Assume that stock market returns have the market index as a common factor, and that all stocks in the economy have a beta of 1 on the market index. Firm-specific returns all have a standard deviation of 30%.

   Suppose that an analyst studies 20 stocks, and finds that one-half have an alpha of 2%, and the other half an alpha of −2%. Suppose the analyst buys $1 million of an equally weighted portfolio of the positive alpha stocks, and shorts $1 million of an equally weighted portfolio of the negative alpha stocks.

   a. What is the expected profit (in dollars) and standard deviation of the analyst's profit?
   b. How does your answer change if the analyst examines 50 stocks instead of 20 stocks? 100 stocks?

7. Assume that security returns are generated by the single-index model,

$$R_i = \alpha_i + \beta_i R_M + e_i$$

where R_i is the excess return for security i and R_M is the market's excess return. The risk-free rate is 2%. Suppose also that there are three securities A, B, and C, characterized by the following data:

Security	β_i	$E(R_i)$	$\sigma(e_i)$
A	0.8	10%	25%
B	1.0	12	10
C	1.2	14	20

   a. If $\sigma_M = 20\%$, calculate the variance of returns of Securities A, B, and C.
   b. Now assume that there are an infinite number of assets with return characteristics identical to those of A, B, and C respectively. If one forms a well-diversified portfolio of type A securities, what will be the mean and variance of the portfolio's excess returns? What about portfolios composed only of type B or C stocks?

    c. Is there an arbitrage opportunity in this market? What is it? Analyze the opportunity graphically.

8. The SML relationship states that the expected risk premium on a security in a one-factor model must be directly proportional to the security's beta. Suppose that this were not the case. For example, suppose that expected return rises more than proportionately with beta as in the figure below.

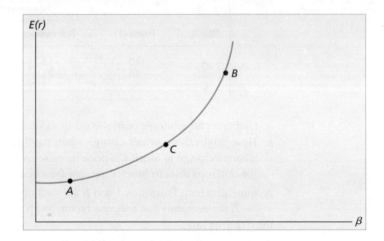

    a. How could you construct an arbitrage portfolio? (Hint: Consider combinations of Portfolios *A* and *B*, and compare the resultant portfolio to *C*.)

    b. We will see in Chapter 13 that some researchers have examined the relationship between average return on diversified portfolios and the β and β^2 of those portfolios. What should they have discovered about the effect of β^2 on portfolio return?

9. If the APT is to be a useful theory, the number of systematic factors in the economy must be small. Why?

10. The APT itself does not provide guidance concerning the factors that one might expect to determine risk premiums. How should researchers decide which factors to investigate? Why, for example, is industrial production a reasonable factor to test for a risk premium?

11. Consider the following multifactor (APT) model of security returns for a particular stock.

Factor	Factor Beta	Factor Risk Premium
Inflation	1.2	6%
Industrial production	0.5	8
Oil prices	0.3	3

    a. If T-bills currently offer a 6% yield, find the expected rate of return on this stock if the market views the stock as fairly priced.

    b. Suppose that the market expected the values for the three macro factors given in Column 1 below, but that the actual values turn out as given in Column 2. Calculate the revised expectations for the rate of return on the stock once the "surprises" become known.

Factor	Expected Rate of Change	Actual Rate of Change
Inflation	5%	4%
Industrial production	3	6
Oil prices	2	0

12. Suppose that the market can be described by the following three sources of systematic risk with associated risk premiums.

Factor	Risk Premium
Industrial production (I)	6%
Interest rates (R)	2
Consumer confidence (C)	4

The return on a particular stock is generated according to the following equation:

$$r = 15\% + 1.0I + .5R + .75C + e$$

Find the equilibrium rate of return on this stock using the APT. The T-bill rate is 6%. Is the stock over- or underpriced? Explain.

 13. Assume that both X and Y are well-diversified portfolios and the risk-free rate is 8%.

Portfolio	Expected Return	Beta
X	16%	1.00
Y	12%	0.25

In this situation you would conclude that Portfolios X and Y:
a. Are in equilibrium.
b. Offer an arbitrage opportunity.
c. Are both underpriced.
d. Are both fairly priced.

 14. According to the theory of arbitrage:
a. High-beta stocks are consistently overpriced.
b. Low-beta stocks are consistently overpriced.
c. Positive alpha stocks will quickly disappear.
d. Rational investors will pursue arbitrage consistent with their risk tolerance.

 15. A zero-investment portfolio with a positive alpha could arise if:
a. The expected return of the portfolio equals zero.
b. The capital market line is tangent to the opportunity set.
c. The law of one price remains unviolated.
d. A risk-free arbitrage opportunity exists.

 16. The arbitrage pricing theory (APT) differs from the single-factor capital asset pricing model (CAPM) because the APT:
a. Places more emphasis on market risk.
b. Minimizes the importance of diversification.
c. Recognizes multiple unsystematic risk factors.
d. Recognizes multiple systematic risk factors.

17. An investor takes as large a position as possible when an equilibrium price relationship is violated. This is an example of:
    a. A dominance argument.
    b. The mean-variance efficient frontier.
    c. A risk-free arbitrage.
    d. The capital asset pricing model.

18. The feature of arbitrage pricing theory (APT) that offers the greatest potential advantage over the simple CAPM is the:
    a. Identification of anticipated changes in production, inflation, and term structure of interest rates as key factors explaining the risk–return relationship.
    b. Superior measurement of the risk-free rate of return over historical time periods.
    c. Variability of coefficients of sensitivity to the APT factors for a given asset over time.
    d. Use of several factors instead of a single market index to explain the risk–return relationship.

19. In contrast to the capital asset pricing model, arbitrage pricing theory:
    a. Requires that markets be in equilibrium.
    b. Uses risk premiums based on micro variables.
    c. Specifies the number and identifies specific factors that determine expected returns.
    d. Does not require the restrictive assumptions concerning the market portfolio.

solutions to

Concept   CHECKS

1. The least profitable scenario currently yields a profit of $10,000 and gross proceeds from the equally weighted portfolio of $700,000. As the price of Dreck falls, less of the equally weighted portfolio can be purchased from the proceeds of the short sale. When Dreck's price falls by more than a factor of 10,000/700,000, arbitrage no longer will be feasible, because the profits in the worst state will be driven below zero.

   To see this, suppose that Dreck's price falls to $10 \times (1 - 1/70)$. The short sale of 300,000 shares now yields $2,957,142, which allows dollar investments of only $985,714 in each of the other shares. In the high real interest rate–low inflation scenario, profits will be driven to zero:

Stock	Dollar Investment	Rate of Return	Dollar Return
Apex	$ 985,714	.20	$197,143
Bull	985,714	.70	690,000
Crush	985,714	−.20	−197,143
Dreck	−2,957,142	.23	−690,000
Total	0		0

   At any price for Dreck stock *below* $10 \times (1 - 1/70) = \$9.857$, profits are negative, which means this arbitrage opportunity is eliminated. *Note:* $9.857 is not the equilibrium price of Dreck. It is simply the upper bound on Dreck's price that rules out the simple arbitrage opportunity.

2. $\sigma(e_p) = \sigma^2(e_i)/n$
    a. $\sqrt{30/10} = 1.732\%$
    b. $\sqrt{30/100} = .548\%$
    c. $\sqrt{30/1,000} = .173\%$
    d. $\sqrt{30/10,000} = .055\%$

We conclude that nonsystematic volatility can be driven to arbitrarily low levels in well-diversified portfolios.

3. A portfolio consisting of two-thirds of Portfolio A and one-third of the risk-free asset will have the same beta as Portfolio E, but an expected return of $(\frac{1}{3} \times 4) + (\frac{2}{3} \times 10) = 8\%$, less than that of Portfolio E. Therefore, one can earn arbitrage profits by shorting the combination of Portfolio A and the safe asset, and buying Portfolio E.

4. *a.* For Portfolio P,

$$K = \frac{E(r_P) - r_f}{\beta_P} = \frac{10 - 5}{.5} = 10$$

For Portfolio Q,

$$K = \frac{15 - 5}{1} = 10$$

b. The equally weighted portfolio has an expected return of 12.5% and a beta of .75. $K = (12.5 - 5)/.75 = 10$.

5. Using equation 11.6, the expected return is

$$4 + .2(6) + 1.4(8) = 16.4\%$$

MARKET EFFICIENCY

One of the early applications of computers in economics in the 1950s was to analyze economic time series. Business cycle theorists felt that tracing the evolution of several economic variables over time would clarify and predict the progress of the economy through boom and bust periods. A natural candidate for analysis was the behavior of stock market prices over time. Assuming that stock prices reflect the prospects of the firm, recurrent patterns of peaks and troughs in economic performance ought to show up in those prices. Maurice Kendall examined this proposition in 1953.[1] He found to his great surprise that he could identify *no* predictable patterns in stock prices. Prices seemed to evolve randomly. They were as likely to go up as they were to go down on any particular day, regardless of past performance. The data provided no way to predict price movements. At first blush, Kendall's results were disturbing to some financial economists. They seemed to imply that the stock market is dominated by erratic market psychology, or "animal spirits"—that it follows no logical rules. In short, the results appeared to confirm the irrationality of the market. On further reflection, however, economists came to reverse their interpretation of Kendall's study. It soon became apparent that random price movements indicated a well-functioning or efficient market, not an irrational one. In this chapter we explore the reasoning behind what may seem a surprising conclusion. We show how competition among analysts leads naturally to market efficiency, and we examine the implications of the efficient market hypothesis for investment policy. We also consider empirical evidence that supports and contradicts the notion of market efficiency.

---

[1] Maurice Kendall, "The Analysis of Economic Time Series, Part I: Prices," *Journal of the Royal Statistical Society* 96 (1953).

12.1   RANDOM WALKS AND THE EFFICIENT MARKET HYPOTHESIS

Suppose Kendall had discovered that stock prices are predictable. What a gold mine this would have been for investors! If they could use Kendall's equations to predict stock prices, investors would reap unending profits simply by purchasing stocks that the computer model implied were about to increase in price and by selling those stocks about to fall in price.

A moment's reflection should be enough to convince yourself that this situation could not persist for long. For example, suppose that the model predicts with great confidence that XYZ stock price, currently at $100 per share, will rise dramatically in three days to $110. What would all investors with access to the model's prediction do today? Obviously, they would place a great wave of immediate buy orders to cash in on the prospective increase in stock price. No one holding XYZ, however, would be willing to sell. The net effect would be an *immediate* jump in the stock price to $110. The forecast of a future price increase will lead instead to an immediate price increase. In other words, the stock price will immediately reflect the "good news" implicit in the model's forecast.

This simple example illustrates why Kendall's attempt to find recurrent patterns in stock price movements was doomed to failure. A forecast about favorable *future* performance leads instead to favorable *current* performance, as market participants all try to get in on the action before the price jump.

More generally, one might say that any information that could be used to predict stock performance should already be reflected in stock prices. As soon as there is any information indicating that a stock is underpriced and therefore offers a profit opportunity, investors flock to buy the stock and immediately bid up its price to a fair level, where only ordinary rates of return can be expected. These "ordinary rates" are simply rates of return commensurate with the risk of the stock.

However, if prices are bid immediately to fair levels, given all available information, it must be that they increase or decrease only in response to new information. New information, by definition, must be unpredictable; if it could be predicted, then the prediction would be part of today's information. Thus stock prices that change in response to new (unpredictable) information also must move unpredictably.

This is the essence of the argument that stock prices should follow a **random walk**, that is, that price changes should be random and unpredictable.[2] Far from a proof of market irrationality, randomly evolving stock prices are the necessary consequence of intelligent investors competing to discover relevant information on which to buy or sell stocks before the rest of the market becomes aware of that information.

Don't confuse randomness in price *changes* with irrationality in the *level* of prices. If prices are determined rationally, then only new information will cause them to change, Therefore, a random walk would be the natural result of prices that always reflect all current knowledge. Indeed, if stock price movements were predictable, that would be damning evidence of stock market inefficiency, because the ability to predict prices would indicate that all available information was not already reflected in stock prices. Therefore,

---

[2]Actually, we are being a little loose with terminology here. Strictly speaking, we should characterize stock prices as following a submartingale, meaning that the expected change in the price can be positive, presumably as compensation for the time value of money and systematic risk. Moreover, the expected return may change over time as risk factors change. A random walk is more restrictive in that it constrains successive stock returns to be independent *and* identically distributed. Nevertheless, the term "random walk" is commonly used in the looser sense that price changes are essentially unpredictable. We will follow this convention.

the notion that stocks already reflect all available information is referred to as the **efficient market hypothesis** (EMH).[3]

Competition as the Source of Efficiency

Why should we expect stock prices to reflect "all available information"? After all, if you are willing to spend time and money on gathering information, it might seem reasonable that you could turn up something that has been overlooked by the rest of the investment community. When information is costly to uncover and analyze, one would expect investment analysis calling for such expenditures to result in an increased expected return.

This point has been stressed by Grossman and Stiglitz.[4] They argued that investors will have an incentive to spend time and resources to analyze and uncover new information only if such activity is likely to generate higher investment returns. Thus, in market equilibrium, efficient information-gathering activity should be fruitful. Moreover, it would not be surprising to find that the degree of efficiency differs across various markets. For example, emerging markets that are less intensively analyzed than U.S. markets and in which accounting disclosure requirements are much less rigorous may be less efficient than U.S. markets. Small stocks which receive relatively little coverage by Wall Street analysts may be less efficiently priced than large ones. Still, while we would not, therefore, go so far as to say that you absolutely cannot come up with new information, it still makes sense to consider and respect your competition.

Consider an investment management fund currently managing a $5 billion portfolio. Suppose that the fund manager can devise a research program that could increase the portfolio rate of return by one-tenth of 1% per year, a seemingly modest amount. This program would increase the dollar return to the portfolio by $5 billion $\times$ .001, or $5 million. Therefore, the fund would be willing to spend up to $5 million per year on research to increase stock returns by a mere tenth of 1% per year. With such large rewards for such small increases in investment performance, it should not be surprising that professional portfolio managers are willing to spend large sums on industry analysts, computer support, and research effort, and therefore that price changes are, generally speaking, difficult to predict.

With so many well-backed analysts willing to spend considerable resources on research, easy pickings in the market are rare. Moreover, the incremental rates of return on research activity are likely to be so small that only managers of the largest portfolios will find them worth pursuing.

Although it may not literally be true that "all" relevant information will be uncovered, it is virtually certain that there are many investigators hot on the trail of most leads that seem likely to improve investment performance. Competition among these many well-backed, highly paid, aggressive analysts ensures that, as a general rule, stock prices ought to reflect available information regarding their proper levels.

Versions of the Efficient Market Hypothesis

It is common to distinguish among three versions of the EMH: the weak, semistrong, and strong forms of the hypothesis. These versions differ by their notions of what is meant by the term "all available information."

---

[3]Market efficiency should not be confused with the idea of efficient portfolios introduced in Chapter 8. An informationally efficient *market* is one in which information is rapidly disseminated and reflected in prices. An efficient *portfolio* is one with the highest expected return for a given level of risk.

[4]Sanford J. Grossman and Joseph E. Stiglitz, "On the Impossibility of Informationally Efficient Markets," *American Economic Review* 70 (June 1980).

The **weak-form** hypothesis asserts that stock prices already reflect all information that can be derived by examining market trading data such as the history of past prices, trading volume, or short interest. This version of the hypothesis implies that trend analysis is fruitless. Past stock price data are publicly available and virtually costless to obtain. The weak-form hypothesis holds that if such data ever conveyed reliable signals about future performance, all investors would have learned already to exploit the signals. Ultimately, the signals lose their value as they become widely known because a buy signal, for instance, would result in an immediate price increase.

The **semistrong-form** hypothesis states that all publicly available information regarding the prospects of a firm must be reflected already in the stock price. Such information includes, in addition to past prices, fundamental data on the firm's product line, quality of management, balance sheet composition, patents held, earning forecasts, and accounting practices. Again, if any investor has access to such information from publicly available sources, one would expect it to be reflected in stock prices.

Finally, the **strong-form** version of the efficient market hypothesis states that stock prices reflect all information relevant to the firm, even including information available only to company insiders. This version of the hypothesis is quite extreme. Few would argue with the proposition that corporate officers have access to pertinent information long enough before public release to enable them to profit from trading on that information. Indeed, much of the activity of the Securities and Exchange Commission is directed toward preventing insiders from profiting by exploiting their privileged situation. Rule 10b-5 of the Security Exchange Act of 1934 sets limits on trading by corporate officers, directors, and substantial owners, requiring them to report trades to the SEC. These insiders, their relatives, and any associates who trade on information supplied by insiders are considered in violation of the law.

Defining insider trading is not always easy, however. After all, stock analysts are in the business of uncovering information not already widely known to market participants. As we saw in Chapter 3, the distinction between private and inside information is sometimes murky.

Concept  **Question 1 •** **If the weak form of the efficient market hypothesis is valid, must the strong form also hold? Conversely, does strong-form efficiency imply weak-form efficiency?**

12.2   IMPLICATIONS OF THE EMH FOR INVESTMENT POLICY

Technical Analysis

Technical analysis is essentially the search for recurrent and predictable patterns in stock prices. Although technicians recognize the value of information regarding future economic prospects of the firm, they believe that such information is not necessary for a successful trading strategy. This is because whatever the fundamental reason for a change in stock price, if the stock price responds slowly enough, the analyst will be able to identify a trend that can be exploited during the adjustment period. The key to successful technical analysis is a sluggish response of stock prices to fundamental supply-and-demand factors. This prerequisite, of course, is diametrically opposed to the notion of an efficient market.

Technical analysts are sometimes called *chartists* because they study records or charts of past stock prices, hoping to find patterns they can exploit to make a profit. Figure 12.1 shows some of the types of patterns a chartist might hope to identify. The chartist may draw lines connecting the high and low prices for the day to examine any trends in the prices

Figure 12.1

Technical analysis. **A**, Momentum (upward). **B**, Breakaway. **C**, Head and shoulders.

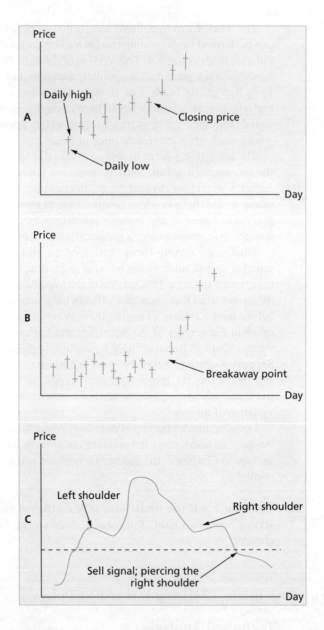

(Figure 12.1, **A**). The crossbars indicate closing prices. This is called a search for "momentum." More complex patterns, such as the "breakaway" (Figure 12.1, **B**) or "head and shoulders" (Figure 12.1, **C**), are also believed to convey clear buy or sell signals. The head and shoulders is named for its rough resemblance to a portrait of a head with surrounding shoulders. Once the right shoulder is penetrated (known as piercing the neckline) chartists believe the stock is on the verge of a major decline in price.

The **Dow theory**, named after its creator Charles Dow (who established *The Wall Street Journal*), is the grandfather of most technical analysis. The aim of the Dow theory is to identify long-term trends in stock market prices. The two indicators used are the Dow Jones Industrial Average (DJIA) and the Dow Jones Transportation Average (DJTA). The DJIA is the key indicator of underlying trends, while the DJTA usually serves as a check to confirm or reject that signal.

Figure 12.2
Dow theory trends.

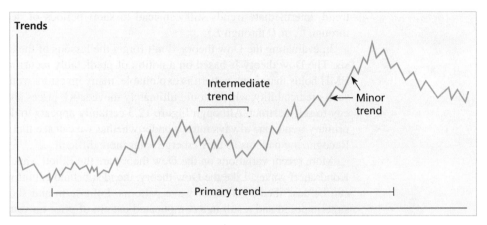

Source: Melanie F. Bowman and Thom Hartle, "Dow Theory," *Technical Analysis of Stocks and Commodities*, September 1990, p. 690.

Figure 12.3
Dow Jones Industrial
Average in 1988.

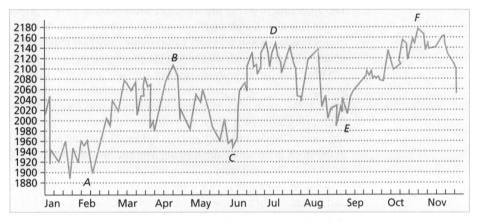

Source: Melanie F. Bowman and Thom Hartle, "Dow Theory," *Technical Analysis of Stocks and Commodities*, September 1990, p. 690.

The Dow theory posits three forces simultaneously affecting stock prices:

1. The *primary trend* is the long-term movement of prices, lasting from several months to several years.
2. *Secondary* or *intermediate trends* are caused by short-term deviations of prices from the underlying trend line. These deviations are eliminated via *corrections*, when prices revert back to trend values.
3. *Tertiary* or *minor trends* are daily fluctuations of little importance.

Figure 12.2 represents these three components of stock price movements. In this figure, the primary trend is upward, but intermediate trends result in short-lived market declines lasting a few weeks. The intraday minor trends have no long-run impact on price.

Figure 12.3 depicts the course of the DJIA during 1988, a year that seems to provide a good example of price patterns consistent with Dow theory. The primary trend is upward, as evidenced by the fact that each market peak is higher than the previous peak (point *F* versus *D* versus *B*). Similarly, each low is higher than the previous low (*E* versus *C* versus *A*). This pattern of upward-moving "tops" and "bottoms" is one of the key ways to identify the underlying primary trend. Notice in Figure 12.3 that, despite the upward primary trend, intermediate trends still can lead to short periods of declining prices (points *B* through *C*, or *D* through *E*).

In evaluating the Dow theory, don't forget the lessons of the efficient market hypothesis. The Dow theory is based on a notion of predictably recurring price patterns. Yet the EMH holds that if any pattern is exploitable, many investors would attempt to profit from such predictability, which would ultimately move stock prices and cause the trading strategy to self-destruct. Although Figure 12.3 certainly appears to describe a classic upward primary trend, one always must wonder whether we can see that trend only *after* the fact. Recognizing patterns as they emerge is far more difficult.

More recent variations on the Dow theory are the Elliott wave theory and the theory of Kondratieff waves. Like the Dow theory, the idea behind Elliott waves is that stock prices can be described by a set of wave patterns. Long-term and short-term wave cycles are superimposed and result in a complicated pattern of price movements, but by interpreting the cycles, one can, according to the theory, predict broad movements. Similarly, Kondratieff waves are named after a Russian economist who asserted that the macroeconomy (and thus the stock market) moves in broad waves lasting between 48 and 60 years. The Kondratieff waves are therefore analogous to Dow's primary trend, although of far longer duration. Kondratieff's assertion is hard to evaluate empirically, however, because cycles that last about 50 years can provide only two independent data points per century, which is hardly enough data to test the predictive power of the theory.

Other chartist techniques involve moving averages. In one version of this approach average prices over the past several months are taken as indicators of the "true value" of the stock. If the stock price is above this value, it may be expected to fall. In another version the moving average is taken as indicative of long-run trends. If the trend has been downward and if the current stock price is below the moving average, then a subsequent increase in the stock price above the moving average line (a "breakthrough") might signal a reversal of the downward trend.

Another technique is called the *relative strength* approach. The chartist compares stock performance over a recent period to performance of the market or other stocks in the same industry. A simple version of relative strength takes the ratio of the stock price to a market indicator such as the S&P 500 index. If the ratio increases over time, the stock is said to exhibit relative strength because its price performance is better than that of the broad market. Such strength presumably may continue for a long enough period of time to offer profit opportunities.

One of the most commonly heard components of technical analysis is the notion of **resistance levels** or **support levels**. These values are said to be price levels above which it is difficult for stock prices to rise, or below which it is unlikely for them to fall, and they are believed to be levels determined by market psychology.

Consider, for example, stock XYZ, which traded for several months at a price of $72, and then declined to $65. If the stock eventually begins to increase in price, $72 is considered a resistance level (according to this theory) because investors who bought originally at $72 will be eager to sell their shares as soon as they can break even on their investment. Therefore, at prices near $72 a wave of selling pressure would exist. Such activity imparts a type of "memory" to the market that allows past price history to influence current stock prospects.

Technical analysts also focus on the volume of trading. The idea is that a price decline accompanied by heavy trading volume signals a more bearish market than if volume were smaller, because the price decline is taken as representing broader-based selling pressure. For example, the trin statistic ("trin" stands for trading index) equals

Figure 12.4
Market diary.

DIARIES

NYSE	WED	TUE	WK AGO
Issues traded	3,401	3,406	3,401
Advances	1,956	2,048	1,373
Declines	903	818	1,476
Unchanged	542	540	552
New highs	190	98	104
New lows	18	14	19
zAdv vol (000)	388,393	402,782	241,061
zDecl vol (000)	107,558	121,525	312,272
zTotal vol (000)	518,143	545,580	587,215
Closing tick[1]	+452	+941	+55
Closing Arms[2] (trin)	.60	.76	1.21
zBlock trades	n.a	10,929	11,548

[1]The net difference of the number of stocks closing higher than their previous trade from those closing lower, NYSE trading only.
[2]A comparison of the number of advancing and declining issues with the volume of shares rising and falling. Generally, a trin of less than 1.00 indicates buying demand; above 1.00 indicates selling pressure.
z-NYSE or Amex only.

Source: *The Wall Street Journal*, August 21, 1997. Reprinted by permission of *The Wall Street Journal*, © 1997 Dow Jones & Company, Inc. All Rights Reserved Worldwide.

$$\text{Trin} = \frac{\text{Volume declining/Number declining}}{\text{Volume advancing/Number advancing}}$$

Therefore, trin is the ratio of average volume in declining issues to average volume in advancing issues. Ratios above 1.0 are considered bearish because the falling stocks would then have higher average volume than the advancing stocks, indicating net selling pressure. *The Wall Street Journal* reports trin every day in the market diary section, as in Figure 12.4.

Note, however, for every buyer there must be a seller of stock. High volume in a falling market should not necessarily indicate a larger imbalance of buyers versus sellers. For example, a trin statistic above 1.0, which is considered bearish, could equally well be interpreted as indicating that there is more *buying* activity in declining issues.

The efficient market hypothesis implies that technical analysis is without merit. The past history of prices and trading volume is publicly available at minimal cost. Therefore, any information that was ever available from analyzing past prices has already been reflected in stock prices. As investors compete to exploit their common knowledge of a stock's price history, they necessarily drive stock prices to levels where expected rates of return are exactly commensurate with risk. At those levels one cannot expect abnormal returns.

As an example of how this process works, consider what would happen if the market believed that a level of $72 truly were a resistance level for stock XYZ. No one would be willing to purchase the stock at a price of $71.50, because it would have almost no room to increase in price, but ample room to fall. However, if no one would buy it at $71.50, then $71.50 would become a resistance level. But then, using a similar analysis, no one would buy it at $71, or $70, and so on. The notion of a resistance level is a logical conundrum. Its simple resolution is the recognition that if the stock is ever to sell at $71.50, investors *must* believe that the price can as easily increase as fall. The fact that investors are willing to purchase (or even hold) the stock at $71.50 is evidence of their belief that they can earn a fair expected rate of return at that price.

Concept
CHECK

Question 2 • If everyone in the market believes in resistance levels, why do these beliefs not become self-fulfilling prophecies?

An interesting question is whether a technical rule that seems to work will continue to work in the future once it becomes widely recognized. A clever analyst may occasionally uncover a profitable trading rule, but the real test of efficient markets is whether the rule itself becomes reflected in stock prices once its value is discovered.

Suppose, for example, that the Dow theory predicts an upward primary trend. If the theory is widely accepted, it follows that many investors will attempt to buy stocks immediately in anticipation of the price increase; the effect would be to bid up prices sharply and immediately rather than at the gradual, long-lived pace initially expected. The Dow theory's predicted trend would be replaced by a sharp jump in prices. It is in this sense that price patterns ought to be *self-destructing*. Once a useful technical rule (or price pattern) is discovered, it ought to be invalidated when the mass of traders attempt to exploit it.

Thus the market dynamic is one of a continual search for profitable trading rules, followed by destruction by overuse of those rules found to be successful, followed by more search for yet-undiscovered rules.

Fundamental Analysis

Fundamental analysis uses earnings and dividend prospects of the firm, expectations of future interest rates, and risk evaluation of the firm to determine proper stock prices. Ultimately, it represents an attempt to determine the present discounted value of all the payments a stockholder will receive from each share of stock. If that value exceeds the stock price, the fundamental analyst would recommend purchasing the stock.

Fundamental analysts usually start with a study of past earnings and an examination of company balance sheets. They supplement this analysis with further detailed economic analysis, ordinarily including an evaluation of the quality of the firm's management, the firm's standing within its industry, and the prospects for the industry as a whole. The hope is to attain insight into future performance of the firm that is not yet recognized by the rest of the market. Chapters 17 through 19 provide a detailed discussion of the types of analyses that underlie fundamental analysis.

Once again, the efficient market hypothesis predicts that *most* fundamental analysis also is doomed to failure. If the analyst relies on publicly available earnings and industry information, his or her evaluation of the firm's prospects is not likely to be significantly more accurate than those of rival analysts. There are many well-informed, well-financed firms conducting such market research, and in the face of such competition it will be difficult to uncover data not also available to other analysts. Only analysts with a unique insight will be rewarded.

Fundamental analysis is much more difficult than merely identifying well-run firms with good prospects. Discovery of good firms does an investor no good in and of itself if the rest of the market also knows those firms are good. If the knowledge is already public, the investor will be forced to pay a high price for those firms and will not realize a superior rate of return.

The trick is not to identify firms that are good, but to find firms that are *better* than everyone else's estimate. Similarly, poorly run firms can be great bargains if they are not quite as bad as their stock prices suggest.

This is why fundamental analysis is difficult. It is not enough to do a good analysis of a firm; you can make money only if your analysis is better than that of your competitors because the market price will already reflect all commonly available information.

Active versus Passive Portfolio Management

By now it is apparent that casual efforts to pick stocks are not likely to pay off. Competition among investors ensures that any easily implemented stock evaluation technique will be used widely enough so that any insights derived will be reflected in stock prices. Only serious analysis and uncommon techniques are likely to generate the *differential* insight necessary to yield trading profits.

Moreover, these techniques are economically feasible only for managers of large portfolios. If you have only $100,000 to invest, even a 1% per year improvement in performance generates only $1,000 per year, hardly enough to justify herculean efforts. The billion-dollar manager, however, reaps extra income of $10 million annually from the same 1% increment.

If small investors are not in a favored position to conduct active portfolio management, what are their choices? The small investor probably is better off investing in mutual funds. By pooling resources in this way, small investors can gain from economies of size.

More difficult decisions remain, though. Can investors be sure that even large mutual funds have the ability or resources to uncover mispriced stocks? Furthermore, will any mispricing be sufficiently large to repay the costs entailed in active portfolio management?

Proponents of the efficient market hypothesis believe that active management is largely wasted effort and unlikely to justify the expenses incurred. Therefore, they advocate a **passive investment strategy** that makes no attempt to outsmart the market. A passive strategy aims only at establishing a well-diversified portfolio of securities without attempting to find under- or overvalued stocks. Passive management is usually characterized by a buy-and-hold strategy. Because the efficient market theory indicates that stock prices are at fair levels, given all available information, it makes no sense to buy and sell securities frequently, which generates large brokerage fees without increasing expected performance.

One common strategy for passive management is to create an **index fund**, which is a fund designed to replicate the performance of a broad-based index of stocks. For example, in 1976 the Vanguard Group of mutual funds introduced a mutual fund called the Index 500 Portfolio, which holds stocks in direct proportion to their weight in the Standard & Poor's 500 stock price index. The performance of the Index 500 fund therefore replicates the performance of the S&P 500. Investors in this fund obtain broad diversification with relatively low management fees. The fees can be kept to a minimum because Vanguard does not need to pay analysts to assess stock prospects and does not incur transaction costs from high portfolio turnover. Indeed, while the typical annual charge for an actively managed equity fund is more than 1% of assets, Vanguard charges a bit less than .2% for the Index 500 Portfolio.

Indexing has grown in appeal considerably since 1976. Vanguard's Index 500 Portfolio was the second-largest mutual fund in early 1998 with more than $50 billion in assets. Several other firms have introduced S&P 500 index funds, but Vanguard still dominates the retail market for indexing. Moreover, corporate pension plans now place more than one-fourth of their equity investments in index funds. Including pension funds and mutual funds, approximately $600 billion was indexed to the S&P 500 by mid-1997. Many institutional investors now hold indexed bond as well as indexed stock portfolios.

Mutual funds offer portfolios that match a wide variety of market indexes. For example, some of the funds offered by the Vanguard Group track the Wilshire 5000 index, the Salomon Brothers Broad Investment Grade Bond Index, the Russell 2000 index of small-capitalization companies, the European equity market, and the Pacific Basin equity market.

A hybrid strategy also is fairly common, where the fund maintains a *passive core*, which is an indexed position, and augments that position with one or more actively managed portfolios.

Concept
CHECK

Question 3 • What would happen to market efficiency if *all* investors attempted to follow a passive strategy?

The Role of Portfolio Management in an Efficient Market

If the market is efficient, why not throw darts at *The Wall Street Journal* instead of trying rationally to choose a stock portfolio? This is a tempting conclusion to draw from the notion that security prices are fairly set, but it is far too facile. There is a role for rational portfolio management, even in perfectly efficient markets.

You have learned that a basic principle in portfolio selection is diversification. Even if all stocks are priced fairly, each still poses firm-specific risk that can be eliminated through diversification. Therefore, rational security selection, even in an efficient market, calls for the selection of a well-diversified portfolio providing the systematic risk level that the investor wants.

Rational investment policy also requires that tax considerations be reflected in security choice. High-tax-bracket investors generally will not want the same securities that low-bracket investors find favorable. At an obvious level high-bracket investors find it advantageous to buy tax-exempt municipal bonds despite their relatively low pretax yields, whereas those same bonds are unattractive to low-tax-bracket investors. At a more subtle level high-bracket investors might want to tilt their portfolios in the direction of capital gains as opposed to dividend or interest income, because the option to defer the realization of capital gain income is more valuable the higher the current tax bracket. Hence these investors may prefer stocks that yield low dividends yet offer greater expected capital gain income. They also will be more attracted to investment opportunities for which returns are sensitive to tax benefits, such as real estate ventures.

A third argument for rational portfolio management relates to the particular risk profile of the investor. For example, a General Motors executive whose annual bonus depends on GM's profits generally should not invest additional amounts in auto stocks. To the extent that his or her compensation already depends on GM's well-being, the executive is already overinvested in GM and should not exacerbate the lack of diversification.

Investors of varying ages also might warrant different portfolio policies with regard to risk bearing. For example, older investors who are essentially living off savings might choose to avoid long-term bonds whose market values fluctuate dramatically with changes in interest rates (discussed in Part IV). Because these investors are living off accumulated savings, they require conservation of principal. In contrast, younger investors might be more inclined toward long-term bonds. The steady flow of income over long periods of time that is locked in with long-term bonds can be more important than preservation of principal to those with long life expectancies.

In conclusion, there is a role for portfolio management even in an efficient market. Investors' optimal positions will vary according to factors such as age, tax bracket, risk aversion, and employment. The role of the portfolio manager in an efficient market is to tailor the portfolio to these needs, rather than to beat the market.

12.3   EVENT STUDIES

The notion of informationally efficient markets leads to a powerful research methodology. If security prices reflect all currently available information, then price changes must reflect new information. Therefore, it seems that one should be able to measure the importance of an event of interest by examining price changes during the period in which the event occurs.

An **event study** describes a technique of empirical financial research that enables an observer to assess the impact of a particular event on a firm's stock price. A stock market analyst might want to study the impact of dividend changes on stock prices, for example. An event study would quantify the relationship between dividend changes and stock returns. Using the results of such a study together with a superior means of predicting dividend changes, the analyst could in principle earn superior trading profits.

Analyzing the impact of an announced change in dividends is more difficult than it might at first appear. On any particular day stock prices respond to a wide range of economic news such as updated forecasts for GDP, inflation rates, interest rates, or corporate profitability. Isolating the part of a stock price movement that is attributable to a dividend announcement is not a trivial exercise.

The statistical approach that researchers commonly use to measure the impact of a particular information release, such as the announcement of a dividend change, is a marriage of efficient market theory with the index model discussed in Chapter 10. We want to measure the unexpected return that results from an event. This is the difference between the actual stock return and the return that might have been expected given the performance of the market. This expected return can be calculated using the index model.

Recall that the index model holds that stock returns are determined by a market factor and a firm-specific factor. The stock return, r_t, during a given period t, would be expressed mathematically as

$$r_t = a + b r_{Mt} + e_t \tag{12.1}$$

where r_{Mt} is the market's rate of return during the period and e_t is the part of a security's return resulting from firm-specific events. The parameter b measures sensitivity to the market return, and a is the average rate of return the stock would realize in a period with a zero market return.[5] Equation 12.1 therefore provides a decomposition of r_t into market and firm-specific factors. The firm-specific return may be interpreted as the unexpected return that results from the event.

Determination of the firm-specific return in a given period requires that we obtain an estimate of the term e_t. Therefore, we rewrite equation 12.1:

$$e_t = r_t - (a + b r_{Mt}) \tag{12.2}$$

Equation 12.2 has a simple interpretation: To determine the firm-specific component of a stock's return, subtract the return that the stock ordinarily would earn for a given level of market performance from the actual rate of return on the stock. The residual, e_t, is the stock's return over and above what one would predict based on broad market movements in that period, given the stock's sensitivity to the market.

For example, suppose that the analyst has estimated that $a = .5\%$ and $b = .8$. On a day that the market goes up by 1%, you would predict from equation 12.1 that the stock should rise by an expected value of $.5\% + .8 \times 1\% = 1.3\%$. If the stock actually rises by 2%, the analyst would infer that firm-specific news that day caused an additional stock return of 2% − 1.3% = .7%. We sometimes refer to the term e_t in equation 12.2 as the **abnormal return**—the return beyond what would be predicted from market movements alone.

The general strategy in event studies is to estimate the abnormal return around the date that new information about a stock is released to the market and attribute the abnormal

---

[5]We know from Chapter 10, Section 10.3, that the CAPM implies that the intercept a in equation 12.1 should equal $r_f(1 - \beta)$. Nevertheless, it is customary to estimate the intercept in this equation empirically rather than imposing the CAPM value. One justification for this practice is that empirically fitted security market lines seem flatter than predicted by the CAPM (see the next chapter), which would make the intercept implied by the CAPM too small.

stock performance to the new information. The first step in the study is to estimate parameters *a* and *b* for each security in the study. These typically are calculated using index model regressions as described in Chapter 10 in a period before that in which the event occurs. The prior period is used for estimation so that the impact of the event will not affect the estimates of the parameters. Next, the information release dates for each firm are recorded. For example, in a study of the impact of merger attempts on the stock prices of target firms, the announcement date is the date on which the public is informed that a merger is to be attempted. Finally, the abnormal returns of each firm surrounding the announcement date are computed, and the statistical significance and magnitude of the typical abnormal return is assessed to determine the impact of the newly released information.

One concern that complicates event studies arises from *leakage* of information. Leakage occurs when information regarding a relevant event is released to a small group of investors before official public release. In this case the stock price might start to increase (in the case of a "good news" announcement) days or weeks before the official announcement date. Any abnormal return on the announcement date is then a poor indicator of the total impact of the information release. A better indicator would be the **cumulative abnormal return**, which is simply the sum of all abnormal returns over the time period of interest. The cumulative abnormal return thus captures the total firm-specific stock movement for an entire period when the market might be responding to new information.

Figure 12.5 presents the results from a fairly typical event study. The authors of this study were interested in leakage of information before merger announcements and constructed a sample of 194 firms that were targets of takeover attempts. In most takeovers, stockholders of the acquired firms sell their shares to the acquirer at substantial premiums

Figure 12.5

Cumulative abnormal returns before takeover attempts: Target companies.

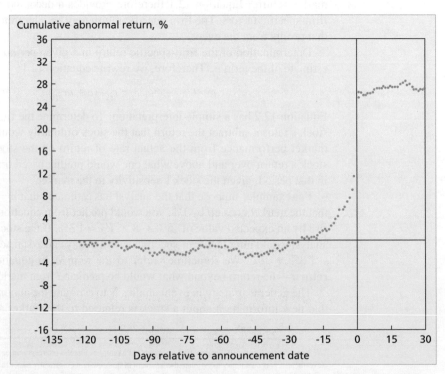

Source: Arthur Keown and John Pinkerton, "Merger Announcements and Insider Trading Activity," *Journal of Finance* 36 (September 1981).

over market value. Announcement of a takeover attempt is good news for shareholders of the target firm and therefore should cause stock prices to jump.

Figure 12.5 confirms the good-news nature of the announcements. On the announcement day, called day 0, the average cumulative abnormal return (CAR) for the sample of takeover candidates increases substantially, indicating a large and positive abnormal return on the announcement date. Notice that immediately after the announcement date the CAR no longer increases or decreases significantly. This is in accord with the efficient market hypothesis. Once the new information became public, the stock prices jumped almost immediately in response to the good news. With prices once again fairly set, reflecting the effect of the new information, further abnormal returns on any particular day are equally likely to be positive or negative. In fact, for a sample of many firms, the average abnormal return will be extremely close to zero, and thus the CAR will show neither upward nor downward drift. This is precisely the pattern shown in Figure 12.5.

The lack of drift in CAR after the public announcement date is perhaps the clearest evidence of an efficient market impounding information into stock prices. This pattern is commonly observed. For example, Figure 12.6 presents results from an event study on dividend announcements. As expected, the firms announcing dividend increases enjoy positive abnormal returns, whereas those with dividend decreases suffer negative abnormal returns. In both cases, however, once the information is made public, the stock price seems to adjust fully, with CARs exhibiting neither upward nor downward drift.

The pattern of returns for the days preceding the public announcement date yields some interesting evidence about efficient markets and information leakage. If insider trading rules were perfectly obeyed and perfectly enforced, stock prices should show no abnormal returns on days before the public release of relevant news, because no special firm-specific information would be available to the market before public announcement. Instead, we should observe a clean jump in the stock price only on the announcement day. In fact, Figure 12.5 shows that the prices of the takeover targets clearly start an upward drift 30 days before the public announcement. There are two possible interpretations of this pattern.

Figure 12.6
Cumulative abnormal returns surrounding dividend announcements.

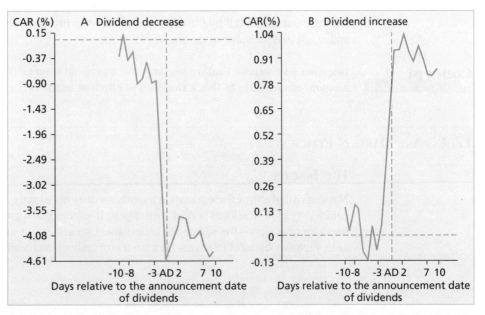

Source: J. Aharony and I. Swary, "Quarterly Dividend and Earnings Announcements and Stockholders' Return: An Empirical Analysis," *Journal of Finance* 35 (March 1980), pp. 1–12.

One is that information is leaking to some market participants who then purchase the stocks before the public announcement. At least some abuse of insider trading rules is occurring.

Another interpretation is that in the days before a takeover attempt the public becomes suspicious of the attempt as it observes someone buying large blocks of stock. As acquisition intentions become more evident, the probability of an attempted merger is gradually revised upward so that we see a gradual increase in CARs. Although this interpretation is certainly a valid possibility, evidence of leakage appears almost universally in event studies, even in cases where the public's access to information is not gradual. For example, the CARs associated with the dividend announcement presented in Figure 12.6 also exhibit leakage. It appears as if insider trading violations do occur.

Actually, the SEC itself can take some comfort from patterns such as that in Figures 12.5 and 12.6. If insider trading rules were widely and flagrantly violated, we would expect to see abnormal returns earlier than they appear in these results. For example, in the case of mergers, the CAR would turn positive as soon as acquiring firms decided on their takeover targets, because insiders would start trading immediately. By the time of the public announcement, the insiders would have bid up the stock prices of target firms to levels reflecting the merger attempt, and the abnormal returns on the actual public announcement date would be close to zero. The dramatic increase in the CAR that we see on the announcement date indicates that a good deal of these announcements are indeed news to the market and that stock prices did not already reflect complete knowledge about the takeovers. It would appear, therefore, that SEC enforcement does have a substantial effect on restricting insider trading, even if some amount of it still persists.

Event study methodology has become a widely accepted tool to measure the economic impact of a wide range of events. For example, the SEC regularly uses event studies to measure illicit gains captured by traders who may have violated insider trading or other securities laws.[6] Event studies are also used in fraud cases, where the courts must assess damages caused by a fraudulent activity. As an example of the technique, suppose that a company with a market value of $100 million suffers an abnormal return of –6% on the day that news of a fraudulent activity surfaces. One might then infer that the damages sustained from the fraud were $6 million, because the value of the firm (after adjusting for general market movements) fell by 6% of $100 million when investors became aware of the news and reassessed the value of the stock.

Concept
CHECK

Question 4 • Suppose that we see negative abnormal returns (declining CARs) after an announcement date. Is this a violation of efficient markets?

12.4   ARE MARKETS EFFICIENT?

The Issues

Not surprisingly, the efficient market hypothesis does not exactly arouse enthusiasm in the community of professional portfolio managers. It implies that a great deal of the activity of portfolio managers—the search for undervalued securities—is at best wasted effort, and quite probably harmful to clients because it costs money and leads to imperfectly diversi-

---

[6]For a review of SEC applications of this technique, see Mark Mitchell and Jeffry Netter, "The Role of Financial Economics in Securities Fraud Cases: Applications at the Securities and Exchange Commission," School of Business Administration, The University of Michigan, working paper No. 93-25, October 1993.

fied portfolios. Consequently, the EMH has never been widely accepted on Wall Street, and debate continues today on the degree to which security analysis can improve investment performance. Before discussing empirical tests of the hypothesis, we want to note three factors that together imply that the debate probably never will be settled: the *magnitude issue*, the *selection bias issue*, and the *lucky event issue*.

The Magnitude Issue   We have noted that an investment manager overseeing a $5 billion portfolio who can improve performance by only .001% per year will increase investment earnings by .001 $\times$ $5 billion = $5 million annually. This manager clearly would be worth her salary! Yet can we, as observers, statistically measure her contribution? Probably not: a .001% contribution would be swamped by the yearly volatility of the market. Remember, the annual standard deviation of the well-diversified S&P 500 index has been more than 20% per year. Against these fluctuations a small increase in performance would be hard to detect. Nevertheless, $5 million remains an extremely valuable improvement in performance.

All might agree that stock prices are very close to fair values, and that only managers of large portfolios can earn enough trading profits to make the exploitation of minor mispricing worth the effort. According to this view, the actions of intelligent investment managers are the driving force behind the constant evolution of market prices to fair levels. Rather than ask the qualitative question "Are markets efficient?" we ought instead to ask a more quantitative question: "How efficient are markets?"

The Selection Bias Issue   Suppose that you discover an investment scheme that could really make money. You have two choices: either publish your technique in *The Wall Street Journal* to win fleeting fame, or keep your technique secret and use it to earn millions of dollars. Most investors would choose the latter option, which presents us with a conundrum. Only investors who find that an investment scheme cannot generate abnormal returns will be willing to report their findings to the whole world. Hence opponents of the efficient markets view of the world always can use evidence that various techniques do not provide investment rewards as proof that the techniques that do work simply are not being reported to the public. This is a problem in *selection bias;* the outcomes we are able to observe have been preselected in favor of failed attempts. Therefore, we cannot fairly evaluate the true ability of portfolio managers to generate winning stock market strategies.

The Lucky Event Issue   In virtually any month it seems we read an article about some investor or investment company with a fantastic investment performance over the recent past. Surely the superior records of such investors disprove the efficient market hypothesis.

Yet this conclusion is far from obvious. As an analogy to the investment game, consider a contest to flip the most number of heads out of 50 trials using a fair coin. The expected outcome for any person is, of course, 50% heads and 50% tails. If 10,000 people, however, compete in this contest, it would not be surprising if at least one or two contestants flipped more than 75% heads. In fact, elementary statistics tells us that the expected number of contestants flipping 75% or more heads would be two. It would be silly, though, to crown these people the "head-flipping champions of the world." Obviously, they are simply the contestants who happened to get lucky on the day of the event. (See the nearby box.)

The analogy to efficient markets is clear. Under the hypothesis that any stock is fairly priced given all available information, any bet on a stock is simply a coin toss. There is equal likelihood of winning or losing the bet. However, if many investors using a variety of schemes make fair bets, statistically speaking, *some* of those investors will be lucky and win a great majority of the bets. For every big winner, there may be many big losers, but we

HOW TO GUARANTEE A SUCCESSFUL MARKET NEWSLETTER

Suppose you want to make your fortune publishing a market newsletter. You need first to convince potential subscribers that you have talent worth paying for. But what if you have no talent? The solution is simple: start eight newsletters.

In year 1, let four of your newsletters predict an up-market and four a down-market. In year 2, let half of the originally optimistic group of newsletters continue to predict an up-market and the other half a down-market. Do the same for the originally pessimistic group. Continue in this manner to obtain the pattern of predictions in the table that follows (U = prediction of an up-market, D = prediction of a down-market).

After three years, no matter what has happened to the market, one of the newsletters would have had a perfect prediction record. This is because after three years there are 2^3 = 8 outcomes for the market, and we have covered all eight possibilities with the eight newsletters. Now, we simply slough off the seven unsuccessful newsletters, and market the eighth newsletter based on its perfect track record. If we want to establish a newsletter with a perfect track record over a four-year period, we need 2^4 = 16 newsletters. A five-year period requires 32 newsletters, and so on.

After the fact, the one newsletter that was always right will attract attention for your uncanny foresight and investors will rush to pay large fees for its advice. Your fortune is made, and you have never even researched the market!

WARNING: This scheme is illegal! The point, however, is that with hundreds of market newsletters, you can find one that has stumbled onto an apparently remarkable string of successful predictions without any real degree of skill. After the fact, *someone's* prediction history can seem to imply great forecasting skill. This person is the one we will read about in *The Wall Street Journal*; the others will be forgotten.

	Newsletter Predictions							
Year	**1**	**2**	**3**	**4**	**5**	**6**	**7**	**8**
1	U	U	U	U	D	D	D	D
2	U	U	D	D	U	U	D	D
3	U	D	U	D	U	D	U	D

---

never hear of these managers. The winners, though, turn up in *The Wall Street Journal* as the latest stock market gurus; then they can make a fortune publishing market newsletters.

Our point is that after the fact there will have been at least one successful investment scheme. A doubter will call the results luck, the successful investor will call it skill. The proper test would be to see whether the successful investors can repeat their performance in another period, yet this approach is rarely taken.

With these caveats in mind, we turn now to some of the empirical tests of the efficient market hypothesis.

Concept CHECK **Question 5 • Fidelity's Magellan Fund outperformed the S&P 500 in 11 of the 13 years that Peter Lynch managed the fund, resulting in an average annual return more than 10% better than that of the index. Is Lynch's performance sufficient to dissuade you from a belief in efficient markets? If not, would *any* performance record be sufficient to dissuade you?**

Tests of Predictability in Stock Market Returns

Returns over Short Horizons Early tests of efficient market were tests of the weak form. Could speculators find trends in past prices that would enable them to earn abnormal profits? This is essentially a test of the efficacy of technical analysis. The already cited work of Kendall and of Roberts,[7] both of whom analyzed the possible existence of patterns in stock prices, suggests that such patterns are not to be found.

---

[7]Harry Roberts, "Stock Market 'Patterns' and Financial Analysis: Methodological Suggestions," *Journal of Finance* 14 (March 1959).

One way of discerning trends in stock prices is by measuring the *serial correlation* of stock market returns. Serial correlation refers to the tendency for stock returns to be related to past returns. Positive serial correlation means that positive returns tend to follow positive returns (a momentum type of property). Negative serial correlation means that positive returns tend to be followed by negative returns (a reversal or "correction" property). Both Conrad and Kaul[8] and Lo and MacKinlay[9] examine weekly returns of NYSE stocks and find positive serial correlation over short horizons. However, the correlation coefficients of weekly returns tend to be fairly small, at least for large stocks for which price data are the most reliably up-to-date. Thus, while these studies demonstrate weak price trends over short periods, the evidence does not clearly suggest the existence of trading opportunities.

A more sophisticated version of trend analysis is a **filter rule**. A filter technique gives a rule for buying or selling a stock depending on past price movements. One rule, for example, might be: "Buy if the last two trades each resulted in a stock price increase." A more conventional one might be: "Buy a security if its price increased by 1%, and hold it until its price falls by more than 1% from the subsequent high." Alexander[10] and Fama and Blume[11] found that such filter rules generally could not generate trading profits.

These very-short-horizon studies suggest momentum in stock market prices, albeit of a magnitude that may be too small to exploit. However, in an investigation of intermediate-horizon stock price behavior (using 3- to 12-month holding periods), Jegadeesh and Titman[12] found that stocks exhibit a momentum property in which good or bad recent performance continues. They conclude that while the performance of individual stocks is highly unpredictable, *portfolios* of the best-performing stocks in the recent past appear to outperform other stocks with enough reliability to offer profit opportunities.

Returns over Long Horizons Although studies of short-horizon returns have detected modest positive serial correlation in stock market prices, tests[13] of long-horizon returns (i.e., returns over multiyear periods) have found suggestions of pronounced negative long-term serial correlation. The latter result has given rise to a "fads hypothesis," which asserts that stock prices might overreact to relevant news. Such overreaction leads to positive serial correlation (momentum) over short time horizons. Subsequent correction of the overreaction leads to poor performance following good performance and vice versa. The corrections mean that a run of positive returns eventually will tend to be followed by negative returns, leading to negative serial correlation over longer horizons. These episodes of apparent overshooting followed by correction give stock prices the appearance of fluctuating around their fair values.

These long-horizon results are dramatic, but the studies offer far from conclusive evidence regarding efficient markets. First, the study results need not be interpreted as

[8]Jennifer Conrad and Gautam Kaul, "Time-Variation in Expected Returns," *Journal of Business* 61 (October 1988), pp. 409–25.

[9]Andrew W. Lo and A. Craig MacKinlay, "Stock Market Prices Do Not Follow Random Walks: Evidence from a Simple Specification Test," *Review of Financial Studies* 1 (1988), pp. 41–66.

[10]Sidney Alexander, "Price Movements in Speculative Markets: Trends or Random Walks, No. 2," in Paul Cootner, ed., *The Random Character of Stock Market Prices* (Cambridge, Mass.: MIT Press, 1964).

[11]Eugene Fama and Marshall Blume, "Filter Rules and Stock Market Trading Profits," *Journal of Business* 39 (Supplement January 1966).

[12]Narasimhan Jegadeesh and Sheridan Titman, "Returns to Buying Winners and Selling Losers: Implications for Stock Market Efficiency," *Journal of Finance* 48 (March 1993), pp. 65–91.

[13]Eugene F. Fama and Kenneth R. French, "Permanent and Temporary Components of Stock Prices," *Journal of Political Economy* 96 (April 1988), pp. 24–73; James Poterba and Lawrence Summers, "Mean Reversion in Stock Prices: Evidence and Implications," *Journal of Financial Economics* 22 (October 1988), pp. 27–59.

evidence for stock market fads. An alternative interpretation of these results holds that they indicate only that market risk premiums vary over time. The response of market prices to variation in the risk premium can lead one to incorrectly infer the presence of mean reversion and excess volatility in prices. For example, when the risk premium and the required return on the market rises, stock prices will fall. When the market then rises (on average) at this higher rate of return, the data convey the impression of a stock price recovery. The impression of overshooting and correction is in fact no more than a rational response of market prices to changes in discount rates.

Second, these studies suffer from statistical problems. Because they rely on returns measured over long time periods, these tests of necessity are based on few observations of long-horizon returns. Moreover, it appears that much of the statistical support for mean reversion in stock market prices derives from returns during the Great Depression. Other periods do not provide strong support for the fads hypothesis.[14]

Predictors of Broad Market Returns   Several studies have documented the ability of easily observed variables to predict market returns. For example, Fama and French[15] showed that the return on the aggregate stock market tends to be higher when the dividend/price ratio, the dividend yield, is high. Campbell and Shiller[16] found that the earnings yield can predict market returns. Keim and Stambaugh[17] showed that bond market data such as the spread between yields on high- and low-grade corporate bonds also help predict broad market returns.

Again, the interpretation of these results is difficult. On the one hand, they may imply that stock returns can be predicted, in violation of the efficient market hypothesis. More probably, however, these variables are proxying for variation in the market risk premium. For example, given a level of dividends or earnings, stock prices will be lower and dividend and earnings yields will be higher when the risk premium (and therefore the expected market return) is higher. Thus a high dividend or earnings yield will be associated with higher market returns. This does not indicate a violation of market efficiency. The predictability of market returns is due to predictability in the risk premium, not in risk-adjusted abnormal returns.

Fama and French[18] showed that the yield spread between high- and low-grade bonds has greater predictive power for returns on low-grade bonds than for returns on high-grade bonds, and greater predictive power for stock returns than for bond returns, suggesting that the predictability in returns is in fact a risk premium rather than evidence of market inefficiency. Similarly, the fact that the dividend yield on stocks helps to predict bond market returns suggests that the yield captures a risk premium common to both markets rather than mispricing in the equity market.

Portfolio Strategies and Market Anomalies

Fundamental analysis calls on a much wider range of information to create portfolios than does technical analysis, and tests of the value of fundamental analysis are thus correspond-

[14]Myung J. Kim, Charles R. Nelson, and Richard Startz, "Mean Reversion in Stock Prices? A Reappraisal of the Empirical Evidence," National Bureau of Economic Research Working Paper No. 2795, December 1988.

[15]Eugene F. Fama and Kenneth R. French, "Dividend Yields and Expected Stock Returns," *Journal of Financial Economics* 22 (October 1988), pp. 3–25.

[16]John Y. Campbell and Robert Shiller, "Stock Prices, Earnings and Expected Dividends," *Journal of Finance* 43 (July 1988), pp. 661–76.

[17]Donald B. Keim and Robert F. Stambaugh, "Predicting Returns in the Stock and Bond Markets," *Journal of Financial Economics* 17 (1986), pp. 357–90.

[18]Eugene F. Fama and Kenneth R. French, "Business Conditions and Expected Returns on Stocks and Bonds," *Journal of Financial Economics* 25 (November 1989), pp. 3–22.

ingly more difficult to evaluate. They have, however, revealed a number of so-called anomalies, that is, evidence that seems inconsistent with the efficient market hypothesis. We will review several such anomalies in the following pages.

We must note before starting that one major problem with these tests is that most require risk adjustments to portfolio performance and most tests use the CAPM to make the risk adjustments. Although beta seems to be a relevant descriptor of stock risk, the empirically measured quantitative trade-off between risk as measured by beta and expected return differs from the predictions of the CAPM. (We review this evidence in the next chapter.) If we use the CAPM to adjust portfolio returns for risk, inappropriate adjustments may lead to the conclusion that various portfolio strategies can generate superior returns, when in fact it simply is the risk adjustment procedure that has failed.

Another way to put this is to note that tests of risk-adjusted returns are *joint tests* of the efficient market hypothesis *and* the risk adjustment procedure. If it appears that a portfolio strategy can generate superior returns, we must then choose between rejecting the EMH and rejecting the risk adjustment technique. Usually, the risk adjustment technique is based on more questionable assumptions than is the EMH; by opting to reject the procedure, we are left with no conclusion about market efficiency.

An example of this issue is the discovery by Basu[19] that portfolios of low price/earnings ratio stocks have higher returns than do high P/E portfolios. The **P/E effect** holds up even if returns are adjusted for portfolio beta. Is this a confirmation that the market systematically misprices stocks according to P/E ratio? This would be an extremely surprising and, to us, disturbing conclusion, because analysis of P/E ratios is such a simple procedure. Although it may be possible to earn superior returns using hard work and much insight, it hardly seems possible that such a simplistic technique is enough to generate abnormal returns. One possible interpretation of these results is that the model of capital market equilibrium is at fault in that the returns are not properly adjusted for risk.

This makes sense, because if two firms have the same expected earnings, then the riskier stock will sell at a lower price and lower P/E ratio. Because of its higher risk, the low P/E stock also will have higher expected returns. Therefore, unless the CAPM beta fully adjusts for risk, P/E will act as a useful additional descriptor of risk, and will be associated with abnormal returns if the CAPM is used to establish benchmark performance.

The Small-Firm-in-January Effect   One of the most important anomalies with respect to the efficient market hypothesis is the so-called size or **small-firm effect**, originally documented by Banz.[20] Banz found that both total and risk-adjusted rates of return tend to fall with increases in the relative size of the firm, as measured by the market value of the firm's outstanding equity. Dividing all NYSE stocks into five quintiles according to firm size, Banz found that the average annual return of firms in the smallest-size quintile was 19.8% greater than the average return of firms in the largest-size quintile.

This is a huge premium; imagine earning a premium of this size on a billion-dollar portfolio. Yet it is remarkable that following a simple (even simplistic) rule such as "invest in low-capitalization stocks" should enable an investor to earn excess returns. After all, any investor can measure firm size at little cost. One would not expect such minimal effort to yield such large rewards.

---

[19]Sanjoy Basu, "The Investment Performance of Common Stocks in Relation to Their Price-Earnings Ratios: A Test of the Efficient Market Hypothesis," *Journal of Finance* 32 (June 1977), pp. 663–82; and "The Relationship between Earnings Yield, Market Value, and Return for NYSE Common Stocks: Further Evidence," *Journal of Financial Economics* 12 (June 1983).

[20]Rolf Banz, "The Relationship between Return and Market Value of Common Stocks," *Journal of Financial Economics* 9 (March 1981).

Figure 12.7
Average difference
between daily
excess returns (in
percentages) of lowest-
firm-size and highest-
firm-size deciles for
each month between
1963 and 1979.

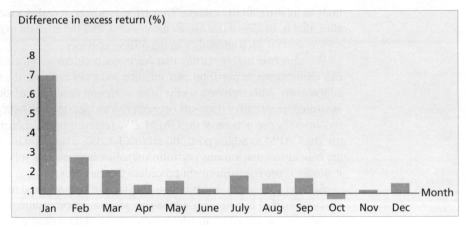

Source: Data from Donald B. Keim, "Size Related Anomalies and Stock Return Seasonality: Further Empirical Evidence," *Journal of Financial Economics* 12 (June 1983).

Later studies (Keim,[21] Reinganum,[22] and Blume and Stambaugh[23]) showed that the small-firm effect occurs virtually entirely in January, in fact, in the first two weeks of January. The size effect is in fact a "small-firm-in-January" effect.

Figure 12.7 illustrates the January effect. Keim ranked firms in order of increasing size as measured by market value of equity and then divided them into 10 portfolios grouped by the size of each firm. In each month of the year, he calculated the difference in the average excess return of firms in the smallest-firm portfolio and largest-firm portfolio. The average monthly differences over the years 1963 to 1979 appear in Figure 12.7. January clearly stands out as an exceptional month for small firms, with an average small-firm premium of .714% *per day*. The results for the first five trading days in January are even more compelling, amounting to an amazing 8.16% over only five trading days.

Some researchers believe that the January effect is tied to tax-loss selling at the end of the year. The hypothesis is that many people sell stocks that have declined in price during the previous months to realize their capital losses before the end of the tax year. Such investors do not put the proceeds from these sales back into the stock market until after the turn of the year. At that point the rush of demand for stock places an upward pressure on prices that results in the January effect. Indeed, Ritter[24] showed that the ratio of stock purchases to sales of individual investors reaches an annual low at the end of December and an annual high at the beginning of January.

The January effect is said to show up most dramatically for the smallest firms because the small-firm group includes, as an empirical matter, stocks with the greatest variability of prices during the year. The group therefore includes a relatively large number of firms that have declined sufficiently to induce tax-loss selling.

From a theoretical standpoint, this theory has substantial flaws. First, if the positive January effect is a manifestation of buying pressure, it should be matched by a symmetric

---

[21]Donald B. Keim, "Size Related Anomalies and Stock Return Seasonality: Further Empirical Evidence," *Journal of Financial Economics* 12 (June 1983).

[22]Marc R. Reinganum, "The Anomalous Stock Market Behavior of Small Firms in January: Empirical Tests for Tax-Loss Effects," *Journal of Financial Economics* 12 (June 1983).

[23]Marshall E. Blume and Robert F. Stambaugh, "Biases in Computed Returns: An Application to the Size Effect," *Journal of Financial Economics*, 1983.

[24]Jay R. Ritter, "The Buying and Selling Behavior of Individual Investors at the Turn of the Year," *Journal of Finance* 43 (July 1988), pp. 701–17.

Figure 12.8

Average daily returns in January for securities in the upper quartile and bottom quartile of the tax-loss selling distribution by market value of portfolio.

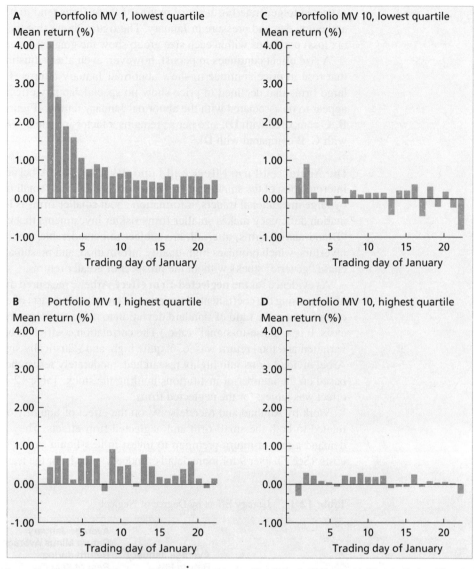

negative December effect when the tax-loss incentives induce selling pressure. Second, the predictable January effect flies in the face of efficient market theory. If investors who do not already hold these firms know that January will bring abnormal returns to the small-firm group, they should rush to purchase stock in December to capture those returns. This would push buying pressure from January to December. Rational investors should not "allow" such predictable abnormal January returns to persist. However, small firms outperform large ones in January in every year of Keim's study, 1963 to 1979.

Despite these theoretical objections, some empirical evidence supports the belief that the January effect is connected to tax-loss selling. For example, Reinganum found that, within size class, firms that had declined more severely in price had larger January returns. This pattern is illustrated in Figure 12.8. Reinganum divided firms into quartiles based on the extent to which stock prices had declined during the year. Big price declines would be expected to generate big January returns if these firms tend to be unloaded in December and enjoy demand pressure in January. The figure shows that the lowest quartile (biggest tax loss) portfolios within each size group show the greatest January effect.

A size effect continues to persist, however, even after adjusting for taxes. Small firms that rose in price continue to show abnormal January returns (Figure 12.8, **B**), whereas large firms that declined in price show no special January effect. Hence, although taxes appear to be associated with the abnormal January returns (Figure 12.8, **A** compared with **B**, **C** compared with **D**), size per se remains a factor in January (Figure 12.8, **A** compared with **C**, **B** compared with **D**).

The Neglected-Firm Effect and Liquidity Effects   Arbel and Strebel[25] gave another interpretation of the small-firm-in-January effect. Because small firms tend to be neglected by large institutional traders, information about smaller firms is less available. This information deficiency makes smaller firms riskier investments that command higher returns. "Brand-name" firms, after all, are subject to considerable monitoring from institutional investors, which promises high-quality information, and presumably investors do not purchase "generic" stocks without the prospect of greater returns.

As evidence for the **neglected-firm effect**, Arbel[26] measured the information deficiency of firms using the coefficient of variation of analysts' forecasts of earnings. (The coefficient of variation is the ratio of standard deviation to mean and measures the dispersion of forecasts. It is a "noise-to-signal" ratio.) The correlation coefficient between the coefficient of variation and total return was .676, quite high, and statistically significant. In a related test Arbel divided firms into highly researched, moderately researched, and neglected groups based on the number of institutions holding the stock. Table 12.1 shows that the January effect was largest for the neglected firms.

Work by Amihud and Mendelson[27] on the effect of liquidity on stock returns might be related to both the small-firm and neglected-firm effects. They argue that investors will demand a rate-of-return premium to invest in less-liquid stocks that entail higher trading costs. (See Chapter 9 for more details.) Indeed, spreads for the least-liquid stocks easily can

Table 12.1   January Effect by Degree of Neglect

	Average January Return (%)	Average January Return Minus Average Return during Rest of Year (%)	Average January Return after Adjusting for Systematic Risk (%)
S&P 500 companies			
Highly researched	2.48	1.63	−1.44
Moderately researched	4.95	4.19	1.69
Neglected	7.62	6.87	5.03
Non–S&P 500 companies			
Neglected	11.32	10.72	7.71

Source: Avner Arbel, "Generic Stocks: An Old Product in a New Package," *Journal of Portfolio Management,* Summer 1985.

[25] Avner Arbel and Paul J. Strebel, "Pay Attention to Neglected Firms," *Journal of Portfolio Management,* Winter 1983.
[26] Avner Arbel, "Generic Stocks: An Old Product in a New Package," *Journal of Portfolio Management,* Summer 1985.
[27] Yakov Amihud and Haim Mendelson, "Asset Pricing and the Bid–Ask Spread," *Journal of Financial Economics* 17 (December 1986), pp. 223–50; and "Liquidity, Asset Prices, and Financial Policy," *Financial Analysts Journal* 47 (November/December 1991), pp. 56–66.

be more than 5% of stock value. In accord with their hypothesis, Amihud and Mendelson showed that these stocks show a strong tendency to exhibit abnormally high risk-adjusted rates of return. Because small and less-analyzed stocks as a rule are less liquid, the liquidity effect might be a partial explanation of their abnormal returns. However, this theory does not explain why the abnormal returns of small firms should be concentrated in January. In any case, exploiting these effects can be more difficult than it would appear. The high trading costs on small stocks can easily wipe out any apparent abnormal profit opportunity.

Book-to-Market Ratios Fama and French and Reinganum[28] showed that a powerful predictor of returns across securities is the ratio of the book value of the firm's equity to the market value of equity. Fama and French stratified firms into 10 groups according to book-to-market ratios and examined the average monthly rate of return of each of the 10 groups during the period July 1963 through December 1990. The decile with the highest book-to-market ratio had an average monthly return of 1.65%, while the lowest-ratio decile averaged only .72% per month. Figure 12.9 shows the pattern of returns across deciles. The dramatic dependence of returns on book-to-market ratio is independent of beta, suggesting either that high book-to-market ratio firms are relatively underpriced, or that the book-to-market ratio is serving as a proxy for a risk factor that affects equilibrium expected returns.

In fact, Fama and French found that after controlling for the size and **book-to-market effects**, beta seemed to have no power to explain average security returns.[29] This finding is an important challenge to the notion of rational markets, since it seems to imply that a factor that should affect returns—systematic risk—seems not to matter, while a factor that should not matter—the book-to-market ratio—seems capable of predicting future returns. We will return to the interpretation of this anomaly.

Figure 12.9

Average rate of return as a function of the book to market ratio.

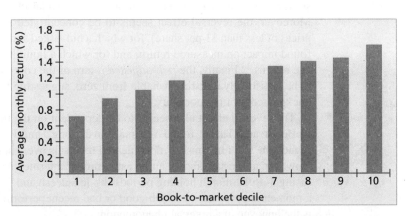

Source: Eugene F. Fama and Kenneth R. French, "The Cross Section of Expected Stock Returns," *Journal of Finance* 47 (1992), pp. 427–65.

---

[28]Eugene F. Fama and Kenneth R. French, "The Cross Section of Expected Stock Returns," *Journal of Finance* 47 (1992), pp. 427–65; Marc R. Reinganum, "The Anatomy of a Stock Market Winner," *Financial Analysts Journal*, March–April 1988, pp. 272–84.

[29]However, a study by S. P. Kothari, Jay Shanken, and Richard G. Sloan, "Another Look at the Cross-Section of Expected Stock Returns," *Journal of Finance* 50 (March 1995), pp. 185–224, finds that when betas are estimated using annual rather than monthly returns, securities with high beta values do in fact have higher average returns. Moreover, the authors find a book-to-market effect that is attenuated compared to the results in Fama and French and furthermore is inconsistent across different samples of securities. They conclude that the empirical case for the importance of the book-to-market ratio may be somewhat weaker than the Fama and French study would suggest.

Reversals   While some of the studies cited earlier suggest momentum in stock market prices over horizons of less than one year, many other studies suggest that over longer horizons, extreme stock market performance tends to reverse itself: The stocks that have performed best in the recent past seem to underperform the rest of the market in following periods, while the worst past performers tend to offer above-average future performance. DeBondt and Thaler[30] and Chopra, Lakonishok, and Ritter[31] find strong tendencies for poorly performing stocks in one period to experience sizable reversals over the subsequent period, while the best-performing stocks in a given period tend to follow with poor performance in the following period.

For example, the DeBondt and Thaler study found that if one were to rank order the performance of stocks over a five-year period and then group stocks into portfolios based on investment performance, the base-period "loser" portfolio (defined as the 35 stocks with the worst investment performance) outperformed the "winner" portfolio (the top 35 stocks) by an average of 25% (cumulative return) in the following three-year period. This **reversal effect**, in which losers rebound and winners fade back, suggests that the stock market overreacts to relevant news. After the overreaction is recognized, extreme investment performance is reversed. This phenomenon would imply that a *contrarian* investment strategy—investing in recent losers and avoiding recent winners—should be profitable.

It would be hard to explain apparent overreaction in the cross section of stocks by appealing to time-varying risk premiums. Moreover, these returns seem pronounced enough to be exploited profitably.

However, a study by Ball, Kothari, and Shanken[32] suggests that the reversal effect may be an illusion. They showed that if portfolios are formed by grouping based on past performance periods ending in mid-year rather than in December (a variation in grouping strategy that ought to be unimportant), the reversal effect is substantially diminished. Moreover, the reversal effect seems to be concentrated in very low-priced stocks (e.g., prices of less than $1 per share), for which a bid–asked spread of even $1/8 can have a profound impact on measured return, and for which a liquidity effect may explain high average returns.[33] Finally, the *risk-adjusted* return of the contrarian strategy actually turns out to be statistically indistinguishable from zero, suggesting that the reversal effect is not an unexploited profit opportunity.

The reversal effect also seems to be dependent on the time horizon of the investment. DeBondt and Thaler found reversals over long (multiyear) horizons, and studies by Jegadeesh[34] and Lehmann[35] documented reversals over short horizons of a month or less. However, as we saw above, an investigation of intermediate-horizon stock price behavior (using 3- to 12-month holding periods) by Jegadeesh and Titman found that stocks exhibit a momentum property in which good or bad recent performance continues. This of course is the opposite of a reversal phenomenon.

---

[30]Werner F. M. DeBondt and Richard Thaler, "Does the Stock Market Overreact?" *Journal of Finance* 40 (1985), pp. 793–805.

[31]Navin Chopra, Josef Lakonishok, and Jay R. Ritter, "Measuring Abnormal Performance: Do Stocks Overreact?" *Journal of Financial Economics* 31 (1992), pp. 235–68.

[32]Ray Ball, S. P. Kothari, and Jan Shanken, "Problems in Measuring Portfolio Performance: An Application in Contrarian Investment Strategies," *Journal of Financial Economics* 37 (1995).

[33]This may explain why the choice of year-end versus mid-year grouping has such a significant impact on the results. Other studies have shown that close-of-year prices on the loser stocks are more likely to be quoted at the bid price. As a result, their initial prices are on average understated, and performance in the follow-up period is correspondingly overstated.

[34]Narasimhan Jegadeesh, "Evidence of Predictable Behavior of Security Returns," *Journal of Finance* 45 (September 1990), pp. 881–98.

[35]Bruce Lehmann, "Fads, Martingales and Market Efficiency," *Quarterly Journal of Economics* 105 (February 1990), pp. 1–28.

Thus it appears that there may be short-run momentum but long-run reversal patterns in price behavior. One interpretation of this pattern is that short-run overreaction (which causes momentum in prices) may lead to long-term reversals (when the market recognizes its past error). This interpretation is emphasized by Haugen.[36]

Risk Premiums or Anomalies?

The small-firm, market-to-book, and long-term reversal effects are currently among the most puzzling phenomena in empirical finance. There are several interpretations of these effects. First note that to some extent, these three phenomena may be related. The feature that small firms, low-market-to-book firms, and recent "losers" seem to have in common is a stock price that has fallen considerably in recent months or years. Indeed, a firm can become a small firm or a low-market-to-book firm by suffering a sharp drop in price. These groups therefore may contain a relatively high proportion of distressed firms that have suffered recent difficulties.

Fama and French[37] argue that these effects can be explained as manifestations of risk premiums. Using an arbitrage pricing type of model they show that stocks with higher "betas" (also known as factor loadings) on size or market-to-book factors have higher average returns; they interpret these returns as evidence of a risk premium associated with the factor. Fama and French propose a *three-factor model*, in the spirit of arbitrage pricing theory. Risk is determined by the sensitivity of a stock to three factors: (1) the market portfolio, (2) a portfolio that reflects the relative returns of small versus large firms, and (3) a portfolio that reflects the relative returns of firms with high versus low ratios of book value to market value. This model does a good job in explaining security returns. While size or book-to-market ratios per se are obviously not risk factors, they perhaps might act as proxies for more fundamental determinants of risk. Fama and French argue that these patterns of returns may therefore be consistent with an efficient market in which expected returns are consistent with risk. We examine this paper in more detail in the next chapter.

The opposite interpretation is offered by Lakonishok, Shleifer, and Vishney,[38] who argue that these phenomena are evidence of inefficient markets, more specifically, of systematic errors in the forecasts of stock analysts. They believe that analysts extrapolate past performance too far into the future, and therefore overprice firms with recent good performance and underprice firms with recent poor performance. Ultimately, when market participants recognize their errors, prices reverse. This explanation is consistent with the reversal effect and also, to a degree, consistent with the small-firm and book-to-market effects because firms with sharp price drops may tend to be small or have high book-to-market ratios.

If Lakonishok, Shleifer, and Vishney are correct, we ought to find that analysts systematically err when forecasting returns of recent "winner" versus "loser" firms. A recent study by La Porta[39] is consistent with this pattern. He finds that equity of firms for which analysts predict low growth rates of earnings actually perform better than those with high expected earnings growth. Analysts seem overly pessimistic about firms with low growth prospects and overly optimistic about firms with high growth prospects. When these too-extreme

---

[36]Robert A. Haugen, *The New Finance: The Case against Efficient Markets* (Englewood Cliffs, N.J.: Prentice Hall, 1995).

[37]Eugene F. Fama and Kenneth R. French, "Common Risk Factors in the Returns on Stocks and Bonds," *Journal of Financial Economics* 33 (1993), pp. 3–56.

[38]Josef Lakonishok, Andrei Shleifer, and Robert W. Vishney, "Contrarian Investment, Extrapolation, and Risk," *Journal of Finance* 50 (1995), pp. 541–78.

[39]Raphael La Porta, "Expectations and the Cross Section of Stock Returns," *Journal of Finance* 51 (December 1996), pp. 1715–42.

expectations are "corrected," the low-expected-growth firms outperform high-expected-growth firms.

Daniel and Titman[40] attempt to test whether the size and book-to-market effects can in fact be explained as risk premia. They first classify firms according to size and book-to-market ratio, and then further stratify portfolios based on the betas of each stock on size and book-to-market factors. They find that once size and book-to-market ratio are held fixed, the betas on these factors do not add any additional information about expected returns. They conclude that the characteristics per se, and not the betas on the size or book-to-market factors influence returns. This result is inconsistent with the Fama-French interpretation that the high returns on these portfolios may reflect risk premia.

The Daniel and Titman results do not *necessarily* imply irrational markets. As noted, it might be that these characteristics per se measure a distressed condition that itself commands a return premium. Moreover, as we have noted, a good part of these apparently abnormal returns may be reflective of an illiquidity premium since small and low-priced firms tend to have bigger bid–asked spreads. Nevertheless, a compelling explanation of these results has yet to be offered.

Inside Information   It would not be surprising if insiders were able to make superior profits trading in their firm's stock. The ability of insiders to trade profitably in their own stock has been documented in studies by Jaffe,[41] Seyhun,[42] Givoly and Palmon,[43] and others. Jaffe's was one of the earlier studies that documented the tendency for stock prices to rise after insiders intensively bought shares and to fall after intensive insider sales.

Can other investors benefit by following insiders' trades? The Securities and Exchange Commission requires all insiders to register their trading activity. The SEC publishes these trades in an *Official Summary of Insider Trading*. Once the *Official Summary* is published, the knowledge of the trades becomes public information. At that point, if markets are efficient, fully and immediately processing the information released in the *Official Summary* of trading, an investor should no longer be able to profit from following the pattern of those trades.

The study by Seyhun, which carefully tracked the public release dates of the *Official Summary*, found that following insider transactions would be to no avail. Although there is some tendency for stock prices to increase even after the *Official Summary* reports insider buying, the abnormal returns are not of sufficient magnitude to overcome transaction costs.

Post–Earnings-Announcement Price Drift   A fundamental principle of efficient markets is that any new information ought to be reflected in stock prices very rapidly. When good news is made public, for example, the stock price should jump immediately. A puzzling anomaly, therefore, is the apparently sluggish response of stock prices to firms' earnings announcements.

The "news content" of an earnings announcement can be evaluated by comparing the announcement of actual earnings to the value previously expected by market participants. The difference is the "earnings surprise." (Market expectations of earnings can be roughly

---

[40]Kent Daniel and Sheridan Titman, "Evidence of the Characteristics of Cross Sectional Variation in Common Stock Returns," *Journal of Finance* 40 (1995), pp. 383–99.

[41]Jeffrey F. Jaffe, "Special Information and Insider Trading," *Journal of Business* 47 (July 1974).

[42]H. Nejat Seyhun, "Insiders' Profits, Costs of Trading and Market Efficiency," *Journal of Financial Economics* 16 (1986).

[43]Dan Givoly and Dan Palmon, "Insider Trading and Exploitation of Inside Information: Some Empirical Evidence," *Journal of Business* 58 (1985).

Figure 12.10

Cumulative abnormal returns in response to earnings announcements.

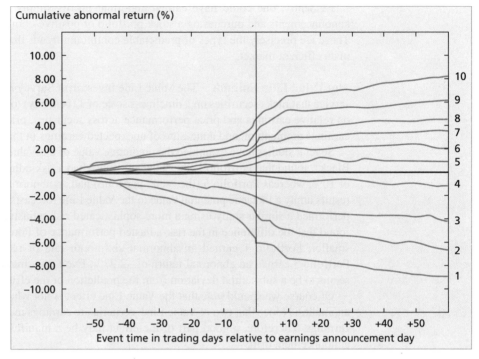

Source: George Foster, Chris Olsen, and Terry Shevlin, "Earnings Releases, Anomalies, and the Behavior of Security Returns," *Accounting Review* 59 (October 1984).

measured by averaging the published earnings forecasts of Wall Street analysts or by applying trend analysis to past earnings.) Foster, Olsen, and Shevlin[44] have examined the impact of earnings announcements on stock returns.

Each earnings announcement for a large sample of firms was placed in 1 of 10 deciles ranked by the magnitude of the earnings surprise, and the abnormal returns of the stock in each decile were calculated. The abnormal return in a period is the return of a portfolio of all stocks in a given decile after adjusting for both the market return in that period and the portfolio beta. It measures return over and above what would be expected given market conditions in that period. Figure 12.10 is a graph of the cumulative abnormal returns for each decile.

The results of this study are dramatic. The correlation between ranking by earnings surprise and abnormal returns across deciles is as predicted. There is a large abnormal return (a large increase in cumulative abnormal return) on the earnings announcement day (time 0). The abnormal return is positive for positive-surprise firms and negative for negative-surprise firms.

The more remarkable, and interesting, result of the study concerns stock price movement *after* the announcement date. The cumulative abnormal returns of positive-surprise stocks continue to grow even after the earnings information becomes public, while the negative-surprise firms continue to suffer negative abnormal returns. The market appears to adjust to the earnings information only gradually, resulting in a sustained period of abnormal returns.

---

[44]George Foster, Chris Olsen, and Terry Shevlin, "Earnings Releases, Anomalies, and the Behavior of Securities Returns," *Accounting Review* 59 (October 1984).

Evidently, one could have earned abnormal profits simply by waiting for earnings announcements and purchasing a stock portfolio of positive-earnings-surprise companies. These are precisely the types of predictable continuing trends that ought to be impossible in an efficient market.

The Value Line Enigma   The Value Line Investment Survey is an investment advisory service that ranks securities on a timeliness scale of 1 (best buy) to 5 (sell). Ranks are based on relative earnings and price performance across securities, price momentum, quarterly earnings momentum, and a measure of unexpected earnings in the most recent quarter.

Several studies have examined the predictive value of the Value Line recommendations. Black[45] found that Portfolio 1 (the "buy" portfolio) had a risk-adjusted excess rate of return of 10%, whereas Portfolio 5 (the "sell" portfolio) had an abnormal return of –10%. These results imply a fantastic potential value to the Value Line forecasts. Copeland and Mayers[46] performed a similar study using a more sophisticated risk-adjustment technique, and they found that the difference in the risk-adjusted performance of Portfolios 1 and 5 was much smaller; Portfolio 1 earned an abnormal six-month rate of return of 1.52%, whereas Portfolio 5 earned an abnormal return of –2.97%. Even this smaller difference, however, seems to be a substantial deviation from the prediction of the efficient market hypothesis.

Of course we should note that the Value Line effect is not wholly independent of other anomalies. Notice that two of Value Line's criteria are earnings momentum and unexpected earnings. Therefore, a good part of the effect may be a manifestation of post–earnings-announcement drift.

Anomalies or Data Mining?   We have covered many of the so-called anomalies cited in the literature, but our list could go on and on. Some wonder whether these anomalies are really unexplained puzzles in financial markets, or whether they instead are an artifact of data mining. After all, if one reruns the computer database of past returns over and over and examines stock returns along enough dimensions, simple chance will cause some criteria to *appear* to predict returns. The nearby box presents a tongue-in-cheek view of the anomalies literature with a "fail-safe" formula for picking stocks based on past "patterns."

Still, even acknowledging the potential for data mining, a common thread seems to run through many of the anomalies we have considered, lending support to the notion that there is a real puzzle to explain. Value stocks—defined by low P/E ratio, high book-to-market ratio, or depressed prices relative to historic levels—seem to have provided higher average returns than "glamour" or growth stocks.

One way to address the problem of data mining is to find a data set that has not already been researched and see whether the relationship in question shows up in the new data. Such studies have revealed size, momentum, and book-to-market effects in other security markets around the world. While these phenomena may be a manifestation of a systematic risk premium, the precise nature of that risk is not fully understood.

The Market Crash of October 1987   The market crash of October 1987 seems to be a glaring counterexample to the efficient market hypothesis. If prices reflect market fundamentals, then defenders of the EMH must look for news on October 19 consistent with the

---

[45]Fischer Black, "Yes, Virginia, There Is Hope: Test of the Value Line Ranking System," Graduate School of Business, University of Chicago, 1971.

[46]Thomas E. Copeland and David Mayers, "The Value Line Enigma (1965–1978): A Case Study of Performance Evaluation Issues," *Journal of Financial Economics* 11 (November 1982).

"NEW" FAIL-SAFE FORMULA FOR STOCK-PICKING

Everyone on Wall Street wants to know how come big stocks are doing so well, and whether they will continue to do so, and whether small stocks haven't done better over time, or at least some of the time, and, meanwhile, have you heard of any good big stocks?

I would like to propose a powerful investment "tool," one that has been overlooked by most of the leading experts and other experts. Simply divide the market into two groups: companies that have their principal headquarters in the Eastern-Seaboard states or within 60 miles of the Gulf of Mexico or at least 24 floors above ground, and all of the others.

You may think this sounds arbitrary, but what if I told you that the eastern, near-Gulf, high-altitude group has typically trailed during the middle and later stages of economic recoveries and yet has outperformed for three straight years? I don't know why. I don't care. My money is on the Western, Bayou-distant, earth-hugging sector. The latter group has never underperformed for more than three years, save for the two times that it did.

I am loath to break the silence, because I know how Wall Street will react. Analysts will get on the case and the opportunity will disappear. In fact, I have it on the QT that a highly paid analyst, who previously discovered that small stocks that outperform in January are stinkers in May and on Tuesdays, is already at work on the thin-air, petroleum-washed, early-statehood effect.

You might think that some wise guy would argue that such distinctions are meaningless, that they have no relation to value, that it doesn't matter if you make your money east or west of the Appalachians any more than it does whether you make it in big stocks or small stocks. Indeed, the apparent significance of such records derives from a statistical conceit: To a man with software, any series of numbers produces apparent "patterns," and any division of past results according to type will result in "overperformance" for one group or another. (Stocks that begin with consonants or vowels? CEOs with sideburns or not?)

Only categories that say something about price and value are relevant to investing, and even there, no group measure will tell you whether any one stock is worth the price. Value doesn't discriminate according to group, religion or market cap. It flows from the future earnings and overall quality of *particular* companies, and is determined by the fundamentals and prospects of particular firms. But analyzing them takes work. It is easier to think about whether stocks are here or there, big or small, elevated or midcap, or not at all.

23% one-day decline in stock prices. Yet no events of such importance seem to have transpired on that date. The fantastic price swing is hard to reconcile with market fundamentals.

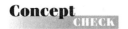

Concept Check

Question 6 • Some say that continued worry concerning the U.S. trade deficit brought down the market on October 19. Is this explanation consistent with EMH?

Mutual Fund Performance   We have documented some of the apparent chinks in the armor of efficient market proponents. Ultimately, however, the issue of market efficiency boils down to whether skilled investors can make consistent abnormal trading profits. The best test is simply to look at the performance of market professionals to see if their performance is superior to that of a passive index fund that buys and holds the market.

As we pointed out in Chapter 4, casual evidence does not support the claim that professionally managed portfolios can consistently beat the market. Figures 4.3 and 4.4 in that chapter demonstrated that between 1972 and 1995 the returns of a passive portfolio indexed to the Wilshire 5000 typically would have been better than those of the average equity fund. On the other hand, there was some (admittedly inconsistent) evidence (see Table 4.3) of persistence in performance, meaning that the better managers in one period tended to be better managers in following periods. Such a pattern would suggest that the better managers can with some consistency outperform their competitors, and it would be inconsistent with the notion that market prices already reflect all relevant information.

The analyses cited in Chapter 4 were based on total returns; they did not properly adjust returns for exposure to systematic risk factors. In this section we revisit the question of

Figure 12.11

Estimates of individual mutual fund alphas, 1972 to 1991.

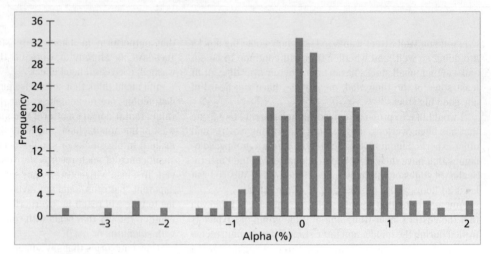

Note: The frequency distribution of estimated alphas for all equity mutual funds with 10-year continuous records.

Source: Burton G. Malkiel, "Returns from Investing in Equity Mutual Funds 1971–1991," *Journal of Finance* 50 (June 1995), pp. 549–72.

mutual fund performance, paying more attention to the benchmark against which performance ought to be evaluated.

As a first pass, we can examine the risk-adjusted returns (i.e., the alpha, or return in excess of required return based on beta and the market return in each period) of a large sample of mutual funds. Malkiel[47] computed these abnormal returns for a large sample of mutual funds between 1972 and 1991. His results, which appear in Figure 12.11, show that the distribution of alphas is roughly bell shaped, with a mean that is slightly negative but statistically indistinguishable from zero.

One problem in interpreting these alphas is that the S&P 500 may not be an adequate benchmark against which to evaluate mutual fund returns. Because mutual funds tend to maintain considerable holdings in equity of small firms, whereas the S&P 500 is exclusively comprised of large firms, mutual funds as a whole will tend to outperform the S&P when small firms outperform large ones and underperform when small firms fare worse. Thus a better benchmark for the performance of funds would be an index that incorporates the stock market performance of smaller firms.

The importance of the benchmark can be illustrated by examining the returns on small stocks in various subperiods.[48] In the 20-year period between 1945 and 1964, a small-stock index underperformed the S&P 500 by about 4% per year (i.e., the alpha of the small stock index after adjusting for systematic risk was –4%). In the more recent 20-year period between 1965 and 1984, small stocks outperformed the S&P index by 10%. Thus if one were to examine mutual fund returns in the earlier period, they would tend to look poor, not necessarily because small-fund managers were poor stock pickers, but simply because mutual funds as a group tend to hold more small stocks than are represented in the S&P 500. In the later period, funds would look better on a risk-adjusted basis relative to the S&P 500 because small funds performed better. The "style choice," that is, the exposure to small

---

[47]Burton G. Malkiel, "Returns from Investing in Equity Mutual Funds 1971–1991," *Journal of Finance* 50 (June 1995), pp. 549–72.

[48]This illustration and the statistics cited are based on E. J. Elton, M. J. Gruber, S. Das, and M. Hlavka, "Efficiency with Costly Information: A Reinterpretation of Evidence from Managed Portfolios," *Review of Financial Studies* 6 (1993), pp. 1–22, which is discussed shortly.

Table 12.2   Performance of Mutual Funds Based on Three-Index Model

Type of Fund (Wiesenberger Classification)	Number of Funds	Alpha	t-Statistic for Alpha
Equity funds			
Maximum capital gain	12	−4.59	−1.87
Growth	33	−1.55	−1.23
Growth and income	40	−0.68	−1.65
Balanced funds	31	−1.27	−2.73

Note: The three-index model calculates the alpha of each fund as the intercept of the following regression:

$$r - r_f = \alpha + \beta_M(r_M - r_f) + \beta_S(r_S - r_f) + \beta_D(r_D - r_f) + e$$

where r is the return on the fund, r_f is the risk-free rate, r_M is the return on the S&P 500 index, r_S is the return on a non–S&P small-stock index, r_D is the return on a bond index, e is the fund's residual return, and the betas measure the sensitivity of fund returns to the various indexes.

Source: E. J. Elton, M. J. Gruber, S. Das, and M. Hlavka, "Efficiency with Costly Information: A Reinterpretation of Evidence from Managed Portfolios," *Review of Financial Studies* 6 (1993), pp. 1–22.

stocks (which is an asset allocation decision) would dominate the evaluation of performance even though it has little to do with managers' stock-picking ability.[49]

Elton, Gruber, Das, and Hlavka attempted to control for the impact of non–S&P assets on mutual fund performance. They used a multifactor version of the index model of security returns (see equation 10.3) and calculated fund alphas using regressions that include as explanatory variables the excess returns of three benchmark portfolios rather than just one proxy for the market index. Their three factors are the excess return on the S&P 500 index, the excess return on an equity index of non–S&P low capitalization (i.e., small) firms, and the excess return on a bond market index. Some of their results are presented in Table 12.2, which shows that average alphas are negative for each type of equity fund, although generally not of statistically significant magnitude. They concluded that after controlling for the relative performance of these three asset classes—large stocks, small stocks, and bonds—mutual fund managers as a group do not demonstrate an ability to beat passive index strategies that would simply mix index funds from among these asset classes. They also found that mutual fund performance is worse for firms that have higher expense ratios and higher turnover ratios. Thus it appears that funds with higher fees do not increase gross returns by enough to justify those fees.

Carhart[50] reexamined the issue of consistency in mutual fund performance—sometimes called the "hot hands" phenomenon—controlling for non–S&P factors in a manner similar to Elton, Gruber, Das, and Hlavka. Carhart used a four-factor extension of the index model in which the four benchmark portfolios are the S&P 500 index and portfolios based on book-to-market ratio, size, and prior-year stock market return. These portfolios capture the impacts of three anomalies discussed earlier: the small-firm effect, the book-to-market effect, and the intermediate-term price momentum documented by Jegadeesh and Titman (cited in footnote 12).

Carhart found that there is persistence in relative performance across managers. However, much of that persistence seems due to expenses and transactions costs rather than

---

[49]Remember that the asset allocation decision is usually in the hands of the individual investor. Investors allocate their investment portfolios to funds in asset classes they desire to hold, and they can reasonably expect only that mutual fund portfolio managers will choose stocks advantageously *within* those asset classes.

[50]Mark M. Carhart, "On Persistence in Mutual Fund Performance," *Journal of Finance* 52 (1997), pp. 57–82.

gross investment returns. This last point is important; while there can be no consistently superior performers in a fully efficient market, there *can* be consistently inferior performers. Repeated weak performance would not be due to an ability to pick bad stocks consistently (that would be impossible in an efficient market!) but could result from a consistently high expense ratio or high portfolio turnover with resulting trading costs. In this regard, it is interesting that in another study documenting apparent consistency across managers, Hendricks, Patel, and Zeckhauser[51] also found the strongest consistency among the weakest performers.

Even allowing for expenses and turnover, some amount of performance persistence seems to be due to differences in investment strategy. Carhart found, however, that the evidence of persistence is concentrated at the two extremes. This suggests that there may be a small group of exceptional managers who can with some consistency outperform a passive strategy, but that for the majority of managers over- or underperformance in any period is largely a matter of chance.

In contrast to the extensive studies of equity fund managers, there have been very few studies on the performance of bond fund managers. In a recent paper, however, Blake, Elton, and Gruber[52] examined the performance of fixed-income mutual funds. They found that, on average, bond funds underperform passive fixed-income indexes by an amount roughly equal to expenses, and that there is no evidence that past performance can predict future performance. Their evidence is consistent with the hypothesis that bond managers operate in an efficient market in which performance before expenses is only as good as that of a passive index.

Thus the evidence on the risk-adjusted performance of professional managers is mixed at best. We conclude that the performance of professional managers is broadly consistent with market efficiency. The amounts by which professional managers as a group beat or are beaten by the market fall within the margin of statistical uncertainty. In any event, it is quite clear that performance superior to passive strategies is far from routine. Studies show either that most managers cannot outperform passive strategies, or that if there is a margin of superiority, it is small.

On the other hand, a small number of investment superstars—Peter Lynch (formerly of Fidelity's Magellan Fund), Warren Buffet (of Berkshire Hathaway), John Templeton (of Templeton Funds), and John Neff (of Vanguard's Windsor Fund) among them—have compiled career records that show a consistency of superior performance hard to reconcile with absolutely efficient markets. Nobel Prize winner Paul Samuelson[53] reviewed this investment hall of fame but pointed out that the records of the vast majority of professional money managers offer convincing evidence that there are no easy strategies to guarantee success in the securities markets. The nearby box points out the perils of trying to identify the next superstar manager.

---

[51]Darryll Hendricks, Jayendu Patel, and Richard Zeckhauser, "Hot Hands in Mutual Funds: Short-Run Persistence of Relative Performance, 1974–1988," *Journal of Finance* 43 (March 1993), pp. 93–130.

[52]Christopher R. Blake, Edwin J. Elton, and Martin J. Gruber, "The Performance of Bond Mutual Funds," *Journal of Business* 66 (July 1993), pp. 371–404.

[53]Paul Samuelson, "The Judgment of Economic Science on Rational Portfolio Management," *Journal of Portfolio Management* 16 (Fall 1989), pp. 4–12.

LOOKING TO FIND THE NEXT PETER LYNCH?

TRY LUCK—AND ASK THE RIGHT QUESTIONS

As manager of Fidelity Magellan Fund from 1977 to 1990, Peter Lynch made a lot of money for shareholders. But he did a big disservice to everybody else.

How so? Mr. Lynch had an astonishing 13-year run, beating the market in every calendar year but two. He did so despite the fund's burgeoning size and despite predictions of failure from many observers, including me.

Mr. Lynch gave hope to amateur investors, who had tried picking stocks themselves and failed. Now they had a new strategy. Instead of picking stocks, they would pick the managers who picked the stocks.

That was the theory. The reality? Every day, thousands of amateur investors, fund analysts, investment advisers and financial journalists pore over the country's 4,000-plus stock funds all looking for the next Peter Lynch.

They are still looking.

Falling Stars

The 44 Wall Street Fund was also a dazzling performer in the 1970s. In the 1970s, 44 Wall Street generated even higher returns than Magellan and it ranked as the third-best-performing stock fund.

But the 1980s weren't quite so kind. It ranked as the worst fund in the 1980s, losing 73.1%. Past performance may be a guide to future results. But it's a mighty tough guide to read.

Fortunately, most stock funds don't self-destruct with quite the vigor of 44 Wall Street. Instead, "superstar" funds follow a rather predictable life cycle. A new fund, or an old fund with a new manager, puts together a decent three-year or five-year record. A great feat? Hardly.

If a manager specializes in, say, blue-chip growth stocks, eventually these shares will catch the market's fancy and—providing the manager doesn't do anything too silly—three or four years of market-beating performance might follow.

This strong performance catches the media's attention and the inevitable profile follows, possibly in Forbes or Money or SmartMoney.

By the time the story reaches print, our manager comes across as opinionated and insightful. The money starts rolling in. That's when blue-chip growth stocks go out of favor. You can guess the rest.

Five Questions

I think it is possible to identify winning managers. But the odds are stacked against you. Over a 10-year period, maybe only a quarter of diversified U.S. stock funds will beat Standard & Poor's 500-stock index, which is why market-tracking index funds make so much sense.

So if you are going to try to identify star managers, what should you do? First, stack the odds in your favor by avoiding funds with high annual expenses and sales commissions. Then kick the tires on those funds that remain. Here are five questions to ask:

• Does the fund make sense for your portfolio?

Start by deciding what sort of stock funds you want. You might opt to buy a large-company fund, a small-company fund, an international fund and an emerging-markets fund. Having settled on your target mix, then buy the best funds to fill each slot in your portfolio.

• How has the manager performed?

Funds don't pick stocks. Fund managers do. If a fund has a great record but a new, untested manager, the record is meaningless. By contrast, a spanking new fund with a veteran manager can be a great investment.

• What explains the manager's good performance?

You want to invest with managers who regularly beat the market by diligently picking one good stock after another. Meanwhile, avoid those who have scored big by switching between stocks and cash or by making hefty bets on one market sector after another.

Why? If a manager performs well by picking stocks, he or she has made the right stock-picking decision on hundreds of occasions, thus suggesting a real skill.

By contrast, managers who score big with market timing or sector rotating may have built their record on just half-a-dozen good calls. With such managers, it's much more difficult to say whether they are truly skillful or just unusually lucky.

• Has the manager performed consistently well?

Look at a manager's record on a year-by-year basis. By doing so, you can see whether the manager has performed consistently well or whether the record is built on just one or two years of sizzling returns.

• Has the fund grown absurdly large?

As investors pile into a top-ranked fund, its stellar returns inevitably dull because the manager can no longer stick with his or her favorite stocks but instead must spread the fund's ballooning assets among a growing group of companies.

So, Are Markets Efficient?

There is a telling joke about two economists walking down the street. They spot a $20 bill on the sidewalk. One starts to pick it up, but the other one says, "Don't bother; if the bill were real someone would have picked it up already."

The lesson is clear. An overly doctrinaire belief in efficient markets can paralyze the investor and make it appear that no research effort can be justified. This extreme view is probably unwarranted. There are enough anomalies in the empirical evidence to justify the search for underpriced securities that clearly goes on.

The bulk of the evidence, however, suggests that any supposedly superior investment strategy should be taken with many grains of salt. The market is competitive *enough* that only differentially superior information or insight will earn money; the easy pickings have been picked. In the end it is likely that the margin of superiority that any professional manager can add is so slight that the statistician will not easily be able to detect it.

We conclude that markets are very efficient, but that rewards to the especially diligent, intelligent, or creative may in fact be waiting.

SUMMARY

1. Statistical research has shown that to a close approximation stock prices seem to follow a random walk with no discernible predictable patterns that investors can exploit. Such findings are now taken to be evidence of market efficiency, that is, evidence that market prices reflect all currently available information. Only new information will move stock prices, and this information is equally likely to be good news or bad news.

2. Market participants distinguish among three forms of the efficient market hypothesis. The weak form asserts that all information to be derived from past stock prices already is reflected in stock prices. The semistrong form claims that all publicly available information is already reflected. The strong form, which generally is acknowledged to be extreme, asserts that all information, including insider information, is reflected in prices.

3. Technical analysis focuses on stock price patterns and on proxies for buy or sell pressure in the market. Fundamental analysis focuses on the determinants of the underlying value of the firm, such as current profitability and growth prospects. Because both types of analysis are based on public information, neither should generate excess profits if markets are operating efficiently.

4. Proponents of the efficient market hypothesis often advocate passive as opposed to active investment strategies. The policy of passive investors is to buy and hold a broad-based market index. They expend resources neither on market research nor on frequent purchase and sale of stocks. Passive strategies may be tailored to meet individual investor requirements.

5. Event studies are used to evaluate the economic impact of events of interest, using abnormal stock returns. Such studies usually show that there is some leakage of inside information to some market participants before the public announcement date. Therefore, insiders do seem to be able to exploit their access to information to at least a limited extent.

6. Empirical studies of technical analysis do not generally support the hypothesis that such analysis can generate superior trading profits. One notable exception to this conclusion is the apparent success of momentum-based strategies over intermediate-term horizons.

7. Several anomalies regarding fundamental analysis have been uncovered. These include the P/E effect, the small-firm-in-January effect, the neglected-firm effect, post–earnings-announcement price drift, the reversal effect, and the book-to-market effect. Whether these anomalies represent market inefficiency or poorly understood risk premia is still a matter of debate.

8. By and large, the performance record of professionally managed funds lends little credence to claims that most professionals can consistently beat the market.

Key Terms

random walk	resistance levels	cumulative abnormal return
efficient market hypothesis	support levels	filter rule
weak-form EMH	fundamental analysis	P/E effect
semistrong-form EMH	passive investment strategy	small-firm effect
strong-form EMH	index fund	neglected-firm effect
technical analysis	event study	book-to-market effect
Dow theory	abnormal return	reversal effect

Selected Readings

One of the best treatments of the efficient market hypothesis is:

Malkiel, Burton G. *A Random Walk Down Wall Street.* 6th ed. New York: W. W. Norton & Co., 1995. This paperback book provides an entertaining and insightful treatment of the ideas presented in this chapter as well as fascinating historical examples of securities markets in action.

A more rigorous introduction to the theoretical underpinnings of the EMH, as well as a review of early empirical work, may be found in:

Fama, Eugene F. "Efficient Capital Markets: A Review of Theory and Empirical Work." *Journal of Finance* 25 (May 1970).

A more recent survey is:

Fama, Eugene F. "Efficient Capital Markets: II." *Journal of Finance* 46 (December 1991).

Problems

1. If markets are efficient, what should be the correlation coefficient between stock returns for two nonoverlapping time periods?

2. Which of the following most appears to contradict the proposition that the stock market is *weakly* efficient? Explain.
   a. Over 25% of mutual funds outperform the market on average.
   b. Insiders earn abnormal trading profits.
   c. Every January, the stock market earns abnormal returns.

3. Suppose that, after conducting an analysis of past stock prices, you come up with the following observations. Which would appear to *contradict* the *weak form* of the efficient market hypothesis? Explain.
   a. The average rate of return is significantly greater than zero.
   b. The correlation between the return during a given week and the return during the following week is zero.
   c. One could have made superior returns by buying stock after a 10% rise in price and selling after a 10% fall.
   d. One could have made higher-than-average capital gains by holding stock with low dividend yields.

4. Which of the following statements are true if the efficient market hypothesis holds?
   a. It implies that future events can be forecast with perfect accuracy.
   b. It implies that prices reflect all available information.
   c. It implies that security prices change for no discernible reason.
   d. It implies that prices do not fluctuate.

5. Which of the following observations would provide evidence *against* the *semistrong form* of the efficient market theory? Explain.
   a. Mutual fund managers do not on average make superior returns.
   b. You cannot make superior profits by buying (or selling) stocks after the announcement of an abnormal rise in dividends.
   c. Low P/E stocks tend to have positive abnormal returns.
   d. In any year approximately 50% of pension funds outperform the market.

Problems 6–12 are taken from past CFA exams.

6. The semistrong form of the efficient market hypothesis asserts that stock prices:
   a. Fully reflect all historical price information.
   b. Fully reflect all publicly available information.
   c. Fully reflect all relevant information including insider information.
   d. May be predictable.

7. Assume that a company announces an unexpectedly large cash dividend to its shareholders. In an efficient market *without* information leakage, one might expect:
   a. An abnormal price change at the announcement.
   b. An abnormal price increase before the announcement.
   c. An abnormal price decrease after the announcement.
   d. No abnormal price change before or after the announcement.

8. Which one of the following would provide evidence *against* the *semistrong form* of the efficient market theory?
   a. About 50% of pension funds outperform the market in any year.
   b. All investors have learned to exploit signals about future performance.
   c. Trend analysis is worthless in determining stock prices.
   d. Low P/E stocks tend to have positive abnormal returns over the long run.

9. According to the efficient market hypothesis:
   a. High-beta stocks are consistently overpriced.
   b. Low-beta stocks are consistently overpriced.
   c. Positive alphas on stocks will quickly disappear.
   d. Negative alpha stocks consistently yield low returns for arbitrageurs.

10. A "random walk" occurs when:
    a. Stock price changes are random but predictable.
    b. Stock prices respond slowly to both new and old information.
    c. Future price changes are uncorrelated with past price changes.
    d. Past information is useful in predicting future prices.

11. Two basic assumptions of technical analysis are that security prices adjust:
    a. Gradually to new information, and study of the economic environment provides an indication of future market movements.
    b. Rapidly to new information, and study of the economic environment provides an indication of future market movements.
    c. Rapidly to new information, and market prices are determined by the interaction between supply and demand.

    d. Gradually to new information, and prices are determined by the interaction between supply and demand.

12. When technical analysts say a stock has good "relative strength," they mean:

    a. The ratio of the price of the stock to a market or industry index has trended upward.

    b. The recent trading volume in the stock has exceeded the normal trading volume.

    c. The total return on the stock has exceeded the total return on T-bills.

    d. The stock has performed well recently compared to its past performance.

13. Which one of the following would be a bullish signal to a technical analyst using contrary opinion rules?

    a. The level of credit balances in investor accounts declines.

    b. The ratio of bearish investment advisors to the number of advisory services expressing an optimistic opinion is historically quite high.

    c. A large proportion of speculators expect the price of stock index futures to rise.

    d. The ratio of over the counter (OTC) volume to New York Stock Exchange (NYSE) volume is relatively high.

14. A successful firm like Microsoft has consistently generated large profits for years. Is this a violation of the EMH?

15. Suppose you find that prices of stocks before large dividend increases show on average consistently positive abnormal returns. Is this a violation of the EMH?

16. "If the business cycle is predictable, and a stock has a positive beta, the stock's returns also must be predictable." Respond.

17. Which of the following phenomena would be either consistent with or a violation of the efficient market hypothesis? Explain briefly.

    a. Nearly half of all professionally managed mutual funds are able to outperform the S&P 500 in a typical year.

    b. Money managers that outperform the market (on a risk-adjusted basis) in one year are likely to outperform in the following year.

    c. Stock prices tend to be predictably more volatile in January than in other months.

    d. Stock prices of companies that announce increased earnings in January tend to outperform the market in February.

    e. Stocks that perform well in one week perform poorly in the following week.

18. "If all securities are fairly priced, all must offer equal expected rates of return." Comment.

19. An index model regression applied to past monthly returns in General Motors' stock price produces the following estimates, which are believed to be stable over time:

$$r_{GM} = .10\% + 1.1 r_M$$

If the market index subsequently rises by 8% and General Motors' stock price rises by 7%, what is the abnormal change in General Motors' stock price?

20. The monthly rate of return on T-bills is 1%. The market went up this month by 1.5%. In addition, AmbChaser, Inc., which has an equity beta of 2, surprisingly just won a lawsuit that awards it $1 million immediately.

    a. If the original value of AmbChaser equity were $100 million, what would you guess was the rate of return of its stock this month?

    b. What is your answer to (*a*) if the market had expected AmbChaser to win $2 million?

21. In a recent closely contested lawsuit, Apex sued Bpex for patent infringement. The jury came back today with its decision. The rate of return on Apex was $r_A = 3.1\%$. The rate

of return on Bpex was only $r_B = 2.5\%$. The market today responded to very encouraging news about the unemployment rate, and $r_M = 3\%$. The historical relationship between returns on these stocks and the market portfolio has been estimated from index model regressions as:

$$\text{Apex:} \quad r_A = .2\% + 1.4r_M$$
$$\text{Bpex:} \quad r_B = -.1\% + .6r_M$$

Based on these data, which company do you think won the lawsuit?

22. Investors *expect* the market rate of return in the coming year to be 12%. The T-bill rate is 4%. Changing Fortunes Industries' stock has a beta of .5. The market value of its outstanding equity is $100 million.

    a. What is your best guess currently as to the expected rate of return on Changing Fortunes' stock? You believe that the stock is fairly priced.

    b. If the market return in the coming year actually turns out to be 10%, what is your best guess as to the rate of return that will be earned on Changing Fortunes' stock?

    c. Suppose now that Changing Fortunes wins a major lawsuit during the year. The settlement is $5 million. Changing Fortunes' stock return during the year turns out to be 10%. What is your best guess as to the settlement the market previously *expected* Changing Fortunes to receive from the lawsuit? (Continue to assume that the market return in the year turned out to be 10%.) The magnitude of the settlement is the only unexpected firm-specific event during the year.

23. Dollar-cost averaging means that you buy equal dollar amounts of a stock every period, for example, $500 per month. The strategy is based on the idea that when the stock price is low, your fixed monthly purchase will buy more shares, and when the price is high, fewer shares. Averaging over time, you will end up buying more shares when the stock is cheaper and fewer when it is relatively expensive. Therefore, by design, you will exhibit good market timing. Evaluate this strategy.

24. Steady Growth Industries has never missed a dividend payment in its 94-year history. Does this make it more attractive to you as a possible purchase for your stock portfolio?

25. We know that the market should respond positively to good news, and that good-news events such as the coming end of a recession can be predicted with at least some accuracy. Why, then, can we not predict that the market will go up as the economy recovers?

26. If prices are as likely to increase as decrease, why do investors earn positive returns from the market on average?

27. You know that firm XYZ is very poorly run. On a scale of 1 (worst) to 10 (best), you would give it a score of 3. The market consensus evaluation is that the management score is only 2. Should you buy or sell the stock?

28. Examine the accompanying figure,[54] which presents cumulative abnormal returns both before and after dates on which insiders buy or sell shares in their firms. How do you interpret this figure? What are we to make of the pattern of CARs before and after the event date?

---

[54]From Nejat H. Seyhun, "Insiders, Profits, Costs of Trading and Market Efficiency," *Journal of Financial Economics* 16 (1986).

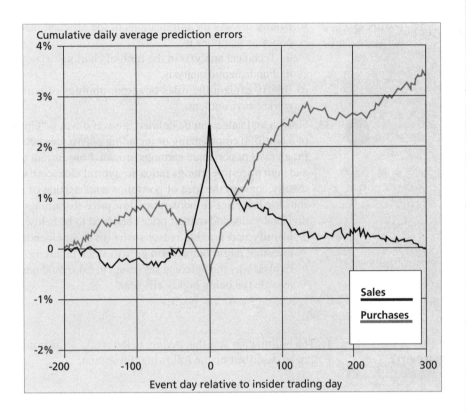

Cumulative daily average prediction errors

Event day relative to insider trading day

29. Suppose that during a certain week the Fed announces a new monetary growth policy, Congress surprisingly passes legislation restricting imports of foreign automobiles, and Ford comes out with a new car model that it believes will increase profits substantially. How might you go about measuring the market's assessment of Ford's new model?

30. Good News, Inc., just announced an increase in its annual earnings, yet its stock price fell. Is there a rational explanation for this phenomenon?

31. Your investment client asks for information concerning the benefits of active portfolio management. She is particularly interested in the question of whether or not active managers can be expected to consistently exploit inefficiencies in the capital markets to produce above-average returns without assuming higher risk.

    The semistrong form of the efficient market hypothesis asserts that all publicly available information is rapidly and correctly reflected in securities prices. This implies that investors cannot expect to derive above-average profits from purchases made after information has become public because security prices already reflect the information's full effects.

    a. Identify and explain two examples of empirical evidence that tend to support the EMH implication stated above.

    b. Identify and explain two examples of empirical evidence that tend to refute the EMH implication stated above.

    c. Discuss reasons why an investor might choose not to index even if the markets were, in fact, semistrong form efficient.

32. a. Briefly explain the concept of the efficient market hypothesis (EMH) and each of its three forms—weak, semistrong, and strong—and briefly discuss the degree to which existing empirical evidence supports each of the three forms of the EMH.

    b. Briefly discuss the implications of the efficient market hypothesis for investment policy as it applies to:
      i. Technical analysis in the form of charting.
      ii. Fundamental analysis.
    c. Briefly explain the roles or responsibilities of portfolio managers in an efficient market environment.

33. Growth and value can be defined in several ways. "Growth" usually conveys the idea of a portfolio emphasizing or including only issues believed to possess above-average future rates of per-share earnings growth. Low current yield, high price-to-book ratios, and high price-to-earnings ratios are typical characteristics of such portfolios. "Value" usually conveys the idea of portfolios emphasizing or including only issues currently showing low price-to-book ratios, low price-to-earnings ratios, above-average levels of dividend yield, and market prices believed to be below the issues' intrinsic values.

    a. Identify and provide reasons why, over an extended period of time, value-stock investing might outperform growth-stock investing.
    b. Explain why the outcome suggested in (*a*) should not be possible in a market widely regarded as being highly efficient.

1. The information sets that pertain to the weak, semistrong, and strong form of the EMH can be described by the following illustration:

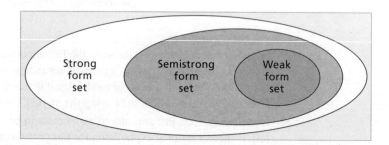

The weak-form information set includes only the history of prices and volumes. The semistrong-form set includes the weak form set *plus* all publicly available information. In turn, the strong-form set includes the semistrong set *plus* insiders' information. It is illegal to act on the incremental information (insiders' private information). The direction of *valid* implication is

$$\text{Strong-form EMH} \Rightarrow \text{Semistrong-form EMH} \Rightarrow \text{Weak-form EMH}$$

The reverse direction implication is *not* valid. For example, stock prices may reflect all past price data (weak-form efficiency) but may not reflect relevant fundamental data (semistrong-form inefficiency).

2. The point we made in the preceding discussion is that the very fact that we observe stock prices near so-called resistance levels belies the assumption that the price can be a resistance level. If a stock is observed to sell *at any price*, then investors must believe that a fair rate of return can be earned if the stock is purchased at that price. It is logically impossible for a stock to have a resistance level *and* offer a fair rate of return at prices just below the resistance level. If we accept that prices are appropriate, we must reject any presumption concerning resistance levels.

3. If *everyone* one follows a passive strategy, sooner or later prices will fail to reflect new information. At this point there are profit opportunities for active investors who uncover mispriced securities. As they buy and sell these assets, prices again will be driven to fair levels.

4. Predictably declining CARs do violate the EMH. If one can predict such a phenomenon, a profit opportunity emerges: Sell (or short sell) the affected stocks on an event date just before their prices are predicted to fall.

5. The answer depends on your prior beliefs about market efficiency. Magellan's record was incredibly strong. On the other hand, with so many funds in existence, it is less surprising that *some* fund would appear to be consistently superior after the fact. Still, Magellan's record was so good that even accounting for its selection as the "winner" of an investment "contest," it still appears to be too good to be attributed to chance.

6. Concern over the deficit was an ongoing issue in 1987. No significant *new* information concerning the deficit was released on October 19. Hence this explanation for the crash is not consistent with the EMH.

CHAPTER THIRTEEN

EMPIRICAL EVIDENCE ON SECURITY RETURNS

In this chapter, we consider the empirical evidence in support of the CAPM and APT. At the outset, however, it is worth noting that many of the implications of these models already have been accepted in widely varying applications. Consider the following:

1. Many professional portfolio managers use the expected return–beta relationship of security returns. Furthermore, many firms rate the performance of portfolio managers according to the reward-to-variability ratios they maintain and the average rates of return they realize relative to the CML or SML.

2. Regulatory commissions use the expected return–beta relationship along with forecasts of the market index return as one factor in determining the cost of capital for regulated firms.

3. Court rulings on torts cases sometimes use the expected return–beta relationship to determine discount rates to evaluate claims of lost future income.

4. Many firms use the SML to obtain a benchmark hurdle rate for capital budgeting decisions.

These practices show that the financial community has passed a favorable judgment on the CAPM and the APT, if only implicitly. In this chapter we consider the evidence along more explicit and rigorous lines. The first part of the chapter presents the methodology that has been deployed in testing the single-factor CAPM and APT and assesses the results. The second part of the chapter provides an overview of current efforts to establish the validity of the multifactor versions of the CAPM and APT. In the third part, we discuss recent literature on so-called anomalies in patterns of security returns and some of the responses to these puzzling findings. Finally, we briefly discuss evidence on how the volatility of asset returns evolves over time. Why lump together empirical works on the CAPM and APT? The CAPM is a theoretical construct that predicts *expected* rates of return on assets, relative to a market portfolio of all risky assets. It is difficult to test these predictions empirically because both expected returns and the exact market portfolio are unobservable (see Chapter 10). To overcome this difficulty, a single-factor or multifactor capital market usually is postulated, where a broad-based market index portfolio (such as the S&P 500) is assumed to represent the factor, or one of the factors. Furthermore, to obtain more reliable statistics, most tests have been conducted with the rates of return on highly diversified portfolios rather than on individual securities. For both of these reasons tests that have been directed at the CAPM actually have been more suitable to establish the validity of the APT. We will see that it is more important to distinguish the empirical work on the basis of the factor structure that is assumed or estimated than to distinguish between tests of the CAPM and the APT.

13.1 THE INDEX MODEL AND THE SINGLE-FACTOR APT

The Expected Return–Beta Relationship

Recall that if the expected return–beta relationship holds with respect to an observable ex ante efficient index, M, the expected rate of return on any security i is

$$E(r_i) = r_f + \beta_i[E(r_M) - r_f] \tag{13.1}$$

where β_i is defined as $\text{Cov}(r_i, r_M)/\sigma_M^2$.

This is the most commonly tested implication of the CAPM. Early simple tests followed three basic steps: establishing sample data, estimating the SCL (security characteristic line), and estimating the SML (security market line).

Setting Up the Sample Data   Determine a sample period of, for example, 60 monthly holding periods (five years). For each of the 60 holding periods collect the rates of return on 100 stocks, a market portfolio proxy (e.g., the S&P 500), and one-month (risk-free) T-bills. Your data thus consist of

r_{it} Returns on the 100 stocks over the 60-month sample period; $i = 1, \ldots, 100$, and $t = 1, \ldots, 60$.

r_{Mt} Returns on the S&P 500 index over the sample period.

r_{ft} Risk-free rate each month.

This constitutes a table of $102 \times 60 = 6,120$ rates of return.

Estimating the SCL   View equation 13.1 as a security characteristic line (SCL), as in Chapter 10. For each stock, i, you estimate the beta coefficient as the slope of a **first-pass**

regression equation. (The terminology *first-pass* regression is due to the fact that the estimated coefficients will be used as input into a **second-pass regression**.)

$$r_{it} - r_{ft} = a_i + b_i(r_{Mt} - r_{ft}) + e_{it}$$

You will use the following statistics in later analysis:

$\overline{r_i - r_f}$ Sample averages (over the 60 observations) of the excess return on each of the 100 stocks.

b_i Sample estimates of the beta coefficients of each of the 100 stocks.

$\overline{r_M - r_f}$ Sample average of the excess return of the market index.

$\sigma^2(e_i)$ Estimates of the variance of the residuals for each of the 100 stocks.

The sample average excess returns on each stock and the market portfolio are taken as estimates of expected excess returns, and the values of b_i are estimates of the true beta coefficients for the 100 stocks during the sample period. The $\sigma^2(e_i)$ estimates the nonsystematic risk of each of the 100 stocks.

Question 1

a. **How many regression estimates of the SCL do we have from the sample?**

b. **How many observations are there in each of the regressions?**

c. **According to the CAPM, what should be the intercept in each of these regressions?**

Estimating the SML   Now view equation 13.1 as a security market line (SML) with 100 observations for the stocks in your sample. You can estimate γ_0 and γ_1 in the following second-pass regression equation with the estimates b_i from the first pass as the independent variable:

$$\overline{r_i - r_f} = \gamma_0 + \gamma_1 b_i \quad i = 1, \dots, 100 \tag{13.2}$$

Compare equations 13.1 and 13.2; you should conclude that if the CAPM is valid, then γ_0 and γ_1 should satisfy

$$\gamma_0 = 0 \quad \gamma_1 = \overline{r_M - r_f}$$

In fact, however, you can go a step further and argue that the key property of the expected return–beta relationship described by the SML is that the expected excess return on securities is determined *only* by the systematic risk (as measured by beta) and should be independent of the nonsystematic risk, as measured by the variance of the residuals, $\sigma^2(e_i)$, which also were estimated from the first-pass regression. These estimates can be added as a variable in equation 13.2 of an expanded SML that now looks like this:

$$\overline{r_i - r_f} = \gamma_0 + \gamma_1 b_i + \gamma_2 \sigma^2(e_i) \tag{13.3}$$

This *second-pass* regression is estimated with the hypotheses

$$\gamma_0 = 0 \quad \gamma_1 = \overline{r_M - r_f} \quad \gamma_2 = 0$$

The hypothesis that $\gamma_2 = 0$ is consistent with the notion that nonsystematic risk should not be "priced," that is, that there is no risk premium earned for bearing nonsystematic risk. More generally, according to the CAPM, the risk premium depends only on beta. Therefore, *any* additional right-hand-side variable in equation 13.3 beyond beta should have a coefficient that is insignificantly different from zero in the second-pass regression.

Tests of the CAPM

Early tests of the CAPM performed by John Lintner,[1] later replicated by Merton Miller and Myron Scholes,[2] used annual data on 631 NYSE stocks for 10 years, 1954 to 1963, and produced the following estimates (with returns expressed as decimals rather than percentages):

Coefficient:	$\gamma_0 = .127$	$\gamma_1 = .042$	$\gamma_2 = .310$
Standard error:	.006	.006	.026
Sample average:		$\overline{r_M - r_f} = .165$	

These results are inconsistent with the CAPM. First, the estimated SML is "too flat"; that is, the γ_1 coefficient is too small. The slope should be $\overline{r_M - r_f} = .165$ (16.5% per year), but it is estimated at only .42. The difference, .122, is about 20 times the standard error of the estimate, .006, which means that the measured slope of the SML is less than it should be by a statistically significant margin. At the same time, the intercept of the estimated SML, γ_0, which is hypothesized to be zero, in fact equals .127, which is more than 20 times its standard error of .006.

Concept CHECK

Question 2

a. **What is the implication of the empirical SML being "too flat"?**
b. **Do high- or low-beta stocks tend to outperform the predictions of the CAPM?**
c. **What is the implication of the estimate of γ_2?**

The two-stage procedure employed by these researchers (i.e., first estimate security betas using a time-series regression and then use those betas to test the SML relationship between risk and average return) seems straightforward, and the rejection of the CAPM using this approach is disappointing. However, it turns out that there are several difficulties with this approach. First and foremost, stock returns are extremely volatile, which lessens the precision of any tests of average return. For example, the average standard deviation of annual returns of the stocks in the S&P 500 is about 40%; the average standard deviation of annual returns of the stocks included in these tests is probably even higher.

In addition, there are fundamental concerns about the validity of the tests. First, the market index used in the tests is surely not the "market portfolio" of the CAPM. Second, in light of asset volatility, the security betas from the first-stage regressions are necessarily estimated with substantial sampling error and therefore cannot readily be used as inputs to the second-stage regression. Finally, investors cannot borrow at the risk-free rate, as assumed by the simple version of the CAPM. Let us investigate the implications of these problems in turn.

The Market Index

In what has become known as *Roll's critique*, Richard Roll[3] pointed out that:

1. There is a single testable hypothesis associated with the CAPM: The market portfolio is mean-variance efficient.

---

[1]John Lintner, "Security Prices, Risk and Maximal Gains from Diversification," *Journal of Finance* 20 (December 1965).
[2]Merton H. Miller and Myron Scholes, "Rate of Return in Relation to Risk: A Reexamination of Some Recent Findings," in Michael C. Jensen, ed., *Studies in the Theory of Capital Markets* (New York: Praeger, 1972).
[3]Richard Roll, "A Critique of the Asset Pricing Theory's Tests: Part I: On Past and Potential Testability of the Theory," *Journal of Financial Economics* 4 (1977).

2. All the other implications of the model, the best-known being the linear relation between expected return and beta, follow from the market portfolio's efficiency and therefore are not independently testable. There is an "if and only if" relation between the expected return–beta relationship and the efficiency of the market portfolio.

3. In any sample of observations of individual returns there will be an infinite number of ex post (i.e., after the fact) mean-variance efficient portfolios using the sample period returns and covariances (as opposed to the ex ante expected returns and covariances). Sample betas calculated between each such portfolio and individual assets will be exactly linearly related to sample average returns. In other words, if betas are calculated against such portfolios, they will satisfy the SML relation exactly whether or not the true market portfolio is mean-variance efficient in an ex ante sense.

4. The CAPM is not testable unless we know the exact composition of the true market portfolio and use it in the tests. This implies that the theory is not testable unless *all* individual assets are included in the sample.

5. Using a proxy such as the S&P 500 for the market portfolio is subject to two difficulties. First, the proxy itself might be mean-variance efficient even when the true market portfolio is not. Conversely, the proxy may turn out to be inefficient, but obviously this alone implies nothing about the true market portfolio's efficiency. Furthermore, most reasonable market proxies will be very highly correlated with each other and with the true market portfolio whether or not they are mean-variance efficient. Such a high degree of correlation will make it seem that the exact composition of the market portfolio is unimportant, whereas the use of different proxies can lead to quite different conclusions. This problem is referred to as **benchmark error**, because it refers to the use of an incorrect benchmark (market proxy) portfolio in the tests of the theory.

Roll and Ross[4] and Kandel and Stambaugh[5] expanded Roll's critique. Essentially, they argued that tests that reject a positive relationship between average return and beta point to inefficiency of the market proxy used in those tests, rather than refuting the theoretical expected return–beta relationship. Their work demonstrates that it is plausible that even highly diversified portfolios, such as the value- or equally weighted portfolios of all stocks in the sample, will fail to produce a significant average return–beta relationship.

Roll and Ross (RR) derived an analytical characterization of market indexes (proxies for the market portfolio) that produce an *arbitrary* cross-sectional slope coefficient in the regression of average asset returns on beta. Their derivation applies to any universe of assets and requires only that the market proxy be constructed from that universe or one of its subsets. They show that the set of indexes that produce a zero second-pass slope lies within a parabola that is tangent to the efficient frontier at the point corresponding to the global minimum variance portfolio.

Figure 13.1 shows one such configuration. In this plausible universe, where "plausible" is taken to mean that the return distribution is not extraordinary, the set of portfolios with

[4]Richard Roll and Stephen A. Ross, "On the Cross-Sectional Relation between Expected Return and Betas," *Journal of Finance* 50 (1995), pp. 185–224.

[5]Schmuel Kandel and Robert F. Stambaugh, "Portfolio Inefficiency and the Cross-Section of Expected Returns," *Journal of Finance* 50 (1995), pp. 185–224; "A Mean-Variance Framework for Tests of Asset Pricing Models," *Review of Financial Studies* 2 (1989), pp. 125–56; "On Correlations and Inferences about Mean-Variance Efficiency," *Journal of Financial Economics* 18 (1987), pp. 61–90.

Figure 13.1

Market index proxies
that produce betas
having no relation to
expected returns.

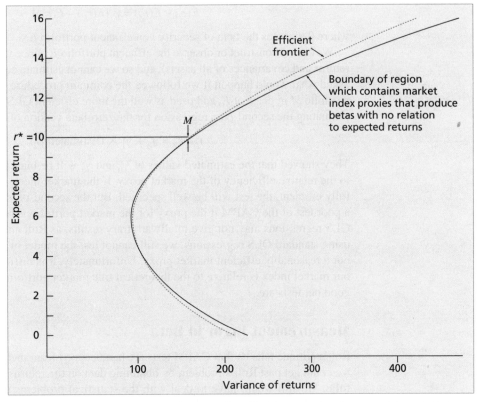

These proxies are located within a restricted region of the mean-variance space, a region bounded by a parabola that lies inside the efficient frontier except for a tangency at the global minimum variance point. The market proxy is located on the boundary at a distance of $M = 22$ basis points below the efficient frontier. While betas against this market proxy have zero cross-sectional correlation with expected returns, a market proxy on the efficient frontier just 22 basis points above it would produce betas that are perfectly positively collinear with expected returns.

Source: Richard Roll and Stephen A. Ross, "On the Cross-Sectional Relation between Expected Return and Betas," *Journal of Finance* 49 (1994), pp. 101–21.

zero slope coefficient in the return–beta regression lies near the efficient frontier. Thus even portfolios that are "nearly efficient" do not necessarily support the expected return–beta relationship.

RR concluded that the slope coefficient in the average return–beta regression cannot be relied on to test the theoretical expected return–beta relationship. It can only indicate that the market proxy that produces this result is inefficient in the second-pass regression. Many studies use the more sophisticated regression procedure called generalized least squares (GLS) to improve on statistical reliability. Can the use of GLS overcome the problems raised by Roll and Ross?

Kandel and Stambaugh (KS) extended this analysis and considered whether the use of generalized least squares regressions can overcome some of the problems identified by Roll and Ross. They found that GLS does help, but only to the extent that the researcher can obtain a nearly efficient market index.

KS considered the properties of the usual two-pass test of the CAPM in an environment in which borrowing is restricted but the zero-beta version of the CAPM holds. In this case, you will recall that the expected return–beta relationship describes the expected returns on a stock, a portfolio E on the efficient frontier, and that portfolio's zero-beta companion, Z (see equation 9.9):

$$E(r_i) - E(r_Z) = \beta_i[E(r_E) - E(r_Z)] \qquad (13.4)$$

where β_i denotes the beta of security i on efficient portfolio E.

We cannot construct or observe the efficient portfolio E (since we do not know expected returns and covariances of all assets), and so we cannot estimate equation 13.4 directly. KS asked what would happen if we followed the common procedure of using a market proxy portfolio M in place of E, and used as well the more efficient GLS regression procedure in estimating the second-pass regression for the zero-beta version of the CAPM, that is,

$$r_i - r_Z = \gamma_0 + \gamma_1 \times (\text{Estimated } \beta_i)$$

They showed that the estimated values of γ_0 and γ_1 will be biased by a term proportional to the relative efficiency of the market proxy. If the market index used in the regression is fully efficient, the test will be well specified. But the second-pass regression will provide a poor test of the CAPM if the proxy for the market portfolio is not efficient. Thus, while GLS regressions may not give totally arbitrary results, as Roll and Ross argue may occur using standard OLS regressions, we still cannot test the model in a meaningful way without a reasonably efficient market proxy. Unfortunately, it is difficult to tell how efficient our market index is relative to the theoretical true market portfolio, so we cannot tell how good our tests are.

Measurement Error in Beta

Roll's critique tells us that CAPM tests are handicapped from the outset. But suppose that we could get past Roll's problem by obtaining data on the returns of the true market portfolio. We still would have to deal with the statistical problems caused by measurement error in the estimates of beta from the first-stage regressions.

It is well known in statistics that if the right-hand-side variable of a regression equation is measured with error (in our case, beta is measured with error and is the right-hand-side variable in the second-pass regression), then the slope coefficient of the regression equation will be biased downward and the intercept biased upward. This is consistent with the findings cited above, which found that the estimate of γ_0 was higher than predicted by the CAPM and that the estimate of γ_1 was lower than predicted.

Indeed, a well-controlled simulation test by Miller and Scholes[6] confirms these arguments. In this test a random-number generator simulated rates of return with covariances similar to observed ones. The average returns were made to agree exactly with the CAPM expected return–beta relationship. Miller and Scholes then used these randomly generated rates of return in the tests we have described as if they were observed from a sample of stock returns. The results of this "simulated" test were virtually identical to those reached using real data, despite the fact that the simulated returns were *constructed* to obey the SML, that is, the true γ coefficients were $\gamma_0 = 0$, $\gamma_1 = r_M - r_f$, and $\gamma_2 = 0$.

This postmortem of the early test gets us back to square one. We can explain away the disappointing test results, but we have no positive results to support the CAPM-APT implications.

The next wave of tests was designed to overcome the measurement error problem that led to biased estimates of the SML. The innovation in these tests, pioneered by Black, Jensen, and Scholes (BJS),[7] was to use portfolios rather than individual securities.

---

[6]Merton H. Miller and Myron Scholes, "Rate of Return in Relation to Risk: A Reexamination of Some Recent Findings," in Michael C. Jensen, ed., *Studies in the Theory of Capital Markets* (New York: Praeger, 1972).

[7]Fischer Black, Michael C. Jensen, and Myron Scholes, "The Capital Asset Pricing Model: Some Empirical Tests," in Michael C. Jensen, ed., *Studies in the Theory of Capital Markets* (New York: Praeger, 1972).

Combining securities into portfolios diversifies away most of the firm-specific part of returns, thereby enhancing the precision of the estimates of beta and the expected rate of return of the portfolio of securities. This mitigates the statistical problems that arise from measurement error in the beta estimates.

Obviously, however, combining stocks into portfolios reduces the number of observations left for the second-pass regression. For example, suppose that we group our sample of 100 stocks into five portfolios of 20 stocks each. If the assumption of a single-factor market is reasonably accurate, then the residuals of the 20 stocks in each portfolio will be practically uncorrelated and, hence, the variance of the portfolio residual will be about one-twentieth the residual variance of the average stock. Thus the portfolio beta in the first-pass regression will be estimated with far better accuracy. However, now consider the second-pass regression. With individual securities we had 100 observations to estimate the second-pass coefficients. With portfolios of 20 stocks each we are left with only five observations for the second-pass regression.

To get the best of this trade-off, we need to construct portfolios with the largest possible dispersion of beta coefficients. Other things being equal, a sample yields more accurate regression estimates the more widely spaced are the observations of the independent variables. Consider the first-pass regressions where we estimate the SCL, that is, the relationship between the excess return on each stock and the market's excess return. If we have a sample with a great dispersion of market returns, we have a greater chance of accurately estimating the effect of a change in the market return on the return of the stock. In our case, however, we have no control over the range of the market returns. But we can control the range of the independent variable of the second-pass regression, the portfolio betas. Rather than allocate 20 stocks to each portfolio randomly, we can rank portfolios by betas. Portfolio 1 will include the 20 highest-beta stocks and Portfolio 5 the 20 lowest-beta stocks. In that case a set of portfolios with small nonsystematic components, e_p, and widely spaced betas will yield reasonably powerful tests of the SML.

Fama and MacBeth[8] used this methodology to verify that the observed relationship between average excess returns and beta is indeed linear and that nonsystematic risk does not explain average excess returns. Using 20 portfolios constructed according to the BJS methodology, Fama and MacBeth expanded the estimation of the SML equation to include the square of the beta coefficient (to test for linearity of the relationship between returns and betas) and the estimated standard deviation of the residual (to test for the explanatory power of nonsystematic risk). For a sequence of many subperiods they estimated for each subperiod, the equation

$$r_i = \gamma_0 + \gamma_1 \beta_i + \gamma_2 \beta_i^2 + \gamma_3 \sigma(e_i) \tag{13.5}$$

The term γ_2 measures potential nonlinearity of return, and γ_3 measures the explanatory power of nonsystematic risk, $\sigma(e_i)$. According to the CAPM, both γ_2 and γ_3 should have coefficients of zero in the second-pass regression.

Fama and MacBeth estimated equation 13.5 for every month of the period January 1935 through June 1968. The results are summarized in Table 13.1, which shows average coefficients and *t*-statistics for the overall period as well as for three subperiods. Fama and MacBeth observed that the coefficients on residual standard deviation (nonsystematic risk), denoted by γ_3, fluctuate greatly from month to month and were insignificant, consistent with the hypothesis that nonsystematic risk is not rewarded by higher average returns. Likewise, the coefficients on the square of beta, denoted by γ_2,

---

[8]Eugene Fama and James MacBeth, "Risk, Return, and Equilibrium: Empirical Tests," *Journal of Political Economy* 81 (March 1973).

Table 13.1   Summary of Fama and MacBeth (1973) Study (all rates in basis points per month)

Period	1935/6–1968	1935–1945	1946–1955	1956/6–1968
Av. r_f	13	2	9	26
Av. $\gamma_0 - r_f$	8	10	8	5
Av. $t(\gamma_0 - r_f)$	0.20	0.11	0.20	0.10
Av. $r_M - r_f$	130	195	103	95
Av. γ_1	114	118	209	34
Av. $t(\gamma_1)$	1.85	0.94	2.39	0.34
Av. γ_2	−26	−9	−76	0
Av. $t(\gamma_2)$	−0.86	−0.14	−2.16	0
Av. γ_3	516	817	−378	960
Av. $t(\gamma_3)$	1.11	0.94	−0.67	1.11
Av. R-SQR	0.31	0.31	0.32	0.29

were insignificant, consistent with the hypothesis that the expected return–beta relationship is linear.

With respect to the expected return–beta relationship, however, the picture is mixed. The estimated SML is too flat, consistent with previous studies, as can be seen from the fact that $\gamma_0 - r_f$ is positive, and that γ_1 is, on average, less than $r_M - r_f$. On the positive side, the difference does not appear to be significant, so that the CAPM is not clearly rejected.

The EMH and the CAPM

Roll's critique also provides a positive avenue to view the empirical content of the CAPM and APT. Recall, as Roll pointed out, that the CAPM and the expected return–beta relationship follow directly from the efficiency of the market portfolio. This means that if we can establish that the market portfolio is efficient, we would have no need to further test the expected return–beta relationship.

As demonstrated in Chapter 12 on the efficient market hypothesis, proxies for the market portfolio such as the S&P 500 and the NYSE index have proven hard to beat by professional investors. This is perhaps the strongest evidence for the empirical content of the CAPM and APT.

Concept

Question 3 • According to the CAPM, what are the predicted values of γ_0, γ_1, γ_2, and γ_3 in the Fama-MacBeth regressions for the period 1946–1955?

In conclusion, these tests of the CAPM provide mixed evidence on the validity of the theory. We can summarize the results as follows:

1. The insights that are supported by the single-factor CAPM and APT are as follows:
   a. Expected rates of return are linear and increase with beta, the measure of systematic risk.
   b. Expected rates of return are not affected by nonsystematic risk.
2. The single-variable expected return–beta relationship predicted by either the risk-free rate or the zero-beta version of the CAPM is not fully consistent with empirical observation.

Thus, although the CAPM seems *qualitatively* correct in that β matters and $\sigma(e_i)$ does not, empirical tests do not validate its *quantitative* predictions.

Concept
CHECK

Question 4 • What would you conclude if you performed the Fama and MacBeth tests and found that the coefficients on β^2 and $\sigma(e)$ were positive?

13.2 TESTS OF MULTIFACTOR CAPM AND APT

The multifactor CAPM and APT are elegant theories of how exposure to systematic risk factors should influence expected returns, but they provide little guidance concerning which factors (sources of risk) ought to result in risk premiums. A full-blown test of the multifactor equilibrium model, with prespecified factors and hedge portfolios, is as yet unavailable. A test of this hypothesis would require three stages:

1. Specification of risk factors.
2. Identification of portfolios that hedge these fundamental risk factors.
3. Test of the explanatory power and risk premiums of the hedge portfolios.

A step in this direction was made by Chen, Roll, and Ross,[9] who hypothesized several possible variables that might proxy for systematic factors:

IP = Growth rate in industrial production

EI = Changes in expected inflation measured by changes in short-term (T-bill) interest rates

UI = Unexpected inflation defined as the difference between actual and expected inflation

CG = Unexpected changes in risk premiums measured by the difference between the returns on corporate Baa-rated bonds and long-term government bonds

GB = Unexpected changes in the term premium measured by the difference between the returns on long- and short-term government bonds

With the identification of these potential economic factors, Chen, Roll, and Ross skipped the procedure of identifying factor portfolios (the portfolios that have the highest correlation with the factors). Instead, by using the factors themselves, they implicitly assumed that factor portfolios exist that can proxy for the factors. The factors are now used in a test similar to that of Fama and MacBeth.

A critical part of the methodology is the grouping of stocks into portfolios. Recall that in the single-factor tests, portfolios were constructed to span a wide range of betas to enhance the power of the test. In a multifactor framework the efficient criterion for grouping is less obvious. Chen, Roll, and Ross chose to group the sample stocks into 20 portfolios by size (market value of outstanding equity), a variable that is known to be associated with stock returns.

They first used five years of monthly data to estimate the factor betas of the 20 portfolios in a first-pass regression. This is accomplished by estimating the following regressions for each portfolio:

$$r = a + \beta_M r_M + \beta_{IP} IP + \beta_{EI} EI + \beta_{UI} UI + \beta_{CG} CG + \beta_{GB} GB + e \qquad (13.6a)$$

where M stands for the stock market index. Chen, Roll, and Ross used as the market index both the value-weighted NYSE index (VWNY) and the equally weighted NYSE index (EWNY).

[9]Nai-Fu Chen, Richard Roll, and Stephen Ross, "Economic Forces and the Stock Market," *Journal of Business* 59 (1986).

Using the 20 sets of first-pass estimates of factor betas as the independent variables, they now estimated the second-pass regression (with 20 observations, one for each portfolio):

$$r = \gamma_0 + \gamma_M \beta_M + \gamma_{IP} \beta_{IP} + \gamma_{EI} \beta_{EI} + \gamma_{UI} \beta_{UI} + \gamma_{CG} \beta_{CG} + \gamma_{GB} \beta_{GB} + e \qquad (13.6b)$$

where the gammas become estimates of the risk premiums on the factors.

Chen, Roll, and Ross ran this second-pass regression for every month of their sample period, reestimating the first-pass factor betas once every 12 months. They ran the second-pass tests in four variations. First (Table 13.2, parts A and B), they excluded the market index altogether and used two alternative measures of industrial production (YP based on annual growth of industrial production and MP based on monthly growth). Finding that MP is a more effective measure, they next included the two versions of the market index, EWNY and VWNY, one at a time (Table 13.2, parts C and D). The estimated risk premiums (the values for the parameters, γ) were averaged over all the second-pass regressions corresponding to each subperiod listed in Table 13.2.

Note in Table 13.2, parts C and D, that the two market indexes EWNY (equally weighted index of NYSE) and VWNY (the value-weighted NYSE index) are not significant (their *t*-statistics of 1.218 and −.633 are less than 2 for the overall sample period and for each subperiod). Note also that the VWNY factor has the wrong sign in that it seems to imply a negative market-risk premium. Industrial production (MP), the risk premium on corporate bonds (CG), and unanticipated inflation (UI) are the factors that appear to have significant explanatory power.

These results must be treated as only preliminary in this line of inquiry, but they indicate that it may be possible to hedge some economic factors that affect future consumption risk with appropriate portfolios. A CAPM or APT multifactor equilibrium expected return–beta relationship may one day supersede the now widely used single-factor model.

It is very difficult to identify the portfolios that serve to hedge common sources of risk to future consumption opportunities. The two lines of research explore the data in search of such portfolios. Factor analysis techniques indicate the portfolios that may be providing hedge services. Researchers can then try to figure out what the source of risk is and how important it is. The second line of research attempts to guess the identity of economic variables that are correlated with consumption risk and determine whether they indeed explain rates of return.

13.3   THE ANOMALIES LITERATURE: RISK PREMIUMS OR INEFFICIENCIES?

The Assault

The search for empirical support for the CAPM and the APT has been frustrating. Study after study has concluded that asset returns do not line up around the hypothesized security market line predicted by the CAPM and APT. Several researchers surmise that even if a positive expected return–beta relationship is valid, a full-blown asset pricing model cannot currently be empirically validated because of a host of statistical problems that, perhaps, can never be fully overcome.

Table 13.2   Economic Variables and Pricing (percent per month × 10), Multivariate Approach

A	Years	YP	IP	EI	UI	CG	GB	Constant
	1958–84	4.341	13.984	−0.111	−0.672	7.941	−5.8	4.112
		(0.538)	(3.727)	(−1.499)	(−2.052)	(2.807)	(−1.844)	(1.334)
	1958–67	0.417	15.760	0.014	−0.133	5.584	0.535	4.868
		(0.032)	(2.270)	(0.191)	(−0.259)	(1.923)	(0.240)	(1.156)
	1968–77	1.819	15.645	−0.264	−1.420	14.352	−14.329	−2.544
		(0.145)	(2.504)	(−3.397)	(−3.470)	(3.161)	(−2.672)	(−0.464)
	1978–84	13.549	8.937	−0.070	−0.373	2.150	−2.941	12.541
		(0.774)	(1.602)	(−0.289)	(−0.442)	(0.279)	(−0.327)	(1.911)

B	Years	IP	EI	UI	CG	GB	Constant
	1958–84	13.589	−0.125	−6.29	7.205	−5.211	4.124
		(3.561)	(−1.640)	(−1.979)	(2.590)	(−1.690)	(1.361)
	1958–67	13.155	0.006	−0.191	5.560	−0.008	4.989
		(1.897)	(0.092)	(−0.382)	(1.935)	(−0.004)	(1.271)
	1968–77	16.966	−0.245	−1.353	12.717	−13.142	−1.889
		(2.638)	(−3.215)	(−3.320)	(2.852)	(−2.554)	(−0.334)
	1978–84	9.383	−0.140	−0.221	1.679	−1.312	11.477
		(1.588)	(−0.552)	(−0.274)	(0.221)	(−0.149)	(1.747)

C	Years	EWNY	IP	EI	UI	CG	GB	Constant
	1958–84	5.021	14.009	−0.128	−0.848	0.130	−5.017	6.409
		(1.218)	(3.774)	(−1.666)	(−2.541)	(2.855)	(−1.576)	(1.848)
	1958–67	6.575	14.936	−0.005	−0.279	5.747	−0.146	7.349
		(1.199)	(2.336)	(−0.060)	(−0.558)	(2.070)	(−0.067)	(1.591)
	1968–77	2.334	17.593	−0.248	−1.501	12.512	−9.904	3.542
		(0.283)	(2.715)	(−3.039)	(−3.366)	(2.758)	(−2.015)	(0.558)
	1978–84	6.638	7.563	−0.132	−0.729	5.273	−4.993	9.164
		(0.906)	(1.253)	(−0.529)	(−0.847)	(0.663)	(−0.520)	(1.245)

D	Years	VWNY	IP	EI	UI	CG	GB	Constant
	1958–84	−2.403	11.756	−0.123	−0.795	8.274	−5.905	10.713
		(−0.633)	(3.054)	(−1.600)	(−2.376)	(2.972)	(−1.879)	(2.755)
	1958–67	1.359	12.394	0.005	−0.209	5.204	−0.086	9.527
		(0.277)	(1.789)	(0.064)	(−0.415)	(1.815)	(−0.040)	(1.984)
	1968–77	−5.269	13.466	−0.255	−1.421	12.897	−11.708	8.582
		(−0.717)	(2.038)	(−3.237)	(−3.106)	(2.955)	(−2.299)	(1.167)
	1978–84	−3.683	8.402	−0.116	−0.739	6.056	−5.928	15.452
		(−0.491)	(1.432)	(−0.458)	(−0.869)	(0.782)	(−0.644)	(1.867)

VWNY = Return on the value-weighted NYSE index; EWNY = Return on the equally weighted NYSE index; IP = Monthly growth rate in industrial production; EI = Change in expected inflation; UI = Unanticipated inflation; CG = Unanticipated change in the risk premium (Baa and under return − long-term government bond return); GB = Unanticipated change in the term structure (long-term government bond return − Treasury-bill rate); and YP = Yearly growth rate in industrial production. Note that *t*-statistics are in parentheses.

Source: Modified from Nai-Fu Chen, Richard Roll, and Stephen Ross, "Economic Forces and the Stock Market," *Journal of Business* 59 (1986); published by the University of Chicago.

BETA BEATEN

A battle between some of the top names in financial economics is attracting attention on Wall Street. Under attack is the famous capital-asset pricing model (CAPM), widely used to assess risk and return. A new paper by two Chicago economists, Eugene Fama and Kenneth French, explodes that model by showing that its key analytical tool does not explain why returns on shares differ.*

According to the CAPM, returns reflect risk. The model uses a measure called beta—shorthand for relative volatility—to compare the riskiness of one share with that of the whole market, on the basis of past price changes. A share with a beta of one is just as risky as the market; one with a beta of 0.5 is less risky. Because investors need to earn more on riskier investments, share prices will reflect the requirement for higher-than-average returns on shares with higher betas.

Whether beta does predict returns has long been debated. Studies have found that market capitalization, price/earnings ratios, leverage and book-to-market ratios do just as well. Messrs. Fama and French are clear: Beta is not a good guide.

The two economists look at all non-financial shares traded on the NYSE, AMEX and NASDAQ between 1963 and 1990. The shares were grouped into portfolios. When grouped solely on the basis of size (i.e., market capitalization), the CAPM worked—but each portfolio contained a wide range of betas. So the authors grouped shares of similar beta and size. Betas now were a bad guide to returns.

Instead of beta, say Messrs. Fama and French, differences in firm size and in the ratio of book value to market value explain differences in returns—especially the latter. When shares were grouped by book-to-market ratios, the gap in returns between the portfolio with the lowest ratio and that with the highest was far wider than when shares were grouped by size.

So should analysts stop using the CAPM? Probably not. Although Mr. Fama and Mr. French have produced intriguing results, they lack a theory to explain them. Their best hope is that size and book-to-market ratios are proxies for other fundamentals. For instance, a high book-to-market ratio may indicate a firm in trouble; its earnings prospects might thus be especially sensitive to economic conditions, so its shares would need to earn a higher return than its beta suggested.

Advocates of CAPM—including Fischer Black, of Goldman Sachs, an investment bank, and William Sharpe of Stanford University, who won the Nobel prize for economics in 1990—reckon the results of the new study can be explained without discarding beta. Investors may irrationally favor big firms. Or they may lack the cash to buy enough shares to spread risk completely, so that risk and return are not perfectly matched in the market.

Those looking for a theoretical alternative to CAPM will find little satisfaction, however. Voguish rivals, such as the "arbitrage-pricing theory," are no better than CAPM and betas at explaining actual share returns. Which leaves Wall Street with an awkward choice: believe the Fama-French evidence, despite its theoretical vacuum, and use size and the book-to-market ratios as a guide to returns; or stick with a theory that, despite the data, is built on impeccable logic.

*Eugene Fama and Kenneth French, "The Cross-Section of Expected Stock Returns," *Journal of Finance* 47 (1992), pp. 427–66.
Source: From *The Economist*, March 7, 1992, p. 87.

It is not surprising that a study by Fama and French,[10] briefly discussed in Chapter 12, received great attention when it reported that:

> Two easily measured variables, size and book-to-market equity, combine to capture the cross-sectional variation in average stock returns associated with market β, size, leverage, book-to-market equity, and earnings-price ratios. Moreover, when the tests allow for variation in β that is unrelated to size, the relation between market β and average returns is flat, even when β is the only explanatory variable.

This is a highly disturbing conclusion. If the empirical evidence suggests that systematic risk is unrelated to expected returns, we must relinquish one of the cornerstones of the theory of finance. Indeed, in Fama and French's words: "In short, our tests do not support the central prediction of the [CAPM and APT], that average stock returns are positively related to β." This conclusion captured the attention of practitioners as well as academic communities, and was reported in *The New York Times* and *The Economist* (see the nearby box).

---

[10]Eugene F. Fama and Kenneth R. French, "The Cross Section of Expected Stock Returns," *Journal of Finance* 47 (1992), pp. 427–66.

The most damning evidence that Fama and French (FF) provide is of the lack of a positive relation between average returns and beta. Table 13.3 best illustrates this point. FF find that both size and beta are positively correlated with average returns. But because these explanatory variables are highly (negatively) correlated, they seek to isolate the effect of beta. They accomplish this by forming 10 portfolios of different betas *within* each of the 10 size groups.

The top row in Panel B of Table 13.3 shows that the portfolio beta of each beta group, averaged across the 10 size portfolios steadily increases from .76 to 1.69. The top row in Panel C shows that the average portfolio size within each beta group is almost identical, ranging from 4.34 to 4.40. This allows us to interpret Panel A as a test of the net effect of beta on average returns holding size fixed.

Panel A of the table clearly shows that, for the period 1941–1990, average returns are not positively related to beta. The two highest-beta portfolios have the two lowest average returns, and the highest average returns occur in the fourth- and fifth-beta portfolios).

The Defense

Fama and French's assault on the CAPM has engendered four responses:

1. Utilize better econometrics in the test procedure.
2. Improve estimates of asset betas.
3. Reconsider the theoretical sources and implications of the Fama and French–type results.
4. Return to the single-index model, accounting for nontraded assets and the cyclical behavior of asset betas.

Improving the econometric procedures employed in tests of asset returns seems the most direct response to the FF results. Amihud, Bent, and Mendelson[11] improve on the FF test procedures, using generalized least squares (GLS) and pooling the time-series and cross-sectional rates of return. For the entire period analyzed by FF, 1941–1990, Amihud, Bent, and Mendelson find a significantly positive relation between average returns and beta, even when controlling for size and book-to-market ratio. The expected return–beta relationship is still not statistically significant for the most recent subperiod, 1972–1990. However, in light of the considerable variability of stock returns, it is perhaps not surprising that it is difficult to obtain statistically significant results over shorter sample periods.

Kothari, Shanken, and Sloan[12] concentrate on the measurement of stock betas. They choose annual intervals for the estimation of stock betas to sidestep problems caused by trading frictions, nonsynchronous trading, and seasonality in monthly returns. As it turns out, this procedure generates results that are more favorable to the expected return–beta hypothesis. Thus they conclude that there has been substantial compensation for beta risk over the 1941–1990 period, and even more over the 1927–1990 period. Table 13.4 shows the coefficient estimates for the average return–beta relationship with and without the presence of the size variable, for five different ways of grouping portfolios and for two periods.

One interpretation of the Fama and French results is that the apparently "irrelevant" variables like firm size and book-to-market ratios are in fact proxies for more fundamental measures of risk that we don't fully understand. In this case, the Fama and French

---

[11]Yakov Amihud, Jesper C. Bent, and Haim Mendelson, "Further Evidence on the Risk-Return Relationship," Working Paper, Graduate School of Business, Standard University (1992).

[12]S. P. Kothari, J. Shanken, and Richard G. Sloan, "Another Look at the Cross Section of Stock Returns," *Journal of Finance* 49 (1994), pp. 101–21.

Table 13.3   Properties of Portfolios Formed on Size and Preranking β: NYSE Stocks Sorted by ME (Down) then Preranking β (Across), 1941–1990

At the end of year $t - 1$, the NYSE stocks on CRSP are assigned to 10 size (ME) portfolios. Each size decile is subdivided into 10 β portfolios using preranking βs of individual stocks, estimated with 24 to 60 monthly returns (as available) ending in December of year $t - 1$. The equal-weighted monthly returns on the resulting 100 portfolios are then calculated for year t. The average returns are the time-series averages of the monthly returns, in percent. The postranking βs use the full 1941–1990 sample of postranking returns for each portfolio. The pre- and postranking βs are the sum of the slopes from a regression of monthly returns on the current and prior month's NYSE value-weighted market return. The average size for a portfolio is the time-series average of each month's average value of ln(ME) for stocks in the portfolio. ME is denominated in millions of dollars. There are, on average, about 10 stocks in each size-β portfolio each month. The All column shows parameter values for equal-weighted size-decile (ME) portfolios. The All rows show parameter values for equal-weighted portfolios of the stocks in each β group.

	All	Low-β	β-2	β-3	β-4	β-5	β-6	β-7	β-8	β-9	High-β
Panel A: Average Monthly Return (in percent)											
All		1.22	1.30	1.32	1.35	1.36	1.34	1.29	1.34	1.14	1.10
Small-ME	1.78	1.74	1.76	2.08	1.91	1.92	1.72	1.77	1.91	1.56	1.46
ME-2	1.44	1.41	1.35	1.33	1.61	1.72	1.59	1.40	1.62	1.24	1.11
ME-3	1.36	1.21	1.40	1.22	1.47	1.34	1.51	1.33	1.57	1.33	1.21
ME-4	1.28	1.26	1.29	1.19	1.27	1.51	1.30	1.19	1.56	1.18	1.00
ME-5	1.24	1.22	1.30	1.28	1.33	1.21	1.37	1.41	1.31	0.92	1.06
ME-6	1.23	1.21	1.32	1.37	1.09	1.34	1.10	1.40	1.21	1.22	1.08
ME-7	1.17	1.08	1.23	1.37	1.27	1.19	1.34	1.10	1.11	0.87	1.17
ME-8	1.15	1.06	1.18	1.26	1.25	1.26	1.17	1.16	1.05	1.08	1.04
ME-9	1.13	0.99	1.13	1.00	1.24	1.28	1.31	1.15	1.11	1.09	1.05
Large-ME	0.95	0.99	1.01	1.12	1.01	0.89	0.95	0.95	1.00	0.90	0.68
Panel B: Postranking β											
All		0.76	0.95	1.05	1.14	1.22	1.26	1.34	1.38	1.49	1.69
Small-ME	1.52	1.17	1.40	1.31	1.50	1.46	1.50	1.69	1.60	1.75	1.92
ME-2	1.37	0.86	1.09	1.12	1.24	1.39	1.42	1.48	1.60	1.69	1.91
ME-3	1.32	0.88	0.96	1.18	1.19	1.33	1.40	1.43	1.56	1.64	1.74
ME-4	1.26	0.69	0.95	1.06	1.15	1.24	1.29	1.46	1.43	1.64	1.83
ME-5	1.23	0.70	0.95	1.04	1.10	1.22	1.32	1.34	1.41	1.56	1.72
ME-6	1.19	0.68	0.86	1.04	1.13	1.20	1.20	1.35	1.36	1.48	1.70
ME-7	1.17	0.67	0.88	0.95	1.14	1.18	1.26	1.27	1.32	1.44	1.68
ME-8	1.12	0.64	0.83	0.99	1.06	1.14	1.14	1.21	1.26	1.39	1.58
ME-9	1.06	0.68	0.81	0.94	0.96	1.06	1.11	1.18	1.22	1.25	1.46
Large-ME	0.97	0.65	0.73	0.90	0.91	0.97	1.01	1.01	1.07	1.12	1.38
Panel C: Average Size (ln(ME))											
All		4.39	4.39	4.40	4.40	4.39	4.40	4.38	4.37	4.37	4.34
Small-ME	1.93	2.04	1.99	2.00	1.96	1.92	1.92	1.91	1.90	1.87	1.80
ME-2	2.80	2.81	2.79	2.81	2.83	2.80	2.79	2.80	2.80	2.79	2.79
ME-3	3.27	3.28	3.27	3.28	3.27	3.27	3.28	3.29	3.27	3.27	3.26
ME-4	3.67	3.67	3.67	3.67	3.68	3.68	3.67	3.68	3.66	3.67	3.67
ME-5	4.06	4.07	4.06	4.05	4.06	4.07	4.06	4.05	4.05	4.06	4.06
ME-6	4.45	4.45	4.44	4.46	4.45	4.45	4.45	4.45	4.44	4.45	4.45
ME-7	4.87	4.86	4.87	4.86	4.87	4.87	4.88	4.87	4.87	4.85	4.87
ME-8	5.36	5.38	5.38	5.38	5.35	5.36	5.37	5.37	5.36	5.35	5.34
ME-9	5.98	5.96	5.98	5.99	6.00	5.98	5.98	5.97	5.95	5.96	5.96
Large-ME	7.12	7.10	7.12	7.16	7.17	7.20	7.29	7.14	7.09	7.04	6.83

Source: Eugene F. Fama and Kenneth R. French, "The Cross Section of Expected Stock Returns," *Journal of Finance* 47 (1992), pp. 427–66.

Table 13.4 Cross-Sectional Regressions of Monthly Returns on Beta and Firm Size: Equally Weighted Market Index, 1927–1990

Time-series averages of estimated coefficients from the following monthly cross-sectional regressions from 1927 to 1990, associated t-statistics, and adjusted R^2s are reported (with and without Size being included in the regressions).

$$R_{pt} = \gamma_{0t} + \gamma_{1t}\beta_p + \gamma_{2t}\text{Size}_{pt-1} + \epsilon_{pt}$$

where R_{pt} is the buy-and-hold return on portfolio p for one month during the year beginning from July 1 of the year t to June 30 of year $t+1$; β_p is the full-period postranking beta of portfolio p and is the slope coefficient from a time-series regression of annual buy-and-hold postranking portfolio returns on the returns on an equally weighted portfolio of all the beta-size portfolios; Size_{pt-1} is the natural log of the average market capitalization in millions of dollars on June 30 of year t of the stocks in portfolio p; γ_{0t}, γ_{1t}, and γ_{2t} are regression parameters; and ϵ_{pt} is the regression error. Portfolios are formed in five different ways: (1) 20 portfolios by grouping on beta alone; (2) 20 portfolios by grouping on size alone; (3) taking intersections of 10 independent beta or size groupings to obtain 100 portfolios; (4) ranking stocks first on beta into 10 portfolios and then on size within each beta group into 10 portfolios; and (5) ranking stocks first on size into 10 portfolios and then on beta within each size group into 10 portfolios. When ranking on beta, the beta for an individual stock is estimated by regressing 24 to 60 monthly portfolio returns ending in June of each year on the Center for Research in Securities Prices (CRSP) equally weighted portfolio. The t-statistic below the average γ_0 value is for the difference between the average γ_0 and the average risk-free rate of return over the 1927–1990 period. The t-statistics below γ_1 and γ_2 are for their average values from zero.

Portfolios	γ_0 / t-statistic	γ_1 / t-statistic	γ_2 / t-statistic	Adj. R^2
20, beta ranked	0.76	0.54		0.32
	3.25	1.94		
	1.76		−0.16	0.27
	2.48		−2.03	
	1.68	0.09	−0.14	0.35
	3.82	0.41	−2.57	
20, size ranked	0.30	1.02		0.32
	−0.18	3.91		
	1.73		−0.18	0.33
	3.70		−3.50	
	−0.05	1.15	0.03	0.40
	−0.85	4.61	0.76	
100, beta and size ranked independently	0.63	0.66		0.07
	1.67	3.65		
	1.72		−0.17	0.09
	3.92		−3.17	
	1.21	0.04	−0.11	0.12
	3.74	2.63	−2.83	
100, first beta, then size ranked	0.57	0.73		0.12
	1.43	3.49		
	1.73		−0.18	0.12
	3.70		−3.48	
	1.12	0.45	−0.10	0.16
	3.43	2.83	−2.65	
100, first size, then beta ranked	0.58	0.71		0.12
	1.54	3.39		
	1.72		−0.18	0.12
	3.66		−3.43	
	1.14	0.43	−0.10	0.16
	3.78	2.58	−2.87	

results would be consistent with a multifactor APT in which the true factors are measured by these proxies. This interpretation requires us to probe more deeply about what these variables are measuring.

Another response to the anomalies literature is to attribute the results to a "data snooping bias." If finance researchers all over the world continually examine data for an apparently successful trading rule, sooner or later they are going to find some variables that appear to predict expected returns. Put another way, if the same data are screened and rescreened for impacts of a wide range of variables, then the *t*-statistics for these tests are overstated.

Fischer Black once commented that "it's a curious fact that just after the small-firm effect was announced, it seems to have vanished. What that sounds like is that people searched over thousands of rules until they found one that worked in the past. . . . As we might expect, in out-of-sample of data, the rule didn't work anymore." The phenomenon of data snooping has been dubbed, only partly in jest, "Darwinian *t*-statistics: survival of the best fit." In other words, countless tests are performed, but only those with statistically significant results are reported in the literature.

It is very hard to estimate expected return even with a stable true mean: We can improve estimates only by taking average returns over long periods. But the longer the period, the less likely it is that expected returns are constant. While historical average is an obvious estimate of expected return, it is highly imprecise. So perhaps we shouldn't be overwhelmed with apparent abnormal returns associated with theoretically irrelevant factors, especially those subject to the data snooping bias. At least with the market portfolio, theory tells us the expected return is positive; we don't have even this small amount of theory to guide us in the interpretation the historical returns on the "irrelevant" factors.

Accounting for Human Capital and Cyclical Variations in Asset Betas

A more recent contribution takes us back to the single-index CAPM and APT. We are reminded of two important deficiencies of the tests of the single-index models:

1. Only a fraction of the value of assets in the United States is traded in capital markets; perhaps the most important nontraded asset is human capital.

2. There is ample evidence that asset betas are cyclical and that accounting for this cyclicality may improve the predictive power of the CAPM.

One of the CAPM assumptions is that all assets are traded and accessible to all investors. Mayers[13] proposed a version of the CAPM that accounts for a violation of this assumption; this requires an additional term in the expected return–beta relationship.

An important nontraded asset that may partly account for the deficiency of standard market proxies such as the S&P 500 is human capital. The value of future wages and compensation for expert services is a significant component of the wealth of investors who expect years of productive careers prior to retirement. Moreover, it is reasonable to expect that changes in human capital are far less than perfectly correlated with asset returns, and hence they diversify the risk of investor portfolios.

Jaganathan and Wang (JW)[14] used a proxy for changes in the value of human capital based on the rate of change in aggregate labor income. In addition to the standard security

[13]David Mayers, "Nonmarketable Assets and Capital Market Equilibrium under Uncertainty," in Michael C. Jensen, ed., *Studies in the Theory of Capital Markets* (New York: Praeger, 1972), pp. 223–48.

[14]Ravi Jaganathan and Zhenyu Wang, "The Conditional CAPM and the Cross-Section of Expected Returns," *Journal of Finance* 51 (March 1996), pp. 3–54.

betas estimated using the value-weighted stock market index, which we denote β^{vw}, JW also estimated the betas of assets with respect to labor income growth, which we denote β^{labor}. Finally, they considered the possibility that business cycles affect asset betas, an issue that has been examined in a number of other studies.[15] They used the difference between the yields on low- and high-grade corporate bonds as a proxy for the state of the business cycle and estimate asset betas relative to this business cycle variable; we denote this beta as β^{prem}.

With the estimates of these three betas for several stock portfolios, JW estimated a second-pass regression which includes firm size (market value of equity, denoted ME):

$$E(R_i) = c_0 + c_{size}\log(ME) + c_{vw}\beta^{vw} + c_{prem}\beta^{prem} + c_{labor}\beta^{labor} \qquad (13.7)$$

Table 13.5 shows the results of various versions of the second-pass estimates for equation 13.7, where each version uses a different subset of the right-hand-side variables. These results are far more supportive of the CAPM than earlier tests. The explanatory power of the equations that include JW's expanded set of explanatory variables (which they call a "conditional" CAPM because beta is conditional on the state of the economy) is much greater than in earlier tests, and the significance of the size variable disappears.

Figures 13.2 to 13.5 show the improvements of these tests more dramatically. Figure 13.2 shows that the conventional CAPM indeed works poorly. The figure compares predicted security returns fitted using the firm's beta versus actual returns. There is obviously

Figure 13.2

Fitted expected returns versus realized average returns.

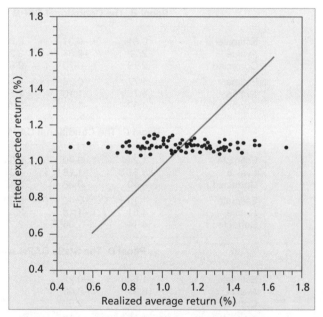

Each scatter point in the graph represents a portfolio, with the realized average return as the horizontal axis and the fitted expected return as the vertical axis. For each portfolio i, the realized average return is the time-series average of the portfolio return, and the fitted expected return is the fitted value for the expected return, $E(R_i)$, in the following regression model:

$$E(R_i) = c_0 + c_{vw}\beta_i^{vw}$$

where β_i^{vw} is the slope coefficient in the OLS regression of the portfolio return on a constant and the return on the value-weighted index portfolio of stocks. The straight line in the graph is the 45° line from the origin.

---

[15]For example, Campbell Harvey, "Time-Varying Conditional Covariances in Tests of Asset Pricing Models," *Journal of Financial Economics* 24 (October 1989), pp. 289–317; Wayne Ferson and Campbell Harvey, "The Variation of Economic Risk Premiums," *Journal of Political Economy* 99 (April 1991), pp. 385–415; and Wayne Ferson and Robert Korajczyk, "Do Arbitrage Pricing Models Explain the Predictability of Stock Returns?" *Journal of Business* 68 (July 1995), pp. 309–49.

Table 13.5   Evaluation of Various CAPM Specifications

This table gives the estimates for the cross-sectional regression model

$$E(R_{it}) = c_0 + c_{size}\log(ME_i) + c_{vw}\beta_i^{vw} + c_{prem}\beta_i^{prem} + c_{labor}\beta_i^{labor}$$

with either a subset or all of the variables. Here, R_{it} is the return on portfolio i ($i = 1, 2, \ldots, 100$) in month t (July 1963–December 1990), R_t^{vw} is the return on the value-weighted index of stocks, R_{t-1}^{prem} is the yield spread between low- and high-grade corporate bonds, and R_t^{labor} is the growth rate in per capita labor income. The β_i^{vw} is the slope coefficient in the OLS regression of R_{it} on a constant and R_t^{vw}. The other betas are estimated in a similar way. The portfolio size, $\log(ME_i)$, is calculated as the equally weighted average of the logarithm of the market value (in millions of dollars) of the stocks in portfolio i. The regression models are estimated by using the Fama-MacBeth procedure. The "corrected t-values" take sampling errors in the estimated betas into account. All R^2s are reported as percentages.

Coefficient	c_0	c_{vw}	c_{prem}	c_{labor}	c_{size}	R^2
Panel A. The Static CAPM without Human Capital						
Estimate	1.24	−0.10				1.35
t-value	5.17	−0.28				
Corrected t	5.16	−0.28				
Estimate	2.08	−0.32			−0.11	57.56
t-value	5.79	−0.94			−2.30	
Corrected t	5.77	−0.94			−2.30	
Panel B. The Conditional CAPM without Human Capital						
Estimate	0.81	−0.31	0.36			29.32
t-value	2.72	−0.87	3.28			
Corrected t	2.19	−0.70	2.67			
Estimate	1.77	−0.38	0.16		−0.10	61.66
t-value	4.75	−1.10	2.50		−1.93	
Corrected t	4.53	−1.05	2.40		−1.84	
Panel C. The Conditional CAPM with Human Capital						
Estimate	1.24	−0.40	0.34	0.22		55.21
t-value	5.51	−1.18	3.31	2.31		
Corrected t	4.10	−0.88	2.48	1.73		
Estimate	1.70	−0.40	0.20	0.10	−0.07	64.73
t-value	4.61	−1.18	3.00	2.09	−1.45	
Corrected t	4.14	−1.06	2.72	1.89	−1.30	
Panel D. The Static CAPM with Human Capital						
Estimate	1.67	−0.22		0.23		30.46
t-value	6.91	−0.63		2.37		
Corrected t	5.71	−0.52		1.97		
Estimate	2.09	−0.32		0.05	−0.10	58.55
t-value	5.80	−0.96		1.22	−2.15	
Corrected t	5.70	−0.95		1.20	−2.11	

almost no relationship between the two. This is indicative of the weak performance of the conventional CAPM in empirical tests. Figure 13.3 shows that adding firm size to the fitting equation improves fit dramatically. This reflects the firm-size anomaly. But if we use the conditional CAPM to compare fitted to actual returns, as in Figure 13.4, we also get a good fit. Moreover, adding firm size to this model, as in Figure 13.5, does nothing to improve the fit. We conclude that firm size does not improve return predictions once we account for the variables addressed in the conditional CAPM.

Figure 13.3

Fitted expected returns versus realized average returns.

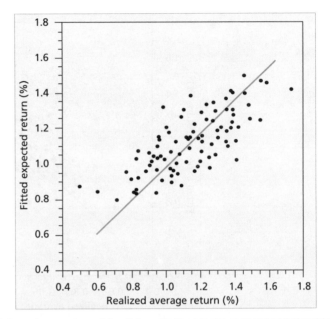

Each scatter point in the graph represents a portfolio, with the realized average return as the horizontal axis and the fitted expected return as the vertical axis. For each portfolio i, the realized average return is the time-series average of the portfolio return, and the fitted expected return is the fitted value for the expected return, $E(R_i)$, in the following regression model:

$$E(R_i) = c_0 + c_{size}\log(ME_i) + c_{vw}\beta_i^{vw}$$

where β_i^{vw} is the slope coefficient in the OLS regression of the portfolio return on a constant and the return on the value-weighted index portfolio of stocks, and the portfolio size, $\log(ME_i)$, is calculated as the equally weighted average of the logarithm of the market value (in million dollars) of the stocks in portfolio i. The straight line in the graph is the 45° line from the origin.

Figure 13.4

Fitted expected returns versus realized average returns.

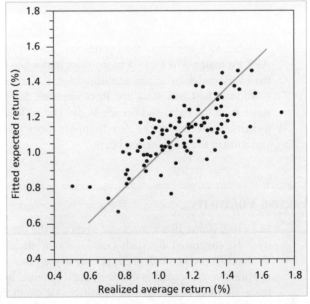

Each scatter point in the graph represents a portfolio, with the realized average return as the horizontal axis and the fitted expected return as the vertical axis. For each portfolio i, the realized average return is the time-series average of the portfolio return, and the fitted expected return is the fitted value for the expected return, $E(R_i)$, in the following regression model:

$$E(R_i) = c_0 + c_{vw}\beta_i^{vw} + c_{prem}\beta_i^{prem} + c_{labor}\beta_i^{labor}$$

where β_i^{vw} is the slope coefficient in the OLS regression of the portfolio return on a constant and the return on the value-weighted index portfolio of stocks, β_i^{prem} is the slope coefficient in the OLS regression of the portfolio return on a constant and the yield spread between low- and high-grade corporate bonds, and β_i^{labor} is the slope coefficient in the OLS regression of the portfolio return on a constant and the growth rate in per capita labor income. The straight line in the graph is the 45° line from the origin.

Figure 13.5
Fitted expected returns
versus realized average
returns.

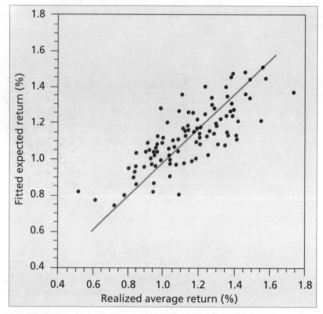

Each scatter point in the graph represents a portfolio, with the realized average return as the horizontal axis and the fitted expected
return as the vertical axis. For each portfolio i, the realized average return is the time-series average of the portfolio return, and the
fitted expected return is the fitted value for the expected return, $E(R_i)$, in the following regression model:

$$E(R_i) = c_0 + c_{size}\log(ME_i) + c_{vw}\beta_i^{vw} + c_{prem}\beta_i^{prem} + c_{labor}\beta_i^{labor}$$

where β_i^{vw} is the slope coefficient in the OLS regression of the portfolio return on a constant and the return on the value-weighted index
portfolio of stocks, β_i^{prem} is the slope coefficient in the OLS regression of the portfolio return on a constant and the yield spread between
low- and high-grade corporate bonds, β_i^{labor} is the slope coefficient in the OLS regression of the portfolio return on a constant and the
growth rate in per capita labor income, and the portfolio size, $\log(ME_i)$, is calculated as the equally weighted average of the logarithm of
the market value (in million dollars) of the stocks in portfolio i. The straight line in the graph is the 45° line from the origin.

Table 13.6 compares the conditional CAPM to the Chen, Roll, and Ross multifactor
APT estimates. The table demonstrates that when human capital and cyclical variation of
the single-index betas are accounted for, the significance of the macroeconomic factors
considered by Chen, Roll, and Ross vanishes. Similarly, Table 13.7 compares results with
those from the Fama and French study. The table shows that the significance of the book-
to-market and size factors also disappears once we account for human capital and cyclical
variation of the single-index betas.

13.4   TIME-VARYING VOLATILITY

In 1976, Fischer Black proposed to model the time-varying nature of asset-return volatility.[16] He suggested that such a model should include three effects. One is that the volatility depends on the stock price. (Generally, an increase in the stock price means a decrease
in volatility.) A second is that the volatility tends to return to a long-term average. Finally,
there are random changes in volatility. Although the idea was well received and widely
cited, little was accomplished for quite a while.

---

[16]Fischer Black, "Studies in Stock Price Volatility Changes," *Proceedings of the 1976 Business Meeting of the Business and
Economic Statistics Sections, American Statistical Association*, pp. 177–81.

Table 13.6   Comparison with the Factors Used by Chen, Roll, and Ross (1986)

This table gives the estimates for the cross-sectional regression model

$$E(R_{it}) = c_0 + c_{vw}\beta_i^{vw} + c_{prem}\beta_i^{prem} + c_{labor}\beta_i^{labor} + c_{GB}\beta_i^{GB} + c_{CG}\beta_i^{CG} + c_{IP}\beta_i^{IP} + c_{UI}\beta_i^{UI}$$

with either a subset or all of the variables. Here, R_{it} is the return on portfolio i ($i = 1, 2, \ldots, 100$) in month t (July 1963–December 1990), R_t^{vw} is the return on the value-weighted index of stocks, R_{t-1}^{prem} is the yield spread between low- and high-grade corporate bonds, R_t^{labor} is the growth rate in per capita labor income, GB_t is the return spread between long-term government bonds and Treasury bills, CG_t is the return differential between long-term corporate and long-term government bonds, IP_t is the growth rate in monthly industrial production in the United States, and UI_t is the change of inflation rate. The β_i^{vw} is the slope coefficient in the OLS regression of R_{it} on a constant and R_t^{vw}. The other betas are estimated in a similar way. The regression models are estimated by using the Fama-MacBeth procedure. The "corrected t-values" take sampling errors in the estimated betas into account. All the R^2 are reported as percentages.

Coefficient	c_0	c_{vw}	c_{prem}	c_{labor}	c_{GB}	c_{CG}	c_{IP}	c_{UI}	R^2
Estimate	1.80	−0.44			−1.07	0.39	−0.02	−0.07	38.96
t-value	7.18	−1.28			−2.44	1.63	−0.17	−1.95	
Corrected t	6.17	−1.10			−2.12	1.41	−0.15	−1.68	
Estimate	1.37	−0.51	0.29	0.18	−0.17	0.19	0.07	−0.03	57.87
t-value	6.33	−1.46	3.54	2.44	−0.46	0.92	0.61	−0.99	
Corrected t	4.97	−1.15	2.81	1.93	−0.36	0.72	0.48	−0.78	

Table 13.7   Comparison with the Factors Used by Fama and French (1993)

This table gives the estimates for the cross-sectional regression model

$$E(R_{it}) = c_0 + c_{vw}\beta_i^{vw} + c_{prem}\beta_i^{prem} + c_{labor}\beta_i^{labor} + c_{SMB}\beta_i^{SMB} + c_{HML}\beta_i^{HML}$$

with either a subset or all of the variables. Here, R_{it} is the return on portfolio i ($i = 1, 2, \ldots, 100$) in month t (July 1963–December 1990), R_t^{vw} is the return on the value-weighted index of stocks, R_{t-1}^{prem} is the yield spread between low- and high-grade corporate bonds, R_t^{labor} is the growth rate in per capita labor income, and SMB_t and HML_t denote the respective Fama and French (1993) factors that are designed to capture the risks related to firm size and book-to-market equity. The β_i^{vw} is the slope coefficient in the OLS regression of R_{it} on a constant and R_t^{vw}. The other betas are estimated in a similar way. The regression models are estimated by using the Fama-MacBeth procedure. The "corrected t-values" take sampling errors in the estimated betas into account. All the R^2 are reported as percentages.

Coefficient	c_0	c_{vw}	c_{prem}	c_{labor}	c_{SMB}	c_{HML}	R^2
Estimate	1.39	−0.45			0.33	0.25	55.12
t-value	6.07	−0.95			1.53	0.96	
Corrected t	5.99	−0.94			1.51	0.95	
Estimate	1.20	−0.38	0.22	0.11	0.16	0.22	64.04
t-value	5.24	−0.80	3.32	2.25	0.78	0.84	
Corrected t	4.60	−0.70	2.95	1.99	0.68	0.74	

    In 1982 Robert F. Engle published a study[17] of U.K. inflation rates that measured their time-varying volatility. His model, named ARCH (autoregressive conditional heteroskedasticity), is based on the idea that a natural way to update a variance forecast is to average it with the most recent squared "surprise" (i.e., the squared deviation of the rate of return from its mean). ARCH is a statistically efficient algorithm to do just that.

---

[17]Robert F. Engle, "Autoregressive Conditional Heteroskedasticity with Estimates of the Variance of U.K. Inflation," *Econometrica* 50 (1982), pp. 987–1008.

This methodology caught fire in empirical research. A survey conducted[18] in May 1990 listed over 250 papers that employ ARCH in financial models. Moreover, an algorithm has been developed[19] to perform a joint estimation of the time-series variances and the relationship between the mean and variance of returns (ARCH-M). By applying this technique to an array of assets, tests that relate mean asset returns to covariances can be devised.

13.5   STOCHASTIC VOLATILITY AND ASSET RETURNS

The price of a stock may change for two reasons: First, the arrival of new information may lead investors to change their assessment of intrinsic value; second, even in the absence of new information, unexpected changes in investor liquidity needs combined with trading frictions may create temporary buying or selling pressures that cause the price to fluctuate around its intrinsic value. Except for the least liquid assets, however, new information should account for the lion's share of price changes, at least when we examine returns for horizons longer than a few weeks. Therefore, we may associate the variance of the rate of return on the stock with the rate of arrival of new information. As a casual survey of the media would indicate, the rate of revision in predictions of business cycles, industry ascents or descents, and the fortunes of individual enterprises fluctuates regularly; in other words, the rate of arrival of new information is time varying. Consequently, we should expect the variances of the rates of return on stocks (as well as the covariances among them) to be time varying.

In an exploratory study of the volatility of NYSE stocks over more than 150 years (using monthly returns over 1835–1987), Pagan and Schwert[20] computed estimates of the variance of monthly returns. Their results, depicted in Figure 13.6, show just how important it may be to consider time variation in stock variance. The centrality of the risk-return trade-off suggests that once we make sufficient progress in the modeling, estimation, and prediction of the time variation in return variances and covariances, we should expect a significant refinement in understanding expected returns as well.

When we consider a time-varying return distribution, we must refer to the *conditional* mean, variance, and covariance, that is, the mean, variance, or covariance conditional on currently available information. The "conditions" that vary over time are the values of variables that determine the level of these parameters. In contrast, the usual estimate of return variance, the average of squared deviations over the sample period, provides an *unconditional* estimate, because it treats the variance as constant over time.

The most widely used model to estimate the conditional (hence time varying) variance of stocks and stock index returns is the generalized autoregressive conditional heteroskedasticity (GARCH) model, pioneered by Robert F. Engle.[21] (The generalized ARCH model allows greater flexibility in the specification of how volatility evolves over time.) Bollerslev, Chou, and Kroner[22] provide an extensive survey of the contribution of this tech-

[18]Tim Bollerslev, Ray Y. Chou, Narayanan Jayaraman, and Kenneth F. Kroner, "ARCH Modeling in Finance: A Selective Review of the Theory and Empirical Evidence, with Suggestions for Future Research," *Journal of Econometrics* 48 (July/August 1992).

[19]Tim Bollerslev, Robert F. Engle, and Jeffrey M. Woolridge, "A Capital Asset Pricing Model with Time-Varying Covariances," *Journal of Political Economy* 96 (1989), pp. 116–31.

[20]Adrian Pagan and G. William Schwert, "Alternative Models for Conditional Stock Volatility," *Journal of Econometrics* 45 (1990), pp. 267–90.

[21]Robert F. Engle, "Autoregressive Conditional Heteroskedasticity with Estimates of the Variance of the U.K. Inflation," *Econometrica* 50 (1982), pp. 987–1008.

[22]Tim Bolerslev, Ray Chou, and Kenneth Kroner, "ARCH Modeling in Finance: A Review of the Theory and Empirical Evidence," *Journal of Econometrics* 52 (1992), pp. 5–59.

Figure 13.6

Estimates of the monthly stock return variance, 1835–1987

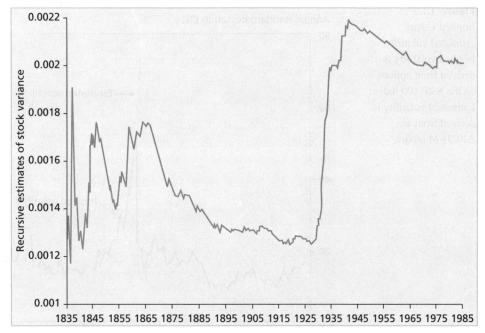

Source: Adrian R. Pagan and G. William Schwert, "Alternative Models for Conditional Stock Volatility," *Journal of Econometrics* 45 (1990), pp. 267–90.

nique to empirical work in finance. The work we present here is illustrative of the issues examined in current lines of research, but is far from exhaustive.

The GARCH model uses rate of return history as the information set used to form our estimates of variance. The model posits that the forecast of market volatility evolves relatively smoothly each period in response to new observations on market returns. The updated estimate of market-return variance in each period depends on both the previous estimate and the most recent squared residual return on the market. The squared residual is an unbiased estimate of variance, so this technique essentially mixes in a statistically efficient manner the previous volatility estimate with an unbiased estimate based on the new observation of market return. The updating formula is

$$\sigma_t^2 = a_0 + a_1 \epsilon_{t-1}^2 + a_2 \sigma_{t-1}^2 \tag{13.8}$$

As noted, equation 13.8 asserts that the updated forecast of variance is a function of the most recent variance forecast σ_{t-1}^2, and the most recent squared prediction error in market return, ϵ_{t-1}^2. The parameters a_0, a_1, and a_2 are estimated from past data.

To estimate the return surprise, ϵ_t, we require an equation for the expected return. One of the extensions of the model, GARCH-Mean, estimates two simultaneous equations for the expected excess return and variance. The first equation is 13.8; the second is an equation for the market excess return:

$$r_t - r_{ft} = b_0 + b_1 \sigma_t^2 + \epsilon_t \tag{13.9}$$

Equation 13.9 asserts that the expected market excess return is an increasing function of predicted variance, with slope coefficient b_1. Therefore, the expected excess return on the stock index is linear in the predicted variance from equation 13.8.

Figure 13.7
Implied versus estimated volatility. Implied volatility is derived from options on the S&P 100 index. Estimated volatility is derived from an ARCH-M model.

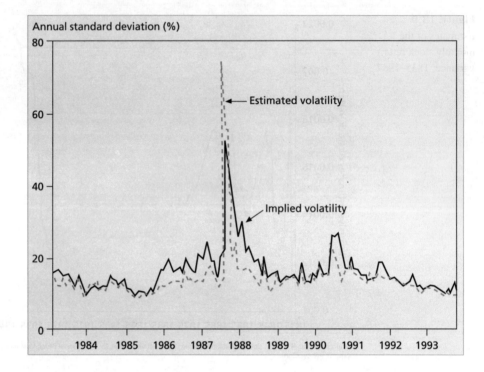

Evidence on the relationship between mean and variance has been mixed. Whitelaw[23] found that average returns and volatility are negatively related, but Kane, Marcus, and Noh[24] found a positive relationship.

ARCH-type models clearly capture much of the variation in stock market volatility. Figure 13.7 compares volatility estimates from an ARCH model to volatility estimates derived from prices on market-index options.[25] The variation in volatility, as well as the close agreement between the estimates, is evident.

SUMMARY

1. Although the single-factor expected return–beta relationship has not yet been confirmed by scientific standards, its use is already commonplace in economic life.

2. Early tests of the single-factor CAPM rejected the SML, finding that nonsystematic risk did explain average security returns.

3. Later tests controlling for the measurement error in beta found that nonsystematic risk does not explain portfolio returns but also that the estimated SML is too flat compared with what the CAPM would predict.

[23]Robert F. Whitelaw, "Time Variation and Covariations in the Expectation and Volatility of Stock Returns," *Journal of Finance* 49 (1994), pp. 515–42.
[24]Alex Kane, Alan J. Marcus, and Jaesun Noh, "The P/E Multiple and Market Volatility," *Financial Analysts Journal* 52 (July–August 1996), pp. 16–24.
[25]We will show you how such estimates can be derived from option prices in Chapter 21.

4. Roll's critique implied that the usual CAPM test is a test only of the mean-variance efficiency of a prespecified market proxy and therefore that tests of the linearity of the expected return–beta relationship do not bear on the validity of the model.

5. Tests of the mean-variance efficiency of professionally managed portfolios against the benchmark of a prespecified market index conform with Roll's critique in that they provide evidence of the efficiency of the prespecific market index.

6. Empirical evidence suggests that most professionally managed portfolios are outperformed by market indexes, which lends weight to acceptance of the efficiency of those indexes and hence the CAPM.

7. Work with economic factors suggests that factors such as unanticipated inflation do play a role in the expected return–beta relationship of security returns.

8. Recent tests of the single-index model, accounting for human capital and cyclical variations in asset betas, are far more consistent with the single-index CAPM and APT. These tests suggest that macroeconomic variables are not necessary to explain expected returns. Moreover, anomalies such as effects of size and book-to-market ratios disappear once these variables are accounted for.

9. Volatility of stock returns is constantly changing. Empirical evidence on stock returns must account for this phenomenon. Contemporary researchers use the variations of the ARCH-M algorithm to estimate the level of volatility and its effect on mean returns.

Key Terms   first-pass regression   second-pass regression   benchmark error

Selected Readings

The key readings concerning tests of the CAPM are still:

Black, Fischer; Michael C. Jensen; and Myron Scholes. "The Capital Asset Pricing Model: Some Empirical Tests." In *Studies in the Theory of Capital Markets*, ed. Michael C. Jensen. New York: Praeger, 1972.

Fama, Eugene; and James MacBeth. "Risk, Return, and Equilibrium: Empirical Tests." *Journal of Political Economy* 81 (1973), pp. 607–36.

Roll, Richard. "A Critique of the Asset Pricing Theory's Tests." *Journal of Financial Economics* 4 (1977).

A test of the model using more recent econometric tools is:

Gibbons, Michael. "Multivariate Tests of Financial Models." *Journal of Financial Economics* 10 (1982).

The factor analysis approach to testing multivariate models is treated in:

Roll, Richard; and Stephen Ross. "An Empirical Investigation of the Arbitrage Pricing Theory." *Journal of Finance* 20 (1980).

Lehman, Bruce; and David Modest. "The Empirical Foundation of the Arbitrage Pricing Theory." *Journal of Financial Economics* 21 (1988).

A good paper that tests the APT with prespecified factors is:

Chen, Nai-Fu; Richard Roll; and Stephen A. Ross. "Economic Forces and the Stock Market." *Journal of Business* 59 (1986).

Problems   The following annual excess rates of return were obtained for nine individual stocks and a market index:

Excess Returns %

	Market					Stocks				
Year	Index	A	B	C	D	E	F	G	H	I
1	29.65	33.88	−25.20	36.48	42.89	−39.89	39.67	74.57	40.22	90.19
2	−11.91	−49.87	24.70	−25.11	−54.39	44.92	−54.33	−79.76	−71.58	−26.64
3	14.73	65.14	−25.04	18.91	−39.86	−3.91	−5.69	26.73	14.49	18.14
4	27.68	14.46	−38.64	−23.31	−0.72	−3.21	92.39	−3.82	13.74	0.09
5	5.18	15.67	61.93	63.95	−32.82	44.26	−42.96	101.67	24.24	8.98
6	25.97	−32.17	44.94	−19.56	69.42	90.43	76.72	1.72	77.22	72.38
7	10.64	−31.55	−74.65	50.18	74.52	15.38	21.95	−43.95	−13.40	28.95
8	1.02	−23.79	47.02	−42.28	28.61	−17.64	28.83	98.01	28.12	39.41
9	18.82	−4.59	28.69	−0.54	2.32	42.36	18.93	−2.45	37.65	94.67
10	23.92	−8.03	48.61	23.65	26.26	−3.65	23.31	15.36	80.59	52.51
11	−41.61	78.22	−85.02	−0.79	−68.70	−85.71	−45.64	2.27	−72.47	−80.26
12	−6.64	4.75	42.95	−48.60	26.27	13.24	−34.34	−54.47	−1.50	−24.46

1. Perform the first-pass regressions and tabulate the summary statistics.

2. Specify the hypotheses for a test of the second-pass regression for the SML.

3. Perform the second-pass SML regression by regressing the average excess return of each portfolio on its beta.

4. Summarize your test results and compare them to the reported results in the text.

5. Group the nine stocks into three portfolios, maximizing the dispersion of the betas of the three resultant portfolios. Repeat the test and explain any changes in the results.

6. Explain Roll's critique as it applies to the tests performed in Problems 1 to 5.

7. Plot the capital market line (CML), the nine stocks, and the three portfolios on a graph of average returns versus standard deviation. Compare the mean-variance efficiency of the three portfolios and the market index. Does the comparison support the CAPM?

Suppose that, in addition to the market factor that has been considered in Problems 1 to 7, a second factor is considered. The values of this factor for years 1 to 12 were as follows:

Year	% Change in Factor Value
1	−9.84
2	6.46
3	16.12
4	−16.51
5	17.82
6	−13.31
7	−3.52
8	8.43
9	8.23
10	7.06
11	−15.74
12	2.03

8. Perform the first-pass regressions as did Chen, Roll, and Ross and tabulate the relevant summary statistics. (Hint: Use a multiple regression as in a standard spreadsheet package. Estimate the betas of the 12 stocks on the two factors.)

9. Specify the hypothesis for a test of a second-pass regression for the two-factor SML.

10. Do the data suggest a two-factor economy?

11. Can you identify a factor portfolio for the second factor?

12. Identify and briefly discuss three criticisms of beta as used in the capital asset pricing model.

13. Richard Roll, in an article on using the capital asset pricing model (CAPM) to evaluate portfolio performance, indicated that it may not be possible to evaluate portfolio management ability if there is an error in the benchmark used.

   a. In evaluating portfolio performance, describe the general procedure, with emphasis on the benchmark employed.

   b. Explain what Roll meant by the benchmark error and identify the specific problem with this benchmark.

   c. Draw a graph that shows how a portfolio that has been judged as superior relative to a "measured" security market line (SML) can be inferior relative to the "true" SML.

   d. Assume that you are informed that a given portfolio manager has been evaluated as superior when compared to the Dow Jones Industrial Average, the S&P 500, and the NYSE Composite Index. Explain whether this consensus would make you feel more comfortable regarding the portfolio manager's true ability.

   e. Although conceding the possible problem with benchmark errors as set forth by Roll, some contend this does not mean the CAPM is incorrect, but only that there is a measurement problem when implementing the theory. Others contend that because of benchmark errors the whole technique should be scrapped. Take and defend one of these positions.

s o l u t i o n s   t o
Concept
CHECKS

1. The SCL is estimated for each stock; hence we need to estimate 100 equations. Our sample consists of 60 monthly rates of return for each of the 100 stocks and for the market index. Thus each regression is estimated with 60 observations. Equation 13.1 in the text shows that when stated in excess return form, the SCL should pass through the origin, that is, have a zero intercept.

2. When the SML has a positive intercept and its slope is less than the mean excess return on the market portfolio, it is flatter than predicted by the CAPM. Low-beta stocks therefore have yielded returns that, on average, were higher than they should have been on the basis of their beta. Conversely, high-beta stocks were found to have yielded, on average, lower returns than they should have on the basis of their betas. The positive coefficient on γ_2 implies that stocks with higher values of firm-specific risk had on average higher returns. This pattern, of course, violates the predictions of the CAPM.

3. According to equation 13.5, γ_0 is the average return earned on a stock with zero beta and zero firm-specific risk. According to the CAPM, this should be the risk-free rate, which for the 1946–1955 period was 9 basis points, or .09% per month (see Table 13.1). According to the CAPM, γ_1 should equal the average market risk premium, which for the 1946–1955 period was 103 basis points, or 1.03% per month. Finally, the CAPM predicts that γ_3, the coefficient on firm-specific risk, should be zero.

4. A positive coefficient on beta-squared would indicate that the relationship between risk and return is nonlinear. High-beta securities would provide expected returns more than proportional to risk. A positive coefficient on $\sigma(e)$ would indicate that firm-specific risk affects expected return, a direct contradiction of the CAPM and APT.

FIXED-INCOME SECURITIES

BOND PRICES AND YIELDS

In the previous chapters on risk and return relationships, we have treated securities at a high level of abstraction. We assumed implicitly that a prior, detailed analysis of each security already had been performed, and that its risk and return features had been assessed. We turn now to specific analyses of particular security markets. We examine valuation principles, determinants of risk and return, and portfolio strategies commonly used within and across the various markets. We begin by analyzing **fixed-income securities**. A fixed-income security is a claim on a specified periodic stream of income. Fixed-income securities have the advantage of being relatively easy to understand because the level of payments is fixed in advance. Risk considerations are minimal as long as the issuer of the security is sufficiently creditworthy. That makes these securities a convenient starting point for our analysis of the universe of potential investment vehicles. The bond is the basic fixed-income security, and this chapter reviews the principles of bond pricing. We show how bond prices are set in accordance with market

interest rates, and why bond prices change with those rates. After examining the Treasury bond market, where default risk may be ignored, we move to the corporate bond sector. Here we look at the determinants of credit risk and the default premium built into bond yields. We examine the impact of call and convertibility provisions on prices and yields. Finally, we discuss certain tax rules that apply to fixed-income investments, and we show how to calculate after-tax returns.

14.1   Bond Characteristics

A **bond** is a security that is issued in connection with a borrowing arrangement. The borrower issues (i.e., sells) a bond to the lender for some amount of cash; the bond is the "IOU" of the borrower. The arrangement obligates the issuer to make specified payments to the bondholder on specified dates. A typical coupon bond obligates the issuer to make semiannual payments of interest to the bondholder for the life of the bond. These are called *coupon payments* because in precomputer days, most bonds had coupons that investors would clip off and mail to the issuer of the bond to claim the interest payment. When the bond matures, the issuer repays the debt by paying the bondholder the bond's **par value** (equivalently, **face value**). The **coupon rate** of the bond serves to determine the interest payment: The annual payment is the coupon rate times the bond's par value. The coupon rate, maturity date, and par value of the bond are part of the **bond indenture**, which is the contract between the issuer and the bondholder.

To illustrate, a bond with par value of $1,000 and coupon rate of 8% might be sold to a buyer for $1,000. The bondholder is then entitled to a payment of 8% of $1,000, or $80 per year, for the stated life of the bond, say 30 years. The $80 payment typically comes in two semiannual installments of $40 each. At the end of the 30-year life of the bond, the issuer also pays the $1,000 par value to the bondholder.

Bonds usually are issued with coupon rates set high enough to induce investors to pay par value to buy the bond. Sometimes, however, **zero-coupon bonds** are issued that make no coupon payments. In this case, investors receive par value at the maturity date but receive no interest payments until then: The bond has a coupon rate of zero. These bonds are issued at prices considerably below par value, and the investor's return comes solely from the difference between issue price and the payment of par value at maturity. We will return to these bonds later.

Treasury Bonds and Notes

Figure 14.1 is an excerpt from the listing of Treasury issues in *The Wall Street Journal*. Treasury note maturities range up to 10 years, whereas Treasury bonds are issued with maturities ranging from 10 to 30 years. Both are issued in denominations of $1,000 or more. Both make semiannual coupon payments. Aside from their differing maturities at issue date, the only major distinction between T-notes and T-bonds is that in the past, some T-bonds were *callable* for a given period, usually during the last five years of the bond's life. The call provision gives the Treasury the right to repurchase the bond at par value during the call period. The Treasury no longer issues callable bonds, but several previously issued bonds still are outstanding.

The callable bonds are easily identified in Figure 14.1 because a range of years appears in the maturity date column. The first date is the time at which the bond is first callable. The second date is the maturity date of the bond. The bond may be called by the Treasury at any coupon date in the call period, but it must be retired by the maturity date.

The highlighted bond in Figure 14.1 matures in November 2021. Its coupon rate is 8%. Par value is $1,000; thus the bond pays interest of $80 per year in two semiannual payments of $40. Payments are made in November and May of each year. The bid and ask prices[1] are quoted in points plus fractions of $\frac{1}{32}$ of a point (the numbers after the colons are

---

[1] Recall that the bid price is the price at which you can sell the bond to a dealer. The ask price, which is slightly higher, is the price at which you can buy the bond from a dealer.

Figure 14.1
Listing of treasury issues.

TREASURY BONDS, NOTES & BILLS

Monday, November 17, 1997

Representative and Indicative Over-the-Counter quotations based on $1 million or more.

Treasury bond, note and bill quotes are as of mid-afternoon. Colons in bond and note bid-and-asked quotes represent 32nds; 101:01 means 101 1/32. Net changes in 32nds. Treasury bill quotes in hundredths, quoted in terms of a rate discount. Days to maturity calculated from settlement date. All yields are based on a one-day settlement and calculated on the offer quote. Current 13-week and 26-week bills are boldfaced. For bonds callable prior to maturity, yields are computed to the earliest call date for issues quoted above par and to the maturity date for issues quoted below par. n-Treasury note. i-Inflation-indexed. wi-When issued. iw-Inflation-indexed when issued; daily change is expressed in basis points.

Source: Dow Jones/Cantor Fitzgerald.

U.S. Treasury strips as of 3 p.m. Eastern time, also based on transactions of $1 million or more. Colons in bid-and-asked quotes represent 32nds; 99:01 means 99 1/32. Net changes in 32nds. Yields calculated on the asked quotation. ci-stripped coupon interest. bp-Treasury bond, stripped principal. np-Treasury note, stripped principal. For bonds callable prior to maturity, yields are computed to the earliest call date for issues quoted above par and to the maturity date for issues below par.

Source: Bear, Stearns & Co. via Street Software Technology Inc.

GOVT. BONDS & NOTES

Rate	Maturity Mo/Yr	Bid	Asked	Chg.	Ask Yld.
5 3/8	Nov 97n	99:30	100:00	....	5.24
6	Nov 97n	99:31	100:01	....	4.91
5 1/4	Dec 97n	99:29	99:31	− 1	5.41
6	Dec 97n	100:00	100:02	− 1	5.34
7 7/8	Jan 98n	100:11	100:13	....	5.14
5	Jan 98n	99:26	99:28	....	5.55
5 5/8	Jan 98n	99:30	100:00	....	5.53
7 3/4	Feb 98n	100:11	100:13	....	5.45
8 1/8	Feb 98n	100:18	100:20	....	5.39
5 1/8	Feb 98n	99:26	99:28	− 1	5.51
5 1/8	Mar 98n	99:26	99:28	....	5.44
6 1/8	Mar 98n	100:06	100:08	....	5.38
7 7/8	Apr 98n	100:29	100:31	− 1	5.40
5 1/8	Apr 98n	99:26	99:28	....	5.40
5 7/8	Apr 98n	100:04	100:06	− 1	5.43
6 1/8	May 98n	100:08	100:10	....	5.47
9	May 98n	101:21	101:23	....	5.41
5 3/8	May 98n	99:27	99:29	....	5.55
6	May 98n	100:06	100:08	....	5.51
5 1/8	Jun 98n	99:22	99:24	− 1	5.53
6 1/4	Jun 98n	100:12	100:14	− 1	5.51
8 1/4	Jul 98n	101:22	101:24	....	5.49
5 1/4	Jul 98n	99:23	99:25	....	5.56
6 1/4	Jul 98n	100:13	100:15	....	5.54
5 7/8	Aug 98n	100:03	100:05	− 1	5.64
9 1/4	Aug 98n	102:18	102:20	− 1	5.57
4 3/4	Aug 98n	99:09	99:11	....	5.61
6 1/8	Aug 98n	100:10	100:12	− 1	5.61
4 3/4	Sep 98n	99:07	99:09	....	5.60
6	Sep 98n	100:09	100:11	....	5.58
7 1/8	Oct 98n	101:09	101:11	− 1	5.58
4 3/4	Oct 98n	99:03	99:05	− 1	5.67
5 7/8	Oct 98n	100:05	100:07	....	5.63
5 1/2	Nov 98n	99:25	99:27	− 1	5.66
8 7/8	Nov 98n	103:02	103:04	....	5.59
5 1/8	Nov 98n	99:14	99:16	....	5.63
5 5/8	Nov 98n	99:29	99:31	− 1	5.65
5 1/8	Dec 98n	99:12	99:14	− 1	5.65
5 3/4	Dec 98n	100:02	100:04	....	5.63
6 3/8	Jan 99n	100:23	100:25	− 1	5.66
5	Jan 99n	99:05	99:07	− 1	5.67
5 7/8	Jan 99n	100:05	100:07	− 1	5.68
5	Feb 99n	99:04	99:06	− 1	5.68
8 7/8	Feb 99n	103:24	103:26	....	5.64
5 1/2	Feb 99n	99:23	99:25	− 1	5.67
5 7/8	Feb 99n	100:06	100:08	....	5.66
5 7/8	Mar 99n	100:06	100:08	− 1	5.68
6 1/4	Mar 99n	100:22	100:24	− 1	5.66
7	Apr 99n	101:23	101:25	− 1	5.66
6 3/8	Apr 99n	101:03	101:05	− 1	5.53
6 1/2	Apr 99n	101:02	101:04	− 1	5.68
6 3/8	May 99n	100:29	100:31	....	5.69
9 1/8	May 99n	104:26	104:28	− 1	5.67
6 1/4	May 99n	100:30	101:00	− 1	5.56
6 3/4	May 99n	101:15	101:17	− 1	5.69
6	Jun 99n	100:13	100:15	− 1	5.69
6 3/4	Jun 99n	101:18	101:20	− 1	5.68
7 1/4	Aug 04n	107:16	107:18	+ 1	5.87
13 3/4	Aug 04	143:02	143:08	+ 1	5.89
7 7/8	Nov 04n	111:05	111:09	+ 1	5.88
11 5/8	Nov 04	132:09	132:15	+ 1	5.89
7 1/2	Feb 05n	109:09	109:11	+ 2	5.89
6 1/2	May 05n	103:18	103:20	+ 1	5.89
8 1/4	May 00-05	105:13	105:15	....	5.86
12	May 05	136:08	136:14	+ 2	5.91
6 1/2	Aug 05n	103:18	103:20	+ 1	5.91
10 3/4	Aug 05	129:16	129:22	+ 2	5.91
5 7/8	Nov 05n	99:23	99:25	+ 2	5.91
5 5/8	Feb 06n	98:02	98:04	+ 2	5.91
9 3/8	Feb 06	122:11	122:17	+ 2	5.88
6 7/8	May 06n	106:09	106:11	+ 2	5.91
7	Jul 06n	107:06	107:08	+ 2	5.92
6 1/2	Oct 06n	103:29	103:31	+ 2	5.92
3 3/8	Jan 07i	98:24	98:25	+ 1	3.53
6 1/4	Feb 07n	102:11	102:13	+ 2	5.91
7 5/8	Feb 02-07	106:05	106:07	+ 2	5.94
6 5/8	May 07n	105:08	105:09	+ 4	5.89
6 1/8	Aug 07n	102:01	102:02	+ 3	5.84
7 7/8	Nov 02-07	108:29	108:31	+ 1	5.78
8 3/8	Aug 03-08	112:06	112:10	+ 2	5.82
8 3/4	Nov 03-08	113:22	113:26	+ 2	5.97
9 1/8	May 04-09	116:20	116:24	+ 3	5.97
10 3/8	Nov 04-09	124:22	124:28	+ 2	5.97
11 3/4	Feb 05-10	133:16	133:22	+ 3	5.96
10	May 05-10	123:28	124:02	+ 3	5.97
12 3/4	Nov 05-10	142:13	142:19	+ 3	5.97
13 7/8	May 06-11	151:27	152:01	+ 4	5.97
14	Nov 06-11	154:31	155:05	+ 3	5.98
10 3/8	Nov 07-12	132:01	132:07	+ 4	6.03
12	Aug 08-13	146:11	146:17	+ 4	6.05
13 1/4	May 09-14	158:23	158:29	+ 4	6.06
12 1/2	Aug 09-14	153:08	153:14	+ 4	6.07
11 3/4	Nov 09-14	147:24	147:30	+ 4	6.07
11 1/4	Feb 15	154:09	154:15	+ 5	6.10
10 5/8	Aug 15	147:29	148:03	+ 5	6.14
9 7/8	Nov 15	140:02	140:08	+ 5	6.15
9 1/4	Feb 16	133:15	133:21	+ 5	6.15
7 1/4	May 16	111:27	111:31	+ 4	6.16
7 1/2	Nov 16	114:19	114:23	+ 5	6.17
8 3/4	May 17	128:26	129:00	+ 5	6.17
8 7/8	Aug 17	130:13	130:19	+ 5	6.17
9 1/8	May 18	133:27	134:01	+ 5	6.18
9	Nov 18	132:24	132:30	+ 6	6.18
8 7/8	Feb 19	131:13	131:19	+ 6	6.18
8 1/8	Aug 19	122:25	122:31	+ 5	6.19
8 1/2	Feb 20	127:17	127:23	+ 5	6.19
8 3/4	May 20	130:22	130:28	+ 6	6.19
8 3/4	Aug 20	130:26	131:00	+ 5	6.19
7 7/8	Feb 21	120:12	120:18	+ 5	6.19
8 1/8	May 21	123:17	123:23	+ 5	6.20
8 1/8	Aug 21	123:21	123:27	+ 6	6.19
8	Nov 21	122:06	122:12	+ 5	6.20
7 1/4	Aug 22	113:04	113:08	+ 5	6.20
7 5/8	Nov 22	117:30	118:02	+ 5	6.19
7 1/8	Feb 23	111:22	111:26	+ 5	6.19
6 1/4	Aug 23	100:25	100:27	+ 5	6.18
7 1/2	Nov 24	117:03	117:07	+ 6	6.18
7 5/8	Feb 25	118:26	118:30	+ 6	6.18
6 7/8	Aug 25	109:05	109:07	+ 5	6.18
6	Feb 26	97:24	97:26	+ 5	6.16
6 3/4	Aug 26	107:29	107:31	+ 5	6.15
6 1/2	Nov 26	104:22	104:24	+ 5	6.15
6 5/8	Feb 27	106:15	106:17	+ 5	6.14
6 3/8	Aug 27	103:14	103:15	+ 5	6.12
6 1/8	Nov 27	100:20	100:21	+ 5	6.08

U.S. TREASURY STRIPS

Mat.	Type	Bid	Asked	Chg.	Ask Yld.
Feb 98	ci	98:22	98:22	....	5.56
Feb 98	np	98:22	98:22	....	5.60
May 98	ci	97:11	97:11	....	5.57
May 98	np	97:11	97:11	....	5.57
Aug 98	ci	95:31	95:31	....	5.64
Aug 98	np	95:31	95:31	....	5.65
Nov 98	ci	94:19	94:20	....	5.67
Nov 98	np	94:19	94:20	....	5.66
Feb 99	ci	93:10	93:10	....	5.66
May 04	np	68:22	68:26	+ 2	5.84
Aug 04	ci	67:20	67:24	+ 2	5.86
Aug 04	np	67:21	67:26	+ 2	5.85
Nov 04	ci	66:15	66:20	+ 2	5.90
Nov 04	bp	66:13	66:18	+ 2	5.91
Nov 04	np	66:18	66:23	+ 2	5.88
Feb 05	ci	65:15	65:19	+ 3	5.91
Feb 05	np	65:19	65:23	+ 3	5.88
May 05	ci	64:14	64:18	+ 3	5.93
May 05	bp	64:13	64:17	+ 3	5.93
May 05	np	64:20	64:25	+ 3	5.88
Aug 05	ci	63:16	63:20	+ 3	5.93
Aug 05	bp	63:16	63:21	+ 5	5.93
Aug 05	np	63:22	63:27	+ 3	5.89
Nov 05	ci	62:17	62:22	+ 3	5.93
Nov 05	np	62:24	62:28	+ 3	5.89
Feb 06	ci	61:16	61:21	+ 3	5.96
Feb 06	bp	61:26	61:30	+ 3	5.90
Feb 06	np	61:29	62:02	+ 3	5.88
May 06	ci	60:17	60:22	+ 3	5.97
Aug 06	ci	59:21	59:26	+ 4	5.97
Nov 06	ci	58:23	58:28	+ 4	5.98
Feb 07	ci	57:25	57:30	+ 4	6.00
May 07	ci	56:27	57:00	+ 4	6.01
Aug 07	ci	56:02	56:07	+ 4	6.00
Nov 07	ci	55:10	55:15	+ 4	5.99
Feb 08	ci	54:07	54:12	+ 5	6.04
May 08	ci	53:11	53:16	+ 5	6.05
Aug 08	ci	52:17	52:23	+ 5	6.05
Nov 08	ci	51:21	51:26	+ 5	6.07
Feb 09	ci	50:26	50:31	+ 5	6.09
May 09	ci	50:00	50:05	+ 5	6.09
Feb 22	ci	22:09	22:14	+ 2	6.26
May 22	ci	21:31	22:04	+ 3	6.26
Aug 22	ci	21:21	21:26	+ 3	6.25
Aug 22	bp	21:23	21:28	+ 3	6.24
Nov 22	ci	21:11	21:16	+ 3	6.25
Nov 22	bp	21:11	21:16	+ 3	6.24
Feb 23	ci	21:02	21:07	+ 3	6.24
Feb 23	bp	21:03	21:08	+ 3	6.23
May 23	ci	20:25	20:30	+ 3	6.23
Aug 23	ci	20:18	20:23	+ 3	6.21
Aug 23	bp	20:19	20:24	+ 3	6.20
Nov 23	ci	20:08	20:13	+ 3	6.21
Feb 24	ci	19:30	20:03	+ 3	6.21
May 24	ci	19:20	19:25	+ 3	6.21
Aug 24	ci	19:12	19:17	+ 3	6.20
Nov 24	ci	19:02	19:07	+ 3	6.20
Nov 24	bp	19:02	19:07	+ 3	6.20
Feb 25	ci	18:25	18:30	+ 3	6.20
Feb 25	bp	18:26	18:31	+ 3	6.20
May 25	ci	18:19	18:24	+ 3	6.18
Aug 25	ci	18:10	18:15	+ 2	6.18
Aug 25	bp	18:11	18:16	+ 2	6.18
Feb 26	ci	17:29	18:02	+ 3	6.15
Feb 26	bp	17:31	18:04	+ 3	6.14
Aug 26	ci	17:14	17:19	+ 3	6.14
Aug 26	bp	17:17	17:22	+ 3	6.12
Nov 26	ci	17:09	17:13	+ 3	6.12
Nov 26	bp	17:11	17:15	+ 3	6.11
Feb 27	ci	16:29	17:02	+ 3	6.14

Source: *The Wall Street Journal*, November 18, 1997. Reprinted by permission of *The Wall Street Journal*, © 1997 Dow Jones & Company, Inc. All Rights Reserved Worldwide.

the fractions of a point). Although bonds are sold in denominations of $1,000 par value, the prices are quoted as a percentage of par value. Therefore, the bid price of the bond is 122:06 = $122\frac{6}{32}$ = 122.1875% of par value, or $1,221.875, whereas the ask price is $122\frac{12}{32}$% of par, or $1,223.75.

The last column, labeled "Ask Yld," is the yield to maturity on the bond based on the ask price. The yield to maturity is a measure of the average rate of return to an investor who purchases the bond for the ask price and holds it until its maturity date. We will have much to say about yield to maturity below.

Accrued Interest and Quoted Bond Prices   The bond prices that you see quoted in the financial pages are not actually the prices that investors pay for the bond. This is because the quoted price does not include the interest that accrues between coupon payment dates.

If a bond is purchased between coupon payments, the buyer must pay the seller for accrued interest, the prorated share of the upcoming semiannual coupon. For example, if 40 days have passed since the last coupon payment, and there are 182 days in the semiannual coupon period, the seller is entitled to a payment of accrued interest of 40/182 of the semiannual coupon. The sale, or *invoice price*, of the bond would equal the stated price plus the accrued interest.

To illustrate, suppose that the coupon rate is 8%. Then the semiannual coupon payment is $40. Because 40 days have passed since the last coupon payment, the accrued interest on the bond is $40 \times (40/182) = \$8.79$. If the quoted price of the bond is $990, then the invoice price will be $990 + $8.79 = $998.79.

The practice of quoting bond prices net of accrued interest explains why the price of a maturing bond is listed at $1,000 rather than $1,000 plus one coupon payment. A purchaser of an 8% coupon bond one day before the bond's maturity would receive $1,040 on the following day and so should be willing to pay a total price of $1,040 for the bond. In fact, $40 of that total payment constitutes the accrued interest for the preceding half-year period. The bond price is quoted net of accrued interest in the financial pages and thus appears as $1,000.

Corporate Bonds

Like the government, corporations borrow money by issuing bonds. Figure 14.2 is a sample of corporate bond listings in *The Wall Street Journal*. The data presented here differ only slightly from U.S. Treasury bond listings. For example, the highlighted AT&T bond pays a coupon rate of 8⅛% and matures in 2022. AT&T's *current yield* is 7.7%, which is simply the annual coupon payment divided by the bond price ($81.25/$1,058.75). Note that current yield measures only the annual interest income the bondholder receives as a percentage of the price paid for the bond. It ignores the fact that an investor who buys the bond for $1,058.75 will be able to redeem it for only $1,000 on the maturity date. Prospective price appreciation or depreciation does not enter the computation of the current yield. The trading volume column shows that 42 bonds traded on that day. The change from yesterday's closing price is given in the last column. Like government bonds, corporate bonds sell in units of $1,000 par value but are quoted as a percentage of par value.

Although the bonds listed in Figure 14.2 trade on a formal exchange operated by the New York Stock Exchange, most bonds are traded over the counter in a loosely organized network of bond dealers linked by a computer quotation system. (See Chapter 3 for a comparison of exchange versus OTC trading.) In practice, the bond market can be quite "thin," in that there are few investors interested in trading a particular bond at any particular time. Figure 14.2 shows that trading volume of many bonds on the New York exchange is quite low. On any day, it could be difficult to find a buyer or seller for a particular issue, which introduces some "liquidity risk" into the bond market. It may be difficult to sell bond holdings quickly if the need arises.

Bonds issued in the United States today are *registered*, meaning that the issuing firm keeps records of the owner of the bond and can mail interest checks to the owner. Registration of bonds is helpful to tax authorities in the enforcement of tax collection. *Bearer bonds* are those traded without any record of ownership. The investor's physical

Figure 14.2
Listing of corporate bonds.

NEW YORK EXCHANGE BONDS

CORPORATION BONDS
Volume, $20,659,000

Bonds	Cur Yld.	Vol.	Close	Net Chg.
AON 6⅞99	6.8	5	100½	...
ATT 4¾98	4.8	6	99⅜	+ 1/16
ATT 6s00	6.0	61	99⅞	...
ATT 5⅛01	5.3	53	96⅞	+ ¼
ATT 7⅛02	6.9	40	103⅝	− ⅛
ATT 7½06	7.0	12	107	...
ATT 8⅛22	7.7	42	105⅞	+ ½
ATT 8⅛24	7.6	25	106½	+ ⅜
ATT 8⅝31	7.9	7	109⅝	+ ⅛
Aames 10½02	10.2	128	103	+ ¼
AlskAr 6⅞14	cv	62	113	− ½
AlldC zr2000	...	15	84¼	− ⅛
AlldC zr01	...	10	79⅝	+ ⅛
AlldC zr03	...	15	70	+ ⅛
AlldC zr09	...	20	46⅜	+ 1⅜

Bonds	Cur Yld.	Vol.	Close	Net Chg.
IBM 7½13	6.9	10	108½	+ ⅛
IntShip 9s03	8.8	10	102½	...
JumboSp 4½00	cv	184	40	...
KaufB 9⅜03	9.0	62	103⅝	...
KentE 4½04	cv	371	76¼	− ¼
LeasSol 6⅞03	cv	18	93	− 3
Loews 3⅛07	cv	7	98	...
LglsLt 7.3s99	7.2	20	101	...
LglsLt 8⅝04	8.4	157	102⅝	...
LglsLt 7½07	7.3	55	102⅜	...
LglsLt 8.9s19	8.4	17	105¾	+ ⅛
LglsLt 9¾21	9.5	65	102⅜	− ⅛
LglsLt 9s22	8.1	1	110¾	− ¼
LglsLt 8.2s23	7.8	2	105¼	+ ⅛
LglsLt 9⅝24	9.4	32	101⅞	...
MacNS 7⅞04	cv	6	100	− ½
Masco 5¼12	cv	9	119⅝	− 2⅜
Mascotch 03	cv	92	86½	− ½

Source: *The Wall Street Journal*, December 19, 1997. Reprinted by permission of *The Wall Street Journal*, © 1997 Dow Jones & Company, Inc. All Rights Reserved Worldwide.

possession of the bond certificate is the only evidence of ownership. These are now rare in the United States, but less rare in Europe.

Call Provisions on Corporate Bonds Although we have seen that the Treasury no longer issues callable bonds, most corporate bonds are issued with call provisions. The call provision allows the issuer to repurchase the bond at a specified *call price* before the maturity date. For example, if a company issues a bond with a high coupon rate when market interest rates are high, and interest rates later fall, the firm might like to retire the high-coupon debt and issue new bonds at a lower coupon rate to reduce interest payments. This is called *refunding*.

The call price of a bond is commonly set at an initial level near par value plus one annual coupon payment. The call price falls as time passes, gradually approaching par value.

Callable bonds typically come with a period of call protection, an initial time during which the bonds are not callable. Such bonds are referred to as *deferred* callable bonds.

The option to call the bond is valuable to the firm, allowing it to buy back the bonds and refinance at lower interest rates when market rates fall. Of course, the firm's benefit is the bondholder's burden. Holders of called bonds forfeit their bonds for the call price, thereby giving up the prospect of an attractive rate of interest on their original investment. To compensate investors for this risk, callable bonds are issued with higher coupons and promised yields to maturity than noncallable bonds.

Concept CHECK

Question 1 • Suppose that General Motors issues two bonds with identical coupon rates and maturity dates. One bond is callable, however, whereas the other is not. Which bond will sell at a higher price?

Convertible Bonds **Convertible bonds** give bondholders an option to exchange each bond for a specified number of shares of common stock of the firm. The *conversion ratio* gives the number of shares for which each bond may be exchanged. To see the value of this right, suppose a convertible bond that is issued at par value of $1,000 is convertible into 40 shares of a firm's stock. The current stock price is $20 per share, so the option to convert is not profitable now. Should the stock price later rise to $30, however, each bond may be converted profitably into $1,200 worth of stock. The *market conversion value* is the current value of the shares for which the bonds may be exchanged. At the $20 stock price, for example, the bond's conversion value is $800. The *conversion premium* is the excess of the bond value over its conversion value. If the bond were selling currently for $950, its premium would be $150.

Convertible bonds give their holders the ability to share in price appreciation of the company's stock. Again, this benefit comes at a price: Convertible bonds offer lower coupon rates and stated or promised yields to maturity than do nonconvertible bonds. At the same time, the actual return on the convertible bond may exceed the stated yield to maturity if the option to convert becomes profitable.

We discuss convertible and callable bonds further in Chapter 20.

Puttable Bonds   A relatively new development is the **put bond**, or extendable bond. Although the callable bond gives the issuer the option to extend or retire the bond at the call date, the put bond gives this option to the bondholder. If the bond's coupon rate exceeds current market yields, for instance, the bondholder will choose to extend the bond's life. If the bond's coupon rate is too low, it will be optimal not to extend; the bondholder instead reclaims principal, which can be invested at current yields.

Floating-Rate Bonds   **Floating-rate bonds** make interest payments that are tied to some measure of current market rates. For example, the rate might be adjusted annually to the current T-bill rate plus 2%. If the one-year T-bill rate at the adjustment date is 5%, the bond's coupon rate over the next year would then be 7%. This arrangement means that the bond always pays approximately current market rates.

The major risk involved in floaters has to do with changes in the firm's financial strength. The yield spread is fixed over the life of the security, which may be many years. If the financial health of the firm deteriorates, then a greater yield premium would be called for than is offered by the security. In this case, the price of the bond would fall. Although the coupon rate on floaters adjusts to changes in the general level of market interest rates, it does not adjust to changes in the financial condition of the firm.

Preferred Stock

Although preferred stock strictly speaking is considered to be equity, it often is included in the fixed-income universe. This is because, like bonds, preferred stock promises to pay a specified stream of dividends. However, unlike bonds, the failure to pay the promised dividend does not result in corporate bankruptcy. Instead, the dividends owed simply cumulate, and the common stockholders may not receive any dividends until the preferred stockholders have been paid in full. In the event of bankruptcy, preferred stockholders' claims to the firm's assets have lower priority than those of bondholders, but higher priority than those of common stockholders.

Most preferred stock pays a fixed dividend. Therefore, it is in effect a perpetuity, providing a level cash flow indefinitely. In the last few years, however, adjustable or floating-rate preferred stock has become popular. Floating-rate preferred stock is much like floating-rate bonds. The dividend rate is linked to a measure of current market interest rates and is adjusted at regular intervals.

Unlike interest payments on bonds, dividends on preferred stock are not considered tax-deductible expenses to the firm. This reduces their attractiveness as a source of capital to issuing firms. On the other hand, there is an offsetting tax advantage to preferred stock. When one corporation buys the preferred stock of another corporation, it pays taxes on only 30% of the dividends received. For example, if the firm's tax bracket is 35%, and it receives $10,000 in preferred dividend payments, it will pay taxes on only $3,000 of that income: Total taxes owed on the income will be $.35 \times \$3,000 = \$1,050$. The firm's effective tax rate on preferred dividends is therefore only $.30 \times 35\% = 10.5\%$. Given this tax rule, it is not surprising that most preferred stock is held by corporations.

Preferred stock rarely gives its holders full voting privileges in the firm. However, if the preferred dividend is skipped, the preferred stockholders will then be provided some voting power.

Other Issuers

There are, of course, several issuers of bonds in addition to the Treasury and private corporations. For example, state and local governments issue municipal bonds. The outstanding feature of these is that interest payments are tax free. We examined municipal bonds and the value of the tax exemption in Chapter 2.

Government agencies such as the Federal Home Loan Bank Board, the Farm Credit agencies, and the mortgage pass-through agencies Ginnie Mae, Fannie Mae, and Freddie Mac, also issue considerable amounts of bonds. These too were reviewed in Chapter 2.

International Bonds

International bonds are commonly divided into two categories, *foreign bonds* and *Eurobonds*. Foreign bonds are issued by a borrower from a country other than the one in which the bond is sold. The bond is denominated in the currency of the country in which it is marketed. For example, if a German firm sells a dollar-denominated bond in the United States, the bond is considered a foreign bond. These bonds are given colorful names based on the countries in which they are marketed. For example, foreign bonds sold in the United States are called *Yankee bonds*. Like other bonds sold in the United States, they are registered with the Securities and Exchange Commission. Yen-denominated bonds sold in Japan by non-Japanese issuers are called *Samurai bonds*. British pound-denominated foreign bonds sold in the United Kingdom are called *bulldog bonds*.

In contrast to foreign bonds, Eurobonds are bonds issued in the currency of one country but sold in other national markets. For example, the Eurodollar market refers to dollar-denominated bonds sold outside the United States (not just in Europe), although London is the largest market for Eurodollar bonds. Because the Eurodollar market falls outside U.S. jurisdiction, these bonds are not regulated by U.S. federal agencies. Similarly, Euroyen bonds are yen-denominated bonds selling outside of Japan, Eurosterling bonds are pound-denominated Eurobonds selling outside the United Kingdom, and so on.

Innovation in the Bond Market

Issuers constantly develop innovative bonds with unusual features; these issues illustrate that bond design can be extremely flexible. For example, issuers of *pay-in-kind* bonds may choose to pay interest either in cash or in additional bonds with the same face value. If the issuer is short on cash, it will likely choose to pay with new bonds rather than scarce cash. *Reverse floaters* are similar to the floating-rate bonds we described above, except that the coupon rate on these bonds *falls* when the general level of interest rates rises.

Even more unusual bonds may be designed. The Walt Disney Company has issued bonds with coupon rates tied to the financial performance of several of its films. Electrolux

DISASTER BONDS HAVE INVESTORS "ROLLING THE DICE WITH GOD"

The next few weeks could determine whether "disaster" bonds become the hottest new offering dreamed up by the wizards of the fixed-income markets.

"There is no reason that, given 10 years or so, this couldn't develop into a $50 billion-plus market," James Tilley, managing director of Morgan Stanley & Co., says of the burgeoning interest in passing along insurance-related risks of natural disasters to bond market investors.

With hurricanes and earthquakes increasingly wreaking not only physical but also financial havoc, the prospect of having to shell out billions of dollars in claims has sent insurance and reinsurance companies in quest of new ways to protect themselves. The latest twist is to offer bond market investors a chance to bet against the likelihood of such catastrophes occurring.

Over the next month or so, Merrill Lynch & Co. will attempt to sell publicly the first major "Act of God" bond issue—as much as $500 million of bonds, Buyers would be betting that USAA, a big seller of car and home insurance based in San Antonio, won't have to cover more than $1 billion in hurricane claims from a single storm over a one-year period.

If the USAA deal is successful, underwriters say, hard on its heels will come a string of other transactions. One megadeal is on the horizon: $3.35 billion of securities to be sold to fund a proposed California Earthquake Authority, a public agency whose creation is pushed by state Insurance Commissioner Charles Quackenbush to alleviate a growing home-insurance availability crunch in that state.

"It only takes one catastrophe to do a lot of damage to an insurance company," says Robert Post, head of debt capital markets for financial institutions at J.P. Morgan & Co. "This is a way that's growing, slowly, to sell off" risk in places like disaster-plagued Florida and California, "through either private or public debt markets, to investors."

But these bonds also could do some heavy damage to holders, too. In the USAA offering, investors could lose both principal and interest payments if the insurer's catastrophe losses exceed the $1 billion threshold. Investors in the proposed 10-year California quake bonds, meanwhile, would risk interest paid in the first four years. "It's like rolling the dice with God," says Jeanne Dunleavy, an assistant vice president with A.M. Best Co., an insurance rating firm.

Source: Suzanne McGre and Leslie Scism, "Disaster Bonds Have Investors 'Rolling the Dice with God,'" *The Wall Street Journal*, August 15, 1996.

once issued a bond with a final payment that depended on whether there had been an earthquake in Japan. The nearby box discusses so-called disaster bonds further.

Indexed bonds make payments that are tied to a general price index or the price of a particular commodity. For example, Mexico has issued 20-year bonds with payments that depend on the price of oil. Bonds tied to the general price level have been common in countries experiencing high inflation. Although Great Britain is not a country experiencing such extreme inflation, about 20% of its government bonds issued in the last decade have been inflation-indexed. The United States Treasury started issuing such inflation-indexed bonds in January 1997. They are called Treasury Inflation Protected Securities (TIPS). By tying the par value of the bond to the general level of prices, coupon payments as well as the final repayment of par value on these bonds will increase in direct proportion to the consumer price index. Therefore, the interest rate on these bonds is a risk-free real rate.

To illustrate how TIPS work, consider one that is maturing in one year. Assume that it offers a risk-free real coupon rate of 3% per year. The *nominal* rate of return is not known with certainty in advance because it depends on the rate of inflation. If the inflation rate turns out to be only 2%, then the realized dollar rate of return will be approximately 5%; if, however, the rate of inflation turns out to be 10%, then the realized dollar rate of return will be approximately 13%, consisting of the 3% coupon plus a 10% increase in the dollar value of the bond, from $1,000 to $1,100. In early 1998, TIPS bonds were trading at real yields to maturity of about 3.75%.

14.2   DEFAULT RISK

Although bonds generally *promise* a fixed flow of income, that income stream is not risk-less unless the investor can be sure the issuer will not default on the obligation. While U.S. government bonds may be treated as free of default risk, this is not true of corporate bonds. If the company goes bankrupt, the bondholders will not receive all the payments they have been promised. Therefore, the actual payments on these bonds are uncertain, for they depend to some degree on the ultimate financial status of the firm.

Bond default risk is measured by Moody's Investor Services, Standard & Poor's Corporation, Duff and Phelps, and Fitch Investors Service, all of which provide financial information on firms as well as quality ratings of large corporate and municipal bond issues. Each firm assigns letter grades to the bonds of corporations and municipalities to reflect their assessment of the safety of the bond issue. The top rating is AAA or Aaa. Moody's modifies each rating class with a 1, 2, or 3 suffix (e.g., Aaa1, Aaa2, Aaa3) to provide a finer gradation of ratings. The other agencies use a + or – modification.

Those rated BBB or above (S&P, Duff and Phelps, Fitch) or Baa and above (Moody's) are considered **investment-grade bonds**, whereas lower-rated bonds are classified as **speculative-grade or junk bonds**. Certain regulated institutional investors such as insurance companies have not always been allowed to invest in speculative grade bonds.

Figure 14.3 provides the definitions of each bond rating classification.

Junk Bonds

Junk bonds, also known as *high-yield bonds*, are nothing more than speculative-grade (low-rated or unrated) bonds. Before 1977, almost all junk bonds were "fallen angels," that is, bonds issued by firms that originally had investment-grade ratings but that had since been downgraded. In 1977, however, firms began to issue "original-issue junk."

Much of the credit for this innovation is given to Drexel Burnham Lambert, and especially its trader Michael Milken. Drexel had long enjoyed a niche as a junk bond trader and had established a network of potential investors in junk bonds. Its reasoning for marketing original-issue junk, so-called emerging credits, lay in the belief that default rates on these bonds did not justify the large yield spreads commonly exhibited in the marketplace. Firms not able to muster an investment-grade rating were happy to have Drexel (and other investment bankers) market their bonds directly to the public, as this opened up a new source of financing. Junk issues were a lower-cost financing alternative than borrowing from banks.

High-yield bonds gained considerable notoriety in the 1980s when they were used as financing vehicles in leveraged buyouts and hostile takeover attempts. Shortly thereafter, however, the junk bond market suffered. The legal difficulties of Drexel and Michael Milken in connection with Wall Street's insider trading scandals of the late 1980s tainted the junk bond market. Drexel agreed to pay $650 million in fines and plead guilty to six felony charges to avoid racketeering charges. Milken was indicted on racketeering and security fraud charges, resigned from Drexel, and eventually agreed in a plea bargain to plead guilty to six felony charges and to pay $600 million in fines. Moreover, as the high-yield bond market tumbled in late 1989, Drexel suffered large losses in its own billion-dollar portfolio of junk bonds. In February 1990, Drexel filed for bankruptcy.

At the height of Drexel's difficulties, the high-yield bond market nearly dried up. Since then, the market has rebounded dramatically. However, it is worth noting that the average credit quality of high-yield debt issued today is higher than the average quality in the boom years of the 1980s.

Figure 14.3
Definitions of each
bond rating class.

Bond Ratings				
	Very High Quality	**High Quality**	**Speculative**	**Very Poor**
Standard & Poor's	AAA AA	A BBB	BB B	CCC D
Moody's	Aaa Aa	A Baa	Ba B	Caa C

At times both Moody's and Standard & Poor's have used adjustments to these ratings: S&P uses plus and minus signs: A+ is the strongest A rating and A– the weakest. Moody's uses a 1, 2, or 3 designation, with 1 indicating the strongest.

Moody's	S&P	
Aaa	AAA	Debt rated Aaa and AAA has the highest rating. Capacity to pay interest and principal is extremely strong.
Aa	AA	Debt rated Aa and AA has a very strong capacity to pay interest and repay principal. Together with the highest rating, this group comprises the high-grade bond class.
A	A	Debt rated A has a strong capacity to pay interest and repay principal, although it is somewhat more susceptible to the adverse effects of changes in circumstances and economic conditions than debt in higher-rated categories.
Baa	BBB	Debt rated Baa and BBB is regarded as having an adequate capacity to pay interest and repay principal. Whereas it normally exhibits adequate protection parameters, adverse economic conditions or changing circumstances are more likely to lead to a weakened capacity to pay interest and repay principal for debt in this category than in higher-rated categories. These bonds are medium-grade obligations.
Ba B Caa Ca	BB B CCC CC	Debt rated in these categories is regarded, on balance, as predominantly speculative with respect to capacity to pay interest and repay principal in accordance with the terms of the obligation. BB and Ba indicate the lowest degree of speculation, and CC and Ca the highest degree of speculation. Although such debt will likely have some quality and protective characteristics, these are outweighed by large uncertainties or major risk exposures to adverse conditions. Some issues may be in default.
C	C	This rating is reserved for income bonds on which no interest is being paid.
D	D	Debt rated D is in default, and payment of interest and/or repayment of principal is in arrears.

Source: Stephen A. Ross and Randolph W. Westerfield, *Corporate Finance* (St. Louis: Times Mirror/Mosby College Publishing, 1988). Data from various editions of *Standard & Poor's Bond Guide* and *Moody's Bond Guide*.

Determinants of Bond Safety

Bond rating agencies base their quality ratings largely on an analysis of the level and trend of some of the issuer's financial ratios. The key ratios used to evaluate safety are:

1. *Coverage ratios*—Ratios of company earnings to fixed costs. For example, the *times-interest-earned ratio* is the ratio of earnings before interest payments and taxes to interest obligations. The *fixed-charge coverage ratio* adds lease payments and sinking fund payments to interest obligations to arrive at the ratio of earnings to all fixed cash obligations (sinking funds are described below). Low or falling coverage ratios signal possible cash flow difficulties.

2. *Leverage ratio*—Debt-to-equity ratio. A too-high leverage ratio indicates excessive indebtedness, signaling the possibility the firm will be unable to earn enough to satisfy the obligations on its bonds.

Table 14.1   Rating Classes and Median Financial Ratios, 1991–1993

Rating Category	Fixed-Charge Coverage Ratio	Cash Flow to Total Debt	Return on Capital (%)	Long-Term Debt to Capital (%)
AAA	6.34	0.49	24.2	11.7
AA	4.48	0.32	18.4	19.1
A	2.93	0.17	13.5	29.4
BBB	1.82	0.04	9.7	39.6
BB	1.33	0.01	9.1	51.1
B	0.78	(0.02)	6.3	61.8

Source: Standard & Poor's *Debt Rating Guide*, 1994. Reprinted by permission of Standard & Poor's Ratings Group.

3. *Liquidity ratios*—The two common liquidity ratios are the *current ratio* (current assets/current liabilities) and the *quick ratio* (current assets excluding inventories/current liabilities). These ratios measure the firm's ability to pay bills coming due with cash currently being collected.

4. *Profitability ratios*—Measures of rates of return on assets or equity. Profitability ratios are indicators of a firm's overall financial health. The *return on assets* (earnings before interest and taxes divided by total assets) is the most popular of these measures. Firms with higher return on assets should be better able to raise money in security markets because they offer prospects for better returns on the firm's investments.

5. *Cash flow–to–debt ratio*—This is the ratio of total cash flow to outstanding debt.

Standard & Poor's periodically computes median values of selected ratios for firms in several rating classes, which we present in Table 14.1. Of course, ratios must be evaluated in the context of industry standards, and analysts differ in the weights they place on particular ratios. Nevertheless, Table 14.1 demonstrates the tendency of ratios to improve along with the firm's rating class.

In fact, the heavy dependence of bond ratings on publicly available financial data is evidence of an interesting phenomenon. You might think that an increase or decrease in bond rating would cause substantial bond price gains or losses, but this is not the case. Weinstein[2] found that bond prices move in *anticipation* of rating changes, which is evidence that investors themselves track the financial status of bond issuers. This is consistent with an efficient market. Rating changes actually largely confirm a change in status that has been reflected in security prices already. Holthausen and Leftwich,[3] however, found that bond rating downgrades (but not upgrades) are associated with abnormal returns in the stock of the affected company.

Many studies have tested whether financial ratios can in fact be used to predict default risk. One of the best-known series of tests was conducted by Edward Altman, who used discriminant analysis to predict bankruptcy. With this technique a firm is assigned a score based on its financial characteristics. If its score exceeds a cutoff value, the firm is deemed creditworthy. A score below the cutoff value indicates significant bankruptcy risk in the near future.

[2]Mark I. Weinstein, "The Effect of a Rating Change Announcement on Bond Price," *Journal of Financial Economics*, December 1977.
[3]Robert W. Holthausen and Richard E. Leftwich, "The Effect of Bond Rating Changes on Common Stock Prices," *Journal of Financial Economics* 17 (September 1986).

Figure 14.4
Discriminant analysis.

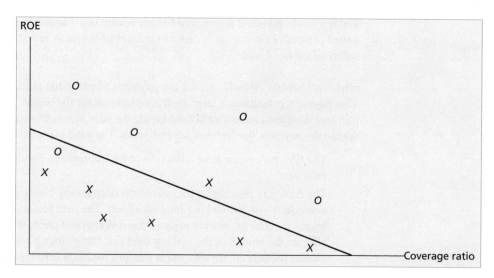

To illustrate the technique, suppose that we were to collect data on the return on equity (ROE) and coverage ratios of a sample of firms, and then keep records of any corporate bankruptcies. In Figure 14.4 we plot the ROE and coverage ratios for each firm using *X* for firms that eventually went bankrupt and *O* for those that remained solvent. Clearly, the *X* and *O* firms show different patterns of data, with the solvent firms typically showing higher values for the two ratios.

The discriminant analysis determines the equation of the line that best separates the *X* and *O* observations. Suppose that the equation of the line is .75 = .9 × ROE + .4 × Coverage. Each firm is assigned a "Z-score" equal to .9 × ROE + .4 × Coverage using the firm's ROE and coverage ratios. If the *Z*-score exceeds .75, the firm plots above the line and is considered a safe bet; *Z*-scores below .75 foretell financial difficulty.

Altman[4] found the following equation to best separate failing and nonfailing firms:

$$Z = 3.3 \frac{\text{EBIT}}{\text{Total assets}} + 99.9 \frac{\text{Sales}}{\text{Assets}} + .6 \frac{\text{Market value of equity}}{\text{Book value of debt}}$$

$$+ 1.4 \frac{\text{Retained earnings}}{\text{Total assets}} + 1.2 \frac{\text{Working capital}}{\text{Total assets}}$$

where EBIT = earnings before interest and taxes.

Concept

Question 2 • Suppose we add a new variable equal to current liabilities/current assets to Altman's equation. Would you expect this variable to receive a positive or negative coefficient?

Bond Indentures

A bond is issued with an *indenture*, which is the contract between the issuer and the bondholder. Part of the indenture is a set of restrictions on the firm issuing the bond to protect the rights of the bondholders. Such restrictions include provisions relating to collateral,

[4]Edward I. Altman, "Financial Ratios, Discriminant Analysis, and the Prediction of Corporate Bankruptcy," *Journal of Finance* 23 (September 1968).

sinking funds, dividend policy, and further borrowing. The issuing firm agrees to these so-called *protective covenants* in order to market its bonds to investors concerned about the safety of the bond issue.

Sinking Funds   Bonds call for the payment of par value at the end of the bond's life. This payment constitutes a large cash commitment for the issuer. To help ensure the commitment does not create a cash flow crisis, the firm agrees to establish a **sinking fund** to spread the payment burden over several years. The fund may operate in one of two ways:

1. The firm may repurchase a fraction of the outstanding bonds in the open market each year.
2. The firm may purchase a fraction of the outstanding bonds at a special call price associated with the sinking fund provision. The firm has an option to purchase the bonds at either the market price or the sinking fund price, whichever is lower. To allocate the burden of the sinking fund call fairly among bondholders, the bonds chosen for the call are selected at random based on serial number.[5]

The sinking fund call differs from a conventional bond call in two important ways. First, the firm can repurchase only a limited fraction of the bond issue at the sinking fund call price. At best, some indentures allow firms to use a *doubling option*, which allows repurchase of double the required number of bonds at the sinking fund call price. Second, the sinking fund call price generally is lower than the call price established by other call provisions in the indenture. The sinking fund call price usually is set at the bond's par value.

Although sinking funds ostensibly protect bondholders by making principal repayment more likely, they can hurt the investor. If interest rates fall and bond prices rise, firms will benefit from the sinking fund provision that enables them to repurchase their bonds at below-market prices. In these circumstances, the firm's gain is the bondholder's loss.

One bond issue that does not require a sinking fund is a *serial bond* issue. In a serial bond issue, the firm sells bonds with staggered maturity dates. As bonds mature sequentially, the principal repayment burden for the firm is spread over time, just as it is with a sinking fund. Serial bonds do not include call provisions. One advantage of serial bonds over sinking fund issues is that there is no uncertainty introduced by the possibility that a particular bond will be called for the sinking fund. The disadvantage of serial bonds, however, is that each maturity date becomes a different bond, which reduces the liquidity of the issue.

Subordination of Further Debt   One of the factors determining bond safety is total outstanding debt of the issuer. If you bought a bond today, you would be understandably distressed to see the firm tripling its outstanding debt tomorrow. Your bond would be of lower quality than it appeared when you bought it. To prevent firms from harming bondholders in this manner, **subordination clauses** restrict the amount of additional borrowing. Additional debt might be required to be subordinated in priority to existing debt; that is, in the event of bankruptcy, *subordinated* or *junior* debtholders will not be paid unless and until the prior senior debt is fully paid off. For this reason, subordination is sometimes called a "me-first rule," meaning the senior (earlier) bondholders are to be paid first in the event of bankruptcy.

Dividend Restrictions   Covenants also limit firms in the amount of dividends they are allowed to pay. These limitations protect the bondholders because they force the firm to

---

[5]Although it is less common, the sinking fund provision also may call for periodic payments to a trustee, with the payments invested so that the accumulated sum can be used for retirement of the entire issue at maturity.

retain assets rather than paying them out to stockholders. A typical restriction disallows payments of dividends if cumulative dividends paid since the firm's inception exceed cumulative net income plus proceeds from sales of stock.

Collateral   Some bonds are issued with specific collateral behind them. **Collateral** can take several forms, but it represents a particular asset of the firm that the bondholders receive if the firm defaults on the bond. If the collateral is property, the bond is called a *mortgage bond*. If the collateral takes the form of other securities held by the firm, the bond is a *collateral trust bond*. In the case of equipment, the bond is known as an *equipment obligation bond*. This last form of collateral is used most commonly by firms such as railroads, where the equipment is fairly standard and can be easily sold to another firm should the firm default and the bondholders acquire the collateral.

Because of the specific collateral that backs them, collaterized bonds generally are considered the safest variety of corporate bonds. General **debenture** bonds by contrast do not provide for specific collateral; they are *unsecured* bonds. The bondholder relies solely on the general earning power of the firm for the bond's safety. If the firm defaults, debenture owners become general creditors of the firm. Because they are safer, collateralized bonds generally offer lower yields than general debentures.

Figure 14.5 shows the terms of a bond issued by Mobil as described in *Moody's Industrial Manual*. The terms of the bond are typical and illustrate many of the indenture provisions we have mentioned. The bond is registered and listed on the NYSE. Although

Figure 14.5

Callable bond issued by Mobil.

```
&. Mobil Corp. debenture 8s, due 2032:
            Rating — Aa2
AUTH — $250,000,000.
OUTSTG — Dec. 31, 1993, $250,000,000.
DATED — Oct. 30, 1991.
INTEREST — F&A 12.
TRUSTEE — Chemical Bank.
DENOMINATION — Fully registered, $1,000 and
integral multiples thereof. Transferable and
exchangeable without service charge.
CALLABLE — As a whole or in part, at any time,
on or after Aug. 12, 2002, at the option of Co. on
at least 30 but not more than 60 days' notice to
each Aug. 11 as follows:
2003........105.007  2004 ........104.756  2005 ........ 104.506
2006........104.256  2007 ........104.005  2008 ........ 103.755
2009........103.505  2010 ........103.254  2011 ........ 103.004
2012........102.754  2013 ........102.503  2014 ........ 102.253
2015........102.003  2016 ........101.752  2017 ........ 101.502
2018........101.252  2019 ........101.001  2020 ........ 100.751
2021........100.501  2022 ........100.250
and thereafter at 100 plus accrued interest.
SECURITY — Not secured. Ranks equally with all
other unsecured and unsubordinated indebtedness
of Co. Co. nor any Affiliate will not incurr any
indebtedness; provided that Co. will not create as
sucurity for any indebtedness for borrowed money,
any mortgage, pledge, security interest or lien on
any stock or indebtedness is directly owned by
Co., without effectively providing that the debt
securities shall be secured equally and ratably with
such indebtedness, so long as such indebtedness
shall be so secured.
INDENTURE    MODIFICATION — Indenture
may be modified, except as provided with, consent
of 66⅔% of debs. outstg.
RIGHTS ON DEFAULT — Trustee, or 25% of
debs. outstg., may declare principal dua nad paya-
ble (30 days' grace for payment of interest).
LISTED — On New York Stock Exchange.
PURPOSE — Proceeds used for general corporate
purposes.
OFFERED — ($250,000,000) at 99.51 plus accrued
interest (proceeds to Co., 99.11) on Aug. 5, 1992
thru Merrill Lynch & Co., Donaldson, Lufkin &
Jenerette Securities Corp., PaineWebber Inc., Pru-
dential Securities Inc., Smith Barney, Harris
Upham & Co. Inc. and associates.
```

Source: *Moody's Industrial Manual*, Moody's Investor Services, 1994.

it was issued in 1991, it is not callable until 2002. Although the call price started at 105.007% of par value, it falls gradually until it reaches par after 2020.

14.3   BOND PRICING

Because a bond's coupon and principal repayments all occur months or years in the future, the price an investor would be willing to pay for a claim to those payments depends on the value of dollars to be received in the future compared to dollars in hand today. This "present value" calculation depends in turn on market interest rates. As we saw in Chapter 5, the nominal risk-free interest rate equals the sum of (1) a real risk-free rate of return and (2) a premium above the real rate to compensate for expected inflation. In addition, because most bonds are not riskless, the discount rate will embody an additional premium that reflects bond-specific characteristics such as default risk, liquidity, tax attributes, call risk, and so on.

We simplify for now by assuming there is one interest rate that is appropriate for discounting cash flows of any maturity, but we can relax this assumption easily. In practice, there may be different discount rates for cash flows accruing in different periods. For the time being, however, we ignore this refinement.

To value a security, we discount its expected cash flows by the appropriate discount rate. The cash flows from a bond consist of coupon payments until the maturity date plus the final payment of par value. Therefore,

Bond value = Present value of coupons + Present value of par value

If we call the maturity date T and call the interest rate r, the bond value can be written as

$$\text{Bond value} = \sum_{t=1}^{T} \frac{\text{Coupon}}{(1 + r)^t} + \frac{\text{Par value}}{(1 + r)^T} \qquad (14.1)$$

The summation sign in equation 14.1 directs us to add the present value of each coupon payment; each coupon is discounted based on the time until it will be paid. The first term on the right-hand side of equation 14.1 is the present value of an annuity. The second term is the present value of a single amount, the final payment of the bond's par value.

An Example: Bond Pricing

We discussed earlier an 8% coupon, 30-year maturity bond with par value of $1,000 paying 60 semiannual coupon payments of $40 each. Suppose that the interest rate is 8% annually, or 4% per six-month period. Then the value of the bond can be written as

$$\text{Price} = \sum_{t=1}^{60} \frac{\$40}{(1.04)^t} + \frac{\$1,000}{(1.04)^{60}} \qquad (14.2)$$

For notational simplicity, we can write equation 14.2 as

Price = $40 × Annuity factor(4%, 60) + $1,000 × PV factor(4%, 60)

where Annuity factor(4%, 60) represents the present value of an annuity of $1 when the semiannual interest rate is 4% and the annuity lasts for 60 six-month periods, and PV factor(4%, 60) is the present value of a single payment of $1 to be received in 60 periods.

It is easy to confirm that the present value of the bond's 60 semiannual coupon payments of $40 each is $904.94, whereas the $1,000 final payment of par value has a present

Figure 14.6

The inverse relationship between bond prices and yields.

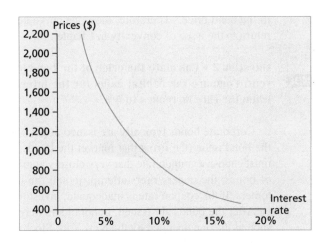

Table 14.2   Bond Prices at Different Interest Rates (8% coupon bond, coupons paid semiannually)

	Bond Price at Given Market Interest Rate				
Time to Maturity	**4%**	**6%**	**8%**	**10%**	**12%**
1 year	1,038.83	1,029.13	1,000.00	981.41	963.33
10 years	1,327.03	1,148.77	1,000.00	875.35	770.60
20 years	1,547.11	1,231.15	1,000.00	828.41	699.07
30 years	1,695.22	1,276.76	1,000.00	810.71	676.77

value of $95.06, for a total bond value of $1,000. You can perform these calculations on any financial calculator or use a set of present value tables.

In this example, the coupon rate equals yield to maturity, and the bond price equals par value. If the interest rate were not equal to the bond's coupon rate, the bond would not sell at par value. For example, if the interest rate were to rise to 10% (5% per six months), the bond's price would fall by $189.29 to $810.71, as follows:

$$\$40 \times \text{Annuity factor}(5\%, 60) + \$1,000 \times \text{PV factor}(5\%, 60)$$
$$= \$757.17 + \$53.54$$
$$= \$810.71$$

At a higher interest rate, the present value of the payments to be received by the bondholder is lower. Therefore, the bond price will fall as market interest rates rise. This illustrates a crucial general rule in bond valuation. When interest rates rise, bond prices must fall because the present value of the bond's payments are obtained by discounting at a higher interest rate.

Figure 14.6 shows the price of the 30-year, 8% coupon bond for a range of interest rates. The negative slope illustrates the inverse relationship between prices and yields. Note also from the figure (and from Table 14.2) that the shape of the curve implies that an increase in the interest rate results in a price decline that is smaller than the price gain resulting from a decrease of equal magnitude in the interest rate. This property of bond prices is called *convexity* because of the convex shape of the bond price curve. This curvature reflects the fact that progressive increases in the interest rate result in progressively smaller reductions in the bond price.[6] Therefore, the price curve becomes flatter at higher interest rates. We return to the issue of convexity in Chapter 16.

Concept

Question 3 • Calculate the price of the bond for a market interest rate of 3% per half year. Compare the capital gains for the interest rate decline to the losses incurred when the rate increases to 5%.

Corporate bonds typically are issued at par value. This means that the underwriters of the bond issue (the firms that market the bonds to the public for the issuing corporation) must choose a coupon rate that very closely approximates market yields. In a primary issue of bonds, the underwriters attempt to sell the newly issued bonds directly to their customers. If the coupon rate is inadequate, investors will not pay par value for the bonds.

After the bonds are issued, bondholders may buy or sell bonds in secondary markets, such as the one operated by the New York Stock Exchange or the over-the-counter market, where most bonds trade. In these secondary markets, bond prices move in accordance with market forces. The bond prices fluctuate inversely with the market interest rate.

The inverse relationship between price and yield is a central feature of fixed-income securities. Interest rate fluctuations represent the main source of risk in the fixed-income market, and we devote considerable attention in Chapter 16 to assessing the sensitivity of bond prices to market yields. For now, however, it is sufficient to highlight one key factor that determines that sensitivity, namely, the maturity of the bond.

A general rule in evaluating bond price risk is that, keeping all other factors the same, the longer the maturity of the bond, the greater the sensitivity of price to fluctuations in the interest rate. For example, consider Table 14.2, which presents the price of an 8% coupon bond at different market yields and times to maturity. For any departure of the interest rate from 8% (the rate at which the bond sells at par value), the change in the bond price is smaller for shorter times to maturity.

This makes sense. If you buy the bond at par with an 8% coupon rate, and market rates subsequently rise, then you suffer a loss: You have tied up your money earning 8% when alternative investments offer higher returns. This is reflected in a capital loss on the bond—a fall in its market price. The longer the period for which your money is tied up, the greater the loss, and correspondingly the greater the drop in the bond price. In Table 14.2, the row for one-year maturity bonds shows little price sensitivity—that is, with only one year's earnings at stake, changes in interest rates are not too threatening. But for 30-year maturity bonds, interest rate swings have a large impact on bond prices.

This is why short-term Treasury securities such as T-bills are considered to be the safest. They are free not only of default risk, but also largely of price risk attributable to interest rate volatility.

14.4   BOND YIELDS

We have noted that the current yield of a bond measures only the cash income provided by the bond as a percentage of bond price and ignores any prospective capital gains or losses. We would like a measure of rate of return that accounts for both current income and the price increase or decrease over the bond's life. The yield to maturity is the standard mea-

---

[6]The progressively smaller impact of interest increases results from the fact that at higher rates the bond is worth less. Therefore, an additional increase in rates operates on a smaller initial base, resulting in a smaller price reduction.

sure of the total rate of return of the bond over its life. However, it is far from a perfect measure, and we will explore several variations of this statistic.

Yield to Maturity

In practice, an investor considering the purchase of a bond is not quoted a promised rate of return. Instead, the investor must use the bond price, maturity date, and coupon payments to infer the return offered by the bond over its life. The **yield to maturity** (YTM) is defined as the interest rate that makes the present value of a bond's payments equal to its price. This interest rate is often viewed as a measure of the average rate of return that will be earned on a bond if it is bought now and held until maturity. To calculate the yield to maturity, we solve the bond price equation for the interest rate given the bond's price.

For example, suppose an 8% coupon, 30-year bond is selling at $1,276.76. What average rate of return would be earned by an investor purchasing the bond at this price? To answer this question, we find the interest rate at which the present value of the remaining bond payments equals the bond price. This is the rate that is consistent with the observed price of the bond. Therefore, we solve for r in the following equation:

$$\$1{,}276.76 = \sum_{t=1}^{60} \frac{\$40}{(1+r)^t} + \frac{\$1{,}000}{(1+r)^{60}}$$

or, equivalently,

$$1{,}276.76 = 40 \times \text{Annuity factor}(r, 60) + 1{,}000 \times \text{PV factor}(r, 60)$$

These equations have only one unknown variable, the interest rate, r. You can use a financial calculator to confirm that the solution to the equation is $r = .03$, or 3% per half year.[7] This is considered the bond's yield to maturity, as the bond would be fairly priced at $1,276.76 if the fair market rate of return on the bond over its entire life were 3% per half year.

The financial press reports yields on an annualized basis, however, and annualizes the bond's semiannual yield using simple interest techniques, resulting in an annual percentage rate, or APR. Yields annualized using simple interest are also called "bond equivalent yields." Therefore, the semiannual yield would be doubled and reported in the newspaper as a bond equivalent yield of 6%. The *effective* annual yield of the bond, however, accounts for compound interest. If one earns 3% interest every six months, then after one year, each dollar invested grows with interest to $1 \times (1.03)^2 = \$1.0609$, and the effective annual interest rate on the bond is 6.09%.

The bond's yield to maturity is the internal rate of return on an investment in the bond. The yield to maturity can be interpreted as the compound rate of return over the life of the bond under the assumption that all bond coupons can be reinvested at an interest rate equal to the bond's yield to maturity.[8] Yield to maturity is widely accepted as a proxy for average return.

Yield to maturity is different from the **current yield** of a bond, which is the bond's annual coupon payment divided by the bond price. For example, for the 8%, 30-year bond currently selling at $1,276.76, the current yield would be $80/\$1,276.76 = .0627$, or 6.27% per year. In contrast, recall that the effective annual yield to maturity is 6.09%. For this

---

[7]Without a financial calculator, you still could solve the equation, but you would need to use a trial-and-error approach.
[8]If the reinvestment rate does not equal the bond's yield to maturity, the compound rate of return will differ from YTM. This is demonstrated later.

bond, which is selling at a premium over par value ($1,276 rather than $1,000), the coupon rate (8%) exceeds the current yield (6.27%), which exceeds the yield to maturity (6.09%). The coupon rate exceeds current yield because the coupon rate divides the coupon payments by par value ($1,000) rather than by the bond price ($1,276). In turn, the current yield exceeds yield to maturity because the yield to maturity accounts for the built-in capital loss on the bond; the bond bought today for $1,276 will eventually fall in value to $1,000 at maturity.

Concept
CHECK

Question 4 • What will be the relationship among coupon rate, current yield, and yield to maturity for bonds selling at discounts from par?

Yield to Call

Yield to maturity is calculated on the assumption that the bond will be held until maturity. What if the bond is callable, however, and may be retired prior to the maturity date? How should we measure average rate of return for bonds subject to a call provision?

Figure 14.7 illustrates the risk of call to the bondholder. The colored line is the value at various market interest rates of a "straight" (i.e., noncallable) bond with par value $1,000, an 8% coupon rate, and a 30-year time to maturity. If interest rates fall, the bond price, which equals the present value of the promised payments, can rise substantially.

Now consider a bond that has the same coupon rate and maturity date but is callable at 110% of par value, or $1,100. When interest rates fall, the present value of the bond's *scheduled* payments rises, but the call provision allows the issuer to repurchase the bond at the call price. If the call price is less than the present value of the scheduled payments, the issuer can call the bond at the expense of the bondholder.

The black line in Figure 14.7 is the value of the callable bond. At high interest rates, the risk of call is negligible, and the values of the straight and callable bonds converge. At lower rates, however, the values of the bonds begin to diverge, with the difference reflecting the value of the firm's option to reclaim the callable bond at the call price. At very low rates, the bond is called, and its value is simply the call price, $1,100.

This analysis suggests that bond market analysts might be more interested in a bond's yield to call rather than yield to maturity if the bond is especially vulnerable to being called. The yield to call is calculated just like the yield to maturity except that the time until call

Figure 14.7
Bond prices: Callable
and straight debt.

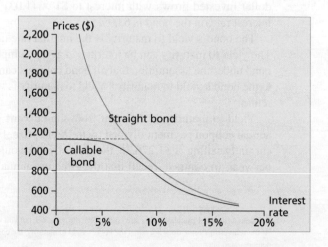

replaces time until maturity, and the call price replaces the par value. This computation is sometimes called "yield to first call," as it assumes the bond will be called as soon as the bond is first callable.

For example, suppose the 8% coupon, 30-year maturity bond sells for $1,150 and is callable in 10 years at a call price of $1,100. Its yield to maturity and yield to call would be calculated using the following inputs:

	Yield to Call	Yield to Maturity
Coupon payment	$40	$40
Number of semiannual periods	20 periods	60 periods
Final payment	$1,100	$1,000
Price	$1,150	$1,150

The yield to call is then 6.64%, whereas yield to maturity is 6.82%.

We have noted that most callable bonds are issued with an initial period of call protection. In addition, an implicit form of call protection operates for bonds selling at deep discounts from their call prices. Even if interest rates fall a bit, deep-discount bonds still will sell below the call price and thus will not be subject to a call.

Premium bonds that might be selling near their call prices, however, are especially apt to be called if rates fall further. If interest rates fall, a callable premium bond is likely to provide a lower return than could be earned on a discount bond whose potential price appreciation is not limited by the likelihood of a call. Investors in premium bonds often are more interested in the bond's yield to call rather than yield to maturity as a consequence, because it may appear to them that the bond will be retired at the call date.

In fact, the yield reported for callable Treasury bonds in the financial pages of the newspaper (see Figure 14.1) is the yield to *call* for premium bonds and the yield to *maturity* for discount bonds. This is because the call price on Treasury issues is simply par value. If the bond is selling at a premium, it is likely that the Treasury will find it advantageous to call the bond when it enters the call period. If the bond is selling at a discount from par, the Treasury will not find it advantageous to exercise its option to call.

Concept CHECK

Question 5 • **The yield to maturity on two 10-year maturity bonds currently is 7%. Each bond has a call price of $1,100. One bond has a coupon rate of 6%, the other 8%. Assume for simplicity that bonds are called as soon as the present value of their remaining payments exceeds their call price. What will be the capital gain on each bond if the market interest rate suddenly falls to 6%?**

Question 6 • **A 20-year maturity 9% coupon bond paying coupons semiannually is callable in five years at a call price of $1,050. The bond currently sells at a yield to maturity of 8%. What is the yield to call?**

Yield to Maturity and Default Risk

Because corporate bonds are subject to default risk, we must distinguish between the bond's promised yield to maturity and its expected yield. The promised or stated yield will be realized only if the firm meets the obligations of the bond issue. Therefore, the stated yield is the *maximum possible* yield to maturity of the bond. The expected yield to maturity must take into account the possibility of a default.

For example, in August 1993, Wang Laboratories, Inc., was in bankruptcy proceedings, and its bonds due in 2009 were selling at about 35% of par value, resulting in a yield to maturity of over 26%. Investors did not really expect these bonds to provide a 26% rate of return. They recognized that bondholders were very unlikely to receive all the payments promised in the bond contract, and that the yield based on *expected* cash flows was far less than the yield based on *promised* cash flows.

To illustrate the difference between expected and promised yield to maturity, suppose a firm issued a 9% coupon bond 20 years ago. The bond now has 10 years left until its maturity date but the firm is having financial difficulties. Investors believe that the firm will be able to make good on the remaining interest payments, but that at the maturity date, the firm will be forced into bankruptcy, and bondholders will receive only 70% of par value. The bond is selling at $750.

Yield to maturity (YTM) would then be calculated using the following inputs:

	Expected YTM	Stated YTM
Coupon payment	$45	$45
Number of semiannual periods	20 periods	20 periods
Final payment	$700	$1,000
Price	$750	$750

The yield to maturity based on promised payments is 13.7%. Based on the expected payment of $700 at maturity, however, the yield to maturity would be only 11.6%. The stated yield to maturity is greater than the yield investors actually expect to receive.

Concept CHECK

Question 7 • What is the expected yield to maturity if the firm is in even worse condition and investors expect a final payment of only $600?

To compensate for the possibility of default, corporate bonds must offer a **default premium**. The default premium is the difference between the promised yield on a corporate bond and the yield of an otherwise-identical government bond that is riskless in terms of default. If the firm remains solvent and actually pays the investor all of the promised cash flows, the investor will realize a higher yield to maturity than would be realized from the government bond. If, however, the firm goes bankrupt, the corporate bond is likely to provide a lower return than the government bond. The corporate bond has the potential for both better and worse performance than the default-free Treasury bond. In other words, it is riskier.

The pattern of default premiums offered on risky bonds is sometimes called the *risk structure of interest rates*. The greater the default risk, the higher the default premium. Figure 14.8 shows yield to maturity of bonds of different risk classes since 1954 and yields on junk bonds since 1986. You can see here clear evidence of default-risk premiums on promised yields.

One particular manner in which yield spreads seem to vary over time is related to the business cycle. Yield spreads tend to be wider when the economy is in a recession. Apparently, investors perceive a higher probability of bankruptcy when the economy is faltering, even holding bond ratings constant. They require a commensurately higher default premium. This is sometimes termed a *flight to quality*, meaning that investors move their funds into safer bonds unless they can obtain larger premiums on lower-rated securities.

Figure 14.8

Yields on long-term bonds.

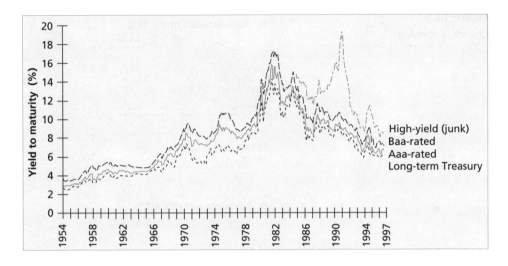

Realized Compound Yield versus Yield to Maturity

We have noted that yield to maturity will equal the rate of return realized over the life of the bond if all coupons are reinvested at an interest rate equal to the bond's yield to maturity. Consider, for example, a two-year bond selling at par value paying a 10% coupon once a year. The yield to maturity is 10%. If the $100 coupon payment is reinvested at an interest rate of 10%, the $1,000 investment in the bond will grow after two years to $1,210, as illustrated in Figure 14.9, **A**. The coupon paid in the first year is reinvested and grows with interest to a second-year value of $110, which together with the second coupon payment and payment of par value in the second year, results in a total value of $1,210. The compound growth rate of invested funds, therefore, is calculated from

$$\$1,000 \,(1 + y_{\text{realized}})^2 = \$1,210$$
$$y_{\text{realized}} = .10 = 10\%$$

With a reinvestment rate equal to the 10% yield to maturity, the *realized* compound yield equals yield to maturity.

But what if the reinvestment rate is not 10%? If the coupon can be invested at more than 10%, funds will grow to more than $1,210, and the realized compound return will exceed 10%. If the reinvestment rate is less than 10%, so will be the realized compound return.

Suppose, for example, that the interest rate at which the coupon can be invested equals 8%. The following calculations are illustrated in Figure 14.9, **B**.

Future value of first coupon payment with interest earnings $100 × 1.08 =	$ 108
Cash payment in second year (final coupon plus par value)	$1,100
Total value of investment with reinvested coupons	$1,208

The realized compound yield is computed by calculating the compound rate of growth of invested funds, assuming that all coupon payments are reinvested. The investor purchased the bond for par at $1,000, and this investment grew to $1,208.

$$\$1,000(1 + y_{\text{realized}})^2 = \$1,208$$
$$y_{\text{realized}} = .0991 = 9.91\%$$

This example highlights the problem with conventional yield to maturity when reinvestment rates can change over time. Conventional yield to maturity will not equal realized

Figure 14.9
Growth of invested funds.

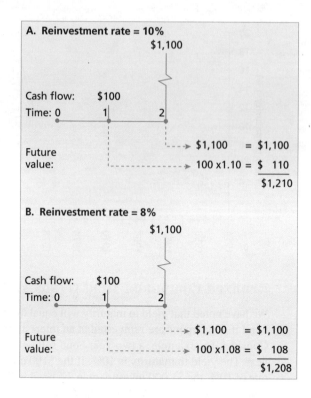

compound return. However, in an economy with future interest rate uncertainty, the rates at which interim coupons will be reinvested are not yet known. Therefore, although realized compound yield can be computed *after* the investment period ends, it cannot be computed in advance without a forecast of future reinvestment rates. This reduces much of the attraction of the realized yield measure.

Yield to Maturity versus Holding Period Return

You should not confuse the rate of return on a bond over any particular holding period with the bond's yield to maturity. The yield to maturity is defined as the single discount rate at which the present value of the payments provided by the bond equals its price. The yield to maturity is a measure of the average rate of return over the bond's life if it is held until maturity. In contrast, the holding period return equals income earned over a period (including capital gains or losses) as a percentage of the bond price at the start of the period. The holding period return can be calculated for any holding period based on the income generated over that period.

For example, if a 30-year bond paying an annual coupon of $80 is purchased for $1,000, its yield to maturity is 8%. If the bond price increases to $1,050 by year end, its yield to maturity will fall below 8% (the bond is now selling above par value, so yield to maturity must be less than the 8% coupon rate), but the holding period return for the year is greater than 8%:

$$\text{Holding period return} = \frac{\$80 + (\$1,050 - \$1,000)}{\$1,000} = .13, \text{ or } 13\%$$

14.5   BOND PRICES OVER TIME

As we noted earlier, a bond will sell at par value when its coupon rate equals the market interest rate. In these circumstances, the investor receives fair compensation for the time value of money in the form of the recurring interest payments. No further capital gain is necessary to provide fair compensation.

When the coupon rate is lower than the market interest rate, the coupon payments alone will not provide investors as high a return as they could earn elsewhere in the market. To receive a fair return on such an investment, investors also need to earn price appreciation on their bonds. The bonds, therefore, would have to sell below par value to provide a "built-in" capital gain on the investment.

To illustrate this point, suppose a bond was issued several years ago when the interest rate was 7%. The bond's annual coupon rate was thus set at 7%. (We will suppose for simplicity that the bond pays its coupon annually.) Now, with three years left in the bond's life, the interest rate is 8% per year. The bond's fair market price is the present value of the remaining annual coupons plus payment of par value. That present value is

$$\$70 \times \text{Annuity factor}(8\%, 3) + \$1,000 \times \text{PV factor}(8\%, 3) = \$974.23$$

which is less than par value.

In another year, after the next coupon is paid, the bond would sell at

$$\$70 \times \text{Annuity factor}(8\%, 2) + \$1,000 \times \text{PV factor}(8\%, 2) = \$982.17$$

thereby yielding a capital gain over the year of $7.94. If an investor had purchased the bond at $974.23, the total return over the year would equal the coupon payment plus capital gain, or $70 + $7.94 = $77.94. This represents a rate of return of $77.94/$974.23, or 8%, exactly the current rate of return available elsewhere in the market.

Concept
CHECK

Question 8 • **What will the bond price be in yet another year, when only one year remains until maturity? What is the rate of return to an investor who purchases the bond at $982.17 and sells it one year hence?**

When bond prices are set according to the present value formula, any discount from par value provides an anticipated capital gain that will augment a below-market coupon rate just sufficiently to provide a fair total rate of return. Conversely, if the coupon rate exceeds the market interest rate, the interest income by itself is greater than that available elsewhere in the market. Investors will bid up the price of these bonds above their par values. As the bonds approach maturity, they will fall in value because fewer of these above-market coupon payments remain. The resulting capital losses offset the large coupon payments so that the bondholder again receives only a fair rate of return.

Problem 12 at the end of the chapter asks you to work through the case of the high-coupon bond. Figure 14.10 traces out the price paths of high- and low-coupon bonds (net of accrued interest) as time to maturity approaches. The low-coupon bond enjoys capital gains, whereas the high-coupon bond suffers capital losses.

We use these examples to show that each bond offers investors the same total rate of return. Although the capital gain versus income components differ, the price of each bond is set to provide competitive rates, as we should expect in well-functioning capital markets. Security returns all should be comparable on an after-tax risk-adjusted basis. It they are not, investors will try to sell low-return securities, thereby driving down the prices until the total return at the now lower price is competitive with other securities. Prices should continue to

Figure 14.10

Price paths of coupon bonds.

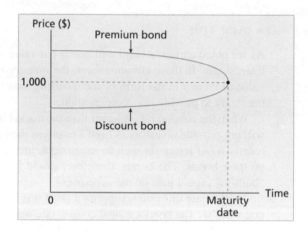

adjust until all securities are fairly priced in that expected returns are appropriate (given necessary risk and tax adjustments).

Zero-Coupon Bonds

Original issue discount bonds are less common than coupon bonds issued at par. These are bonds that are issued intentionally with low coupon rates that cause the bond to sell at a discount from par value. An extreme example of this type of bond is the *zero-coupon bond*, which carries no coupons and must provide all its return in the form of price appreciation. Zeros provide only one cash flow to their owners, and that is on the maturity date of the bond.

U.S. Treasury bills are examples of short-term zero-coupon instruments. The Treasury issues or sells a bill for some amount less than $10,000, agreeing to repay $10,000 at the bill's maturity. All of the investor's return comes in the form of price appreciation over time.

Longer-term zero-coupon bonds are commonly created from coupon-bearing notes and bonds with the help of the U.S. Treasury. A broker which purchases a Treasury coupon bond may ask the Treasury to break down the cash flows to be paid by the bond into a series of independent securities, where each security is a claim to one of the payments of the original bond. For example, a 10-year coupon bond would be "stripped" of its 20 semi-annual coupons, and each coupon payment would be treated as a stand-alone zero-coupon bond. The maturities of these bonds would thus range from 6 months to 20 years. The final payment of principal would be treated as another stand-alone zero-coupon security. Each of the payments is now treated as an independent security and is assigned its own CUSIP number (by the Committee on Uniform Securities Identification Procedures), the security identifier that allows for electronic trading over the Fedwire system, a network that connects all Federal Reserve banks and their branches. The payments are still considered obligations of the U.S. Treasury. The Treasury program under which coupon stripping is performed is called STRIPS (Separate Trading of Registered Interest and Principal of Securities), and these zero-coupon securities are called Treasury *strips*. Turn back to Figure 14.1 to see the listing of these bonds in *The Wall Street Journal*.

What should happen to prices of zeros as time passes? On their maturity dates, zeros must sell for par value. Before maturity, however, they should sell at discounts from par, because of the time value of money. As time passes, price should approach par value. In fact, if the interest rate is constant, a zero's price will increase at exactly the rate of interest.

Figure 14.11

The price of a 30-year zero-coupon bond over time. Price equals $1,000/(1.10)^T$, where T is time until maturity.

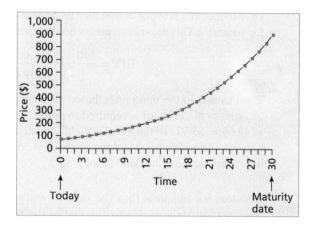

To illustrate this property, consider a zero with 30 years until maturity, and suppose the market interest rate is 10% per year. The price of the bond today will be $1,000/(1.10)^{30} = \$57.31$. Next year, with only 29 years until maturity, the price will be $1,000/(1.10)^{29} = \$63.04$, a 10% increase over its previous-year value. Because the par value of the bond is now discounted for one fewer year, its price has increased by the one-year discount factor.

Figure 14.11 presents the price path of a 30-year zero-coupon bond until its maturity date for an annual market interest rate of 10%. The bond prices rise exponentially, not linearly, until its maturity.

After-Tax Returns

The tax authorities recognize that the "built-in" price appreciation on original issue discount (OID) bonds such as zero-coupon bonds represents an implicit interest payment to the holder of the security. The IRS, therefore, calculates a price appreciation schedule to impute taxable interest income for the built-in appreciation during a tax year, even if the asset is not sold or does not mature until a future year. Any additional gains or losses that arise from changes in market interest rates are treated as capital gains or losses if the OID bond is sold during the tax year.

Let's consider an example. If the interest rate originally is 10%, the 30-year zero would be issued at a price of $1,000/(1.10)^{30} = \$57.31$. The following year, the IRS calculates what the bond price would be if the yield remains at 10%. This is $1,000/(1.10)^{29} = \$63.04$. Therefore, the IRS imputes interest income of $\$63.04 - \$57.31 = \$5.73$. This amount is subject to tax. Notice that the imputed interest income is based on a "constant yield method" that ignores any changes in market interest rates.

If interest rates actually fall, let's say to 9.9%, the bond price actually will be $1,000/(1.099)^{29} = \$64.72$. If the bond is sold, then the difference between $64.72 and $63.04 will be treated as capital gains income and taxed at the capital gains tax rate. If the bond is not sold, then the price difference is an unrealized capital gain and does not result in taxes in that year. In either case, the investor must pay taxes on the $5.73 of imputed interest at the rate on ordinary income.

The same reasoning is applied to the taxation of other original-issue discount bonds, even if they are not zero-coupon bonds. Consider, as an example, a 30-year maturity bond that is issued with a coupon rate of 4% and a yield to maturity of 8%. For simplicity, we will assume that the bond pays coupons once annually. Because of the low coupon rate, the bond will be issued at a price far below par value, specifically at a price of $549.69. If the bond's yield to maturity remains at 8%, then its price in one year will rise to $553.66. (Confirm this for yourself.) This provides a pretax holding period return (HPR) of exactly 8%:

$$HPR = \frac{\$40 + (\$553.66 - \$549.69)}{\$549.69} = .08$$

The increase in the bond price based on a constant yield, however, is treated as interest income, so the investor is required to pay taxes on imputed interest income of $553.66 – $549.69 = $3.97. If the bond's yield actually changes during the year, the difference between the bond's price and the constant-yield value of $553.66 would be treated as capital gains income if the bond is sold.

Concept CHECK

Question 9 • Suppose that the yield to maturity of the 4% coupon, 30-year maturity bond actually falls to 7% by the end of the first year, and that the investor sells the bond after the first year. If the investor's tax rate on interest income is 36% and the tax rate on capital gains is 20%, what is the investor's after-tax rate of return?

SUMMARY

1. Fixed-income securities are distinguished by their promise to pay a fixed or specified stream of income to their holders. The coupon bond is a typical fixed-income security.

2. Treasury notes and bonds have original maturities greater than one year. They are issued at or near par value, with their prices quoted net of accrued interest. T-bonds may be callable during their last five years of life.

3. When bonds are subject to potential default, the stated yield to maturity is the maximum possible yield to maturity that can be realized by the bondholder. In the event of default, however, that promised yield will not be realized. To compensate bond investors for default risk, bonds must offer default premiums, that is, promised yields in excess of those offered by default-free government securities. If the firm remains healthy, its bonds will provide higher returns than government bonds. Otherwise the returns may be lower.

4. Bond safety is often measured using financial ratio analysis. Bond indentures are another safeguard to protect the claims of bondholders. Common indentures specify sinking fund requirements, collateralization of the loan, dividend restrictions, and subordination of future debt.

5. Callable bonds should offer higher promised yields to maturity to compensate investors for the fact that they will not realize full capital gains should the interest rate fall and the bonds be called away from them at the stipulated call price. Bonds often are issued with a period of call protection. In addition, discount bonds selling significantly below their call price offer implicit call protection.

6. Put bonds give the bondholder rather than the issuer the option to terminate or extend the life of the bond.

7. Convertible bonds may be exchanged, at the bondholder's discretion, for a specified number of shares of stock. Convertible bondholders "pay" for this option by accepting a lower coupon rate on the security.

8. Floating-rate bonds pay a fixed premium over a reference short-term interest rate. Risk is limited because the rate paid is tied to current market conditions.

9. The yield to maturity is the single interest rate that equates the present value of a security's cash flows to its price. Bond prices and yields are inversely related. For premium bonds, the coupon rate is greater than the current yield, which is greater than the yield to maturity. The order of these inequalities is reversed for discount bonds.

10. The yield to maturity is often interpreted as an estimate of the average rate of return to an investor who purchases a bond and holds it until maturity. This interpretation is subject to error, however. Related measures are yield to call, realized compound yield, and expected (versus promised) yield to maturity.

11. Prices of zero-coupon bonds rise exponentially over time, providing a rate of appreciation equal to the interest rate. The IRS treats this price appreciation as imputed taxable interest income to the investor.

Key Terms

fixed-income securities	convertible bonds	subordination clauses
bond	put bond	collateral
par value	floating-rate bonds	debenture
face value	investment-grade bonds	yield to maturity
coupon rate	speculative-grade or junk bonds	current yield
bond indenture	sinking fund	default premium
zero-coupon bonds		

Selected Readings

A comprehensive treatment of pricing issues related to fixed-income securities is given in:
  Fabozzi, Frank J. *Bond Markets, Analysis, and Strategies.* 3rd ed. Englewood Cliffs, N.J.:
  Prentice Hall, 1996.
Surveys of fixed-income instruments and investment characteristics are contained in:
  Fabozzi, Frank J.; and T. Dessa Fabozzi. *The Handbook of Fixed Income Securities.* 4th ed.
  Burr Ridge, Ill.: Irwin Professional Publishing, 1995.
  Stigum, Marcia; and Frank J. Fabozzi. *The Dow Jones–Irwin Guide to Bond and Money Market
  Investments.* Homewood, Ill.: Dow Jones-Irwin, 1987.

Problems

1. Which security has a higher *effective* annual interest rate?
    a. A three-month T-bill selling at $97,645 with par value $100,000.
    b. A coupon bond selling at par and paying a 10% coupon semiannually.

2. Treasury bonds paying an 8% coupon rate with *semiannual* payments currently sell at par value. What coupon rate would they have to pay in order to sell at par if they paid their coupons *annually*?

3. Two bonds have identical times to maturity and coupon rates. One is callable at 105, the other at 110. Which should have the higher yield to maturity? Why?

4. Consider a bond with a 10% coupon and with yield to maturity = 8%. If the bond's yield to maturity remains constant, then in one year, will the bond price be higher, lower, or unchanged? Why?

5. Consider an 8% coupon bond selling for $953.10 with three years until maturity making *annual* coupon payments. The interest rates in the next three years will be, with certainty, $r_1 = 8\%$, $r_2 = 10\%$, and $r_3 = 12\%$. Calculate the yield to maturity and realized compound yield of the bond.

6. Philip Morris may issue a 10-year maturity fixed-income security, which might include a sinking fund provision and either refunding or call protection.

a. Describe a sinking fund provision.

b. Explain the impact of a sinking-fund provision on:

  i. The expected average life of the proposed security.

  ii. Total principal and interest payments over the life of the proposed security.

c. From the investor's point of view, explain the rationale for demanding a sinking fund provision.

7. Bonds of Zello Corporation with a par value of $1,000 sell for $960, mature in five years, and have a 7% annual coupon rate paid semiannually.

a. Calculate the:

  i.   Current yield.

  ii. Yield to maturity (to the nearest whole percent, i.e., 3%, 4%, 5%, etc.).

  iii. Realized compound yield for an investor with a three-year holding period and a reinvestment rate of 6% over the period. At the end of three years the 7% coupon bonds with two years remaining will sell to yield 7%.

b. Cite one major shortcoming for each of the following fixed-income yield measures:

  i.   Current yield.

  ii. Yield to maturity.

  iii. Realized compound yield.

8. Assume you have a one-year investment horizon and are trying to choose among three bonds. All have the same degree of default risk and mature in 10 years. The first is a zero-coupon bond that pays $1,000 at maturity. The second has an 8% coupon rate and pays the $80 coupon once per year. The third has a 10% coupon rate and pays the $100 coupon once per year.

a. If all three bonds are now priced to yield 8% to maturity, what are their prices?

b. If you expect their yields to maturity to be 8% at the beginning of next year, what will their prices be then? What is your before-tax holding period return on each bond? If your tax bracket is 30% on ordinary income and 20% on capital gains income, what will your after-tax rate of return be on each?

c. Recalculate your answer to (b) under the assumption that you expect the yields to maturity on each bond to be 7% at the beginning of next year.

9. A 20-year maturity bond with par value of $1,000 makes semiannual coupon payments at a coupon rate of 8%. Find the bond equivalent and effective annual yield to maturity of the bond if the bond price is:

a. $950.

b. $1,000.

c. $1,050.

10. Repeat problem 9 using the same data, but assuming that the bond makes its coupon payments annually. Why are the yields you compute lower in this case?

11. Fill in the table below for the following zero-coupon bonds, all of which have par values of $1,000.

Price	Maturity (years)	Bond-Equivalent Yield to Maturity
$400	20	___
$500	20	___
$500	10	___
___	10	10%
___	10	8%
$400	___	8%

12. Consider a bond paying a coupon rate of 10% per year semiannually when the market interest rate is only 4% per half year. The bond has three years until maturity.

    a. Find the bond's price today and six months from now after the next coupon is paid.

    b. What is the total (six month) rate of return on the bond?

13. A newly issued bond pays its coupons once annually. Its coupon rate is 5%, its maturity is 20 years, and its yield to maturity is 8%.

    a. Find the holding period return for a one-year investment period if the bond is selling at a yield to maturity of 7% by the end of the year.

    b. If you sell the bond after one year, what taxes will you owe if the tax rate on interest income is 40% and the tax rate on capital gains income is 30%? The bond is subject to original-issue discount tax treatment.

    c. What is the after-tax holding period return on the bond?

    d. Find the realized compound yield *before taxes* for a two-year holding period, assuming that (1) you sell the bond after two years, (2) the bond yield is 7% at the end of the second year, and (3) the coupon can be reinvested for one year at a 3% interest rate.

    e. Use the tax rates in (b) above to compute the *after-tax* two-year realized compound yield. Remember to take account of OID tax rules.

14. A bond with a coupon rate of 7% makes semiannual coupon payments on January 15 and July 15 of each year. *The Wall Street Journal* reports the ask price for the bond on January 30 at 100:02. What is the invoice price of the bond? The coupon period has 182 days.

15. A bond has a current yield of 9% and a yield to maturity of 10%. Is the bond selling above or below par value? Explain.

16. Is the coupon rate of the bond in problem 15 more or less than 9%?

17. A newly issued 20-year maturity, zero-coupon bond is issued with a yield to maturity of 8% and face value $1,000. Find the imputed interest income in the first, second, and last year of the bond's life.

18. A newly issued 10-year maturity, 4% coupon bond making *annual* coupon payments is sold to the public at a price of $800. What will be an investor's taxable income from the bond over the coming year? The bond will not be sold at the end of the year. The bond is treated as an original issue discount bond.

19. A 30-year maturity, 8% coupon bond paying coupons semiannually is callable in five years at a call price of $1,100. The bond currently sells at a yield to maturity of 7% (3.5% per half year).

    a. What is the yield to call?

    b. What is the yield to call if the call price is only $1,050?

    c. What is the yield to call if the call price is $1,100, but the bond can be called in two years instead of five years?

20. A 10-year bond of a firm in severe financial distress has a coupon rate of 14% and sells for $900. The firm is currently renegotiating the debt, and it appears that the lenders will allow the firm to reduce coupon payments on the bond to one-half the originally contracted amount. The firm can handle these lower payments. What is the stated and expected yield to maturity of the bonds? The bond makes its coupon payments annually.

21. A two-year bond with par value $1,000 making annual coupon payments of $100 is priced at $1,000. What is the yield to maturity of the bond? What will be the realized compound yield to maturity if the one-year interest rate next year turns out to be (*a*) 8%, (*b*) 10%, (*c*) 12%?

22. The stated yield to maturity and realized compound yield to maturity of a (default-free) zero-coupon bond will always be equal. Why?

23. Suppose that today's date is April 15. A bond with a 10% coupon paid semiannually every January 15 and July 15 is listed in *The Wall Street Journal* as selling at an ask price of 101:04. If you buy the bond from a dealer today, what price will you pay for it?

24. Assume that two firms issue bonds with the following characteristics. Both bonds are issued at par.

	ABC Bonds	XYZ Bonds
Issue size	$1.2 billion	$150 million
Maturity	10 years*	20 years
Coupon	9%	10%
Collateral	First mortgage	General debenture
Callable	Not callable	In 10 years
Call price	None	110
Sinking fund	None	Starting in 5 years

*Bond is extendible at the discretion of the bondholder for an additional 10 years.

Ignoring credit quality, identify four features of these issues that might account for the lower coupon on the ABC debt. Explain.

25. A large corporation issued both fixed and floating-rate notes five years ago, with terms given in the following table:

	9% Coupon Notes	Floating-Rate Note
Issue size	$250 million	$280 million
Maturity	20 years	10 years
Current price (% of par)	93	98
Current coupon	9%	8%
Coupon adjusts	Fixed coupon	Every year
Coupon reset rule	—	1-year T-bill rate + 2%
Callable	10 years after issue	10 years after issue
Call price	106	102
Sinking fund	None	None
Yield to maturity	9.9%	—
Price range since issued	$85 1/8–$112	$97–$102

a. Why is the price range greater for the 9% coupon bond than the floating-rate note?

b. What factors could explain why the floating-rate note is not always sold at par value?

c. Why is the call price for the floating-rate note not of great importance to investors?

d. Is the probability of call for the fixed-rate note high or low?

e. If the firm were to issue a fixed-rate note with a 15-year maturity, what coupon rate would it need to offer to issue the bond at par value?

f. Why is an entry for yield to maturity for the floating-rate note not appropriate?

26. Masters Corp. issues two bonds with 20-year maturities. Both bonds are callable at $1,050. The first bond is issued at a deep discount with a coupon rate of 4% and a price of $580 to yield 8.4%. The second bond is issued at par value with a coupon rate of 8¾%.

a. What is the yield to maturity of the par bond? Why is it higher than the yield of the discount bond?

b. If you expect rates to fall substantially in the next two years, which bond would you prefer to hold?

c. In what sense does the discount bond offer "implicit call protection"?

27. A convertible bond has the following features:

Coupon	5.25%
Maturity	June 15, 2017
Market price of bond	$77.50
Market price of underlying common stock	$28.00
Annual dividend	$ 1.20
Conversion ratio	20.83 shares

Calculate the conversion premium for this bond.

28. a. Explain the impact on the offering yield of adding a call feature to a proposed bond issue.

b. Explain the impact on the bond's expected life of adding a call feature to a proposed bond issue.

c. Describe one advantage and one disadvantage of including callable bonds in a portfolio.

29. The multiple-choice problems following are based on questions that appeared in past CFA examinations.

a. Which bond probably has the highest credit quality?
   i. Sumter, South Carolina, Water and Sewer Revenue Bond.
   ii. Riley County, Kansas, General Obligation Bond.
   iii. University of Kansas Medical Center Refunding Revenue Bonds (insured by American Municipal Bond Assurance Corporation).
   iv. Euless, Texas, General Obligation Bond (refunded and secured by the U.S. government in escrow to maturity).

b. The spread between Treasury and BAA corporate bond yields widens when:
   i. Interest rates are low.
   ii. There is economic uncertainty.
   iii. There is a "flight from quality."
   iv. All of the above.

c. An investment in a coupon bond will provide the investor with a return equal to the bond's yield to maturity at the time of purchase if:
   i. The bond is not called for redemption at a price that exceeds its par value.
   ii. All sinking fund payments are made in a prompt and timely fashion over the life of the issue.
   iii. The reinvestment rate is the same as the bond's yield to maturity and the bond is held until maturity.
   iv. All of the above.

d. A bond with a call feature:
   i. Is attractive because the immediate receipt of principal plus premium produces a high return.
   ii. Is more apt to be called when interest rates are high because the interest saving will be greater.
   iii. Will usually have a higher yield than a similar noncallable bond.
   iv. None of the above.

e. The yield to maturity on a bond is:

    i. Below the coupon rate when the bond sells at a discount, and above the coupon rate when the bond sells at a premium.

    ii. The discount rate that will set the present value of the payments equal to the bond price.

    iii. The current yield plus the average annual capital gain rate.

    iv. Based on the assumption that any payments received are reinvested at the coupon rate.

f. A particular bond has a yield to maturity on an APR basis of 12.00% but makes equal quarterly payments. What is the effective annual yield to maturity?

    i. 11.45%.

    ii. 12.00%.

    iii. 12.55%.

    iv. 37.35%.

g. In which *one* of the following cases is the bond selling at a discount?

    i. Coupon rate is greater than current yield, which is greater than yield to maturity.

    ii. Coupon rate, current yield, and yield to maturity are all the same.

    iii. Coupon rate is less than current yield, which is less than yield to maturity.

    iv. Coupon rate is less than current yield, which is greater than yield to maturity.

h. Consider a five-year bond with a 10% coupon that has a present yield to maturity of 8%. If interest rates remain constant, one year from now the price of this bond will be:

    i. Higher.

    ii. Lower.

    iii. The same.

    iv. Par.

i. A revenue bond is distinguished from a general obligation bond in that revenue bonds:

    i. Are issued by counties, special districts, cities, towns, and state-controlled authorities, whereas general obligation bonds are issued only by the states themselves.

    ii. Are typically secured by limited taxing power, whereas general obligation bonds are secured by unlimited taxing power.

    iii. Are issued to finance specific projects and are secured by the revenues of the project being financed.

    iv. Have first claim to any revenue increase of the tax authority issuing the bonds.

j. Serial obligation bonds differ from *most* other bonds because:

    i. They are secured by the assets and taxing power of the issuer.

    ii. Their par value is usually well below $1,000.

    iii. Their term to maturity is usually very long (30 years or more).

    iv. They possess multiple maturity dates.

k. Which *one* of the following is *not* an advantage of convertible bonds for the investor?

    i. The yield on the convertible will typically be higher than the yield on the underlying common stock.

    ii. The convertible bond will likely participate in a major upward move in the price of the underlying common stock.

    iii. Convertible bonds are typically secured by specific assets of the issuing company.

    iv. Investors normally may convert to the underlying common stock.

l. The call feature of a bond means the:
   i. Investor can call for payment on demand.
   ii. Investor can call only if the firm defaults on an interest payment.
   iii. Issuer can call the bond issue before the maturity date.
   iv. Issuer can call the issue during the first three years.

m. The annual interest paid on a bond relative to its prevailing market price is called its:
   i. Promised yield.
   ii. Yield to maturity.
   iii. Coupon rate.
   iv. Current yield.

n. Which *one* of the following statements about convertible bonds is *false*?
   i. The yield on the convertible will typically be higher than the yield on the underlying common stock.
   ii. The convertible bond will likely participate in a major upward movement in the price of the underlying common stock.
   iii. Convertible bonds are typically secured by specific assets of the issuing company.
   iv. A convertible bond can be valued as a straight bond with an attached option.

o. All else being equal, which *one* of the following bonds *most likely* would sell at the highest yield?
   i. Callable debenture.
   ii. Puttable mortgage bond.
   iii. Callable mortgage bond.
   iv. Puttable debentures.

p. Yields on nonconvertible preferred stock usually are lower than yields on bonds of the same company because of differences in:
   i. Marketability.
   ii. Risk.
   iii. Taxation.
   iv. Call protection.

q. The yield to maturity on a bond is:
   i. Below the coupon rate when the bond sells at a discount and above the coupon rate when the bond sells at a premium.
   ii. The interest rate that makes the present value of the payments equal to the bond price.
   iii. Based on the assumption that all future payments received are reinvested at the coupon rate.
   iv. Based on the assumption that all future payments received are reinvested at future market rates.

solutions to **Concept CHECKS**

1. The callable bond will sell at the *lower* price. Investors will not be willing to pay as much if they know that the firm retains a valuable option to reclaim the bond for the call price if interest rates fall.

2. It should receive a negative coefficient. A high ratio of liabilities to assets is a poor omen for a firm that should lower its credit rating.

3. At a semiannual interest rate of 3%, the bond is worth $40 × Annuity factor(3%, 60) + $1,000 × PV factor(3%, 60) = $1,276.75, which results in a capital gain of $276.75.

This exceeds the capital loss of $189.29 ($1,000 − $810.71) when the interest rate increased to 5%.

4. Yield to maturity exceeds current yield, which exceeds coupon rate. Take as an example the 8% coupon bond with a yield to maturity of 10% per year (5% per half year). Its price is $810.71, and therefore its current yield is 80/810.71 = .0987, or 9.87%, which is higher than the coupon rate but lower than the yield to maturity.

5. The bond with the 6% coupon rate currently sells for 30 × Annuity factor(3.5%, 20) + 1,000 × PV factor(3.5%, 20) = $928.94. If the interest rate immediately drops to 6% (3% per half year), the bond price will rise to $1,000, for a capital gain of $71.06, or 7.65%. The 8% coupon bond currently sells for $1,071.06. If the interest rate falls to 6%, the present value of the *scheduled* payments increases to $1,148.77. However, the bond will be called at $1,100, for a capital gain of only $28.94, or 2.70%.

6. The current price of the bond can be derived from the yield to maturity. Using your calculator, set: n = 40 (semiannual periods); payment = $45 per period; future value = $1,000; interest rate = 4% per semiannual period. Calculate present value as $1,098.96. Now we can calculate yield to call. The time to call is five years, or 10 semiannual periods. The price at which the bond will be called is $1,050. To find yield to call, we set: n = 10 (semiannual periods); payment = $45 per period; future value = $1,050; present value = $1,098.96. Calculate yield to call as 3.72%.

7. The coupon payment is $45. There are 20 semiannual periods. The final payment is assumed to be $600. The present value of expected cash flows is $750. The yield to maturity is 5.42% semiannual or 10.8%.

8. Price = $70 × Annuity factor(8%, 1) + $1,000 × PV factor(8%, 1) = $990.74

$$\text{Rate of return to investor} = \frac{70 + (\$990.74 - \$982.17)}{\$982.17} = .080$$

$$= 8\%$$

9. At the lower yield, the bond price will be $631.67 [n = 29, i = 7%, FV = $1000, PMT = $40]. Therefore, total after-tax income is

Coupon	$40 × (1 − .36) =	$25.60
Imputed interest	($553.66 − $549.69) × (1 − .36) =	2.54
Capital gains	($631.67 − $553.66) × (1 − .20) =	62.41
Total income after taxes		$90.55

Rate of return = 90.55/549.69 = .165 = 16.5%.

THE TERM STRUCTURE OF INTEREST RATES

In Chapter 14 we assumed for the sake of simplicity that the same constant interest rate is used to discount cash flows of any maturity. In the real world this is rarely the case. We have seen, for example, that in late 1994 short-term bonds and notes carried yields to maturity only slightly higher than 5% while the longest-term bonds offered yields above 8%. At the time when these bond prices were quoted, anyway, the longer-term securities had higher yields. This, in fact, is a common empirical pattern. In this chapter we explore the pattern of interest rates for different-term assets. We attempt to identify the factors that account for that pattern and determine what information may be derived from an analysis of the so-called **term structure of interest rates**, the structure of interest rates for discounting cash flows of different maturities.

15.1 THE TERM STRUCTURE UNDER CERTAINTY

What do you conclude from the observation that longer-term bonds offer higher yields to maturity? One possibility is that longer-term bonds are riskier and that the higher yields are evidence of a risk premium that compensates for interest rate risk. Another possibility is that investors expect interest rates to rise and that the higher average yields on long-term bonds reflect the anticipation of high interest rates in the latter years of the bond's life. We start our analysis of these possibilities with the easiest case: a world with no uncertainty where investors already know the path of future interest rates.

Bond Pricing

The interest rate for a given time interval is called the **short interest rate** for that period. Suppose that all participants in the bond market are convinced that the short rates for the next four years will follow the pattern in Table 15.1

Of course, market participants cannot look up such a sequence of short rates in *The Wall Street Journal*. All they observe there are prices and yields of bonds of various maturities. Nevertheless, we can think of the short-rate sequence of Table 15.1 as the series of interest rates that investors keep in the back of their minds when they evaluate the prices of different bonds. Given this pattern of rates, what prices might we observe on various maturity bonds? To keep the algebra simple, for now we will treat only a zero-coupon bond.

A bond paying $1,000 in one year would sell today for $1,000/1.08 = $925.93. Similarly, a two-year maturity bond would sell today at price

$$P = \frac{\$1,000}{(1.08)(1.10)} = \$841.75 \tag{15.1}$$

This is the present value of the future $1,000 cash flow, because $841.75 would need to be set aside now to provide a $1,000 payment in two years. After one year, the $841.75 set aside would grow to $841.75(1.08) = $909.09 and after the second year to $909.09(1.10) = $1,000.

In general we may write the present value of $1 to be received after n periods as

$$\text{PV of \$1 in } n \text{ periods} = \frac{1}{(1 + r_1)(1 + r_2) \ldots (1 + r_n)}$$

where r_i is the one-year interest rate that will prevail in year i. Continuing in this manner, we find the values of the three- and four-year bonds as shown in the middle column of Table 15.2.

Table 15.1 Interest Rates on One-Year Bonds in Coming Years

Year	Interest Rate
0 (Today)	8%
1	10
2	11
3	11

From the bond prices we can calculate the yield to maturity on each bond. Recall that the yield is the *single* interest rate that equates the present value of the bond's payments to the bond's price. Although interest rates may vary over time, the yield to maturity is calculated as one "average" rate that is applied to discount all of the bond's payments. For example, the yield on the two-year zero-coupon bond, which we will call y_2, is the interest rate that satisfies

$$841.75 = 1,000/(1 + y_2)^2 \qquad (15.2)$$

which we solve for $y_2 = .08995$. We repeat the process for the two other bonds, with results as reported in the table. For example, we find y_3 by solving

$$758.33 = 1,000/(1 + y_3)^3$$

Now we can make a graph of the yield to maturity on the four bonds as a function of time to maturity. This graph, which is called the **yield curve**, appears in Figure 15.1.

While the yield curve in Figure 15.1 rises smoothly, a wide range of curves may be observed in practice. Figure 15.2 presents three such curves. Panel **A** is the yield curve from November 1997, which is upward sloping. Panel **B** is a hump-shaped curve, first rising and then falling. The yield curve in Panel **C** is essentially flat.

The yield to maturity on zero-coupon bonds is sometimes called the **spot rate** that prevails today for a period corresponding to the maturity of the zero. The yield curve, or,

Table 15.2   Prices and Yields of Zero-Coupon Bonds

Time to Maturity	Price	Yield to Maturity
1	$925.93	8.000%
2	841.75	8.995
3	758.33	9.660
4	683.18	9.993

Figure 15.1
Yield curve.

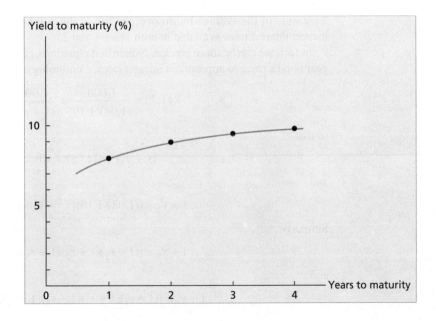

Figure 15.2
Treasury yield curves.

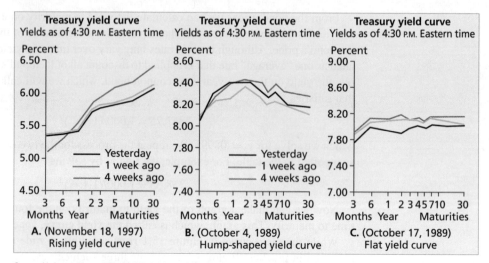

A. (November 18, 1997)
Rising yield curve

B. (October 4, 1989)
Hump-shaped yield curve

C. (October 17, 1989)
Flat yield curve

equivalently, the last column of Table 15.2, thus presents the spot rates for four maturities. Note that the spot rates or yields do *not* equal the one-year interest rates for each year.

To emphasize the difference between the sequence of *short* rates for each future year and *spot* rates for different maturity dates, examine Figure 15.3. The first line of data presents the short rate for each annual period. The lower lines present the spot rates, or equivalently, the yields to maturity, for different holding periods that extend from the present to each relevant maturity date.

The yield on the two-year bond is close to the average of the short rates for years 1 and 2. This makes sense because if interest rates of 8% and 10% will prevail in the next two years, then (ignoring compound interest) a sequence of two one-year investments will provide a cumulative return of 18%. Therefore, we would expect a two-year bond to provide a competitive total return of about 18%, which translates into an annualized yield to maturity of 9%, just about equal to the 8.995% yield we derived in Table 15.2. Because the yield is a measure of the average return over the life of the bond, it should be determined by the market interest rates available in both years 1 and 2.

In fact, we can be more precise. Notice that equations 15.1 and 15.2 each relate the two-year bond's price to appropriate interest rates. Combining equations 15.1 and 15.2, we find

$$841.75 = \frac{1,000}{(1.08)(1.10)} = \frac{1,000}{(1 + y_2)^2}$$

so that

$$(1 + y_2)^2 = (1.08)(1.10)$$

and

$$1 + y_2 = [(1.08)(1.10)]^{1/2} = 1.08995$$

Similarly,

$$1 + y_3 = [(1 + r_1)(1 + r_2)(1 + r_3)]^{1/3}$$

and

$$1 + y_4 = [(1 + r_1)(1 + r_2)(1 + r_3)(1 + r_4)]^{1/4} \tag{15.3}$$

Figure 15.3
Short rates versus spot rates.

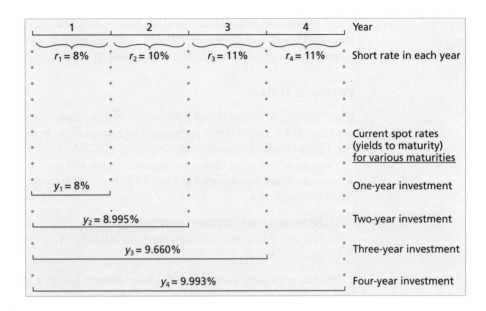

and so on. Thus the yields are in fact averages of the interest rates in each period. However, because of compound interest, the relationship is not an arithmetic average but a geometric one.

Holding-Period Returns

What is the rate of return on each of the four bonds in Table 15.2 over a one-year holding period? You might think at first that higher-yielding bonds would provide higher one-year rates of return, but this is not the case. In our simple world with no uncertainty all bonds must offer identical rates of return over any holding period. Otherwise, at least one bond would be dominated by the others in the sense that it would offer a lower rate of return than would combinations of other bonds; no one would be willing to hold the bond, and its price would fall. In fact, despite their different yields to maturity, each bond will provide a rate of return over the coming year equal to this year's short interest rate.

To confirm this point, we can compute the rates of return on each bond. The one-year bond is bought today for $925.93 and matures in one year to its par value of $1,000. Because the bond pays no coupon, total income is $1,000 – $925.93 = $74.07, and the rate of return is $74.07/$925.93 = .08, or 8 percent. The two-year bond is bought today for $841.75. Next year the interest rate will be 10%, and the bond will have one year left until maturity. It will sell for $1,000/1.10 = $909.09. Thus the *holding-period return* is ($909.09 – $841.75)/$841.75 = .08, again implying an 8% rate of return. Similarly, the three-year bond will be purchased for $758.33 and will be sold at year-end for $1,000/(1.10)(1.11) = $819.00, for a rate of return ($819.00 – $758.33)/$758.33 = .08, again, an 8% return.

Concept

Question 1 • Confirm that the return on the four-year bond also will be 8%.

Therefore, we conclude that when interest rate movements are known with certainty, if all bonds are fairly priced, all will provide equal one-year rates of return. The higher yields on the longer-term bonds merely reflect the fact that future interest rates are higher than current rates, and that the longer bonds are still alive during the higher-rate period. Owners of the short-term bonds receive lower yields to maturity, but they can reinvest, or "roll over," their proceeds for higher yields in later years when rates are higher. In the end, both long-term bonds and short-term rollover strategies provide equal returns over the holding period, at least in a world of interest rate certainty.

Forward Rates

Unfortunately, investors do not have access to short-term interest rate quotations for coming years. What they do have are newspaper quotations of bond prices and yields to maturity. Can they infer future short rates from the available data?

Suppose we are interested in the interest rate that will prevail during year 3, and we have access only to the data reported in Table 15.2. We start by comparing two alternatives, illustrated in Figure 15.4:

1. Invest in a three-year zero-coupon bond.
2. Invest in a two-year zero-coupon bond. After two years reinvest the proceeds in a one-year bond.

Assuming an investment of $100, under strategy 1, with a yield to maturity of 9.660% on three-year zero-coupon bonds, our investment would grow to $100(1.0966)^3 = $131.87. Under strategy 2, the $100 investment in the two-year bond would grow after two years to $100(1.08995)^2 = $118.80. Then in the third year it would grow by an additional factor of $1 + r_3$.

In a world of certainty both of these strategies must yield exactly the same final payoff. If strategy 1 were to dominate strategy 2, no one would hold two-year bonds; their prices would fall and their yields would rise. Likewise, if strategy 2 dominated strategy 1, no one would hold three-year bonds. Therefore, we can conclude that $131.87 = $118.80(1 + r_3)$, which implies that $(1 + r_3) = 1.11$, or $r_3 = 11\%$. This is in fact the rate that will prevail in year 3, as Table 15.1 indicates. Thus our method of obtaining the third-period interest rate does provide the correct solution in the certainty case.

More generally, the comparison of the two strategies establishes that the return on a three-year bond equals that on a two-year bond and rollover strategy:

$$100(1 + y_3)^3 = 100(1 + y_2)^2(1 + r_3)$$

so that $1 + r_3 = (1 + y_3)^3/(1 + y_2)^2$. Generalizing, for the certainty case, a simple rule for inferring a future short interest rate from the yield curve of zero-coupon bonds is to use the following formula:

$$(1 + r_n) = \frac{(1 + y_n)^n}{(1 + y_{n-1})^{n-1}} \tag{15.4}$$

where n denotes the period in question and y_n is the yield to maturity of a zero-coupon bond with an n-period maturity.

Equation 15.4 has a simple interpretation. The numerator on the right-hand side is the total growth factor of an investment in an n-year zero held until maturity. Similarly, the denominator is the growth factor of an investment in an $(n - 1)$-year zero. Because the former investment lasts for one more year than the latter, the difference in these growth factors must be the rate of return available in year n when the $(n - 1)$-year zero can be rolled over into a one-year investment.

Of course, when future interest rates are uncertain, as they are in reality, there is no meaning to inferring "the" future short rate. No one knows today what the future interest rate will be. At best, we can speculate as to its expected value and associated uncertainty. Nevertheless, it still is common to use equation 15.4 to investigate the implications of the

Figure 15.4
Two three-year
investment programs.

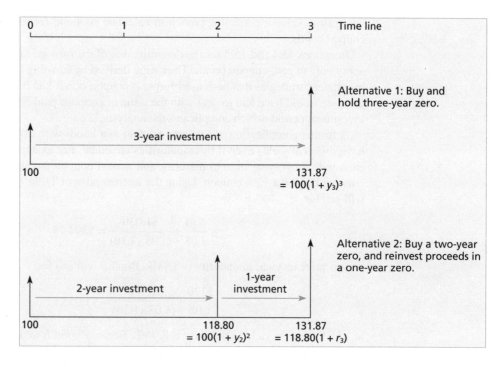

yield curve for future interest rates. In recognition of the fact that future interest rates are uncertain, we call the interest rate that we infer in this matter the **forward interest rate** rather than the *future short rate*, because it need not be the interest rate that actually will prevail at the future date.

If the forward rate for period n is f_n, we then define f_n by the equation

$$1 + f_n = \frac{(1 + y_n)^n}{(1 + y_{n-1})^{n-1}}$$

Equivalently, we may rewrite the equation as

$$(1 + y_n)^n = (1 + y_{n-1})^{n-1}(1 + f_n) \tag{15.5}$$

In this formulation, the forward rate is *defined* as the "break-even" interest rate that equates the return on an n-period zero-coupon bond to that of an $(n - 1)$-period zero-coupon bond rolled over into a one-year bond in year n. The actual total returns on the two n-year strategies will be equal if the spot interest rate in year n turns out to equal f_n.

We emphasize that the interest rate that actually will prevail in the future need not equal the forward rate, which is calculated from today's data. Indeed, it is not even necessarily the case that the forward rate equals the expected value of the future short interest rate. This is an issue that we address in much detail shortly. For now, however, we note that forward rates do equal future short rates in the special case of interest rate certainty.

15.2   MEASURING THE TERM STRUCTURE

Thus far we have focused on default-free zero-coupon bonds. These bonds are easiest to analyze because their maturity is given by their single payment. In practice, however, the great majority of bonds pay coupons, and most available data pertain to coupon bonds, so we must develop a general approach to calculate spot and forward rates from prices of coupon bonds.

Equations 15.4 and 15.5 for the determination of the forward rate from available yields apply only to zero-coupon bonds. They were derived by equating the returns to competing investment strategies that both used zeros. If coupon bonds had been used in those strategies, we would have had to deal with the issue of coupons paid and reinvested during the investment period, which complicates the analysis.

A further complication arises from the fact that bonds with different coupon rates can have different yields even if their maturities are equal. For example, consider two bonds, each with a two-year time to maturity and annual coupon payments. Bond A has a 3% coupon; bond B a 12% coupon. Using the interest rates of Table 15.1, we see that bond A will sell for

$$\frac{\$30}{1.08} + \frac{\$1,030}{(1.08)(1.10)} = \$894.78$$

At this price its yield to maturity is 8.98%. Bond B will sell for

$$\frac{\$120}{1.08} + \frac{\$1,120}{(1.08)(1.10)} = \$1,053.87$$

at which price its yield to maturity is 8.94%. Because bond B makes a greater share of its payments in the first year when the interest rate is lower, its yield to maturity is slightly lower. Because bonds with the same maturity can have different yields, we conclude that a single yield curve relating yields and times to maturity cannot be appropriate for all bonds.

The solution to this ambiguity is to perform all of our analysis using the yield curve for zero-coupon bonds, sometimes called the *pure yield curve*. Our goal, therefore, is to calculate the pure yield curve even if we have to use data on more common coupon-paying bonds.

The trick we use to infer the yield curve from data on coupon bonds is to treat each coupon payment as a separate "mini"–zero-coupon bond. A coupon bond then becomes just a "portfolio" of many zeros. Indeed, we saw in the previous chapter that most zero-coupon bonds are created by stripping coupon payments from coupon bonds and repackaging the separate payments from many bonds into portfolios with common maturity dates. By determining the price of each of these "zeros" we can calculate the yield to that maturity date for a single-payment security and thereby construct the pure yield curve.

As a simple example of this technique, suppose that we observe an 8% coupon bond making semiannual payments with one year until maturity, selling at $986.10, and a 10% coupon bond, also with a year until maturity, selling at $1,004.78. To infer the short rates for the next two six-month periods, we first attempt to find the present value of each coupon payment taken individually, that is, treated as a mini–zero-coupon bond. Call d_1 the present value of $1 to be received in half a year and d_2 the present value of a dollar to be received in one year. (The d stands for discounted values; therefore, $d_1 = 1/(1 + r_1)$, where r_1 is the short rate for the first six-month period.) Then our two bonds must satisfy the simultaneous equations

$$986.10 = d_1 \times 40 + d_2 \times 1,040$$
$$1,004.78 = d_1 \times 50 + d_2 \times 1,050$$

In each equation the bond's price is set equal to the discounted value of all of its remaining cash flows. Solving these equations we find that $d_1 = .95694$ and $d_2 = .91137$. Thus if

r_1 is the short rate for the first six-month period, then $d_1 = 1/(1 + r_1) = .95694$, so that $r_1 = .045$, and $d_2 = 1/[(1 + r_1)(1 + f_2)] = 1/[(1.045)(1 + f_2)] = .91137$, so that $f_2 = .05$. Thus the two short rates are shown to be 4.5% for the first half-year period and 5% for the second.

Concept

Question 2 • **A T-bill with six-month maturity and $10,000 face value sells for $9,700. A one-year maturity T-bond paying semiannual coupons of $40 sells for $1,000. Find the current six-month short rate, and the forward rate for the following six-month period.**

When we analyze many bonds, such an inference procedure is more difficult, in part because of the greater number of bonds and time periods, but also because not all bonds give rise to identical estimates for the discounted value of a future $1 payment. In other words, there seem to be apparent error terms in the pricing relationship.[1] Nevertheless, treating these errors as random aberrations, we can use a statistical approach to infer the pattern of forward rates embedded in the yield curve.

To see how the statistical procedure would operate, suppose that we observe many coupon bonds, indexed by i, selling at prices P_i. The coupon and/or principal payment (the cash flow) of bond i at time t is denoted CF_{it}, and the present value of a $1 payment at time t, which is the implied price of a zero-coupon bond that we are trying to determine, is denoted d_t. Then for each bond we may write the following:

$$P_1 = d_1 CF_{11} + d_2 CF_{12} + d_3 CF_{13} + \ldots + e_1$$
$$P_2 = d_1 CF_{21} + d_2 CF_{22} + d_3 CF_{23} + \ldots + e_2$$
$$P_3 = d_1 CF_{31} + d_2 CF_{32} + d_3 CF_{33} + \ldots + e_3$$
$$\vdots \qquad\qquad\qquad \vdots$$
$$P_n = d_1 CF_{n1} + d_2 CF_{n2} + d_3 CF_{n3} + \ldots + e_n$$

(15.6)

Each line of equation system 15.6 equates the price of the bond to the sum of its cash flows, discounted according to time until payment. The last term in each equation, e_i, represents the error term that accounts for the deviations of a bond's price from the prediction of the equation.

Students of statistics will recognize that equation 15.6 is a simple system of equations that can be estimated by regression analysis. The dependent variables are the bond prices, the independent variables are the cash flows, and the coefficients d_t are to be estimated from the observed data.[2] The estimates of d_t are our inferences of the present value of $1 to be paid at time t. The pattern of d_t for various times to payment is called the *discount function*, because it gives the discounted value of $1 as a function of time until payment. From the discount function, which is equivalent to a list of zero-coupon bond prices for various maturity dates, we can calculate the yields on pure zero-coupon bonds. We would use Treasury securities in this procedure to avoid complications arising from default risk.

Before leaving the issue of the measurement of the yield curve, it is worth pausing briefly to discuss the error terms. Why is it that all bond prices do not conform exactly to

---

[1] We will consider later some of the reasons for the appearance of these error terms.
[2] In practice, variations of regression analysis called "splining techniques" are usually used to estimate the coefficients. This method was first suggested by McCulloch in the following two articles: J. Huston McCulloch, "Measuring the Term Structure of Interest Rates," *Journal of Business* 44 (January 1971); and "The Tax Adjusted Yield Curve," *Journal of Finance* 30 (June 1975).

a common discount function that sets price equal to present value? Two reasons relate to factors not accounted for in the regression analysis of equation 15.6: taxes and options associated with the bond.

Taxes affect bond prices because investors care about their after-tax return on investment. Therefore, the coupon payments should be treated as net of taxes. Similarly, if a bond is not selling at par value, the IRS may impute a "built-in" interest payment by amortizing the difference between the price and the par value of the bond. These considerations are difficult to capture in a mathematical formulation because different individuals are in different tax brackets, meaning that the net-of-tax cash flows from a given bond depend on the identity of the owner. Moreover, the specification of equation 15.6 implicitly assumes that the bond is held until maturity: It discounts *all* the bond's coupon and principal payments. This, of course, ignores the investor's option to sell the bond before maturity and so to realize a different stream of income from that described by equation 15.6. Moreover, it ignores the investor's ability to engage in *tax-timing options*. For example, an investor whose tax bracket is expected to change over time may benefit by realizing capital gains during the period when the tax rate is the lowest.

Another feature affecting bond pricing is the call provision. First, if the bond is callable, how do we know whether to include in equation 15.6 coupon payments in years following the first call date? Similarly, the date of the principal repayment becomes uncertain. More important, one must realize that the issuer of the callable bond will exercise the option to call only when it is profitable to do so. Conversely, the call provision is a transfer of value away from the bondholder who has "sold" the option to call to the bond issuer. The call feature therefore will affect the bond's price and introduce further error terms in the simple specification of equation 15.6.

Finally, we must recognize that the yield curve is based on price quotes that often are somewhat inaccurate. Price quotes used in the financial press may be stale (i.e., out of date), even if only by a few hours. Moreover, they may not represent prices at which dealers actually are willing to trade.

15.3   INTEREST RATE UNCERTAINTY AND FORWARD RATES

Let us turn now to the more difficult analysis of the term structure when future interest rates are uncertain. We have argued so far that, in a certain world, different investment strategies with common terminal dates must provide equal rates of return. For example, two consecutive one-year investments in zeros would need to offer the same total return as an equal-sized investment in a two-year zero. Therefore, under certainty,

$$(1 + r_1)(1 + r_2) = (1 + y_2)^2$$

What can we say when r_2 is not known today?

For example, referring once again to Table 15.1, suppose that today's rate, $r_1 = 8\%$, and that the *expected* short rate next year is $E(r_2) = 10\%$. If bonds were priced based only on the expected value of the interest rate, then a one-year zero would sell for $1,000/1.08 = $925.93, and a two-year zero would sell for $1,000/[(1.08)(1.10)] = $841.75, just as in Table 15.2.

But now consider a short-term investor who wishes to invest only for one year. She can purchase the one-year zero and lock in a riskless 8% return because she knows that at the end of the year, the bond will be worth its maturity value of $1,000. She also can purchase the two-year zero. Its *expected* rate of return also is 8%: Next year, the bond will have one year to maturity, and we expect that the one-year interest rate will be 10%, implying a price of $909.09 and a holding-period return of 8%. But the rate of return on the two-year bond is risky. If next year's interest rate turns out to be above expectations, that is, greater than 10%, the bond price will be below $909.09, and conversely if r_2 turns out to be less than 10%, the bond price will exceed $909.09. Why should this short-term investor buy the risky two-year bond when its expected return is 8%, no better than that of the risk-free one-year bond? Clearly, she would not hold the two-year bond unless it offered an expected rate of return greater than the riskless 8% return available on the competing one-year bond. This requires that the two-year bond sell at a price lower than the $841.75 value we derived when we ignored risk.

Suppose, for example, that most investors have short-term horizons and are willing to hold the two-year bond only if its price falls to $819. At this price, the expected holding-period return on the two-year bond is 11% (because 909.09/819 = 1.11). The risk premium of the two-year bond, therefore, is 3%; it offers an expected rate of return of 11% versus the 8% risk-free return on the one-year bond. At this risk premium, investors are willing to bear the price risk associated with interest rate uncertainty.

In this environment, the forward rate, f_2, no longer equals the expected short rate, $E(r_2)$. Although we have assumed that $E(r_2) = 10\%$, it is easy to confirm that $f_2 = 13\%$. The yield to maturity on the two-year zeros selling at $819 is 10.5%, and

$$1 + f_2 = \frac{(1 + y_2)^2}{1 + y_1} = \frac{1.105^2}{1.08} = 1.13$$

This result—that the forward rate exceeds the expected short rate—should not surprise us. We defined the forward rate as the interest rate that would need to prevail in the second year to make the long- and short-term investments equally attractive, ignoring risk. When we account for risk, it is clear that short-term investors will shy away from the long-term bond unless it offers an expected return greater than that offered by the one-year bond. Another way of putting this is to say that investors will require a risk premium to hold the longer-term bond. The risk-averse investor would be willing to hold the long-term bond only if $E(r_2)$ is less than the break-even value, f_2, because the lower the expectation of r_2 the greater the anticipated return on the long-term bond.

Therefore, if most individuals are short-term investors, bonds must have prices that make f_2 greater than $E(r_2)$. The forward rate will embody a premium compared with the expected future short-interest rate. This **liquidity premium** compensates short-term investors for the uncertainty about the price at which they will be able to sell their long-term bonds at the end of the year.[3]

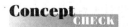

Question 3 • Suppose that the required liquidity premium for the short-term investor is 1%. What must $E(r_2)$ be if f_2 is 10%?

Perhaps surprisingly, we also can imagine scenarios in which long-term bonds can be perceived by investors to be *safer* than short-term bonds. To see how, we now consider a "long-term" investor, who wishes to invest for a full two-year period. Suppose that the investor can purchase a $1,000 par value two-year zero-coupon bond for $841.75 and lock in a guaranteed yield to maturity of $y_2 = 9\%$. Alternatively, the investor can roll over two one-year investments. In this case an investment of $841.75 would grow in two years to $841.75 \times (1.08)(1 + r_2)$, which is an uncertain amount today because r_2 is not yet known.

• [3]*Liquidity* refers to the ability to sell an asset easily at a predictable price. Because long-term bonds have greater price risk, they are considered less liquid in this context and thus must offer a premium.

The break-even year-2 interest rate is, once again, the forward rate, 10%, because the forward rate is defined as the rate that equates the terminal value of the two investment strategies.

The expected value of the payoff of the rollover strategy is $841.75(1.08)[1 + E(r_2)]$. If $E(r_2)$ equals the forward rate, f_2, then the expected value of the payoff from the rollover strategy will equal the *known* payoff from the two-year maturity bond strategy.

Is this a reasonable presumption? Once again, it is only if the investor does not care about the uncertainty surrounding the final value of the rollover strategy. Whenever that risk is important, the long-term investor will not be willing to engage in the rollover strategy unless its expected return exceeds that of the two-year bond. In this case the investor would require that

$$(1.08)[1 + E(r_2)] > (1.09)^2 = (1.08)(1 + f_2)$$

which implies that $E(r_2)$ exceeds f_2. The investor would require that the expected period 2 interest rate exceed the break-even value of 10%, which is the forward rate.

Therefore, if all investors were long-term investors, no one would be willing to hold short-term bonds unless those bonds offered a reward for bearing interest rate risk. In this situation bond prices would be set at levels such that rolling over short bonds resulted in greater expected return than holding long bonds. This would cause the forward rate to be less than the expected future spot rate.

For example, suppose that in fact $E(r_2) = 11\%$. The liquidity premium therefore is negative: $f_2 - E(r_2) = 10\% - 11\% = -1\%$. This is exactly opposite from the conclusion that we drew in the first case of the short-term investor. Clearly, whether forward rates will equal expected future short rates depends on investors' readiness to bear interest rate risk, as well as their willingness to hold bonds that do not correspond to their investment horizons.

15.4   THEORIES OF THE TERM STRUCTURE

The Expectations Hypothesis

The simplest theory of the term structure is the **expectations hypothesis**. A common version of this hypothesis states that the forward rate equals the market consensus expectation of the future short interest rate; in other words, that $f_2 = E(r_2)$, and that liquidity premiums are zero. Because $f_2 = E(r_2)$, we may relate yields on long-term bonds to expectations of future interest rates. In addition, we can use the forward rates derived from the yield curve to infer market expectations of future short rates. For example, with $(1 + y_2)^2 = (1 + r_1)(1 + f_2)$ from equation 15.5, we may also write that $(1 + y_2)^2 = (1 + r_1)[1 + E(r_2)]$ if the expectations hypothesis is correct. The yield to maturity would thus be determined solely by current and expected future one-period interest rates. An upward-sloping yield curve would be clear evidence that investors anticipate increases in interest rates.

 **Concept CHECK**

Question 4• **If the expectations hypothesis is valid, what can we conclude about the premiums necessary to induce investors to hold bonds of different maturities from their investment horizons?**

Liquidity Preference

We noted in our discussion of the long- and short-term investors that short-term investors will be unwilling to hold long-term bonds unless the forward rate exceeds the expected short interest rate, $f_2 > E(r_2)$, whereas long-term investors will be unwilling to hold short bonds unless $E(r_2) > f_2$. In other words, both groups of investors require a premium to induce them to hold bonds with maturities different from their investment horizons. Advocates of the **liquidity preference theory** of the term structure believe that short-term investors dominate the market so that, generally speaking, the forward rate exceeds the expected short rate. The excess of f_2 over $E(r_2)$, the liquidity premium, is predicted to be positive.

Concept
CHECK

Question 5. The liquidity premium hypothesis also holds that *issuers* of bonds prefer to issue long-term bonds. How would this preference contribute to a positive liquidity premium?

To illustrate the differing implications of these theories for the term structure of interest rates, consider a situation in which the short interest rate is expected to be constant indefinitely. Suppose that $r_1 = 10\%$ and that $E(r_2) = 10\%$, $E(r_3) = 10\%$, and so on. Under the expectations hypothesis the two-year yield to maturity could be derived from the following:

$$(1 + y_2)^2 = (1 + r_1)[1 + E(r_2)]$$
$$= (1.10)(1.10)$$

so that y_2 equals 10%. Similarly, yields on all-maturity bonds would equal 10%.

In contrast, under the liquidity preference theory f_2 would exceed $E(r_2)$. To illustrate, suppose that f_2 is 11%, implying a 1% liquidity premium. Then, for two-year bonds:

$$(1 + y_2)^2 = (1 + r_1)(1 + f_2)$$
$$= (1.10)(1.11) = 1.221$$

implying that $1 + y_2 = 1.105$. Similarly, if f_3 also equals 11%, then the yield on three-year bonds would be determined by

$$(1 + y_3)^3 = (1 + r_1)(1 + f_2)(1 + f_3)$$
$$= (1.10)(1.11)(1.11) = 1.35531$$

implying that $1 + y_3 = 1.1067$. The plot of the yield curve in this situation would be given as in Figure 15.5, **A**. Such an upward-sloping yield curve is commonly observed in practice.

If interest rates are expected to change over time, then the liquidity premium may be overlaid on the path of expected spot rates to determine the forward interest rate. Then the yield to maturity for each date will be an average of the single-period forward rates. Several such possibilities for increasing and declining interest rates appear in Figure 15.5 **B** to **D**.

Market Segmentation and Preferred Habitat Theories

Both the liquidity premium and expectations hypothesis of the term structure implicitly view bonds of different maturities as potential substitutes for each other. An investor considering holding bonds of one maturity possibly can be lured instead into holding bonds of another maturity by the prospect of earning a risk premium. In this sense markets for bonds of all maturities are inextricably linked, and yields on short and long bonds are determined jointly in market equilibrium. Forward rates cannot differ from expected short rates by more than a fair liquidity premium, or else investors will reallocate their fixed-income portfolios to exploit what they perceive as abnormal profit opportunities.

In contrast, the **market segmentation theory** holds that long- and short-maturity bonds are traded in essentially distinct or segmented markets, each of which finds its own equilibrium independently. The activities of long-term borrowers and lenders determine rates on long-term bonds. Similarly, short-term traders set short rates independently of long-term

Figure 15.5

Yield curves. **A,** Constant expected short rate. Liquidity premium of 1%. Result is a rising yield curve. **B,** Declining expected short rates. Increasing liquidity premiums. Result is a rising yield curve despite falling expected interest rates.

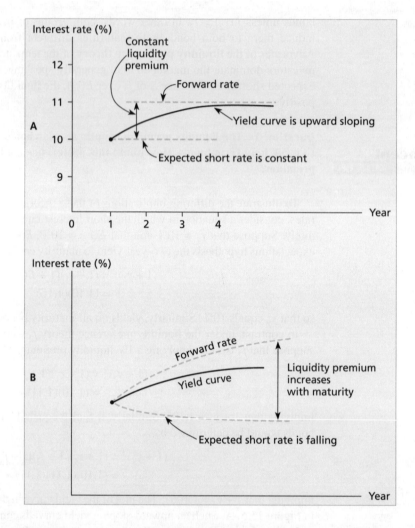

expectations. The term structure of interest rates, in this view, is determined by the equilibrium rates set in the various maturity markets.

This view of the market is not common today. Both borrowers and lenders seem to compare long and short rates, as well as expectations of future rates, before deciding whether to borrow or lend long- or short-term. That they make these comparisons, and are willing to move into a particular maturity if it seems sufficiently profitable to do so, means that bonds of all maturities compete with each other for investors' attention, which implies that the rate on a bond of any given maturity is determined with an eye toward rates on competing bonds. This view of the market is called the **preferred habitat theory:** Investors prefer specific maturity ranges but can be induced to switch if premiums are sufficient. Markets are not so segmented that an appropriate premium cannot attract an investor who prefers one bond maturity to consider a different one.

15.5   INTERPRETING THE TERM STRUCTURE

We have seen that under certainty, 1 plus the yield to maturity on a zero-coupon bond is simply the geometric average of 1 plus the future short rates that will prevail over the life of the bond. This is the meaning of equation 15.3, which we give in general form here:

Figure 15.5

(Concluded)

C, Declining expected short rates. Constant liquidity premiums. Result is a hump-shaped yield curve. **D,** Increasing expected short rates. Increasing liquidity premiums. Result is a sharply increasing yield curve.

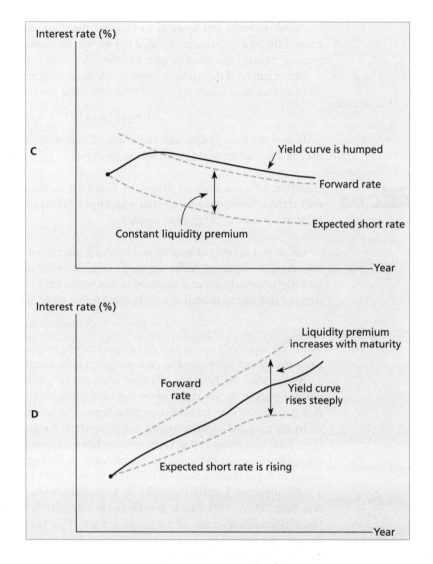

$$1 + y_n = [(1 + r_1)(1 + r_2) \ldots (1 + r_n)]^{1/n}$$

When future rates are uncertain, we modify equation 15.3 by replacing future short rates with forward rates:

$$1 + y_n = [(1 + r_1)(1 + f_2)(1 + f_3) \ldots (1 + f_n)]^{1/n} \tag{15.7}$$

Thus there is a direct relationship between yields on various maturity bonds and forward interest rates. This relationship is the source of the information that can be gleaned from an analysis of the yield curve.

First, we ask what factors can account for a rising yield curve. Mathematically, if the yield curve is rising, f_{n+1} must exceed y_n. In words, the yield curve is upward sloping at any maturity date, n, for which the forward rate for the coming period is greater than the yield at that maturity. This rule follows from the notion of the yield to maturity as an average (albeit a geometric average) of forward rates.

If the yield curve is to rise as one moves to longer maturities, it must be the case that extension to a longer maturity results in the inclusion of a "new" forward rate that is higher than the average of the previously observed rates. This is analogous to the observation that if a new student's test score is to increase the class average, that student's score must exceed the class's average without her score. To raise the yield to maturity, an above-average forward rate must be added to the other rates in the averaging computation.

For example, if the yield to maturity on three-year zero-coupon bonds is 9%, then the yield on four-year bonds will satisfy the following equation:

$$(1 + y_4)^4 = (1.09)^3(1 + f_4)$$

If $f_4 = .09$, then y_4 also will equal .09. (Confirm this!) If f_4 is greater than 9%, y_4 will exceed 9%, and the yield curve will slope upward.

Concept
CHECK

Question 6• Look back at Tables 15.1 and 15.2. Show that y_4 would exceed y_3 if and only if the interest rate for period 4 had been greater than 9.66%, which was the yield to maturity on the three-year bond, y_3.

Given that an upward-sloping yield curve is always associated with a forward rate higher than the spot, or current, yield, we need to ask next what can account for that higher forward rate. Unfortunately, there always are two possible answers to this question. Recall that the forward rate can be related to the expected future short rate according to this equation:

$$f_n = E(r_n) + \text{Liquidity premium}$$

where the liquidity premium might be necessary to induce investors to hold bonds of maturities that do not correspond to their preferred investment horizons.

By the way, the liquidity premium need not be positive, although that is the position generally taken by advocates of the liquidity premium hypothesis. We showed previously that if most investors have long-term horizons, the liquidity premium could be negative.

In any case, the equation shows that there are two reasons that the forward rate could be high. Either investors expect rising interest rates, meaning that $E(r_n)$ is high, or they require a large premium for holding longer-term bonds. Although it is tempting to infer from a rising yield curve that investors believe that interest rates will eventually increase, this is not a valid inference. Indeed, Figure 15.5, **A**, provides a simple counterexample to this line of reasoning. There, the spot rate is expected to stay at 10% forever. Yet there is a constant 1% liquidity premium so that all forward rates are 11%. The result is that the yield curve continually rises, starting at a level of 10% for one-year bonds, but eventually approaching 11% for long-term bonds as more and more forward rates at 11% are averaged into the yields to maturity.

Therefore, although it is true that expectations of increases in future interest rates can result in a rising yield curve, the converse is not true: A rising yield curve does not in and of itself imply expectations of higher future interest rates. This is the heart of the difficulty in drawing conclusions from the yield curve. The effects of possible liquidity premiums confound any simple attempt to extract expectations from the term structure. But estimating the market's expectations is a crucial task, because only by comparing your own expectations to those reflected in market prices can you determine whether you are relatively bullish or bearish on interest rates.

One very rough approach to deriving expected future spot rates is to assume that liquidity premiums are constant. An estimate of that premium can be subtracted from the forward rate to obtain the market's expected interest rate. For example, again making use of the example plotted in Figure 15.5, **A**, the researcher would estimate from historical data that a typical liquidity premium in this economy is 1%. After calculating the forward rate from the yield curve to be 11%, the expectation of the future spot rate would be determined to be 10%.

Figure 15.6

Price volatility of long-term Treasury bonds.

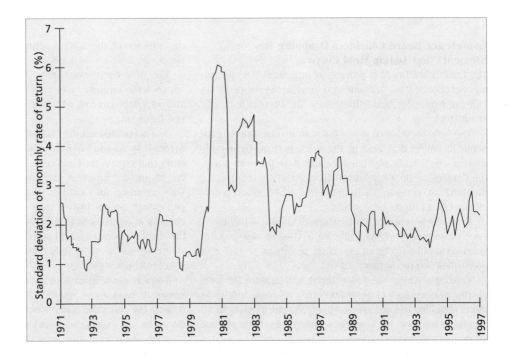

This approach has little to recommend it for two reasons. First, it is next to impossible to obtain precise estimates of a liquidity premium. The general approach to doing so would be to compare forward rates and eventually realized future short rates and to calculate the average difference between the two. However, the deviations between the two values can be quite large and unpredictable because of unanticipated economic events that affect the realized short rate. The data do not contain enough information to calculate a reliable estimate of the expected premium. Second, there is no reason to believe that the liquidity premium should be constant. Figure 15.6 shows the rate of return variability of prices of long-term Treasury bonds since 1971. Interest rate risk fluctuated dramatically during the period. So might we expect risk premiums on various maturity bonds to fluctuate, and empirical evidence suggests that term premiums do in fact fluctuate over time.[4]

Still, as the accompanying box indicates, very steep yield curves are interpreted by many market professionals as warning signs of impending rate increases. In fact, the box points out that the yield curve is a good predictor of the business cycle as a whole, since long-term rates tend to rise in anticipation of an expansion in the economy. When the curve is steep, there is a far lower probability of a recession in the next year than when it is inverted or falling. For this reason, the yield curve has been added to the index of leading economic indicators.

The usually observed upward slope of the yield curve, especially for short maturities, is the empirical basis for the liquidity premium doctrine that long-term bonds offer a positive liquidity premium. In the face of this empirical regularity, perhaps it is valid to interpret a downward-sloping yield curve as evidence that interest rates are expected to decline. If **term premiums**, the spread between yields on long- and short-term bonds, generally are positive, then anticipated declines in rates could account for a downward-sloping yield curve.

---

[4]See, for example, Richard Startz, "Do Forecast Errors or Term Premia Really Make the Difference between Long and Short Rates?" *Journal of Financial Economics* 10 (1982).

MAKEUP OF LEADING INDICATORS MAY SHIFT

Conference Board Considers Dropping Two Elements and Adding Yield Curve

The Conference Board, a provider of important U.S. government economic data, is planning to rewrite the recipe for its index of leading economic indicators, the first such change since 1989.

The New York–based group plans to revamp the 11 economic measures that make up the index, perhaps by as early as year's end. While no final decisions have yet been made, the Conference Board and its advisory panel are considering dropping two components from the mix, while adding a new element that reflects bond yields.

Economists consider the Treasury yield curve—the difference between the interest rate on a 10-year note and on short-term bills—to be an especially promising predictor of recessions and recoveries.

Economists hope the restructuring will improve the forecasting performance of the index, which has done a reliable job of signaling the last six economic downturns eight to 18 months in advance, but also has sounded a few false alarms. "It predicts almost every recession, but . . . there's an extra recession predicted almost every other cycle," says Michael Boldin, the Conference Board's senior economist and director of business-cycle research.

Meantime, there's already broad agreement that a yield-curve component should be added to the index, according to the minutes of the June meeting of the project's advisory panel.

The yield curve would most likely track the differences between the interest rates paid on a 10-year Treasury note and on a one-year bill, or between the 10-year note and the Fed-funds rate.

Two economists at the Federal Reserve Bank of New York, Arturo Estrella and Frederic S. Mishkin, recently published a study that credits the yield curve with strong predictive powers about four quarters prior to the onset of a recession. They calculate, for example, that if the 10-year rate is 1.21 percentage points higher than the three-month rate, the chances of a recession in a year's time are 5%. Conversely, if the short-term rate is 2.40 percentage points above the 10-year rate—an inverted yield curve—the chances of a recession are about 90%.

There are two things they like about the measure. First, it seems to work more reliably than other tools. Second, it reflects the collective wisdom of market participants, whose decisions and expectations—which take political events into account—help determine bond yields. "From a screen at any one point, you can get a very simple prediction as to the status of the economy a year ahead, and somewhat more weakly of the status of inflation two to three years ahead," says Mr. Estrella, senior vice president of the New York Fed's research group.

Figure 15.7 presents a history of yields on 90-day Treasury bills and long-term Treasury bonds. Yields on the longer-term bonds *generally* (roughly two-thirds of the time) exceed those on the bills, meaning that the yield curve generally slopes upward. Moreover, the exceptions to this rule seem to precede episodes of falling short rates, which if anticipated, would induce a downward-sloping yield curve. For example, 1980–82 were years in which 90-day yields exceeded long-term yields. These years preceded a drastic drop in the general level of rates.

Why might interest rates fall? There are two factors to consider: the real rate and the inflation premium. Recall that the nominal interest rate is composed of the real rate plus a factor to compensate for the effect of inflation:

$$1 + \text{Nominal rate} = (1 + \text{Real rate})(1 + \text{Inflation rate})$$

or approximately,

$$\text{Nominal rate} \exists \text{Real rate} + \text{Inflation rate}$$

Therefore, an expected change in interest rates can be due to changes in either expected real rates or expected inflation rates. Usually, it is important to distinguish between these two possibilities because the economic environments associated with them may vary substantially. High real rates may indicate a rapidly expanding economy, high budget deficits, and tight monetary policy. Although high inflation rates also can arise out of a rapidly expand-

Figure 15.7

Yields on long-term versus 90-day Treasury securities: term spread.

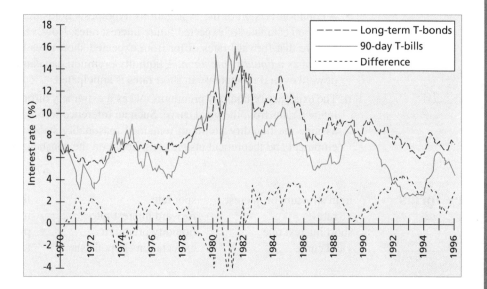

ing economy, inflation also may be caused by rapid expansion of the money supply or supply-side shocks to the economy such as interruptions in oil supplies. These factors have very different implications for investments. Even if we conclude from an analysis of the yield curve that rates will fall, we need to analyze the macroeconomic factors that might cause such a decline.

SUMMARY

1. The term structure of interest rates refers to the interest rates for various terms to maturity embodied in the prices of default-free zero-coupon bonds.

2. In a world of certainty all investments must provide equal total returns for any investment period. Short-term holding-period returns on all bonds would be equal in a risk-free economy, and all equal to the rate available on short-term bonds. Similarly, total returns from rolling over short-term bonds over longer periods would equal the total return available from long-maturity bonds.

3. A pure yield curve could be plotted easily from a complete set of zero-coupon bonds. In practice, however, most bonds carry coupons, payable at different future times, so that yield-curve estimates are often inferred from prices of coupon bonds. Measurement of the term structure is complicated by tax issues such as tax timing options and the different tax brackets of different investors.

4. The forward rate of interest is the break-even future interest rate that would equate the total return from a rollover strategy to that of a longer-term zero-coupon bond. It is defined by the equation

$$(1 + y_n)^n (1 + f_{n+1}) = (1 + y_{n+1})^{n+1}$$

where n is a given number of periods from today. This equation can be used to show that yields to maturity and forward rates are related by the equation

$$(1 + y_n)^n = (1 + r_1)(1 + f_2)(1 + f_3) \ldots (1 + f_n)$$

5. A common version of the expectations hypothesis holds that forward interest rates are unbiased estimates of expected future interest rates. However, there are good reasons to believe that forward rates differ from expected short rates because of a risk premium known as a *liquidity premium*. A liquidity premium can cause the yield curve to slope upward even if no increase in short rates is anticipated.

6. The existence of liquidity premiums makes it extremely difficult to infer expected future interest rates from the yield curve. Such an inference would be made easier if we could assume the liquidity premium remained reasonably stable over time. However, both empirical and theoretical insights cast doubt on the constancy of that premium.

Key Terms

term structure of interest rates	spot rate	liquidity preference theory
short interest rate	forward interest rate	market segmentation theory
yield curve	liquidity premium	preferred habitat theory
	expectations hypothesis	term premiums

Selected Readings

A detailed presentation of yield-curve analytics and relationships among spot rates, yields to maturity, and realized compound yields is contained in:

  Homer, Sidney; and Martin Liebowitz. *Inside the Yield Book: New Tools for Bond Market Strategy*. Englewood Cliffs, N.J.: Prentice Hall, 1972.

A discussion of the various versions of the expectations hypothesis is:

  Cox, John; Jonathan Ingersoll; and Stephen Ross. "A Reexamination of Traditional Hypotheses about the Term Structure of Interest Rates." *Journal of Finance* 36 (September 1981).

Evidence on liquidity premiums may be found in:

  Fama, Eugene. "The Information in the Term Structure." *Journal of Financial Economics* 13 (1984).

  Mankiw, N. Gregory. "The Term Structure of Interest Rates Revisited." *Brookings Papers on Economic Activity* 61 (1986).

Problems in the measurement of the yield curve are treated in:

  McCulloch, J. Houston. "The Tax-Adjusted Yield Curve." *Journal of Finance* 30 (June 1975).

Problems

1. Briefly explain why bonds of different maturities have different yields in terms of the (1) expectations, (2) liquidity, and (3) segmentation hypotheses. Briefly describe the implications of each of the three hypotheses when the yield curve is (1) upward sloping, and (2) downward sloping.

2. Which one of the following statements about the term structure of interest rates is true?
   a. The expectations hypothesis indicates a flat yield curve if anticipated future short-term rates exceed current short-term rates.
   b. The expectations hypothesis contends that the long-term rate is equal to the anticipated short-term rate.
   c. The liquidity premium theory indicates that, all else being equal, longer maturities will have lower yields.
   d. The market segmentation theory contends that borrowers and lenders prefer particular segments of the yield curve.

3. The differences between short and forward rates are most closely associated with which *one* of the following explanations of the term structure of interest rates?
   a. Expectations hypothesis.
   b. Liquidity premium theory.

    c. Preferred habitat hypothesis.

    d. Segmented market theory.

4. Under the expectations hypothesis, if the yield curve is upward sloping, the market must expect an increase in short-term interest rates. True/false/uncertain? Why?

5. Under the liquidity preference theory, if inflation is expected to be falling over the next few years, long-term interest rates will be higher than short-term rates. True/false/uncertain? Why?

6. The following is a list of prices for zero-coupon bonds of various maturities. Calculate the yields to maturity of each bond and the implied sequence of forward rates.

Maturity (Years)	Price of Bond ($)
1	943.40
2	898.47
3	847.62
4	792.16

7. Assuming that the expectations hypothesis is valid, compute the expected price path of the four-year bond in problem 6 as time passes. What is the rate of return of the bond in each year? Show that the expected return equals the forward rate for each year.

8. Suppose the following table shows yields to maturity of U.S. Treasury securities as of January 1, 1996:

Term to Maturity (Years)	Yield to Maturity
1	3.50%
2	4.50
3	5.00
4	5.50
5	6.00
10	6.60

    a. Based on the data in the table, calculate the implied forward one-year rate of interest at January 1, 1999.

    b. Describe the conditions under which the calculated forward rate would be an unbiased estimate of the one-year spot rate of interest at January 1, 1999.

    c. Assume that one year earlier, at January 1, 1995, the prevailing term structure for U.S. Treasury securities was such that the implied forward one-year rate of interest at January 1, 1999, was significantly higher than the corresponding rate implied by the term structure at January 1, 1996. On the basis of the pure expectations theory of the term structure, briefly discuss *two* factors that could account for such a decline in the implied forward rate.

9. Would you expect the yield on a callable bond to lie above or below a yield curve fitted from noncallable bonds?

10. The six-month Treasury bill spot rate is 4%, and the one-year Treasury bill spot rate is 5%. The implied six-month forward rate for six months from now is:

    a. 3.0%

    b. 4.5%

    c. 5.5%

    d. 6.0%

11. The tables below show, respectively, the characteristics of two annual-pay bonds from the same issuer with the same priority in the event of default, and spot interest rates. Neither bond's price is consistent with the spot rates. Using the information in these tables, recommend either bond *A* or bond *B* for purchase. Justify your choice.

Bond Characteristics

	Bond *A*	Bond *B*
Coupons	Annual	Annual
Maturity	3 years	3 years
Coupon rate	10%	6%
Yield to maturity	10.65%	10.75%
Price	98.40	88.34

Spot Interest Rates

Term (Years)	Spot Rates (Zero Coupon)
1	5%
2	8
3	11

12. The current yield curve for default-free zero-coupon bonds is as follows:

Maturity (Years)	YTM
1	10%
2	11
3	12

   a. What are the implied one-year forward rates?
   b. Assume that the pure expectations hypothesis of the term structure is correct. If market expectations are accurate, what will the pure yield curve (that is, the yields to maturity on one- and two-year zero coupon bonds) be next year?
   c. If you purchase a two-year zero-coupon bond now, what is the expected total rate of return over the next year? What if you purchase a three-year zero-coupon bond? (Hint: Compute the current and expected future prices.) Ignore taxes.
   d. What should be the current price of a three-year maturity bond with a 12% coupon rate paid annually? If you purchased it at that price, what would your total expected rate of return be over the next year (coupon plus price change)? Ignore taxes.

13. The term structure for zero-coupon bonds is currently:

Maturity (Years)	YTM
1	4%
2	5
3	6

Next year at this time, *you* expect it to be:

Maturity (Years)	YTM
1	5%
2	6
3	7

a. What do *you* expect the rate of return to be over the coming year on a three-year zero-coupon bond?

b. Under the expectations theory, what yields to maturity does *the market* expect to observe on one- and two-year zeros next year? Is the market's expectation of the return on the three-year bond greater or less than yours?

14. The yield to maturity on one-year zero-coupon bonds is currently 7%; the YTM on two-year zeros is 8%. The Treasury plans to issue a two-year maturity *coupon* bond, paying coupons once per year with a coupon rate of 9%. The face value of the bond is $100.

a. At what price will the bond sell?

b. What will the yield to maturity on the bond be?

c. If the expectations theory of the yield curve is correct, what is the market expectation of the price that the bond will sell for next year?

d. Recalculate your answer to (c) if you believe in the liquidity preference theory and you believe that the liquidity premium is 1%.

15. A portfolio manager at Superior Trust Company is structuring a fixed-income portfolio to meet the objectives of a client. This client plans on retiring in 15 years and wants a substantial lump sum at that time. The client has specified the use of AAA-rated securities.

The portfolio manager compares coupon U.S. Treasuries with zero-coupon stripped U.S. Treasuries and observes a significant yield advantage for the stripped bonds:

Term (Years)	Coupon U.S. Treasuries	Zero-Coupon Stripped U.S. Treasuries
3	5.50%	5.80%
5	6.00	6.60
7	6.75	7.25
10	7.25	7.60
15	7.40	7.80
30	7.75	8.20

Briefly discuss why zero-coupon stripped U.S. Treasuries could yield more than coupon U.S. Treasuries with the same final maturity.

16. Below is a list of prices for zero-coupon bonds of various maturities.

Maturity (Years)	Price of $1,000 Par Bond (Zero Coupon)
1	943.40
2	873.52
3	816.37

a. An 8.5% coupon $1,000 par bond pays an annual coupon and will mature in three years. What should the yield to maturity on the bond be?

b. If at the end of the first year the yield curve flattens out at 8%, what will be the one-year holding-period return on the coupon bond?

17. Prices of zero-coupon bonds reveal the following pattern of forward rates:

Year	Forward Rate
1	5%
2	7
3	8

In addition to the zero-coupon bond, investors also may purchase a three-year bond making annual payments of $60 with par value $1,000.

a. What is the price of the coupon bond?

b. What is the yield to maturity of the coupon bond?

c. Under the expectations hypothesis, what is the expected realized compound yield of the coupon bond?

d. If you forecast that the yield curve in one year will be flat at 7%, what is your forecast for the expected rate of return on the coupon bond for the one-year holding period?

18. You observe the following term structure:

	Effective Annual YTM
1-year zero-coupon bond	6.1%
2-year zero-coupon bond	6.2
3-year zero-coupon bond	6.3
4-year zero-coupon bond	6.4

a. If you believe that the term structure next year will be the same as today's, will the one-year or the four-year zeros provide a greater expected one-year return?

b. What if you believe in the expectations hypothesis?

19. U.S. Treasuries represent a significant holding in many pension portfolios. You decide to analyze the yield curve for U.S. Treasury notes.

a. Using the data in the table below, calculate the five-year spot and forward rates assuming annual compounding. Show your calculations.

U.S. Treasury Note Yield Curve Data

Years to Maturity	Par Coupon Yield to Maturity	Calculated Spot Rates	Calculated Forward Rates
1	5.00	5.00	5.00
2	5.20	5.21	5.42
3	6.00	6.05	7.75
4	7.00	7.16	10.56
5	7.00	?	?

   b. Define and describe each of the following three concepts:
   i.   Yield to maturity.
   ii. Spot rate.
   iii. Forward rate.
   Explain how these concepts are related.
   c. You are considering the purchase of a zero-coupon U.S. Treasury note with four years to maturity. Based on the above yield-curve analysis, calculate both the expected yield to maturity and the price for the security. Show your calculations.

20. The yield to maturity (YTM) on one-year zero-coupon bonds is 5% and the YTM on two-year zeros is 6%. The yield to maturity on two-year-maturity coupon bonds with coupon rates of 12% (paid annually) is 5.8%. What arbitrage opportunity is available for an investment banking firm? What is the profit on the activity?

21. Suppose that a one-year zero-coupon bond with face value $100 currently sells at $94.34, while a two-year zero sells at $84.99. You are considering the purchase of a two-year-maturity bond making *annual* coupon payments. The face value of the bond is $100, and the coupon rate is 12% per year.
   a. What is the yield to maturity of the two-year zero? The two-year coupon bond?
   b. What is the forward rate for the second year?
   c. If the expectations hypothesis is accepted, what are (1) the expected price of the coupon bond at the end of the first year and (2) the expected holding period return on the coupon bond over the first year?
   d. Will the expected rate of return be higher or lower if you accept the liquidity preference hypothesis?

1. The bond sells today for $683.18 (from Table 15.2). Next year, it will sell for $1,000/[(1.10)(1.11)(1.11)] = $737.84, for a return $1 + r = 737.84/683.18 = 1.08$, or $r = 8\%$.

2. The data pertaining to the T-bill imply that the six-month interest rate is $300/$9,700 = .03093, or 3.093%. To obtain the forward rate, we look at the one-year T-bond: The pricing formula

$$1,000 = \frac{40}{1.03093} + \frac{1040}{(1.03093)(1+f)}$$

implies that $f = .04952$, or 4.952%.

3. $10\% - 1\% = 9\%$.

4. The risk premium will be zero.

5. If issuers wish to issue long-term bonds, they will be willing to accept higher expected interest costs on long bonds over short bonds. This willingness combines with investors' demands for higher rates on long-term bonds to reinforce the tendency toward a positive liquidity premium.

6. If r_4 equaled 9.66%, then the four-year bond would sell for $1,000/[(1.08)(1.10)(1.11)(1.0966)] = $691.53. The yield to maturity would satisfy the equation $691.53(1 + y_4)^4 = 1,000$, or $y_4 = 9.66\%$. At a lower value of r_4, the bond would sell for a higher price and offer a lower yield. At a higher value of r_4, the yield would be greater.

FIXED-INCOME PORTFOLIO MANAGEMENT

I n this chapter we turn to various strategies that fixed-income portfolio managers can pursue, making a distinction between passive and active strategies. A *passive investment strategy* takes market prices of securities as fairly set. Rather than attempting to beat the market by exploiting superior information or insight, passive managers act to maintain an appropriate risk-return balance given market opportunities. One special case of passive management is an immunization strategy that attempts to insulate or immunize the portfolio from interest rate risk. A n *active investment strategy* attempts to achieve returns greater than those commensurate with the risk borne. In the context of fixed-income management this style of management can take two forms. Active managers either use interest rate forecasts to predict movements in the entire fixed-income market, or they employ some form of intramarket analysis to identify particular sectors of the fixed-income market or particular bonds that are relatively mispriced. W e start our discussion with an analysis of the sensitivity of bond prices to interest rate fluctuations. The concept of duration, which measures interest rate sensitivity, is basic to formulating both active and passive fixed-income strategies. We turn next to passive strategies and show how duration-matching strategies can be used to immunize the holding-period return of a fixed-income portfolio from interest rate risk. Finally, we explore a variety of active strategies, including intramarket analysis, interest rate forecasting, and interest rate swaps.

16.1   INTEREST RATE RISK

We have seen already that an inverse relationship exists between bond prices and yields, and we know that interest rates can fluctuate substantially. As interest rates rise and fall, bondholders experience capital losses and gains. These gains or losses make fixed-income investments risky, even if the coupon and principal payments are guaranteed, as in the case of Treasury obligations.

Why do bond prices respond to interest rate fluctuations? Remember that in a competitive market all securities must offer investors fair expected rates of return. If a bond is issued with an 8% coupon when competitive yields are 8%, then it will sell at par value. If the market rate rises to 9%, however, who would purchase an 8% coupon bond at par value? The bond price must fall until its expected return increases to the competitive level of 9%. Conversely, if the market rate falls to 7%, the 8% coupon on the bond is attractive compared to yields on alternative investments. In response, investors eager for that return would bid the bond price above its par value until the total rate of return falls to the market rate.

Interest Rate Sensitivity

The sensitivity of bond prices to changes in market rates is obviously of great concern to investors. The determinants of that sensitivity have been described by Malkiel[1] in the following five well-known bond-pricing relationships:

1. Bond prices and yields are inversely related: As yields increase, bond prices fall; as yields fall, bond prices rise.
2. An increase in a bond's yield to maturity results in a smaller price decline than the price gain associated with a decrease of equal magnitude in yield, that is, yield increases cause proportionately smaller price changes than yield decreases.
3. Prices of long-term bonds tend to be more sensitive to interest rate changes than prices of short-term bonds. In other words, long-term bonds tend to have more interest rate risk.
4. As maturity increases, price sensitivity to yield changes increases at a decreasing rate. In other words, bond price sensitivity to changes in yields increases less than proportionately to increases in the maturity of the bond.
5. Interest rate risk is inversely related to the bond's coupon rate. Prices of high-coupon bonds are less sensitive to changes in interest rates than prices of low-coupon bonds.

In addition, a sixth bond-pricing relationship has been demonstrated by Homer and Liebowitz:[2]

6. Bond prices are more sensitive to changes in yields when the bond is selling a lower initial yield to maturity.

These six rules are illustrated in Figure 16.1, which presents the percentage change in price corresponding to changes in yield to maturity for four bonds that differ according to

[1]Burton G. Malkiel, "Expectations, Bond Prices, and the Term Structure of Interest Rates," *Quarterly Journal of Economics* 76 (May 1962), pp. 197–218.
[2]Sidney Homer and Martin L. Liebowitz, *Inside the Yield Book: New Tools for Bond Market Strategy* (Englewood Cliffs, N.J.: Prentice Hall, 1972).

Figure 16.1

Change in bond price
as a function of change
in yield to maturity.

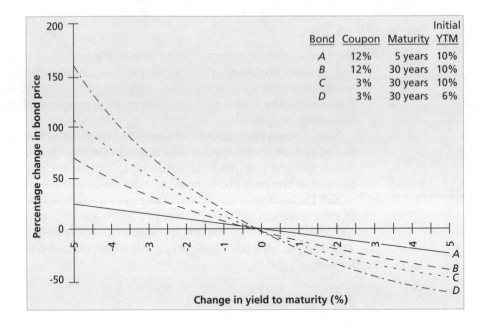

coupon rate, initial yield to maturity, and time to maturity. All four bonds illustrate points 1 and 2: Prices increase when yields fall, and the price curve is convex, meaning that decreases in yields have bigger impacts on price than increases in yields of equal magnitude. Comparing bonds *A* and *B* illustrates the third rule: The price of bond *B*, which has a longer maturity than bond *A*, exhibits greater sensitivity to interest rate changes. In addition, the graph shows that while bond *B* has six times the maturity of bond *A*, it has less than six times the interest rate sensitivity. This is consistent with Malkiel's fourth point: Interest rate sensitivity increases less than proportionately as bond maturity increases. Bonds *B* and *C*, which are alike in all respects except coupon rate, illustrate the fifth point: The lower-coupon bond exhibits greater sensitivity to changes in interest rates. Finally, bonds *C* and *D* are alike except for the yield to maturity at which the bonds currently sell. Consistent with the sixth relationship, the bond with the lower yield is indeed more sensitive to changes in the interest rate.

Malkiel's relationships confirm that maturity is a major determinant of interest rate risk. However, they also show that maturity alone is not sufficient to measure interest rate sensitivity. For example, bonds *B* and *C* in Figure 16.1 have the same maturity, but the higher-coupon bond has less price sensitivity to interest rate changes. Obviously, we need to know more than a bond's maturity to quantify its interest rate risk.

To see why bond characteristics such as coupon rate or yield to maturity affect interest rate sensitivity, let's start with a simple numerical example. Table 16.1 gives bond prices for 8% semiannual coupon bonds at different yields to maturity and times to maturity, *T*. [The interest rates are expressed as annual percentage rates (APRs), meaning that the true six-month yield is doubled to obtain the stated annual yield.] The shortest-term bond falls in value by less than 1% when the interest rate increases from 8% to 9%. The 10-year bond falls by 6.5%, and the 20-year bond by over 9%.

Let us now look at a similar computation using a zero-coupon bond rather than the 8% coupon bond. The results are shown in Table 16.2. Notice that for each maturity, the price of the zero-coupon bond falls by a greater proportional amount than the price of the 8% coupon bond. Because we know that long-term bonds are more sensitive to interest rate

Table 16.1   Prices of 8% Coupon Bond (coupons paid semiannually)

Yield to Maturity (APR)	T = 1 Year	T = 10 Years	T = 20 Years
8%	1,000.00	1,000.00	1,000.00
9%	990.64	934.96	907.99
Change in price (%)*	0.94%	6.50%	9.20%

*Equals value of bond at a 9% yield to maturity divided by value of bond at (the original) 8% yield, minus 1.

Table 16.2   Prices of Zero-Coupon Bond (semiannual compounding)

Yield to Maturity (APR)	T = 1 Year	T = 10 Years	T = 20 Years
8%	924.56	456.39	208.29
9%	915.73	414.64	171.93
Change in price (%)*	0.96%	9.15%	17.46%

*Equals value of bond at a 9% yield to maturity divided by value of bond at (the original) 8% yield, minus 1.

movements than are short-term bonds, this observation suggests that in some sense a zero-coupon bond represents a longer-term bond than an equal-time-to-maturity coupon bond. In fact, this insight about effective maturity is a useful one that we can make mathematically precise.

To start, note that the times to maturity of the two bonds in this example are not perfect measures of the long- or short-term nature of the bonds. The 20-year 8% bond makes many coupon payments, most of which come years before the bond's maturity date. Each of these payments may be considered to have its own "maturity date," and the effective maturity of the bond is therefore some sort of average of the maturities of *all* the cash flows paid out by the bond. The zero-coupon bond, by contrast, makes only one payment at maturity. Its time to maturity is, therefore, a well-defined concept.

Duration

To deal with the ambiguity of the "maturity" of a bond making many payments, we need a measure of the average maturity of the bond's promised cash flows to serve as a useful summary statistic of the effective maturity of the bond. We would like also to use the measure as a guide to the sensitivity of a bond to interest rate changes, because we have noted that price sensitivity tends to increase with time to maturity.

Frederick Macaulay[3] termed the effective maturity concept the **duration** of the bond and suggested that duration be computed as the weighted average of the times to each coupon or principal payment made by the bond. He recommended that the weight associated with each payment time be related to the "importance" of that payment to the value of the bond; specifically, that the weight applied to each payment time be the proportion of the total value of the bond accounted for by that payment. This proportion is just the present value of the payment divided by the bond price.

---

[3]Frederick Macaulay, *Some Theoretical Problems Suggested by the Movements of Interest Rates, Bond Yields, and Stock Prices in the United States since 1856* (New York: National Bureau of Economic Research, 1938).

Table 16.3　Calculating the Duration of Two Bonds

	(1) Time until Payment (Years)	(2) Payment	(3) Payment Discounted at 5% Semiannually	(4) Weight*	(5) Column 1 Multiplied by Column 4
Bond A					
8% bond	0.5	$ 40	$ 38.095	0.0395	0.0198
	1.0	40	36.281	0.0376	0.0376
	1.5	40	34.553	0.0358	0.0537
	2.0	1,040	855.611	0.8871	1.7742
Sum			$964.540	1.0000	1.8853
Bond B					
Zero-coupon bond	0.5–1.5	$ 0	$ 0	0	0
	2.0	1,000	822.70	1.0	2
Sum			$822.70	1.0	2

*Weight = Present value of each payment (column 3) divided by the bond price, $964.54 for bond A and $822.70 for bond B.

Therefore, the weight, denoted w_t, associated with the cash flow made at time t (denoted CF_t) would be

$$w_t = \frac{CF_t/(1 + y)^t}{\text{Bond price}}$$

where y is the bond's yield to maturity. The numerator on the right-hand side of this equation is the present value of the cash flow occurring at time t while the denominator is the value of all the payments forthcoming from the bond. These weights sum to 1.0 because the sum of the cash flows discounted at the yield to maturity equals the bond price.

Using these values to calculate the weighted average of the times until the receipt of each of the bond's payments, we obtain Macaulay's duration formula:`

$$D = \sum_{t=1}^{T} t \times w_t \qquad (16.1)$$

As an example of the application of equation 16.1, we derive in Table 16.3 the durations of an 8% coupon and zero-coupon bond, each with two years to maturity. We assume that the yield to maturity on each bond is 10%, or 5% per half-year.

The numbers in column (5) are the products of time to payment and payment weight. Each of these products corresponds to one of the terms in equation 16.1. According to that equation, we can calculate the duration of each bond by adding the numbers in column (5).

The duration of the zero-coupon bond is exactly equal to its time to maturity, two years. This makes sense, because with only one payment, the average time until payment must be the bond's maturity. In contrast, the two-year coupon bond has a shorter duration of 1.8853 years.

Duration is a key concept in fixed-income portfolio management for at least three reasons. First, it is a simple summary statistic of the effective average maturity of the portfolio. Second, it turns out to be an essential tool in immunizing portfolios from interest rate risk. We explore this application in Section 16.2. Third, duration is a measure of the interest rate sensitivity of a portfolio, which we explore here.

We have already noted that long-term bonds are more sensitive to interest rate movements than are short-term bonds. The duration measure enables us to quantify this relationship. Specifically, it can be shown that when interest rates change, the proportional change in a bond's price can be related to the change in its yield to maturity, y, according to the rule

$$\frac{\Delta P}{P} = -D \times \left[\frac{\Delta(1+y)}{1+y} \right] \tag{16.2}$$

The proportional price change equals the proportional change in 1 plus the bond's yield times the bond's duration. Therefore, bond price volatility is proportional to the bond's duration, and duration becomes a natural measure of interest rate exposure.

Practitioners commonly use equation 16.2 in a slightly different form. They define "modified duration" as $D^* = D/(1+y)$, note that $\Delta(1+y) = \Delta y$, and rewrite equation 16.2 as

$$\frac{\Delta P}{P} = -D^* \Delta y \tag{16.2$'$}$$

The percentage change in bond price is just the product of modified duration and the change in the bond's yield to maturity. Because the percentage change in the bond price is proportional to modified duration, modified duration is a natural measure of the bond's exposure to changes in interest rates.[4]

To confirm the relationship between duration and the sensitivity of bond price to interest rate changes, let's compare the price sensitivity of the two-year coupon bond in Table 16.3, which has a duration of 1.8853 years, to the sensitivity of a zero-coupon bond with maturity *and* duration of 1.8853 years. Both should have equal price sensitivity if duration is a useful measure of interest rate exposure.

The coupon bond sells for $964.5405 at the initial semiannual interest rate of 5%. If the bond's semiannual yield increases by 1 basis point (i.e., .01%) to 5.01%, its price will fall to $964.1942, a percentage decline of .0359%. The zero-coupon bond has a maturity of $1.8853 \times 2 = 3.7706$ half-year periods. (Because we use a half-year interest rate of 5%, we also need to define duration in terms of a number of half-year periods to maintain consistency of units.) At the initial half-year interest rate of 5%, it sells at a price of $831.9623 ($1,000/1.05^{3.7706}$). Its price falls to $831.6636 ($1,000/1.0501^{3.7706}$) when the interest rate increases, for an identical .0359% capital loss. We conclude, therefore, that equal-duration assets are in fact equally sensitive to interest rate movements.

Incidentally, this example confirms the validity of equation 16.2. Note that the equation predicts that the proportional price change of the two bonds should have been $3.7706 \times .0001/1.05 = .000359$, or .0359%, exactly as we found from direct computation.

Concept

Question 1

a. Calculate as in Table 16.3 the price and duration of a two-year maturity, 9% coupon bond making annual coupon payments when the market interest rate is 10%.

b. Now suppose the interest rate increases to 10.05%. Calculate the new value of the bond and the percentage change in the bond's price.

c. Calculate the percentage change in the bond's price predicted by the duration formula in equation 16.2 or 16.2'. Compare this value to your answer for (b).

---

[4]Actually, equation 16.2, or equivalently 16.2', is only approximately valid for large changes in the bond's yield. The approximation becomes exact as one considers smaller, or localized, changes in yields. Students of calculus will recognize that modified duration is proportional to the derivative of the bond's price with respect to changes in the bond's yield:

$$D^* = -\frac{1}{P} \frac{dP}{dy}$$

As such, it gives a measure of the slope of the bond price curve only in the neighborhood of the current price.

Figure 16.2
Bond duration versus bond maturity.

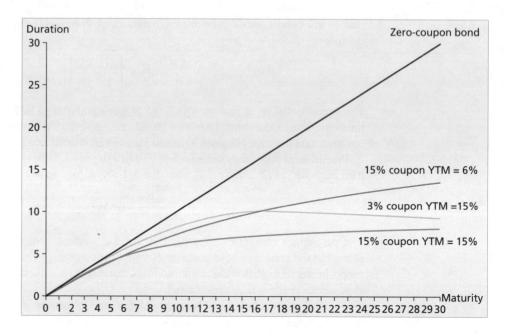

What Determines Duration?

The sensitivity of a bond's price to changes in market interest rates is influenced by three key factors: time to maturity, coupon rate, and yield to maturity. These determinants of price sensitivity are important to fixed-income portfolio management. Therefore, we summarize some of the important relationships in the following eight rules. These rules are also illustrated in Figure 16.2, where durations of bonds of various coupon rates, yields to maturity, and times to maturity are plotted.

We have already established:

Rule 1 for Duration   The duration of a zero-coupon bond equals its time to maturity.

We have also seen that the two-year coupon bond has a lower duration than the two-year zero because coupons early in the bond's life lower the bond's weighted average time until payments. This illustrates another general property:

Rule 2 for Duration   Holding maturity constant, a bond's duration is higher when the coupon rate is lower.

This property corresponds to Malkiel's fifth relationship and is attributable to the impact of early coupon payments on the average maturity of a bond's payments. The higher these coupons, the higher the weights on the early payments and the lower is the weighted average maturity of the payments. Compare the plots in Figure 16.2 of the durations of the 3% coupon and 15% coupon bonds, each with identical yields of 15%. The plot of the duration of the 15% coupon bond lies below the corresponding plot for the 3% coupon bond.

Rule 3 for Duration   Holding the coupon rate constant, a bond's duration generally increases with its time to maturity. Duration always increases with maturity for bonds selling at par or at a premium to par.

This property of duration corresponds to Malkiel's third relationship, and it is fairly intuitive. What is surprising is that duration need not always increase with time to maturity.

It turns out that for some deep-discount bonds, duration may fall with increases in maturity. However, for virtually all traded bonds it is safe to assume that duration increases with maturity.

Notice in Figure 16.2 that for the zero-coupon bond, maturity and duration are equal. However, for coupon bonds duration increases by less than a year with a year's increase in maturity. The slope of the duration graph is less than 1.

Although long-maturity bonds generally will be high-duration bonds, duration is a better measure of the long-term nature of the bond because it also accounts for coupon payments. Time to maturity is an adequate statistic only when the bond pays no coupons; then, maturity and duration are equal.

Notice also in Figure 16.2 that the two 15% coupon bonds have different durations when they sell at different yields to maturity. The lower-yield bond has greater duration. This makes sense, because at lower yields the more distant payments made by the bond have relatively greater present values and account for a greater share of the bond's total value. Thus in the weighted-average calculation of duration the distant payments receive greater weights, which results in a higher duration measure. This establishes rule 4:

Rule 4 for Duration   Holding other factors constant, the duration of a coupon bond is higher when the bond's yield to maturity is lower.

Rule 4, which is the sixth bond-pricing relationship above, applies to coupon bonds. For zeros, of course, duration equals time to maturity, regardless of the yield to maturity.

Finally, we develop some algebraic rules for the duration of securities of special interest. These rules are derived from and consistent with the formula for duration given in equation 16.1 but may be easier to use for long-term bonds.

Rule 5 for Duration   The duration of a level perpetuity is $(1 + y)/y$. For example, at a 10% yield, the duration of a perpetuity that pays $100 once a year forever will equal $1.10/.10 = 11$ years, but at an 8% yield it will equal $1.08/.08 = 13.5$ years.

Rule 5 makes it obvious that maturity and duration can differ substantially. The maturity of the perpetuity is infinite, whereas the duration of the instrument at a 10% yield is only 11 years. The present-value-weighted cash flows early on in the life of the perpetuity dominate the computation of duration.

Notice from Figure 16.2 that as their maturities become ever longer, the durations of the two coupon bonds with yields of 15% both converge to the duration of the perpetuity with the same yield, 7.67 years.

Concept CHECK

Question 2 • Show that the duration of the perpetuity increases as the interest rate decreases in accordance with rule 4.

Rule 6 for Duration   The duration of a level annuity is equal to the following:

$$\frac{1 + y}{y} - \frac{T}{(1 + y)^T - 1}$$

where T is the number of payments and y is the annuity's yield per payment period. For example, a 10-year annual annuity with a yield of 8% will have duration

$$\frac{1.08}{.08} - \frac{10}{1.08^{10} - 1} = 4.87 \text{ years}$$

Table 16.4   Bond Durations (initial bond yield = 8% APR)

Years to Maturity	Coupon Rates (per Year)			
	6%	8%	10%	12%
1	0.985	0.980	0.976	0.972
5	4.361	4.218	4.095	3.990
10	7.454	7.067	6.772	6.541
20	10.922	10.292	9.870	9.568
Infinite (perpetuity)	13.000	13.000	13.000	13.000

Rule 7 for Duration   The duration of a coupon bond equals the following:

$$\frac{1+y}{y} - \frac{(1+y) + T(c-y)}{c[(1+y)^T - 1] + y}$$

where c is the coupon rate per payment period, T is the number of payment periods, and y is the bond's yield per payment period. For example, a 10% coupon bond with 20 years until maturity, paying coupons semiannually, would have a 5% semiannual coupon and 40 payment periods. If the yield to maturity were 4% per half-year period, the bond's duration would be

$$\frac{1.04}{.04} - \frac{1.04 + 40(.05 - .04)}{.05[1.04^{40} - 1] + .04} = 19.74 \text{ half-years} = 9.87 \text{ years}$$

This calculation reminds us again of the importance of maintaining consistency between the time units of the payment period and interest rate. When the bond pays a coupon semi-annually, we must use the effective semiannual interest rate and semiannual coupon rate in all calculations. This unit of time (one half-year) is then carried into the duration measure, when we calculate duration to be 19.74 half-year periods.

Rule 8 for Duration   For coupon bonds selling at par value, rule 7 simplifies to the following formula for duration:

$$\frac{1+y}{y}\left[1 - \frac{1}{(1+y)^T}\right]$$

Durations can vary widely among traded bonds. Table 16.4 presents durations computed from rule 7 for several bonds all assumed to pay semiannual coupons and to yield 4% per half-year. Notice that duration decreases as coupon rates increase, and duration generally increases with time to maturity. According to Table 16.4 and equation 16.2, if the interest rate were to increase from 8% to 8.1%, the 6% coupon 20-year bond would fall in value by about 1.01% (10.922 × .1%/1.08), whereas the 10% coupon one-year bond would fall by only .090%. Notice also from Table 16.4 that duration is independent of coupon rate only for the perpetual bond.

16.2   PASSIVE BOND MANAGEMENT

Passive managers take bond prices as fairly set and seek to control only the risk of their fixed-income portfolio. Two broad classes of passive management are pursued in the fixed-income market. The first is an indexing strategy that attempts to replicate the performance

Table 16.5   The U.S. Fixed-Income Market, 1997

Sector	Size ($ billions)	Percentage of Market
Treasury	$3,830	39.2%
Federal agency	926	9.5
Corporate	1,419	14.5
Tax-exempt*	1,174	12.0
Mortgage-backed	1,740	17.8
Asset-backed	671	6.9
Total	$9,760	100.0%

*Includes private purpose tax-exempt debt.

Source: *Flow of Funds Accounts, Flows and Outstandings*, Board of Governors of the Federal Reserve System, First Quarter, 1997.

of a given bond index. The second broad class of passive strategies is known as immunization techniques; they are used widely by financial institutions such as insurance companies and pension funds. These are designed to shield the overall financial status of the institution from exposure to interest rate fluctuations.

Although indexing and immunization strategies are alike in that they accept market prices as correctly set, they are very different in terms of risk exposure. A bond-index portfolio will have the same risk-reward profile as the bond market index to which it is tied. In contrast, immunization strategies seek to establish a virtually zero-risk profile, in which interest rate movements have no impact on the value of the firm. We discuss both types of strategies in this section.

Bond-Index Funds

In principle, bond market indexing is similar to stock market indexing. The idea is to create a portfolio that mirrors the composition of an index that measures the broad market. In the U.S. equity market, for example, the S&P 500 is the most commonly used index for stock-index funds, and these funds simply buy shares of each firm in the S&P 500 in proportion to the market value of outstanding equity. A similar strategy is used for bond-index funds, but as we shall see shortly, several modifications are required because of difficulties unique to the bond market and its indexes.

Three major indexes of the broad bond market are the Salomon Brothers Broad Investment Grade (BIG) index, the Lehman Brothers Aggregate Index, and the Merrill Lynch Domestic Master Index. All three are market-value-weighted indexes of total returns and are computed daily. All three include government, corporate, mortgage-backed, and Yankee bonds in their universes. (Yankee bonds are dollar-denominated, SEC-registered bonds of foreign issuers sold in the United States.) All three indexes include only bonds with maturities greater than one year. As time passes, and the maturity of a bond falls below one year, the bond is dropped from the index. Table 16.5 presents a breakdown of the fixed-income market in 1997, and Table 16.6 presents some summary statistics pertaining to each index.

The first problem that arises in the formation of a bond index is apparent from Table 16.6. Each of these indexes includes more than 5,000 securities, making it quite difficult to purchase each security in the index in proportion to its market value. Moreover, many bonds are very thinly traded, meaning that identifying their owners and purchasing the securities at a fair market price can be difficult.

Table 16.6 Profile of Bond Indexes

	Lehman Brothers	Merrill Lynch	Salomon Brothers
Number of issues	Over 6,500	Over 5,000	Over 5,000
Maturity of included bonds	≥ 1 year	≥ 1 year	≥ 1 year
Excluded issues	Junk bonds Convertibles Flower bonds Floating-rate bonds	Junk bonds Convertibles Flower bonds	Junk bonds Convertibles Floating-rate bonds
Weighting	Market value	Market value	Market value
Reinvestment of intramonth cash flows	No	Yes (in specific bond)	Yes (at one-month T-bill rate)
Daily availability	Yes	Yes	Yes

Source: Frank K. Reilly, G. Wenchi Kao, and David J. Wright, "Alternative Bond Market Indexes," *Financial Analysts Journal* (May–June 1992), pp. 44–58.

Bond-index funds also present more difficult rebalancing problems than do stock-index funds. Bonds are continually dropped from the index as their maturities fall below one year. Moreover, as new bonds are issued, they are added to the index. Therefore, in contrast to equity indexes, the securities used to compute bond indexes constantly change. As they do, the manager must update or rebalance the portfolio to ensure a close match between the composition of the portfolio and the bonds included in the index. The fact that bonds generate considerable interest income that must be reinvested further complicates the job of the index fund manager.

In practice, it is deemed infeasible to precisely replicate the broad bond indexes. Instead, a stratified sampling or *cellular* approach is often pursued. Figure 16.3 illustrates the idea behind the cellular approach. First, the bond market is stratified into several subclasses. Figure 16.3 shows a simple two-way breakdown by maturity and issuer; in practice, however, criteria such as the bond's coupon rate or the credit risk of the issuer also would be used to form cells. Bonds falling within each cell are then considered reasonably homogeneous. Next, the percentages of the entire universe (i.e., the bonds included in the index that is to be matched) falling within each cell are computed and reported, as we have done for a few cells in Figure 16.3. Finally, the portfolio manager establishes a bond portfolio with representation for each cell that matches the representation of that cell in the bond universe. In this way, the characteristics of the portfolio in terms of maturity, coupon rate, credit risk, industrial representation, and so on, will match the characteristics of the index, and the performance of the portfolio likewise should match the index.

How well does this cellular method track the broad bond indexes? One way to measure the results is to calculate the average absolute value of the *tracking error* between the portfolio and the index. The tracking error in any month is the difference in the performance of the portfolio and the index. A Salomon Brothers study[5] found that a $100 million index fund could track the BIG index with average absolute tracking error of only 4 basis points per month. Not surprisingly, the Corporate subindex, which has the greatest diversity of bonds, was subject to the greatest monthly tracking error, 16 basis points, whereas the government bond subindex could be tracked far more closely, with average absolute error of only 2 basis points per month. Of course, tracking error will also be a function of the size of the index fund. A billion-dollar fund should track the index more closely than a $100

---

[5]Reported in Sharmin Mossavar-Rahmani, *Bond Index Funds* (Chicago: Probus, 1991).

Figure 16.3

Stratification of bonds into cells.

Sector Term to maturity	Treasury	Agency	Mortgage-Backed	Industrial	Finance	Utility	Yankee
<1 year	12.1%						
1-3 years	5.4%						
3-5 years			4.1%				
5-7 years							
7-10 years		0.1%					
10-15 years							
15-30 years			9.2%			3.4%	
30+ years							

million fund since the larger size of the portfolio allows a finer breakdown into smaller and more homogenous cells.

Immunization

In contrast to indexing strategies, many institutions try to insulate their portfolios from interest rate risk altogether. Generally, there are two ways of viewing this risk, depending on the circumstances of the particular investor. Some institutions, such as banks, are concerned with protecting the current net worth or net market value of the firm against interest rate fluctuations. Other investors, such as pension funds, may face an obligation to make payments after a given number of years. These investors are more concerned with protecting the future values of their portfolios.

What is common to the bank and the pension fund, however, is interest rate risk. The net worth of the firm or the ability to meet future obligations fluctuates with interest rates. These institutions presumably might be interested in methods to control that risk. We will see that, by properly adjusting the maturity structure of their portfolios, these institutions can shed their interest rate risk. **Immunization** techniques refer to strategies used by such investors to shield their overall financial status from exposure to interest rate fluctuations.

Net Worth Immunization

Many banks and thrift institutions have a natural mismatch between asset and liability maturity structures. Bank liabilities are primarily the deposits owed to customers, most of which are very short-term in nature and, consequently, of low duration. Bank assets by contrast are composed largely of outstanding commercial and consumer loans or mortgages. These assets are of longer duration than are deposits, and their values are correspondingly more sensitive to interest rate fluctuations. In periods when interest rates increase unexpectedly, banks can suffer serious decreases in net worth—their assets fall in value by more than their liabilities.

The watchword in bank portfolio strategy has become asset and liability management. Techniques called *gap management* were developed to limit the "gap" between asset and liability durations. Adjustable-rate mortgages are one way to reduce the duration of bank asset portfolios. Unlike conventional mortgages, adjustable-rate mortgages do not fall in value when market interest rates rise, because the rates they pay are tied to an index of the current market rate. Even if the indexing is imperfect or entails lags, indexing greatly diminishes sensitivity to interest rate fluctuations. On the other side of the balance sheet, the introduction of bank certificates of deposit with fixed terms to maturity serves to lengthen the duration of bank liabilities, also reducing the duration gap.

One way to view gap management is that the bank is attempting to equate the durations of assets and liabilities to effectively immunize its overall position from interest rate movements. Because bank assets and liabilities are roughly equal in size, if their durations also are equal, any change in interest rates will affect the values of assets and liabilities equally. Interest rates would have no effect on net worth, in other words. Therefore, net worth immunization requires a portfolio duration of zero. This will result if assets and liabilities are equal in both magnitude and duration.

Question 3 • **If assets and liabilities are not equal, then immunization requires that $D_A A = D_L L$ where D denotes duration and A and L denote assets and liabilities, respectively. Explain why the simpler condition, $D_A = D_L$, is no longer valid in this case.**

Target Date Immunization

In contrast to banks, pension funds think more in terms of future commitments than current net worth. Pension funds have an obligation to provide workers with a flow of income upon their retirement, and they must have sufficient funds available to meet these commitments. As interest rates fluctuate, both the value of the assets held by the fund and the rate at which those assets generate income fluctuate. The pension fund manager, therefore, may want to protect, or "immunize," the future accumulated value of the fund at some target date against interest rate movements.

The nearby box illustrates the dangers that pension funds face when they neglect the interest rate exposure of *both* assets and liabilities. The article points out that when interest rates change, the present value of the fund's liabilities change. For example, although pension funds enjoyed excellent investment returns in 1995, they lost ground because as interest rates fell, the value of their liabilities grew even faster than the value of their assets. The article concludes that funds should match the interest rate exposure of assets and liabilities so that the value of assets will track the value of liabilities whether rates rise or fall.

Pension funds are not alone in this concern. Any institution with a future fixed obligation might consider immunization a reasonable risk management policy. Insurance companies, for example, also pursue immunization strategies. Indeed, the notion of immunization was introduced by F. M. Redington,[6] an actuary for a life insurance company. The idea behind immunization is that duration-matched assets and liabilities let the asset portfolio meet the firm's obligations despite interest rate movements. Consider, for example, an insurance company that issues a guaranteed investment contract, or GIC, for $10,000. (Essentially, GICs are zero-coupon bonds issued by the insurance company to its customers. They are popular products for individuals' retirement-saving accounts.) If the GIC has a five-year maturity and a guaranteed interest rate of 8%, the insurance company is obligated to pay $10,000 × (1.08)^5 = $14,693.28 in five years.

Suppose that the insurance company chooses to fund its obligation with $10,000 of 8% *annual* coupon bonds, selling at par value, with six years to maturity. As long as the market interest rate stays at 8%, the company has fully funded the obligation, as the present value of the obligation exactly equals the value of the bonds.

---

[6]F. M. Redington, "Review of the Principle of Life-Office Valuations," *Journal of the Institute of Actuaries* 78 (1952).

HOW PENSION FUNDS LOST IN MARKET BOOM

In one of the happiest reports to come out of Detroit lately, General Motors proclaimed Tuesday that its U.S. pension funds are now "fully funded on an economic basis." Less noticed was GM's admission that, in accounting terms, it is still a few cents—well, $3 billion—shy of the mark.

Wait a minute. If GM's pension plans were $9.3 billion in the hole when 1995 began, and if the company, to its credit, shoveled in $10.4 billion more during the year, how come its pension deficit wasn't wiped out in full?

We'll get to that, but the real news here is broader than GM. According to experts, most pension funds actually *lost* ground in 1995, even though, as you may recall, it was a rather good year for stocks and bonds.

True, pension-fund assets did have a banner year. But as is sometimes overlooked, pension funds also have liabilities (their obligations to retirees). And at most funds, liabilities grew at a rate that put asset growth to shame. At the margin, that means more companies' pension plans will be "underfunded." And down the road, assuming no reversal in the trend, more companies will have to pony up more cash.

What's to blame? The sharp decline in interest rates that brought joy to everyone else. As rates fall, pension funds have to set aside more money today to pay off a fixed obligation tomorrow. In accounting-speak, this "discounted present value" of their liabilities rises.

By now, maybe you sense that pension liabilities swing more, in either direction, than assets. How come? In a phrase, most funds are "mismatched," meaning their liabilities are longer-lived than their investments. The longer an obligation, the more its current value reacts to changes in rates. And at a typical pension fund, even though the average obligation is 15 years away, the average duration of its bond portfolio is roughly five years.

If this seems to defy common sense, it does. No sensible family puts its grocery money (a short-term obligation) into common stocks (a long-term asset). And a college sophomore is unlikely to put his retirement savings into two-year bonds. Ordinary Joes and Janes grasp the principle of "matching" without even thinking about it.

But fund managers—the pros—insist on shorter, unmatching bond portfolios for a simple, stupefying reason. They are graded—usually by consultants—according to how they perform against standard (and shorter-term) bond indexes. Thus, rather than invest to keep up with liabilities, managers are investing so as to avoid lagging behind the popular index in any year. A gutsy exception is AMR (average bond duration: 26 years). Its assets will get hammered if rates rise, but they should track liabilities either way.

Source: Roger Lowenstein, "How Pension Funds Lost in Market Boom," *The Wall Street Journal*, February 1, 1996. Excerpted by permission of *The Wall Street Journal*, © 1996 Dow Jones & Company, Inc. All Rights Reserved Worldwide.

Table 16.7**A** shows that if interest rates remain at 8%, the accumulated funds from the bond will grow to exactly the $14,693.28 obligation. Over the five-year period, the year-end coupon income of $800 is reinvested at the prevailing 8% market interest rate. At the end of the period, the bonds can be sold for $10,000; they still will sell at par value because the coupon rate still equals the market interest rate. Total income after five years from reinvested coupons and the sale of the bond is precisely $14,693.28.

If interest rates change, however, two offsetting influences will affect the ability of the fund to grow to the targeted value of $14,693.28. If interest rates rise, the fund will suffer a capital loss, impairing its ability to satisfy the obligation. The bonds will be worth less in five years than if interest rates had remained at 8%. However, at a higher interest rate, reinvested coupons will grow at a faster rate, offsetting the capital loss. In other words, fixed-income investors face two offsetting types of interest rate risk: *price risk* and *reinvestment rate risk*. Increases in interest rates cause capital losses but at the same time increase the rate at which reinvested income will grow. If the portfolio duration is chosen appropriately, these two effects will cancel out exactly. When the portfolio duration is set equal to the investor's horizon date, the accumulated value of the investment fund at the horizon date will be unaffected by interest rate fluctuations. *For a horizon equal to the portfolio's duration, price risk and reinvestment risk exactly cancel out.*

In the example we are discussing, the duration of the six-year maturity bonds used to fund the GIC is five years. You can confirm this using rule 8. Because the fully funded plan has equal duration for its assets and liabilities, the insurance company should be immu-

Table 16.7 Terminal Value of a Bond Portfolio after Five Years (all proceeds reinvested)

Payment Number	Years Remaining until Obligation	Accumulated Value of Invested Payment		
A. Rates remain at 8%				
1	4	$800 \times (1.08)^4$	=	1,088.39
2	3	$800 \times (1.08)^3$	=	1,007.77
3	2	$800 \times (1.08)^2$	=	933.12
4	1	$800 \times (1.08)^1$	=	864.00
5	0	$800 \times (1.08)^0$	=	800.00
Sale of bond	0	10,800/1.08	=	10,000.00
				14,693.28
B. Rates fall to 7%				
1	4	$800 \times (1.07)^4$	=	1,048.64
2	3	$800 \times (1.07)^3$	=	980.03
3	2	$800 \times (1.07)^2$	=	915.92
4	1	$800 \times (1.07)^1$	=	856.00
5	0	$800 \times (1.07)^0$	=	800.00
Sale of bond	0	10,800/1.07	=	10,093.46
				14,694.05
C. Rates increase to 9%				
1	4	$800 \times (1.09)^4$	=	1,129.27
2	3	$800 \times (1.09)^3$	=	1,036.02
3	2	$800 \times (1.09)^2$	=	950.48
4	1	$800 \times (1.09)^1$	=	872.00
5	0	$800 \times (1.09)^0$	=	800.00
Sale of bond	0	10,800/1.09	=	9,908.26
				14,696.02

Note: The sale price of the bond portfolio equals the portfolio's final payment ($10,800) divided by $1 + r$, because the time to maturity of the bonds will be one year at the time of sale.

nized against interest rate fluctuations. To confirm that this is the case, let us now investigate whether the bond can generate enough income to pay off the obligation five years from now regardless of interest rate movements.

Tables 16.7**B** and **C** consider two possible interest rate scenarios: Rates either fall to 7%, or increase to 9%. In both cases, the annual coupon payments from the bond are reinvested at the new interest rate, which is assumed to change before the first coupon payment, and the bond is sold in year 5 to help satisfy the obligation of the GIC.

Table 16.7**B** shows that if interest rates fall to 7%, the total funds will accumulate to $14,694.05, providing a small surplus of $.77. If rates increase to 9% as in Table 16.7**C**, the fund accumulates to $14,696.02, providing a small surplus of $2.74.

Several points are worth highlighting. First, duration matching balances the difference between the accumulated value of the coupon payments (reinvestment rate risk) and the sale value of the bond (price risk). That is, when interest rates fall, the coupons grow less than in the base case, but the gain on the sale of the bond offsets this. When interest rates rise, the resale value of the bond falls, but the coupons more than make up for this loss because they are reinvested at the higher rate. Figure 16.4 illustrates this case. The solid curve traces out the accumulated value of the bonds if interest rates remain at 8%. The dashed curve shows that value if interest rates happen to increase. The initial impact is a capital loss, but this loss eventually is offset by the now-faster growth rate of reinvested funds. At the five-year horizon date, the two effects just cancel, leaving the company able to satisfy its obligation with the accumulated proceeds from the bond.

Figure 16.4
Growth of invested funds. The solid colored curve represents the growth of portfolio value at the original interest rate. If interest rates increase at time t^*, the portfolio value initially falls but increases thereafter at the faster rate represented by the broken curve. At time D (duration) the curves cross.

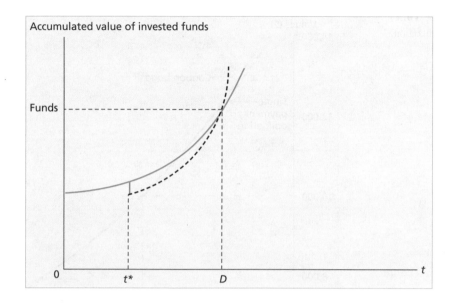

Table 16.8   Market Value Balance Sheet

Assets		Liabilities	
A. Interest rate = 8%			
Bonds	$10,000	Obligation	$10,000
B. Interest rate = 7%			
Bonds	$10,476.65	Obligation	$10,476.11
C. Interest rate = 9%			
Bonds	$ 9,551.41	Obligation	$ 9,549.62

Notes:

Value of bonds = 800 × Annuity factor(r, 6) + 10,000 × PV factor(r, 6)

Value of obligation = $\dfrac{14,693.28}{(1 + r)^5}$ = 14,693.28 × PV factor(r, 5)

We can also analyze immunization in terms of present as opposed to future values. Table 16.8A shows the initial balance sheet for the insurance company's GIC account. Both assets and the obligation have market values of $10,000, so that the plan is just fully funded. Tables 16.8B and C show that whether the interest rate increases or decreases, the value of the bonds funding the GIC and the present value of the company's obligation change by virtually identical amounts. Regardless of the interest rate change, the plan remains fully funded, with the surplus in Table 16.8B and C just about zero. The duration-matching strategy has ensured that both assets and liabilities react equally to interest rate fluctuations.

Figure 16.5 is a graph of the present values of the bond and the single-payment obligation as a function of the interest rate. At the current rate of 8%, the values are equal, and the obligation is fully funded by the bond. Moreover, the two present value curves are tangent at $y = 8\%$. As interest rates change, the change in value of both the asset and the obligation is equal, so the obligation remains fully funded. For greater changes in the interest rate,

Figure 16.5
Immunization.

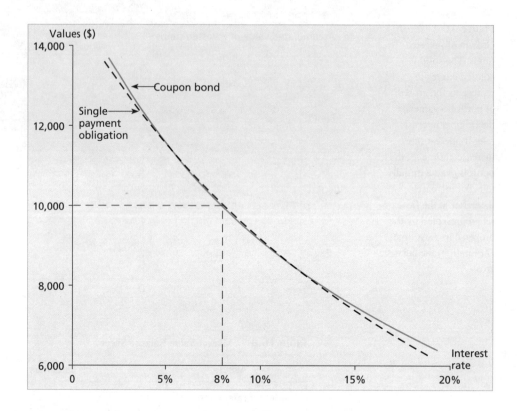

however, the present value curves diverge. This reflects the fact that the fund actually shows a small surplus at market interest rates other than 8%.

Why is there any surplus in the fund? After all, we claimed that a duration-matched asset and liability mix would result in indifference to interest rate shifts. Actually, such a claim is valid only for *small* changes in the interest rate, because as bond yields change, so too does duration. (Recall rule 4 for duration and footnote 4.) In our example, although the duration of the bond is indeed equal to 5 years at a yield to maturity of 8%, it rises to 5.02 years when its yield falls to 7% and drops to 4.97 years at $y = 9\%$; that is, the bond and the obligation were not duration-matched *across* the interest rate shift, so that the position was not fully immunized.

This example highlights the importance of **rebalancing** immunized portfolios. As interest rates and asset durations change, a manager must rebalance the portfolio of fixed-income assets continually to realign its duration with the duration of the obligation. Moreover, even if interest rates do not change, asset durations *will* change solely because of the passage of time. Recall from Figure 16.2 that duration generally decreases less rapidly than does maturity. Thus, even if an obligation is immunized at the outset, as time passes the durations of the asset and liability will fall at different rates. Without portfolio rebalancing, durations will become unmatched and the goals of immunization will not be realized. Obviously, immunization is a passive strategy only in the sense that it does not involve attempts to identify undervalued securities. Immunization managers still actively update and monitor their positions.

As another example of the need for rebalancing, consider a portfolio manager facing an obligation of $19,487 in seven years, which, at a current market interest rate of 10%, has a present value of $10,000. Right now, suppose that the manager wishes to immunize the obligation by holding only three-year zero-coupon bonds and perpetuities paying annual coupons. (Our focus on zeros and perpetuities helps keep the algebra simple.) At current interest rates, the perpetuities have a duration of $1.10/.10 = 11$ years. The duration of the zero is simply three years.

For assets with equal yields, the duration of a portfolio is the weighted average of the durations of the assets comprising the portfolio. To achieve the desired portfolio duration of seven years, the manager would have to choose appropriate values for the weights of the zero and the perpetuity in the overall portfolio. Call w the zero's weight and $(1 - w)$ the perpetuity's weight. Then w must be chosen to satisfy the equation

$$w \times 3 \text{ years} + (1 - w) \times 11 \text{ years} = 7 \text{ years}$$

which implies that $w = \frac{1}{2}$. The manager invests $5,000 in the zero-coupon bond and $5,000 in the perpetuity, providing annual coupon payments of $500 per year indefinitely. The portfolio duration is then seven years, and the position is immunized.

Next year, even if interest rates do not change, rebalancing will be necessary. The present value of the obligation has grown to $11,000, because it is one year closer to maturity. The manager's funds also have grown to $11,000: The zero-coupon bonds have increased in value from $5,000 to $5,500 with the passage of time, while the perpetuity has paid its annual $500 coupon and still is worth $5,000. However, the portfolio weights must be changed. The zero-coupon bond now will have duration of 2 years, while the perpetuity remains at 11 years. The obligation is now due in 6 years. The weights must now satisfy the equation

$$w \times 2 + (1 - w) \times 11 = 6$$

which implies that $w = \frac{5}{9}$. Now, the manager must invest a total of $11,000 \times \frac{5}{9} = $6,111.11$ in the zero. This requires that the entire $500 coupon payment be invested in the zero and that an additional $111.11 of the perpetuity be sold and invested in the zero in order to maintain an immunized position.

Of course, rebalancing of the portfolio entails transaction costs as assets are bought or sold, so one cannot rebalance continuously. In practice, an appropriate compromise must be established between the desire for perfect immunization, which requires continual rebalancing, and the need to control trading costs, which dictates less frequent rebalancing.

Concept

Question 4 • What would be the immunizing weights in the second year if the interest rate had fallen to 8%?

Cash Flow Matching and Dedication

The problems associated with immunization seem to have a simple solution. Why not simply buy a zero-coupon bond that provides a payment in an amount exactly sufficient to cover the projected cash outlay? If we follow the principle of **cash flow matching** we automatically immunize the portfolio from interest rate movement because the cash flow from the bond and the obligation exactly offset each other.

Cash flow matching on a multiperiod basis is referred to as a **dedication strategy**. In this case, the manager selects either zero-coupon or coupon bonds that provide total cash flows in each period that match a series of obligations. The advantage of dedication is that it is a once-and-for-all approach to eliminating interest rate risk. Once the cash flows are matched, there is no need for rebalancing. The dedicated portfolio provides the cash necessary to pay the firm's liabilities regardless of the eventual path of interest rates.

Cash flow matching is not more widely pursued probably because of the constraints that it imposes on bond selection. Immunization-dedication strategies are appealing to firms that do not wish to bet on general movements in interest rates, but these firms may want to immunize using bonds that they perceive are undervalued. Cash flow matching, however, places so many more constraints on the bond selection process that it can be impossible to pursue a dedication strategy using only "underpriced" bonds. Firms looking for underpriced bonds give up exact and easy dedication for the possibility of achieving superior returns from the bond portfolio.

Sometimes, cash flow matching is not possible. To cash-flow-match for a pension fund that is obligated to pay out a perpetual flow of income to current and future retirees, the pension fund would need to purchase fixed-income securities with maturities ranging up to hundreds of years. Such securities do not exist, making exact dedication infeasible.

Concept
CHECK

Question 5 • How would an increase in trading costs affect the attractiveness of dedication versus immunization?

Other Problems with Conventional Immunization

If you look back at the definition of duration in equation 16.1, you note that it uses the bond's yield to maturity to calculate the weight applied to the time until each coupon payment. Given this definition and limitations on the proper use of yield to maturity, it is perhaps not surprising that this notion of duration is strictly valid only for a flat yield curve for which all payments are discounted at a common interest rate.

If the yield curve is not flat, then the definition of duration must be modified and $CF_t/(1 + y)^t$ replaced with the present value of CF_t, where the present value of each cash flow is calculated by discounting with the appropriate interest rate from the yield curve corresponding to the date of the *particular* cash flow, instead of by discounting with the *bond's* yield to maturity. Moreover, even with this modification, duration matching will immunize portfolios only for parallel shifts in the yield curve. Clearly, this sort of restriction is unrealistic. As a result, much work has been devoted to generalizing the notion of duration. Multifactor duration models have been developed to allow for tilts and other distortions in the shape of the yield curve, in addition to shifts in its level. (We refer to some of this work in the suggested readings at the end of this chapter.) However, it does not appear that the added complexity of such models pays off in terms of substantially greater effectiveness.[7]

Finally, immunization can be an inappropriate goal in an inflationary environment. Immunization is essentially a nominal notion and makes sense only for nominal liabilities. It makes no sense to immunize a projected obligation that will grow with the price level using nominal assets such as bonds. For example, if your child will attend college in 15 years and if the annual cost of tuition is expected to be $15,000 at that time, immunizing your portfolio at a locked-in terminal value of $15,000 is not necessarily a risk-reducing strategy. The tuition obligation will vary with the realized inflation rate, whereas the asset portfolio's final value will not. In the end, the tuition obligation will not necessarily be matched by the value of the portfolio.

On this note, it is worth pointing out that immunization is a goal that may well be inappropriate for many investors who would find a zero-risk portfolio strategy unduly conservative. Full immunization is a fairly extreme position for a portfolio manager to pursue.

---

[7]G. O. Bierwag, G. C. Kaufman, and A. Toevs, eds., *Innovations in Bond Portfolio Management: Duration Analysis and Immunization* (Greenwich, CT: JAI Press, 1983).

16.3   CONVEXITY

Duration clearly is a key tool in fixed-income portfolio management. Yet the duration rule for the impact of interest rates on bond prices is only an approximation. Equation 16.2, or its equivalent, 16.2′, which we repeat here, states that the percentage change in the value of a bond approximately equals the product of modified duration times the change in the bond's yield:

$$\frac{\Delta P}{P} = -D^*\Delta y \qquad\qquad (16.2')$$

This rule asserts that the percentage price change is directly proportional to the change in the bond's yield. If this were *exactly* so, however, a graph of the percentage change in bond price as a function of the change in its yield would plot as a straight line, with slope equal to $-D^*$. Yet we know from Figure 16.1, and more generally from Malkiel's five rules (specifically rule 2), that the relationship between bond prices and yields is *not* linear. The duration rule is a good approximation for small changes in bond yield, but it is less accurate for larger changes.

Figure 16.6 illustrates this point. Like Figure 16.1, the figure presents the percentage change in bond price in response to a change in the bond's yield to maturity. The curved line is the percentage price change for a 30-year maturity, 8% coupon bond, selling at an initial yield to maturity of 8%. The straight line is the percentage price change predicted by the duration rule: The modified duration of the bond at its initial yield is 11.26 years, so the straight line is a plot of $-D^*\Delta y = -11.26 \times \Delta y$. Notice that the two plots are tangent at the initial yield. Thus for small changes in the bond's yield to maturity, the duration rule is quite accurate. However, for larger changes in yield, there is progressively more "daylight" between the two plots, demonstrating that the duration rule becomes progressively less accurate.

Notice from Figure 16.6 that the duration approximation (the straight line) always understates the value of the bond; it underestimates the increase in bond price when the

Figure 16.6
Bond price convexity.

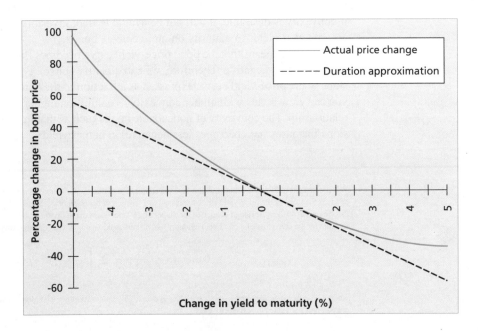

Figure 16.7

Convexity of two bonds.

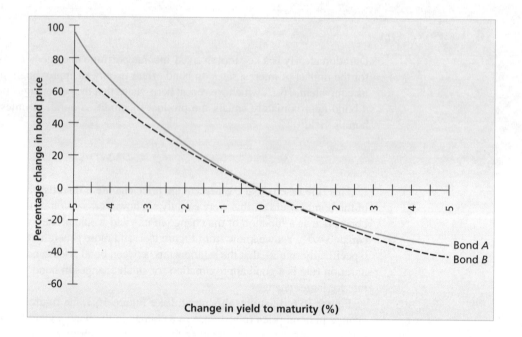

yield falls, and it overestimates the decline in price when the yield rises. This is due to the curvature of the true price-yield relationship. Curves with shapes such as that of the price-yield relationship are said to be *convex*, and the curvature of the price-yield curve is called the **convexity** of the bond. Convexity is generally considered a desirable trait in bonds: Prices of bonds with greater curvature will increase more when yields decrease and fall less when yields increase. For example, in Figure 16.7, bonds *A* and *B* have the same duration at the initial yield: The plots of their proportional price changes as a function of interest rate changes are tangent, meaning that their sensitivities to changes in yields are equal, at least for small changes in yields. However, bond *A* is more convex than bond *B*. It enjoys greater price increases and smaller price declines when rates change by larger amounts. Of course, if convexity is desirable, it will not be available free; investors may have to pay more and accept lower yields to maturity on more convex bonds.

Convexity means that the bond price-yield curve becomes flatter at higher yields, that is, its slope is less negative. Therefore, we can quantify convexity as the rate of change of the slope of the price-yield curve, expressed as a fraction of the bond price.[8] As a practical rule, you can view bonds with higher convexity as exhibiting higher curvature in the price-yield relationship. The convexity of noncallable bonds such as that in Figure 16.6 is positive: The slope increases (i.e., becomes less negative) at higher yields.

---

[8]We pointed out in footnote 4 that equation 16.2 for modified duration can be written as $dP/P = -D^*dy$. Thus $D^* = -1/P \times dP/dy$ is the slope of the price-yield curve expressed as a fraction of the bond price. Similarly, the convexity of a bond equals the second derivative (the rate of change of the slope) of the price-yield curve divided by bond price: $1/P \times d^2P/dy^2$. The formula for the convexity of a bond with a maturity of n years making annual coupon payments is

$$\text{Convexity} = \frac{1}{P \times (1 + y)^2} \sum_{t=1}^{n} \left[\frac{\text{CF}_t}{(1 + y)^t} (t^2 + t) \right]$$

where CF_t is the cash flow paid to the bondholder at date t; CF_t represents either a coupon payment before maturity or final coupon plus par value at the maturity date.

Convexity allows us to improve the duration approximation for bond price changes. Accounting for convexity, equation 16.2 can be modified as follows:[9]

$$\frac{\Delta P}{P} = -D^*\Delta y + \frac{1}{2} \times \text{Convexity} \times (\Delta y)^2 \qquad (16.3)$$

The first term on the right-hand side is the same as the duration rule, equation 16.2. The second term is the modification for convexity. Notice that for a bond with positive convexity, the second term is positive, regardless of whether the yield rises or falls. This insight corresponds to the fact noted just above that the duration rule always underestimates the new value of a bond following a change in its yield. The more accurate equation 16.3, which accounts for convexity, always predicts a higher bond price than equation 16.2. Of course, if the change in yield is small, the convexity term, which is multiplied by $(\Delta y)^2$ in equation 16.3, will be extremely small and will add little to the approximation. In this case, the linear approximation given by the duration rule will be sufficiently accurate. Thus convexity is more important as a practical matter when potential interest rate changes are large.

Convexity is the reason that the immunization examples we considered earlier resulted in small errors. For example, turn back to Figure 16.5 and you will see that the single-payment obligation that was funded with a coupon bond of the same duration was well immunized for small changes in yields. However, for larger yield changes, the two pricing curves diverged a bit, implying that such changes in yields would result in small surpluses. This is due to the greater convexity of the coupon bond.

Let's use a numerical example to examine the impact of convexity. The bond in Figure 16.6 has a 30-year maturity, an 8% coupon, and sells at an initial yield to maturity of 8%. Because the coupon rate equals yield to maturity, the bond sells at par value, or $1,000. The modified duration of the bond at its initial yield is 11.26 years, and its convexity is 212.4 (which can be verified using the formula in footnote 8). If the bond's yield increases from 8% to 10%, the bond price will fall to $811.46, a decline of 18.85%. The duration rule, equation 16.2, would predict a price decline of

$$\frac{\Delta P}{P} = -D^*\Delta y = -11.26 \times .02 = -.2252, \text{ or } -22.52\%$$

which is considerably more than the bond price actually falls. The duration-with-convexity rule, equation 16.3, is more accurate:[10]

$$\frac{\Delta P}{P} = -D^*\Delta y + \frac{1}{2} \times \text{Convexity} \times (\Delta y)^2$$

$$= -11.26 \times .02 + \frac{1}{2} \times 212.4 \times (.02)^2 = -.1827, \text{ or } -18.27\%$$

which is far closer to the exact change in bond price.

Notice that if the change in yield were smaller, say .1%, convexity would matter less. The price of the bond actually would fall to $988.85, a decline of 1.115%. Without accounting for convexity, we would predict a price decline of

$$\frac{\Delta P}{P} = -D^*\Delta y = -11.26 \times .001 = .01126, \text{ or } 1.126\%$$

---

[9]To use the convexity rule, you must express interest rates as decimals rather than percentages.

[10]Notice that when we use equation 16.3, we express interest rates as decimals rather than percentages. The change in rates from 8% to 10% is represented as $\Delta y = .02$.

Accounting for convexity, we get almost the precisely correct answer:

$$\frac{\Delta P}{P} = -11.26 \times .02 + \frac{1}{2} \times 212.4 \times (.001)^2 = .01115, \text{ or } 1.115\%$$

Nevertheless, the duration rule is quite accurate in this case, even without accounting for convexity.

16.4   ACTIVE BOND MANAGEMENT

Sources of Potential Profit

Broadly speaking, there are two sources of potential value in active bond management. The first is interest rate forecasting, which tries to anticipate movements across the entire spectrum of the fixed-income market. If interest rate declines are anticipated, managers will increase portfolio duration (and vice versa). The second source of potential profit is identification of relative mispricing within the fixed-income market. An analyst, for example, might believe that the default premium on one particular bond is unnecessarily large and therefore that the bond is underpriced.

These techniques will generate abnormal returns only if the analyst's information or insight is superior to that of the market. You cannot profit from knowledge that rates are about to fall if everyone else in the market is aware of this. In that case the anticipated decreases in interest rates already are built into bond prices in the sense that long-duration bonds are already selling at higher prices that reflect the anticipated fall in future short rates. If the analyst does not have information before the market does, it will be too late to act on that information—prices will have responded already to the news. You know this from our discussion of market efficiency.

For now we simply repeat that valuable information is differential information. In this context it is worth noting that interest rate forecasters have a notoriously poor track record. If you consider this record, you will approach attempts to time the bond market with caution.

Homer and Liebowitz coined a popular taxonomy of active bond portfolio strategies. They characterize portfolio rebalancing activities as one of four types of *bond swaps*. In the first two swaps the investor typically believes that the yield relationship between bonds or sectors is only temporarily out of alignment. When the aberration is eliminated, gains can be realized on the underpriced bond. The period of realignment is called the *workout period*.

1. The **substitution swap** is an exchange of one bond for a nearly identical substitute. The substituted bonds should be of essentially equal coupon, maturity, quality, call features, sinking fund provisions, and so on. This swap would be motivated by a belief that the market has temporarily mispriced the two bonds, and that the discrepancy between the prices of the bonds represents a profit opportunity.

   An example of a substitution swap would be a sale of a 20-year maturity, 9% coupon Ford Motor Company bond callable after 5 years at $1,050 that is priced to provide a yield to maturity of 9.05%, coupled with a purchase of a 9% coupon Chrysler bond with the same call provisions and time to maturity that yields 9.15%. If the bonds have about the same credit rating, there is no apparent reason for the Chrysler bonds to provide a higher yield. Therefore, the higher yield actually available in the market makes the Chrysler bond seem relatively attractive. Of course, the equality of credit risk is an important condition. If the Chrysler bond is in fact riskier, then its higher yield does not represent a bargain.

2. The **intermarket spread swap** is pursued when an investor believes that the yield spread between two sectors of the bond market is temporarily out of line. For example, if the current spread between corporate and government bonds is considered too wide and is expected to narrow, the investor will shift from government bonds into corporate bonds. If the yield spread does in fact narrow, corporates will outperform governments. For example, if the yield spread between 20-year Treasury bonds and 20-year Baa-rated corporate bonds is now 3%, and the historical spread has been only 2%, an investor might consider selling holdings of Treasury bonds and replacing them with corporates. If the yield spread eventually narrows, the Baa-rated corporate bonds will outperform the Treasuries.

   Of course, the investor must consider carefully whether there is a good reason that the yield spread seems out of alignment. For example, the default premium on corporate bonds might have increased because the market is expecting a severe recession. In this case, the wider spread would not represent attractive pricing of corporates relative to Treasuries, but would simply be an adjustment for a perceived increase in credit risk.

3. The **rate anticipation swap** is pegged to interest rate forecasting. In this case if investors believe that rates will fall, they will swap into bonds of longer duration. Conversely, when rates are expected to rise, they will swap into shorter duration bonds. For example, the investor might sell a 5-year maturity Treasury bond, replacing it with a 25-year maturity Treasury bond. The new bond has the same lack of credit risk as the old one, but has longer duration.

4. The **pure yield pickup swap** is pursued not in response to perceived mispricing, but as a means of increasing return by holding higher-yield bonds. This must be viewed as an attempt to earn an expected term premium in higher-yield bonds. The investor is willing to bear the interest rate risk that this strategy entails.

   A yield pickup swap can be illustrated using the Treasury bond listings in Table 14.1. You can see from that table that a Treasury note maturing in one year yields 5.6%, whereas one maturing in 30 years yields about 6.1%. The investor who swaps the shorter-term bond for the longer one will earn a higher rate of return as long as the yield curve does not shift up during the holding period. Of course if it does, the longer-duration bond will suffer a greater capital loss.

We can add a fifth swap, called a **tax swap**, to this list. This simply refers to a swap to exploit some tax advantage. For example, an investor may swap from one bond that has decreased in price to another if realization of capital losses is advantageous for tax purposes.

Horizon Analysis

One form of interest rate forecasting is called **horizon analysis**. The analyst using this approach selects a particular holding period and predicts the yield curve at the end of that period. Given a bond's time to maturity at the end of the holding period, its yield can be read from the predicted yield curve and its end-of-period price calculated. Then the analyst adds the coupon income and prospective capital gain of the bond to obtain the total return on the bond over the holding period.

For example, suppose that a 20-year maturity, 10% coupon bond currently yields 9% and sells at $1,092.01. An analyst with a five-year time horizon would be concerned about the bond's price and the value of reinvested coupons five years hence. At that time the bond will have a 15-year maturity, so the analyst will predict the yield on 15-year maturity bonds at the end of the 5-year period to determine the bond's expected price. Suppose that the yield is expected to be 8%. Then the bond's end-of-period price will be (assuming 30 semi-annual coupon payments)

$$50 \times \text{Annuity factor}(4\%,30) + 1,000 \times \text{PV factor}(4\%,30) = \$1,172.92$$

The capital gain on the bond therefore will be $80.91.

Meanwhile, the coupons paid by the bond will be reinvested over the five-year period. The analyst must predict a reinvestment rate at which the invested coupons can earn interest. Suppose that the assumed rate is 4% per six-month period. If all coupon payments are reinvested at this rate, the value of the 10 semiannual coupon payments with accumulated interest at the end of the five years will be $600.31. (This amount can be solved for as the future value of a $50 annuity after 10 periods with per-period interest of 4%.) The total return provided by the bond over the five-year period will be $80.91 + $600.31 = $681.22 for a total five-year holding-period return of $681.22/$1,092.01 = .624, or 62.4%.

The analyst repeats this procedure for many bonds and selects the ones promising superior holding-period returns for the portfolio.

Concept
CHECK

Question 6 • Consider a 30-year, 8% coupon bond currently selling at $896.81. The analyst believes that in five years the yield on 25-year bonds will be 8.5%. Should she purchase the 20-year bond just discussed or the 30-year bond?

A particular version of horizon analysis is called **riding the yield curve**, which is a popular strategy among managers of short-term money market securities. If the yield curve is upward sloping *and* if it is projected that the curve will not shift during the investment horizon, then as bond maturities fall with the passage of time, their yields also will fall as they "ride" the yield curve toward the lower yields of shorter-term bonds. The decrease in yields will contribute to capital gains on the bonds.

To illustrate, suppose that the current yield curve is represented by Figure 16.8. For simplicity, we will express all interest rates as effective rates per quarter. A money manager might buy a nine-month bill currently priced to yield 1.5% per quarter, selling at $100/(1.015)^3 = 95.63$. *If* the yield on the bill were to remain unchanged over the quarter, then in three months the bill would sell for $100/(1.015)^2 = 97.07$, providing a holding-period return precisely equal to the 1.5% yield to maturity.

However, remember that in three months the bill will have a maturity of only six months. *If* the yield curve at the end of the quarter is unchanged from today, then the yield on the bill will fall from 1.5% to 1.25% per quarter. As time passes, the bill's maturity falls and its yield rides down the curve, as illustrated in Figure 16.8. Therefore, the bill will provide a holding-period rate of return greater than its original 1.5% yield. Specifically, in three months the bill will be priced at $100/(1.0125)^2 = 97.55$, therefore providing a rate of return of 2.0% [(97.55 − 95.63)/95.63]. Moreover, the longer-term asset will provide a higher rate of return than would the shorter-term one. For example, the three-month bill in Figure 16.8 will mature at the end of the holding period and provide a riskless rate of return of 0.75%.

Thus when the yield curve is upward sloping and the horizon analysis projects an unchanged yield curve, longer-maturity assets will provide greater expected rates of return than shorter-term assets and the expected holding-period rate of return on the fixed-income security will exceed its yield to maturity. Of course, you should always be skeptical of an apparent free lunch. Although extending maturity may increase the expected rate of return, that improvement may come at the price of additional risk. This, in fact, is the trade-off the

Figure 16.8

Riding the yield curve. As time passes and the bond's maturity decreases, its yield to maturity will fall *assuming* the yield curve is unchanged.

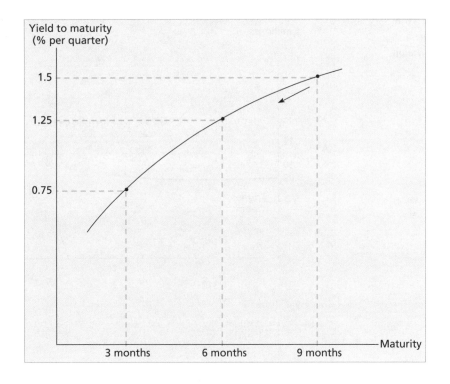

portfolio manager is accepting if the yield curve is sloping upward because of a liquidity premium. The higher expected returns on the longer-term assets are no more than risk premiums.

The danger of riding the yield curve is that the yield curve will in fact rise over time. Indeed, according to the expectations hypothesis, an upward-sloping curve is evidence that market participants expect interest rates to be rising over time.

Contingent Immunization

Contingent immunization is a mixed passive-active strategy suggested by Liebowitz and Weinberger.[11] To illustrate, suppose that interest rates currently are 10% and that a manager's portfolio is worth $10 million right now. At current rates the manager could lock in, via conventional immunization techniques, a future portfolio value of $12.1 million after two years. Now suppose that the manager wishes to pursue active management but is willing to risk losses only to the extent that the terminal value of the portfolio would not drop lower than $11 million. Because only $9.09 million ($11 million/1.10^2) is required to achieve this minimum acceptable terminal value, and the portfolio currently is worth $10 million, the manager can afford to risk some losses at the outset and might start off with an active strategy rather than immediately immunizing.

The key is to calculate the funds required to lock in via immunization a future value of $11 million at current rates. If T denotes the time left until the horizon date, and r is the market interest rate at any particular time, then the value of the fund necessary to guaran-

---

[11]Martin L. Liebowitz and Alfred Weinberger, "Contingent Immunization—Part I: Risk Control Procedures," *Financial Analysts Journal* 38 (November–December 1982).

Figure 16.9
Contingent
immunization.

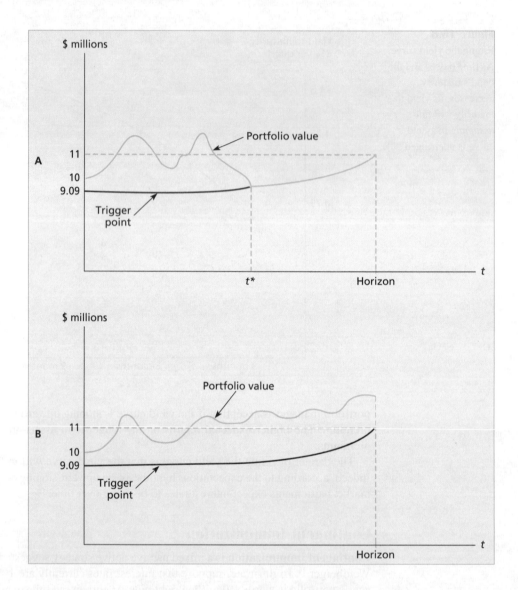

tee an ability to reach the minimum acceptable terminal value is $11 million$/(1 + r)^T$, because this size portfolio, if immunized, will grow risk-free to $11 million by the horizon date. This value becomes the trigger point: If and when the actual portfolio value dips to the trigger point, active management will cease. *Contingent* upon reaching the trigger, an immunization strategy is initiated instead, guaranteeing that the minimal acceptable performance can be realized.

Figure 16.9 illustrates two possible outcomes in a contingent immunization strategy. In Figure 16.9A, the portfolio falls in value and hits the trigger at time t^*. At that point, immunization is pursued and the portfolio rises smoothly to the $11 million terminal value. In Figure 16.9B, the portfolio does well, never reaches the trigger point, and is worth more than $11 million at the horizon date.

Question 7 • What would be the trigger point with a three-year horizon, an interest rate of 12%, and a minimum acceptable terminal value of $10 million?

16.5   INTEREST RATE SWAPS

Interest rate swaps have emerged recently as a major fixed-income tool. An interest rate swap is a contract between two parties to exchange a series of cash flows similar to those that would result if the parties instead were to exchange equal dollar values of different types of bonds. Swaps arose originally as a means of managing interest rate risk. The volume of swaps has increased from virtually zero in 1980 to over $20 trillion today. (Interest rate swaps do not have anything to do with the Homer-Liebowitz bond swap taxonomy set out earlier.)

To illustrate how swaps work, consider the manager of a large portfolio that currently includes $100 million dollars par value of long-term bonds paying an average coupon rate of 7%. The manager believes that interest rates are about to rise. As a result, he would like to sell the bonds and replace them with either short-term or floating-rate issues. However, it would be exceedingly expensive in terms of transaction costs to replace the portfolio every time the forecast for interest rates is updated. A cheaper and more flexible way to modify the portfolio is for the managers to "swap" the $7 million a year in interest income the portfolio currently generates for an amount of money that is tied to the short-term interest rate. That way, if rates do rise, so will the portfolio's interest income.

A swap dealer might advertise its willingness to exchange, or "swap," a cash flow based on the six-month LIBOR rate for one based on a fixed rate of 7%. (The LIBOR, or London Interbank Offered Rate, is the interest rate at which banks borrow from each other in the Eurodollar market. It is the most commonly used short-term interest rate in the swap market.) The portfolio manager would then enter into a swap agreement with the dealer to *pay* 7% on **notional principal** of $100 million and *receive* payment of the LIBOR rate on that amount of notional principal.[12] In other words, the manager swaps a payment of .07 × $100 million for a payment of LIBOR × $100 million. The manager's *net* cash flow from the swap agreement is therefore (LIBOR – .07) × $100 million.

Note that the swap arrangement does not mean that a loan has been made. The participants have agreed only to exchange a fixed cash flow for a variable one.

Now consider the net cash flow to the manager's portfolio in three interest rate scenarios:

	LIBOR Rate		
	6.5%	**7.0%**	**7.5%**
Interest income from bond portfolio (= 7% of $100 million bond portfolio)	$7,000,000	$7,000,000	$7,000,000
Cash flow from swap [= (LIBOR – 7%) × notional principal of $100 million]	(500,000)	0	500,000
Total (= LIBOR x $100 million)	$6,500,000	$7,000,000	$7,500,000

Notice that the total income on the overall position—bonds plus swap agreement—is now equal to the LIBOR rate in each scenario times $100 million. The manager has, in effect, converted a fixed-rate bond portfolio into a synthetic floating-rate portfolio.

---

[12]The participants to the swap do not loan each other money. They agree only to exchange a fixed cash flow for a variable cash flow that depends on the short-term interest rate. This is why the principal is described as *notional*. The notional principal is simply a way to describe the size of the swap agreement. In this example, the parties to the swap exchange a 7% fixed rate for the LIBOR rate; the difference between LIBOR and 7% is multiplied by notional principal to determine the cash flow exchanged by the parties.

You can see now that swaps can be immensely useful for firms in a variety of applications. For example, a corporation that has issued fixed-rate debt can convert it into synthetic floating-rate debt by entering a swap to receive a fixed interest rate (offsetting its fixed-rate coupon obligation) and pay a floating rate. Or a bank that pays current market interest rates to its depositors might enter a swap to receive a floating rate and pay a fixed rate on some amount of notional principal. This swap position, added to its floating-rate deposit liability, would result in a net liability of a fixed stream of cash. The bank might then be able to invest in long-term fixed-rate loans without encountering interest rate risk.

What about the swap dealer? Why is the dealer, which is typically a financial intermediary such as a bank, willing to take on the opposite side of the swaps desired by these participants?

Consider a dealer who takes on one side of a swap, let's say paying LIBOR and receiving a fixed rate. The dealer will search for another trader in the swap market who wishes to receive a fixed rate and pay LIBOR. For example, Company A may have issued a 7% coupon fixed-rate bond that it wishes to convert into synthetic floating-rate debt, while Company B may have issued a floating-rate bond tied to LIBOR that it wishes to convert into synthetic fixed-rate debt. The dealer will enter a swap with Company A in which it pays a fixed rate and receives LIBOR, and will enter another swap with Company B in which it pays LIBOR and receives a fixed rate. When the two swaps are combined, the dealer's position is effectively neutral on interest rates, paying LIBOR on one swap and receiving it on another. Similarly, the dealer pays a fixed rate on one swap and receives it on another. The dealer becomes little more than an intermediary, funneling payments from one party to the other.[13] The dealer finds this activity profitable because he or she will charge a bid–asked spread on the transaction.

This rearrangement is illustrated in Figure 16.10. Company A has issued 7% fixed-rate debt (the leftmost arrow in the figure), but enters a swap to pay the dealer LIBOR and receive a 6.95% fixed rate. Therefore, the company's net payment is 7% + (LIBOR − 6.95%) = LIBOR + .05%. It has thus transformed its fixed-rate debt into synthetic floating-rate debt. Conversely, Company B has issued floating-rate debt paying LIBOR (the rightmost arrow), but enters a swap to pay a 7.05% fixed rate in return for LIBOR. Therefore, its net payment is LIBOR + (7.05% − LIBOR) = 7.05%. It has thus transformed its floating-rate debt into synthetic fixed-rate debt. The bid–asked spread in the example illustrated in Figure 16.10 is .10% of notional principal each year.

Figure 16.10

Interest rate swap. Company B pays a fixed rate of 7.05% to the swap dealer in return for LIBOR. Company A receives 6.95% from the dealer in return for LIBOR. The swap dealer realizes a cash flow each period equal to .10% of notional principal.

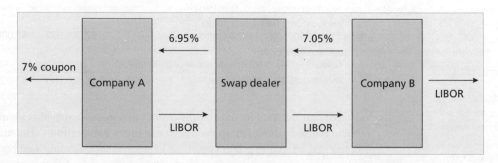

---

[13]Actually, things are a bit more complicated. The dealer is more than just an intermediary because he or she bears the credit risk that one or the other of the parties to the swap might default on the obligation. Referring to Figure 16.10, if firm A defaults on its obligation, for example, the swap dealer still must maintain its commitment to firm B. In this sense, the dealer does more than simply pass through cash flows to the other swap participants.

Concept
Question 8 • A pension fund holds a portfolio of money market securities that the manager believes are paying excellent yields compared to other comparable-risk short-term securities. However, the manager believes that interest rates are about to fall. What type of swap will allow the fund to continue to hold its portfolio of short-term securities while at the same time benefiting from a decline in rates?

One might ask why firms go to the trouble of arranging swaps. For example, why wouldn't a corporation originally borrow short-term instead of borrowing long and entering a swap? In the early years of the swap market the answer seemed to lie in systematic differences in the perceived credit ratings in different markets. Participants in these markets claimed that European banks placed more weight than did U.S. banks on a firm's size, name recognition, and product line compared with its credit rating. Thus it could have paid for a firm that wanted to borrow long-term to instead borrow short-term in the United States and swap into long-term obligations with a European trading partner. The practice exploited a type of market inefficiency—specifically, differences in credit assessments across national markets. Now, however, these inefficiencies seem to have been arbitraged away. Swaps simply provide a means to restructure balance sheets and manage risk very quickly with low transaction costs. We return to the role of swaps in risk management in Chapter 23.

Swaps create an interesting problem for financial statement analysis. Firms are not required to disclose interest rate swaps in corporate financial statements unless they have a "material impact" on the firm, and even then they appear only in the footnotes. Therefore, the firm's true net obligations may be quite different from its apparent or present debt structure.

16.6   FINANCIAL ENGINEERING AND INTEREST-RATE DERIVATIVES

New financial instruments created through financial engineering can have highly unusual risk and return characteristics that offer both opportunities and challenges for fixed-income portfolio managers. To illustrate the possibilities opened up by financial engineering, consider the inverse floater, which is a bond that pays a *lower* coupon payment when a reference interest rate rises. For example, an inverse floater may pay a coupon rate equal to 10% *minus* the rate on one-year Treasury bills. Therefore, if the T-bill rate is 4%, the bond will pay interest income equal to 10% − 4% = 6% of par value. You can see that such a bond will have an interest rate sensitivity much greater than that of a fixed-rate bond with comparable maturity. If the T-bill rate rises, say to 7%, the inverse floater's coupon payments fall to 3% of par value; in addition, as other interest rates rise along with the T-bill rate, the bond price falls as well for the usual reason that future cash flows are discounted at higher rates. Therefore, there is a dual impact on value and these securities perform especially poorly when interest rates rise. Conversely, inverse floaters perform especially well when rates fall: Coupon payments rise, even as the discount rate falls.

While firms do not commonly issue inverse floaters, they may be created synthetically by allocating the cash flows from a fixed-rate security into two *derivative* securities. An investment banking firm can buy a bond issue and carve the original security into a floating-rate note and an inverse floater. The floater will receive interest payments that rise when the T-bill rate rises; the inverse floater will receive interest payments that fall when the T-bill rate rises. The sum of the interest payments due to the two classes of securities is fixed and equal to the interest from the original bond, the primary asset.

As a concrete example, consider a $100 million par value, 20-year maturity bond with a coupon rate of 8%. The bond issue therefore pays total interest of $8 million annually. An investment banking firm might arrange to use the cash flows from the underlying bond to support issues of a floating-rate note and an inverse floater.[14] The floating-rate notes might be issued with aggregate par value of $60 million and a coupon level equal to the T-bill rate plus 1%. If the T-bill rate currently is 6%, therefore, the coupon rate on the floater would be 7% and total interest payments would be .07 × $60 million = $4.2 million. This leaves $8 million – $4.2 million = $3.8 million available to pay interest on the interest floater. The coupon rate on the inverse floater might be set at 18.5% – 1.5 × (T-bill rate), which at the current T-bill rate equals 9.5%. Therefore, the coupon income flowing to the inverse floater is 9.5% of $40 million, or $3.8 million, which just absorbs the remaining interest flowing from the original bond.

Now suppose that in one year, the T-bill rate has increased by 1%. The coupon rate on the floater increases to 8%, while the coupon rate on the inverse floater falls to 18.5% – 1.5 × 7% = 8%. Again, total interest paid on the two derivative securities sums to $8 million: .08 × $60 million + .08 × $40 million = $8 million. However, the value of the inverse floater falls precipitously: Not only are market interest rates higher (which makes the present value of any future cash flow lower), but the coupon rate on the bond has fallen from 9.5% to 8%.[15] Therefore, the inverse floater will have extreme interest rate sensitivity. When rates fall, its performance will be spectacular, but when rates rise, its performance will be disastrous.

The inverse floater is an example of an interest rate derivative product created by financial engineering in which the cash flows from the original bond are unbundled and reallocated to the floater and inverse floater. Because of the impact of interest rates on its coupon rate, the inverse floater will have a very large effective duration,[16] in fact much longer than the maturity of the bond. This property can be useful to investors who wish to immunize very long duration liabilities; it is also obviously useful to investors who wish to speculate on decreases in interest rates.

Investors who speculated on interest rate declines were served well by inverse floaters in 1992 and 1993. For example, Piper Jaffray, a large mutual fund company, sponsored one of the best-performing government bond mutual funds in these years. Part of that performance was due to its positions in inverse floaters. When rates increased rapidly in 1994, however, the fund suffered losses estimated at about $700 million. Unfortunately, this experience was replicated by many other investors.

Inverse floaters are not the only financially engineered products with dramatic dependence on interest rates. In Chapters 1 and 2, we introduced you to derivative securities created by allocating the cash flows from mortgage-backed securities into various CMO (collateralized mortgage obligation) tranches. Some of the more popular mortgage derivative products are interest-only and principal-only strips. The interest-only (IO) strip gets all the interest payments from the mortgage pool and the principal-only (PO) strip gets all the

---

[14]In practice, inverse floaters are often engineered from mortgage-backed securities rather than conventional bonds. While the prepayment risk of the underlying mortgage pool presents another complication, the general structure of these bonds is similar to the one described here.

[15]If the T-bill rate increases beyond 12.33%, the formula for the inverse floater's coupon would call for a negative coupon rate. However, in practice, the inverse floater provides that the coupon rate may never fall below zero. This floor on the coupon rate of the inverse floater necessitates a ceiling on the coupon rate of the floater. The total interest paid by the two securities is constrained to equal the interest provided by the underlying bond.

[16]Strictly speaking, the Macaulay duration (that is, the weighted average of the times until payment of each cash flow) of an inverse floater is not well defined, since the cash flows accruing from the bond are not fixed but instead vary with the level of interest rates. The *effective* duration of a security therefore does not have the interpretation of an average maturity; it is defined instead as the percentage change in the price of a security given a one percentage point increase in yield. Therefore, effective duration, like Macaulay duration, measures interest rate sensitivity.

principal payments. Both of these mortgage strips have extreme and interesting interest rate exposures. In both cases, the sensitivity is due to the effect of mortgage prepayments on the cash flows accruing to the securityholder.

PO securities, like inverse floaters, exhibit very long effective durations, that is, their values are very sensitive to interest rate fluctuations. When interest rates fall and mortgage holders prepay their mortgages, PO holders receive their principal payments much earlier than initially anticipated. Therefore, the payments are discounted for fewer years than expected and have much higher present value. Hence PO strips perform extremely well when rates fall. Conversely, interest rate increases slow mortgage prepayments and reduce the value of PO strips. Investors who speculated on rate decreases in the early 1990s tended to hold POs along with inverse floaters. These securities performed well when rates fell through 1993, but resulted in large losses in 1994 when interest rates rose dramatically.

The prices of interest-only strips, on the other hand, fall when interest rates fall. This is because mortgage prepayments abruptly end the flow of interest payments accruing to IO securityholders. Because rising rates discourage prepayments, they increase the value of IO strips. Thus IOs have effective *negative* durations. They are good investments for an investor who wishes to bet on an increase in rates, or they can be useful for hedging the value of a conventional fixed-income portfolio.

There are still other ways to make highly sensitive bets on the direction of interest rates. Some of these are custom-designed swaps in which the cash flow paid by one party to the swap varies dramatically with the level of some reference interest rate. Such swaps made news in 1994 when Procter & Gamble lost more than $100 million in an interest rate swap that obligated it to make payments that exploded when interest rates increased. In the wake of its losses, P&G sued Bankers Trust, which sold it the swap, claiming that it was misled about the risks of the swap.

Interest rate derivatives are not necessarily bad, or even dangerous, investments. The dramatic sensitivity of their prices to interest rate fluctuations can be useful for hedging as well as for speculation. They can be potent risk management as well as risk-increasing tools. One Wall Street observer has compared them to power tools: When used well by a trained expert, they can serve a valuable function, but in untrained hands, they can lead to severe damage.

SUMMARY

1. Even default-free bonds such as Treasury issues are subject to interest rate risk. Longer-term bonds generally are more sensitive to interest rate shifts than are short-term bonds. A measure of the average life of a bond is Macaulay's duration, defined as the weighted average of the times until each payment made by the security, with weights proportional to the present value of the payment.

2. Duration is a direct measure of the sensitivity of a bond's price to a change in its yield. The proportional change in a bond's price equals the negative of duration multiplied by the proportional change in $1 + y$.

3. Immunization strategies are characteristic of passive fixed-income portfolio management. Such strategies attempt to render the individual or firm immune from movements in interest rates. This may take the form of immunizing net worth or, instead, immunizing the future accumulated value of a fixed-income portfolio.

4. Immunization of a fully funded plan is accomplished by matching the durations of assets and liabilities. To maintain an immunized position as time passes and interest

rates change, the portfolio must be periodically rebalanced. Classic immunization also depends on parallel shifts in a flat yield curve. Given that this assumption is unrealistic, immunization generally will be less than complete. To mitigate the problem, multifactor duration models can be used to allow for variation in the shape of the yield curve.

5. A more direct form of immunization is dedication, or cash flow matching. If a portfolio is perfectly matched in cash flow with projected liabilities, rebalancing will be unnecessary.

6. Convexity refers to the curvature of a bond's price-yield relationship. Accounting for convexity can substantially improve on the accuracy of the duration approximation for bond price sensitivity to changes in yields.

7. Active bond management consists of interest rate forecasting techniques and intermarket spread analysis. One popular taxonomy classifies active strategies as substitution swaps, intermarket spread swaps, rate anticipation swaps, or pure yield pickup swaps.

8. Horizon analysis is a type of interest rate forecasting. In this procedure the analyst forecasts the position of the yield curve at the end of some holding period, and from that yield curve predicts corresponding bond prices. Bonds then can be ranked according to expected total returns (coupon plus capital gain) over the holding period.

9. Interest rate swaps are major recent developments in the fixed-income market. In these arrangements parties trade the cash flows of different securities without actually exchanging any securities directly. This is a useful tool to manage the duration of a portfolio. It also has been used by corporations to borrow at advantageous interest rates in foreign credit markets that are viewed as more hospitable than are domestic credit markets.

10. Financial engineering has created many new fixed-income derivative assets with novel risk characteristics.

Key Terms

duration	substitution swap	horizon analysis
immunization	intermarket spread swap	riding the yield curve
rebalancing	rate anticipation swap	contingent immunization
cash flow matching	pure yield pickup swap	interest rate swaps
dedication strategy	tax swap	notional principal
convexity		

Selected Readings

Duration and immunization are analyzed in a very extensive literature. Good treatments are:

Bierwag, G. O. *Duration Analysis.* Cambridge, MA: Ballinger, 1987.

Weil, Roman. "Macaulay's Duration: An Appreciation." *Journal of Business* 46 (October 1973).

Useful general references to techniques of fixed-income portfolio management may be found in a book of readings used by the Institute of Chartered Financial Analysts:

Fong, H. Gifford. "Portfolio Construction: Fixed Income." In John L. Maginn and Donald L. Tuttle, eds., *Managing Investment Portfolios: A Dynamic Process.* 2nd ed. Boston: Warren, Gorham & Lamont, 1990.

Active bond management strategies are discussed in:

Fabozzi, Frank J. *Bond Markets, Analysis and Strategies.* 3rd ed. Englewood Cliffs, NJ: Prentice Hall, 1996.

For a detailed analysis of swaps see:

Brown, Keith C.; and Donald J. Smith. *Interest Rate and Currency Swaps: A Tutorial.* Charlottesville, VA: Institute of Chartered Financial Analysts, 1995.

Problems

1. A nine-year bond has a yield of 10% and a duration of 7.194 years. If the market yield changes by 50 basis points, what is the percentage change in the bond's price?

2. Find the duration of a 6% coupon bond making *annual* coupon payments if it has three years until maturity and has a yield to maturity of 6%. What is the duration if the yield to maturity is 10%?

3. Find the duration of the bond in problem 2 if the coupons are paid semiannually.

4. Rank the durations of the following pairs of bonds:
   a. Bond A is an 8% coupon bond, with a 20-year time to maturity selling at par value. Bond B is an 8% coupon bond, with a 20-year maturity time selling below par value.
   b. Bond A is a 20-year noncallable coupon bond with a coupon rate of 8%, selling at par. Bond B is a 20-year callable bond with a coupon rate of 9%, also selling at par.

5. An insurance company must make payments to a customer of $10 million in one year and $4 million in five years. The yield curve is flat at 10%.
   a. If it wants to fully fund and immunize its obligation to this customer with a *single* issue of a zero-coupon bond, what maturity bond must it purchase?
   b. What must be the face value and market value of that zero-coupon bond?

6. a. Explain the impact on the offering yield of adding a call feature to a proposed bond issue.
   b. Explain the impact on *both* bond duration and convexity of adding a call feature to a proposed bond issue.

7. Long-term Treasury bonds currently are selling at yields to maturity of nearly 8%. You expect interest rates to fall. The rest of the market thinks that they will remain unchanged over the coming year. In each question, choose the bond that will provide the higher holding-period return over the next year if you are correct. Briefly explain your answer.
   a. i. A Baa-rated bond with coupon rate 8% and time to maturity 20 years.
       ii. An Aaa-rated bond with coupon rate of 8% and time to maturity 20 years.
   b. i. An A-rated bond with coupon rate 4% and maturity 20 years, callable at 105.
       ii. An A-rated bond with coupon rate 8% and maturity 20 years, callable at 105.
   c. i. A 6% coupon noncallable T-bond with maturity 20 years and YTM = 8%.
       ii. A 9% coupon noncallable T-bond with maturity 20 years and YTM = 8%.

8. The following questions are from past CFA examinations.
   a. A 6% coupon bond paying interest annually has a modified duration of 10 years, sells for $800, and is priced at a yield to maturity of 8%. If the YTM increases to 9%, the predicted change in price, using the duration concept, decreases by:
       i. $76.56.
       ii. $76.92.
       iii. $77.67.
       iv. $80.00.
   b. A 6% coupon bond with semiannual coupons has a convexity (in years) of 120, sells for 80% of par, and is priced at a yield to maturity of 8%. If the YTM increases to 9.5%, the predicted contribution to the percentage change in price, due to convexity, would be:
       i. 1.08%.
       ii. 1.35%.
       iii. 2.48%.
       iv. 7.35%.

c. Which statement is true for the Macaulay duration of a zero-coupon bond? The Macaulay duration of a zero-coupon bond:
   i. Is equal to the bond's maturity in years.
   ii. Is equal to one-half the bond's maturity in years.
   iii. Is equal to the bond's maturity in years divided by its yield to maturity.
   iv. Cannot be calculated because of the lack of coupons.

d. A bond with annual coupon payments has a coupon rate of 8%, yield to maturity of 10%, and Macaulay duration of 9. The bond's modified duration is:
   i. 8.18.
   ii. 8.33.
   iii. 9.78.
   iv. 10.00.

e. The interest rate risk of a bond normally is:
   i. Greater for shorter maturities.
   ii. Lower for longer duration.
   iii. Lower for higher coupons.
   iv. None of the above.

f. When interest rates decline, the duration of a 30-year bond selling at a premium:
   i. Increases.
   ii. Decreases.
   iii. Remains the same.
   iv. Increases at first, then declines.

g. If a bond manager swaps a bond for one that is identical in terms of coupon rate, maturity, and credit quality but offers a higher yield to maturity, the swap is:
   i. A substitution swap.
   ii. An interest rate anticipation swap.
   iii. A tax swap.
   iv. An intermarket spread swap.

h. Which bond has the longest duration?
   i. 8-year maturity, 6% coupon.
   ii. 8-year maturity, 11% coupon.
   iii. 15-year maturity, 6% coupon.
   iv. 15-year maturity, 11% coupon.

9. Currently, the term structure is as follows: One-year bonds yield 7%, two-year bonds yield 8%, three-year bonds and greater maturity bonds all yield 9%. An investor is choosing between one-, two-, and three-year maturity bonds all paying annual coupons of 8%, once a year. Which bond should you buy if you strongly believe that at year-end the yield curve will be flat at 9%?

10. Philip Morris has issued bonds that pay semiannually with the following characteristics:

Coupon	Yield to Maturity	Maturity	Macaulay Duration
8%	8%	15 years	10 years

a. Calculate modified duration using the information above.
b. Explain why modified duration is a better measure than maturity when calculating the bond's sensitivity to changes in interest rates.
c. Identify the direction of change in modified duration if:
   i. The coupon of the bond were 4%, not 8%.
   ii. The maturity of the bond were 7 years, not 15 years.

  d. Define convexity and explain how modified duration and convexity are used to approximate the bond's percentage change in price, given a change in interest rates.

11. You will be paying $10,000 a year in tuition expenses at the end of the next two years. Bonds currently yield 8%.
   a. What is the present value and duration of your obligation?
   b. What maturity zero-coupon bond would immunize your obligation?
   c. Suppose you buy a zero-coupon bond with value and duration equal to your obligation. Now suppose that rates immediately increase to 9%. What happens to your net position, that is, to the difference between the value of the bond and that of your tuition obligation? What if rates fall to 7%?

12. Several Investment Committee members have asked about interest rate swap agreements and how are they used in the management of domestic fixed-income portfolios.
   a. Define an interest rate swap and briefly describe the obligation of each party involved.
   b. Cite and explain two examples of how interest rate swaps could be used by a fixed-income portfolio manager to control risk or improve return.

13. What type of interest rate swap would be appropriate for a corporation holding long-term assets that it funded with floating-rate bonds?

14. A corporation has issued a $10 million issue of floating-rate bonds on which it pays an interest rate 1% over the LIBOR rate. The bonds are selling at par value. The firm is worried that rates are about to rise, and it would like to lock in a fixed interest rate on its borrowings. The firm sees that dealers in the swap market are offering swaps of LIBOR for 7%. What interest rate swap will convert the firm's interest obligation into one resembling a synthetic fixed-rate loan? What interest rate will it pay on that synthetic fixed-rate loan?

15. Pension funds pay lifetime annuities to recipients. If a firm will remain in business indefinitely, the pension obligation will resemble a perpetuity. Suppose, therefore, that you are managing a pension fund with obligations to make perpetual payments of $2 million per year to beneficiaries. The yield to maturity on all bonds is 16%.
   a. If the duration of 5-year maturity bonds with coupon rates of 12% (paid annually) is 4 years and the duration of 20-year maturity bonds with coupon rates of 6% (paid annually) is 11 years, how much of each of these coupon bonds (in market value) will you want to hold to both fully fund and immunize your obligation?
   b. What will be the par value of your holdings in the 20-year coupon bond?

16. You are managing a portfolio of $1 million. Your target duration is 10 years, and you can choose from two bonds: a zero-coupon bond with maturity of 5 years, and a perpetuity, each currently yielding 5%.
   a. How much of each bond will you hold in your portfolio?
   b. How will these fractions change *next year* if target duration is now nine years?

17. My pension plan will pay me $10,000 once a year for a 10-year period. The first payment will come in exactly five years. The pension fund wants to immunize its position.
   a. What is the duration of its obligation to me? The current interest rate is 10% per year.
   b. If the plan uses 5-year and 20-year zero-coupon bonds to construct the immunized position, how much money ought to be placed in each bond? What will be the *face value* of the holdings in each zero?

18. A 30-year maturity bond making annual coupon payments with a coupon rate of 12% has duration of 11.54 years and convexity of 192.4. The bond currently sells at a yield to maturity of 8%. Use a financial calculator to find the price of the bond if its yield to

maturity falls to 7% or rises to 9%. What prices for the bond at these new yields would be predicted by the duration rule and the duration-with-convexity rule? What is the percentage error for each rule? What do you conclude about the accuracy of the two rules?

19. A 12.75-year maturity zero-coupon bond selling at a yield to maturity of 8% (effective annual yield) has convexity of 150.3 and modified duration of 11.81 years. A 30-year maturity 6% coupon bond making annual coupon payments also selling at a yield to maturity of 8% has nearly identical duration—11.79 years—but considerably higher convexity of 231.2.

    a. Suppose the yield to maturity on both bonds increases to 9%. What will be the actual percentage capital loss on each bond? What percentage capital loss would be predicted by the duration-with-convexity rule?

    b. Repeat part (*a*), but this time assume the yield to maturity decreases to 7%.

    c. Compare the performance of the two bonds in the two scenarios, one involving an increase in rates, the other a decrease. Based on the comparative investment performance, explain the attraction of convexity.

    d. In view of your answer to (*c*), do you think it would be possible for two bonds with equal duration but different convexity to be priced initially at the same yield to maturity if the yields on both bonds always increased or decreased by equal amounts, as in this example? Would anyone be willing to buy the bond with lower convexity under these circumstances?

20. A newly issued bond has a maturity of 10 years and pays a 7% coupon rate (with coupon payments coming once annually). The bond sells at par value.

    a. What are the convexity and the duration of the bond? Use the formula for convexity in footnote 8.

    b. Find the actual price of the bond assuming that its yield to maturity immediately increases from 7% to 8% (with maturity still 10 years).

    c. What price would be predicted by the duration rule (equation 16.2)? What is the percentage error of that rule?

    d. What price would be predicted by the duration-with-convexity rule (equation 16.3)? What is the percentage error of that rule?

21. You are the manager for the bond portfolio of a pension fund. The policies of the fund allow for the use of active strategies in managing the bond portfolio.

    It appears that the economic cycle is beginning to mature, inflation is expected to accelerate, and in an effort to contain the economic expansion, central bank policy is moving toward constraint. For each of the situations below, state which one of the two bonds you would prefer. Briefly justify your answer in each case.

    a. Government of Canada (Canadian pay) 10% due in 2001 and priced at 98.75 to yield 10.50% to maturity.

    or

    Government of Canada (Canadian pay) 10% due in 2009 and priced at 91.75 to yield 11.19% to maturity.

    b. Texas Power and Light Co., 7½ due in 2002, rated AAA, and priced at 85 to yield 10.02% to maturity.

    or

    Arizona Public Service Co. 7.45 due in 2002, rated A–, and priced at 75 to yield 12.05% to maturity.

    c. Commonwealth Edison 2¾ due in 2000, rated Baa, and priced at 61 to yield 12.2% to maturity.

    or

Commonwealth Edison 15⅝ due in 2000, rated Baa, and priced at 114.40 to yield 12.2% to maturity.

    d. Shell Oil Co. 8½ sinking fund debentures due in 2015, rated AAA (sinking fund begins September 1999 at par), and priced at 68 to yield 12.91% to maturity.

or

Warner-Lambert 8⅞ sinking fund debentures due in 2015, rated AAA (sinking fund begins April 2004 at par), and priced at 74 to yield 12.31% to maturity.

    e. Bank of Montreal (Canadian pay) 8% certificates of deposit due in 1999, rated AAA, and priced at 100 to yield 8% to maturity.

or

Bank of Montreal (Canadian pay) floating rate-note due in 2004, rated AAA. Coupon currently set at 7.1% and priced at 100 (coupon adjusted semiannually to .5% above the three-month Government of Canada Treasury bill rate).

22. A member of a firm's investment committee is very interested in learning about the management of fixed-income portfolios. He would like to know how fixed-income managers position portfolios to capitalize on their expectations concerning three factors which influence interest rates:

    a. Changes in the level of interest rates.

    b. Changes in yield spreads across/between sectors.

    c. Changes in yield spreads as to a particular instrument.

    Assuming that no investment policy limitations apply, formulate and describe a fixed-income portfolio management strategy for each of these factors that could be used to exploit a portfolio manager's expectations about that factor. (Note: Three strategies are required, one for each of the listed factors.)

23. Prices of long-term bonds are more volatile than prices of short-term bonds. However, yields to maturity of short-term bonds fluctuate more than yields of long-term bonds. How do you reconcile these two empirical observations?

24. A fixed-income portfolio manager is unwilling to realize a rate of return of less than 3% annually over a five-year investment period on a portfolio currently valued at $1 million. Three years later, the interest rate is 8%. What is the trigger point of the portfolio at this time, that is, how low can the value of the portfolio fall before the manager will be forced to immunize to be assured of achieving the minimum acceptable return?

25. A 30-year maturity bond has a 7% coupon rate, paid annually. It sells today for $867.42. A 20-year maturity bond has 6.5% coupon rate, also paid annually. It sells today for $879.50. A bond market analyst forecasts that in 5 years, 25-year maturity bonds will sell at yields to maturity of 8% and 15-year maturity bonds will sell at yields of 7.5%. Because the yield curve is upward sloping, the analyst believes that coupons will be invested in short-term securities at a rate of 6%. Which bond offers the higher expected rate of return over the five-year period?

26. Your firm, TMP, is to be interviewed as a possible manager for the $100 million indexed fixed-income portfolio being considered by the investment committee of a large endowment fund. Because the committee has not yet decided which of three indexes to use as their benchmark portfolio, the interview will focus on this issue. Information regarding each of the three indexes to be discussed is presented in the following table. By way of background, TMP is told that the committee has adopted an aggressive overall investment policy with a long-term horizon and an above-average risk tolerance.

	Sector Mix Information		
	Index 1	Index 2	Index 3
U.S. Treasuries	50%	50%	80%
U.S. agencies	10	10	10
Corporates			
Investment grade	10	10	5
Below-investment grade	5	5	0
Residential mortgages	20	25	5
Yankee bonds	5	0	0
Total	100%	100%	100%
Index modified duration	5.0	8.0	8.0
Index yield to maturity	7.50%	8.05%	8.00%

Both the level and the volatility of interest rates have been declining for the past several years. The committee believes these trends are unlikely to continue, and is seeking insight as to how the indexed portfolio might perform under a variety of alternative interest-rate scenarios. Two such scenarios are:

    i. A cycle over which interest rates generally decline, but are accompanied by generally rising volatility; and

    ii. A cycle over which interest rates are generally flat from beginning to end, but in which volatility is high throughout.

  a. Using only the data from the table, rank the three indexes in order of relative attractiveness under each of the two scenarios above, and justify your rankings by citing the factors that support your conclusions.

  b. Recommend and justify one index to the committee for use as its benchmark portfolio. Take into account your answer to part (*a*) and the information which you have been provided about the committee's investment policy.

  c. Assume that the committee has selected an index to use as its benchmark and that TMP has been hired to construct and manage the indexed portfolio. Explain the practical problems associated with construction of an indexed fixed-income portfolio. Identify and briefly discuss two methods of such construction, including in your discussion one strength and one weakness of each method.

27. As part of your analysis of debt issued by Monticello Corporation, you are asked to evaluate two specific bond issues, shown in the table below.

	Monticello Corporation Bond Information	
	Bond *A* (Callable)	Bond *B* (Noncallable)
Maturity	2005	2005
Coupon	11.50%	7.25%
Current price	125.75	100.00
Yield to maturity	7.70%	7.25%
Modified duration to maturity	6.20	6.80
Call date	1999	—
Call price	105	—
Yield to call	5.10%	—
Modified duration to call	3.10	—

a. Using the duration and yield information in the table, compare the price and yield behavior of the two bonds under each of the following two scenarios:
  i. Strong economic recovery with rising inflation expectations.
  ii. Economic recession with reduced inflation expectations.
b. Using the information in the table, calculate the projected price change for bond B if the yield-to-maturity for this bond falls by 75 basis points.
c. Describe the shortcoming of analyzing bond A strictly to call or to maturity.

solutions to
Concept
CHECKS

1. a.

(1) Time until Payment	(2) Payment	(3) Payment Discounted at 10%	(4) Weight	(5) Column (1) × Column (4)
1	$ 90	$ 81.8182	0.0833	0.0833
2	1,090	900.8264	0.9167	1.8334
		$982.6446	1.0	1.9167

Duration is 1.1967 years. Price is $982.6446.

b. At an interest rate of 10.05%, the bond's price is

90 × Annuity factor(10.05%, 2) + 1,000 × PV factor(10.05%, 2) = 981.7891
The percentage change in price is –.087%.

c. The duration formula would predict a price change of

$$-\frac{1.9167}{1.10} \times .0005 = -.00087, \text{ or } -.087\%$$

which is the same answer that we obtained from direct computation in (b).

2. The duration of a level perpetuity is $(1 + y)/y$ or $1 + 1/y$, which clearly falls as y increases. Tabulating duration as a function of y we get

y	D
.01	101 years
.02	51
.05	21
.10	11
.20	6
.25	5
.40	3.5

3. Potential gains and losses are proportional to both duration *and* portfolio size. The dollar loss on a fixed-income portfolio resulting from an increase in the portfolio's yield to maturity is, from equation 16.2, $D \times P \times \Delta y/(1 + y)$, where P is the initial market value of the portfolio. Hence $D \times P$ must be equated for immunization.

4. The perpetuity's duration now would be $1.08/.08 = 13.5$. We need to solve the following equation for w:

$$w \times 2 + (1 - w) \times 13.5 = 6$$

Therefore $w = .6522$

5. Dedication would be more attractive. Cash flow matching eliminates the need for rebalancing and thus saves transaction costs.

6. The 30-year 8% coupon bond will provide a stream of coupons of $40 per half-year, which invested at the assumed rate of 4% per half-year will accumulate to $480.24. The bond will sell in five years at a price equal to $40 × Annuity factor(4.25%, 50) + $1,000 × PV factor(4.25%, 50), or $948.52, for a capital gain of $51.71. The total five-year income is $51.71 + $480.24 = $531.95, for a five-year return of $531.95/$896.81 = .5932, or 59.32%. Based on this scenario, the 20-year 10% coupon bond offers a higher return for a five-year horizon.

7. The trigger point is $10 million/$(1.12)^3$ = $7.118 million.

8. The manager would like to hold on to the money market securities because of their attractive relative pricing compared to other short-term assets. However, there is an expectation that rates will fall. The manager can hold this *particular* portfolio of short-term assets and still benefit from the drop in interest rates by entering a swap to pay a short-term interest rate and receive a fixed interest rate. The resulting synthetic fixed-rate portfolio will increase in value if rates do fall.

SECURITY ANALYSIS

MACROECONOMIC AND INDUSTRY ANALYSIS

To determine a proper price for a firm's stock, the security analyst must forecast the dividend and earnings that can be expected from the firm. This is the heart of **fundamental analysis**—that is, the analysis of the determinants of value such as earnings prospects. Ultimately, the business success of the firm determines the dividends it can pay to shareholders and the price it will command in the stock market. Because the prospects of the firm are tied to those of the broader economy, however, fundamental analysis must consider the business environment in which the firm operates. For some firms, macroeconomic and industry circumstances might have a greater influence on profits than the firm's relative performance within its industry. It often makes sense to do a "top-down" analysis of a firm's prospects. One starts with the broad economic environment, examining the state of the aggregate economy and even the international economy. From there, one considers the implications of the outside environment on the industry in which the firm operates. Finally, the firm's position within the industry is examined. This chapter treats the broad-based aspects of fundamental analysis—macroeconomic and industry analysis. The two chapters following cover firm-specific analysis. We begin with a discussion of international factors relevant to firm performance, and move on to an overview of the significance of the key variables usually used to summarize the state of the macroeconomy. We then discuss government macroeconomic policy. We conclude the analysis of the macro environment with a discussion of business cycles. Finally, we move to industry analysis, treating issues concerning the sensitivity of the firm to the business cycle, the typical life cycle of an industry, and strategic issues that affect industry performance.

17.1   THE GLOBAL ECONOMY

A top-down analysis of a firm's prospects must start with the global economy. The international economy might affect a firm's export prospects, the price competition it faces from competitors, or the profits it makes on investments abroad. Certainly, despite the fact that the economies of most countries are linked in a global macroeconomy, there is considerable variation in the economic performance across countries at any time. Consider, for example, Table 17.1, which presents data on several so-called emerging economies. The table documents striking variation in growth rates of economic output in 1997. For example, while the Chinese economy grew by 8.1% in 1997, Venezuelan output fell by 1.6%. Similarly, there was considerable variation in stock market returns in these countries in 1997, ranging from a 75.9% loss in Thailand (in dollar terms) to a 110.2% gain in Russia.

These data illustrate that the national economic environment can be a crucial determinant of industry performance. It is far harder for businesses to succeed in a contracting economy than in an expanding one.

In addition, the global environment presents political risks of far greater magnitude than is typically encountered in U.S.-based investments. For example, the Hong Kong stock market was extremely sensitive to political developments concerning the transfer of governance to China. In 1992 and 1993, the Mexican stock market responded dramatically to changing assessments regarding the prospects of passage of the North American Free Trade Agreement by the U.S. Congress. A major economic issue with substantial political risk for European countries in 1998 concerns the progress that will be made toward monetary union.

Table 17.1   Economic Performance in Selected Emerging Markets

		Stock Market Return in 1997	
	Growth in Real GDP, 1997 (%)	In Local Currency	In $ Terms
China	+ 8.1	+ 30.3	+ 30.7
Hong Kong	+ 6.4	− 20.0	− 20.2
India	+ 6.8	+ 17.9	+ 7.7
Indonesia	+ 8.0	− 37.0	− 73.3
Malaysia	+ 7.4	− 52.4	− 69.1
Philippines	+ 4.9	− 41.0	− 61.7
Singapore	+10.1	− 31.7	− 43.1
South Korea	+ 6.3	− 42.2	− 70.2
Taiwan	+ 6.9	+ 17.5	− 0.9
Thailand	+ 6.7	− 56.0	− 75.9
Argentina	+ 8.6	+ 5.9	+ 5.8
Brazil	+ 2.8	+ 44.8	+ 34.4
Chile	+ 8.1	− 2.5	− 5.9
Colombia	+ 4.7	+ 69.6	+ 32.1
Mexico	+ 8.1	+ 54.9	+ 51.6
Venezuela	− 1.6	+ 27.2	+ 20.0
Greece	+ 2.6	+ 57.4	+ 36.2
Israel	+ 2.0	+ 36.6	+ 25.7
Portugal	+ 3.0	+ 74.6	+ 47.8
South Africa	+ 1.2	− 7.3	− 10.7
Turkey	+ 5.4	+254.4	+ 86.8
Czech Republic	+ 0.8	− 8.2	− 27.7
Hungary	+ 4.3	+ 93.5	+ 53.6
Poland	+ 7.6	+ 1.5	− 16.8
Russia	+ 1.0	+125.8	+110.2

Source: *The Economist*, January 3, 1998.

THE ASIAN EFFECT

For most of its history, America has shrugged off economic turmoil abroad. Its economy was so big, and trade played so small a part, that distant upheavals of this sort had little impact. No longer. With remarkable speed, Asia's financial mess has come to seem the biggest threat to America's economic expansion, bringing jitters to Wall Street and Washington alike. In today's globalized world, runs the assumption, Asia's woes will hurt America. The question is, how much?

Most Wall Streeters expect Asia's turmoil to knock around half a percentage point from America's growth rate this year. The more pessimistic expect growth to fall by a full percentage point, with America's trade deficit worsening sharply. As Asia's currencies collapse and its economies slow or contract, so demand for American exports will fall, while (cheaper) imports from Asia will soar. The combination will retard America's growth. The size of the trade effect depends on how much Asia's currencies fall and how much its economies slow.

Evidence that a shift of some kind is under way is already appearing. According to a monthly survey of purchasing managers, orders for exports are down and orders for imports are up.

Many analysts are already cutting their forecasts for companies' 1997 earnings because of the Asia effect. According to Chuck Hill of First Call, a financial research firm in Boston, forecasts for year-on-year earnings growth in the fourth quarter of 1997 for the S&P 500 firms have been slashed from 13.2% to 7.8%. For 1998, the consensus forecast so far is that core earnings will grow by 13.7%—only slightly down from a forecast of 14.8% in October 1997. But Mr. Hill reckons there is a growing risk that these forecasts will soon be savagely cut.

With stockmarket valuations still stretched to, or beyond, reasonable limits, any disappointing news on profits could prompt a disproportionately large correction. So, too, could a suspicion that Asia's crisis was worsening. A devaluation of the Chinese currency, for instance, could make Asian (and western) stockmarkets totter. Any more evidence that the IMF's bail-out packages are not working could also prompt a collapse of market confidence. Some in Washington talk of scenarios in which the stockmarket falls by 20%.

Ten years ago, the market crash caused little real harm. Monetary policy was loosened, shares bounced back, and consumption and investment were unscathed. This would probably happen again. But it might not. More Americans hold shares than they did ten years ago, so the effect of a crash on consumption might be bigger; and spreading global panic would make a quick recovery in confidence less likely. So one risk posed by Asia is that a small (and otherwise desirable) correction on Wall Street could become a crash.

Such a loss of confidence may be as likely to come from Washington as from Wall Street. When it reconvenes in February, Congress will need to decide whether to provide $18 billion of new resources for the IMF. A failure to provide it would not have an immediate effect on the IMF's solvency, but it would point to America's unwillingness to play the role of global economic leader—and that, in turn, could roil the markets.

The other political risk is that a rising trade deficit will arouse protectionist sentiment. But, as the months go by and the trade deficit grows, it may become tempting to be more protectionist. Asia's woes could be seen as a proof of the evils of globalization. That, more than any direct trade impact, is the real risk this far-flung crisis poses for America's economy.

Source: *The Economist*, January 17, 1998.

The biggest international economic story of 1997 and early 1998 has been the turmoil in several Asian economies, notably Thailand, Indonesia, and South Korea. The close interplay between politics and economics is also highlighted by these episodes, as both currency and stock values swung with enormous volatility in response to developments concerning the prospects for aid from the International Monetary Fund and the terms on which any aid would be offered. The nearby box discusses the impact of the Asian economic crisis on the U.S. economy and notes how the resolution of the difficulties will be affected by political as well as economic considerations. The presence of these political considerations adds a dimension of risk to foreign investments beyond the purely economic.

Of course, political developments can be positive as well. For example, the end of regional conflicts can portend great growth for local economies. Political developments (and bumps along the way) offer significant opportunities to make or lose money.

Figure 17.1

Change in real exchange rate: dollar versus major currencies, 1986–1996.

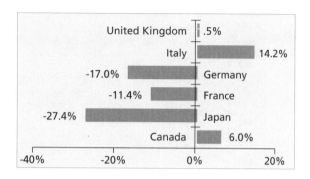

Other political issues that are less sensational but still extremely important to economic growth and investment returns include issues of protectionism and trade policy, the free flow of capital, and the status of a nation's work force.

One obvious factor that affects the international competitiveness of a country's industries is the exchange rate between that country's currency and other currencies. The **exchange rate** is the rate at which domestic currency can be converted into foreign currency. For example, in early 1998, it took about 133 Japanese yen to purchase one U.S. dollar. We would say that the exchange rate is ¥133 per dollar or, equivalently, $.0075 per yen.

As exchange rates fluctuate, the dollar value of goods priced in foreign currency similarly fluctuates. For example, in 1980, the dollar–yen exchange rate was about $.0045 per yen. Because the exchange rate today is $.0075 per yen, a U.S. citizen would need 64% more dollars in 1998 to buy a product selling for ¥10,000 than would have been required in 1980. If the Japanese producer were to maintain a fixed yen price for its product, the price expressed in U.S. dollars would increase by 64%. This would make Japanese products more expensive to U.S. consumers, however, and result in lost sales. Obviously, appreciation of the yen creates a problem for Japanese producers that must compete with U.S. producers.

Figure 17.1 shows the change in the purchasing power of the U.S. dollar relative to the purchasing power of the currencies of several major industrial countries in the decade ending in 1996. The ratio of purchasing powers is called the "real," or inflation-adjusted, exchange rate. The change in the real exchange rate measures how much more or less expensive foreign goods have become to U.S. citizens, accounting for both exchange rate fluctuations and inflation differentials across countries. A positive value in Figure 17.1 means that the dollar has gained purchasing power relative to another currency; a negative number indicates a depreciating dollar. Therefore, the figure shows that goods priced in terms of the German or Japanese currency have become far more expensive to U.S. consumers in the last decade but that goods priced in Italian lire or Canadian dollars have become cheaper. Conversely, goods priced in dollars have become more affordable to Japanese consumers, but more expensive to Italian consumers.

17.2   THE DOMESTIC MACROECONOMY

The macroeconomy is the environment in which all firms operate. The importance of the macroeconomy in determining investment performance is illustrated in Figure 17.2, which compares the level of the S&P 500 stock price index to forecasts of earnings per share of the S&P 500 companies. Stock prices commonly trade at between 8 and 20 times earnings, so the top boundary of the shaded area is drawn at estimated earnings times 20, and the

Figure 17.2

S&P 500 index versus earnings per share forecast.

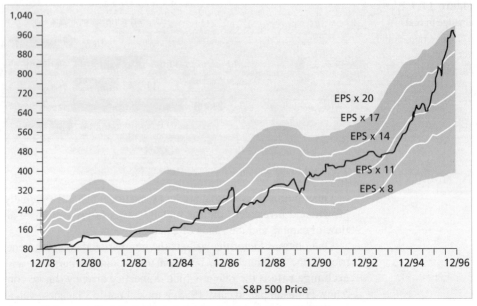

Source: *U.S. Comments*, December 3, 1997. Institutional Brokers Estimate System (I/B/E/S).

bottom boundary is drawn at estimated earnings times 8. Given "normal" price–earnings ratios, we would expect the S&P 500 index to fall within these boundaries. Although the earnings-multiplier rule clearly is not perfect—the price-earnings multiple varies considerably over time—it also seems clear that the level of the broad market and aggregate earnings do trend together. Thus the first step in forecasting the performance of the broad market is to assess the status of the economy as a whole.

The ability to forecast the macroeconomy can translate into spectacular investment performance. But it is not enough to forecast the macroeconomy well. You must forecast it *better* than your competitors to earn abnormal profits.

In this section, we will review some of the key economic statistics used to describe the state of the macroeconomy. Some of these key variables are:

Gross Domestic Product. Gross domestic product, or GDP, is the measure of the economy's total production of goods and services. Rapidly growing GDP indicates an expanding economy with ample opportunity for a firm to increase sales. Another popular measure of the economy's output is *industrial production*. This statistic provides a measure of economic activity more narrowly focused on the manufacturing side of the economy.

Employment. The unemployment rate is the percentage of the total labor force (i.e., those who are either working or actively seeking employment) yet to find work. The unemployment rate measures the extent to which the economy is operating at full capacity. The unemployment rate is a factor related to workers only, but further insight into the strength of the economy can be gleaned from the unemployment rate for other factors of production. Analysts also look at the factory *capacity utilization rate*, which is the ratio of actual output from factories to potential output.

Inflation. Inflation is the rate at which the general level of prices is rising. High rates of inflation often are associated with "overheated" economies, that is, economies where the demand for goods and services is outstripping productive capacity, which leads to upward pressure on prices. Most governments walk a fine line in their economic policies. They hope to stimulate their economics enough to maintain nearly full employment, but not so much as to bring on inflationary pressures. The perceived trade-off between inflation and unemployment is at the heart of many macroeconomic policy disputes. There is considerable room for disagreement as to the relative costs of these policies as well as the economy's relative vulnerability to these pressures at any particular time.

Interest Rates. High interest rates reduce the present value of future cash flows, thereby reducing the attractiveness of investment opportunities. For this reason, real interest rates are key determinants of business investment expenditures. Demand for housing and high-priced consumer durables such as automobiles, which are commonly financed, also is highly sensitive to interest rates because interest rates affect interest payments. (In Chapter 5, Section 5.1, we examined the determinants of interest rates.)

Budget Deficit. The **budget deficit** of the federal government is the difference between government spending and revenues. Any budgetary shortfall must be offset by government borrowing. Large amounts of government borrowing can force up interest rates by increasing the total demand for credit in the economy. Economists generally believe excessive government borrowing will "crowd out" private borrowing and investing by forcing up interest rates and choking off business investment.

Sentiment. Consumers' and producers' optimism or pessimism concerning the economy is an important determinant of economic performance. If consumers have confidence in their future income levels, for example, they will be more willing to spend on big-ticket items. Similarly, businesses will increase production and inventory levels if they anticipate higher demand for their products. In this way, beliefs influence how much consumption and investment will be pursued and affect the aggregate demand for goods and services.

Concept
CHECK

Question 1 • Consider an economy where the dominant industry is automobile production for domestic consumption as well as export. Now suppose the auto market is hurt by an increase in the length of time people use their cars before replacing them. Describe the probable effects of this change on (*a*) GDP, (*b*) unemployment, (*c*) the government budget deficit, and (*d*) interest rates.

17.3   DEMAND AND SUPPLY SHOCKS

A useful way to organize your analysis of the factors that might influence the macroeconomy is to classify any impact as a supply or demand shock. A **demand shock** is an event that affects the demand for goods and services in the economy. Examples of positive demand shocks are reductions in tax rates, increases in the money supply, increases in government spending, or increases in foreign export demand. A **supply shock** is an event that influences production capacity and costs. Examples of supply shocks are changes in the price of imported oil; freezes, floods, or droughts that might destroy large quantities of agricultural crops; changes in the educational level of an economy's work force; or changes in the wage rates at which the labor force is willing to work.

Demand shocks are usually characterized by aggregate output moving in the same direction as interest rates and inflation. For example, a big increase in government spending will tend to stimulate the economy and increase GDP. It also might increase interest rates by increasing the demand for borrowed funds by the government as well as by businesses that might desire to borrow to finance new ventures. Finally, it could increase the inflation rate

CONFLICTING ECONOMIC SIGNALS

Despite last week's return to optimism in the stock market, nagging recession concerns continue to confound Wall Street.

With conflicting economic signals, investors find themselves in a quandary. Is the economy rapidly dropping into recession, or close to one? Or is it simply taking a modest breath before strengthening later this year?

The recession quandary has split Wall Street strategists. One camp, which includes Charles Clough, chief strategist at Merrill Lynch & Co., argues that the economy is slowing much faster than realized. He says rising corporate inventories and a spent consumer are contributing to a steepening slowdown. Moreover, the Federal Reserve is moving too slowly to stave off a period of extended sluggishness, and earnings will probably suffer more than anticipated this year.

The other camp, which includes Abby J. Cohen, market strategist at Goldman, Sachs & Co., believes that the economy will rebound later this year.

Emphasizing Financial Stocks

The divergent views play a crucial role in near-term investing decisions. Mr. Clough has trimmed his exposure to the stock market in favor of bonds and emphasizes financial stocks, which would benefit in a low-rate environment.

Ms. Cohen, conversely, maintains a healthy exposure to the stock market and emphasizes not just financials, but also economically sensitive stocks such as autos and housing-related stocks. She further expects to emphasize later-cyclical commodity stocks as the year unfolds and the economic pace quickens.

James Weiss, deputy chief investment officer for growth equities at State Street in Boston, and David Shulman, chief strategist at Salomon Brothers, concur with much of Mr. Clough's analysis of the economy. Mr. Weiss says the recent uptick in cyclical stocks should be mostly ignored, and he favors steadier growth in defensive sectors like health care and beverages.

Source: Dave Kansas, "Conflicting Economic Signals Are Dividing Strategists," *The Wall Street Journal*, February 26, 1996. Excerpted by permission of *The Wall Street Journal*. © 1996 Dow Jones & Company, Inc. All Rights Reserved Worldwide.

if the demand for goods and services is raised to a level at or beyond the total productive capacity of the economy.

Supply shocks are usually characterized by aggregate output moving in the opposite direction of inflation and interest rates. For example, a big increase in the price of imported oil will be inflationary because costs of production will rise, which eventually will lead to increases in prices of finished goods. The increase in inflation rates over the near term can lead to higher nominal interest rates. Against this background, aggregate output will be falling. With raw materials more expensive, the productive capacity of the economy is reduced, as is the ability of individuals to purchase goods at now-higher prices. GDP, therefore, tends to fall.

How can we relate this framework to investment analysis? You want to identify the industries that will be most helped or hurt in any macroeconomic scenario you envision. For example, if you forecast a tightening of the money supply, you might want to avoid industries such as automobile producers that might be hurt by the likely increase in interest rates. We caution you again that these forecasts are no easy task. Macroeconomic predictions are notoriously unreliable. And again, you must be aware that in all likelihood your forecast will be made using only publicly available information. Any investment advantage you have will be a result only of better analysis—not better information.

An example of how investment advice is tied to macroeconomic forecasts is given in the nearby box. The article focuses on the different advice being given by two prominent analysts with differing views of the economy. The relatively bearish strategists believe the economy is about to slow down. As a result, they recommend asset allocation toward the fixed-income market, which will benefit if interest rates fall in a recession. Within the stock market, they recommend industries with below-average sensitivity to macroeconomic conditions. Two recession-resistant, or "defensive," investments specifically cited are beverage and health care stocks, both of which are expected to outperform the rest of the market as investors become aware of the slowdown in growth. Conversely, the optimistic analysts recommend investments with greater sensitivity to the business cycle.

17.4   FEDERAL GOVERNMENT POLICY

As the previous section would suggest, the government has two broad classes of macro-economic tools—those that affect the demand for goods and services and those that affect the supply. For most of postwar history, demand-side policy has been of primary interest. The focus has been on government spending, tax levels, and monetary policy. Since the 1980s, however, increasing attention has been focused on supply-side economics. Broadly interpreted, supply-side concerns have to do with enhancing the productive capacity of the economy, rather than increasing the demand for the goods and services the economy can produce. In practice, supply-side economists have focused on the appropriateness of the incentives to work, innovate, and take risks that result from our system of taxation. However, issues such as national policies on education, infrastructure (such as communi-cation and transportation systems), and research and development also are properly regarded as part of supply-side macroeconomic policy.

Fiscal Policy

Fiscal policy refers to the government's spending and tax actions and is part of "demand-side management." Fiscal policy is probably the most direct way either to stimulate or to slow the economy. Decreases in government spending directly deflate the demand for goods and services. Similarly, increases in tax rates immediately siphon income from con-sumers and result in fairly rapid decreases in consumption.

Ironically, although fiscal policy has the most immediate impact on the economy, the formulation and implementation of such policy is usually painfully slow and involved. This is because fiscal policy requires enormous amounts of compromise between the executive and legislative branches. Tax and spending policy must be initiated and voted on by Congress, which requires considerable political negotiations, and any legislation passed must be signed by the president, requiring more negotiation. Thus, although the impact of fiscal policy is relatively immediate, its formulation is so cumbersome that fiscal policy cannot in practice be used to fine-tune the economy.

Moreover, much of government spending, such as that for Medicare or social security, is nondiscretionary, meaning that it is determined by formula rather than policy and can-not be changed in response to economic conditions. This places even more rigidity into the formulation of fiscal policy.

A common way to summarize the net impact of government fiscal policy is to look at the government's budget deficit or surplus, which is simply the difference between rev-enues and expenditures. A large deficit means the government is spending considerably more than it is taking in by way of taxes. The net effect is to increase the demand for goods (via spending) by more than it reduces the demand for goods (via taxes), thereby stimulat-ing the economy.

Monetary Policy

Monetary policy refers to the manipulation of the money supply to affect the macroecon-omy and is the other main leg of demand-side policy. Monetary policy works largely through its impact on interest rates. Increases in the money supply lower short-term inter-est rates, ultimately encouraging investment and consumption demand. Over longer peri-ods, however, most economists believe a higher money supply leads only to a higher price level and does not have a permanent effect on economic activity. Thus the monetary authorities face a difficult balancing act. Expansionary monetary policy probably will lower interest rates and thereby stimulate investment and some consumption demand in the short run, but these circumstances ultimately will lead only to higher prices. The stimulation/inflation trade-off is implicit in all debate over proper monetary policy.

Fiscal policy is cumbersome to implement but has a fairly direct impact on the economy, whereas monetary policy is easily formulated and implemented but has a less direct impact. Monetary policy is determined by the Board of Governors of the Federal Reserve System. Board members are appointed by the president for 14-year terms and are reasonably insulated from political pressure. The board is small enough, and often sufficiently dominated by its chairperson, that policy can be formulated and modulated relatively easily.

Implementation of monetary policy also is quite direct. The most widely used tool is the open market operation, in which the Fed buys or sells bonds for its own account. When the Fed buys securities, it simply "writes a check," thereby increasing the money supply. (Unlike us, the Fed can pay for the securities without drawing down funds at a bank account.) Conversely, when the Fed sells a security, the money paid for it leaves the money supply. Open market operations occur daily, allowing the Fed to fine-tune its monetary policy.

Other tools at the Fed's disposal are the discount rate, which is the interest rate it charges banks on short-term loans, and the reserve requirement, which is the fraction of deposits that banks must hold as cash on hand or as deposits with the Fed. Reductions in the discount rate signal a more expansionary monetary policy. Lowering reserve requirements allows banks to make more loans with each dollar of deposits and stimulates the economy by increasing the effective money supply.

Monetary policy affects the economy in a more roundabout way than fiscal policy. Whereas fiscal policy directly stimulates or dampens the economy, monetary policy works largely through its impact on interest rates. Increases in the money supply lower interest rates, which stimulates investment demand. As the quantity of money in the economy increases, investors will find that their portfolios of assets include too much money. They will rebalance their portfolios by buying securities such as bonds, forcing bond prices up and interest rates down. In the longer run, individuals may increase their holdings of stocks as well and ultimately buy real assets, which stimulates consumption demand directly. The ultimate effect of monetary policy on investment and consumption demand, however, is less immediate than that of fiscal policy.

Concept CHECK   **Question 2 • Suppose the government wants to stimulate the economy without increasing interest rates. What combination of fiscal and monetary policy might accomplish this goal?**

Supply-Side Policies

Fiscal and monetary policy are demand-oriented tools that affect the economy by stimulating the total demand for goods and services. The implicit belief is that the economy will not by itself arrive at a full employment equilibrium, and that macroeconomic policy can push the economy toward this goal. In contrast, supply-side policies treat the issue of the productive capacity of the economy. The goal is to create an environment in which workers and owners of capital have the maximum incentive and ability to produce and develop goods.

Supply-side economists also pay considerable attention to tax policy. Whereas demand siders look at the effect of taxes on consumption demand, supply siders focus on incentives and marginal tax rates. They argue that lowering tax rates will elicit more investment and improve incentives to work, thereby enhancing economic growth. Some go so far as to claim that reductions in tax rates can lead to increases in tax revenues because the lower tax rates will cause the economy and the revenue tax base to grow by more than the tax rate is reduced.

Question 3 • **Large tax cuts in the 1980s were followed by rapid growth in GDP. How would demand-side and supply-side economists differ in their interpretations of this phenomenon?**

17.5 BUSINESS CYCLES

We've looked at the tools the government uses to fine-tune the economy, attempting to maintain low unemployment and low inflation. Despite these efforts, economies repeatedly seem to pass through good and bad times. One determinant of the broad asset allocation decision of many analysts is a forecast of whether the macroeconomy is improving or deteriorating. A forecast that differs from the market consensus can have a major impact on investment strategy.

The Business Cycle

The economy recurrently experiences periods of expansion and contraction, although the length and depth of those cycles can be irregular. This recurring pattern of recession and recovery is called the **business cycle**. Figure 17.3 presents graphs of several measures of production and output for the years 1967–1997. The production series all show clear variation around a generally rising trend. The bottom graph of capacity utilization also evidences a clear cyclical (although irregular) pattern.

The transition points across cycles are called peaks and troughs, labeled P and T at the top of the graph. A **peak** is the transition from the end of an expansion to the start of a contraction. A **trough** occurs at the bottom of a recession just as the economy enters a recovery. The shaded areas in Figure 17.3 all represent periods of recession.

As the economy passes through different stages of the business cycle, the relative performance of different industry groups might be expected to vary. For example, at a trough, just before the economy begins to recover from a recession, one would expect that **cyclical industries**, those with above-average sensitivity to the state of the economy, would tend to outperform other industries. Examples of cyclical industries are producers of durable goods such as automobiles or washing machines. Because purchases of these goods can be deferred during a recession, sales are particularly sensitive to macroeconomic conditions. Other cyclical industries are producers of capital goods, that is, goods used by other firms to produce their own products. When demand is slack, few companies will be expanding and purchasing capital goods. Therefore, the capital goods industry bears the brunt of a slowdown but does well in an expansion.

In contrast to cyclical firms, **defensive industries** have little sensitivity to the business cycle. These are industries that produce goods for which sales and profits are least sensitive to the state of the economy. Defensive industries include food producers and processors, pharmaceutical firms, and public utilities. These industries will outperform others when the economy enters a recession.

The cyclical/defensive classification corresponds well to the notion of systematic or market risk introduced in our discussion of portfolio theory. When perceptions about the health of the economy become more optimistic, for example, the prices of most stocks will increase as forecasts of profitability rise. Because the cyclical firms are most sensitive to such developments, their stock prices will rise the most. Thus firms in cyclical industries

Figure 17.3
Cyclical indicators.

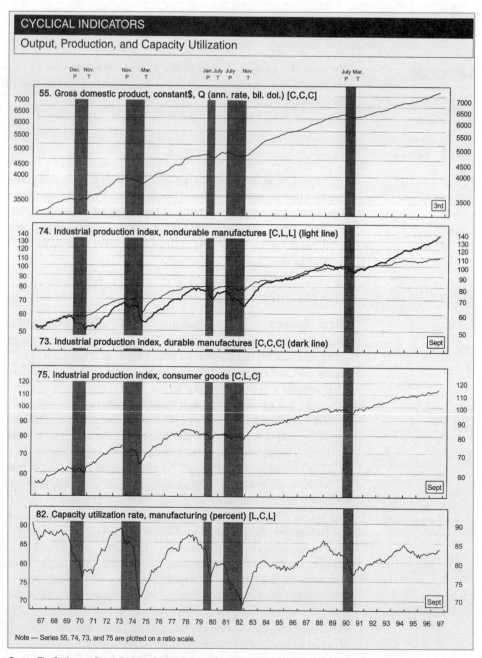

will tend to have high-beta stocks. In general, then, stocks of cyclical firms will show the best results when economic news is positive but the worst results when that news is bad. Conversely, defensive firms will have low betas and performance that is relatively unaffected by overall market conditions.

If your assessments of the state of the business cycle were reliably more accurate than those of other investors, you would simply choose cyclical industries when you are relatively more optimistic about the economy and defensive firms when you are relatively

Table 17.2   Indexes of Economic Indicators

A. Leading indicators

1. Average weekly hours of production workers (manufacturing)
2. Initial claims for unemployment insurance
3. Manufacturers' new orders (consumer goods and materials industries)
4. Vendor performance—slower deliveries diffusion index
5. Contracts and orders for plant and equipment
6. New private housing units authorized by local building permits
7. Interest rate spread, 10-year Treasury minus federal funds rate
8. Stock prices, 500 common stocks
9. Money supply
10. Index of consumer expectations

B. Coincident indicators

1. Employees on nonagricultural payrolls
2. Personal income less transfer payments
3. Industrial production
4. Manufacturing and trade sales

C. Lagging indicators

1. Average duration of unemployment
2. Ratio of trade inventories to sales
3. Change in index of labor cost per unit of output
4. Average prime rate charged by banks
5. Commercial and industrial loans outstanding
6. Ratio of consumer installment credit outstanding to personal income
7. Change in consumer price index for services

Source: The Conference Board, *Business Cycle Indicators*, November 1997.

more pessimistic. Unfortunately, it is not so easy to determine when the economy is passing through a peak or a trough. It if were, choosing between cyclical and defensive industries would be easy. As we know from our discussion of efficient markets, however, attractive investment choices will rarely be obvious. It usually is not apparent that a recession or expansion has started or ended until several months after the fact. With hindsight, the transitions from expansion to recession and back might be apparent, but it is often quite difficult to say whether the economy is heating up or slowing down at any moment.

Economic Indicators

Given the cyclical nature of the business cycle, it is not surprising that to some extent the cycle can be predicted. A set of cyclical indicators computed by the Conference Board helps forecast, measure, and interpret short-term fluctuations in economic activity. **Leading economic indicators** are those economic series that tend to rise or fall in advance of the rest of the economy. *Coincident and lagging indicators*, as their names suggest, move in tandem with or somewhat after the broad economy.

Ten series are grouped into a widely followed composite index of leading economic indicators. Similarly, four coincident and seven lagging indicators form separate indexes. The composition of these indexes appears in Table 17.2.

Figure 17.4 graphs these three series over the period 1958–1997. The numbers on the charts near the turning points of each series indicate the length of the lead time or lag time (in months) from the turning point to the designated peak or trough of the corresponding business cycle. Although the index of leading indicators consistently turns before the rest of the economy, the lead time is somewhat erratic. Moreover, the lead time for peaks is consistently longer than that for troughs.

Figure 17.4
Indexes of leading, coincident, and lagging indicators.

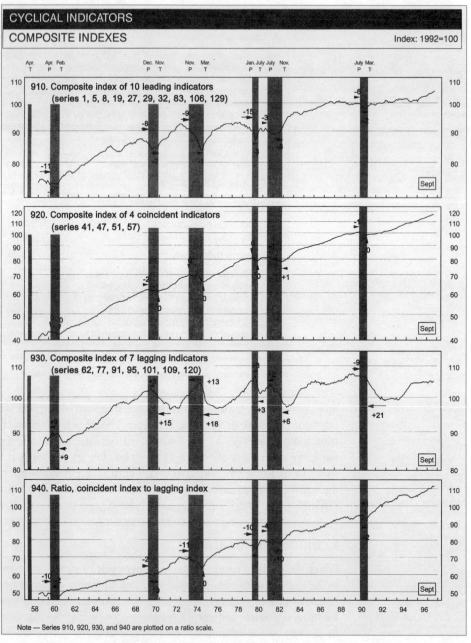

Source: The Conference Board, *Business Cycle Indicators*, November 1997.

The stock market price index is a leading indicator. This is as it should be, as stock prices are forward-looking predictors of future profitability. Unfortunately, this makes the series of leading indicators much less useful for investment policy—by the time the series predicts an upturn, the market his already made its move. Although the business cycle may be somewhat predictable, the stock market may not be. This is just one more manifestation of the efficient markets hypothesis.

Figure 17.5
Earnings growth
estimates in several
industries

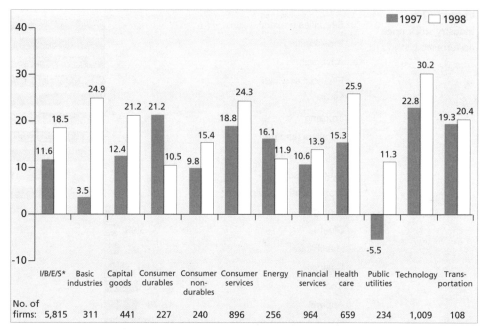

*Institutional Brokers Estimate System.
Source: *U.S. Comments*, December 3, 1997. Institutional Brokers Estimate System (I/B/E/S).

The money supply is another indicator. This makes sense in light of our earlier discussion concerning the lags surrounding the effects of monetary policy on the economy. An expansionary monetary policy can be observed fairly quickly, but it might not affect the economy for several months. Therefore, today's monetary policy might well predict future economic activity.

Other leading indicators focus directly on decisions made today that will affect production in the near future. For example, manufacturers' new orders for goods, contracts and orders for plant and equipment, and housing starts all signal a coming expansion in the economy.

17.6 INDUSTRY ANALYSIS

Industry analysis is important for the same reason that macroeconomic analysis is. Just as it is difficult for an industry to perform well when the macroeconomy is ailing, it is unusual for a firm in a troubled industry to perform well. Similarly, just as we have seen that economic performance can vary widely across countries, performance also can vary widely across industries. Figure 17.5 illustrates the dispersion of industry performance. It shows projected growth in earnings per share in 1998 for several major industry groups. The forecasts, which come from a survey of industry analysts, range from 10.5% for consumer durables to 30.2% for technology firms.

Industry groups show even more dispersion in their stock market performance. Figure 17.6 illustrates the performance of the 10 best- and 10 worst-performing industries in 1997. The spread in performance is remarkable, ranging from an 80.0% return for the security brokerage industry to a 33.5% loss in the footwear industry.

Figure 17.6
Industry stock price
performance, 1997.

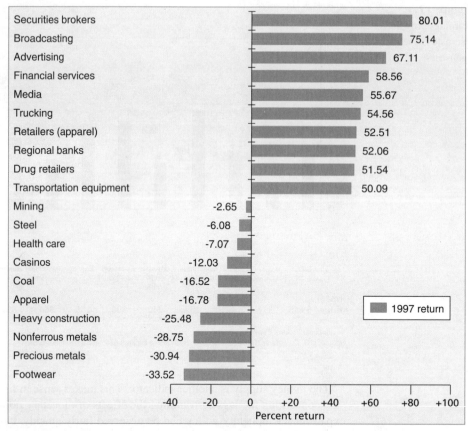

Defining an Industry

Although we know what we mean by an "industry," it can be difficult in practice to decide where to draw the line between one industry and another. Consider, for example, the health care industry. Figure 17.5 shows that the forecast for 1998 growth in industry earnings per share was 25.9%. But the health care "industry" contains firms with widely differing products and prospects. Figure 17.7 breaks down the industry into six subgroups. The forecasted performance on these more narrowly defined groups differs widely, suggesting that they are not members of a homogeneous industry. Similarly, most of these subgroups in Figure 17.7 could be divided into even smaller and more homogeneous groups.

A useful way to define industry groups in practice is given by *Standard Industry Classification*, or **SIC codes**. These are codes assigned by the U.S. government for the purpose of grouping firms for statistical analysis. The first two digits of the SIC codes denote very broad industry classifications. For example, the SIC codes assigned to any type of building contractor all start with 15. The third and fourth digits define the industry grouping more narrowly. For example, codes starting with 152 denote *residential* building contractors, and group 1521 contains *single-family* building contractors. Firms with the same four-digit SIC code, therefore, are commonly taken to be in the same industry. Many statistics are computed for even more narrowly defined five-digit SIC groups.

SIC industry classifications are not perfect. For example, both J.C. Penney and Neiman Marcus are in group 5311, Department Stores. Yet the former is a high-volume "value"

Figure 17.7

Earnings estimates for health care industries.

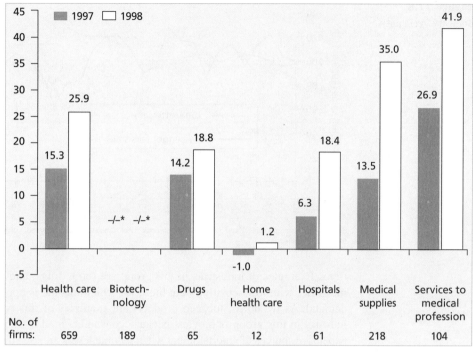

Source: *U.S. Comments*, December 3, 1997. Institutional Brokers Estimate System (I/B/E/S).

store, whereas the latter is a high-margin elite retailer. Are they really in the same industry? Still, SIC classifications are a tremendous aid in conducting industry analysis since they provide a means of focusing on very broad or fairly narrowly defined groups of firms.

Several other industry classifications are provided by other analysts, for example, Standard & Poor's reports on the performance of about 100 industry groups. S&P computes stock price indexes for each group, which is useful in assessing past investment performance. The *Value Line Investment Survey* reports on the conditions and prospects of about 1,700 firms, grouped into about 90 industries. Value Line's analysts prepare forecasts of the performance of industry groups as well as of each firm.

Sensitivity to the Business Cycle

Once the analyst forecasts the state of the macroeconomy, it is necessary to determine the implication of that forecast for specific industries. Not all industries are equally sensitive to the business cycle. For example, consider Figure 17.8, which is a graph of automobile production and shipments of cigarettes, both scaled so that 1963 has a value of 100.

Clearly, the cigarette industry is virtually independent of the business cycle. Demand for cigarettes does not seem affected by the state of the macroeconomy in any meaningful way. This is not surprising. Cigarette consumption is determined largely by habit and is a small enough part of most budgets that it will not be given up in hard times.

Auto production, by contrast, is highly volatile. In recessions, consumers can try to prolong the lives of their cars until their income is higher. For example, the worst year for auto production, according to Figure 17.8, was 1982. This was also a year of deep recession, with the unemployment rate at 9.5%.

Three factors will determine the sensitivity of a firm's earnings to the business cycle. First is the sensitivity of sales. Necessities will show little sensitivity to business condi-

Figure 17.8
Industry cyclicality.

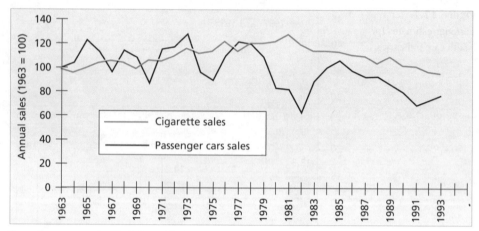

Source: Passenger car sales: *Ward's Automobile Yearbook*, 1994. Cigarette sales: Department of Alcohol, Tobacco, and Firearms Statistical Releases.

tions. Examples of industries in this group are food, drugs, and medical services. Other industries with low sensitivity are those for which income is not a crucial determinant of demand. As we noted, tobacco products are examples of this type of industry. Another industry in this group is movies, because consumers tend to substitute movies for more expensive sources of entertainment when income levels are low. In contrast, firms in industries such as machine tools, steel, autos, and transportation are highly sensitive to the state of the economy.

The second factor determining business cycle sensitivity is operating leverage, which refers to the division between fixed and variable costs. (Fixed costs are those the firm incurs regardless of its production levels. Variable costs are those that rise or fall as the firm produces more or less product.) Firms with greater amounts of variable as opposed to fixed costs will be less sensitive to business conditions. This is because in economic downturns, these firms can reduce costs as output falls in response to falling sales. Profits for firms with high fixed costs will swing more widely with sales because costs do not move to offset revenue variability. Firms with high fixed costs are said to have high operating leverage, as small swings in business conditions can have large impacts on profitability.

An example might help illustrate this concept. Consider two firms operating in the same industry with identical revenues in all phases of the business cycle: recession, normal, and expansion. Firm A has short-term leases on most of its equipment and can reduce its lease expenditures when production slackens. It has fixed costs of $5 million and variable costs of $1 per unit of output. Firm B has long-term leases on most of its equipment and must make lease payments regardless of economic conditions. Its fixed costs are higher, $8 million, but its variable costs are only $.50 per unit. Table 17.3 shows that Firm A will do better in recessions than Firm B, but not as well in expansions. A's costs move in conjunction with its revenues to help performance in downturns and impede performance in upturns.

We can quantify operating leverage by measuring how sensitive profits are to changes in sales. The **degree of operating leverage**, or DOL, is defined as

$$\text{DOL} = \frac{\text{Percentage change in profits}}{\text{Percentage change in sales}}$$

DOL greater than 1 indicates some operating leverage. For example, if DOL = 2, then for every 1% change in sales, profits will change by 2% in the same direction, either up or down.

Table 17.3   Operating Leverage

Scenario:	Recession		Normal		Expansion	
Firm:	**A**	**B**	**A**	**B**	**A**	**B**
Sales (million units)	5	5	6	6	7	7
Price per unit	$ 2	$ 2	$ 2	$ 2	$ 2	$ 2
Revenue ($ million)	10	10	12	12	14	14
Fixed Costs ($ million)	5	8	5	8	5	8
Variable costs ($ million)	5	2.5	6	3	7	3.5
Total costs ($ million)	$10	$10.5	$11	$11	$12	$11.5
Profits	$ 0	$ (0.5)	$ 1	$ 1	$ 2	$ 2.5

We have seen that the degree of operating leverage increases with a firm's exposure to fixed costs. In fact, one can show that DOL depends on fixed costs in the following manner:[1]

$$DOL = 1 + \frac{\text{Fixed costs}}{\text{Profits}}$$

As a concrete example of operating leverage, return to the two firms illustrated in Table 17.3 and compare profits and sales in the "normal" scenario for the economy with those in a recession. Profits of Firm A fall by 100% (from $1 million to zero) when sales fall by 16.7% (from $6 million to $5 million):

$$DOL(\text{Firm A}) = \frac{\text{Percentage change in profits}}{\text{Percentage change in sales}} = \frac{-100\%}{-16.7\%} = 6$$

We can confirm the relationship between DOL and fixed costs as follows:

$$DOL(\text{Firm A}) = 1 + \frac{\text{Fixed costs}}{\text{Profits}} = 1 + \frac{\$5 \text{ million}}{\$1 \text{ million}} = 6$$

Firm B has higher fixed costs, and its operating leverage is higher. Again, compare data for a normal scenario to a recession. Profits for Firm B fall by 150%, from $1 million to –$.5 million. Operating leverage for Firm B is therefore

$$DOL(\text{Firm B}) = \frac{\text{Percentage change in profits}}{\text{Percentage change in sales}} = \frac{-150\%}{-16.7\%} = 9$$

which reflects its higher level of fixed costs:

$$DOL(\text{Firm B}) = 1 + \frac{\text{Fixed costs}}{\text{Profits}} = 1 + \frac{\$8 \text{ million}}{\$1 \text{ million}} = 9$$

The third factor influencing business cycle sensitivity is financial leverage, which is the use of borrowing. Interest payments on debt must be paid regardless of sales. They are fixed costs that also increase the sensitivity of profits to business conditions. (We will have more to say about financial leverage in Chapter 19.)

Investors should not always prefer industries with lower sensitivity to the business cycle. Firms in sensitive industries will have high-beta stocks and are riskier. But while they swing lower in downturns, they also swing higher in upturns. As always, the issue you

---

[1]Operating leverage and DOL are treated in more detail in most corporate finance texts.

need to address is whether the expected return on the investment is fair compensation for the risks borne.

Question 4 • **What will be profits in the three scenarios for Firm C with fixed costs of $2 million and variable costs of $1.50 per unit? What are your conclusions regarding operating leverage and business risk?**

Industry Life Cycles

Examine the biotechnology industry and you will find many firms with high rates of investment, high rates of return on investment, and low dividend payout rates. Do the same for the public utility industry and you will find lower rates of return, lower investment rates, and higher dividend payout rates. Why should this be?

The biotech industry is still new. Recently, available technologies have created opportunities for highly profitable investment of resources. New products are protected by patents, and profit margins are high. With such lucrative investment opportunities, firms find it advantageous to put all profits back into the firm. The companies grow rapidly on average.

Eventually, however, growth must slow. The high profit rates will induce new firms to enter the industry. Increasing competition will hold down prices and profit margins. New technologies become proven and more predictable, risk levels fall, and entry becomes even easier. As internal investment opportunities become less attractive, a lower fraction of profits are reinvested in the firm. Cash dividends increase.

Ultimately, in a mature industry, we observe "cash cows," firms with stable dividends and cash flows and little risk. Growth rates might be similar to that of the overall economy. Industries in early states of their life cycles offer high-risk/high-potential-return investments. Mature industries offer lower-risk, lower-return combinations.

This analysis suggests that a typical **industry life cycle** might be described by four stages: a start-up stage, characterized by extremely rapid growth; a consolidation stage, characterized by growth that is less rapid but still faster than that of the general economy; a maturity state, characterized by growth no faster than the general economy; and a stage of relative decline, in which the industry grows less rapidly than the rest of the economy, or actually shrinks. This industry life cycle is illustrated in Figure 17.9. Let us turn to an elaboration of each of these stages.

Figure 17.9

The industry life cycle.

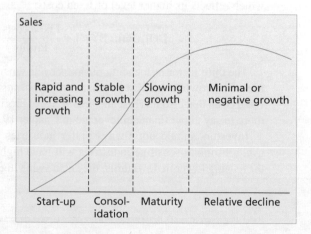

Start-Up Stage   The early stages of an industry are often characterized by a new technology or product such as VCRs or personal computers in the 1980s, or bioengineering in the 1990s. At this stage, it is difficult to predict which firms will emerge as industry leaders. Some firms will turn out to be wildly successful, and others will fail altogether. Therefore, there is considerable risk in selecting one particular firm within the industry.

At the industry level, however, sales and earnings will grow at an extremely rapid rate, because the new product has not yet saturated its market. For example, in 1980 very few households had VCRs. The potential market for the product therefore was the entire set of television-watching households. In contrast to this situation, consider the market for a mature product like refrigerators. Almost all households in the United States already have refrigerators, so the market for this good is primarily comprised of households replacing old refrigerators. Obviously, the growth rate in this market will be far less than for VCRs.

Consolidation Stage   After a product becomes established, industry leaders begin to emerge. The survivors from the start-up stage are more stable, and market share is easier to predict. Therefore, the performance of the surviving firms will more closely track the performance of the overall industry. The industry still grows faster than the rest of the economy as the product penetrates the marketplace and becomes more commonly used.

Maturity Stage   At this point, the product has reached its full potential for use by consumers. Further growth might merely track growth in the general economy. The product has become far more standardized, and producers are forced to compete to a greater extent on the basis of price. This leads to narrower profit margins and further pressure on profits. Firms at this stage sometimes are characterized as cash cows, having reasonably stable cash flow but offering little opportunity for profitable expansion. The cash flow is best "milked from" rather than reinvested in the company.

Relative Decline   In this stage, the industry might grow at less than the rate of the overall economy, or it might even shrink. This could be due to obsolescence of the product, competition from new products, or competition from new low-cost suppliers.

At which stage in the life cycle are investments in an industry most attractive? Conventional wisdom is that investors should seek firms in high-growth industries. This recipe for success is simplistic, however. If the security prices already reflect the likelihood for high growth, then it is too late to make money from that knowledge. Moreover, high growth and fat profits encourage competition from other producers. The exploitation of profit opportunities brings about new sources of supply that eventually reduce prices, profits, investment returns, and finally growth. This is the dynamic behind the progression from one stage of the industry life cycle to another. The famous portfolio manager Peter Lynch makes this point in *One Up on Wall Street*:

> Many people prefer to invest in a high-growth industry, where there's a lot of sound and fury. Not me. I prefer to invest in a low-growth industry. . . . In a low-growth industry, especially one that's boring and upsets people [such as funeral homes or the oil-drum retrieval business], there's no problem with competition. You don't have to protect your flanks from potential rivals . . . and this gives you the leeway to continue to grow. [p. 131]

In fact, Lynch uses an industry classification system in a very similar spirit to the life-cycle approach we have described. He places firms in the following six groups:

Slow Growers   Large and aging companies that will grow only slightly faster than the broad economy. These firms have matured from their earlier fast-growth phase. They usually have steady cash flow and pay a generous dividend, indicating that the firm is generating more cash than can be profitably reinvested in the firm.

Stalwarts   Large, well-known firms like Coca-Cola, Hershey's, or Colgate-Palmolive. They grow faster than the slow growers, but are not in the very rapid growth start-up stage. They also tend to be in noncyclical industries that are relatively unaffected by recessions.

Fast Growers   Small and aggressive new firms with annual growth rates in the neighborhood of 20% to 25%. Company growth can be due to broad industry growth or to an increase in market share in a more mature industry.

Cyclicals   These are firms with sales and profits that regularly expand and contract along with the business cycle. Examples are auto companies (see Figure 17.8 again), steel companies, or the construction industry.

Turnarounds   These are firms that are in bankruptcy or soon might be. If they can recover from what might appear to be imminent disaster, they can offer tremendous investment returns. A good example of this type of firm would be Chrysler in 1982, when it required a government guarantee on its debt to avoid bankruptcy. The stock price rose fifteenfold in the next five years.

Asset Plays   These are firms that have valuable assets not currently reflected in the stock price. For example, a company may own or be located on valuable real estate that is worth as much or more than the company's business enterprises. Sometimes the hidden asset can be tax-loss carryforwards. Other times the assets may be intangible. For example, a cable company might have a valuable list of cable subscribers. These assets do not immediately generate cash flow, and so may be more easily overlooked by other analysts attempting to value the firm.

Industry Structure and Performance

The maturation of an industry involves regular changes in the firm's competitive environment. As a final topic, we examine the relationship among industry structure, competitive strategy, and profitability. Michael Porter[2] has highlighted these five determinants of competition: threat of entry from new competitors, rivalry between existing competitors, price pressure from substitute products, bargaining power of buyers, and bargaining power of suppliers.

Threat of Entry   New entrants to an industry put pressure on price and profits. Even if a firm has not yet entered an industry, the potential for it to do so places pressure on prices, because high prices and profit margins will encourage entry by new competitors. Therefore, barriers to entry can be a key determinant of industry profitability. Barriers can take many forms. For example, existing firms may already have secure distribution channels for their products based on longstanding relationships with customers or suppliers that would be costly for a new entrant to duplicate. Brand loyalty also makes it difficult for new entrants to penetrate a market and gives firms more pricing discretion. Proprietary knowledge or patent protection also may give firms advantages in serving a market. Finally, an

---

[2]Michael Porter, *Competitive Advantage: Creating and Sustaining Superior Performance* (New York: Free Press, 1985).

existing firm's experience in a market may give it cost advantages due to the learning that takes place over time.

Rivalry between Existing Competitors When there are several competitors in an industry, there will generally be more price competition and lower profit margins as competitors seek to expand their share of the market. Slow industry growth contributes to this competition, because expansion must come at the expense of a rival's market share. High fixed costs also create pressure to reduce prices, because fixed costs put greater pressure on firms to operate near full capacity. Industries producing relatively homogeneous goods are also subject to considerable price pressure, because firms cannot compete on the basis of product differentiation.

Pressure from Substitute Products Substitute products means that the industry faces competition from firms in related industries. For example, sugar producers compete with corn syrup producers. Wool producers compete with synthetic fiber producers. The availability of substitutes limits the prices that can be charged to customers.

Bargaining Power of Buyers If a buyer purchases a large fraction of an industry's output, it will have considerable bargaining power and can demand price concessions. For example, auto producers can put pressure on suppliers of auto parts. This reduces the profitability of the auto parts industry.

Bargaining Power of Suppliers If a supplier of a key input has monopolistic control over the product, it can demand higher prices for the good and squeeze profits out of the industry. One special case of this issue pertains to organized labor as a supplier of a key input to the production process. Labor unions engage in collective bargaining to increase the wages paid to workers. When the labor market is highly unionized, a significant share of the potential profits in the industry can be captured by the work force.

The key factor determining the bargaining power of suppliers is the availability of substitute products. If substitutes are available, the supplier has little clout and cannot extract higher prices.

SUMMARY

1. Macroeconomic policy aims to maintain the economy near full employment without aggravating inflationary pressures. The proper trade-off between these two goals is a source of ongoing debate.

2. The traditional tools of macropolicy are government spending and tax collection, which comprise fiscal policy, and manipulation of the money supply via monetary policy. Expansionary fiscal policy can stimulate the economy and increase GDP but tends to increase interest rates. Expansionary monetary policy works by lowering interest rates.

3. The business cycle is the economy's recurring pattern of expansions and recessions. Leading economic indicators can be used to anticipate the evolution of the business cycle because their values tend to change before those of other key economic variables.

4. Industries differ in their sensitivity to the business cycle. More sensitive industries tend to be those producing high-priced durable goods for which the consumer has considerable discretion as to the timing of purchase. Examples are automobiles or consumer durables. Other sensitive industries are those that produce capital equipment for

other firms. Operating leverage and financial leverage increase sensitivity to the business cycle.

Key Terms

fundamental analysis	supply shock	cyclical industries
exchange rate	fiscal policy	defensive industries
gross domestic product	monetary policy	leading economic indicators
unemployment rate	business cycle	SIC codes
inflation	peak	degree of operating leverage
budget deficit	trough	industry life cycle
demand shock		

Selected Readings

Overviews of the macroeconomy appear regularly in several business periodicals. Try, for example:
  Business Week, Financial World, Fortune, or *Forbes*
More formal evaluations of the economy appear in:
  The Economic Report of the President (annually) and the *Survey of Current Business* (weekly).

Problems

1. What monetary and fiscal policies might be prescribed for an economy in a deep recession?

2. Unlike other investors, you believe the Fed is going to loosen monetary policy. What would be your recommendations about investments in the following industries?
   a. Gold mining.
   b. Construction.

3. Briefly discuss what actions the U.S. Federal Reserve would likely take in pursuing an *expansionary* monetary policy using each of the following three monetary tools:
   a. Reserve requirements.
   b. Open market operations.
   c. Discount rate.

4. An unanticipated expansionary monetary policy has been implemented. Indicate the impact of this policy on each of the following four variables:
   a. Inflation rate.
   b. Real output and employment.
   c. Real interest rate.
   d. Nominal interest rate.

5. If you believe the U.S. dollar will depreciate more dramatically than do other investors, what will be your stance on investments in U.S. auto producers?

6. According to supply-side economists, what will be the long-run impact on prices of a reduction in income tax rates?

7. Consider two firms producing videocassette recorders. One uses a highly automated robotics process, whereas the other uses workers on an assembly line and pays overtime when there is heavy production demand.
   a. Which firm will have higher profits in a recession? In a boom?
   b. Which firm's stock will have a higher beta?

8. Here are four industries and four forecasts for the macroeconomy. Match the industry to the scenario in which it is likely to perform best.

Industry	Economic Forecast
a. Housing construction *b.* Health care *c.* Gold mining *d.* Steel production	(i.) *Deep recession:* falling inflation, interest rates, and GDP (ii.) *Superheated economy:* rapidly rising GDP, increasing inflation and interest rates (iii.) *Healthy expansion:* rising GDP, mild inflation, low unemployment (iv.) *Stagflation:* falling GDP, high inflation

9. In which stage of the industry life cycle would you place the following industries? (Warning: There is often considerable room for disagreement concerning the "correct" answers to this question.)
   a. Oil well equipment.
   b. Computer hardware.
   c. Computer software.
   d. Genetic engineering.
   e. Railroads.

10. For each pair of firms, choose the one that you think would be more sensitive to the business cycle.
    a. General Autos or General Pharmaceuticals.
    b. Friendly Airlines or Happy Cinemas.

11. Choose an industry and identify the factors that will determine its performance in the next three years. What is your forecast for performance in that time period?

12. Why do you think the index of consumer expectations is a useful leading indicator of the macroeconomy? (See Table 17.2.)

13. Why do you think the change in the index of labor cost per unit of output is a useful lagging indicator of the macroeconomy? (See Table 17.2.)

14. Universal Auto is a large multinational corporation headquartered in the United States. For segment reporting purposes, the company is engaged in two businesses: production of motor vehicles and information processing services.

    The motor vehicle business is by far the larger of Universal's two segments. It consists mainly of domestic U.S. passenger car production, but it also includes small truck manufacturing operations in the United States and passenger car production in other countries. This segment of Universal has had weak operating results for the past several years, including a large loss in 1996. Although the company does not reveal the operating results of its domestic passenger car segments, that part of Universal's business is generally believed to be primarily responsible for the weak performance of its motor vehicle segment.

    Idata, the information processing services segment of Universal, was started by Universal about 15 years ago. This business has shown strong, steady growth that has been entirely internal; no acquisitions have been made.

    An excerpt from a research report on Universal prepared by Paul Adams, a CFA candidate, states: "Based on our assumption that Universal will be able to increase prices significantly on U.S. passenger cars in 1997, we project a multibillion dollar profit improvement."
    a. Discuss the concept of an industrial life cycle by describing each of its four phases.
    b. Identify where each of Universal's two primary businesses—passenger cars and information processing—is in such a cycle.

c. Discuss how product pricing should differ between Universal's two businesses, based on the location of each in the industrial life cycle.

15. Adams's research report (see the preceding problem) continued as follows: "With a business recovery already under way, the expected profit surge should lead to a much higher price for Universal Auto stock. We strongly recommend purchase."
    a. Discuss the business cycle approach to investment timing. (Your answer should describe actions to be taken on both stocks and bonds at different points over a typical business cycle.)
    b. Assuming Adams's assertion is correct (that a business recovery is already under way), evaluate the timeliness of his recommendation to purchase Universal Auto, a cyclical stock, based on the business cycle approach to investment timing.

16. General Weedkillers dominates the chemical weed control market with its patented product Weed-ex. The patent is about to expire, however. What are your forecasts for changes in the industry? Specifically, what will happen to industry prices, sales, the profit prospects of General Weedkillers, and the profit prospects of its competitors? What stage of the industry life cycle do you think is relevant for the analysis of this market?

17. Your business plan for your proposed start-up firm envisions first-year revenues of $120,000, fixed costs of $30,000, and variable costs equal to one-third of revenue.
    a. What are expected profits based on these expectations?
    b. What is the degree of operating leverage based on the estimate of fixed costs and expected profits?
    c. If sales are 10% below expectation, what will be the decrease in profits?
    d. Show that the percentage decrease in profits equals DOL times the 10% drop in sales.
    e. Based on the DOL, what is the largest percentage shortfall in sales relative to original expectations that the firm can sustain before profits turn negative? What are break-even sales at this point?
    f. Confirm that your answer to (*e*) is correct by calculating profits at the break-even level of sales.

18. As a securities analyst you have been asked to review a valuation of a closely held business, Wigwam Autoparts Heaven, Inc. (WAH), prepared by the Red Rocks Group (RRG). You are to give an opinion on the valuation and to support your opinion by analyzing each part of the valuation. WAH's sole business is automotive parts retailing. The RRG valuation includes a section called "Analysis of the Retail Autoparts Industry," based completely on the data in Table 17A and the following additional information:
    * WAH and its principal competitors each operated more than 150 stores at year-end 1994.
    * The average number of stores operated per company engaged in the retail autoparts industry is 5.3.
    * The major customer base for auto parts sold in retail stores consists of young owners of old vehicles. These owners do their own automotive maintenance out of economic necessity.
    a. One of RRG's conclusions is that the retail autoparts industry as a whole is in the maturity stage of the industry life cycle. Discuss three relevant items of data from Table 17A that support this conclusion.
    b. Another RRG conclusion is that WAH and its principal competitors are in the consolidation stage of their life cycle.

Table 17A   Selected Retail Autoparts Industry Data

	1994	1993	1992	1991	1990	1989	1988	1987	1986	1985
Population 18–29 years old (percentage change)	−1.8%	−2.0%	−2.1%	−1.4%	−0.8%	−0.9%	−1.1%	−0.9%	−0.7%	−0.3%
Number of households with income more than $35,000 (percentage change)	6.0%	4.0%	8.0%	4.5%	2.7%	3.1%	1.6%	3.6%	4.2%	2.2%
Number of households with income less than $35,000 (percentage change)	3.0%	−1.0%	4.9%	2.3%	−1.4%	2.5%	1.4%	−1.3%	0.6%	0.1%
Number of cars 5–15 years old (percentage change)	0.9%	−1.3%	−6.0%	1.9%	3.3%	2.4%	−2.3%	−2.2%	−8.0%	1.6%
Automotive aftermarket industry retail sales (percentage change)	5.7%	1.9%	3.1%	3.7%	4.3%	2.6%	1.3%	0.2%	3.7%	2.4%
Consumer expenditures on automotive parts and accessories (percentage change)	2.4%	1.8%	2.1%	6.5%	3.6%	9.2%	1.3%	6.2%	6.7%	6.5%
Sales growth of retail autoparts companies with 100 or more stores	17.0%	16.0%	16.5%	14.0%	15.5%	16.8%	12.0%	15.7%	19.0%	16.0%
Market share of retail autoparts companies with 100 or more stores	19.0%	18.5%	18.3%	18.1%	17.0%	17.2%	17.0%	16.9%	15.0%	14.0%
Average operating margin of retail autoparts companies with 100 or more stores	12.0%	11.8%	11.2%	11.5%	10.6%	10.6%	10.0%	10.4%	9.8%	9.0%
Average operating margin of all retail autoparts companies	5.5%	5.7%	5.6%	5.8%	6.0%	6.5%	7.0%	7.2%	7.1%	7.2%

     i. Cite three relevant items of data from Table 17A that support this conclusion.

    ii. Explain how WAH and its principal competitors can be in a consolidation stage while their industry as a whole is in the maturity stage.

 19. The following questions appeared on recent CFA examinations.

    a. Which one of the following statements *best* expresses the central idea of counter-cyclical fiscal policy?

      i. Planned government deficits are appropriate during economic booms, and planned surpluses are appropriate during economic recessions.

     ii. The balanced budget approach is the proper criterion for determining annual budget policy.

    iii. Actual deficits should equal actual surpluses during a period of deflation.

    iv. Government deficits are planned during economic recessions, and surpluses are utilized to restrain inflationary booms.

    b. The supply-side view stresses that:

      i. Aggregate demand is the major determinant of real output and aggregate employment.

     ii. An increase in government expenditures and tax rates will cause real income to rise.

    iii. Tax rates are a major determinant of real output and aggregate employment.

    iv. Expansionary monetary policy will cause real output to expand without causing the rate of inflation to accelerate.

    c. In macroeconomics, the crowding-out effect refers to:

      i. The impact of government deficit spending on inflation.

      ii. Increasing population pressures and associated movements toward zero population growth.

      iii. A situation where the unemployment rate is below its natural rate.

      iv. The impact of government borrowing on interest rates and private investment.

  d. If the exchange rate value of the British pound goes from U.S.\$1.80 to U.S.\$1.60, then the pound has:

      i. Appreciated and the British will find U.S. goods cheaper.

      ii. Appreciated and the British will find U.S. goods more expensive.

      iii. Depreciated and the British will find U.S. goods more expensive.

      iv. Depreciated and the British will find U.S. goods cheaper.

  e. The consumer price index is:

      i. A measure of the increase in the prices of the goods that are included in the calculation of GDP.

      ii. The ratio of the average price of a typical market basket of goods compared to the cost of producing those goods during the previous year.

      iii. A comparison of the cost of a typical bundle of goods during a given period with the cost of the same bundle during a prior base period.

      iv. Computed in the same manner as the GDP deflator.

  f. Changes in which of the following are likely to affect interest rates?

      I. Inflation expectations.

      II. Size of the federal deficit.

      III. Money supply.

      i. I and II only.

      ii. II and III only.

      iii. I and III only.

      iv. I, II, and III.

  g. According to the supply-side view of fiscal policy, if the impact of tax revenues is the same, does it make any difference whether the government cuts taxes by either reducing marginal tax rates or increasing the personal exemption allowance?

      i. No, both methods of cutting taxes will exert the same impact on aggregate supply.

      ii. No, people in both cases will increase their saving expecting higher future taxes and thereby offset the stimulus effect of lower current taxes.

      iii. Yes, the lower marginal tax rates alone will increase the incentive to earn marginal income and thereby stimulate aggregate supply.

      iv. Yes, interest rates will increase if marginal tax rates are lowered, whereas they will tend to decrease if the personal exemption allowance is raised.

  h. If the Federal Reserve wanted to reduce the supply of money as part of an anti-inflation policy, it might:

      i. Increase the reserve requirements.

      ii. Buy U.S. securities on the open market.

      iii. Lower the discount rate.

      iv. Buy U.S. securities directly from the Treasury.

solutions to **Concept** CHECKS

1. The downturn in the auto industry will reduce the demand for the product of this economy. The economy will, at least in the short term, enter a recession. This would suggest that:

  a. GDP will fall.

  b. The unemployment rate will rise.

    c. The government deficit will increase. Income tax receipts will fall, and government expenditures on social welfare programs probably will increase.

    d. Interest rates should fall. The contraction in the economy will reduce the demand for credit. Moreover, the lower inflation rate will reduce nominal interest rates.

2. Expansionary fiscal policy coupled with expansionary monetary policy will stimulate the economy, with the loose monetary policy keeping down interest rates.

3. A traditional demand-side interpretation of the tax cuts is that the resulting increase in after-tax income increased consumption demand and stimulated the economy. A supply-side interpretation is that the reduction in marginal tax rates made it more attractive for businesses to invest and for individuals to work, thereby increasing economic output.

4. Firm C has the lowest fixed cost and highest variable costs. It should be least sensitive to the business cycle. In fact, it is. Its profits are highest of the three firms in recessions but lowest in expansions.

	Recession	Normal	Expansion
Revenue	$10	$12	$14
Fixed cost	2	2	2
Variable cost	7.5	9	10.5
Profits	$ 0.5	$ 1	$ 1.5

CHAPTER EIGHTEEN

EQUITY VALUATION MODELS

As our discussion of market efficiency indicated, finding undervalued securities is hardly easy. At the same time, there are enough chinks in the armor of the efficient market hypothesis that the search for such securities should not be dismissed out of hand. Moreover, it is the ongoing search for mispriced securities that maintains a nearly efficient market. Even infrequent discoveries of minor mispricing justify the salary of a stock market analyst. This chapter describes the valuation models that stock market analysts use to uncover mispriced securities. The models presented are those used by *fundamental analysts,* those analysts who use information concerning the current and prospective profitability of a company to assess its fair market value. Fundamental analysts are different from *technical analysts,* who essentially use trend analysis and measures of market conditions to uncover trading opportunities. We start with a discussion of alternative measures of the value of a company. From there, we progress to quantitative tools called *dividend discount models,* which security analysts commonly  use to measure the value of a firm as an ongoing concern. Next we turn to price–earnings, or P/E, ratios, explaining why they are of such interest to analysts but also highlighting some of their shortcomings. We explain how P/E ratios are tied to dividend valuation models and, more generally, to the growth prospects of the firm.

18.1   BALANCE SHEET VALUATION METHODS

A common valuation measure is **book value**, which is the net worth of a company as shown on the balance sheet. Table 18.1 gives the balance sheet totals for Dow Chemical to illustrate how to calculate book value per share.

The book value of Dow stock on December 31, 1996, was $24.35 per share ($7,964 million divided by 327.1 million shares). On that same date, Dow stock had a market price of $78.375. Would it be fair to say Dow stock was overpriced?

The book value is established by applying a set of arbitrary accounting rules to spread the acquisition cost of assets over a specified number of years, whereas the market price of a stock takes account of the firm's value as a going concern. In other words, the market price reflects the present value of its expected future cash flows. It would be unusual if the market price of Dow stock were exactly equal to its book value.

Can book value represent a "floor" for the stock's price, below which level the market price can never fall? Although Dow's book value per share on December 31, 1996, was less than its market price, other evidence disproves this notion. On December 31, 1995, Digital Equipment Corp. stock had a book value of $36.19 per share and a market price of $34.25. Clearly, book value cannot always be a floor for the stock's price.

A better measure of a floor for the stock price is the **liquidation value** per share of the firm. This represents the amount of money that could be realized by breaking up the firm, selling its assets, repaying its debt, and distributing the remainder to the shareholders. The reasoning behind this concept is that if the market price of equity drops below the liquidation value of the firm, the firm becomes attractive as a takeover target. A corporate raider would find it profitable to buy enough shares to gain control and then actually to liquidate, because the liquidation value exceeds the value of the business as a going concern.

Another balance sheet concept that is of interest in valuing a firm is the **replacement cost** of its assets less its liabilities. Some analysts believe the market value of the firm cannot get too far above its replacement cost because if it did, competitors would try to replicate the firm. The competitive pressure of other similar firms entering the same industry would drive down the market value of all firms until they come into equality with replacement cost.

This idea is popular among economists, and the ratio of market price to replacement cost is known as **Tobin's q**, after the Nobel Prize–winning economist James Tobin. In the long run, according to this view, the ratio of market price to replacement cost will tend toward 1, but the evidence is that this ratio can differ significantly from 1 for very long periods of time.

Although focusing on the balance sheet can give some useful information about a firm's liquidation value or its replacement cost, the analyst must usually turn to expected future cash flows for a better estimate of the firm's value as a going concern. We now examine the quantitative models that analysts use to value common stock in terms of the future earnings and dividends the firm will yield.

Table 18.1   Dow Chemical Balance Sheet, December 31, 1996
($ million)

Assets	Liabilities and Owners' Equity	
$24,673	Liabilities	$16,709
	Common equity	$ 7,964
	327.1 million shares outstanding	

18.2   INTRINSIC VALUE VERSUS MARKET PRICE

The most popular model for assessing the value of a firm as a going concern takes off from the observation that an investor in stock expects a return consisting of cash dividends and capital gains or losses. We begin by assuming a one-year holding period and supposing that ABC stock has an expected dividend per share, $E(D_1)$, of \$4, the current price of a share, P_0, is \$48, and the expected price at the end of a year, $E(P_1)$, is \$52.

The holding-period return the investor expects is $E(D_1)$ plus the expected price appreciation, $E(P_1) - P_0$, all divided by the current price, P_0:

$$\text{Expected HPR} = E(r)$$

$$= \frac{E(D_1) + [E(P_1) - P_0]}{P_0}$$

$$= \frac{4 + (52 - 48)}{48} = .167, \text{ or } 16.7\%$$

Note that $E(\ )$ denotes an expected future value. Thus $E(P_1)$ represents the expectation today of the stock price one year from now. $E(r)$ is referred to as the stock's expected holding-period return. It is the sum of the expected dividend yield, $E(D_1)/P_0$, and the expected rate of price appreciation, the capital gains yield, $[E(P_1) - P_0]/P_0$.

But what is the appropriate discount rate for ABC stock? We know from the CAPM that when stock market prices are at equilibrium levels, the rate of return that investors can expect to earn on a security is $r_f + \beta[E(r_M) - r_f]$. Thus the CAPM may be viewed as providing the rate of return an investor can expect to earn on a security given its risk as measured by beta. This is the return that investors will require of any other investment with equivalent risk. We will denote this required rate of return as k. If a stock is priced "correctly," its expected return will equal the required return. Of course, the goal of a security analyst is to find stocks that are mispriced. For example, an underpriced stock will provide an expected return greater than the "fair," or required, return.

Suppose that $r_f = 6\%$, $E(r_M) - r_f = 5\%$, and the beta of ABC is 1.2. Then the value of k is

$$k = 6\% + 1.2 \times 5\% = 12\%$$

The rate of return the investor expects exceeds the required rate based on ABC's risk by a margin of 4.7%. Naturally, the investor will want to include more of ABC stock in the portfolio than a passive strategy would indicate.

Another way to see this is to compare the intrinsic value of a share of stock to its market price. The **intrinsic value**, denoted V_0, of a share of stock is defined as the present value of all cash payments to the investor in the stock, including dividends as well as the proceeds from the ultimate sale of the stock, discounted at the appropriate risk-adjusted interest rate, k. Whenever the intrinsic value, or the investor's own estimate of what the stock is really worth, exceeds the market price, the stock is considered undervalued and a good investment. In the case of ABC, using a one-year investment horizon and a forecast that the stock can be sold at the end of the year at price $P_1 = \$52$, the intrinsic value is

$$V_0 = \frac{E(D_1) + E(P_1)}{1 + k} = \frac{\$4 + \$52}{1.12} = \$50$$

Because intrinsic value, \$50, exceeds current price, \$48, we conclude the stock is undervalued in the market. We again conclude investors will want to buy more ABC than they would following a passive strategy.

If the intrinsic value turns out to be lower than the current market price, investors should buy less of it than under the passive strategy. It might even pay to go short on ABC stock, as we discussed in Chapter 3.

In market equilibrium, the current market price will reflect the intrinsic value estimates of all market participants. This means the individual investor whose V_0 estimate differs from the market price, P_0, in effect must disagree with some or all of the market consensus estimates of $E(D_1)$, $E(P_1)$, or k. A common term for the market consensus value of the required rate of return, k, is the **market capitalization rate**, which we use often throughout this chapter.

Concept

Question 1 • You expect the price of IBX stock to be $59.77 per share a year from now. Its current market price is $50, and you expect it to pay a dividend one year from now of $2.15 per share.
  a. What is the stock's expected dividend yield, rate of price appreciation, and holding-period return?
  b. If the stock has a beta of 1.15, the risk-free rate is 6% per year, and the expected rate of return on the market portfolio is 14% per year, what is the required rate of return on IBX stock?
  c. What is the intrinsic value of IBX stock, and how does it compare to the current market price?

18.3   DIVIDEND DISCOUNT MODELS

Consider an investor who buys a share of Steady State Electronics stock, planning to hold it for one year. The intrinsic value of the share is the present value of the dividend to be received at the end of the first year, D_1, and the expected sales price, P_1. We will henceforth use the simpler notation P_1 instead of $E(P_1)$ to avoid clutter. Keep in mind, though, that future prices and dividends are unknown, and we are dealing with expected values, not certain values. We've already established

$$V_0 = \frac{D_1 + P_1}{1 + k} \tag{18.1}$$

Although this year's dividends are fairly predictable given a company's history, you might ask how we can estimate P_1, the year-end price. According to equation 18.1, V_1 (the year-end intrinsic value) will be

$$V_1 = \frac{D_2 + P_2}{1 + k}$$

If we assume the stock will be selling for its intrinsic value next year, then $V_1 = P_1$, and we can substitute this value for P_1 into equation 18.1 to find

$$V_0 = \frac{D_1}{1 + k} + \frac{D_2 + P_2}{(1 + k)^2}$$

This equation may be interpreted as the present value of dividends plus sales price for a two-year holding period. Of course, now we need to come up with a forecast of P_2. Continuing in the same way, we can replace P_2 by $(D_3 + P_3)/(1 + k)$, which relates P_0 to the value of dividends plus the expected sales price for a three-year holding period.

More generally, for a holding period of H years, we can write the stock value as the present value of dividends over the H years, plus the ultimate sale price, P_H:

$$V_0 = \frac{D_1}{1+k} + \frac{D_2}{(1+k)^2} + \cdots + \frac{D_H + P_H}{(1+k)^H} \tag{18.2}$$

Note the similarity between this formula and the bond valuation formula developed in Chapter 14. Each relates price to the present value of a stream of payments (coupons in the case of bonds, dividends in the case of stocks) and a final payment (the face value of the bond, or the sales price of the stock). The key differences in the case of stocks are the uncertainty of dividends, the lack of a fixed maturity date, and the unknown sales price at the horizon date. Indeed, one can continue to substitute for price indefinitely, to conclude

$$V_0 = \frac{D_1}{1+k} + \frac{D_2}{(1+k)^2} + \frac{D_3}{(1+k)^3} + \cdots \tag{18.3}$$

Equation 18.3 states that the stock price should equal the present value of all expected future dividends into perpetuity. This formula is called the **dividend discount model (DDM)** of stock prices.

It is tempting, but incorrect, to conclude from equation 18.3 that the DDM focuses exclusively on dividends and ignores capital gains as a motive for investing in stock. Indeed, we assume explicitly in equation 18.1 that capital gains (as reflected in the expected sales price, P_1) are part of the stock's value. At the same time, the price at which you can sell a stock in the future depends on dividend forecasts at that time.

The reason only dividends appear in equation 18.3 is not that investors ignore capital gains. It is instead that those capital gains will be determined by dividend forecasts at the time the stock is sold. That is why in equation 18.2 we can write the stock price as the present value of dividends plus sales price for *any* horizon date. P_H is the present value at time H of all dividends expected to be paid after the horizon date. That value is then discounted back to today, time 0. The DDM asserts that stock prices are determined ultimately by the cash flows accruing to stockholders, and those are dividends.[1]

The Constant-Growth DDM

Equation 18.3 as it stands is still not very useful in valuing a stock because it requires dividend forecasts for every year into the indefinite future. To make the DDM practical, we need to introduce some simplifying assumptions. A useful and common first pass at the problem is to assume that dividends are trending upward at a stable growth rate that we will call g. Then if $g = .05$, and the most recently paid dividend was $D_0 = 3.81$, expected future dividends are

$$
\begin{aligned}
D_1 &= D_0(1+g) &= 3.81 \times 1.05 &= 4.00 \\
D_2 &= D_0(1+g)^2 &= 3.81 \times (1.05)^2 &= 4.20 \\
D_3 &= D_0(1+g)^3 &= 3.81 \times (1.05)^3 &= 4.41
\end{aligned}
$$

and so on. Using these dividend forecasts in equation 18.3, we solve for intrinsic value as

$$V_0 = \frac{D_0(1+g)}{1+k} + \frac{D_0(1+g)^2}{(1+k)^2} + \frac{D_0(1+g)^3}{(1+k)^3} + \cdots$$

---

[1]If investors never expected a dividend to be paid, then this model implies that the stock would have no value. To reconcile the fact that non–dividend-paying stocks do have a market value with this model, one must assume that investors expect that some day it may pay out some cash, even if only a liquidating dividend.

This equation can be simplified to[2]

$$V_0 = \frac{D_0(1+g)}{k-g} = \frac{D_1}{k-g} \qquad (18.4)$$

Note in equation 18.4 that we divide D_1 (not D_0) by $k - g$ to calculate intrinsic value. If the market capitalization rate for Steady State is 12%, now we can use equation 18.4 to show that the intrinsic value of a share of Steady State stock is

$$\frac{\$4.00}{.12 - .05} = \$57.14$$

Equation 18.4 is called the **constant-growth DDM**, or the Gordon model, after Myron J. Gordon, who popularized the model. It should remind you of the formula for the present value of a perpetuity. If dividends were expected not to grow, then the dividend stream would be a simple perpetuity, and the valuation formula would be[3] $V_0 = D_1/k$. Equation 18.4 is a generalization of the perpetuity formula to cover the case of a *growing* perpetuity. As g increases (for a given value of D_1), the stock price also rises.

The constant-growth DDM is valid only when g is less than k. If dividends were expected to grow forever at a rate faster than k, the value of the stock would be infinite. If an analyst derives an estimate of g that is greater than k, that growth rate must be unsustainable in the long run. The appropriate valuation model to use in this case is a multistage DDM such as that discussed below.

The constant-growth DDM is so widely used by stock market analysts that it is worth exploring some of its implications and limitations. The constant-growth rate DDM implies that a stock's value will be greater:

1. The larger its expected dividend per share.
2. The lower the market capitalization rate, k.
3. The higher the expected growth rate of dividends.

---

[2]We prove that the intrinsic value, V_0, of a stream of cash dividends growing at a constant rate g is equal to $\dfrac{D_1}{(k-g)}$ as follows. By definition,

$$V_0 = \frac{D_1}{1+k} + \frac{D_1(1+g)}{(1+k)^2} + \frac{D_1(1+g)^2}{(1+k)^3} + \cdots \qquad (a)$$

Multiplying through by $(1 + k)/(1 + g)$, we obtain

$$\frac{(1+k)}{(1+g)} V_0 = \frac{D_1}{(1+g)} + \frac{D_1}{(1+k)} + \frac{D_1(1+g)}{(1+k)^2} + \cdots \qquad (b)$$

Subtracting equation a from equation b, we find that

$$\frac{1+k}{1+g} V_0 - V_0 = \frac{D_1}{(1+g)}$$

which implies

$$\frac{(k-g)V_0}{(1+g)} = \frac{D_1}{(1+g)}$$

$$V_0 = \frac{D_1}{k-g}$$

[3]Recall from introductory finance that the present value of a $1 per year perpetuity is $1/k$. For example, if $k = 10\%$, the value of the perpetuity is $\$1/.10 = \$10$. Notice that if $g = 0$ in equation 18.4, the constant-growth DDM formula is the same as the perpetuity formula.

Another implication of the constant-growth model is that the stock price is expected to grow at the same rate as dividends. To see this, suppose Steady State stock is selling at its intrinsic value of $57.14, so that $V_0 = P_0$. Then

$$P_0 = \frac{D_1}{k - g}$$

Note that price is proportional to dividends. Therefore, next year, when the dividends paid to Steady State stockholders are expected to be higher by $g = 5\%$, price also should increase by 5%. To confirm this, note

$$D_2 = \$4(1.05) = \$4.20$$

$$P_1 = \frac{D_2}{k - g} = \frac{\$4.20}{.12 - .05} = \$60.00$$

which is 5% higher than the current price of $57.14. To generalize,

$$P_1 = \frac{D_2}{k - g} = \frac{D_1(1 + g)}{k - g} = \frac{D_1}{k - g}(1 + g)$$

$$= P_0(1 + g)$$

Therefore, the DDM implies that in the case of constant growth of dividends, the rate of price appreciation in any year will equal that constant-growth rate, g. Note that for a stock whose market price equals its intrinsic value ($V_0 = P_0$), the expected holding-period return will be

$$E(r) = \text{Dividend yield} + \text{Capital gains yield} \qquad (18.5)$$

$$= \frac{D_1}{P_0} + \frac{P_1 - P_0}{P_0} = \frac{D_1}{P_0} + g$$

This formula offers a means to infer the market capitalization rate of a stock, for if the stock is selling at its intrinsic value, then $E(r) = k$, implying that $k = D_1/P_0 + g$. By observing the dividend yield, D_1/P_0, and estimating the growth rate of dividends, we can compute k. This equation is also known as the *discounted cash flow (DCF) formula.*

This is an approach often used in rate hearings for regulated public utilities. The regulatory agency responsible for approving utility pricing decisions is mandated to allow the firms to charge just enough to cover costs plus a "fair" profit, that is, one that allows a competitive return on the investment the firm has made in its productive capacity. In turn, that return is taken to be the expected return investors require on the stock of the firm. The $D_1/P_0 + g$ formula provides a means to infer that required return.

Concept CHECK

Question 2

a. IBX's stock dividend at the end of this year is expected to be $2.15, and it is expected to grow at 11.2% per year forever. If the required rate of return on IBX stock is 15.2% per year, what is its intrinsic value?

b. If IBX's current market price is equal to this intrinsic value, what is next year's expected price?

c. If an investor were to buy IBX stock now and sell it after receiving the $2.15 dividend a year from now, what is the expected capital gain (i.e., price appreciation) in percentage terms? What is the dividend yield, and what would be the holding-period return?

Convergence of Price to Intrinsic Value

Now suppose that the current market price of ABC stock is only $48 per share and, therefore, that the stock now is undervalued by $2 per share. In this case the expected rate of price appreciation depends on an additional assumption about whether the discrepancy between the intrinsic value and the market price will disappear, and if so, when.

One fairly common assumption is that the discrepancy will never disappear and that the market price will continue to grow at rate g forever. This implies that the discrepancy between intrinsic value and market price also will grow at the same rate. In our example:

Now	Next Year
$V_0 = \$50$	$V_1 = \$50 \times 1.04 = \$52$
$P_0 = \$48$	$P_1 = \$48 \times 1.04 = \$49.92$
$V_0 - P_0 = \$2$	$V_1 - P_1 = \$2 \times 1.04 = \$2.08$

Under this assumption the expected HPR will exceed the required rate, because the dividend yield is higher than it would be if P_0 were equal to V_0. In our example the dividend yield would be 8.33% instead of 8%, so that the expected HPR would be 12.33% rather than 12%:

$$E(r) = \frac{D_1}{P_0} + g = \frac{\$4}{\$48} + .04 = .0833 + .04 = .1233$$

An investor who identifies this undervalued stock can get an expected dividend that exceeds the required yield by 33 basis points. This excess return is earned each year, and the market price never catches up to intrinsic value.

A second possible assumption is that the gap between market price and intrinsic value will disappear by the end of the year. In that case we would have $P_1 = V_1 = \$52$, and

$$E(r) = \frac{D_1}{P_0} + \frac{P_1 - P_0}{P_0} = \frac{4}{48} + \frac{52 - 48}{48} = .0833 + .0833 = .1667$$

The assumption of complete catch-up to intrinsic value produces a much larger one-year HPR. In future years the stock is expected to generate only fair rates of return.

Many stock analysts assume that a stock's price will approach its intrinsic value gradually over time—for example, over a five-year period. This puts their expected one-year HPR somewhere between the bounds of 12.33% and 16.67%.

Stock Prices and Investment Opportunities

Consider two companies, Cash Cow, Inc., and Growth Prospects, each with expected earnings in the coming year of $5 per share. Both companies could in principle pay out all of these earnings as dividends, maintaining a perpetual dividend flow of $5 per share. If the market capitalization rate were $k = 12.5\%$, both companies would then be valued at D_1/k = $5/.125 = \$40$ per share. Neither firm would grow in value, because with all earnings paid out as dividends, and no earnings reinvested in the firm, both companies' capital stock and earnings capacity would remain unchanged over time; earnings and dividends would not grow.

Actually, we are referring here to earnings net of the funds necessary to maintain the productivity of the firm's capital, that is, earnings net of "economic depreciation." In other

Figure 18.1
Dividend growth for
two earnings
reinvestment policies.

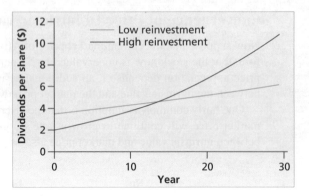

words, the earnings figure should be interpreted as the maximum amount of money the firm could pay out each year in perpetuity without depleting its productive capacity. For this reason, the net earnings number may be quite different from the accounting earnings figure that the firm reports in its financial statements. (We explore this further in the next chapter.)

Now suppose one of the firms, Growth Prospects, engages in projects that generate a return on investment of 15%, which is greater than the required rate of return, $k = 12.5\%$. It would be foolish for such a company to pay out all of its earnings as dividends. If Growth Prospects retains or plows back some of its earnings into its highly profitable projects, it can earn a 15% rate of return for its shareholders, whereas if it pays out all earnings as dividends, it forgoes the projects, leaving shareholders to invest the dividends in other opportunities at a fair market rate of only 12.5%. Suppose, therefore, that Growth Prospects lowers its **dividend payout ratio** (the fraction of earnings paid out as dividends) from 100% to 40%, maintaining a **plowback ratio** (the fraction of earnings reinvested in the firm) at 60%. The plowback ratio is also referred to as the **earnings retention ratio**.

The dividend of the company, therefore, will be $2 (40% of $5 earnings) instead of $5. Will share price fall? No—it will rise! Although dividends initially fall under the earnings reinvestment policy, subsequent growth in the assets of the firm because of reinvested profits will generate growth in future dividends, which will be reflected in today's share price.

Figure 18.1 illustrates the dividend streams generated by Growth Prospects under two dividend policies. A low-investment-rate plan allows the firm to pay higher initial dividends, but results in a lower dividend growth rate. Eventually, a high-reinvestment-rate plan will provide higher dividends. If the dividend growth generated by the reinvested earnings is high enough, the stock will be worth more under the high-reinvestment strategy.

How much growth will be generated? Suppose Growth Prospects starts with plant and equipment of $100 million and is all equity financed. With a return on investment or equity (ROE) of 15%, total earnings are ROE × $100 million = .15 × $100 million = $15 million. There are 3 million shares of stock outstanding, so earnings per share are $5, as posited above. If 60% of the $15 million in this year's earnings is reinvested, then the value of the firm's capital stock will increase by .60 × $15 million = $9 million, or by 9%. The percentage increase in the capital stock is the rate at which income was generated (ROE) times the plowback ratio (the fraction of earnings reinvested in more capital), which we will denote as b.

Now endowed with 9% more capital, the company earns 9% more income, and pays out 9% higher dividends. The growth rate of the dividends, therefore, is

$$g = \text{ROE} \times b = .15 \times .60 = .09$$

If the stock price equals its intrinsic value, it should sell at

$$P_0 = \frac{D_1}{k-g} = \frac{\$2}{.125-.09} = \$57.14$$

When Growth Prospects pursued a no-growth policy and paid out all earnings as dividends, the stock price was only $40. When it reduced current dividends and plowed funds back into the company, the growth rate increased enough to cause the stock price to increase.

The difference between the no-growth price of $40 and the actual price of $57.14 can be ascribed to the present value of the company's excellent investment opportunities. One way to think of the company's value is to describe its stock price as the sum of the no-growth value (the value of current earnings per share, E_1, in perpetuity) plus the present value of these growth opportunities, which we will denote as PVGO. In terms of the example we have been following PVGO = 17.14:

$$\text{Price} = \text{No-growth value per share} + \text{PVGO} \qquad (18.6)$$

$$P_0 = \frac{E_1}{k} + \text{PVGO}$$

$$57.14 = 40 + 17.14$$

It is important to recognize that growth per se is not what investors desire. Growth enhances company value only if it is achieved by investment in projects with attractive profit opportunities (i.e., with ROE > k). To see why, let's now consider Growth Prospects's unfortunate sister company, Cash Cow, Inc. Cash Cow's ROE is only 12.5%, just equal to the required rate of return, k. The net present value of its investment opportunities is zero. We've seen that following a zero-growth strategy with $b = 0$ and $g = 0$, the value of Cash Cow will be $E_1/k = \$5/.125 = \$40$ per share. Now suppose Cash Cow chooses a plowback ratio of $b = .60$, the same as Growth Prospects's plowback. Then g would increase to

$$g = \text{ROE} \times b$$

$$= .125 \times .60 = .075$$

but the stock price is still

$$P_0 = \frac{D_1}{k-g} = \frac{\$2}{.125-.075} = \$40$$

no different from the no-growth strategy.

In the case of Cash Cow, the dividend reduction used to free funds for reinvestment in the firm generates only enough growth to maintain the stock price at the current level. This is as it should be: If the firm's projects yield only what investors can earn on their own, shareholders cannot be made better off by a high reinvestment rate policy. This demonstrates that "growth" is not the same as growth opportunities. To justify reinvestment, the firm must engage in projects with better prospective returns than those shareholders can find elsewhere. Notice also that the PVGO of Cash Cow is zero: PVGO = $P_0 - E_1/k = 40 - 40 = 0$. With ROE = k, there is no advantage to plowing funds back into the firm; this shows up as PVGO of zero. In fact, this is why firms with considerable cash flow but limited investment prospects are called "cash cows." The cash these firms generate is best taken out of, or "milked from," the firm.

Concept CHECK   Question 3 • Calculate the price of a firm with a plowback ratio of .60 if its ROE is 20%. Current earnings, E_1, will be $5 per share, and $k = 12.5\%$. Find the PVGO for this firm. Why is PVGO so high?

Question 4 • **Takeover Target is run by entrenched and incompetent management that insists on reinvesting 60% of its earnings in projects that provide an ROE of 10%, despite the fact that the firm's capitalization rate is $k = 15\%$. The firm's year-end dividend will be $2 per share, paid out of earnings of $5 per share. At what price will the stock sell? What is the present value of growth opportunities? Why would such a firm be a target for a takeover by another firm?**

Life Cycles and Multistage Growth Models

As useful as the constant-growth DDM formula is, you need to remember that it is based on a simplifying assumption, namely, that the dividend growth rate will be constant forever. In fact, firms typically pass through life cycles with very different dividend profiles in different phases. In early years, there are ample opportunities for profitable reinvestment in the company. Payout ratios are low, and growth is correspondingly rapid. In later years, the firm matures, production capacity is sufficient to meet market demand, competitors enter the market, and attractive opportunities for reinvestment may become harder to find. In this mature phase, the firm may choose to increase the dividend payout ratio, rather than retain earnings. The dividend level increases, but thereafter it grows at a slower rate because of fewer growth opportunities.

Table 18.2 illustrates this pattern. It gives Value Line's forecasts of return on assets, dividend payout ratio, and three-year growth rate in earnings per share of a sample of the firms included in the semiconductor industry versus those in the northeast region electric utility group. (We compare return on assets rather than return on equity because the latter is affected by leverage, which tends to be far greater in the electric utility industry than in the semiconductor industry. Return on assets measures operating income per dollar of total

Table 18.2   Financial Ratios in Two Industries

	Return on Assets (%)	Payout Ratio (%)	Growth Rate, 1995–1998
Semiconductors			
Analog Devices	16.5	0.0	11.6%
Cirrus Logic	18.0	0.0	7.7%
Intel	24.0	4.0	9.8%
Micron Technologies	22.5	5.0	9.7%
Motorola	13.5	15.0	4.6%
National Semiconductor	14.0	2.0	13.4%
Novellus	16.0	0.0	11.3%
Teradyne	19.0	0.0	3.1%
Texas Instruments	18.5	13.0	3.4%
Average	18.0	4.3	8.3%
Electric Utilities			
Boston Edison	8.0	73.0	6.3%
Central Maine Power	6.5	67.0	7.2%
Central Vermont	8.0	55.0	6.1%
Commonwealth Energy	8.0	70.0	0.7%
Consolidated Edison	8.0	75.0	1.1%
Eastern Utilities	8.0	69.0	4.2%
Long Island Lighting	6.5	82.0	2.3%
New England Electric	7.5	76.0	1.5%
Northeastern Utilities	8.0	70.0	4.7%
Average	7.6	70.8	3.8%

Source: Value Line Investment Survey, 1997.

assets, regardless of whether the source of the capital supplied is debt or equity. We will return to this issue in the next chapter.)

The semiconductor firms as a group have had attractive investment opportunities. The average return on assets of these firms is forecast to be 18.0%, and the firms have responded with high plowback ratios. Many of these firms pay no dividends at all. The high return on assets and high plowback result in rapid growth. The average growth rate of earnings per share in this group is projected at 8.3%.

In contrast, the electric utilities are more representative of mature firms. Their return on assets is lower, 7.6%; dividend payout is higher, 70.8%; and average growth is lower, 3.8%.

To value companies with temporarily high growth, analysts use a multistage version of the dividend discount model. Dividends in the early high-growth period are forecast and their combined present value is calculated. Then, once the firm is projected to settle down to a steady-growth phase, the constant-growth DDM is applied to value the remaining stream of dividends.

We can illustrate this with a real-life example. Figure 18.2 is a Value Line Investment Survey report on Motorola, a designer and manufacturer of electronic equipment and components. Some of the relevant information in late 1997 is highlighted.

Motorola's beta appears at the circled A, the recent stock price at the B, the per-share dividend payments at the C, the ROE (referred to as percent earned on net worth) at the D, and the dividend payout ratio (referred to as percent of all dividends to net profits) at the E. The rows ending at C, D, and E are historical time series. The bold-faced italicized entries under 1998 are estimates for that year. Similarly, the entries in the far right column (labeled 00–02) are forecasts for some time between 2000 and 2002, which we will take to be 2001.

Note that while dividends were $.54 per share in 1998, dividends forecast for 2001 are $.85; hence Value Line forecasts rapid short-term growth in dividends, about 16.3% per year. If we use linear interpolation between 1998 and 2001, we obtain dividend forecasts as follows:

1998	$.54
1999	$.64
2000	$.74
2001	$.85

Now let us assume the dividend growth rate levels off in 2001. What is a good guess for that steady-state growth rate? Value Line forecasts a dividend payout ratio of .15 and an ROE of 15.0%, implying that long-term growth will be

$$g = \text{ROE} \times b = 15\% \times (1 - .15) = 12.75\%$$

Our estimate of Motorola's intrinsic value using an investment horizon of 2001 is therefore obtained from equation 18.2, which we restate here:

$$V_{1997} = \frac{D_{1998}}{(1+k)} + \frac{D_{1999}}{(1+k)^2} + \frac{D_{2000}}{(1+k)^3} + \frac{D_{2001} + P_{2001}}{(1+k)^4}$$

$$= \frac{.54}{(1+k)} + \frac{.64}{(1+k)^2} + \frac{.74}{(1+k)^3} + \frac{.85 + P_{2001}}{(1+k)^4}$$

Here, P_{2001} represents the forecasted price at which we can sell our shares of Motorola at the end of 2001, when dividends enter their constant-growth phase. That price, according to the constant-growth DDM, should be

$$P_{2001} = \frac{D_{2002}}{k-g} = \frac{D_{2001}(1+g)}{k-g} = \frac{.85(1.1275)}{k - .1275}$$

Figure 18.2

Value Line Investment Survey report on Motorola.

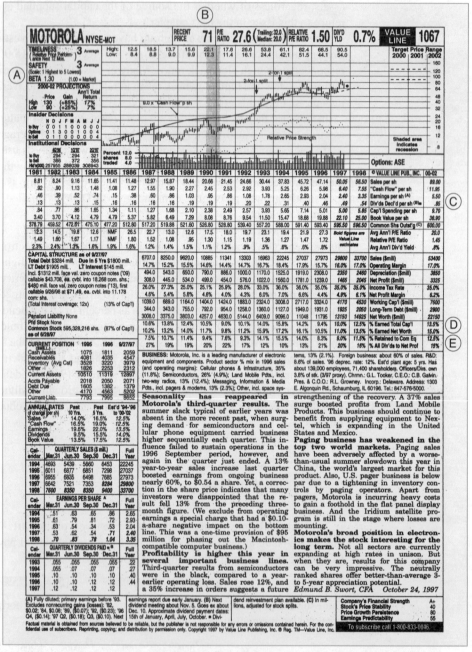

The only variable remaining to be determined in order to calculate intrinsic value is the market capitalization rate, k.

One way to obtain k is from the CAPM. Observe from the Value Line data that Motorola's beta is 1.30. The risk-free rate in late 1997 was about 5.3%. Suppose that the market risk premium were forecast at 7.0%.[4] This would imply that the forecast for the market return was

$$\text{Risk-free rate} + \text{Market risk premium} = 5.3\% + 7.0\% = 12.3\%$$

Therefore, we can solve for the market capitalization rate for Motorola as

$$k = r_f + \beta[E(r_M) - r_f]$$
$$= 5.3\% + 1.3[12.3\% - 5.3\%] = 14.4\%$$

Our guess for the stock price in 2001 is thus

$$P_{2001} = \frac{\$.85(1.1275)}{.144 - .1275} = \$58.08$$

and today's estimate of intrinsic value is

$$V_{2001} = \frac{.54}{(1.144)} + \frac{.64}{(1.144)^2} + \frac{.74}{(1.144)^3} + \frac{.85 + 58.08}{(1.144)^4} = \$35.86$$

We know from the Value Line report that Motorola's actual price was $71 (at the circled B). Our intrinsic value analysis indicates Motorola was overpriced. Should we sell our holdings of Motorola or even sell Motorola short?

Perhaps. But before betting the farm, stop to consider how firm our estimate is. We've had to guess at dividends in the near future, the ultimate growth rate of those dividends, and the appropriate discount rate. Moreover, we've assumed Motorola will follow a relatively simple two-stage growth process. In practice, the growth of dividends can follow more complicated patterns. Even small errors in these approximations could upset a conclusion.

For example, suppose that we have underestimated Motorola's growth prospects and that the actual ROE in the post-2001 period will be 16% rather than 15%, a seemingly minor change. Using the return on equity in the dividend discount model would result in an intrinsic value in 1997 of $72.42, which actually is slightly greater than the stock price. Our conclusion regarding intrinsic value versus price is reversed.

This exercise shows that finding bargains is not as easy as it seems. Although the DDM is easy to apply, establishing its inputs is more of a challenge. This should not be surprising. In even a moderately efficient market, finding profit opportunities has to be more involved than sitting down with Value Line for a half hour.

The exercise also highlights the importance of performing sensitivity analysis when you attempt to value stocks. Your estimates of stock values are no better than your assumptions. Sensitivity analysis will highlight the inputs that need to be most carefully examined. For example, we just found that very small changes in the estimated ROE rate for the post-2001 period would result in big changes in intrinsic value. Similarly, small changes in the assumed capitalization rate would change intrinsic value substantially. On the other hand,

---

[4]The historical risk premium on the market portfolio has been closer to 8.5%. However, after three banner years, stock analysts in late 1997 were increasingly wary about future market performance. Although the historical risk premium is a guide as to the typical risk premium one might expect from the market, there is no reason that the risk premium cannot vary somewhat from period to period.

reasonable changes in the dividends forecast between 1998 and 2001 would have a small impact on intrinsic value.

Concept
CHECK

Question 5 • **Confirm that the intrinsic value of Motorola using ROE = 16% is $72.42. (Hint: First calculate the stock price in 2001. Then calculate the present value of all interim dividends plus the present value of the 2001 sales price.)**

18.4   PRICE–EARNINGS RATIO

The Price–Earnings Ratio and Growth Opportunities

Much of the real-world discussion of stock market valuation concentrates on the firm's **price–earnings multiple,** the ratio of price per share to earnings per share, commonly called the P/E ratio. The nearby box, which asks whether Coke is overvalued at a P/E multiple of nearly 40, illustrates the emphasis placed on this ratio. The article also points out that the P/E ratio that can be justified for a stock can be derived from the dividend discount model of stock valuation; we will show you how to do so in this section.

Our discussion of growth opportunities shows why stock market analysts focus on the P/E ratio. Both companies considered, Cash Cow and Growth Prospects, had earnings per share (EPS) of $5, but Growth Prospects reinvested 60% of earnings in prospects with an ROE of 15%, whereas Cash Cow paid out all earnings as dividends. Cash Cow had a price of $40, giving it a P/E multiple of 40/5 = 8.0, whereas Growth Prospects sold for $57.14, giving it a multiple of 57.14/5 = 11.4. This observation suggests the P/E ratio might serve as a useful indicator of expectations of growth opportunities. We can see this explicitly by rearranging equation 18.6 to

$$\frac{P_0}{E_1} = \frac{1}{k} \left(1 + \frac{\text{PVGO}}{E/k}\right) \tag{18.7}$$

When PVGO = 0, equation 18.7 shows that $P_0 = E_1/k$. The stock is valued like a nongrowing perpetuity of EPS_1. The P/E ratio is just $1/k$. However, as PVGO becomes an increasingly dominant contributor to price, the P/E ratio can rise dramatically. The ratio of PVGO to E/k has a simple interpretation. It is the ratio of the component of firm value due to growth opportunities to the component of value due to assets already in place (i.e., the no-growth value of the firm, E/k). When future growth opportunities dominate the estimate of total value, the firm will command a high price relative to current earnings. Thus a high P/E multiple appears to indicate a firm is endowed with ample growth opportunities.

Let's see if this is so. In early 1998, Motorola's P/E ratio was 33 while Boston Edison's was only 14. These numbers do not necessarily imply Motorola was overpriced compared to Boston Edison. If investors believed at the time that Motorola would grow sufficiently faster than Boston Edison, the higher P/E multiple would be justified. That is, an investor might well pay a higher price per dollar of *current* earnings if he or she expects that earnings stream to grow rapidly. In fact, Motorola's growth rate has been consistent with its higher P/E multiple. Its earnings per share grew more than fivefold between 1981 and 1997, whereas Boston Edison earnings increased by only 32%. Figure 18.4, page 550, shows the EPS history of the two companies.

Clearly, it is differences in expected growth opportunities that justify particular differentials in P/E ratios across firms. The P/E ratio actually is a reflection of the market's optimism concerning a firm's growth prospects. In their use of a P/E ratio, analysts must decide

THE NEW MATH: ARE SOME HIGH P/E STOCKS "BARGAINS"?

Here is something investors haven't heard for a while: Coca-Cola stock is cheap.

Calling a megacapitalization blue chip trading at 38 times earnings cheap is heresy to many investors. But the fact that many strategists and even some conservative investors can now make that argument shows how the lowest interest rates in nearly two years are transforming the stock-valuation landscape.

Lower interest rates raise the present value of a company's future earnings. That is because an investor puts a higher price on future earnings if he or she will earn less in competing investments, like bonds. Furthermore, the effect accelerates the lower rates go. A drop in bond yields from 7% to 6% boosts valuations far more than the drop from 8% to 7%.

At present, all these factors are working in stocks' favor. The 30-year Treasury bond yield has plummeted and is closing in on long-term bond yields' 30-year lows set in October 1993 and December 1995. At the same time, and despite Asia's economic turmoil, long-term S&P 500 earnings growth expectations have risen.

The power of lower interest rates to boost stock valuations is most easily seen by applying the same math for valu-

ing bonds, where falling rates reward those willing to wait longest to get back their principal.

"If you said to me 'I'm bullish on interest rates, how do I get the biggest capital gain?' I'd say buy the longest-maturity security," says Edward Kerschner, chief strategist at PaineWebber.

So even though the S&P 500 today trades at a little more than 21 times current-year operating earnings, far above the average ratio of the past 30 years, that's right around fair value, by Mr. Kerschner's reckoning.

"Why do most people think Coke is expensive? They typically look at a price-earnings ratio based on 1998 earnings estimates and they think 'holy cow, that's expensive.' We look at something else. The present value of earnings in a number of years out, not just next year's earnings. With Coke, or Wrigley's, we're comfortable going out eight or 10 years," because they have consistently managed their businesses well.

Such conclusions are easily derived from the dividend discount models that are part of almost every financial analyst's tool kit.

Source: Greg Ip, "The New Math: Are Some High P/E Stocks "Bargains"? *The Wall Street Journal*, December 1, 1997. Excerpted by permission of *The Wall Street Journal*, © Dow Jones & Company, Inc. All Rights Reserved Worldwide.

whether they are more or less optimistic than the market. If they are more optimistic, they will recommend buying the stock.

There is a way to make these insights more precise. Look again at the constant-growth DDM formula, $P_0 = D_1/(k - g)$. Now recall that dividends equal the earnings that are *not* reinvested in the firm: $D_1 = E_1(1 - b)$. Recall also that $g = \text{ROE} \times b$. Hence, substituting for D_1 and g, we find that

$$P_0 = \frac{E_1(1 - b)}{k - \text{ROE} \times b}$$

implying the P/E ratio is

$$\frac{P_0}{E_1} = \frac{1 - b}{k - \text{ROE} \times b} \qquad (18.8)$$

It is easy to verify that the P/E ratio increases with ROE. This makes sense, because high-ROE projects give the firm good opportunities for growth.[5] We also can verify that the P/E ratio increases for higher b as long as ROE exceeds k. This too makes sense. When a firm has good investment opportunities, the market will reward it with a higher P/E multiple if it exploits those opportunities more aggressively by plowing back more earnings into those opportunities.

---

[5]Note that equation 18.8 is a simple rearrangement of the DDM formula, with $\text{ROE} \times b = g$. Because that formula requires that $g < k$, equation 18.8 is valid only when $\text{ROE} \times b < k$.

Table 18.3   Effect of ROE and Plowback on Growth and the P/E Ratio

	Plowback Rate (*b*)			
ROE	**0**	**.25**	**.50**	**.75**
A. Growth rate, *g*				
10%	0	2.5%	5.0%	7.5%
12	0	3.0	6.0	9.0
14	0	3.5	7.0	10.5
B. P/E ratio				
10%	8.33	7.89	7.14	5.56
12	8.33	8.33	8.33	8.33
14	8.33	8.82	10.00	16.67

Assumption: k = 12% per year.

Remember we noted, however, that growth is not desirable for its own sake. Examine Table 18.3 where we use equation 18.8 to compute both growth rates and P/E ratios for different combinations of ROE and *b*. Although growth always increases with the plowback rate (move across the rows in Table 18.3A), the P/E ratio does not (move across the rows in Panel **B**). In the top row of Table 18.3**B**, the P/E falls as the plowback rate increases. In the middle row, it is unaffected by plowback. In the third row, it increases.

This pattern has a simple interpretation. When the expected ROE is less than the required return, *k*, investors prefer that the firm pay out earnings as dividends rather than reinvest earnings in the firm at an inadequate rate of return. That is, for ROE lower than *k*, the value of the firm falls as plowback increases. Conversely, when ROE exceeds *k*, the firm offers attractive investment opportunities, so the value of the firm is enhanced as those opportunities are more fully exploited by increasing the plowback rate.

Finally, where ROE just equals *k*, the firm offers "break-even" investment opportunities with a fair rate of return. In this case, investors are indifferent between reinvestment of earnings in the firm or elsewhere at the market capitalization rate, because the rate of return in either case is 12%. Therefore, the stock price is unaffected by the plowback rate.

One way to summarize these relationships is to say the higher the plowback rate, the higher the growth rate, but a higher plowback rate does not necessarily mean a higher P/E ratio. A higher plowback rate increases P/E only if investments undertaken by the firm offer an expected rate of return higher than the market capitalization rate. Otherwise, higher plowback hurts investors because it means more money is sunk into projects with inadequate rates of return.

Notwithstanding these fine points, P/E ratios commonly are taken as proxies for the expected growth in dividends or earnings. In fact, a common Wall Street rule of thumb is that the growth rate ought to be roughly equal to the P/E ratio. Peter Lynch, the famous portfolio manager, puts it this way in his book *One Up on Wall Street*:

> The P/E ratio of any company that's fairly priced will equal its growth rate. I'm talking here about growth rate of earnings here. . . . If the P/E ratio of Coca Cola is 15, you'd expect the company to be growing at about 15% per year, etc. But if the P/E ratio is less than the growth rate, you may have found yourself a bargain. [p. 198]

Let's try his rule of thumb. Assume

$$r_f = 8\% \qquad \text{(roughly the value when Peter Lynch was writing)}$$
$$r_M - r_f = 8\% \qquad \text{(about the historical average market risk premium)}$$
$$b = .4 \qquad \text{(a typical value for the plowback ratio in the United States)}$$

Therefore, $r_M = r_f +$ Market risk premium $= 8\% + 8\% = 16\%$, and $k = 16\%$ for an average ($\beta = 1$) company. If we also accept as reasonable that ROE $= 16\%$ (the same value as the expected return on the stock), we conclude that

$$g = \text{ROE} \times b = 16\% \times .4 = 6.4\%$$

and

$$\frac{P}{E} = \frac{1 - .4}{.16 - .064} = 6.26$$

Thus the P/E ratio and g are about equal using these assumptions, consistent with the rule of thumb.

However, note that this rule of thumb, like almost all others, will not work in all circumstances. For example, the value of r_f today is more like 5%, so a comparable forecast of r_M today would be

$$r_f + \text{Market risk premium} = 5\% + 8\% = 13\%$$

If we continue to focus on a firm with $\beta = 1$, and if ROE still is about the same as k, then

$$g = 13\% \times .4 = 5.2\%$$

while

$$\frac{P}{E} = \frac{1 - .4}{.13 - .052} = 7.69$$

The P/E ratio and g now diverge. Nevertheless, it still is the case that high P/E stocks are almost invariably expected to show rapid earnings growth, even if the expected growth rate does not equal the P/E ratio.

Concept
CHECK

Question 6 • ABC stock has an expected ROE of 12% per year, expected earnings per share of \$2, and expected dividends of \$1.50 per share. Its market capitalization rate is 10% per year.
a. **What are its expected growth rate, its price, and its P/E ratio?**
b. **If the plowback rate were .4, what would be the expected dividend per share, the growth rate, price, and the P/E ratio?**

P/E Ratios and Stock Risk

One important implication of any stock valuation model is that (holding all else equal) riskier stocks will have lower P/E multiples. We can see this quite easily in the context of the constant-growth model by examining the formula for the P/E ratio (equation 18.8):

$$\frac{P}{E} = \frac{1 - b}{k - g}$$

Riskier firms will have higher required rates of return, that is, higher values of k. Therefore, the P/E multiple will be lower. This is true even outside the context of the constant-growth model. For *any* expected earnings and dividend stream, the present value of those cash flows will be lower when the stream is perceived to be riskier. Hence the stock price and the ratio of price to earnings will be lower.

Of course, if you scan *The Wall Street Journal*, you will observe many small, risky, start-up companies with very high P/E multiples. This does not contradict our claim that

Figure 18.3

P/E ratios and inflation.

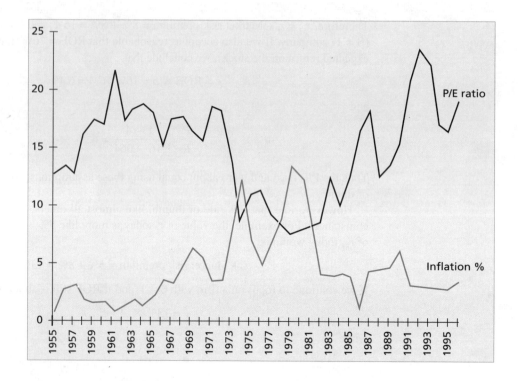

P/E multiples should fall with risk; instead it is evidence of the market's expectations of high growth rates for those companies. This is why we said that high-risk firms will have lower P/E ratios *holding all else equal.* Holding the projection of growth fixed, the P/E multiple will be lower when risk is perceived to be higher.

Pitfalls in P/E Analysis

No description of P/E analysis is complete without mentioning some of its pitfalls. First, consider that the denominator in the P/E ratio is accounting earnings, which are influenced by somewhat arbitrary accounting rules such as the use of historical cost in depreciation and inventory valuation. In times of high inflation, historic cost depreciation and inventory costs will tend to underrepresent true economic values, because the replacement cost of both goods and capital equipment will rise with the general level of prices. As Figure 18.3 demonstrates, P/E ratios have tended to be lower when inflation has been higher. This reflects the market's assessment that earnings in these periods are of "lower quality," artificially distorted by inflation, and warranting lower P/E ratios.

Another confounding factor in the use of P/E ratios is related to the business cycle. We were careful in deriving the DDM to define earnings as being net of *economic* depreciation, that is, the maximum flow of income that the firm could pay out without depleting its productive capacity. And reported earnings, as we note above, are computed in accordance with generally accepted accounting principles and need not correspond to economic earnings. Beyond this, however, notions of a normal or justified P/E ratio, as in equations 18.7 or 18.8, assume implicitly that earnings rise at a constant rate, or, put another way, on a smooth trend line. In contrast, reported earnings can fluctuate dramatically around a trend line over the course of the business cycle.

Another way to make this point is to note that the "normal" P/E ratio predicted by equation 18.8 is the ratio of today's price to the trend value of future earnings, E_1. The P/E ratio reported in the financial pages of the newspaper, by contrast, is the ratio of price to the most recent *past* accounting earnings. Current accounting earnings can differ considerably from future economic earnings. Because ownership of stock conveys the right to future as well as current earnings, the ratio of price to most recent earnings can vary substantially over the business cycle, as accounting earnings and the trend value of economic earnings diverge by greater and lesser amounts.

As an example, Figure 18.4 graphs the earnings per share of Motorola and Boston Edison since 1980. Note that Motorola's EPS fluctuate considerably. This reflects the company's relatively high degree of sensitivity to the business cycle. Value Line estimates its beta at 1.30. Boston Edison, by contrast, shows much less variation in earnings per share around a smoother and flatter trend line. Its beta was only .75.

Because the market values the entire stream of future dividends generated by the company, when earnings are temporarily depressed, the P/E ratio should tend to be high—that is, the denominator of the ratio responds more sensitively to the business cycle than the numerator. This pattern is borne out well.

Figure 18.5 graphs the Motorola and Boston Edison P/E ratios. Motorola, with the more volatile earnings profile, also has a more volatile P/E profile. For example, in 1985, when EPS fell to a far-below-trend value of \$.31, the P/E rose to 56.3. The market clearly recognized that earnings were depressed only temporarily.

This example shows why analysts must be careful in using P/E ratios. There is no way to say P/E ratio is overly high or low without referring to the company's long-run growth prospects, as well as to current earnings per share relative to the long-run trend line.

Nevertheless, Figures 18.4 and 18.5 demonstrate a clear relationship between P/E ratios and growth. Despite considerable short-run fluctuations, Motorola's EPS clearly trended upward over the period. Its compound rate of growth between 1980 and 1997 was 9.7%. Boston Edison's earnings grew less rapidly, with an average growth rate of 2.4%. The growth prospects of Motorola are reflected in its consistently higher P/E multiple.

This analysis suggests that P/E ratios should vary across industries, and in fact they do. Figure 18.6 shows P/E ratios at the end of 1997 for a sample of industries. P/E ratios for each industry are computed in two ways: by taking the ratio of price to previous year (i.e., 1997) earnings, and projected next-year earnings. Notice that although the ratios based on 1997 earnings appear quite high, the ratios are far more moderate when prices are compared to forecasted 1998 earnings. This should not surprise you, because stock market prices are based on firms' future earnings prospects.

Combining P/E Analysis and the DDM

Some analysts use P/E ratios in conjunction with earnings forecasts to estimate the price of a stock at an investor's horizon date. The Motorola analysis in Figure 18.2 shows that Value Line forecasted a P/E ratio for 2001 of 20.0. EPS for 2001 were forecast at \$5.50, implying a price in 2001 of $20 \times \$5.50 = \$110$. Given an estimate of \$110 for the 2001 sales price, we would compute Motorola's intrinsic value as

$$V_{1997} = \frac{\$.54}{(1.144)} + \frac{\$.64}{(1.144)^2} + \frac{\$.74}{(1.144)^3} + \frac{\$.85 + \$110}{(1.144)^4} = \$66.17$$

which turns out to be quite close to the \$71 market price.

Figure 18.4
Earnings per share.

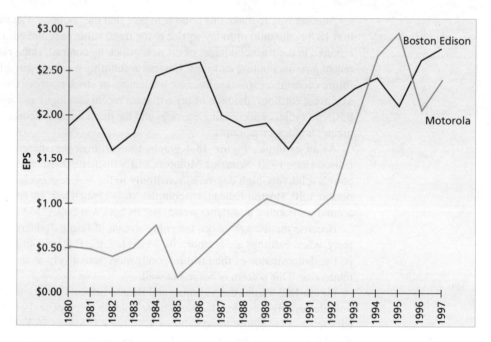

Figure 18.5
Price/earnings ratios.

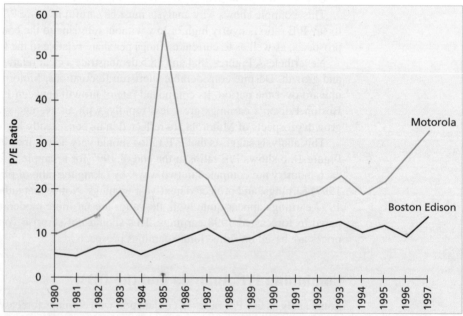

18.5 CORPORATE FINANCE AND THE FREE CASH FLOW APPROACH

In both the discounted dividend and capitalized earnings approaches to equity valuation we made the assumption that the only source of financing of new equity investment in the firm was retained earnings. How would our results be affected if we allowed external equity financing of new investments? How would they be affected if we assumed debt financing of new investments? In other words, how do dividend policy and capital structure affect the value of a firm's shares?

Figure 18.6

P/E ratios based on
1997 and 1998 EPS.

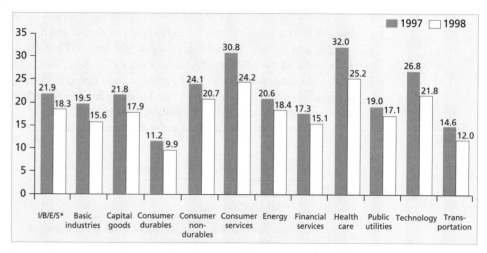

*Data for entire universe.

Source: Institutional Brokers Estimate System (I/B/E/S), *U.S. Comments*, December 3, 1997.

The classic answer to these questions was provided by Modigliani and Miller (MM) in a series of articles that have become the foundation for the modern theory of corporate finance,[6] and we will briefly explain their theory.[7]

MM claim that if we take as given a firm's future investments, then the value of its existing common stock is not affected by how those investments are financed. Therefore, neither the firm's dividend policy nor its capital structure should affect the value of a share of its equity.

The reasoning underlying the MM theory is that the intrinsic value of the equity in a firm is the present value of the net cash flows to shareholders that can be produced by the firm's existing assets plus the net present value of any investments to be made in the future. Given those existing and expected future investments, the firm's dividend and financing decisions will affect only the form in which existing shareholders will receive their future returns, that is, as dividends or capital gains, but not their present value.

As a by-product of their proof of these propositions, MM show the equivalence of three seemingly different approaches to valuing the equity in a firm. The first two are the discounted dividend and capitalized earnings approaches presented in the earlier parts of this chapter. The third is the free cash flow approach.

This third approach starts with an estimate of the value of the firm as a whole and derives the value of the equity by subtracting the market value of all nonequity claims. The estimate of the value of the firm is found as the present value of cash flows, assuming all-equity financing plus the net present value of tax shields created by using debt. This approach is similar to that used by the firm's own management in capital budgeting, or the valuation approach that another firm would use in assessing the firm as a possible acquisition target.

---

[6]The original two papers are M. Miller and F. Modigliani, "Dividend Policy, Growth and the Valuation of Shares," *Journal of Business*, October 1961; and F. Modigliani and M. Miller, "The Cost of Capital, Corporation Finance, and the Theory of Investment," *American Economic Review*, June 1958. Miller has revised his views in "Debt and Taxes," *Journal of Finance*, May 1976, and Modigliani his in "Debt, Dividend Policy, Taxes, Inflation and Market Valuation," *Journal of Finance*, May 1982.
[7]For a more complete treatment see Stephen A. Ross, Randolph W. Westerfield, and Jeffrey F. Jaffe, *Corporate Finance,* 5th ed. (Burr Ridge, IL: Irwin/McGraw-Hill, 1999), Chapters 15 and 16; or Richard A. Brealey and Stewart C. Myers, *Principles of Corporate Finance*, 5th ed. (New York: McGraw-Hill, 1996), Chapters 17 and 18.

For example, consider the MiMo Corporation. Its cash flow from operations before interest and taxes was $1 million in the year just ended, and it expects that this will grow by 6% per year forever. To make this happen, the firm will have to invest an amount equal to 15% of pretax cash flow each year. The tax rate is 30%. Depreciation was $100,000 in the year just ended and is expected to grow at the same rate as the operating cash flow. The appropriate market capitalization rate for the unleveraged cash flow is 10% per year, and the firm currently has debt of $2 million outstanding.

MiMo's projected free cash flow for the coming year is

Before-tax cash flow from operations	$1,060,000
Depreciation	106,000
Taxable income	954,000
Taxes (at 30%)	286,200
After-tax unleveraged income	667,800
After-tax cash flow from operations (after-tax unleveraged income plus depreciation)	773,800
New investment (15% of cash flow from operations)	159,000
Free cash flow (after-tax cash flow from operations minus new investment)	614,800

It is important to realize that this projected free cash flow is what the firm's cash flow would be under all-equity financing. It ignores the interest expense on the debt, as well as any tax savings resulting from the deductibility of the interest expense.

The present value of all future free cash flows is

$$V_0 = \frac{C_1}{k - g} = \frac{\$614,800}{.10 - .06} = \$15,370,000$$

Thus the value of the whole firm, debt plus equity, is $15,370,000. Because the value of the debt is $2 million, the value of the equity is $13,370,000.

If we believe that the use of financial leverage enhances the total value of the firm, then we should add to the $15,370,000 estimate of the firm's unleveraged value the gain from leverage. Thus if in our example we believe that the tax shield provided by the deductibility of interest payments on the debt increases the firm's total value by $.5 million, the value of the firm would be $15,870,000 and the value of the equity $13,870,000.

In reconciling this free cash flow approach with either the discounted dividend or the capitalized earnings approach, it is important to realize that the capitalization rate to be used in the present value calculation is different. In the free cash flow approach it is the rate appropriate for unleveraged equity, whereas in the other two approaches, it is the rate appropriate for leveraged equity. Because leverage affects the stock's beta, these two capitalization rates will be different.

18.6   INFLATION AND EQUITY VALUATION

What about the effects of inflation on stock prices? We start with an "inflation-neutral" case in which all *real* variables, and therefore the stock price, are unaffected by inflation. We then explore the ways in which reality might differ.

Consider the case of Inflatotrend, a firm that in the absence of inflation pays out all earnings as dividends. Earnings and dividends per share are $1, and there is no growth. We will use asterisked (*) letters to denote variables in the no-inflation case, or what represents the real value of variables. We consider an equilibrium real capitalization rate, k^*, of 10% per year. The price per share of this stock should be $10:

$$P_0 = \frac{\$1}{.10} = \$10$$

Now imagine that inflation, i, is 6% per year, but that the values of the other economic variables adjust so as to leave their real values unchanged. Specifically, the *nominal* capitalization rate, k, becomes $(1 + k^*)(1 + i) - 1 = 1.10 \times 1.06 - 1 = .166$, or 16.6%, and the expected nominal growth rate of dividends, g, is now 6%, which is necessary to maintain a constant level of real dividends. The *nominal* dividend expected at the end of this year is therefore $1.06 per share.

If we apply the constant-growth DDM to these nominal variables we get the same price as in the no-inflation case:

$$P_0 = \frac{D_1}{k - g} = \frac{\$1.06}{.166 - .060} = \$10$$

Thus as long as real values are unaffected, the stock's current price is unaffected by inflation.

Note that the expected nominal dividend yield, D_1/P_0, is 10.6% and the expected nominal capital gains rate, $(P_1 - P_0)/P_0$, is 6%. Almost the entire 6.6% increase in nominal return comes in the form of expected capital gains. A capital gain is necessary if the real value of the stock is to remain unaffected by inflation.

Let us see how these assumptions affect the other variables: earnings and the plowback ratio. To illuminate what otherwise may be confusing implications, we can explore a simplified story behind the examples above.

Inflatotrend produces a product that requires purchase of inventory at the beginning of each year, and sells the finished product at the end of the year. Last year there was no inflation. The inventory cost $10 million. Labor, rent, and other processing costs (paid at year-end) were $1 million, and revenue was $12 million. Assuming no taxes, earnings were $1 million:

Revenue	$12 million
− Labor and rent	1 million
− Cost of goods sold	10 million
Earnings	$ 1 million

All earnings are distributed as dividends to the 1 million shareholders. Because the only invested capital is the $10 million in inventory, the ROE is 10%.

This year, inflation of 6% is expected, and all prices are expected to rise at that rate. Because inventory is paid for at the beginning of the year, it will still cost $10 million. However, revenue will be $12.72 million instead of $12 million, and other costs will be $1.06 million.

Nominal Earnings	
Revenue	$12.72 million
− Labor and rent	1.06 million
− Cost of goods sold	10.00 million
Earnings	$ 1.66 million
ROE	16.6%

Note that the amount required to *replace* inventory at year's end is $10.6 million, rather than the beginning *cost* of $10 million, so the amount of cash available to distribute as dividends is $1.06 million, not the reported earnings of $1.66 million.

A dividend of $1.06 million would be just enough to keep the real value of dividends unchanged and at the same time allow for maintenance of the same real value of inventory. The reported earnings of $1.66 million overstate true economic earnings, in other words.

We thus have the following set of relationships:

	No Inflation	6% Inflation
Dividends	$1 million	$1.06 million
Reported earnings	$1 million	$1.66 million
ROE	10%	16.6%
Plowback ratio	0	.36145
Price of a share	$10	$10
P/E ratio	10	6.0241

There are some surprising findings in this case of "neutral" inflation, that is, inflation that leaves the real interest rate and real earnings unaffected. Although nominal dividends rise at the rate of inflation, 6%, reported earnings increase initially by 66%. In subsequent years, as long as inflation remains at a constant rate of 6%, earnings will grow at 6%.

Note also that the plowback ratio rises from 0 to .36145. Although plowback in the no-inflation case was zero, positive plowback of reported earnings now becomes necessary to maintain the level of inventory at a constant real value. Inventory must rise from a nominal level of $10 million to a level of $10.6 million to maintain its real value. This inventory investment requires reinvested earnings of $.6 million.

Thus the proportion of reported income that must be retained and reinvested to keep the real growth rate of earnings at zero is .36145 if inflation is 6% per year. Multiplying this plowback ratio by the nominal ROE of 16.6% produces a nominal growth rate of dividends of 6%, which is equal to the inflation rate:

$$g = b \times \text{ROE}$$
$$= .36145 \times 16.6\% = 6\% \text{ per year}$$

More generally, the relationship between nominal and real variables is:

Variable	Real	Nominal
Growth rate	g^*	$g = (1 + g^*)(1 + i) - 1$
Capitalization rate	k^*	$k = (1 + k^*)(1 + i) - 1$
Return on equity	ROE^*	$\text{ROE} = (1 + \text{ROE}^*)(1 + i) - 1$
Expected dividend	D_1^*	$D_1 = (1 + i)D_1^*$
Plowback ratio	b^*	$b = \dfrac{(1 + b^* \times \text{ROE}^*)(1 + i) - 1}{(1 + \text{ROE}^*)(1 + i) - 1}$

Note that it is not true that $E_1 = (1 + i)E_1^*$. That is, expected reported earnings do not, in general, equal expected real earnings times one plus the inflation rate. The reason, as you have seen, is that stated earnings do not accurately measure the cost of replenishing assets.

For example, cost of goods sold is treated as if it were $10 million, even though it now costs $10.6 million to replace the inventory. Historical cost accounting in this case distorts the measured cost of goods sold, which in turn distorts the reported earnings figures. We will return to this point in Chapter 19.

Note also the effect of inflation on the P/E ratio. In our example the P/E ratio drops from 10 in the no-inflation scenario to 6.0241 in the 6% inflation scenario. This is entirely a result of the fact that the reported earnings figure gets distorted by inflation and overstates true economic earnings.

This is true in the real world too, not just in our simplified example. Look back at Figure 18.3 and you will see that P/E ratios fall dramatically when the inflation rate increases. Many companies show gains in reported earnings during inflationary periods, even though real earnings may be unaffected. This is one reason analysts must interpret data on the past behavior of P/E ratios over time with great care.

Concept
CHECK

Question 7 • Assume that Inflatotrend has a 4% annual expected constant growth rate of earnings if there is no inflation. $E_1^* = \$1$ per share; ROE* = 10% per year; $b^* = .4$; and $k^* = 10\%$ per year.

a. What is the current price of a share?
b. What are the expected real dividend yield and rate of capital appreciation?
c. If the firm's real revenues and dividends are unaffected by inflation, and expected inflation is 6% per year, what should be the nominal growth rate of dividends, the expected nominal dividend yield, the expected ROE, and the nominal plowback ratio?

For many years economists thought that stocks ought to be an inflation-neutral investment in the sense that we have described. They believed, and many of them still believe, that changes in the rate of inflation, whether expected or unexpected, ought to have no effect on the expected real rate of return on common stocks.

Recent empirical research, however, seems to indicate that real rates of return are negatively correlated with inflation. In terms of the simple constant-growth-rate DDM, this would mean that an increase in inflation is associated with a decrease in D_1, an increase in k, a decrease in g, or some combination of all three.

One school of thought[8] believes that economic "shocks" such as oil price hikes can cause a simultaneous increase in the inflation rate and decline of expected real earnings (and dividends). This would result in a negative correlation between inflation and real stock returns.

A second view[9] is that the higher the rate of inflation, the riskier real stock returns are perceived to be. The reasoning here is that higher inflation is associated with greater uncertainty about the economy, which tends to induce a higher required rate of return on equity. In addition, a higher k implies a lower level of stock prices.

A third perspective[10] is that higher inflation results in lower real dividends because our tax system results in lower after-tax real earnings as the inflation rate rises.

Finally, there is the view[11] that many investors in the stock market suffer from a form of "money illusion." Investors mistake the rise in nominal rate of interest for a rise in the real rate. As a result, they undervalue stocks in a period of higher inflation.

---

[8]See Eugene F. Fama, "Stock Returns, Real Activity, Inflation, and Money," *American Economic Review*, September 1981.
[9]See Burton Malkiel, *A Random Walk Down Wall Street*, 6th ed. (New York: W. W. Norton, 1996).
[10]See Martin Feldstein, "Inflation and the Stock Market," *American Economic Review*, December 1980.
[11]See Franco Modigliani and Richard Cohn, "Inflation, Rational Valuation, and the Market," *Financial Analysts Journal*, March–April 1979.

Figure 18.7
Earnings yield of S&P
500 versus Treasury
bond yield.

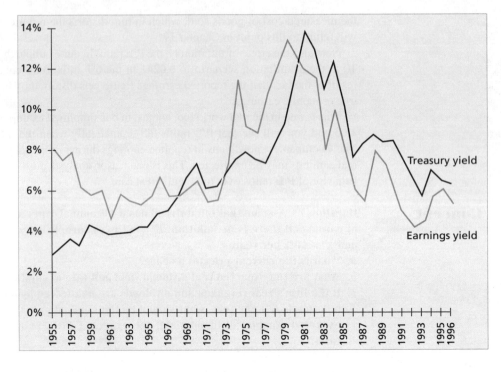

18.7   BEHAVIOR OF THE AGGREGATE STOCK MARKET

Explaining Past Behavior

It has been well documented that the stock market is a leading economic indicator.[12] This means that it tends to fall before a recession and to rise before an economic recovery. However, the relationship is far from perfectly reliable.

Most scholars and serious analysts would agree that, although the stock market appears to have a substantial life of its own, responding perhaps to bouts of mass euphoria and then panic, economic events and the anticipation of such events do have a substantial effect on stock prices.[13] Perhaps the two factors with the greatest impact are interest rates and corporate profits.

Figure 18.7 shows the behavior of the earnings-to-price ratio (i.e., the earnings yield) of the S&P 500 stock index versus the yield to maturity on long-term Treasury bonds since 1955. Clearly, the two series track each other quite closely. This is to be expected: The two variables that affect a firm's value are earnings (and implicitly the dividends they can support) and the discount rate, which "translates" future income into present value. Thus it should not be surprising that the ratio of earnings to stock price (the inverse of the P/E ratio) varies with the interest rate. Indeed, the nearby box is an article from *The Wall Street Journal* that argues that earnings (or, as we pointed out above, free cash flow) and interest rates are the two forces that "drive the stock market engine."

---

[12]See, for example, Stanley Fischer and Robert C. Merton, "Macroeconomics and Finance: The Role of the Stock Market," *Carnegie-Rochester Conference Series on Public Policy* 21 (1984).

[13]For a discussion of the current debate on the rationality of the stock market, see the suggested readings at the end of this chapter.

TWO FORCES DRIVE THE STOCK-MARKET ENGINE

Recent milestones racked up by the Standard & Poor's 500 stocks and Dow Jones industrials demonstrate one thing: Over any longish term, stock-market values are driven by two, repeat two, fundamental factors—interest rates and expected earnings.

You can skip the rest. Forget all of those indicators of bearish and bullish sentiment; ditto, the plotted pictures of "resistance levels" and 100-day moving averages. Trash the stats on mutual-fund inflows.

Even yardsticks such as book value and dividends are inconsistent measures of broad groups of stocks. We will get to the reasons. First, take a look at the chart.*

What it shows is that, in the past 10 years anyway, the broad market values stocks so that the implicit return on stocks—that is, the expected earnings of companies divided by their stock prices—very closely tracks the yield in the bond market.

How so? The chart depicts the expected earnings of the S&P companies divided by their stock prices—known as the "earnings yield." The earnings yield has moved more or less in lockstep with long-term bond rates. When interest rates fell, so did the earnings yield, meaning that investors were demanding less in terms of earnings for every dollar they were willing to pay for a stock. The flip side: The P/E multiple (not shown on the chart) was rising.

Nothing has decoupled broad market prices from underlying earnings and interest rates for long. Over long periods, prices of stocks ought to mimic the underlying business values of companies. This underlying or *intrinsic* value is what counts to an investor who is in for keeps, such as a private owner of a whole business.

Investors' return, if any, will come from the cash their businesses throw off. They figure value today by estimating future free cash flow (or earnings), discounted by an appropriate rate of interest. Similarly, for a publicly traded stock, intrinsic value is the per-share value to the owner, or to some ultimate future owner, who is in for keeps.

Dividends tell us only about the *portion* of earnings that managers have chosen to pay out. This point is controversial, but if companies opt to reinvest more of their earnings—as many have—it doesn't make those earnings worth less. Thus, says Abby Joseph Cohen of Goldman Sachs, stock prices should bear more relation to total cash flow or earnings than to dividends.

Book value probably is even less useful as a broad check on markets. Book tells us what has been invested in a business, but may say little about the company's future earning power. This is especially true for the many companies that have written off chunks of book value in restructurings.

The one trouble with the chart is that—save for an unusual period such as 1987—it isn't predictive. It explains why stocks have risen, but it is silent on whether earnings expectations will be as high—or interest rates as low—next year.

*The chart mentioned is identical to Figure 18.7.

Source: Roger Lowenstein, "Two Forces Drive the Stock-Market Engine," *The Wall Street Journal*, November 30, 1995. Excerpted by permission of *The Wall Street Journal*, © 1995 Dow Jones & Company, Inc. All Rights Reserved Worldwide.

Forecasting the Stock Market

What can we learn from all of this about the future rate of return on stocks? First, a note of optimism. Although timing the stock market is a very difficult and risky game, it may not be impossible. For example, we saw in Chapter 12 that some variables such as the market dividend yield seem to predict market returns.

However, if market history teaches us anything at all, it is that the market has great variability. Thus, although we can use a variety of methods to derive a best forecast of the expected holding-period return on the market, the uncertainty surrounding that forecast will always be high.

The most popular approach to forecasting the overall stock market is the earnings multiplier approach applied at the aggregate level. The first step is to forecast corporate profits for the coming period. Then we derive an estimate of the earnings multiplier, the aggregate P/E ratio, based on a forecast of long-term interest rates. The product of the two forecasts is the estimate of the end-of-period level of the market.

The forecast of the P/E ratio of the market is sometimes derived from a graph similar to that in Figure 18.7, which plots the *earnings yield* (earnings per share divided by price per share, the reciprocal of the P/E ratio) of the S&P 500 and the yield to maturity on 10-year Treasury bonds. The figure shows that both yields rose dramatically in the 1970s. In the

Table 18.4   S&P 500 Price Forecasts under Various Scenarious

	Most Likely Scenario	Pessimistic Scenario	Optimistic Scenario
Treasury bond yield	5.7%	6.2%	5.2%
Earnings yield	4.7%	5.2%	4.2%
Resulting P/E ratio	21.3	19.2	23.8
EPS forecast	$ 51.51	$ 51.51	$ 51.51
Forecast for S&P 500	1,097	989	1,226

Forecast for the earnings yield on the S&P 500 equals Treasury bond yield minus 1%. The P/E ratio is the reciprocal of the forecasted earnings yield.

case of Treasury bonds, this was because of an increase in the inflationary expectations built into interest rates. The earnings yield on the S&P 500, however, probably rose because of inflationary distortions that artificially increased reported earnings. We have already seen that P/E ratios tend to fall when inflation rates increase. For most of the 1980s and 1990s, the earnings yield ran about one percentage point below the T-bond rate.

One might use this relationship and the current yield on 10-year Treasury bonds to forecast the earnings yield on the S&P 500. Given that earnings yield, a forecast of earnings could be used to predict the level of the S&P in some future period. Let's consider a simple example of this procedure.

The 1997 forecast for 1998 earnings per share for the S&P 500 portfolio was about $51.51.[14] The 10-year Treasury bond yield at the end of 1997 was about 5.7%. Because the earnings yield on the S&P 500 has been about one percentage point below the 10-year Treasury yield, a first guess for the earnings yield on the S&P 500 might be 4.7%. This would imply a P/E ratio of 1/.047 = 21.3. Our forecast for the S&P 500 index would then be 21.3 × 51.51 = 1,097.

Of course, there is uncertainty regarding all three inputs into this analysis: the actual earnings on the S&P 500 stocks, the level of Treasury yields at year end, and the spread between the Treasury yield and the earnings yield. One would wish to perform sensitivity or scenario analysis to examine the impact of changes in all of these variables. To illustrate, consider Table 18.4, which shows a simple scenario analysis treating possible effects of variation in the Treasury bond yield. The scenario analysis shows that forecasted level of the stock market varies inversely and with dramatic sensitivity to interest rate changes.

Some analysts use an aggregate version of the dividend discount model rather than an earnings multiplier approach. All of these models, however, rely heavily on forecasts of such macroeconomic variables as GDP, interest rates, and the rate of inflation, which are difficult to predict accurately.

Because stock prices reflect expectations of future dividends, which are tied to the economic fortunes of firms, it is not surprising that the performance of a broad-based stock index like the S&P 500 is taken as a leading economic indicator, that is, a predictor of the performance of the aggregate economy. Stock prices are viewed as embodying consensus forecasts of economic activity and are assumed to move up or down in anticipation of movements in the economy. The government's index of leading economic indicators, which is taken to predict the progress of the business cycle, is made up in part of recent stock market performance. However, the predictive value of the market is far from perfect.

---

[14]According to Institutional Brokers Estimate System (I/B/E/S) as of December 1997. I/B/E/S surveys a large sample of stock analysts and reports several analyses of their forecasts for both the economy and individual stocks.

A well-known joke, often attributed to Paul Samuelson, is that the market has forecast eight of the last five recessions.

SUMMARY

1. One approach to firm valuation is to focus on the firm's book value, either as it appears on the balance sheet or as adjusted to reflect current replacement cost of assets or liquidation value. Another approach is to focus on the present value of expected future dividends.

2. The dividend discount model holds that the price of a share of stock should equal the present value of all future dividends per share, discounted at an interest rate commensurate with the risk of the stock.

3. The constant-growth version of the DDM asserts that if dividends are expected to grow at a constant rate forever, then the intrinsic value of the stock is determined by the formula

$$V_0 = \frac{D_1}{k - g}$$

This version of the DDM is simplistic in its assumption of a constant value of g. There are more sophisticated multistage versions of the model for more complex environments. When the constant-growth assumption is reasonably satisfied, the formula can be inverted to infer the market capitalization rate for the stock:

$$k = \frac{D_1}{P_0} + g$$

4. Stock market analysts devote considerable attention to a company's price-to-earnings ratio. The P/E ratio is a useful measure of the market's assessment of the firm's growth opportunities. Firms with no growth opportunities should have a P/E ratio that is just the reciprocal of the capitalization rate, k. As growth opportunities become a progressively more important component of the total value of the firm, the P/E ratio will increase.

5. The expected growth rate of earnings is related both to the firm's expected profitability and to its dividend policy. The relationship can be expressed as

$g =$ (ROE on new investment) $\times$ (1 − Dividend payout ratio)

6. You can relate any DDM to a simple capitalized earnings model by comparing the expected ROE on future investments to the market capitalization rate, k. If the two rates are equal, then the stock's intrinsic value reduces to expected earnings per share (EPS) divided by k.

7. Many analysts form their estimate of a stock's value by multiplying their forecast of next year's EPS by a P/E multiple derived from some empirical rule. This rule can be consistent with some version of the DDM, although often it is not.

8. The free cash flow approach is the one used most often in corporate finance. The analyst first estimates the value of the entire firm as the present value of expected future free cash flows, assuming all-equity financing, then adds the value of tax shields arising from debt financing, and finally subtracts the value of all claims other than equity. This approach will be consistent with the DDM and capitalized earnings approaches as long as the capitalization rate is adjusted to reflect financial leverage.

9. We explored the effects of inflation on stock prices in the context of the constant-growth DDM. Although traditional theory has been that inflation should have a neutral effect on real stock returns, recent historical evidence shows a striking negative correlation between inflation and real stock market returns. There are four different explanations that may account for this negative correlation:

   a. Economic "shocks" that simultaneously produce high inflation and lower real earnings.

   b. Increased riskiness of stocks in a more inflationary environment.

   c. Lower real after-tax earnings and dividends attributable to inflation-induced distortions in the tax system.

   d. Money "illusion."

10. The models presented in this chapter can be used to explain and forecast the behavior of the aggregate stock market. The key macroeconomic variables that determine the level of stock prices in the aggregate are interest rates and corporate profits.

Key Terms

book value	intrinsic value	dividend payout ratio
liquidation value	market capitalization rate	plowback ratio
replacement cost	dividend discount model (DDM)	earnings retention ratio
Tobin's q	constant-growth DDM	price–earnings multiple

Selected Readings

For the key issues in the debate about the link between fundamentals and stock prices see:

Merton, Robert C. "On the Current State of the Stock Market Rationality Hypothesis." In *Macroeconomics and Finance, Essays in Honor of Franco Modigliani,* eds. Rudiger Dornbusch, Stanley Fischer, and John Bossons. Cambridge, MA: MIT Press, 1986.

Cutler, David M.; James M. Poterba; and Lawrence H. Summers. "What Moves Stock Prices?" *Journal of Portfolio Management* 15 (Spring 1989), pp. 4–12.

West, Kenneth D. "Bubbles, Fads, and Stock Price Volatility Tests: A Partial Evaluation." *Journal of Finance* 43 (July 1988), pp. 639–55.

Problems

1. *a.* Computer stocks currently provide an expected rate of return of 16%. MBI, a large computer company, will pay a year-end dividend of $2 per share. If the stock is selling at $50 per share, what must be the market's expectation of the growth rate of MBI dividends?

   b. If dividend growth forecasts for MBI are revised downward to 5% per year, what will happen to the price of MBI stock? What (qualitatively) will happen to the company's price–earnings ratio?

2. *a.* MF Corp. has an ROE of 16% and a plowback ratio of 50%. If the coming year's earnings are expected to be $2 per share, at what price will the stock sell? The market capitalization rate is 12%.

   b. What price do you expect MF shares to sell for in three years?

3. At Litchfield Chemical Corp. (LCC), a director of the company said that the use of dividend discount models by investors is "proof" that the higher the dividend, the higher the stock price.

   a. Using a constant-growth dividend discount model as a basis of reference, evaluate the director's statement.

   b. Explain how an increase in dividend payout would affect each of the following (holding all other factors constant):

        i. Sustainable growth rate.

       ii. Growth in book value.

4. The market consensus is that Analog Electronic Corporation has an ROE = 9%, a beta of 1.25, and it plans to maintain indefinitely its traditional plowback ratio of 2/3. This year's earnings were $3 per share. The annual dividend was just paid. The consensus estimate of the coming year's market return is 14%, and T-bills currently offer a 6% return.

  a. Find the price at which Analog stock should sell.

  b. Calculate the P/E ratio.

  c. Calculate the present value of growth opportunities.

  d. Suppose your research convinces you Analog will announce momentarily that it will immediately reduce its plowback ratio to 1/3. Find the intrinsic value of the stock. The market is still unaware of this decision. Explain why V_0 no longer equals P_0 and why V_0 is greater or less than P_0.

5. If the expected rate of return of the market portfolio is 15% and a stock with a beta of 1.0 pays a dividend yield of 4%, what must the market believe is the expected rate of price appreciation on that stock?

6. The FI Corporation's dividends per share are expected to grow indefinitely by 5% per year.

  a. If this year's year-end dividend is $8 and the market capitalization rate is 10% per year, what must the current stock price be according to the DDM?

  b. If the expected earnings per share are $12, what is the implied value of the ROE on future investment opportunities?

  c. How much is the market paying per share for growth opportunities (i.e., for an ROE on future investments that exceeds the market capitalization rate)?

7. Imelda Emma, a financial analyst at Del Advisors, Inc. (DAI), has been asked to assess the impact that construction of Disney's new theme parks might have on its stock. DAI uses a dividend discount valuation model that incorporates beta in the derivation of risk-adjusted required rates of return on stocks.

    Until now, Emma has been using a five-year earnings and dividends per share growth rate of 15% and a beta estimate of 1.00 for Disney. Taking construction of the new theme parks into account, however, she has raised her growth rate and beta estimates to 25% and 1.15, respectively. The complete set of Emma's current assumptions is:

Current stock price	$37.75
Beta	1.15
Risk-free rate of return (T-bill)	4.0%
Required rate of return on the market	10.0%
Short-term growth rate (five years) for earnings and dividends	25.0%
Long-term growth rate (beyond five years) for earnings and dividends	9.3%
Dividend forecast for 1994 (per share)	$.287

  a. Calculate the risk-adjusted required rate of return on Disney stock using Emma's current beta assumption.

  b. Using the results of part (*a*), Emma's current assumptions, and DAI's dividend discount model, calculate the intrinsic, or fair, value of Disney stock at September 30, 1993.

  c. After calculating the intrinsic value of Disney stock using her new assumptions and DAI's dividend discount model, Emma finds that her recommendation for Disney should be changed from a "buy" to a "sell." Explain how the construction of the new theme parks could have such a negative impact on the valuation of Disney stock, despite Emma's assumption of sharply higher growth rates (25%).

8. The risk-free rate of return is 10%, the required rate of return on the market is 15%, and High-Flyer stock has a beta coefficient of 1.5. If the dividend per share expected during the coming year, D_1, is $2.50 and $g = 5\%$, at what price should a share sell?

9. Your preliminary analysis of two stocks has yielded the information set forth below. The market capitalization rate for both Stock A and Stock B is 10% per year.

	Stock A	Stock B
Expected return on equity, ROE	14%	12%
Estimated earnings per share, E_1	$ 2.00	$ 1.65
Estimated dividends per share, D_1	$ 1.00	$ 1.00
Current market price per share, P_0	$27.00	$25.00

a. What are the expected dividend payout ratios for the two stocks?
b. What are the expected dividend growth rates of each?
c. What is the intrinsic value of each stock?
d. In which, if either, of the two stocks would you choose to invest?

10. Phoebe Black's investment club wants to buy the stock of either NewSoft Inc. or Capital Corp. In this connection, Black prepared the following table. You have been asked to help her interpret the data, based on your forecast for a healthy economy and a strong stock market over the next 12 months.

	NewSoft Inc.	Capital Corp.	S&P 500 Index
Current price	$30	$32	
Industry	Computer software	Capital goods	
P/E ratio (current)	25	14	16
P/E ratio (5-year average)	27	16	16
P/B ratio (current)	10	3	3
P/B ratio (5-year average)	12	4	2
Beta	1.5	1.1	1.0
Dividend yield	.3%	2.7%	2.8%

a. Newsoft's shares have higher price–earnings (P/E) and price–book value (P/B) ratios than those of Capital Corp. (The price–book ratio is the ratio of market value to book value.) Briefly discuss why the disparity in ratios may not indicate that NewSoft's shares are overvalued relative to the shares of Capital Corp. Answer the question in terms of the two ratios, and assume that there have been no extraordinary events affecting either company.
b. Using a constant-growth dividend discount model, Black estimated the value of NewSoft to be $28 per share and the value of Capital Corp. to be $34 per share. Briefly discuss weaknesses of this dividend discount model and explain why this model may be less suitable for valuing NewSoft than for valuing Capital Corp.
c. Recommend and justify a more appropriate dividend discount model for valuing NewSoft's common stock.

11. The stock of Nogro Corporation is currently selling for $10 per share. Earnings per share in the coming year are expected to be $2. The company has a policy of paying

out 50% of its earnings each year in dividends. The rest is retained and invested in projects that earn a 20% rate of return per year. This situation is expected to continue indefinitely.

a. Assuming the current market price of the stock reflects its intrinsic value as computed using the constant-growth DDM, what rate of return do Nogro's investors require?

b. By how much does its value exceed what it would be if all earnings were paid as dividends and nothing were reinvested?

c. If Nogro were to cut its dividend payout ratio to 25%, what would happen to its stock price? What if Nogro eliminated the dividend?

12. Chiptech, Inc., is an established computer chip firm with several profitable existing products as well as some promising new products in development. The company earned $1 a share last year, and just paid out a dividend of $.50 per share. Investors believe the company plans to maintain its dividend payout ratio at 50%. ROE equals 20%. Everyone in the market expects this situation to persist indefinitely.

a. What is the market price of Chiptech stock? The required return for the computer chip industry is 15%, and the company has just gone ex-dividend (i.e., the next dividend will be paid a year from now, at $t = 1$).

b. Suppose you discover that Chiptech's competitor has developed a new chip that will eliminate Chiptech's current technological advantage in this market. This new product, which will be ready to come to the market in two years, will force Chiptech to reduce the prices of its chips to remain competitive. This will decrease ROE to 15%, and, because of falling demand for its product, Chiptech will decrease the plowback ratio to .40. The plowback ratio will be decreased at the end of the second year, at $t = 2$: The annual year-end dividend for the second year (paid at $t = 2$) will be 60% of that year's earnings. What is your estimate of Chiptech's intrinsic value per share? (Hint: Carefully prepare a table of Chiptech's earnings and dividends for each of the next three years. Pay close attention to the change in the payout ratio in $t = 2$.)

c. No one else in the market perceives the threat to Chiptech's market. In fact, you are confident that no one else will become aware of the change in Chiptech's competitive status until the competitor firm publicly announces its discovery near the end of year 2. What will be the rate of return on Chiptech stock in the coming year (i.e., between $t = 0$ and $t = 1$)? In the second year (between $t = 1$ and $t = 2$)? The third year (between $t = 2$ and $t = 3$)? (Hint: Pay attention to when the *market* catches on to the new situation. A table of dividends and market prices over time might help.)

13. The risk-free rate of return is 8%, the expected rate of return on the market portfolio is 15%, and the stock of Xyrong Corporation has a beta coefficient of 1.2. Xyrong pays out 40% of its earnings in dividends, and the latest earnings announced were $10 per share. Dividends were just paid and are expected to be paid annually. You expect that Xyrong will earn an ROE of 20% per year on all reinvested earnings forever.

a. What is the intrinsic value of a share of Xyrong stock?

b. If the market price of a share is currently $100, and you expect the market price to be equal to the intrinsic value one year from now, what is your expected one-year holding-period return on Xyrong stock?

14. The Digital Electronic Quotation System (DEQS) Corporation pays no cash dividends currently and is not expected to for the next five years. Its latest EPS was $10, all of which was reinvested in the company. The firm's expected ROE for the next five years is 20% per year, and during this time it is expected to continue to reinvest all of its earnings. Starting six years from now the firm's ROE on new investments is expected

to fall to 15%, and the company is expected to start paying out 40% of its earnings in cash dividends, which it will continue to do forever after. DEQS's market capitalization rate is 15% per year.

a. What is your estimate of DEQS's intrinsic value per share?

b. Assuming its current market price is equal to its intrinsic value, what do you expect to happen to its price over the next year? The year after?

c. What effect would it have on your estimate of DEQS's intrinsic value if you expected DEQS to pay out only 20% of earnings starting in year 6?

15. At year-end 1991, the Wall Street consensus was that Philip Morris's earnings and dividends would grow at 20% for five years, after which growth would fall to a market-like 7%. Analysts also projected a required rate of return of 10% for the U.S. equity market.

a. Using the data in the accompanying table and the multistage dividend discount model, calculate the intrinsic value of Philip Morris stock at year-end 1991. Assume a similar level of risk for Philip Morris stock as for the typical U.S. stock.

b. Using the data in the accompanying table, calculate Philip Morris's price–earnings ratio and the price–earnings ratio relative to the S&P 500 Stock Index as of December 31, 1991.

c. Using the data in the accompanying table, calculate Philip Morris's price–book ratio (i.e., ratio of market value to book value) and the price–book ratio relative to the S&P 500 Stock Index as of December 31, 1991.

Philip Morris Corporation
Selected Financial Data
Years Ending December 31
($ millions except per share data)

	1991	1981
Earnings per share	$4.24	$0.66
Dividends per share	$1.91	$0.25
Stockholders' equity	12,512	3,234
Total liabilities and stockholders' equity	$47,384	$9,180
Other data		
Philip Morris		
Common shares outstanding (millions)	920	1,003
Closing price common stock	$80.250	$6.125
S&P 500 Stock Index:		
Closing price	417.09	122.55
Earnings per share	16.29	15.36
Book value per share	161.08	109.43

16. a. State one major advantage and one major disadvantage of each of the three valuation methodologies you used to value Philip Morris in the previous problem.

b. State whether Philip Morris stock is undervalued or overvalued as of December 31, 1991. Support your conclusion using your answers to previous questions and any data provided. (The past 10-year average S&P 500 Stock Index relative price–earnings and price–book ratios for Philip Morris were .80 and 1.61, respectively.)

17. The Duo Growth Company just paid a dividend of $1 per share. The dividend is expected to grow at a rate of 25% per year for the next three years and then to level off to 5% per year forever. You think the appropriate market capitalization rate is 20% per year.

    a. What is your estimate of the intrinsic value of a share of the stock?

    b. If the market price of a share is equal to this intrinsic value, what is the expected dividend yield?

    c. What do you expect its price to be one year from now? Is the implied capital gain consistent with your estimate of the dividend yield and the market capitalization rate?

18. The Generic Genetic (GG) Corporation pays no cash dividends currently and is not expected to for the next four years. Its latest EPS was $5, all of which was reinvested in the company. The firm's expected ROE for the next four years is 20% per year, during which time it is expected to continue to reinvest all of its earnings. Starting five years from now, the firm's ROE on new investments is expected to fall to 15% per year. GG's market capitalization rate is 15% per year.

    a. What is your estimate of GG's intrinsic value per share?

    b. Assuming its current market price is equal to its intrinsic value, what do you expect to happen to its price over the next year?

19. The MoMi Corporation's cash flow from operations before interest and taxes was $2 million in the year just ended, and it expects that this will grow by 5% per year forever. To make this happen, the firm will have to invest an amount equal to 20% of pretax cash flow each year. The tax rate is 34%. Depreciation was $200,000 in the year just ended and is expected to grow at the same rate as the operating cash flow. The appropriate market capitalization rate for the unleveraged cash flow is 12% per year, and the firm currently has debt of $4 million outstanding. Use the free cash flow approach to value the firm's equity.

20. The CPI Corporation is expected to pay a real dividend of $1 per share this year. Its expected growth rate of real dividends is 4% per year, and its current market price per share is $20.

    a. Assuming the constant-growth DDM is applicable, what must be the real market capitalization rate for CPI?

    b. If the expected rate of inflation is 6% per year, what must be the nominal capitalization rate, the nominal dividend yield, and the growth rate of nominal dividends?

    c. It the expected real earnings per share are $1.80, what would be your estimate of intrinsic value if you used a simple capitalized earnings model?

21. The following questions are from past CFA examinations.

    a. The constant-growth DDM will not produce a finite value if the dividend growth rate is:

       i. Above its historical average.

       ii. Above the market capitalization rate.

       iii. Below its historical average.

       iv. Below the market capitalization rate.

    b. In theory, a firm wanting to maximize share value should pay out as much of its earnings in dividends as possible if it believes that:

       i. Investors are indifferent to the form of their return.

       ii. The company's future growth rate will be below its historical average.

       iii. The company will still have positive cash flow.

       iv. The company's future return on equity will be below its market capitalization rate.

    c. According to the constant-growth DDM, a fall in the market capitalization rate will cause a stock's intrinsic value to:

       i. Decrease.

       ii. Increase.

iii. Remain unchanged.

iv. Decrease or increase, depending on other factors.

d. You plan to buy a common stock and hold it for one year. You expect to receive both $1.50 in dividends and $26 from the sale of stock at the end of the year. If you wanted to earn a 15% return, the maximum price you would pay for the stock today is:

i. $22.61.

ii. $23.91.

iii. $24.50.

iv. $27.50.

e. In the dividend discount model, a factor *not* affecting the discount rate, k, is the:

i. Real risk-free rate.

ii. Risk premium for stocks.

iii. Return on assets.

iv. Expected inflation rate.

f. If the return on equity of a firm is 15% and the retention ratio is 40%, the sustainable growth rate of the firm's earnings and dividends should be:

i. 6%.

ii. 9%.

iii. 15%.

iv. 40%.

g. A share of stock is expected to pay a dividend of $1.00 one year from now and grow at 5% thereafter. In the context of a dividend discount model, the stock is correctly priced today at $10. According to the single-stage, constant-growth DDM, if the required return is 15%, the value of the stock two years from now should be:

i. $11.03.

ii. $12.10.

iii. $13.23.

iv. $14.40.

h. After selling its common stock for $20 per share, a company has 5 million shares issued and outstanding. The firm's balance sheet after the sale of the stock is as follows:

Assets ($ Millions)		Liabilities and Equity ($ Millions)	
Current assets	$20	Current liabilities	$12
Net plant and equipment	42	Long-term debt	5
Total	$62	Common equity	45
		Total	$62

The book value per share is:

i. $ 5.63.

ii. $ 7.75.

iii. $ 9.00.

iv. $12.40.

i. A stock is not expected to pay dividends until three years from now. The dividend is then expected to be $2.00 per share, the dividend payout ratio is expected to be 40%, and the return on equity is expected to be 15%. If the required rate of return is 12%, the value of the stock today is closest to:

      i. $27.

     ii. $33.

    iii. $53.

    iv. $67.

j. In its latest annual report, a company reported the following:

Net income	$1,000,000
Total equity	$5,000,000
Total assets	$10,000,000
Dividend payout ratio	40%

Based on the sustainable growth model, the most likely forecast of the company's future earnings growth rate is:

      i. 4%.

     ii. 6%.

    iii. 8%.

    iv. 12%.

k. The constant-growth DDM would typically be most appropriate in valuing the stock of a:

      i. New venture expected to retain all earnings for several years.

     ii. Rapidly growing company.

    iii. Moderate-growth, "mature" company.

    iv. Company with valuable assets not yet generating profits.

l. A stock has a required return of 15%, a constant-growth rate of 10%, and a dividend payout ratio of 45%. The stock's price–earnings ratio should be:

      i. 3.

     ii. 4.5.

    iii. 9.

    iv. 11.

s o l u t i o n s   t o
Concept CHECKS

1. *a.* Dividend yield = $2.15/$50 = 4.3%.

Capital gains yield = (59.77 − 50)/50 = 19.54%.

Total return = 4.3% + 19.54% = 23.84%.

b. $k = 6\% + 1.15(14\% - 6\%) = 15.2\%$.

c. $V_0 = (\$2.15 + \$59.77)/1.152 = \$53.75$, which exceeds the market price. This would indicate a "buy" opportunity.

2. *a.* $D_1/(k - g) = \$2.15/(.152 - .112) = \$53.75$.

b. $P_1 = P_0(1 + g) = \$53.75(1.112) = \$59.77$.

c. The expected capital gain equals $59.77 − $53.75 = $6.02, for a percentage gain of 11.2%. The dividend yield is $D_1/P_0 = 2.15/53.75 = 4\%$, for a holding-period return of 4% + 11.2% = 15.2%.

3. $g = \text{ROE} \times b = 20\% \times .60 = 12\%$.

$D_1 = .4 \times E_1 = .4 \times \$5 = \$2$.

$P_0 = 2/(.125 - .12) = 400$.

$\text{PVGO} = P_0 - E_1/k = 400 - 5/.125 = 360$. PVGO represents an extremely high fraction of the total value of the firm. This is because the assumed dividend growth rate, 12%, is nearly as high as the discount rate, 12.5%. The assumption that the growth rate can remain so close to the discount rate for an indefinitely long period represents an extremely optimistic (and probably unrealistic) view of the long-term growth prospects of the firm.

4. Given current management's investment policy, the dividend growth rate will be

$$g = \text{ROE} \times b = 10\% \times .6 = 6\%$$

and the stock price should be

$$P_0 = \frac{\$2}{.15 - .06} = \$22.22$$

The present value of growth opportunities is

$$\text{PVGO} = \text{Price per share} - \text{No-growth value per share}$$
$$= \$22.22 - E_1/k$$
$$= \$22.22 - \$5/.15$$
$$= -\$11.11$$

PVGO is *negative*. This is because the net present value of the firm's projects is negative: The rate of return on those assets is less than the opportunity cost of capital.

Such a firm would be subject to takeover, because another firm could buy the firm for the market price of $22.22 per share and increase the value of the firm by changing its investment policy. For example, if the new management simply paid out all earnings as dividends, the value of the firm would increase to its no-growth value, $E_1/k = \$5/.15 = \$33.33$.

5. $$V_{1997} = \frac{.54}{(1.144)} + \frac{.64}{(1.144)^2} + \frac{.74}{(1.144)^3} + \frac{.85 + P_{2001}}{(1.144)^4}$$

Now compute the sales price in 2001 using the constant-growth dividend discount model. The growth rate will be $g = \text{ROE} \times b = 16\% \times .85 = 13.6\%$.

$$P_{2001} = \frac{.85 \times (1 + g)}{k - g} = \frac{\$.85 \times 1.136}{.144 - .136} = \$120.70$$

Therefore, $V_{1997} = \$72.42$.

6. *a.* ROE = 12%.

   $b = \$.50/\$2.00 = .25$.

   $g = \text{ROE} \times b = 12\% \times .25 = 3\%$.

   $P_0 = D_1/(k - g) = \$1.50/(.10 - .03) = \$21.43$.

   $P_0/E_1 = \$21.43/\$2.00 = 10.71$.

b. If $b = .4$, then $.4 \times \$2 = \$.80$ would be reinvested and the remainder of earnings, or $1.20, would be paid as dividends.

   $g = 12\% \times .4 = 4.8\%$.

   $P_0 = D_1/(k - g) = \$1.20/(.10 - .048) = \$23.08$.

   $P_0/E_1 = \$23.08/\$2.00 = 11.54$.

7. *a.* $P_0 = \dfrac{(1-b)E_1}{k-g} = \dfrac{.6 \times \$1}{.10 - .04} = \$10.$

b. $\dfrac{D_1^*}{P_0} = \dfrac{(1-b)E_1^*}{P_0} = \dfrac{(1-.4) \times \$1}{\$10} = .06,$ or 6% per year. The rate of price

appreciation $= g^* = b^* \times \text{ROE}^* = 4\%$ per year.

c. i. $g = (1.04)(1.06) - 1 = .1024,$ or 10.24%.

ii. $\dfrac{D_1}{P_0} = \dfrac{D_1^*(1+i)}{P_0} = .06 \times 1.06 = .0636,$ or 6.36%.

iii. ROE = 16.6%.

iv. $b = \dfrac{g}{\text{ROE}} = \dfrac{.1024}{.166} = .6169.$

FINANCIAL STATEMENT ANALYSIS

In the previous chapter, we explored equity valuation techniques. These techniques take the firm's dividends and earnings prospects as inputs. Although the valuation analyst is interested in economic earnings streams, only financial accounting data are readily available. What can we learn from a company's accounting data that can help us estimate the intrinsic value of its common stock? In this chapter, we show how investors can use financial data as inputs into stock valuation analysis. We start by reviewing the basic sources of such data—the income statement, the balance sheet, and the statement of cash flows. We next discuss the difference between economic and accounting earnings. Although economic earnings are more important for issues of valuation, we examine evidence suggesting that, whatever their shortcomings, accounting data still are useful in assessing the economic prospects of the firm. We show how analysts use financial ratios to explore the sources of a firm's profitability and evaluate the "quality" of its earnings in a systematic fashion. We also examine the impact of debt policy on various

ious financial ratios. Finally, we conclude with a discussion of the limitations of financial statement analysis as a tool in uncovering mispriced securities. Some of these limitations are due to differences in firms' accounting procedures. Others arise from inflation-induced distortions in accounting numbers.

19.1 THE MAJOR FINANCIAL STATEMENTS

The Income Statement

The **income statement** is a summary of the profitability of the firm over a period of time, such as a year. It presents revenues generated during the operating period, the expenses incurred during that same period, and the company's net earnings or profits, which are simply the difference between revenues and expenses.

It is useful to distinguish four broad classes of expenses: cost of goods sold, which is the direct cost attributable to producing the product sold by the firm; general and administrative expenses, which correspond to overhead expenses, salaries, advertising, and other costs of operating the firm that are not directly attributable to production; interest expense on the firm's debt; and taxes on earnings owed to federal and local governments.

Table 19.1 presents a 1996 income statement for PepsiCo. At the top are revenues from operations. Next come operating expenses, the costs incurred in the course of generating those revenues, including a depreciation allowance. The difference between operating revenues and operating costs is called *operating income*. Income or expenses from other, primarily nonrecurring, sources are then added or subtracted to obtain earnings before interest and taxes (EBIT), which is what the firm would have earned if not for obligations to its creditors and the tax authorities. EBIT is a measure of the profitability of the firm's operations, ignoring any interest burden attributable to debt financing. The income statement then goes on to subtract net interest expense from EBIT to arrive at taxable income. Finally, the income tax due the government is subtracted to arrive at net income, the "bottom line" of the income statement.

Table 19.1 Consolidated Statement of Income for PepsiCo, Inc., for the year ended December 31, 1996 (figures in millions)

Operating Revenues	
Net sales	$31,645
Operating Expenses	
Cost of sales	$15,383
Selling, general, and administrative expenses	11,175
Depreciation and amortization	1,719
Other expenses	822
Total operating expenses	$29,099
Operating income	$ 2,546
Nonoperating income and expenses	0
Earnings before interest and income taxes	2,546
Net interest expense	499
Earnings before income taxes	2,047
Income taxes	898
Net income	$ 1,149

Note: Column sums subject to rounding error.

Source: PepsiCo Annual Report, 1996.

The Balance Sheet

While the income statement provides a measure of profitability over a period of time, the **balance sheet** provides a "snapshot" of the financial condition of the firm at a particular time. The balance sheet is a list of the firm's assets and liabilities at that moment. The difference in assets and liabilities is the net worth of the firm, also called *shareholders'* or *stockholders' equity*. Like income statements, balance sheets are reasonably standardized in presentation. Table 19.2 is the balance sheet of PepsiCo for the year-end 1996.

The first section of the balance sheet gives a listing of the assets of the firm. Current assets are presented first. These are cash and other items such as accounts receivable or inventories that will be converted into cash within one year. Next comes a listing of long-term assets, which consists primarily of the company's property, plant, and equipment. The sum of current and long-term assets is total assets, the last line of the assets section of the balance sheet.

The liability and stockholders' equity section is arranged similarly. First come short-term, or "current," liabilities such as accounts payable, accrued taxes, and debts that are due within one year. Following this is long-term debt and other liabilities due in more than one year. The difference between total assets and total liabilities is stockholders' equity. This is the net worth, or book value, of the firm. Stockholders' equity is divided into par value of stock, additional paid-in capital, and retained earnings, although this division is usually unimportant. Briefly, par value plus additional paid-in capital represent the proceeds realized from the sale of stock to the public, whereas retained earnings represent the buildup of equity from profits plowed back into the firm. Even if the firm issues no new equity, book value will increase each year by the earnings plowed back into the firm.

The first column of numbers in the balance sheet in Table 19.2 presents the dollar value of each asset. To make it easier to compare firms of different sizes, analysts sometimes present each item on the balance sheet as a percentage of total assets. This is called a *common-size balance sheet*, and it is presented in the last column of the table.

The Statement of Cash Flows

The **statement of cash flows** details the cash flow generated by the firm's operations, investments, and financial activities. This statement was mandated by the Financial Accounting Standards Board in 1987 and is sometimes called the *FASB Statement No. 95*, or *FAS 95*.

Although the income statement and balance sheets are based on accrual methods of accounting, which means that revenues and expenses are recognized when incurred even if no cash has yet been exchanged, the statement of cash flows recognizes only transactions in which cash changes hands. For example, if goods are sold now, with payment due in 60 days, the income statement will treat the revenue as generated when the sale occurs, and the balance sheet will be immediately augmented by accounts receivable, but the statement of cash flows will not recognize the transaction until the bill is paid and the cash is in hand.

Table 19.3 is the 1996 statement of cash flows for PepsiCo. The first entry listed under cash flows from operations is net income. The next entries modify that figure by components of income that have been recognized but for which cash has not yet changed hands. Increases in accounts receivable, for example, mean that income has been claimed on the income statement, but cash has not yet been collected. Hence increases in accounts receivable reduce the cash flows realized from operations in this period. Similarly, increases in accounts payable mean that expenses have been incurred, but cash has not yet left the firm. Any payment delay increases the company's net cash flows in this period.

Table 19.2   Consolidated Balance Sheet for Pepsico, Inc., as of December 31, 1996

	Dollars (millions)	Percentage of Total Assets
Assets		
Current assets		
Cash and cash equivalents	$ 447	2
Other short-term investments	339	1
Receivables	2,516	10
Inventories	1,038	4
Prepaid taxes and other expenses	799	3
Total current assets	$ 5,139	21
Property, plant, and equipment (net of depreciation)	$10,191	42
Net intangible assets	7,136	29
Other assets	2,046	8
Total assets	$24,512	100
Liabilities and Stockholders' Equity		
Current liabilities		
Loans payable	$ 26	0
Accounts payable and other current liabilities	4,626	19
Income taxes due	487	2
Total current liabilities	$ 5,139	21
Long-term debt	$ 8,439	34
Deferred income taxes	1,778	7
Other long-term liabilities	2,533	10
Total liabilities	$17,889	73
Stockholders' equity		
Common stock, par value	$ 29	0
Additional paid-in capital	1,201	5
Retained earnings	9,184	37
Cumulative foreign currency adjustments	(768)	(3)
Treasury stock (at cost)	(3,023)	(12)
Total stockholders' equity	$ 6,623	27
Total liabilities and stockholders' equity	$24,512	100

Note: Column sums subject to rounding error.

Source: PepsiCo Annual Report, 1996.

Another major difference between the income statement and the statement of cash flows involves depreciation, which is a major addition to income in the adjustment section of the statement of cash flows in Table 19.3. The income statement attempts to "smooth" large capital expenditures over time to reflect a measure of profitability not distorted by large, infrequent expenditures. The depreciation expense on the income statement is a way of doing this by recognizing capital expenditures over a period of many years rather than at the specific time of those expenditures.

The statement of cash flows, however, recognizes the cash implication of a capital expenditure when it occurs. It will ignore the depreciation "expense" over time but will account for the full capital expenditure when it is paid.

Rather than smooth or allocate expenses over time, as in the income statement, the statement of cash flows reports cash flows separately for operations, investing, and financing activities. This way, any large cash flows, such as those for big investments, can be recog-

Table 19.3   Consolidated Statement of Cash Flows for PepsiCo for the year ended December 31, 1996 (figures in millions)

Cash Flows from Operating Activities	
Net income	$ 1,149
Adjustments to reconcile net income to net cash provided by operating activities:	
Depreciation and amortization	1,719
Other	1,147
Changes in operating assets and liabilities	
Decrease (increase) in accounts receivable	(70)
Decrease (increase) in inventories	(28)
Increase (decrease) in accounts payable	427
Decrease (increase) in other current assets	(30)
Increase (decrease) in taxes payable	(120)
Total adjustments	$ 3,045
Net cash provided by operating activities	$ 4,194
Cash Flows from Investing Activities	
Cash provided (used) by disposal of (for additions to) property, plant, and equipment	$ (2,230)
Acquisitions of businesses	(75)
Short-term investments	775
Other	255
Net cash provided (used) in investing activities	$ (1,275)
Cash Flows from Financing Activities	
Proceeds from exercise of stock option and purchase plans	$ 323
Proceeds from issuance of long-term debt	1,773
Repayment of long-term debt	(1,424)
Increase (decrease) in loans payable	(1,150)
Dividends paid	(675)
Share repurchases	(1,651)
Other	(46)
Net cash provided by (used in) financing activities	$ (2,850)
Effect of exchange rate changes	$ (4)
Net increase (decrease) in cash and cash equivalents	$ 65

Note: Column sums subject to rounding error.

Source: PepsiCo Annual Report, 1996.

nized explicitly as nonrecurring without affecting the measure of cash flow generated by operating activities.

The second section of the statement of cash flows is the accounting of cash flows from investing activities. These entries are investments in the capital stock necessary for the firm to maintain or enhance its productive capacity.

Finally, the last section of the statement lists the cash flows realized from financing activities. Issuance of securities will contribute positive cash flows, and redemption of outstanding securities will use up cash. For example, PepsiCo repaid $1,424 million of outstanding debt during 1996, which was a use of cash. However, it issued new long-term debt amounting to $1,773 million, which was a major source of cash. The $675 million it paid in dividends reduced net cash flow. Notice that although dividends paid are included in the cash flows from financing section, interest on debt is included with operating activities, presumably because unlike dividends, interest payments are not discretionary.

The statement of cash flows provides evidence on the well-being of a firm. If a company cannot pay its dividends and maintain the productivity of its capital stock out of cash flow from operations, for example, and it must resort to borrowing to meet these demands, this is a serious warning that the firm cannot maintain the dividend payout at its current level in the long run. The statement of cash flows will reveal this developing problem when it shows that cash flow from operations is inadequate and that borrowing is being used to maintain dividend payments at unsustainable levels.

19.2 ACCOUNTING VERSUS ECONOMIC EARNINGS

We've seen that stock valuation models require a measure of **economic earnings**—the sustainable cash flow that can be paid out to stockholders without impairing the productive capacity of the firm. In contrast, **accounting earnings** are affected by several conventions regarding the valuation of assets such as inventories (e.g., LIFO versus FIFO treatment), and by the way some expenditures such as capital investments are recognized over time (as depreciation expenses). We discuss problems with some of these accounting conventions in greater detail later in the chapter. In addition to these accounting issues, as the firm makes its way through the business cycle, its earnings will rise above or fall below the trend line that might more accurately reflect sustainable economic earnings. This introduces an added complication in interpreting net income figures. One might wonder how closely accounting earnings approximate economic earnings and, correspondingly, how useful accounting data might be to investors attempting to value the firm.

In fact, the net income figure on the firm's income statement does convey considerable information concerning a firm's prospects. We see this in the fact that stock prices tend to increase when firms announce earnings greater than market analysis or investors had anticipated. There are several studies to this effect. We noted one such study in Chapter 12; Figure 12.10 documented that firms which announced accounting earnings in excess of market expectations enjoyed increases in stock prices, while shares of firms that announced below-expected earnings fell in price.

19.3 RETURN ON EQUITY

Past versus Future ROE

We noted in Chapter 18 that **return on equity** (ROE) is one of the two basic factors in determining a firm's growth rate of earnings. There are two sides to using ROE. Sometimes it is reasonable to assume that future ROE will approximate its past value, but a high ROE in the past does not necessarily imply a firm's future ROE will be high.

A declining ROE, on the other hand, is evidence that the firm's new investments have offered a lower ROE than its past investments. The best forecast of future ROE in this case may be lower than the most recent ROE. The vital point for an analyst is not to accept historical values as indicators of future values. Data from the recent past may provide information regarding future performance, but the analyst should always keep an eye on the future. It is expectations of future dividends and earnings that determine the intrinsic value of the company's stock.

Financial Leverage and ROE

An analyst interpreting the past behavior of a firm's ROE or forecasting its future value must pay careful attention to the firm's debt-equity mix and to the interest rate on its debt. An example will show why. Suppose Nodett is a firm that is all-equity financed and has total assets of $100 million. Assume it pays corporate taxes at the rate of 40% of taxable earnings.

Table 19.4 shows the behavior of sales, earnings before interest and taxes, and net profits under three scenarios representing phases of the business cycle. It also shows the behavior of two of the most commonly used profitability measures: operating **return on assets** (ROA), which equals EBIT/assets, and ROE, which equals net profits/equity.

Somdett is an otherwise identical firm to Nodett, but $40 million of its $100 million of assets are financed with debt bearing an interest rate of 8%. It pays annual interest expenses of $3.2 million. Table 19.5 shows how Somdett's ROE differs from Nodett's.

Note that annual sales, EBIT, and therefore ROA for both firms are the same in each of the three scenarios; that is, business risk for the two companies is identical. It is their financial risk that differs. Although Nodett and Somdett have the same ROA in each scenario, Somdett's ROE exceeds that of Nodett in normal and good years and is lower in bad years.

We can summarize the exact relationship among ROE, ROA, and leverage in the following equation:[1]

$$\text{ROE} = (1 - \text{Tax rate})\left[\text{ROA} + (\text{ROA} - \text{Interest rate})\,\frac{\text{Debt}}{\text{Equity}}\right] \qquad (19.1)$$

The relationship has the following implications. If there is no debt or if the firm's ROA equals the interest rate on its debt, its ROE will simply equal (1 minus the tax rate) times ROA. If its ROA exceeds the interest rate, then its ROE will exceed (1 minus the tax rate) times ROA by an amount that will be greater the higher the debt-to-equity ratio.

This result makes intuitive sense: If ROA exceeds the borrowing rate, the firm earns more on its money than it pays out to creditors. The surplus earnings are available to the firm's owners, the equityholders, which raises ROE. If, on the other hand, ROA is less than the interest rate, then ROE will decline by an amount that depends on the debt-to-equity ratio.

---

[1]The derivation of equation 19.1 is as follows:

$$\text{ROE} = \frac{\text{Net profit}}{\text{Equity}}$$

$$= \frac{\text{EBIT} - \text{Interest} - \text{Taxes}}{\text{Equity}}$$

$$= \frac{(1 - \text{Tax rate})(\text{EBIT} - \text{Interest})}{\text{Equity}}$$

$$= (1-\text{Tax rate})\left[\frac{(\text{ROA} \times \text{Assets}) - (\text{Interest rate} \times \text{Debt})}{\text{Equity}}\right]$$

$$= (1 - \text{Tax rate})\left[\text{ROA} \times \frac{(\text{Equity} + \text{Debt})}{\text{Equity}} - \text{Interest Rate} \times \frac{\text{Debt}}{\text{Equity}}\right]$$

$$= (1 - \text{Tax rate})\left[\text{ROA} + (\text{ROA} - \text{Interest rate})\,\frac{\text{Debt}}{\text{Equity}}\right]$$

Table 19.4   Nodett's Profitability over the Business Cycle

Scenario	Sales ($ Millions)	EBIT ($ Millions)	ROA (% per Year)	Net Profit ($ Millions)	ROE (% per Year)
Bad year	80	5	5	3	3
Normal year	100	10	10	6	6
Good year	120	15	15	9	9

Table 19.5   Impact of Financial Leverage on ROE

Scenario	Nodett EBIT ($ Millions)	Nodett Net Profits ($ Millions)	Nodett ROE (%)	Somdett Net Profit* ($ Millions)	Somdett ROE† (%)
Bad year	5	3	3	1.08	1.8
Normal year	10	6	6	4.08	6.8
Good year	15	9	9	7.08	11.8

*Somdett's after-tax profits are given by .6(EBIT − $3.2 million).

†Somdett's equity is only $60 million.

To illustrate the application of equation 19.1, we can use the numerical example in Table 19.5. In a normal year, Nodett has an ROE of 6%, which is .6 (i.e., 1 minus the tax rate) times its ROA of 10%. However, Somdett, which borrows at an interest rate of 8% and maintains a debt-to-equity ratio of ⅔, has an ROE of 6.8%. The calculation using equation 19.1 is

$$ROE = .6[10\% + (10\% - 8\%)\tfrac{2}{3}]$$
$$= .6[10\% + \tfrac{4}{3}\%] = 6.8\%$$

The important point to remember is that increased debt will make a positive contribution to a firm's ROE only if the firm's ROA exceeds the interest rate on the debt.

Note also that financial leverage increases the risk of the equityholder returns. Table 19.5 shows that ROE on Somdett is worse than that of Nodett in bad years. Conversely, in good years, Somdett outperforms Nodett because the excess of ROA over ROE provides additional funds for equityholders. The presence of debt makes Somdett more sensitive to the business cycle than Nodett. Even though the two companies have equal business risk (reflected in their identical EBITs in all three scenarios), Somdett carries greater financial risk than Nodett.

Even if financial leverage increases the expected ROE of Somdett relative to Nodett (as it seems to in Table 19.5), this does not imply that the market value of Somdett's equity will be higher. Financial leverage increases the risk of the firm's equity as surely as it raises the expected ROE.

Concept **CHECK**

Question 1• Mordett is a company with the same assets as Nodett and Somdett but a debt-to-equity ratio of 1.0 and an interest rate of 9%. What would its net profit and ROE be in a bad year, a normal year, and a good year?

19.4   RATIO ANALYSIS

Decomposition of ROE

To understand the factors affecting a firm's ROE, including its trend over time and its performance relative to competitors, analysts often "decompose" ROE into the product of a series of ratios. Each component ratio is in itself meaningful, and the process serves to focus the analyst's attention on the separate factors influencing performance. This kind of decomposition of ROE is often called the **Du Pont system**.

One useful decomposition of ROE is

$$ROE = \frac{\text{Net profits}}{\text{Pretax profits}} \times \frac{\text{Pretax profits}}{\text{EBIT}} \times \frac{\text{EBIT}}{\text{Sales}} \times \frac{\text{Sales}}{\text{Assets}} \times \frac{\text{Assets}}{\text{Equity}}$$
$$(1) \quad \times \quad (2) \quad \times \quad (3) \times (4) \times (5)$$

Table 19.6 shows all these ratios for Nodett and Somdett Corporations under the three different economic scenarios.

Let us first focus on factors 3 and 4. Notice that their product, EBIT/Assets, gives us the firm's ROA.

Factor 3 is known as the firm's operating **profit margin** or **return on sales** (ROS). ROS shows operating profit per dollar of sales. In an average year, ROS is .10, or 10%; in a bad year, it is .0625, or 6.25%, and in a good year, .125, or 12.5%.

Factor 4, the ratio of sales to assets, is known as **asset turnover** (ATO). It indicates the efficiency of the firm's use of assets in the sense that it measures the annual sales generated by each dollar of assets. In a normal year, Nodett's ATO is 1.0 per year, meaning that sales of $1 per year were generated per dollar of assets. In a bad year, this ratio declines to .8 per year, and in a good year, it rises to 1.2 per year.

Comparing Nodett and Somdett, we see that factors 3 and 4 do not depend on a firm's financial leverage. The firms' ratios are equal to each other in all three scenarios.

Similarly, factor 1, the ratio of net income after taxes to pretax profit, is the same for both firms. We call this the *tax-burden ratio*. Its value reflects both the government's tax code and the policies pursued by the firm in trying to minimize its tax burden. In our example it does not change over the business cycle, remaining a constant .6.

Table 19.6   Ratio Decomposition Analysis for Nodett and Somdett

	ROE	(1) Net Profit/ Pretax Profit	(2) Pretax Profit/EBIT	(3) EBIT/Sales (ROS)	(4) Sales/Assets (ATO)	(5) Assets/ Equity	(6) Compound Leverage Factor (2) × (5)
Bad year							
Nodett	.030	.6	1.000	.0625	0.800	1.000	1.000
Somdett	.018	.6	0.360	.0625	0.800	1.667	0.600
Normal year							
Nodett	.060	.6	1.000	.1000	1.000	1.000	1.000
Somdett	.068	.6	0.680	.1000	1.000	1.667	1.134
Good year							
Nodett	.090	.6	1.000	.1250	1.200	1.000	1.000
Somdett	.118	.6	0.787	.1250	1.200	1.667	1.311

Although factors 1, 3, and 4 are not affected by a firm's capital structure, factors 2 and 5 are. Factor 2 is the ratio of pretax profits to EBIT. The firm's pretax profits will be greatest when there are no interest payments to be made to debtholders. In fact, another way to express this ratio is

$$\frac{\text{Pretax profits}}{\text{EBIT}} = \frac{\text{EBIT} - \text{Interest expense}}{\text{EBIT}}$$

We will call this factor the *interest-burden ratio* (*IB*). It takes on its highest possible value, 1, for Nodett, which has no financial leverage. The higher the degree of financial leverage, the lower the IB ratio. Nodett's IB ratio does not vary over the business cycle. It is fixed at 1.0, reflecting the total absence of interest payments. For Somdett, however, because interest expense is fixed in a dollar amount while EBIT varies, the IB ratio varies from a low of .36 in a bad year to a high of .787 in a good year.

Factor 5, the ratio of assets to equity, is a measure of the firm's degree of financial leverage. It is called the **leverage ratio** and is equal to 1 plus the debt-to-equity ratio.[2] In our numerical example in Table 19.6, Nodett has a leverage ratio of 1, while Somdett's is 1.667.

From our discussion in Section 19.2, we know that financial leverage helps boost ROE only if ROA is greater than the interest rate on the firm's debt. How is this fact reflected in the ratios of Table 19.6?

The answer is that to measure the full impact of leverage in this framework, the analyst must take the product of the IB and leverage ratios (i.e., factors 2 and 5, shown in Table 19.6 as column 6). For Nodett, factor 6, which we call the *compound leverage factor*, remains a constant 1.0 under all three scenarios. But for Somdett, we see that the compound leverage factor is greater than 1 in normal years (1.134) and in good years (1.311), indicating the positive contribution of financial leverage to ROE. It is less than 1 in bad years, reflecting the fact that when ROA falls below the interest rate, ROE falls with increased use of debt.

We can summarize all of these relationships as follows:

ROE = Tax burden × Interest burden × Margin × Turnover × Leverage

Because

ROA = Margin × Turnover

and

Compound leverage factor = Interest burden × Leverage

we can decompose ROE equivalently as follows:

ROE = Tax burden × ROA × Compound leverage factor

Table 19.6 compares firms with the same ROS and ATO but different degrees of financial leverage.

Comparison of ROS and ATO usually is meaningful only in evaluating firms in the same industry. Cross-industry comparisons of these two ratios are often meaningless and can even be misleading. For example, let us take two firms with the same ROA of 10% per year. The first is a supermarket chain, the second is a gas and electric utility.

---

[2] $\dfrac{\text{Assets}}{\text{Equity}} = \dfrac{\text{Equity} + \text{Debt}}{\text{Equity}} = 1 + \dfrac{\text{Debt}}{\text{Equity}}$

Table 19.7   Differences between ROS and ATO across Industries

	ROS	×	ATO	=	ROA
Supermarket chain	2%		5.0		10%
Utility	20%		0.5		10%

As Table 19.7 shows, the supermarket chain has a "low" ROS of 2% and achieves a 10% ROA by "turning over" its assets five times per year. The capital-intensive utility, on the other hand, has a "low" ATO of only .5 times per year and achieves its 10% ROA by having an ROS of 20%. The point here is that a "low" ROS or ATO ratio need not indicate a troubled firm. Each ratio must be interpreted in light of industry norms.

Even within an industry, ROS and ATO sometimes can differ markedly among firms pursuing different marketing strategies. In the retailing industry, for example, Neiman Marcus pursues a high-margin, low-ATO policy compared to Wal-Mart, which pursues a low-margin, high-ATO policy.

Concept CHECK

Question 2 • Do a ratio decomposition analysis for the Mordett corporation of Question 1, preparing a table similar to Table 19.6.

Turnover and Other Asset Utilization Ratios

It is often helpful in understanding a firm's ratio of sales to assets to compute comparable efficiency-of-utilization, or turnover, ratios for subcategories of assets. For example, *fixed-asset turnover* would be

$$\frac{\text{Sales}}{\text{Fixed assets}}$$

This ratio measures sales per dollar of the firm's money tied up in fixed assets.

To illustrate how you can compute this and other ratios from a firm's financial statements, consider Growth Industries, Inc. (GI). GI's income statement and opening and closing balance sheets for the years 19X1, 19X2, and 19X3 appear in Table 19.8.

GI's total asset turnover in 19X3 was .303, which was below the industry average of .4. To understand better why GI underperformed, we decide to compute asset utilization ratios separately for fixed assets, inventories, and accounts receivable.

GI's sales in 19X3 were $144 million. Its only fixed assets were plant and equipment, which were $216 million at the beginning of the year and $259.2 million at year's end. Average fixed assets for the year were, therefore, $237.6 million [($216 million + $259.2 million)/2]. GI's fixed-asset turnover for 19X3 therefore was $144 million per year/$237.6 million = .606 per year. In other words, for every dollar of fixed assets, there were $.606 in sales during the year 19X3.

Comparable figures for the fixed-asset turnover ratio for 19X1 and 19X2 and the 19X3 industry average are

19X1	19X2	19X3	19X3 Industry Average
.606	.606	.606	.700

GI's fixed asset turnover has been stable over time and below the industry average.

Table 19.8   Growth Industries Financial Statements, 19X1–19X3 ($ thousands)

	19X0	19X1	19X2	19X3
Income Statements				
Sales revenue		$100,000	$120,000	$144,000
Cost of goods sold (including depreciation)		55,000	66,000	79,200
Depreciation		15,000	18,000	21,600
Selling and administrative expenses		15,000	18,000	21,600
Operating income		30,000	36,000	43,200
Interest expense		10,500	19,095	34,391
Taxable income		19,500	16,905	8,809
Income tax (40% rate)		7,800	6,762	3,524
Net income		$ 11,700	$ 10,143	$ 5,285
Balance Sheets (end of year)				
Cash and marketable securities	$ 50,000	60,000	72,000	86,400
Accounts receivable	25,000	30,000	36,000	43,200
Inventories	75,000	90,000	108,000	129,600
Net plant and equipment	150,000	180,000	216,000	259,200
Total assets	$300,000	$360,000	$432,000	$518,400
Accounts payable	$ 30,000	$ 36,000	$ 43,200	$ 51,840
Short-term debt	45,000	87,300	141,957	214,432
Long-term debt (8% bonds maturing in 19X7)	75,000	75,000	75,000	75,000
Total liabilities	$150,000	$198,300	$260,157	341,272
Shareholders' equity (1 million shares outstanding)	$150,000	$161,700	$171,843	$177,128
Other Data				
Market price per common share at year-end		$93.60	$61.00	$21.00

Whenever a financial ratio includes one item from the income statement, which covers a period of time, and another from a balance sheet, which is a "snapshot" at a particular time, the practice is to take the average of the beginning and end-of-year balance sheet figures. Thus in computing the fixed-asset turnover ratio you divided sales (from the income statement) by average fixed assets (from the balance sheet).

Another widely followed turnover ratio is the inventory turnover ratio, which is the ratio of cost of goods sold per dollar of average inventory. The numerator is cost of goods sold instead of sales revenue because inventory is valued at cost. This ratio measures the speed with which inventory is turned over.

In 19X1, GI's cost of goods sold (less depreciation) was $40 million, and its average inventory was $82.5 million [($75 million + $90 million)/2]. Its inventory turnover was .485 per year ($40 million/$82.5 million). In 19X2 and 19X3, inventory turnover remained the same, which was below the industry average of .5 per year.

Another measure of efficiency is the ratio of accounts receivable to sales. The accounts receivable ratio usually is computed as average accounts receivable/sales × 365. The result is a number called the **average collection period**, or **days receivables**, which equals the total credit extended to customers per dollar of daily sales. It is the number of days' worth of sales tied up in accounts receivable. You can also think of it as the average lag between the date of sale and the date payment is received.

For GI in 19X3 this number was 100.4 days:

$$\frac{(\$36 \text{ million} + \$43.2 \text{ million})/2}{\$144 \text{ million}} \times 365 = 100.4 \text{ days}$$

The industry average was 60 days.

In summary, use of these ratios lets us see that GI's poor total asset turnover relative to the industry is in part caused by lower-than-average fixed-asset turnover and inventory turnover and higher-than-average days receivables. This suggests GI may be having problems with excess plant capacity along with poor inventory and receivables management procedures.

Liquidity and Coverage Ratios

Liquidity and interest coverage ratios are of great importance in evaluating the riskiness of a firm's securities. They aid in assessing the financial strength of the firm. Liquidity ratios include the current ratio, quick ratio, and interest coverage ratio.

1. **Current ratio:** Current assets/current liabilities. This ratio measures the ability of the firm to pay off its current liabilities by liquidating its current assets (i.e., turning them into cash). It indicates the firm's ability to avoid insolvency in the short run. GI's current ratio in 19X1, for example, was $(60 + 30 + 90)/(36 + 87.3) = 1.46$. In other years, it was

19X1	19X2	19X3	19X3 Industry Average
1.46	1.17	.97	2.0

This represents an unfavorable time trend and poor standing relative to the industry.

2. **Quick ratio:** (Cash + receivables)/current liabilities. This ratio is also called the **acid test ratio**. It has the same denominator as the current ratio, but its numerator includes only cash, cash equivalents, and receivables. The quick ratio is a better measure of liquidity than the current ratio for firms whose inventory is not really convertible into cash. GI's quick ratio shows the same disturbing trends as its current ratio:

19X1	19X2	19X3	19X3 Industry Average
.73	.58	.49	1.0

3. **Interest coverage ratio:** EBIT/interest expense. This ratio is often called **times interest earned**. It is closely related to the interest-burden ratio discussed in the previous section. A high coverage ratio tells the firm's shareholders and lenders that the likelihood of bankruptcy is low because annual earnings are significantly greater than annual interest obligations. It is widely used by both lenders and borrowers in determining the firm's debt capacity and is a major determinant of the firm's bond rating. GI's interest coverage ratios are

19X1	19X2	19X3	19X3 Industry Average
2.86	1.89	19X1	5

GI's interest coverage ratio has fallen dramatically over this three-year period, and by 19X3 it is far below the industry average. Probably its credit rating has been declining as well, and no doubt GI is considered a relatively poor credit risk in 19X3.

Market Price Ratios

There are two market price ratios: the market–book-value ratio and the price–earnings ratio.

The **market–book-value ratio** (P/B) equals the market price of a share of the firm's common stock divided by its *book value*, that is, shareholders' equity per share. Analysts sometimes consider the stock of a firm with a low market–book value to be a "safer" investment, seeing the book value as a "floor" supporting the market price.

Analysts presumably view book value as the level below which market price will not fall because the firm always has the option to liquidate, or sell, its assets for their book values. However, this view is questionable. In fact, some firms sell for less than book value. Nevertheless, low market–book-value ratio is seen by some as providing a "margin of safety," and some analysts will screen out or reject high P/B firms in their stock selection process.

Proponents of the P/B screen would argue that if all other relevant attributes are the same for two stocks, the one with the lower P/B ratio is safer. Although there may be firms for which this approach has some validity, book value does not necessarily represent liquidation value, which renders the margin of safety notion unreliable.

The theory of equity valuation offers some insight into the significance of the P/B ratio. A high P/B ratio is an indication that investors think a firm has opportunities of earning a rate of return on their investment in excess of the market capitalization rate, k.

To illustrate this point, we can return to the numerical example in Chapter 18, Table 18.3. That example assumes the market capitalization rate is 12% per year. Now add the assumptions that the book value per share is $8.33 and that the coming year's expected EPS is $1, so that in the case for which the expected ROE on future investments also is 12%, the stock will sell at $1/.12 = $8.33, and the P/B ratio will be 1.

Table 19.9 shows the P/B ratio for alternative assumptions about future ROE and plowback ratio. Reading down any column, you can see how the P/B ratio changes with ROE. The numbers reveal that for a given plowback ratio, the P/B ratio is higher, the higher the expected ROE. This makes sense, because the greater the expected profitability of the firm's future investment opportunities, the greater its market value as an ongoing enterprise compared with the cost of acquiring its assets.

Table 19.9   Effect of ROE and Plowback Ratio on P/B

ROE	Plowback Ratio, *b*			
	0	25%	50%	75%
10%	1.00	0.95	0.86	0.67
12%	1.00	1.00	1.00	1.00
14%	1.00	1.06	1.20	2.00

The assumptions and formulas underlying this table are: $E_1 = \$1$; book value per share = $8.33; $k = 12\%$ per year; and

$$g = b \times \text{ROE} \qquad P_0 = \frac{(1-b)E}{k-g} \qquad \text{P/B} = \frac{P_0}{\$8.33}$$

We've noted that the **price–earnings ratio** that is based on the firm's financial statements and reported in newspaper stock listings is not the same as the price–earnings multiple that emerges from a discounted dividend model. The numerator is the same (the market price of the stock), but the denominator is different. The reported P/E ratio uses the most recent past accountings earnings, whereas the P/E multiple predicted by valuation models uses expected future economic earnings.

Many security analysts pay careful attention to the accounting P/E ratio in the belief that among low P/E stocks they are more likely to find bargains than with high P/E stocks. The idea is that you can acquire a claim on a dollar of earnings more cheaply if the P/E ratio is low. For example, if the P/E ratio is 8, you pay $8 per share per $1 of *current* earnings, whereas if P/E is 12, you must pay $12 for a claim on $1 of current earnings.

Note, however, that current earnings may differ substantially from future earnings. The higher P/E stock still may be a bargain relative to the low P/E stock if its earnings and dividends are expected to grow at a faster rate. Our point is that ownership of the stock conveys the right to future earnings, as well as to current earnings. An exclusive focus on the commonly reported accounting P/E ratio can he shortsighted, because by its nature it ignores future growth in earnings.

An efficient markets adherent will be skeptical of the notion that a strategy of investment in low P/E stocks would result in an expected rate of return greater than that of investing in high or medium P/E stocks having the same risk. The empirical evidence on this question is mixed, but even if the strategy has worked in the past, it still should not work in the future because too many investors would be following it. This is the lesson of market efficiency.

Before leaving the P/B and P/E ratios, it is worth pointing out the relationship among these ratios and ROE:

$$\text{ROE} = \frac{\text{Earnings}}{\text{Book value}}$$

$$= \frac{\text{Market price}}{\text{Book value}} \div \frac{\text{Market price}}{\text{Earnings}}$$

$$= \text{P/B ratio} \div \text{P/E ratio}$$

By rearranging the terms, we find that a firm's **earnings yield**, the ratio of earnings to price, is equal to its ROE divided by the market–book-value ratio:

$$\frac{E}{P} = \frac{\text{ROE}}{\text{P/B}}$$

Thus a company with a high ROE can have a relatively low earnings yield because its P/B ratio is high. This indicates that a high ROE does not in and of itself imply the stock is a good buy: The price of the stock already may be bid up to reflect an attractive ROE. If so, the P/B ratio will be above 1.0, and the earnings yield to stockholders will be below the ROE, as the equation demonstrates. The relationship shows that a strategy of investing in the stock of high ROE firms may produce a lower holding-period return than investing in those with a low ROE.

Clayman[3] found that investing in the stocks of 29 "excellent" companies, with mean reported ROE of 19.05% during the period of 1976 to 1980, produced results much inferior to investing in 39 "unexcellent" companies, those with a mean ROE of 7.09% during the

---

[3]Michelle Clayman, "In Search of Excellence: The Investor's Viewpoint," *Financial Analysts Journal*, May–June 1987.

period. An investor putting equal dollar amounts in the stocks of unexcellent companies would have earned a portfolio rate of return over the 1981 to 1985 period that was 11.3% higher per year than the rate of return on a comparable portfolio of excellent company stocks.

Concept
CHECK

Question 3 • What were GI's ROE, P/E, and P/B ratios in the year 19X3? How do they compare to the industry average ratios, which were:

$$\text{ROE} = 8.64\% \qquad \text{P/E} = 8 \qquad \text{P/B} = .69$$

How does GI's earnings yield in 19X3 compare to the industry average?

19.5   AN ILLUSTRATION OF FINANCIAL STATEMENT ANALYSIS

In her 19X3 annual report to the shareholders of Growth Industries, Inc., the president wrote: "19X3 was another successful year for Growth Industries. As in 19X2, sales, assets, and operating income all continued to grow at a rate of 20%."

Is she right?

We can evaluate her statement by conducting a full-scale ratio analysis of Growth Industries. Our purpose is to assess GI's performance in the recent past, to evaluate its future prospects, and to determine whether its market price reflects its intrinsic value.

Table 19.10 shows the key financial ratios we can compute from GI's financial statements. The president is certainly right about the growth rate in sales, assets, and operating income. Inspection of GI's key financial ratios, however, contradicts her first sentence: 19X3 was not another successful year for GI—it appears to have been another miserable one.

ROE has been declining steadily from 7.51% in 19X1 to 3.03% in 19X3. A comparison of GI's 19X3 ROE to the 19X3 industry average of 8.64% makes the deteriorating time trend appear especially alarming. The low and falling market–book-value ratio and the falling price–earnings ratio indicate investors are less and less optimistic about the firm's future profitability.

The fact that ROA has not been declining, however, tells us that the source of the declining time trend in GI's ROE must be inappropriate use of financial leverage. And we see that as GI's leverage ratio climbed from 2.117 in 19X1 to 2.723 in 19X3, its interest-burden ratio fell from .650 to .204—with the net result that the compound leverage factor fell from 1.376 to .556.

The rapid increase in short-term debt from year to year and the concurrent increase in interest expense make it clear that to finance its 20% growth rate in sales, GI has incurred sizable amounts of short-term debt at high interest rates. The firm is paying rates of inter-

Table 19.10   Key Financial Ratios of Growth Industries, Inc.

Year	ROE	(1) Net Profit/ Pretax Profit	(2) Pretax Profit/ EBIT	(3) EBIT/ Sales (ROS)	(4) Sales/ Assets (ATO)	(5) Assets/ Equity	(6) Compound Leverage Factor (2) × (5)	(7) ROA (3) × (4)	P/E	P/B
19X1	7.51%	.6	.650	30%	.303	2.117	1.376	9.09%	8	.58
19X2	6.08	.6	.470	30	.303	2.375	1.116	9.09	6	.35
19X3	3.03	.6	.204	30	.303	2.723	0.556	9.09	4	.12
Industry average	8.64%	.6	.800	30%	.400	1.500	1.200	12.00%	8	.69

Table 19.11   Growth Industries Statement of Cash Flows ($ thousands)

	19X1	19X2	19X3
Cash Flow from Operating Activities			
Net income	$ 11,700	$ 10,143	$ 5,285
+ Depreciation	15,000	18,000	21,600
+ Decrease (increase) in accounts receivable	(5,000)	(6,000)	(7,200)
+ Decrease (increase) in inventories	(15,000)	(18,000)	(21,600)
+ Increase in accounts payable	6,000	7,200	8,640
	$ 12,700	$ 11,343	$ 6,725
Cash Flow from Investing Activities			
Investment in plant and equipment*	$(45,000)	$(54,000)	$(64,800)
Cash Flow from Financing Activities			
Dividends paid†	$ 0	$ 0	$ 0
Short-term debt issued	$ 42,300	$ 54,657	$ 72,475
Change in cash and marketable securities‡	$ 10,000	$ 12,000	$ 14,400

*Gross investment equals increase in net plant and equipment plus depreciation.

†We can conclude that no dividends are paid because stockholders' equity increases each year by the full amount of net income, implying a plowback ratio of 1.0.

‡Equals cash flow from operations plus cash flow from investment activities plus cash flow from financing activities. Note that this equals the yearly change in cash and marketable securities on the balance sheet.

est greater than the ROA it is earning on the investment financed with the new borrowing. As the firm has expanded, its situation has become ever more precarious.

In 19X3, for example, the average interest rate on short-term debt was 20% versus an ROA of 9.09%. (We compute the average interest rate on short-term debt by taking the total interest expense of $34,391,000, subtracting the $6 million in interest on the long-term bonds, and dividing by the beginning-of-year short-term debt of $141,957,000.)

GI's problems become clear when we examine its statement of cash flows in Table 19.11. The statement is derived from the income statement and balance sheet in Table 19.8. GI's cash flow from operations is falling steadily, from $12,700,000 in 19X1 to $6,725,000 in 19X3. The firm's investment in plant and equipment, by contrast, has increased greatly. Net plant and equipment (i.e., net of depreciation) rose from $150,000,000 in 19X0 to $259,200,000 in 19X3. This near doubling of the capital assets makes the decrease in cash flow from operations all the more troubling.

The source of the difficulty is GI's enormous amount of short-term borrowing. In a sense, the company is being run as a pyramid scheme. It borrows more and more each year to maintain its 20% growth rate in assets and income. However, the new assets are not generating enough cash flow to support the extra interest burden of the debt, as the falling cash flow from operations indicates. Eventually, when the firm loses its ability to borrow further, its growth will be at an end.

At this point GI stock might be an attractive investment. Its market price is only 12% of its book value, and with a P/E ratio of 4 its earnings yield is 25% per year. GI is a likely candidate for a takeover by another firm that might replace GI's management and build shareholder value through a radical change in policy.

Concept

Question 4 • You have the following information for IBX Corporation for the years 1998 and 1996 (all figures are in $ millions):

	1998	1996
Net income	$ 253.7	$ 239.0
Pretax income	411.9	375.6
EBIT	517.6	403.1
Average assets	4,857.9	3,459.7
Sales	6,679.3	4,537.0
Shareholders' equity	2,233.3	2,347.3

What is the trend in IBX's ROE, and how can you account for it in terms of tax burden, margin, turnover, and financial leverage?

19.6   COMPARABILITY PROBLEMS

Financial statement analysis gives us a good amount of ammunition for evaluating a company's performance and future prospects. But comparing financial results of different companies is not so simple. There is more than one acceptable way to represent various items of revenue and expense according to generally accepted accounting principles (GAAP). This means two firms may have exactly the same economic income yet very different accounting incomes.

Furthermore, interpreting a single firm's performance over time is complicated when inflation distorts the dollar measuring rod. Comparability problems are especially acute in this case because the impact of inflation on reported results often depends on the particular method the firm adopts to account for inventories and depreciation. The security analyst must adjust the earnings and the financial ratio figures to a uniform standard before attempting to compare financial results across firms and over time.

Comparability problems can arise out of the flexibility of GAAP guidelines in accounting for inventories and depreciation and in adjusting for the effects of inflation. Other important potential sources of noncomparability include the capitalization of leases and other expenses and the treatment of pension costs, but they are beyond the scope of this book. The nearby box illustrates the types of problems an analyst must be aware of in using financial statements to identify bargain stocks.

Inventory Valuation

There are two commonly used ways to value inventories: **LIFO** (last-in first-out) and **FIFO** (first-in first-out). We can explain the difference using a numerical example.

Suppose Generic Products, Inc. (GPI), has a constant inventory of 1 million units of generic goods. The inventory turns over once per year, meaning the ratio of cost of goods sold to inventory is 1.

The LIFO system calls for valuing the million units used up during the year at the current cost of production, so that the last goods produced are considered the first ones to be sold. They are valued at today's cost.

The FIFO system assumes that the units used up or sold are the ones that were added to inventory first, and goods sold should be valued at original cost.

THE MANY WAYS OF FIGURING FINANCIAL RESULTS

An investor in First Boston Corp. might have had a pleasant surprise while reading the investment banking company's 1987 financial statement. Despite taking heavy hits in the volatile bond markets and October's stock crash, First Boston reported earnings of $3.12 per share—down 40 percent from the heights of 1986, but about the same as profits in 1984.

But hold on. Looking through Value Line's *Investment Survey*, the same investor would be dismayed to find that First Boston's earnings for last year were only 59¢ a share. What gives? In this case the explanation is fairly simple. Value Line doesn't take into account the profits First Boston made in selling its Park Avenue headquarters, while the company and other reporting services such as Standard & Poor's do.

This type of discrepancy in reported financial figures is very common (table) and points to a general rule: Where the bottom line falls depends on who's drawing it. S&P's *Stock Report* generally follows the company's accounting in regard to nonrecurring items, but Value Line doesn't. For example, Union Carbide's reserve for Bhopal [chemical spill] litigation amounted to 40¢ per share. S&P and Carbide subtracted it from earnings, but Value Line left it in.

THE BOTTOM LINE: TAKE YOUR CHOICE

	1987 Earnings per Share	
	S&P	Value Line
Alcoa	$2.52	$4.14
Affiliated Publ.	4.08	0.61
First Boston	3.12	0.59
Merrill Lynch	3.58	1.52
Union Carbide	1.76	2.17

Source: Data from Standard & Poor's Corp., Value Line Inc.

Source: Reprinted from April 11, 1988, issue of *Business Week* by special permission, copyright © 1988 by McGraw-Hill, Inc.

Forecast Tool

With the rash of mergers, acquisitions, and divestitures in recent years, the varying approaches of reporting services can result in enormous differences. In 1985, for example, when Warner-Lambert cut its losses by selling three hospital-supply units, S&P showed the company losing $4.05 per share for the year, while Value Line reported a gain of $3.05 per share.

To try to get a "clear-cut number," Value Line will remove from earnings such items as gains or losses from discontinued operations and other special items, says a senior analyst at the firm. He says such a number is more useful to investors looking at the future earning power of a company. Similarly, *Business Week's* Corporate Scoreboard shows earnings from continuing operations, excluding special, non-recurring, or extraordinary items. Dan Mayper at S&P says S&P's philosophy is to reflect all the special items in the figures and explain their significance in the narrative of the report.

There are also wide variations when it comes to computing a company's book value. That's basically what's left over when you subtract liabilities from assets. Unlike Value Line, S&P gives no credit to such intangible assets as customer lists, patents, trademarks, or franchises. Companies with many intangibles on their books, such as broadcasters and publishers, are bound to look a lot worse in S&P's calculations. For example, Capital Cities/ABC had a 1986 per-share book value of $120.82, said Value Line, while S&P showed a negative net worth of $24.26 per share.

Value Line analyst Marc Gerstein believes that including the intangibles on the balance sheet gives the best idea of a company's value as an ongoing concern. S&P regards its approach as more conservative, designed to approximate the company's liquidation value.

If the price of generic goods has been constant, at the level of $1, say, the book value of inventory and the cost of goods sold would be the same, $1 million under both systems. But suppose the price of generic goods rises by 10 cents per unit during the year as a result of general inflation.

LIFO accounting would result in a cost of goods sold of $1.1 million, whereas the end-of-year balance sheet value of the 1 million units in inventory remains $1 million. The balance sheet value of inventories is given as the cost of the goods still in inventory. Under LIFO the last goods produced are assumed to be sold at the current cost of $1.10; the goods remaining are the previously produced goods, at a cost of only $1. You can see that although LIFO accounting accurately measures the cost of goods sold today, it understates the current value of the remaining inventory in an inflationary environment.

In contrast, under FIFO accounting, the cost of goods sold would be $1 million, and the end-of-year balance sheet value of the inventory would be $1.1 million. The result is that the LIFO firm has both a lower reported profit and a lower balance sheet value of inventories than the FIFO firm.

LIFO is preferred over FIFO in computing economic earnings (i.e., real sustainable cash flow), because it uses up-to-date prices to evaluate the cost of goods sold. A disadvantage is that LIFO accounting induces balance sheet distortions when it values investment in inventories at original cost. This practice results in an upward bias in ROE because the investment base on which return is earned is undervalued.

In computing the gross national product, the U.S. Department of Commerce has to make an inventory valuation adjustment (IVA) to eliminate the effects of FIFO accounting on the cost of goods sold. In effect, it puts all firms in the aggregate onto a LIFO basis.

Depreciation

Another source of problems is the measurement of depreciation, which is a key factor in computing true earnings. The accounting and economic measures of depreciation can differ markedly. According to the *economic* definition, depreciation is the amount of a firm's operating cash flow that must be reinvested in the firm to sustain its real productive capacity at the current level.

The *accounting* measurement is quite different. Accounting depreciation is the amount of the original acquisition cost of an asset that is allocated to each accounting period over an arbitrarily specified life of the asset. This is the figure reported in financial statements.

Assume, for example, that a firm buys machines with a useful economic life of 20 years at $100,000 apiece. In its financial statements, however, the firm can depreciate the machines over 10 years using the straight-line method, for $10,000 per year in depreciation. Thus after 10 years a machine will be fully depreciated on the books, even though it remains a productive asset that will not need replacement for another 10 years.

In computing accounting earnings, this firm will overestimate depreciation in the first 10 years of the machine's economic life and underestimate it in the last 10 years. This will cause reported earnings to be understated compared with economic earnings in the first 10 years and overstated in the last 10 years.

If the management of the firm had a zero-plowback policy and distributed as cash dividends only its accounting earnings, it would pay out too little in the first 10 years relative to the sustainable cash flow. Similarly, a security analyst who relied on the (unadjusted) reported earnings figure during the first few years would see understated economic earnings and would underestimate the firm's intrinsic value.

Depreciation comparability problems add one more wrinkle. A firm can use different depreciation methods for tax purposes than for other reporting purposes. Most firms use accelerated depreciation methods for tax purposes and straight-line depreciation in published financial statements. There also are differences across firms in their estimates of the depreciable life of plant, equipment, and other depreciable assets.

The major problem related to depreciation, however, is caused by inflation. Because conventional depreciation is based on historical costs rather than on the current replacement cost of assets, measured depreciation in periods of inflation is understated relative to replacement cost, and *real* economic income (sustainable cash flow) is correspondingly overstated.

The situation is similar to what happens in FIFO inventory accounting. Conventional depreciation and FIFO both result in an inflation-induced overstatement of real income because both use original cost instead of current cost to calculate net income.

For example, suppose Generic Products, Inc., has a machine with a three-year useful life that originally cost $3 million. Annual straight-line depreciation is $1 million, regardless of what happens to the replacement cost of the machine. Suppose inflation in the first year turns out to be 10%. Then the true annual depreciation expense is $1.1 million in current terms, whereas conventionally measured depreciation remains fixed at $1 million per year. Accounting income overstates *real* economic income by $.1 million.

As it does in the case of inventory valuation, the Commerce Department in its computation of GDP tries to adjust aggregate depreciation. It does this by applying "capital consumption allowances" (CCA), to account for the distorting effects of conventional depreciation techniques.

Inflation and Interest Expense

Although inflation can cause distortions in the measurement of a firm's inventory and depreciation costs, it has perhaps an even greater effect on calculation of *real* interest expense. Nominal interest rates include an inflation premium that compensates the lender for inflation-induced erosion in the real value of principal. From the perspective of both lender and borrower, therefore, part of what is conventionally measured as interest expense should be treated more properly as repayment of principal.

For example, suppose Generic Products has debt outstanding with a face value of $10 million at an interest rate of 10% per year. Interest expense as conventionally measured is $1 million per year. However, suppose inflation during the year is 6%, so that the real interest rate is 4%. Then $.6 million of what appears as interest expense on the income statement is really an inflation premium, or compensation for the anticipated reduction in the real value of the $10 million principal; only $.4 million is *real* interest expense. The $.6 million reduction in the purchasing power of the outstanding principal may be thought of as repayment of principal, rather than as an interest expense. Real income of the firm is, therefore, understated by $.6 million.

This mismeasurement of real interest means inflation deflates the statement of real income. The effects of inflation on the reported values of inventories and depreciation that we have discussed work in the opposite direction.

Concept CHECK

Question 5 • In a period of rapid inflation, companies ABC and XYZ have the same *reported* earnings. ABC uses LIFO inventory accounting, has relatively fewer depreciable assets, and has more debt than XYZ. XYZ uses FIFO inventory accounting. Which company has the higher *real* income, and why?

International Accounting Conventions

The examples cited above illustrate some of the problems that analysts can encounter when attempting to interpret financial data. Even greater problems arise in the interpretation of the financial statements of foreign firms. This is because these firms do not follow GAAP guidelines. Accounting practices in various countries differ to greater or lesser extents from U.S. standards. Here are some of the major issues that you should be aware of when using the financial statements of foreign firms:

Reserving Practices. Many countries allow firms considerably more discretion in setting aside reserves for future contingencies than is typical in the United States. Because additions to reserves result in a charge against income, reported earnings are far more subject to managerial discretion than in the United States.

Germany is a country that allows particularly wide discretion in reserve practice. When Daimler-Benz AG (producer of the Mercedes-Benz) decided to issue shares on

Figure 19.1

Adjusted versus
reported
price–earnings ratios.

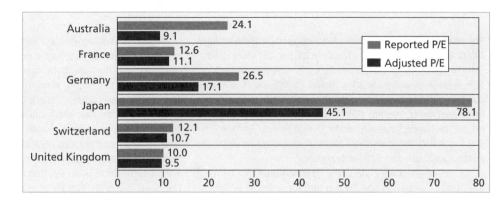

the New York Stock Exchange in 1993, it had to revise its accounting statements in accordance with U.S. standards. The revisions transformed a small profit for the first half of 1993 using German accounting rules into a *loss* of a $592 million under more stringent U.S. rules.

Depreciation. In the United States, firms typically maintain separate sets of accounts for tax and reporting purposes. For example, accelerated depreciation is typically used for tax purposes, whereas straight-line depreciation is used for reporting purposes. In contrast, most other countries do not allow dual sets of accounts, and most firms in foreign countries use accelerated depreciation to minimize taxes despite the fact that it results in lower reported earnings. This makes reported earnings of foreign firms lower than they would be if the firms were allowed to use the U.S. practice.

Intangibles. Treatment of intangibles such as goodwill can vary widely. Are they amortized or expensed? If amortized, over what period? Such issues can have a large impact on reported profits.

The effect of different accounting practices can be substantial. A study by Speidell and Bavishi[4] recalculated the financial statements of firms in several countries using common accounting rules. Figure 19.1, from their study, compares P/E ratios as reported and restated on a common basis. The variation is considerable.

Such differences in international accounting standards become more of a problem as the drive to globally integrated capital markets progresses. For example, many foreign firms would like to list their shares on the New York Stock Exchange in order to more easily tap U.S. equity markets, and the NYSE would like to have those firms listed. But the SEC will not allow such shares to be listed unless the firms prepare their financial statements in accordance with U.S. GAAP standards. This has limited listing of non-U.S. companies dramatically.

In contrast to the United States, most other large national stock exchanges allow foreign firms to be listed if their financial statements conform to International Accounting Standards (IAS) rules. IAS disclosure requirements tend to be far more rigorous than those of most countries, and these standards impose greater uniformity in accounting practices. Its advocates argue that IAS rules are already fairly similar to GAAP rules, providing nearly the same quality financial information about the firm. While the SEC does not yet deem IAS standards acceptable for listing in U.S. markets, negotiations are currently under

---

[4]Lawrence S. Speidell and Vinod Bavishi, "GAAP Arbitrage: Valuation Opportunities in International Accounting Standards," *Financial Analysts Journal*, November–December 1992, pp. 58–66.

A HILL OF BEANS

The world cannot have a truly global financial system without the help of its accountants. They are letting investors down.

The biggest impediment to a global capital market is not volatile exchange rates, nor timid investors. It is that firms from one country are not allowed to sell their shares in many others, including, crucially, in the United States. And the reason for that is the inability of different countries to settle on an international standard for reporting.

In order to change this, the International Accounting Standards Committee has been trying for years to persuade as many companies as possible to adopt its standards, and to convince securities regulators such as America's Securities and Exchange Commission to let such firms list on their stock exchanges. But the IASC has so far failed to produce standards that the SEC is willing to endorse. It should produce them now.

The purpose of accounting standards is simple: to help investors keep track of what managers are doing with their money. Countries such as America and Britain, in which managers are accountable to lots of dispersed investors, have had to develop standards that are more transparent and rigorous than those of other countries. And since the purpose of international standards is to encourage such markets on a global scale, it makes sense to use these countries' standards as a guide.

British and American accounting standards have their respective flaws, debated ad nauseam by accountancy's aficionados. But they are both superior to the IASC's existing standards in two main ways. First, they promote transparency by making firms attach to their aggregate financial tables (such as the profit-and-loss statement) a set of detailed notes disclosing exactly how the main items (such as inventories and pension liabilities) are calculated. Second, they lay down rules on how to record certain transactions. In many cases, there is no intellectually "right" way to do this. The point is simply that there is a standard method, so that managers cannot mislead investors by choosing the method for themselves.

Let the Markets Do the Talking

If the merits of Anglo-American accounting are so obvious, why has the IASC not adopted its standards? Even in their present state, the international standards are more rigorous than many domestic ones, and therefore unpopular with local firms. But by introducing a rigorous set of international standards, acceptable to the SEC, the committee could unleash some interesting competition. Companies which adopted the new standards would enjoy the huge advantage of being able to sell their shares anywhere; those opting for less disclosure would be punished by investors. It is amazing how persuasive the financial markets can be.

Source: *The Economist*, January 17, 1998.

---

way to change that situation. The nearby box reports on the various initiatives to enhance global standardization of accounting rules.

Inflation Accounting

In recognition of the need to adjust for the effects of inflation, the Financial Accounting Standards Board in 1980 issued Rule No. 33 (FASB 33). It required large public corporations to supplement their customary financial statements with data pertaining to the effect of inflation.

A survey reported by Norby,[5] however, indicated that security analysts, by and large, were ignoring the inflation-adjusted data. One possible reason is that analysts believed FASB 33 just added another element of noncomparability. In other words, analysts may have judged the inflation-adjusted earnings to be poorer estimates of real economic earnings than the original unadjusted figures.

In 1987, after a lengthy evaluation of the effects of FASB 33, the FASB decided to discontinue it. Today, analysts interested in adjusting reported financial statements for inflation are on their own.

---

[5]W. C. Norby, "Applications of Inflation-Adjusted Accounting Data," *Financial Analysts Journal*, March–April 1983.

19.7 VALUE INVESTING: THE GRAHAM TECHNIQUE

No presentation of fundamental security analysis would be complete without a discussion of the ideas of Benjamin Graham, the greatest of the investment "gurus." Until the evolution of modern portfolio theory in the latter half of this century, Graham was the single most important thinker, writer, and teacher in the field of investment analysis. His influence on investment professionals remains very strong.

Graham's magnum opus is *Security Analysis*, written with Columbia Professor David Dodd in 1934. Its message is similar to the ideas presented in this chapter. Graham believed careful analysis of a firm's financial statements could turn up bargain stocks. Over the years, he developed many different rules for determining the most important financial ratios and the critical values for judging a stock to be undervalued. Through many editions, his book has had a profound influence on investment professionals. It has been so influential and successful, in fact, that widespread adoption of Graham's techniques has led to elimination of the very bargains they are designed to identify.

In a 1976 seminar Graham said:[6]

> I am no longer an advocate of elaborate techniques of security analysis in order to find superior value opportunities. This was a rewarding activity, say, forty years ago, when our textbook "Graham and Dodd" was first published; but the situation has changed a good deal since then. In the old days any well-trained security analyst could do a good professional job of selecting undervalued issues through detailed studies; but in the light of the enormous amount of research now being carried on, I doubt whether in most cases such extensive efforts will generate sufficiently superior selections to justify their cost. To that very limited extent I'm on the side of the "efficient market" school of thought now generally accepted by the professors.

Nonetheless, in that same seminar, Graham suggested a simplified approach to identify bargain stocks:

> My first, more limited, technique confines itself to the purchase of common stocks at less than their working-capital value, or net current-asset value, giving no weight to the plant and other fixed assets, and deducting all liabilities in full from the current assets. We used this approach extensively in managing investment funds, and over a 30-odd-year period we must have earned an average of some 20 percent per year from this source. For a while, however, after the mid-1950s, this brand of buying opportunity became very scarce because of the pervasive bull market. But it has returned in quantity since the 1973–1974 decline. In January 1976 we counted over 100 such issues in the Standard & Poor's *Stock Guide*—about 10 percent of the total. I consider it a foolproof method of systematic investment—once again, not on the basis of individual results but in terms of the expectable group income.

There are two convenient sources of information for those interested in trying out the Graham technique: Both Standard & Poor's *Outlook* and *The Value Line Investment Survey* carry lists of stocks selling below net working capital value.

SUMMARY

1. The primary focus of the security analyst should be the firm's real economic earnings rather than its reported earnings. Accounting earnings as reported in financial statements can be a biased estimate of real economic earnings, although empirical studies

---

[6]As cited by John Train in *Money Masters* (New York: Harper & Row, 1987).

reveal that reported earnings convey considerable information concerning a firm's prospects.

2. A firm's ROE is a key determinant of the growth rate of its earnings. ROE is affected profoundly by the firm's degree of financial leverage. An increase in a firm's debt-to-equity ratio will raise its ROE and hence its growth rate only if the interest rate on the debt is less than the firm's return on assets.

3. It is often helpful to the analyst to decompose a firm's ROE ratio into the product of several accounting ratios and to analyze their separate behavior over time and across companies within an industry. A useful breakdown is

$$\text{ROE} = \frac{\text{Net profits}}{\text{Pretax profits}} \times \frac{\text{Pretax profits}}{\text{EBIT}} \times \frac{\text{EBIT}}{\text{Sales}} \times \frac{\text{Sales}}{\text{Assets}} \times \frac{\text{Assets}}{\text{Equity}}$$

4. Other accounting ratios that have a bearing on a firm's profitability and/or risk are fixed-asset turnover, inventory turnover, days receivables, and the current, quick, and interest coverage ratios.

5. Two ratios that make use of the market price of the firm's common stock in addition to its financial statements are the ratios of market to book value and price to earnings. Analysts sometimes take low values for these ratios as a margin of safety or a sign that the stock is a bargain.

6. A strategy of investing in stocks with high reported ROE seems to have produced a lower rate of return to the investor than investing in low ROE stocks. This implies that high reported ROE stocks were overpriced compared with low ROE stocks.

7. A major problem in the use of data obtained from a firm's financial statements is comparability. Firms have a great deal of latitude in how they choose to compute various items of revenue and expense. It is, therefore, necessary for the security analyst to adjust accounting earnings and financial ratios to a uniform standard before attempting to compare financial results across firms.

8. Comparability problems can be acute in a period of inflation. Inflation can create distortions in accounting for inventories, depreciation, and interest expense.

Key Terms

income statement	profit margin	acid test ratio
balance sheet	return on sales	interest coverage ratio
statement of cash flows	asset turnover	times interest earned
economic earnings	leverage ratio	market–book-value ratio
accounting earnings	average collection period	price–earnings ratio
return on equity	days receivables	earnings yield
return on assets	current ratio	LIFO
Du Pont system	quick ratio	FIFO

Selected Readings

The classic book on the use of financial statements in equity valuation, now in its fifth edition, is:
Cottle, S.; R. Murray; and F. Block. *Graham and Dodd's Security Analysis.* New York: McGraw-Hill, 1996.

Problems

1. The Crusty Pie Co., which specializes in apple turnovers, has a return on sales higher than the industry average, yet its ROA is the same as the industry average. How can you explain this?

2. The ABC Corporation has a profit margin on sales below the industry average, yet its ROA is above the industry average. What does this imply about its asset turnover?

3. Firm A and Firm B have the same ROA, yet Firm A's ROE is higher. How can you explain this?

Problems 4 through 20 are from past CFA examinations.

4. The cash flow data of Palomba Pizza Stores for the year ended December 31, 1991, are as follows:

Cash payment of dividends	$ 35,000
Purchase of land	14,000
Cash payments for interest	10,000
Cash payments for salaries	45,000
Sale of equipment	38,000
Retirement of common stock	25,000
Purchase of equipment	30,000
Cash payments to suppliers	85,000
Cash collections from customers	250,000
Cash at beginning of year	50,000

   a. Prepare a statement of cash flows for Palomba in accordance with FAS 95 showing:

   • Net cash provided by operating activities.
   • Net cash provided by or used in investing activities.
   • Net cash provided by or used in financing activities.

   b. Discuss, from an analyst's viewpoint, the purpose of classifying cash flows into the three categories listed above.

5. This problem should be solved according to the provisions of FAS 95 and using the following data:

Cash payments for interest	$(12)
Retirement of common stock	(32)
Cash payments to merchandise suppliers	(85)
Purchase of land	(8)
Sale of equipment	30
Payments of dividends	(37)
Cash payment for salaries	(35)
Cash collection from customers	260
Purchase of equipment	(40)

   a. What are cash flows from operating activities?
   b. Using the data above, calculate cash flows from investing activities.
   c. Using the data above, calculate cash flows from financing activities.

6. The Walt Disney Company (Disney) is a diversified international entertainment company with operations in three business segments. Revenue and operating income data for the three segments are presented in Table 19A.

   The profitability of the leisure-time industry is influenced by various factors including economic conditions, the amount of available leisure time, oil and transportation prices, and weather patterns. Attendance at Disney's U.S. theme parks was soft in the early 1990s because a weak economy reduced consumer discretionary spending. Also, Disney management was very aggressive in raising theme park admission prices. For

Table 19A   The Walt Disney Company Business Segment Data, years ending September 30 ($ millions)

Business Segments	1993		1989	
	Revenue	Operating Income	Revenue	Operating Income
Theme parks and resorts	$3,441	$ 747	$2,595	$ 785
Film entertainment	3,673	622	1,588	256
Consumer products	1,415	355	411	188
	$8,529	$1,724	$4,594	$1,229

the 10-year period ending in 1993, admission prices increased at an annual rate of 8% to 9% compared to less than 4% for U.S. consumer price inflation.

Disney's film entertainment business has grown rapidly because of increasing acceptance of The Disney Channel and, importantly, management efforts to exploit the expanding distribution opportunities available for its extensive video library. Disney's consumer products revenue has also grown meaningfully as the company moved its product mix aggressively toward direct publishing and direct retail (239 new Disney stores were open by the end of 1993) and away from higher-margined licensing and royalty income sources.

Disney has a 49% ownership interest in Euro Disney, a publicly traded French company, which operates a theme park and resort complex on a 4,800-acre site near Paris. The investment is accounted for using the equity method. Recessionary conditions in Europe have plagued Euro Disney since it opened in 1992, and attendance has been poor. Theme park profitability is generally characterized by high operating leverage due to a proportionally large fixed cost structure. In the case of Euro Disney, high operating leverage and very high financial leverage have combined to produce significant losses. During the fourth quarter of fiscal year 1993 (ending September 30, 1993), Disney management made the decision to write off the full carrying value of Euro Disney. The charge was $350 million ($218 million after tax).

After the close of fiscal year 1993, Disney management indicated its intention to pursue aggressive expansion of the theme park and resort business. Disney planned to build a new park, named Disney's America, in Virginia, at an estimated cost of $500 million to $800 million. Management was also considering a new resort in California, called Westcot, with a planned cost of $3.0 billion, and the company expected to announce another new theme park at Disney World in Florida.

a. Using the Du Pont method, identify and calculate the five primary components of Disney's return on equity for the fiscal years ending September 30, 1989, and September 30, 1993. Using these components, calculate Disney's return on equity for each year.

b. Drawing only on your answers to part (a) and the data given earlier and in Table 19B, identify the two components that contributed most to the observed change in Disney's return on equity between 1989 and 1993. State two reasons for the observed change in each of the two components.

7. Calculate the ratios listed below for Disney as of September 30, 1993 (use ending balance sheet amounts from Table 19B). Briefly explain the use of each ratio in evaluating a company's operations.

Table 19B   The Walt Disney Company Selected Financial Statement and Other
Data, years ending September 30 ($ millions except per-share data)

	1993	1989
Income Statement		
Revenue	$ 8,529	$ 4,594
Operating expenses	(6,805)	(3,365)
Operating income	$ 1,724	$ 1,229
General and administrative expenses	(163)	(119)
Interest expense	(158)	(24)
Investment and interest income	186	67
Income (loss) from Euro Disney	(515)	0
Pretax income	$ 1,074	$ 1,153
Taxes	(403)	(450)
Net income	$ 671	$ 703
Earnings per share	$ 1.23	$ 1.27
Dividends per share	$ 0.23	$ 0.11
Balance Sheet		
Cash	$ 363	$ 381
Receivables	1,390	224
Inventories	609	909
Other	1,889	662
Current assets	$ 4,251	$ 2,176
Property, plant, and equipment, net	5,228	3,397
Other assets	2,272	1,084
Total assets	$11,751	$ 6,657
Current liabilities	$ 2,821	$ 1,262
Borrowings	2,386	861
Other liabilities	1,514	1,490
Stockholders' equity	5,030	3,044
Total liabilities and stockholders' equity	$11,751	$ 6,657
Cash Flow from Operations		
Net income	$ 671	$ 703
Depreciation	364	272
Goodwill	0	0
Other	1,110	300
Total	$ 2,145	$ 1,275
Other Data		
Common shares outstanding (millions)	544	552
Closing price common stock per share	$ 37.75	$ 30.22

a. Average number of days receivables are outstanding.
b. Cash flow from operations ratio (= cash flow from operations/current liabilities).
c. Long-term debt to total capital (with capital defined as long-term debt plus equity valued at market).
d. Times interest earned (interest coverage).

Table 19C   Eastover Company ($ millions, except shares outstanding)

	1986	1987	1988	1989	1990
Income Statement Summary					
Sales	$5,652	$6,990	$7,863	$8,281	$7,406
Earnings before interest and taxes (EBIT)	$ 568	$ 901	$1,037	$ 708	$ 795
Interest expense (net)	(147)	(188)	(186)	(194)	(195)
Income before taxes	$ 421	$ 713	$ 851	$ 514	$ 600
Income taxes	(144)	(266)	(286)	(173)	(206)
Tax rate	34%	37%	33%	34%	34%
Net income	$ 277	$ 447	$ 565	$ 341	$ 394
Preferred dividends	(28)	(17)	(17)	(17)	(0)
Net income to common	$ 249	$ 430	$ 548	$ 324	$ 394
Common shares outstanding (millions)	196	204	204	205	201
Balance Sheet Summary					
Current assets	$1,235	$1,491	$1,702	$1,585	$1,367
Timberland assets	649	625	621	612	615
Property, plant, and equipment	4,370	4,571	5,056	5,430	5,854
Other assets	360	555	473	472	429
Total assets	$6,614	$7,242	$7,852	$8,099	$8,265
Current liabilities	$1,226	$1,186	$1,206	$1,606	$1,816
Long-term debt	1,120	1,340	1,585	1,346	1,585
Deferred taxes	1,000	1,000	1,016	1,000	1,000
Equity-preferred	364	350	350	400	0
Equity-common	2,904	3,366	3,695	3,747	3,864
Total liabilities and equity	$6,614	$7,242	$7,852	$8,099	$8,265

The following case should be used to solve problems 8–11.

8. Eastover Company (EO) is a large, diversified forest products company. Approximately 75% of its sales are from paper and forest products, with the remainder from financial services and real estate. The company owns 5.6 million acres of timberland, which is carried at very low historical cost on the balance sheet.

   Peggy Mulroney, CFA, is an analyst at the investment counseling firm of Centurion Investments. She is assigned the task of assessing the outlook for Eastover, which is being considered for purchase, and comparing it to another forest products company in Centurion's portfolios, Southampton Corporation (SHC). SHC is a major producer of lumber products in the United States. Building products, primarily lumber and plywood, account for 89% of SHC's sales, with pulp accounting for the remainder. SHC owns 1.4 million acres of timberland, which is also carried at historical cost on the balance sheet. In SHC's case, however, that cost is not as far below current market as Eastover's.

   Mulroney began her examination of Eastover and Southampton by looking at the five components of return on equity (ROE) for each company. For her analysis, Mulroney elected to define equity as total shareholders' equity, including preferred stock. She also elected to use year-end data rather than averages for the balance sheet items.

   a. Based on the data shown in Tables 19C and 19D, calculate each of the five ROE components for Eastover and Southampton in 1990. Using the five components, calculate ROE for both companies in 1990.

Table 19D   Southampton Corporation ($ millions, except shares outstanding)

	1986	1987	1988	1989	1990
Income Statement Summary					
Sales	$1,306	$1,654	$1,799	$2,010	$1,793
Earnings before interest and taxes (EBIT)	$ 120	$ 230	$ 221	$ 304	$ 145
Interest expense (net)	(13)	(36)	(7)	(12)	(8)
Income before taxes	$ 107	$ 194	$ 214	$ 292	$ 137
Income taxes	(44)	(75)	(79)	(99)	(46)
Tax rate	41%	39%	37%	34%	34%
Net income	$ 63	$ 119	$ 135	$ 193	$ 91
Common shares outstanding (millions)	38	38	38	38	38
Balance Sheet Summary					
Current assets	$ 487	$ 504	$ 536	$ 654	$ 509
Timberland assets	512	513	508	513	518
Property, plant, and equipment	648	681	718	827	1,037
Other assets	141	151	34	38	40
Total assets	$1,788	$1,849	$1,796	$2,032	$2,104
Current liabilities	$ 185	$ 176	$ 162	$ 180	$195
Long-term debt	536	493	370	530	589
Deferred taxes	123	136	127	146	153
Equity	944	1,044	1,137	1,176	1,167
Total liabilities and equity	$1,788	$1,849	$1,796	$2,032	$2,104

 b. Referring to the components calculated in part (*b*), explain the difference in ROE for Eastover and Southampton in 1990.

 c. Using 1990 data, calculate the sustainable growth rate for both Eastover and Southampton. Discuss the appropriateness of using these calculations as a basis for estimating future growth.

9. *a.* Mulroney (see the previous problem) recalled from her CFA studies that the constant-growth discounted dividend model was one way to arrive at a valuation for a company's common stock. She collected current dividend and stock price data for Eastover and Southampton, shown in Table 19E. Using 11% as the required rate of return (i.e., discount rate) and a projected growth rate of 8%, compute a constant-growth DDM value for Eastover's stock and compare the computed value for Eastover to its stock price indicated in Table 19F.

 b. Mulroney's supervisor commented that a two-stage DDM may be more appropriate for companies such as Eastover and Southampton. Mulroney believes that Eastover and Southampton could grow more rapidly over the next three years and then settle in at a lower but sustainable rate of growth beyond 1994. Her estimates are indicated in Table 19G. Using 11% as the required rate of return, compute the two-stage DDM value of Eastover's stock and compare that value to its stock price indicated in Table 19F.

 c. Discuss advantages and disadvantages of using a constant-growth DDM. Briefly discuss how the two-stage DDM improves upon the constant-growth DDM.

10. In addition to the discounted dividend model approach, Mulroney (see previous problem) decided to look at the price–earnings ratio and price–book ratio, relative to the

Table 19E   Valuation of Eastover Company and Southampton Corporation Compared to S&P 500

	1986	1987	1988	1989	1990	1991	Five-Year Average (1987–1991)
Eastover Company							
Earnings per share	$ 1.27	$ 2.12	$ 2.68	$ 1.56	$ 1.87	$ 0.90	
Dividends per share	0.87	0.90	1.15	1.20	1.20	1.20	
Book value per share	14.82	16.54	18.14	18.55	19.21	17.21	
Stock price							
High	28	40	30	33	28	30	
Low	20	20	23	25	18	20	
Close	25	26	25	28	22	27	
Average P/E	18.9	14.2	9.9	18.6	12.3	27.8	
Average P/B	1.6	1.8	1.5	1.6	1.2	1.5	
Southampton Corporation							
Earnings per share	$ 1.66	$ 3.13	$ 3.55	$ 5.08	$ 2.46	$ 1.75	
Dividends per share	0.77	0.79	0.89	0.98	1.04	1.08	
Book value per share	24.84	27.47	29.92	30.95	31.54	32.21	
Stock price							
High	34	40	38	43	45	46	
Low	21	22	26	28	20	26	
Close	31	27	28	39	27	44	
Average P/E	16.6	9.9	9.0	7.0	13.2	20.6	
Average P/B	1.1	1.1	1.1	1.2	1.0	1.1	
S&P 500							
Average P/E	15.8	16.0	11.1	13.9	15.6	19.2	15.2
Average P/B	1.8	2.1	1.9	2.2	2.1	2.3	2.1

Table 19F   Current Information

	Current Share Price	Current Dividends Per Share	1992 EPS Estimate	Current Book Value Per Share
Eastover	$ 28	$ 1.20	$ 1.60	$ 17.32
Southampton	48	1.08	3.00	32.21
S&P 500	415	12.00	20.54	159.83

Table 19G   Projected Growth Rates

	Next Three Years (1992, 1993, 1994)	Growth Beyond 1994
Eastover	12%	8%
Southampton	13%	7%

S&P 500, for both Eastover and Southampton. Mulroney elected to perform this analysis using 1987–1991 and current data.

   a. Using the data in Tables 19E and 19F, compute both the current and the five-year (1987–1991) average relative price–earnings ratios and relative price–book ratios for Eastover and Southampton (i.e., ratios relative to those for the S&P 500). Discuss each company's current relative price–earnings ratio compared to its five-year average relative price–earnings ratio and each company's current relative price–book ratio as compared to its five-year average relative price–book ratio.

   b. Briefly discuss one disadvantage for each of the relative price–earnings and relative price–book approaches to valuation.

 11. Mulroney (see Problems 8–10) previously calculated a valuation for Southampton for both the constant-growth and two-stage DDM as shown below:

Constant Growth Approach	Two-Stage Approach
$29	$35.50

Using only the information provided and your answers to Problems 8–10, select the stock (EO or SHC) that Mulroney should recommend as the better value, and justify your selection.

 12. Philip Morris Corporation is a major consumer products company operating worldwide. The company's brand names have immediate recognition in most markets and include Marlboro, Benson & Hedges, Kraft, Kool-Aid, Jell-O, Miller, and Maxwell House. Some of these brands were the result of acquisitions, but many of them have been established through years of marketing effort and advertising expenditures.

   Philip Morris is the world leader in tobacco products, and this line is its primary source of profits. Tobacco product sales are growing slowly, particularly in the United States, for both health and economic reasons. However, cigarette prices have increased much faster than the rate of inflation in the United States due to a combination of excise tax pressure and aggressive pricing by Philip Morris and other tobacco companies. One justification for this trend put forth by the tobacco industry is that the price increases are necessary to cover the extensive legal fees arising from the large number of negligence and liability suits now pending against tobacco companies.

   For many years, Philip Morris has been redeploying the growing excess cash flow from operations (defined as cash over and above that necessary to sustain the intrinsic growth of the basic business). The strategy has been to consistently increase dividends, repurchase common shares, and make acquisitions in consumer nondurable businesses. Dividends have been raised in every year over the past decade, and shares have been steadily repurchased at prices well above book value. Some repurchased stock is held as treasury stock, and the remainder has been retired. Philip Morris has also made many sizable acquisitions (almost all on a purchase basis), which have added substantial goodwill to the balance sheet.

   Philip Morris uses the LIFO method for costing all domestic inventories and the straight-line method for recording depreciation. Goodwill and other intangibles are amortized on a straight-line basis over 40 years. The company was an early adopter of FAS 106, "Employers' Accounting for Postretirement Benefits Other than Pensions," doing so on the immediate recognition basis on January 1, 1991, for all U.S. employee benefit plans. The 1991 year-end accrued postretirement health care cost

Table 19H   Philip Morris Corporation Selected Financial Statement and Other Data, years ending December 31 ($ millions except per share data)

	1991	1981
Income Statement		
Operating revenue	$56,458	$10,886
Cost of sales	25,612	5,253
Excise taxes on products	8,394	2,580
Gross profit	$22,452	$ 3,053
Selling, general, and administrative expenses	13,830	1,741
Operating income	$ 8,622	$ 1,312
Interest expense	1,651	232
Pretax earnings	$ 6,971	$ 1,080
Provision for income taxes	3,044	420
Net earnings	$ 3,927	$ 660
Earnings per share	$4.24	$0.66
Dividends per share	$1.91	$0.25
Balance Sheet		
Current assets	$12,594	$ 3,733
Property, plant, and equipment, net	9,946	3,583
Goodwill	18,624	634
Other assets	6,220	1,230
	$47,384	$ 9,180
Current liabilities	$11,824	$ 1,936
Long-term debt	14,213	3,499
Deferred taxes	1,803	455
Other liabilities	7,032	56
Stockholders' equity	12,512	3,234
Total liabilities and stockholders' equity	$47,384	$ 9,180
Other Data		
Philip Morris:		
Common shares outstanding (millions)	920	1,003
Closing price common stock	$80.250	$6.125
S&P 500 Stock Index:		
Closing price	417.09	122.55
Earnings per share	16.29	15.36
Book value per share	161.08	109.43

liability amounted to $1,854 million. Table 19H presents other pertinent information on the firm.

a. Using the Du Pont method, identify and calculate Philip Morris's five primary components of return on equity for the years 1981 and 1991. Using these components, calculate and return on equity for both years.

b. Using your answers to part (*a*), identify the two most significant components contributing to the observed difference in Philip Morris's ROE between 1981 and 1991. Briefly discuss the likely reasons for the changes in those components.

c. Calculate Philip Morris's sustainable growth rate (i.e., ROE × *b*) using the 1981 data. The company's actual compound annual growth rate in earnings per share over the 1981–91 period was 20.4%. Discuss why the sustainable growth rate was or was not a good predictor of actual growth over the 1981–91 period.

 13. In reviewing the financial statements of the Graceland Rock Company, you note that net income increased while cash flow from operations decreased from 1997 to 1998.

    a. Explain how net income could increase for Graceland Rock Company while cash flow from operations decreased. Give some illustrative examples.

    b. Explain why cash flow from operations may be a good indicator of a firm's "quality of earnings."

 14. A firm has net sales of $3,000, cash expenses (including taxes) of $1,400, and depreciation of $500. If accounts receivable increase over the period by $400, cash flow from operations equals:

    a. $1,200.

    b. $1,600.

    c. $1,700.

    d. $2,100.

 15. Under LIFO accounting, when a firm sells a greater quantity of its inventory than it produces or acquires, the result is:

    a. An understatement of the cost of goods sold.

    b. Lower earnings during a period of inflation.

    c. Lower earnings than would have occurred under FIFO.

    d. None of the above.

 16. During a period of rising prices, the financial statements of a firm using FIFO reporting instead of LIFO reporting would show:

    a. Higher total assets and higher net income.

    b. Higher total assets and lower net income.

    c. Lower total assets and higher net income.

    d. Lower total assets and lower net income.

 17. In an inflationary period, the use of FIFO will make which one of the following more realistic than the use of LIFO?

    a. Balance sheet.

    b. Income statement.

    c. Cash flow statement.

    d. None of the above.

 18. Cash flow from operating activities includes:

    a. Inventory increases resulting from acquisitions.

    b. Inventory changes due to changing exchange rates.

    c. Interest paid to bondholders.

    d. Dividends paid to stockholders.

 19. All other thing being equal, what effect will the payment of a cash dividend have on the following ratios?

	Times Interest Earned	Debt/Equity Ratio
a.	Increase	Increase
b.	No effect	Increase
c.	No effect	No effect
d.	Decrease	Decrease

Table 19I   Income Statements and Balance Sheets

	1996	1999
Income Statement Data		
Revenues	$542	$979
Operating income	38	76
Depreciation and amortization	3	9
Interest expense	3	0
Pretax income	32	67
Income taxes	13	37
Net income after tax	19	30
Balance Sheet Data		
Fixed assets	$ 41	$ 70
Total assets	245	291
Working capital	123	157
Total debt	16	0
Total shareholders' equity	159	220

20. The Du Pont formula defines the net return on shareholders' equity as a function of the following components:

- Operating margin.
- Asset turnover.
- Interest burden.
- Financial leverage.
- Income tax rate.

Using only the data in Table 19I:

a. Calculate each of the five components listed above for 1996 and 1999, and calculate the return on equity (ROE) for 1996 and 1999, using all of the five components.

b. Briefly discuss the impact of the changes in asset turnover and financial leverage on the change in ROE from 1996 and 1999.

1. A debt-to-equity ratio of 1 implies that Mordett will have $50 million of debt and $50 million of equity. Interest expense will be .09 × $50 million, or $4.5 million per year. Mordett's net profits and ROE over the business cycle will therefore be

		Nodett		Mordett	
Scenario	**EBIT**	**Net Profits**	**ROE**	**Net Profits***	**ROE†**
Bad year	$ 5 million	$3 million	3%	$0.3 million	.6%
Normal year	10	6	6	3.3	6.6
Good year	15	9	9	6.3	12.6

*Mordett's after-tax profits are given by .6(EBIT − $4.5 million).

†Mordett's equity is only $50 million.

2.

		(1) Net Profit/ Pretax Profit	(2) Pretax Profit/ EBIT	(3) EBIT/ Sales (ROS)	(4) Sales/ Assets (ATO)	(5) Assets/ Equity	(6) Combined Leverage Factor (2) × (5)
	ROE						

Ratio Decomposition Analysis for Mordett Corporation

	ROE	(1)	(2)	(3)	(4)	(5)	(6)
Bad year							
Nodett	.030	.6	1.000	.0625	0.800	1.000	1.000
Somdett	.018	.6	0.360	.0625	0.800	1.667	0.600
Mordett	.006	.6	0.100	.0625	0.800	2.000	0.200
Normal year							
Nodett	.060	.6	1.000	.100	1.000	1.000	1.000
Somdett	.068	.6	0.680	.100	1.000	1.667	1.134
Mordett	.066	.6	0.550	.100	1.000	2.000	1.100
Good year							
Nodett	.090	.6	1.000	.125	1.200	1.000	1.000
Somdett	.118	.6	0.787	.125	1.200	1.667	1.311
Mordett	.126	.6	0.700	.125	1.200	2.000	1.400

3. GI's ROE in 19X3 was 3.03%, computed as follows:

$$ROE = \frac{\$5,285}{.5(\$171,843 + \$177,128)} = .0303, \text{ or } 3.03\%$$

Its P/E ratio was 4 = $21/$5.285 and its P/B ratio was .12 = $21/$177. Its earnings yield was 25% compared with an industry average of 12.5%.

Note that in our calculations the earnings yields will not equal ROE/(P/B) because we have computed ROE with average shareholders' equity in the denominator and P/B with end-of-year shareholders' equity in the denominator.

4.

IBX Ratio Analysis

Year	ROE	(1) Net Profit/ Pretax Profit	(2) Pretax Profit/ EBIT	(3) EBIT/ Sales (ROS)	(4) Sales/ Assets (ATO)	(5) Assets/ Equity	(6) Combined Leverage Factor (2) × (5)	(7) ROA (3) × (4)
1998	11.4%	.616	.796	7.75%	1.375	2.175	1.731	10.65%
1996	10.2	.636	.932	8.88	1.311	1.474	1.374	11.65

ROE went up despite a decline in operating margin and a decline in the tax burden ratio because of increased leverage and turnover. Note that ROA declined from 11.65% in 1996 to 10.65% in 1998.

5. LIFO accounting results in lower reported earnings than does FIFO. Fewer assets to depreciate results in lower reported earnings because there is less bias associated with the use of historic cost. More debt results in lower reported earnings because the inflation premium in the interest rate is treated as part of interest expense and not as repayment of principal. If ABC has the same reported earnings as XYZ despite these three sources of downward bias, its real earnings must be greater.

OPTIONS, FUTURES, AND OTHER DERIVATIVES

OPTIONS MARKETS: INTRODUCTION

A relatively recent, but extremely important class of financial assets is derivative securities, or simply *derivatives*. These are securities whose prices are determined by, or "derive from," the prices of other securities. These assets are also called *contingent claims* because their payoffs are contingent on the prices of other securities.   Options and futures contracts are both derivative securities. We will see that their payoffs depend on the value of other securities. Swaps, which we discussed in Chapter 16, also are derivatives. Because the value of derivatives depends on the value of other securities, they can be powerful tools for both hedging and speculation. We will investigate these applications in the next four chapters, starting in this chapter with options.   Trading of standardized options contracts on a national exchange started in 1973 when the Chicago Board Options Exchange (CBOE) began listing call options. These contracts were almost immediately a great success, crowding out the previously existing over-the-counter trading in stock options. Figure 20.1 documents the incredible

growth in trading on the CBOE. Trading volume rose rapidly and steadily between 1973 and 1987. While volume fell off considerably in the wake of the 1987 stock market crash, it has since recovered.   Option contracts are traded now on several exchanges. They are written on common stock, stock indexes, foreign exchange, agricultural commodities, precious metals, and interest rate futures. In addition, the over-the-counter market has enjoyed a tremendous resurgence in recent years as trading in custom-tailored options has exploded. Popular and potent tools in modifying portfolio characteristics, options have become essential tools a portfolio manager must understand.   This chapter is an

Figure 20.1
CBOE fiscal year
average daily volume
(contracts).

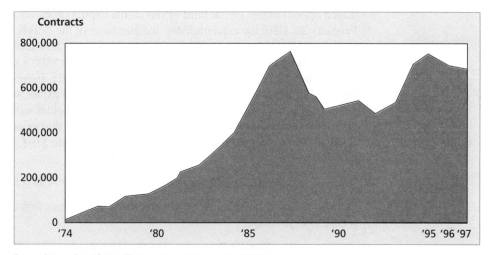

Source: Chicago Board Options Exchange *Annual Reports*, 1995 and 1997.

introduction to options markets. It explains how puts and calls work and examines their investment characteristics. Popular option strategies are considered next. Finally, we examine a range of securities with embedded options such as callable or convertible bonds, and we take a quick look at so-called exotic options.

20.1   THE OPTION CONTRACT

A **call option** gives its holder the right to purchase an asset for a specified price, called the **exercise**, or **strike price**, on or before some specified expiration date. For example, a February call option on IBM stock with exercise price $105 entitles its owner to purchase IBM stock for a price of $105 at any time up to and including the expiration date in February. The holder of the call is not required to exercise the option. It will pay to exercise the call only if the market value of the asset to be purchased exceeds the exercise price. When the market price does exceed the exercise price, the optionholder may either sell the option or "call away" the asset for the exercise price and reap a profit. Otherwise, the option may be left unexercised. If it is not exercised before the expiration date of the contract, a call option simply expires and no longer has value.

The purchase price of the option is called the *premium*. It represents the compensation the purchaser of the call must pay for the right to exercise the option if exercise becomes profitable. Sellers of call options, who are said to *write* calls, receive premium income now as payment against the possibility they will be required at some later date to deliver the asset in return for an exercise price lower than the market value of the asset. If the option is left to expire worthless because the exercise price remains above the market price of the asset, then the writer of the call clears a profit equal to the premium income derived from the sale of the option.

To illustrate, consider the February 1998 maturity call option on a share of IBM stock with an exercise price of $105 per share selling on January 8, 1998, for $5. Exchange-traded options expire on the third Friday of the expiration month, which for this option is February 20. Until the expiration day, the purchaser of the calls is entitled to buy shares of IBM for $105. On January 8, IBM stock sells for $104.3125, which is less than the exercise price. Because the stock price is currently a bit less than $105 a share, it would not make sense at the moment to exercise the option to buy at $105. Indeed, if IBM stock remains below $105 by the expiration date, the call will be left to expire worthless. If, on the other hand, IBM is selling above $105 at expiration, the callholder will find it optimal to exercise. For example, if IBM sells for $108 on February 20, the option will be exercised since it will give its holder the right to pay $105 for a stock worth $108. The proceeds from exercise will be

$$\text{Proceeds} = \text{Stock price} - \text{Exercise price} = \$108 - \$105 = \$3$$

Despite the $3 payoff at maturity, the investor still realizes a loss of $2 on the call because it cost $5 to purchase:

$$\text{Profit} = \text{Proceeds} - \text{Original investment} = \$3 - \$5 = -\$2$$

Nevertheless, exercise of the call will be optimal at maturity if the stock price is above the exercise price because the exercise proceeds will offset at least part of the investment in the option. The investor in the call will clear a profit if IBM is selling above $110 at the maturity date. At that stock price, the proceeds from exercise will just cover the original cost of the call.

A **put option** gives its holder the right to *sell* an asset for a specified exercise or strike price on or before some expiration date. A February put on IBM with exercise price $105 entitles its owner to sell IBM stock to the put writer at a price of $105 at any time before expiration in February even if the market price of IBM is less than $105. While profits on call options increase when the asset increases in value, profits on put options increase when the asset value falls. A put will be exercised only if the exercise price is greater than the price of the underlying asset, that is, only if its holder can deliver for the exercise price an asset with market value less than the exercise price. (One doesn't need to own the shares of IBM to exercise the IBM put option. Upon exercise, the investor's broker purchases the necessary shares of IBM at the market price and immediately delivers, or "puts them," to an option writer for the exercise price. The owner of the put profits by the difference between the exercise price and market price.)

To illustrate, consider the February 1998 maturity put option on IBM with an exercise price of $105 selling on January 8, 1998, for $5.25. It entitles its owner to sell a share of IBM for $105 at any time until February 20. If the optionholder bought a share of IBM and immediately exercised the right to sell at $105, net proceeds would be $105 - $104.3125 = $.6875. Obviously, an investor who pays $5.25 for the put has no intention of exercising it immediately. If, on the other hand, IBM is selling at $96 at expiration, the put will turn out to be a profitable investment. The proceeds from exercise would be

$$\text{Proceeds} = \text{Exercise price} - \text{Stock price} = \$105 - \$96 = \$9$$

and profit would be $9 - $5.25 = $4.75. This is a holding period return of $4.75/$5.25 = .905, or 90.5%—over only 43 days! Obviously, put option sellers on January 8 did not consider this outcome very likely.

An option is described as **in the money** when its exercise would produce profits for its holder. An option is **out of the money** when exercise would be unprofitable. A call option is in the money when the exercise price is below the asset's value because purchase at the exercise price would be profitable. It is out of the money when the exercise price exceeds the asset value; no one would exercise the right to purchase for the strike price an asset worth less than that price. Conversely, put options are in the money when the exercise price exceeds the asset's value, because delivery of the lower-valued asset in exchange for the exercise price is profitable for the holder. Options are **at the money** when the exercise price and asset price are equal.

Options Trading

Some options trade on over-the-counter markets. The OTC market offers the advantage that the terms of the option contract—the exercise price, maturity date, and number of shares committed—can be tailored to the needs of the traders. The costs of establishing an OTC option contract, however, are higher than for exchange-traded options. Today, most option trading occurs on organized exchanges, but the OTC market in customized options is also thriving.

Options contracts traded on exchanges are standardized by allowable maturity dates and exercise prices for each listed option. Each stock option contract provides for the right to buy or sell 100 shares of stock (except when stock splits occur after the contract is listed and the contract is adjusted for the terms of the split).

Standardization of the terms of listed option contracts means all market participants trade in a limited and uniform set of securities. This increases the depth of trading in any particular option, which lowers trading costs and results in a more competitive market. Exchanges, therefore, offer two important benefits: ease of trading, which flows from a central marketplace where buyers and sellers or their representatives congregate; and a liquid secondary market where buyers and sellers of options can transact quickly and cheaply.

Figure 20.2 is a reproduction of listed stock option quotations from *The Wall Street Journal*. The highlighted options are for shares of IBM. The numbers in the column below the company name represent the last recorded price on the New York Stock Exchange for IBM stock, $104\frac{5}{16} = \$104.3125$ per share.[1] The first column shows that options are traded on IBM at exercise prices of $80 through $120. These values are also called the *strike price*.

The exercise or strike prices bracket the stock price. While exercise prices generally are set at five-point intervals for stocks, larger intervals may be set for stocks selling above $100, and intervals of $2½ may be used for stocks selling below $30. If the stock price moves outside the range of exercise prices of the existing set of options, new options with appropriate exercise prices may be offered. Therefore, at any time, both in-the-money and out-of-the-money options will be listed, as in the IBM example.

The next column in Figure 20.2 gives the maturity month of each contract, followed by two pairs of columns showing the number of contracts traded on that day and the closing price for the call and put, respectively. When we compare prices of call options with the same maturity date but different exercise prices in Figure 20.2, we see that the value of call is lower when the exercise price is higher. This makes sense, because the right to purchase a share at a given exercise price is not as valuable when the purchase price is higher. Thus the February maturity IBM call option with strike price $105 sells for $5, whereas the $110 exercise price February call sells for only $2\frac{15}{16}$. Conversely, put options are worth *more* when the exercise price is higher: You would rather have the right to sell IBM shares for

---

[1]Occasionally, this price may not match the closing price listed for the stock on the stock market page. This is because some NYSE stocks also trade on the Pacific Stock Exchange, which closes after the NYSE, and the stock pages may reflect the more recent Pacific Exchange closing price. The options exchanges, however, close with the NYSE, so the closing NYSE stock price is appropriate for comparison with the closing option price.

Figure 20.2

Stock options.

LISTED OPTIONS QUOTATIONS

Option/Strike	Exp.	Call Vol.	Call Last	Put Vol.	Put Last
86 3/16 75	Jan	263	12	725	3/8
86 3/16 75	Feb	10	14	329	2 1/8
86 3/16 80	Jan	...	...	587	3/4
86 3/16 80	Feb	119	9 7/8	245	3 1/4
86 3/16 80	May	28	14 1/2	1106	7 3/8
86 3/16 85	Jan	629	3 1/4	624	2
86 3/16 85	Feb	297	6 3/4	500	5 1/2
86 3/16 90	Feb	329	4 5/8	80	8 1/2
86 3/16 95	Jan	284	1/4	105	8 1/8
86 3/16 95	Feb	324	3	150	10 3/4
86 3/16 100	Jan	67	3/16	770	13
86 3/16 100	Feb	221	2 1/16	680	14 7/8
Deluxe 35	Jan	385	1/4	...	...
33 1/16 35	Jul	385	1 3/8	...	...
DiamMult 7 1/2	Jan	340	3 7/8	...	...
11 1/4 10	Jan	399	1 1/2	20	1/4
11 1/4 10	Feb	350	2 3/16	10	1/2
11 1/4 12 1/2	Jan	223	1/8	60	1 3/8
11 1/4 12 1/2	Feb	1040	15/16	100	1 7/8
Dig Eq 30	Jan	318	8 5/8	...	...
38 5/8 35	Jul	400	7 7/8	5	3
38 5/8 37 1/2	Jul	445	6 1/2	...	...
38 5/8 40	Jan	1066	7/8	43	2 3/8
Disney 50	Jan	325	4 7/8	...	...
97 11/16 90	Jan	354	8	53	1/4
Dressr 40	Feb	1108	1 3/8	...	...
DuPont 57 1/2	Jan	225	7/8	106	1
56 7/8 60	Jan	212	5/16	65	3 1/4
ETradeGr 20	Jan	...	...	215	7/8
24 7/16 25	Jan	207	1 11/16	5	1 1/2
EMC 22 1/2	Jan	500	4 3/4	...	...
27 1/4 25	Jan	238	2 7/16	9	5/8
EstnEn 30	Mar	500	7/16	...	...
EKodak 65	Jan	146	1	374	2 1/4
63 5/8 65	Feb	56	2 1/4	279	3 1/2
63 5/8 70	Jan	25	1/16	320	6 5/8
Elan 45	Feb	300	7 1/8	...	...
50 7/8 50	Feb	250	3 1/8	...	...
50 7/8 55	Feb	300	1	...	...
EDS 40	Jan	420	5	10	3/16
44 15/16 45	Feb	85	2 5/16	504	2 5/8
44 15/16 45	Mar	62	3 1/8	300	2 7/8
44 15/16 47 1/2	Feb	250	1 1/4	...	...
EmplySt 5	Feb	266	1	...	...
Exxon 60	Jan	527	1 13/16	1368	1 3/8
59 9/16 60	Feb	386	2 1/16	129	2 1/8
59 9/16 65	Jan	50	1/16	365	5
59 9/16 65	Feb	83	1/2	350	5 5/8
FedExp 65	Feb	217	3 1/8	435	3 1/4
FedDSt 37 1/2	Jan	700	5 1/2	...	...
FileNt 30	Feb	257	4 7/8	...	...
FtATn 50	Jun	270	2	...	...
FChNBD 70	Jan	...	...	269	1/4
75 90	Apr	280	1 1/8	...	...

Option/Strike	Exp.	Call Vol.	Call Last	Put Vol.	Put Last
5 5/32 7 1/2	Feb	746	3/16	...	...
Infoseek 12 1/2	Feb	247	5/8	10	2 1/16
Innovex 20	May	...	...	554	3 1/4
Intel 55	Jan	77	19 5/8	486	1/16
74 5/16 60	Apr	35	15 7/8	209	1 1/8
74 5/16 60	Jul	208	18 1/2	52	2
74 5/16 65	Jan	449	9 5/8	1264	1/4
74 5/16 65	Feb	67	10 3/8	637	1 1/16
74 5/16 65	Apr	16	12	336	2 1/8
74 5/16 67 1/2	Jan	101	7 5/8	2531	1/2
74 5/16 70	Jan	1923	5	2459	13/16
74 5/16 70	Feb	350	6 1/2	1212	2 1/8
74 5/16 70	Apr	243	8 3/4	337	3 7/8
74 5/16 72 1/2	Jan	1609	3 1/4	1151	1 1/4
74 5/16 75	Jan	6663	1 5/8	1411	2 1/2
74 5/16 75	Feb	1849	3 5/8	3253	3 7/8
74 5/16 75	Apr	150	6	461	5 5/8
74 5/16 77 1/2	Jan	2331	7/8	81	3 3/4
74 5/16 80	Jan	3972	5/16	533	6 1/4
74 5/16 80	Feb	2987	1 3/4	70	7 1/2
74 5/16 80	Apr	388	4	95	8 3/4
74 5/16 80	Jul	277	6 3/8	29	10 1/8
74 5/16 82 1/2	Jan	317	3/16	67	8 5/8
74 5/16 85	Jan	1116	3/16	155	11
74 5/16 85	Feb	549	5/8	4	10 5/8
74 5/16 85	Apr	218	2 1/2	245	11 7/8
74 5/16 90	Apr	368	1 1/2	10	16 1/4
74 5/16 95	Jul	333	2 5/8	...	...
74 5/16 100	Jul	415	1 3/4	...	...
I B M 80	Feb	...	...	275	7/16
104 5/16 80	Apr	30	25 7/8	234	1 1/16
104 5/16 85	Jan	1069	20 5/8	42	1/16
104 5/16 90	Jan	45	14 7/8	206	1/8
104 5/16 95	Jan	216	9 5/8	741	1/4
104 5/16 95	Feb	10	12 3/8	261	1 7/8
104 5/16 100	Jan	911	5 1/4	2021	3/4
104 5/16 100	Apr	29	11	319	4 3/4
104 5/16 100	Jul	5	13 3/8	225	6 5/8
104 5/16 105	Jan	3109	1 3/4	2357	2 1/4
104 5/16 105	Feb	358	5	339	5 1/4
104 5/16 105	Apr	231	7 3/4	527	6 1/2
104 5/16 110	Jan	1986	3/8	80	5 3/4
104 5/16 110	Feb	1025	2 15/16	27	7 1/2
104 5/16 110	Apr	421	5 3/8	21	9 1/4
104 5/16 115	Jan	689	1/8	...	...
104 5/16 115	Feb	313	1 5/8	4	12 3/4
104 5/16 120	Feb	956	13/16	...	...
104 5/16 120	Jul	26	5	360	18 1/2
IGame 25	Jan	35	7/16	315	11/16
In Pap 40	Jan	1780	4 3/4	3	1/16
44 3/4 40	Jul	1775	7	...	...
Iomega 12 1/2	Jan	764	7/16	286	5/8
12 3/8 12 1/2	Feb	471	15/16	195	1 1/4
12 3/8 15	Jan	1350	1/16	24	2 5/8

Option/Strike	Exp.	Call Vol.	Call Last	Put Vol.	Put Last
106 3/16 110	Jan	523	1/2	...	...
106 3/16 110	Feb	330	2 3/8	...	...
106 3/16 110	Apr	514	4 1/2	...	...
Merril 60	Jan	322	8 5/8	10	3/16
67 3/4 65	Feb	216	5 3/8	94	2 3/8
67 3/4 65	Apr	297	7 5/8	52	4
67 3/4 70	Jan	1006	1	107	2 7/8
67 3/4 70	Feb	306	2 7/8	25	4 7/8
MicrTc 20	Apr	817	9 3/4	356	5/8
28 3/8 22 1/2	Jul	405	8 3/8	...	...
28 3/8 25	Jan	2677	3 5/8	4187	1/4
28 3/8 25	Feb	229	4 7/8	197	1
28 3/8 25	Apr	320	6	277	1 7/8
28 3/8 27 1/2	Jan	1538	1 5/8	1064	13/16
28 3/8 27 1/2	Feb	462	3	215	2 1/2
28 3/8 27 1/2	Apr	453	4 3/4	23	3
28 3/8 27 1/2	Jul	425	6	2	4 3/8
28 3/8 30	Jan	4938	5/8	1121	2 1/8
28 3/8 30	Feb	1505	1 7/8	73	3 1/8
28 3/8 30	Apr	561	3 1/4	64	4 1/4
28 3/8 32 1/2	Jan	341	1/4	85	3 7/8
28 3/8 32 1/2	Feb	1596	1 1/8	32	4 5/8
28 3/8 35	Jan	206	1/8	119	6 1/4
28 3/8 35	Apr	639	1 3/4	127	7 1/2
28 3/8 40	Jan	227	1	12	11 3/4
Micsft 80	Jan	275	49	...	...
130 1/2 110	Apr	22	24	405	2 1/8
130 1/2 115	Jan	32	16	269	3/16
130 1/2 120	Feb	222	11 1/2	405	1/2
130 1/2 120	Apr	1	13 7/8	252	2 1/4
130 1/2 120	Apr	...	...	750	4
130 1/2 125	Jan	441	6 5/8	963	1
130 1/2 125	Feb	97	10	256	3 1/2
130 1/2 130	Jan	1753	2 1/2	1288	2 3/8
130 1/2 130	Feb	...	...	245	5 3/8
130 1/2 135	Jan	1419	3/4	563	5 1/4
130 1/2 135	Feb	511	4	40	7 1/2
130 1/2 140	Jan	728	3/16	329	9 1/2
130 1/2 145	Feb	318	1 1/8	24	15
Millerin 40	Jan	230	2 1/8	...	...
MMM 65	Jan	266	18 1/4	...	...
83 5/16 80	Jul	351	3 1/2	3	9 1/2
MirRst 20	Feb	43	2	212	5/8
Mobil 70	Feb	250	1 1/2	3	3 3/4
MoneySt 17 1/2	Feb	...	...	500	1 1/2
Monsanto 35	Jan	400	7 1/8	...	...
MSDWDis 55	Feb	204	5 3/8	631	1 1/2
58 15/16 60	Feb	209	2 5/16	90	3 5/8
Motorola 50	Jan	43	8	712	1/4
57 3/4 55	Jan	194	3 5/8	545	1
57 3/4 55	Feb	38	5 1/4	275	2 1/4
57 3/4 60	Jan	871	7/8	361	3
57 3/4 60	Feb	525	2 1/2	75	4 3/8
57 3/4 60	Jul	1174	6 3/4	37	7 1/2

Source: *The Wall Street Journal*, January 9, 1998. Reprinted by permission of *The Wall Street Journal*, © 1998 Dow Jones & Company, Inc. All Rights Reserved Worldwide.

$110 than for $105, and this is reflected in the prices of the puts. The February maturity put options with strike price $110 sells for $7.50, whereas the $105 exercise price February put sells for only $5.25.

Throughout Figure 20.2, you will see that many options may go an entire day without trading. Lack of trading is denoted by three dots in the volume and price columns. Because trading is infrequent, it is not unusual to find option prices that appear out of line with other prices. You might see, for example, two calls with different exercise prices that seem to sell for the same price. This discrepancy arises because the last trades for these options may have occurred at different times during the day. At any moment, the call with the lower exercise price must be worth more than an otherwise-identical call with a higher exercise price.

Figure 20.2 illustrates that the maturities of most exchange-traded options tend to be fairly short, ranging up to only several months. For larger firms and some stock indexes, however, longer-term options are traded with maturities ranging up to several years. These options are called LEAPS (for *L*ong-*T*erm *E*quity *A*ntici*P*ation *S*ecurities).

Question 1

a. **What will be the proceeds and net profits to an investor who purchases the February maturity IBM calls with exercise price $105 if the stock price at maturity is $115? What if the stock price at maturity is $95?**

b. **Now answer part (*a*) for an investor who purchases a January maturity IBM put option with exercise price $105.**

American and European Options

An **American option** allows its holder to exercise the right to purchase (if a call) or sell (if a put) the underlying asset on *or before* the expiration date. **European options** allow for exercise of the option only on the expiration date. American options, because they allow more leeway than their European counterparts, generally will be more valuable. Virtually all traded options in this country are American style. Foreign currency options and stock index options traded on the Chicago Board Options Exchange are notable exceptions to this rule, however.

Adjustments in Option Contract Terms

Because options convey the right to buy or sell shares at a stated price, stock splits would radically alter their value if the terms of the options contract were not adjusted to account for the stock split. For example, reconsider the IBM call options in Figure 20.2. If IBM were to announce a 10-for-1 split, its share price would fall from over $100 to about $10. A call option with exercise price $105 would be just about worthless, with virtually no possibility that the stock would sell at more than $105 before the options expired.

To account for a stock split, the exercise price is reduced by a factor of the split, and the number of options held is increased by that factor. For example, the original IBM call option with exercise price of $105 would be altered after a 10-for-1 split to 10 new options, with each option carrying an exercise price of $10.50. A similar adjustment is made for stock dividends of more than 10%; the number of shares covered by each option is increased in proportion to the stock dividend, and the exercise price is reduced by that proportion.

In contrast to stock dividends, cash dividends do not affect the terms of an option contract. Because payment of a cash dividend reduces the selling price of the stock without inducing offsetting adjustments in the option contract, the value of the option is affected by dividend policy. Other things being equal, call option values are lower for high-dividend-payout policies, because such policies slow the rate of increase of stock prices; conversely, put values are higher for high-dividend payouts. (Of course, the option values do not necessarily rise or fall on the dividend payment or ex-dividend dates. Dividend payments are anticipated, so the effect of the payment already is built into the original option price.)

Question 2 • Suppose that IBM's stock price at the exercise date is $120, and the exercise price of the call is $105. What is the profit on one option contract? After a 10-for-1 split, the stock price is $12, the exercise price is $10.50, and the option holder now can purchase 1,000 shares. Show that the split leaves option profits unaffected.

The Option Clearing Corporation

The Option Clearing Corporation (OCC), the clearinghouse for options trading, is jointly owned by the exchanges on which stock options are traded. Buyers and sellers of options who agree on a price will strike a deal. At this point, the OCC steps in. The OCC places itself between the two traders, becoming the effective buyer of the option from the writer and the effective writer of the option to the buyer. All individuals, therefore, deal only with the OCC, which effectively guarantees contract performance.

When an optionholder exercises an option, the OCC arranges for a member firm with clients who have written that option to make good on the option obligation. The member firm selects from its clients who have written that option to fulfill the contract. The selected client must deliver 100 shares of stock at a price equal to the exercise price for each call option contract written or must purchase 100 shares at the exercise price for each put option contract written.

Because the OCC guarantees contract performance, option writers are required to post margin amounts to guarantee that they can fulfill their contract obligations. The margin required is determined in part by the amount by which the option is in the money, because that value is an indicator of the potential obligation of the option writer upon exercise of the option. When the required margin exceeds the posted margin, the writer will receive a margin call. The holder of the option need not post margin because the holder will exercise the option only if it is profitable to do so. After purchasing the option, no further money is at risk.

Margin requirements are determined in part by the other securities held in the investor's portfolio. For example, a call option writer owning the stock against which the option is written can satisfy the margin requirement simply by allowing a broker to hold that stock in the brokerage account. The stock is then guaranteed to be available for delivery should the call option be exercised. If the underlying security is not owned, however, the margin requirement is determined by the value of the underlying security as well as by the amount by which the option is in or out of the money. Out-of-the-money options require less margin from the writer, for expected payouts are lower.

Other Listed Options

Options on assets other than stocks are also widely traded. These include options on market indexes and industry indexes, on foreign currency, and even on the futures prices of agricultural products, gold, silver, fixed-income securities, and stock indexes. We will discuss these in turn.

Index options   An index option is a call or put based on a stock market index such as the S&P 500 or the New York Stock Exchange Index. Index options are traded on several broad-based indexes as well as on a few industry-specific indexes and even commodity price indexes. We discussed many of these indexes in Chapter 2.

The construction of the indexes can vary across contracts or exchanges. For example, the S&P 100 index is a value-weighted average of the 100 stocks in the Standard & Poor's 100 stock group. The weights are proportional to the market value of outstanding equity for each stock. The Dow Jones Industrial Index, by contrast, is a price-weighted average of 30 stocks, whereas the Value Line Index is an equally weighted average of roughly 1,700 stocks.

Option contracts on many foreign stock indexes also trade. For example, options on the (Japanese) Nikkei 225 stock average trade on the Chicago Mercantile Exchange and options on the Hong Kong and Japan indexes trade on the American Stock Exchange. The Chicago Board Options Exchange lists options on the Mexican, Israeli, and Nikkei 300 stock indexes. European stock index options trade in London.

Figure 20.3 is a reproduction of the listings of index options from *The Wall Street Journal*. The listings for index options are similar to those of stock options. However, instead of supplying separate columns for puts and calls, the index options are all listed in

Figure 20.3 Index options.

INDEX OPTIONS TRADING

Tuesday, January 13, 1998

Volume, last, net change and open interest for all contracts. Volume figures are unofficial. Open interest reflects previous trading day. p-Put c-Call

CHICAGO

CB MEXICO INDEX(MEX)

	Strike	Vol.	Last	Net Chg.	Open Int.
Feb	100p	11	2 1/8	− 1 1/8	7
Mar	100p	1	3 1/4	− 5/8	81
Feb	110c	75	9	+ 1 1/4	95
Feb	110p	75	5 1/2	− 7/8	17
Mar	110c	2	11	+ 2 3/8	58
Mar	120c	10	6 1/4	− 1/8	5
Mar	120p	5	10 3/8	+ 2 3/4	45
Mar	130p	3	17 1/8	− 5 1/4	20
Mar	140p	2	25 1/2	+ 10	62
Call Vol.		87	Open Int.		634
Put Vol.		97	Open Int.		578

CB TECHNOLOGY(TXX)

	Strike	Vol.	Last	Net Chg.	Open Int.
Jan	190c	1	24 1/2	+ 7	11
Feb	200p	5	4	− 3 1/2	...
Jan	205c	1	7	+ 1 7/8	1
Jan	210c	10	4 1/8	+ 1	10
Feb	210c	1	12 3/8	− 8	5
Feb	215c	2	9	− 1 1/8	...
Feb	215p	3	11 1/4	− 3 1/2	3
Jan	230p	1	17 1/8	+ 4 1/8	5
Call Vol.		15	Open Int.		1,469
Put Vol.		11	Open Int.		232

DJ INDUS AVG(DJX)

	Strike	Vol.	Last	Net Chg.	Open Int.
Feb	64p	115	1/4	− 3/16	107
Feb	68p	103	1/2	− 1/4	183
Jan	70c	10	7	+ 7/8	136
Jan	72p	35	1/16	− 5/16	2,416
Feb	72p	15	7/8	− 5/16	1,436
Mar	72c	7	7	+ 1	768
Mar	72p	56	1 7/16	− 3/8	3,253
Jun	72c	30	8 3/4	− 1 3/4	137
Jun	72p	8	2 3/4	− 3/8	1,269
Mar	88c	95	3/16	− 1/16	333
Call Vol.		17,094	Open Int.		152,585
Put Vol.		19,783	Open Int.		191,532

DJ TRANP AVG(DTX)

	Strike	Vol.	Last	Net Chg.	Open Int.
Feb	295p	10	1 15/16	...	...
Feb	305c	10	23 3/4	− 2	25
Jan	310c	15	14 1/2	+ 4 3/4	50
Feb	310c	15	19 3/8	...	...
Jan	325c	10	2 9/16	+ 3/4	42
Jan	325p	10	3 3/4	− 2 1/8	28
Jan	330p	5	6	− 5 3/4	6
Mar	330p	1	12 1/4	− 1 3/4	28
Jun	330c	15	17 7/8	− 5/8	115
Call Vol.		65	Open Int.		1,064
Put Vol.		26	Open Int.		1,593

DJ UTIL AVG(DUX)

	Strike	Vol.	Last	Net Chg.	Open Int.
Jan	270c	10	5/16	− 3/4	12
Call Vol.		10	Open Int.		48
Put Vol.		0	Open Int.		35

MS MULTINATIONAL(NFT)

	Strike	Vol.	Last	Net Chg.	Open Int.
Feb	485p	1,275	5 1/2	...	...
Jan	540p	10	12 1/2	+ 4	100
Mar	540p	4	25 5/8	− 5 1/8	9
Call Vol.		0	Open Int.		544
Put Vol.		1,289	Open Int.		1,474

NASDAQ-100(NDX)

	Strike	Vol.	Last	Net Chg.	Open Int.
Feb	850p	3	5 3/4	− 6 3/8	200
Feb	860p	1	7 7/8	− 2 1/8	30
Jan	1040c	2	1/4	− 1/8	743
Feb	1040c	31	19 5/8	+ 9 5/8	997
Feb	1120c	5	3 1/4	...	...
Mar	1130c	200	7 3/4	+ 3	745
Feb	1150c	5	1 1/16	− 1/16	494
Mar	1170c	15	4	− 2 3/8	20
Mar	1200c	5	2 1/8	+ 1 1/16	466
Call Vol.		5,169	Open Int.		20,681
Put Vol.		3,952	Open Int.		20,753

RUSSELL 2000(RUT)

	Strike	Vol.	Last	Net Chg.	Open Int.
Mar	390p	250	8 3/4	− 3/4	500
Jan	405c	43	13 3/8	+ 1 1/2	275
Jan	405p	32	1	− 1 7/16	34
Feb	405c	24	20 1/8	+ 1/4	703
Jan	410c	60	8 1/2	+ 3 1/8	200
Jan	410p	19	1 7/16	− 2 7/16	1,659
Mar	445p	1	31 3/4	+ 6 5/8	37
Feb	450c	23	1 3/4	− 2 1/4	1,514
Mar	450p	4	35 1/2	+ 20 1/2	54
Call Vol.		622	Open Int.		18,104
Put Vol.		884	Open Int.		15,831

S & P 100 INDEX(OEX)

	Strike	Vol.	Last	Net Chg.	Open Int.
Jan	380p	416	1/16	− 1/16	15,016
Feb	380p	1,884	1 3/4	− 7/8	5,507
Jan	390p	665	1/16	− 1/8	8,336
Feb	390p	412	2 1/4	− 1 1/8	826
Mar	390p	75	4 5/8	...	...
Jan	400p	770	1/16	− 5/16	9,778
Feb	400p	302	3	− 1 1/8	2,946
Jan	455c	11,026	2 1/8	+ 5/16	14,940
Jan	455p	2,721	6	− 4 7/8	6,193
Feb	500c	132	3/8	...	5,185
Feb	505c	180	5/16	+ 1/16	3,928
Feb	510c	2	1/8	− 1/16	4,468
Mar	510c	20	1	+ 1/8	480
Call Vol.		75,944	Open Int.		322,627
Put Vol.		84,288	Open Int.		265,013

S & P 500 INDEX-AM(SPX)

	Strike	Vol.	Last	Net Chg.	Open Int.
Mar	40c	300	5 1/2	− 5 3/4	1,000
Mar	500c	349	452	+ 22	219
Mar	500p	337	1/8	− 1/16	2,394
Mar	575p	3	5/8	− 1/8	142
Mar	600p	25	13/16	+ 3/16	3,821
Mar	650p	100	1 1/4	− 3/4	5,652
Feb	700p	601	5/8	− 3/8	7,558
Mar	700p	164	2 1/8	− 1 5/8	9,297
Feb	720p	110	1	− 1 1/2	20
Feb	910c	31	59	+ 10	108
Feb	910p	142	13 1/2	− 6 1/2	1,188
Mar	910p	6	24 1/2	− 3 3/8	630
Jan	915c	50	35 1/2	+ 5	70
Jan	915p	203	1	− 2 3/4	1,317
Mar	915p	40	23	− 11 1/2	5,426
Jan	920c	68	33 1/2	+ 9	5,459
Mar	1050c	11	4 1/4	+ 1	5,059
Mar	1050p	4	94 1/2	− 22 1/2	7,139
Jan	1075c	20	1/16	...	894
Jan	1075p	10	127 3/4	− 10 1/4	439
Mar	1075p	65	117	− 11	3,042
Mar	1100c	365	1	...	1,808
Mar	1100p	337	143	− 6 1/4	1,126
Call Vol.		42,489	Open Int.		730,205
Put Vol.		70,696	Open Int.		1,119,545

AMERICAN

AM MEXICO INDEX(MXY)

	Strike	Vol.	Last	Net Chg.	Open Int.
Feb	100p	10	1	− 9/16	150
Mar	150c	10	1	− 8 1/8	10
Call Vol.		10	Open Int.		82
Put Vol.		10	Open Int.		270

COMP TECH(XCI)

	Strike	Vol.	Last	Net Chg.	Open Int.
Mar	390p	6	6 5/8	...	...
Jan	425c	2	18 1/4	+ 4 1/8	20
Mar	430p	6	16 5/8	...	...
Jan	435c	9	14 1/2	+ 8	3
Jan	435p	5	2	− 5 3/4	60
Call Vol.		11	Open Int.		1,091
Put Vol.		17	Open Int.		808

HONG KONG INDEX(HKO)

	Strike	Vol.	Last	Net Chg.	Open Int.
Mar	170p	2	13 3/8	− 6 3/8	9
Jan	180c	20	1 3/4	+ 5/8	322
Jan	180p	10	8 3/8	− 6 7/8	351
Mar	180p	2	19 3/4	− 1 1/4	507
Jan	200p	1	26 1/8	− 3 3/8	480
Mar	220p	6	45 5/8	+ 8 3/8	88
Jan	270p	30	97	+ 32	20
Mar	400c	500	1/16	...	...
Call Vol.		521	Open Int.		14,857
Put Vol.		82	Open Int.		6,595

INTERNET(IIX)

	Strike	Vol.	Last	Net Chg.	Open Int.
Feb	230p	20	3 1/2	+ 1/2	20
Feb	240p	15	6 1/2	− 3/4	5
Jan	245p	10	9/16	− 9 13/16	10
Jan	255c	20	4 1/8	+ 2 3/16	10
Jan	255p	30	1 15/16	− 8 9/16	...
Jan	270p	5	13 3/4	− 12 1/2	5
Jan	280p	20	25 3/4	− 6 3/4	20
Feb	280p	20	26 7/8	...	...
Call Vol.		20	Open Int.		649
Put Vol.		120	Open Int.		450

JAPAN INDEX(JPN)

	Strike	Vol.	Last	Net Chg.	Open Int.
Feb	120p	250	3/4	...	...
Feb	130p	20	2	3/4	590
Jan	135p	3	1/4	− 1 1/4	36
Jan	145p	266	3/8	− 3/8	709
Jan	150p	15	7/8	− 7/8	565
Feb	150c	4	10 1/2	+ 1	50
Call Vol.		1,941	Open Int.		26,596
Put Vol.		1,962	Open Int.		14,830

MAJOR MARKET(XMI)

	Strike	Vol.	Last	Net Chg.	Open Int.
Jan	760p	10	3/4	− 3 7/8	58
Feb	760p	50	8 3/8	− 5	2
Feb	780p	2	11	...	...
Jan	800p	20	3 3/8	− 3/4	129
Jan	820c	31	8 5/8	+ 3/8	254
Jan	830c	16	3 1/2	− 5/8	40
Jan	840c	15	1 5/16	+ 3/16	230
Jan	840p	10	21 5/8	− 17 3/8	189
Feb	840c	10	14	+ 1/2	22
Call Vol.		72	Open Int.		1,693
Put Vol.		232	Open Int.		2,740

MS HITECH 35(MSH)

	Strike	Vol.	Last	Net Chg.	Open Int.
Feb	395c	2	45 7/8	+ 5 3/4	2
Jan	400p	253	3/8	− 5/8	987
Jan	410p	255	3/4	− 3 3/4	227
Jan	415p	103	15/16	− 4 1/16	4,970
Jan	420c	12	24 1/8	+ 15	309
Jan	420p	12	2	− 3 1/4	412
Call Vol.		5,238	Open Int.		15,918
Put Vol.		2,321	Open Int.		28,913

PHARMACEUTICAL(DRG)

	Strike	Vol.	Last	Net Chg.	Open Int.
Feb	450p	15	11/16	− 1 3/16	15
Feb	480p	5	2 3/4	− 2 1/4	5
Jan	500p	20	1/4	− 1 5/8	40
Jan	510p	5	5/16	− 1 1/16	25
Jan	530c	20	11 1/8	+ 7/8	24
Jan	530p	3	1 3/8	− 2 3/8	4
Feb	530c	500	24	+ 5 1/4	2
Feb	530p	500	15	+ 1/4	1
Jan	540c	40	3 1/4	− 2 1/8	11
Jan	540p	30	5 1/4	− 5 1/8	30
Jan	550c	25	1 1/4	− 1 5/8	37
Feb	580c	25	4	...	5
Call Vol.		610	Open Int.		1,396
Put Vol.		578	Open Int.		2,401

S & P MIDCAP(MID)

	Strike	Vol.	Last	Net Chg.	Open Int.
Feb	280p	25	2 3/8	...	...
Feb	310p	2	6 1/8	+ 1 1/8	5
Jan	320c	20	3/4	− 1 1/16	50
Jan	320p	50	4	− 4 5/8	444
Call Vol.		120	Open Int.		1,254
Put Vol.		77	Open Int.		2,799

PHILADELPHIA

GOLD/SILVER(XAU)

	Strike	Vol.	Last	Net Chg.	Open Int.
Mar	50p	2	13/16	− 1/8	4
Mar	55p	10	1 3/4	+ 11/16	34
Jan	60c	237	6 3/8	+ 3 7/8	218
Feb	60c	16	7 3/4	+ 3	146
Mar	100c	3	3/8	+ 1/4	2,128
Call Vol.		2,884	Open Int.		26,210
Put Vol.		1,534	Open Int.		7,990

OIL SERVICE(OSX)

	Strike	Vol.	Last	Net Chg.	Open Int.
Mar	10c	200	4 1/4	+ 1 1/8	279
Feb	80c	50	17 3/4	+ 2 3/4	50
Feb	80p	1	1 3/4	− 1/4	1,000
Feb	85c	600	12 1/4	+ 2 5/8	980
Feb	85p	1	3 5/8	+ 3/8	1,705
Mar	125c	3	1 3/16	− 1/16	360
Feb	135c	10	1/4	− 2 3/16	50
Call Vol.		2,258	Open Int.		32,280
Put Vol.		7,269	Open Int.		33,758

OTC INDEX(XOC)

	Strike	Vol.	Last	Net Chg.	Open Int.
Feb	780c	8	8 3/4	...	...
Feb	790c	3	7 3/8	...	...
Feb	800c	5	4 7/8	− 22 5/8	5
Call Vol.		16	Open Int.		284
Put Vol.		0	Open Int.		158

PHLX KBW BANK(BKX)

	Strike	Vol.	Last	Net Chg.	Open Int.
Feb	640p	20	11 1/4	− 2 5/8	356
Jan	650p	1	3/8	− 1 1/8	406
Jan	670p	140	1 3/8	− 1 5/8	213
Jan	675p	4	1 9/16	− 3 1/16	2

SEMICONDUCTOR(SOX)

	Strike	Vol.	Last	Net Chg.	Open Int.
Feb	200p	20	1 15/16	+ 13/16	53
Feb	205p	1	2	...	...
Feb	210p	1	2 1/2	− 1 3/8	20
Feb	310c	17	3 1/8	+ 1 1/4	64
Feb	320c	5	2 1/8	− 5/8	9
Call Vol.		1,216	Open Int.		10,231
Put Vol.		795	Open Int.		8,427

TOP 100 INDEX(TPX)

	Strike	Vol.	Last	Net Chg.	Open Int.
Mar	910c	2	30 1/8	− 22 7/8	1
Call Vol.		2	Open Int.		2,024
Put Vol.		0	Open Int.		3,350

UTILITY INDEX(UTY)

	Strike	Vol.	Last	Net Chg.	Open Int.
Feb	305p	5	7 3/8	− 1	320
Call Vol.		0	Open Int.		2,093
Put Vol.		5	Open Int.		1,754

VALUE LINE(VLE)

	Strike	Vol.	Last	Net Chg.	Open Int.
Jan	810p	12	15/16	− 4 1/16	200
Jan	840p	5	5 7/8	...	...
Jan	850c	6	5 3/4	+ 2	208
Jan	850p	5	11 7/8	− 6 5/8	200
Feb	880c	5	9	...	...
Call Vol.		11	Open Int.		537
Put Vol.		22	Open Int.		617

LEAPS-LONG TERM

DJ INDUS AVG – CB

	Strike	Vol.	Last	Net Chg.	Open Int.
Dec 00	60p	10	4 1/4	+ 1/8	46
Dec 99	80p	85	8	...	15278
Dec 00	80p	3	8 3/4	− 1/4	11611
Dec 99	84p	3	9 7/8	− 1 1/2	16
Dec 00	88c	1200	10 1/8	+ 5/8	26102
Dec 00	88p	10	12	+ 7/8	2656
Dec 00	100c	75	6 1/4	+ 1/2	154
Dec 00	100p	30	18	− 1	338
Call vol.		1,275	Open Int.		66,922
Put vol.		141	Open Int.		114,589

S & P 100 INDEX – CB

	Strike	Vol.	Last	Net Chg.	Open Int.
Dec 98	55p	10	5/8	+ 1/16	2786
Dec 98	60p	4	7/8	− 1/4	4907
Dec 98	65p	10	1 1/8	− 1/4	6094
Dec 98	80p	13	3 1/2	− 5/8	2967
Dec 99	80p	40	5 3/4	+ 1/8	1207
Dec 98	85p	5	5 1/2	...	15401
Dec 98	90c	5	9 1/2	+ 1 1/4	1804
Dec 98	90p	7	7	− 1/2	5152
Dec 98	95p	10	10	+ 1/8	4420
Dec 98	100c	11	4 1/2	+ 3/8	4080
Call vol.		16	Open Int.		17,629
Put vol.		99	Open Int.		81,001

S & P 500 INDEX – CB

	Strike	Vol.	Last	Net Chg.	Open Int.
Dec 98	55p	40	5/16	...	15443
Dec 98	60p	9	1/2	− 1/8	21340
Dec 98	65p	14	15/16	− 1/16	26066
Dec 98	67 1/2p	7	15/16	+ 1/8	4399
Dec 98	70p	70	1 3/8	− 1/8	22596
Dec 98	72 1/2p	110	1 1/2	− 3/8	3296

SEMICONDUCTOR(SOX)

	Strike	Vol.	Last	Net Chg.	Open Int.
Feb	200p	20	1 15/16	+ 13/16	53
Feb	205p	1	2	...	...
Feb	210p	1	2 1/2	− 1 3/8	20
Dec 98	102 1/2c	2	6	− 1	134
Dec 00	105p	2	13	− 1/2	103
Dec 98	110p	2	13 3/4	− 7/8	387
Dec 98	110p	4	14 1/2	− 3/8	246
Call vol.		30	Open Int.		58,681
Put vol.		1,365	Open Int.		327,903

Source: *The Wall Street Journal*, January 14, 1998. Reprinted by permission of *The Wall Street Journal*,

one column, and the letter *p* or *c* is used to denote puts or calls. The index options listings also report the *open interest* for each contract, which is the number of contracts currently outstanding. Notice from the trading volume and open interest columns that the S&P 100 options contract, often called the *OEX* after its ticker symbol, is the most actively traded contract on the CBOE, although volume on S&P 500 index contracts is also quite high. Together, these contracts dominate CBOE volume.

In contrast to stock options, index options do not require that the call writer actually "deliver the index" upon exercise or that the put writer "purchase the index." Instead, a cash settlement procedure is used. The payoff that would accrue upon exercise of the option is calculated, and the option writer simply pays that amount to the option holder. The payoff is equal to the difference between the exercise price of the option and the value of the index. For example, if the S&P index is at 1,050 when a call option on the index with exercise price 1,040 is exercised, the holder of the call receives a cash payment of the difference, 1,050 – 1,040, times the contract multiplier of $100, or $1,000 per contract.

Futures Options Futures options give their holders the right to buy or sell a specified futures contract, using as a futures price the exercise price of the option. Although the delivery process is slightly complicated, the terms of futures options contracts are designed in effect to allow the option to be written on the futures price itself. The optionholder receives upon exercise a net payoff equal to the difference between the current futures price on the specified asset and the exercise price of the option. Thus if the futures price is, say, $37, and the call has an exercise price of $35, the holder who exercises the call option on the futures gets a payoff of $2. Many of the futures options in Figure 20.4 are foreign

Figure 20.4
Futures options.

FUTURES OPTIONS PRICES

Tuesday, January 13, 1998

AGRICULTURAL

CORN (CBT)
5,000 bu.; cents per bu.

Strike	Calls-Settle			Puts-Settle		
Price	Mar	May	Jly	Mar	May	Jly
250	20⅞	27½	34¼	⅞	1⅝	4
260	12⅞	19¾	27¼	2½	3¾	7
270	7¼	14¼	22	6⅞	7½	11
280	4	10	17	13⅜	13	16
290	2¼	7	13½	21¾	19½	22½
300	1½	4¾	10¾	30⅞	27¾	29¼

Est vol 25,000 Mn 12,336 calls 8,501 puts
Op int Mon 184,821 calls 105,668 puts

SOYBEANS (CBT)
5,000 bu.; cents per bu.

Strike	Calls-Settle			Puts-Settle		
Price	Mar	May	Jly	Mar	May	Jly
625	49	57½	65½	1¾	5½	10½
650	28½	39	49	6	12	18¼
675	14¼	25½	36½	16½	23	30½
700	7	17	27	34	39	45½
725	3¼	11	21	55	58	63¾
750	1¾	7¼	15¾	78½	79	83½

Est vol 12,000 Mn 9,088 calls 3,239 puts
Op int Mon 106,128 calls 51,389 puts

SOYBEAN MEAL (CBT)
100 tons; $ per ton

Strike	Calls-Settle			Puts-Settle		
Price	Mar	May	Jly	Mar	May	Jly
185	....	....	1.50	3.00	4.75
190	9.25	11.00	14.25	2.50	5.00	6.00
195	6.25	8.15	....	4.50	7.00	8.50
200	4.00	6.25	9.50	7.10	9.75	11.40
210	1.90	3.40	5.80	14.85	17.00	17.75
220	1.00	2.00	4.00	24.00	25.50	25.50

Est vol 2,800 Mn 2,487 calls 1,045 puts

LIVESTOCK

CATTLE-FEEDER (CME)
50,000 lbs.; cents per lb.

Strike	Calls-Settle			Puts-Settle		
Price	Jan	Mar	Apr	Jan	Mar	Apr
75	2.50	2.67	....	.10	.97	....
76	1.60	2.07	2.75	.20	1.35	1.35
77	.85	1.55	....	.45	1.82	....
78	.40	1.07	1.60	.90	2.32	2.20
79	.15	.72	....	1.75	....	....
80	.02	.52	1.42	2.62	3.77	3.40

Est vol 742 Mn 220 calls 340 puts
Op int Mon 5,000 calls 8,086 puts

CATTLE-LIVE (CME)
40,000 lbs.; cents per lb.

Strike	Calls-Settle			Puts-Settle		
Price	Feb	Apr	Jun	Feb	Apr	Jun
63	2.40	....	....	.30	.37	....
64	1.67	....	....	.52	.55	.70
65	1.00	....	....	.87	.75	....
66	.57	2.72	3.40	1.42	1.05	1.20
67	.30	2.10	....	2.15	1.42	....
68	.12	1.60	2.20	2.97	1.90	1.95

Est vol 2,537 Mn 463 calls 2,470 puts
Op int Mon 18,614 calls 28,312 puts

HOGS-LEAN (CME)
40,000 lbs.; cents per lb.

Strike	Calls-Settle			Puts-Settle		
Price	Feb	Apr	Jun	Feb	Apr	Jun
56	2.35	2.30	....	.45	1.55	....
57	1.65	1.80	....	.75	2.05	....
58	1.12	1.37	....	1.22	2.60	....
59	.72	1.00	....	1.82	....	....
60	.45	.75	....	2.55	3.95	....
61	.22	.55	....	3.30	....	....

Est vol 260 Mn 899 calls 480 puts
Op int Mon 12,165 calls 7,354 puts

CURRENCY

JAPANESE YEN (CME)
12,500,000 yen; cents per 100 yen

Strike	Calls-Settle			Puts-Settle		
Price	Feb	Mar	Apr	Feb	Mar	Apr
7550	1.74	2.19	....	0.65	1.11	....
7600	1.43	1.90	....	0.84	1.31	....
7650	1.14	1.63	....	1.06	1.54	....
7700	0.93	1.40	....	1.34	1.81	....
7750	0.74	1.19	....	1.65	2.09	..
7800	0.57	1.01	....	1.98	2.41	....

Est vol 5,527 Mon 4,119 calls 3,907 puts
Op int Mon 42,236 calls 57,381 puts

DEUTSCHEMARK (CME)
125,000 marks; cents per mark

Strike	Calls-Settle			Puts-Settle		
Price	Feb	Mar	Apr	Feb	Mar	Apr
5400	1.38	1.58	....	0.24	0.45	....
5450	....	0.00	....	0.35	0.61	....
5500	0.69	0.96	....	0.55	0.82	....
5550	0.44	0.72	....	0.80	1.08	....
5600	0.27	0.53	....	1.12	1.38	....
5650	0.17	0.39	....	1.52	1.74	....

Est vol 1,637 Mon 481 calls 740 puts
Op int Mon 19,947 calls 27,962 puts

SWISS FRANC (CME)
125,000 francs; cents per franc

Strike	Calls-Settle			Puts-Settle		
Price	Feb	Mar	Apr	Feb	Mar	Apr
6700	1.50	1.82	....	0.34	0.67	....
6750	0.00	....	....	0.48	0.85	....
6800	0.85	1.22	....	0.69	1.06	....
6850	0.61	0.98	....	0.00	1.32	....
6900	0.43	0.78	....	1.27	1.61	....
6950	0.30	0.61	....	....	1.94	....

Est vol 628 Mon 448 calls 218 puts
Op int Mon 11,335 calls 9,849 puts

exchange futures options; they are written on the futures price of foreign exchange rather than on the actual or spot exchange rate.

Foreign Currency Options A currency option offers the right to buy or sell a quantity of foreign currency for a specified amount of domestic currency. Foreign currency options have traded on the Philadelphia Stock Exchange since December 1982. Since then, the Chicago Board Options Exchange and the Chicago Mercantile Exchange have listed foreign currency options. Currency option contracts call for purchase or sale of the currency in exchange for a specified number of U.S. dollars. Contracts are quoted in cents or fractions of a cent per unit of foreign currency.

Figure 20.5 shows a listing from *The Wall Street Journal* of some of these contracts. The size of each option contract is specified for each listing. The call option on the Swiss franc, for example, entitles its holder to purchase 62,500 francs for a specified number of cents per franc on or before the expiration date. The March call option with strike price of 68 cents sells for .99 cent, which means each contract costs \$.0099 × 62,500 = \$618.75.

There is an important difference between the options traded on the Philadelphia exchange and the futures options traded on the International Monetary Market (IMM). The former provide payoffs that depend on the difference between the exercise price and the exchange rate at maturity. The latter are foreign exchange futures options that provide payoffs that depend on the difference between the exercise price and the exchange rate *futures price* at maturity. Because exchange rates and exchange rate futures prices generally are not equal, the options and futures-options contracts will have different values, even with identical expiration dates and exercise prices. For example, in Figure 20.4, the call option on the Swiss franc with strike price 68 cents and March maturity is quoted at 1.22 cents. The corresponding futures option in Figure 20.5 with the same strike price and maturity is quoted at .99 cent.

Interest Rate Options Options on particular U.S. Treasury notes and bonds are listed on the Amex and the CBOE. Options also are traded on Treasury bills, certificates of deposit, GNMA pass-through certificates, and yields on Treasury securities of various maturities. Options on several interest rate futures also trade. Among these are contracts on Treasury bond, Treasury note, municipal bond, LIBOR, Eurodollar, and Euromark futures.

Figure 20.5
Foreign currency options.

Tuesday, January 13, 1998

OPTIONS

PHILADELPHIA EXCHANGE

		Calls Vol.	Calls Last	Puts Vol.	Puts Last
Australian Dollar					**64.79**
50,000 Australian Dollars-cents per unit.					
65	Mar	1	1.01	...	...
British Pound					**163.33**
31,250 Brit. Pound EOM-European					
165	Jan	20	0.70	...	...
31,250 Brit. Pounds-European Style.					
159	Mar	...	...	20	1.07
160	Mar	...	...	20	1.33
161	Feb	...	...	100	0.95
163	Jan	...	...	140	0.57
167	Feb	100	0.58	...	...
31,250 Brit. Pounds-cents per unit.					
164	Jan	600	0.50	...	...
165	Feb	40	1.25	...	...
165	Mar	26	1.70	5	3.93
166	Feb	4	0.85	...	...
British Pound-GMark					**297.20**
31,250 British Pound-German Mark cross.					
298	Jan	10	0.78	...	...
300	Jan	20	0.36	...	...
Canadian Dollar					**69.66**
50,000 Canadian Dollars-cents per unit.					
70½	Jan	...	...	36	0.83
71	Jan	...	...	42	1.32
71½	Mar	10	0.15	...	...
72	Jan	...	...	9	2.31
GMark-JYen					**72.35**
62,500 German Mark-Japanese Yen cross.					
70½	Feb	...	...	10	0.42
72	Mar	...	...	20	1.58
74	Feb	10	0.50	...	...
German Mark					**54.96**
62,500 German Marks-cents per unit.					
55	Mar	...	...	1	0.90
57	Feb	7	0.17	...	...
58	Jan	...	...	3	3.13
Japanese Yen					**75.97**
6,250,000J.Yen EOM 100ths of a cent per unit.					
74½	Jan	...	...	250	0.40
6,250,000J.Yen-100ths of a cent per unit.					
75	Mar	10	2.60	27	1.10
76	Jan	...	...	35	0.51
77	Jan	...	...	5	1.01
78½	Feb	45	0.57	...	...
6,250,000J.Yen-EuropeanStyle.					
78	Feb	5	0.55	...	...
79	Feb	30	0.35	...	...
Swiss Franc					**67.69**
62,500 Swiss Francs-European Style.					
65	Feb	6	3.11	...	...
65	Mar	67	3.54	...	...
66	Mar	9	2.56	...	...
67	Feb	16	1.60	49	0.44
67	Mar	22	1.98	...	...
68	Feb	33	0.99	...	...
68	Mar	58	1.44	...	...
68½	Mar	4	1.15	...	...
69	Feb	...	...	6	1.40
69	Mar	...	...	12	1.65
70	Feb	...	...	10	2.27
70	Mar	320	0.55	...	...
71	Feb	...	...	6	3.04
62,500 Swiss Francs-cents per unit.					
68	Feb	...	...	50	0.96
68	Mar	...	...	2	1.18
Call Vol 1,878				**Open Int ... 94,627**	
Put Vol 3,017				**Open Int ... 99,908**	

Source: *The Wall Street Journal*, January 14, 1998. Reprinted by permission of *The Wall Street Journal*,

20.2   VALUES OF OPTIONS AT EXPIRATION

Call Options

Recall that a call option gives the right to purchase a security at the exercise price. If you hold a call option on IBM stock with an exercise price of $100, and IBM is now selling at $110, you can exercise your option to purchase the stock at $100 and simultaneously sell the shares at the market price of $110, clearing $10 per share. Yet if the shares sell below $100, you can sit on the option and do nothing, realizing no further gain or loss. The value of the call option at expiration equals

$$\text{Payoff to callholder} = \begin{array}{ll} S_T - X & \text{if } S_T > X \\ 0 & \text{if } S_T \leq X \end{array}$$

where S_T is the value of the stock at expiration and X is the exercise price. This formula emphasizes the option property because the payoff cannot be negative. That is, the option is exercised only if S_T exceeds X. If S_T is less than X, exercise does not occur, and the option expires with zero value. The loss to the optionholder in this case equals the price originally paid for the right to buy at the exercise price. More generally, the *profit* to the optionholder is the value of the option at expiration minus the original purchase price.

The value at expiration of the call on IBM with exercise price $100 is given by the schedule:

IBM value:	$90	$100	$110	$120	$130
Option value:	0	0	10	20	30

For IBM prices at or below $100, the option is worthless. Above $100, the option is worth the excess of IBM's price over $100. The option's value increases by one dollar for each dollar increase in the IBM stock price. This relationship can be depicted graphically as in Figure 20.6.

The solid line in Figure 20.6 depicts the value of the call at maturity. The net *profit* to the holder of the call equals the gross payoff less the initial investment in the call. Suppose the call cost $14. Then the profit to the callholder would be as given in the dashed (bottom) line of Figure 20.6. At option expiration, the investor has suffered a loss of $14 if the stock price is less than or equal to $100.

Profits do not become positive unless the stock price at expiration exceeds $114. The break-even point is $114, because at that price the payoff to the call, $S_T - X = \$114 - \$100 = \$14$, equals the cost paid to acquire the call. Hence the callholder shows a profit only if the stock price is higher.

Conversely, the writer of the call incurs losses if the stock price is high. In that scenario, the writer will receive a call and will be obligated to deliver a stock worth S_T for only X dollars:

$$\text{Payoff to callholder} = \begin{array}{ll} -(S_T - X) & \text{if } S_T > X \\ 0 & \text{if } S_T \leq X \end{array}$$

The call writer, who is exposed to losses if IBM increases in price, is willing to bear this risk in return for the option premium.

Figure 20.7 depicts the payoff and profit diagrams for the call writer. These are the mirror images of the corresponding diagrams for callholders. The break-even point for the

Figure 20.6
Payoff and profit to
call option at
expiration.

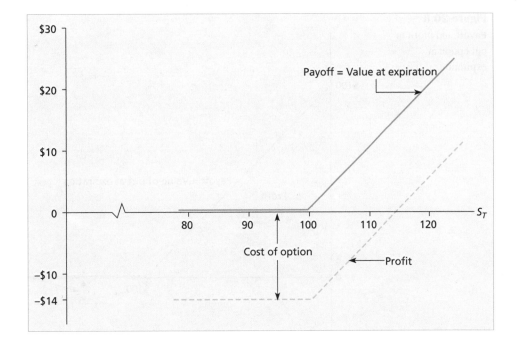

Figure 20.7
Payoff and profit to
call writers at
expiration.

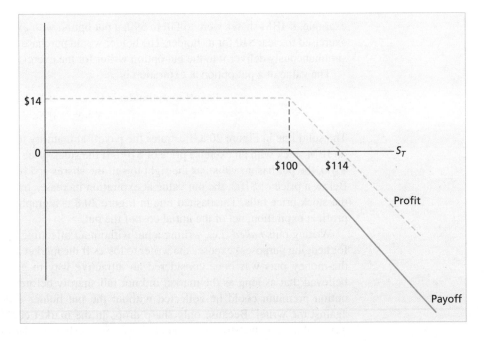

option writer also is $114. The (negative) payoff at that point just offsets the premium orig-
inally received when the option was written.

Put Options

A put option conveys the right to sell an asset at the exercise price. In this case, the holder
will not exercise the option unless the asset sells for *less* than the exercise price. For

Figure 20.8
Payoff and profit to
put option at
expiration.

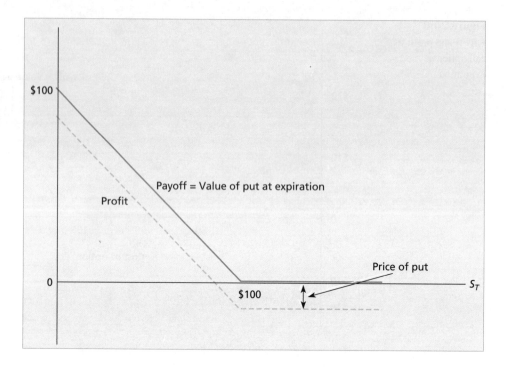

example, if IBM shares were to fall to $90, a put option with exercise price $100 could be
exercised to clear $10 for its holder. The holder would purchase a share of IBM for $90 and
simultaneously deliver it to the put option writer for the exercise price of $100.

The value of a put option at expiration is

$$\text{Payoff to putholder} = \begin{array}{ll} 0 & \text{if } S_T \geq X \\ X - S_T & \text{if } S_T < X \end{array}$$

The solid line in Figure 20.8 illustrates the payoff at maturity to the holder of a put option
on IBM stock with an exercise price of $100. If the stock price at option maturity is above
$100, the put has no value, as the right to sell the shares at $100 would not be exercised.
Below a price of $100, the put value at expiration increases by one dollar for each dollar
the stock price falls. The dashed line in Figure 20.8 is a graph of the put option owner's
profit at expiration, net of the initial cost of the put.

Writing puts *naked* (i.e., writing a put without an offsetting short position in the stock
for hedging purposes) exposes the writer to losses if the market falls. Writing naked out-of-
the-money puts was once considered an attractive way to generate income, as it was
believed that as long as the market did not fall sharply before the option expiration, the
option premium could be collected without the put holder ever exercising the option
against the writer. Because only sharp drops in the market could result in losses to the
writer of the put, the strategy was not viewed as overly risky. However, in the wake of the
market crash of October 1987, such put writers suffered huge losses. Participants now perceive much greater risk to this strategy.

Concept    **Question 3° Analyze the strategy of put writing.**
a. **What is the payoff to a put writer as a function of the stock price?**
b. **What is the profit?**
c. **Draw the payoff and profit graphs.**
d. **When do put writers do well? When do they do poorly?**

Option versus Stock Investments

Purchasing call options is a bullish strategy; that is, the calls provide profits when stock prices increase. Purchasing puts, in contrast, is a bearish strategy. Symmetrically, writing calls is bearish, whereas writing puts is bullish. Because option values depend on the price of the underlying stock, purchase of options may be viewed as a substitute for direct purchase or sale of a stock. Why might an option strategy be preferable to direct stock transactions?

For example, why would you purchase a call option rather than buy IBM stock directly? Maybe you have some information that leads you to believe IBM stock will increase in value from its current level, which in our examples we will take to be $100. You know your analysis could be incorrect, however, and that IBM also could fall in price. Suppose a six-month maturity call option with exercise price $100 currently sells for $10, and the interest rate for the period is 3%. Consider these three strategies for investing a sum of money, say, $10,000. For simplicity, suppose IBM will not pay any dividends until after the six-month period.

Strategy A: Purchase 100 shares of IBM stock.

Strategy B: Purchase 1,000 call options on IBM with exercise price $100. (This would require 10 contracts, each for 100 shares.)

Strategy C: Purchase 100 call options for $1,000. Invest the remaining $9,000 in six-month T-bills, to earn 3% interest. The bills will grow in value from $9,000 to $9,000 × 1.03 = $9,270.

Let us trace the possible values of these three portfolios when the options expire in six months as a function of IBM stock price at that time:

	IBM Price					
Portfolio	$95	$100	$105	$110	$115	$120
Portfolio A: All stock	$9,500	$10,000	$10,500	$11,000	$11,500	$12,000
Portfolio B: All options	0	0	5,000	10,000	15,000	20,000
Portfolio C: Call plus bills	9,270	9,270	9,770	10,270	10,770	11,270

Portfolio A will be worth 100 times the share value of IBM. Portfolio B is worthless unless IBM sells for more than the exercise price of the call. Once that point is reached, the portfolio is worth 1,000 times the excess of the stock price over the exercise price. Finally, Portfolio C is worth $9,270 from the investment in T-bills plus any profits from the 100 call options. Remember that each of these portfolios involves the same $10,000 initial investment. The rates of return on these three portfolios are as follows:

	IBM Price					
Portfolio	$95	$100	$105	$110	$115	$120
Portfolio A: All stock	− 5.0%	0.0%	5.0%	10.0%	15.0%	20.0%
Portfolio B: All options	−100.0	−100.0	− 50.0	0.0	50.0	100.0
Portfolio C: Call plus bills	− 7.3	− 7.3	− 2.3	2.7	7.7	12.7

These rates of return are graphed in Figure 20.9.

Figure 20.9

Rate of return to three strategies.

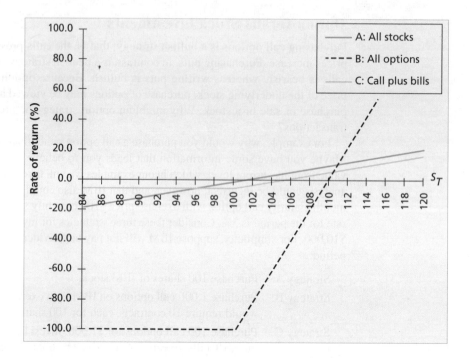

Comparing the returns of Portfolios B and C to those of the simple investment in IBM stock represented by Portfolio A, we see that options offer two interesting features. First, an option offers leverage. Compare the returns of Portfolios B and A. Unless IBM stock increases from its initial value of $100, the value of Portfolio B falls precipitously to zero—a rate of return of negative 100%. Conversely, modest increases in the rate of return on the stock result in disproportionate increases in the option rate of return. For example, a 4.3% increase in the stock price from $115 to $120 would increase the rate of return on the call from 50% to 100%. In this sense, calls are a levered investment on the stock. Their values respond more than proportionately to changes in the stock value.

Figure 20.9 vividly illustrates this point. The slope of the all-option portfolio is far steeper than that for the all-stock portfolio, reflecting its greater proportional sensitivity to the value of the underlying security. The leverage factor is the reason investors (illegally) exploiting inside information commonly choose options as their investment vehicle.

The potential insurance value of options is the second interesting feature, as Portfolio C shows. The T-bill-plus-option portfolio cannot be worth less than $9,270 after six months, as the option can always be left to expire worthless. The worst possible rate of return on Portfolio C is −7.3%, compared to a (theoretically) worst possible rate of return of IBM stock of −100% if the company were to go bankrupt. Of course, this insurance comes at a price: When IBM does well, Portfolio C, the option-plus-bills portfolio, does not perform quite as well as Portfolio A, the all-stock portfolio.

This simple example makes an important point. Although options can be used by speculators as effectively leveraged stock positions, as in Portfolio B, they also can be used by investors who desire to tailor their risk exposures in creative ways, as in Portfolio C. For example, the call-plus-bills strategy of Portfolio C provides a rate of return profile quite unlike that of the stock alone. The absolute limitation on downside risk is a novel and attractive feature of this strategy. We next discuss several option strategies that provide other novel risk profiles that might be attractive to hedgers and other investors.

20.3   OPTION STRATEGIES

An unlimited variety of payoff patterns can be achieved by combining puts and calls with various exercise prices. We explain in this section the motivation and structure of some of the more popular ones.

Protective Put

Imagine you would like to invest in a stock, but you are unwilling to bear potential losses beyond some given level. Investing in the stock alone seems risky to you because in principle you could lose all the money you invest. You might consider instead investing in stock and purchasing a put option on the stock. Table 20.1 shows the total value of your portfolio at option expiration: Whatever happens to the stock price, you are guaranteed a payoff equal to the put option's exercise price because the put gives you the right to sell IBM for the exercise price even if the stock price is below that value.

For example, if the strike price is $X = \$100$ and IBM is selling at $97 at option expiration, then the value of your total portfolio is $100. The stock is worth $97 and the value of the expiring put option is

$$X - S_T = \$100 - \$97 = \$3$$

Another way to look at it is that you are holding the stock and a put contract giving you the right to sell the stock for $100. The right to sell locks in a minimum portfolio value of $100. On the other hand, if the stock price is above $100, say $104, then the right to sell a share at $100 is worthless. You allow the put to expire unexercised, ending up with a share of stock worth $S_T = \$104$.

Figure 20.10 illustrates the payoff and profit to this **protective put** strategy. The solid line in Figure 20.10C is the total payoff. The dashed line is displaced downward by the cost of establishing the position, $S_0 + P$. Notice that potential losses are limited. See the nearby box for further discussion of this strategy.

It is instructive to compare the profit on the protective put strategy with that of the stock investment. For simplicity, consider an at-the-money protective put, so that $X = S_0$. Figure 20.11 compares the profits for the two strategies. The profit on the stock is zero if the stock price remains unchanged and $S_T = S_0$. It rises or falls by $1 for every dollar swing in the ultimate stock price. The profit on the protective put is negative and equal to the cost of the put if S_T is below S_0. The profit on the protective put increases one for one with increases in the stock price once S_T exceeds S_0.

Figure 20.11 makes it clear that the protective put offers some insurance against stock price declines in that it limits losses. Therefore, protective put strategies provide a form of *portfolio insurance*. The cost of the protection is that, in the case of stock price increases, your profit is reduced by the cost of the put, which turned out to be unneeded.

This example also shows that despite the common perception that derivatives mean risk, derivative securities can be used effectively for *risk management*. In fact, such risk management is becoming accepted as part of the fiduciary responsibility of financial managers. Indeed, in a recent court case, *Brane* v. *Roth*, a company's board of directors was successfully sued for failing to use derivatives to hedge the price risk of grain held in storage. Such hedging might have been accomplished using protective puts. Some observers believe that this case will soon lead to a broad legal obligation for firms to use derivatives and other techniques to manage risk.

Table 20.1   Value of Protective Put Portfolio
at Option Expiration

	$S_T \leq X$	$S_T > X$
Stock	S_T	S_T
+ Put	$X - S_T$	0
= Total	X	S_T

Figure 20.10

Value of a protective
put position at option
expiration.

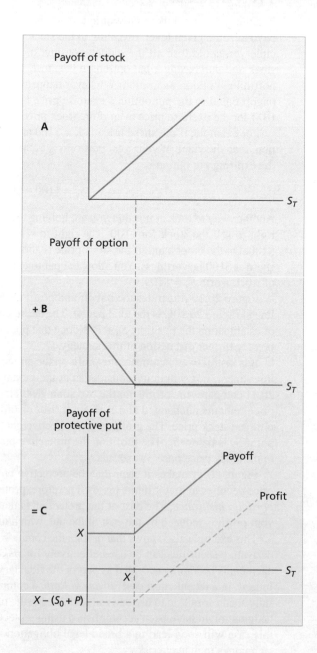

PROTECTIVE PUTS VERSUS STOP-LOSS ORDERS

We have seen that protective puts guarantee that the end-of-period value of a portfolio will equal or exceed the put's exercise price. As a specific example, consider a share of stock protected by a European put option with one year maturity and an exercise price of $40. Even if the stock at year-end is selling below $40, the put can be exercised and the stock can be sold for the exercise price, locking in a minimum payoff of $40.

Another common tool to protect a portfolio position is the stop-loss order. This is an order to your broker to sell your stock when and if its price falls to some lower boundary such as $40 per share. Thus, should the stock price fall substantially, your shares will be sold before losses mount, so that your proceeds will not fall below $40 per share.

It would seem that the stop-loss order provides the same stock price insurance offered by the protective put. However, the stop-loss order can be executed by your broker for no extra cost. Does this mean that the stop-loss order is effectively a free put option? What does the put offer that the stop-loss order does not?

To resolve this seeming paradox, look at the accompanying figure, which graphs one possible path for the stock price over the course of the year. Notice that, although the stock price falls below $40 at time t, it ultimately recovers and ends the year at $60. The protective put position will end the year worth $60—the put will expire worthless, but the stock will be worth $60. The stop-loss order, however, required that the stock be sold at time t as soon as its price fell below $40. This strategy will yield by year-end only $40 plus any interest accumulated between time t and the end of the year, far less than the payoff on the protective put strategy.

The protective put strategy does offer an advantage over the stop-loss strategy. With a stop-loss order in force, the investor realizes the $40 lower bound if the stock price *ever* reaches that boundary because the stock is sold as soon as the boundary is reached. Even if the stock price rebounds from the $40 limit, the investor using the stop-loss order will not share in the gain. The holder of the put option, on the other hand, need not exercise when the stock hits $40. Instead, the optionholder may wait until the end of the year to exercise the option, knowing that the $40 exercise price is guaranteed regardless of how far the stock falls, but that, should the stock price recover, the stock still will be held and any gain will be captured.*

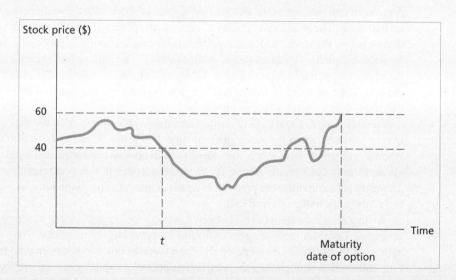

*Another disadvantage of the stop-loss order, which is of a more practical nature, is that the selling price is not guaranteed. Problems in executing trades could lead to a transaction at a price lower than $40.

Figure 20.11
Protective put versus
stock investment.

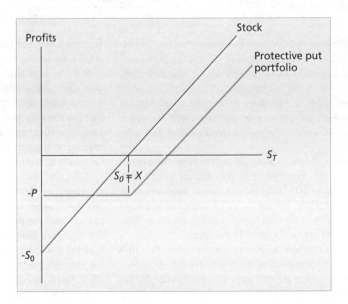

Covered Calls

A **covered call** position is the purchase of a share of stock with a simultaneous sale of a call on that stock. The position is "covered" because the potential obligation to deliver the stock is covered by the stock held in the portfolio. Writing an option without an offsetting stock position is called by contrast *naked option writing*. The value of a covered call position at the expiration of the call, presented in Table 20.2, equals the stock value minus the value of the call. The call value is *subtracted* because the covered call position involves issuing a call to another investor who can choose to exercise it to profit at your expense.

The solid line in Figure 20.12C illustrates the payoff pattern. You see that the total position is worth S_T when the stock price at time T is below X and rises to a maximum of X when S_T exceeds X. In essence, the sale of the call options means the call writer has sold the claim to any stock value above X in return for the initial premium (the call price). Therefore, at expiration, the position is worth at most X. The dashed line of Figure 20.12C is the net profit to the covered call.

Writing covered call options has been a popular investment strategy among institutional investors. Consider the managers of a fund invested largely in stocks. They might find it appealing to write calls on some or all of the stock in order to boost income by the premiums collected. Although they thereby forfeit potential capital gains should the stock price rise above the exercise price, if they view X as the price at which they plan to sell the stock anyway, then the call may be viewed as a kind of "sell discipline." The written call guarantees the stock sale will occur as planned.

For example, assume a pension fund holds 1,000 shares of IBM stock, with a current price of $100 per share. Suppose management intends to sell all 1,000 shares if the share price hits $110, and a call expiring in 60 days with an exercise price of $110 currently sells for $5. By writing 10 IBM call contracts (100 shares each) the fund can pick up $5,000 in extra income. The fund would lose its share of profits from any movement of IBM stock above $110 per share, but given that it would have sold its shares at $110, it would not have realized those profits anyway.

Table 20.2   Value of Covered Call Position
at Option Expiration

	$S_T \leq X$	$S_T > X$
Payoff of stock	S_T	S_T
+ Payoff of written call	-0	$-(S_T - X)$
= Total	S_T	X

Figure 20.12

Value of a covered call
position at expiration.

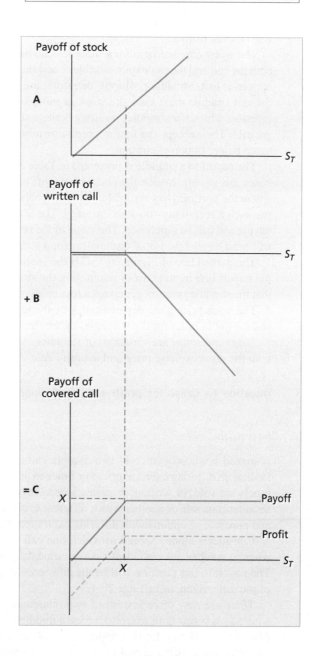

Straddle

A long **straddle** is established by buying both a call and a put on a stock, each with the same exercise price, X, and the same expiration date, T. Straddles are useful strategies for investors who believe a stock will move a lot in price but are uncertain about the direction of the move. For example, suppose you believe an important court case that will make or break a company is about to be settled, and the market is not yet aware of the situation. The stock will either double in value if the case is settled favorably or will drop by half if the settlement goes against the company. The straddle position will do well regardless of the outcome because its value is highest when the stock price makes extreme upward or downward moves from X.

The worst-case scenario for a straddle is no movement in the stock price. If S_T equals X, both the call and the put expire worthless, and the investor's outlay for the purchase of both options is lost. Straddle positions, therefore, are bets on volatility. An investor who establishes a straddle must view the stock as more volatile than the market does. Conversely, investors who *write* straddles—selling both a call and a put—must believe the stock is less volatile. They accept the option premiums now, hoping the stock price will not change much before option expiration.

The payoff to a straddle is presented in Table 20.3. The solid line of Figure 20.13C illustrates this payoff. Notice the portfolio payoff is always positive, except at the one point where the portfolio has zero value, $S_T = X$. You might wonder why all investors don't pursue such a seemingly "no-lose" strategy. The reason is that the straddle requires that both the put and call be purchased. The value of the portfolio at expiration, while never negative, still must exceed the initial cash outlay for a straddle investor to clear a profit.

The dashed line of Figure 20.13C is the profit to the straddle. The profit line lies below the payoff line by the cost of purchasing the straddle, $P + C$. It is clear from the diagram that the straddle position generates a loss unless the stock price deviates substantially from X. The stock price must depart from X by the total amount expended to purchase the call and the put in order for the purchaser of the straddle to clear a profit.

Strips and *straps* are variations of straddles. A strip is two puts and one call on a security with the same exercise price and maturity date. A strap is two calls and one put.

Concept

Question 4 • Graph the profit and payoff diagrams for strips and straps.

Spreads

A **spread** is a combination of two or more call options (or two or more puts) on the same stock with differing exercise prices or times to maturity. Some options are bought, whereas others are sold, or written. A *money spread* involves the purchase of one option and the simultaneous sale of another with a different exercise price. A *time spread* refers to the sale and purchase of options with differing expiration dates.

Consider a money spread in which one call option is bought at an exercise price X_1, whereas another call with identical expiration date, but higher exercise price, X_2, is written. The payoff to this position will be the difference in the value of the call held and the value of the call written, as in Table 20.4.

There are now three instead of two outcomes to distinguish: the lowest-price region where S_T is below both exercise prices, a middle region where S_T is between the two exercise prices, and a high-price region where S_T exceeds both exercise prices. Figure 20.14 illustrates the payoff and profit to this strategy, which is called a *bullish spread* because the

Table 20.3   Value of a Straddle Position
at Option Expiration

	$S_T < X$	$S_T \geq X$
Payoff of call	0	$S_T - X$
+ Payoff of put	$X - S_T$	0
= Total	$\overline{X - S_T}$	$\overline{S_T - X}$

Figure 20.13
Value of a straddle at
expiration.

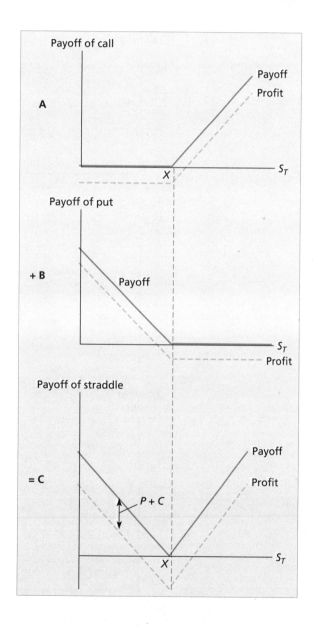

Table 20.4   Value of a Bullish Vertical Spread Position at Expiration

	$S_T \leq X_1$	$X_1 < S_T \leq X_2$	$S_T \geq X_2$
Payoff of purchased call, exercise price = X_1	0	$S_T - X_1$	$S_T - X_1$
+ Payoff of written call, exercise price = X_2	-0	-0	$-(S_T - X_2)$
= Total	0	$S_T - X_1$	$X_2 - X_1$

Figure 20.14

Value of a bullish spread position at expiration.

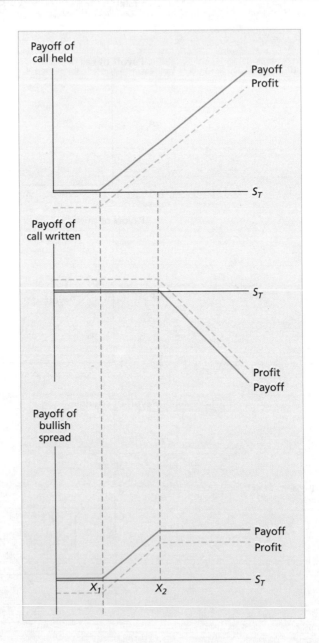

payoff either increases or is unaffected by stock price increases. Holders of bullish spreads benefit from stock price increases.

One motivation for a bullish spread might be that the investor thinks one option is over-priced relative to another. For example, an investor who believes an $X = \$100$ call is cheap compared to an $X = \$110$ call might establish the spread, even without a strong desire to take a bullish position in the stock.

Collars

A **collar** is an options strategy that brackets the value of a portfolio between two bounds. Suppose that an investor currently is holding a large position in IBM, which is currently selling at $100 per share. A lower bound of $90 can be placed on the value of the portfolio by buying a protective put with exercise price $90. This protection, however, requires that the investor pay the put premium. To raise the money to pay for the put, the investor might write a call option, say with exercise price $110. The call might sell for roughly the same price as the put, meaning that the net outlay for the two options positions is approximately zero. Writing the call limits the portfolio's upside potential. Even if the stock price moves above $110, the investor will do no better than $110, because at a higher price the stock will be called away. Thus the investor obtains the downside protection represented by the exercise price of the put by selling her claim to any upside potential beyond the exercise price of the call.

A collar would be appropriate for an investor who has a target wealth goal in mind but is unwilling to risk losses beyond a certain level. If you are contemplating buying a house for $150,000, for example, you might set this figure as your goal. Your current wealth may be $140,000, and you are unwilling to risk losing more than $10,000. A collar established by (1) purchasing 1,000 shares of stock currently selling at $140 per share, (2) purchasing 1,000 put options (10 option contracts) with exercise price $130, and (3) writing 1,000 calls with exercise price $150 would give you a good chance to realize the $10,000 capital gain without risking a loss of more than $10,000.

The nearby box discusses the increasingly popular use of collars among those corporate insiders who have large grants of company stock and wish to limit their exposure to the risk of the firm. A collar allows them to limit their risk without selling any shares; thus they avoid triggering capital gains taxes. Moreover, since the shares are not sold, the insiders retain their voting rights in the firm.

Concept
CHECK
Question 5 • Graph the payoff diagram for the IBM collar just described with exercise price of the put equal to $90, and exercise price of the call equal to $110.

20.4   THE PUT-CALL PARITY RELATIONSHIP

We saw in the previous section that a protective put portfolio, comprising a stock position and a put option on that position, provides a payoff with a guaranteed minimum value, but with unlimited upside potential. This is not the only way to achieve such protection, however. A call-plus-bills portfolio also can provide limited downside risk with unlimited upside potential.

Consider the strategy of buying a call option and, in addition, buying Treasury bills with face value equal to the exercise price of the call, and with maturity date equal to the expiration date of the option. For example, if the exercise price of the call option is $100, then each option contract (which is written on 100 shares) would require payment of $10,000 upon exercise. Therefore, you would purchase one T-bill, which also has a maturity value of $10,000. More generally, for each option that you hold with exercise price X, you would purchase a risk-free zero-coupon bond with face value X.

Examine the value of this position at time T, when the options expire and the zero-coupon bond matures:

	$S_T \leq X$	$S_T > X$
Value of call option	0	$S_T - X$
Value of riskless bond	X	X
Total	X	S_T

If the stock price is below the exercise price, the call is worthless, but the riskless bond matures to its face value, X. The bond therefore provides a floor value to the portfolio. If the stock price exceeds X, then the payoff to the call, $S_T - X$, is added to the face value of the bond to provide a total payoff of S_T. The payoff to this portfolio is precisely identical to the payoff of the protective put that we derived in Table 20.1.

If two portfolios always provide equal values, then they must cost the same amount to establish. Therefore, the call-plus-bond portfolio must cost the same as the stock-plus-put portfolio. Each call costs C. The riskless zero-coupon bond costs $X/(1 + r_f)^T$. Therefore, the call-plus-bond portfolio costs $C + X/(1 + r_f)^T$ to establish. The stock costs S_0 to purchase now (at time zero), while the put costs P. Therefore, we conclude that

$$C + \frac{X}{(1 + r_f)^T} = S_0 + P \tag{20.1}$$

Equation 20.1 is called the **put-call parity theorem** because it represents the proper relationship between put and call prices. If the parity relation is ever violated, an arbitrage opportunity arises. For example, suppose you confront these data for a certain stock:

Stock price	$110
Call price (six-month maturity, $X = \$105$)	$\ 17
Put price (six-month maturity, $X = \$105$)	$\ \ 5
Risk-free interest rate	10.25% per year

We can use these data in equation 20.1 to see if parity is violated:

$$C + \frac{X}{(1 + r_f)^T} \overset{?}{=} S_0 + P$$

$$17 + \frac{105}{1.025^{1/2}} \overset{?}{=} 110 + 5$$

$$117 \overset{?}{=} 115$$

This result, a violation of parity—117 does not equal 115—indicates mispricing. To exploit the mispricing you buy the relatively cheap portfolio (the stock-plus-put position represented on the right-hand side of the equation), and sell the relatively expensive portfolio (the call-plus-bond position corresponding to the left-hand side). Therefore, if you *buy* the stock, *buy* the put, *write* the call, and *borrow* $100 for six months (because borrowing money is the opposite of buying a bond), you should earn arbitrage profits.

Let's examine the payoff to this strategy. In six months, the stock will be worth S_T. The $100 borrowed will be paid back with interest, resulting in a cash flow of $105. The written call will result in a cash outflow of $S_T - \$105$ if S_T exceeds $105. The purchased put pays off $105 - S_T$ if the stock price is below $105.

Table 20.5 summarizes the outcome. The immediate cash inflow is $2. In six months, the various positions provide exactly offsetting cash flows: The $2 inflow is realized without any offsetting outflows. This is an arbitrage opportunity that investors will pursue on a large scale until buying and selling pressure restores the parity condition expressed in equation 20.1.

Equation 20.1 actually applies only to options on stocks that pay no dividends before the maturity date of the option. The extension of the parity condition for European call options on dividend-paying stocks is, however, straightforward. Problem 5 at the end of the chapter leads you through the extension of the parity relationship. The more general formulation of the *put-call parity* condition is

$$P = C - S_0 + \text{PV}(X) + \text{PV}(\text{dividends}) \qquad (20.2)$$

Table 20.5   Arbitrage Strategy

Position	Immediate Cash Flow	Cash Flow in Six Months	
		$S_T < 105$	$S_T \geq 105$
Buy stock	−110	S_T	S_T
Borrow $105/1.1025^{1/2} = \$100$	+100	−105	−105
Sell call	+ 17	0	$-(S_T - 105)$
Buy put	− 5	$105 - S_T$	0
Total	2	0	0

where PV(dividends) is the present value of the dividends that will be paid by the stock during the life of the option. If the stock does not pay dividends, equation 20.2 becomes identical to equation 20.1.

Notice that this generalization would apply as well to European options on assets other than stocks. Instead of using dividend income per se in equation 20.2, we would let any income paid out by the underlying asset play the role of the stock dividends. For example, European put and call options on bonds would satisfy the same parity relationship, except that the bond's coupon income would replace the stock's dividend payments in the parity formula.

Even this generalization, however, applies only to European options, as the cash flow streams from the two portfolios represented by the two sides of equation 20.2 will match only if each position is held until maturity. If a call and a put may be optimally exercised at different times before their common expiration date, then the equality of payoffs cannot be assured, or even expected, and the portfolios will have different values.

Let's see how well parity works using real data on the IBM options in Figure 20.2. The February maturity call with exercise price $105 and time to expiration of 43 days cost $5 while the corresponding put option cost $5.25. IBM was selling for $104.3125, and the annualized short-term interest rate on this date was 4.9%. There are no dividends to be paid to a stock purchaser between the date of the listing, January 8, and the option maturity date. According to parity, we should find that

$$P = C + PV(X) - S_0 + PV(\text{dividends})$$

$$5.25 = 5.00 + \frac{105}{(1.049)^{43/365}} - 104.3125 + 0$$

$$5.25 = 5.00 + 104.41 - 104.3125$$

$$5.25 = 5.0975$$

So parity is violated by about $.15 per share. Is this a big enough difference to exploit? Probably not. You have to weigh the potential profit against the trading costs of the call, put, and stock. More important, given the fact that options trade relatively infrequently, this deviation from parity might not be "real," but may instead be attributable to "stale" price quotes at which you cannot actually trade.

20.5   OPTIONLIKE SECURITIES

Suppose you never traded an option directly. Why do you need to appreciate the properties of options in formulating an investment plan? Many financial instruments and agreements have features that convey implicit or explicit options to one or more parties. If you are to value and use these securities correctly, you must understand these embedded option attributes.

Callable Bonds

You know from Chapter 14 that most corporate bonds are issued with call provisions entitling the issuer to buy bonds back from bondholders at some time in the future at a specified call price. A call provision conveys a call option to the issuer, where the exercise price is equal to the price at which the bond can be repurchased. A callable bond arrangement is essentially a sale of a *straight bond* (a bond with no option features such as callability or convertibility) to the investor and the concurrent issuance of a call option by the investor to the bond-issuing firm.

Figure 20.15

Values of callable
bonds compared with
straight bonds.

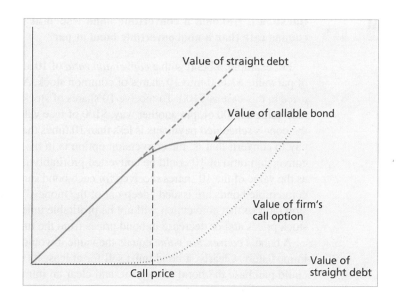

There must be some compensation for conveying this implicit call option to the firm. If the callable bond were issued with the same coupon rate as a straight bond, we would expect it to sell at a lower price than the straight bond. In fact, we would expect the price difference to equal the value of the call. To sell callable bonds at par, firms must issue them with coupon rates higher than the coupons on straight debt. The higher coupons are the investor's compensation for the call option retained by the issuer. Coupon rates usually are selected so that the newly issued bond will sell at par value.

Figure 20.15 illustrates this optionlike property. The horizontal axis is the value of a straight bond with otherwise identical terms as the callable bond. The dashed 45-degree line represents the value of straight debt. The solid line is the value of the callable bond, and the dotted line is the value of the call option retained by the firm. A callable bond's potential for capital gains is limited by the firm's option to repurchase at the call price.

Question 6 • **How is a callable bond similar to a covered call strategy on a straight bond?**

The option inherent in callable bonds actually is more complex than an ordinary call option, because usually it may be exercised only after some initial period of call protection. The price at which the bond is callable may change over time also. Unlike exchange-listed options, these features are defined in the initial bond covenant and will depend on the needs of the issuing firm and its perception of the market's tastes.

Concept CHECK

Question 7 • **Suppose the period of call protection is extended. How will the coupon rate the company needs to offer on its bonds change to enable the issuer to sell the bonds at par value?**

Convertible Securities

Convertible bonds and convertible preferred stock convey options to the holder of the security rather than to the issuing firm. A convertible security typically gives its holder the right to exchange each bond or share of preferred stock for a fixed number of shares of common stock, regardless of the market prices of the securities at the time.

Question 8 • Should a convertible bond issued at par value have a higher or lower coupon rate than a nonconvertible bond at par?

For example, a bond with a *conversion ratio* of 10 allows its holder to convert one bond of par value $1,000 into 10 shares of common stock. Alternatively, we say the *conversion price* in this case is $100: To receive 10 shares of stock, the investor sacrifices bonds with face value $1,000 or, put another way, $100 of face value per share. If the present value of the bond's scheduled payments is less than 10 times the value of one share of stock, it may pay to convert; that is, the conversion option is in the money. A bond worth $950 with a conversion ratio of 10 could be converted profitably if the stock were selling above $95, as the value of the 10 shares received for each bond surrendered would exceed $950. Most convertible bonds are issued "deep out of the money." That is, the issuer sets the conversion ratio so that conversion will not be profitable unless there is a substantial increase in stock prices and/or decrease in bond prices from the time of issue.

A bond's *conversion value* equals the value it would have if you converted it into stock immediately. Clearly, a bond must sell for at least its conversion value. If it did not, you could purchase the bond, convert it, and clear an immediate profit. This condition could never persist, for all investors would pursue such a strategy and ultimately would bid up the price of the bond.

The straight bond value, or "bond floor," is the value the bond would have if it were not convertible into stock. The bond must sell for more than its straight bond value because a convertible bond has more value; it is in fact a straight bond plus a valuable call option. Therefore, the convertible bond has two lower bounds on its market price: the conversion value and the straight bond value.

Figure 20.16 illustrates the optionlike properties of the convertible bond. Figure 20.16A shows the value of the straight debt as a function of the stock price of the issuing firm. For healthy firms, the straight debt value is almost independent of the value of the stock because default risk is small. However, if the firm is close to bankruptcy (stock prices are low), default risk increases, and the straight bond value falls. Panel B shows the conversion value of the bond. Panel C compares the value of the convertible bond to these two lower bounds.

When stock prices are low, the straight bond value is the effective lower bound, and the conversion option is nearly irrelevant. The convertible will trade like straight debt. When stock prices are high, the bond's price is determined by its conversion value. With conversion all but guaranteed, the bond is essentially equity in disguise.

We can illustrate with two examples:

	Bond A	Bond B
Annual coupon	$80	$80
Maturity date	10 years	10 years
Quality rating	Baa	Baa
Conversion ratio	20	25
Stock price	$30	$50
Conversion value	$600	$1,250
Market yield on 10-year Baa-rated bonds	8.5%	8.5%
Value as straight debt	$967	$967
Actual bond price	$972	$1,255
Reported yield to maturity	8.42%	4.76%

Bond A has a conversion value of only $600. Its value as straight debt, in contrast, is $967. This is the present value of the coupon and principal payments at a market rate for straight debt of 8.5%. The bond's price is $972, so the premium over straight bond value is only $5,

Figure 20.16

Value of a convertible bond as a function of stock price. **A**, Straight debt value, or bond floor. **B**, Conversion value of the bond. **C**, Total value of convertible bond.

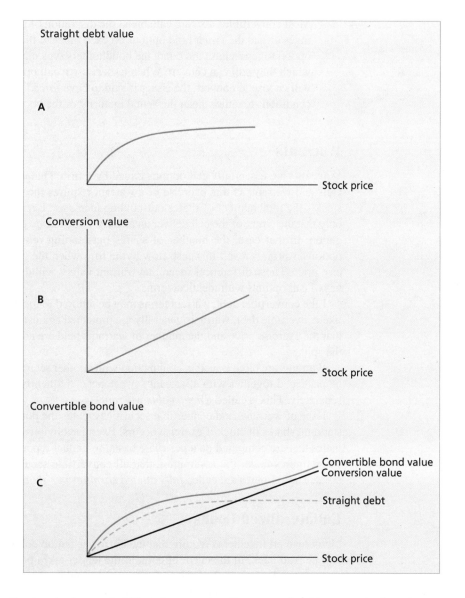

reflecting the low probability of conversion. Its reported yield to maturity based on scheduled coupon payments and the market price of $972 is 8.42%, close to that of straight debt.

The conversion option on Bond B is in the money. Conversion value is $1,250, and the bond's price, $1,255, reflects its value as equity (plus $5 for the protection the bond offers against stock price declines). The bond's reported yield is 4.76%, far below the comparable yield on straight debt. The big yield sacrifice is attributable to the far greater value of the conversion option.

In theory, we could value convertible bonds by treating them as straight debt plus call options. In practice, however, this approach is often impractical for several reasons:

1. The conversion price frequently increases over time, which means the exercise price of the option changes.
2. Stocks may pay several dividends over the life of the bond, further complicating the option valuation analysis.

3. Most convertibles also are callable at the discretion of the firm. In essence, both the investor and the issuer hold options on each other. If the issuer exercises its call option to repurchase the bond, the bondholders typically have a month during which they still can convert. When issuers use a call option, knowing bondholders will choose to convert, the issuer is said to have *forced a conversion*. These conditions together mean the actual maturity of the bond is indeterminate.

Warrants

Warrants are essentially call options issued by a firm. One important difference between calls and warrants is that exercise of a warrant requires the firm to issue a new share of stock—the total number of shares outstanding increases. Exercise of a call option requires only that the writer of the call deliver an already-issued share of stock to discharge the obligation. In that case, the number of shares outstanding remains fixed. Also unlike call options, warrants result in a cash flow to the firm when the warrant holder pays the exercise price. These differences mean that warrant values will differ somewhat from the values of call options with identical terms.

Like convertible debt, warrant terms may be tailored to meet the needs of the firm. Also like convertible debt, warrants generally are protected against stock splits and dividends in that the exercise price and the number of warrants held are adjusted to offset the effects of the split.

Warrants are often issued in conjunction with another security. Bonds, for example, may be packaged together with a warrant "sweetener," frequently a warrant that may be sold separately. This is called a *detachable warrant*.

Issue of warrants and convertible securities creates the potential for an increase in outstanding shares of stock if exercise occurs. Exercise obviously would affect financial statistics that are computed on a per-share basis, so annual reports must provide earnings per share figures under the assumption that all convertible securities and warrants are exercised. These figures are called *fully diluted earnings per share*.[2]

Collateralized Loans

Many loan arrangements require that the borrower put up collateral to guarantee the loan will be paid back. In the event of default, the lender takes possession of the collateral. A nonrecourse loan gives the lender no recourse beyond the right to the collateral. That is, the lender may not sue the borrower for further payment if the collateral turns out not to be valuable enough to repay the loan.

This arrangement gives an implicit call option to the borrower. Assume the borrower is obligated to pay back L dollars at the maturity of the loan. The collateral will be worth S_T dollars at maturity. (Its value today is S_0.) The borrower has the option to wait until loan maturity and repay the loan only if the collateral is worth more than the L dollars necessary to satisfy the loan. If the collateral is worth less than L, the borrower can default on the loan, discharging the obligation by forfeiting the collateral, which is worth only S_T.[3]

---

[2] We should note that the exercise of a convertible bond need not reduce EPS. Diluted EPS will be less than undiluted EPS only if interest saved (per share) on the convertible bonds is less than the prior EPS.

[3] In reality, of course, defaulting on a loan is not so simple. There are losses of reputation involved as well as considerations of ethical behavior. This is a description of a pure nonrecourse loan where both parties agree from the outset that only the collateral backs the loan and that default is not to be taken as a sign of bad faith if the collateral is insufficient to repay the loan.

Another way of describing such a loan is to view the borrower as turning over the collateral to the lender but retaining the right to reclaim it by paying off the loan. The transfer of the collateral with the right to reclaim it is equivalent to a payment of S_0 dollars, less a simultaneous recovery of a sum that resembles a call option with exercise price L. Basically, the borrower turns over collateral and keeps an option to "repurchase" it for L dollars at the maturity of the loan if L turns out to be less than S_T. This is a call option.

A third way to look at a collateralized loan is to assume that the borrower will repay the L dollars with certainty but also retain the option to sell the collateral to the lender for L dollars, even if S_T is less than L. In this case, the sale of the collateral would generate the cash necessary to satisfy the loan. The ability to "sell" the collateral for a price of L dollars represents a put option, which guarantees the borrower can raise enough money to satisfy the loan simply by turning over the collateral.

It is perhaps surprising to realize that we can describe the same loan as involving either a put option or a call option, as the payoffs to calls and puts are so different. Yet the equivalence of the two approaches is nothing more than a reflection of the put-call parity relationship. In our call-option description of the loan, the value of the borrower's liability is $S_0 - C$: The borrower turns over the asset, which is a transfer of S_0 dollars, but retains a call worth C dollars. In the put-option description, the borrower is obligated to pay L dollars but retains the put, which is worth P: The present value of this net obligation is $L/(1 + r_f)^T - P$. Because these alternative descriptions are equivalent ways of viewing the same loan, the value of the obligations must be equal:

$$S_0 - C = \frac{L}{(1 + r_f)^T} - P \qquad (20.3)$$

Treating L as the exercise price of the option, equation 20.3 is simply the put-call parity relationship.

Figure 20.17 illustrates this fact. Figure 20.17A is the value of the payment to be received by the lender, which equals the minimum of S_T or L. Panel B shows that this amount can be expressed as S_T minus the payoff of the call implicitly written by the lender and held by the borrower. Panel C shows it also can be viewed as a receipt of L dollars minus the proceeds of a put option.

Levered Equity and Risky Debt

Investors holding stock in incorporated firms are protected by limited liability, which means that if the firm cannot pay its debts, the firm's creditors may attach only the firm's assets, not sue the corporation's equityholders for further payment. In effect, any time the corporation borrows money, the maximum possible collateral for the loan is the total of the firm's assets. If the firm declares bankruptcy, we can interpret this as an admission that the assets of the firm are insufficient to satisfy the claims against it. The corporation may discharge its obligations by transferring ownership of the firm's assets to the creditors.

Just as is true for nonrecourse collateralized loans, the required payment to the creditors represents the exercise price of the implicit option, while the value of the firm is the underlying asset. The equityholders have a put option to transfer their ownership claims on the firm to the creditors in return for the face value of the firm's debt.

Alternatively, we may view the equityholders as retaining a call option. They have, in effect, already transferred their ownership claim to the firm to the creditors but have retained the right to reacquire that claim by paying off the loan. Hence the equityholders have the option to "buy back" the firm for a specified price: They have a call option.

Figure 20.17
Collateralized loan.

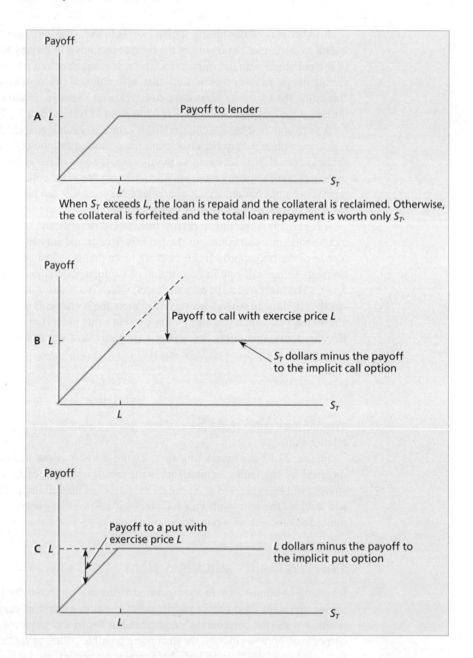

When S_T exceeds L, the loan is repaid and the collateral is reclaimed. Otherwise, the collateral is forfeited and the total loan repayment is worth only S_T.

The significance of this observation is that analysts can value corporate bonds using option pricing techniques. The default premium required of risky debt in principle can be estimated using option valuation models. We consider some of these models in the next chapter.

20.6   FINANCIAL ENGINEERING

One of the attractions of options is the ability they provide to create investment positions with payoffs that depend in a variety of ways on the values of other securities. We have seen evidence of this capability in the various options strategies examined in Section 20.4. Options also can be used to custom design new securities or portfolios with desired patterns of exposure to the price of an underlying security. In this sense, options (and futures contracts, to be discussed in Chapters 22 and 23) provide the ability to engage in *financial engineering*, the creation of portfolios with specified payoff patterns.

Most financial engineering takes place for institutional investors. However, some applications have been designed for the retail market. One highly successful retail product of financial engineering, first introduced by Merrill Lynch in 1985, is the liquid-yield option note, or LYON.[4] A LYON is a *zero-coupon, convertible, callable*, and *puttable* bond. To illustrate how the bond works, consider the first LYON issued, by Waste Management, Inc. The bond paid no coupon income and was priced at $250 in 1985, with a maturity value of $1,000 in 2001. If the security is not called, converted, or redeemed, it provides a yield to maturity of about 9%. However, three options may result in early retirement of the issue.

First, the investor can convert each bond into 4.36 shares of Waste Management stock. Second, the investor can put (sell) the bond back to Waste Management at a predetermined exercise price that rises over time according to a schedule detailed in the bond indenture. Finally, Waste Management can call the bond back from the investor at fixed exercise prices that also increase over time.

This combination of option results in risk-sharing attributes that seem to be attractive to both the issuer and investors. The convertibility feature provides the opportunity to profit from price advances in Waste Management stock. At the same time, the embedded put option provides the LYON holder a protective floor. Finally, the call feature allows Waste Management to call the bonds back for refinancing if interest rates drop considerably. The Waste Management LYON was a big success for Merrill Lynch. Although only 10% of a convertible bond typically is purchased by individual investors, they purchased approximately 40% of the LYON issue. Although other underwriters have since brought LYON competitors to the market, Merrill Lynch remains dominant in the field.

A simpler product also engineered with options is the "bull" certificate of deposit. Bull CDs enable retail investors to take small positions in index options. Unlike conventional CDs, which pay a fixed rate of interest, bull CDs pay depositors a specified fraction of the rate of return on a market index such as the S&P 500, while guaranteeing a minimum rate of return should the market fall. A bull CD may offer 70% of any market increase, but protect its holder from any market decrease by guaranteeing at least no loss. The nearby box notes that this product has become one of the fastest-growing products in the life insurance industry, which markets it as an "equity-indexed annuity."

The bull CD is clearly a type of call option. If the market rises, the depositor profits according to the *participation rate* or *multiplier*, in this case 70%; if the market falls, the investor is insured against loss. Just as clearly, the bank offering these CDs is in effect writing call options and can hedge its position by buying index calls in the options market. Figure 20.18 shows the nature of the bank's obligation to its depositors.

How might the bank set the appropriate multiplier? To answer this, note various features of the option:

1. The price the depositor is paying for the options is the forgone interest on the conventional CD that could be purchased. Because interest is received at the end of the period, the present value of the interest payment on each dollar invested is $r_f/(1 + r_f)$. Therefore, the depositor trades a sure payment with present value per dollar invested of $r_f/(1 + r_f)$ for a return that depends on the market's performance. Conversely, the bank can fund its obligation using the interest that it would have paid on a conventional CD.

[4]This discussion is based on a paper by John J. McConnell and Eduardo S. Schwartz, "The Origins of LYONs: A Case Study in Financial Innovation," *Journal of Applied Corporate Finance*, Winter 1992.

EQUITY-INDEXED ANNUITIES SCORE BIG HIT

An index is an index is an index. Or is it?

Not when it is an "equity-indexed annuity," a newfangled investment designed by insurance companies to attract risk-averse individuals.

Index investments, such as the hugely successful index mutual funds, typically seek to match the performance of some underlying market index, or benchmark, like Standard & Poor's 500 index of big, blue-chip stocks.

But equity-index annuities are a different breed. These are so-called fixed annuities, which means that they promise a fixed minimum return and protection of an investor's principal. With this variation, investors also get a chance to benefit from an increase in some market index. But the big draw is the protection in a falling stock market that the guaranteed minimum return provides.

Introduced in 1995, equity-indexed annuities are considered the fastest-growing product in the life-insurance industry and perhaps the financial services field. About 30 companies now sell this hot product, which had sales of $2 billion in 1996 and is projected to hit as much as $10 billion this year.

"Fundamentally, it is delivering to retail customers what's available to sophisticated investors on Wall Street all the time" in terms of hedging and asset protection, says John Rosensteel, president of Keyport Life Insurance Co., the industry leader in indexed annuities. "Here's a product that lets you throw a floor under the gains, take the volatility out of what you made and continue to give some upside."

There is, however, a cost to the very protection that investors find so appealing—and it can significantly limit what they can make.

Unlike indexed investments in variable-annuity contracts, which typically mimic the performance of an index mutual fund, equity-index annuities generally give investors only a *portion* of an index's increase—and that doesn't include dividends.

Peter Katt, a fee-only life-insurance adviser whose Katt & Co. is in Mattawan, Mich., calls an indexed annuity "the perfect greed-without-fear product" from an insurer's perspective, playing on consumers' desires for the upside gains of the stock market, but the security of a fixed-income security. He calls it a "feathered fish—it's somebody's attempt to have the best of both worlds."

Source: Bridget O'Brian and Leslie Scism, "Equity-Indexed Annuities Score Big Hit, But They Put a High Price on Protection," *The Wall Street Journal*, May 30, 1997. Excerpted by permission of *The Wall Street Journal*, © 1997 Dow Jones & Company, Inc. All Rights Reserved Worldwide.

Figure 20.18
Bull CD.

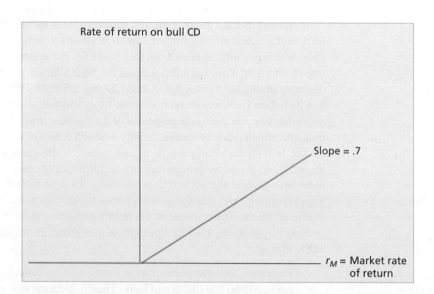

2. The option we have described is an at-the-money option, meaning that the exercise price equals the current value of the stock index. The option goes into the money as soon as the market index increases from its level at the inception of the contract.

3. We can analyze the option on a per-dollar-invested basis. For example, the option costs the depositor $r_f/(1 + r_f)$ dollars per dollar placed in the bull CD. The market price of the option per dollar invested is C/S_0: The at-the-money option costs C dollars and is written on one unit of the market index, currently at S_0.

Now it is easy to determine the multiplier that the bank can offer on its bull CDs. It receives from its depositors a "payment" of $r_f/(1 + r_f)$ per dollar invested. It costs the bank C/S_0 to purchase the call option on a \$1 investment in the market index. Therefore, if $r_f/(1 + r_f)$ is, for example, 70% of C/S_0, the bank can purchase at most .7 call option on the \$1 investment and the multiplier will be .7. More generally, the multiplier on a bull CD is $r_f/(1 + r_f)$ divided by C/S_0.

As an example, suppose that $r_f = 6\%$ per year, and that six-month maturity at-the-money calls on the market index currently cost \$50. The index is at 1,000. Then the option costs $50/1,000 = \$.05$ per dollar of market value. The CD rate is 3% per six months, meaning that $r_f/(1 + r_f) = .03/1.03 = .0291$. Therefore, the multiplier would be $.0291/.05 = .5825$.

This version of the bull CD has several variants. Investors can purchase bull CDs that guarantee a positive minimum return if they are willing to settle for a smaller multiplier. In this case, the option is "purchased" by the depositor for $(r_f - r_{min})/(1 + r_f)$ dollars per dollar invested, where r_{min} is the guaranteed minimum return. Because the purchase price is lower, fewer options can be purchased, which results in a lower multiplier. Another variant is the *bear CD*, which pays depositors a fraction of any *fall* in the market index. For example, a bear CD might offer a rate of return of .6 times any percentage decline in the S&P 500.

Concept   **CHECK**   **Question 9** •Continue to assume that $r_f = 3\%$ per half-year, that at-the-money calls sell for \$50, and that the market index is at 1,000. What would be the multiplier for six-month bull CDs offering a guaranteed minimum return of .5% over the term of the CD?

20.7   EXOTIC OPTIONS

Options markets have been tremendously successful. Investors clearly value the portfolio strategies made possible by trading options; this is reflected in the heavy trading volume in these markets. Success breeds imitation, and in recent years we have witnessed considerable innovation in the range of option instruments available to investors. Part of this innovation has occurred in the market for customized options, which now trade in active over-the-counter markets. Many of these options have terms that would have been highly unusual even a few years ago; they are therefore called "exotic options." In this section we survey some of the more interesting variants of these new instruments.

Asian Options

You already have been introduced to American and European options. Asian options are options with payoffs that depend on the *average* price of the underlying asset during at least some portion of the life of the option. For example, an Asian call option may have a payoff equal to the average stock price over the last three months minus the strike price if that value is positive, and zero otherwise. These options may be of interest, for example, to firms that wish to hedge a profit stream that depends on the average price of a commodity over some period of time.

Barrier Options

Barrier options have payoffs that depend not only on some asset price at option expiration, but also on whether the underlying asset price has crossed through some "barrier." For example, a down-and-out option is one type of barrier option that automatically expires worthless if and when the stock price falls below some barrier price. Similarly, down-and-in options will not provide a payoff unless the stock price *does* fall below some barrier at least once during the life of the option. These options also are referred to as knock-out and knock-in options.

Lookback Options

Lookback options have payoffs that depend in part on the minimum or maximum price of the underlying asset during the life of the option. For example, a lookback call option might provide a payoff equal to the maximum stock price during the life of the option minus the exercise price, instead of the *closing* stock price minus the exercise price. Such an option provides (for a fee, of course) a form of perfect market timing, providing the callholder with a payoff equal to the one that would accrue if the asset were purchased for *X* dollars and later sold at what turns out to be its high price.

Currency-Translated Options

Currency-translated options have either asset or exercise prices denominated in a foreign currency. A good example of such an option is the *quanto*, which allows an investor to fix in advance the exchange rate at which an investment in a foreign currency can be converted back into dollars. The right to translate a fixed amount of foreign currency into dollars at a given exchange rate is a simple foreign exchange option. Quantos are more interesting, however, because the amount of currency that will be translated into dollars depends on the investment performance of the foreign security. Therefore, a quanto in effect provides a *random number* of options.

Binary Options

Binary, or "bet," options have fixed payoffs that depend on whether a condition is satisfied by the price of the underlying asset. For example, a binary call option might pay off a fixed amount of $100 if the stock price at maturity exceeds the exercise price.

There are many more exotic options that we do not have room to discuss, and new ones are continually being created. For an extensive review of these options and their valuation (which is far more complex than the valuation of the simple options emphasized in this chapter), we refer you to the collection of articles compiled by *RISK Magazine* listed in the Selected Readings at the end of the chapter.

SUMMARY

1. A call option is the right to buy an asset at an agreed-upon exercise price. A put option is the right to sell an asset at a given exercise price.

2. American options allow exercise on or before the exercise date. European options allow exercise only on the expiration date. Most traded options are American in nature.

3. Options are traded on stocks, stock indexes, foreign currencies, fixed-income securities, and several futures contracts.

4. Options can be used either to lever up an investor's exposure to an asset price or to provide insurance against volatility of asset prices. Popular option strategies include covered calls, protective puts, straddles, spreads, and collars.

5. The put-call parity theorem relates the prices of put and call options. If the relationship is violated, arbitrage opportunities will result. Specifically, the relationship that must be satisfied is

$$P = C - S_0 + PV(X) + PV(dividends)$$

where X is the exercise price of both the call and the put options, $PV(X)$ is the present value of a claim to X dollars to be paid at the expiration date of the options. and PV(dividends) is the present value of dividends to be paid before option expiration.

6. Many commonly traded securities embody option characteristics. Examples of these securities are callable bonds, convertible bonds, and warrants. Other arrangements such as collateralized loans and limited-liability borrowing can be analyzed as conveying implicit options to one or more parties.

7. Trading in so-called exotic options now takes place in an active over-the-counter market.

Key Terms

call option	at the money	straddle
exercise or strike price	American option	spread
put option	European option	collar
in the money	protective put	put-call parity theorem
out of the money	covered call	warrant

Selected Readings

A good treatment of the institutional organization of option markets is in the Chicago Board Options Exchange Reference Manual. The CBOE also publishes a Margin Manual that provides an overview of margin requirements on many option positions.
> *An excellent discussion of option trading strategies is:*
> Black, Fischer. "Fact and Fantasy in the Use of Options." *Financial Analysts Journal*,
>   July–August 1975, pp. 3–20.

RISK Magazine *is an excellent source of material on current developments in option pricing, applications of derivative instruments, and new developments in the derivatives markets. It has assembled a collection of articles that have appeared in its previous issues on option pricing generally and exotic options in particular in:*
> *From Black-Scholes to Black Holes: New Frontiers in Options.* London: RISK Magazine, 1992.

Problems

1. Turn back to Figure 20.2, which lists prices of various IBM options. Use the data in the figure to calculate the payoff and the profits for investments in each of the following January maturity options, assuming that the stock price on the maturity date is $105.
   a. Call option, $X = \$100$.
   b. Put option, $X = \$100$.
   c. Call option, $X = \$105$.
   d. Put option, $X = \$105$.
   e. Call option, $X = \$110$.
   f. Put option, $X = \$110$.

2. Suppose you think Wal-Mart stock is going to appreciate substantially in value in the next six months. Say the stock's current price, S_0, is $100, and the call option expiring in six months has an exercise price, X, of $100 and is selling at a price, C, of $10. With $10,000 to invest, you are considering three alternatives.
   a. Invest all $10,000 in the stock, buying 100 shares.
   b. Invest all $10,000 in 1,000 options (10 contracts).

c. Buy 100 options (one contract) for $1,000, and invest the remaining $9,000 in a money market fund paying 4% in interest over six months (8% per year).

What is your rate of return for each alternative for the following four stock prices six months from now? Summarize your results in the table and diagram below.

		Price of Stock Six Months from Now			
		$80	$100	$110	$120
a.	All stocks (100 shares)				
b.	All options (1,000 shares)				
c.	Bills + 100 options				

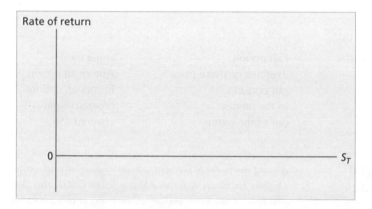

3. The common stock of the P.U.T.T. Corporation has been trading in a narrow price range for the past month, and you are convinced it is going to break far out of that range in the next three months. You do not know whether it will go up or down, however. The current price of the stock is $100 per share, and the price of a three-month call option at an exercise price of $100 is $10.

a. If the risk-free interest rate is 10% per year, what must be the price of a three-month put option on P.U.T.T. stock at an exercise price of $100? (The stock pays no dividends.)

b. What would be a simple options strategy to exploit your conviction about the stock price's future movements? How far would it have to move in either direction for you to make a profit on your initial investment?

4. The common stock of the C.A.L.L. Corporation has been trading in a narrow range around $50 per share for months, and you believe it is going to stay in that range for the next three months. The price of a three-month put option with an exercise price of $50 is $4.

a. If the risk-free interest rate is 10% per year, what must be the price of a three-month call option on C.A.L.L. stock at an exercise price of $50 if it is at the money? (The stock pays no dividends.)

b. What would be a simple options strategy using a put and a call to exploit your conviction about the stock price's future movement? What is the most money you can make on this position? How far can the stock price move in either direction before you lose money?

c. How can you create a position involving a put, a call, and riskless lending that would have the same payoff structure as the stock at expiration? What is the net cost of establishing that position now?

5. In this problem, we derive the put-call parity relationship for European options on stocks that pay dividends before option expiration. For simplicity, assume that the stock makes one dividend payment of $D per share at the expiration date of the option.

   a. What is the value of a stock-plus-put position on the expiration date of the option?

   b. Now consider a portfolio comprising a call option and a zero-coupon bond with the same maturity date as the option and with face value $(X + D)$. What is the value of this portfolio on the option expiration date? You should find that its value equals that of the stock-plus-put portfolio regardless of the stock price.

   c. What is the cost of establishing the two portfolios in parts (*a*) and (*b*)? Equate the costs of these portfolios, and you will derive the put-call parity relationship, equation 20.2.

6. a. A butterfly spread is the purchase of one call at exercise price X_1, the sale of two calls at exercise price X_2, and the purchase of one call at exercise price X_3. X_1 is less than X_2, and X_2 is less than X_3 by equal amounts, and all calls have the same expiration date. Graph the payoff diagram to this strategy.

   b. A vertical combination is the purchase of a call with exercise price X_2 and a put with exercise price X_1, with X_2 greater than X_1. Graph the payoff to this strategy.

7. A bearish spread is the purchase of a call with exercise price X_2 and the sale of a call with exercise price X_1, with X_2 greater than X_1. Graph the payoff to this strategy and compare it to Figure 20.14.

8. Joseph Jones, a manager at Computer Science, Inc. (CSI), received 10,000 shares of company stock as part of his compensation package. The stock currently sells at $40 a share. Joseph would like to defer selling the stock until the next tax year. In January, however, he will need to sell all his holdings to provide for a down payment on his new house. Joseph is worried about the price risk involved in keeping his shares. At current prices, he would receive $40,000 for the stock. If the value of his stock holdings falls below $35,000, his ability to come up with the necessary down payment would be jeopardized. On the other hand, if the stock value rises to $45,000, he would be able to maintain a small cash reserve even after making the down payment. Joseph considers three investment strategies:

   a. Strategy A is to write January call options on the CSI shares with strike price $45. These calls are currently selling for $3 each.

   b. Strategy B is to buy January put options on CSI with strike price $35. These options also sell for $3 each.

   c. Strategy C is to establish a zero-cost collar by writing the January calls and buying the January puts.

   Evaluate each of these strategies with respect to Joseph's investment goals. What are the advantages and disadvantages of each? Which would you recommend?

9. You are attempting to formulate an investment strategy. On the one hand, you think there is great upward potential in the stock market and would like to participate in the upward move if it materializes. However, you are not able to afford substantial stock market losses and so cannot run the risk of a stock market collapse, which you also think is a possibility. Your investment adviser suggests a protective put position: Buy both shares in a market index stock fund and put options on those shares with three-month maturity and exercise price of $780. The stock index is currently selling for $900. However, your uncle suggests you instead buy a three-month call option on the index fund with exercise price $840 and buy three-month T-bills with face value $840.

   a. On the same graph, draw the *payoffs* to each of these strategies as a function of the stock fund value in three months. (Hint: Think of the options as being on one "share" of the stock index fund, with the current price of each share of the index equal to $900.)

    b. Which portfolio must require a greater initial outlay to establish? (Hint: Does either portfolio provide a final payout that is always at least as great as the payoff of the other portfolio?)

    c. Suppose the market prices of the securities are as follows:

Stock fund	$900
T-bill (face value 840)	$810
Call (exercise price 840)	$120
Put (exercise price 780)	$ 6

    Make a table of the profits realized for each portfolio for the following values of the stock price in three months: $S_T = \$700, \$840, \$900, \$960$.

       Graph the profits to each portfolio as a function S_T on a single graph.

    d. Which strategy is riskier? Which should have a higher beta?

    e. Explain why the data for the securities given in part (*c*) do *not* violate the put-call parity relationship.

10. The agricultural price support system guarantees farmers a minimum price for their output. Describe the program provisions as an option. What is the asset? The exercise price?

11. In what ways is owning a corporate bond similar to writing a put option? A call option?

12. A executive compensation scheme might provide a manager a bonus of $1,000 for every dollar by which the company's stock price exceeds some cutoff level. In what way is this arrangement equivalent to issuing the manager call options on the firm's stock?

13. A member of an investment committee, interested in learning more about fixed-income investment procedures, recalls that a fixed-income manager recently stated that derivative instruments could be used to control portfolio duration, saying "a futures-like position can be created in a portfolio by using put and call options on Treasury bonds."

    a. Identify the options market exposure or exposures that create a "futures-like position" similar to being long Treasury bond futures. Explain why the position you created is similar to being long Treasury bond futures.

    b. Explain in which direction and why the exposure(s) you identified in part (*a*) would affect portfolio duration.

    c. Assume that a pension plan's investment policy requires the fixed-income manager to hold portfolio duration within a narrow range. Identify and briefly explain circumstances or transactions in which the use of Treasury bond futures would be helpful in managing a fixed-income portfolio when duration is constrained.

14. Consider the following options portfolio. You write a January maturity call option on IBM with exercise price 105. You write a January IBM put option with exercise price 100.

    a. Graph the payoff of this portfolio at option expiration as a function of IBM's stock price at that time.

    b. What will be the profit/loss on this position if IBM is selling at 102 on the option maturity date? What if IBM is selling at 115? Use *The Wall Street Journal* listing from Figure 20.2 to answer this question.

    c. At what two stock prices will you just break even on your investment?

    d. What kind of "bet" is this investor making; that is, what must this investor believe about IBM's stock price in order to justify this position?

15. Consider the following portfolio. You write a put option with exercise price 90 and buy a put option on the same stock with the same maturity date with exercise price 95.

a. Plot the value of the portfolio at the maturity date of the options.

b. On the same graph, plot the profit of the portfolio. Which option must cost more?

16. A Ford put option with strike price 60 trading on the Acme options exchange sells for $2. To your amazement, a Ford put with the same maturity selling on the Apex options exchange but with strike price 62 also sells for $2. If you plan to hold the options positions to maturity, devise a zero-net-investment arbitrage strategy to exploit the pricing anomaly. Draw the profit diagram at maturity for your position.

17. Using the IBM option prices in Figure 20.2, calculate the market price of a riskless zero-coupon bond with face value $100 that matures in January on the same date as the listed options.

18. You buy a share of stock, write a one-year call option with $X = \$10$, and buy a one-year put option with $X = \$10$. Your net outlay to establish the entire portfolio is $9.50. What is the risk-free interest rate? The stock pays no dividends.

19. Demonstrate that an at-the-money call option on a given stock must cost more than an at-the-money put option on that stock with the same maturity. (Hint: Use put-call parity.)

20. You write a put option with $X = 100$ and buy a put with $X = 110$. The puts are on the same stock and have the same maturity date.
    a. Draw the payoff graph for this strategy.
    b. Draw the profit graph for this strategy.
    c. If the underlying stock has positive beta, does this portfolio have positive or negative beta?

21. Joe Finance has just purchased a stock index fund, currently selling at $400 per share. To protect against losses, Joe also purchased an at-the-money European put option on the fund for $20, with exercise price $400, and three-month time to expiration. Sally Calm, Joe's financial adviser, points out that Joe is spending a lot of money on the put. She notes that three-month puts with strike prices of $390 cost only $15, and suggests that Joe use the cheaper put.
    a. Analyze Joe's and Sally's strategies by drawing the *profit* diagrams for the stock-plus-put positions for various values of the stock fund in three months.
    b. When does Sally's strategy do better? When does it do worse?
    c. Which strategy entails greater systematic risk?

22. You write a call option with $X = 50$ and buy a call with $X = 60$. The options are on the same stock and have the same maturity date. One of the calls sells for $3; the other sells for $9.
    a. Draw the payoff graph for this strategy at the option maturity date.
    b. Draw the profit graph for this strategy.
    c. What is the break-even point for this strategy? Is the investor bullish or bearish on the stock?

23. Devise a portfolio using only call options and shares of stock with the following value (payoff) at the option maturity date. If the stock price is currently 53, what kind of bet is the investor making?

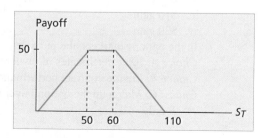

24. The following questions appeared in past CFA Level I examinations.

   a. Which one of the following comparative statements about common stock call options and warrants is correct?

		Call Option	Warrant
i.	Issued by the company	No	Yes
ii.	Sometimes attached to bonds	Yes	Yes
iii.	Maturity greater than one year	Yes	No
iv.	Convertible into the stock	Yes	No

   b. Consider a bullish spread option strategy using a call option with a $25 exercise price priced at $4 and a call option with a $40 exercise price priced at $2.50. If the price of the stock increases to $50 at expiration and the option is exercised on the expiration date, the net profit per share at expiration (ignoring transaction costs) is:
      i. $8.50.
      ii. $13.50.
      iii. $16.50.
      iv. $23.50.

   c. A convertible bond sells at $1,000 par with a conversion ratio of 40 and an accompanying stock price of $20 per share. The conversion premium and (percentage) conversion premium, respectively, are:
      i. $200 and 20%.
      ii. $200 and 25%.
      iii. $250 and 20%.
      iv. $250 and 25%.

   d. A put on XYZ stock with a strike price of $40 is priced at $2.00 per share, while a call with a strike price of $40 is priced at $3.50. What is the maximum per-share loss to the writer of the uncovered put and the maximum per-share gain to the writer of the uncovered call?

	Maximum Loss to Put Writer	Maximum Gain to Call Writer
i.	$38.00	$ 3.50
ii.	$38.00	$36.50
iii.	$40.00	$ 3.50
iv.	$40.00	$40.00

   e. You create a strap by buying two calls and one put on ABC stock, all with a strike price of $45. The calls cost $5 each, and the put costs $4. If you close your position when ABC is priced at $55, your per share gain or loss is:
      i. $4 loss.
      ii. $6 gain.
      iii. $10 gain.
      iv. $20 gain.

   f. In the options markets, the purpose of the clearinghouse is to:
      Choice A: Issue certificates of ownership.
      Choice B: Ensure contract performance.
      Choice C: Match up the option buyer who exercises with the original option writer.
      i. *B* only.

  ii. *B* and *C* only.
  iii. *C* only.
  iv. *A, B,* and *C.*

s o l u t i o n s t o
Concept
    CHECKS

1. *a.* Denote the stock price at option expiration by S_T, and the exercise price by X. Proceeds = $S_T - X = S_T - \$105$ if this value is positive; otherwise the call expires worthless. Profit = Proceeds – Price of call option = Proceeds – $5.

	$S_T = \$95$	$S_T = \$115$
Proceeds	$0	$10
Profits	–$5	$ 5

 b. Proceeds = $X - S_T = \$105 - S_T$ if this value is positive; otherwise the put expires worthless.
  Profit = Proceeds – Price of put option = Proceeds – $5.25.

	$S_T = \$95$	$S_T = \$115$
Proceeds	$10.00	$0
Profits	$ 4.75	–$5.25

2. Before the split, profits would have been $100 \times (\$120 - \$105) = \$1{,}500$. After the split, profits are $1{,}000 \times (\$12 - \$10.50) = \$1{,}500$. Profits are unaffected.

3. *a.* Payoff to put writer = 0 if $S_T \geq X$
$$-(X - S_T) \text{ if } S_T < X$$

 b. Profit = Initial premium realized + Ultimate payoff

$$= P \qquad\qquad \text{if } S_T \geq X$$
$$P - (X - S_T) \text{ if } S_T < X$$

 c.

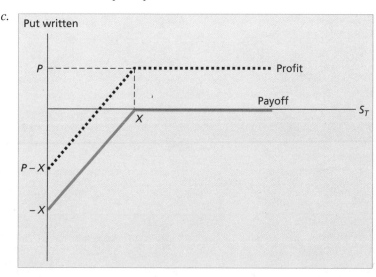

 d. Put writers do well when the stock price increases and poorly when it falls.

4.

	Payoff to a Strip	
	$S_T \leq X$	$S_T > X$
2 Puts	$2(X - S_T)$	0
1 Call	0	$S_T - X$

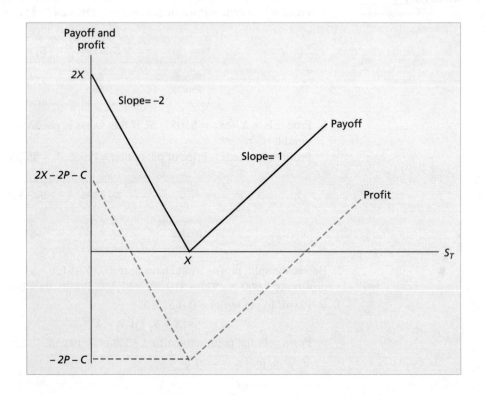

Payoff to a Strap		
	$S_T \le X$	$S_T > X$
1 Put	$X - S_T$	0
2 Calls	0	$2(S_T - X)$

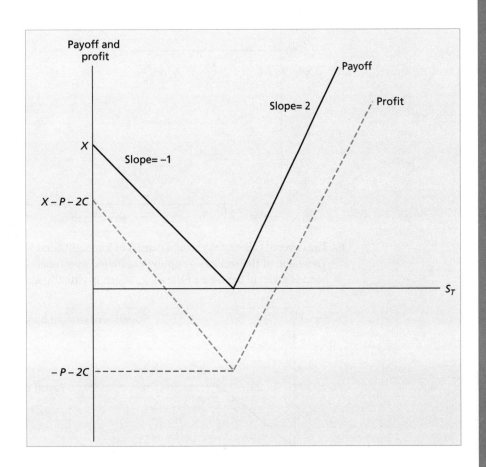

5.

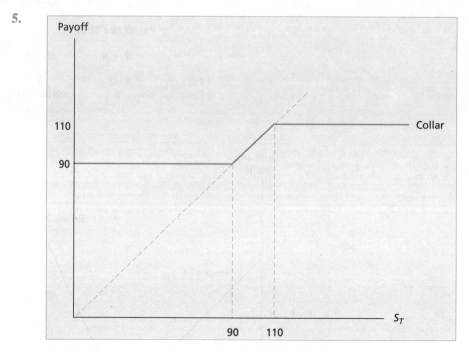

6. The covered call strategy would consist of a straight bond with a call written on the bond. The value of the strategy at option expiration as a function of the value of the straight bond is given in the figure following, which is virtually identical to Figure 20.15.

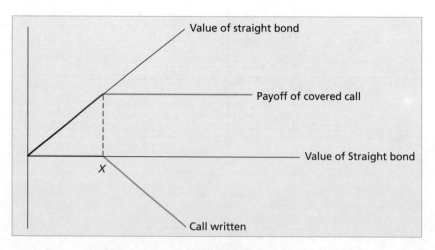

7. The call option is worth less as call protection is expanded. Therefore, the coupon rate need not be as high.

8. Lower. Investors will accept a lower coupon rate in return for the conversion option.

9. The depositor's implicit cost per dollar invested is now only ($.03 − $.005)/1.03 = $.02427 per six-month period. Calls cost 50/1,000 = $.05 per dollar invested in the index. The multiplier falls to .02427/.05 = .4854.

CHAPTER TWENTY-ONE

OPTION VALUATION

In the previous chapter we examined option markets and strategies. We noted that many securities contain embedded options that affect both their values and their risk-return characteristics. In this chapter, we turn our attention to option valuation issues. To understand most option valuation models requires considerable mathematical and sta-

tistical background. Still, many of the ideas and insights of these models can be demonstrated in simple examples, and we will concentrate on these. We start with a discussion of the factors that ought to affect option prices. After this discussion, we present several bounds within which option prices must lie. Next we turn to quantitative models, starting with a simple "two-state" option valuation model, and then showing how this approach can be generalized into a useful and accurate pricing tool. We then move on to one particular valuation formula, the famous Black-Scholes model, one of the most significant breakthroughs in finance theory in the past three decades. Finally, we look at some of the more important applications of option-pricing theory in portfolio management and control.

21.1   OPTION VALUATION: INTRODUCTION

Intrinsic and Time Values

Consider a call option that is out of the money at the moment, with the stock price below the exercise price. This does not mean the option is valueless. Even though immediate exercise today would be unprofitable, the call retains a positive value because there is always a chance the stock price will increase sufficiently by the expiration date to allow for profitable exercise. If not, the worst that can happen is that the option will expire with zero value.

The value $S_0 - X$ is sometimes called the **intrinsic value** of in-the-money call options because it gives the payoff that could be obtained by immediate exercise. Intrinsic value is set equal to zero for out-of-the-money or at-the-money options. The difference between the actual call price and the intrinsic value is commonly called the *time value* of the option.

"Time value" is an unfortunate choice of terminology, because it may confuse the option's time value with the time value of money. Time value in the options context refers simply to the difference between the option's price and the value the option would have if it were expiring immediately. It is the part of the option's value that may be attributed to the fact that it still has positive time to expiration.

Most of an option's time value typically is a type of "volatility value." As long as the optionholder can choose not to exercise, the payoff cannot be worse than zero. Even if a call option is out of the money now, it still will sell for a positive price because it offers the potential for a profit if the stock price increases, while imposing no risk of additional loss should the stock price fall. The volatility value lies in the value of the right *not* to exercise the call if that action would be unprofitable. The option to exercise, as opposed to the obligation to exercise, provides insurance against poor stock price performance.

As the stock price increases substantially, it becomes more likely that the call option will be exercised by expiration. In this case, with exercise all but assured, the volatility value becomes minimal. As the stock price gets ever larger, the option value approaches the "adjusted" intrinsic value, the stock price minus the present value of the exercise price, $S_0 - PV(X)$.

Why should this be? If you are virtually certain the option will be exercised and the stock purchased for X dollars, it is as though you own the stock already. The stock certificate, with a value today of S_0, might as well be sitting in your safe-deposit box now, as it will be there in only a few months. You just haven't paid for it yet. The present value of your obligation is the present value of X, so the net value of the call option is $S_0 - PV(X)$.[1]

Figure 21.1 illustrates the call option valuation function. The value curve shows that when the stock price is very low, the option is nearly worthless, because there is almost no chance that it will be exercised. When the stock price is very high, the option value approaches adjusted intrinsic value. In the midrange case, where the option is approximately at the money, the option curve diverges from the straight lines corresponding to adjusted intrinsic value. This is because although exercise today would have a negligible (or negative) payoff, the volatility value of the option is quite high in this region.

---

[1] This discussion presumes that the stock pays no dividends until after option expiration. If the stock does pay dividends before maturity, then there *is* a reason you would care about getting the stock now rather than at expiration—getting it now entitles you to the interim dividend payments. In this case, the adjusted intrinsic value of the option must subtract the value of the dividends the stock will pay out before the call is exercised. Adjusted intrinsic value would more generally be defined as $S_0 - PV(X) - PV(D)$ where D is the dividend to be paid before option expiration.

Figure 21.1

Call option value before expiration.

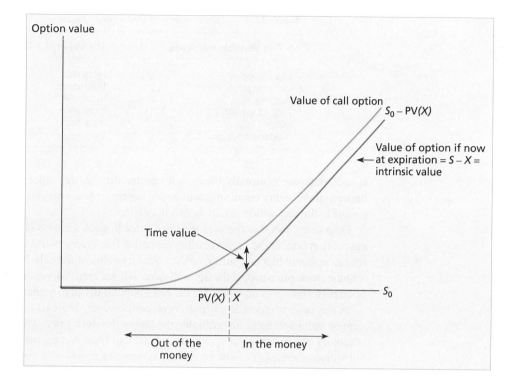

The option always increases in value with the stock price. The slope is greatest, however, when the option is deep in the money. In this case, exercise is all but assured, and the option increases in price one for one with the stock price.

Determinants of Option Values

We can identify at least six factors that should affect the value of a call option: the stock price, the exercise price, the volatility of the stock price, the time to expiration, the interest rate, and the dividend rate of the stock. The call option should increase in value with the stock price and decrease in value with the exercise price because the payoff to a call, if exercised, equals $S_T - X$. The magnitude of the expected payoff from the call increases with the difference $S_0 - X$.

Call option values also increase with the volatility of the underlying stock price. To see why, consider circumstances where possible stock prices at expiration may range from $10 to $50 compared to a situation where stock prices may range only from $20 to $40. In both cases, the expected, or average, stock price will be $30. Suppose the exercise price on a call option is also $30. What are the option payoffs?

High-Volatility Scenario					
Stock price	$10	$20	$30	$40	$50
Option payoff	0	0	0	10	20
Low-Volatility Scenario					
Stock price	$20	$25	$30	$35	$40
Option payoff	0	0	0	5	10

Table 21.1   Determinants of Call Option Values

If This Variable Increases . . .	The Value of a Call Option
Stock price, S	Increases
Exercise price, X	Decreases
Volatility, σ	Increases
Time to expiration, T	Increases
Interest rate, r_f	Increases
Dividend payouts	Decreases

If each outcome is equally likely, with probability .2, the expected payoff to the option under high-volatility conditions will be $6, but under low-volatility conditions the expected payoff to the call option is half as much, only $3.

Despite the fact that the average stock price in each scenario is $30, the average option payoff is greater in the high-volatility scenario. The source of this extra value is the limited loss an optionholder can suffer, or the volatility value of the call. No matter how far below $30 the stock price drops, the optionholder will get zero. Obviously, extremely poor stock price performance is no worse for the call optionholder than moderately poor performance.

In the case of good stock performance, however, the call option will expire in the money, and it will be more profitable the higher the stock price. Thus extremely good stock outcomes can improve the option payoff without limit, but extremely poor outcomes cannot worsen the payoff below zero. This asymmetry means that volatility in the underlying stock price increases the expected payoff to the option, thereby enhancing its value.

Concept CHECK   **Question 1 • Should a put option increase in value with the volatility of the stock?**

Similarly, longer time to expiration increases the value of a call option. For more distant expiration dates, there is more time for unpredictable future events to affect prices, and the range of likely stock prices increases. This has an effect similar to that of increased volatility. Moreover, as time to expiration lengthens, the present value of the exercise price falls, thereby benefiting the call optionholder and increasing the option value. As a corollary to this issue, call option values are higher when interest rates rise (holding the stock price constant) because higher interest rates also reduce the present value of the exercise price.

Finally, the dividend payout policy of the firm affects option values. A high-dividend payout policy puts a drag on the rate of growth of the stock price. For any expected total rate of return on the stock, a higher dividend yield must imply a lower expected rate of capital gain. This drag on stock price appreciation decreases the potential payoff from the call option, thereby lowering the call value. Table 21.1 summarizes these relationships.

Concept CHECK   **Question 2 • Prepare a table like Table 21.1 for the determinants of put option values. How should put values respond to increases in S, X, σ, T, r_f, and dividend payouts?**

21.2   RESTRICTIONS ON OPTION VALUES

Several quantitative models of option pricing have been devised, and we will examine some of them in this chapter. All models, however, rely on simplifying assumptions. You might wonder which properties of option values are truly general and which depend on the particular simplifications. To start with, we will consider some of the more important general properties of option prices. Some of these properties have important implications for the effect of stock dividends on option values and the possible profitability of early exercise of an American option.

Restrictions on the Value of a Call Option

The most obvious restriction on the value of a call option is that its value cannot be negative. Because the option need not be exercised, it cannot impose any liability on its holder; moreover, as long as there is any possibility that at some point the option can be exercised profitably, the option will command a positive price. Its payoff is zero at worst, and possibly positive, so that investors are willing to pay some amount to purchase it.

We can place another lower bound on the value of a call option. Suppose that the stock will pay a dividend of D dollars just before the expiration date of the option, denoted by T (where today is time zero). Now compare two portfolios, one consisting of a call option on one share of stock and the other a leveraged equity position consisting of that share and borrowing of $(X + D)/(1 + r_f)^T$ dollars. The loan repayment is $X + D$ dollars, due on the expiration date of the option. For example, for a half-year maturity option with exercise price \$70, dividends to be paid of \$5, and effective annual interest of 10%, you would purchase one share of stock and borrow $75/(1.10)^{1/2} = \$71.51$. In six months, when the loan matures, the payment due is \$75.

At that time, the payoff to the leveraged equity position would be

	In General	Our Numbers
Stock value	$S_T + D$	$S_T + 5$
− Payback of loan	$-(X + D)$	-75
Total	$S_T - X$	$S_T - 70$

where S_T denotes the stock price at the option expiration date. Notice that the payoff to the stock is the ex-dividend stock value plus dividends received. Whether the total payoff to the stock-plus-borrowing position is positive or negative depends on whether S_T exceeds X. The net cash outlay required to establish this leveraged equity position is $S_0 - \$71.51$, or, more generally, $S_0 - (X + D)/(1 + r_f)^T$, that is, the current price of the stock, S_0, less the initial cash inflow from the borrowing position.

The payoff to the call option will be $S_T - X$ if the option expires in the money and zero otherwise. Thus the option payoff is equal to the leveraged equity payoff when that payoff is positive and is greater when the leveraged equity position has a negative payoff. Because the option payoff is always greater than or equal to that of the leveraged equity position, the option price must exceed the cost of establishing that position.

Therefore, the value of the call must be greater than $S_0 - (X + D)/(1 + r_f)^T$, or, more generally,

$$C \geq S_0 - \text{PV}(X) - \text{PV}(D)$$

where PV(X) denotes the present value of the exercise and PV(D) is the present value of the dividends the stock will pay at the option's expiration. More generally, we can interpret PV(D) as the present value of any and all dividends to be paid prior to the option expiration date. Because we know already that the value of a call option must be nonnegative, we may conclude that C is greater than the *maximum* of either 0 or $S_0 - \text{PV}(X) - \text{PV}(D)$.

We also can place an upper bound on the possible value of the call; this bound is simply the stock price. No one would pay more than S_0 dollars for the right to purchase a stock currently worth S_0 dollars. Thus $C \leq S_0$.

Figure 21.2
Range of possible call
option values.

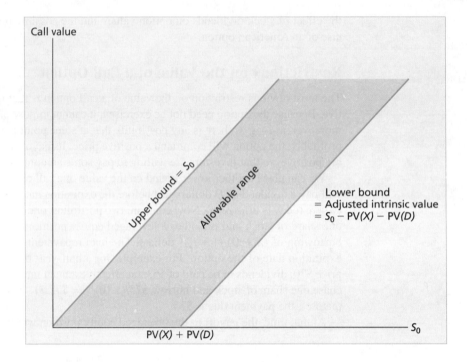

Figure 21.2 demonstrates graphically the range of prices that is ruled out by these upper and lower bounds for the value of a call option. Any option value outside the shaded area is not possible according to the restrictions we have derived. Before expiration, the call option value normally will be *within* the allowable range, touching neither the upper nor lower bound, as in Figure 21.3.

Early Exercise and Dividends

A call optionholder who wants to close out that position has two choices: exercise the call or sell it. If the holder exercises at time t, the call will provide a profit of $S_t - X$, assuming, of course, that the option is in the money. We have just seen that the option can be sold for at least $S_t - PV(X) - PV(D)$. Therefore, for an option on a nondividend paying stock, C is greater than $S_t - PV(X)$. Because the present value of X is less than X itself, it follows that

$$C \geq S_t - PV(X) \geq S_t - X$$

The implication here is that the proceeds from a sale of the option (at price C) must exceed the proceeds from an exercise ($S_t - X$). It is economically more attractive to sell the call, which keeps it alive, than to exercise and thereby end the option. In other words, calls on non–dividend-paying stocks are "worth more alive than dead."

If it never pays to exercise a call option before maturity, the right to exercise early actually must be valueless. The right to exercise an American call early is irrelevant because it will never pay to exercise early. We therefore conclude that the values of otherwise identical American and European call options on stocks paying no dividends are equal. If we can find the value for the European call, we also will have found the value of the American call. This simplifies matters, because any valuation formula that applies to the European call, for which only one exercise date need be considered, also must apply to an American call.

As most stocks do pay dividends, you may wonder whether this result is just a theoretical curiosity. It is not: Reconsider our argument and you will see that all that we really

Figure 21.3

Call option value as a function of the current stock price.

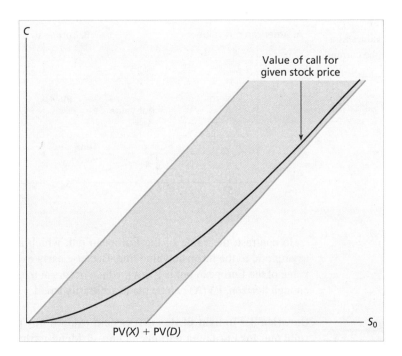

require is that the stock pay no dividends *until the option expires*. This condition will be true for many real-world options.

Early Exercise of American Puts

For American *put options*, the optimality of early exercise is most definitely a possibility. To see why, consider a simple example. Suppose that you purchase a put option on a stock. Soon the firm goes bankrupt, and the stock price falls to zero. Of course you want to exercise now, because the stock price can fall no lower. Immediate exercise gives you immediate receipt of the exercise price, which can be invested to start generating income. Delay in exercise means a time-value-of-money cost. The right to exercise a put option before maturity must have value.

Now suppose instead that the firm is only *nearly* bankrupt, with the stock selling at just a few cents. Immediate exercise may still be optimal. After all, the stock price can fall by only a very small amount, meaning that the proceeds from future exercise cannot be more than a few cents greater than the proceeds from immediate exercise. Against this possibility of a tiny increase in proceeds must be weighed the time-value-of-money cost of deferring exercise. Clearly, there is some stock price below which early exercise is optimal.

This argument also proves that the American put must be worth more than its European counterpart. The American put allows you to exercise anytime before maturity. Because the right to exercise early may be useful in some circumstances, it will command a positive price in the capital market. The American put therefore will sell for a higher price than a European put with otherwise identical terms.

Figure 21.4A illustrates the value of an American put option as a function of the current stock price, S_0. Once the stock price drops below a critical value, denoted S^* in the figure, exercise becomes optimal. At that point the option-pricing curve is tangent to the straight line depicting the intrinsic value of the option. If and when the stock price reaches S^*, the put option is exercised and its payoff equals its intrinsic value.

Figure 21.4
Put option values as a function of the current stock price.

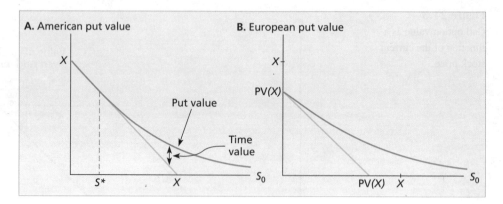

In contrast, the value of the European put, which is graphed in Figure 21.4**B**, is not asymptotic to the intrinsic value line. Because early exercise is prohibited, the maximum value of the European put is PV(X), which occurs at the point $S_0 = 0$. Obviously, for a long enough horizon, PV(X) can be made arbitrarily small.

Concept CHECK

Question 3 • In light of this discussion, explain why the put-call parity relationship is valid only for European options on non–dividend-paying stocks. If the stock pays no dividends, what *inequality* for American options would correspond to the parity theorem?

21.3   BINOMIAL OPTION PRICING

Two-State Option Pricing

A complete understanding of commonly used option valuation formulas is difficult without a substantial mathematics background. Nevertheless, we can develop valuable insight into option valuation by considering a simple special case. Assume that a stock price can take only two possible values at option expiration: The stock will either increase to a given higher price or decrease to a given lower price. Although this may seem an extreme simplification, it allows us to come closer to understanding more complicated and realistic models. Moreover, we can extend this approach to describe far more reasonable specifications of stock price behavior. In fact, several major financial firms employ variants of this simple model to value options and securities with optionlike features.

Suppose the stock now sells at $100, and the price will either double to $200 or fall in half to $50 by year-end. A call option on the stock might specify an exercise price of $125 and a time to expiration of one year. The interest rate is 8%. At year-end, the payoff to the holder of the call option will be either zero, if the stock falls, or $75, if the stock price goes to $200.

These possibilities are illustrated by the following "trees":

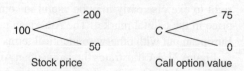

Compare the payoff of the call to that of a portfolio consisting of one share of the stock and borrowing of $46.30 at the interest rate of 8%. The payoff of this portfolio also depends on the stock price at year-end:

Value of stock at year-end	$50	$200
− Repayment of loan with interest	− 50	− 50
Total	$ 0	$150

We know the cash outlay to establish the portfolio is $53.70: $100 for the stock, less the $46.30 proceeds from borrowing. Therefore the portfolio's value tree is

The payoff of this portfolio is exactly twice that of the call option for either value of the stock price. In other words, two call options will exactly replicate the payoff to the portfolio; it follows that two call options should have the same price as the cost of establishing the portfolio. Hence the two calls should sell for the same price as the "replicating portfolio." Therefore,

$$2C = \$53.70$$

or each call should sell at $C = \$26.85$. Thus, given the stock price, exercise price, interest rate, and volatility of the stock price (as represented by the magnitude of the up or down movements), we can derive the fair value for the call option.

This valuation approach relies heavily on the notion of *replication*. With only two possible end-of-year values of the stock, the payoffs to the levered stock portfolio replicate the payoffs to two call options and, therefore, command the same market price. This notion of replication is behind most option-pricing formulas. For more complex price distributions for stocks, the replication technique is correspondingly more complex, but the principles remain the same.

One way to view the role of replication is to note that, using the numbers assumed for this example, a portfolio made up of one share of stock and two call options written is perfectly hedged. Its year-end value is independent of the ultimate stock price:

Stock value	$50	$200
− Obligations from 2 calls written	− 0	− 150
Net payoff	$50	$ 50

The investor has formed a riskless portfolio, with a payout of $50. Its value must be the present value of $50, or $50/1.08 = $46.30. The value of the portfolio, which equals $100 from the stock held long, minus $2C$ from the two calls written, should equal $46.30. Hence $100 − 2C = \$46.30$, or $C = \$26.85$.

The ability to create a perfect hedge is the key to this argument. The hedge locks in the end-of-year payout, which can be discounted using the risk-free interest rate. To find the value of the option in terms of the value of the stock, we do not need to know either the option's or the stock's beta or expected rate of return. The perfect hedging, or replication, approach enables us to express the value of the option in terms of the current value of the stock without this information. With a hedged position, the final stock price does not affect the investor's payoff, so the stock's risk and return parameters have no bearing.

The hedge ratio of this example is one share of stock to two calls, or one-half. For every call option written, one-half share of stock must be held in the portfolio to hedge away risk. This ratio has an easy interpretation in this context: It is the ratio of the range of the values of the option to those of the stock across the two possible outcomes. The option is worth either zero or $75, for a range of $75. The stock is worth either $50 or $200, for a range of $150. The ratio of ranges, 75/150, is one-half, which is the hedge ratio we have established.

The hedge ratio equals the ratio of ranges because the option and stock are perfectly correlated in this two-state example. When the returns of the option and stock are perfectly correlated, a perfect hedge requires that the option and stock be held in a fraction determined only by relative volatility.

We can generalize the hedge ratio for other two-state option problems as

$$H = \frac{C^+ - C^-}{S^+ - S^-}$$

where C^+ or C^- refers to the call option's value when the stock goes up or down, respectively, and S^+ and S^- are the stock prices in the two states. The hedge ratio, H, is the ratio of the swings in the possible end-of-period values of the option and the stock. If the investor writes one option and holds H shares of stock, the value of the portfolio will be unaffected by the stock price. In this case, option pricing is easy: Simply set the value of the hedged portfolio equal to the present value of the known payoff.

Using our example, the option-pricing technique would proceed as follows:

1. Given the possible end-of-year stock prices, $S^+ = 200$ and $S^- = 50$, and the exercise price of 125, calculate that $C^+ = 75$ and $C^- = 0$. The stock price range is 150, while the option price range is 75.

2. Find that the hedge ratio of 75/150 = .5.

3. Find that a portfolio made up of .5 share with one written option would have an end-of-year value of $25 with certainty.

4. Show that the present value of $25 with a one-year interest rate of 8% is $23.15.

5. Set the value of the hedged position to the present value of the certain payoff:

$$.5S_0 - C_0 = \$23.15$$
$$\$50 - C_0 = \$23.15$$

6. Solve for the call's value, $C_0 = \$26.85$.

What if the option were overpriced, perhaps selling for $30? Then you can make arbitrage profits. Here is how:

	Initial Cash Flow	Cash Flow in One Year for Each Possible Stock Price	
		$S = 50$	$S = 200$
1. Write 2 options	$ 60	$ 0	$–150
2. Purchase 1 share	–100	50	200
3. Borrow $40 at 8% interest Repay in 1 year	40	–43.20	–43.20
Total	$ 0	$ 6.80	$ 6.80

Although the net initial investment is zero, the payoff in one year is positive and riskless. If the option were underpriced, one would simply reverse this arbitrage strategy: Buy the option, and sell the stock short to eliminate price risk. Note, by the way, that the present value of the profit to the arbitrage strategy above exactly equals twice the amount by which the option is overpriced. The present value of the risk-free profit of $6.80 at an 8% interest rate is $6.30. With two options written in the strategy above, this translates to a profit of $3.15 per option, exactly the amount by which the option was overpriced: $30 versus the "fair value" of $26.85.

Concept CHECK

Question 4 • Suppose the call option had been underpriced, selling at $24. Formulate the arbitrage strategy to exploit the mispricing, and show that it provides a riskless cash flow in one year of $3.08 per option purchased.

Generalizing the Two-State Approach

Although the two-state stock price model seems simplistic, we can generalize it to incorporate more realistic assumptions. To start, suppose we were to break up the year into two six-month segments, and then assert that over each half-year segment the stock price could take on two values. Here we will say it can increase 10% or decrease 5%. A stock initially selling at 100 could follow these possible paths over the course of the year:

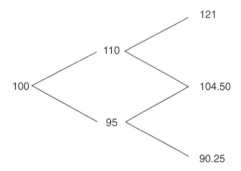

The midrange value of 104.50 can be attained by two paths: an increase of 10% followed by a decrease of 5%, or a decrease of 5% followed by a 10% increase.

There are now three possible end-of-year values for the stock and three for the option:

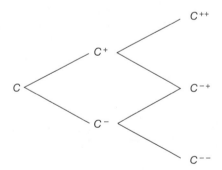

Using methods similar to those we followed above, we could value C^+ from knowledge of C^{++} and C^{+-}, then value C^- from knowledge of C^{-+} and C^{--}, and finally value C from knowledge of C^+ and C^-. And there is no reason to stop at six-month intervals. We could next break the year into four three-month units, or 12 one-month units, or 365 one-day units, each of which would be posited to have a two-state process. Although the calculations become quite numerous and correspondingly tedious, they are easy to program into a computer, and such computer programs are used widely by participants in the options market.

As we break the year into progressively finer subintervals, the range of possible year-end stock prices expands and, in fact, will ultimately take on a familiar bell-shaped distribution. This can be seen from an analysis of the event tree for the stock for a period with three subintervals:

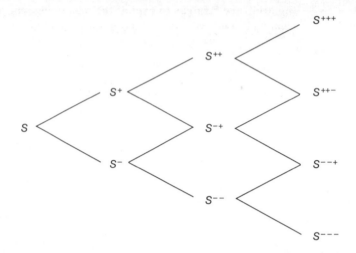

First, notice that as the number of subintervals increases, the number of possible stock prices also increases. Second, notice that extreme events such as S^{+++} or S^{---} are relatively rare, as they require either three consecutive increases or decreases in the three subintervals. More moderate, or midrange, results such as S^{++-} can be arrived at by more than one path—any combination of two price increases and one decrease will result in stock price S^{++-}. Thus the midrange values will be more likely. The probability of each outcome is described by the binomial distribution, and this multiperiod approach to option pricing is called the **binomial model.**

For example, using our initial stock price of $100, equal probability of stock price increases or decreases, and three intervals for which the possible price increase is 5% and decrease is 3%, we can obtain the probability distribution of stock prices from the calculations following. There are eight possible combinations for the stock price movements in the three periods: $+++, ++-, +-+, -++, +--, -+-, --+, ---$. Each has probability of 1/8. Therefore, the probability distribution of stock prices at the end of the last interval would be:

Event	Probability	Stock Price	
3 up movements	1/8	100×1.05^3	= 115.76
2 up and 1 down	3/8	$100 \times 1.05^2 \times .97$	= 106.94
1 up and 2 down	3/8	$100 \times 1.05 \times .97^2$	= 98.79
3 down movements	1/8	$100 \times .97^3$	= 91.27

The midrange values are three times as likely to occur as the extreme values. Figure 21.5A is a graph of the frequency distribution for this example. The graph approaches the appearance of the familiar bell-shaped curve. In fact, as the number of intervals increases,

Figure 21.5
Probability
distributions.
A, Possible outcomes
and associated
probabilities for stock
prices after three
periods. The stock
price starts at $100,
and in each period it
can increase by 5% or
decrease by 3%.
B, Each period is
subdivided into two
smaller subperiods.
Now there are six
periods, and in each of
these the stock price
can increase by 2.5%
or fall by 1.5%. As the
number of periods
increases, the stock
price distribution
approaches the
familiar bell-shaped
curve.

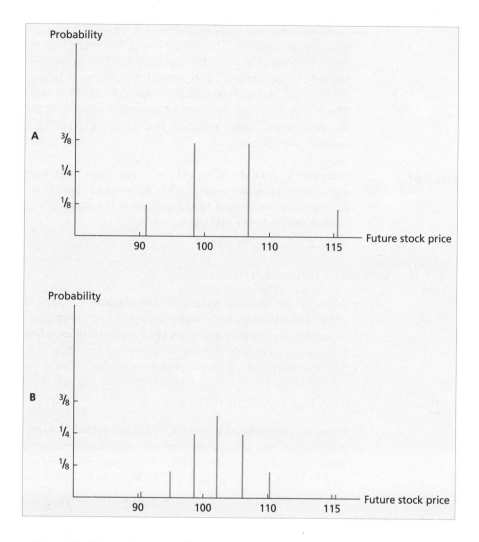

as in Figure 21.5**B**, the frequency distribution progressively approaches the lognormal distribution rather than the normal distribution.[2]

Suppose we were to continue subdividing the interval in which stock prices are posited to move up or down. Eventually, each node of the event tree would correspond to an infinitesimally small time interval. The possible stock price movement within that time interval would be correspondingly small. As those many intervals passed, the end-of-period stock price would more and more closely resemble a lognormal distribution. Thus the apparent oversimplification of the two-state model can be overcome by progressively subdividing any period into many subperiods.

---

[2]Actually, more complex considerations enter here. The limit of this process is lognormal only if we assume also that stock prices move continuously, by which we mean that over small time intervals only small price movements can occur. This rules out rare events such as sudden, extreme price moves in response to dramatic information (like a takeover attempt). For a treatment of this type of "jump process," see John C. Cox and Stephen A. Ross, "The Valuation of Options for Alternative Stochastic Processes," *Journal of Financial Economics* 3 (January–March 1976), pp. 145–66, or Robert C. Merton, "Option Pricing when Underlying Stock Returns Are Discontinuous," *Journal of Financial Economics* 3 (January–March 1976), pp. 125–44.

At any node, one still could set up a portfolio that would be perfectly hedged over the next tiny time interval. Then, at the end of that interval, on reaching the next node, a new hedge ratio could be computed and the portfolio composition could be revised to remain hedged over the coming small interval. By continuously revising the hedge position, the portfolio would remain hedged and would earn a riskless rate of return over each interval. This is called *dynamic hedging*, the continued updating of the hedge ratio as time passes. As the dynamic hedge becomes ever finer, the resulting option valuation procedure becomes more precise.

Concept CHECK

Question 5 * Would you expect the hedge ratio to be higher or lower when the call option is more in the money? (Hint: Remember that the hedge ratio is the change in the option price divided by the change in the stock price. When is the option price most sensitive to the stock price?)

21.4   BLACK-SCHOLES OPTION VALUATION

Although the binomial model we have described is extremely flexible, a computer is needed for it to be useful in actual trading. An option-pricing *formula* would be far easier to use than the complex algorithm involved in the binomial model. It turns out that such a formula can be derived if one is willing to make just two more assumptions: that both the risk-free interest rate and stock price volatility are constant over the life of the option.

The Black-Scholes Formula

Financial economists searched for years for a workable option-pricing model before Black and Scholes[3] and Merton[4] derived a formula for the value of a call option. Scholes and Merton shared the 1997 Nobel Prize in economics for their accomplishment.[5] Now widely used by options market participants, the **Black-Scholes pricing formula** for a call option is

$$C_0 = S_0 N(d_1) - Xe^{-rT} N(d_2) \tag{21.1}$$

where

$$d_1 = \frac{\ln(S_0/X) + (r + \sigma^2/2)T}{\sigma\sqrt{T}}$$

$$d_2 = d_1 - \sigma\sqrt{T}$$

and where

C_0 = Current call option value.

S_0 = Current stock price.

$N(d)$ = The probability that a random draw from a standard normal distribution will be less than d. This equals the area under the normal curve up to d, as in the shaded area of Figure 21.6.

---

[3]Fischer Black and Myron Scholes, "The Pricing of Options and Corporate Liabilities," *Journal of Political Economy* 81 (May–June 1973).
[4]Robert C. Merton, "Theory of Rational Option Pricing," *Bell Journal of Economics and Management Science* 4 (Spring 1973).
[5]Fischer Black died in 1995.

Figure 21.6

A standard normal curve.

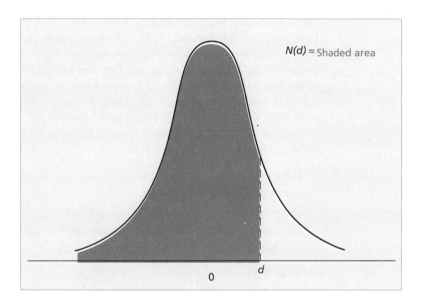

X	=	Exercise price.
e	=	2.71828, the base of the natural log function.
r	=	Risk-free interest rate (the annualized continuously compounded rate on a safe asset with the same maturity as the expiration of the option, which is to be distinguished from r_f, the discrete period interest rate).
T	=	Time to maturity of option, in years.
ln	=	Natural logarithm function.
σ	=	Standard deviation of the annualized continuously compounded rate of return of the stock.

The option value does *not* depend on the expected rate of return on the stock. In a sense, this information is already built into the formula with the inclusion of the stock price, which itself depends on the stock's risk and return characteristics. This version of the Black-Scholes formula is predicated on the assumption that the stock pays no dividends.

Although you may find the Black-Scholes formula intimidating, we can explain it at a somewhat intuitive level. The trick is to view the $N(d)$ terms (loosely) as risk-adjusted probabilities that the call option will expire in the money. First, look at equation 21.1 assuming both $N(d)$ terms are close to 1.0, that is, when there is a very high probability the option will be exercised. Then the call option value is equal to $S_0 - Xe^{-rT}$, which is what we called earlier the adjusted intrinsic value, $S_0 - PV(X)$. This makes sense; if exercise is certain, we have a claim on a stock with current value S_0, and an obligation with present value $PV(X)$, or, with continuous compounding, Xe^{-rT}.

Now look at equation 21.1 assuming the $N(d)$ terms are close to zero, meaning the option almost certainly will not be exercised. Then the equation confirms that the call is worth nothing. For middle-range values of $N(d)$ between 0 and 1, equation 21.1 tells us that the call value can be viewed as the present value of the call's potential payoff adjusting for the probability of in-the-money expiration.

How do the $N(d)$ terms serve as risk-adjusted probabilities? This question quickly leads us into advanced statistics. Notice, however, that $\ln(S_0/X)$, which appears in the numerator of d_1 and d_2, is approximately the percentage amount by which the option is currently in or out of the money. For example, if $S_0 = 105$ and $X = 100$, the option is 5% in the money, and $\ln(105/100) = .049$. Similarly, if $S_0 = 95$, the option is 5% out of the money, and $\ln(95/100) = -.051$. The denominator, $\sigma\sqrt{T}$, adjusts the amount by which the option is in or out of the money for the volatility of the stock price over the remaining life of the option. An option in the money by a given percent is more likely to stay in the money if both stock price volatility and time to maturity are small. Therefore, $N(d_1)$ and $N(d_2)$ increase with the probability that the option will expire in the money.

You can use the Black-Scholes formula fairly easily. Suppose you want to value a call option under the following circumstances:

Stock price	$S_0 = 100$
Exercise price	$X = 95$
Interest rate	$r = .10$ (10% per year)
Time to expiration	$T = .25$ (one-quarter of a year)
Standard deviation	$\sigma = .50$ (50% per year)

First calculate

$$d_1 = \frac{\ln(100/95) + (.10 + .5^2/2).25}{.5\sqrt{.25}} = .43$$

$$d_2 = .43 - .5\sqrt{.25} = .18$$

Next find $N(d_1)$ and $N(d_2)$. The values of the normal distribution are tabulated and may be found in many statistics textbooks. A table of $N(d)$ is provided here as Table 21.2. The normal distribution function, $N(d)$, is also provided in any spreadsheet program. In Microsoft Excel, for example, the function name is NORMSDIST. Table 21.2 reveals (using interpolation for .43) that

$$N(.43) = .6664$$
$$N(.18) = .5714$$

Thus the value of the call option is

$$C = 100 \times .6664 - 95e^{-.10 \times .25} \times .5714$$
$$= 66.64 - 52.94 = \$13.70$$

Concept  **Question 6** • **Calculate the call option value if the standard deviation on the stock were .6 instead of .5. Confirm that the option is worth more using this higher volatility.**

What if the option price in our example were $15 rather than $13.70? Is the option mispriced? Maybe, but before betting your fortune on that, you may want to reconsider the valuation analysis. First, like all models, the Black-Scholes formula is based on some simplifying abstractions that make the formula only approximately valid.

Some of the important assumptions underlying the formula are the following:

1. The stock will pay no dividends until after the option expiration date.
2. Both the interest rate, r, and variance rate, σ^2, of the stock are constant (or in slightly more general versions of the formula, both are *known* functions of time—any changes are perfectly predictable).
3. Stock prices are continuous, meaning that sudden extreme jumps such as those in the aftermath of an announcement of a takeover attempt are ruled out.

Variants of the Black-Scholes formula have been developed to deal with some of these limitations.

Second, even within the context of the Black-Scholes model, you must be sure of the accuracy of the parameters used in the formula. Four of these—S_0, X, T, and r—are straightforward. The stock price, exercise price, and time to maturity are readily determined. The interest rate used is the money market rate for a maturity equal to that of the option.

The last input, though, the standard deviation of the stock return, is not directly observable. It must be estimated from historical data, from scenario analysis, or from the prices of other options, as we will describe momentarily.

We saw in Chapter 5 that the historical variance of stock market returns can be calculated from n observations as follows:

$$\sigma^2 = \frac{n}{n-1} \sum_{t=1}^{n} \frac{(r_t - \bar{r})^2}{n}$$

where $\bar{r}$ is the average return over the sample period. The rate of return on day t is defined to be consistent with continuous compounding as $r_t = \ln(S_t/S_{t-1})$. [We note again that the natural logarithm of a ratio is approximately the percentage difference between the numerator and denominator so that $\ln(S_t/S_{t-1})$ is a measure of the rate of return of the stock from time $t - 1$ to time t.] Historical variance commonly is computed using daily returns over periods of several months. Because the standard deviation of stock returns must be estimated, however, it is always possible that discrepancies between an option price and its Black-Scholes value are simply artifacts of error in the estimation of the stock's volatility.

In fact, market participants often give the option valuation problem a different twist. Rather than calculating a Black-Scholes option value for a given stock's standard deviation, they ask instead: "What standard deviation would be necessary for the option price that I observe to be consistent with the Black-Scholes formula?" This is called the **implied volatility** of the option, the volatility level for the stock that the option price implies.[6] Investors can then judge whether they think the actual stock standard deviation exceeds the implied volatility. If it does, the option is considered a good buy; if actual volatility seems greater than the implied volatility, its fair price would exceed the observed price.

Another variation is to compare two options on the same stock with equal expiration dates but different exercise prices. The option with the higher implied volatility would be considered relatively expensive, because a higher standard deviation is required to justify its price. The analyst might consider buying the option with the lower implied volatility and writing the option with the higher implied volatility.

Figure 21.7 presents plots of the historical and implied standard deviation of the rate of return on the S&P 500 Index. The implied volatility is derived from prices of option contracts traded on the index. Notice that although both series have considerable tendency to move together, there is some slippage between the two estimates of volatility. Notice also that both volatility series vary considerably over time. Therefore, choosing the proper volatility value to use in any option-pricing model always presents a formidable challenge. A considerable amount of recent research has been devoted to new techniques to predict changes in volatility. These techniques, which go by the name ARCH models, posit that changes in stock volatility are partially predictable, and that by analyzing recent levels and trends in volatility, one can improve predictions of future volatility.

Concept
CHECK

Question 7 • Consider the option in the example selling for $15 with Black-Scholes value of $13.70. Is its implied volatility more or less than 50%?

---

[6]This concept was introduced in Richard E. Schmalensee and Robert R. Trippi, "Common Stock Volatility Expectations Implied by Option Premia," *Journal of Finance* 33 (March 1978), pp. 129–47.

Table 21.2   Cumulative Normal Distribution

d	N(d)	d	N(d)	d	N(d)
−3.00	.0013	−1.58	.0571	−0.76	.2236
−2.95	.0016	−1.56	.0594	−0.74	.2297
−2.90	.0019	−1.54	.0618	−0.72	.2358
−2.85	.0022	−1.52	.0643	−0.70	.2420
−2.80	.0026	−1.50	.0668	−0.68	.2483
−2.75	.0030	−1.48	.0694	−0.66	.2546
−2.70	.0035	−1.46	.0721	−0.64	.2611
−2.65	.0040	−1.44	.0749	−0.62	.2676
−2.60	.0047	−1.42	.0778	−0.60	.2743
−2.55	.0054	−1.40	.0808	−0.58	.2810
−2.50	.0062	−1.38	.0838	−0.56	.2877
−2.45	.0071	−1.36	.0869	−0.54	.2946
−2.40	.0082	−1.34	.0901	−0.52	.3015
−2.35	.0094	−1.32	.0934	−0.50	.3085
−2.30	.0107	−1.30	.0968	−0.48	.3156
−2.25	.0122	−1.28	.1003	−0.46	.3228
−2.20	.0139	−1.26	.1038	−0.44	.3300
−2.15	.0158	−1.24	.1075	−0.42	.3373
−2.10	.0179	−1.22	.1112	−0.40	.3446
−2.05	.0202	−1.20	.1151	−0.38	.3520
−2.00	.0228	−1.18	.1190	−0.36	.3594
−1.98	.0239	−1.16	.1230	−0.34	.3669
−1.96	.0250	−1.14	.1271	−0.32	.3745
−1.94	.0262	−1.12	.1314	−0.30	.3821
−1.92	.0274	−1.10	.1357	−0.28	.3897
−1.90	.0287	−1.08	.1401	−0.26	.3974
−1.88	.0301	−1.06	.1446	−0.24	.4052
−1.86	.0314	−1.04	.1492	−0.22	.4129
−1.84	.0329	−1.02	.1539	−0.20	.4207
−1.82	.0344	−1.00	.1587	−0.18	.4286
−1.80	.0359	−0.98	.1635	−0.16	.4365
−1.78	.0375	−0.96	.1685	−0.14	.4443
−1.76	.0392	−0.94	.1736	−0.12	.4523
−1.74	.0409	−0.92	.1788	−0.10	.4602
−1.72	.0427	−0.90	.1841	−0.08	.4681
−1.70	.0446	−0.88	.1894	−0.06	.4761
−1.68	.0465	−0.86	.1949	−0.04	.4841
−1.66	.0485	−0.84	.2005	−0.02	.4920
−1.64	.0505	−0.82	.2061	0.00	.5000
−1.62	.0526	−0.80	.2119	0.02	.5080
−1.60	.0548	−0.78	.2177	0.04	.5160

Dividends and Call Option Valuation

We noted earlier that the Black-Scholes call option formula applies to stocks that do not pay dividends. When dividends are to be paid before the option expires, we need to adjust the formula. The payment of dividends raises the possibility of early exercise, and for most realistic dividend payout schemes the valuation formula becomes significantly more complex than the Black-Scholes equation.

We can apply some simple rules of thumb to approximate the option value, however. One popular approach, originally suggested by Black, calls for adjusting the stock price downward by the present value of any dividends that are to be paid before option expiration.[7]

---

[7]Fischer Black, "Fact and Fantasy in the Use of Options," *Financial Analysts Journal* 31 (July–August 1975).

Table 21.2   *(Concluded)*

d	N(d)	d	N(d)	d	N(d)
0.06	.5239	0.86	.8051	1.66	.9515
0.08	.5319	0.88	.8106	1.68	.9535
0.10	.5398	0.90	.8159	1.70	.9554
0.12	.5478	0.92	.8212	1.72	.9573
0.14	.5557	0.94	.8264	1.74	.9591
0.16	.5636	0.96	.8315	1.76	.9608
0.18	.5714	0.98	.8365	1.78	.9625
0.20	.5793	1.00	.8414	1.80	.9641
0.22	.5871	1.02	.8461	1.82	.9656
0.24	.5948	1.04	.8508	1.84	.9671
0.26	.6026	1.06	.8554	1.86	.9686
0.28	.6103	1.08	.8599	1.88	.9699
0.30	.6179	1.10	.8643	1.90	.9713
0.32	.6255	1.12	.8686	1.92	.9726
0.34	.6331	1.14	.8729	1.94	.9738
0.36	.6406	1.16	.8770	1.96	.9750
0.38	.6480	1.18	.8810	1.98	.9761
0.40	.6554	1.20	.8849	2.00	.9772
0.42	.6628	1.22	.8888	2.05	.9798
0.44	.6700	1.24	.8925	2.10	.9821
0.46	.6773	1.26	.8962	2.15	.9842
0.48	.6844	1.28	.8997	2.20	.9861
0.50	.6915	1.30	.9032	2.25	.9878
0.52	.6985	1.32	.9066	2.30	.9893
0.54	.7054	1.34	.9099	2.35	.9906
0.56	.7123	1.36	.9131	2.40	.9918
0.58	.7191	1.38	.9162	2.45	.9929
0.60	.7258	1.40	.9192	2.50	.9938
0.62	.7324	1.42	.9222	2.55	.9946
0.64	.7389	1.44	.9251	2.60	.9953
0.66	.7454	1.46	.9279	2.65	.9960
0.68	.7518	1.48	.9306	2.70	.9965
0.70	.7580	1.50	.9332	2.75	.9970
0.72	.7642	1.52	.9357	2.80	.9974
0.74	.7704	1.54	.9382	2.85	.9978
0.76	.7764	1.56	.9406	2.90	.9981
0.78	.7823	1.58	.9429	2.95	.9984
0.80	.7882	1.60	.9452	3.00	.9986
0.82	.7939	1.62	.9474	3.05	.9989
0.84	.7996	1.64	.9495		

Therefore, we would simply replace S_0 with $S_0 - $ PV(dividends) in the Black-Scholes formula. Such an adjustment will take dividends into account by reflecting their eventual impact on the stock price. The option value then may be computed as before, assuming that the option will he held to expiration.

This procedure would yield a very good approximation of option value for European call options that must be held until maturity, but it does not allow for the fact that the holder of an American call option might choose to exercise the option just before a dividend. The current value of a call option, assuming that the option will be exercised just before the ex-dividend date, might be greater than the value of the option assuming it will be held until maturity. Although holding the option until maturity allows greater effective time to expiration, which increases the option value, it also entails more dividend payments, lowering the expected stock price at maturity and thereby lowering the current option value.

For example, suppose that a stock selling at $20 will pay a $1 dividend in four months, whereas the call option on the stock does not expire for six months. The effective annual

Figure 21.7
S&P 500 implied and historical volatility comparison.

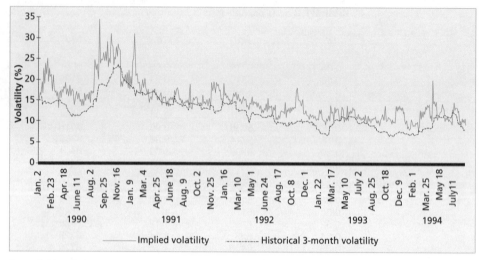

Source: Goldman Sachs, reported in Roger G. Clarke, "Estimating and Using Volatility, Part 2," *Derivatives Quarterly,* Winter 1994, p. 39.

interest rate is 10%, so that the present value of the dividend is $\$1/(1.10)^{1/3} = \$0.97$. Black suggests that we can compute the option value in one of two ways:

1. Apply the Black-Scholes formula assuming early exercise, thus using the actual stock price of $20 and a time to expiration of four months (the time until the dividend payment).

2. Apply the Black-Scholes formula assuming no early exercise, using the dividend-adjusted stock price of $20 − $.97 = $19.03 and a time to expiration of six months.

The greater of the two values is the estimate of the option value, recognizing that early exercise might be optimal. In other words, the so-called **pseudo-American call option value** is the maximum of the value derived by assuming that the option will be held until expiration and the value derived by assuming that the option will be exercised just before an ex-dividend date. Even this technique is not exact, however, for it assumes that the optionholder makes an irrevocable decision now on when to exercise, when in fact the decision is not binding until exercise notice is given.[8]

Put Option Valuation

We have concentrated so far on call option valuation. We can derive Black-Scholes European put option values from call option values using the put-call parity theorem. To value the put option, we simply calculate the value of the corresponding call option in equation 21.1 from the Black-Scholes formula, and solve for the put option value as

$$P = C + \mathrm{PV}(X) - S_0$$
$$= C + Xe^{-rT} - S_0$$

(21.2)

---

[8]An exact formula for American call valuation on dividend-paying stocks has been developed in Richard Roll, "An Analytic Valuation Formula for Unprotected American Call Options on Stocks with Known Dividends," *Journal of Financial Economics* 5 (November 1977). The technique has been discussed and revised in Robert Geske, "A Note on an Analytical Formula for Unprotected American Call Options on Stocks with Known Dividends," *Journal of Financial Economics* 7 (December 1979), and Robert E. Whaley, "On the Valuation of American Call Options on Stocks with Known Dividends," *Journal of Financial Economics* 9 (June 1981). These are difficult papers, however.

We must calculate the present value of the exercise price using continuous compounding to be consistent with the Black-Scholes formula.

Using data from the Black-Scholes call option example ($C = \$13.70$, $X = \$95$, $S = \$100$, $r = .10$, $\sigma = .50$, and $T = .25$), we find that a European put option on that stock with identical exercise price and time to maturity is worth

$$P = \$13.70 + \$95e^{-.10 \times .25} - \$100 = \$6.35$$

As we noted traders can do, we might then compare this formula value to the actual put price as one step in formulating a trading strategy.

Equation 21.2 is valid for European puts on non–dividend-paying stocks. Listed put options are American options that offer the opportunity of early exercise, however, and we have seen that the right to exercise puts early can turn out to be valuable. This means that an American option must be worth more than the corresponding European option. Therefore, equation 21.2 describes only the lower bound on the true value of the American put. However, in many applications the approximation is very accurate.[9]

21.5   USING THE BLACK-SCHOLES FORMULA

Hedge Ratios and the Black-Scholes Formula

In the last chapter, we considered two investments in IBM: 1,000 shares of IBM stock or 10,000 call options on IBM. We saw that the call option position was more sensitive to swings in IBM's stock price than was the all-stock position. To analyze the overall exposure to a stock price more precisely, however, it is necessary to quantify these relative sensitivities. A tool that enables us to summarize the overall exposure of portfolios of options with various exercise prices and times to maturity is the hedge ratio. An option's **hedge ratio** is the change in the price of an option for a $1 increase in the stock price. A call option, therefore, has a positive hedge ratio and a put option a negative hedge ratio. The hedge ratio is commonly called the option's **delta**.

If you were to graph the option value as a function of the stock value as we have done for a call option in Figure 21.8, the hedge ratio is simply the slope of the value curve evaluated at the current stock price. For example, suppose the slope of the curve at $S_0 = \$120$ equals .60. As the stock increases in value by $1, the option increases by approximately $.60, as the figure shows.

For every call option written, .60 share of stock would be needed to hedge the investor's portfolio. For example, if one writes 10 options and holds six shares of stock, according to the hedge ratio of .6, a $1 increase in stock price will result in a gain of $6 on the stock holdings, whereas the loss on the 10 options written will be $10 \times \$.60$, an equivalent $6. The stock price movement leaves total wealth unaltered, which is what a hedged position is intended to do. The investor holding the stock and an option in proportions dictated by their relative price movements hedges the portfolio.

Black-Scholes hedge ratios are particularly easy to compute. The hedge ratio for a call is $N(d_1)$, whereas the hedge ratio for a put is $N(d_1) - 1$. We defined $N(d_1)$ as part of the Black-Scholes formula in equation 21.1. Recall that $N(d)$ stands for the area under the standard normal curve up to d. Therefore, the call option hedge ratio must be positive and

---

[9]For a more complete treatment of American put valuation, see R. Geske and H. E. Johnson, "The American Put Valued Analytically," *Journal of Finance* 39 (December 1984), pp. 1511–24.

Figure 21.8
Call option value and hedge ratio.

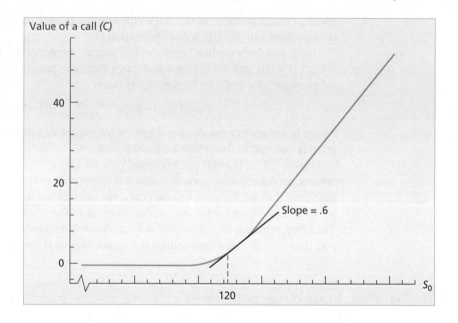

less than 1.0, whereas the put option hedge ratio is negative and of smaller absolute value than 1.0.

Figure 21.8 verifies the insight that the slope of the call option valuation function is less than 1.0, approaching 1.0 only as the stock price becomes much greater than the exercise price. This tells us that option values change less than one for one with changes in stock prices. Why should this be? Suppose an option is so far in the money that you are absolutely certain it will be exercised. In that case, every dollar increase in the stock price would increase the option value by one dollar. But if there is a reasonable chance the call option will expire out of the money, even after a moderate stock price gain, a $1 increase in the stock price will not necessarily increase the ultimate payoff to the call; therefore, the call price will not respond by a full dollar.

The fact that hedge ratios are less than 1.0 does not contradict our earlier observation that options offer leverage and are sensitive to stock price movements. Although *dollar* movements in option prices are slighter than dollar movements in the stock price, the *rate of return* volatility of options remains greater than stock return volatility because options sell at lower prices. In our example, with the stock selling at $120, and a hedge ratio of .6, an option with exercise price $120 may sell for $5. If the stock price increases to $121, the call price would be expected to increase by only $.60 to $5.60. The percentage increase in the option value is $.60/$5.00 = 12%, however, whereas the stock price increase is only $1/$120 = .83%. The ratio of the percentage changes is 12%/.83% = 14.4. For every 1% increase in the stock price, the option price increases by 14.4%. This ratio, the percentage change in option price per percentage change in stock price, is called the **option elasticity.**

The hedge ratio is an essential tool in portfolio management and control. An example will show why. Consider two portfolios, one holding 750 IBM calls and 200 shares of IBM and the other holding 800 shares of IBM. Which portfolio has greater dollar exposure to IBM price movements? You can answer this question easily using the hedge ratio.

Each option changes in value by H dollars for each dollar change in stock price, where H stands for the hedge ratio. Thus, if H equals .6, the 750 options are equivalent to $.6 \times 750 = 450$ shares in terms of the response of their market value to IBM stock price movements. The first portfolio has less dollar sensitivity to stock price change because the 450 share-

Figure 21.9

Profit on a protective put strategy.

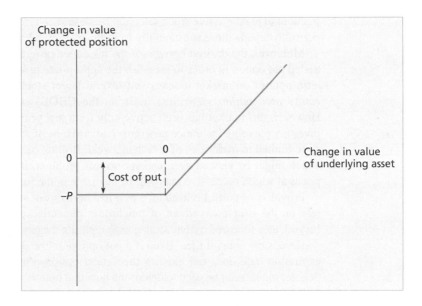

equivalents of the options plus the 200 shares actually held are less than the 800 shares held in the second portfolio.

This is not to say, however, that the first portfolio is less sensitive to the stock's rate of return. As we noted in discussing option elasticities, the first portfolio may be of lower total value than the second, so despite its lower sensitivity in terms of total market value, it might have greater rate of return sensitivity. Because a call option has a lower market value than the stock, its price changes more than proportionally with stock price changes, even though its hedge ratio is less than 1.0.

Concept    **Question 8 • What is the elasticity of a put option currently selling for $4 with exercise price $120 and hedge ratio −.4 if the stock price is currently $122?**

Portfolio Insurance

In Chapter 20, we showed that protective put strategies offer a sort of insurance policy on an asset. The protective put has proved to be extremely popular with investors. Even if the asset price falls, the put conveys the right to sell the asset for the exercise price, which is a way to lock in a minimum portfolio value. With an at-the-money put ($X = S_0$), the maximum loss that can be realized is the cost of the put. The asset can be sold for X, which equals its original value, so even if the asset price falls, the investor's net loss over the period is just the cost of the put. If the asset value increases, however, upside potential is unlimited. Figure 21.9 graphs the profit or loss on a protective put position as a function of the change in the value of the underlying asset, P.

While the protective put is a simple and convenient way to achieve **portfolio insurance,** that is, to limit the worst-case portfolio rate of return, there are practical difficulties in trying to insure a portfolio of stocks. First, unless the investor's portfolio corresponds to a standard market index for which puts are traded, a put option on the portfolio will not be available for purchase. And if index puts are used to protect a non-indexed portfolio, tracking error can result. For example, if the portfolio falls in value while the market index rises, the put will fail to provide the intended protection. Tracking error limits the investor's freedom to pursue active stock selection because such error will be greater as the managed portfolio departs more substantially from the market index.

Moreover, the desired horizon of the insurance program must match the maturity of a traded put option in order to establish the appropriate protective put position. Today long-term options on market indexes and several larger stocks called LEAPS (for *long-term equity anticipation securities*) trade on the CBOE with maturities of several years. However, this market has been active only for a few years. In the mid-1980s, while most investors pursuing insurance programs had horizons of several years, actively traded puts were limited to maturities of less than a year. Rolling over a sequence of short-term puts, which might be viewed as a response to this problem, introduces new risks because the prices at which successive puts will be available in the future are not known today.

Providers of portfolio insurance who had horizons of several years, therefore, could not rely on the simple expedient of purchasing protective puts for their clients' portfolios. Instead, they followed trading strategies to replicate the payoffs to the protective put position.

Here is the general idea. Even if a put option on the desired portfolio with the desired expiration date does not exist, a theoretical option-pricing model (such as the Black-Scholes model) can be used to determine how that option's price would respond to the portfolio's value if the option did trade. For example, if stock prices were to fall, the put option would increase in value. The option model could quantify this relationship. The net exposure of the (hypothetical) protective put portfolio to swings in stock prices is the sum of the exposures of the two components of the portfolio, the stock and the put. The net exposure of the portfolio equals the equity exposure less the (offsetting) put option exposure.

We can create "synthetic" protective put positions by holding a quantity of stocks with the same net exposure to market swings as the hypothetical protective put position. The key to this strategy is the option delta, or hedge ratio, that is, the change in the price of the protective put option per change in the value of the underlying stock portfolio.

An example will clarify the procedure. Suppose a portfolio is currently valued at $100 million. An at-the-money put option on the portfolio might have a hedge ratio or delta of $-.6$, meaning the option's value swings $.60 for every dollar change in portfolio value, but in an opposite direction. Suppose the stock portfolio falls in value by 2%. The profit on a hypothetical protective put position (if the put existed) would be as follows (in millions of dollars):

Loss on stocks:	2% of $100 =	$2.00
+ Gain on put:	.6 × $2.00 =	1.20
Net loss		= $ .80

We create the synthetic option position by selling a proportion of shares equal to the put option's delta (i.e., selling 60% of the shares) and placing the proceeds in risk-free T-bills. The rationale is that the hypothetical put option would have offset 60% of any change in the stock portfolio's value, so one must reduce portfolio risk directly by selling 60% of the equity and putting the proceeds into a risk-free asset. Total return on a synthetic protective put position with $60 million in risk-free investments such as T-bills and $40 million in equity is

Loss on stocks:	2% of $40 =	$ .80
+ Loss on bills:	=	0
Net loss		= $ .80

Figure 21.10

Hedge ratios change
as the stock price
fluctuates.

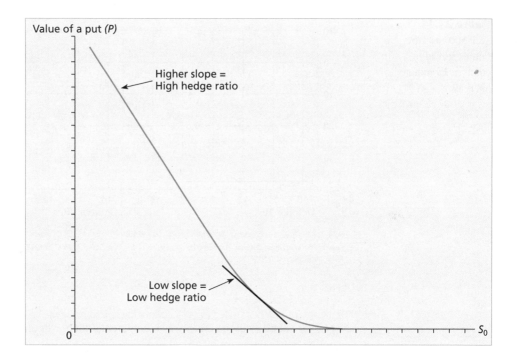

The synthetic and actual protective put positions have equal returns. We conclude that if you sell a proportion of shares equal to the put option's delta and place the proceeds in cash equivalents, your exposure to the stock market will equal that of the desired protective put position.

The difficulty with this procedure is that deltas constantly change. Figure 21.10 shows that as the stock price falls, the magnitude of the appropriate hedge ratio increases. Therefore, market declines require extra hedging, that is, additional conversion of equity into cash. This constant updating of the hedge ratio is called **dynamic hedging.**

Dynamic hedging is one reason portfolio insurance has been said to contribute to market volatility. Market declines trigger additional sales of stock as portfolio insurers strive to increase their hedging. These additional sales are seen as reinforcing or exaggerating market downturns.

In practice, portfolio insurers do not actually buy or sell stocks directly when they update their hedge positions. Instead, they minimize trading costs by buying or selling stock index futures as a substitute for sale of the stocks themselves. As you will see in the next chapter, stock prices and index futures prices usually are very tightly linked by cross-market arbitrageurs so that futures transactions can be used as reliable proxies for stock transactions. Instead of selling equities based on the put option's delta, insurers will sell an equivalent number of futures contracts.[10]

Several portfolio insurers suffered great setbacks during the market crash of October 19, 1987, when the market suffered unprecedented one-day loss of about 20%. A description of what happened then should let you appreciate the complexities of applying a seemingly straightforward hedging concept.

---

[10]Notice, however, that the use of index futures reintroduces the problem of tracking error between the portfolio and the market index.

Figure 21.11

S&P 500 cash-to-
futures spread in
points at 15-minute
intervals.

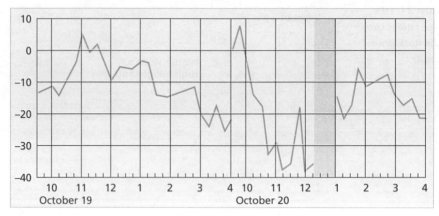

Note: Trading in futures contracts halted between 12:15 and 1:05.

Source: *The Wall Street Journal.* Reprinted by permission of *The Wall Street Journal*, © 1987 Dow Jones & Company, Inc.
All Rights Reserved Worldwide.

1. Market volatility at the crash was much greater than ever encountered before. Put
   option deltas based on historical experience were too low; insurers underhedged,
   held too much equity, and suffered excessive losses.

2. Prices moved so fast that insurers could not keep up with the necessary
   rebalancing. They were "chasing deltas" that kept getting away from them. The
   futures market saw a "gap" opening, where the opening price was nearly 10%
   below the previous day's close. The price dropped before insurers could update
   their hedge ratios.

3. Execution problems were severe. First, current market prices were unavailable,
   with trade execution and the price quotation system hours behind, which made
   computation of correct hedge ratios impossible. Moreover, trading in stocks and
   stock futures ceased during some periods. The continuous rebalancing capability
   that is essential for a viable insurance program vanished during the precipitous
   market collapse.

4. Futures prices traded at steep discounts to their proper levels compared to reported
   stock prices, thereby making the sale of futures (as a proxy for equity sales) seem
   expensive. Although you will see in the next chapter that stock index futures prices
   normally exceed the value of the stock index, Figure 21.11 shows that on October
   19, futures sold far below the stock index level. The so-called cash-to-futures
   spread was negative most of the day. When some insurers gambled that the futures
   price would recover to its usual premium over the stock index, and chose to defer
   sales, they remained underhedged. As the market fell farther, their portfolios
   experienced substantial losses.

Although most observers believe that the portfolio insurance industry will never recover
from the market crash, the nearby box points out that delta hedging is still alive and well on
Wall Street. Dynamic hedges are widely used by large firms to hedge potential losses from
the options they write. The article also points out, however, that these traders are increasingly aware of the practical difficulties in implementing dynamic hedges in very volatile
markets.

DELTA-HEDGING: THE NEW NAME IN PORTFOLIO INSURANCE

Portfolio insurance, the high-tech hedging strategy that helped grease the slide in the 1987 stock-market crash, is alive and well.

And just as in 1987, it doesn't always work out as planned, as some financial institutions found out in the recent European bond-market turmoil.

Banks, securities firms, and other big traders rely heavily on portfolio insurance to contain their potential losses when they buy and sell options. But since portfolio insurance got a bad name after it backfired on investors in 1987, it goes by an alias these days—the sexier, Star Trek moniker of "delta-hedging."

Whatever you call it, the recent turmoil in European bond markets taught some practitioners—including banks and securities firms that were hedging options sales to hedge funds and other investors—the same painful lessons of earlier portfolio insurers: Delta-hedging can break down in volatile markets, just when it is needed most.

What's more, at such times, it can actually feed volatility. The complexities of hedging certain hot-selling "exotic" options may only compound such glitches.

"The tried-and-true strategies for hedging [these products] work fine when the markets aren't subject to sharp moves or large shocks," says Victor S. Filatov, president of Smith Barney Global Capital Management in London. But turbulent times can start "causing problems for people who normally have these risks under control."

Options are financial arrangements that give buyers the right to buy, or sell, securities or other assets at prearranged prices over some future period. An option can gyrate wildly in value with even modest changes in the underlying security's price; the relationship between the two is known as the option's "delta." Thus, dealers in these instruments need some way to hedge their delta to contain the risk.

How you delta-hedge depends on the bets you're trying to hedge. For instance, delta-hedging would prompt options sellers to sell into falling markets and buy into rallies. It would give the opposite directions to options buyers, such as dealers who might hold big options inventories.

In theory, delta-hedging takes place with computer-timed precision, and there aren't any snags. But in real life, it doesn't always work so smoothly.

"When volatility ends up being much greater than anticipated, you can't get your delta trades off at the right points," says an executive at one big derivatives dealer.

A Scenario in Treasuries

How does this happen? Take the relatively simple case of dealers who sell "call" options on long-term Treasury bonds. Such options give buyers the right to buy bonds at a fixed price over a specific time period. And compared with buying bonds outright, these options are much more sensitive to market moves.

Because selling the calls made those dealers vulnerable to a rally, they delta-hedged by buying bonds. As bond prices turned south [and option deltas fell] the dealers shed their hedges by selling bonds, adding to the selling orgy. The plunging markets forced them to sell at lower prices than expected, causing unexpected losses on their hedges.

To be sure, traders say delta-hedging wasn't the main source of selling in the markets' fall. That dubious honor goes to the huge dumping by speculators of bond and stock holdings that were purchased with borrowed money. While experts may agree that delta-hedging doesn't actually cause crashes, in some cases it can speed the decline once prices slip.

By the same token, delta-hedging also tends to buoy prices once they turn up—which may be one reason why markets correct so suddenly these days.

21.6 EMPIRICAL EVIDENCE

There have been an enormous number of empirical tests of the Black-Scholes option-pricing model. For the most part, the results of the studies have been positive in that the Black-Scholes model generates option values fairly close to the actual prices at which options trade. At the same time, some regular empirical failures of the model have been noted. For example, the Black-Scholes model tends to undervalue deep in-the-money calls and overvalue deep out-of-the-money calls. Geske and Roll[11] have argued that these empirical

---

[11]Robert Geske and Richard Roll, "On Valuing American Call Options with the Black-Scholes European Formula," *Journal of Finance* 39 (June 1984).

results can be attributed to the failure of the Black-Scholes model to account for the possible early exercise of American calls on stocks that pay dividends. They show that the theoretical bias induced by this failure corresponds exactly to the actual "mispricing" observed empirically.

Whaley[12] examined the performance of the Black-Scholes formula relative to that of more complicated option formulas that allow for early exercise. His findings indicate that formulas allowing for the possibility of early exercise do better at pricing than the Black-Scholes formula. The Black-Scholes formula seems to perform worst for options on stocks with high dividend payouts. The true American call option formula, on the other hand, seems to fare equally well in the prediction of option prices on stocks with high or low dividend payouts.

In a recent paper, Rubinstein[13] pointed out that the performance of the Black-Scholes model has deteriorated in recent years in the sense that options on the same stock with the same strike price that *should* have the same implied volatility actually exhibit progressively different implied volatilities. He attributed this to an increasing fear of another market crash like that in 1987, and noted that, consistent with this hypothesis, out-of-the-money put options are priced higher (i.e., with higher implied volatilities) than are other puts. He suggested a method to extend the option valuation framework to allow for these issues.

SUMMARY

1. Option values may be viewed as the sum of intrinsic value plus time or "volatility" value. The volatility value is the right to choose not to exercise if the stock price moves against the holder. Thus optionholders cannot lose more than the cost of the option regardless of stock price performance.

2. Call options are more valuable when the exercise price is lower, when the stock price is higher, when the interest rate is higher, when the time to maturity is greater, when the stock's volatility is greater, and when dividends are lower.

3. Call options must sell for at least the stock price less the present value of the exercise price and dividends to be paid before maturity. This implies that a call option on a non–dividend-paying stock may be sold for more than the proceeds from immediate exercise. Thus European calls are worth as much as American calls on stocks that pay no dividends, because the right to exercise the American call early has no value.

4. Options may be priced relative to the underlying stock price using a simple two-period, two-state pricing model. As the number of periods increases, the model can approximate more realistic stock price distributions. The Black-Scholes formula may be seen as a limiting case of the binomial option model, as the holding period is divided into progressively smaller subperiods when the interest rate and stock volatility are constant.

5. The Black-Scholes formula is valid for options on stocks that pay no dividends. Dividend adjustments may be adequate to price European calls on dividend-paying stocks, but the proper treatment of American calls on dividend-paying stocks requires more complex formulas.

6. Put options may be exercised early, whether the stock pays dividends or not. Therefore, American puts generally are worth more than are European puts.

[12]Robert E. Whaley, "Valuation of American Call Options on Dividend-Paying Stocks: Empirical Tests," *Journal of Financial Economics* 10 (1982).
[13]Mark Rubinstein, "Implied Binomial Trees," *Journal of Finance* 49 (July 1994), pp. 771–818.

7. European put values can be derived from the call value and the put-call parity relationship. This technique cannot be applied to American puts for which early exercise is a possibility.

8. The hedge ratio is the number of shares of stock required to hedge the price risk involved in writing one option. Hedge ratios are near zero for deep out-of-the-money call options and approach 1.0 for deep in-the-money calls.

9. Although hedge ratios are less than 1.0, call options have elasticities greater than 1.0. The rate of return on a call (as opposed to the dollar return) responds more than one for one with stock price movements.

10. Portfolio insurance can be obtained by purchasing a protective put option on an equity position. When the appropriate put is not traded, portfolio insurance entails a dynamic hedge strategy where a fraction of the equity portfolio equal to the desired put option's delta is sold and placed in risk-free securities.

Key Terms

intrinsic value	implied volatility	delta
binomial model	pseudo-American call option	option elasticity
Black-Scholes pricing	value	portfolio insurance
formula	hedge ratio	dynamic hedging

Selected Readings

The breakthrough articles in option pricing are:
  Black, Fischer; and Myron Scholes. "The Pricing of Options and Corporate Liabilities." *Journal of Political Economy* 81 (May–June 1973), pp. 637–59.
  Merton, Robert C. "Theory of Rational Option Pricing." *Bell Journal of Economics and Management Science* 4 (Spring 1973), pp. 141–83.
The two-state approach was first suggested in:
  Sharpe, William F. *Investments.* Englewood Cliffs, NJ: Prentice Hall, 1978.
The approach was developed more fully in:
  Rendelman, Richard J., Jr.; and Brit J. Bartter. "Two-State Option Pricing." *Journal of Finance* 34 (December 1979), pp. 1093–1110.
  Cox, John C.; Stephen Ross; and Mark Rubinstein. "Option Pricing: A Simplified Approach." *Journal of Financial Economics* 7 (September 1979), pp. 229–63.
A popular textbook on option valuation models is:
  Hull, John C. *Options, Futures, and Other Derivative Securities*, 3rd ed. Englewood Cliffs, NJ: Prentice Hall, 1997.

Problems

1. We showed in the text that the value of a call option increases with the volatility of the stock. Is this also true of put option values? Use the put-call parity theorem as well as a numerical example to prove your answer.

2. In each of the following questions, you are asked to compare two options with parameters as given. The risk-free interest rate for *all* cases should be assumed to be 6%. Assume the stocks on which these options are written pay no dividends.

a.

Put	T	X	σ	Price of Option
A	.5	50	.20	$10
B	.5	50	.25	$10

Which put option is written on the stock with the lower price?
  i. A.
  ii. B.
  iii. Not enough information.

b.

Put	T	X	σ	Price of Option
A	.5	50	.2	$10
B	.5	50	.2	$12

Which put option must be written on the stock with the lower price?
  i. A.
  ii. B.
  iii. Not enough information.

c.

Call	S	X	σ	Price of Option
A	50	50	.20	$12
B	55	50	.20	$10

Which call option must have the lower time to maturity?
  i. A.
  ii. B.
  iii. Not enough information.

d.

Call	T	X	S	Price of Option
A	.5	50	55	$10
B	.5	50	55	$12

Which call option is written on the stock with higher volatility?
  i. A.
  ii. B.
  iii. Not enough information.

e.

Call	T	X	S	Price of Option
A	.5	50	55	$10
B	.5	50	55	$ 7

Which call option is written on the stock with higher volatility?
  i. A.
  ii. B.
  iii. Not enough information.

3. Reconsider the determination of the hedge ratio in the two-state model (page 662), where we showed that one-half share of stock would hedge one option. What is the hedge ratio at the following exercise prices: 115, 100, 75, 50, 25, 10? What do you

conclude about the hedge ratio as the option becomes progressively more in the money?

4. Show that Black-Scholes call option hedge ratios also increase as the stock price increases. Consider a one-year option with exercise price $50, on a stock with annual standard deviation 20%. The T-bill rate is 8% per year. Find $N(d_1)$ for stock prices $45, $50, and $55.

5. We will derive a two-state put option value in this problem. Data: $S_0 = 100$; $X = 110$; $1 + r = 1.10$. The two possibilities for S_T are 130 and 80.
   a. Show that the range of S is 50, whereas that of P is 30 across the two states. What is the hedge ratio of the put?
   b. Form a portfolio of three shares of stock and five puts. What is the (nonrandom) payoff to this portfolio? What is the present value of the portfolio?
   c. Given that the stock currently is selling at 100, solve for the value of the put.

6. Calculate the value of call option on the stock in the previous problem with an exercise price of 110. Verify that the put-call parity theorem is satisfied by your answers to problems 5 and 6. (Do not use continuous compounding to calculate the present value of X in this example because we are using a two-state model here, not a continuous-time Black-Scholes model.)

7. Use the Black-Scholes formula to find the value of a call option on the following stock:

Time to maturity:	6 months
Standard deviation:	50% per year
Exercise price:	$50
Stock price:	$50
Interest rate:	10%

8. Recalculate the value of the option in problem 7, successively substituting one of the changes below while keeping the other parameters as in problem 7:
   a. Time to maturity = 3 months.
   b. Standard deviation = 25% per year.
   c. Exercise price = $55.
   d. Stock price = $55.
   e. Interest rate = 15%.
   Consider each scenario independently. Confirm that the option value changes in accordance with the prediction of Table 21.1.

9. A call option with $X = \$50$ on a stock currently priced at $S = \$55$ is selling for $10. Using a volatility estimate of $\sigma = .30$, you find that $N(d_1) = .6$ and $N(d_2) = .5$. The risk-free interest rate is zero. Is the implied volatility based on the option price more or less than .30? Explain.

10. Would you expect a $1 increase in a call option's exercise price to lead to a decrease in the option's value of more or less than $1?

11. Is a put option on a high-beta stock worth more than one on a low-beta stock? The stocks have identical firm-specific risk.

12. All else equal, is a call option on a stock with a lot of firm-specific risk worth more than one on a stock with little firm-specific risk? The betas of the two stocks are equal.

13. All else equal, will a call option with a high exercise price have a higher or lower hedge ratio than one with a low exercise price?

14. Should the rate of return of a call option on a long-term Treasury bond be more or less sensitive to changes in interest rates than is the rate of return of the underlying bond?

15. If the stock price falls and the call price rises, then what has happened to the call option's implied volatility?

16. If the time to maturity falls and the put price rises, then what has happened to the put option's implied volatility?

17. According to the Black-Scholes formula, what will be the value of the hedge ratio of a call option as the stock price becomes infinitely large? Explain briefly.

18. According to the Black-Scholes formula, what will be the value of the hedge ratio of a put option for a very small exercise price?

19. The hedge ratio of an at-the-money call option on IBM is .4. The hedge ratio of an at-the-money put option is –.6. What is the hedge ratio of an at-the-money straddle position on IBM?

20. A collar is established by buying a share of stock for $50, buying a six-month put option with exercise price $45, and writing a six-month call option with exercise price $55. Based on the volatility of the stock, you calculate that for a strike price of $45 and maturity of six months, $N(d_1) = .60$, whereas for the exercise price of $55, $N(d_1) = .35$.
    a. What will be the gain or loss on the collar if the stock price increases by $1?
    b. What happens to the delta of the portfolio if the stock price becomes very large? Very small?

21. These three put options are all written on the same stock. One has a delta of –.9, one a delta of –.5, and one a delta of –.1. Assign deltas to the three puts by filling in this table.

Put	X	Delta
A	10	
B	20	
C	30	

22. You are *very* bullish (optimistic) on stock EFG, much more so than the rest of the market. In each question, choose the portfolio strategy that will give you the biggest dollar profit if your bullish forecast turns out to be correct. Explain your answer.
    a. *Choice A:* $10,000 invested in calls with $X = 50$.
       Choice B: $10,000 invested in EFG stock.
    b. *Choice A:* 10 call options contracts (for 100 shares each), with $X = 50$.
       Choice B: 1,000 shares of EFG stock.

23. Imagine you are a provider of portfolio insurance. You are establishing a four-year program. The portfolio you manage is currently worth $100 million, and you hope to provide a minimum return of 0%. The equity portfolio has a standard deviation of 25% per year, and T-bills pay 5% per year. Assume for simplicity that the portfolio pays no dividends (or that all dividends are reinvested).
    a. How much should be placed in bills? How much in equity?
    b. What should the manager do if the stock portfolio falls by 3% on the first day of trading?

24. You would like to be holding a protective put position on the stock of XYZ Co. to lock in a guaranteed minimum value of $100 at year-end. XYZ currently sells for $100. Over the next year the stock price will increase by 10% or decrease by 10%. The T-bill rate is 5%. Unfortunately, no put options are traded on XYZ Co.
    a. Suppose the desired put option were traded. How much would it cost to purchase?
    b. What would have been the cost of the protective put portfolio?

c. What portfolio position in stock and T-bills will ensure you a payoff equal to the payoff that would be provided by a protective put with $X = 100$? Show that the payoff to this portfolio and the cost of establishing the portfolio matches that of the desired protective put.

25. Suppose that the risk-free interest rate is zero. Would an American put option ever be exercised early? Explain.

26. Let $p(S, T, X)$ denote the value of a European put on a stock selling at S dollars, with time to maturity T, and with exercise price X, and let $P(S, T, X)$ be the value of an American put.
    a. Evaluate $p(0, T, X)$.
    b. Evaluate $P(0, T, X)$.
    c. Evaluate $p(S, T, 0)$.
    d. Evaluate $P(S, T, 0)$.
    e. What does your answer to (*b*) tell you about the possibility that American puts may be exercised early?

27. You are attempting to value a call option with an exercise price of $100 and one year to expiration. The underlying stock pays no dividends, its current price is $100, and you believe it has a 50% chance of increasing to $120 and a 50% change of decreasing to $80. The risk-free rate of interest is 10%. Calculate the call option's value using the two-state stock price model.

28. Consider an increase in the volatility of the stock in problem 27. Suppose that if the stock increases in price, it will increase to $130, and that if it falls, it will fall to $70. Show that the value of the call option is now higher than the value derived in problem 27.

29. Calculate the value of a put option with exercise price $100 using the data in problem 27. Show that put-call parity is satisfied by your solution.

30. XYZ Corp. will pay a $2 per share dividend in two months. Its stock price currently is $60 per share. A call option on XYZ has an exercise price of $55 and three-month time to maturity. The risk-free interest rate is .5% per month, and the stock's volatility (standard deviation) = 7% per month. Find the pseudo-American option value. (Hint: Try defining one "period" as a month, rather than as a year.)

31. "The beta of a call option on General Motors is greater than the beta of a share of General Motors." True or false?

32. "The beta of a call option on the S&P 500 index with an exercise price of 1,030 is greater than the beta of a call on the index with an exercise price of 1,040." True or false?

33. What will happen to the hedge ratio of a convertible bond as the stock price becomes very large?

Concept CHECKS

1. Yes. Consider the same scenarios as for the call

Stock price	$10	$20	$30	$40	$50
Put payoff	$20	$10	$ 0	$ 0	$ 0
Stock price	$20	$25	$30	$35	$40
Put payoff	$10	$ 5	$ 0	$ 0	$ 0

The low volatility scenario yields a lower expected payoff.

2.

If This Variable Increases	...	The Value of a Put Option
S		Decreases
X		Increases
σ		Increases
T		Increases
r_f		Decreases
Dividend payouts		Increases

3. The parity relationship assumes that all options are held until expiration and that there are no cash flows until expiration. These assumptions are valid only in the special case of European options on non–dividend-paying stocks. If the stock pays no dividends, the American and European calls are equally valuable, whereas the American put is worth more than the European put. Therefore, although the parity theorem for European options states that

$$P = C + S_0 - PV(X)$$

in fact, P will be *greater* than this value if the put is American.

4. Because the option now is underpriced, we want to reverse our previous strategy.

	Initial Cash Flow	Cash Flow in 1 Year for Each Possible Stock Price	
		$S = 50$	$S = 200$
Buy 2 options	−48	0	150
Short-sell 1 share	100	−50	−200
Lend $52 at 8% interest rate	52	56.16	56.16
Total	0	6.16	6.16

5. Higher. For deep out-of-the-money options, an increase in the stock price still leaves the option unlikely to be exercised. Its value increases only fractionally. For deep in-the-money options, exercise is likely, and optionholders benefit by a full dollar for each dollar increase in the stock, as though they already own the stock.

6. Because $\sigma = .6$, $\sigma^2 = .36$.

$$d_1 = \frac{\ln(100/95) + (.10 + .36/2)\,.25}{.6\sqrt{.25}} = .4043$$

$$d_2 = d_1 - .6\sqrt{.25} = .1043$$

Using Table 21.2 and interpolation,

$N(d_1) = .6570$

$N(d_2) = .5415$

$C = 100 \times .6570 - 95e^{-.10 \times .25} \times .5415$

$\quad = 15.53$

7. Implied volatility exceeds .5. Given a standard deviation of .5, the option value is $13.70. A higher volatility is needed to justify the actual $15 price.

8. A $1 increase in stock price is a percentage increase of $1/122 = .82\%$. The put option will fall by $(.4 \times \$1) = \$.40$, a percentage decrease of $\$.40/\$4 = 10\%$. Elasticity is $-10/.82 = -12.2$.

CHAPTER TWENTY-TWO

FUTURES MARKETS

Futures and forward contracts are like options in that they specify purchase or sale of some underlying security at some future date. The key difference is that the holder of an option to buy is not compelled to buy and will not do so if the trade is unprofitable. A futures or forward contract, however, carries the obligation to go through with the agreed-upon transaction. A forward contract is not an investment in the strict sense that funds are paid for an asset. It is only a commitment today to transact in the future. Forward arrangements are part of our study of investments, however, because they offer powerful means to hedge other investments and generally modify portfolio characteristics. Forward markets for future delivery of various commodities go back at least to ancient Greece. Organized *futures markets*, though, are a relatively modern development, dating only to the 19th century. Futures markets replace informal forward contracts with highly standardized, exchange-traded securities.

This chapter describes the workings of futures markets and the mechanics of trading in these markets. We show how futures contracts are useful investment vehicles for both hedgers and speculators and how the futures price relates to the spot price of an asset. Chapter 22 deals with general principles of future markets. Chapter 23 describes specific futures markets in greater detail.

22.1 THE FUTURES CONTRACT

To see how futures and forwards work and how they might be useful, consider the portfolio diversification problem facing a farmer growing a single crop, let us say wheat. The entire planting season's revenue depends critically on the highly volatile crop price. The farmer can't easily diversify his position because virtually his entire wealth is tied up in the crop.

The miller who must purchase wheat for processing faces a portfolio problem that is the mirror image of the farmer's. He is subject to profit uncertainty because of the unpredictable future cost of the wheat.

Both parties can reduce this source of risk if they enter into a **forward contract** requiring the farmer to deliver the wheat when harvested at a price agreed upon now, regardless of the market price at harvest time. No money need change hands at this time. A forward contract is simply a deferred-delivery sale of some asset with the sales price agreed on now. All that is required is that each party be willing to lock in the ultimate price to be paid or received for delivery of the commodity. A forward contract protects each party from future price fluctuations.

Futures markets formalize and standardize forward contracting. Buyers and sellers trade in a centralized futures exchange. The exchange standardizes the types of contracts that may be traded: It establishes contract size, the acceptable grade of commodity, contract delivery dates, and so forth. Although standardization eliminates much of the flexibility available in forward contracting, it has the offsetting advantage of liquidity because many traders will concentrate on the same small set of contracts. Futures contracts also differ from forward contracts in that they call for a daily settling up of any gains or losses on the contract. In the case of forward contracts, no money changes hands until the delivery date.

The centralized market, standardization of contracts, and depth of trading in each contract allows futures positions to be liquidated easily through a broker rather than personally renegotiated with the other party to the contract. Because the exchange guarantees the performance of each party to the contract, costly credit checks on other traders are not necessary. Instead, each trader simply posts a good-faith deposit, called the *margin*, in order to guarantee contract performance.

The Basics of Futures Contracts

The futures contract calls for delivery of a commodity at a specified delivery or maturity date, for an agreed-upon price, called the **futures price**, to be paid at contract maturity. The contract specifies precise requirements for the commodity. For agricultural commodities, the exchange sets allowable grades (e.g., No. 2 hard winter wheat or No. 1 soft red wheat). The place or means of delivery of the commodity is specified as well. Delivery of agricultural commodities is made by transfer of warehouse receipts issued by approved warehouses. In the case of financial futures, delivery may be made by wire transfer; in the case of index futures, delivery may be accomplished by a cash settlement procedure such as those for index options. (Although the futures contract technically calls for delivery of an asset, delivery rarely occurs. Instead, parties to the contract much more commonly close out their positions before contract maturity, taking gains or losses in cash.)

Because the futures exchange specifies all the terms of the contract, the traders need bargain only over the futures price. The trader taking the **long position** commits to purchasing the commodity on the delivery date. The trader who takes the **short position** commits to delivering the commodity at contract maturity. The trader in the long position is said to "buy" a contract; the short-side trader "sells" a contract. The words *buy* and *sell* are figurative only, because a contract is not really bought or sold like a stock or bond; it is entered into by mutual agreement. At the time the contract is entered into, no money changes hands.

Figure 22.1 shows prices for several futures contracts as they appear in *The Wall Street Journal*. The boldface heading lists in each case the commodity, the exchange where the futures contract is traded in parentheses, the contract size, and the pricing unit. The first contract listed is for corn, traded on the Chicago Board of Trade (CBT). Each contract calls for delivery of 5,000 bushels, and prices in the entry are quoted in cents per bushel.

The next several rows detail price data for contracts expiring on various dates. The March 1998 maturity corn contract, for example, opened during the day at a futures price of 270¼ cents per bushel. The highest futures price during the day was 278, the lowest was 270¼, and the settlement price (a representative trading price during the last few minutes of trading) was 273¾. The settlement price increased by 3½ cents from the previous trading day. The highest futures price over the contract's life to date was 305, the lowest 236 cents. Finally, open interest, or the number of outstanding contracts, was 159,366. Similar information is given for each maturity date.

The trader holding the long position, that is, the person who will purchase the good, profits from price increases. Suppose that when the contract matures in March, the price of corn turns out to be 278¾ cents per bushel. The long-position trader who entered the contract at the futures price of 273¾ cents earns a profit of 5 cents per bushel: The eventual price is 5 cents higher than the originally agreed-to futures price. As each contract calls for delivery of 5,000 bushels (ignoring brokerage fees), the profit to the long position equals 5,000 × $.05 = $250 per contract. Conversely, the short position loses 5 cents per bushel. The short position's loss equals the long position's gain.

To summarize, at maturity:

$$\text{Profit to long} = \text{Spot price at maturity} - \text{Original futures price}$$
$$\text{Profit to short} = \text{Original futures price} - \text{Spot price at maturity}$$

where the spot price is the actual market price of the commodity at the time of the delivery.

The futures contract is, therefore, a zero-sum game, with losses and gains to all positions netting out to zero. Every long position is offset by a short position. The aggregate profits to futures trading, summing over all investors, also must be zero, as is the net exposure to changes in the commodity price. For this reason, the establishment of a futures market in a commodity should not have a major impact on prices in the spot market for that commodity.

Concept
CHECK

Question 1 • Graph the profit realized by an investor who enters the long side of a futures contract as a function of the price of the asset on the maturity date. Compare this graph to a graph of the profits realized by the purchaser of the asset itself. Next, try the same exercise for a short futures position and a short sale of the asset.

Existing Contracts

Futures and forward contracts are traded on a wide variety of goods in four broad categories: agricultural commodities, metals and minerals (including energy commodities), foreign currencies, and financial futures (fixed-income securities and stock market indexes). The financial futures contracts are a relatively recent innovation, for which trading was introduced in 1975. Innovation in financial futures has been rapid and is ongoing. Figure 22.2 illustrates both the tremendous growth in futures trading in the last decade and the preeminent role of financial futures. Table 22.1 enumerates some of the various contracts trading in 1998.

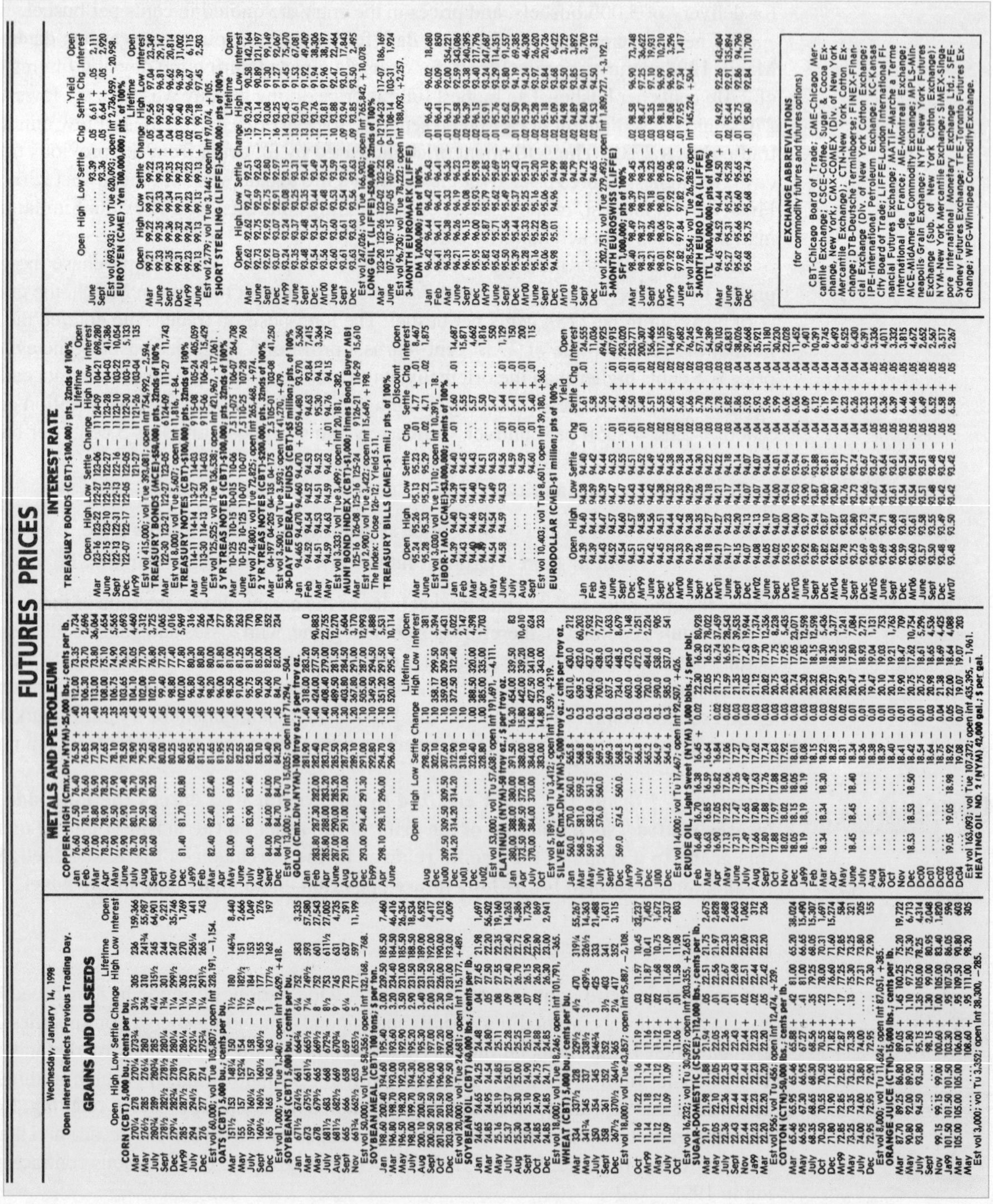

Figure 22.1   Futures listings.

OTHER FUTURES

Figure 22.2

Trading volume in futures contracts.

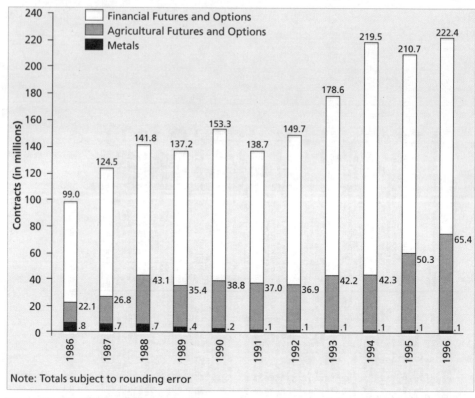

Note: Totals subject to rounding error

Source: Chicago Board of Trade *Annual Report*, 1997.

Table 22.1 Sample of Futures Contracts

Foreign Currencies	Agricultural	Metals and Energy	Interest Rate Futures	Equity Indexes
British pound	Corn	Copper	Euroyen	Dow Jones Industrials
Canadian dollar	Oats	Aluminum	Eurodollars	S&P 500
Japanese yen	Soybeans	Gold	Euromark	S&P midcap 400
Swiss franc	Soybean meal	Platinum	Eurolira	NYSE index
French franc	Soybean oil	Palladium	Euroswiss	Value Line index
Deutschemark	Wheat	Silver	Treasury bonds	Major market index
U.S. dollar index	Barley	Crude oil	Treasury bills	Nasdaq 100
Australian dollar	Flaxseed	Heating oil	Treasury notes	Russell 2000
Brazilian real	Canola	Gas oil	Municipal bond index	Nikkei 225
Mexican peso	Rye	Natural gas	LIBOR	Eurotop 100
Mark/Yen cross rate	Cattle (feeder)	Gasoline	Federal funds rate	FTSE index (London)
Sterling/Mark cross rate	Cattle (live)	Propane	Short gilt[†]	CAC-40 (French index)
Mark/Franc cross rate	Hogs	Electricity	Long gilt[†]	Australia ordinary share
	Pork bellies	CRB index*	Australian government bond	Toronto 35
	Cocoa		German government bond	DAX-30 (German index)
	Coffee		Canadian government bond	
	Cotton		Italian government bond	
	Orange juice		French government bond	
	Sugar			
	Lumber			
	Rice			

*The Commodity Research Bureau's index of futures prices of agricultural as well as metal and energy prices.

[†]Gilts are British government bonds.

Outside the futures markets, a well-developed network of banks and brokers has established a forward market in foreign exchange. This forward market is not a formal exchange in the sense that the exchange specifies the terms of the traded contract. Instead, participants in a forward contract may negotiate for delivery of any quantity of goods, whereas in the formal futures markets contract size is set by the exchange. In forward arrangements, banks and brokers simply negotiate contracts for clients (or themselves) as needed.

22.2 MECHANICS OF TRADING IN FUTURES MARKETS

The Clearinghouse and Open Interest

The mechanics of trading in futures contracts is more complex than are ordinary stock transactions. If you want to make a stock purchase, your broker simply acts as an intermediary to enable you to buy shares from or sell to another individual through the stock exchange. In futures trading, however, the clearinghouse plays a more active role.

When an investor contacts a broker to establish a futures position, the brokerage firm wires the order to the firm's trader on the floor of the futures exchange. In contrast to stock trading, which involves either specialists or market makers in each security, most futures trades in the United States occur among floor traders in the "trading pit" for each contract. Traders use voice or hand signals to signify their desire to buy or sell. Once a trader willing to accept the opposite side of a trade is located, the trade is recorded and the investor is notified.

At this point, just as is true for options contracts, the **clearinghouse** enters the picture. Rather than having the long and short traders hold contracts with each other, the clearinghouse becomes the seller of the contract for the long position and the buyer of the contract for the short position. The clearinghouse is obligated to deliver the commodity to the long position and to pay for delivery from the short; consequently, the clearinghouse's position nets to zero. This arrangement makes the clearinghouse the trading partner of each trader, both long and short. The clearinghouse, bound to perform on its side of each contract, is the only party that can be hurt by the failure of any trader to observe the obligations of the futures contract. This arrangement is necessary because a futures contract calls for future performance, which cannot be as easily guaranteed as an immediate stock transaction.

Figure 22.3 illustrates the role of the clearinghouse. Panel **A** shows what would happen in the absence of the clearinghouse. The trader in the long position would be obligated to pay the futures price to the short-position trader, and the trader in the short position would be obligated to deliver the commodity. Panel **B** shows how the clearinghouse becomes an intermediary, acting as the trading partner for each side of the contract. The clearinghouse's position is neutral, as it takes a long and a short position for each transaction.

The clearinghouse makes it possible for traders to liquidate positions easily. If you are currently long in a contract and want to undo your position, you simply instruct your broker to enter the short side of a contract to close out your position. This is called a *reversing trade*. The exchange nets out your long and short positions, reducing your net position to zero. Your zero net position with the clearinghouse eliminates the need to fulfill at maturity either the original long or reversing short position.

The **open interest** on the contract is the number of contracts outstanding. (Long and short positions are not counted separately, meaning that open interest can be defined as the number of either long or short contracts outstanding.) The clearinghouse's position nets out to zero, and so is not counted in the computation of open interest. When contracts begin trading, open interest is zero. As time passes, open interest increases as progressively more

Figure 22.3
A, Trading without a
clearinghouse.
B, Trading with a
clearinghouse.

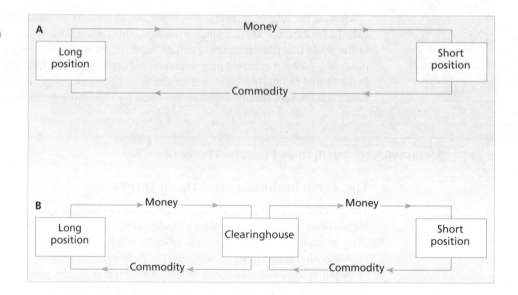

contracts are entered. Almost all traders, however, liquidate their positions before the contract maturity date.

Instead of actually taking or making delivery of the commodity, virtually all market participants enter reversing trades to cancel their original positions, thereby realizing the profits or losses on the contract. Actual deliveries and purchases of commodities are then made via regular channels of supply, usually via warehouse receipts. The fraction of contracts that result in actual delivery is estimated to range from less than 1% to 3%, depending on the commodity and the activity in the contract. The image of a trader awakening one delivery date with a mountain of wheat in the front yard is amusing, but only fanciful.

You can see the typical pattern of open interest in Figure 22.1. In the soybean or soybean meal contracts, for example, the January delivery contract is close to maturity, and open interest is relatively small; most contracts have been reversed already. The next few maturities have significant open interest. Finally, the most distant maturity contracts have little open interest, as they have been available only recently, and few participants have yet traded. For other contracts, for example, corn or wheat, for which March is the nearest maturity, open interest is typically highest in the nearest contract.

Marking to Market and the Margin Account

Anyone who saw the film *Trading Places* knows that Eddie Murphy as a trader in orange juice futures had no intention of purchasing or delivering orange juice. Traders simply bet on the futures price of juice. The total profit or loss realized by the long trader who buys a contract at time 0 and closes, or reverses, it at time t is just the change in the futures price over the period, $F_t - F_0$. Symmetrically, the short trader earns $F_0 - F_t$.

The process by which profits or losses accrue to traders is called *marking to market*. At initial execution of a trade, each trader establishes a margin account. The margin is a security account consisting of cash or near-cash securities, such as Treasury bills, that ensures the trader is able to satisfy the obligations of the futures contract. Because both parties to a futures contract are exposed to losses, both must post margin. If the initial margin on corn, for example, is 10%, then the trader must post $1,368.75 per contract of the margin account. This is 10% of the value of the contract (2.7375 per bushel × 5,000 bushels per contract).

Because the initial margin may be satisfied by posting interest-earning securities, the requirement does not impose a significant opportunity cost of funds on the trader. The initial margin is usually set between 5% and 15% of the total value of the contract. Contracts written on assets with more volatile prices require higher margins.

On any day that futures contracts trade, futures prices may rise or may fall. Instead of waiting until the maturity date for traders to realize all gains and losses, the clearinghouse requires all positions to recognize profits as they accrue daily. If the futures price of corn rises from 273¾ to 275¾ cents per bushel, the clearinghouse credits the margin account of the long position for 5,000 bushels times 2 cents per bushel, or $100 per contract. Conversely, for the short position, the clearinghouse takes this amount from the margin account for each contract held. Although the price of corn has changed by only 2/273.75 = .73%, the percentage return on the long corn position on that day is 10 times greater: $100/$1,368.75 = 7.3%. The 10-to-1 ratio of percentage changes reflects the leverage inherent in the futures position, since the corn contract was established with an initial margin of one-tenth the value of the underlying asset.

This daily settling is called **marking to market**. It means the maturity date of the contract does not govern realization of profit or loss. Marking to market ensures that, as futures prices change, the proceeds accrue to the trader's margin account immediately. We will provide a more detailed example of this process shortly.

Concept
CHECK

Question 2 • What must be the net inflow or outlay from marking to market for the clearinghouse?

If a trader accrues sustained losses from daily marking to market, the margin account may fall below a critical value called the **maintenance**, or **variation, margin**. Once the value of the account falls below this value, the trader receives a margin call. For example, if the maintenance margin on corn is 5%, then the margin call will go out when the 10% margin initially posted has fallen about in half, to $684 per contract. (This requires that the futures price fall only about 14 cents as each 1-cent drop in the futures price results in a loss of $50 to the long position.) Either new funds must be transferred into the margin account, or the broker will close out enough of the trader's position to meet the required margin for that position. This procedure safeguards the position of the clearinghouse. Positions are closed out before the margin account is exhausted—the trader's losses are covered, and the clearinghouse is not affected.

Marking to market is the major way in which futures and forward contracts differ, besides contract standardization. Futures follow this pay- (or receive-) as-you-go method. Forward contracts are simply held until maturity, and no funds are transferred until that date, although the contracts may be traded.

It is important to note that the futures price on the delivery date will equal the spot price of the commodity on that date. As a maturing contract calls for immediate delivery, the futures price on that day must equal the spot price—the cost of the commodity from the two competing sources is equalized in a competitive market.[1] You may obtain delivery of the commodity either by purchasing it directly in the spot market or by entering the long side of a futures contract.

A commodity available from two sources (spot or futures market) must be priced identically, or else investors will rush to purchase it from the cheap source in order to sell it in

---

[1]Small differences between the spot and futures price at maturity may persist because of transportation costs, but this is a minor factor.

the high-priced market. Such arbitrage activity could not persist without prices adjusting to eliminate the arbitrage opportunity. Therefore, the futures price and the spot price must converge at maturity. This is called the **convergence property**.

For an investor who establishes a long position in a contract now (time 0) and holds that position until maturity (time T), the sum of all daily settlements will equal $F_T - F_0$, where F_T stands for the futures price at contract maturity. Because of convergence, however, the futures price at maturity, F_T, equals the spot price, P_T, so total futures profits also may be expressed as $P_T - F_0$. Thus we see that profits on a futures contract held to maturity perfectly track changes in the value of the underlying asset.

A concrete example can illustrate the time profile of returns to a futures contract. Assume the current futures price for silver for delivery five days from today is $5.10 per ounce. Suppose that over the next five days, the futures price evolves as follows:

Day	Futures Price
0 (today)	$5.10
1	5.20
2	5.25
3	5.18
4	5.18
5 (delivery)	5.21

The spot price of silver on the delivery date is $5.21: The convergence property implies that the price of silver in the spot market must equal the futures price on the delivery day.

The daily mark-to-market settlements for each contract held by the long position will be as follows:

Day	Profit (Loss) per Ounce	× 5,000 Ounces/Contract = Daily Proceeds
1	5.20 − 5.10 = .10	$500
2	5.25 − 5.20 = .05	250
3	5.18 − 5.25 = −.07	−350
4	5.18 − 5.18 = 0	0
5	5.21 − 5.18 = .03	150
		Sum = $550

The profit on Day 1 is the increase in the futures price from the previous day, or ($5.20 − $5.10) per ounce. Because each silver contract on the Commodity Exchange (CMX) calls for purchase and delivery of 5,000 ounces, the total profit per contract is 5,000 times $.10, or $500. On Day 3, when the futures price falls, the long position's margin account will be debited by $350. By Day 5, the sum of all daily proceeds is $550. This is exactly equal to 5,000 times the difference between the final futures price of $5.21 and original futures price of $5.10. Thus the sum of all the daily proceeds (per ounce of silver held long) equals $P_T - F_0$.

Cash versus Actual Delivery

Most futures tickets call for delivery of an actual commodity such as a particular grade of wheat or a specified amount of foreign currency if the contract is not reversed before maturity. For agricultural commodities, where quality of the delivered good may vary, the exchange sets quality standards as part of the futures contract. In some cases, contracts may be settled with higher- or lower-grade commodities. In these cases, a premium or discount is applied to the delivered commodity to adjust for the quality difference.

Some futures contracts call for **cash delivery**. An example is a stock index futures contract where the underlying asset is an index such as the Standard & Poor's 500 or the New York Stock Exchange Index. Delivery of every stock in the index clearly would be impractical. Hence the contract calls for "delivery" of a cash amount equal to the value that the index attains on the maturity date of the contract. The sum of all the daily settlements from marking to market results in the long position realizing total profits or losses of $S_T - F_0$, where S_T is the value of the stock index on the maturity date T, and F_0 is the original futures price. Cash settlement closely mimics actual delivery, except the cash value of the asset rather than the asset itself is delivered by the short position in exchange for the futures price.

More concretely, the S&P 500 index contract calls for delivery of $250 times the value of the index. At maturity, the index might list at 950, the market-value-weighted index of the prices of all 500 stocks in the index. The cash settlement contract calls for delivery of 250×950, or $237,500 cash in return for 250 times the futures price. This yields exactly the same profit as would result from directly purchasing 250 units of the index for $237,500 and then delivering it for 250 times the original futures price.

Regulations

Futures markets are regulated by the Commodities Futures Trading Commission, a federal agency. The CFTC sets capital requirements for member firms of the futures exchanges, authorizes trading in new contracts, and oversees maintenance of daily trading records.

The futures exchange may set limits on the amount by which futures prices may change from one day to the next. For example, if the price limit on silver contracts traded on the Chicago Board of Trade is $1 and silver futures close today at $5.10 per ounce, then trades in silver tomorrow may vary only between $6.10 and $4.10 per ounce. The exchanges may increase or reduce price limits in response to perceived changes in price volatility of the contract. Price limits are often eliminated as contracts approach maturity, usually in the last month of trading.

Price limits traditionally are viewed as a means to limit violent price fluctuations. This reasoning seems dubious. Suppose an international monetary crisis overnight drives up the spot price of silver to $8.00. No one would sell silver futures at prices for future delivery as low as $5.10. Instead, the futures price would rise each day by the $1 limit, although the quoted price would represent only an unfilled bid order—no contracts would trade at the low quoted price. After several days of limit moves of $1 per day, the futures price would finally reach its equilibrium level, and trading would occur again. This process means no one could unload a position until the price reached its equilibrium level. This example shows that price limits offer no real protection against fluctuations in equilibrium prices.

Taxation

Because of the mark-to-market procedure, investors do not have control over the tax year in which they realize gains or losses. Instead, price changes are realized gradually, with each daily settlement. Therefore, taxes are paid at year-end on cumulated profits or losses regardless of whether the position has been closed out.

22.3   FUTURES MARKETS STRATEGIES

Hedging and Speculation

Hedging and speculating are two polar uses of futures markets. A speculator uses a futures contract to profit from movements in futures prices, a hedger to protect against price movement.

If speculators believe prices will increase, they will take a long position for expected profits. Conversely, they exploit expected price declines by taking a short position. As an example of a speculative strategy, let's consider the use of the T-bond futures contract, the listing for which appear in Figure 22.1. Each T-bond contract on the Chicago Board of Trade (CBT) calls for delivery of $100,000 par value of bonds. The listed futures price of 123-06 (i.e., 123%₃₂) means the market price of the underlying bonds is 123.1875% of par, or $123,187.50. Therefore, for every increase of one point in the T-bond futures price (e.g., to 124-06), the long position gains $1,000, and the short loses that amount. Therefore, if you are bullish on bond prices, you might speculate by buying T-bond futures contracts.

If the T-bond futures price increases by one point to 124-06, then you profit by your speculation by $1,000 per contract. If the forecast is incorrect, and T-bond futures prices decline, you lose $1,000 times the decrease in the futures price for each contract purchased. Speculators bet on the direction of futures price movements.

Why does a speculator buy a T-bond futures contract? Why not buy T-bonds directly? One reason lies in transaction costs, which are far smaller in futures markets.

Another reason is the leverage futures trading provides. Recall that each T-bond contract calls for delivery of $100,000 par value, worth about $123,187 in our example. The initial margin required for this account might be only $10,000. The $1,000 per contract gain translates into a $1,000/$10,000 = 10% return on the money put up, despite the fact that the T-bond futures price increases only 1/123.1875 = .8%. Futures margins, therefore, allow speculators to achieve much greater leverage than is available from direct trading in a commodity.

Hedgers by contrast use futures markets to protect themselves against price movements. An investor holding a T-bond portfolio, for example, might anticipate a period of interest rate volatility and want to protect the value of the portfolio against price fluctuations. In this case, the investor has no desire to bet on price movements in either direction. To achieve such protection, a hedger takes a short position in T-bond futures, which obligates the investor to deliver T-bonds at the contract maturity date for the current futures price. This locks in the sales price for the bonds and guarantees that the total value of the bond-plus-futures position at the maturity date is the futures price.[2]

For illustration, suppose as in Figure 22.1 that the futures price for March delivery is $123.19 per $100 par value (rounded off to the nearest penny), and that the only three possible T-bond prices in March are $122.19, $123.19, and $124.19. If investors currently hold 200 bonds, each with par value $1,000, they would take short positions in two contracts, each for $100,000 par value. Protecting the value of a portfolio with short futures positions is called *short hedging*. Taking the futures position requires no current investment. (The initial margin requirement is small relative to the size of the contract, and because it may

---

[2]To keep things simple, we will assume that the T-bond futures contract calls for delivery of a bond with the same coupon and maturity as that in the investor's portfolio. In practice, a variety of bonds may be delivered to satisfy the contract, and a "conversion factor" is used to adjust for the relative values of the eligible delivery bonds. We will ignore this complication.

be posted in interest-bearing securities, it does not represent a time-value or opportunity cost to the hedger.)

The profits in March from each of the two short futures contracts will be 1,000 times any decrease in the futures price. At maturity, the convergence property ensures that the final futures price will equal the spot price of the T-bonds. Hence the futures profit will be 2,000 times $(F_0 - P_T)$, where P_T is the price of the bonds on the delivery date, and F_0 is the original futures price, $123.19.

Now consider the hedged portfolio consisting of the bonds and the short futures positions. The portfolio value as a function of the bond price in March can be computed as follows:

	T-Bond Price in March		
	$122.19	**$123.19**	**$124.19**
Bond holdings (value = $2,000P_T$)	$244,380	$246,380	$248,380
Futures profits or losses	2,000	0	− 2,000
Total	$246,380	$246,380	$246,380

The total portfolio value is unaffected by the eventual bond price, which is what the hedger wants. The gains or losses on the bond holdings are exactly offset by those on the two contracts held short.

For example, if bond prices fall to $122.19, the losses on the bond portfolio are offset by the $2,000 gain on the futures contracts. That profit equals the difference between the futures price on the maturity date (which equals the spot price on that date of $122.19) and the originally contracted futures price of $123.19. For short contracts, a profit of $1 per $100 par value is realized from the fall in the spot price. Because two contracts call for delivery of $200,000 par value, this results in a $2,000 gain that offsets the decline in the value of the bonds held in portfolio. In contrast to a speculator, a hedger is indifferent to the ultimate price of the asset. The short hedger who has in essence arranged to sell the asset for an agreed-upon price need not be concerned about further developments in the market price.

To generalize this numerical example, you can note that the bond will be worth P_T at maturity, whereas the profit on the futures contract is $F_0 - P_T$. The sum of the two positions is F_0 dollars, which is independent of the eventual bond price.

A *long hedge* is the analogue to a short hedge for a purchaser of an asset. Consider, for example, a pension fund manager who anticipates a cash inflow in two months that will be invested in fixed-income securities. The manager views T-bonds as very attractively priced now and would like to lock in current prices and yields until the investment actually can be made two months hence. The manager can lock in the effective cost of the purchase by entering the long side of a contract, which commits her to purchasing at the current futures price.

Question 3 • **Suppose, as in our example, that T-bonds will be priced at $122.19, $123.19, or $124.19 in two months. Show that the cost in March of purchasing $200,000 par value of T-bonds net of the profit/loss on two long T-bond contracts will be $246,380 regardless of the eventual bond price.**

Exact futures hedging may be impossible for some goods because the necessary futures contract is not traded. For example, miners of bauxite, the ore from which aluminum is extracted, might like to trade in bauxite futures, but they cannot because such contracts are not listed. Because bauxite and aluminum prices are highly correlated, however, a close hedge may be established by shorting aluminum futures. Hedging a position using futures on another commodity is called *cross-hedging*.

Concept CHECK

Question 4 • What are the sources of risk to an investor who uses aluminum futures to hedge an inventory of bauxite?

Futures contracts may be used also as general portfolio hedges. Bodie and Rosansky[3] found that commodity futures returns have had a negative correlation with the stock market. Investors therefore may add a diversified portfolio of futures contracts to a diversified stock portfolio to lower the standard deviation of the overall rate of return. In their study, the correlation coefficient between the two portfolios during the estimation period (1950–1976) was –.24. This implies that long positions in commodity futures would add substantial diversification benefits to a stock portfolio.

Commodity futures are also inflation hedges. When commodity prices increase because of unanticipated inflation, returns from long futures positions will increase because the contracts call for delivery of goods for the price agreed on before the high inflation rate became a reality.

Basis Risk and Hedging

The **basis** is the difference between the futures price and the spot price.[4] As we have noted, on the maturity date of a contract, the basis must be zero: The convergence property implies that $F_T - P_T = 0$. Before maturity, however, the futures price for later delivery may differ substantially from the current spot price.

We discussed the case of a short hedger who holds an asset (T-bonds, in our example) and a short position to deliver that asset in the future. If the asset and futures contract are held until maturity, the hedger bears no risk, as the ultimate value of the portfolio on the delivery date is determined by the current futures price. Risk is eliminated because the futures price and spot price at contract maturity must be equal: Gains and losses on the futures and the commodity position will exactly cancel. If the contract and asset are to be liquidated early, before contract maturity, however, the hedger bears **basis risk**, because the futures price and spot price need not move in perfect lockstep at all times before the delivery date. In this case, gains and losses on the contract and the asset need not exactly offset each other.

Some speculators try to profit from movements in the basis. Rather than betting on the direction of the futures or spot prices per se, they bet on the changes in the difference between the two. A long spot–short futures position will profit when the basis narrows. For example, consider an investor holding 100 ounces of gold, who is short one gold-futures contract. Suppose that gold today sells for $391 an ounce, and the futures price for June delivery is $396 an ounce. Therefore, the basis is currently $5. Tomorrow, the spot price might increase to $394, while the futures price increases to $398.50, so the basis narrows to $4.50. The investor gains $3 per ounce on the gold holdings, but loses $2.50 an ounce on the short futures position. The net gain is the decrease in the basis, or $.50 an ounce.

[3]Zvi Bodie and Victor Rosansky, "Risk and Return in Commodity Futures." *Financial Analysts Journal*, May–June 1980.
[4]Usage of the word *basis* is somewhat loose. It sometimes is used to refer to the futures-spot difference $F - P$, and sometimes to the spot-futures difference $P - F$. We will consistently call the basis $F - P$.

A related strategy is a **spread** position, where the investor takes a long position in a futures contract of one maturity and a short position in a contract on the same commodity, but with a different maturity. Profits accrue if the difference in futures prices between the two contracts changes in the hoped-for direction; that is, if the futures price on the contract held long increases by more (or decreases by less) than the futures price on the contract held short.

Consider an investor who holds a September maturity contract long and a June contract short. If the September futures price increases by 5 cents while the June futures price increases by 4 cents, the net gain will be 5 cents – 4 cents, or 1 cent. Like basis strategies, spread positions aim to exploit movements in relative price structures rather than to profit from movements in the general level of prices.

22.4 THE DETERMINATION OF FUTURES PRICES

The Spot-Futures Parity Theorem

We have seen that a futures contract can be used to hedge changes in the value of the underlying asset. If the hedge is perfect, meaning that the asset-plus-futures portfolio has no risk, then the hedged position must provide a rate of return equal to the rate on other risk-free investments. Otherwise, there will be arbitrage opportunities that investors will exploit until prices are brought back into line. This insight can be used to derive the theoretical relationship between a futures price and the price of its underlying asset.

Suppose, for example, that the S&P 500 index currently is at 960 and an investor who holds $960 in a mutual fund indexed to the S&P 500 wishes to temporarily hedge her exposure to market risk. Assume that the indexed portfolio pays dividends totaling $18 over the course of the year, and for simplicity, that all dividends are paid at year-end. Finally, assume that the futures price for year-end delivery of the S&P 500 contract is $990.[5] Let's examine the end-of-year proceeds for various values of the stock index if the investor hedges her portfolio by entering the short side of the futures contract.

Value of stock portfolio	$940	$960	$ 980	$1,000	$1,020	$1,040
Payoff from short futures position (equals $F_0 - F_T = \$990 - S_T$)	50	30	10	– 10	– 30	– 50
Dividend income	18	18	18	18	18	18
Total	$1,008	$1,008	$1,008	$1,008	$1,008	$1,008

The payoff from the short futures position equals the difference between the original futures price, $990, and the year-end stock price. This is because of convergence: The futures price at contract maturity will equal the stock price at that time.

Notice that the overall position is perfectly hedged. Any increase in the value of the indexed stock portfolio is offset by an equal decrease in the payoff of the short futures position, resulting in a final value independent of the stock price. The $1,008 payoff is the sum of the current futures price, $F_0 = \$990$, and the $18 dividend. It is as though the investor

---

[5]Actually, the futures contract calls for delivery of $250 times the value of the S&P 500 index, so that each contract would be settled for $250 times the index. We will simplify by assuming that you can buy a contract for one unit rather than 250 units of the index. In practice, one contract would hedge about $250 × 960 = $240,000 worth of stock. Of course, institutional investors would consider a stock portfolio of this size to be quite small.

arranged to sell the stock at year-end for the current futures price, thereby eliminating price risk and locking in total proceeds equal to the sales price plus dividends paid before the sale.

What rate of return is earned on this riskless position? The stock investment requires an initial outlay of $960, whereas the futures position is established without an initial cash outflow. Therefore, the $960 portfolio grows to a year-end value of $1,008, providing a rate of return of 5%. More generally, a total investment of S_0, the current stock price, grows to a final value of $F_0 + D$, where D is the dividend payout on the portfolio. The rate of return is therefore

$$\text{Rate of return on perfectly hedged stock portfolio} = \frac{(F_0 + D) - S_0}{S_0}$$

This return is essentially riskless. We observe F_0 at the beginning of the period when we enter the futures contract. While dividend payouts are not perfectly riskless, they are highly predictable over short periods, especially for diversified portfolios. Any uncertainty is *extremely* small compared to the uncertainty in stock prices.

Presumably, 5% must be the rate of return available on other riskless investments. If not, then investors would face two competing risk-free strategies with different rates of return, a situation that could not last. Therefore, we conclude that

$$\frac{(F_0 + D) - S_0}{S_0} = r_f$$

Rearranging, we find that the futures price must be

$$F_0 = S_0(1 + r_f) - D = S_0(1 + r_f - d) \tag{22.1}$$

where d is the dividend yield on the stock portfolio, defined as D/S_0. This result is called the **spot-futures parity theorem**. It gives the normal or theoretically correct relationship between spot and futures prices.

Suppose that parity were violated. For example, suppose the risk-free interest rate in the economy were only 4% so that according to parity, the futures price should be $960(1.04) - 18 = \$980.40$. The actual futures price, $F_0 = \$990$, is $9.60 higher than its "appropriate" value. This implies that an investor can make arbitrage profits by shorting the relatively overpriced futures contract and buying the relatively underpriced stock portfolio using money borrowed at the 4% market interest rate. The proceeds from this strategy would be as follows:

Action	Initial Cash Flow	Cash Flow in One Year
Borrow $960, repay with interest in one year	+960	$-960(1.04) = -\$998.40$
Buy stock for $960	−960	$S_T + \$18$ dividend
Enter short futures position ($F_0 = \$990$)	0	$\$990 - S_T$
Total	0	$9.60

The net initial investment of the strategy is zero. But its cash flow in one year is positive and riskless. The payoff is $9.60 regardless of the stock price. This payoff is precisely equal to the mispricing of the futures contract relative to its parity value.

When parity is violated, the strategy to exploit the mispricing produces an arbitrage profit—a riskless profit requiring no initial net investment. If such an opportunity existed, all market participants would rush to take advantage of it. The results? The stock price would be bid up, and/or the futures price offered down until equation 22.1 is satisfied. A similar analysis applies to the possibility that F_0 is less than $980.40. In this case, you simply reverse the strategy above to earn riskless profits. We conclude, therefore, that in a well-functioning market in which arbitrage opportunities are competed away, $F_0 = S_0(1 + r_f) - D$.

Concept CHECK

Question 5 • Return to the arbitrage strategy just laid out. What would be the three steps of the strategy if F_0 were too low, say $975? Work out the cash flows of the strategy now and in one year in a table like the one in the text.

The arbitrage strategy can be represented more generally as follows:

Action	Initial Cash Flow	Cash Flow in One Year
1. Borrow S_0	S_0	$-S_0(1 + r_f)$
2. Buy stock for S_0	$-S_0$	$S_T + D$
3. Enter short futures position	0	$F_0 - S_T$
Total	0	$F_0 - S_0(1 + r_f) + D$

The initial cash flow is zero by construction: The money necessary to purchase the stock in Step 1 is borrowed in Step 2, and the futures position in Step 3, which is used to hedge the value of the stock position, does not require an initial outlay. Moreover, the total cash flow to the strategy at year-end is riskless because it involves only terms that are already known when the contract is entered. This situation could not persist, as all investors would try to cash in on the arbitrage opportunity. Ultimately prices would change until the year-end cash flow is reduced to zero, at which point F_0 would once again equal $S_0(1 + r_f) - D$.

The parity relationship also is called the **cost-of-carry relationship** because it asserts that the futures price is determined by the relative costs of buying a stock with deferred delivery in the futures market versus buying it in the spot market with immediate delivery and "carrying" it in inventory. If you buy stock now, you tie up your funds and incur a time-value-of-money cost of r_f per period. On the other hand, you receive dividend payments with a current yield of d. The net carrying cost advantage of deferring delivery of the stock is therefore $r_f - d$ per period. This advantage must be offset by a differential between the futures price and the spot price. The price differential just offsets the cost-of-carry advantage when $F_0 = S_0(1 + r_f - d)$.

The parity relationship is easily generalized to multiperiod applications. We simply recognize that the difference between the futures and spot price will be larger as the maturity of the contract is longer. This reflects the longer period to which we apply the net cost of carry. For contract maturity of T periods, the parity relationship is

$$F_0 = S_0(1 + r_f - d)^T \tag{22.2}$$

Although we have described parity in terms of stocks and stock index futures, it should be clear that the logic applies as well to any financial futures contract. For gold futures, for example, we would simply set the dividend yield to zero. For bond contracts, we would let the coupon income on the bond play the role of dividend payments. In both cases, the parity relationship would be essentially the same as equation 22.2.

The arbitrage strategy described above should convince you that these parity relationships are more than just theoretical results. Any violations of the parity relationship give rise to arbitrage opportunities that can provide large profits to traders. We will see in the next chapter that index arbitrage in the stock market is a tool to exploit violations of the parity relationship for stock index futures contracts.

Spreads

Just as we can predict the relationship between spot and futures prices, there are similar ways to determine the proper relationships among futures prices for contracts of different maturity dates. Equation 22.2 shows that the futures price is in part determined by time to maturity. If $r_f > d$, as typically is the case for stock index futures, then the futures price will be higher on longer-maturity contracts. For futures on assets like gold, which pay no "dividend yield," we call set $d = 0$ and conclude that F must increase as time to maturity increases.

To be more precise about spread pricing, call $F(T_1)$ the current futures price for delivery at date T_1, and $F(T_2)$ the futures price for delivery at T_2. Let d be the dividend yield of the stock. We know from the parity equation 22.2 that

$$F(T_1) = S_0(1 + r_f - d)^{T_1}$$
$$F(T_1) = S_0(1 + r_f - d)^{T_2}$$

As a result,

$$F(T_2)/F(T_1) = (1 + r_f - d)^{(T_2 - T_1)}$$

Therefore, the basic parity relationship for spreads is

$$F(T_2) = F(T_1)(1 + r_f - d)^{(T_2 - T_1)} \tag{22.3}$$

Note that equation 22.3 is quite similar to the spot-futures parity relationship. The major difference is in the substitution of $F(T_1)$ for the current spot price. The intuition is also similar. Delaying delivery from T_1 to T_2 provides the long position the knowledge that the stock will be purchased for $F(T_2)$ dollars at T_2 but does not require that money be tied up in the stock until T_2. The savings realized are the net cost of carry between T_1 and T_2. Delaying delivery from T_1 until T_2 frees up $F(T_1)$ dollars, which earn risk-free interest at r_f. The delayed delivery of the stock also results in the lost dividend yield between T_1 and T_2. The net cost of carry saved by delaying the delivery is thus $r_f - d$. This gives the proportional increase in the futures price that is required to compensate market participants for the delayed delivery of the stock and postponement of the payment of the futures price. If the parity condition for spreads is violated, arbitrage opportunities will arise. (Problem 19 at the end of the chapter explores this possibility.)

To see how to use equation 22.3, consider the following data for a hypothetical contract:

Contract Maturity Data	Futures Price
January 15	$105.00
March 15	$105.10

Suppose that the effective annual T-bill rate is expected to persist at 5% and that the dividend yield is 4% per year. The "correct" March futures price relative to the January price is, according to equation 22.3,

$$105(1 + .05 - .04)^{1/6} = 105.174$$

Figure 22.4

Gold futures prices, September 1997.

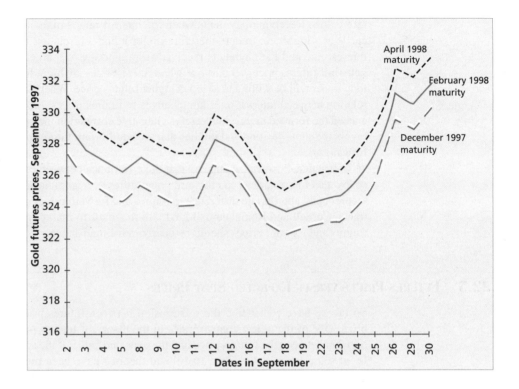

The actual March futures price is 105.10, meaning that the March futures price is slightly underpriced compared to the January futures, and that, aside from transaction costs, an arbitrage opportunity seems to be present.

Equation 22.3 shows that futures prices should all move together. Actually, it is not surprising that futures prices for different maturity dates move in unison, because all are linked to the same spot price through the parity relationship. Figure 22.4 plots futures prices on gold for three maturity dates. It is apparent that the prices move in virtual lockstep and that the more distant delivery dates require higher futures prices, as equation 22.3 predicts.

Forward versus Futures Pricing

Until now we have paid little attention to the differing time profile of returns of futures and forward contracts. Instead, we have taken the sum of daily mark-to-market proceeds to the long position as $P_T - F_0$ and assumed for convenience that the entire profit to the futures contract accrues on the delivery date. The parity theorems we have derived apply strictly to forward pricing because they are predicated on the assumption that contract proceeds are realized only on delivery. Although this treatment is appropriate for a forward contract, the actual timing of cash flows influences the determination of the futures price.

Futures prices will deviate from parity values when marking to market gives a systematic advantage to either the long or short position. If marking to market tends to favor the long position, for example, the futures price should exceed the forward price, since the long position will be willing to pay a premium for the advantage of marking to market.

When will marking to market favor either a long or short trader? A trader will benefit if daily settlements are received when the interest rate is high and are paid when the interest rate is low. Receiving payments when the interest rate is high allows investment of proceeds at a high rate; traders therefore prefer a high correlation between the level of the interest rate and the payments received from marking to market. The long position will benefit if futures prices tend to rise when interest rates are high. In such circumstances the long trader will be willing to accept a higher futures price. Whenever there is a positive correlation between interest rates and changes in futures prices, the "fair" futures price will exceed the forward price. Conversely, a negative correlation means that marking to market favors the short position and implies that the equilibrium futures price should be below the forward price.

In practice, however, it appears that the covariance between prices and interest rates is so low that futures prices and forward prices differ by negligible amounts. In estimating the theoretically appropriate difference in futures and forward prices on foreign exchange contracts, Cornell and Reinganum[6] found that the mark-to-market premium is so small that futures and forward prices should be nearly indistinguishable.

22.5 FUTURES PRICES VERSUS EXPECTED SPOT PRICES

So far we have considered the relationship between futures prices and the current spot price. One of the oldest controversies in the theory of futures pricing concerns the relationship between the futures price and the expected value of the spot price of the commodity at some *future* date. Three traditional theories have been put forth: the expectations hypothesis, normal backwardation, and contango. Today's consensus is that all of these traditional hypotheses are subsumed by the insights provided by modern portfolio theory. Figure 22.5 shows the expected path of futures under the three traditional hypotheses.

Expectations Hypothesis

The *expectations hypothesis* is the simplest theory of futures pricing. It states that the futures price equals the expected value of the future spot price of the asset: $F_0 = E(P_T)$. Under this theory the expected profit to either position of a futures contract would equal zero: The short position's expected profit is $F_0 = E(P_T)$, whereas the long's is $E(P_T) - F_0$. With $F_0 = E(P_T)$, the expected profit to either side is zero. This hypothesis relies on a notion of risk neutrality. If all market participants are risk neutral, they should agree on a futures price that provides an expected profit of zero to all parties.

The expectations hypothesis bears a resemblance to market equilibrium in a world with no uncertainty; that is, if prices of goods at all future dates are currently known, then the futures price for delivery at any particular date would equal the currently known future spot price for that date. It is a tempting but incorrect leap to assert next that under uncertainty the futures price should equal the currently expected spot price. This view ignores the risk premiums that must be built into futures prices when ultimate spot prices are uncertain.

Normal Backwardation

This theory is associated with the famous British economists John Maynard Keynes and John Hicks. They argued that for most commodities there are natural hedgers who desire

---

[6]Bradford Cornell and Marc R. Reinganum, "Forward and Futures Prices: Evidence from the Foreign Exchange Markets," *Journal of Finance* 36 (December 1981).

Figure 22.5
Futures price over time, in the special case that the expected spot price remains unchanged.

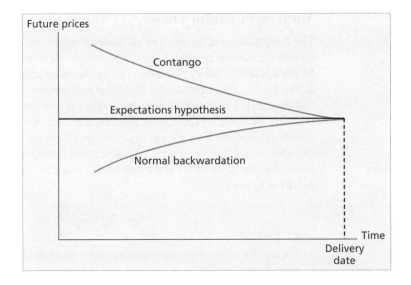

to shed risk. For example, wheat farmers will desire to shed the risk of uncertain wheat prices. These farmers will take short positions to deliver wheat in the future at a guaranteed price; they will short hedge. In order to induce speculators to take the corresponding long positions, the farmers need to offer speculators an expectation of profit. Speculators will enter the long side of the contract only if the futures price is below the expected spot price of wheat, for an expected profit of $E(P_T) - F_0$. The speculators' expected profit is the farmers' expected loss, but farmers are willing to bear the expected loss on the contract in order to shed the risk of uncertain wheat prices. The theory of *normal backwardation* thus suggests that the futures price will be bid down to a level below the expected spot price, and will rise over the life of the contract until the maturity date, at which point $F_T = P_T$.

Although this theory recognizes the important role of risk premiums in futures markets, it is based on total variability rather than on systematic risk. (This is not surprising, as Keynes wrote almost 40 years before the development of modern portfolio theory.) The modern view refines the measure of risk used to determine appropriate risk premiums.

Contango

The polar hypothesis to backwardation holds that the natural hedgers are the purchasers of a commodity, rather than the suppliers. In the case of wheat, for example, we would view grain processors as willing to pay a premium to lock in the price that they must pay for wheat. These processors hedge by taking a long position in the futures market; they are long hedgers, whereas farmers are short hedgers. Because long hedgers will agree to pay high futures prices to shed risk, and because speculators must be paid a premium to enter into the short position, the *contango* theory holds that F_0 must exceed $E(P_T)$.

It is clear that any commodity will have both natural long hedgers and short hedgers. The compromise traditional view, called the "net hedging hypothesis," is that F_0 will be less than $E(P_T)$ when short hedgers outnumber long hedgers and vice versa. The strong side of the market will be the side (short or long) that has more natural hedgers. The strong side must pay a premium to induce speculators to enter into enough contracts to balance the "natural" supply of long and short hedgers.

Modern Portfolio Theory

The three traditional hypotheses all envision a mass of speculators willing to enter either side of the futures market if they are sufficiently compensated for the risk they incur. Modern portfolio theory fine-tunes this approach by refining the notion of risk used in the determination of risk premiums. Simply put, if commodity prices pose positive systematic risk, futures prices must be lower than expected spot prices.

As an example of the use of modern portfolio theory to determine the equilibrium futures price, consider once again a stock paying no dividends. If $E(P_T)$ denotes today's expectation of the time T price of the stock, and k denotes the required rate of return on the stock, then the price of the stock today must equal the present value of its expected future payoff as follows:

$$P_0 = \frac{E(P_T)}{(1 + k)^T} \tag{22.4}$$

We also know from the spot-futures parity relationship that

$$P_0 = \frac{F_0}{(1 + r_f)^T} \tag{22.5}$$

Therefore, the right-hand sides of equations 22.4 and 22.5 must be equal. Equating these terms allows us to solve for F_0:

$$F_0 = E(P_T)\left(\frac{1 + r_f}{1 + k}\right)^T \tag{22.6}$$

You can see immediately from equation 22.6 that F_0 will be less than the expectation of P_T whenever k is greater than r_f, which will be the case for any positive-beta asset. This means that the long side of the contract will make an expected profit [F_0 will be lower than $E(P_T)$] when the commodity exhibits positive systematic risk (k is greater than r_f).

Why should this be? A long futures position will provide a profit (or loss) of $P_T - F_0$. If the ultimate realization of P_T involves positive systematic risk, the profit to the long position also involves such risk. Speculators with well-diversified portfolios will be willing to enter long futures positions only if they receive compensation for bearing that risk in the form of positive expected profits. Their expected profits will be positive only if $E(P_T)$ is greater than F_0. The converse is that the short position's profit is the negative of the long's and will have negative systematic risk. Diversified investors in the short position will be willing to suffer an expected loss in order to lower portfolio risk and will be willing to enter the contract even when F_0 is less than $E(P_T)$. Therefore, if P_T has positive beta, F_0 must be less than the expectation of P_T. The analysis is reversed for negative-beta commodities.

Concept CHECK

Question 6 . What must be true of the risk of the spot price of an asset if the futures price is an unbiased estimate of the ultimate spot price?

SUMMARY

1. Forward contracts are arrangements that call for future delivery of an asset at a currently agreed-on price. The long trader is obligated to purchase the good, and the short trader is obligated to deliver it. If the price of the asset at the maturity of the contract exceeds the forward price, the long side benefits by virtue of acquiring the good at the contract price.

2. A futures contract is similar to a forward contract, differing most importantly in the aspects of standardization and marking to market, which is the process by which gains and losses on futures contract positions are settled daily. In contrast, forward contracts call for no cash transfers until contract maturity.

3. Futures contracts are traded on organized exchanges that standardize the size of the contract, the grade of the deliverable asset, the delivery date, and the delivery location. Traders negotiate only over the contract price. This standardization creates increased liquidity in the marketplace and means that buyers and sellers can easily find many traders for a desired purchase or sale.

4. The clearinghouse acts as an intermediary between each pair of traders, acting as the short position for each long, and as the long position for each short. In this way traders need not be concerned about the performance of the trader on the opposite side of the contract. In turn, traders post margins to guarantee their own performance on the contracts.

5. The gain or loss to the long side for the futures contract held between time 0 and t is $F_t - F_0$. Because $F_T = P_T$, the long's profit if the contract is held until maturity is $P_T - F_0$, where P_T is the spot price at time T and F_0 is the original futures price. The gain or loss to the short position is $F_0 - P_T$.

6. Futures contracts may be used for hedging or speculating. Speculators use the contracts to take a stand on the ultimate price of an asset. Short hedgers take short positions in contracts to offset any gains or losses on the value of an asset already held in inventory. Long hedgers take long positions to offset gains or losses in the purchase price of a good.

7. The spot-futures parity relationship states that the equilibrium futures price on an asset providing no service or payments (such as dividends) is $F_0 = P_0(1 + r_f)^T$. If the futures price deviates from this value, then market participants can earn arbitrage profits.

8. If the asset provides services or payments with yield d, the parity relationship becomes $F_0 = P_0(1 + r_f - d)^T$. This model is also called the cost-of-carry model, because it states that futures price must exceed the spot price by the net cost of carrying the asset until maturity date T.

9. The equilibrium futures price will be less than the currently expected time T spot price if the spot price exhibits systematic risk. This provides an expected profit for the long position who bears the risk and imposes an expected loss on the short position who is willing to accept that expected loss as a means to shed risk.

Key Terms

forward contract	marking to market	basis
futures price	maintenance margin	basis risk
long position	variation margin	spread
short position	convergence property	spot-futures parity theorem
clearinghouse	cash delivery	cost-of-carry relationship
open interest		

Selected Readings

An extensive treatment of the institutional background of several futures markets is provided in:

Stoll, Hans R.; and Robert E. Whaley, *Futures and Options*. Cincinnati: Southwestern Publishing, 1993.

Excellent, although challenging, treatments of the differences between futures and forward markets and the pricing of each type of contract are in:

Jarrow, Robert; and George Oldfield. "Forward Contracts and Futures Contracts." *Journal of Financial Economics* 9 (December 1981).

Cox, John; Jonathan Ingersoll; and Stephen A. Ross. "The Relation between Forward Prices and Futures Prices." *Journal of Financial Economics* 9 (December 1981).

Black, Fischer. "The Pricing of Commodity Contracts." *Journal of Financial Economics* 3 (January–March 1976).

For a treatment of backwardation/contango debate, see:

Cootner, Paul H. "Speculation and Hedging." Food Research Institute Studies, Supplement, Stanford, CA, 1967.

Keynes, John Maynard. *Treatise on Money.* 2nd ed. London: Macmillan, 1930.

Working, Holbrook. "The Theory of Price Storage." *American Economic Review* 39 (December 1949).

Hicks, J. R. *Value and Capital.* 2nd ed. London: Oxford University Press, 1946.

The use of futures contracts in risk management is treated in:

Smith, Clifford W., Jr; Charles W. Smithson; with D. Sykes Wilford. *Managing Financial Risk.* Burr Ridge, IL: Irwin Professional Publishing, 1995.

Problems

1. *a.* Using Figure 22.1, compute the dollar value of the stocks traded on one contract on the Standard & Poor's 500 index. The closing spot price of the S&P 500 index is given in the last line of the listing. If the margin requirement is 10% of the futures price times the multiplier of $250, how much must you deposit with your broker to trade the March contract?

   b. If the March futures price were to increase to 970, what percentage return would you earn on your net investment if you entered the long side of the contract at the price shown in the figure?

   c. If the March futures price falls by 1%, what is your percentage return?

2. Why is there no futures market in cement?

3. Why might individuals purchase futures contracts rather than the underlying asset?

4. What is the difference in cash flow between short-selling an asset and entering a short futures position?

5. Are the following statements true or false? Why?

   a. All else equal, the futures price on a stock index with a high dividend yield should be higher than the futures price on an index with a low dividend yield.

   b. All else equal, the futures price on a high-beta stock would be higher than the futures price on a low-beta stock.

   c. The beta of a short position in the S&P 500 futures contract is negative.

6. *a.* A hypothetical futures contract on a non–dividend-paying stock with current price $150 has a maturity of one year. If the T-bill rate is 6%, what should the futures price be?

   b. What should the futures price be if the maturity of the contract is three years?

   c. What if the interest rate is 8% and the maturity of the contract is three years?

7. Your analysis leads you to believe the stock market is about to rise substantially. The market is unaware of this situation. What should you do?

8. How might a portfolio manager use financial futures to hedge risk in each of the following circumstances:

   a. You own a large position in a relatively illiquid bond that you want to sell.

   b. You have a large gain on one of your Treasuries and want to sell it, but you would like to defer the gain until the next tax year.

   c. You will receive your annual bonus next month that you hope to invest in long-term corporate bonds. You believe that bonds today are selling at quite attractive yields, and you are concerned that bond prices will rise over the next few weeks.

9. Suppose the value of the S&P 500 stock index is currently 950. If the one-year T-bill rate is 6% and the expected dividend yield on the S&P 500 is 2%, what should the one-year maturity futures price be?

10. Consider a stock that pays no dividends on which a futures contract, a call option, and a put option trade. The maturity date for all three contracts is T, the exercise price of the put and the call are both X, and the futures price is F. Show that if $X = F$, then the call price equals the put price. Use parity conditions to guide your demonstration.

11. It is now January. The current interest rate is 5%. The June futures price for gold is $346.30, whereas the December futures price is $360.00. Is there an arbitrage opportunity here? If so, how would you exploit it?

12. The Chicago Board of Trade has just introduced a new futures contract on Brandex stock, a company that currently pays no dividends. Each contract calls for delivery of 1,000 shares of stock in one year. The T-bill rate is 6% per year.
    a. If Brandex stock now sells at $120 per share, what should the futures price be?
    b. If the Brandex price drops by 3%, what will be the change in the futures price and the change in the investor's margin account?
    c. If the margin on the contract is $12,000, what is the percentage return on the investor's position?

13. The multiplier for a futures contract on the stock market index is $250. The maturity of the contract is one year, the current level of the index is 950, and the risk-free interest rate is .5% per month. The dividend yield on the index is .2% per month. Suppose that after one month, the stock index is at 960.
    a. Find the cash flow from the mark-to-market proceeds on the contract. Assume that the parity condition always holds exactly.
    b. Find the holding period return if the initial margin on the contract is $15,000.

14. Michelle Industries issued a Swiss franc–denominated five-year discount note for SFr200 million. The proceeds were converted to U.S. dollars to purchase capital equipment in the United States. The company wants to hedge this currency exposure and is considering the following alternatives:
    • At-the-money Swiss franc call options.
    • Swiss franc forwards.
    • Swiss franc futures.
    a. Contrast the essential characteristics of each of these three derivative instruments.
    b. Evaluate the suitability of each in relation to Michelle's hedging objective, including both advantages and disadvantages.

15. You are a corporate treasurer who will purchase $1 million of bonds for the sinking fund in three months. You believe rates will soon fall, and you would like to repurchase the company's sinking fund bonds (which currently are selling below par) in advance of requirements. Unfortunately, you must obtain approval from the board of directors for such a purchase, and this can take up to two months. What action can you take in the futures market to hedge any adverse movements in bond yields and prices until you can actually buy the bonds? Will you be long or short? Why? A qualitative answer is fine.

16. Identify the fundamental distinction between a futures contract and an option contract, and briefly explain the difference in the manner that futures and options modify portfolio risk.

17. The S&P portfolio pays a dividend yield of 2% annually. Its current value is 950. The T-bill rate is 5%. Suppose the S&P futures price for delivery in one year is 980.

Construct an arbitrage strategy to exploit the mispricing and show that your profits one year hence will equal the mispricing in the futures market.

18. *a.* How should the parity condition (equation 22.2) for stocks be modified for futures contracts on Treasury bonds? What should play the role of the dividend yield in that equation?

   b. In an environment with an upward-sloping yield curve, should T-bond futures prices on more distant contracts be higher or lower than those on near-term contracts?

   c. Confirm your intuition by examining Figure 22.1.

19. Consider this arbitrage strategy to derive the parity relationship for spreads: (1) enter a long futures position with maturity date T_1 and futures price $F(T_1)$; (2) enter a short position with maturity T_2 and futures price $F(T_2)$; (3) at T_1, when the first contract expires, buy the asset and borrow $F(T_1)$ dollars at rate r_f; (4) pay back the loan with interest at time T_2.

   a. What are the total cash flows to this strategy at times 0, T_1, and T_2?

   b. Why must profits at time T_2 be zero if no arbitrage opportunities are present?

   c. What must the relationship between $F(T_1)$ and $F(T_2)$ be for the profits at T_2 to be equal to zero? This relationship is the parity relationship for spreads.

20. What is the difference between the futures price and the value of the futures contract?

21. Evaluate the criticism that futures markets siphon off capital from more productive uses.

Concept

1.

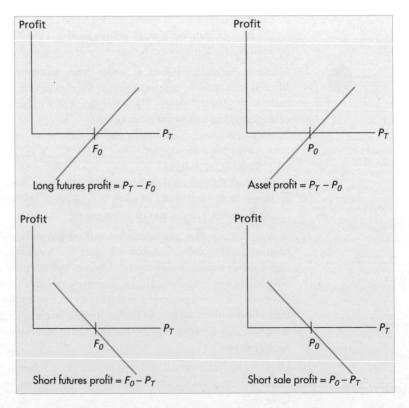

Long futures profit = $P_T - F_0$

Asset profit = $P_T - P_0$

Short futures profit = $F_0 - P_T$

Short sale profit = $P_0 - P_T$

2. The clearinghouse has a zero net position in all contracts. Its long and short positions are offsetting, so that net cash flow from marking to market must be zero.

3.

	T-Bond Price in March		
	$122.19	**$123.19**	**$124.19**
Cash flow to purchase bonds ($= -2{,}000\ P_T$)	−$244,380	−$246,380	−$248,380
Profits on long futures position	−2,000	0	2,000
Total cash flow	−$246,380	−$246,380	−$246,380

4. The risk would be that aluminum and bauxite prices do not move perfectly together. Thus basis risk involving the spread between the futures price and bauxite spot prices could persist even if the aluminum futures price were set perfectly relative to aluminum itself.

5.

Action	Initial Cash Flow	Cash Flow in One Year
Lend S_0	−960	$960(1.04) = 998.40$
Short stock	+960	$-S_T - 18$
Long futures	0	$S_T - 975$
Total	0	$5.40 risklessly

6. It must have zero beta. If the futures price is an unbiased estimator, then we infer that it has a zero risk premium, which means that beta must be zero.

FUTURES AND SWAPS: A CLOSER LOOK

The previous chapter provided a basic introduction to the operation of futures markets and the principles of futures pricing. This chapter explores selected futures markets in more depth. Most of the growth has been in financial futures, which now dominate trading, so we emphasize these contracts. We begin by discussing stock-index futures, where we focus on program trading and index arbitrage. That is followed by a treatment of foreign exchange futures. Next, we move on to the most actively traded markets, those for interest rate futures. Finally, we turn to the swap markets in foreign exchange and fixed-income securities. We will see that swaps can be interpreted as portfolios of forward contracts and valued accordingly.

23.1   STOCK-INDEX FUTURES

The Contracts

In contrast to most futures contracts, which call for delivery of a specified commodity, stock-index contracts are settled by a cash amount equal to the value of the stock index in question on the contract maturity date times a multiplier that scales the size of the contract. The total profit to the long position is $S_T - F_0$, where S_T is the value of the stock index on the maturity date. Cash settlement avoids the costs that would be incurred if the short trader had to purchase the stocks in the index and deliver them to the long position, and if the long position then had to sell the stocks for cash. Instead, the long trader's profit is $S_T - F_0$ dollars, and the short trader's is $F_0 - S_T$ dollars. These profits duplicate those that would arise with actual delivery.

There are several stock-index futures contracts currently traded. Table 23.1 lists some of the major ones, showing under contract size the multiplier used to calculate contract settlements. An S&P 500 contract, for example, with a futures price of 950 and a final index value of 955 would result in a profit for the long side of $\$250 \times (955 - 950) = \$1,250$. The S&P contract by far dominates the market in stock index futures.

The broad-based stock market indexes are all highly correlated. Table 23.2 presents a correlation matrix for four U.S. indexes. The only index whose correlation with the others is below .90 is the Value Line Index. This index uses an equally weighted geometric average of 1,700 firms, as opposed to the NYSE or S&P indexes, which use market weights. (See Chapter 2, Section 2.4, for a review of geometric averages.) This means that the Value

Table 23.1   Major Stock-Index Futures

Contract	Underlying Market Index	Contract Size	Exchange
S&P 500	Standard & Poor's 500 index. A value-weighted arithmetic average of 500 stocks.	$250 times the S&P 500 index	Chicago Mercantile Exchange
Dow Jones Industrial Average (DJIA)	Dow Jones Industrial Average. Price-weighted average of 30 firms.	$10 times the index	Chicago Board of Trade
NYSE	NYSE Composite Index. Value-weighted arithmetic average of all stocks listed on the NYSE.	$500 times the NYSE index	New York Futures Exchange
Russell 2000	Index of 2,000 smaller firms.	$500 times index	Chicago Mercantile Exchange
S&P Mid-Cap	Index of 400 firms of midrange market value.	$500 times the index	Chicago Mercantile Exchange
Nasdaq 100	Value-weighted arithmetic average of 100 of the largest over-the-counter stocks.	$100 times the index	Chicago Mercantile Exchange
Nikkei	Nikkei 225 stock average.	$5 times the Nikkei Index	Chicago Mercantile Exchange
FT-SE 100	Financial Times–Share Exchange Index of 100 U.K. firms.	£10 times the FT-SE Index	London International Financial Futures Exchange
DAX-30	Index of 30 German stocks.	100 deutschemarks times the index	DTB (Deutsche Terminboerse)
CAC-40	Index of 40 French stocks.	200 French francs times the index	MATIF (Marché à Terme International de France)

Table 23.2   Correlations among Major U.S. Stock Market Indexes

Index	DJIA	S&P 500	Value Line	NYSE
DJIA	1.0000	0.9774	0.8880	0.9750
S&P 500		1.0000	0.9137	0.9972
Value Line			1.0000	0.9337
NYSE				1.0000

Note: Correlations were computed from weekly percentage rates of price appreciation during calendar year 1989.

Source: Hans R. Stoll and Robert E. Whaley, *Futures and Options: Theory and Applications* (Cincinnati: South-Western Publishing, 1993).

Line contract overweights small firms compared to the other indexes, which may explain the lower observed correlation.

Creating Synthetic Stock Positions: An Asset Allocation Tool

One reason stock-index futures are so popular is that they substitute for holdings in the underlying stocks themselves. Index futures let investors participate in broad market movements without actually buying or selling large numbers of stocks.

Because of this, we say futures represent "synthetic" holdings of the market portfolio. Instead of holding the market directly, the investor takes a long futures position in the index. Such a strategy is attractive because the transaction costs involved in establishing and liquidating futures positions are much lower than taking actual spot positions. Investors who wish to frequently buy and sell market positions find it much less costly to play the futures market rather than the underlying spot market. "Market timers," who speculate on broad market moves rather than on individual securities, are large players in stock-index futures for this reason.

One means to market time, for example, is to shift between Treasury bills and broad-based stock market holdings. Timers attempt to shift from bills into the market before market upturns, and to shift back into bills to avoid market downturns, thereby profiting from broad market movements. Market timing of this sort, however, can result in huge brokerage fees with the frequent purchase and sale of many stocks. An attractive alternative is to invest in Treasury bills and hold varying amounts of market-index futures contracts.

The strategy works like this. When timers are bullish, they will establish many long futures positions that they can liquidate quickly and cheaply when expectations turn bearish. Rather than shifting back and forth between T-bills and stocks, they buy and hold T-bills and adjust only the futures position. This minimizes transaction costs. An advantage of this technique for timing is that investors can implicitly buy or sell the market index in its entirety, whereas market timing in the spot market would require the simultaneous purchase or sale of all the stocks in the index. This is technically difficult to coordinate and can lead to slippage in execution of a timing strategy.

You can construct a T-bill plus index futures position that duplicates the payoff to holding the stock index itself. Here is how:

1. Hold as many market-index futures contracts long as you need to purchase your desired stock position. A desired holding of $1,000 multiplied by the S&P 500 index, for example, would require the purchase of four contracts because each contract calls for delivery of $250 multiplied by the index.

2. Invest enough money in T-bills to cover the payment of the futures price at the contract's maturity date. The necessary investment will equal the present value of the futures price that will be paid to satisfy the contracts. The T-bill holdings will grow by the maturity date to a level equal to the futures price.

For example, suppose that an institutional investor wants to invest $45 million in the market for one month and, to minimize trading costs, chooses to buy the S&P 500 futures contracts as a substitute for actual stock holdings. If the index is now at 900, the one-month delivery futures price is 909, and the T-bill rate is 1% per month, it would buy 200 contracts. (Each contract controls $250 × 900 = $225,000 worth of stock, and $45 million/$225,000 = 200.) The institution thus has a long position on 50,000 times the S&P 500 index (200 contracts times the contract multiplier of 250). To cover payment of the futures price, it must invest 50,000 times the present value of the futures price in T-bills. This equals 50,000 × (909/1.01) = $45 million market value of bills. Notice that the $45 million outlay in bills is precisely equal to the amount that would have been needed to buy the stock directly. (The face value of the bills will be 50,000 × 909 = $45.45 million.)

This is an artificial, or synthetic, stock position. What is the value of this portfolio at the maturity date? Call S_T the value of the stock index on the maturity date T, and as usual, let F_0 be the original futures price:

	In General (Per Unit of the Index)	Our Numbers
1. Profits from contract	$S_T - F_0$	$50,000(S_T - 909)$
2. Value of T-bills	F_0	$45,450,000$
Total	S_T	$50,000 S_T$

The total payoff on the contract maturity date is exactly proportional to the value of the stock index. In other words, adopting this portfolio strategy is equivalent to holding the stock index itself, aside from the issue of interim dividend distributions and tax treatment.

This bills-plus-futures contracts strategy may be viewed as a 100% stock strategy. At the other extreme, investing in zero futures results in a 100% bills position. Moreover, a short futures position will result in a portfolio equivalent to that obtained by short selling the stock market index, because in both cases the investor gains from decreases in the stock price. Bills-plus-futures mixtures clearly allow for a flexible and low-transaction-cost approach to market timing. The futures positions may be established or reversed quickly and cheaply. Also, since the short futures position allows the investor to earn interest on T-bills, it is superior to a conventional short sale of the stock, where the investor may earn little or no interest on the proceeds of the short sale.

The nearby box illustrates that it is now commonplace for money managers to use futures contracts to create synthetic equity positions in stock markets. The article notes that futures positions can be particularly helpful in establishing synthetic positions in foreign equities, where trading costs tend to be greater and markets tend to be less liquid.

Concept CHECK   **Question 1 • As the payoffs of the synthetic and actual stock positions are identical, so should be their costs. What does this say about the spot-futures parity relationship?**

Empirical Evidence on Pricing of Stock-Index Futures

Recall the spot-futures parity relationship between the futures and spot stock price:

$$F_0 = S_0(1 + r_f - d)^T \tag{23.1}$$

Several investigators have tested this relationship empirically. The general procedure has been to calculate the theoretically appropriate futures price using the current value of the stock index and equation 23.1. The dividend yield of the index in question is approximated

GOT A BUNDLE TO INVEST FAST? THINK STOCK-INDEX FUTURES

As investors go increasingly global and market turbulence grows, stock-index futures are emerging as the favorite way for nimble money managers to deploy their funds.

Indeed, research from Goldman, Sachs & Co. shows that, in most major markets, trading in stock futures now exceeds the buying and selling of actual shares. In the U.S., for instance, average daily trading volume of futures based on the Standard & Poor's 500 stock-index was a whopping $16.8 billion in 1994. By contrast, New York Stock Exchange trading averaged only $10.56 billion a day.

What's the big appeal? Speed, ease and cheapness. For most major markets, stock futures not only boast greater liquidity but also lower transaction costs than traditional trading methods.

Portfolio managers stress that in today's fast-moving markets, it's critical to implement decisions quickly. For giant mutual and pension funds eager to keep assets fully invested, shifting billions around through stock-index futures is much easier than trying to identify individual stocks to buy and sell.

"When I decide it's time to move into France, Germany or Britain, I don't necessarily want to wait around until I find exactly the right stocks," says Fabrizio Pierallini, manager of New York–based Vontobel Ltd.'s Euro Pacific Fund.

Mr. Pierallini, who has $120 million invested in stocks in Europe, Asia and Latin America, says he later fine-tunes his market picks by gradually shifting out of futures into favorite stocks. To the extent Mr. Pierallini's stocks outperform the market, futures provide a means to preserve those gains, even while hedging against market declines.

For instance, by selling futures equal to the value of the underlying portfolio, a manager can almost completely insulate a portfolio from market moves. Say a manager succeeds in outperforming the market, but still loses 3% while the

market as a whole falls 10%. Hedging with futures would capture that margin of outperformance, transforming the loss into a profit of roughly 7%. Demand for such protection helped account for stock futures' surging popularity in last year's difficult markets, Goldman said in its report.

"You can get all the value your managers are going to add" relative to the market, "and you don't need to worry about the costs of trading" actual securities, said David Leinweber, director of research at First Quadrant Corp., a Pasadena, Calif., investment firm that traded some $59 billion of futures in 1994.

Among First Quadrant's futures-intensive strategies is "global tactical asset allocation," which involves trading whole markets worldwide as traditional managers might trade stocks. The growing popularity of such asset-allocation strategies has given futures a big boost in recent years.

To capitalize on global market swings, "futures do the job for us better than stocks, and they're cheaper," said Jarrod Wilcox, director of global investments at PanAgora Asset Management, a Boston-based asset allocator. Even when PanAgora does take positions in individual stocks, it often employs futures to modify its position, such as by hedging part of its exposure to that particular stock market.

When it comes to investing overseas, Mr. Wilcox noted, futures are often the only vehicle that makes sense from a cost standpoint. Abroad, transaction taxes and sky-high commissions can wipe out more than 1% of the money deployed on each trade. By contrast, a comparable trade in futures costs as little as 0.05%.

"Futures allow us to convert [even] modest opportunities into profits for our clients," Mr. Wilcox said. If trading actual stocks "costs 1% in fees to get in and another 1% to get out, it's too costly to do."

Source: Suzanne McGee, *The Wall Street Journal*, February 21, 1995. Reprinted by permission of *The Wall Street Journal*, © 1995 Dow Jones & Company, Inc. All Rights Reserved Worldwide.

using historical data. Although dividends of individual securities may fluctuate unpredictably, the annualized dividend yield of a broad-based index such as the S&P 500 is fairly stable, recently in the neighborhood of 2% per year. The yield is seasonal with regular and predictable peaks and troughs, however, so the dividend yield for the relevant months must be the one used. Figure 23.1 illustrates the dividend yield of the S&P 500 index from 1994 to 1996. Notice that some months, such as January or April, have consistently low yields. Others, such as May or August, have consistently high yields.

If the actual futures price deviates from the value dictated by the parity relationship, then (aside from transaction costs), an arbitrage opportunity arises. Given an estimate of transaction costs, we can bracket the theoretically correct futures price within a band. If the actual futures price lies within that band, the discrepancy between the actual and the proper futures price is too small to exploit because of the transaction costs; if the actual price lies outside the no-arbitrage band, profit opportunities are worth exploiting.

Figure 23.1
Monthly dividend
yield of the S&P 500.

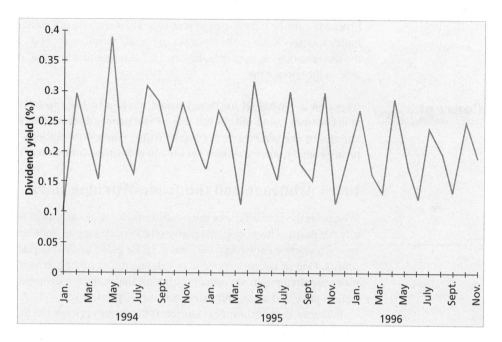

Figure 23.2
Prices of S&P 500
contract maturing June
1982. Data plotted for
April 21–June 16,
1982.

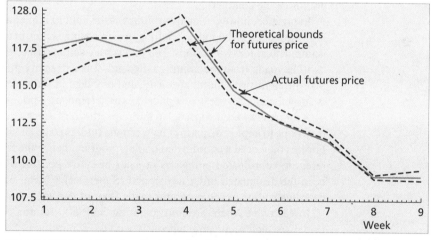

Source: David Modest and Mahadevan Sundaresan, "The Relationship between Spot and Futures Prices in Stock Index Futures Markets: Some Preliminary Evidence," *Journal of Futures Markets* 3 (Spring 1983). © John Wiley & Sons, Inc., 1983.

Modest and Sundaresan[1] constructed such a test. Figure 23.2 replicates an example of their results. The figure shows that the futures prices generally did lie in the theoretically determined no-arbitrage band, but that profit opportunities occasionally were possible for low-cost transactors.

Modest and Sundaresan pointed out that much of the cost of short selling shares is attributable to the investor's inability to invest the entire proceeds from the short sale.

---

[1]David Modest and Mahadevan Sundaresan, "The Relationship between Spot and Futures Prices in Stock Index Futures Markets: Some Preliminary Evidence," *Journal of Futures Markets* 3 (Spring 1983).

Proceeds must be left on margin account, where they do not earn interest. Arbitrage opportunities, or the width of the no-arbitrage band, therefore depend on assumptions regarding the use of short-sale proceeds. Figure 23.2 assumes that one-half of the proceeds are available to the short seller.

Concept CHECK

Question 2 • **What (if anything) would happen to the top of the no-arbitrage band if short sellers could obtain full use of the proceeds from the short sale? What would happen to the low end of the band? (Hint: When do violations of parity call for a long futures–short stock position versus short futures–long stock?)**

Index Arbitrage and the Triple-Witching Hour

Whenever the actual futures price falls outside the no-arbitrage band, there is an opportunity for profit. This is why the parity relationships are so important. Far from being theoretical academic constructs, they are in fact a guide to trading rules that can generate large profits. One of the most notable developments in trading activity his been the advent of **index arbitrage**, an investment strategy that exploits divergences between the actual futures price and its theoretically correct parity value.

In theory, index arbitrage is simple. If the futures price is too high, short the futures contract and buy the stocks in the index. If it is too low, go long in futures and short the stocks. You can perfectly hedge your position and should earn arbitrage profits equal to the mispricing of the contract.

In practice, however, index arbitrage is difficult to implement. The problem lies in buying "the stocks in the index." Selling or purchasing shares in all 500 stocks in the S&P 500 is impractical for two reasons. The first is transaction costs, which may outweigh any profits to be made from the arbitrage. Second, it is extremely difficult to buy or sell stock of 500 different firms simultaneously, and any lags in the execution of such a strategy can destroy the effectiveness of a plan to exploit temporary price discrepancies.

Arbitrageurs need to trade an entire portfolio of stocks quickly and simultaneously if they hope to exploit disparities between the futures price and its corresponding stock index. For this they need a coordinated trading program; hence the term **program trading**, which refers to coordinated purchases or sales of entire portfolios of stocks. The response has been the designated order turnaround (SuperDot) system, which enables traders to send coordinated buy or sell programs to the floor of the stock exchange via computer.

In each year, there are four maturing S&P 500 futures contracts. Each of these four Fridays, which occur simultaneously with the expiration of S&P index options and options on some individual stocks, is called a **triple-witching hour** because of the volatility believed to be associated with the expirations in the three types of contracts.

Expiration-day volatility can be explained by program trading to exploit arbitrage opportunities. Suppose that some time before a stock-index future contract matures, the futures price is a little above its parity value. Arbitrageurs will attempt to lock in superior profits by buying the stocks in the index (the program trading buy order) and taking an offsetting short futures position. If and when the pricing disparity reverses, the position can be unwound at a profit. Alternatively, arbitrageurs can wait until contract maturity day and realize a profit by simultaneously closing out the offsetting stock and futures positions. By waiting until contract maturity, arbitrageurs can be assured that the futures price and stock-index price will be aligned—they rely on the convergence property.

Obviously, when many program traders follow such a strategy at contract expiration, a wave of program selling passes over the market. The result? Prices go down. This is the *expiration-day effect.* If execution of the arbitrage strategy calls for an initial sale (or short sale) of stocks, unwinding on expiration day requires repurchase of the stocks, with the opposite effect: Prices will increase.

The success of these arbitrage positions and associated program trades depends on only two things: the relative levels of spot and futures prices and synchronized trading in the two markets. Because arbitrageurs exploit disparities in futures and spot prices, absolute price levels are unimportant. This means that large buy or sell programs can hit the floor even if stock prices are at "fair" levels, that is, at levels consistent with fundamental information. The markets in individual stocks may not be sufficiently deep to absorb the arbitrage-based program trades without significant price movements despite the fact that those trades are not informationally motivated.

In an investigation of expiration-day effects on stock prices Stoll and Whaley[2] found that the market is in fact somewhat more volatile at contract expirations. For example, in their study, the standard deviation of the last-hour return on the S&P 500 index is .641% on expirations of the S&P 500 futures contract, compared to only .211% on nonexpiration days. Interestingly, the last-hour volatility of non–S&P 500 stocks appears unaffected by expiration days, consistent with the hypothesis that the effect is related to program trading of the stocks in the index.

If these price swings are based only on temporary market pressure coming from simultaneous program trades, we should expect price declines or advances to reverse after the trades are executed, when profit seekers attempt to buy or sell stocks that are subsequently mispriced according to fundamental information. For this reason, reversals might be the best measure of the price impact of expiration-day trading. To the extent that Monday returns tend to be positive following negative Friday returns, or negative following positive Friday returns, we have evidence that prices were pushed beyond their equilibrium or intrinsic values by program traders, and returned to their equilibrium values on the next trading day. In fact, Stoll and Whaley found some tendency for large price swings to be reversed on the day following the expiration activity.

In an attempt to mitigate expiration-day effects, expiring futures contracts on the S&P 500, S&P 100, and NYSE indexes now cease trading on Thursday afternoon rather than Friday. The contracts are marked to market for the last time on Friday using the stock index value at market *opening*. Because the final futures price is based on market opening prices, arbitrageurs must use market-on-open orders (instead of market-on-close orders) to ensure convergence and lock in a profit from earlier futures mispricing.

The purported advantage of the morning settlement is that supply-demand imbalances can be more easily rectified when they occur before market opening. Arbitrageurs must submit their market-on-open unwinding orders before 9 A.M. on the expiration day, while the market is closed. When buy-sell imbalances emerge, other participants will be aware of them, and can take the opposite side of the trade for only slight price concessions if they are convinced the imbalance is due only to index arbitrage and not to changes in intrinsic values.

Stoll and Whaley[3] later updated their original study to measure expiration-day effects before and after the change in the contract settlement procedures. Before settlement procedures changed in June 1987, average reversals of price movements at market close on expiration days were greater than either typical reversals at market open or reversals

---

[2]Hans R. Stoll and Robert E. Whaley, "Program Trading and Expiration-Day Effect," *Financial Analysts Journal*, March–April 1987.
[3]Hans R. Stoll and Robert E. Whaley, "Expiration-Day Effects: What Has Changed?" *Financial Analysts Journal*, January–February 1991.

Figure 23.3
Program trading
activity.

PROGRAM TRADING

NEW YORK—Program trading in the week ended Jan. 9, accounted for 16.2%, or an average 107.7 million daily shares, of New York Stock Exchange volume.

Brokerage firms executed an additional 31.6 million daily shares of program trading away from the Big Board, mostly on foreign markets. Program trading is the simultaneous purchase or sale of at least 15 different stocks with a total value of $1 million or more.

Of the program total on the Big Board, 16.6% involved stock index arbitrage, up from 12% the prior week. In this strategy, traders dart between stocks and stock-index options and futures to capture fleeting price differences.

NYSE PROGRAM TRADING
Volume (in millions of shares) for the week ending
January 9, 1998

Top 15 Firms	Index Arbitrage	Derivative-Related*	Other Strategies	Total
BNP Securities	....	....	114.8	114.8
Goldman Sachs	0.1	....	45.6	45.7
Morgan Stanley	7.7	....	36.9	44.6
First Boston	6.1	....	33.5	39.6
Salomon Smith Barney	0.4	0.6	33.0	34.0
Susquehanna Bkrg Srvs	13.3	....	19.0	32.3
NatWest	10.0	2.1	19.8	31.9
W&D Securities	....	....	26.0	26.0
Nomura Securities	7.1	....	13.8	20.9
BT Alex Brown	....	....	20.6	20.6
Interactive Brokers	....	....	18.3	18.3
Merrill Lynch	7.6	2.0	8.0	17.6
Lehman Brothers	2.0	0.2	11.5	13.7
Lawrence Helfant	....	....	11.0	11.0
RBC Dominion	9.2	....	0.6	9.8
OVERALL TOTAL	**89.5**	**5.4**	**443.8**	**538.7**

*Other derivative-related strategies besides index arbitrage
Source: New York Stock Exchange

experienced on nonexpiration days. After June 1987, reversals at closing have been smaller than their pre-June levels. However, reversals at market opening are now larger, signifying that the expiration-day price pressure simply shifted to the earlier settlement time.

Stoll and Whaley noted, however, that any expiration-day effects detected in their sample are quite mild. A reversal of .3%, a typical value in their study, corresponds to a price movement of only 12 cents on a $40 stock, less than the bid–asked spread. They concluded that expiration-day effects are small, and that the market seems to handle expirations of index futures contracts reasonably well. Index arbitrage probably does not have a major impact on stock prices, and any impact it does have appears to be extremely short-lived.

The program trading activity associated with index arbitrage commonly accounts for more than 10% of NYSE daily volume. *The Wall Street Journal* regularly reports on program trading, both in aggregate and for the largest traders, Figure 23.3 is a reproduction of one such report.

23.2   FOREIGN EXCHANGE FUTURES

The Markets

Exchange rates between currencies vary continually and often substantially. This variability can be a source of concern for anyone involved in international business. A U.S. exporter who sells goods in England, for example, will be paid in British pounds, and the dollar value of those pounds depends on the exchange rate at the time payment is made. Until that date, the U.S. exporter is exposed to foreign exchange rate risk. This risk can be hedged through currency futures or forward markets. For example, if you know you will

Figure 23.4

Spot and forward prices in foreign exchange.

CURRENCY TRADING

Monday, January 19, 1998

EXCHANGE RATES

The New York foreign exchange selling rates below apply to trading among banks in amounts of $1 million and more, as quoted at 3 p.m. Eastern time by Dow Jones and other sources. Retail transactions provide fewer units of foreign currency per dollar.

Country	U.S. $ equiv. Mon	Fri	Currency per U.S. $ Mon	Fri
Argentina (Peso)	1.0010	1.0001	.9990	.9999
Australia (Dollar)	.6682	.6661	1.4966	1.5013
Austria (Schilling)	.07740	.07792	12.920	12.833
Bahrain (Dinar)	2.6525	2.6525	.3770	.3770
Belgium (Franc)	.02639	.02647	37.895	37.775
Brazil (Real)	.8935	.8929	1.1192	1.1199
Britain (Pound)	1.6365	1.6342	.6111	.6119
1-month forward	1.6339	1.6317	.6120	.6129
3-months forward	1.6290	1.6267	.6139	.6147
6-months forward	1.6213	1.6190	.6168	.6177
Canada (Dollar)	.6955	.6969	1.4379	1.4349
1-month forward	.6961	.6976	1.4365	1.4335
3-months forward	.6971	.6986	1.4345	1.4314
6-months forward	.6982	.6999	1.4322	1.4288
Chile (Peso)	.002186	.002186	457.50	457.50
China (Renminbi)	.1204	.1204	8.3089	8.3089
Colombia (Peso)	.0007563	.0007580	1322.16	1319.21
Czech. Rep. (Koruna)	....	....	....	....
Commercial rate	.02810	.02824	35.585	35.408
Denmark (Krone)	.1430	.1432	6.9915	6.9815
Ecuador (Sucre)	....	....	....	....
Floating rate	.0002223	.0002223	4498.00	4498.00
Finland (Markka)	.1801	.1807	5.5515	5.5330
France (Franc)	.1627	.1629	6.1480	6.1405
1-month forward	.1630	.1631	6.1364	6.1297
3-months forward	.1635	.1637	6.1175	6.1101
6-months forward	.1642	.1644	6.0894	6.0821
Germany (Mark)	.5447	.5456	1.8360	1.8330
1-month forward	.5457	.5465	1.8326	1.8297
3-months forward	.5474	.5483	1.8267	1.8238
6-months forward	.5500	.5509	1.8183	1.8153
Greece (Drachma)	.003462	.003463	288.83	288.75
Hong Kong (Dollar)	.1293	.1291	7.7355	7.7480
Hungary (Forint)	.004799	.004828	208.38	207.14
India (Rupee)	.02562	.02513	39.025	39.800
Indonesia (Rupiah)	.0001044	.0001183	9575.00	8450.00
Ireland (Punt)	1.3774	1.3795	.7260	.7249
Israel (Shekel)	.2777	.2765	3.6010	3.6167
Italy (Lira)	.0005537	.0005543	1806.00	1804.00
Japan (Yen)	.007764	.007737	128.80	129.25
1-month forward	.007800	.007771	128.20	128.68
3-months forward	.007864	.007837	127.16	127.60
6-months forward	.007965	.007937	125.56	125.98
Jordan (Dinar)	1.4134	1.4134	.7075	.7075
Kuwait (Dinar)	3.2680	3.2701	.3060	.3058
Lebanon (Pound)	.0006553	.0006553	1526.00	1526.00
Malaysia (Ringgit)	.2407	.2395	4.1553	4.1750
Malta (Lira)	2.5157	2.5094	.3975	.3985
Mexico (Peso)	....	....	....	....
Floating rate	.1222	.1220	8.1850	8.1950
Netherland (Guilder)	.4833	.4841	2.0689	2.0655
New Zealand (Dollar)	.5900	.5890	1.6949	1.6978
Norway (Krone)	.1322	.1323	7.5616	7.5598
Pakistan (Rupee)	.02296	.02296	43.560	43.560
Peru (new Sol)	.3668	.3668	2.7263	2.7263
Philippines (Peso)	.02432	.02417	41.125	41.380
Poland (Zloty)	.2822	.2821	3.5433	3.5450
Portugal (Escudo)	.005327	.005337	187.74	187.38
Russia (Ruble) (a)	.1667	.1667	5.9975	5.9975
Saudi Arabia (Riyal)	.2666	.2666	3.7508	3.7513
Singapore (Dollar)	.5724	.5770	1.7470	1.7330
Slovak Rep. (Koruna)	.02818	.02838	35.485	35.240
South Africa (Rand)	.2009	.2013	4.9780	4.9675
South Korea (Won)	.0006303	.0006180	1586.50	1618.00
Spain (Peseta)	.006429	.006438	155.55	155.32
Sweden (Krona)	.1242	.1244	8.0488	8.0357
Switzerland (Franc)	.6681	.6680	1.4967	1.4970
1-month forward	.6707	.6704	1.4909	1.4916
3-months forward	.6751	.6749	1.4813	1.4817
6-months forward	.6815	.6815	1.4668	1.4673
Taiwan (Dollar)	.02977	.02959	33.586	33.792
Thailand (Baht)	.01903	.01932	52.550	51.750
Turkey (Lira)	.00000465	.00000469	215105.00	213185.00
United Arab (Dirham)	.2723	.2723	3.6730	3.6725
Uruguay (New Peso)	....	....	....	....
Financial	.1002	.1002	9.9800	9.9800
Venezuela (Bolivar)	.001967	.001968	508.43	508.07
SDR	1.3416	1.3416	.7454	.7454
ECU	1.0775	1.0791	....	....

Special Drawing Rights (SDR) are based on exchange rates for the U.S., German, British, French, and Japanese currencies. Source: International Monetary Fund.

European Currency Unit (ECU) is based on a basket of community currencies.

a-fixing, Moscow Interbank Currency Exchange. Ruble newly-denominated Jan. 1998.

The Wall Street Journal daily foreign exchange data for 1996 and 1997 may be purchased through the Readers' Reference Service (413) 592-3600.

Source: *The Wall Street Journal*, January 20, 1998. Reprinted by permission of *The Wall Street Journal*, © 1998 Dow Jones & Company, Inc. All Rights Reserved Worldwide.

receive £100,000 in 90 days, you can sell those pounds forward today in the forward market and lock in an exchange rate equal to today's forward price.

The forward market in foreign exchange is fairly informal. It is simply a network of banks and brokers that allows customers to enter forward contracts to purchase or sell currency in the future at a currently agreed-upon rate of exchange. The bank market in currencies is among the largest in the world, and most large traders with sufficient creditworthiness execute their trades here rather than in futures markets. Unlike those in futures markets, contracts in forward markets are not standardized in a formal market setting. Instead, each is negotiated separately. Moreover, there is no marking to market, as would occur in futures markets. Currency forward contracts call for execution only at the maturity date.

For currency *futures*, however, there are formal markets established by the Chicago Mercantile Exchange (International Monetary Market), the London International Financial Futures Exchange, and the MidAmerica Commodity Exchange. Here, contracts are standardized by size, and daily marking to market is observed. Moreover, there are standard clearing arrangements that allow traders to enter or reverse positions easily.

Figure 23.4 reproduces *The Wall Street Journal* listing of foreign exchange spot and forward rates. The listing gives the number of U.S. dollars required to purchase some unit of

Figure 23.5

Foreign exchange futures.

CURRENCY								
	Open	High	Low	Settle	Change	Lifetime High	Low	Open Interest
JAPAN YEN (CME)-12.5 million yen; $ per yen (.00)								
Mar	.7625	.7656	.7577	.7597	− .0038	.9375	.7512	91,239
June	.7715	.7715	.7676	.5769	− .0040	.9090	.7637	2,170
Sept	....	....	....	.7787	− .0042	.8695	.7735	326
Est vol 17,263; vol Fr 27,465; open int 93,739, −2,010.								
DEUTSCHEMARK (CME)-125,000 marks; $ per mark								
Mar	.5497	.5542	.5487	.5514	+ .0007	.6160	.5383	106,287
June	.5553	.5563	.5533	.5539	+ .0007	.5995	.5490	3,321
Sept	....	....	....	.5561	+ .0007	.5944	.5560	1,633
Est vol 13,712; vol Fr 20,663; open int 111,244, −1,358.								
CANADIAN DOLLAR (CME)-100,000 dlrs.; $ per Can $								
Mar	.7003	.7004	.6980	.6985	− .0021	.7670	.6954	55,153
June	.7013	.7015	.8995	.7000	− .0021	.7470	.6966	4,222
Sept	.7025	.7025	.7005	.7011	− .0021	.7463	.6978	1,034
Dec	.7025	.7025	.7020	.7022	− .0021	.7400	.6990	687
Mr99	....	....	....	.7032	− .0021	.7247	.6986	181
Est vol 7,869; vol Fr 12,501; open int 61,277, −609.								
BRITISH POUND (CME)-62,500 pds.; $ per pound								
Mar	1.6070	1.6186	1.6064	1.6168	+ .0100	1.7020	1.5680	33,588
June	1.6040	1.6100	1.6030	1.6094	+ .0100	1.6940	1.5610	1,333
Est vol 6,318; vol Fr 6,651; open int 34,936, −821.								
SWISS FRANC (CME)-125,000 francs; $ per franc								
Mar	.6807	.6862	.6800	.6825	+ .0004	.7450	.6754	57,766
June	.6920	.6922	.6885	.6891	+ .0003	.7304	.6750	997
Sept	....	....	....	.6956	+ .0002	.7310	.6965	1,102
Est vol 10,220; vol Fr 8,923; open int 59,870, +71.								
AUSTRALIAN DOLLAR (CME)-100,000 dlrs.; $ per A.$								
Mar	.6440	.6450	.6398	.6434	− .0009	.7590	.6328	18,853
Est vol 538; vol Fr 1,867; open int 18,894, +545.								
MEXICAN PESO (CME)-500,000 new Mex. peso, $ per MP								
Mar	.11550	.11850	.11200	.11732	− 00092	.12340	.09700	15,857
June	.10850	.11430	.10700	.11322	− 00107	.11985	09200	3,838
Sept	.10730	.11090	.10500	.10970	− 00850	.11680	.08000	5,198
Dec	.10250	.10790	.10200	.10632	− 00122	.11440	.08000	1,302
Est vol 8,562; vol Fr 8,398; open int 26,190, +672.								

foreign currency and then the amount of foreign currency needed to purchase $1. Figure 23.5 reproduces futures listings, which show the number of dollars needed to purchase a given unit of foreign currency. In Figure 23.4, both spot and forward exchange rates are listed for various delivery dates.

The forward quotations always apply to rolling delivery in 30, 90, or 180 days. Thus tomorrow's forward listings will apply to a maturity date one day later than today's listing. In contrast, the futures contracts mature at specified dates in March, June, September, and December; these four maturity days are the only dates each year when futures contracts settle.

Interest Rate Parity

As is true of stocks and stock futures, there is a spot-futures exchange rate relationship that will prevail in well-functioning markets. Should this so-called interest rate parity relationship be violated, arbitrageurs will be able to make risk-free profits in foreign exchange markets with zero net investment. Their actions will force futures and spot exchange rate back into alignment.

We can illustrate the **interest rate parity theorem** by using two currencies, the U.S. dollar and the British (U.K.) pound. Call E_0 the current exchange rate between the two currencies, that is, E_0 dollars are required to purchase one pound. F_0, the forward price, is the number of dollars that is agreed to today for purchase of one pound at time T in the future. Call the risk-free rates in the United States and United Kingdom r_{US} and r_{UK}, respectively.

The interest rate parity theorem then states that the proper relationship between E_0 and F_0 is given as

$$F_0 = E_0 \left(\frac{1 + r_{US}}{1 + r_{UK}} \right)^T \tag{23.2}$$

For example, if $r_{US} = .05$ and $r_{UK} = .06$ annually, while $E_0 = \$1.60$ per pound, then the proper futures price for a one-year contract would be

$$\$1.60 \left(\frac{1.05}{1.06} \right) = \$1.585 \text{ per pound}$$

Consider the intuition behind this result. If r_{US} is less than r_{UK}, money invested in the United States will grow at a slower rate than money invested in the United Kingdom. If this is so, why wouldn't all investors decide to invest their money in the United Kingdom? One important reason why not is that the dollar may be appreciating relative to the pound. Although dollar investments in the United States grow slower than pound investments in the United Kingdom, each dollar is worth progressively more pounds as time passes. Such an effect will exactly offset the advantage of the higher U.K. interest rate.

To complete the argument, we need only determine how an appreciating dollar will show up in equation 23.2. If the dollar is appreciating, meaning that progressively fewer dollars are required to purchase each pound, then the forward exchange rate F_0 (which equals the dollars required to purchase one pound for delivery in one year) must be less than E_0, the current exchange rate. This is exactly what equation 23.2 tells us: When r_{US} is less than r_{UK}, F_0 must be less than E_0. The appreciation of the dollar embodied in the ratio of F_0 to E_0 exactly compensates for the difference in interest rates available in the two countries. Of course, the argument also works in reverse: If r_{US} is greater than r_{UK}, then F_0 is greater than E_0.

What if the interest rate parity relationship is violated? For example, suppose the futures price is \$1.57 instead of \$1.585. You could adopt the following strategy to reap arbitrage profits. In this example let E_1 denote the exchange rate that will prevail in one year. E_1 is, of course, a random variable from the perspective of today's investors.

Action	Initial Cash Flow ($)	CF in 1 Year ($)
1. Borrow 1 U.K. pound in London. Convert to dollars.	1.60	$-E_1(1.06)$
2. Lend \$1.60 in the United States.	-1.60	$1.60(1.05)$
3. Enter a contract to purchase 1.06 pounds at a (futures) price of $F_0 = \$1.57$	0	$1.06(E_1 - 1.57)$
Total	0	\$.0158

In Step 1, you exchange the one pound borrowed in the United Kingdom for \$1.60 at the current exchange rate. After one year you must repay the pound borrowed with interest. Because the loan is made in the United Kingdom at the U.K. interest rate, you would repay 1.06 pounds, which would be worth $E_1(1.06)$ dollars. The U.S. loan in Step 2 is made at the U.S. interest rate of 5%. The futures position in Step 3 results in receipt of 1.06 pounds, for which you would first pay F_0 dollars each, and then convert into dollars at exchange rate E_1.

Note that the exchange rate risk here is exactly offset between the pound obligation in Step 1 and the futures position in Step 3. The profit from the strategy is therefore risk-free and requires no net investment.

To generalize this strategy:

Action	Initial CF ($)	CF in 1 Year ($)
1. Borrow 1 U.K. pound in London. Convert to dollars.	E_0	$-\$E_1(1 + r_{UK})$
2. Use proceeds of borrowing in London to lend in the U.S.	$-\$E_0$	$\$E_0(1 + r_{US})$
3. Enter $(1 + r_{UK})$ futures positions to purchase 1 pound for F_0 dollars.	0	$(1 + r_{UK})(E_1 - F_0)$
Total	0	$E_0(1 + r_{US}) - F_0(1 + r_{UK})$

Let us again review the stages of the arbitrage operation. The first step requires borrowing one pound in the United Kingdom. With a current exchange rate of E_0, the one pound is converted into E_0 dollars, which is a cash inflow. In one year the British loan must be paid off with interest, requiring a payment in pounds of $(1 + r_{UK})$, or in dollars of $E_1(1 + r_{UK})$. In the second step the proceeds of the British loan are invested in the United States. This involves an initial cash outflow of $\$E_0$, and a cash inflow of $\$E_0(1 + r_{US})$ in one year. Finally, the exchange risk involved in the British borrowing is hedged in Step 3. Here, the $(1 + r_{UK})$ pounds that will need to be delivered to satisfy the British loan are purchased ahead in the futures contract.

The net proceeds to the arbitrage portfolio are risk-free and given by $E_0(1 + r_{US}) - F_0(1 + r_{UK})$. If this value is positive, borrow in the United Kingdom, lend in the United States, and enter a long futures position to eliminate foreign exchange risk. If the value is negative, borrow in the United States, lend in the United Kingdom, and take a short position in pound futures. When prices are aligned properly to preclude arbitrage opportunities, the expression must equal zero. If it were positive, investors would pursue the arbitrage portfolio. If it were negative, they would pursue the reverse positions.

Rearranging this expression gives us the relationship

$$F_0 = \frac{1 + r_{US}}{1 + r_{UK}} E_0 \tag{23.3}$$

which is the interest rate parity theorem for a one-year horizon, known also as the **covered interest arbitrage relationship**.

Concept CHECK

Question 3 • What are the arbitrage strategy and associated profits if the initial futures price is $F_0 = \$1.62$/pound?

Ample empirical evidence bears out this relationship. For example, on January 12, 1998, the interest rate on U.S. money market securities with maturity of three months was 5.38%, whereas the comparable rate in the United Kingdom was 7.44%. The spot exchange rate was $\$1.6215/£$. Using these values, we find that interest rate parity implies that the forward exchange rate for delivery in one-half year should have been $1.6215 \times (1.0538/1.0744)^{1/4} = \$1.6137/£$. The actual forward rate was $\$1.6143/£$, which was so close to the parity value that transaction costs would have prevented arbitrageurs from profiting from the discrepancy.

23.3   INTEREST RATE FUTURES

The late 1970s and 1980s saw a dramatic increase in the volatility of interest rates, leading to investor desire to hedge returns on fixed-income securities against changes in interest rates. As one example, thrift institutions that had loaned money on home mortgages before

1975 suffered substantial capital losses on those loans when interest rates later increased. An interest rate futures contract could have protected banks against such large swings in yields. The significance of these losses has spurred trading in interest rate futures.

The major contracts on U.S. interest rates are on Treasury bills, Treasury notes, Treasury bonds, and a municipal bond index. The range of these securities provides an opportunity to hedge against a wide spectrum of maturities from very short (T-bills) to long term (T-bonds). In addition, futures contracts trade on Eurodollar rates and interest rates in Germany, Japan, Switzerland, Italy, Canada, France, and the United Kingdom. Figure 22.1 from Chapter 22 includes listings of some of these contracts.

The Treasury contracts call for delivery of a Treasury bond, bill, or note. Should interest rates rise, the market value of the security at delivery will be less than the original futures price, and the deliverer will profit. Hence the short position in the interest rate futures contract gains when interest rates rise.

Similarly, Treasury bond futures can be useful hedging vehicles for bond dealers or underwriters. We saw earlier, for example, how the T-bond contract could be used by an investor to hedge the value of a T-bond portfolio or by a pension fund manager who anticipates the purchase of a Treasury bond. The contract on the municipal bond index allows for more direct hedging of long-term bonds other than Treasury issues.

An episode that occurred in October 1979 illustrates the potential hedging value offered by T-bond contracts. Salomon Brothers, Merrill Lynch, and other underwriters brought out a $1 billion issue of IBM bonds. As is typical, the underwriting syndicate quoted an interest rate at which it guaranteed the bonds could be sold. (In essence, the syndicate buys the company's bonds at an agreed-upon price and then takes the responsibility of reselling them in the open market. If interest rates increase before the bonds can be sold to the public, the syndicate, not the issuer, bears the capital loss from the fall in the value of the bonds.)

In this case, the syndicate led by Salomon Brothers and Merrill Lynch brought out the IBM debt to sell at yields of 9.62% for $500 million of 7-year notes and 9.41% for $500 million of 25-year bonds. These yields were only about four basis points above comparable maturity U.S. government bond yields, reflecting IBM's excellent credit rating. The debt issue was brought to market on Thursday, October 4, when the underwriters began placing the bonds with customers. Interest rates, however, rose slightly that Thursday, making the IBM yields less attractive, and only about 70% of the issue had been placed by Friday afternoon, leaving the syndicate still holding between $250 million and $300 million of bonds.

Then on Saturday, October 6, the Federal Reserve Board announced a major credit-tightening policy. Interest rates jumped by almost a full percentage point. The underwriting syndicate realized the balance of the IBM bonds could not be placed to its regular customers at the original offering price and decided to sell them in the open bond market. By that time, the bonds had fallen nearly 5% in value, so that the underwriters' loss was about $12 million on the unsold bonds. The net loss on the underwriting operation came to about $7 million, after the profit of $5 million that had been realized on the bonds that were placed.

As the major underwriter with the lion's share of the bonds, Salomon lost about $3.5 million on the bond issue. Yet, although most of the other underwriters were vulnerable to the interest rate movement, Salomon had hedged its bond holdings by shorting about $100 million in GNMA and Treasury bond futures. Holding a short position, Salomon Brothers realized profits on the contracts when interest rates increased. The profits on the short futures position resulted because the value of the bonds required to be delivered to satisfy the contracts decreased when interest rates rose. Salomon Brothers probably about broke even on the entire transaction, making estimated gains on the futures position of about $3.5 million, which largely offset the capital loss on the bonds it was holding.

How could Salomon Brothers have constructed the proper hedge ratio, that is, the proper number of futures contracts per bond held in its inventory? The T-bond futures contract nominally calls for delivery of an 8% coupon, 20-year maturity government bond in return for the futures price. (In practice, other bonds may be substituted for this standard bond to settle the contract, but we will use the 8% bond for illustration.) Suppose the market interest rate is 10% and Salomon is holding $100 million worth of bonds, with a coupon rate of 10% and 20 years to maturity. The bonds currently sell at 100% of par value. If the interest rate were to jump to 11%, the bonds would fall in value to a market value of $91.98 per $100 of par value, a loss of $8.02 million. (We use semiannual compounding in this calculation.)

To hedge this risk, Salomon would need to short enough futures so that the profits on the futures position would offset the loss on the bonds. The 8%, 20-year bond of the futures contract would sell for $82.84 at an interest rate of 10%. If the interest rate were to jump to 11%, the bond price would fall to $75.93, and the fall in the price of the 8% bond, $6.91, would approximately equal the profit on the short futures position per $100 par value.[4] Because each contract calls for delivery of $100,000 par value of bonds, the gain on each short position would equal $6,910. Thus, to offset the $8.02 million loss on the value of the bonds, Salomon theoretically would need to hold $8.02 million/$6,910 = 1,161 contracts short. The total gain on the contracts would offset the loss on the bonds and leave Salomon unaffected by interest rate swings.

The actual hedging problem is more difficult for several reasons: (1) Salomon probably would hold more than one issue of bonds in its inventory; (2) interest rates on government and corporate bonds will not be equal and need not move in lockstep; (3) the T-bond contract may be settled with any of several bonds instead of the 8% benchmark bond; and (4) taxes could complicate the picture. Nevertheless, the principles illustrated here underlie all hedging activity.

23.4 COMMODITY FUTURES PRICING

Commodity futures prices are governed by the same general considerations as stock futures. One difference, however, is that the cost of carrying commodities, especially those subject to spoilage, is greater than the cost of carrying financial assets. Moreover, spot prices for some commodities demonstrate marked seasonal patterns that can affect futures pricing.

Pricing with Storage Costs

The cost of carrying commodities includes, in addition to interest costs, storage costs, insurance costs, and an allowance for spoilage of goods in storage. To price commodity futures, let us reconsider the earlier arbitrage strategy that calls for holding both the asset and a short position in the futures contract on the asset. In this case we will denote the price of the commodity at time T as P_T, and assume for simplicity that all non–interest carrying costs (C) are paid in one lump sum at time T, the contract maturity. Carrying costs appear in the final cash flow.

---

[4]We say approximately because the exact figure depends on the time to maturity of the contract. We assume here that the maturity date is less than a month away so that the futures price and the bond price move in virtual lockstep.

Action	Initial Cash Flow	CF at Time T
Buy asset; pay carrying costs at T	$-P_0$	$P_T - C$
Borrow P_0; repay with interest at time T	P_0	$-P_0(1 + r_f)$
Short futures position	0	$F_0 - P_T$
Total	0	$F_0 - P_0(1 + r_f) - C$

Because market prices should not allow for arbitrage opportunities, the terminal cash flow of this zero net investment, risk-free strategy should be zero.

If the cash flow were positive, this strategy would yield guaranteed profits for no investment. If the cash flow were negative, the reverse of this strategy also would yield profits. In practice, the reverse strategy would involve a short sale of the commodity. This is unusual but may be done as long as the short sale contract appropriately accounts for storage costs.[5] Thus, we conclude that

$$F_0 = P_0(1 + r_f) + C$$

Finally, if we define $c = C/P_0$, and interpret c as the percentage "rate" of carrying costs, we may write

$$F_0 = P_0(1 + r_f + c) \tag{23.4}$$

which is a (one-year) parity relationship for futures involving storage costs. Compare equation 23.4 to the first parity relation for stocks, equation 23.1, and you will see that they are extremely similar. In fact, if we think of carrying costs as a "negative dividend," the equations are identical. This treatment makes intuitive sense because, instead of receiving a dividend yield of d, the storer of the commodity must pay a storage cost of c. Obviously, this parity relationship is simply an extension of those we have seen already.

Actually, although we have called c the carrying cost of the commodity, we may interpret it more generally as the *net* carrying cost, that is, the carrying cost net of the benefits derived from holding the commodity in inventory. For example, part of the "convenience yield" of goods held in inventory is the protection against stocking out, which may result in lost production or sales.

It is vital to note that we derive equation 23.4 assuming that the asset will be bought and stored; it therefore applies only to goods that currently *are* being stored. Two kinds of commodities cannot be expected to be stored. The first is highly perishable goods, such as fresh strawberries, for which storage is technologically not feasible. The second includes goods that are not stored for economic reasons. For example, it would be foolish to buy wheat now, planning to store it for ultimate use in three years. Instead, it is clearly preferable to delay the purchase of the wheat until after the harvest of the third year. The wheat is then obtained without incurring the storage costs. Moreover, if the wheat harvest in the third year is comparable to this year's, you could obtain it at roughly the same price as you would pay this year. By waiting to purchase, you avoid both interest and storage costs.

In fact, it is generally not reasonable to hold large quantities of agricultural goods across a harvesting period. Why pay to store this year's wheat, when you can purchase next year's wheat when it is harvested? Maintaining large wheat inventories across harvests makes

[5]Robert A. Jarrow and George S. Oldfield, "Forward Contracts and Futures Contracts," *Journal of Financial Economics* 9 (1981).

Figure 23.6

Futures prices for corn and gold.

```
                  GRAINS AND OILSEEDS
                                        Lifetime     Open
             Open High Low Settle Change High Low Interest
   CORN (CBT) 5,000 bu.; cents per bu.
   Mar  259½ 260¾ 257   258¼  – 1½  305   236  164,223
   May  265  266¾ 263   264¼  – 2   310   241¾  55,260
   July 269¾ 271¼ 267¼  268¾  – 1½  315½  245   63,622
   Sept 268½ 270  268   268½  – 2   301   244    9,064
   Dec  272¾ 273¾ 271   272   – 1¾  299½  247   35,516
   Mr99 271½ 278¾ 277½  278   – 1¾  305   277½   1,643
   July 283¾ 285  283¾  285   – 2   312   256¼    449
   Dec  268  269½ 268   268   – 2   291½  265     714
      Est vol 45,000; vol Fri 39,956; open int 330,502, +5.

   GOLD (Cmx.Div.NYM)-100 troy oz.; $ per troy oz.
   Jan   ....  ....      278.30  – .20 318.00 283.20      0
   Feb  279.10 280.40 278.30 278.90 – .20 424.00 278.00 103,789
   Apr  280.60 281.90 280.00 280.40 – .30 408.40 280.00  16,782
   June 282.00 283.50 282.00 282.10 – .40 489.50 282.00  12,360
   Aug  284.50 284.50 284.50 283.90 – .50 403.80 284.50   5,520
   Oct   ....  ....      285.60  – .60 367.80 291.00   3,085
   Dec  288.30 289.20 287.20 287.30 – .80 505.00 287.20  13,129
   Fb99  ....  ....      289.10  – .90 349.50 294.50   4,456
   Apr  291.50 291.50 291.50 291.00 – .90 351.20 291.50   5,529
   June  ....  ....      292.90  – .90 520.00 295.40  10,109
   Dec  299.50 300.00 299.50 298.40 – .90 506.00 299.50   5,486
```

Source: *The Wall Street Journal*, January 13, 1998. Reprinted by permission of *The Wall Street Journal*, © 1998 Dow Jones & Company, Inc. All Rights Reserved Worldwide.

sense only if such a small wheat crop is forecast that wheat prices will not fall when the new supply is harvested.

Concept CHECK

Question 4 • **People are willing to buy and "store" shares of stock despite the fact that their purchase ties up capital. Most people, however, are not willing to buy and store wheat. What is the difference in the properties of the expected evolution of stock prices versus wheat prices that accounts for this result?**

Because storage across harvests is costly, equation 23.4 should not be expected to apply for holding periods that span harvest times, nor should it apply to perishable goods that are available only "in season." You can see that this is so if you look at the futures markets page of the newspaper. Figure 23.6, for example, gives futures prices for several times to maturity for corn and for gold. Whereas the futures price for gold, which is a stored commodity, increases steadily with the maturity of the contract, the futures price for corn is seasonal; it rises within a harvest period as equation 23.4 would predict, but the price then falls across harvests as new supplies become available. Compare, for example, the corn futures price for delivery in July 1998 versus December 1999.

Futures pricing across seasons requires a different approach that is not based on storage across harvest periods. In place of general no-arbitrage restrictions we rely instead on risk premium theory and discounted cash flow (DCF) analysis.

Discounted Cash Flow Analysis for Commodity Futures

We have said that most agricultural commodities follow seasonal price patterns; prices rise before a harvest and then fall at the harvest when the new crop becomes available for consumption. Figure 23.7 graphs this pattern. The price of the commodity following the harvest must rise at the rate of the total cost of carry (interest plus noninterest carrying costs) to induce holders of the commodity to store it willingly for future sale instead of selling it immediately. Inventories will be run down to near zero just before the next harvest.

Clearly, this pattern differs sharply from financial assets such as stocks or gold, for which there is no seasonal price movement. For financial assets, the current price is set in

Figure 23.7

Typical commodity price pattern over the season. Prices adjusted for inflation.

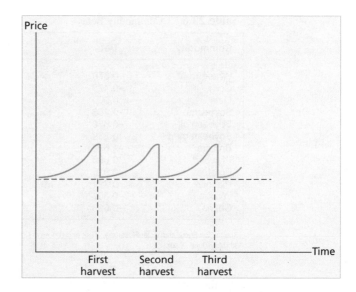

market equilibrium at a level that promises an expected rate of capital gains plus dividends equal to the required rate of return on the asset. Financial assets are stored only if their economic rate of return compensates for the cost of carry. In other words, financial assets are priced so that storing them produces a fair return. Agricultural prices, by contrast, are subject to steep periodic drops as each crop is harvested, which makes storage across harvests consequently unprofitable.

Of course, neither the exact size of the harvest nor the demand for the good is known in advance, so the spot price of the commodity cannot be perfectly predicted. As weather forecasts change, for example, the expected size of the crop and the expected future spot price of the commodity are updated continually.

Given the current expectation of the spot price of the commodity at some future date and a measure of the risk characteristics of that price, we can measure the present value of a claim to receive the commodity at that future date. We simply calculate the appropriate risk premium from a model such as the CAPM or APT and discount the expected spot price at the appropriate risk-adjusted interest rate.

Table 23.3, which presents betas on a variety of commodities, shows that the beta of orange juice, for example, was estimated to be .117 over the period. If the T-bill rate is currently 5.5% and the historical market risk premium has been about 8.5%, the appropriate discount rate for orange juice would be given by the CAPM as

$$5.5\% + .117(8.5\%) = 6.49\%$$

If the expected spot price for orange juice six months from now is $1.45 per pound, the present value of a six-month deferred claim to a pound of orange juice is simply

$$\$1.45/(1.0649)^{1/2} = \$1.405$$

What would the proper futures price for orange juice be? The contract calls for the ultimate exchange of orange juice for the futures price. We have just shown that the present value of the juice is $1.405. This should equal the present value of the futures price that will be paid for the juice. A commitment to a payment of F_0 dollars in six months has a present value of $F_0/(1.055)^{1/2} = .974 \times F_0$. (Note that the discount rate is the risk-free rate of 5.5%, because the promised payment is fixed and therefore independent of market conditions.)

Table 23.3   Commodity Betas

Commodity	Beta	Commodity	Beta
Wheat	−0.370	Orange juice	0.117
Corn	−0.429	Propane	−3.851
Oats	0.000	Cocoa	−0.291
Soybeans	−0.266	Silver	−0.272
Soybean oil	−0.650	Copper	0.005
Soybean meal	0.239	Cattle	0.365
Broilers	−1.692	Hogs	−0.148
Plywood	0.660	Pork bellies	−0.062
Potatoes	−0.610	Egg	−0.293
Platinum	0.221	Lumber	−0.131
Wool	0.307	Sugar	−2.403
Cotton	−0.015		

Source: Zvi Bodie and Victor Rosansky, "Risk and Return in Commodity Futures," *Financial Analysts Journal* 36 (May–June 1980).

To equate the present values of the promised payment of F_0 and the promised receipt of orange juice, we would set

$$.974F_0 = \$1.405$$

or $F_0 = \$1.443$.

The general rule, then, to determine the appropriate futures price is to equate the present value of the future payment of F_0 and the present value of the commodity to be received. This gives us

$$\frac{F_0}{(1 + r_f)^T} = \frac{E(P_T)}{(1 + k)^T}$$

or

$$F_0 = E(P_T)\left(\frac{1 + r_f}{1 + k}\right)^T \tag{23.5}$$

where k is the required rate of return on the commodity, which may be obtained from a model of asset market equilibrium such as the CAPM.

Note that equation 23.5 is perfectly consistent with the spot-futures parity relationship. For example, apply equation 23.5 to the futures price for a stock paying no dividends. Because the entire return on the stock is in the form of capital gains, the expected rate of capital gains must equal k, the required rate of return on the stock. Consequently, the expected price of the stock will be its current price times $(1 + k)^T$, or $E(P_T) = P_0(1 + k)^T$. Substituting this expression into equation 23.5 results in $F_0 = P_0(1 + r_f)^T$, which is exactly the parity relationship. This equilibrium derivation of the parity relationship simply reinforces the no-arbitrage restrictions we derived earlier. The spot-futures parity relationship may be obtained from the equilibrium condition that all portfolios earn fair expected rates of return.

The advantage of the arbitrage proofs that we have explored is that they do not rely on the validity of any particular model of security market equilibrium. The absence of arbitrage opportunities is a much more robust basis for argument than the CAPM, for example. Moreover, arbitrage proofs clearly demonstrate how an investor can exploit any misalignment in the spot-futures relationship. To their disadvantage, arbitrage restrictions may be less precise than desirable in the face of storage costs or costs of short selling.

We can summarize by saying that the actions of arbitrageurs force the futures prices of financial assets to maintain a precise relationship with the price of the underlying financial asset. This relationship is described by the spot-futures parity formula. Opportunities for arbitrage are more limited in the case of commodity futures because such commodities often are not stored. Hence, to make a precise prediction for the correct relationship between futures and spot prices, we must rely on a model of security market equilibrium such as the CAPM or APT and estimate the unobservables, the expected spot price, and the appropriate interest rate. Such models will be perfectly consistent with the parity relationships in the benchmark case where investors willingly store the commodity.

Question 5 • **Suppose that the systematic risk of orange juice were to increase, holding the expected time *T* price of juice constant. If the expected spot price is unchanged, would the futures price change? In what direction? What is the intuition behind your answer?**

23.5   SWAPS

We noted in Chapter 16 that interest rate swaps have become common tools for interest rate risk management. A large and active market also exists for foreign exchange swaps. Recall that a swap arrangement obligates two counterparties to exchange cash flows at one or more future dates. To illustrate, a **foreign exchange swap** might call for one party to exchange $1.6 million for 1 million British pounds in each of the next five years. An **interest rate swap** with notional principal of $1 million might call for one party to exchange a variable cash flow equal to $1 million times the LIBOR rate for $1 million times a fixed rate of 8%. In this way the two parties exchange the cash flows corresponding to interest payments on a fixed-rate 8% coupon bond for those corresponding to payments on a floating-rate bond paying LIBOR.

Swaps offer participants easy ways to restructure their balance sheets. Consider, for example, a firm that has issued long-term bonds with total par value of $10 million at a fixed interest rate of 8%. The firm is obligated to make interest payments of $800,000 per year. However, it can change the nature of its interest obligations from fixed rate to floating rate by entering a swap agreement to pay a floating rate of interest and receive a fixed rate.

A swap with notional principal of $10 million that exchanges LIBOR for an 8% fixed rate will bring the firm fixed cash inflows of $800,000 per year and obligate it to pay instead $10 million $\times r_{LIBOR}$. The receipt of the fixed payments from the swap agreement offsets the firm's interest obligations on the outstanding bond issue, leaving it with a net obligation to make floating-rate payments. The swap, therefore, is a way for the firm to effectively convert its outstanding fixed-rate debt into synthetic floating-rate debt.

To illustrate the mechanics of the swap agreement, suppose that the swap is for three years and the LIBOR rates turn out to be 7%, 8%, and 9% in the next three years. The cash flow streams called for by the swap would be as illustrated in Figure 23.8. In the first year, when LIBOR is 7%, the fixed-rate payer would be owed a cash flow equal to .07 $\times$ $10 million = $700,000, and would owe the 8% fixed rate on the notional principal, or $800,000. Actually, instead of two cash payments, the parties would simply exchange one payment equal to the difference in required payments. Here, the fixed-rate payer would pay $100,000 to the fixed-rate receiver. In the second year, when LIBOR equals 8%, no net payments would be exchanged. In the third year, the fixed-rate payer would receive a net cash flow of $100,000.

Figure 23.8
Three-year interest
rate swap.

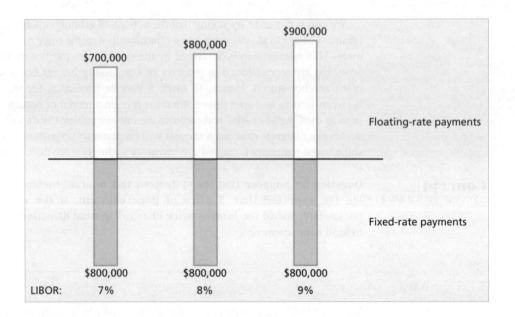

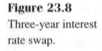

Question 6 • Suppose that two parties enter a three-year swap agreement to exchange the LIBOR rate for a 7% fixed rate on $20 million of notional principal. If LIBOR in the three years turns out to be 8%, 7%, and 9%, what cash flows will be exchanged between the two counterparties?

Instead of entering the swap, the firm could have retired its outstanding debt and issued floating-rate notes. The swap agreement is a far cheaper and quicker way to restructure the balance sheet, however. The swap does not entail trading costs to buy back outstanding bonds or underwriting fees and lengthy registration procedures to issue new debt. In addition, if the firm perceives price advantages in either the fixed- or floating-rate markets, the swap market allows it to issue its debt in the cheaper of the two markets and then "convert" to the financing mode it feels best suits its business needs.

Foreign exchange swaps also enable the firm to quickly and cheaply restructure its balance sheet. Suppose, for example, that the firm that issued the $10 million in debt actually preferred that its interest obligations be denominated in British pounds. For example, the issuing firm might have been a British corporation that perceived advantageous financing opportunities in the United States but prefers pound-denominated liabilities. Then the firm, whose debt currently obliges it to make dollar-denominated payments of $800,000, can agree to swap a given number of pounds each year for $800,000. By so doing, it effectively covers its dollar obligation and replaces it with a new pound-denominated obligation.

How can the fair swap rate be determined? For example, do we know that an exchange of LIBOR is a fair trade for a fixed rate of 8%? Or, what is the fair swap rate between dollars and pounds for the foreign exchange swap we considered? To answer these questions we can exploit the analogy between a swap agreement and forward or futures contract.

Consider a swap agreement to exchange dollars for pounds for one period only. Next year, for example, one might exchange $1 million for £.6 million. This is no more than a simple forward contract in foreign exchange. The dollar-paying party is contracting to buy British pounds in one year for a number of dollars agreed to today. The forward exchange rate for one-year delivery is $F_1 = \$1.67/\text{pound}$. We know from the interest rate parity rela-

Figure 23.9
Forward contracts
versus swaps.

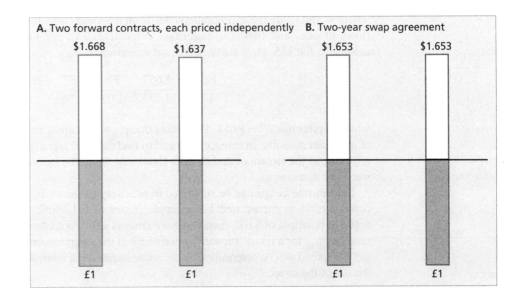

tionship that this forward price should be related to the spot exchange rate, E_0, by the formula $F_1 = E_0(1 + r_{US})/(1 + r_{UK})$. Because a one-period swap is in fact a forward contract, the fair swap rate is also given by the parity relationship.

Now consider an agreement to trade foreign exchange for two periods. This agreement could be structured as a portfolio of two separate forward contracts. If so, the forward price for the exchange of currencies in one year would be $F_1 = E_0(1 + r_{US})/(1 + r_{UK})$, while the forward price for the exchange in the second year would be $F_2 = E_0[(1 + r_{US})/(1 + r_{UK})]^2$. As an example, suppose that $E_0 = \$1.70$/pound, $r_{US} = 5\%$, and $r_{UK} = 7\%$. Then, using the parity relationship, we would have prices for forward delivery of $F_1 = \$1.70/£ \times (1.05/1.07) = \$1.668/£$ and $F_2 = \$1.70/£ \times (1.05/1.07)^2 = \$1.637/£$. Figure 23.9A illustrates this sequence of cash exchanges assuming that the swap calls for delivery of one pound in each year. Although the dollars to be paid in each of the two years are known today, they differ from year to year.

In contrast, a swap agreement to exchange currency for two years would call for a fixed exchange rate to be used for the duration of the swap. This means that the same number of dollars would be paid per pound in each year, as illustrated in Figure 23.9**B**. Because the forward prices for delivery in each of the next two years are $\$1.668/£$ and $\$1.637/£$, the fixed exchange rate that makes the two-period swap a fair deal must be between these two values. Therefore, the dollar payer underpays for the pound in the first year (compared to the forward exchange rate) and overpays in the second year. Thus the swap can be viewed as a portfolio of forward transactions, but instead of each transaction being priced independently, one forward price is applied to all of the transactions.

Given this insight, it is easy to determine the fair swap price. If we were to purchase one pound per year for two years using two independent forward rate agreements, we would pay F_1 dollars in one year and F_2 dollars in two years. If instead we enter a swap, we pay a constant rate of F^* dollars per pound. Because both strategies must be equally costly, we conclude that

$$\frac{F_1}{1 + y_1} + \frac{F_2}{(1 + y_2)^2} = \frac{F^*}{1 + y_1} + \frac{F^*}{(1 + y_2)^2}$$

where y_1 and y_2 are the appropriate yields from the yield curve for discounting dollar cash flows of one- and two-year maturities, respectively. In our example, where we have assumed a flat U.S. yield curve at 5%, we would solve

$$\frac{1.668}{1.05} + \frac{1.637}{1.05^2} = \frac{F^*}{1.05} + \frac{F^*}{1.05^2}$$

which implies that $F^* = 1.653$. The same principle would apply to a foreign exchange swap of any other maturity. In essence, we need to find the level annuity, F^*, with the same present value as the stream of annual cash flows that would be incurred in a sequence of forward rate agreements.

Interest rate swaps can be subjected to precisely the same analysis. Here, the forward contract is on an interest rate. For example, if you swap LIBOR for an 8% fixed rate with notional principal of $100, then you have entered a forward contract for delivery of $100 times r_{LIBOR} for a fixed "forward" price of $8. If the swap agreement is for many periods, the fair spread will be determined by the entire sequence of interest rate forward prices over the life of the swap.

Credit Risk in the Swap Market

The rapid growth of the swap market has given rise to increasing concern about credit risk in these markets and the possibility of a default by a major swap trader. Actually, although credit risk in the swap market certainly is not trivial, it is not nearly as large as the magnitude of notional principal in these markets would suggest. To see why, consider a simple interest rate swap of LIBOR for a fixed rate. At the time the transaction is initiated, it has zero net present value to both parties for the same reason that a futures contract has zero value at inception: Both are simply contracts to exchange cash in the future at terms established today that make both parties willing to enter into the deal. Even if one party were to back out of the deal at this moment, it would not cost the counterparty anything, because another trader could be found to take its place.

Once interest or exchange rates change, however, the situation is not as simple. Suppose, for example, that interest rates increase shortly after an interest-rate swap agreement has begun. The floating-rate payer therefore suffers a loss, while the fixed-rate payer enjoys a gain. If the floating-rate payer reneges on its commitment at this point, the fixed-rate payer suffers a loss. However, that loss is not as large as the notional principal of the swap, for the default of the floating-rate payer relieves the fixed-rate payer from its obligation as well. The loss is only the *difference* between the values of the fixed-rate and floating-rate obligations, not the *total* value of the payments that the floating-rate payer was obligated to make.

Let's illustrate with an example. Consider a swap written on $1 million of notional principal that calls for exchange of LIBOR for a fixed rate of 8% for five years. Suppose, for simplicity, that the yield curve is currently flat at 8%. With LIBOR thus equal to 8%, no cash flows will be exchanged unless interest rates change. But now suppose that the yield curve immediately shifts up to 9%. The floating-rate payer now is obligated to pay a cash flow of $(.09 - .08) \times \$1$ million $= \$10,000$ each year to the fixed-rate payer (as long as rates remain at 9%). If the floating-rate payer defaults on the swap, the fixed-rate payer loses the prospect of that five-year annuity. The present value of that annuity is $10,000 $\times$ Annuity factor(9%, 5 years) = $38,897. This loss may not be trivial, but it is less than 4% of notional principal. We conclude that the credit risk of the swap is far less than notional principal. Again, this is because the default by the floating-rate payer costs the counterparty only the net difference between the LIBOR rate and the fixed rate.

Swap Variations

Swaps have given rise to a wide range of spinoff products. Many of these add option features to the basic swap agreement. For example, an *interest rate cap* is an agreement in which the buyer makes a payment today in exchange for possible future payments if a reference interest rate (usually LIBOR) exceeds a specified limit—the cap—on a series of settlement dates. For example, if the limit rate is 7%, then the cap holder receives (r_{LIBOR} – .07) for each dollar of notional principal if the LIBOR rate exceeds 7%. The purchaser of the cap in effect has entered a swap agreement to exchange the LIBOR rate for a fixed rate of 7% with an option not to do the swap in any period that the transaction is unprofitable. The payoff to the holder of the cap is

(Reference rate – Limit rate) × Notional principal *if* this value is positive

and zero otherwise. This, of course, is the payoff of an option to purchase a cash flow proportional to the LIBOR rate for an exercise price proportional to the limit rate.

An *interest rate floor*, on the other hand, pays its holder in any period that the reference interest rate falls *below* some limit. This is analogous to a sequence of options to sell the reference rate for a stipulated "strike rate."

A *collar* combines interest rate caps and floors. A collar entails the purchase of a cap with one limit rate, and the sale of a floor with a lower limit rate. If a firm starts with a floating-rate liability and buys the cap, it achieves protection against rates rising. If rates do rise, the cap provides a cash flow equal to the reference interest rate in exchange for a payment equal to the limit rate. Therefore, the cap places an upper bound equal to the limit rate on the firm's net interest rate expense. The written floor places a limit on how much the firm can benefit from rate declines. Even if interest rates fall dramatically, the firm's savings on its floating-rate obligation will be offset by its obligation to pay the difference between the reference rate and the limit rate. Therefore, the collar limits the firm's net cost of funds to a value between the limit rate on the cap and the limit rate on the floor.

Other option-based variations on the basic swap arrangement are *swaptions*. A swaption is an option on a swap. The buyer of the swaption has the right to enter an interest rate swap on some reference interest rate at a specified fixed interest rate on or before some expiration date. A call swaption (often called a *payer swaption*) is the right to pay the fixed rate in a swap and receive the floating rate. A put swaption is the right to receive the fixed rate and pay the floating rate. An exit option is the right to walk away from a swap without penalty. Swaptions can be European or American.

There also are futures and forward variations on swaps. A forward swap, for example, obligates both traders to enter a swap at some date in the future with terms agreed to today.

SUMMARY

1. Futures contracts calling for cash settlement are traded on various stock market indexes. The contracts may be mixed with Treasury bills to construct artificial equity positions, which makes them potentially valuable tools for market timers. Market index contracts are used also by arbitrageurs who attempt to profit from violations of the parity relationship.

2. Foreign exchange futures trade on several foreign currencies, as well as on a European currency index. The interest rate parity relationship for foreign exchange futures is

$$F_0 = E_0 \left(\frac{1 + r_{US}}{1 + r_{foreign}} \right)^T$$

with exchange rates quoted as dollars per foreign currency.

Deviations of the futures price from this value imply arbitrage opportunity. Empirical evidence, however, suggests that generally the parity relationship is satisfied.

3. Interest rate futures allow for hedging against interest rate fluctuations in several different markets.

4. Commodity futures pricing is complicated by costs for storage of the underlying commodity. When the asset is willingly stored by investors, then the storage costs net of convenience yield enter the futures pricing equation as follows:

$$F_0 = P_0(1 + r_f + c)$$

The non–interest net carrying costs, c, play the role of a "negative dividend" in this context.

5. When commodities are not stored for investment purposes, the correct futures price must be determined using general risk-return principles. In this event,

$$F_0 = E(P_T)\left(\frac{1 + r_f}{1 + k}\right)^T$$

The equilibrium (risk-return) and the no-arbitrage predictions of the proper futures price are consistent with one another.

6. Swaps, which call for the exchange of a series of cash flows, may be viewed as portfolios of forward contracts. Each transaction may be viewed as a separate forward agreement. However, instead of pricing each exchange independently, the swap sets one "forward price" that applies to all of the transactions. Therefore, the swap price will be an average of the forward prices that would prevail if each exchange were priced separately.

Key Terms

index arbitrage	interest rate parity theorem	foreign exchange swap
program trading	covered interest arbitrage	interest rate swap
triple-witching hour	relationship	

Selected Readings

A good treatment of futures markets is in:
  Stoll, Hans R.; and Robert E. Whaley. *Futures and Options.* Cincinnati: Southwestern Publishing, 1993.
Evidence on the effects of index arbitrage on stock market prices and volatility is given in:
  Stoll, Hans R.; and Robert E. Whaley. "Expiration-Day Effects: What Has Changed?" *Financial Analysts Journal*, January–February 1991.
The use of futures contracts in the management of interest rate risk is explored in several articles in:
  Fabozzi, Frank J.; and T. Dessa Fabozzi, eds. *The Handbook of Fixed Income Securities*, 4th ed. Burr Ridge, IL: Irwin Professional Publishing, 1995.
A good introduction to swaps is:
  Brown, Keith C.; and Donald J. Smith. *Interest Rate and Currency Swaps: A Tutorial.* Charlottesville, VA: Research Foundation of the Institute of Chartered Financial Analysts, 1995.

Problems

1. Consider the futures contract written on the S&P 500 index, and maturing in six months. The interest rate is 3% per six-month period, and the future value of dividends expected to be paid over the next six months is $10. The current index level is 950. Assume that you can short sell the S&P index.

    a. Suppose the expected rate of return on the market is 6% per six-month period. What is the expected level of the index in six months?

    b. What is the theoretical no-arbitrage price for a six-month futures contract on the S&P 500 stock index?

    c. Suppose the futures price is 948. Is there an arbitrage opportunity here? If so, how would you exploit it?

2. Suppose that the value of the S&P 500 stock index is 900.

    a. If each futures contract costs $25 to trade with a discount broker, how much is the transaction cost per dollar of stock controlled by the futures contract?

    b. If the average price of a share on the NYSE is about $40, how much is the transaction cost per "typical share" controlled by one futures contract?

    c. For small investors, the typical transaction cost per share in stocks directly is about 30 cents per share. How many times the transactions costs in futures markets is this?

3. Suppose the one-year futures price on a stock-index portfolio is 812, the stock index currently is 800, the one-year risk-free interest rate is 3%, and the year-end dividend that will be paid on an $800 investment in the market index portfolio is $10.

    a. By how much is the contract mispriced?

    b. Formulate a zero-net-investment arbitrage portfolio and show that you can lock in riskless profits equal to the futures mispricing.

    c. Now assume (as is true for small investors) that if you short sell the stocks in the market index, the proceeds of the short sale are kept with the broker, and you do not receive any interest income on the funds. Is there still an arbitrage opportunity (assuming that you don't already own the shares in the index)? Explain.

    d. Given the short-sale rules, what is the no-arbitrage *band* for the stock-futures price relationship? That is, given a stock index of 800, how high and how low can the futures price be without giving rise to arbitrage opportunities?

4. Consider these futures market data for the June delivery S&P 500 contract, exactly six months hence. The S&P 500 index is at 900, and the June maturity contract is at $F_0 = 901$.

    a. If the current interest rate is 2.2% semiannually, and the average dividend rate of the stocks in the index is 1.2% semiannually, what fraction of the proceeds of stock short sales would need to be available to you to earn arbitrage profits?

    b. Suppose that you in fact have access to 90% of the proceeds from a short sale. What is the lower bound on the futures price that rules out arbitrage opportunities? By how much does the actual futures price fall below the no-arbitrage bound? Formulate the appropriate arbitrage strategy, and calculate the profits to that strategy.

5. You manage a $4.5 million portfolio, currently all invested in equities, and believe that you have extraordinary market-timing skills. You believe that the market is on the verge of a big but short-lived downturn; you would move your portfolio temporarily into T-bills, but you do not want to incur the transaction costs of liquidating and reestablishing your equity position. Instead, you decide to temporarily hedge your equity holdings with S&P 500 index futures contracts.

    a. Should you be long or short the contracts? Why?

    b. If your equity holdings are invested in a market-index fund, into how many contracts should you enter? The S&P 500 index is now at 900 and the contract multiplier is $250.

    c. How does your answer to (*b*) change if the beta of your portfolio is .6?

6. Suppose your client says, "I am invested in Japanese stocks but want to eliminate my exposure to this market for a period of time. Can I accomplish this without the cost and inconvenience of selling out and buying back in again if my expectations change?"

    a. Briefly describe a strategy to hedge both the local market risk and the currency risk of investing in Japanese stocks.

    b. Briefly explain why the hedge strategy you described in part (*a*) might not be fully effective.

7. Suppose that the spot price of the Swiss franc is currently 65 cents. The one-year futures price is 68 cents. Is the interest rate higher in the United States or Switzerland?

8. *a.* The spot price of the British pound is currently $1.60. If the risk-free interest rate on one-year government bonds is 4% in the United States and 8% in the United Kingdom, what must the forward price of the pound be for delivery one year from now?

    b. How could an investor make risk-free arbitrage profits if the forward price were higher than the price you gave in answer to (*a*)? Give a numerical example.

9. Consider the following information:

$$r_{US} = 4\% \qquad r_{UK} = 7\%$$
$$E_0 = 1.60 \text{ dollars per pound}$$
$$F_0 = 1.58 \text{ (one-year delivery)}$$

    where the interest rates are annual yields on U.S. or U.K. bills. Given this information:

    a. Where would you lend?

    b. Where would you borrow?

    c. How could you arbitrage?

10. René Michaels, CFA, plans to invest $1 million in U.S. government cash equivalents for the next 90 days. Michaels's client has authorized her to use non-U.S. government cash equivalents, but only if the currency risk is hedged to U.S. dollars by using forward currency contracts.

    a. Calculate the U.S. dollar value of the hedged investment at the end of 90 days for each of the two cash equivalents in the table below. Show all calculations.

    b. Briefly explain the theory that best accounts for your results.

    c. Based on this theory, estimate the implied interest rate for a 90-day U.S. government cash equivalent.

Interest Rates 90-Day Cash Equivalents	
Japanese government	7.6%
German government	8.6%

Exchange Rates Currency Units per U.S. Dollar		
	Spot	90-Day Forward
Japanese yen	133.05	133.47
German deutschemark	1.5260	1.5348

11. You believe that the spread between municipal bond yields and U.S. Treasury bond yields is going to narrow in the coming month. How can you profit from such a change using the municipal bond and T-bond futures contracts?

12. Salomon Brothers is underwriting an issue of a 30-year zero-coupon corporate bonds with a face value of $100 million and a current market value of $5.354 million (a yield of 5% per six-month period). The firm must hold the bonds for a few days before issuing them to the public, which exposes it to interest rate risk. Salomon wishes to hedge its position by using T-bond futures contracts. The current T-bond futures price is $90.80 per $100 par value, and the T-bond contract will be settled using a 20-year, 8% coupon bond paying interest semiannually. The contract is due to expire in a few days, so the T-bond price and the T-bond futures price are virtually identical. The yield implied on the bond is therefore 4.5% per six-month period. (Confirm this as a first step.) Assume that the yield curve is flat and that the corporate bond will continue to yield .5% more than T-bonds per six-month period, even if the general level of interest rates should change. What hedge ratio should Salomon Brothers use to hedge its bond holdings against possible interest rate fluctuations over the next few days?

13. If the spot price of gold is $350 per troy ounce, the risk-free interest rate is 10%, and storage and insurance costs are zero, what should the forward price of gold be for delivery in one year? Use an arbitrage argument to prove your answer. Include a numerical example showing how you could make risk-free arbitrage profits if the forward price exceeded its upper bound value.

14. If the corn harvest today is poor, would you expect this fact to have any effect on today's futures prices for corn to be delivered (postharvest) two years from today? Under what circumstances will there be no effect?

15. Suppose that the price of corn is risky, with a beta of .5. The monthly storage cost is $.03, and the current spot price is $2.75, with an expected spot price in three months of $2.94. If the expected rate of return on the market is 1.8% per month, with a risk-free rate of 1% per month, would you store corn for three months?

16. You are provided the information outlined as follows to be used in solving this problem.

Issue	Price	Yield to Maturity	Modified Duration*
U.S. Treasury bond 11¾% maturing Nov. 15, 2014	100	11.75%	7.6 years
U.S. Treasury long bond futures contract (contract expiration date December 1986)	63.33	11.85%	8.0 years
XYZ Corporation bond 12½% maturing June 1, 2005 (sinking fund debenture, rated AAA)	93	13.50%	7.2 years
Volatility of AAA corporate bond yields relative to U.S. Treasury bond yields = 1.25 to 1.0 (1.25 times)			
Assume no commission and no margin requirements on U.S. Treasury long bond futures contracts. Assume no taxes.			
One U.S. Treasury long bond futures contract is a claim on $100,000 par value long-term U.S. Treasury bonds.			

*Modified duration = Duration/(1 + y).

Situation A   A fixed-income manager holding a $20 million market value position of U.S. Treasury 11¾% bonds maturing November 15, 2014, expects the economic growth rate and the inflation rate to be above market expectations in the near future. Institutional rigidities prevent any existing bonds in the portfolio from being sold in the cash market.

Situation B   The treasurer of XYZ Corporation has recently become convinced that interest rates will decline in the near future. He believes it is an opportune time to purchase his company's sinking fund bonds in advance of requirements since these bonds are trading at a discount from par value. He is preparing to purchase in the open market $20 million par value XYZ Corporation 12½% bonds maturing June 1, 2005. A $20 million par value position of these bonds is currently offered in the open market at 93. Unfortunately, the treasurer must obtain approval from the board of directors for such a purchase, and this approval process can take up to two months. The board of directors' approval in this instance is only a formality.

For each of these two situations, outline and calculate how the interest rate risk can be hedged using the Treasury long bond futures. Show all calculations, including the total number of futures contracts used.

17. The U.S. yield curve is flat at 5% and the German yield curve is flat at 8%. The current exchange rate is $.65 per mark. What will be the swap rate on an agreement to exchange currency over a three-year period? The swap will call for the exchange of 1 million deutschemarks for a given number of dollars in each year.

18. Firm ABC enters a five-year swap with firm XYZ to pay LIBOR in return for a fixed 8% rate on notional principal of $10 million. Two years from now, the market rate on three-year swaps is LIBOR for 7%; at this time, firm XYZ goes bankrupt and defaults on its swap obligation.
    a. Why is firm ABC harmed by the default?
    b. What is the market value of the loss incurred by ABC as a result of the default?
    c. Suppose instead that ABC had gone bankrupt. How do you think the swap would be treated in the reorganization of the firm?

19. At the present time, one can enter five-year swaps that exchange LIBOR for 8%. Five-year caps with limit rates of 8% sell for $.30 per dollar of notional principal. What must be the price of five-year floors with a limit rate of 8%?

20. At the present time, one can enter five-year swaps that exchange LIBOR for 8%. An *off-market swap* would then be defined as a swap of LIBOR for a fixed rate other than 8%. For example, a firm with 10% coupon debt outstanding might like to convert to synthetic floating-rate debt by entering a swap in which it pays LIBOR and receives a fixed rate of 10%. What up-front payment will be required to induce a counterparty to take the other side of this swap? Assume notional principal is $10 million.

solutions to Concept CHECKS

1. As the payoffs to the two strategies are identical, so should be the costs of establishing them. The synthetic stock strategy costs $F_0/(1 + r_f)^T$ to establish, this being the present value of the futures price. The stock index purchased directly costs S_0. Therefore, we conclude that $S_0 = F_0/(1 + r_f)^T$, or $F_0 = S_0(1 + r_f)^T$, which is the parity relationship in the case of no dividends.

2. If the futures price is above the parity level, investors would sell futures and buy stocks. Short selling would not be necessary. Therefore, the top of the no-arbitrage band would be unaffected by the use of the proceeds. If the futures price is too low, investors would want to short sell stocks and buy futures. Now the costs of short selling are important. If proceeds from the short sale become available, short selling becomes less costly and the bottom of the band will move up.

3. According to interest rate parity, F_0 should be $1.585. Since the futures price is too high, we should reverse the arbitrage strategy just considered.

	CF Now ($)	CF in 1 Year
1. Borrow $1.60 in the U.S. Convert to one pound.	+1.60	$-1.60(1.05)$
2. Lend the one pound in the U.K.	−1.60	$1.06E_1$
3. Enter a contract to sell 1.05 pounds at a futures price of 1.62.	0	$(1.06)(1.62 - E_1)$
Total	0	.0372

4. Stocks offer a total return (capital gain plus dividends) large enough to compensate investors for the time value of the money tied up in the stock. Wheat prices do not necessarily increase over time. In fact, across a harvest, wheat prices will fall. The returns necessary to make storage economically attractive are lacking.

5. If systematic risk were higher, the appropriate discount rate, k, would increase. Referring to equation 23.5, we conclude that F_0 would fall. Intuitively, the claim to 1 pound of orange juice is worth less today if its expected price is unchanged, but the risk associated with the value of the claim increases. Therefore, the amount investors are willing to pay today for future delivery is lower.

6. *Year 1*. LIBOR − 7% = 1%. Therefore, fixed-rate payer receives .01 × $20 million = $200,000 from counterparty.
Year 2. LIBOR = 7%. No payments are exchanged.
Year 3. Fixed-rate payer receives .02 × 20 million = $400,000.

ACTIVE PORTFOLIO MANAGEMENT

CHAPTER TWENTY-FOUR

PORTFOLIO PERFORMANCE EVALUATION

How can we evaluate the performance of a portfolio manager? It turns out that even average portfolio return is not as straightforward to measure as it might seem. In addition, adjusting average returns for risk presents a host of other problems. We begin with the measurement of portfolio returns. From there we move on to conventional approaches to risk adjustment. We identify the problems with these approaches when applied in various situations. Finally, we discuss some promising developments in the theory of performance evaluation and examine evaluation procedures used in the field.

24.1   MEASURING INVESTMENT RETURNS

The rate of return of an investment is a simple concept in the case of a one-period investment. It is simply the total proceeds derived from the investment per dollar initially invested. Proceeds must be defined broadly to include both cash distributions and capital gains. For stocks, total returns are dividends plus capital gains. For bonds, total returns are coupon or interest paid plus capital gains.

To set the stage for discussing the more subtle issues that follow, let us start with a trivial example. Consider a stock paying a dividend of $2 annually that currently sells for $50. You purchase the stock today and collect the $2 dividend, and then you sell the stock for $53 at year-end. Your rate of return is

$$\frac{\text{Total proceeds}}{\text{Initial investment}} = \frac{\text{Income} + \text{Capital gain}}{50}$$

$$= \frac{2 + 3}{50} = .10, \text{ or } 10\%$$

Another way to derive the rate of return that is useful in the more difficult multiperiod case is to set up the investment as a discounted cash flow problem. Call r the rate of return that equates the present value of all cash flows from the investment with the initial outlay. In our example the stock is purchased for $50 and generates cash flows at year-end of $2 (dividend) plus $53 (sale of stock). Therefore, we solve $50 = (2 + 53)/(1 + r)$ to find again that $r = 10\%$.

Time-Weighted Returns versus Dollar-Weighted Returns

When we consider investments over a period during which cash was added to or withdrawn from the portfolio, measuring the rate of return becomes more difficult. To continue our example, suppose that you were to purchase a second share of the same stock at the end of the first year, and hold both shares until the end of Year 2, at which point you sell each share for $54.

Total cash outlays are

Time	Outlay
0	$50 to purchase first share
1	$53 to purchase second share a year later
	Proceeds
1	$2 dividend from initially purchased share
2	$4 dividend from the 2 shares held in the second year, plus $108 received from selling both shares at $54 each

Using the discounted cash flow (DCF) approach, we can solve for the average return over the two years by equating the present values of the cash inflows and outflows:

$$50 + \frac{53}{1 + r} = \frac{2}{1 + r} + \frac{112}{(1 + r)^2}$$

resulting in $r = 7.117\%$.

This value is called the internal rate of return, or the **dollar-weighted rate of return** on the investment. It is "dollar weighted" because the stock's performance in the second year, when two shares of stock are held, has a greater influence on the average overall return than the first-year return, when only one share is held.

An alternative to the internal, or dollar-weighted, return is the **time-weighted return.** This method ignores the number of shares of stock held in each period. The stock return in the first year was 10%. In the second year the stock had a starting value of $53 and sold at year-end for $54, for a total one-period rate of return of $3 ($2 dividend plus $1 capital gain) divided by $53 (the stock price at the start of the second year), or 5.66%. The time-weighted return is the average of 10% and 5.66%, which is 7.83%. This average return considers only the period-by-period returns without regard to the amounts invested in the stock in each period.

Note that the dollar-weighted return is less than the time-weighted return in this example. The reason is that the stock fared relatively poorly in the second year, when the investor was holding more shares. The greater weight that the dollar-weighted average places on the second-year return results in a lower measure of investment performance. In general, dollar- and time-weighted returns will differ, and the difference can be positive or negative, depending on the configuration of period returns and portfolio composition.

Which measure of performance is superior? At first, it appears that the dollar-weighted return must be more relevant. After all, the more money you invest in a stock when its performance is superior, the more money you end up with. Certainly your performance measure should reflect this fact.

Time-weighted returns have their own use, however, especially in the money management industry. This is so because in many important applications a portfolio manager may not directly control the timing or the amount of money invested in securities. Pension fund management is a good example. A pension fund manager faces cash inflows into the fund when pension contributions are made, and cash outflows when pension benefits are paid. Obviously, the amount of money invested at any time can vary for reasons beyond the manager's control. Because dollars invested do not depend on the manager's choice, it is inappropriate to weight returns by dollars invested when measuring the investment ability of the manager. Consequently, the money management industry normally uses time-weighted returns for performance evaluation.

Concept
CHECK

Question 1 • Shares of XYZ Corp. pay a $2 dividend at the end of every year on December 31. An investor buys two shares of the stock on January 1 at a price of $20 each, sells one of those shares for $22 a year later on the next January 1, and sells the second share an additional year later for $19. Find the time- and dollar-weighted rates of return on the two-year investment.

Arithmetic versus Geometric Averages

Our example takes the arithmetic average of the two annual returns, 10% and 5.66%, as the time-weighted average, 7.83%. Another approach is to take a geometric average, denoted r_G.

The motivation for this calculation comes from the principle of compounding. If dividend proceeds are reinvested, the accumulated value of an investment in the stock will grow by a factor of 1.10 in the first year and by an additional factor of 1.0566 in the second year. The compound average growth rate, r_G, is then calculated as the solution to the following equation:

$$(1 + r_G)^2 = (1.10)(1.0566)$$

Table 24.1   Average Annual Returns by Investment Class, 1926–1996

	Arithmetic Average	Geometric Average	Difference	Standard Deviation
Common stocks of small firms*	19.0	12.6	6.4	40.4
Common stocks of large firms	12.5	10.5	2.0	20.4
Long-term Treasury bonds	5.3	5.0	0.3	8.0
U.S. Treasury bills	3.8	3.7	0.1	3.3

*These are firms with relatively low market values of equity. Market capitalization is computed as price per share times shares outstanding.

Source: Authors' calculations based on data in Table 5.2.

This approach would entail computing

$$1 + r_G = [(1.10)(1.0566)]^{1/2} = 1.0781$$

or $r_G = 7.81\%$.

More generally, for an n-period investment, the geometric average rate of return is given by

$$1 + r_G = [(1 + r_1)(1 + r_2) \ldots (1 + r_n)]^{1/n}$$

where r_t is the return in each time period.

The geometric average return in this example, 7.81%, is slightly less than the arithmetic average return, 7.83%. This is a general property: Geometric averages never exceed arithmetic ones. To see the intuition behind this result, consider a stock that doubles in price in period 1 ($r_1 = 100\%$) and halves in price in period 2 ($r_2 = -50\%$). The arithmetic average is $r_A = [100 + (-50)]/2 = 25\%$, whereas the geometric average is $r_G = [(1 + 1)(1 - .5)]^{1/2} - 1 = 0$. The effect of the –50% return in period 2 fully offsets the 100% return in period 1 in the calculation of the geometric average, resulting in an average return of zero. This is not true of the arithmetic average. In general, the bad returns have a greater influence on the averaging process in the geometric technique. Therefore, geometric averages are lower.

Moreover, the difference in the two averaging techniques will be greater the greater is the variability of period-by-period returns. The general rule when returns are expressed as decimals (rather than percentages) is as follows:

$$r_G \approx r_A - \frac{1}{2}\sigma^2 \tag{24.1}$$

where σ^2 is the variance of returns. Equation 24.1 is exact when returns are normally distributed.

For example, consider Table 24.1, which presents arithmetic and geometric returns over the 1926–1996 period for a variety of investments. The arithmetic averages all exceed the geometric ones, with the difference greatest in the case of stocks of small firms, where annual returns exhibit the greatest standard deviation. The difference between the two averages falls to zero only when there is no variation in yearly returns. The table indicates that when the standard deviation falls to a level characteristic of T-bills, the difference is quite small.

To illustrate equation 24.1, consider the average returns for large stocks. According to the equation,

$$.105 \approx .125 - \frac{1}{2}(.204)^2 = .1042$$
$$.105 \approx .1042$$

As predicted, the arithmetic mean (.125) exceeded the geometric mean (.105) by approximately one-half the variance in returns. Clearly, when comparing returns, one never should mix and match the two averaging techniques.[1]

This last point leads to another question. Which is the superior measure of investment performance, the arithmetic average or the geometric average? The geometric average has considerable appeal because it represents the constant rate of return we would have needed to earn in each year to match actual performance over some past investment period. It is an excellent measure of *past* performance. However, if our focus is on future performance, then the arithmetic average is the statistic of interest because it is an unbiased estimate of the portfolio's expected future return (assuming, of course, that the expected return does not change over time). In contrast, because the geometric return over a sample period is always less than the arithmetic mean, it constitutes a downward-biased estimator of the stock's expected return in any future year.

To illustrate this concept, consider again a stock that will either double in value ($r = 100\%$) with probability of .5, or halve in value ($r = -50\%$) with probability .5. The following table illustrates these outcomes:

Investment Outcome	Final Value of Each Dollar Invested	One-Year Rate of Return
Double	$2.00	100%
Halve	$0.50	−50%

Suppose that the stock's performance over a two-year period is characteristic of the probability distribution, doubling in one year and halving in the other. The stock's price ends up exactly where it started, and the geometric average annual return is zero:

$$1 + r_G = [(1 + r_1)(1 + r_2)]^{1/2}$$
$$= [(1 + 1)(1 - .50)]^{1/2}$$
$$= 1$$
$$r_G = 0$$

which confirms that a zero year-by-year return would have replicated the total return earned on the stock.

The expected annual future rate of return on the stock, however, is *not* zero; it is the arithmetic average of 100% and −50%: $(100 - 50)/2 = 25\%$. There are two equally likely outcomes per dollar invested: either a gain of $1 (when $r = 100\%$) or a loss of $.50 (when $r = -50\%$). The expected profit is $(\$1 - \$.50)/2 = \$.25$, for a 25% expected rate of return. The profit in the good year more than offsets the loss in the bad year, despite the fact that the geometric return is zero. The arithmetic average return thus provides the best guide to expected future returns.

This argument carries forward into multiperiod investments. Consider, for example, all the possible outcomes over a two-year period:

Investment Outcome	Final Value of Each Dollar Invested	Total Return over Two Years
Double, double	$4.00	300%
Double, halve	$1.00	0
Halve, double	$1.00	0
Halve, halve	$0.25	−75%

[1] In the case of small stocks, $\frac{1}{2}(.404)^2 = .082$ exceeds the difference, $r_A - r_G = .064$, because extreme values in small stock returns are more frequent than would be predicted from a normal distribution.

The expected final value of each dollar invested is $(4 + 1 + 1 + .25)/4 = \$1.5625$ for two years, again indicating an average rate of return of 25% per year, equal to the arithmetic average. Note that an investment yielding 25% per year with certainty will yield the same final compounded value as the expected final value of this investment, as $1.25^2 = 1.5625$. The arithmetic average return on the stock is $[300 + 0 + 0 + (-75)]/4 = 56.25\%$ per two years, for an effective annual return of 25%, that is, $1.5625^{1/2} - 1$. In contrast, the geometric mean return is zero:

$$[(1 + 3)(1 + 0)(1 + 0)(1 - .75)]^{1/4} = 1.0$$

Again, the arithmetic average is the better guide to *future* performance.

Question 2 • **Suppose that a stock now selling for $100 will either increase in value by 15% by year-end with probability .5, or fall in value by 5% with probability .5. The stock pays no dividends.**
a. **What are the geometric and arithmetic mean returns on the stock?**
b. **What is the expected end-of-year value of the share?**
c. **Which measure of expected return is superior?**

24.2   THE CONVENTIONAL THEORY OF PERFORMANCE EVALUATION

Calculating average portfolio returns does not mean the task is done. Returns must be adjusted for risk before they can be compared meaningfully. The simplest and most popular way to adjust returns for portfolio risk is to compare rates of return with those of other investment funds with similar risk characteristics. For example, high-yield bond portfolios are grouped into one "universe," growth stock equity funds are grouped into another universe, and so on. Then the (usually time-weighted) average returns of each fund within the universe are ordered, and each portfolio manager receives a percentile ranking depending on relative performance with the **comparison universe**. For example, the manager with the ninth-best performance in a universe of 100 funds would be the 90th percentile manager: Her performance was better than 90% of all competing funds over the evaluation period.

These relative rankings are usually displayed in a chart such as that in Figure 24.1. The chart summarizes performance rankings over four periods: 1 quarter, 1 year, 3 years, and 5 years. The top and bottom lines of each box are drawn at the rate of return of the 95th and 5th percentile managers. The three dashed lines correspond to the rates of return of the 75th, 50th (median), and 25th percentile managers. The diamond is drawn at the average return of a particular fund and the square is drawn at the return of a benchmark index such as the S&P 500. The placement of the diamond within the box is an easy-to-read representation of the performance of the fund relative to the comparison universe.

This comparison of performance with other managers of similar investment style is a useful first step in evaluating performance. However, such rankings can be misleading. For example, within a particular universe, some managers may concentrate on particular subgroups, so that portfolio characteristics are not truly comparable. For example, within the equity universe, one manager may concentrate on high-beta stocks. Similarly, within fixed-income universes, durations can vary across managers. These considerations suggest that a more precise means for risk adjustment is desirable.

Methods of risk-adjusted performance evaluation using mean-variance criteria came on stage simultaneously with the capital asset pricing model. Jack Treynor,[2] William Sharpe,[3]

---

[2]Jack L. Treynor, "How to Rate Management Investment Funds," *Harvard Business Review* 43 (January–February 1966).
[3]William F. Sharpe, "Mutual Fund Performance," *Journal of Business* 39 (January 1966).

Figure 24.1
Universe comparison.
Periods ending
December 31, 1998.

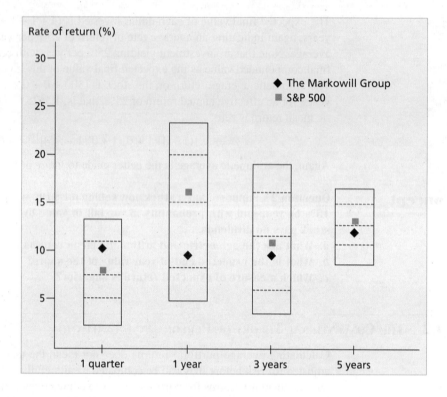

and Michael Jensen[4] recognized immediately the implications of the CAPM for rating the performance of managers. Within a short time, academicians were in command of a battery of performance measures, and a bounty of scholarly investigation of mutual fund performance was pouring from ivory towers. Shortly thereafter, agents emerged who were willing to supply rating services to portfolio managers eager for regular feedback. This trend has since lost some of its steam.

One explanation for the lagging popularity of risk-adjusted performance measures is the generally negative cast to the performance statistics. In nearly efficient markets it is extremely difficult for analysts to perform well enough to offset costs of research and transaction costs. Indeed, we have seen that most professionally managed equity funds generally underperform the S&P 500 index on both risk-adjusted and raw return measures.

Another reason mean-variance criteria may have suffered relates to intrinsic problems in the measures. We will explore these problems, as well as some innovations suggested to overcome them.

For now, however, we can catalog some possible risk-adjusted performance measures and examine the circumstances in which each measure might be most relevant.

1. *Sharpe's measure:* $(\bar{r}_P - \bar{r}_f)/\sigma_P$
   Sharpe's measure divides average portfolio excess return over the sample period by the standard deviation of returns over that period. It measures the reward to (total) volatility trade-off.[5]

---

[4]Michael C. Jensen, "The Performance of Mutual Funds in the Period 1945–1964," *Journal of Finance*, May 1968; and "Risk, the Pricing of Capital Assets, and the Evaluation of Investment Portfolios," *Journal of Business*, April 1969.

[5]We place bars over r_f as well as r_P to denote the fact that since the risk-free rate may not be constant over the measurement period, we are taking a sample average, just as we do for r_P.

2. *Treynor's measure:* $(\bar{r}_P - \bar{r}_f)/\beta_P$

   Like Sharpe's, **Treynor's measure** gives excess return per unit of risk, but it uses systematic risk instead of total risk.

3. *Jensen's measure:* $\alpha_P = \bar{r}_P - [\bar{r}_f + \beta_P(r_M - \bar{r}_f)]$

   Jensen's measure is the average return on the portfolio over and above that predicted by the CAPM, given the portfolio's beta and the average market return. Jensen's measure is the portfolio's alpha value.

4. *Appraisal ratio:* $\alpha_P/\sigma(e_P)$

   The **appraisal ratio** divides the alpha of the portfolio by the nonsystematic risk of the portfolio. It measures abnormal return per unit of risk that in principle could be diversified away from holding a market index portfolio.

Each measure has some appeal. But each does not necessarily provide consistent assessments of performance, since the risk measures used to adjust returns differ substantially.

Concept
CHECK

Question 3 • Consider the following data for a particular sample period:

	Portfolio *P*	Market *M*
Average return	35%	28%
Beta	1.20	1.00
Standard deviation	42%	30%
Nonsystematic risk, $\sigma(e)$	18%	0

Calculate the following performance measures for portfolio *P* and the market: Sharpe, Jensen (alpha), Treynor, appraisal ratio. The T-bill rate during the period was 6%. By which measures did portfolio *P* outperform the market?

The M^2 Measure of Performance

While the Sharpe ratio can be used to rank portfolio performance, its numerical value is not easy to interpret. Comparing the ratios for portfolios *M* and *P* in Concept Check 3, you should have found that $S_P = .69$ and $S_M = .73$. This suggests that portfolio *P* underperformed the market index. But is a difference of .04 in the Sharpe ratio economically meaningful? We are used to comparing rates of return, but these ratios are difficult to interpret.

A variant of Sharpe's measure was recently introduced by Leah Modigliani of Morgan Stanley and her grandfather Franco Modigliani, past winner of the Nobel Prize for economics.[6] Their approach has been dubbed the M^2 measure (for Modigliani-squared). Like the Sharpe ratio, the M^2 measure focuses on total volatility as a measure of risk, but its risk-adjusted measure of performance has the easy interpretation of a differential return relative to the benchmark index.

To compute the M^2 measure, we imagine that a managed portfolio, *P*, is mixed with a position in T-bills so that the complete, or "adjusted," portfolio matches the volatility of a market index such as the S&P 500. For example, if the managed portfolio has 1.5 times the standard deviation of the index, the adjusted portfolio would be two-thirds invested in the managed portfolio and one-third invested in bills. The adjusted portfolio, which we call *P**,

---

[6]Franco Modigliani and Leah Modigliani, "Risk-Adjusted Performance," *Journal of Portfolio Management*, Winter 1997, pp. 45–54.

Figure 24.2

M^2 of portfolio P.

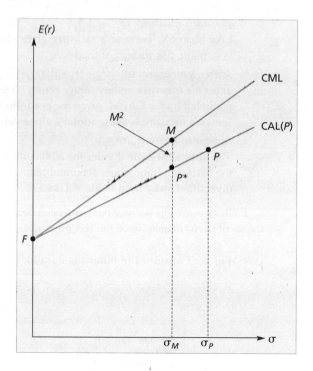

would then have the same standard deviation as the index. (If the managed portfolio had *lower* standard deviation than the index, it would be leveraged by borrowing money and investing the proceeds in the portfolio.) Because the market index and portfolio P^* have the same standard deviation, we may compare their performance simply by comparing returns. This is the M^2 measure:

$$M^2 = r_{P*} - r_M$$

In the example of Concept Check 3, P has a standard deviation of 30% versus a market standard deviation of 42%. Therefore, the adjusted portfolio P^* would be formed by mixing bills and portfolio P with weights $30/42 = .714$ in P and $1 - .714 = .286$ in bills. The expected return on this portfolio would be $(.286 \times 6\%) + (.714 \times 35\%) = 26.7\%$, which is 1.3% less than the market return. Thus portfolio P has an M^2 measure of -1.3%.

A graphical representation of the M^2 measure appears in Figure 24.2. We move down the capital allocation line corresponding to portfolio P (by mixing P with T-bills) until we reduce the standard deviation of the adjusted portfolio to match that of the market index. The M^2 measure is then the vertical distance (i.e., the difference in expected returns) between portfolios P^* and M. You can see from Figure 24.2 that P will have an M^2 measure below that of the market when its capital allocation line is less steep than the capital market line, that is, when its Sharpe ratio is less than that of the market index.[7]

The nearby box reports on the growing popularity of the M^2 measure in the investment community.

---

[7]In fact you use Figure 24.2 to show that the M^2 and Sharpe measures are directly related. Letting R denote excess returns, the geometry of the figure implies that $R_{P*} = S_P \sigma_M$, and therefore that

$$M^2 = r_{P*} - r_M = R_{P*} - R_M = S_P \sigma_M - R_M$$

NEW GAUGE MEASURES MUTUAL-FUND RISK

Fidelity Select Electronics Portfolio boasts the best five-year record in the mutual-fund business. But take volatility into account, and it tumbles to 40th place among the top 50 five-year winners. What gives?

At *The Wall Street Journal*'s request, Morgan Stanley Dean Witter strategist Leah Modigliani reshuffled the 50 best-performing funds of the past five years, using a new gauge of risk-adjusted performance she developed with her grandfather, Nobel laureate Franco Modigliani.

Her purpose: to encourage investors to consider not only raw performance but also volatility along the way, and to identify funds that have delivered the best results relative to the risks they took.

The need for fund investors to weigh risk along with potential reward has gotten a lot of attention from investment advisers and fund regulators in recent years. Many fret that investors aren't paying enough attention to risk—even at this juncture, when high stock prices and the still-unfolding Asian crisis have some market watchers worrying about the possibility of a steep U.S. stock-market slide. Hence, the appeal of risk-adjusted measures such as the recently developed M-squared.

The Modiglianis define risk as the variability, or unpredictability, in a fund's quarterly returns. They adjust each fund's risk to that of a market benchmark such as the Standard & Poor's 500-stock average. How? By hypothetically blending shares of a volatile fund with cash or by using borrowed money to leverage up the jumpiness of a more sedate fund.

The M-squared figure is the return an investor would have earned in a particular period if the fund had been diluted or leveraged to match the benchmark's risk.

Though there's nothing inherently superior about a high-risk or a low-risk fund, Ms. Modigliani says investors should favor mutual funds that are the most efficient in delivering high returns for the amount of risk they take. Over the past five years, she notes, an aggressive, risk-tolerant investor would have done better by shunning Fidelity Select Electronics in favor of a leveraged bet on an index fund that tracks the S&P 500, or on a fund such as Safeco Equity Fund that has a high M-squared.

Like many other performance and risk measures, M-squared is backward-looking. Steve Lipper, vice president of fund researchers Lipper Analytical Services, in Summit, N.J., complains that risk-adjusted returns can be deceptive because the volatility of an industry or type of investment doesn't stay constant. Several years ago, he says, technology funds appeared to have great risk-adjusted returns. Now they look terrible on a risk-adjusted basis, as the stocks have been soaring and plunging in quick succession.

One final thought for investors: While these M-squared rankings address the risk-adjusted performance of individual funds, risky funds can be skillfully blended into a low-risk diversified portfolio. "You should be thinking about the risk of your whole portfolio, not the individual pieces," says Susan Belden of the *No-Load Fund Analyst*.

Source: Karen Damato and Robert McGough, "New Gauge Measures Mutual-Fund Risk," *The Wall Street Journal*, January 9, 1998. Excerpted by permission of *The Wall Street Journal*, © 1998 Dow Jones & Company, Inc. All Rights Reserved Worldwide.

Sharpe's Measure as the Criterion for Overall Portfolios

Suppose that Jane Close constructs a portfolio and holds it for a considerable period of time. She makes no changes in portfolio composition during the period. In addition, suppose that the daily rates of return on all securities have constant means, variances, and covariances. This assures that the portfolio rate of return also has a constant mean and variance. These assumptions are unrealistic, but they make it easier to highlight the important issues. They are also crucial to understanding the shortcoming of conventional applications of performance measurement.

Now we want to evaluate the performance of Jane's portfolio. Has she made a good choice of securities? This is really a three-pronged question. First, "good choice" compared with what alternatives? Second, in choosing between two distinct alternative portfolios, what are the appropriate criteria to evaluate performance? Finally, having identified the performance criteria, is there a rule that will separate basic ability from the random luck of the draw?

Earlier chapters of this text help to determine portfolio choice criteria. If investor preferences can be summarized by a mean-variance utility function such as that introduced in

Chapter 6, we can arrive at a relatively simple criterion. The particular utility function that we used is

$$U = E(r_P) - .005A\sigma_P^2$$

where A is the coefficient of risk aversion. With mean-variance preferences, Jane wants to maximize the Sharpe measure (i.e., the ratio $[E(r_P) - r_f]/\sigma_P$). Recall that this criterion led to the selection of the tangency portfolio in Chapter 8. Jane's problem reduces to the achievement of the highest possible Sharpe ratio.

Appropriate Performance Measures in Three Scenarios

To evaluate Jane's portfolio choice, we first ask whether she intends this portfolio to be her exclusive investment vehicle. If the answer is no, we need to know her "complementary" portfolio. The appropriate measure of portfolio performance depends critically on whether the portfolio is the entire investment fund or only a portion of the investor's overall wealth.

Jane's Portfolio Represents Her Entire Risky Investment Fund   In this simplest case we need to ascertain only whether Jane's portfolio has the highest Sharpe measure. We can proceed in four steps:

1. Assume that past security performance is representative of expected performance, meaning that realized security returns over Jane's holding period exhibit similar averages and covariances that Jane had anticipated.
2. Estimate the efficient frontier of risky assets from return data over Jane's holding period.
3. Using the risk-free rate at the time of decision, find the portfolio with the highest Sharpe measure.
4. Compare Jane's Sharpe measure to that of the best portfolio.

This comprehensive approach, however, is problematic. It not only requires an extensive database and optimization techniques, but it also exacerbates the problem of inference from sample data. We have to rely on a limited sample to estimate the means and covariances of a very large set of securities. The verdict on Jane's choice will be subject to estimation errors. The very complexity of the procedure makes it hard to assess the reliability and significance of the verdict. Is there a second-best alternative?

It makes sense to compare Jane's choice to a restricted set of alternative portfolios that were easy for her to assess and invest in at the time of her decision. An obvious candidate for this set is the passive strategy, the market index portfolio. Other candidates are professionally managed active funds. The method is the same: Compare Sharpe measures.

In sum, when Jane's portfolio represents her entire investment fund, the benchmark is the market index or another specific portfolio. The performance criterion is the Sharpe measure of the actual portfolio versus the benchmark.

Jane's Portfolio Is an Active Portfolio and Is Mixed with the Market-Index Portfolio   How do we evaluate the optimal mix in this case? Call Jane's portfolio P, and denote the market portfolio by M. When the two portfolios are mixed optimally, we will see in Chapter 28 that the square of the Sharpe measure of the composite portfolio, C, is given by

$$S_C^2 = S_M^2 + \left[\frac{\alpha_P}{\sigma(e_P)} \right]^2$$

where α_P is the abnormal return of the active portfolio relative to the market-index, and $\sigma(e_P)$ is the diversifiable risk. The ratio $\alpha_P/\sigma(e_P)$ is thus the correct performance measure for P in this case, since it gives the improvement in the Sharpe measure of the overall portfolio.

To see this result intuitively, recall the single-index model:

$$r_P - r_f = \alpha_P + \beta_P(r_M - r_f) + e_P$$

If P is fairly priced, then $\alpha_P = 0$, and e_P is just diversifiable risk that can be avoided. If P is mispriced, however, α_P no longer equals zero. Instead, it represents the expected abnormal return. Holding P in addition to the market portfolio thus brings a reward of α_P against the nonsystematic risk voluntarily incurred, $\sigma(e_P)$. Therefore, the ratio of $\alpha_P/\sigma(e_P)$ is the natural benefit-to-cost ratio for portfolio P. This performance measurement is sometimes called the *appraisal ratio*:

$$AR_P = \frac{\alpha_P}{\sigma(e_P)}$$

Jane's Choice Portfolio Is One of Many Portfolios Combined into a Large Investment Fund   This third case might describe a situation where Jane, as a corporate financial officer, manages the corporate pension fund. She parcels out the entire fund to a number of portfolio managers. Then she evaluates the performance of individual managers to reallocate the fund to improve future performance. What is the correct performance measure?

We would use the appraisal ratio if the complementary portfolio to P (i.e., the part of the fund managed by others) were approximated by the market index. But you can expect other portfolio managers to take offense at this assumption. Jane, too, is likely to respond, "Do you think I am exerting all this effort just to end up with a passive portfolio?"

We can, however, approximate the benefit of portfolio P to the entire diversified fund by P's alpha value. Although α_P is not a full measure of portfolio P's performance value, it will give Jane some indication of P's potential contribution to the overall portfolio. An even better solution, however, is to use Treynor's measure.

Suppose you determine that portfolio P exhibits an alpha value of 2%. "Not bad," you tell Jane. But she pulls out of her desk a report and informs you that another portfolio, Q, has an alpha of 3%. "One hundred basis points is significant," says Jane. "Should I transfer some of my funds from P's manager to Q's?"

You tabulate the relevant data, as in Table 24.2, and graph the results as in Figure 24.3. Note that we plot P and Q in the expected return–beta (rather than the expected return–standard deviation) plane, because we assume that P and Q are two of many subportfolios

Table 24.2   Portfolio Performance

	Portfolio P	**Portfolio Q**	**Market**
Beta	.90	1.60	1.0
Excess return $(\bar{r} - \bar{r}_f)$	11%	19%	10%
Alpha*	2%	3%	0

*Alpha = Excess return − (Beta × Market excess return)
   $= (\bar{r} - \bar{r}_f) - \beta(\bar{r}_M - \bar{r}_f)$
   $= \bar{r} - [\bar{r}_f + \beta(\bar{r}_M - \bar{r}_f)]$

Figure 24.3
Treynor's measure.

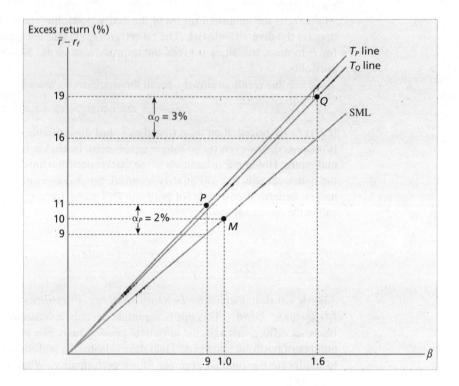

in the fund, and thus that nonsystematic risk will be largely diversified away, leaving beta as the appropriate risk measure. The security market line (SML) shows the value of α_P and α_Q as the distance of P and Q above the SML.

Suppose portfolio Q can be mixed with T-bills. Specifically, if we invest w_Q in Q and $w_F = 1 - w_Q$ in T-bills, the resulting portfolio, Q^*, will have alpha and beta values proportional to Q's alpha and beta scaled down by w_Q:

$$\alpha_{Q^*} = w_Q\alpha_Q$$
$$\beta_{Q^*} = w_Q\beta_Q$$

Thus all portfolios Q^* generated from mixing Q with T-bills plot on a straight line from the origin through Q. We call it the T-line for the Treynor measure, which is the slope of this line.

Figure 24.3 shows the T-line for portfolio P as well. P has a steeper T-line; despite its lower alpha, P is a better portfolio after all. For any *given* beta, a mixture of P with T-bills will give a better alpha than a mixture of Q with T-bills.

To see this, suppose that we choose to mix Q with T-bills to create a portfolio Q^* with a beta equal to that of P. We find the necessary proportion by solving for w_Q:

$$\beta_{Q^*} = w_Q\beta_Q = 1.6w_Q = \beta_P = .9$$
$$w_Q = \%_{16}$$

Portfolio Q^* therefore has an alpha of

$$\alpha_{Q^*} = \%_{16} \times 3 = 1.69\%$$

which is less than that of P.

In other words, the slope of the T-line is the appropriate performance criterion for the third case. The slope of the T-line for P, denoted by T_P, is given by

$$T_P = \frac{\bar{r}_P - \bar{r}_f}{\beta_P}$$

Treynor's performance measure is appealing because when an asset is part of a large investment portfolio, one should weigh its mean excess return against its *systematic* risk rather than against total risk to evaluate contribution to performance.

Like M^2, Treynor's measure is a percentage. If you subtract the market excess return from Treynor's measure, you will obtain the difference between the return on the T_P line in Figure 24.3 and the SML, at the point where $\beta = 1$. We might dub this difference the Treynor-square, or T^2, measure (analogous to M^2). Be aware though that M^2 and T^2 are as different as Sharpe's measure is from Treynor's measure. They may well rank portfolios differently.

Relationships among the Various Performance Measures

We have shown that under various scenarios one of four different performance measures is appropriate:

Sharpe: $\dfrac{E(r_P) - r_f}{\sigma_P}$

Treynor: $\dfrac{E(r_P) - r_f}{\beta_P}$

Jensen, or alpha: α_P

Appraisal ratio: $\dfrac{\alpha_P}{\sigma(e_P)}$

It is interesting to see how these measures are related to one another. Beginning with Treynor's measure, note that as the market index beta is 1.0, Treynor's measure for the market index is

$$T_M = \bar{r}_M - \bar{r}_f$$

The mean excess return of portfolio P is

$$\bar{r}_P - \bar{r}_f = \alpha_P + \beta_P(\bar{r}_M - \bar{r}_f)$$

and thus its Treynor measure is

$$T_P = \frac{\alpha_P + \beta_P(\bar{r}_M - \bar{r}_f)}{\beta_P} \tag{24.2}$$

$$= \frac{\alpha_P}{\beta_P} + \bar{r}_M - \bar{r}_f$$

$$= \frac{\alpha_P}{\beta_P} + T_M$$

Hence, the "Treynor-square" measure is

$$T^2 = T_P - T_M = \frac{\alpha_P}{\beta_P}$$

Treynor's measure compares portfolios on the basis of the alpha-to-beta ratio.[8] Note that this is very different in numerical value *and spirit* from the appraisal ratio, which is the ratio of alpha to residual risk.

Sharpe's measure for the market index portfolio is

$$S_M = \frac{\overline{r}_M - \overline{r}_f}{\sigma_M}$$

For portfolio *P* we have

$$S_P = \frac{\overline{r}_P - \overline{r}_f}{\sigma_P} = \frac{\alpha_P + \beta_P(\overline{r}_M - \overline{r}_f)}{\sigma_P}$$

With some algebra that relies on the fact that ρ^2 between *P* and *M* is

$$\rho^2 = \frac{\beta^2 \sigma_M^2}{\beta^2 \sigma_M^2 + \sigma^2(e)} = \frac{\beta^2 \sigma_M^2}{\sigma_P^2}$$

we find that

$$S_P = \frac{\alpha_P}{\sigma_P} + \frac{\beta_P(\overline{r}_M - \overline{r}_f)}{\sigma_P}$$

$$= \frac{\alpha_P}{\sigma_P} + \rho S_M$$

This expression yields some insight into the process of generating valuable performance with active management. It is obvious that one needs to find significant-alpha stocks to establish potential value. A higher portfolio alpha, however, has to be tempered by the increase in standard deviation that arises when one departs from full diversification. The more we tilt toward high-alpha stocks, the lower the correlation with the market index, ρ, and the greater the potential loss of performance value.

We conclude that it is important to use the performance measure that fits the relevant scenario. Evaluating portfolios by different performance measures may yield quite different results.

Actual Performance Measurement: An Example

Now that we have examined possible criteria for performance evaluation, we need to deal with a statistical issue: Can we assess the quality of ex ante decisions using ex post data? Before we plunge into a discussion of this problem, let us look at the rate of return on Jane's portfolio over the last 12 months. Table 24.3 shows the excess return recorded each month for Jane's portfolio *P*, one of her alternative portfolios *Q*, and the benchmark index portfolio *M*. The last rows in Table 24.3 give sample average and standard deviations. From these, and regressions of *P* and *Q* on *M*, we obtain the necessary performance statistics.

---

[8]Interestingly, although our definition of Treynor's measure is conventional, Treynor himself initially worked with the alpha-to-beta ratio. In this form the measure is independent of the market. Either measure will rank-order portfolio performance identically, because they differ by a constant (the market's Treynor value). Some call the ratio of alpha to beta "modified alpha" or "modified Jensen's measure," not realizing that this is really Treynor's measure.

Table 24.3   Excess Returns for Portfolios *P* and *Q* and the Benchmark *M* over 12 Months

Month	Jane's Portfolio *P*	Alternative *Q*	Benchmark *M*
1	3.58%	2.81%	2.20%
2	−4.91	−1.15	−8.41
3	6.51	2.53	3.27
4	11.13	37.09	14.41
5	8.78	12.88	7.71
6	9.38	39.08	14.36
7	−3.66	−8.84	−6.15
8	5.56	0.83	2.74
9	−7.72	0.85	−15.27
10	7.76	12.09	6.49
11	−4.01	−5.68	−3.13
12	0.78	−1.77	1.41
Year's average	2.76	7.56	1.63
Standard deviation	6.17	14.89	8.48

Table 24.4   Performance Statistics

	Portfolio *P*	Portfolio *Q*	Portfolio *M*
Sharpe's measure	0.45	0.51	0.19
M^2	2.19	2.69	0.00
SCL regression statistics			
Alpha	1.63	5.28	0.00
Beta	0.69	1.40	1.00
Treynor	4.00	3.77	1.63
T^2	2.37	2.14	0.00
$\sigma(e)$	1.95	8.98	0.00
Appraisal ratio	0.84	0.59	0.00
R-SQR	0.91	0.64	1.00

The performance statistics in Table 24.4 show that portfolio *Q* is more aggressive than *P*, in the sense that its beta is significantly higher (1.40 vs. .69). On the other hand, from its residual standard deviation *P* appears better diversified (1.95% vs. 8.98%). Both portfolios outperformed the benchmark market index, as is evident from their larger Sharpe measures (and thus positive M^2) and their positive alphas.

Which portfolio is more attractive based on reported performance? If *P* or *Q* represents the entire investment fund, *Q* would be preferable on the basis of its higher Sharpe measure (.51 vs. .45) and better M^2 (2.69% vs. 2.19%). On the other hand, as an active portfolio to be mixed with the market index, *P* is preferable to *Q*, as is evident from its appraisal ratio (. 84 vs. .59). For the third scenario, where *P* and *Q* are competing for a role as one of a number of subportfolios, the inadequacy of alpha as a performance measure is evident. Whereas *Q*'s alpha is larger (5.28% vs. 1.63%), *P*'s beta is low enough to give it a better Treynor measure (4.00 vs. 3.77), suggesting that it is superior to *Q* as one portfolio to be mixed with others.

This analysis is based on 12 months of data only, a period too short to lend statistical significance to the conclusions. Even longer observation intervals may not be enough to make the decision clear-cut, which represents a further problem.

Realized Returns versus Expected Returns

When evaluating a portfolio, the evaluator knows neither the portfolio manager's original expectations nor whether those expectations made sense. One can only observe performance after the fact and hope that random results are not taken for, or do not hide, true underlying ability. But risky asset returns are "noisy," which complicates the inference problem. To avoid making mistakes, we have to determine the "significance level" of a performance measure to know whether it reliably indicates ability.

Consider Joe Dart, a portfolio manager. Suppose that his portfolio has an alpha of 20 basis points per month, which makes for a hefty 2.4% per year before compounding. Let us assume that the return distribution of Joe's portfolio has constant mean, beta, and alpha, a heroic assumption, but one that is in line with the usual treatment of performance measurement. Suppose that for the measurement period Joe's portfolio beta is 1.2 and the monthly standard deviation of the residual (nonsystematic risk) is .02 (2%). With a market index standard deviation of 6.5% per month (22.5% per year), Joe's portfolio systematic variance is

$$\beta^2 \sigma_M^2 = 1.2^2 \times 6.5^2 = 60.84$$

and hence the correlation coefficient between his portfolio and the market index is

$$\rho = \left[\frac{\beta^2 \sigma_M^2}{\beta^2 \sigma_M^2 + \sigma^2(e)} \right]^{1/2}$$

$$= \left[\frac{60.84}{60.84 + 4} \right]^{1/2} = .97$$

which shows that his portfolio is quite well diversified.

To estimate Joe's portfolio alpha from the security characteristic line (SCL), we regress the portfolio excess returns on the market index. Suppose that we are in luck and the regression estimates yield the true parameters. That means that our SCL estimates for the N months are

$$\hat{\alpha} = .2\%, \qquad \hat{\beta} = 1.2, \qquad \hat{\sigma}(e) = 2\%$$

The evaluator who runs such a regression, however, does not know the true values, and hence must compute the t-statistic of the alpha estimate to determine whether to reject the hypothesis that Joe's alpha is zero, that is, that he has no superior ability.

The standard error of the alpha estimate in the SCL regression is approximately

$$\sigma(\hat{\alpha}) = \frac{\hat{\sigma}(e)}{\sqrt{N}}$$

where N is the number of observations and $\hat{\sigma}(e)$ is the sample estimate of nonsystematic risk. The t-statistic for the alpha estimate is then

$$t(\hat{\alpha}) = \frac{\hat{\alpha}}{\hat{\sigma}(\alpha)} \tag{24.3}$$

$$= \frac{\hat{\alpha}\sqrt{N}}{\hat{\sigma}(e)}$$

Suppose that we require a significance level of 5%. This requires a $t(\hat{\alpha})$ value of 1.96 if N is large. With $\hat{\alpha} = .2$ and $\hat{\sigma}(e) = 2$, we solve equation 24.3 for N and find that

$$1.96 = \frac{.2\sqrt{N}}{2}$$

$$N = 384 \text{ months}$$

or 32 years!

What have we shown? Here is an analyst who has very substantial ability. The example is biased in his favor in the sense that we have assumed away statistical problems. Nothing changes in the parameters over a long period of time. Furthermore, the sample period "behaves" perfectly. Regression estimates are all perfect. Still, it will take Joe's entire working career to get to the point where statistics will confirm his true ability. We have to conclude that the problem of statistical inference makes performance evaluation extremely difficult in practice.

Concept
CHECK

Question 4 • Suppose an analyst has a measured alpha of .2% with a standard error of 2%, as in our example. What is the probability that the positive alpha is due to luck of the draw and that true ability is zero?

24.3   PERFORMANCE MEASUREMENT WITH CHANGING PORTFOLIO COMPOSITION

We have seen already that the high variance of stock returns requires a very long observation period to determine performance levels with any statistical significance, even if portfolio returns are distributed with constant mean and variance. Imagine how this problem is compounded when portfolio return distributions are constantly changing.

It is acceptable to assume that the return distributions of passive strategies have constant mean and variance when the measurement interval is not too long. However, under an active strategy return distributions change by design, as the portfolio manager updates the portfolio in accordance with the dictates of financial analysis. In such a case estimating various statistics from a sample period assuming a constant mean and variance may lead to substantial errors. Let us look at an example.

Suppose that the Sharpe measure of the market index is .4. Over an initial period of 52 weeks, the portfolio manager executes a low-risk strategy with an annualized mean excess return of 1% and standard deviation of 2%. This makes for a Sharpe measure of .5, which beats the passive strategy. Over the next 52-week period this manager finds that a *high*-risk strategy is optimal, with an annual mean excess return of 9% and standard deviation of 18%. Here, again, the Sharpe measure is .5. Over the two-year period our manager maintains a better-than-passive Sharpe measure.

Figure 24.4 shows a pattern of (annualized) quarterly returns that are consistent with our description of the manager's strategy of two years. In the first four quarters the excess returns are –1%, 3%, –1%, and 3%, making for an average of 1% and standard deviation of 2%. In the next four quarters the returns are –9%, 27%, –9%, 27%, making for an average of 9% and standard deviation of 18%. Thus *both* years exhibit a Sharpe measure of .5. However, over the eight-quarter sequence the mean and standard deviation are 5% and 13.42%, respectively, making for a Sharpe measure of only .37, apparently inferior to the passive strategy!

What happened? The shift of the mean from the first four quarters to the next was not recognized as a shift in strategy. Instead, the difference in mean returns in the two years added to the *appearance* of volatility in portfolio returns. The active strategy with shifting means appears riskier than it really is and biases the estimate of the Sharpe measure down-

Figure 24.4
Portfolio returns.

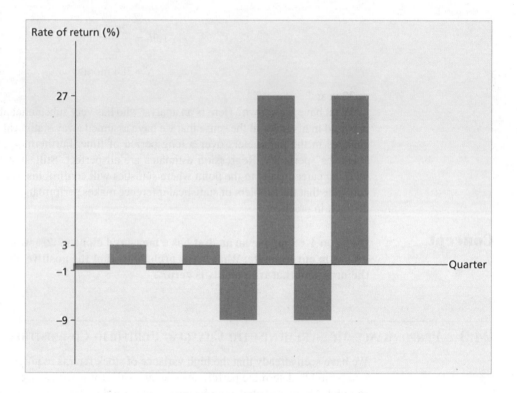

ward. We conclude that for actively managed portfolios it is helpful to keep track of port-folio composition and changes in portfolio mean and risk. We will see another example of this problem in the next section, which deals with market timing.

24.4   MARKET TIMING

In its pure form, market timing involves shifting funds between a market-index portfolio and a safe asset, such as T-bills or a money market fund, depending on whether the market as a whole is expected to outperform the safe asset. In practice, of course, most managers do not shift fully between T-bills and the market. How can we account for partial shifts into the market when it is expected to perform well?

To simplify, suppose that an investor holds only the market-index portfolio and T-bills. If the weight of the market were constant, say, .6, then portfolio beta would also be con-stant, and the SCL would plot as a straight line with slope .6, as in Figure 24.5A. If, how-ever, the investor could correctly time the market and shift funds into it in periods when the market does well, the S would plot as in Figure 24.5B. If bull and bear markets can be pre-dicted, the investor will shift more into the market when the market is about to go up. The portfolio beta and the slope of the SCL will be higher when r_M is higher, resulting in the curved line that appears in Figure 24.5B.

Treynor and Mazuy[9] were the first to propose that such a line can be estimated by adding a squared term to the usual linear index model:

---

[9]Jack L. Treynor and Kay Mazuy, "Can Mutual Funds Outguess the Market?" *Harvard Business Review* 43 (July–August 1966).

Figure 24.5
Characteristic lines. **A**, No market timing, beta is constant. **B**, Market timing, beta increases with expected market excess return. **C**, Market timing with only two values of beta.

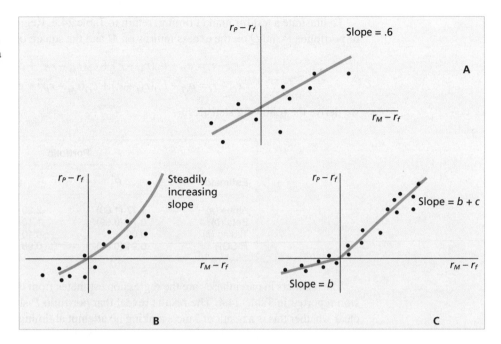

$$r_P - r_f = a + b(r_M - r_f) + c(r_M - r_f)^2 + e_P$$

where r_P is the portfolio return, and a, b, and c are estimated by regression analysis. If c turns out to be positive, we have evidence of timing ability, because this last term will make the characteristic line steeper as $r_M - r_f$ is larger. Treynor and Mazuy estimated this equation for a number of mutual funds, but found little evidence of timing ability.

A similar and simpler methodology was proposed by Henriksson and Merton.[10] These authors suggested that the beta of the portfolio take only two values: a large value if the market is expected to do well and a small value otherwise. Under this scheme the portfolio characteristic line appears as Figure 24.5C. Such a line appears in regression form as

$$r_P - r_f = a + b(r_M - r_f) + c(r_M - r_f)D + e_P$$

where D is a dummy variable that equals 1 for $r_M > r_f$ and zero otherwise. Hence the beta of the portfolio is b in bear markets and $b + c$ in bull markets. Again, a positive value of c implies market timing ability.

Henriksson[11] estimated this equation for 116 mutual funds over the period 1968 to 1980. He found that the average value of c for the funds was *negative*, and equal to $-.07$, although the value was not statistically significant at the conventional 5% level. Eleven funds had significantly positive values of c, while eight had significantly negative values. Overall, 62% of the funds had negative point estimates of timing ability. In sum, the results showed little evidence of market timing ability. Perhaps this should be expected; given the tremendous values to be reaped by a successful market timer, it would be surprising in nearly efficient markets to uncover clear-cut evidence of such skills.

[10]Roy D. Henriksson and R. C. Merton, "On Market Timing and Investment Performance. II. Statistical Procedures for Evaluating Forecast Skills," *Journal of Business* 54 (October 1981).

[11]Roy D. Henriksson, "Market Timing and Mutual Fund Performance: An Empirical Investigation," *Journal of Business* 57 (January 1984).

To illustrate a test for market timing, return to Table 24.3. Regressing the excess returns of portfolios P and Q on the excess returns on M and the square of these returns,

$$r_P - r_f = a_P + b_P(r_M - r_f) + c_P(r_M - r_f)^2 + e_P$$
$$r_Q - r_f = a_Q + b_Q(r_M - r_f) + c_Q(r_M - r_f)^2 + e_Q$$

we derive the following statistics:

		Portfolio	
Estimate		**P**	**Q**
Alpha (*a*)		1.77 (1.63)	−2.29 (5.28)
Beta (*b*)		0.70 (0.69)	1.10 (1.40)
Timing (*c*)		0.00	0.10
R-SQR		0.91 (0.91)	0.98 (0.64)

The numbers in parentheses are the regression estimates from the single variable regression reported in Table 24.4. The results reveal that portfolio P shows no timing. It is not clear whether this is a result of Jane's making no attempt at timing or that the effort to time the market was in vain and served only to increase portfolio variance unnecessarily.

The results for portfolio Q, however, reveal that timing has, in all likelihood, successfully been attempted. The timing coefficient, c, is estimated at .10. This describes a successful timing effort that was offset by unsuccessful stock selection. Note that the alpha estimate, a, is now −2.29% as opposed to the 5.28% estimate derived from the regression equation that did not allow for the possibility of timing activity.

This is an example of the inadequacy of conventional performance evaluation techniques that assume constant mean returns and constant risk. The market timer constantly shifts beta and mean return, moving into and out of the market. Whereas the expanded regression captures this phenomenon, the simple SCL does not. The relative desirability of portfolios P and Q remains unclear in the sense that the value of the timing success and selectivity failure of Q compared with P has yet to be evaluated. The important point for performance evaluation, however, is that expanded regressions can capture many of the effects of portfolio composition change that would confound the more conventional mean-variance measures.

24.5   PERFORMANCE ATTRIBUTION PROCEDURES

Rather than focus on risk-adjusted returns, practitioners often want simply to ascertain which decisions resulted in superior or inferior performance. Superior investment performance depends on an ability to be in the "right" securities at the right time. Such timing and selection ability may be considered broadly, such as being in equities as opposed to fixed-income securities when the stock market is performing well. Or it may be defined at a more detailed level, such as choosing the relatively better-performing stocks within a particular industry.

Portfolio managers constantly make broad-brush asset allocation decisions as well as more detailed sector and security allocation decisions within asset class. Performance attribution studies attempt to decompose overall performance into discrete components that may be identified with a particular level of the portfolio selection process.

Attribution studies start from the broadest asset allocation choices and progressively focus on ever-finer details of portfolio choice. The difference between a managed portfolio's performance and that of a benchmark portfolio then may be expressed as the sum of the contributions to performance of a series of decisions made at the various levels of the portfolio construction process. For example, one common attribution system decomposes performance into three components: (1) broad asset market allocation choices across equity, fixed-income, and money markets; (2) industry (sector) choice within each market; and (3) security choice within each sector.

The attribution method explains the difference in returns between a managed portfolio, *P*, and a selected benchmark portfolio, *B*, called the **bogey**. Suppose that the universe of assets for *P* and *B* includes *n* asset classes such as equities, bonds, and bills. For each asset class, a benchmark index portfolio is determined. For example, the S&P 500 may be chosen as benchmark for equities. The bogey portfolio is set to have fixed weights in each asset class, and its rate of return is given by

$$r_B = \sum_{i=1}^{n} w_{Bi} r_{Bi}$$

where w_{Bi} is the weight of the bogey in asset class *i*, and r_{Bi} is the return on the benchmark portfolio of that class over the evaluation period. The portfolio managers choose weights in each class, w_{Pi}, based on their capital market expectations, and they choose a portfolio of the securities within each class based on their security analysis, which earns r_{Pi} over the evaluation period. Thus the return of the managed portfolio will be

$$r_P = \sum_{i=1}^{n} w_{Pi} r_{Pi}$$

The difference between the two rates of return, therefore, is

$$r_P - r_B = \sum_{i=1}^{n} w_{Pi} r_{Pi} - \sum_{i=1}^{n} w_{Bi} r_{Bi} = \sum_{i=1}^{n} (w_{Pi} r_{Pi} - w_{Bi} r_{Bi}) \tag{24.4}$$

Each term in the summation of equation 24.4 can be rewritten in a way that shows how asset allocation decisions versus security selection decisions for each asset class contributed to overall performance. We decompose each term of the summation into a sum of two terms as follows. Note that the two terms we have labeled contributions from asset allocation and security selection in the following decomposition do in fact sum to the total contribution of each asset class to overall performance.

Contribution from asset allocation	$(w_{Pi} - w_{Bi}) r_{Bi}$
+ Contribution from security selection	$w_{Pi}(r_{Pi} - r_{Bi})$
= Total contribution from asset class *i*	$w_{Pi} r_{Pi} - w_{Bi} r_{Bi}$

The first term of the sum measures the impact of asset allocation because it shows how deviations of the actual weight from the benchmark weight for that asset class multiplied by the index return for the asset class added to or subtracted from total performance. The second term of the sum measures the impact of security selection because it shows how the manager's excess return *within* the asset class compared to the benchmark return for that class multiplied by the portfolio weight for that class added to or subtracted from total performance. Figure 24.6 presents a graphical interpretation of the attribution of overall performance into security selection versus asset allocation.

Figure 24.6
Performance
attribution of *i*th asset
class. Enclosed area
indicates total rate of
return.

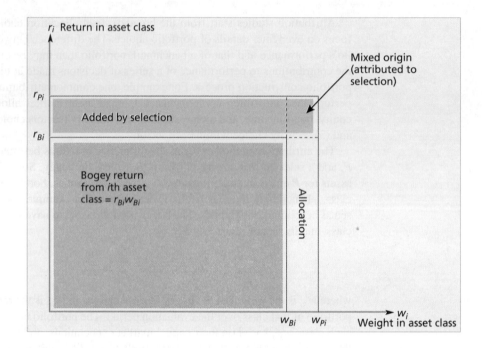

To illustrate this method, consider the attribution results for a hypothetical portfolio. The portfolio invests in stocks, bonds, and money market securities. An attribution analysis appears in Tables 24.5 through 24.8. The portfolio return over the month is 5.34%.

The first step is to establish a benchmark level of performance against which performance ought to be compared. This benchmark, again, is called the bogey. It is designed to measure the returns the portfolio manager would earn if he or she were to follow a completely passive strategy. "Passive" in this context has two attributes. First, it means that the allocation of funds across broad asset classes is set in accord with a notion of "usual," or neutral, allocation across sectors. This would be considered a passive asset market allocation. Second, it means that within each asset class, the portfolio manager holds an indexed portfolio such as the S&P 500 index for the equity sector. In such a manner, the passive strategy used as a performance benchmark rules out asset allocation as well as security selection decisions. Any departure of the manager's return from the passive benchmark must be due to either asset allocation bets (departures from the neutral allocation across markets) or security selection bets (departures from the passive index within asset classes.)

While we have already discussed in earlier chapters the justification for indexing within sectors, it is worth briefly explaining the determination of the neutral allocation of funds across the broad asset classes. Weights that are designated as "neutral" will depend on the risk tolerance of the investor and must be determined in consultation with the client. For example, risk-tolerant clients may place a large fraction of their portfolio in the equity market, perhaps directing the fund manager to set neutral weights of 75% equity, 15% bonds, and 10% cash equivalents. Any deviation from these weights must be justified by a belief that one or another market will either over- or underperform its usual risk-return profile. In contrast, more risk-averse clients may set neutral weights of 45%/35%/20% for the three markets. Therefore, their portfolios in normal circumstances will be exposed to less risk than that of the risk-tolerant client. Only intentional bets on market performance will result in departures from this profile.

Table 24.5   Performance of the Managed Portfolio

	Bogey Performance and Excess Return	
Component	Benchmark Weight	Return of Index during Month (percent)
Equity (S&P 500)	.60	5.81
Bonds (Lehman Brothers Index)	.30	1.45
Cash (money market)	.10	0.48
Bogey = (.60 × 5.81) + (.30 × 1.45) + (.10 × 0.48) = 3.97%		
Return of managed portfolio	5.34%	
− Return of bogey portfolio	3.97	
Excess return of managed portfolio	1.37%	

In Table 24.5, the neutral weights have been set at 60% equity, 30% fixed income, and 10% cash (money market securities). The bogey portfolio, comprised of investments in each index with the 60/30/10 weights, returned 3.97%. The managed portfolio's measure of performance is positive and equal to its actual return less the return of the bogey: 5.34 − 3.97 = 1.37%. The next step is to allocate the 1.37% excess return to the separate decisions that contributed to it.

Asset Allocation Decisions

Our hypothetical managed portfolio is invested in the equity, fixed-income, and money markets with weights of 70%, 7%, and 23%, respectively. The portfolio's performance could have to do with the departure of this weighting scheme from the benchmark 60/30/10 weights and/or to superior or inferior results *within* each of the three broad markets.

To isolate the effect of the manager's asset allocation choice, we measure the performance of a hypothetical portfolio that would have been invested in the indexes for each market with weights 70/7/23. This return measures the effect of the shift away from the benchmark 60/30/10 weights without allowing for any effects attributable to active management of the securities selected within each market.

Superior performance relative to the bogey is achieved by overweighting investments in markets that turn out to perform well and by underweighting those in poorly performing markets. The contribution of asset allocation to superior performance equals the sum over all markets of the excess weight in each market times the return of the market index.

Table 24.6**A** demonstrates that asset allocation contributed 31 basis points to the portfolio's overall excess return of 137 basis points. The major factor contributing to superior performance in this month is the heavy weighting of the equity market in a month when the equity market has an excellent return of 5.81%.

Sector and Security Selection Decisions

If .31% of the excess performance can be attributed to advantageous asset allocation across markets, the remaining 1.06% then must be attributable to sector selection and security selection within each market. Table 24.6**B** details the contribution of the managed portfolio's sector and security selection to total performance.

Panel **B** shows that the equity component of the managed portfolio has a return of 7.28% versus a return of 5.81% for the S&P 500. The fixed-income return is 1.89% versus 1.45% for the Lehman Brothers Index. The superior performance in both equity and

Table 24.6   Performance Attribution

A. Contribution of Asset Allocation to Performance				
Market	**(1) Actual Weight in Market**	**(2) Benchmark Weight in Market**	**(3) Excess Weight**	**(4) Market Return (%)**	**(5) = (3) × (4) Contribution to Performance (%)**
Equity	.70	.60	.10	5.81	.5810
Fixed-income	.07	.30	−.23	1.45	−.3335
Cash	.23	.10	.13	.48	.0624
Contribution of asset allocation					.3099

B. Contribution of Selection to Total Performance				
Market	**(1) Portfolio Performance (%)**	**(2) Index Performance (%)**	**(3) Excess Performance (%)**	**(4) Portfolio Weight**	**(5) = (3) × (4) Contribution (%)**
Equity	7.28	5.81	1.47	.70	1.03
Fixed-income	1.89	1.45	0.44	.07	0.03
Contribution of selection within markets					1.06

Table 24.7   Sector Selection within the Equity Market

Sector	**(1) Beginning of Month Weights (%)** Portfolio	**(2) Beginning of Month Weights (%)** S&P 500	**(3) Difference in Weights (%)**	**(4) Sector Return**	**(5) = (3) × (4) Sector Allocation Contribution**
Basic materials	1.96	8.3	−6.34	6.4	−0.4058
Business services	7.84	4.1	3.74	6.5	0.2431
Capital goods	1.87	7.8	−5.93	3.7	−0.2194
Consumer cyclical	8.47	12.5	−4.03	8.4	−0.3385
Consumer noncyclical	40.37	20.4	19.97	9.4	1.8772
Credit sensitive	24.01	21.8	2.21	4.6	0.1017
Energy	13.53	14.2	−0.67	2.1	−0.0141
Technology	1.95	10.9	−8.95	−0.1	0.0090
Total					1.2532

fixed-income markets weighted by the portfolio proportions invested in each market sums to the 1.06% contribution to performance attributable to sector and security selection.

Table 24.7 documents the sources of the equity market performance by each sector within the market. The first three columns detail the allocation of funds within the equity market compared to their representation in the S&P 500. Column (4) shows the rate of return of each sector. The contribution of each sector's allocation presented in Column (5) equals the product of the difference in the sector weight and the sector's performance.

Note that good performance (a positive contribution) derives from overweighting well-performing sectors such as consumer noncyclicals, as well as underweighting poorly performing sectors such as technology. The excess return of the equity component of the portfolio attributable to sector allocation alone is 1.25%. Table 24.6**B**, Column (3) shows

Table 24.8   Portfolio Attribution: Summary

		Contribution (basis points)
1. Asset allocation		31
2. Selection		
a. Equity excess return (basis points)		
i. Sector allocation	125	
ii. Security selection	22	
	147 × .70 (portfolio weight) =	102.9
b. Fixed-income excess return	44 × .07 (portfolio weight) =	3.1
Total excess return of portfolio		137.0

that the equity component of the portfolio outperformed the S&P 500 by 1.47%. We conclude that the effect of security selection *within* sectors must have contributed an additional 1.47 − 1.25, or .22%, to the performance of the equity component of the portfolio.

A similar sector analysis can be applied to the fixed-income portion of the portfolio, but we do not show those results here.

Summing Up Component Contributions

In this particular month, all facets of the portfolio selection process were successful. Table 24.8 details the contribution of each aspect of performance. Asset allocation across the major security markets contributes 31 basis points. Sector and security allocation within those markets contributes 106 basis points, for total excess portfolio performance of 137 basis points.

The sector and security allocation of 106 basis points can be partitioned further. Sector allocation within the equity market results in excess performance of 125 basis points, and security selection within sectors contributes 22 basis points. (The total equity excess performance of 147 basis points is multiplied by the 70% weight in equity to obtain contribution to portfolio performance.) Similar partitioning could be done for the fixed-income sector.

Concept    **Question 5**

a. **Suppose the benchmark weights had been set at 70% equity, 25% fixed-income, and 5% cash equivalents. What then are the contributions of the manager's asset allocation choices?**

b. **Suppose the S&P 500 return is 5%. Compute the new value of the manager's security selection choices.**

24.6   EVALUATING PERFORMANCE EVALUATION

Performance evaluation has two very basic problems:

1. Many observations are needed for significant results even when portfolio mean and variance are constant.

2. Shifting parameters when portfolios are actively managed make accurate performance evaluation all the more elusive.

Although these objective difficulties cannot be overcome completely, it is clear that to obtain reasonably reliable performance measures we need to do the following:

1. Maximize the number of observations by taking more frequent return readings.
2. Specify the exact makeup of the portfolio to obtain better estimates of the risk parameters at each observation period.

Suppose an evaluator knows the exact portfolio composition at the opening of each day. Because the daily return on each security is available, the total daily return on the portfolio can be calculated. Furthermore, the exact portfolio composition allows the evaluator to estimate the risk characteristics (variance, beta, residual variance) for each day. Thus daily risk-adjusted rates of return can be obtained. Although a performance measure for one day is statistically unreliable, the number of days with such rich data accumulates quickly. Performance evaluation that accounts for frequent revision in portfolio composition is superior by far to evaluation that assumes constant risk characteristics over the entire measurement period.

What sort of evaluation takes place in practice? Performance reports for portfolio managers traditionally have been based on quarterly data over 5 to 10 years. Currently, managers of mutual funds are required to disclose the exact composition of their portfolios only quarterly. Trading activity that immediately precedes the reporting date is known as "window dressing." Rumor has it that window dressing involves changes in portfolio composition to make it look as if the manager chose successful stocks. If IBM performed well over the quarter, for example, a portfolio manager will make sure that his or her portfolio includes a lot of IBM on the reporting date whether or not it did during the quarter and whether or not IBM is expected to perform as well over the next quarter. Of course, portfolio managers deny such activity, and we know of no published evidence to substantiate the allegation. However, if window dressing is quantitatively significant, even the reported quarterly composition data can be misleading. Mutual funds publish portfolio values on a daily basis, which means the rate of return for each day is publicly available, but portfolio composition is not.

Moreover, mutual fund managers have had considerable leeway in the presentation of both past investment performance and fees charged for management services. The resultant noncomparability of net-of-expense performance numbers has made it difficult to meaningfully compare funds.

This situation may be changing, however. The money management industry is beginning to respond to demands for more complete and easily interpretable data on historical performance. For example, the Association of Investment Management and Research (AIMR) recently published an extensive set of *Performance Presentation Standards* (see the selected readings). The nearby box briefly summarizes some of the highlights of these recommendations. The thrust of these recommendations is that firms are not allowed to "cherry pick" when presenting their performance history: A complete record of performance is required. For example, firms must present returns for all years, as opposed to strategically choosing a starting date that makes subsequent performance look best. They also should provide the investment performance of an index against which their performance may reasonably be compared. Similarly, composite results for the firm must include returns of all of its managers, even those who have since left the firm. The firm, therefore, may not ignore the results of its unsuccessful managers who have since been replaced. The firm, not the individual manager, has the responsibility for performance. Finally, the firm is encouraged to supply risk measures such as beta or duration to make risk-return trade-offs easier to evaluate. Although the AIMR guidelines do not have the force of law, it nevertheless is expected that they will form the basis for industry performance presentation practices.

Traditional academic research uses monthly, weekly, and more recently even daily data. But such research makes no use of changes in portfolio composition because the data usu-

HIGHLIGHTS OF AIMR PERFORMANCE PRESENTATION STANDARDS

- Returns must be total returns, including income and capital appreciation. Income should include accrued interest on securities.

- Annual returns should be reported for all years individually, as well as for longer periods. Firms should present time-weighted average rates of return (with portfolios valued at least quarterly, but preferably monthly or more frequently where feasible) and present geometric average linked returns (compound annualized returns) to summarize average performance. Portfolios should be revalued whenever large cash flows (e.g., more than 10% of the portfolio's value) might affect performance.

- Performance should be reported before fees, except where SEC advertising requirements mandate after-fee performance (because fees are often a function of size of assets). Fee schedules should be clearly presented.

- Composite results should reflect the record of the firm, not of individual managers. A portfolio's return should be included in the firm's composite performance as of the first full reporting period for which the portfolio is under management. Asset weighting within a composite should use beginning-of-period weights based on market value. Composite returns may not be biased by excluding selected portfolios. For example, portfolios no longer under management must be included in historical composites. Composite results may not be adjusted because of changes in the firm's organization or personnel.

- Composite returns should be reported for at least a 10-year period; 20 years is preferable if the company has been in existence for that period. Firms may not link simulated (or model) portfolio returns based on some trading strategy with actual performance.

- Performance results must be presented, including positions in cash and cash equivalents. Cash positions must be assigned to various portfolios at the beginning of each reporting period.

- The total return of multiple-asset portfolios (e.g., balanced accounts) must be included in composite results. If segment returns (i.e., individual asset class returns) from multiple-asset composite portfolios are included in the performance of a single asset class composite, a cash allocation to each segment must be made at the beginning of each reporting period.

- Risk measures such as beta, duration, or standard deviation are encouraged. In addition, benchmarks for performance evaluation such as returns on market indexes or normal portfolios should be chosen to reflect the expected risk or investment style of the client portfolio. Rebalancing of the benchmark asset allocation of multiple-asset portfolios should be agreed to by managers and clients in advance.

- In addition to actual results, performance for accounts utilizing leverage should be restated to an all-cash (no leverage) basis.

ally are unavailable. Therefore, performance evaluation is unsatisfactory in both the academic and practitioner communities.

Portfolio managers reveal their portfolio composition only when they have to, which so far is quarterly. This is not nearly sufficient for adequate evaluation. However, current computer and communication technology makes it easy to use daily composition data for evaluation purposes. If the technology required for meaningful evaluation is in place, implementation of more accurate performance measurement techniques could improve welfare by enabling the public to identify the truly talented investment managers.

SUMMARY

1. The appropriate performance measure depends on the role of the portfolio to be evaluated. Appropriate performance measures are as follows:
   a. Sharpe: when the portfolio represents the entire investment fund.
   b. Appraisal ratio: when the portfolio represents the active portfolio to be optimally mixed with the passive portfolio.
   c. Treynor or Jensen: when the portfolio represents one subportfolio of many.

2. Many observations are required to eliminate the effect of the "luck of the draw" from the evaluation process because portfolio returns commonly are very "noisy."

3. The shifting mean and variance of actively managed portfolios make it even harder to assess performance. A typical example is the attempt of portfolio managers to time the market, resulting in ever-changing portfolio betas.

4. A simple way to measure timing and selection success simultaneously is to estimate an expanded security characteristic line, with a quadratic term added to the usual index model.

5. Common attribution procedures partition performance improvements to asset allocation, sector selection, and security selection. Performance is assessed by calculating departures of portfolio composition from a benchmark or neutral portfolio.

Key Terms

dollar-weighted rate of return	comparison universe	Jensen's measure
time-weighted return	Sharpe's measure	appraisal ratio
	Treynor's measure	bogey

Selected Readings

The mean-variance–based performance evaluation literature is based on early papers by:
Sharpe, William. "Mutual Fund Performance." *Journal of Business* 39 (January 1966).
Treynor, Jack L. "How to Rate Management Investment Funds." *Harvard Business Review* 43 (January–February 1966).
Jensen, Michael C. "The Performance of Mutual Funds in the Period 1945–1964." *Journal of Finance*, May 1968.
Jensen, Michael C. "Risk, the Pricing of Capital Assets, and the Evaluation of Investment Portfolios." *Journal of Business*, April 1969.

The problems that arise when conventional mean-variance measures are calculated in the presence of a shifting return distribution are treated in:
Dybvig, Philip H.; and Stephen A. Ross. "Differential Information and Performance Measurement Using a Security Market Line." *Journal of Finance* 40 (June 1985).

The separation of investment ability into timing versus selection activity derives from:
Fama, Eugene. "Components of Investment Performance." *Journal of Finance* 25 (June 1970).

The Association for Investment Management and Research, the parent of the ICFA, has proposed a set of standards for reporting investment performance. See:
Performance Presentation Standards. Charlottesville, VA: AIMR, 1993.

Problems

1. Consider the rate of return of stocks ABC and XYZ.

Year	r_{ABC}	r_{XYZ}
1	20%	30%
2	12	12
3	14	18
4	3	0
5	1	−10

a. Calculate the arithmetic average return on these stocks over the sample period.
b. Which stock has greater dispersion around the mean?
c. Calculate the geometric average returns of each stock. What do you conclude?
d. If you were equally likely to earn a return of 20%, 12%, 14%, 3%, or 1%, in each of the five annual returns for stock ABC, what would be your expected rate of return? What if the five possible outcomes were those of stock XYZ?

2. XYZ stock price and dividend history are as follows:

Year	Beginning-of-Year Price	Dividend Paid at Year-End
1995	$100	$4
1996	$120	$4
1997	$ 90	$4
1998	$100	$4

An investor buys three shares of XYZ at the beginning of 1995, buys another two shares at the beginning of 1996, sells one share at the beginning of 1997 and sells all four remaining shares at the beginning of 1998.

a. What are the arithmetic and geometric average time-weighted rates of return for the investor?

b. What is the dollar-weighted rate of return? (Hint: Carefully prepare a chart of cash flows for the *four* dates corresponding to the turns of the year for January 1, 1995 to January 1, 1998. If your calculator cannot calculate internal rate of return, you will have to use trial and error.)

3. A manager buys three shares of stock today, and then sells one of those shares each year for the next three years. His actions and the price history of the stock are summarized below. The stock pays no dividends.

Time	Price	Action
0	90	Buy 3 shares
1	100	Sell 1 share
2	100	Sell 1 share
3	100	Sell 1 share

a. Calculate the time-weighted geometric average return on this "portfolio."

b. Calculate the time-weighted arithmetic average return on this portfolio.

c. Calculate the dollar-weighted average return on this portfolio.

4. Based on current dividend yields and expected capital gains, the expected rates of return on portfolios A and B are 12% and 16%, respectively. The beta of A is .7, while that of B is 1.4. The T-bill rate is currently 5%, whereas the expected rate of return of the S&P 500 index is 13%. The standard deviation of portfolio A is 12% annually, that of B is 31%, and that of the S&P 500 index is 18%.

a. If you currently hold a market-index portfolio, would you choose to add either of these portfolios to your holdings? Explain.

b. If instead you could invest *only* in T-bills and *one* of these portfolios, which would you choose?

5. Consider the two (excess return) index-model regression results for stocks A and B. The risk-free rate over the period was 6%, and the market's average return was 14%. Performance is measured using an index model regression on excess returns.

	Stock A	Stock B
Index model regression estimates	$1\% + 1.2(r_M - r_f)$	$2\% + .8(r_M - r_f)$
R-square	.576	.436
Residual standard deviation, $\sigma(e)$	10.3%	19.1%
Standard deviation of excess returns	21.6%	24.9%

    a. Calculate the following statistics for each stock:
      i. Alpha.
      ii. Appraisal ratio.
      iii. Sharpe measure.
      iv. Treynor measure.
    b. Which stock is the best choice under the following circumstances?
      i. This is the only risky asset to be held by the investor.
      ii. This stock will be mixed with the rest of the investor's portfolio, currently composed solely of holdings in the market index fund.
      iii. This is one of many stocks that the investor is analyzing to form an actively managed stock portfolio.

6. Evaluate the market timing and security selection abilities of four managers whose performances are plotted in the accompanying diagrams.

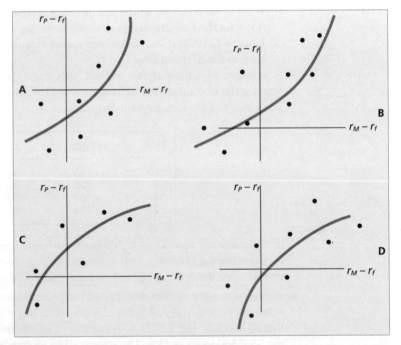

7. Consider the following information regarding the performance of a money manager in a recent month. The table represents the actual return of each sector of the manager's portfolio in column 1, the fraction of the portfolio allocated to each sector in column 2, the benchmark or neutral sector allocations in column 3, and the returns of sector indices in column 4.

	Actual Return	Actual Weight	Benchmark Weight	Index Return
Equity	2%	.70	.60	2.5% (S&P 500)
Bonds	1	.20	.30	1.2 (Salomon Brothers Index)
Cash	0.5	.10	.10	0.5

    a. What was the manager's return in the month? What was her overperformance or underperformance?

b. What was the contribution of security selection to relative performance?

c. What was the contribution of asset allocation to relative performance? Confirm that the sum of selection and allocation contributions equals her total "excess" return relative to the bogey.

8. A global equity manager is assigned to select stocks from a universe of large stocks throughout the world. The manager will be evaluated by comparing her returns to the return on the MSCI World Market Portfolio, but she is free to hold stocks from various countries in whatever proportions she finds desirable. Results for a given month are contained in the following table:

Country	Weight In MSCI Index	Manager's Weight	Manager's Return in Country	Return of Stock Index for That Country
U.K.	.15	.30	20%	12%
Japan	.30	.10	15	15
U.S.	.45	.40	10	14
Germany	.10	.20	5	12

a. Calculate the total value added of all the manager's decisions this period.

b. Calculate the value added (or subtracted) by her *country* allocation decisions.

c. Calculate the value added from her stock selection ability within countries. Confirm that the sum of the contributions to value added from her country allocation plus security selection decisions equals total over- or underperformance.

9. Conventional wisdom says that one should measure a manager's investment performance over an entire market cycle. What arguments support this convention? What arguments contradict it?

10. Does the use of universes of managers with similar investment styles to evaluate relative investment performance overcome the statistical problems associated with instability of beta or total variability?

11. During a particular year, the T-bill rate was 6%, the market return was 14%, and a portfolio manager with beta of .5 realized a return of 10%.

a. Evaluate the manager based on the portfolio alpha.

b. Reconsider your answer to part (*a*) in view of the Black-Jensen-Scholes finding that the security market line is too flat. Now how do you assess the manager's performance?

12. You and a prospective client are considering the measurement of investment performance, particularly with respect to international portfolios for the past five years. The data you discussed are presented in the following table:

International Manager or Index	Total Return	Country and Security Return	Currency Return
Manager A	−6.0%	2.0%	−8.0%
Manager B	−2.0	−1.0	−1.0
International Index	−5.0	0.2	−5.2

a. Assume that the data for Manager A and Manager B accurately reflect their investment skills and that both managers actively manage currency exposure. Briefly describe one strength and one weakness for each manager.

    b. Recommend and justify a strategy that would enable your fund to take advantage of the strengths of each of the two managers while minimizing their weaknesses.

13. Carl Karl, a portfolio manager for the Alpine Trust Company, has been responsible since 2010 for the City of Alpine's Employee Retirement Plan, a municipal pension fund. Alpine is a growing community, and city services and employee payrolls have expanded in each of the past 10 years. Contributions to the plan in fiscal 2015 exceeded benefit payments by a three-to-one ratio.

    The plan board of trustees directed Karl five years ago to invest for total return over the long term. However, as trustees of this highly visible public fund, they cautioned him that volatile or erratic results could cause them embarrassment. They also noted a state statute that mandated that not more than 25% of the plan's assets (at cost) be invested in common stocks.

    At the annual meeting of the Trustees in November 2015, Karl presented the following portfolio and performance report to the Board:

Alpine Employee Retirement Plan

Asset Mix as of 9/30/15	At Cost (millions)		At Market (millions)	
Fixed-income assets:				
Short-term securities	$ 4.5	11.0%	$ 4.5	11.4%
Long-term bonds and mortgages	26.5	64.7	23.5	59.5
Common stocks	10.0	24.3	11.5	29.1
	$41.0	100.0%	$39.5	100.0%

Investment Performance

	Annual Rates of Return for Periods Ending 9/30/15	
	5 Years	1 Year
Total Alpine Fund:		
Time-weighted	8.2%	5.2%
Dollar-weighted (internal)	7.7%	4.8%
Assumed actuarial return	6.0%	6.0%
U.S. Treasury bills	7.5%	11.3%

Large sample of pension funds		
(average 60% equities, 40% fixed income)	10.1%	14.3%
Common stocks—Alpine Fund	13.3%	14.3%
Average portfolio beta coefficient	0.90	0.89
Standard & Poor's 500 Stock Index	13.8%	21.1%
Fixed-income securities—Alpine Fund	6.7%	1.0%
Salomon Brothers' Bond Index	4.0%	−11.4%

    Karl was proud of his performance and was chagrined when a trustee made the following critical observations:

    a. "Our one-year results were terrible, and it's what you've done for us lately that counts most."

    b. "Our total fund performance was clearly inferior compared to the large sample of other pension funds for the last five years. What else could this reflect except poor management judgment?"

  c. "Our common stock performance was especially poor for the five-year period."

  d. "Why bother to compare your returns to the return from Treasury bills and the actuarial assumption rate? What your competition could have earned for us or how we would have fared if invested in a passive index (which doesn't charge a fee) are the only relevant measures of performance."

  e. "Who cares about time-weighted return? If it can't pay pensions, what good is it!"

  Appraise the merits of each of these statements and give counterarguments that Mr. Karl can use.

14. The Retired Fund is an open-ended mutual fund composed of $500 million in U.S. bonds and U.S. Treasury bills. This fund has had a portfolio duration (including T-bills) of between three and nine years. Retired has shown first-quartile performance over the past five years, as measured by an independent fixed-income measurement service. However, the directors of the fund would like to measure the market timing skill of the fund's sole bond investor manager. An external consulting firm has suggested the following three methods:

  a. Method I examines the value of the bond portfolio at the beginning of every year, then calculates the return that would have been achieved had that same portfolio been held throughout the year. This return would then be compared with the return actually obtained by the fund.

  b. Method II calculates the average weighting of the portfolio in bonds and T-bills for each year. Instead of using the actual bond portfolio, the return on a long-bond market index and T-bill index would be used. For example, if the portfolio on average was 65% in bonds and 35% in T-bills, the annual return on a portfolio invested 65% in a long-bond index and 35% in T-bills would be calculated. This return is compared with the annual return that would have been generated using the indexes and the manager's actual bond/T-bill weighting for each quarter of the year.

  c. Method III examines the net bond purchase activity (market value of purchases less sales) for each quarter of the year. If net purchases were positive (negative) in any quarter, the performance of the bonds would be evaluated until the net purchase activity became negative (positive). Positive (negative) net purchases would be viewed as a bullish (bearish) view taken by the manager. The correctness of this view would be measured.

  Critique *each* method with regard to market timing measurement problems.

Use the following data in solving problems 15 and 16.

  The administrator of a large pension fund wants to evaluate the performance of four portfolio managers. Each portfolio manager invests only in U.S. common stocks. Assume that during the most recent five-year period, the average annual total rate of return including dividends on the S&P 500 was 14%, and the average nominal rate of return on government Treasury bills was 8%. The following table shows risk and return measures for each portfolio:

Portfolio	Average Annual Rate of Return	Standard Deviation	Beta
P	17%	20%	1.1
Q	24	18	2.1
R	11	10	0.5
S	16	14	1.5
S&P 500	14	12	1.0

15. The Treynor performance measure for Portfolio P is:
   a. .082.
   b. .099.
   c. .155.
   d. .450.

16. The Sharpe performance measure for Portfolio Q is:
   a. .076.
   b. .126.
   c. .336.
   d. .888.

17. An analyst wants to evaluate Portfolio X, consisting entirely of U.S. common stocks, using both the Treynor and Sharpe measures of portfolio performance. The following table provides the average annual rate of return for Portfolio X, the market portfolio (as measured by the S&P 500), and U.S. Treasury bills during the past eight years:

	Average Annual Rate of Return	Standard Deviation of Return	Beta
Portfolio X	10%	18%	0.60
S&P 500	12	13	1.00
T-bills	6	N/A	N/A

   a. Calculate the Treynor and Sharpe measures for both Portfolio X and the S&P 500. Briefly explain whether Portfolio X underperformed, equaled, or outperformed the S&P 500 on a risk-adjusted basis using both the Treynor measure and the Sharpe measure.
   b. Based on the performance of Portfolio X relative to the S&P 500 calculated in part (*a*), briefly explain the reason for the conflicting results when using the Treynor measure versus the Sharpe measure.

18. A plan sponsor with a portfolio manager who invests in small-capitalization, high-growth stocks should have the plan sponsor's performance measured against which one of the following?
   a. S&P 500 index.
   b. Wilshire 5000 index.
   c. Dow Jones Industrial Average.
   d. S&P 400 index.

19. In measuring the comparative performance of different fund managers, the preferred method of calculating rate of return is:
   a. Internal.
   b. Time-weighted.
   c. Dollar-weighted.
   d. Income.

20. Which *one* of the following is a valid benchmark against which a portfolio's performance can be measured over a given time period?
   a. The portfolio's dollar-weighted rate of return.
   b. The portfolio's time-weighted rate of return.
   c. The portfolio manager's "normal" portfolio.
   d. The average beta of the portfolio.

21. Assume you invested in an asset for two years. The first year you earned a 15% return, and the second year you earned a negative 10% return. What was your annual geometric return?
    a. 1.7%.
    b. 2.5%.
    c. 3.5%.
    d. 5.0%.

22. Assume you purchased a rental property for $50,000 and sold it one year later for $55,000 (there was no mortgage on the property). At the time of the sale, you paid $2,000 in commissions and $600 in taxes. If you received $6,000 in rental income (all of it received at the end of the year), what annual rate of return did you earn?
    a. 15.3%.
    b. 15.9%.
    c. 16.8%.
    d. 17.1%.

23. A portfolio of stocks generates a –9% return in 1996, a 23% return in 1997, and a 17% return in 1998. The annualized return (geometric mean) for the entire period is:
    a. 7.2%.
    b. 9.4%.
    c. 10.3%.
    d. None of the above.

24. A two-year investment of $2,000 results in a return of $150 at the end of the first year and a return of $150 at the end of the second year, in addition to the return of the original investment. The internal rate of return on the investment is:
    a. 6.4%.
    b. 7.5%.
    c. 15.0%.
    d. None of the above.

25. In measuring the performance of a portfolio, the time-weighted rate of return is superior to the dollar-weighted rate of return because:
    a. When the rate of return varies, the time-weighted return is higher.
    b. The dollar-weighted return assumes all portfolio deposits are made on Day 1.
    c. The dollar-weighted return can only be estimated.
    d. The time-weighted return is unaffected by the timing of portfolio contributions and withdrawals.

26. The annual rate of return for JSI's common stock has been:

	1995	1996	1997	1998
Return	14%	19%	–10%	14%

    a. What is the arithmetic mean of the rate of return for JSI's common stock over the four years?
       i. 8.62%.
       ii. 9.25%.
       iii. 14.25%.
       iv. None of the above.

b. What is the geometric mean of the rate of return for JSI's common stock over the four years?

   i. 8.62%.

   ii. 9.25%.

   iii. 14.21%.

   iv. Cannot be calculated due to the negative return in 1997.

 27. A pension fund portfolio begins with $500,000 and earns 15% the first year and 10% the second year. At the beginning of the second year, the sponsor contributes another $500,000. The time-weighted and dollar-weighted rates of return were:

   a. 12.5% and 11.7%.

   b. 8.7% and 11.7%.

   c. 12.5% and 15.0%.

   d. 15.0% and 11.7%.

 28. Strict market timers attempt to maintain a _____ portfolio beta and a _____ portfolio alpha.

   a. Constant; shifting.

   b. Shifting; zero.

   c. Shifting; shifting.

   d. Zero; zero.

 29. Which one of the following methods measures the reward to volatility trade-off by dividing the average portfolio excess return over the standard deviation of returns?

   a. Sharpe's measure.

   b. Treynor's measure.

   c. Jensen's measure.

   d. Appraisal ratio.

 30. The difference between an arithmetic average and a geometric average of returns

   a. Increases as the variability of the returns increases.

   b. Increases as the variability of the returns decreases.

   c. Is always negative.

   d. Depends on the specific returns being averaged, but is not necessarily sensitive to their variability.

solutions to Concept CHECKS

1.

Time	Action	Cash Flow
0	Buy two shares	–40
1	Collect dividends; then sell one of the shares	4 + 22
2	Collect dividend on remaining share, then sell it	2 + 19

a. Dollar-weighted return:

$$-40 + \frac{26}{1+r} + \frac{21}{(1+r)^2} = 0$$

$$r = .1191, \text{ or } 11.91\%$$

b. Time-weighted return:

The rates of return on the stock in the two years were:

$$r_1 = \frac{2 + (22 - 20)}{22} = .20$$

$$r_2 = \frac{2 + (19 - 22)}{22} = -.045$$

$$(r_1 + r_2)/2 = .077, \text{ or } 7.7\%$$

2. *a.* $E(r_A) = [.15 + (-.05)]/2 = .05$
   $E(r_G) = [(1.15)(.95)]^{1/2} - 1 = .045$
   b. The expected stock price is $(115 + 95)/2 = 105$.
   c. The expected rate of return on the stock is 5%, equal to r_A.

3. Sharpe: $(\bar{r} - \bar{r}_f)/\sigma$
   $S_P = (35 - 6)/42 = .69$
   $S_M = (28 - 6)/30 = .733$
   Alpha: $\bar{r} - [r_f + \beta(\bar{r}_M - \bar{r}_f)]$
   $\alpha_P = 35 - [6 + 1.2(28 - 6)] = 2.6$
   $\alpha_M = 0$
   Treynor: $(\bar{r} - \bar{r}_f)/\beta$
   $T_P = (35 - 6)/1.2 = 24.2$
   $T_M = (28 - 6)/1.0 = 22$
   Appraisal ratio: $\alpha/\sigma(e)$
   $A_P = 2.6/18 = .144$
   $A_M = 0$

4. The *t*-statistic on α is $.2/2 = .1$. The probability that a manager with a true alpha of zero could obtain a sample period alpha with a *t*-statistic of .1 or better by pure luck can be calculated approximately from a table of the normal distribution. The probability is 46%.

5. Performance Attribution
   First compute the new bogey performance as $(.70 \times 5.81) + (.25 \times 1.45) + (.05 \times .48) = 4.45$.

   a. Contribution of asset allocation to performance:

Market	(1) Actual Weight in Market	(2) Benchmark Weight in Market	(3) Excess Weight	(4) Market Return (%)	(5) = (3) × (4) Contribution to Performance (%)
Equity	.70	.70	.00	5.81	.00
Fixed-income	.07	.25	−.18	1.45	−.26
Cash	.23	.05	.18	0.48	.09
Contribution of asset allocation					−.17

   b. Contribution of selection to total performance:

Market	(1) Portfolio Performance (%)	(2) Index Performance (%)	(3) Excess Performance (%)	(4) Portfolio Weight	(5) = (3) × (4) Contribution (%)
Equity	7.28	5.00	2.28	.70	1.60
Fixed-income	1.89	1.45	0.44	.07	0.03
Contribution of selection within markets					1.63

INTERNATIONAL DIVERSIFICATION

Although we in the United States customarily treat the S&P 500 as the market-index portfolio, the practice is increasingly inappropriate. U.S. equities represent less than 50% of world equities. In this chapter, we look beyond domestic markets to survey issues of international and extended diversification.   In one sense, international invest-

ing may be viewed as no more than a straightforward generalization of our earlier treatment of portfolio selection with a larger menu of assets from which to construct a portfolio. Similar issues of diversification, security analysis, security selection, and asset allocation face the investor. On the other hand, international investments pose some problems not encountered in domestic markets. Among these are the presence of exchange rate risk, restrictions on capital flows across national boundaries, an added dimension of political risk and country-specific regulations, and differing accounting practices in different countries.   Therefore, in this chapter we review the major topics covered in the rest of the book, emphasizing their international aspects. We start with the central concept of portfolio theory—diversification. We will see that global diversification offers dramatic opportunities for improving portfolio risk-return trade-offs, and that investors are beginning to take advantage of these opportunities. We also will see how exchange rate fluctuations affect the risk of international investments. We next turn to passive and active investment styles in the international context. We will consider some of the special problems involved in the interpretation of passive index portfolios, and we will show how active asset allocation can be generalized to incorporate country and currency choices in addition to traditional domestic asset–class choices.

25.1   INTERNATIONAL INVESTMENTS

The World Equity Portfolio

To appreciate the folly of focusing exclusively on U.S. investments, consider in Table 25.1 and in Figure 25.1 the market capitalization (in U.S. dollars) and market share of the world's 48 largest organized equity markets. While the total capitalization of U.S. equities is by far the largest, its share of total world capitalization is only 47.8%.

Only three countries—the United States, Japan, and the United Kingdom—have an equity market share greater than 4% and capture in aggregate only 70% of the total market value of world equity. The average country market share is 2%, and to diversify into the last 10% of market capitalization an investor would have to include stocks of 35 countries.

International Diversification

From the discussion of diversification in Chapter 8, you know that adding to a portfolio assets that are not perfectly correlated will enhance the reward-to-volatility ratio. Increasing globalization lets us take advantage of foreign securities as a feasible way to extend diversification.

The evidence in Figure 25.2 is clear. The figure presents the standard deviation of equally weighted portfolios of various sizes as a percentage of the average standard devia-

Table 25.1   Global Equity Market Capitalization and Global Portfolio Shares, 1997

Country	Market Capitalization (US $ Millions)	Portfolio Share	Country	Market Capitalization (US $ Millions)	Portfolio Share
Argentina	55,458	0.27%	Netherlands	459,078	2.22%
Australia	257,166	1.24%	New Zealand	31,468	0.15%
Austria	28,444	0.14%	Norway	70,399	0.34%
Belgium	134,849	0.65%	Pakistan	9,940	0.05%
Brazil	369,279	1.79%	Peru	10,338	0.05%
Canada	400,003	1.93%	Philippines	28,930	0.14%
Chile	60,744	0.29%	Poland	9,990	0.05%
China	15,692	0.08%	Portugal	34,738	0.17%
Colombia	12,213	0.06%	Russia	87,122	0.42%
Czech Republic	15,106	0.07%	Singapore	114,755	0.56%
Denmark	69,112	0.33%	Slovakia	1,530	0.01%
Finland	60,956	0.29%	South Africa	195,526	0.95%
France	630,545	3.05%	Spain	207,115	1.00%
Germany	779,926	3.77%	Sri Lanka	1,515	0.01%
Greece	29,815	0.14%	Sweden	195,004	0.94%
Hong Kong	332,481	1.61%	Switzerland	377,710	1.83%
Hungary	8,356	0.04%	Taiwan	233,946	1.13%
India	101,761	0.49%	Thailand	37,136	0.18%
Indonesia	45,283	0.22%	Turkey	51,305	0.25%
Ireland	45,927	0.22%	United Kingdom	1,919,410	9.28%
Israel	21,491	0.10%	United States	9,890,470	47.84%
Italy	288,202	1.39%	Venezuela	11,412	0.06%
Japan	2,673,900	12.93%			
Korea	74,950	0.36%	Total market	20,675,377	100.00%
Malaysia	99,113	0.48%	Country average	430,737	2.08%
Mexico	85,768	0.41%			

Source: I/B/E/S.

Figure 25.1
Country Shares of
World Equity
Capitalization, 1997.

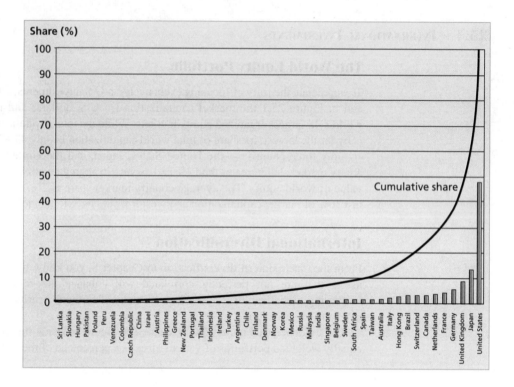

Figure 25.2
International
diversification.

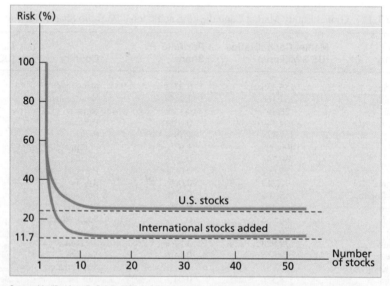

Source: Modified from B. Solnik, "Why Not Diversify Internationally Rather Than Domestically?" *Financial Analysts Journal*, July–August 1994.

tion of a one-stock portfolio. For example, a value of 20 means the diversified portfolio has only 20% the standard deviation of a typical stock.

There is a marked reduction in risk for a portfolio that includes foreign as well as U.S. stocks, so rational investors should invest across borders. Adding international to national investments enhances the power of portfolio diversification. Indeed, the figure indicates that the risk of an internationally diversified portfolio can be reduced to less than half the

GLOBAL INVESTING IS STILL SMART

Kick 'em when they're down.

That may make sense in a barroom brawl, but it's a lousy approach to making money. Which brings me to the current demonization of international investing.

After 1997's foreign-stock-market drubbing, some folks are arguing that American investors should keep their money close to home. I think they're dead wrong.

Here are just some of the dubious arguments getting tossed around by the isolationist crowd:

History Has Spoken

Foreign investing makes no sense, the detractors maintain, and the recent performance proves it.

If you find this argument convincing, cast your mind back to year-end 1978. Over the previous eight years, Standard & Poor's 500-stock index had spluttered along at 4.6% a year, while foreign stocks had gained 13.5% annually.

A sell signal for U.S. stocks? Of course not. It was a great time to buy. Today, the tables are turned.

Those who head abroad should do just fine—as long as they give it time.

There's No Place Like Home

Stick with what you know, say the isolationists. Keep your money at home, they argue.

Sure, overseas markets involve greater uncertainty. True, you may have a better sense of your local economy and local companies. But there is no guarantee that this greater knowledge will translate into greater returns.

After all, U.S. stock-fund managers spend their days ripping apart the balance sheets of corporate America, projecting earnings and scouring the 50 states for new investment opportunities. Result? Most of them still end up lagging far behind the market averages. Familiarity may be comforting, but it doesn't seem to lead to superior stock-picking.

Currencies Can Kill

As detractors are quick to note, not only did foreign stocks take it on the chin in 1997, but the dollar soared as well. That made foreign shares even less valuable for U.S. holders.

Another argument for avoiding foreign stocks? Hardly. In fact, you want to own foreign stocks *because* of their contrary performance. As 1997 made clear, foreign markets can perform quite unlike U.S. stocks, and a big reason is currency fluctuations. Last year, the contrary performance worked against you. In 1998, it may help.

The real value in owning foreign stocks comes when U.S. shares are struggling, not soaring. World stock markets are more closely linked than ever before, and when there are big jolts, U.S. and foreign stocks tend to sink simultaneously. But over longer periods, U.S. and foreign shares don't rise and fall in lock step, so you get smoother portfolio performance by owning both.

America the Bountiful

Invest with the best, say the xenophobes. Buy American.

This notion may ring a bell with the Japanese. Remember 1989? Tokyo was going to rule the world, Japanese management techniques were all the rage, and yuppies everywhere were gagging down sushi. It was, of course, a terrible time to buy Japanese stocks.

America now reigns triumphant, and the rest of the world appears to be in economic meltdown. Is this really the time to wash our hands of foreign markets and load up on U.S. stocks?

Source: Jonathan Clements, "No Bunk: Global Investing Is Still Smart Despite Foreign Stocks' Drubbing in '97," *The Wall Street Journal*, January 6, 1998. Excerpted by permission of *The Wall Street Journal*, © 1998 Dow Jones & Company, Inc. All Rights Reserved Worldwide.

level of a diversified U.S. portfolio. The nearby box provides additional discussion of the benefits of international diversification.

Table 25.2 presents results from a study of equity returns showing that although the correlation coefficients between the U.S. stock index and stock- and bond-index portfolios of other large industrialized economies are typically positive, they are much smaller than 1.0. Most correlations are below .5. In contrast, correlation coefficients between diversified U.S. portfolios, say, with 40 to 50 securities, typically exceed .9. This imperfect correlation across national boundaries allows for the improvement in diversification potential that shows up in Figure 25.2.

 **Concept CHECK**

Question 1 • What would Figure 25.2 look like if we allowed the possibility of diversifying into real estate investments in addition to foreign equity?

Table 25.2   Correlations of Unhedged Asset Returns, 1980–1993

Asset/Country	Stocks							Bonds						
	U.S.	Ger.	U.K.	Jap.	Aus.	Can.	Fra.	U.S.	Ger.	U.K.	Jap.	Aus.	Can.	Fra.
Stocks														
United States	1.00													
Germany	0.37	1.00												
United Kingdom	0.53	0.47	1.00											
Japan	0.26	0.36	0.43	1.00										
Australia	0.43	0.29	0.50	0.26	1.00									
Canada	0.73	0.36	0.54	0.29	0.56	1.00								
France	0.44	0.63	0.51	0.42	0.34	0.39	1.00							
Bonds														
United States	0.35	0.28	0.17	0.15	0.00	0.27	0.19	1.00						
Germany	0.08	0.56	0.30	0.35	0.05	0.13	0.46	0.40	1.00					
United Kingdom	0.13	0.34	0.61	0.36	0.19	0.27	0.33	0.34	0.60	1.00				
Japan	0.03	0.31	0.27	0.63	0.10	0.11	0.36	0.33	0.67	0.54	1.00			
Australia	0.19	0.20	0.31	0.12	0.67	0.32	0.16	0.13	0.17	0.25	0.17	1.00		
Canada	0.31	0.26	0.21	0.19	0.18	0.52	0.23	0.69	0.36	0.41	0.35	0.25	1.00	
France	0.12	0.53	0.33	037	0.10	0.16	0.58	0.36	0.90	0.57	0.65	0.21	0.33	1.00

Note: Data represent the U.S. dollar perspective.

Source: Roger G. Clarke and Mark P. Kritzman, *Currency Management Concepts and Practices* (Charlottesville, VA: Research Foundation of the Institute of Chartered Financial Analysts, 1996).

Figure 25.3 gives yet a different perspective on opportunities for international diversification. It shows risk-return opportunities offered by equity indexes of several countries, alone and combined into portfolios. (All returns here are calculated in terms of U.S. dollars.) The efficient frontiers generated from the full set of assets offers the best possible risk-return pairs; they are far superior to the risk-return profile of U.S. stocks alone.

Lest you think that mean-variance analysis is too "academic," consider Figure 25.4, which is reproduced from a paper in *Journal of Portfolio Management* and was written by a portfolio manager at Batterymarch Financial Management.[1] It is from an article devoted to the management of "risk for international portfolios." The entire analysis of risk management is performed in terms of efficient frontiers that exploit international diversification. In this exhibit, the author examines the efficiency of one index of non-U.S. stocks, the EAFE index (which we will describe in detail later).

Techniques for Investing Internationally

U.S. investors have several avenues through which they can invest internationally. The most obvious method, which is available in practice primarily to larger institutional investors, is to purchase securities directly in the capital markets of other countries. However, even small investors now may take advantage of several investment vehicles with an international focus.

Shares of several foreign firms are traded in U.S. markets in the form of **American depository receipts**, or ADRs. A U.S. financial institution like a bank will purchase shares of a foreign firm in that firm's country, then issue claims to those shares in the United

---

[1] Jarrod W. Wilcox, "EAFE Is for Wimps," *Journal of Portfolio Management*, Spring 1994.

Figure 25.3
The minimum-variance frontier. The minimum-variance frontier is calculated from the unconditional means, variances, and covariances of 17 country returns. The returns are in U.S. dollars and are from Morgan Stanley Capital International. The data are from 1970:2 to 1989:5 (232 observations).

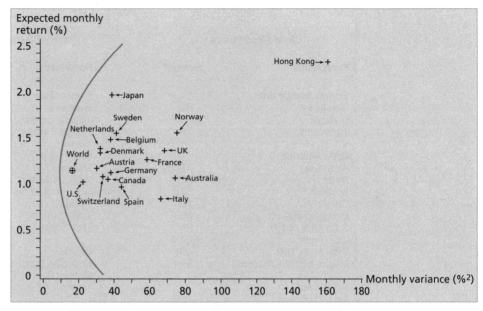

Source: Campbell R. Harvey, "The World Price of Covariance Risk," *Journal of Finance* 46 (March 1991), pp. 111–58.

Figure 25.4
Passive efficient frontier versus EAFE (return based on country risk).

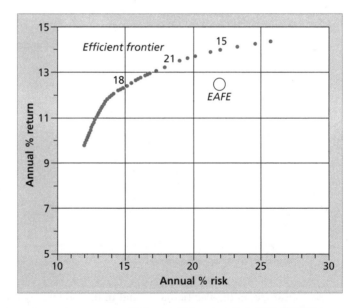

States. Each ADR is then a claim on a given number of the shares of stock held by the bank. In this way, the stock of foreign companies can be traded on U.S. stock exchanges. Trading foreign stocks with ADRs has become increasingly easy.

There are also a wide array of mutual funds with an international focus. **Single-country funds** are mutual funds that invest in the shares of only one country. These tend to be closed-end funds, as the listing of these funds in Table 25.3 indicates. In addition to single-country funds, there are several open-end mutual funds with an international focus. For example, Fidelity offers funds with investments concentrated overseas, generally in

Table 25.3   Sampling of Emerging Country Funds, 1997

Closed-End Funds		Closed-End Funds	
Fund Name	**Symbol**	**Fund Name**	**Symbol**
Europe/Middle East		**Pacific/Asia**	
First Israel	ISL	Indonesia	IF
Portugal	PGF	Jakarta Growth	JGF
Turkish Inv.	TKF	Jardine Fleming China	JFC
		Korea	KF
Latin America		Korean Inv.	KIF
Argentina	AF	Malaysia	MF
Brazil	BZF	R.O.C. Taiwan	ROC
Brazilian Eqty.	BZL	Scudder New Asia	SAF
Chile	CH	Taiwan	TWN
Emerging Mexico	MEF	Thai	TTF
Latin Amer. Eqty.	LAQ	Thai Capital	TC
Latin Amer. Inv.	LAM		
Latin Amer. Disc.	LDF	**Global**	
Mexico Equity & Income	MXF	Emerging Markets Tele.	ETF
		Morgan Stanley EM	MSF
Pacific/Asia		Templeton Emerging	EMF
Asia Pacific	APB		
China	CHN	**Income**	
First Philippine	FPF	Alliance World	AWG
Greater China	GCH	Emerging Markets	
India Growth	IGF	Income	EMD
		Latin Amer. Dollar	LBF

Open-End Funds	
Fund Name	**Assets (millions), 1997**
Fidelity Emerging Markets	$1,283
G.T. Global Emerging Market A	197
G.T. Latin Amer. Growth A	166
Govett Emerging Markets	60
Lexington Worldwide EM	265
Merrill Develop Cap. Market	309
Merrill Latin Amer. A	519
Montgomery Emerging Mkt.	907
Morgan Stanley EM	1,292
Scudder Emerging Market Income	324
Templeton Dev. Mkts.	3,206
Vanguard Int'l Index: Emerging	622

Source: *The Wall Street Journal*, January 9, 1997.

Europe, in the Pacific basin, and in developing economies in an emerging opportunities fund. Vanguard, consistent with its indexing philosophy, offers separate index funds for Europe and the Pacific basin. The nearby box discusses a wide range of single-country index funds.

U.S. investors also can trade derivative securities based on prices in foreign security markets. For example, they can trade options and futures on the Nikkei stock index of 225 stocks traded on the Tokyo stock exchange, or on FTSE (Financial Times Share Exchange) indexes of U.K. and European stocks.

NEW FUNDS THAT TRACK FOREIGN MARKETS

Low-Cost Foreign Index Funds Called WEBS and CountryBaskets Eliminate Some of the Guesswork and Costs of Investing Abroad

With foreign markets generally stronger this year, a new way to invest abroad has appeared at a good time. Two competing products, WEBS and CountryBaskets, are shares of open-end mutual funds that replicate the price and yield performance of foreign stock market indexes and trade on a stock exchange like stocks. You sell these shares rather than redeeming them, but there the similarity to closed-end country funds ends. The new funds create and redeem shares in large blocks as needed, thus preventing the big premiums or discounts to net asset value typical of closed-end country funds. As index funds, foreign index baskets are passively managed, so their expenses run much lower than for current open- or closed-end country funds.

Both products are continuously priced, an advantage over open-end international funds, which are priced once a day. They can be bought on margin and sold short even in a falling market. Like any listed stock, they can be used as part of a hedging strategy. While these features make them useful to traders, they offer conservative, long-term investors a convenient and relatively economical means of diversifying into foreign markets.

The two products track their foreign indexes differently. WEBS portfolio managers use a mix of stocks and derivative investments such as listed futures, options, and swaps on OTC equity derivatives to maintain performance close to their underlying foreign indexes. CountryBaskets achieve more precise tracking by holding nearly all the equities in each of the underlying indexes and making minor adjust-ments with listed futures and options. WEBS trade at 1/16 of a point increments and CountryBaskets at eighths of a point.

As diversified portfolios representing foreign markets as a whole, WEBS and CountryBaskets are less volatile than many of the equities they hold, and, by investing in the market, you avoid the problems ADR investors often have in getting information and evaluating shares subject to different accounting rules. WEBS and CountryBaskets are also useful to investors who want to target specific countries as part of portfolio balancing.

Investors may prefer the active management, diversity, and flexibility of open-end international equity index funds as a way to limit currency and political risks of investing in foreign markets. As conventional open-end funds, however, the international funds are sometimes forced by net redemptions to sell stocks at inopportune times, which can be a particular problem in foreign markets with highly volatile stocks.

Foreign index baskets pay dividends at least annually on realized capital gains and the accumulated cash dividends of the underlying stocks less accumulated fund expenses. As index funds, they can be expected to have low turnover, so their taxable capital gains distributions are expected to be minimal.

You pay brokerage commissions on purchase and sale of WEBS and CountryBasket shares, but since their portfolios are passively managed, their management and administrative fees are relatively low and they eliminate most of the transaction charges typical of managed funds. WEBS and CountryBaskets average annual expenses are expected to be around 0.8% versus 1.8% for open-end international funds and 1.6% for closed-end funds.

FOREIGN INDEX BASKETS

WEBS	Symbol (Amex)	WEBS	Symbol (Amex)	Country Baskets	Symbol (NYSE)
Australia	EWA	Malaysia	EWM	Australia	GXA
Austria	EWO	Mexico	EWW	France	GXF
Belgium	EWK	Netherlands	EWN	Germany	GXG
Canada	EWC	Singapore	EWS	Hong Kong	GXH
France	EWQ	Spain	EWP	Italy	GXI
Germany	EWG	Sweden	EWD	Japan	GXJ
Hong Kong	EWH	Switzerland	EWL	South Africa	GXR
Italy	EWI	U.K.	EWU	U.K.	GXK
Japan	EWJ			U.S.	GXU

Source: From *The Outlook*, May 22, 1996.

Exchange Rate Risk

International investing poses unique challenges and a variety of new risks for U.S. investors. Information in foreign markets may be less timely and more difficult to come by. In smaller economies with correspondingly smaller securities markets, there may be higher transaction costs and liquidity problems. Figure 25.5 illustrates that trading costs in the United States tend to be quite low by international standards. Investment advisors also need special expertise concerning **political risk**, by which we mean the possibility of the expropriation of assets, changes in tax policy, the institution of restrictions on the exchange of foreign currency for domestic currency, or other changes in the business climate of a country. A good example of political risk surrounds the Gulf War in early 1991, when investors in Kuwait saw their investments destroyed by the war.

Beyond these risks, international investing entails **exchange rate risk**. The dollar return from a foreign investment depends not only on the returns in the foreign currency, but also on the exchange rate between the dollar and that currency.

To see this, consider an investment in England in risk-free British government bills paying 10% annual interest in British pounds. Although these U.K. bills would be the risk-free asset to a British investor, this is not the case for a U.S. investor. Suppose, for example, the current exchange rate is $2 per pound, and the U.S. investor starts with $20,000. That amount can be exchanged for £10,000 and invested at a riskless 10% rate in the United Kingdom to provide £11,000 in one year.

What happens if the dollar–pound exchange rate varies over the year? Say that during the year, the pound depreciates relative to the dollar, so that by year-end only $1.80 is required to purchase £1. The £11,000 can be exchanged at the year-end exchange rate for only $19,800 (£11,000 × $1.80/£), resulting in a loss of $200 relative to the initial $20,000 investment. Despite the positive 10% pound-denominated return, the dollar-denominated return is a negative 1%.

Figure 25.5

Cost estimates for one-way trades.

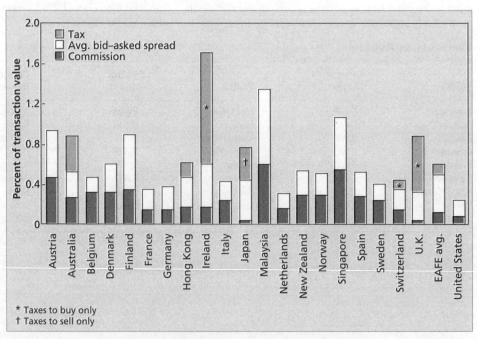

* Taxes to buy only
† Taxes to sell only

Source: Bruno Solnik, *International Investments,* 3rd ed. (Reading, MA: Addison-Wesley, 1996).

We can generalize from these results. The $20,000 is exchanged for $20,000/$E_0$ pounds, where E_0 denotes the original exchange rate ($2/£). The U.K. investment grows to $(20,000/E_0)[1 + r_f(\text{UK})]$ British pounds, where $r_f(\text{UK})$ is the risk-free rate in the United Kingdom. The pound proceeds ultimately are converted back to dollars at the subsequent exchange rate E_1, for total dollar proceeds of $20,000(E_1/E_0)[1 + r_f(\text{UK})]$. The dollar-denominated return on the investment in British bills, therefore, is

$$1 + r(\text{US}) = [1 + r_f(\text{UK})]E_1/E_0 \qquad (25.1)$$

We see in equation 25.1 that the dollar-denominated return for a U.S. investor equals the pound-denominated return times the exchange rate "return." For a U.S. investor, the investment in the British bill is a combination of a safe investment in the United Kingdom and a risky investment in the performance of the pound relative to the dollar. Here, the pound fared poorly, falling from a value of $2.00 to only $1.80. The loss on the pound more than offsets the earnings on the British bill.

Figure 25.6 illustrates this point. It presents returns on stock market indexes in some of the larger emerging stock markets for a 15-month period ending in March 1997. The light boxes depict returns in local currencies, whereas the dark boxes depict returns in dollars, adjusting for exchange rate movements. It is clear that exchange rate fluctuations over this period had large effects on dollar-denominated returns. For example, Turkey showed a 41% gain in local currency, but only 22% in dollars.

Question 2 • **Calculate the rate of return in dollars to a U.S. investor holding the British bill if the year-end exchange rate is:** (*a*) $E_1 = \$2.00/£$; (*b*) $E_1 = \$2.20/£$.

The investor in our example could have hedged the exchange rate risk using a forward or futures contract in foreign exchange. Recall that a forward or futures contract on foreign exchange calls for delivery or acceptance of one currency for another at a stipulated exchange rate. Here, the U.S. investor would agree to deliver pounds for dollars at a fixed exchange rate, thereby eliminating the future risk involved with conversion of the pound investment back into dollars.

Figure 25.6
Stock market returns in dollars and local currencies.

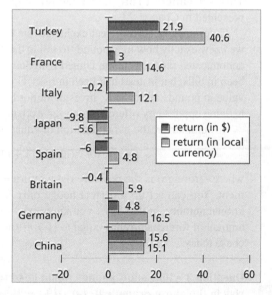

Source: *The Economist*, March 8–14, 1997.

If the futures exchange rate had been $F_0 = \$1.93/\pounds$ when the investment was made, the U.S. investor could have assured a riskless dollar-denominated return by locking in the year-end exchange rate at $\$1.93/\pounds$. In this case, the riskless U.S. return would have been 6.15%:

$$[1 + r_f(\text{UK})]F_0/E_0 = (1.10)\ 1.93/2.00 = 1.0615$$

Here are the steps to take to lock in the dollar-denominated returns. The futures contract entered in the second step exactly offsets the exchange rate risk incurred in Step 1.

Initial Transaction	End-of-Year Proceeds in Dollars
Exchange $20,000 for £10,000 and invest at 10% in the United Kingdom	£11,000 $\times E_1$
Enter a contract to deliver £11,000 for dollars at the (forward) exchange rate $1.93/£	£11,000(1.93 – E_1)
Total	£11,000 $\times$ $1.93/£ = $21,320

You may recall that this is the same type of hedging strategy at the heart of the interest rate parity relationship discussed in Chapter 23, where futures markets are used to eliminate the risk of holding another asset. The U.S. investor can lock in a riskless dollar-denominated return either by investing in the United Kingdom and hedging exchange rate risk or by investing in riskless U.S. assets. Because the returns on two riskless strategies must provide equal returns, we conclude

$$[1 + r_f(\text{UK})]\ \frac{F_0}{E_0} = 1 + r_f(\text{US})$$

Rearranging,

$$\frac{F_0}{E_0} = \frac{1 + r_f(\text{US})}{1 + r_f(\text{UK})} \tag{25.2}$$

This is the **interest rate parity relationship** or **covered interest arbitrage relationship** presented in Chapter 23.

Unfortunately, such perfect exchange rate hedging is usually not so easy. In our example, we knew exactly how may pounds to sell in the forward or futures market because the pound-denominated proceeds in the United Kingdom were riskless. If the U.K. investment had not been in bills, but instead had been in risky U.K. equity, we would know neither the ultimate value in pounds of our U.K. investment nor how many pounds to sell forward. That is, the hedging opportunity offered by foreign exchange forward contracts would be imperfect.

To summarize, the generalization of equation 25.1 is

$$1 + r(\text{US}) = [1 + r(\text{foreign})]\ E_1/E_0 \tag{25.3}$$

where $r(\text{foreign})$ is the possibly risky return earned in the currency of the foreign investment. You can set up a perfect hedge only in the special case that $r(\text{foreign})$ is itself a known number. In that case, you know you must sell in the forward or futures market an amount of foreign currency equal to $[1 + r(\text{foreign})]$ for each unit of that currency you purchase today.

Concept CHECK

Question 3 • How many pounds would need to be sold forward to hedge exchange rate risk in the above example if: (a) $r(\text{UK}) = 20\%$; (b) $r(\text{UK}) = 30\%$?

Passive and Active International Investing

Passive Benchmarks   When we discussed investment strategies in the purely domestic context, we used a market index portfolio like the S&P 500 as a benchmark passive equity investment. This suggests a world market index might be a useful starting point for a passive international strategy.

One widely used index of non-U.S. stocks is the **Europe, Australia, Far East (EAFE) index** computed by Morgan Stanley. Table 2.5 (Chapter 2) presented a sample of the extensive set of Morgan Stanley Capital International indexes. Additional indexes of world equity performance are published by Salomon Brothers, First Boston, and Goldman, Sachs. Portfolios designed to mirror or even replicate the country, currency, and company representation of these indexes would be the obvious generalization of the purely domestic passive equity strategy.

An issue that sometimes arises in the international context is the appropriateness of market-capitalization weighting schemes in the construction of international indexes. Although this is far and away the most common approach, some argue that it might not be the best weighting scheme in an international context. This is in part because different countries have differing proportions of their corporate sector organized as publicly traded firms. For example, Table 25.4 shows that U.K. firms received a total weighting of 16.7% of the EAFE index in terms of market value of equity but accounted for only 8% of the gross domestic product (GDP) of the EAFE countries. In contrast, French firms represented 5.8% of the market-value weighted index despite that fact that France accounted for fully 11.4% of EAFE GDP.

Some argue that it is more appropriate to weight international indexes by GDP rather than market capitalization because an internationally diversified portfolio should purchase shares in proportion to the broad asset base of each country, and GDP might be a better measure of the importance of a country in the international economy than the value of its

Table 25.4   Weighting Schemes for EAFE Countries

Country	Market Capitalization	Gross Domestic Product (GDP)
Australia	2.4%	2.4%
Austria	0.4	1.6
Belgium	1.1	1.9
Denmark	0.6	1.2
Finland	0.3	0.8
France	5.8	11.4
Germany	6.7	15.4
Hong Kong	3.3	0.9
Italy	1.9	9.2
Ireland	0.2	0.4
Japan	48.3	33.4
Malaysia	1.6	0.5
New Zealand	0.3	0.3
Netherlands	2.9	2.8
Norway	0.3	0.9
Singapore	0.9	1.4
Spain	1.8	4.6
Sweden	1.3	1.8
Switzerland	4.2	2.1
U.K.	16.7	8.0

Source: Bruce Clarke and Anthony W. Ryan, "Proper Overseas Benchmark a Critical Choice," *Pensions and Investments*, May 30, 1994, p. 28.

INTERNATIONAL INVESTING RAISES QUESTIONS

As Yogi Berra might say, the problem with international investing is that it's so darn foreign.

Currency swings? Hedging? International diversification? What's that?

Here are answers to five questions that I'm often asked:

- Foreign stocks account for some 60% of world stock-market value, so shouldn't you have 60% of your stock-market money overseas?

The main reason to invest abroad isn't to replicate the global market or to boost returns. Instead, "what we're trying to do by adding foreign stocks is to reduce volatility," explains Robert Ludwig, chief investment officer at money manager SEI Investments.

Foreign stocks don't move in sync with U.S. shares and, thus, they may provide offsetting gains when the U.S. market is falling. But to get the resulting risk reduction, you don't need anything like 60% of your money abroad.

- So, how much foreign exposure do you need to get decent diversification?

"Based on the volatility of foreign markets and the correlation between markets, we think an optimal portfolio is 70% in the U.S., 20% in developed foreign markets and 10% in emerging markets," Mr. Ludwig says.

Even with a third of your stock-market money in foreign issues, you may find that the risk-reduction benefits aren't all that reliable. Unfortunately, when U.S. stocks get really pounded, it seems foreign shares also tend to tumble.

- Can U.S. companies with global operations give you international diversification?

"When you look at these multinationals, the factor that drives their performance is their home market," says Mark Riepe, a vice president with Ibbotson Associates, a Chicago research firm.

How come? U.S. multinationals tend to be owned by U.S. investors, who will be swayed by the ups and downs of the U.S. market. In addition, Mr. Riepe notes that while multinationals may derive substantial profits and revenue abroad, most of their costs—especially labor costs—will be incurred in the U.S.

- Does international diversification come from the foreign stocks or the foreign currency?

"It comes from both in roughly equal pieces," Mr. Riepe says. "Those who choose to hedge their foreign currency raise the correlation with U.S. stocks, and so the diversification benefit won't be nearly as great."

Indeed, you may want to think twice before investing in a foreign-stock fund that frequently hedges its currency exposure in an effort to mute the impact of—and make money from—changes in foreign-exchange rates.

"The studies that we've done show that stock managers have hurt themselves more than they've helped themselves by actively managing currencies," Mr. Ludwig says.

- Should you divvy up your money among foreign countries depending on the size of each national stock market?

At issue is the nagging question of how much to put in Japan. If you replicated the market weightings of Morgan Stanley Capital International's Europe, Australasia and Far East index, you would currently have around a third of your overseas money in Japan.

That's the sort of weighting you find in international index funds, which seek to track the performance of the EAFE or similar international indexes. Actively managed foreign-stock funds, by contrast, pay less attention to market weights and, on average, these days have just 14% in Japan.

If your focus is risk reduction rather than performance, the index—and the funds that track it—are the clear winners. Japan performs quite unlike the U.S. market, so it provides good diversification for U.S. investors, says Tricia Rothschild, international editor at Morningstar Mutual Funds, a Chicago newsletter.

"But correlations aren't static," she adds. "There's always a problem with taking what happened over the past 20 years and projecting it out over the next 20 years."

outstanding stocks. Others have even suggested weights proportional to the import share of various countries. The argument is that investors who wish to hedge the price of imported goods might choose to hold securities in foreign firms in proportion to the goods imported from those countries. The nearby box considers the question of global asset allocation for investors seeking effective international diversification.

Another problem with market capitalization weights arises from the practice of **cross-holdings** that tend to overstate the aggregate value of outstanding equity. Cross-holdings refer to equity investments that firms make in other firms. These purchases can increase

Table 25.5   The Effect of Cross-Holding on Market Value of Equity (all dollar values in millions)

Firm A			Firm B		
Assets		Liabilities and NW	Assets		Liabilities and NW
A. Before the Cross-Holding					
Plant, equipment, other assets $10	Equity	$10	Plant, equipment, other assets $10	Equity	$10
B. After the Cross-Holding					
Plant, equipment, other assets $10	Equity	$15	Plant, equipment, other assets $10	Equity	$10
Shares in Firm B $5					

the sum of the market values of outstanding equity. To see how, consider the following example.

Firms A and B each have $10 million in plant and equipment and no debt outstanding: therefore, each has $10 million in equity. This situation is illustrated in panel A of Table 25.5. Now suppose that Firm A issues $5 million of new equity to buy shares in Firm B. The new balance sheets of the two firms are illustrated in panel B. Although the market value of Firm B is unchanged, Firm A now has a market value of $15 million. One of its assets is a claim on Firm B, however, meaning that half the physical assets of Firm B are now counted in the computation of the values of *both* Firm A and Firm B. What has not changed is the value of equity held by the noncorporate sector. Private shareholders still have a total claim of $20 million: $15 million in Firm A and $5 million in Firm B. (The other $5 million of Firm B is held by Firm A.) To measure the aggregate value of the productive assets of the two firms, we must net out the intercorporate shareholdings that result in the double counting and measure only the value of noncorporate equity holdings. This number is unaffected by cross-holdings.

French and Poterba[2] calculated the effect of cross-holdings on the U.S. and Japanese equity markets. They found that in mid-1990, the value of the Japanese equity market fell from $3,266 billion to $1,623 billion when cross-holdings were netted out. In contrast, in the United States, where cross-holdings are minimal, the value of equity fell only slightly, from $3,044 billion to $3,006 billion.

Table 25.4 illustrates the different weightings that would emerge for the EAFE countries using market capitalization and GDP. The differing methodologies result in substantially different weights for some countries. In particular, Japan had a market-value weight of 48.3% despite the fact that its GDP was only 33.4% of the EAFE total. This disproportionate weight was due primarily to much higher price earnings ratios in Japan and the more common practice of cross-holdings in Japan.

Asset Allocation   Active portfolio management in an international context may be viewed similarly as an extension of active domestic management. In principle, one would form an efficient frontier from the full menu of world securities and determine the optimal risky portfolio. We saw in Chapter 8 that even in the domestic context, the need for

---

[2]Kenneth R. French and James M. Poterba, "Were Japanese Stock Prices Too High?" *Journal of Financial Economics* 29 (October 1991), pp. 337–63.

specialization in various asset classes usually calls for a two-step procedure in which asset allocation is fixed initially, and then security selection within each asset class is determined. The complexities of the international market argue even more strongly for the primacy of asset allocation, and this is the perspective often taken in the evaluation of active portfolio management. Performance attribution of international managers focuses on these potential sources of abnormal returns: currency selection, country selection, stock selection within countries, and cash-bond selection within countries.

We can measure the contribution of each of these factors following a manner similar to the performance attribution techniques introduced in Chapter 24.

1. **Currency selection** measures the contribution to total portfolio performance attributable to exchange rate fluctuations relative to the investor's benchmark currency, which we will take to be the U.S. dollar. We might use a benchmark like the EAFE index to compare a portfolio's currency selection for a particular period to a passive benchmark. EAFE currency selection would be computed as the weighted average of the currency appreciation of the currencies represented in the EAFE portfolio using as weights the fraction of the EAFE portfolio invested in each currency.

2. **Country selection** measures the contribution to performance attributable to investing in the better-performing stock markets of the world. It can be measured as the weighted average of the equity *index* returns of each country using as weights the share of the manager's portfolio in each country. We use index returns to abstract from the effect of security selection within countries. To measure a manager's contribution relative to a passive strategy, we might compare country selection to the weighted average across countries of equity index returns using as weights the share of the EAFE portfolio in each country.

3. Stock selection ability may, as in Chapter 24, be measured as the weighted average of equity returns *in excess of the equity index* in each country. Here, we would use local currency returns and use as weights the investments in each country.

4. Cash/bond selection may be measured as the excess return derived from weighting bonds and bills differently from some benchmark weights.

Table 25.6 gives an example of how to measure the contribution of the decisions an international portfolio manager might make.

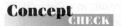

Question 4 • Using the data in Table 25.6, compute the manager's country and currency selection if portfolio weights had been 40% in Europe, 20% in Australia, and 40% in the Far East.

Security Analysis   Security analysis of non-U.S. companies is complicated by noncomparabilities in accounting data. Security analysts must attempt to place accounting statements on an equal footing before comparing companies. Some of the major issues are:

1. *Depreciation:* The United States allows firms to use different financial reports for tax and reporting purposes. As a result, even firms that use accelerated depreciation for tax purposes in the United States tend to use straight-line depreciation for reporting purposes. This use of dual statements is uncommon elsewhere. Non-U.S. firms tend to use accelerated depreciation for reporting as well as taxes, which affects both earnings and book values of assets.

Table 25.6 Example of Performance Attribution: International

	EAFE Weight	Return on Equity Index	Currency Application $E_1/E_0 - 1$	Manager's Weight	Manager's Return
Europe	.30	10%	10%	.35	8%
Australia	.10	5	−10	.10	7
Far East	.60	15	30	.55	18

Currency Selection

EAFE: $(.30 \times 10\%) + (.10 \times -10\%) + (.60 \times 30\%) = 20\%$ appreciation
Manager: $(.35 \times 10\%) + (.10 \times -10\%) + (.55 \times 30\%) = 19\%$ appreciation
Loss of 1% relative to EAFE

Country Selection

EAFE: $(.30 \times 10\%) + (.10 \times 5\%) + (.60 \times 15\%) = 12.5\%$
Manager: $(.35 \times 10\%) + (.10 \times 5\%) + (.55 \times 15\%) = 12.25\%$
Loss of .25% relative to EAFE

Stock Selection

$(8\% - 10\%).35 + (7\% - 5\%).10 + (18\% - 15\%).55 = 1.15\%$
Contribution of 1.15% relative to EAFE

2. *Reserves:* U.S. standards generally allow lower discretionary reserves for possible losses, resulting in higher reported earnings than in other countries. There are also big differences in how firms reserve for pension liabilities.

3. *Consolidation:* Accounting practice in some countries does not call for all subsidiaries to be consolidated in the corporation's income statement.

4. *Taxes:* Taxes may be reported either as paid or accrued.

5. *P/E ratios:* There may be different practices for calculating the number of shares used to calculate P/E ratios. Firms may use end-of-year shares, year-average shares, or even beginning-of-year shares.

Factor Models and International Investing

International investing presents a good opportunity to demonstrate an application of multifactor models of security returns such as those considered in connection with the arbitrage pricing model. Natural factors might include:

1. A world stock index.
2. A national (domestic) stock index.
3. Industrial-sector indexes.
4. Currency movements.

Solnik and de Freitas[3] used such a framework, and Table 25.7 shows some of their results for several countries. The first four columns of numbers present the *R*-square of various one-factor regressions. Recall that the *R*-square, or R^2, measures the percentage of return volatility of a company's stock that can be explained by the particular factor treated as the independent or explanatory variable. Solnik and de Freitas estimated the factor regressions

---

[3]Bruno Solnik and A. de Freitas, "International Factors of Stock Price Behavior," in S. Khoury and A. Ghosh, eds., *Recent Developments in International Finance and Banking* (Lexington, MA: Lexington Books, 1988). Cited in Bruno Solnik, *International Investments,* 2nd ed. (Reading, MA: Addison-Wesley, 1991).

Table 25.7   Relative Importance of World, Industrial, Currency, and Domestic Factors
in Explaining Return of a Stock

	Average R-SQR of Regression on Factors				
	Single-Factor Tests				Joint Test All Four Factors
Locality	World	Industrial	Currency	Domestic	
Switzerland	.18	.17	.00	.38	.39
West Germany	.08	.10	.00	.41	.42
Australia	.24	.26	.01	.72	.72
Belgium	.07	.08	.00	.42	.43
Canada	.27	.24	.07	.45	.48
Spain	.22	.03	.00	.45	.45
United States	.26	.47	.01	.35	.55
France	.13	.08	.01	.45	.60
United Kingdom	.20	.17	.01	.53	.55
Hong Kong	.06	.25	.17	.79	.81
Italy	.05	.03	.00	.35	.35
Japan	.09	.16	.01	.26	.33
Norway	.17	.28	.00	.84	.85
Netherlands	.12	.07	.01	.34	.31
Singapore	.16	.15	.02	.32	.33
Sweden	.19	.06	.01	.42	.43
All countries	.18	.23	.01	.42	.46

Source: Bruno Solnik, *International Investments,* 3rd ed. (p. 37), © 1996 by Addison-Wesley Publishing Company, Inc. Reprinted by permission of the publisher.

for many firms in a given country and reported the average R-square across the firms in that country.

In this case, the table reveals that the domestic factor seems to be the dominant influence on stock returns. While the domestic index alone generates an average R-square of .42 across all countries, adding the three additional factors (in the last column of the table) increases average R-square only to .46. This is consistent with the low cross-country correlation coefficients in Table 25.2, reiterating the value of international diversification.

At the same time, there is clear evidence of a world market factor in results of the market crash of October 1987. Even though we have said equity returns across borders show only moderate correlation, a study by Richard Roll[4] showed negative October 1987 equity index returns in all 23 countries considered. Figure 25.7, reproduced from Roll's study, shows the values he found for regional equity indexes during that month. The obvious correlation among returns suggests some underlying world factor common to all economies. Roll found that the beta of a country's equity index on a world index (estimated through September 1987) was the best predictor of that index's response to the October 1987 crash, which lends further support to the presence of a world factor.

Equilibrium in International Capital Markets

We can use the CAPM or the APT to predict expected rates of return in an international capital market equilibrium, just as we can for domestic assets. The models need some adaptation for international use, however.

---

[4]Richard Roll, "The International Crash of October 1987," *Financial Analysts Journal,* September–October 1988.

Figure 25.7

Regional indexes around the crash, October 14–October 26, 1987.

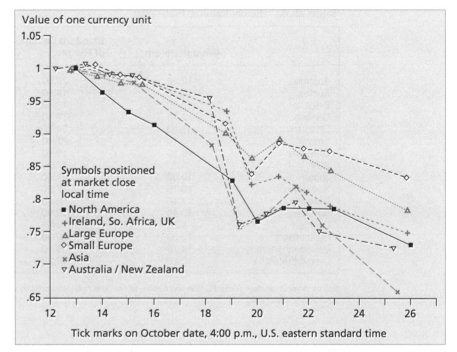

Source: Richard Roll, "The International Crash of October 1987," *Financial Analysts Journal*, September–October 1988.

For example, one might expect that a world CAPM would result simply by replacing a narrow domestic market portfolio with a broad world market portfolio and measuring betas relative to the world portfolio. This approach was pursued in part of a paper by Ibbotson, Carr, and Robinson,[5] who calculated betas of equity indexes of several countries against a world equity index. Their results appear in Table 25.8. The betas for different countries show surprising variability.

Although such a straightforward generalization of the simple CAPM seems like a reasonable first step, it is subject to some problems:

1. Taxes, transaction costs, and capital barriers across countries make it difficult and not always attractive for investors to hold a world index portfolio. Some assets are simply unavailable to foreign investors.

2. Investors in different countries view exchange rate risk from the perspective of their different domestic currencies. Thus they will not agree on the risk characteristics of various securities and therefore will not derive identical efficient frontiers.

3. Investors in different countries tend to consume different baskets of goods, either because of differing tastes or because of tariffs, transportation costs, or taxes. If relative prices of goods vary over time, the inflation risk perceived by investors in different countries will also differ.

These problems suggest that the simple CAPM will not work as well in an international context as it would if all markets were fully integrated. Some evidence suggests that assets

---

[5]Roger G. Ibbotson, Richard C. Carr, and Anthony W. Robinson, "International Equity and Bond Returns," *Financial Analysts Journal*, July–August 1982.

Table 25.8   Equity Returns, 1960–1980

	Average Return	Standard Deviation of Return	Beta	Alpha
Australia	12.20	22.80	1.02	1.52
Austria	10.30	16.90	0.01	4.86
Belgium	10.10	13.80	0.45	2.44
Canada	12.10	17.50	0.77	2.75
Denmark	11.40	24.20	0.60	2.91
France	8.10	21.40	0.50	0.17
Germany	10.10	19.90	0.45	2.41
Italy	5.60	27.20	0.41	−1.92
Japan	19.00	31.40	0.81	9.49
Netherlands	10.70	17.80	0.90	0.65
Norway	17.40	49.00	−0.27	13.39
Spain	10.40	19.80	0.04	4.73
Sweden	9.70	16.70	0.51	1.69
Switzerland	12.50	22.90	0.87	2.66
United Kingdom	14.70	33.60	1.47	1.76
United States	10.20	17.70	1.08	−0.69

Source: Roger G. Ibbotson, Richard C. Carr, and Anthony W. Robinson, "International Equity and Bond Returns," *Financial Analysts Journal*, July–August 1982.

that are less accessible to foreign investors carry higher risk premiums than a simple CAPM would predict.[6]

The APT seems better designed for use in an international context than the CAPM, as the special risk factors that arise in international investing can be treated much like any other risk factor. World economic activity and currency movements might simply be included in a list of factors already used in a domestic APT model.

Summary

1. U.S. equities are only a small fraction of the world equity portfolio. International capital markets offer important opportunities for portfolio diversification with enhanced risk-return characteristics.

2. Exchange rate risk imparts an extra source of uncertainty to investments denominated in foreign currencies. Much of that risk can be hedged in foreign exchange futures or forward markets, but a perfect hedge is not feasible unless the foreign currency rate of return is known.

3. Several world market indexes can form a basis for passive international investing. Active international management can be partitioned into currency selection, country selection, stock selection, and cash/bond selection.

4. A factor model applied to international investing would include a world factor as well as the usual domestic factors. Although some evidence suggests domestic factors dominate stock returns, effects of the October 1987 crash demonstrate existence of an important international factor.

[6]Vihang Errunza and Etienne Losq, "International Asset Pricing under Mild Segmentation: Theory and Test," *Journal of Finance* 40 (March 1985), pp. 105–24.

Key Terms

American depository
  receipts (ADRs)
single-country funds
political risk
exchange rate risk

interest rate parity relationship
covered interest arbitrage
  relationship
Europe, Australia, Far East
  (EAFE) index

cross-holdings
currency selection
country selection

**Selected
Readings**

Two textbooks on international investing ad capital markets are:
  Giddy, Ian H. *Global Financial Markets.* Lexington, MA: D.C. Heath, 1993.
  Solnik, Bruno. *International Investments.* 3rd ed. Reading, MA: Addison-Wesley, 1996.

Problems

1. You are a U.S. investor who purchased British securities for £2,000 one year ago when
   the British pound cost U.S.$1.50. What is your total return (based on U.S. dollars) if
   the value of the securities is now £2,400 and the pound is worth $1.75? No dividends
   or interest was paid during this period.
   a. 16.7%.
   b. 20.0%.
   c. 28.6%.
   d. 40.0%.

2. The correlation coefficient between the returns on a broad index of U.S. stocks and the
   returns on indexes of the stocks of other industrialized countries is mostly _____,
   and the correlation coefficient between the returns on various diversified portfolios of
   U.S. stocks is mostly _____.
   a. less than .8; greater than .8.
   b. greater than .8; less than .8.
   c. less than 0: greater than 0.
   d. greater than 0; less than 0.

3. An investor in the common stock of companies in a foreign country may wish to hedge
   against the _____ of the investor's home currency and can do so by _____ the
   foreign currency in the forward market.
   a. depreciation; selling.
   b. appreciation; purchasing.
   c. appreciation; selling.
   d. depreciation; purchasing.

4. Suppose a U.S. investor wishes to invest in a British firm currently selling for £40 per
   share. The investor has $10,000 to invest, and the current exchange rate is $2/£.
   a. How many shares can the investor purchase?
   b. Fill in the table below for rates of return after one year in each of the nine scenar-
       ios (three possible prices per share in pounds times three possible exchange rates).

Price per Share (£)	Pound-Denominated Return (%)	Dollar-Denominated Return for Year-End Exchange Rate		
		$1.80/£	$2/£	$2.20/£
£35				
£40				
£45				

   c. When is the dollar-denominated return equal to the pound-denominated return?

5. If each of the nine outcomes in problem 4 is equally likely, find the standard deviation of both the pound- and dollar-denominated rates of return.

6. Now suppose that the investor in problem 4 also sells forward £5,000 at a forward exchange rate of $2.10/£.

   a. Recalculate the dollar-denominated returns of each scenario.

   b. What happens to the standard deviation of the dollar-denominated return? Compare it both to its old value and the standard deviation of the pound-denominated return.

7. Calculate the contribution to total performance from currency, country, and stock selection for the manager in the example below:

	EAFE Weight	Return on Equity Index	$E_1/E_0 - 1$	Manager's Weight	Manager's Return
Europe	.30	20%	−10%	.35	18%
Australia	.10	15	0	.15	20
Far East	.60	25	+10	.50	20

8. If the current exchange rate is $1.75/£, the one-year forward exchange rate is $1.85/£, and the interest rate on British government bills is 8% per year, what risk-free dollar-denominated return can be locked in by investing in the British bills?

9. If you were to invest $10,000 in the British bills of problem 8, how would you lock in the dollar-denominated return?

10. John Irish, CFA, is an independent investment adviser who is assisting Alfred Darwin, the head of the Investment Committee of General Technology Corporation, to establish a new pension fund. Darwin asks Irish about international equities and whether the Investment Committee should consider them as an additional asset for the pension fund.

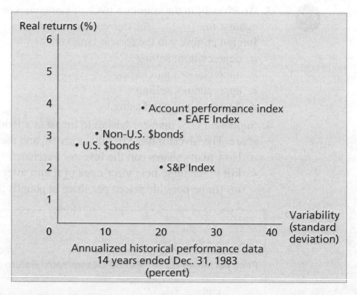

   a. Explain the rationale for including international equities in General's equity portfolio. Identify and describe three relevant considerations in formulating your answer.

   b. List three possible arguments against international equity investment and briefly discuss the significance of each.

c. To illustrate several aspects of the performance of international securities over time, Irish shows Darwin the accompanying graph of investment results experienced by a U.S. pension fund in the 1970–83 period. Compare the performance of the U.S. dollar and non–U.S. dollar equity and fixed-income asset categories, and explain the significance of the result of the Account Performance Index relative to the results of the four individual asset class indexes.

11. You are a U.S. investor considering purchase of one of the following securities. Assume that the currency risk of the German government bond will be hedged, and the six-month discount on deutschemark forward contracts is –.75% versus the U.S. dollar.

Bond	Maturity	Coupon	Price
U.S. government	June 1, 2003	6.50%	100.00
German government	June 1, 2003	7.50%	100.00

Calculate the expected price change required in the German government bond which would result in the two bonds having equal total returns in U.S. dollars over a six-month horizon. Assume that the yield on the U.S. bond is expected to remain unchanged.

12. A global manager plans to invest $1 million in U.S. government cash equivalents for the next 90 days. However, she is also authorized to use non-U.S. government cash equivalents, as long as the currency risk is hedged to U.S. dollars using forward currency contracts.
  a. What rate of return will the manager earn if she invests in money market instruments in either Canada or Japan and hedges the dollar value of her investment? Use the data in the following tables.
  b. What must be the approximate value of the 90-day interest rate available on U.S. government securities?

Interest Rates (APR) 90-Day Cash Equivalents	
Japanese government	2.52%
Canadian government	6.74%

Exchange Rates Dollars per Unit of Foreign Currency		
	Spot	90-Day Forward
Japanese yen	.0119	.0120
Canadian dollar	.7284	.7269

13. Suppose two all-equity-financed firms, ABC and XYZ, both have $100 million of equity outstanding. Each firm now issues $10 million of new stock and uses the proceeds to purchase the other's shares.
  a. What happens to the sum of the value of outstanding equity of the two firms?
  b. What happens to the value of the equity in these firms held by the noncorporate sector of the economy?
  c. Prepare the balance sheet for these two firms before and after the stock issues.
  d. If both of these firms were in the S&P 500, what would happen to their weights in the index?

14. After much research on the developing economy and capital markets of the country of Otunia, your firm, GAC, has decided to include an investment in the Otunia stock market in its Emerging Markets Commingled Fund. However, GAC has not yet decided whether to invest actively or by indexing. Your opinion on the active versus indexing decision has been solicited. The following is a summary of the research findings:

> Otunia's economy is fairly well diversified across agricultural and natural resources, manufacturing (both consumer and durable goods), and a growing finance sector. Transaction costs in securities markets are relatively large in Otunia because of high commissions and government "stamp taxes" on securities trades. Accounting standards and disclosure regulations are quite detailed, resulting in wide public availability of reliable information about companies' financial performance.
>
> Capital flows into and out of Otunia, and foreign ownership of Otunia securities is strictly regulated by an agency of the national government. The settlement procedures under these ownership rules often cause long delays in settling trades made by nonresidents. Senior finance officials in the government are working to deregulate capital flows and foreign ownership, but GAC's political consultant believes that isolationist sentiment may prevent much real progress in the short run.

a. Briefly discuss aspects of the Otunia environment that favor investing actively, and aspects that favor indexing.

b. Recommend whether GAC should invest in Otunia actively or by indexing. Justify your recommendation based on the factors identified in part (a).

1. The graph would asymptote to a lower level, as shown in the figure on page 809, reflecting the improved opportunities for diversification. There still would be a positive level of nondiversifiable risk.

2. $1 + r(\text{US}) = [(1 + r_f(\text{UK})]E_1/E_0$.
   a. $1 + r(\text{US}) = 1.1 \times 1.0 = 1.10$. Therefore, $r(\text{US}) = 10\%$.
   b. $1 + r(\text{US}) = 1.1 \times 1.1 = 1.21$. Therefore, $r(\text{US}) = 21\%$.

3. You must sell forward the number of pounds you will end up with at the end of the year. This value cannot be known with certainty, however, unless the rate of return of the pound-denominated investment is known.
   a. $10,000 \times 1.20 = £12,000$.
   b. $10,000 \times 1.30 = £13,000$.

4. *Country selection:*

$$(.40 \times 10) + (.20 \times 5) + (.40 \times 15) = 11\%$$

This is a loss of 1.5% relative to the EAFE passive benchmark.
Currency selection:

$$(.40 \times 10\%) + (.20 \times -10\%) + (.40 \times 30\%) = 14\%$$

This is a loss of 6% relative to the EAFE benchmark.

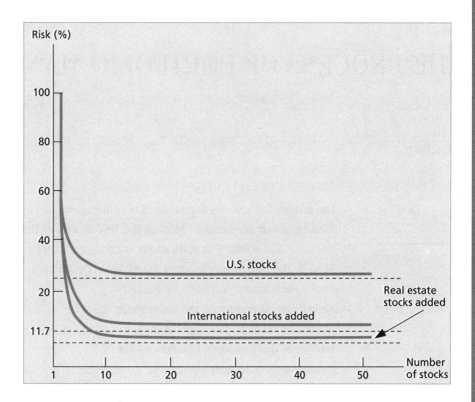

CHAPTER TWENTY SIX

THE PROCESS OF PORTFOLIO MANAGEMENT

The investment process is a chain of considerations and actions for an individual, from thinking about investing to placing the buy or sell order for investment assets such as stocks and bonds. For institutions such as insurance companies and pension funds as well, the investment process starts with a mission and a budget and ends with a detailed investment portfolio. Establishing a clear hierarchy of the investment process is useful. The first step is to determine the investor's objectives. The second step is to identify all the constraints, that is, the qualifications and requirements of the resultant portfolio. Finally, the objectives and constraints must be translated into investment policies. These steps are necessary for both individual and institutional investors. Objectives and constraints are greatly affected by the investor's stage in the life cycle. A young father's goals are very different from a retired widow's. Institutional investors do the lion's share of investing. However, their constraints are often compounded by legal restrictions and regulations.

26.1 MAKING INVESTMENT DECISIONS

Translating the aspirations and circumstances of diverse households into desirable investment decisions is a daunting task. Accomplishing the same task for institutions with many stakeholders, which are regulated by various authorities, is equally perplexing. Put simply, the investment process is not easily programmable into an efficient procedure.

A natural place to look for quality investment procedures is in the offices of professional investors. Better yet, we choose to examine the approach of the Association for Investment Management and Research (AIMR), which was established by a merger of the Financial Analysts Federation (FAF) with the Institute of Chartered Financial Analysts (ICFA).

The AIMR administers three examinations for those who wish to be certified as chartered financial analysts (CFAs). To become a CFA, a candidate must pass exams at Levels I, II, and III, and show a satisfactory record of experience. The AIMR helps CFA candidates by organizing classes and compiling reading materials. Our analysis in this chapter is compiled along the lines of the AIMR model.

The basic idea is to subdivide the major steps (objectives, constraints, and policies) into concrete considerations of the various aspects, making the task of organization more tractable. The standard format appears in Table 26.1. In the next sections, we elaborate briefly (there is a lot more to be said than this text will allow) on the construction of the three parts of the investment process, along the lines of Table 26.1.

Objectives

Portfolio objectives center on the **risk-return trade-off** between the expected return the investors want (*return requirements* in the first column of Table 26.1) and how much risk they are willing to assume (*risk tolerance*). Investment managers must know the level of risk that can be tolerated in the pursuit of a better expected rate of return. Table 26.2 lists factors governing return requirements and risk attitudes for each of the seven major investor categories discussed.

Individual Investors

The basic factors affecting individual investor return requirements and risk tolerance are life-cycle stage and individual preferences (see the nearby box). We will have much more to say about individual investor objectives later in this chapter.

Personal Trusts

Personal trusts are established when an individual confers legal title to property to another person or institution (the trustee) to manage that property for one or more beneficiaries.

Table 26.1   Determination of Portfolio Policies

Objectives	Constraints	Policies
Return requirements	Liquidity	Asset allocation
Risk tolerance	Horizon	Diversification
	Regulations	Risk positioning
	Taxes	Tax positioning
	Unique needs	Income generation

MERRILL LYNCH ASKS: HOW MUCH RISK CAN YOU TAKE?

When it comes to investing how much risk can you stomach?

Merrill Lynch & Co. wants to know.

In coming weeks, the nation's biggest brokerage firm will begin asking the individual investors behind its 7.2 million retail accounts to decide for themselves just how aggressive they're really willing to be in buying stocks, bonds, and other investments.

With the new setup, individual investors will be asked to put themselves in one of four risk categories: "conservative for income," "conservative for growth," "moderate risk," and "aggressive risk." Each category will have its own recommended asset allocation, or investment mix.

Merrill Lynch isn't the only securities firm that wants investors to state more explicitly how willing they are to risk losing money in the pursuit of profit. Some other brokerage firms say they're looking at such setups, too.

Getting investors to pigeonhole themselves in this way can be a good thing because it forces them to come to grips with their feelings about risk. And it gives their stockbrokers formal written notice about these desires. The customer's choice goes into the record.

At the same time, getting investors on record about their risk tolerances is likely to make it easier for a brokerage firm to defend itself if it gets hit with lawsuits or arbitration claims by investors who don't like what their brokers are doing.

An investor who picks the "aggressive risk" category, for example, is agreeing to "move aggressively among asset classes" and deal in "speculative and high-risk issues," according to guidelines distributed to Merrill Lynch brokers last week. Such an investor might have a difficult time claiming that his or her broker was *too* aggressive.

Legal issues like that are a growing concern on Wall Street. Over the past year, brokerage firms have been forced to pay increasingly stiff punitive-damage awards in arbitration cases brought by disgruntled investors.

Brokers are required by securities law to make sure customers are put into "suitable" investments. Unsuitability lawsuits are brought when it's alleged that a broker knew, or should have known, that an investment wasn't consistent with a client's investment objectives.

Merrill Lynch officials stress that such legal concerns aren't the main reason for the new system, although they don't deny they are a factor. The officials say they mainly wanted to be more "flexible" with the firm's asset-allocation recommendations, tailoring the research department's advice on the markets to an investor's general profile.

Avoiding customer disputes is "one of the side benefits, but that's not why it was created in the first place," says John Steffens, president of Merrill Lynch's individual-investor operations. "'The Street,' in my view, in general has dealt with this whole asset-allocation subject a little bit too simplistically," he says.

Sam Scott Miller, a New York securities lawyer, says getting investors to segment themselves according to risk preferences is a "sound and prudent approach" to heading off legal disputes, providing the firms monitor the systems well. Not only should it protect the firm in disputes with customers, it might also be an early warning to a securities firm if one of its brokers is pushing customers into unsuitable investments. If a certain broker "brings in all 'aggressive' accounts, they're going to want to take a look at it," he says.

Table 26.2 Matrix of Objectives

Type of Investor	Return Requirement	Risk Tolerance
Individual and personal trusts	Life cycle (education, children, retirement)	Life cycle (younger are more risk tolerant)
Mutual funds	Variable	Variable
Pension funds	Assumed actuarial rate	Depends on proximity of payouts
Endowment funds	Determined by current income needs and need for asset growth to maintain real value	Generally conservative
Life insurance companies	Should exceed new money rate by sufficient margin to meet expenses and profit objectives; also actuarial rates important	Conservative
Nonlife insurance companies	No minimum	Conservative
Banks	Interest spread	Variable

Some of Merrill Lynch's competitors have less-formal ways of tailoring asset-allocation recommendations. Firms including St. Louis–based A. G. Edwards & Sons Inc. and Raymond James & Associates Inc., St. Petersburg, Fla., already have more than one asset-allocation model for different investor profiles. But they don't ask investors to commit formally to one or the other.

"There is a temptation with asset allocation to put the retail client into a profile," says Raymond Worseck, investment strategy coordinator at A. G. Edwards, which has decided not to institute a formal system like Merrill Lynch's. Such a system has "compliance pluses" for brokerage firms, "because it protects them legally from a risk standpoint." But the investor can sometimes be better served with a more personalized approach, he says.

Merrill Lynch emphasizes that getting investors to specify their risk tolerance is only a beginning for grooming an investor's portfolio. Once an investor picks a risk category, the broker uses computer models and other tools to build a portfolio of appropriate stocks and bonds. Investors can switch risk categories, but frequent switching isn't encouraged, Merrill Lynch officials say.

Charles Clough, Merrill Lynch's chief investment strategist, says he realizes there are critics of his firm's plan. "You could say a multitude of asset guidelines just adds to the confusion of the issue," he says. But Mr. Clough adds that having the set categories helps to organize investors whose risk profiles otherwise would be "all over the map."

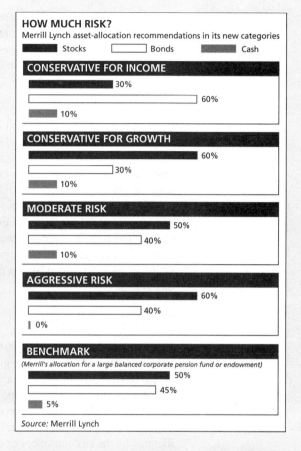

Beneficiaries customarily are divided into **income beneficiaries**, who receive the interest and dividend income from the trust during their lifetimes, and **remaindermen**, who receive the principal of the trust when the income beneficiary dies and the trust is dissolved. The trustee is usually a bank, a savings and loan association, a lawyer, or an investment professional. Investment of a trust is subject to trust laws, as well as "prudent man" rules that limit the types of allowable trust investment to those that a prudent person would select.

Objectives in the case of personal trusts normally are more limited in scope than those of the individual investor. Because of their fiduciary responsibility, personal trust managers typically are more risk averse than are individual investors. Certain asset classes such as options and futures contracts, for example, and strategies such as short-selling or buying on margin are ruled out.

When there are both income beneficiaries and remaindermen, the trustee faces a built-in conflict between the interests of the two sets of beneficiaries because greater current income inherently entails a sacrifice of future capital gain. For the typical case where the life beneficiary has substantial income requirements, there is pressure on the trustee to invest heavily in fixed-income securities or high-dividend-yielding common stocks.

Mutual Funds

Mutual funds are pools of investors' money. They invest in ways specified in their prospectuses and issue shares to investors entitling them to a pro rata portion of the income generated by the funds. The objectives of a mutual fund are spelled out in its prospectus. We discuss mutual funds in detail in Chapter 4.

Pension Funds

Pension fund objectives depend on the type of pension plan. There are two basic types: **defined contribution plans** and **defined benefit plans**. Defined contribution plans are in effect tax-deferred retirement savings accounts established by the firm in trust for its employees, with the employee bearing all the risk and receiving all the return from the plan's assets.

The largest pension funds, however, are defined benefit plans. In these plans the assets serve as collateral for the liabilities that the firm sponsoring the plan owes to plan beneficiaries. The liabilities are life annuities, earned during the employee's working years, that start at the plan participant's retirement. Thus it is the sponsoring firm's shareholders who bear the risk in a defined benefit pension plan. We discuss pension plans more fully later in this chapter.

Endowment Funds

Endowment funds are organizations chartered to use their money for specific nonprofit purposes. They are financed by gifts from one or more sponsors and are typically managed by educational, cultural, and charitable organizations or by independent foundations established solely to carry out the fund's specific purposes. Generally, the investment objectives of an endowment fund are to produce a steady flow of income subject to only a moderate degree of risk. Trustees of an endowment fund, however, can specify other objectives as dictated by the circumstances of the particular endowment fund.

Life Insurance Companies

Life insurance companies generally try to invest so as to hedge their liabilities, which are defined by the policies they write. Thus there are as many objectives as there are distinct types of policies. Until a decade or so ago there were only two types of life insurance policies available for individuals: whole-life and term.

A **whole-life insurance policy** combines a death benefit with a kind of savings plan that provides for a gradual buildup of cash value that the policyholder can withdraw at a later point in life, usually at age 65. **Term insurance**, on the other hand, provides death benefits only, with no buildup of cash value.

The interest rate that is embedded in the schedule of cash value accumulation promised under a whole-life policy is a fixed rate, and life insurance companies try to hedge this liability by investing in long-term bonds. Often the insured individual has the right to borrow at a prespecified fixed interest rate against the cash value of the policy.

During the inflationary years of the 1970s and early 1980s, when many older whole-life policies carried contractual borrowing rates as low as 4% or 5% per year, policyholders borrowed heavily against the cash value to invest in money market mutual funds paying double-digit yields. Other actual and potential policyholders abandoned whole-life policies and took out term insurance, investing the difference in the premiums on their own. By 1981, term insurance accounted for more than half the volume of new sales of individual life policies.

In response to these developments the insurance industry came up with two new policy types: **variable life** and **universal life**. Under a variable life policy the insured's premium buys a fixed death benefit plus a cash value that can be invested in a variety of mutual funds from which the policyholder can choose. With a universal life policy, policyholders can increase or reduce the premium or death benefit according to their needs. Furthermore, the interest rate on the cash value component changes with market interest rates.

The great advantage of variable and universal life insurance policies is that earnings on the cash value are not taxed until the money is withdrawn. Since the Tax Reform Act of 1986 these policies are one of the few tax-advantaged investments left.

The life insurance industry also provides products for pension plans. The two major products are insured defined benefit pensions and **guaranteed insurance contracts (GICs)**.

In the case of insured defined benefit pensions, the firm sponsoring the pension plan enters into a contractual agreement by which the life insurance company assumes all liability for the benefits accrued under the plan. The insurance company provides this service in return for an annual premium based on the benefit formula, and the number and characteristics of the employees covered by the plan. In the case of GICs the insurance company sells to a pension plan a contract promising a stated nominal interest rate over some specified period of time, usually several years. A GIC is in effect a zero-coupon bond issued by an insurance company. With respect to both types of product the insurance company usually pursues an investment policy designed to hedge the associated risk.

Life insurance companies may be organized as either mutual companies or stock companies. In principle, the organizational form should affect the investment objectives of the company. Mutual companies are supposed to be run solely for the benefit of their policyholders, whereas stock companies have as their objective the maximization of shareholder value.

In actuality, it is hard to discern from its investment policies which organizational form a particular insurance company has. Some examples of mutual insurance companies are Prudential and Mutual of Omaha. Examples of stock companies are Travelers and Aetna.

Non–Life Insurance Companies

Non–life insurance companies such as property and casualty insurers have investable funds primarily because they pay claims *after* they collect policy premiums. Typically, they are conservative in their attitude toward risk. As with life insurers, non–life insurance companies can be either stock companies or mutual companies.

Banks

The defining characteristic of banks is that most of their investments are loans to businesses and consumers and most of their liabilities are accounts of depositors. As investors, the objective of banks is to try to match the risk of assets to liabilities while earning a profitable spread between the lending and borrowing rates.

26.2 CONSTRAINTS

Both individuals and institutional investors restrict their choice of investment assets. These restrictions arise from their specific circumstances. Identifying these restrictions/constraints will affect the choice of investment policy. Five common types of constraints are described below. Table 26.3 presents a matrix summarizing the main constraints in each category for each of the seven types of investors.

Table 26.3   Matrix of Constraints

Type of Investor	Liquidity	Horizon	Regulations	Taxes
Individuals and personal trusts	Variable	Life cycle	None	Variable
Mutual funds	High	Variable	Few	None
Pension funds	Young, low; mature, high	Long	ERISA	None
Endowment funds	Low	Long	Few	None
Life insurance companies	Low	Long	Complex	Yes
Non–life insurance companies	High	Short	Few	Yes
Banks	High	Short	Changing	Yes

Liquidity

Liquidity is the ease (speed) with which an asset can be sold and still fetch a fair price. It is a relationship between the time dimension (how long will it take to dispose) and the price dimension (any discount from fair market price) of an investment asset.

When an actual concrete measure of liquidity is necessary, one thinks of the discount when an immediate sale is unavoidable. Cash and money market instruments such as Treasury bills and commercial paper, where the bid–asked spread is a fraction of 1%, are the most liquid assets, and real estate is among the least liquid.[1] Office buildings and manufacturing structures can potentially experience a 50% liquidity discount.

Both individual and institutional investors must consider how likely they are to dispose of assets at short notice. From this likelihood, they establish the minimum level of liquid assets they want in the investment portfolio.

Investment Horizon

This is the *planned* liquidation date of the investment or part of it. Examples of an individual **investment horizon** could be the time to fund a child's college education or the retirement date for a wage earner. For a university endowment, an investment horizon could relate to the time to fund a major campus construction project. Horizon needs to be considered when investors choose between assets of various maturities, such as bonds, which pay off at specified future dates.

Regulations

Only professional and institutional investors are constrained by regulations. First and foremost is the **prudent man law**. That is, professional investors who manage other people's money have a fiduciary responsibility to restrict investment to assets that would have been approved by a prudent investor. The law is purposefully nonspecific. Every professional investor must stand ready to defend an investment policy in a court of law, and interpretation may differ according to the standards of the times.

Also, specific regulations apply to various institutional investors. For instance, U.S. mutual funds (institutions that pool individual investor money under professional manage-

---

[1]In most cases it is impossible to know the liquidity of an asset with certainty before it is put up for sale. In dealer markets (described in Chapter 3), however, the liquidity of the traded assets can be observed from the bid–asked spread that is quoted by the dealers, that is, the difference between the "bid" quote (the lower price the dealer will pay the owner), and the "asked" quote (the higher price a buyer would have to pay the dealer).

ment) may not hold more than 5% of the shares of any publicly traded corporation. This regulation keeps professional investors from getting involved in the actual management of corporations.

Tax Considerations

Tax consequences are central to investment decisions. The performance of any investment strategy is measured by how much it yields after taxes. For household and institutional investors who face significant tax rates, tax sheltering and deferral of tax obligations may be pivotal in their investment strategy.

Unique Needs

Virtually every investor faces special circumstances. Imagine husband-and-wife aeronautical engineers holding high-paying jobs in the same aerospace corporation. The entire human capital of that household is tied to a single player in a rather cyclical industry. This couple would need to hedge the risk of a deterioration of the economic well-being of the aerospace industry by investing in assets that will yield more if such deterioration materializes.

An example of a unique need for an institutional investor is a university whose trustees let the administration use only cash income from the endowment fund. This constraint would translate into a preference for high-dividend-paying assets.

26.3   ASSET ALLOCATION

Consideration of their objectives and constraints leads investors to a set of investment policies. The policies column in Table 26.1 lists the various dimensions of portfolio management policymaking—asset allocation, diversification, risk and tax positioning, and income generation. By far the most important part of policy determination is asset allocation, that is, deciding how much of the portfolio to invest in each major asset category.

We can view the process of asset allocation as consisting of the following steps:

1. Specify asset classes to be included in the portfolio. The major classes usually considered are the following:
    a. Money market instruments (usually called *cash*).
    b. Fixed-income securities (usually called *bonds*).
    c. Stocks.
    d. Real estate.
    e. Precious metals.
    f. Other.
    Institutional investors will rarely invest in more than the first four categories, whereas individual investors frequently will include precious metals and other more exotic types of investments in their portfolios.
2. Specify capital market expectations. This step consists of using both historical data and economic analysis to determine your expectations of future rates of return over the relevant holding period on the assets to be considered for inclusion in the portfolio.
3. Derive the efficient portfolio frontier. This step consists of finding portfolios that achieve the maximum expected return for any given degree of risk.

4. Find the optimal asset mix. This step consists of selecting the efficient portfolio that best meets your risk and return objectives while satisfying the constraints you face.

Taxes and Asset Allocation

Until this point we have glossed over the issue of income taxes in discussing asset allocation. Of course, to the extent that you are a tax-exempt investor such as a pension fund, or if all of your investment portfolio is in a tax-sheltered account such as an individual retirement account (IRA), then taxes are irrelevant to your portfolio decisions.

But let us say that at least some of your investment income is subject to income taxes at a rate of 39.6%, the highest rate under current U.S. law. You are interested in the after-tax holding-period return (HPR) on your portfolio. At first glance it might appear to be a simple matter to figure out what the after-tax HPRs on stocks, bonds, and cash are if you know what they are before taxes. However, there are several complicating factors.

The first is the fact that you can choose between tax-exempt and taxable bonds. We discussed this issue in Chapter 2 and concluded there that you will choose to invest in tax-exempt bonds (i.e., munis) if your personal tax rate is such that the after-tax rate of interest on taxable bonds is less than the interest rate on munis.

Because we are assuming that you are in the highest tax bracket, it is fair to assume that you will prefer to invest in munis for both the short maturities (cash) and the long maturities (bonds). As a practical matter, this means that cash for you will probably be a tax-exempt money market fund.

The second complication is not quite so easy to deal with. It arises from the fact that part of your HPR is in the form of a capital gain or loss. Under the current tax system you pay income taxes on a capital gain only if you *realize* it by selling the asset during the holding period. This applies to bonds as well as stocks, and it makes the after-tax HPR a function of whether the security will actually be sold at the end of the holding period. Sophisticated investors time the realization of their sales of securities to minimize their tax burden. This often calls for selling securities that are losing money at the end of the tax year and holding on to those that are making money.

Furthermore, because cash dividends on stocks are fully taxable and capital gains taxes can be deferred by not selling stocks that appreciate in value, the after-tax HPR on stocks will depend on the dividend payout policies of the corporations that issued the stock.

These tax complications make the process of portfolio selection for a taxable investor a lot harder than for the tax-exempt investor. There is a whole branch of the money management industry that deals with ways to defer or avoid paying taxes through special investment strategies. Unfortunately, many of these strategies contradict the principles of efficient diversification.

We will discuss these and related issues in greater detail later in this chapter.

26.4   MANAGING PORTFOLIOS OF INDIVIDUAL INVESTORS

The overriding consideration in individual investor goal-setting is one's stage in the life cycle. Most young people start their adult lives with only one asset—their earning power. In this early stage of the life cycle an individual may not have much interest in investing in stocks and bonds. The needs for liquidity and preserving safety of principal dictate a conservative policy of putting savings in a bank or a money market fund. If and when a person gets married, the purchase of life and disability insurance will be required to protect the value of human capital.

When a married couple's labor income grows to the point at which insurance and housing needs are met, the couple may start to save for their children's college education and their own retirement, especially if the government provides tax incentives for retirement savings. Retirement savings typically constitute a family's first pool of investable funds. This is money that can be invested in stocks, bonds, and real estate (other than the primary home).

Human Capital and Insurance

The first significant investment decision for most individuals concerns education, building up their human capital. The major asset most people have during their early working years is the earning power that draws on their human capital. In these circumstances, the risk of illness or injury is far greater than the risk associated with financial wealth.

The most direct way of hedging human capital risk is to purchase insurance. Viewing the combination of your labor income and a disability insurance policy as a portfolio, the rate of return on this portfolio is less risky than the labor income by itself. Life insurance is a hedge against the complete loss of income as a result of death of any of the family's income earners.

Investment in Residence

The first major economic asset many people acquire is their own house. Deciding to buy rather than rent a residence qualifies as an investment decision.

An important consideration in assessing the risk and return aspects of this investment is the value of a house as a hedge against two kinds of risk. The first kind is the risk of increases in rental rates. If you own a house, any increase in rental rates will increase the return on your investment.

The second kind of risk is that the particular house or apartment where you live may not always be available to you. By buying, you guarantee its availability.

Saving for Retirement and the Assumption of Risk

People save and invest money to provide for future consumption and leave an estate. The primary aim of lifetime savings is to allow maintenance of the customary standard of living after retirement. Life expectancy, when one makes it to retirement at age 65, approaches 85 years, so the average retiree needs to prepare a 20-year nest egg and sufficient savings to cover unexpected health-care costs. Investment income may also increase the welfare of one's heirs, favorite charity, or both.

The leisure that investment income can be expected to produce depends on the degree of risk the household is willing to take with its investment portfolio. Empirical observation summarized in Table 26.4 indicates a person's age and stage in the life cycle affect attitude toward risk.

The evidence in Table 26.4 supports the life-cycle view of investment behavior. Questionnaires suggest that attitudes shift away from risk tolerance and toward risk aversion as investors near retirement age. With age, individuals lose the potential to recover from a disastrous investment performance. When they are young, investors can respond to a loss by working harder and saving more of their income. But as retirement approaches, investors realize there will be less time to recover. Hence the shift to safe assets.

The "right" portfolio for an individual also depends on unique circumstances. The accompanying box discusses some of these.

DIVERSITY IS MORE THAN STOCKS AND BONDS

Every investor has heard about how crucial it is to diversify, but many people—even some with varied stock and bond holdings—probably don't realize how *un*diversified they really are.

"Individuals rarely take an overall view" when it comes to diversification, says Michael Lipper, who heads Lipper Analytical Services. "They think of it in terms of different chunks of money" they have invested in stocks, bonds, cash, and other assets. In reality, "securities are only one part of the total [diversification] picture—and not even the most important one at that."

Take the case of a young Wall Street executive with a mortgaged cooperative apartment in lower Manhattan. A diversified stock portfolio would actually compound, not lessen, such an individual's risk because all those "assets"— job, home, and savings—are heavily exposed to the vagaries of the stock market.

The way the professionals see it, diversification for individuals isn't driven by fancy theories about market volatility. Instead, they say, it starts with a basic grasp of personal economic risk.

At different points in an individual's investing lifetime, diversification has two roles to play, the pros say. Initially, its function is to protect the individual from being hit hard by losses in basic "assets," such as job, home, and purchasing power.

"Most people don't think of their job as their No. 1 investment," says Mr. Lipper. "But over their lifetime, it's salary, insurance, and pension benefits that will wind up setting their whole investment picture."

The second purpose of diversification is to protect against the long-term risk of "outliving one's capital" once the job ends, says Mr. Lipper. In this context, says Owen Quattlebaum, head of personal financial services at Brown Brothers Harriman & Co., diversification means "branching out into other, risky assets" such as stocks and bonds. In other words, it becomes "something genuinely defined as a way to make money," he says.

What strategies should the individual use to hedge these risks? The pros offer some advice:

Job Risk

At the end of a long economic expansion, especially in this age of corporate restructurings and increasing foreign competition, job risk—unemployment and other factors that threaten income and benefits—is relatively high. In such a hazardous environment, individuals should safeguard their option of seeking new opportunity elsewhere.

Depending on how marketable a person's skills are and how vulnerable his or her industry is, everyone should hold between three months' and a year's worth of after-tax salary in short-term cash investments, such as bank deposits and money market funds, the specialists say.

Additionally, says Mr. Lipper, an individual should hedge against the loss of 3 to 12 months of pension and other benefits—a sum usually equal to about a third of pretax salary. That money should be invested in risky assets, such as stocks and long-term bonds.

House Risk

A mortgaged home is probably the individual's major exposure to "the factors in the local area that will vibrate with the job risk and, in effect, double up the job risk," says Mr. Quattlebaum of Brown Brothers.

The risk of having to meet house payments while searching for a new job would probably be covered by the cash reserves mentioned above. However, says Mr. Lipper, people who think they might have to sell their home and move to find employment in another area should consider protecting themselves against potential losses.

A "short-term weakness in housing prices might entail a 10 percent to 20 percent hit to the equity in your house," compared with what it would cost to buy a comparable home in a more-vibrant area, he says. He recommends setting aside money to cover that potential shortage and buying "intermediate bonds of one to five years' maturity and roll them over—so that you get a reasonable interest rate."

Source: Barbara Donnelly, "Diversity Is More Than Stocks and Bonds," *The Wall Street Journal*, September 14, 1989. Reprinted by permission of *The Wall Street Journal*, © 1989 Dow Jones & Company, Inc. All Rights Reserved Worldwide.

Table 26.4 Amount of Risk Investors Said They Were Willing to Take by Age

	Under 35	35–54	55 and Over
No risk	54%	57%	71%
A little risk	30	30	21
Some risk	14	18	8
A lot of risk	2	1	1

Source: Market Facts, Inc., Chicago, IL.

Concept

Question 1

a. **Think about the financial circumstances of your closest relative in your parents' generation (preferably your parents' household if you are fortunate enough to have them around). Write down the objectives and constraints for their investment decisions.**

b. **Now consider the financial situation of your closest relative who is in his or her 30s. Write down the objectives and constraints that would fit his or her investment decision.**

c. **How much of the difference between the two statements is due to the age of the investors?**

Manage Your Own Portfolio or Rely on Others?

Lots of people have assets such as social security benefits, pension and group insurance plans, and savings components of life insurance policies. Yet they exercise limited control, if any, on the investment decisions of these plans. The funds that secure pension and life insurance plans are managed by institutional investors.

Outside of the "forced savings" plans, however, individuals can manage their own investment portfolios. As the population grows richer, more and more people face this decision.

Managing your own portfolio *appears* to be the lowest-cost solution. Conceptually, there is little difference between managing one's own investments and professional financial planning/investment management.

Against the fees and charges that financial planners and professional investment managers impose, you will want to offset the value of your time and energy expended on diligent portfolio management. People with a suitable background may even look at investment as recreation. Most of all, you must recognize the *potential* difference in investment results.

Besides the need to deliver better-performing investments, professional managers face two added difficulties. First, getting clients to communicate their objectives and constraints requires considerable skill. This is not a one-time task because objectives and constraints are forever changing. Second, the professional needs to articulate the financial plan and keep the client abreast of outcomes. Professional management of large portfolios is complicated further by the need to set up an efficient organization where decisions can be decentralized and information properly disseminated.

The task of life-cycle financial planning is a formidable one for most people. It is not surprising that a whole industry has sprung up to provide personal financial advice.

Tax Sheltering

In this section we explain three important tax sheltering options that can radically affect optimal asset allocation for individual investors. The first is the tax-deferral option, which arises from the fact that you do not have to pay tax on a capital gain until you choose to realize the gain. The second is tax-deferred retirement plans such as individual retirement accounts, and the third is tax-deferred annuities offered by life insurance companies. Not treated here at all is the possibility of investing in the tax-exempt instruments discussed in Chapter 2.

The Tax-Deferral Option   A fundamental feature of the U.S. Internal Revenue Code is that tax on a capital gain on an asset is payable only when the asset is sold;[2] this is its **tax-**

---

[2]The only exception to this rule occurs in futures investing, where the IRS treats a gain as taxable in the year it occurs regardless of whether the investor closes his or her position.

deferral option. The investor therefore can control the timing of the tax payment. From a tax perspective this option makes stocks in general preferable to fixed-income securities.

To see this, compare IBM stock with an IBM bond. Suppose both offer an expected total return of 15% this year. The stock has a dividend yield of 5% and an expected appreciation in price of 10%, whereas the bond has an interest rate of 15%. The bond investor must pay tax on the bond's interest in the year it is earned, whereas the IBM stockholder pays tax only on the dividend and defers paying tax on the capital gain until the stock is sold.

Suppose the investor is investing $2,000 for five years and is in a 28% tax bracket. An investment in the bond will earn an after-tax return of 10.8% per year (.72 × 15%). The amount of money available after taxes at the end of five years is

$$\$1,000 \times 1.108^5 = \$1,669.93$$

For the stock, the dividend yield after taxes will be 3.6% per year (.72 × 5%). Because no taxes are paid on the capital gain until Year 5, the return before paying the capital gains tax is

$$\$1,000 \times (1 + .036 + .10)^5 = 1,000(1.136)^5$$
$$= \$1,891.87$$

In Year 5 the capital gain is

$$\$1,891.87 - \$1,000(1.036)^5 = 1,891.87 - 1,193.44$$
$$= \$698.43$$

Taxes due are $195.56, leaving $1,696.31, which is $26.38 more than the bond investment yields. Deferral of the capital gains tax allows the investment to compound at a faster rate until the tax is actually paid.

Note that the more of one's total return that is in the form of price appreciation, the greater the value of the tax-deferral option.

Tax-Deferred Retirement Plans   Recent years have seen increased use of **tax-deferred retirement plans** in which investors can choose how to allocate assets. Such plans include IRAs, Keogh plans, and employer sponsored "tax-qualified" defined contribution plans. A feature they have in common is that contributions and earnings are not subject to federal income tax until the individual withdraws them as benefits.

Typically, an individual may have some investment in the form of such qualified retirement accounts and some in the form of ordinary taxable accounts. The basic investment principle that applies is to hold whatever bonds you want to hold in the retirement account while holding equities in the ordinary account. You maximize the tax advantage of the retirement account by holding it in the security that is the least tax advantaged.

To see this point, consider the following example. Suppose Eloise has $200,000 of wealth, $100,000 of it in a tax-qualified retirement account. She has decided to invest half of her wealth in bonds and half in stocks, so she allocates half of her retirement account and half of her nonretirement funds to each. By doing this, Eloise is not maximizing her after-tax returns. She could reduce her tax bill with no change in before-tax returns by simply shifting her bonds into the retirement account and holding all her stocks outside the retirement account.

Concept
CHECK

Question 2 • **Suppose Eloise earns a 10% per year rate of interest on bonds and 15% per year on stocks, all in the form of price appreciation. In five years she will withdraw all her funds and spend them. By how much will she increase her final accumulation if she shifts all bonds into the retirement account and holds all stocks outside the retirement account? She is in a 28% tax bracket.**

Deferred Annuities   **Deferred annuities** are essentially tax-sheltered accounts offered by life insurance companies. They combine the same kind of deferral of taxes available on IRAs with the option of withdrawing one's funds in the form of a life annuity. Variable annuity contracts offer the additional advantage of mutual fund investing. One major difference between an IRA and a variable annuity contract is that whereas the amount one can contribute to an IRA is tax-deductible and extremely limited as to maximum amount, the amount one can contribute to a deferred annuity is unlimited, but not tax-deductible.

The defining characteristic of a life annuity is that its payments continue as long as the recipient is alive, although virtually all deferred annuity contracts have several withdrawal options, including a lump sum of cash paid out at any time. You need not worry about running out of money before you die. Like social security, therefore, life annuities offer longevity insurance and thus would seem to be an ideal asset for someone in the retirement years. Indeed, theory suggests that where there are no bequest motives, it would be optimal for people to invest heavily in actuarially fair life annuities.[3]

There are two types of life annuities, **fixed annuities** and **variable annuities**. A fixed annuity pays a fixed nominal sum of money per period (usually each month), whereas a variable annuity pays a periodic amount linked to the investment performance of some underlying portfolio.

In pricing annuities, insurance companies use **mortality tables** that show the probabilities that individuals of various ages will die within a year. These tables enable the insurer to compute with reasonable accuracy how many of a large number of people in a given age group will die in each future year. If it sells life annuities to a large group, the insurance company can estimate fairly accurately the amount of money it will have to pay in each future year to meet its obligations.

Variable annuities are structured so that the investment risk of the underlying asset portfolio is passed through to the recipient, much as shareholders bear the risk of a mutual fund. There are two stages in a variable annuity contract: an accumulation phase and a payout phase. During the *accumulation* phase, the investor contributes money periodically to one or more open-end mutual funds and accumulates shares. The second, or *payout*, stage usually starts at retirement, when the investor typically has several options, including the following:

1. Taking the market value of the shares in a lump sum payment.
2. Receiving a fixed annuity until death.
3. Receiving a variable amount of money each period that is computed according to a certain procedure.

This procedure is best explained by the following example. Assume that at retirement John Shortlife has $100,000 accumulated in a variable annuity contract. The initial annuity payment is determined by setting an assumed investment return (AIR), 4% per year in this example, and an assumption about mortality probabilities. In Shortlife's case we assume he will live for only three years after retirement and will receive three annual payments starting one year from now.

The benefit payment in each year, B_t, is given by the recursive formula:

$$B_t = B_{t-1} \frac{1 + R_t}{1 + \text{AIR}} \tag{26.1}$$

---

[3]For an elaboration of this point see Laurence J. Kotlikoff and Avia Spivak, "The Family as an Incomplete Annuities Market," *Journal of Political Economy* 89 (April 1981).

ILLUSTRATION OF A VARIABLE ANNUITY

Starting accumulation = $100,000

R_t = Rate of return on underlying portfolio in year t

Assumed investment return (AIR) = 4% per year

B_t = Benefit received at end of year $t = B_{t-1} \dfrac{1 + R_t}{1 + \text{AIR}}$

B_0 = $36,035; this is the hypothetical constant payment, which has a present value of $100,000, using a discount rate of 4% per year

A_t = Remaining balance after B_t is withdrawn

t	R_t	B_t	Remaining balance = $A_t = A_{t-1} \times (1 + R_t) - B_t$
0			$100,000
1	6%	$36,728	69,272
2	2	36,022	34,635
3	4	36,022	0

where R_t is the actual holding-period return on the underlying portfolio in year t. In other words, each year the amount Shortlife receives equals the previous year's benefit multiplied by a factor that reflects the actual investment return compared with the assumed investment return. In our example, if the actual return equals 4%, the factor will be one, and this year's benefits will equal last year's. If R_t is greater than 4%, the benefit will increase, and if R_t is less than 4%, the benefit will decrease.

The starting benefit is found by computing a hypothetical constant payment with a present value of $100,000 using the 4% AIR to discount future values and multiplying it by the first year's performance factor. In our example the hypothetical constant payment is $36,035.

The nearby box summarizes the computation and shows what the payment will be in each of three years if R_t is 6%, then 2% and 4%. The last column shows the balance in the fund after each payment.

This method guarantees that the initial $100,000 will be sufficient to pay all benefits due regardless of what actual holding-period returns turn out to be. In this way the variable annuity contract passes all portfolio risk through to the annuitant.

By selecting an appropriate mix of underlying assets, such as stocks, bonds, and cash, an investor can create a stream of variable annuity payments with a wide variety of risk-return combinations. Naturally, the investor wants to select a combination on the efficient frontier, that is, a combination that offers the highest expected level of payments for any specified level of risk.[4]

Question 3 • Assume Victor is now 75 years old and is expected to live until age 80. He has $100,000 in a variable annuity account. If the assumed investment return is 4% per year, what is the initial annuity payment? Suppose the annuity's asset base is the S&P 500 equity portfolio and its holding-period return for the next five years is each of the following: 4%, 10%, –8%, 25%, and 0. How much would Victor receive each year? Verify that the insurance company would wind up using exactly $100,000 to fund Victor's benefits.

Variable and Universal Life Insurance   Variable life insurance is another tax-deferred investment vehicle offered by the life insurance industry. A variable life insurance policy combines life insurance with the tax-deferred annuities described earlier.

---

[4]For an elaboration on possible combinations see Zvi Bodie, "An Innovation for Stable Real Retirement Income," *Journal of Portfolio Management*, Fall 1980; and Zvi Bodie and James E. Pesando, "Retirement Annuity Design in an Inflationary Climate," in Zvi Bodie and J. B. Shoven, *Financial Aspects of the United States Pension System* (Chicago: University of Chicago Press, 1983), chapter 11.

To invest in this product, you pay either a single premium or a series of premiums. In each case there is a stated death benefit, and the policyholder can allocate the money invested to several portfolios, which generally include a money market fund, a bond fund, and at least one common stock fund. The allocation can be changed at any time.

A variable life policy has a cash surrender value equal to the investment base minus any surrender charges. Typically, there is a surrender charge (about 6% of the purchase payments) if you surrender the policy during the first several years, but not thereafter. At policy surrender income taxes become due on all investment gains.

Variable life insurance policies offer a death benefit that is the greater of the stated face value or the market value of the investment base. In other words, the death benefit may rise with favorable investment performance, but it will not go below the guaranteed face value. Furthermore, the surviving beneficiary is not subject to income tax on the death benefit.

The policyholder can choose from a number of income options to convert the policy into a stream of income, either on surrender of the contract or as a partial withdrawal. In all cases income taxes are payable on the part of any distribution representing investment gains.

The insured can gain access to the investment without having to pay income tax by borrowing against the cash surrender value. Policy loans of up to 90% of the cash value are available at any time at a contractually specified interest rate.

A universal life insurance policy is similar to a variable life policy except that, instead of having a choice of portfolios to invest in, the policyholder earns a rate of interest that is set by the insurance company and changed periodically as market conditions change. The disadvantage of universal life insurance is that the company controls the rate of return to the policyholder, and, although companies may change the rate in response to competitive pressures, changes are not automatic. Different companies offer different rates, so it often pays to shop around for the best.

Since the passage of the Tax Reform Act of 1986, the investment products offered by the life insurance industry—tax-deferred annuities and variable and universal life insurance—are among the most attractive of the remaining tax-advantaged opportunities.

26.5   PENSION FUNDS

By far the most important institution in the retirement income system is the employer-sponsored pension plan. These plans vary in form and complexity, but they all share certain common elements in every country. In general, investment strategy depends on the type of plan.

Pension plans are defined by the terms specifying the "who," "when," and "how much," for both the plan benefits and the plan contributions used to pay for those benefits. The *pension fund* of the plan is the cumulation of assets created from contributions and the investment earnings on those contributions, less any payments of benefits from the fund. In the United States, contributions to the fund by either employer or employee are tax-deductible, and investment income of the fund is not taxed. Distributions from the fund, whether to the employer or the employee, are taxed as ordinary income. There are two "pure" types of pension plans: *defined contribution* and *defined benefit*.

Defined Contribution Plans

In a defined contribution plan, a formula specifies contributions but not benefit payments. Contribution rules usually are specified as a predetermined fraction of salary (e.g., the employer contributes 15% of the employee's annual wages to the plan), although that fraction need not be constant over the course of an employee's career. The pension fund consists of a set of individual investment accounts, one for each employee. Pension benefits are not specified, other than that at retirement the employee applies that total accumulated value of contributions and earnings on those contributions to purchase an annuity. The employee often has some choice over both the level of contributions and the way the account is invested.

In principle, contributions could be invested in any security, although in practice most plans limit investment choices to bond, stock, and money market funds. The employee bears all the investment risk; the retirement account is, by definition, fully funded by the contributions, and the employer has no legal obligation beyond making its periodic contributions.

For defined contribution plans, investment policy is essentially the same as for a tax-qualified individual retirement account. Indeed, the main providers of investment products for these plans are the same institutions such as mutual funds and insurance companies that serve the general investment needs of individuals. Therefore, in a defined contribution plan much of the task of setting and achieving the income-replacement goal falls on the employee.

Defined Benefit Plans

In a defined benefit plan, a formula specifies benefits, but not the manner, including contributions, in which these benefits are funded. The benefit formula typically takes into account years of service for the employer and level of wages or salary (e.g., the employer pays the employee for life, beginning at age 65, a yearly amount equal to 1% of his final annual wage for each year of service). The employer (called the "plan sponsor") or an insurance company hired by the sponsor guarantees the benefits and thus absorbs the investment risk. The obligation of the plan sponsor to pay the promised benefits is like a long-term debt liability of the employer.

As measured both by number of plan participants and the value of total pension liabilities, the defined benefit form dominates in most countries around the world. This is so in the United States, although the trend since the mid-1970s is for sponsors to choose the defined contribution form when starting new plans. But the two plan types are not mutually exclusive. Many sponsors adopt defined benefit plans as their primary plan, in which participation is mandatory, and supplement them with voluntary defined contribution plans.

With defined benefit plans, there is an important distinction between the pension *plan* and the pension *fund*. The plan is the contractual arrangement setting out the rights and obligations of all parties; the fund is a separate pool of assets set aside to provide collateral for the promised benefits. In defined contribution plans, by definition, the value of the benefits equals that of the assets, so the plan is always fully funded. But in defined benefit plans, there is a continuum of possibilities. There may be no separate fund, in which case the plan is said to be unfunded. When there is a separate fund with assets worth less than the present value of the promised benefits, the plan is underfunded. And if the plan's assets have a market value that exceeds the present value of the plan's liabilities, it is said to be overfunded.

Alternative Perspectives on Defined Benefit Pension Obligations

As previously described, in a defined benefit plan, the pension benefit is determined by a formula that takes into account the employee's history of service and wages or salary. The plan sponsor provides this benefit regardless of the investment performance of the pension fund assets. The annuity promised to the employee is therefore the employer's liability. What is the nature of this liability?

Private-sector defined benefit pension plans in the United States offer an *explicit* benefit determined by the plan's benefit formula. However, many plan sponsors have from time to time provided voluntary increases in benefits to their retired employees, depending on the financial condition of the sponsor and increases in the cost of living. Some observers have interpreted such increases as evidence of *implicit* cost-of-living indexation. These voluntary ad hoc benefit increases, however, are very different from a formal COLA (cost-of-living adjustment). Under current laws in the United States, the plan sponsor is not legally obligated to pay more than the amount promised explicitly under the plan's benefit formula.

There is a widespread belief that in final-pay formula plans, pension benefits are protected against inflation at least up to the date of retirement. But this is a misperception. Unlike social security benefits, whose starting value is indexed to a general index of wages, pension benefits even in final-pay private-sector plans are "indexed" only to the extent that (1) the employee continues to work for the same employer, (2) the employee's own wage or salary keeps pace with the general index, and (3) the employer continues to maintain the same plan. Very few private corporations in the United States offer pension benefits that are automatically indexed for inflation; thus workers who change jobs wind up with lower pension benefits at retirement than otherwise identical workers who stay with the same employer, even if the employers have defined benefit plans with the same final-pay benefit formula. This is referred to as the *portability problem.*

Both the rule-making body of the accounting profession (the Financial Accounting Standards Board) and Congress have adopted the present value of the nominal benefits as the appropriate measure of a sponsor's pension liability. FASB Statement 87 specifies that the measure of corporate pension liabilities to be used on the corporate balance sheet in external reports is the accumulated benefit obligation (ABO)—that is, the present value of pension benefits owed to employees under the plan's benefit formula absent any salary projections and discounted at a nominal rate of interest. Similarly, in its Omnibus Budget Reconciliation Act (OBRA) of 1987, Congress defined the current liability as the measure of a corporation's pension liability and set limits on the amount of tax-qualified contributions a corporation could make as a proportion of the current liability. OBRA's definition of the current liability is essentially the same as FASB Statement 87's definition of the ABO.

The ABO is thus a key element in a pension fund's investment strategy. It not only affects a corporation's reported balance sheet liabilities; it also reflects economic reality.

Statement 87, however, recognizes an additional measure of a defined benefit plan's liability: the projected benefit obligation (PBO). The PBO is a measure of the sponsor's pension liability that includes projected increases in salary up to the expected age of retirement. Statement 87 requires corporations to use the PBO in computing pension expense reported in their income statements. This is perhaps useful for financial analysts, in that the amount may help them to derive an appropriate estimate of expected future labor costs for discounted cash flow valuation models of the firm as a going concern. The PBO is not, however, an appropriate measure of the benefits that the employer has explicitly guaranteed. The difference between the PBO and the ABO should not be treated as a liability of the firm, because these additional pension costs will be realized only if the employees continue to work in the future. If these future contingent labor costs are to be treated as a liability of the firm, then why not book the entire future wage bill as a liability? If this is done, then shouldn't one add as an asset the present value of future revenues generated by these labor activities? It is indeed difficult to see either the accounting or economic logic for using the PBO as a measure of pension liabilities.

The PBO would be the correct number to use for the firm's liability if benefits were tied to some index of wages up to the age of retirement, independently of whether the employee stays with the employer. Because private plans in the United States do not offer such automatic indexation, however, it is a mistake to use the PBO as the measure of what the sponsor is contractually obliged to pay to employees.[5] Hence it may not be an appropriate target for the pension fund to hedge in its investment strategy.

Concept CHECK

Question 4 • An employee is 40 years old and has been working for the firm for 15 years. If normal retirement age is 65, the interest rate is 8%, and the employee's life expectancy is 80, what is the present value of the accrued pension benefit?

Pension Investment Strategies

The special tax status of pension funds creates the same incentive for both defined contribution and defined benefit plans to tilt their asset mix toward assets with the largest spread between pretax and after-tax rates of return. In a defined contribution plan, because the participant bears all the investment risk, the optimal asset mix also depends on the risk tolerance of the participant.

In defined benefit plans, optimal investment policy may be different because the sponsor absorbs the investment risk. If the sponsor has to share some of the upside potential of the pension assets with plan participants, there is in incentive to eliminate all investment risk by investing in securities that match the promised benefits. If, for example, the plan sponsor has to pay $100 per year for the next five years, it can provide this stream of benefit payments by buying a set of five zero-coupon bonds each with a face value of $100 and maturing sequentially. By so doing, the sponsor eliminates the risk of a shortfall. This is called **immunization** of the pension liability.

If a corporate pension fund has an ABO that exceeds the market value of its assets, FASB Statement 87 requires that the corporation recognize the unfunded liability on its balance sheet. If, however, the pension assets exceed the ABO, the corporation cannot include the surplus on its balance sheet. This asymmetric accounting treatment expresses a deeply held view about defined benefit pension funds. Representatives of organized labor, some politicians, and even a few pension professionals believe that the sponsoring corporation, as guarantor of the accumulated pension benefits, is liable for pension asset shortfalls but does not have a clear right to the entire surplus in case of pension overfunding.

If the pension fund is overfunded, then a 100% fixed-income portfolio is no longer required to minimize the cost of the corporate pension guarantee. Management can invest surplus pension assets in equities, provided it reduces the proportion so invested when the market value of pension assets comes close to the value of the ABO. Such an investment strategy is a type of portfolio insurance known as *contingent immunization*.

To understand how contingent immunization works, consider a simple version of it that makes use of a stop-loss order. Imagine that the ABO is $100 and that the fund has $120 of assets entirely invested in equities. The fund can protect itself against downside risk by maintaining a stop-loss order on all its equities at a price of $100. This means that should the price of the stocks fall to $100, the fund manager would liquidate all the stocks and

---

[5]In contrast to the situation in the United States, current law in the United Kingdom requires pension sponsors to index accrued pension benefits for inflation to the age of retirement, subject to a cap of 5% per year. Thus even a terminated employee has indexation for general inflation up to retirement age, as long as the benefit is vested. Therefore, under the U.K. system, the PBO is the appropriate measure of the sponsor's liability.

immunize the ABO. A stop-loss order at $100 is not a perfect hedge because there is no guarantee that the sell order can be executed at a price of $100. The result of a series of stop-loss orders at prices starting well above $100 is even better protection against downside risk.

Investing in Equities   If the only goal guiding corporate pension policy were shareholder wealth maximization, it is hard to understand why a financially sound pension sponsor would invest in equities at all. A policy of 100% bond investment would minimize the cost of guaranteeing the defined benefits.

In addition to the reasons given for a fully funded pension plan to invest only in fixed-income securities, there is a tax reason for doing so too. The tax advantage of a pension fund stems from the ability of the sponsor to earn the pretax interest rate on pension investments. To maximize the value of this tax shelter, it is necessary to invest entirely in assets offering the highest pretax interest rate. Because capital gains on stocks can be deferred and dividends are taxed at a much lower rate than interest on bonds, corporate pension funds should invest entirely in taxable bonds and other fixed-income investments.

Yet we know that in general pension funds invest from 40% to 60% of their portfolios in equity securities. Even a casual perusal of the practitioner literature suggests that they do so for a variety of reasons—some right and some wrong. There are three possible correct reasons.

The first is that corporate management views the pension plan as a trust for the employees and manages fund assets as if it were a defined contribution plan. It believes that a successful policy of investment in equities might allow it to pay extra benefits to employees and is therefore worth taking the risk. As explained before, if the plan is overfunded, then the sponsor can invest in stocks and still minimize the cost of providing the benefit guarantee by pursuing a contingent immunization strategy.

The second possible correct reason is that management believes that through superior market timing and security selection it is possible to create value in excess of management fees and expenses. Many executives in nonfinancial corporations are used to creating value in excess of cost in their businesses. They assume that it can also be done in the area of portfolio management. Of course, if that is true, then one must ask why they do not do it on their corporate account rather than in the pension fund. That way they could have their tax shelter "cake" and eat it too. It is important to realize, however, that to accomplish this feat, the plan must beat the market, not merely match it.

Note that a very weak form of the efficient markets hypothesis would imply that management cannot create shareholder value simply by shifting the pension portfolio out of bonds and into stocks. Even when the entire pension surplus belongs to the shareholders, investing in stocks just moves the shareholders along the capital market line (the market trade-off between risk and return for passive investors) and does not create value. When the net cost of providing plan beneficiaries with shortfall risk insurance is taken into account, increasing the pension fund equity exposure reduces shareholder value unless the equity investment can put the firm above the capital market line. This implies that it makes sense for a pension fund to invest in equities only *if* it intends to pursue an active strategy of beating the market either through superior timing or security selection. A completely passive strategy will add no value to shareholders.

For an underfunded plan of a corporation in financial distress there is another possible reason for investing in stocks and other risky assets—federal pension insurance. Firms in financial distress have an incentive to invest pension fund money in the riskiest assets, just as troubled thrift institutions insured by the Federal Savings and Loan Insurance Corporation (FSLIC) in the 1980s had similar motivation with respect to their loan portfolios.

Wrong Reasons to Invest in Equities The wrong reasons for a pension fund to invest in equities stem from several interrelated fallacies. The first is the notion that stocks are not risky in the long run. This fallacy was discussed at length in Appendix C to Chapter 8. Another related fallacy is the notion that stocks are a hedge against inflation. The reasoning behind this fallacy is that stocks are an ownership claim over real physical capital. Real profits are either unaffected or enhanced when there is unanticipated inflation, so owners of real capital should not be hurt by it.

Let us assume that this proposition is true, and that the real rate of return on stocks is uncorrelated or slightly positively correlated with inflation. If stocks are to be a good hedge against inflation risk in the conventional sense, however, the nominal return on stocks has to be *highly* positively correlated with inflation.

To see this, suppose that the benefit the sponsor is obliged to pay is indexed for inflation. The way to immunize an inflation-protected pension obligation is with zero-coupon bonds linked to the price index, not by investing in an equity portfolio. Although stocks may be free of inflation risk, they are not free of stock market risk.

Alternatively, suppose that you are a pensioner living on a money-fixed pension and therefore concerned about inflation risk. You could eliminate this risk to your real income stream by hedging with CPI-linked bonds. You might want to invest some of your money in stocks to increase your expected return, but by doing so you increase your exposure to market risk. There is no way to use stocks to reduce your risk in any significant way.

To have any valid economic content, the proposition that stocks are a good inflation hedge can mean only that nominal stock returns tend to rise and fall in proportion to changes in the rate of inflation. Even if this were true, the explanatory power of the relation (R^2) would have to be high for stocks to be useful as a vehicle for hedging against inflation risk. Empirical studies show that stock returns have been negatively correlated with inflation in the past with a low R^2. Thus even in the best of circumstances, stocks can offer only a limited hedge against inflation risk.

SUMMARY

1. When discussing the principles of portfolio management, it is useful to distinguish among seven classes of investors:
   a. Individual investors and personal trusts.
   b. Mutual funds.
   c. Pension funds.
   d. Endowment funds.
   e. Life insurance companies.
   f. Non–life insurance companies.
   g. Banks.
   In general, these groups have somewhat different investment objectives, constraints, and portfolio policies.

2. To some extent, most institutional investors seek to match the risk-and-return characteristics of their investment portfolios to the characteristics of their liabilities.

3. The process of asset allocation consists of the following steps:
   a. Specifying the asset classes to be included.
   b. Defining capital market expectations.
   c. Finding the efficient portfolio frontier.
   d. Determining the optimal mix.

4. People living on money-fixed incomes are vulnerable to inflation risk and may want to hedge against it. The effectiveness of an asset as an inflation hedge is related to its correlation with unanticipated inflation.

5. For investors who must pay taxes on their investment income, the process of asset allocation is complicated by the fact that they pay income taxes only on certain kinds of investment income. Interest income on munis is exempt from tax, and high-tax-bracket investors will prefer to hold them rather than short- and long-term taxable bonds. However, the really difficult part of the tax effect to deal with is the fact that capital gains are taxable only if realized through the sale of an asset during the holding period. Investment strategies designed to avoid taxes may contradict the principles of efficient diversification.

6. The life-cycle approach to the management of an individual's investment portfolio views the individual as passing through a series of stages, becoming more risk averse in later years. The rationale underlying this approach is that as we age, we use up our human capital and have less time remaining to recoup possible portfolio losses through increased labor supply.

7. People buy life and disability insurance during their prime earning years to hedge against the risk associated with loss of their human capital, that is, their future earning power.

8. There are three ways to shelter investment income from federal income taxes besides investing in tax-exempt bonds. The first is by investing in assets whose returns take the form of appreciation in value, such as common stocks or real estate. As long as capital gains taxes are not paid until the asset is sold, the tax can be deferred indefinitely.

   The second way of tax sheltering is through investing in tax-deferred retirement plans such as IRAs. The general investment rule is to hold the least tax-advantaged assets in the plan and the most tax-advantaged assets outside of it.

   The third way of sheltering is to invest in the tax-advantaged products offered by the life insurance industry—tax-deferred annuities and variable and universal life insurance. They combine the flexibility of mutual fund investing with the tax advantages of tax deferral.

9. Pension plans are either defined contribution plans or defined benefit plans. Defined contribution plans are in effect retirement funds held in trust for the employee by the employer. The employees in such plans bear all the risk of the plan's assets and often have some choice in the allocation of those assets. Defined benefit plans give the employees a claim to a money-fixed annuity at retirement. The annuity level is determined by a formula that takes into account years of service and the employee's wage or salary history.

10. If the only goal guiding corporate pension policy were shareholder wealth maximization, it would be hard to understand why a financially sound pension sponsor would invest in equities at all. A policy of 100% bond investment would both maximize the tax advantage of funding the pension plan and minimize the costs of guaranteeing the defined benefits.

11. If sponsors viewed their pension liabilities as indexed for inflation, then the appropriate way for them to minimize the cost of providing benefit guarantees would be to hedge using securities whose returns are highly correlated with inflation. Common stocks would not be an appropriate hedge because they have a low correlation with inflation.

Key Terms

risk-return trade-off	term insurance	tax-deferral option
personal trusts	variable life	tax-deferred retirement
income beneficiaries	universal life	plans
remaindermen	guaranteed insurance	deferred annuities
defined contribution plans	contracts (GICs)	fixed annuities
defined benefit plans	liquidity	variable annuities
endowment funds	investment horizon	mortality tables
whole-life insurance policy	prudent man law	immunization

Selected Readings

For a collection of essays presenting the Institute of Chartered Financial Analysts approach to portfolio management see:

Maginn, John L.; and Donald L. Tuttle, eds. *Managing Investment Portfolios.* 2nd ed. New York: Warren, Gorham, & Lamont, 1990.

A good discussion of asset allocation in practice is:

Brinson, G. P.; J. J. Diermeier; and G. G. Schlarbaum. "A Composite Portfolio Benchmark for Pension Plans." *Financial Analysts Journal*, March–April 1986.

For a further discussion of the theory and evidence regarding the investment policies of corporate defined benefit pension plans see:

Bodie, Z.; J. Light; R. Morck; and R. A. Taggart. "Corporate Pension Policy: An Empirical Investigation." *Financial Analysts Journal*, September–October 1985.

Bodie, Z. "Managing Pension and Retirement Assets: An International Perspective." *Journal of Financial Services Research*, December 1990.

Bodie, Z.; and D. Crane. "Personal Investing: Advice, Theory, and Evidence." *Financial Analysts Journal*, November–December 1997.

Problems

1. Several discussion meetings have provided the following information about one of your firm's new advisory clients, a charitable endowment fund recently created by means of a one-time $10,000,000 gift.

Objectives

Return requirement. Planning is based on a minimum total return of 8% per year, including an initial current income component of $500,000 (5% of beginning capital). Realizing this current income target is the endowment fund's primary return goal. (See "Unique needs" following.)

Constraints

Time horizon. Perpetuity, except for requirement to make an $8,500,000 cash distribution on June 30, 1998. (See "Unique needs.")

Liquidity needs. None of a day-to-day nature until 1998. Income is distributed annually after year-end. (See "Unique needs" below.)

Tax considerations. None; this endowment fund is exempt from taxes.

Legal and regulatory considerations. Minimal, but the prudent man rule applies to all investment actions.

Unique needs, circumstances, and preferences. The endowment fund must pay out to another tax-exempt entity the sum of $8,500,000 in cash on June 30, 1998. The assets remaining after this distribution will be retained by the fund in perpetuity. The endowment fund has adopted a "spending rule" requiring a first-year current income payout of $500,000; thereafter the annual payout is to rise by 3% in real terms. Until 1998, annual income in excess of that required by the spending rule is to be reinvested. After 1998, the spending rate will be reset at 5% of the then-existing capital.

With this information and information found in this chapter, do the following:
a. Formulate an appropriate investment policy statement for the endowment fund.
b. Identify and briefly explain three major ways in which your firm's initial asset allocation decisions for the endowment fund will be affected by the circumstances of the account.

2. Your client says, "With the unrealized gains in my portfolio, I have almost saved enough money for my daughter to go to college in eight years, but educational costs keep going up." Based on this statement alone, which one of the following appears to be least important to your client's investment policy?
a. Time horizon.
b. Purchasing power risk.
c. Liquidity.
d. Taxes.

3. The common stock investments of the defined contribution plan of a corporation are being managed by the trust department of a national bank. The risk of investment loss is borne by the
a. Pension Benefit Guarantee Corporation.
b. Employees.
c. Corporation.
d. Federal Deposit Insurance Corporation.

4. The aspect least likely to be included in the portfolio management process is
a. Identifying an investor's objectives, constraints, and preferences.
b. Organizing the management process itself.
c. Implementing strategies regarding the choice of assets to be used.
d. Monitoring market conditions, relative values, and investor circumstances.

5. Investors in high marginal tax brackets probably would be least interested in a
a. Portfolio of diversified stocks.
b. Tax-free bond fund.
c. Commodity pool.
d. High-income bond fund.

6. Sam Short, CFA, has recently joined the investment management firm of Green, Spence, and Smith (GSS). For several years, GSS has worked for a broad array of clients, including employee benefit plans, wealthy individuals, and charitable organizations. Also, the firm expresses expertise in managing stocks, bonds, cash reserves, real estate, venture capital, and international securities. To date, the firm has not utilized a formal asset allocation process but instead has relied on the individual wishes of clients or the particular preferences of its portfolio managers. Short recommends to GSS management that a formal asset allocation process would be beneficial and emphasizes that a large part of a portfolio's ultimate return depends on asset allocation. He is asked to take his conviction an additional step by making a proposal to executive management.
a. Recommend and justify an approach to asset allocation that could be used by GSS.
b. Apply the approach to a middle-aged, wealthy individual characterized as a fairly conservative investor (sometimes referred to as a "guardian investor").

7. Ambrose Green, 63, is a retired engineer and a client of Clayton Asset Management Associates ("Associates"). His accumulated savings are invested in Diversified Global

Fund ("the Fund"), an in-house investment vehicle with multiple portfolio managers through which Associates manage nearly all client assets on a pooled basis. Dividend and capital gain distributions have produced an annual average return to Green of about 8% on his $900,000 original investment in the Fund, made six years ago. The $1,000,000 current value of his Fund interest represents virtually all of Green's net worth.

Green is a widower whose daughter is a single parent living with her young son. While not an extravagant person, Green's spending has exceeded his after-tax income by a considerable margin since his retirement. As a result, his non-Fund financial resources have steadily diminished and now amount to $10,000. Green does not have retirement income from a private pension plan, but he does receive taxable government benefits of about $1,000 per month. His marginal tax rate is 40%. He lives comfortably in a rented apartment, travels extensively, and makes frequent cash gifts to his daughter and grandson, to whom he wants to leave an estate of at least $1,000,000.

Green realizes that he needs more income to maintain his lifestyle. He also believes his assets should provide an after-tax cash flow sufficient to meet his present $80,000 annual spending needs, which he is unwilling to reduce. He is uncertain as to how to proceed and has engaged you, a CFA Charterholder with an independent advisory practice, to counsel him.

a. Your first task is to review Green's investment policy statement:

Objectives

I need a maximum return that includes enough income to meet my spending needs, so about a 10% total return is required.

I want low risk, to minimize the possibility of large losses and preserve the value of my assets for eventual use by my daughter and grandson.

Constraints

With my spending needs averaging about $80,000 per year and only $10,000 of cash remaining, I will probably have to sell something soon.

I am in good health and my noncancelable health insurance will cover my future medical expenses.

  i. Identify and briefly discuss four key constraints present in Green's situation not adequately treated in his investment policy statement.
  ii. Based on your assessment of his situation and the information presented in the introduction, create and justify appropriate return and risk objectives for Green.

b. Green has asked you to review the existing asset allocation of Diversified Global Fund. He wonders if a 60:30:10 allocation to stocks, bonds, and cash equivalents would be better than the present 40:40:20 allocation. Green also wonders if the Fund is appropriate as his primary investment asset. To address his concerns you decide to do a scenario forecasting exercise using the facts presented in the introduction and the data in Tables 26A and 26B provided by Associates.

Under the "degearing" scenario, the U.S.–Europe–Far East trading nations experience an extended period of slow economic growth while they reduce prior debt excesses. This scenario is assigned a probability of .50, while each of the other two scenarios—"disinflation" and "inflation"—is assigned a probability of .25. The asset classes shown in Table 26A reflect the diversification strategy used by Associates in managing its Diversified Global Fund.

Table 26A   Associates' Diversified Global Fund Current Asset Allocation

Asset Class	Percentage of Total Assets				
	United States	Europe	Far East	Other	Total
Stocks	15%	10%	12%	3%	40%
Bonds	20	12	8	0	40
Cash equivalents	10	5	5	0	20
Totals	45%	27%	25%	3%	100%

Table 26B   Projected Returns by Economic Scenario, 1996–99 (All data have been weighted to reflect the geographic mix shown in Table 26A)

	Scenario		
	Degearing	Disinflation	Inflation
Real economic growth	2.5%	1.0%	3.0%
Inflation rate	3.0	1.0	6.0
Nominal total returns			
Stocks	8.25%	−8.00%	4.00%
Bonds	6.25	7.50	2.00
Cash equivalents	4.50	2.50	6.50
Real total returns			
Stocks	5.25%	−9.00%	−2.00%
Bonds	3.25	6.50	−4.00
Cash equivalents	1.50	1.50	0.50

    i. Calculate the expected total returns associated with the existing 40:40:20 asset allocation and with the alternative 60:30:10 mix, given the three scenarios shown in Table 26B.

    ii. Justify the 40:40:20 asset allocation shown for the Fund in Table 26A versus the alternative 60:30:10 mix and explain your conclusion. In formulating your response, use the data in Tables 26A and 26B, your knowledge of multiple scenario forecasting, and your part (i) calculations.

    iii. Evaluate the appropriateness of the Fund as a primary investment asset for Green, citing and explaining characteristics that relate directly to his needs and goals.

  c. Continuing your discussion with Green, you explain that historical return and risk premiums of the type presented in Table 26C are frequently used in forming estimates of future returns for various types of financial assets. While such historical data are helpful in forecasting returns, most users know that history is an imperfect guide to the future. Thus they recognize that there are reasons why these data should be adjusted if they are to be employed in the forecasting process.

     As shown in Table 26C, the historical real interest rate for Treasury bills was .5% per year and the maturity premium on Treasury bonds over Treasury bills was .8%. Briefly describe and justify one adjustment to each of these two data items that should be made before they can be used to form expectations about future real interest rates and Treasury bond maturity premiums.

Table 26C   U.S. Historical Annualized Return and Risk Premiums, 1926–1994

Inflation rate	3.0%
Real interest rate on Treasury bills	0.5%
Maturity premium of long-term T-bonds over T-bills	0.8%
Default premium of long-term corporate bonds over long-term T-bonds	0.6%
Risk premium on stocks over long-term T-bonds	5.6%
Return on T-bills	3.5%
Return on long-term corporate bonds	4.9%
Return on large-cap stocks	9.9%

 d. You recognize that even adjusted historical economic and capital markets data may be of limited use when estimating future returns. Independent of your response to (*c*), briefly describe three key circumstances that should be considered when forming expectations about future returns.

8. Susan Fairfax is president of Reston Industries, a U.S.-based company whose sales are entirely domestic and whose shares are listed on the New York Stock Exchange. The following are additional facts concerning her current situation:

 Fairfax is single, aged 58. She has no immediate family, no debts, and does not own a residence. She is in excellent health and covered by Reston-paid health insurance that continues after her expected retirement at age 65.

 Her base salary of $500,000/year, inflation-protected, is sufficient to support her present lifestyle but can no longer generate any excess for savings.

 She has $2,000,000 of savings from prior years held in the form of short-term instruments.

 Reston rewards key employees through a generous stock-bonus incentive plan but provides no pension plan and pays no dividend.

 Fairfax's incentive plan participation has resulted in her ownership of Reston stock worth $10 million (current market value). The stock, received tax-free but subject to tax at a 35% rate (on entire proceeds) if sold, is expected to be held at least until her retirement.

 Her present level of spending and the current annual inflation rate of 4% are expected to continue after her retirement.

 Fairfax is taxed at 35% on all salary, investment income, and realized capital gains. Assume her composite tax rate will continue at this level indefinitely.

Fairfax's orientation is patient, careful, and conservative in all things. She has stated that an annual after-tax real total return of 3% would be completely acceptable to her if it was achieved in a context where an investment portfolio created from her accumulated savings was not subject to a decline of more than 10% in nominal terms in any given 12-month period. To obtain the benefits of professional assistance, she has approached two investment advisory firms—HH Counselors ("HH") and Coastal Advisors ("Coastal")—for recommendations on allocation of the investment portfolio to be created from her existing savings assets (the "Savings Portfolio") as well as for advice concerning investing in general.

 a. Create and justify an investment policy statement for Fairfax based only on the information provided thus far. Be specific and complete in presenting objectives and constraints. (An asset allocation is not required in answering this question.)

 b. Coastal has proposed the asset allocation shown in Table 26D for investment of Fairfax's $2 million of savings assets. Assume that only the current yield portion of

Table 26D   Susan Fairfax Proposed Asset Allocation, Prepared by Coastal Advisors

Asset Class	Proposed Allocation (%)	Current Yield (%)	Projected Total Return (%)
Cash equivalents	15.0	4.5	4.5
Corporate bonds	10.0	7.5	7.5
Municipal bonds	10.0	5.5	5.5
Large-cap U.S. stocks	0.0	3.5	11.0
Small-cap U.S. stocks	0.0	2.5	13.0
International stocks (EAFE)	35.0	2.0	13.5
Real estate investment trusts (REITs)	25.0	9.0	12.0
Venture capital	5.0	0.0	20.0
Total	100.0	4.9	10.7
Inflation (CPI), projected			4.0

Table 26E   Alternative Asset Allocations, Prepared by HH Counselors

Asset Class	Projected Total Return	Expected Standard Deviation	Asset Allocation A	Asset Allocation B	Asset Allocation C	Asset Allocation D	Asset Allocation E
Cash equivalents	4.5%	2.5%	10%	20%	25%	5%	10%
Corporate bonds	6.0	11.0	0	25	0	0	0
Municipal bonds	7.2	10.8	40	0	30	0	30
Large-cap U.S. stocks	13.0	17.0	20	15	35	25	5
Small-cap U.S. stocks	15.0	21.0	10	10	0	15	5
International stocks (EAFE)	15.0	21.0	10	10	0	15	10
Real estate investment trusts (REITs)	10.0	15.0	10	10	10	25	35
Venture capital	26.0	64.0	0	10	0	15	5
Total			100	100	100	100	100
Summary Data							
			Asset Allocation A	Asset Allocation B	Asset Allocation C	Asset Allocation D	Asset Allocation E
Projected total return			9.9%	11.0%	8.8%	14.4%	10.3%
Projected after-tax total return			7.4%	7.2%	6.5%	9.4%	7.4%
Expected standard deviation			9.4%	12.4%	8.5%	18.1%	10.1%
Sharpe ratio			0.574	0.524	0.506	—	0.574

projected total return (comprised of both investment income and realized capital gains) is taxable to Fairfax and that the municipal bond income is entirely tax-exempt.

Critique the Coastal proposal. Include in your answer three weaknesses in the Coastal proposal from the standpoint of the investment policy statement you created for her in (*a*).

c. HH Counselors has developed five alternative asset allocations (shown in Table 26E) for client portfolios. Answer the following questions based on Table 26E and the investment policy statement you created for Fairfax in (*a*).

  i. Determine which of the asset allocations in Table 26E meet or exceed Fairfax's stated return objective.

  ii. Determine the three asset allocations in Table 26E that meet Fairfax's risk tolerance criterion. Assume a 95% confidence interval is required, with 2 standard deviations serving as an approximation of that requirement.

    d. Assume that the risk-free rate is 4.5%.
        i. Calculate the Sharpe ratio for Asset Allocation D.
        ii. Determine the two asset allocations in Table 26E having the best risk-adjusted
           returns, based only on the Sharpe ratio measure.
    e. Recommend and justify the one asset allocation in Table 26E you believe would be
       the best model for Fairfax's savings portfolio.

9. John Franklin is a recent widower with some experience in investing for his own
account. Following his wife's recent death and settlement of the estate, Mr. Franklin
owns a controlling interest in a successful privately held manufacturing company in
which Mrs. Franklin was formerly active, a recently completed warehouse property,
the family residence, and his personal holdings of stocks and bonds. He has decided to
retain the warehouse property as a diversifying investment but intends to sell the private company interest, giving half of the proceeds to a medical research foundation in
memory of his deceased wife. Actual transfer of this gift is expected to take place about
three months from now. You have been engaged to assist him with the valuations, planning, and portfolio building required to structure his investment program appropriately.

    Mr. Franklin has introduced you to the finance committee of the medical research
foundation that is to receive his $45 million cash gift three months hence (and will
eventually receive the assets of his estate). This gift will greatly increase the size of the
foundation's endowment (from $10 million to $55 million) as well as enable it to make
larger grants to researchers. The foundation's grant-making (spending) policy has been
to pay out virtually all of its annual net investment income. As its investment approach
has been very conservative, the endowment portfolio now consists almost entirely of
fixed-income assets. The finance committee understands that these actions are causing
the real value of foundation assets and the real value of future grants to decline due to
the effects of inflation. Until now, the finance committee has believed that it had no
alternative to these actions, given the large immediate cash needs of the research programs being funded and the small size of the foundation's capital base. The foundation's annual grants must at least equal 5% of its assets' market value to maintain its
U.S. tax-exempt status, a requirement that is expected to continue indefinitely. No
additional gifts or fund-raising activities are expected over the foreseeable future.

    Given the change in circumstances that Mr. Franklin's gift will make, the finance
committee wishes to develop new grant-making and investment policies. Annual
spending must at least meet the level of 5% of market value that is required to maintain
the foundation's tax-exempt status, but the committee is unsure about how much
higher than 5% it can or should be. The committee wants to pay out as much as possible because of the critical nature of the research being funded; however, it understands
that preserving the real value of the foundation's assets is equally important in order to
preserve its future grant-making capabilities. You have been asked to assist the committee in developing appropriate policies.

    a. Identify and briefly discuss the three key elements that should determine the foun-
       dation's grant-making (spending) policy.
    b. Formulate and justify an investment policy statement for the foundation, taking into
       account the increased size of its assets arising from Mr. Franklin's gift. Your policy
       statement must encompass all relevant objectives, constraints, and the key elements
       identified in your answer to part (*a*).
    c. Recommend and justify a long-term asset allocation that is consistent with the
       investment policy statement you created in part (*b*). Explain how your allocation's
       expected return meets the requirements of a feasible grant-making (spending) pol-

Table 26F   Capital Markets Annnualized Return Data

	1926–1992 Averages	1993–2000 Consensus Forecast
U.S. Treasury bills	3.7%	4.2%
Intermediate-term U.S. T-bonds	5.2	5.8
Long-term U.S. T-bonds	4.8	7.7
U.S. corporate bonds (AAA)	5.5	8.8
Non-U.S. bonds (AAA)	N/A	8.4
U.S. common stocks (all)	10.3	9.0
U.S. common stocks (small-cap)	12.2	12.0
Non-U.S. common stocks (all)	N/A	10.1
U.S. inflation	3.1	3.5

icy for the foundation. (Your allocation must sum to 100% and should use the economic/market data presented in Table 26F and your knowledge of historical asset-class characteristics.)

10. The foundation's grant-making and investment policy issues have been finalized. Receipt of the expected $45 million Franklin cash gift will not occur for 90 days, yet the committee believes current stock and bond prices are unusually attractive and wishes to take advantage of this perceived opportunity.

    a. Briefly describe two strategies that utilize derivative financial instruments and could be implemented to take advantage of the committee's market expectations.

    b. Evaluate whether or not it is appropriate for the foundation to undertake a derivatives-based hedge to bridge the expected 90-day time gap, considering both positive and negative factors.

11. Your neighbor has heard that you successfully completed a course in investments and has come to seek your advice. She and her husband are both 50 years old. They just finished making their last payments for their condominium and their children's college education and are planning for retirement. What advice on investing their retirement savings would you give them? If they are very risk averse, what would you advise?

12. C. B. Snow, deceased president of Highway Cartage Company, left a net estate of $300,000 in the late 1970s. Under his will, a trust of $300,000 was created for his surviving spouse, with Peninsular Trust Company named trustee. A daughter is the remainderman of her mother's trust. The widow's trust is composed of the following assets:

	Proportion of Portfolio	Amount at Market	Current Yield (%)
Money market fund	25%	$ 75,000	14.7
Tax-exempt municipal bonds	35%	105,000	8.0*
Highway Cartage Co. common stock	40%	120,000	7.9
	100%	$300,000	

*Yield to maturity equals 12.0%.

As a portfolio manager with Peninsular, you have just attended a meeting with the widow and learned the following:

She is 65 and in good health (mortality tables indicate an expected life span of 18 years). As a retirement benefit, she is eligible for Highway's generous group medical insurance plan for the remainder of her life.

Table 26G   Market Data

Category	Beta Coefficient	Implied Total Return	Current Yield
Fixed-income Securities			
Money market funds			14.7%
Government bonds			
Intermediate term			14.4
Long term			14.0
Corporate bonds (A-rated)			
Intermediate term			15.1
Long term			16.0
Tax-exempt municipals			
Intermediate term			10.2
Long term			11.1
Common Stocks			
Industrials	1.0	17.0%	5.2%
Trucking	1.1	14.8	4.0
Highway Cartage Co.	1.3	14.8	7.9
Consumer Price Index (Average Annual Index)			
8.9% projected current year	8.0% projected next year	5%–15% range next 5 years	7%–10% most probable next 5 years

Her estimated household and other expenses last year, adjusted to allow for inflation this year, are $19,600. In the absence of her husband's salary, her tax bracket will decline substantially to 30%. Next week she will be eligible to receive social security payments of $600 per month. (See the note at the end of this question on the taxation of social security benefits.)

She plans to purchase a $60,000 condominium as a vacation residence within the next six months, using $15,000 in deferred compensation (after taxes) due her husband as a down payment. Conventional mortgage financing is available for 75% of the cost at 17.5% for 30 years. She anticipates that any tax savings from the credit for mortgage interest payments will be consumed by maintenance fees charged to the owner. She also intends to join an adjacent golf club where the dues are $125 per month.

She wishes to retain all of the Highway common stock, because "It's the only stock C. B. ever owned and he had such great confidence in the company's future. Also, the yield is very generous, I think, despite the dividend reduction last year when the economy sagged."

At the conclusion of the meeting, Mrs. Snow requested that the assets in her trust be left intact, if possible. Mrs. Snow is cotrustee of her trust and can veto any of your recommendations.

a. Calculate Mrs. Snow's income sources and expenses, assuming her request is honored, and state whether her income requirements can be met.

b. Identify and discuss the investment objectives and constraints that appear applicable to Mrs. Snow's situation.

c. Recommend and justify changes in her present trust portfolio that are consistent with the objectives and constraints in part (b). (Use the information in Table 26G.)

Note on the taxation of social security benefits at the time:

If the sum of all income (including interest on municipal bonds) plus one-half of social security benefits is greater than $32,000 (for the couple filing jointly; $25,000 for an individual), then either one-half of the social security benefit or the excess of total income over $32,000 is taxable as ordinary income.

13. George More is a participant in a defined contribution pension plan that offers a fixed-income fund and a common stock fund as investment choices. He is 40 years old and has an accumulation of $100,000 in each of the funds. He currently contributes $1,500 per year to each. He plans to retire at age 65, and his life expectancy is age 80.

    a. Assuming a 3% per year real earnings rate for the fixed-income fund and 6% per year for common stocks, what will be George's expected accumulation in each account at age 65?

    b. What will be the expected real retirement annuity from each account, assuming these same real earnings rates?

    c. If George wanted a retirement annuity of $30,000 per year from the fixed-income fund, by how much would he have to increase his annual contributions?

14. A firm has a defined benefit pension plan that pays an annual retirement benefit of 1.5% of final salary per year of service. Joe Loyal is 60 years old and has been working for the firm for the last 35 years. His current salary is $40,000 per year.

    a. If normal retirement age is 65, the interest rate is 8%, and Joe's life expectancy is 80, what is the present value of his accrued pension benefit?

    b. If Joe wanted to retire now, what would be an actuarially fair annual pension benefit? (Assume the first payment would be made one year from now.)

15. Food Processors Inc. (FPI) is a mature U.S. company reporting declining earnings and a weak balance sheet. Its ERISA-qualified defined benefit pension plan has total assets of $750 million. However, the plan is underfunded by $200 million by U.S. standards, a cause for concern by shareholders, management, and the board.

    The average age of plan participants is 45 years. FPI's annual contribution to the plan and the earnings on its assets are sufficient to meet pension payments to present retirees. The pension portfolio's holdings are equally divided between large-capitalization U.S. equities and high-quality, long-maturity U.S. corporate bonds. For actuarial purposes, the assumed long-term rate of return on plan assets is 9% per year; the discount rate applied to plan liabilities, all of which are U.S.-based, is 8%. As FPI's treasurer, you are responsible for oversight of the plan's investments and managers and for liaison with the board's pension investment committee.

    At the committee's last meeting, its chairman observed that both U.S. stocks and U.S. bonds had recorded total returns in excess of 12% per year over the past decade. He then made a pointed comment: "Given this experience, we seem to be overly conservative in using only a 9% future return assumption. Why don't we raise the rate to 10%? This would be consistent with the recent record, would help our earnings, and should make the stockholders feel a lot better."

    You have been directed to examine the situation and prepare a recommendation for next week's committee meeting. In this connection, your assistant has provided you with the background information shown in Table 26H.

    a. In response to the chairman's observations and based solely on the data shown in Table 26H, recommend and justify the long-term rate of return assumption you believe is most appropriate for FPI's plan. Prepare an asset allocation summing to 100% and calculate the expected return on the portfolio resulting from that allocation.

    b. You read that other companies in your industry recently reduced the discount rate used in their pension plan calculations. Briefly describe the capital markets conditions that would be consistent with a decision to reduce the discount rate and relate your response to the FPI situation described in the introduction.

Table 26H   Capital Markets Data

	Total Return, 1929–1993	Total Return, 1984–1993	Annualized Monthly Standard Deviation, 1984–1993	Consensus Forecast Total Return, 1994–2000
U.S. Treasury bills	3.7%	6.4%	2.2%	3.5%
Intermediate-term T-bonds	5.3	11.4	5.6	5.0
Long-term T-bonds	5.0	14.4	11.7	6.0
U.S. corporate bonds (AAA)	5.6	14.0	8.9	6.5
Non-U.S. bonds (AAA)	n/a	15.4	14.5	6.5
U.S. common stocks (S&P 500)	9.5	14.9	18.0	8.5
U.S. common stocks (small-cap)	12.0	10.0	19.9	10.5
Non-U.S. common stocks (in $ terms)	n/a	17.9	23.7	9.5
U.S. real estate*	n/a	9.3	2.4	7.5
U.S. inflation (annual rate)	3.2	5.5	n/a	3.3

*Business, residential, and agricultural appraisal data.

Note: Neither U.S. venture capital nor emerging-market data have been included in the table on instructions from the chairman; neither may be considered for plan investment at present.

    c. Explain what is meant when a pension plan is said to be "underfunded" and relate your response to the FPI situation described in the introduction.

    d. Explain how the underfunded condition of FPI's plan would be affected if the discount rate were reduced to 7% from the current 8%.

The following information pertains to problems 16–18.

    Planet Trade Company (PTC) is a major U.S.-based import/export firm. Headquartered in New York City, PTC also has offices and employees in Tokyo, Sydney, Madrid, Bangkok, and several other non-U.S. locations. Permanent employees in all locations are covered by a defined-benefit pension plan whose liabilities reflect the following background facts:

- Wages are inflation adjusted, and retirement benefits (which are based on final pay levels) provide for automatic postretirement inflation adjustment.

- Because the average age of the work force is relatively young, company contributions into the fund are expected to exceed annual plan operating expenses and benefit payments for at least the next 10 years.

- An estimated 30% of benefit payments will be non-U.S. dollar–based for an extended period of time. The current non-U.S. liabilities breakdown by country is as follows:

    7% Australia.
    6% Japan.
    6% Singapore.
    4% Thailand.
    4% Spain.
    3% Malaysia.

    PTC's internal investment committee is assisted in administration of the company's employee benefits program by Benefits Advisory Group (BAG), a well-known pension consulting organization. To provide guidance to its Investment Committee and to its investment managers, PTC's board has adopted the investment policy statement shown in Figure 26A for its pension plan.

Figure 26A

Planet Trade Company
defined benefit
pension plan,
Investment Policy
Statement (6/1/92).

> The plan should emphasize production of adequate levels of real return as its primary return objective, giving special attention to the inflation-related aspects of the plan. To the extent consistent with appropriate control of portfolio risk, investment action should seek to maintain or increase the surplus of plan assets relative to benefit liabilities over time. Five-year periods, updated annually, shall be employed in planning for investment decision making; the plan's actuary shall update the benefit liabilities breakdown by country every three years.
>
> The orientation of investment planning shall be long term in nature. In addition, minimal liquidity reserves shall be maintained so long as annual company funding contributions and investment income exceed annual benefit payments to retirees and the operating expenses of the plan. The plan's actuary shall update plan cash flow projections annually. Plan administration shall ensure compliance with all laws and regulations related to maintenance of the plan's tax-exempt status and with all requirements of the Employee Retirement Income Security Act (ERISA).

16. PTC's Investment Committee intends to adopt a set of long-term asset allocation ranges for the firm's defined benefit pension plan that takes into consideration the plan's liability structure as set forth in the introduction. In addition, the committee requires a set of short-term asset allocation targets that will position the fund's current exposure within the long-term setting. As a principal of BAG, this strategic and tactical goal-setting assignment has been given to you. You intend to preface your recommendations to the committee with a brief review of three alternative methods that may be used for determining appropriate asset allocations, including:

Extrapolation and adjustment of long-term historical asset class data.
Multiple-scenario forecasting.
Asset/liability forecasting.

a. Briefly describe the three alternatives listed above. In your discussion, cite one strength and one weakness of each method relative to the purpose of determining long-term pension portfolio asset allocation ranges.

b. Based on the information provided in the introduction and Figure 26A, and your general knowledge of asset class characteristics, create a set of long-term asset allocation ranges for the PTC pension portfolio using the format presented below, and justify your range selection for each asset class.

	Range	Midpoint
U.S. equities	_____ – _____ %	_____ %
Non-U.S. equities	_____ – _____ %	_____ %
Equity real estate	_____ – _____ %	_____ %
U.S. bonds	_____ – _____ %	_____ %
Non-U.S. bonds	_____ – _____ %	_____ %
Cash equivalents	_____ – _____ %	_____ %
		100%

c. i. Table 26I provides expected return data for six asset classes under three alternative economic scenarios. Identify two other asset-class statistics not shown in Table 26I that are essential for making effective asset allocation decisions, and explain the importance of each of these two statistics in the asset allocation process.

ii. Based solely on the data contained in Table 26I, calculate the expected return for each asset class using the multiple scenario forecasting method. Show all your calculations.

iii. Considering the scenario weightings in Table 26I, the expected returns calculated in part (ii), and your general knowledge about the two missing asset class

Table 26I   Expected Annual Asset Class Returns over the Next Three Years under Different Global Economic Scenarios (in U.S. dollar terms)

	Scenario I: Recession/ Deflation	Scenario II: Slow Growth/ Low Inflation	Scenario III: Rapid Growth/ High Inflation
Probability of occurrence	30%	50%	20%
Asset Class Expected Annual Returns			
U.S. equities	7%	12%	8%
Non-U.S. equities	4	10	9
Equity real estate	0	9	14
U.S. bonds	15	8	3
Non-U.S. bonds	10	9	2
Cash equivalents	3	5	9

statistics, create and justify a short-term asset allocation for the PTC pension portfolio. Your allocation must sum to 100%.

 d. Explain how you could use derivative securities to make short-term asset allocation adjustments away from long-term targets, and cite one reason for and one reason against using derivative securities to do so.

17. As PTC's new chief financial officer, you have recently assumed responsibility for internal administration of the firm's pension plan. In this capacity, you have completed a detailed review of the portfolio assets and the minutes of the investment committee meetings at which the policies determining the broad outline for plan investment actions were discussed and adopted. You note that the investment committee's decision to accept equity real estate investments for the portfolio followed a discussion in which two assertions were offered as key favorable considerations:

- Equity real estate provides its owners with a prime means for offsetting inflation's erosive effects on both investment value and the income stream.

- Inclusion of an equity real estate component in a portfolio significantly reduces total portfolio risk as a result of the low standard deviation of real estate returns.

 a. Evaluate these assertions, including in your response two observations that support them and two observations that dispute them.

Among the holdings of the PTC pension portfolio's equity real estate component, which is well diversified geographically and across property types, is a 12-story Class A office building situated in the downtown center of a major U.S. city. Built in 1983, the building is 95% leased at an average of $23 per square foot. All leases call for rent escalation at a rate matching the U.S. Consumer Price Index (CPI). The key tenant in the building, occupying 45% of rentable space, has given notice that it will vacate the space at the end of its current lease in December 1993.

The area's economy, highly sensitive to conditions in the energy industry in the past, has benefited recently from the arrival of new businesses that have diversified the city's industrial base. Demographic projections indicate a 500,000-person increase in metropolitan-area population by the year 2010, with job growth gaining proportionally at approximately 2.5% per year.

The downtown center vacancy rate in the city is currently 22%; in the suburban area, it approaches 30%. New leases in Class A buildings are being written at $12 per square foot, with some inducement concessions being offered as well. No new office buildings have been completed in the immediate area since 1987. This lack of new construction, and the arrival of new businesses, has permitted about 10% of previously available space to be absorbed within the past 12 months.

  b. Evaluate the above-described property in terms of its ability to provide the inflation protection and diversification benefits stated in part (*a*). Segment your discussion into 5-year and 20-year time frames.

18. In the 1970s, when PTC was a much smaller company and all employees were U.S.-based, its retirement plan consisted solely of a tax-exempt defined contribution (profit-sharing) arrangement. Annual contributions to employees' accounts under this plan ceased some years ago, when the company's present tax-exempt defined benefit (pension) program was adopted. As a result, all participants in the profit-sharing plan are older U.S. employees who are also covered by PTC's newer pension plan. Their profit-sharing interests are "frozen" in the sense that withdrawals are permitted only on their retirement or an earlier termination of PTC employment, and then only in lump-sum form.

    On review, BAG has discovered that the original investment policy statement for the profit-sharing plan has not been updated since inception, despite the passage of time and changes in the company's retirement program. The investment committee intends to adopt a new statement to recognize current circumstances and obligations and has requested your recommendations. It has been suggested that you use an objectives/constraints approach in your presentation.

  a. Prepare and justify an appropriate investment policy statement for the PTC profit-sharing plan.
  b. Compare the elements in your part (*a*) profit-sharing policy statement to those of the PTC pension plan statement presented in Figure 26A and briefly comment on any major differences between the two.

    The chairman of the investment committee has proposed that an international securities component be added to the present U.S.-only securities portfolio in which the interests of the profit-sharing plan's participants are invested. However, another member of the committee is strongly opposed to doing so, basing his objection on the fact that the profit-sharing plan has only U.S.-dollar liabilities and all participants are U.S.-based.

  c. Critique the opposing committee member's position on this issue, including in your response specific reference to the grounds he has cited for his objection.

solutions to Concept CHECKS

1. Identify the elements that are life-cycle driven in the two schemes of objectives and constraints.

2. If Eloise keeps her present asset allocation, she will have the following amounts to spend after taxes five years from now:

Tax-qualified account:

Banks: $50,000(1.1)^5 \times .72$	= $ 57,978.36
Stocks: $50,000(1.15)^5 \times .72$	= $ 72,408.86
Subtotal	$130,387.22

Nonretirement account:

Bonds: $50,000(1.072)^5$	= $ 70,785.44
Stocks: $50,000(1.15)^5 - .28 \times [50,000(1.15)^5 - 50,000]$	= $ 86,408.86
Subtotal	$157,194.30
Total	$287,581.52

If Eloise shifts all of the bonds into the retirement account and all of the stock into the nonretirement account, she will have the following amounts to spend after taxes five years from now:

Tax-qualified account:

Bonds: $100,000(1.1)^5 \times .72$ = \$115,956.72

Nonretirement account:

Stocks: $100,000(1.15)^5 - .28 \times [100,000(1.15)^5 - 100,000]$ = \$172,817.72

      Total   = \$288,774.44

Her spending budget will increase by $1,192.92.

3. $B_0 \times$ Annuity factor(4%, 5 years) = 100,000 implies that $B_0 = \$22,462.71$.

t	B_t	B_t	A_t
0			$100,000.00
1	4%	$22,462.71	$ 81,537.29
2	10%	$23,758.64	$ 65,923.38
3	−8%	$21,017.26	$ 39,640.53
4	25%	$25,261.12	$ 24,289.54
5	0	$24,289.54	0

4. He has accrued an annuity of $.01 \times 15 \times 15,000 = \$2,250$ per year for 15 years, starting in 25 years. The present value of this annuity is $2,812.13:

$$PV = 2,250 \times \text{Annuity factor}(8\%, 15) \times \text{PV factor}(8\%, 25) = 2812.13$$

APPENDIX: POPULAR ADVICE AND SURVEY EVIDENCE

Potential investors can sift through an abundance of advice, with sources ranging from newspaper columns on personal investing to information offered by mutual fund groups and other providers of financial products. We summarize this advice here, in a set of practical guidelines that we call generally accepted investment principles.

Generally Accepted Investment Principles

Investors should have an emergency fund invested in short-term, safe assets. This fund should be held outside one's retirement account to avoid the tax and other penalties generally assessed when assets are withdrawn prematurely from a retirement account.

Funds saved for retirement should be invested primarily in equities and longer-term fixed-income securities.

The proportion of assets invested in equities should decline with age. A popular rule of thumb regarding the age–equity relationship is that the percentage of one's portfolio invested in equities should be 100 minus the investor's age: A person 30 years old should invest 70% in equities, and a person aged 70 should invest 30% in equities.

The fraction invested in equities should increase with wealth because a wealthier individual should be able to handle more risk.

Tax-advantaged assets, such as municipal bonds, should be held outside one's retirement account, and only investors in high tax brackets should invest in them at all. More generally, assets that are taxed relatively heavily (such as taxable bonds) should be held inside one's retirement account, while those that are taxed less heavily (such as non–dividend-paying equities) should be held outside one's retirement account.

All investors should diversify their total portfolio across asset classes, and the equity portion should be well-diversified across industries and companies.

Most popular sources of advice recognize that the optimal asset mix for a particular household might differ from the general mix they recommend because of the special circumstances or risk-preferences of the given household. For example, married couples with both partners working might want to invest a larger fraction of their wealth in equities than otherwise identical single people. Or people with uncertain job prospects might want to invest less in equities than people with relatively predictable labor income.

The Survey

In 1996 Bodie and Crane carried out a survey in cooperation with the research department of the Teachers Insurance and Annuity Association–College Retirement Equities Fund (TIAA-CREF) to collect information about the asset mix held by that organization's members both inside and outside their retirement accounts. Most TIAA-CREF members work in institutions that have offered self-directed retirement accounts for many years. The survey respondents are likely to be better informed and more experienced about investing than their counterparts at other places of employment who may not have had similar exposure. Furthermore, current growth trends in self-directed investment accounts indicate that the future population of the United States will be more widely exposed to these accounts and may be more fully informed about investing. Thus data from the TIAA-CREF respondents can provide some clues about future behavior of the general population.

They group investments into three broad asset classes: cash (including bank deposits and shares in money market funds), equities, and fixed-income securities. This classification scheme follows the one generally used in the investment-advisory business. They also classify an individual's assets according to whether they are held in a tax-deferred retirement account.

Findings   The findings of the survey conform well to the generally accepted investment principles. They found the following:

Short-term, safe assets (called cash in the investment business) are held outside retirement accounts. The fraction held in cash varies with an individual's net worth but not with age.

The fraction of assets held in tax-exempt bonds increases with wealth but not with age.

The percentage of equity in total financial assets declines with age and rises with wealth.

Controlling for the effects of age and wealth, there are still substantial differences among individuals in the fraction of their total assets invested in equity. Factors reflecting the value and riskiness of human capital help explain these differences.

There is some evidence that elderly individuals are trying to maximize the tax advantage of their retirement accounts by "tilting" them more toward taxable fixed-income investments than their assets in nonretirement accounts, but other hypotheses for this behavior are also credible.

Conclusions   They conclude that the TIAA-CREF respondents, on average, appear to follow the generally accepted investment principles recommended by experts. While TIAA-CREF participants are on average better informed and more experienced at making their own investment choices than the general population, the survey findings suggest that, given enough education, information, and experience, people will tend to manage their self-directed investment accounts in an appropriate manner.

CHAPTER TWENTY-SEVEN

RISK MANAGEMENT AND HEDGING

You might wonder what could be left to say about risk management after our extensive discussion of portfolio theory. This chapter, however, treats risk in a very different manner than portfolio theory does. Portfolio theory deals with the big picture—the risk and return attributes of the investor's overall portfolio of assets. Here we focus much more narrowly on how investors can eliminate their vulnerability to one particular source of risk. For example, an exporter may want to offset a large exposure to foreign exchange fluctuations, or a farmer may want to reduce his dependence on the price of wheat. **Hedging** is understood as a technique to offset particular sources of risk rather than as a more ambitious search for the optimal risk-return profile for the entire portfolio. In examining basic hedging strategies, we start with a discussion of the general principles of hedging, illustrating with an example of an exporting firm that seeks to manage its exposure to exchange rate fluctuations. Then we turn to specific applications. We demonstrate how stock index futures can be used to hedge against market risk and allow portfolio managers to separate bets on firm-specific versus marketwide performance. We turn next to hedging tools in the fixed-income market and see how interest rate futures contracts can be used to offset interest rate risk. Finally, we show how the hedge ratios that emerge from option-pricing models like the Black-Scholes formula can be used to allow options traders to speculate on perceived option mispricing without inadvertently taking a position on the performance of the underlying stock. In the last section, we explore the ramifications of hedging demands on capital market equilibrium. We will see that when many individuals hedge particular risks to their consumption or

investment opportunities, these demands can affect equilibrium rates of return. Thus these hedging demands provide a foundation for the multifactor CAPM and the multifactor APT.

27.1 HEDGING TECHNIQUES

General Principles

Consider a U.S. firm that exports most of its product to Great Britain. The firm is vulnerable to fluctuations in the dollar/pound exchange rate for several reasons. First, the dollar value of the pound-denominated revenue derived from its customers will fluctuate with the exchange rate. Second, the pound price that the firm can charge its customers in the United Kingdom will itself be affected by the exchange rate. For example, if the pound depreciates by 10% relative to the dollar, the firm would need to increase the pound price of its goods by 10% in order to maintain the dollar-equivalent price. However, the firm might not be able to raise the price by 10% if it faces competition from British producers, or if it believes the higher pound-denominated price would reduce demand for its product.

To offset its foreign exchange exposure, the firm might engage in transactions that bring it profits when the pound depreciates. The lost profits from business operations resulting from a depreciation will then be offset by gains on its financial transactions. Suppose, for example, that the firm enters a futures contract to deliver pounds for dollars at an exchange rate agreed to today. As the deliverer of the currency, the firm enters the short side of the pound futures contract. Therefore, if the pound depreciates, the futures position will yield a profit.

For example, suppose that the futures price is currently $1.70 per pound for delivery in three months. If the firm enters a futures contract with a futures price of $1.70 per pound, and the exchange rate in three months is $1.60 per pound, then the profit on the transaction is $.10 per pound. The futures price converges at the maturity date to the spot exchange rate of $1.60 and the profit to the short position is therefore $F_0 - F_T = \$1.70 - \$1.60 = \$.10$ per pound.

How many pounds should be sold in the futures market to most fully offset the exposure to exchange rate fluctuations? Suppose the dollar value of profits in the next quarter will fall by $200,000 for every $.10 depreciation of the pound. Given this information, the proper hedge position is easy to calculate. We need to find the number of pounds we should commit to delivering in order to provide a $200,000 profit for every $.10 that the pound depreciates. Therefore, we need a futures position to deliver 2,000,000 pounds. As we have just seen, the profit per pound on the futures contract equals the difference in the current futures price and the ultimate exchange rate; therefore, the foreign exchange profits resulting from a $.10 depreciation[1] will equal $.10 × 2,000,000 = $200,000.

The proper hedge position in pound futures is independent of the actual depreciation in the pound as long as the relationship between profits and exchange rates is approximately linear. For example, if the pound depreciates by only half as much, $.05, the firm would

---

[1] Actually, the profit on the contract depends on the change in the futures price, not the spot exchange rate. For simplicity, we call the decline in the futures price the depreciation in the pound.

lose only $100,000 in operating profits. The futures position would also return half the profits: $.05 × 2,000,000 = $100,000, again just offsetting the operating exposure. If the pound *appreciates*, the hedge position still (unfortunately in this case) offsets the operating exposure. If the pound appreciates by $.05, the firm might gain $100,000 from the enhanced value of the pound; however, it will lose that amount on its obligation to deliver the pounds for the original futures price.

The hedge ratio is the number of futures positions necessary to hedge the risk of the unprotected portfolio, in this case the firm's export business. In general, we can think of the **hedge ratio** as the number of hedging vehicles (e.g., futures contracts) one would establish to offset the risk of a particular unprotected position. The hedge ratio, H, in this case is

$$H = \frac{\text{Change in value of unprotected position for a given change in exchange rate}}{\text{Profit derived from one futures position for the same change in exchange rate}}$$

$$= \frac{\$200,000 \text{ per } \$.10 \text{ change in } \$/£ \text{ exchange rate}}{\$.10 \text{ profit } per pound \text{ delivered per } \$.10 \text{ change in } \$/£ \text{ exchange rate}}$$

$$= 2,000,000 \text{ pounds to be delivered}$$

Because each pound-futures contract on the International Monetary Market (a division of the Chicago Mercantile Exchange) calls for delivery of 62,500 pounds, you would need to short 2,000,000/62,500 per contract = 32 contracts.

One interpretation of the hedge ratio is as a ratio of sensitivities to the underlying source of uncertainty. The sensitivity of operating profits is $200,000 per swing of $.10 in the exchange rate. The sensitivity of futures profits is $.10 per pound to be delivered per swing of $.10 in the exchange rate. Therefore, the hedge ratio is 200,000/.10 = 2,000,000 pounds.

We could just as easily have defined the hedge ratio in terms of futures contracts rather than in terms of pounds. Because each contract calls for delivery of 62,500 pounds, the profit on each contract per swing of $.10 in the exchange rate is $6,250. Therefore, the hedge ratio defined in units of futures contracts is $200,000/$6,250 = 32 contracts, as derived above.

Concept
CHECK

Question 1 • Suppose a multinational firm is harmed when the *dollar* depreciates. Specifically, suppose that its profits decrease by $200,000 for every $.05 rise in the dollar/pound exchange rate. How many contracts should the firm enter? Should it take the long side or the short side of the contracts?

Once you know the sensitivity of the unhedged position to changes in the exchange rate, calculating the risk-minimizing hedge position is easy. Far more difficult is the determination of that sensitivity. For the exporting firm, for example, a naive view might hold that one need only estimate the expected pound-denominated revenue, and then contract to deliver that number of pounds in the futures or forward market. This approach, however, fails to recognize that pound revenue is itself a function of the exchange rate by virtue of the fact that the U.S. firm's competitive position in the United Kingdom is determined in part by the exchange rate. In fact, estimating the sensitivity of business exposure to the exchange rate requires considerable judgment.

One approach relies, in part, on historical relationships. Suppose, for example, that the firm prepares a scatter diagram as in Figure 27.1 that relates its business profits (measured in dollars) in each of the last 40 quarters to the dollar/pound exchange rate in that quarter. The general tendency is that profits are lower when the exchange rate is lower, that is, when the pound depreciates. To quantify that sensitivity, we might draw a line to represent the

Figure 27.1

Profits as a function of the exchange rate.

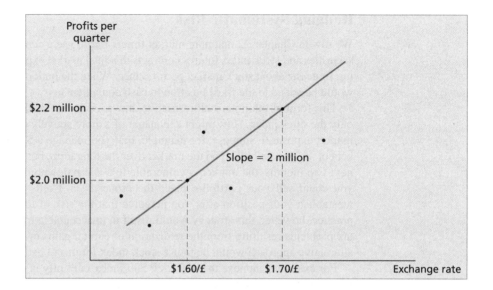

average tendency through the scatter diagram, or even better, estimate the following regression equation:

$$\text{Profits} = a + b \ (\$/\pounds \text{ exchange rate})$$

The slope of the regression, the estimate of b, is the sensitivity of quarterly profits to the exchange rate. For example, if the estimate of b turns out to be 2,000,000, as in Figure 27.1, then the regression equation is interpreted as stating that on average, the relationship between profits and the exchange rate is that a one-dollar *increase* in the value of the pound results in a \$2,000,000 *increase* in quarterly profits. This, of course, is the sensitivity we posited when we asserted that a \$.10 drop in the dollar/pound exchange rate would decrease profits by \$200,000.

Of course, one must interpret regression output with care. For example, one would not want to extrapolate the historical relationship between profitability and exchange rates exhibited in a period when the exchange rate hovered between \$1.60 and \$1.90 per pound to scenarios in which the exchange rate might be forecast at below \$1.20 per pound or above \$2.50 per pound.

In addition, one always must use care when extrapolating past relationships into the future. We saw in Chapter 10 that regression betas from the index model tend to vary across time; such problems are not unique to the index model. Moreover, regression estimates are just that—estimates. Parameters of a regression equation are sometimes measured with considerable imprecision.

Still, historical relationships are often a good place to start when looking for the average sensitivity of one variable to another. These slope coefficients are not perfect, but they are still useful indicators of hedge ratios.

Concept

Question 2 • United Millers purchases corn to make cornflakes. When the price of corn increases, the cost of making cereal increases, resulting in lower profits. Historically, profits per quarter have been related to the price of corn according to the equation: Profits = \$8 million – 1 million × price per bushel. How many bushels of corn should United Millers purchase in the corn futures market to hedge its corn-price risk?

Hedging Systematic Risk

We saw in Chapter 22 that pure market timers might use a combination of money market securities and stock index futures contracts to adjust market exposure in response to changing forecasts about stock market performance. When the outlook is bullish, more contracts would be added to the fixed position in cash equivalents.

This form of timing is a bit restrictive, however, in that it allows for equity positions in only the stock index. How might a manager of a more actively constructed portfolio hedge market exposure? Suppose, for example, that you manage a $30 million portfolio with a beta of .8. You are bullish on the market over the long term, but you are afraid that over the next two months, the market is vulnerable to a sharp downturn. If trading were costless, you could sell your portfolio, place the proceeds in T-bills for two months, and then reestablish your position after you perceive that the risk of the downturn has passed. In practice, however, this strategy would result in unacceptable trading costs, not to mention tax problems resulting from the realization of capital gains or losses on the portfolio. An alternative approach would be to use stock index futures to hedge your market exposure.

For example, suppose that the S&P 500 index currently is at 1,000. A decrease in the index to 975 would represent a drop of 2.5%. Given the beta of your portfolio, you would expect a loss of .8 × 2.5% = 2%, or in dollar terms, .02 × $30 million = $600,000. Therefore, the sensitivity of your portfolio value to market movements is $600,000 per 25-point movement in the S&P 500 index.

To hedge this risk, you could sell stock index futures. When your portfolio falls in value along with declines in the broad market, the futures contract will provide an offsetting profit.

The sensitivity of a futures contract to market movements is easy to determine. With its contract multiplier of $250, the profit on the S&P 500 futures contract varies by $6,250 for every 25-point swing in the index. Therefore, to hedge your market exposure for two months, you could calculate the hedge ratio as follows:

$$H = \frac{\text{Change in portfolio value}}{\text{Profit on one futures contract}} = \frac{\$600,000}{\$6,250} = 96 \text{ contracts (short)}$$

You would enter the short side of the contracts, because you want profits from the contract to offset the exposure of your portfolio to the market. Because your portfolio does poorly when the market falls, you need a position that will do well when the market falls.

We also could approach the hedging problem using the regression procedure illustrated above. The predicted value of the portfolio is graphed in Figure 27.2 as a function of the value of the S&P 500 index. With a beta of .8, the slope of the relationship is 24,000: A 2.5% increase in the index, from 1,000 to 1,025 results in a capital gain of 2% of $30 million, or $600,000. Therefore, your portfolio will increase in value by $24,000 for each increase of one point in the index. As a result, you should enter a short position on 24,000 units of the S&P 500 index to fully offset your exposure to marketwide movements. Because the contract multiplier is $250 times the index, you need to sell 24,000/250 = 96 contracts.

Notice that when the slope of the regression line relating your unprotected position to the value of an asset is positive, your hedge strategy calls for a *short* position in that asset. The hedge ratio is the negative of the regression slope. This is because the hedge position should offset your initial exposure. If you do poorly when the asset value falls, you need a hedge vehicle that will do well when the asset value falls. This calls for a short position in the asset.

Active managers sometimes believe that a particular asset is underpriced, but that the market as a whole is about to fall. Even if the asset is a good buy relative to other stocks in

Figure 27.2

Predicted value of the portfolio as a function of the market index.

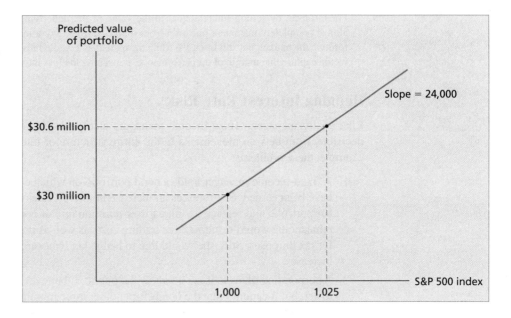

the market, it still might perform poorly in a broad market downturn. To solve this problem, the manager would like to separate the bet on the firm from the bet on the market: The bet on the company must be offset with a hedge against the market exposure that normally would accompany a purchase of the stock.

Here again, the stock's beta is the key to the hedging strategy. Suppose the beta of the stock is 2/3, and the manager purchases $375,000 worth of the stock. For every 3% drop in the broad market, the stock would be expected to respond with a drop of $2/3 \times 3\% = 2\%$, or $7,500. The S&P 500 contract will fall by 30 points from a current value of 1,000 if the market drops 3%. With the contract multiplier of $250, this would entail a profit to a short futures position of $30 \times \$250 = \$7,500$ per contract. Therefore, the market risk of the stock can be offset by shorting one S&P contract. More formally, we could calculate the hedge ratio as

$$H = \frac{\text{Expected change in stock value per 3\% market drop}}{\text{Profit on one short contract per 3\% market drop}}$$

$$= \frac{\$7,500 \text{ swing in unprotected position}}{\$7,500 \text{ profit per contract}}$$

$$= 1 \text{ contract}$$

Now that market risk is hedged, the only source of variability in the performance of the stock-plus-futures portfolio will be the firm-specific performance of the stock.

By allowing investors to bet on market performance, the futures contract allows the portfolio manager to make stock picks without concern for the market exposure of the stocks chosen. After the stocks are chosen, the resulting systematic risk of the portfolio can be modulated to any degree using the stock futures contracts.

Portfolio managers actually do use futures to separate firm-specific bets from bets on overall market performance. The article from *The Wall Street Journal* reproduced in Chapter 23 (page 720) cited a Goldman Sachs study on stock futures' trading that cited such motives as responsible in part for the rapid increase in stock futures' trading volume. The article noted that

For instance, by selling futures equal to the value of the underlying portfolio, a manager can almost completely insulate a portfolio from market moves. Say a manager succeeds in outperforming the market, but still loses 3% while the market as a whole falls 10%. Hedging with futures would capture that margin of outperformance, translating the loss into a profit of roughly 7%.

Hedging Interest Rate Risk

Like equity managers, fixed-income managers also desire to separate security-specific decisions from bets on movements in the entire structure of interest rates. Consider, for example, these problems:

1. A fixed-income manager holds a bond portfolio on which considerable capital gains have been earned. She foresees an increase in interest rates but is reluctant to sell her portfolio and replace it with a lower-duration mix of bonds because such rebalancing would result in large trading costs as well as realization of capital gains for tax purposes. Still, she would like to hedge her exposure to interest rate increases.

2. A corporation plans to issue bonds to the public. It believes that now is a good time to act, but it cannot issue the bonds for another three months because of the lags inherent in SEC registration. It would like to hedge the uncertainty surrounding the yield at which it eventually will be able to sell the bonds.

3. A pension fund will receive a large cash inflow next month that it plans to invest in long-term bonds. It is concerned that interest rates may fall by the time it can make the investment, and would like to lock in the yield currently available on long-term issues.

In each of these cases, the investment manager wishes to hedge interest rate uncertainty. To illustrate the procedures that might be followed, we will focus on the first example, and suppose that the portfolio manager has a $10 million bond portfolio with a modified duration of nine years.[2] If, as feared, market interest rates increase and the bond portfolio's yield also rises, say by 10 basis points (.1%), the fund will suffer a capital loss. Recall from Chapter 16 that the capital loss in percentage terms will be the product of modified duration, D^*, and the change in the portfolio yield. Therefore, the loss will be

$$D^* \times \Delta y = 9 \times .1\% = .9\%$$

or $90,000. This establishes that the sensitivity of the value of the unprotected portfolio to changes in market yields is $9,000 per one basis point change in the yield. Market practitioners call this ratio the **price value of a basis point**, or PVBP. The PVBP represents the sensitivity of the dollar value of the portfolio to changes in interest rates. Here, we've shown that

$$\text{PVBP} = \frac{\text{Change in portfolio value}}{\text{Predicted change in yield}} = \frac{\$90,000}{10 \text{ basis points}} = \$9,000 \text{ per basis point}$$

One way to hedge this risk is to take an offsetting position in an interest rate futures contract. The Treasury bond contract is the most widely traded contract. The bond nominally calls for delivery of $100,000 par value T-bonds with 8% coupons and 20-year maturity. In

---

[2]Recall that modified duration, D^*, is related to duration, D, by the formula $D^* = D/(1 + y)$, where y is the bond's yield to maturity. If the bond pays coupons semiannually, then y should be measured as a semiannual yield. For simplicity, we will assume annual coupon payments, and treat y as the effective annual yield to maturity.

Figure 27.3

Yield spread between
long-term government
and Aaa-rated
corporate bonds.

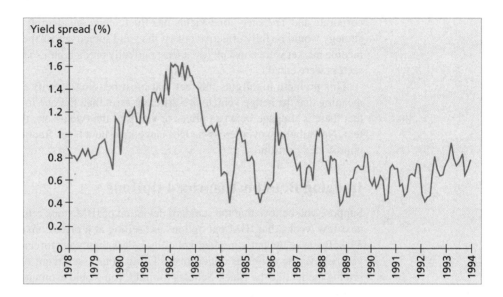

practice, the contract delivery terms are fairly complicated because many bonds with different coupon rates and maturities may be substituted to settle the contract. However, we will assume that the bond to be delivered on the contract already is known and has a modified duration of 10 years. Finally, suppose that the futures price currently is $90 per $100 par value. Because the contract requires delivery of $100,000 par value of bonds, the contract multiplier is $1,000.

Given these data, we can calculate the PVBP for the futures contract. If the yield on the delivery bond increases by 10 basis points, the bond value will fall by $D^* \times .1\% = 10 \times .1\% = 1\%$. The futures price also will decline 1% from 90 to 89.10.[3] Because the contract multiplier is $1,000, the gain on each short contract will be $1,000 \times .90 = $900. Therefore, the PVBP for one futures contract is $900/10-basis-point change, or $90 for a change in yield of one basis point.

Now we can easily calculate the hedge ratio as follows:

$$H = \frac{\text{PVBP of portfolio}}{\text{PVBP of hedge vehicle}} = \frac{\$9,000}{\$90 \text{ per contract}} = 100 \text{ contracts}$$

Therefore, 100 T-bond futures contracts will serve to offset the portfolio's exposure to interest rate fluctuations.

Concept

Question 3 • Suppose the bond portfolio is twice as large, $20 million, but that its modified duration is only 4.5 years. Show that the proper hedge position in T-bond futures is the same as the value just calculated, 100 contracts.

Although the hedge ratio is easy to compute, the hedging problem in practice is more difficult. We assumed in our example that the yields on the T-bond contract and the bond portfolio would move perfectly in unison. Although interest rates on various fixed-income instruments do tend to vary in tandem, there is considerable slippage across sectors of the fixed-income market. For example, Figure 27.3 shows that the spread between long-term

---

[3]This assumes the futures price will be exactly proportional to the bond price, which ought to be nearly true.

corporate and Treasury bond yields has fluctuated considerably over time. Our hedging strategy would be fully effective only if the yield spread across the two sectors of the fixed-income market were constant (or at least perfectly predictable) so that yield changes in both sectors were equal.

This problem highlights the fact that most hedging activity is in fact **cross-hedging**, meaning that the hedge vehicle is a different asset than the one to be hedged. To the extent that there is slippage between prices or yields of the two assets, the hedge will not be perfect. Nevertheless, even cross-hedges can eliminate a large fraction of the total risk of the unprotected portfolio.

Hedging Bets on Mispriced Options

Suppose you believe that the standard deviation of IBM stock returns will be 35% over the next few weeks, but IBM put options are selling at a price consistent with a volatility of 33%. Because the put's implied volatility is less than your forecast of the stock volatility, you believe the option is underpriced. Using your assessment of volatility in an option-pricing model like the Black-Scholes formula, you would estimate that the fair price for the puts exceeds the actual price.

Does this mean that you ought to buy put options? Perhaps it does, but by doing so, you risk great losses if IBM stock performs well, *even if* you are correct about the volatility. You would like to separate your bet on volatility from the "attached" bet inherent in purchasing a put that IBM's stock price will fall. In other words, you would like to speculate on the option mispricing by purchasing the put option, but hedge the resulting exposure to the performance of IBM stock.

We saw in Chapter 21 that the option *delta* is in fact a hedge ratio that can be used for this purpose. The delta was defined as

$$\text{Delta} = \frac{\text{Change in value of option}}{\text{Change in value of stock}}$$

Therefore, delta is the slope of the option-pricing curve.

This ratio tells us precisely how many shares of stock we must hold to offset our exposure to IBM. For example, if the delta is −.6, then the put will fall by $.60 in value for every one-point increase in IBM stock, and we need to hold .6 share of stock to hedge each put. If we purchase 10 option contracts, each for 100 shares, we would need to buy 600 shares of stock. If the stock price rises by $1, each put option will decrease in value by $.60, resulting in a loss of $600. However, the loss on the puts will be offset by a gain on the stock holdings of $1 per share × 600 shares.

To see how the profits on this strategy might develop, let's use the following example:

Option maturity, T	60 days
Put price, P	$4.495
Exercise price, X	$90
Stock price, S	$90
Risk-free rate, r	4%

We assume that the stock will not pay a dividend in the next 60 days. Given these data, the implied volatility on the option is 33%, as we posited. However, you believe the true volatility is 35%, implying that the fair put price is $4.785. Therefore, if the market assessment of volatility is revised to the value you believe is correct, your profit will be $.29 per put purchased.

Table 27.1   Profit on Hedged Put Portfolio

A. Cost to establish hedged position

1,000 put options @ $4.495/option	$ 4,495
453 shares @ $90/share	40,770
Total outlay	$45,265

B. Value of put option as a function of the stock price at implied volatility of 35%

Stock Price:	89	90	91
Put price	$5.254	$4.785	$4.347
Profit (loss) on each put	0.759	0.290	(0.148)

C. Value of and profit on hedged put portfolio

Stock Price:	89	90	91
Value of 1,000 put options	$ 5,254	$ 4,785	$ 4,347
Value of 453 shares	40,317	40,770	41,223
Total	$45,571	$45,555	$45,570
Profit (= Value − Cost from Panel A)	306	290	305

Recall from Chapter 21 that the hedge ratio, or delta, of a put option equals $N(d_1) - 1$, where $N (\bullet)$ is the cumulative normal distribution function and

$$d_1 = \frac{\ln(S/X) + (r + \sigma^2/2)T}{\sigma\sqrt{T}}$$

Using your estimate of $\sigma = .35$, you find that the hedge ratio, $N(d_1) - 1 = -.453$.

Suppose, therefore, that you purchase 10 option contracts (1,000 puts) and purchase 453 shares of stock. Once the market "catches up" to your presumably better volatility estimate, the put options purchased will increase in value. If the market assessment of volatility changes as soon as you purchase the options, your profits should equal 1,000 × $.29 = $290. The option price will be affected as well by any change in the stock price, but this part of your exposure will be eliminated if the hedge ratio is chosen properly. Your profit should be based solely on the effect of the change in the implied volatility of the put, with the impact of the stock price hedged away.

Table 27.1 illustrates your profits as a function of the stock price assuming that the put price changes to reflect *your* estimate of volatility. Panel B shows that the put option alone can provide profits or losses depending on whether the stock price falls or rises. We see in Panel C, however, that each *hedged* put option provides profits nearly equal to the original mispricing, regardless of the change in the stock price.[4]

This hedging strategy is similar in spirit to the strategy used by the active equity manager who wishes to make a firm-specific bet without taking a position on the direction of the broad market. The equity manager buys the stock perceived to be underpriced and uses

---

[4]The profit is not exactly independent of the stock price. This is because as the stock price changes, so do the deltas used to calculate the hedge ratio. The hedge ratio in principle would need to be continually adjusted as deltas evolve. The sensitivity of the delta to the stock price is called the *gamma* of the option. Option gammas are analogous to bond convexity. In both cases, the curvature of the value function means that hedge ratios or durations change with market conditions, making rebalancing a necessary part of hedging strategies.

stock-index futures to hedge the stock's market exposure. Here, the options manager buys the option perceived to be underpriced and uses the stock to hedge the exposure of the option to changes in the price of the stock.

Concept

Question 4 • Suppose you bet on volatility by purchasing calls instead of puts. How would you hedge your exposure to stock-price fluctuations? What is the hedge ratio?

A variant of this strategy involves cross-option speculation. Suppose you observe a 45-day maturity call option on IBM with strike price 95 selling at a price consistent with a volatility of $\sigma = 33\%$ while another 45-day call with strike price 90 has an implied volatility of only 27%. Because the underlying asset and maturity date are identical, you conclude that the call with the higher implied volatility is relatively overpriced. To exploit the mispricing, you might buy the cheap calls (with strike price 90 and implied volatility of 27%) and write the expensive calls (with strike price 95 and implied volatility of 33%). If the risk-free rate is 4% and IBM is selling at $90 per share, the calls purchased will be priced at $3.6202 and the calls written will be priced at $2.3735.

Despite the fact that you are long one call and short another, your exposure to IBM stock-price uncertainty will not be hedged using this strategy. This is because calls with different strike prices have different sensitivities to the price of the underlying asset. The lower-strike-price call has a higher delta and therefore greater exposure to the price of IBM. If you take an equal number of positions in these two options, you will inadvertently establish a bullish position in IBM, as the calls you purchase have higher deltas than the calls you write. In fact, you may recall from Chapter 20 that this portfolio (long call with low exercise price and short call with high exercise price) is called a *bullish spread*.

To establish a hedged position, we can use the hedge ratio approach as follows. Consider the 95-strike-price options you write as the asset that hedges your exposure to the 90-strike-price options you purchase. Then the hedge ratio is

$$H = \frac{\text{Change in value of 90-strike-price call for \$1 change in IBM}}{\text{Change in value of 95-strike-price call for \$1 change in IBM}}$$

$$= \frac{\text{Delta of 90-strike-price call}}{\text{Delta of 95-strike-price call}} > 1$$

You need to write *more* than one call with the higher strike price to hedge the purchase of each call with the lower strike price. Because the prices of higher-strike-price calls are less sensitive to IBM prices, more of them are required to offset the exposure.

Suppose the true annual volatility of the stock is midway between the two implied volatilities, so $\sigma = 30\%$. We know from Chapter 21 that the delta of a call option is $N(d_1)$. Therefore, the deltas of the two options and the hedge ratio are computed as follows:

Option with strike price 90:

$$d_1 = \frac{\ln(90/90) + (.04 + .30^2/2) \times 45/365}{.30\sqrt{45/365}} = .0995$$

$$N(d_1) = .5396$$

Option with strike price 95:

$$d_1 = \frac{\ln(90/95) + (.04 + .30^2/2) \times 45/365}{.30\sqrt{45/365}} = -.4138$$

$$N(d_1) = .3395$$

Table 27.2   Profits on Delta-Neutral Options Portfolio

A. Cash flow when portfolio is established

Purchase 1,000 calls ($X = 90$) @ $3.6202
(option priced at implied volatility of 27%) $3,620.20 cash outflow

Write 1,589 calls ($X = 95$) @ $2.3735
(option priced at implied volatility of 33%)   3,771.50 cash inflow

Total $ 151.30 net cash inflow

B. Option prices at implied volatility of 30%

Stock Price:	89	90	91
90-strike-price calls	$3.478	$3.997	$4.557
95-strike-price calls	1.703	2.023	2.382

C. Value of portfolio after implied volatilities converge to 30%

Stock Price:	89	90	91
Value of 1,000 calls held	$3,478	$3,997	$ 4,557
− Value of 1,589 calls written	2,705	3,214	3,785
Total	$ 773	$ 782	$ 772

Hedge ratio:

$$\frac{.5396}{.3395} = 1.589$$

Therefore, for every 1,000 call options purchased with strike price 90, we need to write 1,589 call options with strike price 95. Following this strategy enables us to bet on the relative mispricing of the two options without taking a position on IBM. Panel A of Table 27.2 shows that the position will result in a cash inflow of $151.30. The premium income on the calls written exceeds the cost of the calls purchased.

When you establish a position in stocks and options that is hedged with respect to fluctuations in the price of the underlying asset, your portfolio is said to be **delta neutral,** meaning that the portfolio has no tendency to either increase or decrease in value when the stock price fluctuates.

Let's check that our options position is in fact delta neutral. Suppose that the implied volatilities of the two options come back into alignment just after you establish your position, so that both options are priced at implied volatilities of 30%. You expect to profit from the increase in the value of the call purchased as well as from the decrease in the value of the call written. The option prices at 30% volatility are given in Panel B of Table 27.2 and the values of your position for various stock prices are presented in Panel C. Although the profit or loss on each option is affected by the stock price, the value of the delta-neutral option portfolio is positive and essentially independent of the price of IBM. Moreover, we saw in Panel A that the portfolio would have been established without ever requiring a cash outlay. You would have cash inflows both when you establish the portfolio *and* when you liquidate it after the implied volatilities converge to 30%.

This unusual profit opportunity arises because you have identified prices out of alignment. Such opportunities could not arise if prices were at equilibrium levels. By exploiting the pricing discrepancy using a delta-neutral strategy, you should earn profits regardless of the price movement in IBM stock.

Delta-neutral hedging strategies are also subject to practical problems, the most important of which is the difficulty in assessing the proper volatility for the coming period. If the volatility estimate is incorrect, so will be the deltas, and the overall position will not truly be hedged. Moreover, option or option-plus-stock positions generally will not be neutral with respect to changes in volatility. For example, a put option hedged by a stock might be delta neutral, but it is not volatility neutral. Changes in the market assessments of volatility will affect the option price even if the stock price is unchanged.

These problems can be serious, because volatility estimates are never fully reliable. First, volatility cannot be observed directly, and must be estimated from past data which imparts measurement error to the forecast. Second, we've seen that both historical and implied volatilities fluctuate over time. Therefore, we are always shooting at a moving target. Although delta-neutral positions are hedged against changes in the price of the underlying asset, they still are subject to **volatility risk**, the risk incurred from unpredictable changes in volatility. Thus, although delta-neutral option hedges might eliminate exposure to risk from fluctuations in the value of the underlying asset, they do not eliminate volatility risk.

27.2   EFFECTS OF HEDGING DEMANDS ON CAPITAL MARKET EQUILIBRIUM

One implication of the capital asset pricing model was that all investors would decide that the same portfolio of risky assets, the market portfolio, provides the best risk-to-reward ratio. The CAPM, however, assumes that investors face only one source of risk—namely, uncertainty about future values of securities—and that the dollar value of wealth is the only determinant of economic welfare.

In reality, of course, investors must deal with many other sources of risk. Among these are:

1. Uncertain labor income.
2. Uncertain prices of consumption goods, for example, energy, or housing price uncertainty.
3. Uncertain life expectancy.
4. Uncertainty about future investment opportunities, for example, uncertainty in future interest rates.

Naturally, investors will attempt to hedge these risks to the greatest extent possible. For example, life insurance policies may be viewed as hedging vehicles for the uncertainty in life expectancy. Extramarket hedging demands against various sources of risk mean that our earlier treatment of portfolio demands must be modified. We can illustrate with an example.

The dramatic fluctuations in oil prices in the 1970s and 1980s illustrated the vulnerability of the economy to oil price shocks. In addition to the direct effect of oil prices on stock market values, consumers and investors found that oil prices had substantial effects on unemployment and inflation rates as well as on the cost of heating their homes and commuting to work. The important effect of oil price uncertainty for most investors had more to do with their activities as consumers and employees than with the impact of oil prices on the value of energy stocks such as Exxon.

It would not be surprising for individuals to search for investment vehicles to offset, or hedge, the risk they face from oil price uncertainty. A natural hedge security would be shares of energy sector stocks that should do well when the rest of the economy is harmed by an oil price shock. Investors would thus form hedge portfolios of stocks like Exxon to offset their oil price exposure. Therefore, the optimal risky portfolio would no longer be just the market portfolio. Investors would add to the market portfolio an additional position in the hedge portfolio.

But if many investors tilt their portfolios away from the market portfolio toward a specific sector such as energy stocks, the relative prices of those securities will change to reflect this extra hedging demand. For example, the prices of energy stocks will be bid up by the hedging demand, and their rates of return will be driven down. Investors will be willing to hold these stocks even with an expected rate of return lower than that dictated by the expected return–beta relationship of the CAPM because of the hedging value of the securities. The simple expected return–beta relationship therefore needs to be generalized to account for the effects of extramarket hedging demands on equilibrium rates of return.

Merton[5] has shown that these hedging demands will result in an expanded or "multifactor" version of the CAPM that recognizes the multidimensional nature of risk. The focal point of Merton's model is not dollar returns per se but the consumption and investment made possible by the investor's wealth. Each source of risk to consumption or investment opportunities may in principle command its own risk premium.

In the case of oil price risk, for example, Merton's model would imply that the expected return–beta relationship of the single-factor CAPM would be generalized to the following two-factor relationship:

$$E(r_i) - r_f = \beta_{iM}[E(r_M) - r_f] + \beta_{io}[E(r_o) - r_f]$$

where β_{iM} is the beta of security i with respect to the market portfolio and β_{io} is the beta with respect to oil price risk. Just as we measure the beta in the traditional index model using simple regression analysis, we can measure the multiple betas in this extended model in a multiple regression that allows for several explanatory or systematic factors. Similarly, $[E(r_o) - r_f]$ is the risk premium associated with exposure to oil price uncertainty. The rate of return on the portfolio that best hedges the oil price uncertainty is r_o. This equation, therefore, is a two-factor CAPM. More generally, we will have a beta and a risk premium for every significant source of risk that consumers try to hedge.

Notice that this expanded version of the CAPM provides a prediction for security returns identical to that of the multifactor APT. Therefore, there is no contradiction between these two theories of risk premiums. They provide complementary but consistent ways of deriving determinants of risk premiums. The CAPM approach does offer one notable advantage, however. In contrast to the APT, which takes the systematic factors in the economy as given, the CAPM provides guidance as to where to look for those factors. The important factors will be those sources of risk that large groups of investors try to offset by establishing extramarket hedge portfolios. By specifying the likely sources of risk against which dominant groups of investors attempt to hedge, we identify the dimensions along which the CAPM needs to be generalized. Therefore, we might specify that some important sources of extramarket risk are uncertainty in interest rates, inflation rates, and prices of goods in major sectors of the economy such as energy or housing.

Concept
CHECK

Question 5 • Consider the following regression results for stock X:

$$r_X = 2\% + 1.2 \text{ (percentage change in oil prices)}$$

a. **If I live in Louisiana, where the local economy is heavily dependent on oil industry profits, does stock X represent a useful asset to hedge my overall economic well-being?**

---

[5]Robert C. Merton, "An Intertemporal Capital Asset Pricing Model," *Econometrica* 41 (1973).

b. What if I live in Massachusetts, where most individuals and firms are energy consumers?

c. If energy consumers are far more numerous than energy producers, will high oil-beta stocks have higher or lower expected rates of return in market equilibrium than low oil-beta stocks?

SUMMARY

1. Hedging requires investors to purchase assets that will offset the sensitivity of their portfolios to particular sources of risk. A hedged position requires that the hedging vehicle provide profits that vary inversely with the value of the position to be protected.

2. The hedge ratio is the number of hedging vehicles such as futures contracts required to offset the risk of the unprotected position.

3. The hedge ratio for systematic market risk is proportional to the size and beta of the underlying stock portfolio. The hedge ratio for fixed-income portfolios is proportional to the price value of a basis point, which in turn is proportional to modified duration and the size of the portfolio.

4. The option delta is used to determine the hedge ratio for options positions. Delta-neutral portfolios are independent of price changes in the underlying asset. Even delta-neutral option portfolios are subject to volatility risk, however.

5. Investors are concerned with a host of extramarket sources of uncertainty pertaining to future consumption and investment opportunities. These concerns give rise to demands for securities that hedge these risks. Hedge portfolios with high correlation with one of the relevant sources of uncertainty will be sought to offset those sources of risk.

6. With the extra hedging demands, equilibrium security returns will satisfy a multifactor generalization of the expected return–beta relationship. This relationship is identical to the one predicted by the multifactor APT. A risk premium will arise if there is an aggregate desire to hedge an extramarket risk.

Key Terms

hedging	price value of a basis point	delta neutral
hedge ratio	cross-hedging	volatility risk

Selected Readings

A good book devoted to risk management is:
Smithson, Charles H.; Clifford W. Smith; with D. Sykes Wilford. *Managing Financial Risk.* Burr Ridge, IL: Irwin Professional Publishing, 1995.

Problems

1. A manager is holding a $1 million stock portfolio with a beta of 1.25. She would like to hedge the risk of the portfolio using the S&P 500 stock index futures contract. How many dollars' worth of the index should she sell in the futures market to minimize the volatility of her position?

2. A manager is holding a $1 million bond portfolio with a modified duration of eight years. She would like to hedge the risk of the portfolio by short-selling Treasury bonds. The modified duration of T-bonds is 10 years. How many dollars' worth of T-bonds should she sell to minimize the variance of her position?

3. Farmer Brown grows Number 1 red corn and would like to hedge the value of the coming harvest. However, the futures contract is traded on the Number 2 yellow grade of corn. Suppose that yellow corn typically sells for 90% of the price of red corn. If he grows 100,000 bushels, and each futures contract calls for delivery of 5,000 bushels, how many contracts should Farmer Brown buy or sell to hedge his position?

4. Yields on short-term bonds tend to be more volatile than yields on long-term bonds. Suppose that you have estimated that the yield on 20-year bonds changes by 10 basis points for every 15-basis-point move in the yield on five-year bonds. You hold a $1 million portfolio of five-year maturity bonds with modified duration four years and desire to hedge your interest rate exposure with T-bond futures, which currently have modified duration nine years and sell at $F_0 = \$95$. How many futures contracts should you sell?

5. A corporation plans to issue $10 million of 10-year bonds in three months. At current yields the bonds would have modified duration of eight years. The T-note futures contract is selling at $F_0 = 100$ and has modified duration of six years. How can the firm use this futures contract to hedge the risk surrounding the yield at which it will be able to sell its bonds? Both the bond and the contract are at par value.

6. You hold an $8 million stock portfolio with a beta of 1.0. You believe that the risk-adjusted abnormal return on the portfolio (the alpha) over the next three months is 2%. The S&P 500 index currently is at 800 and the risk-free rate is 1% per quarter.
   a. What will be the futures price on the three-month maturity S&P 500 futures contract?
   b. How many S&P 500 futures contracts are needed to hedge the stock portfolio?
   c. What will be the profit on that futures position in three months as a function of the value of the S&P 500 index on the maturity date?
   d. If the alpha of the portfolio is 2%, show that the expected rate of return (in decimal form) on the portfolio as a function of the market return is $r_p = .03 + 1.0 \times (r_M - .01)$.
   e. Call S_T the value of the index in three months. Then $S_T/S_0 = S_T/800 = 1 + r_M$. (We are ignoring dividends here to keep things simple.) Substitute this expression in the equation for the portfolio return, r_p, and calculate the expected value of the hedged stock-plus-futures portfolio in three months as a function of the value of the index.
   f. Show that the hedged portfolio provides an expected rate of return of 3% over the next three months.
   g. What is the beta of the hedged portfolio? What is the alpha of the hedged portfolio?

7. Suppose that the relationship between the rate of return on IBM stock, the market index, and a computer industry index can be described by the following regression equation: $r_{IBM} = .5r_M + .75r_{Industry}$. If a futures contract on the computer industry is traded, how would you hedge the exposure to the systematic and industry factors affecting the performance of IBM stock? How many dollars' worth of the market and industry index contracts would you buy or sell for each dollar held in IBM?

8. Salomon Brothers believes that market volatility will be 20% annually for the next three years. Three-year at-the-money call and put options on the market index sell at an implied volatility of 22%. What options portfolio can Salomon Brothers establish to speculate on its volatility belief without taking a bullish or bearish position on the market? Using Salomon's estimate of volatility, three-year at-the-money options have $N(d_1) = .6$.

9. Suppose that call options on Exxon stock with time to maturity three months and strike price $60 are selling at an implied volatility of 30%. Exxon stock currently is $60 per share, and the risk-free rate is 4%. If you believe the true volatility of the stock is 32%,

how can you trade on your belief without taking on exposure to the performance of Exxon? How many shares of stock will you hold for each option contract purchased or sold?

10. Using the same data in problem 9, suppose that three-month put options with a strike price of $60 are selling at an implied volatility of 34%. Construct a delta-neutral portfolio comprising positions in calls and puts that will profit when the option prices come back into alignment.

11. Suppose that Salomon Brothers sells call options on $1.25 million worth of a stock portfolio with beta = 1.5. The option delta is .8. It wishes to hedge out its resultant exposure to a market advance by buying market index futures contracts.

    a. If the current value of the market index is 1,000 and the contract multiplier is $250, how many contracts should it buy?

    b. What if Salomon instead uses market index puts to hedge its exposure? Should it buy or sell puts? Each put option is on 100 units of the index, and the index at current prices represents $1,000 worth of stock.

12. You are holding call options on a stock. The stock's beta is .75, and you are concerned that the stock market is about to fall. The stock is currently selling for $5 and you hold 1 million options on the stock (i.e., you hold 10,000 contracts for 100 shares each). The option delta is .8. How many market index futures contracts must you buy or sell to hedge your market exposure if the current value of the market index is 1,000 and the contract multiplier is $250?

13. Suppose that everyone agrees that uncertainty in the relative price of coal energy versus oil energy is an important factor to hedge, but that because energy-supply companies are diversified, no securities have returns correlated with the ratio of oil to coal prices. Would the multifactor CAPM in this case predict any departures from the simple CAPM?

14. Consider the following regression results for stock X:

$$R_X = .01 + 1.7 \times \text{Inflation rate}$$

    a. If I am retired and live on my pension, which provides a fixed number of dollars each month, does stock X represent a useful asset to hedge my overall economic well-being? Why or why not?

    b. What if I am a gold producer, and I am aware that gold prices increase when inflation accelerates?

    c. If retirees are far more numerous than gold producers in this economy, will high inflation-beta stocks have higher or lower expected rates of return in market equilibrium than low inflation-beta stocks?

15. An example of a factor that might be identified as explaining stock returns, but not appear in the multifactor CAPM, is the return on a particular industry group such as machine tools.

    a. Why might this industry factor seem to be a useful explanatory variable in describing security returns, yet still not appear in the multifactor CAPM?

    b. Would you expect this factor to command a significant risk premium? More generally, what types of factors will not command such premiums?

16. On June 1, 1989, Byron Henry was examining a new fixed-income account that his firm, Hawaiian Advisors, had accepted. Included in the new portfolio was a $10 million par value position in Procter & Gamble (PG) 8⅝% bonds due April 1, 2016.

    Henry was concerned about this position for three reasons: (1) There was an unrealized loss on the PG bonds due to a widening in the yield spread between U.S.

Table 27A   Bonds

Name	Coupon	Maturity	Price	Yield	Duration (years)	Price Value of a Basis Point
Procter & Gamble	8⅝%	4/1/16	86.36	10.10%	10.08	0.08286
U.S. Treasury bond	9⅛%	5/15/13	99.125	9.21%	9.25	0.08766

Table 27B   Futures (contract size = $100,000)

Contract	Expiration	Settlement Price	Yield	Price Value of a Basis Point	Conversion Factor
U.S. Treasury bond future	Dec. 1989	86.3125	9.51%	0.0902	1.1257

Treasuries and high-grade corporate bonds; (2) he felt that the PG bonds represented too large a portion of the $100 million portfolio; and (3) he feared that interest rates would move higher over the short term.

Hawaiian Advisors has the capability to do short sales and to use financial futures as well as options on futures. With this in mind, Henry collected some information on the PG bonds and on some alternative vehicles, shown in Tables 27A and 27B.

Henry recalled that the formula for calculating a hedge ratio is

$$\text{Hedge ratio} = \text{Yield beta} \times \frac{\text{PVBP}(y)}{\text{PVBP}(x)}$$

where

$\text{PVBP}(y)$ = the price change for a one-basis-point change (PVBP) in the target vehicle (the PG bond)

$\text{PVBP}(x)$ = the price change for a one-basis-point change (PVBP) in the hedge vehicle (the U.S. Treasury bond or the U.S. Treasury bond future)

Henry did a regression using Y (the dependent variable) as the yield of the PG bonds, and X (the independent variable) as the yield of the U.S. Treasury bonds. The result was the following equation:

$$Y = 1.75 + .89X \qquad (R\text{-squared} = .81)$$

Henry did a second regression using Y (the dependent variable) as the yield of the PG bonds, and X (the independent variable) as the yield on the futures contract. The result was the following equation:

$$Y = 5.25 + .47X \qquad (R\text{-squared} = .49)$$

For tax reasons, Henry does not want to sell the PG bonds now but would like to protect the portfolio from any further price decline. Formulate two hedging strategies, using only the investment vehicles cited in Tables 27A and 27B, that would protect against any further decline in the price of the PG bonds. Calculate the relevant hedge ratio for each strategy. Comment on the appropriateness of each of these strategies for this portfolio.

1. Because the firm does poorly when the dollar depreciates, it hedges with a futures contract that will provide profits in that scenario. It needs to enter a *long* position in pound futures, which means that it will earn profits on the contract when the futures price increases, that is, when more dollars are required to purchase one pound. The specific hedge ratio is determined by noting that if the number of dollars required to buy one pound rises by $.05, profits decrease by $200,000 at the same time that the profit on a long future contract would be $.05 × 62,500 = $3,125. The hedge ratio is

$$\frac{\$200,000 \text{ per } \$.05 \text{ depreciation in the dollar}}{\$3,125 \text{ per contract per } \$.05 \text{ depreciation}} = 64 \text{ contracts long}$$

2. Each $1 increase in the price of corn reduces profits by $1 million. Therefore, the firm needs to enter futures contracts to purchase 1 million bushels at a price stipulated today. The futures position will profit by $1 million for each increase of $1 in the price of corn. The profit on the contract will offset the lost profits on operations.

3. The price value of a basis point is still $900,000, as a one-basis-point change in the interest rate reduces the value of the $20 million portfolio by .01% × 4.5 = .0045%. Therefore, the number of futures needed to hedge the interest rate risk is the same as for a portfolio half the size with double the modified duration.

4. The delta for a call option is $N(d_1)$, which is positive, and in this case is .547. Therefore, for every 10 option contracts, you would need to *short* 547 shares of stock.

5. *a.* For Louisiana residents, the stock is not a hedge. When their economy does poorly (low oil prices) the stock also does poorly, thereby aggravating their problems.

   b. For Massachusetts residents, the stock is a hedge. When energy prices increase, the stock will provide greater wealth with which to purchase energy.

   c. If energy consumers (who are willing to bid up the price of the stock for its hedge value) dominate the economy, then high oil-beta stocks will have lower expected rates of return than would be predicted by the simple CAPM.

THE THEORY OF ACTIVE PORTFOLIO MANAGEMENT

Thus far we have alluded to active portfolio management in only three instances: the Markowitz methodology of generating the optimal risky portfolio (Chapter 8); security analysis that generates forecasts to use as inputs with the Markowitz procedure (Chapters 17 through 19); and fixed-income portfolio management (Chapter 16). These brief analyses are not adequate to guide investment managers in a comprehensive enterprise of active portfolio management. You may also be wondering about the seeming contradiction between our equilibrium analysis in Part III—in particular, the theory of efficient markets—and the real-world environment where profit-seeking investment managers use active management to exploit perceived market inefficiencies. Despite the efficient market hypothesis, it is clear that markets cannot be perfectly efficient; hence there are reasons to believe that active management can have effective results, and we discuss these at the outset.

Next we consider the objectives of active portfolio management. We analyze two forms of active management: market timing, which is based solely on macroeconomic factors; and security selection, which includes microeconomic forecasting. We show the use of multifactor models in active portfolio management, and we end with a discussion of the use of imperfect forecasts and the implementation of security analysis in industry.

28.1   THE LURE OF ACTIVE MANAGEMENT

How can a theory of active portfolio management be reconciled with the notion that markets are in equilibrium? You may want to look back at the analysis in Chapter 12, but we can interpret our conclusions as follows.

Market efficiency prevails when many investors are willing to depart from maximum diversification, or a passive strategy, by adding mispriced securities to their portfolios in the hope of realizing abnormal returns. The competition for such returns ensures that prices will be near their "fair" values. Most managers will not beat the passive strategy on a risk-adjusted basis. However, in the competition for rewards to investing, exceptional managers might beat the average forecasts built into market prices.

There is both economic logic and some empirical evidence to indicate that exceptional portfolio managers can beat the average forecast. Let us discuss economic logic first. We must assume that if no analyst can beat the passive strategy, investors will be smart enough to divert their funds from strategies entailing expensive analysis to less expensive passive strategies. In that case funds under active management will dry up, and prices will no longer reflect sophisticated forecasts. The consequent profit opportunities will lure back active managers who once again will become successful.[1] Of course, the critical assumption is that investors allocate management funds wisely. Direct evidence on that has yet to be produced.

As for empirical evidence, consider the following: (1) Some portfolio managers have produced streaks of abnormal returns that are hard to label as lucky outcomes; (2) the "noise" in realized rates is enough to prevent us from rejecting outright the hypothesis that some money managers have beaten the passive strategy by a statistically small, yet economically significant, margin; and (3) some anomalies in realized returns have been sufficiently persistent to suggest that portfolio managers who identified them in a timely fashion could have beaten the passive strategy over prolonged periods.

These conclusions persuade us that there is a role for a theory of active portfolio management. Active management has an inevitable lure even if investors agree that security markets are nearly efficient.

Suppose that capital markets are perfectly efficient, that an easily accessible market-index portfolio is available, and that this portfolio is for all practical purposes the efficient risky portfolio. Clearly, in this case security selection would be a futile endeavor. You would be better off with a passive strategy of allocating funds to a money market fund (the safe asset) and the market-index portfolio. Under these simplifying assumptions the optimal investment strategy seems to require no effort or know-how.

Such a conclusion, however, is too hasty. Recall that the proper allocation of investment funds to the risk-free and risky portfolios requires some analysis because y, the fraction to be invested in the risky market portfolio, M, is given by

$$y = \frac{E(r_M) - r_f}{.01A\sigma_M^2} \tag{28.1}$$

where $E(r_M) - r_f$ is the risk premium on M, σ_M^2 its variance, and A is the investor's coefficient of risk aversion. Any rational allocation therefore requires an estimate of σ_M and $E(r_M)$. Even a passive investor needs to do some forecasting, in other words.

Forecasting $E(r_M)$ and σ_M is further complicated by the existence of security classes that are affected by different environmental factors. Long-term bond returns, for example, are

---

[1]This point is worked out fully in Sanford J. Grossman and Joseph E. Stiglitz, "On the Impossibility of Informationally Efficient Markets," *American Economic Review* 70 (June 1980).

driven largely by changes in the term structure of interest rates, whereas equity returns depend on changes in the broader economic environment, including macroeconomic factors beyond interest rates. Once our investor determines relevant forecasts for separate sorts of investments, she might as well use an optimization program to determine the proper mix for the portfolio. It is easy to see how the investor may be lured away from a purely passive strategy, and we have not even considered temptations such as international stock and bond portfolios or sector portfolios.

In fact, even the definition of a "purely passive strategy" is problematic, because simple strategies involving only the market-index portfolio and risk-free assets now seem to call for market analysis. For our purposes we define purely passive strategies as those that use only index funds *and* weight those funds by fixed proportions that do not vary in response to perceived market conditions. For example, a portfolio strategy that always places 60% in a stock market–index fund, 30% in a bond-index fund, and 10% in a money market fund is a purely passive strategy.

More important, the lure into active management may be extremely strong because the potential profit from active strategies is enormous. At the same time, competition among the multitude of active managers creates the force driving market prices to near efficiency levels. Although enormous profits may be increasingly difficult to earn, decent profits to diligent analysts must always be the rule rather than the exception. For prices to remain efficient to some degree, some analysts must be able to eke out a reasonable profit. Absence of profits would decimate the active investment management industry, eventually allowing prices to stray from informationally efficient levels. The theory of managing active portfolios is the concern of this chapter.

28.2   OBJECTIVES OF ACTIVE PORTFOLIOS

What does an investor expect from a professional portfolio manager, and how does this expectation affect the operation of the manager? If the client were risk neutral, that is, indifferent to risk, the answer would be straightforward. The investor would expect the portfolio manager to construct a portfolio with the highest possible expected rate of return. The portfolio manager follows this dictum and is judged by the realized average rate of return.

When the client is risk averse, the answer is more difficult. Without a normative theory of portfolio management, the manager would have to consult each client before making any portfolio decision in order to ascertain that reward (average return) is commensurate with risk. Massive and constant input would be needed from the client-investors, and the economic value of professional management would be questionable.

Fortunately, the theory of mean-variance efficient portfolio management allows us to separate the "product decision," which is how to construct a mean-variance efficient risky portfolio, and the "consumption decision," or the investor's allocation of funds between the efficient risky portfolio and the safe asset. We have seen that construction of the optimal risky portfolio is purely a technical problem, resulting in a single optimal risky portfolio appropriate for all investors. Investors will differ only in how they apportion investment to that risky portfolio and the safe asset. For evidence that the theory of efficient frontiers has been seeping through to the practitioner community, see the nearby box, which presents an advertisement by J.P. Morgan.

Another feature of the mean-variance theory that affects portfolio management decisions is the criterion for choosing the optimal risky portfolio. In Chapter 8 we established that the optimal risky portfolio for any investor is the one that maximizes the reward-to-variability ratio, or the expected excess rate of return (over the risk-free rate) divided by the

International fixed-income securities account for nearly half the world's $5.4 trillion bond market—and offer plan sponsors increasingly attractive opportunities. J.P. Morgan Investment, the leader in this field, manages more than $3 billion of international fixed-income securities. We believe you should consider including international bonds in your pension portfolio.

Estimated market value $5.4 trillion (publicly issued securities)

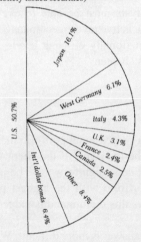

Shown at J.P. Morgan Investment's London headquarters are international fixed income team members (left to right) Anthony G. Bird, Hans K-E Danielsson, Bernard A. Wagenmann, and Adrian F. Lee

standard deviation. A manager who uses this Markowitz methodology to construct the optimal risky portfolio will satisfy all clients regardless of risk aversion. Clients, for their part, can evaluate managers using statistical methods to draw inferences from realized rates of return about prospective, or ex-ante, reward-to-variability ratios.

William Sharpe's assessment of mutual fund performance[2] is the seminal work in the area of portfolio performance evaluation (see Chapter 24). The reward-to-variability ratio has come to be known as **Sharpe's measure:**

---

[2]William F. Sharpe, "Mutual Fund Performance," *Journal of Business, Supplement on Security Prices* 39 (January 1966).

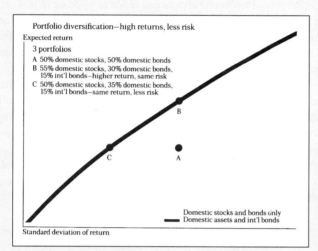
$$S = \frac{E(r_P) - r_f}{\sigma_P}$$

It is now a common criterion for tracking performance of professionally managed portfolios.

Briefly, mean-variance portfolio theory implies that the objective of professional portfolio managers is to maximize the (ex-ante) Sharpe measure, which entails maximizing the slope of the CAL (capital allocation line). A "good" manager is one whose CAL is steeper than the CAL representing the passive strategy of holding a market-index portfolio. Clients can observe rates of return and compute the realized Sharpe measure (the ex-post CAL) to evaluate the relative performance of their manager.

Ideally, clients would like to invest their funds with the most able manager, one who consistently obtains the highest Sharpe measure and presumably has real forecasting ability. This is true for all clients regardless of their degree of risk aversion. At the same time, each client must decide what fraction of investment funds to allocate to this manager, placing the remainder in a safe fund. If the manager's Sharpe measure is constant over time (and can be estimated by clients), the investor can compute the optimal fraction to be invested with the manager from equation 28.1, based on the portfolio long-term average return and variance. The remainder will be invested in a money market fund.

The manager's ex-ante Sharpe measure from updated forecasts will be constantly varying. Clients would have liked to increase their allocation to the risky portfolio when the forecasts are optimistic, and vice versa. However, it would be impractical to constantly communicate updated forecasts to clients and for them to constantly revise their allocation between the risky portfolios and risk-free asset.

Allowing managers to shift funds between their optimal risky portfolio and a safe asset according to their forecasts alleviates the problem. Indeed, many stock funds allow the managers reasonable flexibility to do just that.

28.3 MARKET TIMING

Consider the results of the following two different investment strategies:

1. An investor who put $1,000 in 30-day commercial paper on January 1, 1927, and rolled over all proceeds into 30-day paper (or into 30-day T-bills after they were introduced) would have ended on December 31, 1978, fifty-two years later, with $3,600.

2. An investor who put $1,000 in the NYSE index on January 1, 1927, and reinvested all dividends in that portfolio would have ended on December 31, 1978, with $67,500.

Suppose we defined perfect **market timing** as the ability to tell (with certainty) at the beginning of each month whether the NYSE portfolio will outperform the 30-day paper portfolio. Accordingly, at the beginning of each month, the market timer shifts all funds into either cash equivalents (30-day paper) or equities (the NYSE portfolio), whichever is predicted to do better. Beginning with $1,000 on the same date, how would the perfect timer have ended up 52 years later?

This is how Professor Robert Merton began a seminar with finance professors several years ago. As he collected responses, the boldest guess was a few million dollars. The correct answer: $5.36 *billion*.[3]

Question 1 • What was the monthly and annual compounded rate of return for the three strategies over the period 1926 to 1978?

These numbers have some lessons for us. The first has to do with the power of compounding. Its effect is particularly important because more and more of the funds under management represent pension savings. The horizons of such investments may not be as long as 52 years, but by and large they are measured in decades, making compounding a significant factor.

Another result that may seem surprising at first is the huge difference between the end-of-period value of the all-safe asset strategy ($3,600) and that of the all-equity strategy

---

[3]This demonstration has been extended to recent data with similar results.

($67,500). Why would anyone invest in safe assets given this historical record? If you have internalized the lessons of previous chapters, you know the reason: risk. The average rates of return and the standard deviations on the all-bills and all-equity strategies for this period are:

	Arithmetic Mean	Standard Deviation
Bills	2.55	2.10
Equities	10.70	22.14

The significantly higher standard deviation of the rate of return on the equity portfolio is commensurate with its significantly higher average return.

Can we also view the rate-of-return premium on the perfect-timing fund as a risk premium? The answer must be "no," because the perfect timer never does worse than either bills or the market. The extra return is not compensation for the possibility of poor returns but is attributable to superior analysis. It is the value of superior information that is reflected in the tremendous end-of-period value of the portfolio.

The monthly rate-of-return statistics for the all-equity portfolio and the timing portfolio are

Per Month	All Equities (%)	Perfect Timer No Charge (%)	Perfect Timer Fair Charge (%)
Average rate of return	0.85	2.58	0.55
Average excess return over return on safe asset	0.64	2.37	0.34
Standard deviation	5.89	3.82	3.55
Highest return	38.55	38.55	30.14
Lowest return	−29.12	0.06	−7.06
Coefficient of skewness	0.42	4.28	2.84

Ignore for the moment the fourth column ("Perfect Timer—Fair Charge"). The results of rows one and two are self-explanatory. The third item, standard deviation, requires some discussion. The standard deviation of the rate of return earned by the perfect market timer was 3.82%, far greater than the volatility of T-bill returns over the same period. Does this imply that (perfect) timing is a riskier strategy than investing in bills? No. For this analysis standard deviation is a misleading measure of risk.

To see why, consider how you might choose between two hypothetical strategies: The first offers a sure rate of return of 5%; the second strategy offers an uncertain return that is given by 5% *plus* a random number that is zero with probability .5 and 5% with probability .5. The characteristics of each strategy are

	Strategy 1 (%)	Strategy 2 (%)
Expected return	5	7.5
Standard deviation	0	2.5
Highest return	5	10.0
Lowest return	5	5.0

Clearly, Strategy 2 dominates Strategy 1 because its rate of return is *at least* equal to that of Strategy 1 and sometimes greater. No matter how risk averse you are, you will always prefer Strategy 2 to Strategy 1, despite the significant standard deviation of Strategy 2.

Compared to Strategy 1, Strategy 2 provides only "good surprises," so the standard deviation in this case cannot be a measure of risk.

These results are analogous to the case of the perfect timer compared with an all-equity or all-bills strategy. In every period the perfect timer obtains at least as good a return, in some cases a better one. Therefore the timer's standard deviation is a misleading measure of risk compared to an all-equity or all-bills strategy.

Returning to the empirical results, you can see that the highest rate of return is identical for the all-equity and the timing strategies, whereas the lowest rate of return is positive for the perfect timer and disastrous for all the all-equity portfolio. Another reflection of this is seen in the coefficient of skewness, which measures the asymmetry of the distribution of returns. Because the equity portfolio is almost (but not exactly) normally distributed, its coefficient of skewness is very low at .42. In contrast, the perfect timing strategy effectively eliminates the negative tail of the distribution of portfolio returns (the part below the risk-free rate). Its returns are "skewed to the right," and its coefficient of skewness is therefore quite large, 4.28.

Now for the fourth column, "Perfect Timer—Fair Charge," which is perhaps the most interesting of the three results columns. Most assuredly, the perfect timer will charge clients for such a valuable service. (The perfect timer may have otherwordly predictive powers, but saintly benevolence is unlikely.)

Subtracting a fair fee (discussed later) from the monthly rate of return of the timer's portfolio gives us an average rate of return lower than that of the passive, all-equity strategy. However, because the fee is *assumed* to be fair, the two portfolios (the all-equity strategy and the market timing with fee strategy) must be equally attractive after risk adjustment. In this case, again, the standard deviation of the market timing strategy (with fee) is of no help in adjusting for risk because the coefficient of skewness remains high, 2.84. In other words, standard mean-variance analysis is quite complicated for valuing market timing. We need an alternative approach.

Valuing Market Timing as an Option

The key to analyzing the pattern of returns to the perfect market timer is to recognize that perfect foresight is equivalent to holding a call option on the equity portfolio. The perfect timer invests 100% in either the safe asset or the equity portfolio, whichever will yield the higher return. This is shown in Figure 28.1. The rate of return is bounded from below by r_f.

To see the value of information as an option, suppose that the market index currently is at S_0, and that a call option on the index has an exercise price of $X = S_0(1 + r_f)$. If the market outperforms bills over the coming period, S_T will exceed X, whereas it will be less than X otherwise. Now look at the payoff to a portfolio consisting of this option and S_0 dollars invested in bills:

	$S_T < X$	$S_T \geq X$
Bills	$S_0(1 + r_f)$	$S_0(1 + r_f)$
Option	0	$S_T - X$
Total	$S_0(1 + r_f)$	S_T

The portfolio pays the risk-free return when the market is bearish (i.e., the market return is less than the risk-free rate), and it pays the market return when the market is bullish and beats bills. Such a portfolio is a perfect market timer. Consequently, we can measure the

Figure 28.1

Rate of return of a perfect market timer.

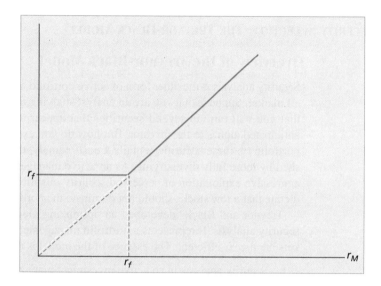

value of perfect ability as the value of the call option, because a call enables the investor to earn the market return only when it exceeds r_f.

This insight lets Merton[4] value timing ability using the theory of option of valuation, and from this we calculate our fair charge for timing.

The Value of Imperfect Forecasting

Unfortunately, managers are not perfect forecasters, as you and Merton know. It seems pretty obvious that if managers are right most of the time, they are doing very well. However, when we say right "most of the time," we cannot mean merely the percentage of the time a manager is right. The weather forecaster in Tucson, Arizona, who *always* predicts no rain, may be right 90% of the time. But a high success rate for a "stopped-clock" strategy clearly is not evidence of forecasting ability.

Similarly, the appropriate measure of market forecasting ability is not the overall proportion of correct forecasts. If the market is up two days out of three and a forecaster always predicts market advance, the two-thirds success rate is not a measure of forecasting ability. We need to examine the proportion of bull markets ($r_M > r_f$) correctly forecast *and* the proportion of bear markets ($r_M < r_f$) correctly forecast.

If we call P_1 the proportion of the correct forecasts of bull markets and P_2 the proportion for bear markets, then $P_1 + P_2 - 1$ is the correct measure of timing ability. For example, a forecaster who always guesses correctly will have $P_1 = P_2 = 1$, and will show ability of 1 (100%). An analyst who always bets on a bear market will mispredict all bull markets ($P_1 = 0$), will correctly "predict" all bear markets ($P_2 = 1$), and will end up with timing ability of $P_1 + P_2 - 1 = 0$. If C denotes the (call option) value of a perfect market timer, then $(P_1 + P_2 - 1)C$ measures the value of imperfect forecasting ability. In Chapter 24, "Portfolio Performance Evaluation," we saw how market timing ability can be detected and measured.

Concept
CHECK

Question 2 • What is the market timing score of someone who flips a fair coin to predict the market?

---

[4]Robert C. Merton, "On Market Timing and Investment Performance: An Equilibrium Theory of Value for Market Forecasts," *Journal of Business,* July 1981.

28.4 SECURITY SELECTION: THE TREYNOR-BLACK MODEL

Overview of the Treynor-Black Model

Security analysis is the other form of active portfolio management besides timing the overall market. Suppose that you are an analyst studying individual securities. It is quite likely that you will turn up several securities that appear to be mispriced. They offer positive anticipated alphas to the investor. But how do you exploit your analysis? Concentrating a portfolio on these securities entails a cost, namely, the firm-specific risk that you could shed by more fully diversifying. As an active manager you must strike a balance between aggressive exploitation of perceived security mispricing and diversification motives that dictate that a few stocks should not dominate the portfolio.

Treynor and Black[5] developed an optimizing model for portfolio managers who use security analysis. It represents a portfolio management theory that assumes security markets are *nearly* efficient. The essence of the model is this:

1. Security analysis in an active investment management organization can analyze in depth only a relatively small number of stocks out of the entire universe of securities. The securities not analyzed are assumed to be fairly priced.

2. For the purpose of efficient diversification, the market index portfolio is the baseline portfolio, which the model treats as the passive portfolio.

3. The macro forecasting unit of the investment management firm provides forecasts of the expected rate of return and variance of the passive (market-index) portfolio.

4. The objective of security analysis is to form an active portfolio of a necessarily limited number of securities. Perceived mispricing of the analyzed securities is what guides the composition of this active portfolio.

5. Analysts follow several steps to make up the active portfolio and evaluate its expected performance:
   a. Estimate the beta of each analyzed security and its residual risk. From the beta and macro forecast, $E(r_M) - r_f$, determine the *required* rate of return of the security.
   b. Given the degree of mispricing of each security, determine its expected return and expected *abnormal* return (alpha).
   c. The cost of less than full diversification comes from the nonsystematic risk of the mispriced stock, the variance of the stock's residual, which offsets the benefit (alpha) of specializing in an underpriced security.
   d. Use the estimates for the values of alpha, beta, and residual risk to determine the optimal weight of each security in the active portfolio.
   e. Estimate the alpha, beta, and residual risk for the active portfolio according to the weights of the securities in the portfolio.

6. The macroeconomic forecasts for the passive index portfolio and the composite forecasts for the active portfolio are used to determine the optimal risky portfolio, which will be a combination of the passive and active portfolios.

Treynor and Black's model did not take the industry by storm. This is unfortunate for several reasons:

---

[5] Jack Treynor and Fischer Black, "How to Use Security Analysis to Improve Portfolio Selection," *Journal of Business,* January 1973.

1. Just as even imperfect market timing ability has enormous value, security analysis of the sort Treynor and Black proposed has similar potential value. Even with far from perfect security analysis, proper active management can add value.

2. The Treynor-Black model is conceptually easy to implement. Moreover, it is useful even when some of its simplifying assumptions are relaxed.

3. The model lends itself to use in decentralized organizations. This property is essential to efficiency in complex organizations.

Portfolio Construction

Assuming that all securities are fairly priced, and using the index model as a guideline for the rate of return on fairly priced securities, the rate of return on the ith security is given by

$$r_i = r_f + \beta_i(r_M - r_f) + e_i \tag{28.2}$$

where e_i is the zero mean, firm-specific disturbance.

Absent security analysis, Treynor and Black (TB) took equation 28.2 to represent the rate of return on all securities and assumed that the market portfolio, M, is the efficient portfolio. For simplicity, they also assumed that the nonsystematic components of returns, e_i, are independent across securities. As for market timing, TB assumed that the forecast for the **passive portfolio** already has been made, so that the expected return on the market index, r_M, as well as the variance, σ_M^2, has been assessed.

Now a portfolio manager unleashes a team of security analysts to investigate a subset of the universe of available securities. The objective is to form an active portfolio of positions in the analyzed securities to be mixed with the index portfolio. For each security, k, that is researched, we write the rate of return as

$$r_k = r_f + \beta_k(r_M - r_f) + e_k + \alpha_k \tag{28.3}$$

where α_k represents the extra expected return (called the *abnormal return*) attributable to any perceived mispricing of the security. Thus for each security analyzed the research team estimates the parameters

$$\alpha_k, \qquad \beta_k, \qquad \sigma^2(e_k)$$

If all the α_k turn out to be zero, there would be no reason to depart from the passive strategy and the index portfolio M would remain the manager's choice. However, this is a remote possibility. In general, there will be a significant number of nonzero alpha values, some positive and some negative.

One way to get an overview of the TB methodology is to examine what we should do with the active portfolio once we determine it. Suppose that the **active portfolio** (A) has been constructed somehow and has the parameters

$$\alpha_A, \qquad \beta_A, \qquad \sigma^2(e_A)$$

Its total variance is the sum of its systematic variance, $\beta_A^2 \sigma_M^2$, plus the nonsystematic variance, $\sigma^2(e_A)$. Its covariance with the market index portfolio, M, is

$$\text{Cov}(r_A, r_M) = \beta_A \sigma_M^2$$

Figure 28.2 shows the optimization process with the active and passive portfolios. The dashed efficient frontier represents the universe of all securities assuming that they are all fairly priced, that is, that all alphas are zero. By definition, the market index, M, is on this efficient frontier and is tangent to the (dashed) capital market line (CML). In practice the

Figure 28.2

The optimization process with active and passive portfolios.

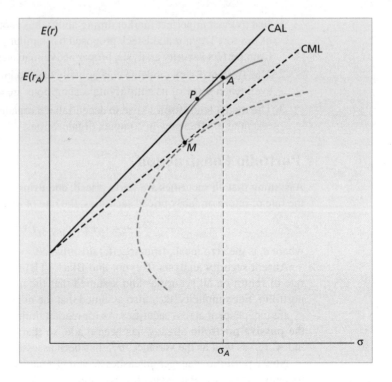

analysts do not need to know this frontier. They need only to observe the market-index portfolio and construct a portfolio resulting in a capital allocation line that lies above the CML. Given their perceived superior analysis, they will view the market-index portfolio as inefficient: The active portfolio, *A,* constructed from mispriced securities, must lie, by design, above the CML.

To locate the active portfolio *A* in Figure 28.2, we need its expected return and standard deviation. The standard deviation is

$$\sigma_A = [\beta_A^2 \sigma_M^2 + \sigma^2(e_A)]^{1/2}$$

Because of the positive alpha value that is forecast for *A,* it may plot above the (dashed) CML with expected return

$$E(r_A) = \alpha_A + r_f + \beta_A[E(r_M) - r_f]$$

The optimal combination of the active portfolio, *A,* with the passive portfolio, *M,* is a simple application of the construction of optimal risky portfolios from two component assets that we first encountered in Chapter 8. Because the active portfolio is not perfectly correlated with the market-index portfolio, we need to account for their mutual correlation in the determination of the optimal allocation between the two portfolios. This is evident from the solid efficient frontier that passes through *M* and *A* in Figure 28.2. It supports the optimal capital allocation line (CAL) and identifies the optimal risky portfolio, *P,* which combines portfolios *A* and *M* and is the tangency point of the CAL to the efficient frontier. The active portfolio *A* in this example is not the ultimate efficient portfolio, because we need to mix *A* with the passive market portfolio to achieve greater diversification.

Let us now outline the algebraic approach to this optimization problem. If we invest a proportion, *w,* in the active portfolio and $1 - w$ in the market index, the portfolio return will be

$$r_p(w) = wr_A + (1 - w)r_M$$

We can use this equation to calculate Sharpe's measure (dividing the mean excess return by the standard deviation of the return) as a function of the weight, w, and then find the optimal weight, w^*, that maximizes the measure. This is the value of w that makes P the optimal tangency portfolio in Figure 28.2. This maximization ultimately leads to the solution

$$w^* = \frac{w_0}{1 + (1 - \beta_A)w_0} \tag{28.4}$$

where

$$w_0 = \frac{\alpha_A/\sigma^2(e_A)}{[E(r_M) - r_f]/\sigma_M^2}$$

Equation 28.4 is actually a restatement of the formula for determining the optimal weights to invest in two risky assets that you first encountered in Chapter 8. Here we state the equation in terms of portfolio alphas relative to the CAPM, but the approach is identical.

First look at w_0. This would be the optimal weight in the active portfolio *if* its beta (β_A) were 1.0. This weight is a ratio of two measures. In the numerator is the reward from the active portfolio, α_A, reflecting its mispricing, against the nonsystematic risk, $\sigma^2(e_A)$, incurred in holding it. This ratio is divided by an analogous measure for the index portfolio

$$\frac{E(r_M) - r_f}{\sigma_M^2}$$

which is the ratio of the reward from holding the index, $E(r_M) - r_f$, to its risk, σ_M^2.

The intuition here is straightforward. We mix the active portfolio with the index for the benefit of diversification. The position to take in the active portfolio relative to the market portfolio depends on the ratio of the active portfolio's abnormal return, α_A, to its potentially diversifiable risk, $\sigma^2(e_A)$. The optimal weights also will depend on the opportunities for diversification, which in turn depend on the correlation between the two portfolios and can be measured by β_A. To adjust the optimal weight for the fact that the beta of the active portfolio may not be 1.0, we compute w^* in equation 28.4.

What is the reward-to-variability ratio of the optimal risky portfolio once we find the best mix, w^*, of the active and passive index portfolios? It turns out that if we compute the square of Sharpe's measure of the risky portfolio, we can separate the contributions of the index and active portfolios as follows:

$$S_P^2 = S_M^2 + \frac{\alpha_A^2}{\sigma^2(e_A)} = \left[\frac{E(r_M) - r_f}{\sigma_M}\right]^2 + \left[\frac{\alpha_A}{\sigma(e_A)}\right]^2 \tag{28.5}$$

This decomposition of the Sharpe measure of the optimal risky portfolio, which by the way is valid *only* for the optimal portfolio, tells us how to construct the active portfolio. Look at the last equality in equation 28.5. It shows that the highest Sharpe measure for the risky portfolio will be attained when we construct an active portfolio that maximizes the value of $\alpha_A/\sigma^2(e_A)$. The ratio of alpha to residual standard deviation of the active portfolio will be maximized when we choose a weight for the kth analyzed security as follows:

$$w_k = \frac{\alpha_k/\sigma^2(e_k)}{\sum_{i=1}^{n} \alpha_i/\sigma^2(e_i)} \tag{28.6}$$

This makes sense: The weight of a security in the active portfolio depends on the ratio of the degree of mispricing, α_k, to the nonsystematic risk, $\sigma^2(e_k)$, of the security. The denominator, the sum of the ratio across securities, is a scale factor to guarantee that the weights sum to one.

Note from equation 28.5 that the square of Sharpe's measure of the optimal risky portfolio is increased over the square of the Sharpe measure of the passive (market-index) portfolio by the amount

$$\left[\frac{\alpha_A}{\sigma(e_A)}\right]^2$$

The ratio of the degree of mispricing, α_A, to the nonsystematic standard deviation, $\sigma(e_A)$, becomes a natural performance measure of the active component of the risky portfolio. Sometimes this is called the **appraisal ratio.**

We can calculate the contribution of a single security in the active portfolio to the portfolio's overall performance. When the active portfolio contains n analyzed securities, the total improvement in the squared Sharpe measure equals the sum of the squared appraisal ratios of the analyzed securities,

$$\left[\frac{\alpha_A}{\sigma(e_A)}\right]^2 = \sum_{i=1}^{n}\left[\frac{\alpha_i}{\sigma(e_i)}\right]^2 \tag{28.7}$$

The appraisal ratio for each security, $\alpha_i/\sigma(e_i)$, is a measure of the contribution of that security to the performance of the active portfolio.

The best way to illustrate the Treynor-Black process is through an example. Suppose that the macroforecasting unit of Drex Portfolio Inc. (DPF) issues a forecast for a 15% market return. The forecast's standard error is 20%. The risk-free rate is 7%. The macro data can be summarized as follows:

$$E(r_M) - r_f = 8\%; \qquad \sigma_M = 20\%$$

At the same time the security analysis division submits to the portfolio manager the following forecast of annual returns for the three securities that it covers:

Stock	α	β	$\sigma(e)$	$\alpha/\sigma(e)$
1	7%	1.6	45%	.1556
2	−5	1.0	32	−.1563
3	3	0.5	26	.1154

Note that the alpha estimates appear reasonably moderate. The estimates of the residual standard deviations are correlated with the betas, just as they are in reality. The magnitudes also reflect typical values for NYSE stocks. Equation 28.7 and the analyst input table allow a quick calculation of the DPF portfolio's Sharpe measure. We sum the squares of the market and individual-security appraisal ratios,

$$(S_P)^2 = [(8/20)^2 + .1556^2 + .1563^2 + .1154^2]^{1/2} = .2220$$

and compare the result with the squared Sharpe ratio for the market-index portfolio, which is only $(8/20)^2 = .16$. We now proceed to compute the composition and performance of the active portfolio.

First, let us construct the optimal active portfolio implied by the security analyst input list. To do so we compute the appraisal ratios as follows (remember to use decimal representations of returns in the formulas):

Stock	$\alpha/\sigma^2(e)$	$\dfrac{\alpha_k}{\sigma^2(e_k)} \Bigg/ \displaystyle\sum_{i=1}^{3} \dfrac{\alpha_i}{\sigma^2(e_i)}$
1	$.07/.45^2 =$ .3457	$.3457/.3012 =$ 1.1477
2	$-.05/.32^2 = -.4883$	$-.4883/.3012 = -1.6212$
3	$.03/.26^2 =$ .4438	$.4438/.3012 =$ 1.4735
Total	.3012	1.0000

The last column presents the optimal positions of each of the three securities in the active portfolio. Obviously, Stock 2, with a negative alpha, has a negative weight. The magnitudes of the individual positions in the active portfolio (e.g., 114.77% in Stock 1) seem quite extreme. However, this should not concern us because the active portfolio will later be mixed with the well-diversified market-index portfolio, resulting in much more moderate positions, as we shall see shortly.

The forecasts for the stocks, together with the proposed composition of the active portfolio, lead to the following parameter estimates (in decimal form) for the active portfolio:

$$\alpha_A = 1.1477 \times .07 + (-1.6212) \times (-.05) + 1.4735 \times .03$$
$$= .2056 = 20.56\%$$
$$\beta_A = 1.1477 \times 1.6 + (-1.6212) \times 1.0 + 1.4735 \times .5 = .9519$$
$$\sigma(e_A) = [1.1477^2 \times .45^2 + (-1.6212)^2 \times .32^2 + 1.4735^2 \times .26^2]^{1/2}$$
$$= .8262 = 82.62\%$$
$$\sigma^2(e_A) = .8262^2 = .6826$$

Note that the negative weight (short position) on the negative alpha stock results in a positive contribution to the alpha of the active portfolio. Note also that because of the assumption that the stock residuals are uncorrelated, the active portfolio's residual variance is simply the weighted sum of the individual stock residual variances, with the squared portfolio proportions as weights.

The parameters of the active portfolio are now used to determine its proportion in the overall risky portfolio:

$$w_0 = \frac{\alpha_A/\sigma^2(e_A)}{[E(r_M) - r_f]/\sigma_M^2}$$

$$= \frac{.2056/.6826}{.08/.04} = .1506$$

$$w^* = \frac{w_0}{1 + (1 - \beta_A)w_0}$$

$$= \frac{.1506}{1 + (1 - .9519) \times .1506} = .1495$$

Although the active portfolio's alpha is impressive (20.56%), its proportion in the overall risky portfolio, before adjustment for beta, is only 15.06%, because of its large nonsystematic standard deviation (82.62%). Such is the importance of diversification. As it happens, the beta of the active portfolio is almost 1.0, and hence the correction for beta (from w_0 to w^*) is small, from 15.06% to 14.95%. The direction of the change makes sense. If the beta of the active portfolio is low (less than 1.0), there are more potential gains from diversification, hence a smaller position in the active portfolio is called for. If the beta of the active portfolio were significantly greater than 1.0, a larger correction in the opposite direction would be called for.

The proportions of the individual stocks in the active portfolio, together with the proportion of the active portfolio in the overall risky portfolio, determine the proportions of each individual stock in the overall risky portfolio.

Stock	Final Position		
1	.1495 ×	1.1477 =	.1716
2	.1495 ×	(−1.6212) =	−.2424
3	.1495 ×	1.4735 =	.2202
Active portfolio			.1495
Market portfolio			.8505
			1.0000

The parameters of the active portfolio and market-index portfolio are now used to forecast the performance of the optimal, overall risky portfolio. When optimized, a property of the risky portfolio is that its squared Sharpe measure increases by the square of the active portfolio's appraisal ratio:

$$S_P^2 = \left[\frac{E(r_M) - r_f}{\sigma_M} \right]^2 + \left[\frac{\alpha_A}{\sigma(e_A)} \right]^2$$

$$= .16 + .0619 = .2219$$

and hence the Sharpe measure of the DPF portfolio is $\sqrt{.2219} = .4711$, compared with .40 for the passive portfolio.

Another measure of the gain from increasing the Sharpe measure is the M^2 statistic, as described in Chapter 24. M^2 is calculated by comparing the expected return of a portfolio on the capital allocation line supported by portfolio P, CAL(P), with a standard deviation equal to that of the market index, to the expected return on the market index. In other words, we mix portfolio P with the risk-free asset to obtain a new portfolio P^* that has the same standard deviation as the market portfolio. Since both portfolios have equal risk, we can compare their expected returns. The M^2 statistic is the difference in expected returns.

Portfolio P^* can be obtained by investing a fraction σ_M/σ_P in P and a fraction $(1 - \sigma_M/\sigma_P)$ in the risk-free asset.

The risk premium on CAL(P^*) with total risk σ_M is given by

$$E(r_{P*}) - r_f = S_P \sigma_M = .4711 \times .20 = .0942, \text{ or } 9.42\% \tag{28.8}$$

and

$$M^2 = [E(r_{P*}) - r_f] - [E(r_M) - r_f] = 9.42 - 8 = 1.42\% \tag{28.9}$$

At first blush, an incremental expected return of 1.42% seems paltry compared with the alpha values submitted by the analyst. This seemingly modest improvement is the result of diversification motives: To mitigate the large risk of individual stocks (verify that the standard deviation of stock 1 is 55%) and maximize the portfolio Sharpe measure (which compares excess return to total volatility), we must diversify the active portfolio by mixing it with M. Note also that this improvement has been achieved with only three stocks, and with forecasts and portfolio rebalancing only once a year. Increasing the number of stocks and the frequency of forecasts can improve the results dramatically.

For example, suppose the analyst covers three more stocks that turn out to have alphas and risk levels identical to the first three. Use equation 28.7 to show that the squared appraisal ratio of the active portfolio will double. By using equation 28.5, it is easy to show that the new Sharpe measure will rise to .5327. Equation 28.9 then implies that M^2 rises to 2.65%, almost double the previous value. Increasing the frequency of forecasts and portfolio rebalancing will deploy the power of compounding to improve annual performance even more.

Concept
CHECK

Question 3

a. **When short positions are prohibited, the manager simply discards stocks with negative alphas. Using the preceding example, what would be the composition of the active portfolio if short sales were disallowed? Find the cost of the short-sale restriction in terms of the decline in performance (M^2) of the new overall risky portfolio.**

b. **How would your answer change if the macro forecast is adjusted upward, for example, to $E(r_M) - r_f = 12\%$, and short sales are again allowed?**

28.5   MULTIFACTOR MODELS AND ACTIVE PORTFOLIO MANAGEMENT

Perhaps in the foreseeable future a multifactor structure of security returns will be developed and accepted as conventional wisdom. So far our analytical framework for active portfolio management seems to rest on the validity of the index model, that is, on a single-factor security model. Despite this appearance, a multifactor structure will not affect the construction of the active portfolio because the entire TB analysis focuses on the residuals of the index model. If we were to replace the one-factor model with a multifactor model, we would continue to form the active portfolio by calculating each security's alpha relative to its fair return (given its betas on *all* factors), and again we would combine the active portfolio with the portfolio that would be formed in the absence of security analysis. The multifactor framework, however, does raise several new issues in portfolio management.

You saw in Chapter 10 how the index model simplifies the construction of the input list necessary for portfolio optimization programs. If

$$r_i - r_f = \alpha_i + \beta_i(r_M - r_f) + e_i$$

adequately describes the security market, then the variance of any asset is the sum of systematic and nonsystematic risk: $\sigma^2(r_i) = \beta_i^2\sigma_M^2 + \sigma^2(e_i)$, and the covariance between any two assets is $\beta_i\beta_j\sigma_M^2$.

How do we generalize this rule to use in a multifactor model? To simplify, let us consider a two-factor world, and let us call the two factor portfolios M and H. Then we generalize the index model to

$$r_i - r_f = \beta_{iM}(r_M - r_f) + \beta_{iH}(r_H - r_f) + \alpha_i + e_i$$
$$= r_\beta + \alpha_i + e_i \tag{28.10}$$

β_{iM} and β_{iH} are the betas of the security relative to portfolios M and H. Given the rates of return on the factor portfolios, r_M and r_H, the fair excess rate of return over r_f on a security is denoted r_β and its expected abnormal return is α_i.

How can we use equation 28.10 to form optimal portfolios? Suppose that investors wish to maximize the Sharpe measures of their portfolios. The factor structure of equation 28.10 can be used to generate the inputs for the Markowitz portfolio selection algorithm. The variance and covariance estimates are now more complex, however:

$$\sigma^2(r_i) = \beta_{iM}^2\sigma_M^2 + \beta_{iH}^2\sigma_H^2 + 2\beta_{iM}\beta_{iH}\text{Cov}(r_M, r_H) + \sigma^2(e_i)$$
$$\text{Cov}(r_i, r_j) = \beta_{iM}\beta_{jM}\sigma_M^2 + \beta_{iH}\beta_{jH}\sigma_H^2 + (\beta_{iM}\beta_{jH} + \beta_{jM}\beta_{iH})\text{Cov}(r_M, r_H)$$

Nevertheless, the informational economy of the factor model still is valuable, because we can estimate a covariance matrix for an *n*-security portfolio from

n estimates of β_{iM}

n estimates of β_{iH}

n estimates of $\sigma^2(e_i)$

1 estimate of σ_M^2

1 estimate of σ_H^2

rather than $n(n + 1)/2$ separate variance and covariance estimates. Thus the factor structure continues to simplify portfolio construction issues.

The factor structure also suggests an efficient method to allocate research effort. Analysts can specialize in forecasting means and variances of different factor portfolios. Having established factor betas, they can form a covariance matrix to be used together with expected security returns generated by the CAPM or APT to construct an optimal passive risky portfolio. If active analysis of individual stocks also is attempted, the procedure of constructing the optimal active portfolio and its optimal combination with the passive portfolio is identical to that followed in the single-factor case.

In the case of the multifactor market even passive investors (meaning those who accept market prices as "fair") need to do a considerable amount of work. They need forecasts of the expected return and volatility of each factor return, *and* they need to determine the appropriate weights on each factor portfolio to maximize their expected utility. Such a process is straightforward in principle, but it quickly becomes computationally demanding.

28.6   IMPERFECT FORECASTS OF ALPHA VALUES AND THE USE OF THE TREYNOR-BLACK MODEL IN INDUSTRY

Estimating alphas is much more difficult than estimating beta and residual variance. Competition among analysts is expected to constantly drive alpha values toward zero. As a result, past abnormal returns on securities do not persist, and extrapolation methods are therefore ineffective. New information is needed for each new forecast. No such force operates on the correlation of a stock with the market index or on its variance. Statistical methods can be utilized quite effectively to forecast stock beta and residual variance from past data. As a result, we expect greater precision in forecasts of beta and residual variance. Thus we must address the issue of quality of alpha forecasts.

The accuracy of analyst forecasts can be monitored and the statistical properties of the errors can be used to improve future forecasts. Suppose we use the history of forecasted alphas predicted by an analyst to estimate the following regression (where a hat over a variable denotes an estimated variable):

$$\text{Abnormal return} = r - [r_f + \hat{\beta}(r_M - r_f)] = \alpha + e = a + b\hat{\alpha} + \hat{e} \qquad (28.11a)$$

and we use the estimated equation to adjust future forecasts by

$$\text{Adjusted forecasts} = \alpha^* = a + b\hat{\alpha} \qquad (28.11b)$$

Equations 28.11 are in linear form with a bias coefficient, *a*, and a precision coefficient, *b*. A more general form would be a straightforward extension. In equations 28.11a and b,

$\hat{\beta}$ is the forecast of beta corresponding to the alpha forecast. Notice that given the forecasts $\hat{\alpha}$ and $\hat{\beta}$, $\hat{e}$ is the stock residual, and its variance—the residual variance of the regression—is to be used in the optimization procedure.

The intercept in equation 28.11 corrects for bias: excessive optimism if a is negative or excessive pessimism if a is positive. Suppose the correlation coefficient between α and $\hat{\alpha}$ is ρ. The slope coefficient of the regression can then be written as

$$b = \frac{\text{Cov}(\alpha + e, \hat{\alpha})}{\sigma^2(\hat{\alpha})} = \frac{\text{Cov}(\alpha, \hat{\alpha})\sigma(\alpha)}{\sigma(\alpha)\sigma^2(\hat{\alpha})} = \rho\frac{\sigma(\alpha)}{\sigma(\hat{\alpha})} \qquad (28.12)$$

This equation corrects for precision. The adjustment is proportional to the correlation coefficient between forecasts and realizations and to the variation in true alphas relative to forecasts. Equation 28.11b is applied to the raw forecast and the resulting adjusted alpha is used in constructing the active portfolio. Since the prior expectation for α (in the absence of security analysis) is zero, the precision coefficient, b in equation 28.12, is in effect the weight we use to average the forecast of alpha with our prior expectation of zero. To obtain a higher weight and thus more effectively contribute to a better portfolio, a forecaster needs to increase the correlation between forecasts and actual abnormal returns.

The resistance to implementation of the Treynor-Black model in industry arises in part from the need to require analysts to submit numerical forecasts and subject them to regular tests of bias and precision. It is only natural that analysts would object strenuously to the risk of being judged ineffective. Moreover, tests are bound to show low precision of alpha forecasts, which could make analysts uncomfortable. However, even low precision can contribute handsomely to superior performance and justify a very handsome analyst salary. One hopes that portfolio managers in time will recognize the power of this methodology.

The inevitably low forecast precision also adds to scale economies in portfolio management, since it is necessary to cover many securities to achieve superior performance. Moreover, the econometric work of estimating betas and residual variance, and of analyzing the quality of analysts' forecasts, is not very sensitive to the number of securities covered.

SUMMARY

1. A truly passive portfolio strategy entails holding the market-index portfolio and a money market fund. Determining the optimal allocation to the market portfolio requires an estimate of its expected return and variance, which in turn suggests delegating some analysis to professionals.

2. Active portfolio managers attempt to construct a risky portfolio that maximizes the reward-to-variability (Sharpe) ratio.

3. The value of perfect market timing ability is considerable. The rate of return to a perfect market timer will be uncertain. However, its risk characteristics are not measurable by standard measures of portfolio risk, because perfect timing dominates a passive strategy, providing "good" surprises only.

4. Perfect timing ability is equivalent to the possession of a call option on the market portfolio, whose value can be determined using option valuation techniques such as the Black-Scholes formula.

5. With imperfect timing, the value of a timer who attempts to forecast whether stocks will outperform bills is given by the conditional probabilities of the true outcome given the forecasts $P_1 + P_2 - 1$. Thus if the value of perfect timing is given by the option value, C, then imperfect timing has the value $(P_1 + P_2 - 1)C$.

6. The Treynor-Black security selection model envisions that a macroeconomic forecast for market performance is available and that security analysts estimate abnormal expected rates of return, α, for various securities. Alpha is the expected rate of return on a security beyond that explained by its beta and the security market line.

7. In the Treynor-Black model the weight of each analyzed security is proportional to the ratio of its alpha to its nonsystematic risk, $\sigma^2(e)$.

8. Once the active portfolio is constructed, its alpha value, nonsystematic risk, and beta can be determined from the properties of the component securities. The optimal risky portfolio, P, is then constructed by holding a position in the active portfolio according to the ratio of α_A to $\sigma^2(e_A)$, divided by the analogous ratio for the market-index portfolio. Finally, this position is adjusted by the beta of the active portfolio.

9. When the overall risky portfolio is constructed using the optimal proportions of the active portfolio and passive portfolio, its performance, as measured by the square of Sharpe's measure, is improved (over that of the passive, market-index, portfolio) by the amount $[\alpha_A/\sigma(e_A)]^2$.

10. The contribution of each security to the overall improvement in the performance of the active portfolio is determined by its degree of mispricing and nonsystematic risk. The contribution of each security to portfolio performance equals $[\alpha_i/\sigma(e_i)]^2$, so that for the optimal risky portfolio,

$$S_P^2 = \left[\frac{E(r_M) - r_f}{\sigma_M}\right]^2 + \sum_{i=1}^{n}\left[\frac{\alpha_i}{\sigma(e_i)}\right]^2$$

11. Applying the Treynor-Black model to a multifactor framework is straightforward. The forecast of the market-index mean and standard deviation must be replaced with forecasts for an optimized passive portfolio based on the multifactor model equation. The proportions of the factor portfolios are calculated using the familiar efficient frontier program. The active portfolio is constructed on the basis of residuals from the multifactor model, in the same way a single-index model is.

12. Implementing the model with imperfect forecasts requires estimation of bias and precision of raw forecasts. The adjusted forecast is obtained by applying the estimated coefficients to the raw forecasts.

Key Terms	Sharpe's measure	passive portfolio	appraisal ratio
	market timing	active portfolio	

Selected Readings

The valuation of market timing ability using the option-pricing framework was developed in:
  Merton, Robert C. "On Market Timing and Investment Performance: An Equilibrium Theory of Value for Market Forecasts." *Journal of Business,* July 1981.
The Treynor-Black model was laid out in:
  Treynor, Jack; and Fischer Black. "How to Use Security Analysis to Improve Portfolio Selection." *Journal of Business,* January 1973.
The applicability of the model is demonstrated in:
  Ambachtsheen, Keith. "Profit Potential in an Almost Efficient Market." *Journal of Portfolio Management,* Fall 1974.

Problems

1. The five-year history of annual rates of return in excess of the T-bill rate for two competing stock funds is

The Bull Fund	The Unicorn Fund
−21.7%	−1.3%
28.7	15.5
17.0	14.4
2.9	−11.9
28.9	25.4

   a. How would these funds compare in the eye of a risk-neutral potential client?
   b. How would these funds compare by Sharpe's measure?
   c. If a risk-averse investor (with a coefficient of risk aversion $A = 3$) had to choose one of these funds to mix with T-bills, which fund should he choose, and how much should be invested in that fund on the basis of available data?

2. Historical data suggest that the standard deviation of an all-equity strategy is about 5.5% per month. Suppose that the risk-free rate is now 1% per month and that market volatility is at its historical level. What would be a fair monthly fee to a perfect market timer, based on the Black-Scholes formula?

3. In scrutinizing the record of two market timers, a fund manager comes up with the following table:

Number of months that $r_M > r_f$	135	
Correctly predicted by timer *A*		78
Correctly predicted by timer *B*		86
Number of months that $r_M < r_f$	92	
Correctly predicted by timer *A*		57
Correctly predicted by timer *B*		50

   a. What are the conditional probabilities, P_1 and P_2, and the total ability parameters for timers *A* and *B*?
   b. Using the historical data of problem 2, what is a fair monthly fee for the two timers?

4. A portfolio manager summarizes the input from the macro and micro forecasters in the following table:

	Micro Forecasts		
Asset	Expected Return (%)	Beta	Residual Standard Deviation (%)
Stock A	20	1.3	58
Stock B	18	1.8	71
Stock C	17	0.7	60
Stock D	12	1.0	55

	Macro Forecasts	
Asset	Expected Return (%)	Standard Deviation (%)
T-bills	8	0
Passive equity portfolio	16	23

    a. Calculate expected excess returns, alpha values, and residual variances for these stocks.

    b. Construct the optimal risky portfolio.

    c. What is Sharpe's measure for the optimal portfolio and how much of it is contributed by the active portfolio? What is the M^2?

    d. What should be the exact makeup of the complete portfolio for an investor with a coefficient of risk aversion of 2.8?

5. Recalculate problem 4 for a portfolio manager who is not allowed to short-sell securities.

    a. What is the cost of the restriction in terms of Sharpe's measure and M^2?

    b. What is the utility loss to the investor ($A = 2.8$) given his new complete portfolio?

6. A portfolio management house approximates the return-generating process by a two-factor model and uses two factor portfolios to construct its passive portfolio. The input table that is constructed by the house analysts looks as follows:

Micro Forecasts			
Asset	**Expected Return (%)**	**Beta on *M***	**Beta on *H***	**Residual Standard Deviation (%)**
Stock A	20	1.2	1.8	58
Stock B	18	1.4	1.1	71
Stock C	17	0.5	1.5	60
Stock D	12	1.0	0.2	55

Macro Forecasts		
Asset	**Expected Return (%)**	**Standard Deviation (%)**
T-bills	8	0
Factor *M* portfolio	16	23
Factor *H* portfolio	10	18

The correlation coefficient between the two factor portfolios is .6.

    a. What is the optimal passive portfolio?

    b. By how much is the optimal passive portfolio superior to the single-factor passive portfolio, *M,* in terms of Sharpe's measure?

    c. Analyze the utility improvement to the $A = 2.8$ investor relative to holding portfolio *M* as the sole risky asset that arises from the expanded macro model of the portfolio manager.

7. Construct the optimal active and overall risky portfolio with the data of problem 6 with no restrictions on short sales.

    a. What is the Sharpe measure of the optimal risky portfolio and what is the contribution of the active portfolio?

    b. Analyze the utility value of the optimal risky portfolio for the $A = 2.8$ investor. Compare to that of problem 6.

8. Recalculate problem 7 with a short-sale restriction. Compare the results to those from problem 7.

9. Suppose that based on the analyst's past record, you estimate that the relationship between forecast and actual alpha is:

$$\text{Actual abnormal return} = .3 \times \text{Forecast of alpha}$$

Use the alphas from problem 4. How much is expected performance affected by recognizing the imprecision of alpha forecasts?

solutions to
Concept
CHECKS

1. We show the answer for the annual compounded rate of return for each strategy and leave the monthly rate for you to compute.
   Beginning-of-period fund:

$$F_0 = \$1,000$$

End-of-period fund for each strategy:

$$F_1 = \begin{cases} \$3,600 & \text{Strategy} = \text{Bills only} \\ \$67,500 & \text{Strategy} = \text{Market only} \\ \$5,360,000,000 & \text{Strategy} = \text{Perfect timing} \end{cases}$$

Number of periods: $N = 52$ years
Annual compounded rate:

$$[1 + r_A]^N = \frac{F_1}{F_0}$$

$$r_A = \left(\frac{F_1}{F_0}\right)^{1/N} - 1$$

$$r_A = \begin{cases} 2.49\% & \text{Strategy} = \text{Bills only} \\ 8.44\% & \text{Strategy} = \text{Market only} \\ 34.71\% & \text{Strategy} = \text{Perfect timing} \end{cases}$$

2. The timer will guess bear or bull markets completely randomly. One-half of all bull markets will be preceded by a correct forecast, and similarly for bear markets. Hence $P_1 + P_2 - 1 = \frac{1}{2} + \frac{1}{2} - 1 = 0$.

3. *a.* When short positions are prohibited, the analysis is identical except that negative-alpha stocks are dropped from the list. In that case the sum of the ratios of alpha to residual variance for the remaining two stocks is .7895. This leads to the new composition of the active portfolio:

$$x_1 = .3457/.7895 = .4379$$
$$x_2 = .4438/.7895 = .5621$$

The alpha, beta, and residual standard deviation of the active portfolio are now

$$\alpha_A = .4379 \times .07 + .5621 \times .03 = .0475$$
$$\beta_A = .4379 \times 1.6 + .5621 \times .5 = .9817$$
$$\sigma(e_A) = [.4379^2 \times .45^2 + .5621^2 \times .26^2]^{1/2} = .2453$$

The cost of the short sale restriction is already apparent. The alpha has shrunk from 20.56% to 4.75%, while the reduction in the residual standard deviation is more moderate, from 82.62% to 24.53%. In fact, a negative-alpha stock is potentially more attractive than a positive-alpha one: Since most stocks are positively correlated, the negative position that is required for the negative-alpha stock creates a better diversified active portfolio.

The optimal allocation of the new active portfolio is

$$w_0 = \frac{.0475/.6019}{.08/.04} = .3946$$

$$w^* = \frac{.3946}{1 + (1 - .9817) \times .3946} = .3918$$

Here, too, the beta correction is essentially irrelevant because the portfolio beta is so close to 1.0.

Finally, the performance of the overall risky portfolio is estimated at

$$S_P^2 = .16 + \left[\frac{.0475}{.2453}\right]^2 = .1975; \qquad S_P = .44$$

It is clear that in this case we have lost about half of the original improvement in the Sharpe measure. Note, however, that this is an artifact of the limited coverage of the security analysis division. When more stocks are covered, then a good number of positive-alpha stocks will keep the residual risk of the active portfolio low. This is the key to extracting large gains from the active strategy.

We calculate the "Modigliani-square," or M^2 measure, as follows:

$$E(r_{P*}) = r_f + S_P \, \sigma_M = .07 + .44 \times .20 = .158 \text{ or } 15.8\%$$
$$M^2 = E(r_{P*}) - E(r_M) = 15.8\% - 15\% = 0.8\%$$

which is a bit less than half the M^2 value of the unconstrained portfolio.

b. When the forecast for the market-index portfolio is more optimistic, the position in the active portfolio will be smaller and the contribution of the active portfolio to the Sharpe measure of the risky portfolio will be of a smaller magnitude. In the original example the allocation to the active portfolio would be

$$w_0 = \frac{.2056/.6826}{.12/.04} = .1004$$

$$w^* = \frac{.1004}{1 + (1 - .9519) \times .1004} = .0999$$

Although the Sharpe measure of the market is now better, the improvement derived from security analysis is smaller:

$$S_P^2 = \left(\frac{.12}{.20}\right)^2 + \left(\frac{.2056}{.8262}\right)^2 = .4219$$
$$S_P = .65; \qquad S_M = .60$$

APPENDICES

QUANTITATIVE REVIEW

Students in management and investment courses typically come from a variety of backgrounds. Some, who have had strong quantitative training, may feel perfectly comfortable with formal mathematical presentation of material. Others, who have had less technical training, may easily be overwhelmed by mathematical formalism. Most students, however, will benefit from some coaching to make the study of investment easier and more efficient. If you had a good introductory quantitative methods course, and like the text that was used, you may want to refer to it whenever you feel in need of a refresher. If you feel uncomfortable with standard quantitative texts, this reference is for you. Our aim is to present the essential quantitative concepts and methods in a self-contained, nontechnical, and intuitive way. Our approach is structured in line with requirements for the CFA program. The material included is relevant to investment management by the ICFA, the Institute of Chartered Financial Analysts. We hope you find this appendix helpful. Use it to make your venture into investments more enjoyable. *Note:* If you do not already have a financial calculator, we strongly advise you get one. Many financial calculators have a statistical mode that allows you to compute expected values, standard deviations, and regressions with ease. Actually, working through the user manual is a helpful exercise by itself. If you are interested in investments, you should look at a financial calculator as a good initial investment.

A.1   PROBABILITY DISTRIBUTIONS

Statisticians talk about "experiments," or "trials," and refer to possible outcomes as "events." In a roll of a die, for example, the "elementary events" are the numbers 1 through 6. Turning up one side represents the most disaggregate *mutually exclusive* outcome. Other events are *compound,* that is, they consist of more than one elementary event, such as the result "odd number" or "less than 4." In this case "odd" and "less than 4" are not mutually exclusive. Compound events can be mutually exclusive outcomes, however, such as "less than 4" and "equal to or greater than 4."

In decision making, "experiments" are circumstances in which you contemplate a decision that will affect the set of possible events (outcomes) and their likelihood (probabilities). Decision theory calls for you to identify optimal decisions under various sets of circumstances (experiments), which you may do by determining losses from departures from optimal decisions.

When the outcomes of a decision (experiment) can be quantified, that is, when a numerical value can be assigned to each elementary event, the decision outcome is called a *random variable.* In the context of investment decision making, the random variable (the payoff to the investment decision) is denominated either in dollars or as a percentage rate of return.

The set or list of all possible values of a random variable, *with* their associated probabilities, is called the *probability distribution* of the random variable. Values that are impossible for the random variable to take on are sometimes listed with probabilities of zero. All possible elementary events are assigned values and probabilities, and thus the probabilities have to sum to 1.0.

Sometime the values of a random variable are *uncountable,* meaning that you cannot make a list of all possible values. For example, suppose you roll a ball on a line and report the distance it rolls before it comes to rest. Any distance is possible, and the precision of the report will depend on the need of the roller and/or the quality of the measuring device. Another uncountable random variable is one that describes the weight of a newborn baby. Any positive weight (with some upper bound) is possible.

We call uncountable probability distributions *continuous,* for the obvious reason that, at least within a range, the possible outcomes (those with positive probabilities) lie anywhere on a continuum of values. Because there is an infinite number of possible values for the random variable in any continuous distribution, such a probability distribution has to be described by a formula that relates the values of the random variable and their associated probabilities, instead of by a simple list of outcomes and probabilities. We discuss continuous distributions later in this section.

Even countable probability distributions can be complicated. For example, on the New York Stock Exchange stock prices are quoted in eighths. This means the price of a stock at some future date is a *countable* random variable. Probability distributions of countable random variables are called *discrete distributions.* Although a stock price cannot dip below zero, it has no upper bound. Therefore a stock price is a random variable that can take on infinitely many values, even though they are countable, and its discrete probability distribution will have to be given by a formula just like a continuous distribution.

There are random variables that are both discrete and finite. When the probability distribution of the relevant random variable is countable and finite, decision making is tractable and relatively easy to analyze. One example is the decision to call a coin toss "heads" or "tails," with a payoff of zero for guessing wrong and 1 for guessing right. The random variable of the decision to guess "heads" has a discrete, finite probability distribution. It can be written as

Event	Value	Probability
Heads	1	.5
Tails	0	.5

This type of analysis usually is referred to as *scenario analysis*. Because scenario analysis is relatively simple, it is used sometimes even when the actual random variable is infinite and uncountable. You can do this by specifying values and probabilities for a set of compound, yet exhaustive and mutually exclusive, events. Because it is simple and has important uses, we handle this case first.

Here is a problem from the 1988 CFA examination.

Mr. Arnold, an Investment Committee member, has confidence in the forecasting ability of the analysts in the firm's research department. However, he is concerned that analysts may not appreciate risk as an important investment consideration. This is especially true in an increasingly volatile investment environment. In addition, he is conservative and risk averse. He asks for your risk analysis for Anheuser-Busch stock.

1. Using Table A.1, calculate the following measures of dispersion of returns for Anheuser-Busch stock under each of the three outcomes displayed. Show calculations.
  a. Range.
  b. Variance: $\Sigma \Pr(i)[r_i - E(r)]^2$.
  c. Standard deviation.
  d. Coefficient of variation: $CV = \sigma/E(r)$.
2. Discuss the usefulness of each of the four measures listed in quantifying risk.

The examination questions require very specific answers. We use the questions as framework for exposition of scenario analysis.

Table A.1 specifies a three-scenario decision problem. The random variable is the rate of return on investing in Anheuser-Busch stock. However, the third column, which specifies the value of the random variable, does not say simply "Return"—it says "Expected Return." This tells us that the scenario description is a compound event consisting of many elementary events, as is almost always the case. We streamline or simplify reality in order to gain tractability.

Analysts who prepare input lists must decide on the number of scenarios with which to describe the entire probability distribution, as well as the rates of return to allocate to each one. This process calls for determining the probability of occurrence of each scenario, *and* the expected rate of return *within* (conditional on) each scenario, which governs the out-

Table A.1   Anheuser-Busch Companies, Inc.,
            Dispersion of Potential Returns

Outcome	Probability	Expected Return*
Number 1	.20	20%
Number 2	.50	30
Number 3	.30	50

*Assume for the moment that the expected return in each scenario will be realized with certainty. This is the way returns were expressed in the original question.

come of each scenario. Once you become familiar with scenario analysis, you will be able to build a simple scenario description from any probability distribution.

Expected Returns

The expected value of a random variable is the answer to the question, "What would be the average value of the variable if the 'experiment' (the circumstances and the decision) were repeated infinitely?" In the case of an investment decision, your answer is meant to describe the reward from making the decision.

Note that the question is hypothetical and abstract. It is hypothetical because, practically, the exact circumstances of a decision (the "experiment") often cannot be repeated even once, much less infinitely. It is abstract because, even if the experiment were to be repeated many times (short of infinitely), the *average* rate of return may not be one of the possible outcomes. To demonstrate, suppose that the probability distribution of the rate of return on a proposed investment project is +20% or –20%, with equal probabilities of .5. Intuition indicates that repeating this investment decision will get us ever closer to an average rate of return of zero. But a one-time investment cannot produce a rate of return of zero. Is the "expected" return still a useful concept when the proposed investment represents a one-time decision?

One argument for using expected return to measure the reward from making investment decisions is that, although a specific investment decision may be made only once, the decision maker will be making many (although different) investment decisions over time. Over time, then, the average rate of return will come close to the average of the expected values of all the individual decisions. Another reason for using the expected value is that admittedly we lack a better measure.[1]

The probabilities of the scenarios in Table A.1 predict the relative frequencies of the outcomes. If the current investment in Anheuser-Busch could be replicated many times, a 20% return would occur 20% of the time, a 30% return would occur 50% of the time, and 50% return would occur the remaining 30% of the time. This notion of probabilities and the definition of the expected return tells us how to calculate the expected return.[2]

$$E(r) = .20 \times .20 + .50 \times .30 + .30 \times .50 = .34 \text{ (or } 34\%)$$

Labeling each scenario $i = 1, 2, 3$, and using the summation sign, Σ, we can write the formula for the expected return:

$$E(r) = \Pr(1)r_1 + \Pr(2)r_2 + \Pr(3)r_3 \qquad \text{(A.1)}$$
$$= \sum_{i=1}^{3} \Pr(i)r_i$$

The definition of the expectation in equation A.1 reveals two important properties of random variables. First, if you add a constant to a random variable, its expectation is also increased by the same constant. If, for example, the return in each scenario in Table A.1 were increased by 5%, the expectation would increase to 39%. Try this, using equation A.1. If a random variable is multiplied by a constant, its expectation will change by that same proportion. If you multiply the return in each scenario by 1.5, $E(r)$ would change to $1.5 \times .34 = .51$ (or 51%).

---

[1] Another case where we use a less-than-ideal measure is the case of yield to maturity on a bond. The YTM measures the rate of return from investing in a bond *if* it is held to maturity and *if* the coupons can be reinvested at the same yield to maturity over the life of the bond.

[2] We will consistently perform calculations in decimal fractions to avoid confusion.

Second, the deviation of a random variable from its expected value is itself a random variable. Take any rate of return r_1 in Table A.1 and define its deviation from the expected value by

$$d_i = r_i - E(r)$$

What is the expected value of d? $E(d)$ is the expected deviation from the expected value, and by equation A.1 it is necessarily zero because

$$E(d) = \Sigma \operatorname{Pr}(i)d_i = \Sigma \operatorname{Pr}(i)[r_i - E(r)]$$
$$= \Sigma \operatorname{Pr}(i)r_i - E(r)\Sigma \operatorname{Pr}(i)$$
$$= E(r) - E(r) = 0$$

Measures of Dispersion

The Range   Assume for a moment that the expected return for each scenario in Table A.1 will be realized with certainty in the event that scenario occurs. Then the set of possible return outcomes is unambiguously 20%, 30%, and 50%. The *range* is the difference between the maximum and the minimum values of the random variable, 50% – 20% = 30% in this case. Range is clearly a crude measure of dispersion. Here it is particularly inappropriate because the scenario returns themselves are given as expected values, and therefore the true range is unknown. There is a variant of the range, the *interquartile range,* that we explain in the discussion of descriptive statistics.

The Variance   One interpretation of variance is that it measures the "expected surprises." Although that may sound like a contradiction in terms, it really is not. First, think of a surprise as a deviation from expectation. The surprise is not in the *fact* that expectation has not been realized, but rather in the *direction* and *magnitude* of the deviation.

The example in Table A.1 leads us to *expect* a rate of return of 34% from investing in Anheuser-Busch stock. A second look at the scenario returns, however, tells us that we should stand ready to be surprised because the probability of earning exactly 34% is zero. Being sure that our expectation will not be realized does not mean that we can be sure what the realization is going to be. The element of surprise lies in the direction and magnitude of the deviation of the actual return from expectation, and that is the relevant random variable for the measurement of uncertainty. Its probability distribution adds to our understanding of the nature of the uncertainty that we are facing.

We measure the reward by the expected return. Intuition suggests that we measure uncertainty by the expected *deviation* of the rate of return from expectation. We showed in the previous section, however, that the expected deviation from expectation must be zero. Positive deviations, when weighted by probabilities, are exactly offset by negative deviations. To get around this problem, we replace the random variable "deviation from expectations" (denoted earlier by d) with its square, which must be positive even if d itself is negative.

We define the *variance,* our measure of surprise or dispersion, by the *expected squared deviation of the rate of return from its expectation.* With the Greek letter sigma square denoting variance, the formal definition is

$$\sigma^2(r) = E(d^2) = E[r_i - E(r)]^2 = \Sigma \operatorname{Pr}(i)[r_i - E(r)]^2 \qquad (A.2)$$

Squaring each deviation eliminates the sign, which eliminates the offsetting effects of positive and negative deviations.

In the case of Anheuser-Busch, the variance of the rate of return on the stock is

$$\sigma^2(r) = .2(.20 - .34)^2 + .5(.30 - .34)^2 + .3(.50 - .34)^2 = .0124$$

Remember that if you add a constant to a random variable, the variance does not change at all. This is because the expectation also changes by the same constant, and hence deviations from expectation remain unchanged. You can test this by using the data from Table A.1.

Multiplying the random variable by a constant, however, *will* change the variance. Suppose that each return is multiplied by the factor k. The new random variable, kr, has expectation of $E(kr) = kE(r)$. Therefore, the deviation of kr from its expectation is

$$d(kr) = kr - E(kr) = kr - kE(r) = k[r - E(r)] = kd(r)$$

If each deviation is multiplied by k, the squared deviations are multiplied by the square of k:

$$\sigma^2(kr) = k^2\sigma^2(r)$$

To summarize, adding a constant to a random variable does not affect the variance. Multiplying a random variable by a constant, though, will cause the variance to be multiplied by the square of that constant.

The Standard Deviation   A closer look at the variance will reveal that its dimension is different from that of the expected return. Recall that we squared deviations from the expected return in order to make all values positive. This alters the *dimension* (units of measure) of the variance to "square percents." To transform the variance into terms of percentage return, we simply take the square root of the variance. This measure is the *standard deviation*. In the case of Anheuser-Busch's stock return, the standard deviation is

$$\sigma = (\sigma^2)^{1/2} = \sqrt{.0124} = .1114 \text{ (or } 11.14\%) \tag{A.3}$$

Note that you always need to calculate the variance first before you can get the standard deviation. The standard deviation conveys the same information as the variance but in a different form.

We know already that adding a constant to r will not affect its variance, and it will not affect the standard deviation either. We also know that multiplying a random variable by a constant multiplies the variance by the square of that constant. From the definition of the standard deviation in equation A.3, it should be clear that multiplying a random variable by a constant will multiply the standard deviation by the (absolute value of this) constant. The absolute value is needed because the sign of the constant is lost through squaring the deviations in the computation of the variance. Formally,

$$\sigma(kr) = \text{Abs}(k)\,\sigma(r)$$

Try a transformation of your choice using the data in Table A.1.

The Coefficient of Variation   To evaluate the magnitude of dispersion of a random variable, it is useful to compare it to the expected value. The ratio of the standard deviation to the expectation is called the *coefficient of variation*. In the case of returns on Anheuser-Busch stock, it is

$$CV = \frac{\sigma}{E(r)} = \frac{.1114}{.3400} = .3285 \tag{A.4}$$

The standard deviation of the Anheuser-Busch return is about one-third of the expected return (reward). Whether this value for the coefficient of variation represents a big risk depends on what can be obtained with alternative investments.

The coefficient of variation is far from an ideal measure of dispersion. Suppose that a plausible expected value for a random variable is zero. In this case, regardless of the magnitude of the standard deviation, the coefficient of variation will be infinite. Clearly, this measure is not applicable in all cases. Generally, the analyst must choose a measure of dispersion that fits the particular decision at hand. In finance, the standard deviation is the measure of choice in most cases where overall risk is concerned. (For individual assets, the measure β, explained in the text, is the measure used.)

Skewness

So far, we have described the measures of dispersion as indicating the size of the average surprise, loosely speaking. The standard deviation is not exactly equal to the average surprise though, because squaring deviations and then taking the square root of the average square deviation results in greater weight (emphasis) placed on larger deviations. Other than that, it is simply a measure that tells us how big a deviation from expectation can be expected.

Most decision makers agree that the expected value and standard deviation of a random variable are the most important statistics. However, once we calculate them another question about risk (the nature of the random variable describing deviations from expectations) is pertinent: Are the larger deviations (surprises) more likely to be positive? Risk-averse decision makers worry about bad surprises, and the standard deviation does not distinguish good from bad ones. Most risk avoiders are believed to prefer random variables with likely *small negative surprises* and *less* likely *large positive surprises,* to the reverse, likely *small good surprises* and *less* likely *large bad surprises.* More than anything, risk is really defined by the possibility of disaster (large bad surprises).

One measure that distinguishes between the likelihood of large good-vs.-bad surprises is the "third moment." It builds on the behavior of deviations from the expectation, the random variable we have denoted by d. Denoting the *third moment* by M_3, we define it:

$$M_3 = E(d^3) = E[r_i - E(r)]^3 = \Sigma \operatorname{Pr}(i)[r_i - E(r)]^3 \qquad (A.5)$$

Cubing each value of d (taking it to the third power) magnifies larger deviations more than smaller ones. Raising values to an odd power causes them to retain their sign. Recall that the sum of all deviations multiplied by their probabilities is zero because positive deviations weighted by their probabilities exactly offset the negative. When *cubed* deviations are multiplied by their probabilities and then added up, however, large deviations will dominate. The sign will tell us in this case whether *large positive* deviations dominate (positive M_3) or whether *large negative* deviations dominate (negative M_3).

Incidentally, it is obvious why this measure of skewness is call the third moment; it refers to cubing. Similarly, the variance is often referred to as the second moment because it requires squaring.

Returning to the investment decision described in Table A.1, with the expected value of 34%, the third moment is

$$M_3 = .2(.20 - .34)^3 + .5(.30 - .34)^3 + .3(.50 - .34)^3 = .000648$$

The sign of the third moment tells us that larger *positive* surprises dominate in this case. You might have guessed this by looking at the deviations from expectation and their probabilities; that is, the most likely event is a return of 30%, which makes for a small negative surprise. The other negative surprise (20% − 34% = −14%) is smaller in magnitude than the positive surprise (50% − 34% = 16%) *and* is also *less* likely (probability .20) relative to the positive surprise, 30% (probability .30). The difference appears small, however, and we do not know whether the third moment may be an important issue for the decision to invest in Anheuser-Busch.

It is difficult to judge the importance of the third moment, here .000648, without a benchmark. Following the same reasoning we applied to the standard deviation, we can take the *third root* of M_3 (which we denote m_3) and compare it to the standard deviation. This yields $m_3 = .0865 = 8.65\%$, which is not trivial compared with the standard deviation (11.14%).

Another Example: Options on Anheuser-Busch Stock

Suppose that the current price of Anheuser-Busch stock is $30. A call option on the stock is selling for 60 cents, and a put is selling for $4. Both have an exercise price of $42 and maturity date to match the scenarios in Table A.1.

The call option allows you to buy the stock at the exercise price. You will choose to do so if the call ends up "in the money," that is, the stock price is above the exercise price. The profit in this case is the difference between the stock price and the exercise price, less cost of the call. Even if you exercise the call, your profit may still be negative if the cash flow from the exercise of the call does not cover the initial cost of the call. If the call ends up "out of the money," that is, the stock price is below the exercise price, you will let the call expire worthless and suffer a loss equal to the cost of the call.

The put option allows you to sell the stock at the exercise price. You will choose to do so if the put ends up "in the money," that is, the stock price is below the exercise price. Your profit is then the difference between the exercise price and the stock price, less the initial cost of the put. Here again, if the cash flow is not sufficient to cover the cost of the put, the investment will show a loss. If the put ends up "out of the money," you again let it expire worthless, taking a loss equal to the initial cost of the put.

The scenario analysis of these alternative investments is described in Table A.2.

The expected rates of return on the call and put are

$$E(r_{call}) = .2(-1) + .5(-1) + .3(4) = .5 \text{ (or } 50\%)$$
$$E(r_{put}) = .2(.5) + .5(-.25) + .3(-1) = -.325 \text{ (or } -32.5\%)$$

Table A.2   Scenario Analysis for Investment in Options on Anheuser-Busch Stock

	Scenario 1	Scenario 2	Scenario 3
Probability	.20	.50	.30
Event			
1. Return on stock	20%	30%	50%
Stock price (initial price = $30)	$36.00	$39.00	$45.00
2. Cash flow from call (exercise price = $42)	0	0	$3.00
Call profit (initial price = $.60)	−$.60	−$.60	$2.40
Call rate of return	−100%	−100%	400%
3. Cash flow from put (exercise price = $42)	$6.00	$3.00	0
Put profit (initial price = $4)	$2.00	−$1.00	−$4.00
Put rate of return	50%	−25%	−100%

The negative expected return on the put may be justified by the fact that it is a hedge asset, in this case an insurance policy against losses from holding Anheuser-Busch stock. The variance and standard deviation of the two investments are

$$\sigma^2_{call} = .2(-1 - .5)^2 + .5(-1 - .5)^2 + .3(4 - .5)^2 = 5.25$$
$$\sigma^2_{put} = .2[.5 - (-.325)]^2 + .5[-.25 - (-.325)]^2 + .3[-1 - (-.325)]^2 = .2756$$
$$\sigma_{call} = \sqrt{5.25} = 2.2913 \text{ (or } 229.13\%)$$
$$\sigma_{put} = \sqrt{.2756} = .525 \text{ (or } 52.5\%)$$

These are very large standard deviations. Comparing the standard deviation of the call's return to its expected value, we get the coefficient of variation:

$$CV_{call} = \frac{2.2913}{.5} = 4.5826$$

Refer back to the coefficient of variation for the stock itself, .3275, and it is clear that these instruments have high standard deviations. This is quite common for stock options. The negative expected return of the put illustrates again the problem in interpreting the magnitude of the "surprise" indicated by the coefficient of variation.

Moving to the third moments of the two probability distributions:

$$M_3(call) = .2(-1 - .5)^3 + .5(-1 - .5)^3 + .3(4 - .5)^3 = 10.5$$
$$M_3(put) = .2[.5 - (-.325)]^3 + .5[-.25 - (-.325)]^3 + .3[-1 - (-.325)]^3$$
$$= .02025$$

Both instruments are positively skewed, which is typical of options and one part of their attractiveness. In this particular circumstance the call is more skewed than the put. To establish this fact, note the third root of the third moment:

$$m_3(call) = M_3(call)^{1/3} = 2.1898 \text{ (or } 218.98\%)$$
$$m_3(put) = .02^{1/3} = .2725 \text{ (or } 27.25\%)$$

Compare these figures to the standard deviations, 229.13% for the call and 52.5% for the put, and you can see that a large part of the standard deviation of the option is driven by the possibility of large good surprises instead of by the more likely, yet smaller, bad surprises.[3]

So far we have described discrete probability distributions using scenario analysis. We shall come back to decision making in a scenario analysis framework in Section A.3 on multivariate statistics.

Continuous Distributions: Normal and Lognormal Distributions

When a compact scenario analysis is possible and acceptable, decisions may be quite simple. Often, however, so many relevant scenarios must be specified that scenario analysis is impossible for practical reasons. Even in the case of Anheuser-Busch, as we were careful to specify, the individual scenarios considered actually represented compound events.

When many possible values of rate of return have to be considered, we must use a formula that describes the probability distribution (relates values to probabilities). As we noted earlier, there are two types of probability distributions: discrete and continuous.

---

[3]Note that the expected return of the put is –32.5%; hence the worst surprise is –67.5%, and the best is 82.5%. The middle scenario is also a positive deviation of 7.5% (with a high probability of .50). These two elements explain the positive skewness of the put.

Figure A.1
Probabilities under the
normal density.

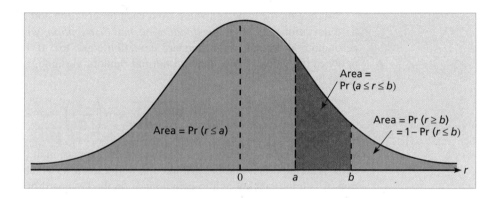

Scenario analysis involves a discrete distribution. However, the two most useful distributions in investments, the normal and lognormal, are continuous. At the same time they are often used to approximate variables with distributions that are known to be discrete, such as stock prices. The probability distribution of future prices and returns is discrete—prices are quoted in eighths. Yet the industry norm is to approximate these distributions by the normal or lognormal distribution.

Standard Normal Distribution   The normal distribution, also known as Gaussian (after the mathematician Gauss) or bell-shaped, describes random variables with the following properties and is shown in Figure A.1:

- The expected value is the mode (the most frequent elementary event) and also the median (the middle value in the sense that half the elementary events are greater and half smaller). Note that the expected value, unlike the median or mode, requires weighting by probabilities to produce the concept of central value.
- The normal probability distribution is symmetric around the expected value. In other words, the likelihood of equal absolute-positive and negative deviations from expectation is equal. Larger deviations from the expected value are less likely than are smaller deviations. In fact, the essence of the normal distribution is that the probability of deviations decreases exponentially with the magnitude of the deviation (positive and negative alike).
- A normal distribution is identified completely by two parameters, the expected value and the standard deviation. The property of the normal distribution that makes it most convenient for portfolio analysis is that any weighted sum or normally distributed random variables produce a random variable that also is normally distributed. This property is called *stability*. It is also true that if you add a constant to a "normal" random variable (meaning a random variable with a normal probability distribution) or multiply it by a constant, then the transformed random variable also will be normally distributed.

Suppose that n is any random variable (not necessarily normal) with expectation μ and standard deviation σ. As we showed earlier, if you add a constant c to n, the standard deviation is not affected at all, but the mean will change to $\mu + c$. If you multiply n by a constant b, its mean and standard deviation will change by the same proportion to $b\mu$ and $b\sigma$. If n is normal, the transformed variable also will be normal.

Stability, together with the property that a normal variable is completely characterized by its expectation and standard deviation, implies that if we know one normal probability distribution with a given expectation and standard deviation, we know them all.

Subtracting the expected value from each observation and then dividing by the standard deviation we obtain the *standard normal distribution,* which has an expectation of zero and both variance and standard deviation equal to 1.0. Formally, the relationship between the value of the standard normal random variable, z, and its probability, f, is given by

$$f(z) = \frac{1}{\sqrt{2\pi}} \exp\left(\frac{-z^2}{2}\right) \tag{A.6}$$

where "exp" is the quantity e to the power of the expression in the parentheses. The quantity e is an important number just like the well-known π, which also appears in the function. It is important enough to earn a place on the keyboard of your financial calculator, mostly because it is used also in continuous compounding.

Probability functions of continuous distributions are called *densities* and denoted by f, rather than by the "Pr" of scenario analysis. The reason is that the probability of any of the infinitely many possible values of z is infinitesimally small. Density is a function that allows us to obtain the probability of a *range of values* by integrating it over a desired range. In other words, whenever we want the probability that a standard normal variate (a random variable) will fall in the range from $z = a$ to $z = b$, we have to add up the density values, $f(z)$, for all zs from a to b. There are infinitely many zs in that range, regardless how close a is to b. *Integration* is the mathematical operation that achieves this task.

Consider first the probability that a standard normal variate will take on a value less than or equal to a, that is, z is in the range $[-\infty, a]$. We have to integrate the density from ∞ to a. The result is called the *cumulative (normal) distribution,* denoted by $N(a)$. When a approaches infinity, any value is allowed for z; hence the probability that z will end up in that range approaches 1.0. It is a property of any density that when it is integrated over the entire range of the random variable, the cumulative distribution is 1.0.

In the same way, the probability that a standard normal variate will take on a value less than or equal to b is $N(b)$. The probability that a standard normal variate will take on a value in the range $[a, b]$ is just the difference between $N(b)$ and $N(a)$. Formally,

$$\Pr(a \leq z \leq b) = N(b) - N(a)$$

These concepts are illustrated in Figure A.1. The graph shows the normal density. It demonstrates the symmetry of the normal density around the expected value (zero for the standard normal variate, which is also the mode and the median), and the smaller likelihood of larger deviations from expectation. As is true for any density, the entire area under the density graph adds up to 1.0. The values a and b are chosen to be positive, so they are to the right of the expected value. The leftmost blue shaded area is the proportion of the area under the density for which the value of z is less than or equal to a. Thus this area yields the cumulative distribution for a, the probability that z will be smaller than or equal to a. The gray shaded area is the area under the density graph between a and b. If we add that area to the cumulative distribution of a, we get the entire area up to b, that is, the probability that z will be anywhere to the left of b. Thus the area between a and b has to be the probability that z will fall between a and b.

Applying the same logic, we find the probability that z will take on a value greater than b. We know already that the probability that z will be smaller than or equal to b is $N(b)$. The compound events "smaller than or equal to b" and "greater than b" are mutually exclusive *and* "exhaustive," meaning that they include all possible outcomes. Thus their probabilities sum to 1.0, and the probability that z is greater than b is simply equal to one minus the probability that z is less than or equal to b. Formally, $\Pr(z > b) = 1 - N(b)$.

Figure A.2

Probabilities and the
cumulative normal
distribution.

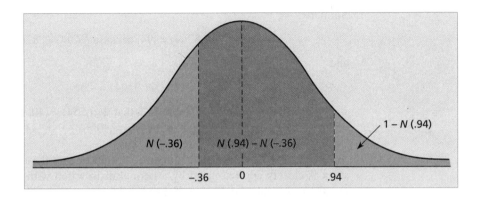

Look again at Figure A.1. The area under the density graph between b and infinity is just the difference between the entire area under the graph (equal to 1.0) and the area between minus infinity and b, that is, $N(b)$.

The normal density is sufficiently complex that its cumulative distribution, its integral, does not have an exact formulaic closed-form solution. It must be obtained by numerical (approximation) methods. These values are produced in tables that give the value $N(z)$ for any z, such as Table 21.2 of this text.

To illustrate, let us find the following probabilities for a standard normal variate:

$$\Pr(z \leq -.36) = N(-.36) = \text{Probability that } z \text{ is less than or equal to } -.36$$
$$\Pr(z \leq .94) = N(.94) = \text{Probability that } z \text{ is less than or equal to } .94$$
$$\Pr(-.36 \leq z \leq .94) = N(.94) - N(-.36) = \text{Probability that } z \text{ will be in the range } [-.36, .94]$$
$$\Pr(z > .94) = 1 - N(.94) = \text{Probability that } z \text{ is greater than } .94$$

Use Table 21.2 of the cumulative standard normal (sometimes called the area under the normal density) and Figure A.2. The table shows that

$$N(-.36) = .3594$$
$$N(.94) = .8264$$

In Figure A.2 the area under the graph between $-.36$ and $.94$ is the probability that z will fall between $-.36$ and $.94$. Hence

$$\Pr(-.36 \leq z \leq .94) = N(.94) - N(-.36) = .8264 - .3594 = .4670$$

The probability that z is greater than $.94$ is the area under the graph in Figure A.2, between $.94$ and infinity. Thus it is equal to the entire area (1.0) less the area from minus infinity to $.94$. Hence

$$\Pr(z > .94) = 1 - N(.94) = 1 - .8264 = .1736$$

Finally, one can ask, What is the value a for which z will be smaller than or equal to a with probability P? The notation for the function that yields the desired value of a is $\Phi(P)$, so that

$$\text{If } \Phi(P) = a, \text{ then } P = N(a) \tag{A.7}$$

For instance, suppose the question is, Which value has a cumulative density of $.50$? A glance at Figure A.2 reminds us that the area between minus infinity and zero (the expected value) is $.5$. Thus we can write

$$\Phi(.5) = 0, \text{ because } N(0) = .5$$

Similarly,

$$\Phi(.8264) = .94, \text{ because } N(.94) = .8264$$

and

$$\Phi(.3594) = -.36$$

For practice, confirm with Table 21.2 that $\Phi(.6554) = .40$, meaning that the value of z with a cumulative distribution of .6554 is $z = .40$.

Nonstandard Normal Distributions   Suppose that the monthly rate of return on a stock is closely approximated by a normal distribution with a mean of .015 (1.5% per month), and standard deviation of .127 (12.7% per month). What is the probability that the rate of return will fall below zero in a given month? Recall that because the rate is a normal variate, its cumulative density has to be computed by numerical methods. The standard normal table can be used for any normal variate.

Any random variable, x, may be transformed into a new standardized variable, x^*, by the following rule:

$$x^* = \frac{x - E(x)}{\sigma(x)} \tag{A.8}$$

Note that all we have done to x was (1) *subtract* its expectation and (2) *multiply* by one over its standard deviation, $1/[\sigma(x)]$. According to our earlier discussion, the effect of transforming a random variable by adding and multiplying by a constant is such that the expectation and standard deviation of the transformed variable are

$$E(x^*) = \frac{E(x) - E(x)}{\sigma(x)} = 0; \qquad \sigma(x^*) = \frac{\sigma(x)}{\sigma(x)} = 1 \tag{A.9}$$

From the stability property of the normal distribution we also know that if x is normal, so is x^*. A normal variate is characterized completely by two parameters: its expectation and standard deviation. For x^*, these are zero and 1.0, respectively. When we subtract the expectation and then divide a normal variate by its standard deviation, we standardize it; that is, we transform it to a standard normal variate. This trick is used extensively in working with normal (and approximately normal) random variables.

Returning to our stock, we have learned that if we subtract .015 and then divide the monthly returns by .127, the resultant random variable will be standard normal. We can now determine the probability that the rate of return will be zero or less in a given month. We know that

$$z = \frac{r - .015}{.127}$$

where z is standard normal and r the return on our stock. Thus if r is zero, z has to be

$$z(r = 0) = \frac{0 - .015}{.127} = -.1181$$

For r to be zero, the corresponding standard normal has to be -11.81%, a negative number. The event "r will be zero or less" is identical to the event "z will be $-.1181$ or less." Calculating the probability of the latter will solve our problem. That probability is simply $N(-.1181)$. Visit the standard normal table and find that

$$\Pr(r \leq 0) = N(-.1181) = .5 - .047 = .453$$

The answer makes sense. Recall that the expectation of r is 1.5%. Thus, whereas the probability that r will be 1.5% or less is .5, the probability that it will be *zero* or less has to be close, but somewhat lower.

Confidence Intervals   Given the large standard deviation of our stock, it is logical to be concerned about the likelihood of extreme values for the monthly rate of return. One way to quantify this concern is to ask: "What is the interval (range) within which the stock return will fall in a given month, with a probability of .95?" Such an interval is called the *95% confidence interval.*

Logic dictates that this interval be centered on the expected value, .015, because r is a normal variate (has a normal distribution) which is symmetric around the expectation. Denote the desired interval by

$$[E(r) - a, E(r) + a] = [.015 - a, .015 + a]$$

which has a length of $2a$. The probability that r will fall within this interval is described by the following expression:

$$\Pr(.015 - a \leq r \leq .015 + a) = .95$$

To find this probability, we start with a simpler problem, involving the *standard normal variate,* that is, a normal with expectation of zero and standard deviation of 1.0.

What is the 95% confidence interval for the standard normal variate, z? The variable will be centered on zero, so the expression is

$$\Pr(-a^* \leq z \leq a^*) = N(a^*) - N(-a^*) = .95$$

You might best understand the substitution of the difference of the appropriate cumulative distributions for the probability with the aid of Figure A.3. The probability of falling outside of the interval is $1 - .95 = .05$. By the symmetry of the normal distribution, z will be equal to or less than $-a^*$ with probability of .025, and with probability .025, z will be greater than a^*. Thus we solve for a^* using

$$-a^* = \Phi(.025), \text{ which is equivalent to } N(-a^*) = .025$$

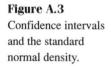

Figure A.3
Confidence intervals
and the standard
normal density.

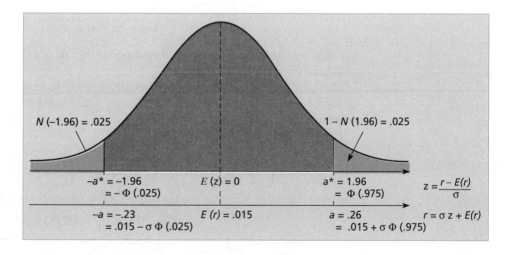

We can summarize the chain that we have pursued so far as follows. If we seek a $P = .95$ level confidence interval, we define α as the probability that r will fall outside the confidence interval. Because of the symmetry, α will be split so that half of it is the probability of falling to the right of the confidence interval, while the other half is the probability of falling to the left of the confidence interval. Therefore, the relation between α and P is

$$\alpha = 1 - P = .05; \qquad \frac{\alpha}{2} = \frac{1 - P}{2} = .025$$

We use $\alpha/2$ to indicate that the area that is excluded for r is equally divided between the tails of the distributions. Each tail that is excluded for r has an area of $\alpha/2$. The value $\alpha = 1 - P$ represents the entire value that is excluded for r.

To find $z = \Phi(\alpha/2)$, which is the lower boundary of the confidence interval for the standard normal variate, we have to locate the z value for which the standard normal cumulative distribution is .025, finding $z = -1.96$. Thus we conclude that $-a^* = -1.96$ and $a^* = 1.96$. The confidence interval for z is

$$[E(z) - \Phi(\alpha/2), E(z) + \Phi(\alpha/2)] = [-\Phi(.025), \Phi(.025)]$$
$$= [-1.96, .196]$$

To get the interval boundaries for the nonstandard normal variate r, we transform the boundaries for z by the usual relationship, $r = z\sigma(r) + E(r) = \Phi(\alpha/2)\sigma(r) + E(r)$. Note that all we are doing is setting the expectation at the center of the confidence interval and extending it by a number of standard deviations. The number of standard deviations is determined by the probability that we allow for falling outside the confidence interval (α), or, equivalently, the probability of falling in it (P). Using minus and plus 1.96 for $z = \pm \Phi(\emptyset.25)$, the distance on each side of the expectation is $\pm 1.96 \times .127 = .249$. Thus we obtain the confidence interval

$$[E(r) - \sigma(r)\Phi(\alpha/2), E(r) + \sigma(r)\Phi(\alpha/2)] = [E(r) - .249, E(r) + .249]$$
$$= [-.234, .264]$$

so that

$$P = 1 - \alpha = \Pr[E(r) - \sigma(r)\Phi(\alpha/2) \leq r \leq E(r) + \sigma(r)\Phi(\alpha/2)]$$

which, for our stock (with expectation .015 and standard deviation .127), amounts to

$$\Pr[-.234 \leq r \leq .264] = .95$$

Note that because of the large standard deviation of the rate of return on the stock, the 95% confidence interval is 49% wide.

To reiterate with a variation on this example, suppose we seek a 90% confidence interval for the annual rate of return on a portfolio, r_p, with a monthly expected return of 1.2% and standard deviation of 5.2%.

The solution is simply

$$\Pr\left[E(r) - \sigma(r)\,\Phi\left(\frac{1-P}{2}\right) \leq r_p \leq E(r) + \sigma(r)\,\Phi\left(\frac{1-P}{2}\right)\right]$$
$$= \Pr[.012 - .052 \times 1.645) \leq r_p \leq .012 + .052 \times 1.645)]$$
$$= \Pr[-.0735 \leq r_p \leq .0975] = .90$$

Because the portfolio is of low risk this time (and we require only a 90% rather than a 95% probability of falling within the interval, the 90% confidence interval is only 2.4% wide.

The Lognormal Distribution   The normal distribution is not adequate to describe stock prices and returns for two reasons. First, whereas the normal distribution admits any value, including negative values, actual stock prices cannot be negative. Second, the normal distribution does not account for compounding. The lognormal distribution addresses these two problems.

The lognormal distribution describes a random variable that grows, *every instant,* by a rate that is a normal random variable. Thus the progression of a lognormal random variable reflects continuous compounding.

Suppose that the *annual continuously compounded* (ACC) rate of return on a stock is normally distributed with expectation $\mu = .12$ and standard deviation $\sigma = .42$. The stock price at the beginning of the year is $P_0 = \$10$. With continuous compounding (see appendix to Chapter 5), if the ACC rate of return, r_C, turns out to be .23, then the end-of-year price will be

$$P_1 = P_0 \exp(r_C) = 10e^{.23} = \$12.586$$

representing an effective annual rate of return of

$$r = \frac{P_1 - P_0}{P_0} = e^{r_C} - 1 = .2586 \text{ (or } 25.86\%)$$

This is the practical meaning of r, the annual rate on the stock, being lognormally distributed. Note that however negative the ACC rate of return (r_C) is, the price, P_1, cannot become negative.

Two properties of lognormally distributed financial assets are important: their expected return and the allowance for changes in measurement period.

Expected Return of a Lognormally Distributed Asset   The expected annual rate of return of a lognormally distributed stock (as in our example) is

$$E(r) = \exp(\mu + \sigma^2/2) - 1 = \exp(.12 + .42^2/2) - 1 = e^{.2082} - 1$$
$$= .2315 \text{ (or } 23.15\%)$$

This is just a statistical property of the distribution. For this reason, a useful statistic is

$$\mu^* = \mu + \sigma^2/2 = .2082$$

When analysts refer to the expected ACC return on a lognormal asset, frequently they are really referring to μ^*. Often the asset is said to have a normal distribution of the ACC return with expectation μ^* and standard deviation σ.

Change of Frequency of Measured Returns   The lognormal distribution allows for easy change of the holding period of returns. Suppose that we want to calculate returns monthly instead of annually. We use the parameter t to indicate the fraction of the year that is desired; in the case of monthly periods, $t = 1/12$. To transform the annual distribution to a t-period (monthly) distribution, it is necessary merely to multiply the expectation and variance of the ACC return by t (in this case, 1/12).

The monthly continuously compounded return on the stock in our example has the expectation and standard deviation of

$$\mu\text{(monthly)} = .12/12 = .01 \text{ (1\% per month)}$$
$$\sigma\text{(monthly)} = .42/\sqrt{12} = .1212 \text{ (or 12.12\% per month)}$$
$$\mu^*\text{(monthly)} = .2082/12 = .01735 \text{ (or 1.735\% per month)}$$

Note that we divide variance by 12 when changing from annual to monthly frequency; the standard deviation therefore is divided by the square root of 12.

Similarly, we can convert a nonannual distribution to an annual distribution by following the same routine. For example, suppose that the weekly continuously compounded rate of return on a stock is normally distributed with $\mu^* = .003$ and $\sigma = .07$. Then the ACC return is distributed with

$$\mu^* = 52 \times .003 = .156 \text{ (or 15.6\% per year)}$$
$$\sigma = \sqrt{52} \times .07 = .5048 \text{ (or 50.48\% per year)}$$

In practice, to obtain normally distributed, continuously compounded returns, R, we take the log of 1.0 plus the raw returns:

$$R = \log(1 + r)$$

For short intervals, raw returns are small, and the continuously compounded returns, R, will be practically identical to the raw returns, r. The rule of thumb is that this conversion is not necessary for periods of 1 month or less. That is, approximating stock returns as normal will be accurate enough. For longer intervals, however, the transformation may be necessary.

A.2   DESCRIPTIVE STATISTICS

Our analysis so far has been forward looking, or, as economists like to say, ex ante. We have been concerned with probabilities, expected values, and surprises. We made our analysis more tractable by assuming that decision outcomes are distributed according to relatively simple formulas, and that we know the parameters of these distributions.

Investment managers must satisfy themselves that these assumptions are reasonable, which they do by constantly analyzing observations from relevant random variables that accumulate over time. Distribution of past rates of return on a stock is one element they need to know in order to make optimal decisions. True, the distribution of the rate of return itself changes over time. However, a sample that is not too old does yield information relevant to the next-period probability distribution and its parameters. In this section we explain descriptive statistics, or the organization and analysis of such historic samples.

Histograms, Boxplots, and Time Series Plots

Table A.3 shows the annual excess returns (over the T-bill rate) for two major classes of assets, the S&P 500 index and a portfolio of long-term government bonds, for the period 1926 to 1993.

One way to understand the data is to present it graphically, commonly in a *histogram* or frequency distribution. Histograms of the 68 observations in Table A.3 are shown in Figure A.4. We construct a histogram according to the following principles:

Table A.3   Excess Return (Risk Premiums) on Stocks and Long-Term Treasury Bonds (Maturity Premiums)

Year	Equity Risk Premium	Maturity Premium	Year	Equity Risk Premium	Maturity Premium
1926	8.35	4.50	1963	19.68	−1.91
1927	34.37	5.81	1964	12.94	−0.03
1928	40.37	−3.14	1965	8.52	−3.22
1929	−13.17	−1.33	1966	−14.82	−1.11
1930	−27.31	2.25	1967	19.77	−13.40
1931	−44.41	−6.38	1968	5.85	−5.47
1932	−9.15	15.88	1969	−15.08	−11.66
1933	53.69	−0.38	1970	−2.52	5.57
1934	−1.60	9.86	1971	9.92	8.84
1935	47.50	4.81	1972	15.14	1.84
1936	33.74	7.33	1973	−21.59	−8.04
1937	−35.34	−0.08	1974	−34.47	−3.65
1938	31.14	5.55	1975	31.40	3.39
1939	−0.43	5.92	1976	18.76	11.67
1940	−9.78	6.09	1977	−12.30	−5.79
1941	−11.65	0.87	1978	−0.62	−8.34
1942	20.07	2.95	1979	8.06	−11.60
1943	25.55	1.73	1980	21.18	−15.19
1944	19.42	2.48	1981	−19.62	−12.86
1945	36.11	10.40	1982	10.87	29.81
1946	−8.42	−0.45	1983	13.71	−8.12
1947	5.21	−3.13	1984	−3.58	5.58
1948	4.69	2.59	1985	24.44	23.25
1949	17.69	5.35	1986	12.31	18.28
1950	30.51	−1.14	1987	−0.24	−8.16
1951	22.53	−5.43	1988	10.46	3.32
1952	16.71	−0.50	1989	23.12	9.74
1953	−2.81	1.81	1990	−10.98	−1.63
1954	51.76	6.33	1991	24.95	13.70
1955	29.99	−2.87	1992	4.16	4.54
1956	4.10	−8.05	1993	7.09	15.34
1957	−13.92	4.31			
1958	41.82	−7.64	Average	8.57	1.62
1959	9.01	−5.21	Standard deviation	20.90	8.50
1960	−3.13	11.12	Minimum	−44.41	−15.19
1961	24.76	−1.16	Maximum	53.69	29.81
1962	−11.46	4.16			

Source: Data from the Center for Research of Security Prices, University of Chicago.

- The range (of values) of the random variable is divided into a relatively small number of equal-sized intervals. The number of intervals that makes sense depends on the number of available observations. The data in Table A.3 provide 68 observations, and thus deciles (10 intervals) seem adequate.
- A rectangle is drawn over each interval. The height of the rectangle represents the frequency of observations for each interval.
- If the observations are concentrated in one part of the range, the range may be divided to unequal intervals. In that case the rectangles are scaled to that their *area* represents the frequency of the observations for each interval. (This is not the case in our samples, however.)
- If the sample is representative, the shape of the histogram will reveal the probability distribution of the random variable. Our total of 68 observations is not a large

Figure A.4
A. Histogram of the
equity risk premium.
B. Histogram of the
bond maturity
premium.

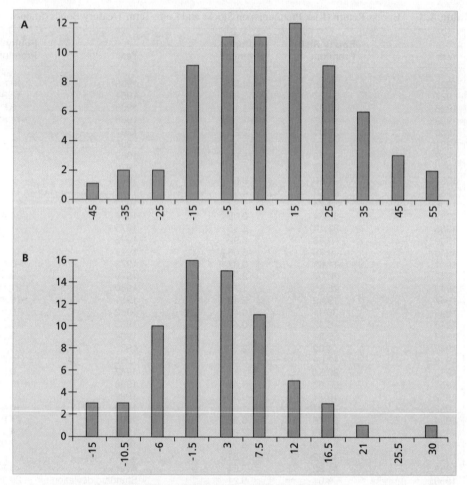

Source: *The Wall Street Journal*. October 15, 1997. Reprinted by permission of *The Wall Street Journal*, © 199x Dow Jones & Company, Inc. All Rights Reserved Worldwide.

sample, but a look at the histogram does suggest that the returns may be reasonably approximated by a normal or lognormal distribution.

Another way to represent sample information graphically is by *boxplots*. Figure A.5 is an example that uses the same data as in Table A.3. Boxplots are most useful to show the dispersion of the sample distribution. A commonly used measure of dispersion is the *interquartile range*. Recall that the range, a crude measure of dispersion, is defined as the distance between the largest and smallest observations. By its nature, this measure is unreliable because it will be determined by the two most extreme outliers of the sample.

The interquartile range, a more satisfactory variant of the simple range, is defined as the difference between the lower and upper quartiles. Below the *lower* quartile lies 25% of the sample; similarly, above the *upper* quartile lies 25% of the sample. The interquartile range therefore is confined to the central 50% of the sample. The greater the dispersion of a sample, the greater the distance between these two values.

Figure A.5

Boxplots of annual
equity risk premium
and long-term bond
(maturity) risk
premium (1926–1993).

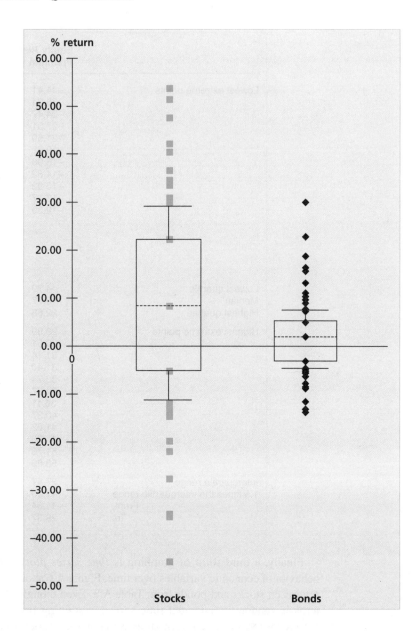

In the boxplot the horizontal broken line represents the median, the box the interquartile range, and the vertical lines extending from the box the range. The vertical lines representing the range often are restricted (if necessary) to extend only to 1.5 times the interquartile range, so that the more extreme observations can be shown separately (by points) as outliers.

As a concept check, verify from Table A.3 that the points on the boxplot of Figure A.5 correspond to the following list:

	Equity Risk Premium	Bond Maturity Premium
Lowest extreme points	−44.41	−15.19
	−35.34	−13.40
	−34.47	−12.86
	−27.31	−11.66
	−21.59	−11.60
	−19.62	−8.34
	−15.08	−8.16
	−14.82	−8.12
	−13.92	−8.05
	−13.17	−8.04
	−12.30	−7.64
		−6.38
		−5.79
		−5.47
		−5.43
		−5.21
Lowest quartile	−4.79	−3.33
Median	8.77	1.77
Highest quartile	22.68	5.64
Highest extreme points	29.99	8.84
	30.51	9.74
	31.14	9.86
	31.40	10.40
	33.74	11.12
	34.37	11.67
	36.11	13.70
	40.37	15.34
	41.82	15.88
	47.50	18.28
	51.76	23.25
	53.69	29.81
Interquartile range	27.47	8.97
1.5 times the interquartile range	41.20	13.45
From:	−11.84	−4.95
To:	29.37	8.49

Finally, a third form of graphing is *time series plots,* which are used to convey the behavior of economic variables over time. Figure A.6 shows a time series plot of the excess returns on stocks and bonds from Table A.3. Even though the human eye is apt to see patterns in randomly generated time series, examining time series' evolution over a long period does yield some information. Sometimes, such examination can be as revealing as that provided by formal statistical analysis.

Sample Statistics

Suppose we can assume that the probability distribution of stock returns has not changed over the 68 years from 1926 to 1993. We wish to draw inferences about the probability distribution of stock returns from the sample of 68 observations of annual stock excess returns in Table A.3.

A central question is whether given observations represent independent observations from the underlying distribution. If they do, statistical analysis is quite straightforward. Our analysis assumes that this is indeed the case. Empiricism in financial markets tends to confirm this assumption in most cases.

Figure A.6
A. Equity risk premium, 1926–1993.
B. Bond maturity premium, 1926–1993.

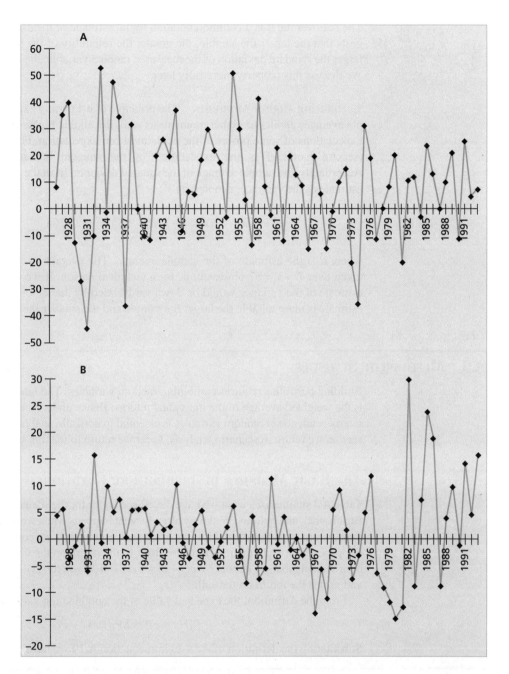

Estimating Expected Returns from the Sample Average   The definition of expected returns suggests that the sample average be used as an estimate of the expected value. Indeed, one definition of the expected return is the average of a sample when the number of observations tends to infinity.

Denoting the sample returns in Table A.3 by R_t, $t = 1, \ldots, T = 68$, the estimate of the annual expected excess rate of return is

$$\bar{R} = \frac{1}{T}\Sigma R_t = 8.57\%$$

The bar over the R is a common notation for an estimate of the expectation. Intuition suggests that the larger the sample, the greater the reliability of the sample average, and the larger the standard deviation of the measured random variable, the less reliable the average. We discuss this property more fully later.

Estimating Higher Moments   The principle of estimating expected values from sample averages applies to higher moments as well. Recall that higher moments are defined as expectations of some power of the deviation from expectation. For example, the variance (second moment) is the expectation of the squared deviation from expectation. Accordingly, the sample average of the squared deviation from the average will serve as the estimate of the variance, denoted by s^2:

$$s^2 = \frac{1}{T-1}\Sigma(R_t - \bar{R})^2 = \frac{1}{67}\Sigma(R_t - .0857)^2 = .04368 \qquad (s = 20.90\%)$$

where $\bar{R}$ is the estimate of the sample average. The average of the squared deviation is taken over $T - 1 = 67$ observations for a technical reason. If we were to divide by T, the estimate of the variance would be downward-biased by the factor $(T - 1)/T$. Here too, the estimate is more reliable the larger the sample and the smaller the true standard deviation.

A.3   MULTIVARIATE STATISTICS

Building portfolios requires combining random variables. The rate of return on a portfolio is the weighted average of the individual returns. Hence understanding and quantifying the interdependence of random variables is essential to portfolio analysis. In the first part of this section we return to scenario analysis. Later we return to making inferences from samples.

The Basic Measure of Association: Covariance

Table A.4 summarizes what we have developed so far for the scenario returns on Anheuser-Busch stock and options. We know already what happens when we add a constant to one of these return variables or multiply by a constant. But what if we combine any two of them? Suppose that we add the return on the stock to the return on the call. We create a new random variable that we denote by $r(s + c) = r(s) + r(c)$, where $r(s)$ is the return on the stock and $r(c)$ is the return on the call.

From the definition, the expected value of the combination variable is

$$E[r(s + c)] = \Sigma Pr(i)r_i(s + c) \qquad (A.10)$$

Substituting the definition of $r(s + c)$ into equation A.10 we have

$$E[r(s + c)] = \Sigma Pr(i)[r_i(s) + r_i(c)] = \Sigma Pr(i)r_i(s) + \Sigma Pr(i)r_i(c) \qquad (A.11)$$
$$= E[r(s)] + E[r(c)]$$

In words, the expectation of the sum of two random variables is just the sum of the expectations of the component random variables. Can the same be true about the variance? The answer is "no," which is, perhaps, the most important fact in portfolio theory. The reason lies in the statistical association between the combined random variables.

As a first step, we introduce the *covariance,* the basic measure of association. Although the expressions that follow may look intimidating, they are merely squares of sums; that is, $(a + b)^2 = a^2 + b^2 + 2ab$, and $(a - b)^2 = a^2 + b^2 - 2ab$, where the as and bs might stand for

Table A.4   Probability Distribution of Anheuser-Busch Stock and Options

	Scenario 1	Scenario 2	Scenario 3
Probability	.20	.50	.30
Rates of return (%)			
Stock	20	30	50
Call option	−100	−100	400
Put option	50	−25	−100
	E(r)	**σ**	**σ²**
Stock	.340	0.1114	0.0124
Call option	.500	2.2913	5.2500
Put option	−.325	0.5250	0.2756

random variables, their expectations or their deviations from expectations. From the definition of the variance

$$\sigma^2_{s+c} = E[r_{s+c} - E(r_{s+c})]^2 \tag{A.12}$$

To make equations A.12 through A.20 easier to read, we will identify the variables by subscripts s and c and drop the subscript i for scenarios. Substitute the definition of $r(s + c)$ and its expectation into equation A.12:

$$\sigma^2_{s+c} = E[r_s + r_c - E(r_s) - E(r_c)]^2 \tag{A.13}$$

Changing the order of variables within the brackets in equation A.13,

$$\sigma^2_{s+c} = E[r_s - E(r_s) + r_c - E(r_c)]^2$$

Within the square brackets we have the sum of the deviations from expectations of the two variables, which we denote by d. Writing this out,

$$\sigma^2_{s+c} = E[(d_s + d_c)^2] \tag{A.14}$$

Equation A.14 is the expectation of a complete square. Taking the square, we find

$$\sigma^2_{s+c} = E(d^2_s + d^2_c + 2d_s d_c) \tag{A.15}$$

The term in parentheses in equation A.15 is the summation of three random variables. Because the expectation of a sum is the sum of the expectations, we can write equation A.15 as

$$\sigma^2_{s+c} = E(d^2_s) + E(d^2_c) + 2E(d_s d_c) \tag{A.16}$$

In equation A.16 the first two terms on the right-hand side are the variance of the stock (the expectation of its squared deviation from expectation) plus the variance of the call. The third term is twice the expression that is the definition of the covariance discussed in equation A.17. (Note that the expectation is multiplied by 2 because expectation of twice a variable is twice the variable's expectation.)

In other words, the variance of a sum of random variables is the sum of the variances *plus* twice the covariance, which we denote by $\text{Cov}(r_s, r_c)$, or the covariance between the return on s and the return on c. Specifically,

$$\text{Cov}(r_s, r_c) = E(d_s d_c) = E\{[r_s - E(r_s)][r_c - E(r_c)]\} \tag{A.17}$$

Table A.5   Deviations, Squared Deviations, and Weighted Products of Deviations from Expectations of Anheuser-Busch Stock and Options

	Scenario 1	Scenario 2	Scenario 3	Probability-Weighted Sum
Probability	0.20	0.50	0.30	
Deviation of stock	−0.14	−0.04	0.16	
Squared deviation	0.0196	0.0016	0.0256	0.0124
Deviation of call	−1.50	−1.50	3.50	
Squared deviation	2.25	2.25	12.25	5.25
Deviation of put	0.825	0.75	−0.675	
Squared deviation	0.680625	0.005625	0.455635	0.275628
Product of deviations $(d_s d_c)$	0.21	0.06	0.56	0.24
Product of deviations $(d_s d_p)$	−0.1155	−0.003	−0.108	−0.057
Product of deviations $(d_c d_p)$	−1.2375	−0.1125	−2.3625	−1.0125

The sequence of the variables in the expression for the covariance is of no consequence. Because the order of multiplication makes no difference, the definition of the covariance in equation A.17 shows that it will not affect the covariance either.

We use the data in Table A.4 to set up the input table for the calculation of the covariance, as shown in Table A.5.

First, we analyze the covariance between the stock and the call. In Scenarios 1 and 2, both assets show *negative* deviations from expectation. This is an indication of *positive co-movement.* When these two negative deviations are multiplied, the product, which eventually contributes to the covariance between the returns, is positive. Multiplying deviations leads to positive covariance when the variables move in the same direction and negative covariance when they move in opposite directions. In Scenario 3 both assets show *positive* deviations, reinforcing the inference that the co-movement is positive. The magnitude of the products of the deviations, weighted by the probability of each scenario, when added up, results in a covariance that shows not only the direction of the co-movement (by its sign) but also the degree of the co-movement.

The covariance is a variance-like statistic. Whereas the variance shows the degree of the movement of a random variable about its expectation, the covariance shows the degree of the co-movement of two variables about their expectations. It is important for portfolio analysis that the covariance of a variable with itself is equal to its variance. You can see this by substituting the appropriate deviations in equation A.17; the result is the expectation of the variable's squared deviation from expectation.

The first three values in the last column of Table A.5 are the familiar variances of the three assets, the stock, the call, and the put. The last three are the covariances; two of them are negative. Examine the covariance between the stock and the put, for example. In the first two scenarios the stock realizes negative deviations, while the put realizes positive deviations. When we multiply such deviations, the sign becomes negative. The same happens in the third scenario, except that the stock realizes a positive deviation and the put a negative one. Again, the product is negative, adding to the inference of negative co-movement.

With other assets and scenarios the product of the deviations can be negative in some scenarios, positive in others. The *magnitude* of the products, when *weighted* by the probabilities, determines which co-movements dominate. However, whenever the sign of the products varies from scenario to scenario, the results will offset one another, contributing to a small, close-to-zero covariance. In such cases we may conclude that the returns have either a small, or no, average co-movement.

Covariance between Transformed Variables   Because the covariance is the expectation of the product of deviations from expectation of two variables, analyzing the effect of transformations on deviations from expectation will show the effect of the transformation on the covariance.

Suppose that we add a constant to one of the variables. We know already that the expectation of the variable increases by that constant, so deviations from expectation will remain unchanged. Just as adding a constant to a random variable does not affect its variance, it also will not affect its covariance with other variables.

Multiplying a random variable by a constant also multiplies its expectation, as well as its deviation from expectation. Therefore, the covariance with any other variable will also be multiplied by that constant. Using the definition of the covariance, check that this summation of the foregoing discussion is true:

$$Cov(a_1 + b_1 r_s, a_2 + b_2 r_c) = b_1 b_2 Cov(r_s, r_c) \qquad (A.18)$$

The covariance allows us to calculate the variance of sums of random variables, and eventually the variance of portfolio returns.

A Pure Measure of Association: The Correlation Coefficient

If we tell you that the covariance between the rates of return of the stock and the call is .24 (see Table A.5), what have you learned? Because the sign is positive, you know that the returns generally move in the same direction. However, the number .24 adds nothing to your knowledge of the closeness of co-movement of the stock and the call.

To obtain a measure of association that conveys the degree of intensity of the co-movement, we relate the covariance to the standard deviations of the two variables. Each standard deviation is the square root of the variance. Thus the product of the standard deviations has the dimensions of the variance that is also shared by the covariance. Therefore, we can define the correlation coefficient, denoted by ρ, as

$$\rho_{sc} = \frac{Cov(r_s, r_c)}{\sigma_s \sigma_c} \qquad (A.19)$$

where the subscripts on ρ identify the two variables involved. Because the order of the variables in the expression of the covariance is of no consequence, equation A.19 shows that the order does not affect the correlation coefficient either.

We use the covariances in Table A.5 to show the *correlation matrix* for the three variables:

	Stock	Call	Put
Stock	1.00	0.94	−0.97
Call	0.94	1.00	−0.84
Put	−0.97	−0.84	1.00

The highest (in absolute value) correlation coefficient is between the stock and the put, −.97, although the absolute value of the covariance between them is the lowest by far. The reason is attributable to the effect of the standard deviations. The following properties of the correlation coefficient are important:

- Because the correlation coefficient, just as the covariance, measures only the degree of association, it tells us nothing about causality. The direction of causality has to come from theory and be supported by specialized tests.

- The correlation coefficient is determined completely by deviations from expectations, as are the components in equation A.19. We expect, therefore, that it is not affected by adding constants to the associated random variables. However, the correlation coefficient is invariant also to multiplying the variables by constants. You can verify this property by referring to the effect of multiplication by a constant on the covariance and standard deviation.

- The correlation coefficient can vary from −1.0, perfect negative correlation, to 1.0, perfect positive correlation. This can be seen by calculating the correlation coefficient of a variable with itself. You expect it to be 1.0. Recalling that the covariance of a variable with itself is its own variance, you can verify this using equation A.19. The more ambitious can verify that the correlation between a variable and the negative of itself is equal to −1.0. First, find from equation A.17 that the covariance between a variable and its negative equals the negative of the variance. Then check equation A.19.

Because the correlation between x and y is the same as the correlation between y and x, the *correlation matrix is symmetric about the diagonal*. The diagonal entries are all 1.0 because they represent the correlations of returns with themselves. Therefore, it is customary to present only the lower triangle of the correlation matrix.

Reexamine equation A.19. You can invert it so that the covariance is presented in terms of the correlation coefficient and the standard deviations as in equation A.20:

$$\text{Cov}(r_s r_c) = \rho_{sc}\sigma_s\sigma_c \tag{A.20}$$

This formulation can be useful, because many think in terms of correlations rather than covariances.

Estimating Correlation Coefficients from Sample Returns   Assuming that a sample consists of independent observations, we assign equal weights to all observations and use simple averages to estimate expectations. When estimating variances and covariances, we get an average by dividing by the number of observations minus one.

Suppose that you are interested in estimating the correlation between stock and long-term default-free government bonds. Assume that the sample of 68 annual excess returns for the period 1926 to 1993 in Table A.3 is representative.

Using the definition for the correlation coefficient in equation A.19, you estimate the following statistics (using the subscripts s for stocks, b for bonds, and t for time):

$$\bar{R}_s = \frac{1}{68}\sum_{t=1}^{68} R_{s,t} = .0857; \qquad \bar{R}_b = \frac{1}{68}\sum R_{b,t} = 0.162$$

$$\sigma_s = \left[\frac{1}{67}\sum (R_{s,t} - \bar{R}_s)^2\right]^{1/2} = .2090$$

$$\sigma_b = \left[\frac{1}{67}\sum (R_{b,t} - \bar{R}_b)^2\right]^{1/2} = .0850$$

$$\text{Cov}(R_s,R_b) = \frac{1}{67}\sum [(R_{s,t} - \bar{R}_s)(R_{b,t} - \bar{R}_b)] = .00314$$

$$\rho_{sb} = \frac{\text{Cov}(R_s,R_b)}{\sigma_s\sigma_b} = .17916$$

Here is one example of how problematic estimation can be. Recall that we predicate our use of the sample on the assumption that the probability distributions have not changed over the sample period. To see the problem with this assumption, suppose that we reestimate the correlation between stocks and bonds over a more recent period—for example, beginning in 1965, about the time of onset of government debt financing of both the war in Vietnam and the Great Society programs.

Repeating the previous calculations for the period 1965 to 1987, we find

$$\bar{R}_s = .0312; \qquad \bar{R}_b = -.00317$$
$$\sigma_s = .15565; \qquad \sigma_b = .11217$$
$$\text{Cov}(R_s, R_b) = .0057; \qquad \rho_{sb} = .32647$$

A comparison of the two sets of numbers suggests that it is likely, but by no means certain, that the underlying probability distributions have changed. The variance in the rates of return and the size of the sample are why we cannot be sure. We shall return to the issue of testing the sample statistics shortly.

Regression Analysis

We will use a problem from the CFA examination (Level I, 1986) to represent the degree of understanding of regression analysis that is required for the ground level. However, first let us develop some background.

In analyzing measures of association so far, we have ignored the question of causality, identifying simply *independent* and *dependent* variables. Suppose that theory (in its most basic form) tells us that all asset excess returns are driven by the same economic force whose movements are captured by a broad-based market index, such as excess return on the S&P 500 stock index.

Suppose further that our theory predicts a simple, linear relationship between the excess return of any asset and the market index. A linear relationship, one that can be described by a straight line, takes on this form:

$$R_{j,t} = a_j + b_j R_{M,t} + e_{j,t} \tag{A.21}$$

where the subscript j represents any asset, M represents the market index (the S&P 500), and t represents variables that change over time. (In the following discussion we omit subscripts when possible.) On the left-hand side of equation A.21 is the dependent variable, the excess return on asset j. The right-hand side has two parts, the explained and unexplained (by the relationship) components of the dependent variable.

The explained component of R_j is the $a + bR_M$ part. It is plotted in Figure A.7. The quantity a, also called the intercept, gives the value of R_j when the *independent* variable is zero. This relationship assumes that it is a constant. The second term in the explained part of the return represents the driving force, R_M, times the sensitivity coefficient, b, that transmits movements in R_M to movements in R_j. The term b is also assumed to be constant. Figure A.7 shows that b is the slope of the regression line.

The unexplained component of R_j is represented by the *disturbance* term, e_j. The disturbance is assumed to be uncorrelated with the explanatory variable, R_M, and of zero expectation. Such a variable is also called a noise variable because it contributes to the variance but not to the expectation of the dependent variable, R_j.

A relationship such as that shown in equation A.21 applied to data, with coefficients estimated, is called a *regression equation*. A relationship including only one explanatory variable is called *simple regression*. The parameters a and b are called (simple) *regression coefficients*. Because every value of R_j is explained by the regression, the expectation and variance of R_j are also determined by it. Using the expectation of the expression in equation A.21, we get

$$E(R_j) = a + bE(R_M) \tag{A.22}$$

Figure A.7

Simple regression estimates and residuals. The intercept and slope are chosen so as to minimize the sum of the squared deviations from the regression line.

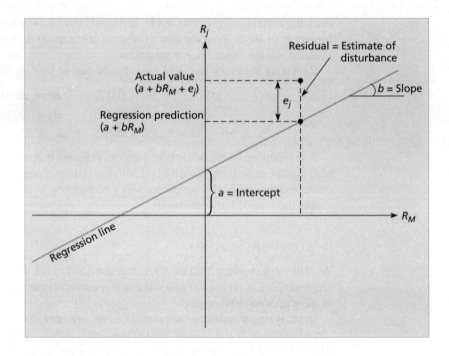

The constant a has no effect on the variance of R_j. Because the variables r_M and e_j are uncorrelated, the variance of the sum, $bR_m + e$, is the sum of the variances. Accounting for the parameter b multiplying R_M, the variance of R_j will be

$$\sigma_j^2 = b^2\sigma_M^2 + \sigma_e^2 \tag{A.23}$$

Equation A.23 tells us that the contribution of the variance of R_M to that of R_j depends on the regression (slope) coefficient b. The term $(b\sigma_M)^2$ is called the *explained variance*. The variance of the disturbance makes up the *unexplained variance*.

The covariance between R_j and R_M is also given by the regression equation. Setting up the expression, we have

$$\begin{aligned}\text{Cov}(R_j, R_M) &= \text{Cov}(a + bR_M + e, R_M)\\ &= \text{Cov}(bR_M, R_M) = b\text{Cov}(R_M, R_M) = b\sigma_M^2\end{aligned} \tag{A.24}$$

The intercept, a, is dropped because a constant added to a random variable does not affect the covariance with any other variable. The disturbance term, e, is dropped because it is, by assumption, uncorrelated with the market return.

Equation A.24 shows that the slope coefficient of the regression, b, is equal to

$$b = \frac{\text{Cov}(R_j, R_M)}{\sigma_M^2}$$

The slope thereby measures the co-movements of j and M as a fraction of the movement of the driving force, the explanatory variable M.

One way to measure the explanatory power of the regression is by the fraction of the variance of R_j that it explains. This fraction is called the *coefficient of determination* and denoted by ρ^2.

$$\rho_{jM}^2 = \frac{b^2\sigma_M^2}{\sigma_j^2} = \frac{b^2\sigma_M^2}{b_M^2\sigma_M^2 + \sigma_e^2} \tag{A.25}$$

Note that the unexplained variance, σ_e^2, has to make up the difference between the coefficient of determination and 1.0. Therefore, another way to represent the coefficient of determination is by

$$\rho_{jM}^2 = 1 - \frac{\sigma_e^2}{\sigma_j^2}$$

Some algebra shows that the coefficient of determination is the square of the correlation coefficient. Finally, squaring the correlation coefficient tells us what proportion of the variance of the dependent variable is explained by the independent (the explanatory) variable.

Estimation of the regression coefficients a and b is based on minimizing the sum of the square deviation of the observations from the estimated regression line (see Figure A.7). Your calculator, as well as any spreadsheet program, can compute regression estimates.

The CFA 1986 examination for Level I included this question:

Question.

Pension plan sponsors place a great deal of emphasis on universe rankings when evaluating money managers. In fact, it appears that sponsors assume implicitly that managers who rank in the top quartile of a representative sample of peer managers are more likely to generate superior relative performance in the future than managers who rank in the bottom quartile.

The validity of this assumption can be tested by regressing percentile rankings of managers in one period on their percentile rankings from the prior period.

1. Given that the implicit assumption of plan sponsors is true to the extent that there is perfect correlation in percentile rankings from one period to the next, list the numerical values you would expect to observe for the slope of the regression, and the R-squared of the regression.
2. Given that there is no correlation in percentile rankings from period to period, list the numerical values you would expect to observe for the intercept of the regression, the slope of the regression, and the R-squared of the regression.
3. Upon performing such a regression, you observe an intercept of .51, a slope of $-.05$, and an R-squared of .01. Based on this regression, state your best estimate of a manager's percentile ranking next period if his percentile ranking this period were .15.
4. Some pension plan sponsors have agreed that a good practice is to terminate managers who are in the top quartile and to hire those who are in the bottom quartile. State what those who advocate such a practice expect implicitly about the correlation and slope from a regression of the managers' subsequent ranking on their current ranking.

Answer.

1. Intercept = 0
   Slope   = 1
   R-squared = 1
2. Intercept = .50
   Slope   = 0.0
   R-squared = 0.0
3. 50th percentile, derived as follows:
   $y = a + bx$
   $\quad = .51 - 0.05(.15)$
   $\quad = .51 - .0075$
   $\quad = .5025$
   Given the very low R-squared, it would be difficult to estimate what the manager's rank would be.
4. Sponsors who advocate firing top-performance managers and hiring the poorest implicitly expect that both the correlation and slope would be significantly negative.

Multiple Regression Analysis

In many cases, theory suggests that a number of independent, explanatory variables drive a dependent variable. This concept becomes clear enough when demonstrated by a two-variable case. A real estate analyst offers the following regression equation to explain the return on a nationally diversified real estate portfolio:

$$RE_t = a + b_1 RE_{t-1} + b_2 NVR_t + e_t \qquad (A.26)$$

The dependent variable is the period t real estate portfolio, RE_t. The model specifies that the explained part of that return is driven by two independent variables. The first is the previous period return, RE_{t-1}, representing persistence of momentum. The second explanatory variable is the current national vacancy rate, NVR_t.

As in the simple regression, a is the intercept, representing the value that RE is expected to take when the explanatory variables are zero. The (slope) regression coefficients, b_1 and b_2, represent the *marginal* effect of the explanatory variables.

The coefficient of determination is defined exactly as before. The ratio of the variance of the disturbance, e, to the total variance of RE is 1.0 *minus* the coefficient of determination. The regression coefficients are estimated here, too, by finding coefficients that minimize the sum of squared deviations of the observations from the prediction of the regression.

A.4   HYPOTHESIS TESTING

The central hypothesis of investment theory is that nondiversifiable (systematic) risk is rewarded by a higher *expected* return. But do the data support the theory? Consider the data on the excess return on stocks in Table A.3. The estimate of the expected excess return (the sample average) is 8.57%. This appears to be a hefty risk premium, but so is the risk—the estimate of the standard deviation for the same sample is 20.9%. Could it be that the positive average is just the luck of the draw? Hypothesis testing supplies probabilistic answers to such concerns.

The first step in hypothesis testing is to state the claim that is to be tested. This is called the *null hypothesis* (or simply the *null*), denoted by H_0. Against the null, an alternative claim (hypothesis) is stated, which is denoted by H_1. The objective of hypothesis testing is to decide whether to reject the null in favor of the alternative while identifying the probabilities of the possible errors in the determination.

A hypothesis is *specified* if it assigns a value to a variable. A claim that the risk premium on stocks is zero is one example of a specified hypothesis. Often, however, a hypothesis is general. A claim that the risk premium on stocks is not zero would be a completely general alternative against the specified hypothesis that the risk premium is zero. It amounts to "anything but the null." The alternative that the risk premium is *positive,* although not completely general, is still unspecified. Although it is sometimes desirable to test two unspecified hypotheses (e.g., the claim that the risk premium is zero or negative, against the claim that it is positive), unspecified hypotheses complicate the task of determining the probabilities of errors in judgment.

What are the possible errors? There are two, called Type I and Type II errors. Type I is the event that we will *reject* the null when it is *true.* The probability of Type I error is called the *significance level.* Type II is the event that we will *accept* the null when it is *false.*

Suppose we set a criterion for acceptance of H_0 that is so lax that we know for certain we will accept the null. In doing so we will drive the significance level to zero (which is good). If we will never reject the null, we will also never reject it when it is true. At the same time the probability of Type II error will become 1 (which is bad). If we will accept the null for certain, we must also do so when it is false.

The reverse is to set a criterion for acceptance of the null that is so stringent that we know for certain that we will reject it. This drives the probability of Type II error to zero (which is good). By never accepting the null, we avoid accepting it when it is false. Now, however, the significance level will go to 1 (which is bad). If we always reject the null, we will reject it even when it is true.

To compromise between the two evils, hypothesis testing fixes the significance level; that is, it limits the probability of Type I error. Then, subject to this present constraint, the ideal test will minimize the probability of Type II error. If we *avoid* Type II error (accepting the null when it is false) we actually *reject* the null when it is indeed *false*. The probability of doing so is one minus the probability of Type II error, which is called the *power of the test*. Minimizing the probability of Type II error maximizes the power of the test.

Testing the claim that stocks earn a risk premium, we set the hypotheses as

$$H_0 : E(R) = 0 \qquad \text{The expected excess return is zero}$$
$$H_1 : E(R) > 0 \qquad \text{The expected excess return is positive}$$

H_1 is an *unspecified alternative*. When a null is tested against a completely general alternative, it is called a *two-tailed test* because you may reject the null in favor of both greater or smaller values.

When both hypotheses are unspecified, the test is difficult because the calculation of the probabilities of Type I and II errors is complicated. Usually, at least one hypothesis is simple (specified) and set as the null. In that case it is relatively easy to calculate the significance level of the test. Calculating the power of the test that assumes the *unspecified* alternative is true remains complicated; often it is left unsolved.

As we will show, setting the hypothesis that we wish to reject, $E(R) = 0$ as the null (the "straw man"), makes it harder to accept the alternative that we favor, our theoretical bias, which is appropriate.

In testing $E(R) = 0$, suppose we fix the significance level at 5%. This means that we will reject the null (and accept that there is a positive premium) *only* when the data suggest that the probability the null is true is 5% or less. To do so, we must find a critical value, denoted z_α (or critical values in the case of two-tailed tests), that corresponds to $\alpha = .05$, which will create two regions, an acceptance region and a rejection region. Look at Figure A.8 as an illustration.

If the sample average is to the right of the critical value (in the rejection region), the null is rejected; otherwise, it is accepted. In the latter case it is too likely (i.e., the probability is greater than 5%) that the sample average is positive simply because of sampling error. If the sample average is greater than the critical value, we will reject the null in favor of the alternative. The probability that the positive value of the sample average results from sampling error is 5% or less.

If the alternative is one-sided (one-tailed), as in our case, the acceptance region covers the entire area from minus infinity to a positive value, above which lies 5% of the distribution (see Figure A.8). The critical value is z_α in Figure A.8. When the alternative is two-tailed, the area of 5% lies at both extremes of the distribution and is equally divided between them, 2.5% on each side. A two-tailed test is more stringent (it is harder to reject the null). In a one-tailed test the fact that our theory predicts the direction in which the average will deviate from the value under the null is weighted in favor of the alternative. The upshot is that for a significance level of 5%, with a one-tailed test, we use a confidence interval of $\alpha = .05$, instead of $\alpha/2 = .025$ as with a two-tailed test.

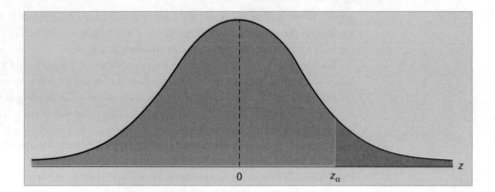

Hypothesis testing requires assessment of the probabilities of the test statistics, such as the sample average and variance. Therefore, it calls for some assumption about the probability distribution of the underlying variable. Such an assumption becomes an integral part of the null hypothesis, often an implicit one.

In this case we assume that the stock portfolio excess return is normally distributed. The distribution of the test statistic is derived from its mathematical definition and the assumption of the underlying distribution for the random variable. In our case the test statistic is the sample average.

The sample average is obtained by summing all observations ($T = 68$) and then multiplying by $1/T = 1/68$. Each observation is a random variable, drawn independently from the same underlying distribution, with an unknown expectation μ, and standard deviation σ. The expectation of the sum of all observations is the sum of the T expectations (all equal to μ) divided by T, therefore equal to the population expectation. The result is 8.57%, which is equal to the true expectation *plus* sampling errors. Under the null hypothesis, the expectation is zero, and the entire 8.57% constitutes sampling error.

To calculate the variance of the sample average, recall that we assumed that all observations were independent, or uncorrelated. Hence the variance of the sum is the sum of the variances, that is, T times the population variance. However, we also transform the sum, multiplying it by $1/T$; therefore, we have to divide the variance of the sum $T\sigma^2$ by T^2. We end up with the variance of the sample average as the population variance divided by T. The standard deviation of the sample average, which is called the *standard error,* is

$$\sigma(\text{average}) = \left(\frac{1}{T^2}\Sigma\sigma^2\right)^{1/2} = \left(\frac{1}{T^2}T\sigma^2\right)^{1/2} = \frac{\sigma}{\sqrt{T}} = \frac{.2090}{\sqrt{68}} = .0253 \qquad \text{(A.27)}$$

Our test statistic has a standard error of 2.53%. It makes sense that the larger the number of observations, the *smaller* the *standard error* of the estimate of the expectation. However, note that it is the variance that goes down by the proportion $T = 68$. The standard error goes down by a much smaller proportion, $\sqrt{T} = 8.25$.

Now that we have the sample mean, 8.57%, its standard deviation, 2.53%, and know that the distribution under the null is normal, we are ready to perform the test. We want to determine whether 8.57% is significantly positive. We achieve this by standardizing our statistic, which means that we subtract from it its expected value under the null hypothesis and divide by its standard deviation. This standardized statistic can now be compared to z values from the standard normal tables. We ask whether

$$\frac{\bar{R} - E(R)}{\sigma} > z_\alpha$$

We would be finished except for another caveat. The assumption of normality is all right in that the test statistic is a weighted sum of normals (according to our assumption about returns). Therefore, it is also normally distributed. However, the analysis also requires that we *know* the variance. Here we are using a sample variance that is only an *estimate* of the true variance.

The solution to this problem turns out to be quite simple. The normal distribution is replaced with *Student-t* (or *t,* for short) *distribution.* Like the normal, the *t* distribution is symmetric. It depends on degrees of freedom, that is, the number of observations less one. Thus, here we replace z_α with $t_{\alpha,T-1}$.

The test is then

$$\frac{\overline{R} - E(R)}{\sigma} > t_{\alpha,T-1}$$

When we substitute in sample results, the left-hand side is a standardized statistic and the right-hand side is a *t*-value derived from *t* tables for $\alpha = .05$ and $T - 1 = 68 - 1 = 67$. We ask whether the inequality holds. If it does, we *reject* the null hypothesis with a 5% significance level; if it does not, we *cannot reject* the null hypothesis. (In this example, $t_{.05,67} = 1.67$.) Proceeding, we find that

$$\frac{.0857 - 0}{.0253} = 3.39 > 1.67$$

In our sample the inequality holds, and we reject the null hypothesis in favor of the alternative that the risk premium is positive.

A repeat of the test of this hypothesis for the 1965-to-1987 period may make a skeptic out of you. For that period the sample average is 3.12%, the sample standard deviation is 15.57%, and there are $23 - 1 = 22$ degrees of freedom. Does that give you second thoughts?

The *t*-Test of Regression Coefficients

Suppose that we apply the simple regression model (equation A.21) to the relationship between the long-term government bond portfolio and the stock market index, using the sample in Table A.3. The estimation result (% per year) is

$$a = .9913, \quad b = .0729, \quad R\text{-squared} = .0321$$

We interpret these coefficients as follows. For periods when the excess return on the market index is zero, we expect the bonds to earn an excess return of 99.13 basis points. This is the role of the intercept. As for the slope, for each percentage return of the stock portfolio in any year, the bond portfolio is expected to earn, *additionally,* 7.29 basis points. With the average equity risk premium for the sample period of 8.57%, the sample average for bonds is $.9913 + (.0729 \times 8.57) = 1.62\%$. From the squared correlation coefficient you know that the variation in stocks explains 3.21% of the variation in bonds.

Can we rely on these statistics? One way to find out is to set up a hypothesis test, presented here for the regression coefficient *b*.

H_0: $b = 0$ The regression slope coefficient is zero, meaning that changes in the independent variable do not explain changes in the dependent variable

H_1: $b > 0$ The dependent variable is sensitive to changes in the independent variable (with a *positive* covariance)

Any decent regression software supplies the statistics to test this hypothesis. The regression customarily assumes that the dependent variable and the disturbance are normally distributed, with an unknown variance that is estimated from the sample. Thus the regression coefficient b is normally distributed. Because once again the null is that $b = 0$, all we need is an estimate of the standard error of this statistic.

The estimated standard error of the regression coefficient is computed from the estimated standard deviation of the disturbance and the standard deviation of the explanatory variable. For the regression at hand, that estimate is $s(b) = .0493$. Just as in the previous exercise, the critical value of the test is

$$s(b)t_{\alpha,T-1}$$

Compare this value to the value of the estimated coefficient b. We will reject the null in favor of $b > 0$ if

$$b > s(b)t_{\alpha,T-1}$$

which, because the standard deviation $s(b)$ is positive, is equivalent to the following condition:

$$\frac{b}{s(b)} > t_{\alpha,T-1}$$

The t-test reports the ratio of the estimated coefficient to its estimated standard deviation. Armed with this t-ratio, the number of observations, T, and a table of the *Student-t* distribution, you can perform the test at the desired significance level.

The t-ratio for our example is $.0729/.0493 = 1.4787$. The t-table for 68 degrees of freedom shows we cannot reject the null at a significance level of 5%, for which the critical value is 1.67.

A question from the CFA 1987 exam calls for understanding of regression analysis and hypothesis testing.

Question.

An academic suggests to you that the returns on common stocks differ based on a company's market capitalization, its historical earnings growth, the stock's current yield, and whether or not the company's employees are unionized. You are skeptical that there are any attributes other than market exposure as measured by beta that explain differences in returns across a sample of securities.

Nonetheless, you decide to test whether or not these other attributes account for the differences in returns. You select the S&P 500 stocks as your sample, and regress their returns each month for the past five years against the company's market capitalization at the beginning of each month, the company's growth in earnings throughout the previous 12 months, the prior year's dividend divided by the stock price at the beginning of each month, and a dummy variable that has a value of 1 if employees are unionized and 0 if not.

1. The average R-squared from the regression is .15, and it varies very little from month to month. Discuss the significance of this result.
2. You note that all of the coefficients of the attributes have t-statistics greater than 2 in most of the months in which the regressions were run. Discuss the significance of these attributes in terms of explaining differences in common stock returns.
3. You observe in most of the regressions that the coefficient of the dummy variable is $-.14$ and the t-statistic is -4.74. Discuss the implication of the coefficient regarding the relationship between unionization and the return on a company's common stock.

Answer.

1. Differences in the attributes' values together explain about 15% of the differences in return among the stocks in the S&P 500 index. The remaining unexplained differences in return may be attributable to omitted attributes, industry affiliations, or stock-specific factors. This information by itself is not sufficient to form any qualitative conclusions. The fact that R-squared varied little from month to month implies that the relationship is stable and the observed results are not sample specific.

2. Given a t-statistic greater than 2 in most of the months, one would regard the attribute coefficients as statistically significant. If the attribute coefficients were not significantly different from zero, one would expect t-statistics greater than 2 in fewer than 5% of the regressions for each attribute coefficient. Because the t-statistics are greater than 2 much more frequently, one should conclude that they are definitely significant in terms of explaining differences in stock returns.

3. Because the coefficient for the dummy variable representing unionization has persistently been negative and since it persistently has been statistically significant, one would conclude that disregarding all other factors, unionization lowers a company's common stock return. That is, everything else being equal, nonunionized companies will have higher returns than companies whose employees are unionized. Of course, one would want to test the model further to see if there are omitted variables of other problems that might account for this apparent relationship.

REFERENCES TO CFA QUESTIONS

Each end-of-chapter CFA question is reprinted with permission from the Association for Investment Management and Research (AIMR), Charlottesville, VA. Following is a list of the CFA questions in the end-of-chapter material and the exams and study guides from which they were taken and updated.

Chapter 2
1. 1996 Level I CFA Study Guide, © 1996
7. 1994 Level I CFA Study Guide, © 1994
14. 1994 Level I CFA Study Guide, © 1994

Chapter 3
16. 1986 Level I CFA Study Guide, © 1986
17. 1986 Level I CFA Study Guide, © 1986
18. 1986 Level I CFA Study Guide, © 1986

Chapter 5
13. 1992 Level I CFA Study Guide, © 1992
14. 1992 Level I CFA Study Guide, © 1992
15. 1993 Level I CFA Study Guide, © 1993
16. 1993 Level I CFA Study Guide, © 1993
17. 1993 Level I CFA Study Guide, © 1993

Chapter 6
7. 1991 Level I CFA Study Guide, © 1991
8. 1991 Level I CFA Study Guide, © 1991
9. 1991 Level I CFA Study Guide, © 1991

Chapter 7
14. 1991 Level I CFA Study Guide, © 1991
19. 1993 Level I CFA Study Guide, © 1993
20. 1993 Level I CFA Study Guide, © 1993

Chapter 8
15. 1982 Level III CFA Study Guide, © 1982
16. 1982 Level III CFA Study Guide, © 1982
17. 1982 Level III CFA Study Guide, © 1982
21. 1993 Level I CFA Study Guide, © 1993
22. 1993 Level I CFA Study Guide, © 1993
23. 1992 Level I CFA Study Guide, © 1992
24. 1992 Level I CFA Study Guide, © 1992

25. 1994 Level I CFA Study Guide, © 1994
26. 1994 Level I CFA Study Guide, © 1994
27. 1994 Level I CFA Study Guide, © 1994

Chapter 9
21. 1993 Level I CFA Study Guide, © 1993
22. 1993 Level I CFA Study Guide, © 1993
23. 1993 Level I CFA Study Guide, © 1993
24. 1992 Level I CFA Study Guide, © 1992
25. 1994 Level I CFA Study Guide, © 1994
26. 1993 Level I CFA Study Guide, © 1993
27. 1994 Level I CFA Study Guide, © 1994
28. 1994 Level I CFA Study Guide, © 1994

Chapter 10
14. 1982 Level I CFA Study Guide, © 1982
16. 1993 Level I CFA Study Guide, © 1993
17. 1993 Level I CFA Study Guide, © 1993
18. 1993 Level I CFA Study Guide, © 1993
19. 1994 Level I CFA Study Guide, © 1994

Chapter 11
13–18. 1991–1993 Level I CFA study guides

Chapter 12
6. 1993 Level I CFA Study Guide, © 1993
7. 1993 Level I CFA Study Guide, © 1993
8. 1993 Level I CFA Study Guide, © 1993
9. 1993 Level I CFA Study Guide, © 1993
10. 1993 Level I CFA Study Guide, © 1993
11. 1992 Level I CFA Study Guide, © 1992
12. 1992 Level I CFA Study Guide, © 1992
28. 1996 Level III CFA Study Guide, © 1996
29. 1995 Level II CFA Study Guide, © 1995
30. 1996 Level III CFA Study Guide, © 1996

Chapter 13
12. 1993 Level I CFA Study Guide, © 1993
13. 1993 Level I CFA Study Guide, © 1993

Chapter 14
6. 1993 Level I CFA Study Guide, © 1993
7. 1994 Level I CFA Study Guide, © 1994
27. 1992 Level I CFA Study Guide, © 1992
28. 1993 Level I CFA Study Guide, © 1993
29. 1992 Level I CFA Study Guide, © 1992
30. From various Level I study guides

Chapter 15
1. 1993 Level II CFA Study Guide, © 1993
2. 1993 Level I CFA Study Guide, © 1993
3. 1992 Level I CFA Study Guide, © 1992
8. 1993 Level II CFA Study Guide, © 1993
10. 1994 Level I CFA Study Guide, © 1994
11. 1994 Level II CFA Study Guide, © 1994
15. 1992 Level I CFA Study Guide, © 1992
19. 1993 Level II CFA Study Guide, © 1993

Chapter 16
6. 1993 Level II CFA Study Guide, © 1993
8. 1992–1994 Level I CFA study guides
10. 1993 Level I CFA Study Guide, © 1993
12. 1993 Level I CFA Study Guide, © 1993
21. From various Level I study guides
22. 1994 Level III CFA Study Guide, © 1994
26. 1993 Level III CFA Study Guide, © 1993
27. 1992 Level II CFA Study Guide, © 1992

Chapter 17
3. 1993 Level I CFA Study Guide, © 1993
4. 1993 Level I CFA Study Guide, © 1993
14. 1993 Level II CFA Study Guide, © 1993
16. 1993 Level II CFA Study Guide, © 1993
19. 1993 Level I CFA Study Guide, © 1993

Chapter 18
3. 1995 Level II CFA Study Guide, © 1995
7. 1994 Level I CFA Study Guide, © 1994
10. 1995 Level III CFA Study Guide, © 1995
15. 1993 Level I CFA Study Guide, © 1993
16. 1993 Level I CFA Study Guide, © 1993
21. 1994 Level I CFA Study Guide, © 1994

Chapter 19
4. 1992 Level I CFA Study Guide, © 1992
5. 1994 Level I CFA Study Guide, © 1994
6. 1994 Level I CFA Study Guide, © 1994
7. 1994 Level I CFA Study Guide, © 1994
8. 1992 Level I CFA Study Guide, © 1992

9. 1992 Level I CFA Study Guide, © 1992
10. 1992 Level I CFA Study Guide, © 1992
11. 1992 Level I CFA Study Guide, © 1992
13. 1994 Level I CFA Study Guide, © 1994
14. 1994 Level I CFA Study Guide, © 1994
15. 1992 Level I CFA Study Guide, © 1992
16. 1993 Level II CFA Study Guide, © 1993

Chapter 20
13. 1994 Level III CFA Study Guide, © 1994
24. From various Level I study guides

Chapter 22
17. 1993 Level II CFA Study Guide, © 1993

Chapter 23
6. 1995 Level III CFA Study Guide, © 1995
10. 1991 Level III CFA Study Guide, © 1991
16. 1985 Level III CFA Study Guide, © 1985

Chapter 25
1. 1992 Level I CFA Study Guide, © 1992
2. 1992 Level I CFA Study Guide, © 1992
3. 1992 Level I CFA Study Guide, © 1992
10. 1986 Level III CFA Study Guide, © 1986
11. 1993 Level I CFA Study Guide, © 1993
14. 1992 Level III CFA Study Guide, © 1992

Chapter 26
1. 1988 Level I CFA Study Guide, © 1988
2. 1988 Level I CFA Study Guide, © 1988
3. 1988 Level I CFA Study Guide, © 1988
4. 1988 Level I CFA Study Guide, © 1988
5. 1988 Level I CFA Study Guide, © 1988
6. 1988 Level I CFA Study Guide, © 1988
7. 1995 Level III CFA Study Guide, © 1995
8. 1996 Level III CFA Study Guide, © 1996
10. 1993 Level III CFA Study Guide, © 1993
13. 1982 Level I CFA Study Guide, © 1982
16. 1994 Level III CFA Study Guide, © 1994
17. 1992 Level III CFA Study Guide, © 1992
18. 1992 Level III CFA Study Guide, © 1992
20. 1992 Level III CFA Study Guide, © 1992

Chapter 27
16. From various Level I study guides

Abnormal return. Return on a stock beyond what would be predicted by market movements alone. Cumulative abnormal return (CAR) is the total abnormal return for the period surrounding an announcement or the release of information.

Accounting earnings. Earnings of a firm as reported on its income statement.

Acid test ratio. See quick ratio.

Active management. Attempts to achieve portfolio returns more than commensurate with risk, either by forecasting broad market trends or by identifying particular mispriced sectors of a market or securities in a market.

Active portfolio. In the context of the Treynor-Black model, the portfolio formed by mixing analyzed stocks of perceived nonzero alpha values. This portfolio is ultimately mixed with the passive market index portfolio.

Adjustable-rate mortgage. A mortgage whose interest rate varies according to some specified measure of the current market interest rate.

Adjusted forecast. A (micro or macro) forecast that has been adjusted for the imprecision of the forecast.

Agency problem. Conflicts of interest among stockholders, bondholders, and managers.

Alpha. The abnormal rate of return on a security in excess of what would be predicted by an equilibrium model like CAPM or APT.

American depository receipts (ADRs). Domestically traded securities representing claims to shares of foreign stocks.

American option, European option. An American option can be exercised before and up to its expiration date. Compare with a *European option,* which can be exercised only on the expiration date.

Announcement date. Date on which particular news concerning a given company is announced to the public. Used in *event studies,* which researchers use to evaluate the economic impact of events of interest.

Appraisal ratio. The signal-to-noise ratio of an analyst's forecasts. The ratio of alpha to residual standard deviation.

Arbitrage. A zero-risk, zero-net investment strategy that still generates profits.

Arbitrage pricing theory. An asset pricing theory that is derived from a factor model, using diversification and arbitrage arguments. The theory describes the relationship between expected returns on securities, given that there are no opportunities to create wealth through risk-free arbitrage investments.

Asked price. The price at which a dealer will sell a security.

Asset allocation decision. Choosing among broad asset classes such as stocks versus bonds.

Asset turnover (ATO). The annual sales generated by each dollar of assets (sales/assets).

Auction market. A market where all traders in a good meet at one place to buy or sell an asset. The NYSE is an example.

Average collection period, or days' receivables. The ratio of accounts receivable to sales, or the total amount of credit extended per dollar of daily sales (average AR/sales $\times$ 365).

Balance sheet. An accounting statement of a firm's financial position at a specified time.

Bank discount yield. An annualized interest rate assuming simple interest, a 360-day year, and using the face value of the security rather than purchase price to compute return per dollar invested.

Banker's acceptance. A money market asset consisting of an order to a bank by a customer to pay a sum of money at a future date.

Basis. The difference between the futures price and the spot price.

Basis risk. Risk attributable to uncertain movements in the spread between a futures price and a spot price.

Benchmark error. Use of an inappropriate proxy for the true market portfolio.

Beta. The measure of the systematic risk of a security. The tendency of a security's returns to respond to swings in the broad market.

Bid–asked spread. The difference between a dealer's bid and asked price.

Bid price. The price at which a dealer is willing to purchase a security.

Binomial model. An option valuation model predicated on the assumption that stock prices can move to only two values over any short time period.

Black-Scholes formula. An equation to value a call option that uses the stock price, the exercise price, the risk-free interest rate, the time to maturity, and the standard deviation of the stock return.

Block house. Brokerage firms that help to find potential buyers or sellers of large block trades.

Block sale. A transaction of more than 10,000 shares of stock.

Block transactions. Large transactions in which at least 10,000 shares of stock are bought or sold. Brokers or "block houses" often search directly for other large traders rather than bringing the trade to the stock exchange.

Bogey. The return an investment manager is compared to for performance evaluation.

Bond. A security issued by a borrower that obligates the issuer to make specified payments to the holder over a specific period. A *coupon bond* obligates the issuer to make interest payments called coupon payments over the life of the bond, then to repay the *face value* at maturity.

Bond equivalent yield. Bond yield calculated on an annual percentage rate method. Differs from effective annual yield.

Book value. An accounting measure describing the net worth of common equity according to a firm's balance sheet.

Brokered market. A market where an intermediary (a broker) offers search services to buyers and sellers.

Budget deficit. The amount by which government spending exceeds government revenues.

Bull CD, bear CD. A *bull CD* pays its holder a specified percentage of the increase in return on a specified market index while guaranteeing a minimum rate of return. A *bear CD* pays the holder a fraction of any fall in a given market index.

Bullish, bearish. Words used to describe investor attitudes. *Bullish* means optimistic; *bearish* means pessimistic. Also used in bull market and bear market.

Bundling, unbundling. A trend allowing creation of securities either by combining primitive and derivative securities into one composite hybrid or by separating returns on an asset into classes.

Business cycle. Repetitive cycles of recession and recovery.

Callable bond. A bond that the issuer may repurchase at a given price in some specified period.

Call option. The right to buy an asset at a specified exercise price on or before a specified expiration date.

Call protection. An initial period during which a callable bond may not be called.

Capital allocation decision. Allocation of invested funds between risk-free assets versus the risky portfolio.

Capital allocation line (CAL). A graph showing all feasible risk-return combinations of a risky and risk-free asset.

Capital gains. The amount by which the sale price of a security exceeds the purchase price.

Capital market line (CML). A capital allocation line provided by the market index portfolio.

Capital markets. Includes longer-term, relatively riskier securities.

Cash/bond selection. Asset allocation in which the choice is between short-term cash equivalents and longer-term bonds.

Cash delivery. The provision of some futures contracts that requires not delivery of the underlying assets (as in agricultural futures) but settlement according to the cash value of the asset.

Cash equivalents. Short-term money-market securities.

Cash flow matching. A form of immunization, matching cash flows from a bond portfolio with an obligation.

Certainty equivalent. The certain return providing the same utility as a risky portfolio.

Certificate of deposit. A bank time deposit.

Clearinghouse. Established by exchanges to facilitate transfer of securities resulting from trades. For options and futures contracts, the clearinghouse may interpose itself as a middleman between two traders.

Closed-end (mutual) fund. A fund whose shares are traded through brokers at market prices; the fund will not redeem shares at their net asset value. The market price of the fund can differ from the net asset value.

Collateral. A specific asset pledged against possible default on a bond. *Mortgage* bonds are backed by claims on property. *Collateral trust bonds* are backed by claims on other securities. *Equipment obligation bonds* are backed by claims on equipment.

Collateralized mortgage obligation (CMO). A mortgage pass-through security that partitions cash flows from underlying mortgages into classes called *tranches,* that receive principal payments according to stipulated rules.

Commercial paper. Short-term unsecured debt issued by large corporations.

Commission broker. A broker on the floor of the exchange who executes orders for other members.

Common stock. Equities, or equity securities, issued as ownership shares in a publicly held corporation. Shareholders have voting rights and may receive dividends based on their proportionate ownership.

Comparison universe. The collection of money managers of similar investment style used for assessing relative performance of a portfolio manager.

Complete portfolio. The entire portfolio, including risky and risk-free assets.

Constant growth model. A form of the dividend discount model that assumes dividends will grow at a constant rate.

Contango theory. Holds that the futures price must exceed the expected future spot price.

Contingent claim. Claim whose value is directly dependent on or is contingent on the value of some underlying assets.

Contingent immunization. A mixed passive-active strategy that immunizes a portfolio if necessary to guarantee a minimum acceptable return but otherwise allows active management.

Convergence property. The convergence of futures prices and spot prices at the maturity of the futures contract.

Convertible bond. A bond with an option allowing the bondholder to exchange the bond for a specified number of shares of common stock in the firm. A *conversion ratio* specifies the number of shares. The *market conversion price* is the current value of the shares for which the bond may be exchanged. The *conversion premium* is the excess of the bond's value over the conversion price.

Corporate bonds. Long-term debt issued by private corporations typically paying semiannual coupons and returning the face value of the bond at maturity.

Correlation coefficient. A statistic in which the covariance is scaled to a value between minus one (perfect negative correlation) and plus one (perfect positive correlation).

Cost-of-carry relationship. See spot-futures parity theorem.

Country selection. A type of active international management that measures the contribution to performance attributable to investing in the better-performing stock markets of the world.

Coupon rate. A bond's interest payments per dollar of par value.

Covariance. A measure of the degree to which returns on two risky assets move in tandem. A positive covariance means that asset returns move together. A negative covariance means they vary inversely.

Covered call. A combination of selling a call on a stock together with buying the stock.

Covered interest arbitrage relationship. See interest rate parity theorem.

Credit enhancement. Purchase of the financial guarantee of a large insurance company to raise funds.

Cross hedge. Hedging a position in one asset using futures on another commodity.

Cross holdings. One corporation holds shares in another firm.

Cumulative abnormal return. See abnormal return.

Currency selection. Asset allocation in which the investor chooses among investments denominated in different currencies.

Current account. The difference between imports and exports, including merchandise, services, and transfers such as foreign aid.

Current ratio. A ratio representing the ability of the firm to pay off its current liabilities by liquidating current assets (current assets/current liabilities).

Current yield. A bond's annual coupon payment divided by its price. Differs from yield to maturity.

Day order. A buy order or a sell order expiring at the close of the trading day.

Days' receivables. See average collection period.

Dealer market. A market where traders specializing in particular commodities buy and sell assets for their own accounts. The OTC market is an example.

Debenture or unsecured bond. A bond not backed by specific collateral.

Dedication strategy. Refers to multiperiod cash flow matching.

Default premium. A differential in promised yield that compensates the investor for the risk inherent in purchasing a corporate bond that entails some risk of default.

Deferred annuities. Tax-advantaged life insurance product. Deferred annuities offer deferral of taxes with the option of withdrawing one's funds in the form of a life annuity.

Defined benefit plans. Pension plans in which retirement benefits are set according to a fixed formula.

Defined contribution plans. Pension plans in which the employer is committed to making contributions according to a fixed formula.

Delta (of option). See hedge ratio.

Delta neutral. The value of the portfolio is not affected by changes in the value of the asset on which the options are written.

Demand shock. An event that affects the demand for goods and services in the economy.

Derivative asset/contingent claim. Securities providing payoffs that depend on or are contingent on the values of other assets such as commodity prices, bond and stock prices, or market index values. Examples are futures and options.

Derivative security. See primitive security.

Detachable warrant. A warrant entitles the holder to buy a given number of shares of stock at a stipulated price. A detachable warrant is one that may be sold separately from the package it may have originally been issued with (usually a bond).

Direct search market. Buyers and sellers seek each other directly and transact directly.

Discounted dividend model (DDM). A formula to estimate the intrinsic value of a firm by figuring the present value of all expected future dividends.

Discount function. The discounted value of $1 as a function of time until payment.

Discretionary account. An account of a customer who gives a broker the authority to make buy and sell decisions on the customer's behalf.

Diversifiable risk. Risk attributable to firm-specific risk, or nonmarket risk. *Nondiversifiable* risk refers to systematic or market risk.

Diversification. Spreading a portfolio over many investments to avoid excessive exposure to any one source of risk.

Dividend payout ratio. Percentage of earnings paid out as dividends.

Dollar-weighted return. The internal rate of return on an investment.

Doubling option. A sinking fund provision that may allow repurchase of twice the required number of bonds at the sinking fund call price.

Dow theory. A technique that attempts to discern long- and short-term trends in stock market prices.

Dual funds. Funds in which income and capital shares on a portfolio of stocks are sold separately.

Duration. A measure of the average life of a bond, defined as the weighted average of the times until each payment is made, with weights proportional to the present value of the payment.

Dynamic hedging. Constant updating of hedge positions as market conditions change.

EAFE index. The European, Australian, Far East index, computed by Morgan Stanley, is a widely used index of non-U.S. stocks.

Earnings retention ratio. Plowback ratio.

Earnings yield. The ratio of earnings to price, E/P.

Economic earnings. The real flow of cash that a firm could pay out forever in the absence of any change in the firm's productive capacity.

Effective annual yield. Annualized interest rate on a security computed using compound interest techniques.

Efficient diversification. The organizing principle of modern portfolio theory, which maintains that any risk-averse investor will search for the highest expected return for any level of portfolio risk.

Efficient frontier. Graph representing a set of portfolios that maximize expected return at each level of portfolio risk.

Efficient market hypothesis. The prices of securities fully reflect available information. Investors buying securities in an efficient market should expect to obtain an equilibrium rate of return. Weak-form EMH asserts that stock prices already reflect all information contained in the history of past prices. The semistrong-form hypothesis asserts that stock prices already reflect all publicly available information. The strong-form hypothesis asserts that stock prices reflect all relevant information including insider information.

Elasticity (of an option). Percentage change in the value of an option accompanying a 1 percent change in the value of a stock.

Endowment funds. Organizations chartered to invest money for specific purposes.

Equivalent taxable yield. The pretax yield on a taxable bond providing an after-tax yield equal to the rate on a tax-exempt municipal bond.

Eurodollars. Dollar-denominated deposits at foreign banks or foreign branches of American banks.

European, Australian, Far East (EAFE) index. A widely used index of non-U.S. stocks computed by Morgan Stanley.

European option. A European option can be exercised only on the expiration date. Compare with an American option, which can be exercised before, up to, and including its expiration date.

Event study. Research methodology designed to measure the impact of an event of interest on stock returns.

Excess return. Rate of return in excess of the risk-free rate.

Exchange rate. Price of a unit of one country's currency in terms of another country's currency.

Exchange rate risk. The uncertainty in asset returns due to movements in the exchange rates between the dollar and foreign currencies.

Exchanges. National or regional auction markets providing a facility for members to trade securities. A seat is a membership on an exchange.

Exercise or strike price. Price set for calling (buying) an asset or putting (selling) an asset.

Expectations hypothesis (of interest rates). Theory that forward interest rates are unbiased estimates of expected future interest rates.

Expected return. The probability-weighted average of the possible outcomes.

Expected return–beta relationship. Implication of the CAPM that security risk premiums (expected excess returns) will be proportional to beta.

Face value. The maturity value of a bond.

Factor model.   A way of decomposing the factors that influence a security's rate of return into common and firm-specific influences.

Factor portfolio.   A well-diversified portfolio constructed to have a beta of 1.0 on one factor and a beta of zero on any other factor.

Fair game.   An investment prospect that has a zero risk premium.

FIFO.   The first-in first-out accounting method of inventory valuation.

Filter rule.   A technical analysis technique stated as a rule for buying or selling stock according to past price movements.

Financial assets.   Financial assets such as stocks and bonds are claims to the income generated by real assets or claims on income from the government.

Financial intermediary.   An institution such as a bank, mutual fund, investment company, or insurance company that serves to connect the household and business sectors so households can invest and businesses can finance production.

Firm-specific risk.   See diversifiable risk.

First-pass regression.   A time series regression to estimate the betas of securities or portfolios.

Fiscal policy.   The use of government spending and taxing for the specific purpose of stabilizing the economy.

Fixed annuities.   Annuity contracts in which the insurance company pays a fixed dollar amount of money per period.

Fixed-charge coverage ratio.   Ratio of earnings to all fixed cash obligations, including lease payments and sinking fund payments.

Fixed-income security.   A security such as a bond that pays a specified cash flow over a specific period.

Flight to quality.   Describes the tendency of investors to require larger default premiums on investments under uncertain economic conditions.

Floating-rate bond.   A bond whose interest rate is reset periodically according to a specified market rate.

Floor broker.   A member of the exchange who can execute orders for commission brokers.

Flower bond.   Special Treasury bond (no longer issued) that may be used to settle federal estate taxes at par value under certain conditions.

Forced conversion.   Use of a firm's call option on a callable convertible bond when the firm knows that bondholders will exercise their option to convert.

Foreign exchange market.   An informal network of banks and brokers that allows customers to enter forward contracts to purchase or sell currencies in the future at a rate of exchange agreed upon now.

Foreign exchange swap.   An agreement to exchange stipulated amounts of one currency for another at one or more future dates.

Forward contract.   An agreement calling for future delivery of an asset at an agreed-upon price. Also see futures contract.

Forward interest rate.   Rate of interest for a future period that would equate the total return of a long-term bond with that of a strategy of rolling over shorter-term bonds. The forward rate is inferred from the term structure.

Fourth market.   Direct trading in exchange-listed securities between one investor and another without the benefit of a broker.

Fully diluted earnings per share.   Earnings per share expressed as if all outstanding convertible securities and warrants have been exercised.

Fundamental analysis.   Research to predict stock value that focuses on such determinants as earnings and dividends prospects, expectations for future interest rates, and risk evaluation of the firm.

Futures contract.   Obliges traders to purchase or sell an asset at an agreed-upon price on a specified future date. The long position is held by the trader who commits to purchase. The short position is held by the trader who commits to sell. Futures differ from forward contracts in their standardization, exchange trading, margin requirements, and daily settling (marking to market).

Futures option.   The right to enter a specified futures contract at a futures price equal to the stipulated exercise price.

Futures price.   The price at which a futures trader commits to make or take delivery of the underlying asset.

Geometric average.   The nth root of the product of n numbers. It is used to measure the compound rate of return over time.

Globalization.   Tendency toward a worldwide investment environment, and the integration of national capital markets.

Gross domestic product (GDP).   The market value of goods and services produced over time including the income of foreign corporations and foreign residents working in the United States, but excluding the income of U.S. residents and corporations overseas.

Guaranteed insurance contract.   A contract promising a stated nominal rate of interest over some specific time period, usually several years.

Hedge ratio (for an option).   The number of stocks required to hedge against the price risk of holding one option. Also called the option's delta.

Hedging.   Investing in an asset to reduce the overall risk of a portfolio.

Hedging demands. Demands for securities to hedge particular sources of consumption risk, beyond the usual mean-variance diversification motivation.

Holding-period return. The rate of return over a given period.

Homogenous expectations. The assumption that all investors use the same expected returns and covariance matrix of security returns as inputs in security analysis.

Horizon analysis. Interest rate forecasting that uses a forecast yield curve to predict bond prices.

Immunization. A strategy that matches durations of assets and liabilities so as to make net worth unaffected by interest rate movements.

Implied volatility. The standard deviation of stock returns that is consistent with an option's market value.

Income beneficiary. One who receives income from a trust.

Income fund. A mutual fund providing for liberal current income from investments.

Income statement. A financial statement showing a firm's revenues and expenses during a specified period.

Indenture. The document defining the contract between the bond issuer and the bondholder.

Index arbitrage. An investment strategy that exploits divergences between actual futures prices and their theoretically correct parity values to make a profit.

Index fund. A mutual fund holding shares in proportion to their representation in a market index such as the S&P 500.

Index model. A model of stock returns using a market index such as the S&P 500 to represent common or systematic risk factors.

Index option. A call or put option based on a stock market index.

Indifference curve. A curve connecting all portfolios with the same utility according to their means and standard deviations.

Inflation. The rate at which the general level of prices for goods and services is rising.

Initial public offering. Stock issued to the public for the first time by a formerly privately owned company.

Input list. List of parameters such as expected returns, variances, and covariances necessary to determine the optimal risky portfolio.

Inside information. Nonpublic knowledge about a corporation possessed by corporate officers, major owners, or other individuals with privileged access to information about a firm.

Insider trading. Trading by officers, directors, major stockholders, or others who hold private inside information allowing them to benefit from buying or selling stock.

Insurance principle. The law of averages. The average outcome for many independent trials of an experiment will approach the expected value of the experiment.

Interest coverage ratio, or times interest earned. A financial leverage measure (EBIT divided by interest expense).

Interest rate. The number of dollars earned per dollar invested per period.

Interest rate parity theorem. The spot-futures exchange rate relationship that prevails in well-functioning markets.

Interest rate swaps. A method to manage interest rate risk where parties trade the cash flows corresponding to different securities without actually exchanging securities directly.

Intermarket spread swap. Switching from one segment of the bond market to another (from Treasuries to corporates, for example).

In the money. In the money describes an option whose exercise would produce profits. Out of the money describes an option where exercise would not be profitable.

Intrinsic value (of a firm). The present value of a firm's expected future net cash flows discounted by the required rate of return.

Intrinsic value of an option. Stock price minus exercise price, or the profit that could be attained by immediate exercise of an in-the-money option.

Investment bankers. Firms specializing in the sale of new securities to the public, typically by underwriting the issue.

Investment company. Firm managing funds for investors. An investment company may manage several mutual funds.

Investment-grade bond. Bond rated BBB and above or Baa and above. Lower-rated bonds are classified as speculative-grade or junk bonds.

Investment portfolio. Set of securities chosen by an investor.

Jensen's measure. The alpha of an investment.

Junk bond. See speculative-grade bond.

Law of one price. The rule stipulating that equivalent securities or bundles of securities must sell at equal prices to preclude arbitrage opportunities.

Leading economic indicators. Economic series that tend to risk or fall in advance of the rest of the economy.

Leakage. Release of information to some persons before official public announcement.

Leverage ratio. Ratio of debt to total capitalization of a firm.

LIFO. The last-in first-out accounting method of valuing inventories.

Limit order. An order specifying a price at which an investor is willing to buy or sell a security.

Limited liability. The fact that shareholders have no personal liability to the creditors of the corporation in the event of bankruptcy.

Liquidation value. Net amount that could be realized by selling the assets of a firm after paying the debt.

Liquidity. Liquidity refers to the speed and ease with which an asset can be converted to cash.

Liquidity preference theory. Theory that the forward rate exceeds expected future interest rates.

Liquidity premium. Forward rate minus expected future short interest rate.

Load fund. A mutual fund with a sales commission, or load.

London Interbank Offered Rate (LIBOR). Rate that most creditworthy banks charge one another for large loans of Eurodollars in the London market.

Long hedge. Protecting the future cost of a purchase by taking a long futures position to protect against changes in the price of the asset.

Maintenance, or variation, margin. An established value below which a trader's margin cannot fall. Reaching the maintenance margin triggers a margin call.

Margin. Describes securities purchased with money borrowed from a broker. Current maximum margin is 50 percent.

Market-book ratio. Market price of a share divided by book value per share.

Market capitalization rate. The market-consensus estimate of the appropriate discount rate for a firm's cash flows.

Market model. Another version of the index model that breaks down return uncertainty into systematic and nonsystematic components.

Market or systematic risk, firm-specific risk. Market risk is risk attributable to common macroeconomic factors. Firm-specific risk reflects risk peculiar to an individual firm that is independent of market risk.

Market order. A buy or sell order to be executed immediately at current market prices.

Market portfolio. The portfolio for which each security is held in proportion to its market value.

Market price of risk. A measure of the extra return, or risk premium, that investors demand to bear risk. The reward-to-risk ratio of the market portfolio.

Market segmentation or preferred habitat theory. The theory that long- and short-maturity bonds are traded in essentially distinct or segmented markets and that prices in one market do not affect those in the other.

Market timer. An investor who speculates on broad market moves rather than on specific securities.

Market timing. Asset allocation in which the investment in the market is increased if one forecasts that the market will outperform T-bills.

Market-value-weighted index. An index of a group of securities computed by calculating a weighted average of the returns of each security in the index, with weights proportional to outstanding market value.

Marking to market. Describes the daily settlement of obligations on futures positions.

Mean-variance analysis. Evaluation of risky prospects based on the expected value and variance of possible outcomes.

Mean-variance criterion. The selection of portfolios based on the means and variances of their returns. The choice of the higher expected return portfolio for a given level of variance or the lower variance portfolio for a given expected return.

Measurement error. Errors in measuring an explanatory variable in a regression that leads to biases in estimated parameters.

Membership or seat on an exchange. A limited number of exchange positions that enable the holder to trade for the holder's own accounts and charge clients for the execution of trades for their accounts.

Minimum-variance frontier. Graph of the lowest possible portfolio variance that is attainable for a given portfolio expected return.

Minimum-variance portfolio. The portfolio of risky assets with lowest variance.

Modern portfolio theory (MPT). Principles underlying analysis and evaluation of rational portfolio choices based on risk-return trade-offs and efficient diversification.

Monetary policy. Actions taken by the Board of Governors of the Federal Reserve System to influence the money supply or interest rates.

Money market. Includes short-term, highly liquid, and relatively low-risk debt instruments.

Mortality tables. Tables of probability that individuals of various ages will die within a year.

Mortgage-backed security. Ownership claim in a pool of mortgages or an obligation that is secured by such a pool. Also called a *pass-through,* because payments are passed along from the mortgage originator to the purchaser of the mortgage-backed security.

Multifactor CAPM. Generalization of the basic CAPM that accounts for extra-market hedging demands.

Municipal bonds. Tax-exempt bonds issued by state and local governments, generally to finance capital improvement projects. General obligation bonds are backed by the general taxing power of the issuer. Revenue bonds are backed by the proceeds from the project or agency they are issued to finance.

Mutual fund.   A firm pooling and managing funds of investors.

Mutual fund theorem.   A result associated with the CAPM, asserting that investors will choose to invest their entire risky portfolio in a market-index mutual fund.

Naked option writing.   Writing an option without an offsetting stock position.

Nasdaq.   The automated quotation system for the OTC market, showing current bid–asked prices for thousands of stocks.

Neglected-firm effect.   That investments in stock of less well-known firms have generated abnormal returns.

Nominal interest rate.   The interest rate in terms of nominal (not adjusted for purchasing power) dollars.

Nonsystematic risk.   Nonmarket or firm-specific risk factors that can be eliminated by diversification. Also called unique risk or diversifiable risk. Systematic risk refers to risk factors common to the entire economy.

Normal backwardation theory.   Holds that the futures price will be bid down to a level below the expected spot price.

Open-end (mutual) fund.   A fund that issues or redeems its own shares at their net asset value (NAV).

Open (good-till-canceled) order.   A buy or sell order remaining in force for up to six months unless canceled.

Open interest.   The number of futures contracts outstanding.

Optimal risky portfolio.   An investor's best combination of risky assets to be mixed with safe assets to form the complete portfolio.

Option elasticity.   The percentage increase in an option's value given a 1 percent change in the value of the underlying security.

Original issue discount bond.   A bond issued with a low coupon rate that sells at a discount from par value.

Out of the money.   Out of the money describes an option where exercise would not be profitable. In the money describes an option where exercise would produce profits.

Over-the-counter market.   An informal network of brokers and dealers who negotiate sales of securities (not a formal exchange).

Par value.   The face value of the bond.

Passive investment strategy.   See passive management.

Passive management.   Buying a well-diversified portfolio to represent a broad-based market index without attempting to search out mispriced securities.

Passive portfolio.   A market index portfolio.

Passive strategy.   See passive management.

Pass-through security.   Pools of loans (such as home mortgage loans) sold in one package. Owners of pass-throughs receive all principal and interest payments made by the borrowers.

Peak.   The transition from the end of an expansion to the start of a contraction.

P/E effect.   That portfolios of low P/E stocks have exhibited higher average risk-adjusted returns than high P/E stocks.

Personal trust.   An interest in an asset held by a trustee for the benefit of another person.

Plowback ratio.   The proportion of the firm's earnings that is reinvested in the business (and not paid out as dividends). The plowback ratio equals 1 minus the dividend payout ratio.

Political risk.   Possibility of the expropriation of assets, changes in tax policy, restrictions on the exchange of foreign currency for domestic currency, or other changes in the business climate of a country.

Portfolio insurance.   The practice of using options or dynamic hedge strategies to provide protection against investment losses while maintaining upside potential.

Portfolio management.   Process of combining securities in a portfolio tailored to the investor's preferences and needs, monitoring that portfolio, and evaluating its performance.

Portfolio opportunity set.   The expected return–standard deviation pairs of all portfolios that can be constructed from a given set of assets.

Preferred habitat theory.   Holds that investors prefer specific maturity ranges but can be induced to switch if risk premiums are sufficient.

Preferred stock.   Nonvoting shares in a corporation, paying a fixed or variable stream of dividends.

Premium.   The purchase price of an option.

Price value of a basis point.   The change in the value of a fixed-income asset resulting from a one basis point change in the asset's yield to maturity.

Price–earnings multiple.   See price–earnings ratio.

Price–earnings ratio.   The ratio of a stock's price to its earnings per share. Also referred to as the P/E multiple.

Primary market.   New issues of securities are offered to the public here.

Primitive security, derivative security.   A *primitive security* is an instrument such as a stock or bond for which payments depend only on the financial status of its issuer. A *derivative security* is created from the set of primitive securities to yield returns that depend on factors beyond the characteristics of the issuer and that may be related to prices of other assets.

Principal.   The outstanding balance on a loan.

Profit margin.   See return on sales.

Program trading.   Coordinated buy orders and sell orders of entire portfolios, usually with the aid of computers, often to achieve index arbitrage objectives.

Prospectus.   A final and approved registration statement including the price at which the security issue is offered.

Protective covenant.   A provision specifying requirements of collateral, sinking fund, dividend policy, etc., designed to protect the interests of bondholders.

Protective put.   Purchase of stock combined with a put option that guarantees minimum proceeds equal to the put's exercise price.

Proxy.   An instrument empowering an agent to vote in the name of the shareholder.

Public offering, private placement.   A *public offering* consists of bonds sold in the primary market to the general public; a *private placement* is sold directly to a limited number of institutional investors.

Pure yield pickup swap.   Moving to higher yield bonds.

Put bond.   A bond that the holder may choose either to exchange for par value at some date or to extend for a given number of years.

Put-call parity theorem.   An equation representing the proper relationship between put and call prices. Violation of parity allows arbitrage opportunities.

Put option.   The right to sell an asset at a specified exercise price on or before a specified expiration date.

Quick ratio.   A measure of liquidity similar to the current ratio except for exclusion of inventories (cash plus receivables divided by current liabilities).

Random walk.   Describes the notion that stock price changes are random and unpredictable.

Rate anticipation swap.   A switch made in response to forecasts of interest rates.

Real assets, financial assets.   *Real assets* are land, buildings, and equipment that are used to produce goods and services. *Financial assets* are claims such as securities to the income generated by real assets.

Real interest rate.   The excess of the interest rate over the inflation rate. The growth rate of purchasing power derived from an investment.

Realized compound yield.   Yield assuming that coupon payments are invested at the going market interest rate at the time of their receipt and rolled over until the bond matures.

Rebalancing.   Realigning the proportions of assets in a portfolio as needed.

Registered bond.   A bond whose issuer records ownership and interest payments. Differs from a bearer bond, which is traded without record of ownership and whose possession is its only evidence of ownership.

Registered trader.   A member of the exchange who executes frequent trades for his or her own account.

Registration statement.   Required to be filed with the SEC to describe the issue of a new security.

Regression equation.   An equation that describes the average relationship between a dependent variable and a set of explanatory variables.

REIT.   Real estate investment trust, which is similar to a closed-end mutual fund. REITs invest in real estate or loans secured by real estate and issue shares in such investments.

Remainderman.   One who receives the principal of a trust when it is dissolved.

Replacement cost.   Cost to replace a firm's assets. "Reproduction" cost.

Repurchase agreements (repos).   Short-term, often overnight, sales of government securities with an agreement to repurchase the securities at a slightly higher price. A *reverse repo* is a purchase with an agreement to resell at a specified price on a future date.

Residual claim.   Refers to the fact that shareholders are at the bottom of the list of claimants to assets of a corporation in the event of failure or bankruptcy.

Residuals.   Parts of stock returns not explained by the explanatory variable (the market-index return). They measure the impact of firm-specific events during a particular period.

Resistance level.   A price level above which it is supposedly difficult for a stock or stock index to rise.

Return on assets (ROA).   A profitability ratio; earnings before interest and taxes divided by total assets.

Return on equity (ROE).   An accounting ratio of net profits divided by equity.

Return on sales (ROS), or profit margin.   The ratio of operating profits per dollar of sales (EBIT divided by sales).

Reversing trade.   Entering the opposite side of a currently held futures position to close out the position.

Reward-to-volatility ratio.   Ratio of excess return to portfolio standard deviation.

Riding the yield curve.   Buying long-term bonds in anticipation of capital gains as yields fall with the declining maturity of the bonds.

Risk arbitrage.   Speculation on perceived mispriced securities, usually in connection with merger and acquisition targets.

Risk-averse, risk-neutral, risk lover.   A *risk-averse* investor will consider risky portfolios only if they provide compensation for risk via a risk premium. A *risk-neutral* investor finds the level of risk irrelevant and considers only the expected return of risk prospects. A *risk lover* is willing to accept lower expected returns on prospects with higher amounts of risk.

Risk-free asset. An asset with a certain rate of return; often taken to be short-term T-bills.

Risk-free rate. The interest rate that can be earned with certainty.

Risk lover. See risk-averse.

Risk-neutral. See risk-averse.

Risk premium. An expected return in excess of that on risk-free securities. The premium provides compensation for the risk of an investment.

Risk–return trade-off. If an investor is willing to take on risk, there is the reward of higher expected returns.

Risky asset. An asset with an uncertain rate of return.

Seasoned new issue. Stock issued by companies that already have stock on the market.

Secondary market. Already-existing securities are bought and sold on the exchanges or in the OTC market.

Second-pass regression. A cross-sectional regression of portfolio returns on betas. The estimated slope is the measurement of the reward for bearing systematic risk during the period.

Securitization. Pooling loans for various purposes into standardized securities backed by those loans, which can then be traded like any other security.

Security analysis. Determining correct value of a security in the marketplace.

Security characteristic line. A plot of the excess return on a security over the risk-free rate as a function of the excess return on the market.

Security market line. Graphical representation of the expected return–beta relationship of the CAPM.

Security selection. See security selection decision.

Security selection decision. Choosing the particular securities to include in a portfolio.

Semistrong-form EMH. See efficient market hypothesis.

Separation property. The property that portfolio choice can be separated into two independent tasks: (1) determination of the optimal risky portfolio, which is a purely technical problem, and (2) the personal choice of the best mix of the risky portfolio and the risk-free asset.

Serial bond issue. An issue of bonds with staggered maturity dates that spreads out the principal repayment burden over time.

Sharpe's measure. Reward-to-volatility ratio; ratio of portfolio excess return to standard deviation.

Shelf registration. Advance registration of securities with the SEC for sale up to two years following initial registration.

Short interest rate. A one-period interest rate.

Short position or hedge. Protecting the value of an asset held by taking a short position in a futures contract.

Short sale. The sale of shares not owned by the investor but borrowed through a broker and later repurchased to replace the loan. Profit is earned if the initial sale is at a higher price than the repurchase price.

Simple prospect. An investment opportunity where a certain initial wealth is placed at risk and only two outcomes are possible.

Single-country funds. Mutual funds that invest in securities of only one country.

Single-factor model. A model of security returns that acknowledges only one common factor. See factor model.

Single index model. A model of stock returns that decomposes influences on returns into a systematic factor, as measured by the return on a broad market index, and firm-specific factors.

Sinking fund. A procedure that allows for the repayment of principal at maturity by calling for the bond issuer to repurchase some proportion of the outstanding bonds either in the open market or at a special call price associated with the sinking fund provision.

Skip-day settlement. A convention for calculating yield that assumes a T-bill sale is not settled until two days after quotation of the T-bill price.

Small-firm effect. That investments in stocks of small firms appear to have earned abnormal returns.

Soft dollars. The value of research services that brokerage houses supply to investment managers "free of charge" in exchange for the investment managers' business.

Specialist. A trader who makes a market in the shares of one or more firms and who maintains a "fair and orderly market" by dealing personally in the stock.

Speculation. Undertaking a risky investment with the objective of earning a greater profit than an investment in a risk-free alternative (a risk premium).

Speculative-grade bond. Bond rated Ba or lower by Moody's, or BB or lower by Standard & Poor's, or an unrated bond.

Spot-futures parity theorem, or cost-of-carry relationship. Describes the theoretically correct relationship between spot and futures prices. Violation of the parity relationship gives rise to arbitrage opportunities.

Spot rate. The current interest rate appropriate for discounting a cash flow of some given maturity.

Spread (futures). Taking a long position in a futures contract of one maturity and a short position in a contract of different maturity, both on the same commodity.

Spread (options). A combination of two or more call options or put options on the same stock with differing exercise prices or times to expiration. A money spread refers to a spread with different exercise price; a time spread refers to differing expiration date.

Squeeze.   The possibility that enough long positions hold their contracts to maturity that supplies of the commodity are not adequate to cover all contracts. A *short squeeze* describes the reverse: short positions threaten to deliver an expensive-to-store commodity.

Standard deviation.   Square root of the variance.

Statement of cash flows.   A financial statement showing a firm's cash receipts and cash payments during a specified period.

Stock exchanges.   Secondary markets where already-issued securities are bought and sold by members.

Stock selection.   An active portfolio management technique that focuses on advantageous selection of particular stocks rather than on broad asset allocation choices.

Stock split.   Issue by a corporation of a given number of shares in exchange for the current number of shares held by stockholders. Splits may go in either direction, either increasing or decreasing the number of shares outstanding. A *reverse split* decreases the number outstanding.

Stop-loss order.   A sell order to be executed if the price of the stock falls below a stipulated level.

Straddle.   A combination of buying both a call and a put on the same asset, each with the same exercise price and expiration date. The purpose is to profit from expected volatility.

Straight bond.   A bond with no option features such as callability or convertibility.

Street name.   Describes securities held by a broker on behalf of a client but registered in the name of the firm.

Strike price.   See exercise price.

Strip, strap.   Variants of a straddle. A *strip* is two puts and one call on a stock; a *strap* is two calls and one put, both with the same exercise price and expiration date.

Stripped of coupons.   Describes the practice of some investment banks that sell "synthetic" zero coupon bonds by marketing the rights to a single payment backed by a coupon-paying Treasury bond.

Strong-form EMH.   See efficient market hypothesis.

Subordination clause.   A provision in a bond indenture that restricts the issuer's future borrowing by subordinating the new leaders' claims on the firm to those of the existing bond holders. Claims of *subordinated* or *junior* debtholders are not paid until the prior debt is paid.

Substitution swap.   Exchange of one bond for a bond with similar attributes but more attractively priced.

Supply shock.   An event that influences production capacity and costs in the economy.

Support level.   A price level below which it is supposedly difficult for a stock or stock index to fall.

Swaption.   An option on a swap.

Systematic risk.   Risk factors common to the whole economy, for example, nondiversifiable risk; see market risk.

Tax anticipation notes.   Short-term municipal debt to raise funds to pay for expenses before actual collection of taxes.

Tax deferral option.   The feature of the U.S. Internal Revenue Code that the capital gains tax on an asset is payable only when the gain is realized by selling the asset.

Tax-deferred retirement plans.   Employer-sponsored and other plans that allow contributions and earnings to be made and accumulate tax free until they are paid out as benefits.

Tax-timing option.   Describes the investor's ability to shift the realization of investment gains or losses and their tax implications from one period to another.

Tax swap.   Swapping two similar bonds to receive a tax benefit.

Technical analysis.   Research to identify mispriced securities that focuses on recurrent and predictable stock price patterns and on proxies for buy or sell pressure in the market.

Tender offer.   An offer from an outside investor to shareholders of a company to purchase their shares at a stipulated price, usually substantially above the market price, so that the investor may amass enough shares to obtain control of the company.

Term insurance.   Provides a death benefit only, no build-up of cash value.

Term premiums.   Excess of the yields to maturity on long-term bonds over those of short-term bonds.

Term structure of interest rates.   The pattern of interest rates appropriate for discounting cash flows of various maturities.

Third market.   Trading of exchange-listed securities on the OTC market.

Times interest earned.   See interest coverage ratio.

Time value (of an option).   The part of the value of an option that is due to its positive time to expiration. Not to be confused with present value or the time value of money.

Time-weighted return.   An average of the period-by-period holding-period returns of an investment.

Tobin's q.   Ratio of market value of the firm to replacement cost.

Tranche.   See collateralized mortgage obligation.

Treasury bill.   Short-term, highly liquid government securities issued at a discount from the face value and returning the face amount at maturity.

Treasury bond or note.   Debt obligations of the federal government that make semiannual coupon payments and are issued at or near par value.

Treynor's measure.   Ratio of excess return to beta.

Triple-witching hour. The four times a year that the S&P 500 futures contract expires at the same time as the S&P 100 index option contract and option contracts on individual stocks.

Trough. The transition point between recession and recovery.

Unbundling. See bundling.

Underwriting, underwriting syndicate. Underwriters (investment bankers) purchase securities from the issuing company and resell them. Usually a syndicate of investment bankers is organized behind a lead firm.

Unemployment rate. The ratio of the number of people classified as unemployed to the total labor force.

Unique risk. See diversifiable risk.

Unit investment trust. Money invested in a portfolio whose composition is fixed for the life of the fund. Shares in a unit trust are called redeemable trust certificates, and they are sold at a premium above net asset value.

Universal life policy. An insurance policy that allows for a varying death benefit and premium level over the term of the policy, with an interest rate on the cash value that changes with market interest rates.

Uptick, or zero-plus tick. A trade resulting in a positive change in a stock price, or a trade at a constant price following a preceding price increase.

Utility. The measure of the welfare or satisfaction of an investor.

Utility value. The welfare a given investor assigns to an investment with a particular return and risk.

Variable annuities. Annuity contracts in which the insurance company pays a periodic amount linked to the investment performance of an underlying portfolio.

Variable life policy. An insurance policy that provides a fixed death benefit plus a cash value that can be invested in a variety of funds from which the policyholder can choose.

Variance. A measure of the dispersion of a random variable. Equals the expected value of the squared deviation from the mean.

Variation margin. See maintenance margin.

Volatility risk. The risk in the value of options portfolios due to unpredictable changes in the volatility of the underlying asset.

Warrant. An option issued by the firm to purchase shares of the firm's stock.

Weak-form EMH. See efficient market hypothesis.

Weekend effect. The common recurrent negative average return from Friday to Monday in the stock market.

Well-diversified portfolio. A portfolio spread out over many securities in such a way that the weight in any security is close to zero.

Whole-life insurance policy. Provides a death benefit and a kind of savings plan that builds up cash value for possible future withdrawal.

Workout period. Realignment period of a temporary misaligned yield relationship.

World investable wealth. The part of world wealth that is traded and is therefore accessible to investors.

Writing a call. Selling a call option.

Yield curve. A graph of yield to maturity as a function of time to maturity.

Yield to maturity. A measure of the average rate of return that will be earned on a bond if held to maturity.

Zero-beta portfolio. The minimum-variance portfolio uncorrelated with a chosen efficient portfolio.

Zero coupon bond. A bond paying no coupons that sells at a discount and provides payment of face value only at maturity.

Zero-investment portfolio. A portfolio of zero net value, established by buying and shorting component securities, usually in the context of an arbitrage strategy.

Useful Formulas

Measures of Risk

Variance of returns: $\sigma^2 = E[r - E(r)]^2$

Standard deviation: $\sqrt{\sigma^2}$

Covariance between returns: $\mathrm{Cov}(r_i, r_j) = E\{[r_i - E(r_i)][r_j - E(r_j)]\}$

Beta of security i: $\beta_i = \dfrac{\mathrm{Cov}\,(r_i, r_M)}{\mathrm{Var}(r_M)}$

Portfolio Theory

Expected rate of return on a portfolio with weights w_i in each security:

$$E(r_p) = \sum_{i=1}^{n} w_i E(r_i)$$

Variance of portfolio rate or return: $\sigma_p^2 = \sum_{j=1}^{n} \sum_{i=1}^{n} w_j w_i \, \mathrm{Cov}(r_i, r_j)$

Optimal fraction of the complete portfolio to place in the optimal risky

portfolio: $y = \dfrac{E(r_p) - r_f}{A\sigma_p^2}$

Market Equilibrium

The security market line: $E(r_i) = r_f + \beta_i[E(r_M) - r_f]$

Fixed-Income Analysis

Present value of $1

Discrete period compounding: $PV = 1/(1 + r)^T$

Continuous compounding: $PV = e^{-rT}$

Forward rate of interest for period T: $f_T = \dfrac{(1 + y_T)^T}{(1 + y_{T-1})^{T-1}}$

Real interest rate: $R = \dfrac{1 + r}{1 + i} - 1$

where r is the nominal interest rate
and i is the inflation rate

Duration of a security: $D = \sum_{t=1}^{T} t \times \dfrac{CF_t}{(1 + y)^t} / \text{Price}$

Equity Analysis

Constant growth dividend discount model: $V_o = \dfrac{D_1}{k - g}$

Growth rate of dividends: $g = \text{ROE} \times b$

Price-earnings multiple: $P/E = \dfrac{1 - b}{k - \text{ROE} \times b}$

$\text{ROE} = (1 - \text{tax rate}) \left[\text{ROA} + (\text{ROA} - \text{interest rate}) \dfrac{\text{debt}}{\text{equity}} \right]$

Derivative Assets

Put-call parity: $P = C - S_0 + \text{PV}(X)$

Black-Scholes formula: $C = SN(d_1) - Xe^{-rT} N(d_2)$

$$d_1 = \frac{\ln (S/X) + (r + \sigma^2/2)T}{\sigma\sqrt{T}}$$

$$d_2 = d_1 - \sigma\sqrt{T}$$

Spot-futures parity: $F_0 = S_0(1 + r - d)^T$

Interest rate parity: $F_0 = E_0 \left(\dfrac{1 + r_{\text{US}}}{1 + r_{\text{foreign}}} \right)^T$

Performance Evaluation

Sharpe's measure: $S_p = \dfrac{\bar{r}_p - \bar{r}_f}{\sigma_p}$

Treynor's measure: $T_p = \dfrac{\bar{r}_p - \bar{r}_f}{\beta_p}$

Jensen's measure, or alpha: $\alpha_p = \bar{r}_p - [\bar{r}_f + \beta_p(\bar{r}_M - \bar{r}_f)]$

Appraisal ratio: $A_p = \dfrac{\alpha_p}{\sigma(e_p)}$